THE VICTORIA HISTORY
OF THE
COUNTIES OF ENGLAND

A HISTORY OF
SHROPSHIRE

VOLUME XI

THE VICTORIA HISTORY
OF THE
COUNTIES OF ENGLAND

EDITED BY C. R. ELRINGTON

THE UNIVERSITY OF LONDON
INSTITUTE OF
HISTORICAL RESEARCH

Oxford University Press, Walton Street, Oxford OX2 6DP
London New York Toronto
Delhi Bombay Calcutta Madras Karachi
Kuala Lumpur Singapore Hong Kong Tokyo
Nairobi Dar es Salaam Cape Town
Melbourne Auckland

and associated companies in
Beirut Berlin Ibadan Mexico City Nicosia

Oxford is a trade mark of Oxford University Press

Published in the United States by
Oxford University Press, New York

© University of London 1985

ISBN 0 19 722763 5

Produced by Alan Sutton Publishing Limited, Gloucester
Printed in Great Britain

INSCRIBED TO THE
MEMORY OF HER LATE MAJESTY
QUEEN VICTORIA
WHO GRACIOUSLY GAVE THE TITLE TO
AND ACCEPTED THE DEDICATION
OF THIS HISTORY

A HISTORY OF
SHROPSHIRE

EDITED BY G. C. BAUGH

VOLUME XI

TELFORD

PUBLISHED FOR

THE INSTITUTE OF HISTORICAL RESEARCH

BY

OXFORD UNIVERSITY PRESS

1985

R 942.45

Distributed by Oxford University Press until 1 January 1988
thereafter by Dawsons of Pall Mall

CONTENTS OF VOLUME ELEVEN

LIST OF ILLUSTRATIONS

For permission to reproduce material in their copyright, custody, or possession and for the loan of prints, thanks are offered to Aerofilms Ltd. (plate 31), the British Waterways Board (plate 8), Dr. I. J. Brown (plate 28), the Committee for Aerial Photography of the University of Cambridge (plate 32), Mr. A. M. Carr (plates 40, 54), the Department of Defence (plate 32), the Rt. Hon. the Lord Forester (plates 3, 48, 50, 56), the Hon. J. L. Hamilton and the Trustees of the Apley Park Estate (plate 23), the Ironbridge Gorge Museum Trust (I.G.M.T., plates 12, 14, 25–7, 41), the National Monuments Record (N.M.R.) of the Royal Commission on Historical Monuments (England) (plates 19, 39, 42, 52), Moorland Publishing Co. (plate 28), the National Portrait Gallery (plate 21), the Scottish National Portrait Gallery (plate 22), the Shropshire Archaeological Society (plates 6, 34), Shropshire Libraries (Local Studies Department, Shrewsbury, formerly Shrewsbury Public Library (S.P.L.), plates 4, 9, 17, 29–30, 33, 35–8, 51), the Shropshire Record Office (S.R.O., plates 11, 18, 20, 24), the *Shropshire Star* (plates 1, 44–7), the Stourbridge Preparative Meeting of the Society of Friends (plate 21), the Rt. Hon. the Countess of Sutherland (plate 22), the Department of Transport (plates 2, 55), and Sir Owen Williams & Partners (plates 2, 55).

LIST OF MAPS AND PLANS

The maps were drawn by K. J. Wass of the Department of Geography, University College, London, from drafts by G. C. Baugh (pages 14, 24, 49, and 98), D. C. Cox (pages 20, 79, 148, 196, 199, 200, and 204), H. D. G. Foxall (page 94), P. A. Stamper (facing page 1 and pages 137, 176, 179, 186, 202, 283, 287, 307, 324, and 327), and A. J. L. Winchester (pages 108 and 116); the maps on page 3 were drafted by A. J. L. Winchester and P. A. Stamper. Where sources are not specified the maps should be understood as based on sources cited in the text. The plans on pages 37, 90, and 168 were drawn by A. P. Baggs. Telford Development Corporation is thanked for permission to reproduce the map on page 210.

EDITORIAL NOTE

VOLUME XI is the fifth volume of the *Victoria History of Shropshire* to be published, and the fourth since the revival of the project outlined in the Editorial Note to Volume VIII (1968). The partnership there described between the Salop (since 1980 Shropshire) County Council and the University of London has continued, local responsibility for the Shropshire *History* having been borne since 1977 by the County Council's Leisure Activities Committee under the chairmanship of Mr. V. M. E. Holt. As explained in the Editorial Note to Volume III (1979), the Committee devolved supervision of the *History*'s work on the Victoria County History Advisory Board, chaired by Mr. Holt until 1981 and since then by Sir Jasper More. The University expresses its gratitude to the County Council for its continued support, and indeed for an increase in support since 1983 to maintain an additional editorial post. In that connexion the University has also to thank first the Walker Trust, which in 1979 increased the generous support it has given the *History* since 1961, and secondly two new patrons, the Telford Development Corporation and the Bridgnorth District Council. In 1979 the Corporation, interested in the *History*'s work on Telford and learning of the County Council's wish to increase the editorial staff, offered a contribution for the duration of work on the present volume, thereby enabling an additional Assistant County Editor to be appointed. In 1981 the Bridgnorth District Council, aware that work on parishes in the district was to succeed work on the Telford area, promised a contribution to the new post: that contribution and the County Council's increase in support began, with work on Volume X, in 1983. The University is most grateful to the Development Corporation and the District Council for the assistance they have rendered, in co-operation with the County Council, to promote the *History*'s progress.

The local staff mentioned in the Editorial Note to Volume III have continued in their posts, Mr. G. C. Baugh as County Editor, Dr. D. C. Cox as Assistant County Editor. Dr. A. J. L. Winchester was appointed an Assistant County Editor in 1979 and left in 1981. In succession to him Dr. P. A. Stamper has been Assistant County Editor since 1981. Mrs. J. McFall began to work voluntarily for the *History* in 1980 and continues to prepare contributions for future volumes.

Many people have helped during the preparation of this volume. In the first instance thanks are offered to Mr. E. Thomas, C.B.E., general manager of the Telford Development Corporation 1969–80; his regard for the *History* and its progress have been fruitful in many ways and are very gratefully acknowledged. Special thanks are also rendered to Miss U. B. M. Rayska, the Corporation's Archivist 1975–83, to her successor Miss S. J. Bramley, and to Mr. D. G. Fenter, successively the Corporation's Director of Architecture and Assistant Technical Director 1972–81. Among the record offices and libraries whose resources have been drawn upon particular mention must be made of the Shropshire Record Office under Mrs. L. B. Halford, County Archivist; the Hereford and Worcester Record Office at Hereford; the Lichfield Joint Record Office; the John Rylands University Library of Manchester; the Staffordshire Record Office; Shropshire Libraries, especially the Local Studies Library, Shrewsbury, under Mr. A. M. Carr, and the Central Information and Reference Services; the Ironbridge Gorge Museum Library under Mr. J. Powell; and the *Shropshire Star* Library. Lord Barnard very kindly made his deeds at Raby Castle available; his courtesy and the help of Mrs. E. Steele, the curator at Raby, are very greatly appreciated. The late G. G. Colton and Mrs. P. A. Downes, successive town clerks of Much Wenlock, Mr. H. M. Colvin, C.B.E., Fellow of St. John's College, Oxford, Mr. M. B. S. Exham, Lichfield Diocesan Registrar, the late P. Gwynne James, Hereford Diocesan Registrar, Mr. J. B. Lawson,

Shrewsbury School Librarian, Mr. B. E. Poole of Johnson, Poole & Bloomer, the County Education Officer, the County Planning Officer, the Chief Executive and the Director of Planning and Environmental Services of the Wrekin District Council, some incumbents, and many head teachers are thanked for facilitating the use of material in their custody; the Craven estate papers at St. John's College were moved to the Bodleian Library after this volume was written. Much general help and information have also been given by the Revd. Prebendary C. Hill and Dr. B. S. Trinder. A very special debt of gratitude is owed to Mr. H. D. G. Foxall. Over many years he has prepared field-name maps from tithe apportionments and tithe and estate maps for the use of the *History*; his work, now almost complete, will endure as an indispensable aid to the historian, topographer, and onomastic of Shropshire. Thanks are also offered to many private householders who have courteously allowed the interior examination of their houses and to others who helped with particular articles and are named in appropriate footnotes.

The *General Introduction* to the *History* (1970) outlines the structure and aims of the series as a whole.

LIST OF CLASSES OF DOCUMENTS
IN THE PUBLIC RECORD OFFICE
USED IN THIS VOLUME
WITH THEIR CLASS NUMBERS

Board of Trade
BT 31   Files of Dissolved Companies

Chancery
            Proceedings
C 1   Early
C 2   Series I
            Six Clerks Series
C 5   Bridges
C 6   Collins
C 54   Close Rolls
C 66   Patent Rolls
            Inquisitions post mortem
C 136   Series I, Ric. II
C 137   Hen. IV
C 138   Hen. V
C 139   Hen. VI
C 140   Edw. IV
C 142   Series II, Hen. VII–Chas. II
C 143   Inquisitions ad quod damnum

Court of Common Pleas
            Feet of Fines
CP 25(1)   Series I
CP 25(2)   Series II
CP 40   Plea Rolls, Placita de Banco, or De Banco Rolls
CP 43   Recovery Rolls

Exchequer of Pleas
E 13   Plea Rolls

Exchequer, Treasury of the Receipt
E 32   Forest Proceedings
E 36   Miscellaneous Books

Exchequer, King's Remembrancer
E 134   Depositions taken by Commission
E 156   Original Letters Patent
E 163   Miscellanea of the Exchequer
E 178   Special Commissions of Inquiry
E 179   Subsidy Rolls, etc.
E 199   Sheriffs' Accounts, etc.
E 210   Ancient Deeds, Series D

Exchequer, Augmentation Office
E 315   Miscellaneous Books
E 317   Parliamentary Surveys
E 318   Particulars for Grants of Crown Lands
E 321   Proceedings of the Court of Augmentations

Exchequer, Lord Treasurer's Remembrancer's and Pipe Offices
E 370   Miscellaneous Rolls
E 372   Pipe Rolls

Ministry of Education
ED 7   Public Elementary Schools, Preliminary Statements

Home Office
HO 67   Acreage Returns
            Various, Census Papers
HO 107   Population Returns
HO 129   Ecclesiastical Returns

Justices Itinerant, Assize and Gaol Delivery Justices, etc.
JUST 1   Eyre Rolls, Assize Rolls, etc.

Exchequer, Office of the Auditors of Land Revenue
LR 2   Miscellaneous Books

Ministry of Agriculture, Fisheries and Food
MAF 68   Various, Agricultural Returns, Parish Summaries

Probate
PROB 5   Paper Inventories

Registrar General
            Census Records
RG 9   1861 Census Returns
RG 10   1871 Census Returns
RG 31   Registers of Places of Worship

Special Collections
SC 2   Court Rolls
SC 5   Hundred Rolls
SC 6   Ministers' and Receivers' Accounts
SC 12   Rentals and Surveys

State Paper Office
            State Papers Domestic
SP 16   Chas. I
SP 23   Interregnum, Committee for Compounding with Delinquents

Court of Wards and Liveries
WARD 2   Deeds and Evidences

SELECT LIST OF ACCUMULATIONS AND COLLECTIONS IN THE SHROPSHIRE RECORD OFFICE

USED IN THIS VOLUME

Official Archives

	Shropshire (formerly Salop) County Council
119,215	Miscellanea
559	County Treasurer
725,803	Electoral Registration Officer
1240,1604, 2699,2782, 2879,3346, 3593	Education Department
2981	Clerk's Department
3763	Victoria History of Shropshire
77, 78	Newport and Wellington boards of guardians
1206	Chester District Probate Registry
1335	Shifnal parish
1491,2990	West Midlands Gas Board
1560,4084	Dawley Magna parish
1910	Newport parish
2079,4044	Board of Inland Revenue
2142,3331	Little Wenlock parish
2280	Madeley parish
2732	Malinslee parish
3279	Wrekin district
3499	Wellington, Christ Church parish
3916,3937	Archdeacon of Salop
4105	Lawley parish
4462	Lilleshall parish
4472	Wrockwardine parish
4510	Hadley parish
4608	Preston upon the Weald Moors parish
DA 6	Wenlock corporation
DA 8	Dawley urban district
DA 12	Oakengates urban district
DA 13	Wellington urban district
DA 23	Newport rural district
DA 26	Wellington rural district
DA 34	Wrekin district
QR	Quarter sessions rolls

Family and Estate Archives

38,673, 972	Duke of Sutherland

Family and Estate Archives (*cont.*)

81	Leeke of Longford
327	Corbet of Adderley
513	Cure of Badger
567	Corbett of Longnor
625, 676, 3882	Charlton-Meyrick of Apley Castle
665, 746	Eyton of Eyton upon the Weald Moors
796	Mrs. M. E. M. Dyas
999	Orleton estate
1036	More of Linley
1224	Lord Forester
1952, 2224, 2374	Kenyon-Slaney of Hatton Grange
1981	Lady Labouchere
2919	Corser of Bletchley

Other Archives

436	Shropshire Provident Society
1861	Wrockwardine Wood Primitive Methodist circuit
1936, 2533, 3038,3543, 3840,4286	Methodist records, various
3027,4113	Shifnal Methodist circuit
3129	Paterson & Son of Wellington
3605	Methodist Archives and Research Centre, Manchester
3767	Wellington Methodist circuit

Solicitors' Accumulations

14	R. D. Newill of Wellington
407	Mayler, Teasdale & Co. of Old Jewry
604	Potts & Potts of Broseley
1011,1300, 3288,3651	Salt & Sons of Shrewsbury
1101	Liddle & Heane of Newport
1150	Farrer & Co. of Lincoln's Inn Fields
1190	Pitt & Cooksey of Bridgnorth
1265	Littlewood, Peace & Lanyon of Wellington

NOTE ON ABBREVIATIONS

Among the abbreviations and short titles used the following, in addition to those listed in the Victoria History's *Handbook for Editors and Authors* (1970), may require elucidation:

B.L.	British Library
Bye-Gones	*Bye-Gones relating to Wales and the Border Counties* (Oswestry, [1871–1940])
C.S.	Cantilupe Society
Cranage	D. H. S. Cranage, *Architectural Account of the Churches of Shropshire* (Wellington; 2 vols. 1901 and 1912, published in 10 parts 1894–1912). Cited by part number.
Eyton	R.W. Eyton, *Antiquities of Shropshire* (12 vols. 1854–60)
G.R.O.	General Register Office
H.W.R.O.(H.)	Hereford and Worcester Record Office (Hereford)
H.W.R.O.(W.)	Hereford and Worcester Record Office (Worcester)
I.G.M.T.	Ironbridge Gorge Museum Trust
L.J.R.O.	Lichfield Joint Record Office
M.U.L.	John Rylands University Library of Manchester
Montg. Coll.	*Montgomeryshire Collections: Journal of the Powysland Club*
N.M.R.	National Monuments Record
Orders of Q. Sess.	*Abstract of the Orders made by the Court of Quarter Sessions for Shropshire*, ed. R. Ll. Kenyon and Sir Offley Wakeman (Shropshire County Records nos. 2–5, 7, 9, 11–17 [Shrewsbury, 1901–16])
Pevsner, *Shropshire*	N. Pevsner, *Shropshire* (The Buildings of England, 1958)
Q. Sess. Rolls	*Full List and Partial Abstract of . . . the Quarter Sessions Rolls*, 1696–1820, ed. L. J. Lee and R. G. Venables (Shropshire County Records nos. 6, 10 [Shrewsbury, 1901–5])
R.O.	Record Office
SA	See below, S.M.R.
S.C.C.	Shropshire (formerly Salop) County Council
S.C.C. Mins.	*Shropshire (formerly Salop) County Council Reports and Minutes*
S.H.C.	Staffordshire Record Society (formerly William Salt Archaeological Society), *Collections for a History of Staffordshire*
S.M.R.	Shropshire Sites and Monuments Record, S.C.C. Planning Department. Information cited by primary record number prefixed with SA.
S.P.L.	Shropshire Libraries, Local Studies Department, Shrewsbury (formerly Shrewsbury Public Library)
S.P.R.	*Shropshire Parish Registers*
S.R.O.	Shropshire Record Office
Salop. Agric. Returns, 1905	Board of Agriculture Returns for Shropshire 1905, copy in possession of *V.C.H.*
Salop. N. & Q.	*Shropshire Notes & Queries*
T.C.S.V.F.C.	*Transactions of the Caradoc and Severn Valley Field Club*
T.D.C.	Telford Development Corporation
T.S.A.S.	*Transactions of the Shropshire Archaeological Society*
Trinder, *Ind. Rev. Salop.*	B. Trinder, *Industrial Revolution in Shropshire* (1973; 2nd edn. 1981). References to the 2nd edition are dated.
W.B.R.	Wenlock borough records
W.S.L.	William Salt Library, Stafford

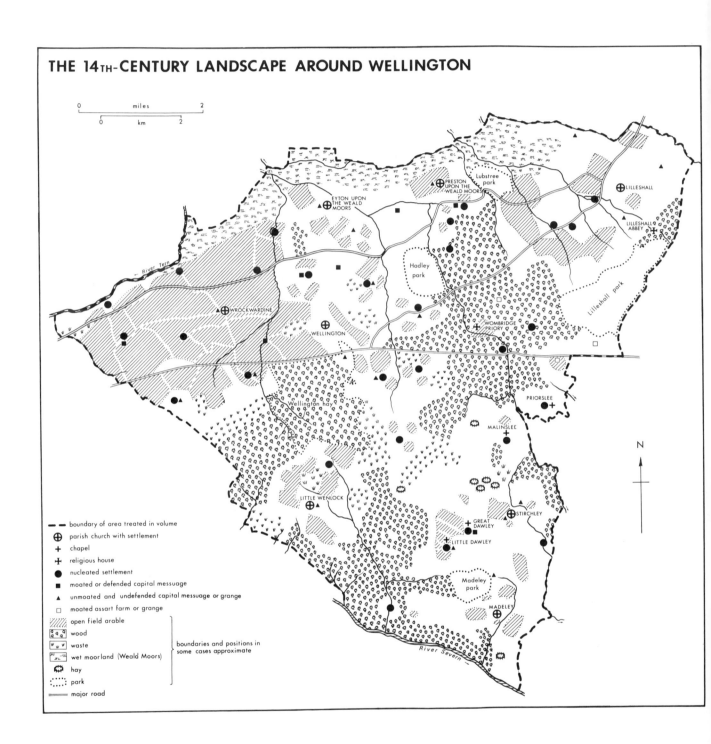

THE 14TH-CENTURY LANDSCAPE AROUND WELLINGTON

0   miles   2
0   km   2

LILLESHALL
LILLESHALL ABBEY
Lubstree park
PRESTON UPON THE WEALD MOORS
EYTON UPON THE WEALD MOORS
Hadley park
Lilleshall park
River Tern
WROCKWARDINE
WELLINGTON
WOMBRIDGE PRIORY
PRIORSLEE
MALINSLEE
Wellington hay
LITTLE WENLOCK
STIRCHLEY
GREAT DAWLEY
LITTLE DAWLEY
Madeley park
MADELEY
River Severn

N

boundary of area treated in volume
⊕ parish church with settlement
+ chapel
✚ religious house
● nucleated settlement
■ moated or defended capital messuage
▲ unmoated and undefended capital messuage or grange
□ moated assart farm or grange
open field arable
wood
waste
wet moorland (Weald Moors)
hay
park
major road

boundaries and positions in
some cases approximate

TELFORD

TELFORD town centre lies *c.* 21 km. east-south-east of Shrewsbury and *c.* 24 km. north-west of Wolverhampton. The town comprises 7,803 ha.[1] and its southern and eastern parts, between the Severn Gorge and Donnington Wood, include the worked-out east Shropshire coalfield. North and north-west Telford lie beyond the coalfield's Boundary fault on the Bunter Pebble Beds which, with other Triassic formations, prevail over much of north Shropshire. The town centre stands on a watershed; south of it the land is an undulating plateau crossed by deeply incised valleys whose streams drain south to the Severn or south-east to its tributary the Worfe; to the north the land slopes gently down towards the Weald Moors, which lie two kilometres or so north of the Telford boundary. Scenically Telford is dominated by the Wrekin, south-west of Wellington and outside the Telford boundary.

Most early settlement in the area was probably on the land that sloped up from the Weald Moors towards the line along which the Roman Watling Street was built. Extensive arable surrounded three large estates, which existed there by the 10th century: the royal estates at Wellington and Wrockwardine and the ecclesiastical estate at Lilleshall. Wellington town and nearby Dothill, with Walcot township and the main part of Wrockwardine parish, lay outside the royal forest of Mount Gilbert or the Wrekin; the rest of the area's townships were disafforested in 1301. From the 14th century the only considerable tract of woodland extending north of Watling Street was that which stretched north from the confines of Priorslee to Horton's wood and east from Hadley wood to Donnington wood; parcelled out among various manors in the 13th century, that area, save perhaps for some clearing around Wombridge priory, remained wood pasture until the 17th century or later. In the hilly southern part of the area later-established settlements lay in cleared woodland, arable fields were smaller, and woodland lasted longer.

From the 13th century urban developments were fostered in Wellington and also at Madeley, where Wenlock priory founded a new town. Six monastic houses, founded in the 11th and 12th centuries, had large interests in the area's economic growth. They acquired the rectorial tithes of all its larger parishes,[2] owned manorial rights over almost half of the area,[3] and profited from coal and ironstone mines and iron smithies on their estates. Coal and iron industries on a large scale, however, grew up only from the mid 17th century. The mid 18th-century transformation of local industry by technological and business enterprise was a development of national importance. By 1806 the area boasted Britain's second largest ironworks.[4] The landscape was transformed by clearance of much of the remaining woodland and the spread of mining spoil, canals, new roads, railways, and sprawling industrial settlements. Some small towns grew up, but municipal institutions were acquired slowly or not at all. Prosperity ebbed away from the southern end of the coalfield after

[1] *Census*, 1971, *Co. Rep. Salop.* i. 15. Thanks are offered to Mr. D. G. Fenter (successively director of architecture and asst. technical director T.D.C. 1972–81) and Mr. N. R. Boden (S.C.C. Planning Dept.) for much valuable help during the writing of this art. (1983–4) and to Mr. E. Thomas (gen. manager T.D.C. 1969–80) and Mr. C. Griffiths (chief architect–planner 1964–72) for commenting on it in draft.

[2] And one of the small ones: Lilleshall, Madeley, Wellington, Wombridge, and Wrockwardine.

[3] Aston, Lilleshall, Madeley, Stirchley, Walcot, L. Wenlock, and Wombridge.

[4] Old Pk.: Trinder, *Ind. Rev. Salop.* (1981), 46.

the mid 19th century and, after some recovery in the 1940s and 1950s, the whole area was seriously affected by a national recession, which deepened from the later 1960s.

The area had no administrative unity before 1974; even Telford new town's smaller predecessor, Dawley new town (3,698 ha.),[5] came only briefly (1966–8) within the area of a single local authority. Although Telford included the most important industrial area of Shropshire within its boundaries, its constituent towns and villages were, and long had been, remarkably diverse.[6] Wellington, an old market town off the coalfield and with a considerable middle class,[7] had become the area's shopping and service centre by the mid 20th century. Oakengates had grown from virtually nothing in the mid 19th century to a small, densely built town by 1898 when, by a federation of four adjoining civil parishes, it acquired municipal institutions. Madeley parish, containing the town of Ironbridge, was a ward of the borough of Wenlock until 1966. Dawley, the central part of Telford, contained the greatest concentration of the area's most derelict and impoverished parts: old basic industries were in decline, leaving a ravaged landscape,[8] a residual population, and inadequate local resources to effect improvements. Symptomatic of the long neglect of the area was the late provision (1956) of secondary schools in Dawley, where measures taken to remedy social and intellectual impoverishment in the 1970s included the government-aided establishment of nursery classes.[9] More or less all the settlements in the southern part of the coalfield, and some in the north, were afflicted by the same problems, even if not on the same scale. It was to provide resources for rehabilitating the area, and also to contribute to the working-out of regional planning policies in the west Midlands, that Dawley new town was designated in 1963; in 1968 it was extended north and renamed Telford.

Post-war hopes of containing the growth of Birmingham[10] and its conurbation[11] included plans to house some of the overspill population in new towns, economically and socially balanced communities beyond a surrounding green belt.[12] From time to time various places in the west Midlands were considered as sites for new towns but besides Dawley only Redditch (1964) was designated. Both designations were commitments to develop the economic and social self-sufficiency characteristic of a new town, but the Conservatives' failure to make use of the New Towns Act[13] in the prosperous 1950s[14] meant that the commitments were undertaken as circumstances were becoming less favourable. In the harsher economic climate of the later 1960s Redditch's proximity to Birmingham conferred the advantages of a satellite town[15] but Dawley had a harder task: its greater distance from the conurbation made it, within the west Midlands, a unique[16] indicator of the commitment of government and regional planners to the ideal of dispersing population widely to new and independent communities. In the event successive changes in planning strategy, not least because of their timing, had profound effects upon Telford.

In 1963 Dawley new town was intended to take 50,000 people from the conurbation and so to grow to a town of 70,000 or more. By 1968 Telford was intended to take an

[5] Census, 1971, Co. Rep. Salop. i. 15.

[6] Below; cf. The Victorian Countryside, ed. G.E. Mingay (1981), i. 359.   [7] V.C.H. Salop. iii. 345.

[8] Below, Dawley; Madeley; Wellington; Wombridge.

[9] Under the urban aid programme: S.C.C. Educ. Dept., Schools subcttee. min. bk. 1967–71, pp. 4–5, 67–9, 176–7, 341–5; S.C.C. Mins. (Educ.) 1969–70, 11–12; 1970–1, 146–8; below, Dawley, Educ. Cf. J. McFall, 'Educ. in Madeley Union of Salop. in 19th Cent.' (Keele Univ. M.A. (Educ.) thesis, 1973), 48.

[10] For this para. see P. Hall and others, The Containment of Urban Eng. (1973), i. 504–50; ii. 332–8; A. Sutcliffe and R.

Smith, Birmingham 1939–70 (Hist. of Birm. iii, 1974), cap. 4.

[11] Dept. of Econ. Affairs, The W. Midlands: a regional study (1965), 3–4, 84.

[12] The long-proposed W. Midlands green belt (ibid. 72) was formally designated from 1974: The Times, 15 Aug. 1974.

[13] 9 & 10 Geo. VI, c. 68.

[14] Hall, Containment of Urban Eng. ii. 334–5.

[15] Dept. of Econ. Affairs, W. Midlands regional study, 64–6; J. B. Cullingworth, New Towns Policy (Environmental Planning 1939–69, iii, 1979), 173.

[16] R. S. Tolley, 'Post-War Changes in Ind. Geog. of E. Salop.' (Keele Univ. M.A. thesis, 1970), 192–3.

THE AREA AROUND WELLINGTON

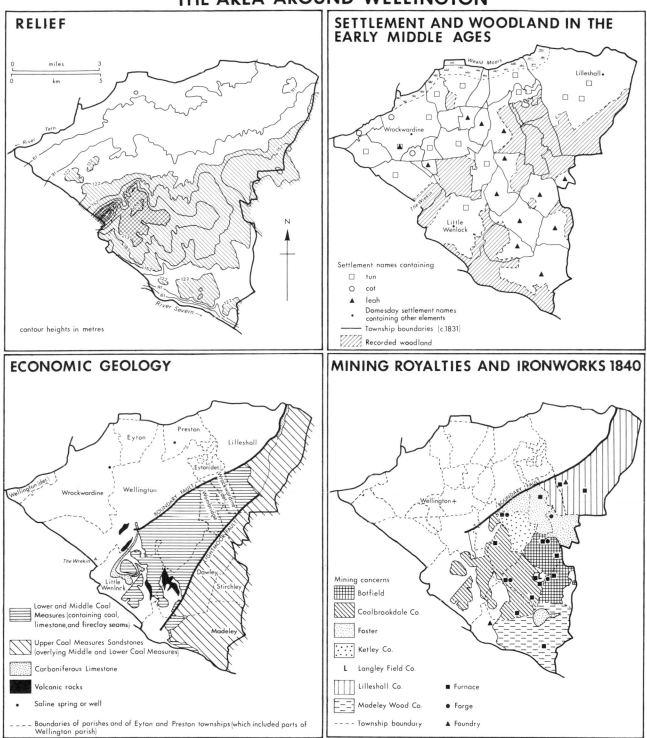

RELIEF

miles 0 — 3
km 0 — 5

River Tern

The Wrekin

N

contour heights in metres

SETTLEMENT AND WOODLAND IN THE EARLY MIDDLE AGES

Weald Moors

Lilleshall.

Wrockwardine

The Wrekin

Little Wenlock

Settlement names containing
☐ tun
○ cot
▲ leah
• Domesday settlement names containing other elements
— Township boundaries (c.1831)
▨ Recorded woodland

ECONOMIC GEOLOGY

Preston
Eyton
Lilleshall
Eyton (det.)
Wellington (det.)
Wrockwardine   Wellington
Wombridge
BOUNDARY FAULT
Wrockwardine
LIGHTMOOR FAULT
The Wrekin
Little Wenlock
Dawley
Stirchley
Madeley

▦ Lower and Middle Coal Measures (containing coal, limestone, and fireclay seams)
▧ Upper Coal Measures Sandstones (overlying Middle and Lower Coal Measures)
⠒ Carboniferous Limestone
■ Volcanic rocks
• Saline spring or well
---- Boundaries of parishes and of Eyton and Preston townships (which included parts of Wellington parish)

MINING ROYALTIES AND IRONWORKS 1840

Wellington+

BOUNDARY FAULT

Mining concerns
▦ Botfield
▨ Coalbrookdale Co.
⠒ Foster
⠿ Ketley Co.
L Langley Field Co.
▥ Lilleshall Co.
▤ Madeley Wood Co.
---- Township boundary

■ Furnace
● Forge
▲ Foundry

Settlement and Woodland: Woodland is indicated from sources cited in the notes and from surviving old woodland. *Economic Geology*: the ancient metamorphic rocks around the Wrekin and Leaton, quarried for road stone, are not shown. *Mining Royalties*: potentially productive royalties (but not others) are distinguished, except for an area in eastern Stirchley, owned by the duke of Cleveland and several freeholders.

3

additional 50,000 and grow to a town of 220,000 or more by 1991. By 1983, however, Telford's population was just under 108,000, and it was generally thought that it might not reach 120,000 by the time of the development corporation's demise, expected in the late 1980s. Thus the effects of immigration were offset by a fall in the national birth rate and by a national economic recession, which deepened throughout the 1970s and beyond. In the mid 1960s, when those changes began[17] but were not yet detected, regional and Ministry of Housing and Local Government planners began to work out Dawley's expansion by incorporating into their plan for Telford optimistic rates of employment growth unparalleled[18] since the growth of the first-generation London new towns in the 1950s.[19] Soon afterwards, however, the planners began to favour the contrary strategy of allowing growth within Birmingham and its satellite towns. Even before the change of strategy, and certainly for long after, other government departments accorded Telford low priority. Job creation there was hampered by inflexible policies at the Board of Trade (later the Department of Trade and Industry), while the minister of Transport's original (1962) undertaking to improve road communications with the conurbation[20] took 21 years to fulfil.

The rehousing of Birmingham people in Dawley urban district began in the late 1950s with assistance from the city of Birmingham under the 1952 Town Development Act,[21] the Conservatives' alternative in the 1950s to designations under the New Towns Act.[22] In 1955, following up an article by the *Birmingham Gazette*'s Dawley correspondent A.W. Bowdler,[23] Dawley U.D.C. made approaches to the city of Birmingham and the Shropshire county planning officer[24] with the result that 100 dwellings were provided in Dawley for Birmingham people between 1958 and 1961,[25] a small scheme in the context of the city's problems. Meanwhile, however, Birmingham's ruling Labour group, which had proclaimed that Birmingham's people and industry had 'a right to remain in the city', had seen the apparently final defeat of its plans for expansion on the city's southern edge. At the same time the Conservative government was realizing that procedure under the 1952 Act was too slow. Accordingly when the minister of Housing and Local Government rejected Birmingham's expansion plan in April 1960, he immediately offered help in working out new overspill arrangements; reports on Dawley were called for in the summer, and in November the minister announced the possibility of a new town there. In 1961 the Midlands New Towns Society also suggested a new town at Dawley, and the minister commissioned the Birmingham city architect[26] to advise on the feasibility of a new town there, publicly confirming that a designation was being considered.[27] Development in Dawley and Madeley, which were to be combined in the new town, was restricted, at first while the government's decision was being made, later until the new town master plan was completed in 1965.[28]

Dawley new town was designated in January 1963.[29] Besides the rehousing of 50,000 overspill population from the Birmingham conurbation, the other main

[17] See e.g. Office of Pop. Censuses and Surveys, *Birth Stats. Eng. and Wales, 1980* (1982), for the declining rate of pop. increase from 1964; J. L. Hanson, *Dict. of Economics and Commerce* (1974), 146, 346, for the destruction of the 1965 National Plan by the 1966–7 credit restrictions. Later, planning for lower density development also helped to depress pop. targets: see below.
[18] R. S. Tolley, 'Telford New Town', *Town Planning Rev.* xliii. 348.
[19] Cf. (for Harlow) Hall, *Containment of Urban Eng.* ii. 301; *V.C.H. Essex*, viii. 151–4.
[20] Cullingworth, *New Towns Policy*, 173–4.
[21] 15 & 16 Geo. VI and 1 Eliz. II, c. 54.
[22] Hall, *Containment of Urban Eng.* ii. 335.
[23] *Birm. Gaz.* 16 Feb. 1955.
[24] *V.C.H. Salop.* iii. 220; E. Thomas, 'Telford—the Last Fifteen Yrs.' (TS. 1978), pp. 6–8 (copy in S.R.O. 3763). Mr. Thomas is thanked for making the text of his lecture available.
[25] Below, Dawley, Growth of Settlement.
[26] A. G. Sheppard Fidler, previously Crawley new town architect: Sutcliffe and Smith, *Birm. 1939–70*, 430.
[27] Ibid. 143–7; Hall, *Containment of Urban Eng.* i. 528–9; ii. 335; T.D.C., Constitutional Doc. i.
[28] S.R.O., DA 6/119/1, pp. 537, 543, 556–8, 583, 587; DA 8/100/7, pp. 2095, 2537, 2748; *Shropshire Star*, 5 Nov. 1964; 20 Jan. 1965.
[29] Under the New Towns Act, 1946: *Dawley New Town (Designation) Order 1963* (Stat. Instr. 1963, no. 64).

objective was the rehabilitation of the depressed area of the east Shropshire coalfield, an essential part of which was the reclamation of extensive derelict land. Some 41 per cent (1,528 ha.) of the new town, mainly in the old Dawley area, was affected by shallow mining, spoil heaps, or geological instability. From the outset the government accepted the principle of bearing the additional costs of building a new town on reclaimed land, thus reducing, as the minister of Agriculture emphasized, the need to take agricultural land.[30] Agricultural interests nevertheless worked hard to restrict the designated area narrowly around the area of old industry and settlement. They were only partly successful,[31] and to the east tracts of grade 3 agricultural land were included in the new town.[32] In the south also much of Madeley was still agricultural and it was there, on relatively good agricultural land, that the new town's first estate, Sutton Hill (1,233 houses 1966–9), was built next to the new Hills Lane council estate. Other early development around Madeley, however, was on low-grade agricultural land,[33] derelict industrial land,[34] or a mixture of the two.[35] In the later 1960s, when proposals to enlarge Dawley were made, and in the later 1970s, when Telford's population target and development proposals were being scaled down,[36] farmers[37] and the county council[38] remained vigilant for the preservation of agricultural land or pressed for the return of undeveloped land to farming.

A master plan for Dawley, prepared by John H. D. Madin & Partners, of Birmingham, and published in January 1965, provided for a horseshoe-shaped primary road looping south from the Shifnal–Priorslee road at Priorslee and from a long-proposed southern bypass of Wellington and Oakengates at Ketley; the bypass was to form the new town's northern border. Under the town's first, and only, chief architect–planner, Ceri Griffiths (1964–72), the applicability of Gordon Cullen's theoretical new town 'Alcan' was urged. 'Alcan' was a linear town built either side of a primary road designed to motorway standard; Dawley, with its road loop, was conceived as 'curvilinear'. Residential areas, in which pedestrian and vehicle routes were to be separate,[39] were to be grouped mainly on the inside of the loop, around a new town centre and town park. Nevertheless much new housing was planned south of the loop, around Madeley, and some east of it, north and south of Nedge Farm in Shifnal parish. New residential areas inside the western arm of the loop were to be grafted on existing settlements at Dawley Bank, Dawley, and Little Dawley. Inside the eastern arm of the loop, in Stirchley parish, there were no old settlements of any size. Industry was to be located outside the loop, on land unaffected by instability. The natural beauty and historic importance of the Severn Gorge area were recognized as high-quality amenities, and a nearby site between Lincoln Hill and Roughpark Farm was reserved for a proposed university.[40]

The development corporation intended to fulfil the plan by building first along the new town's eastern edge. Until its new sewage works at Gitchfield (in Broseley) came

[30] Cullingworth, *New Towns Policy*, 167–8, 172–4, 571; *The Times*, 17 Mar. 1976, Special Rep.; T.D.C., Constitutional Doc. i, engineering insp.'s rep. 31 Aug. 1960, p. 3; J. H. D. Madin & Partners, *Dawley New Town Rep. No. 2: Interim Proposals* (Sept. 1964), para. 2:29.

[31] T.D.C., Constitutional Doc. i, Rep. of Inq. into Draft Dawley New Town Designation Order, 16 Jan. 1963; S.R.O., DA 6/119/1, p. 592.

[32] Cf. *Dawley New Town (Designation) Order 1963*, accompanying map (copy in S.R.O. 2981, parcel VI); Min. of Ag., Fish. and Food, *Agric. Land Classificn.* map 1", sheet 119 (1970 edn.).

[33] Woodside housing est.   [34] Tweedale ind. est.

[35] Halesfield ind. est. See below, Madeley; S.R.O. 2685/1;

D. G. Fenter, 'Bldg. Development carried out in Telford by the Development Corp.' (TS. in S.R.O. 3763).

[36] Below.

[37] See e.g. *Shropshire Star*, 18 Nov. 1966; 22 Dec. 1979; S.R.O. 4417.

[38] Private inf.; *S.C.C. Mins.* 1962–3, 35–6, 148, 297; 1966–7, 273, 297; 1967–8, 323.

[39] The Radburn principle, later modified: below.

[40] J. H. D. Madin & Partners, *Dawley New Town: Short Memo. on Draft Master Plan* (Oct. 1964); *Shropshire Star*, 20 Jan. 1965; inf. from T.D.C.; Thomas, 'Telford', 20. For 'Alcan' see *Architectural Rev.* May–Sept. 1964. For the Wellington–Oakengates bypass see T.D.C., Constitutional Doc. i, Sheppard Fidler's rep. p. 4.

into use new building had to use the borough of Wenlock's works south of Cuckoo Oak. Accordingly the first industrial estate was laid out at Tweedale, where the first factory was occupied in the autumn of 1966,[41] and house building began at Sutton Hill, where the corporation's first tenants were visited by Elizabeth II in 1967.[42] The corporation's plan was to build northwards thereafter, keeping pace with the northward extension of sewerage: there, on largely agricultural land in Sutton Maddock, Kemberton, Stirchley, and Shifnal, development could proceed most easily and quickly while to the west derelict land was reclaimed and changes to the old centres of Madeley and Dawley were planned.[43]

Barely was the Dawley plan published, however, when, later in 1965, the Department of Economic Affairs[44] produced a new *Regional Study* of the West Midlands economic planning region.[45] It identified the planned expansion of Wellington and Oakengates as an essential part of the region's strategy for dispersing 500,000 people from the Birmingham and Black Country conurbation. The future relationship between Wellington and Oakengates on the one hand and Dawley new town on the other was not defined[46] but in July 1965 Richard Crossman, minister of Housing and Local Government, visited Dawley with his permanent under-secretary Dame Evelyn Sharp[47] and, as she intended, he ordered the suspension of the master plan. At the ministry's behest Dawley development corporation produced a Continuity Plan, published April 1966, to enable the building of the southern part of the new town to proceed, though restricted to Madeley, while the ministry's consultants, the John Madin Design Group, prepared proposals for the development of Dawley, Wellington, and Oakengates.[48] Moreover, within the restricted area where work could go on the development corporation's problems were made more acute and its responsibilities increased. Reconsideration of the new town evoked scepticism among government officials about its economic prospects and Treasury arguments for its cancellation.[49] The corporation accordingly came under very great pressure. Though much essential construction work had been put in hand in the early years, in 1967 Dawley was publicly criticized for slow progress by Crossman's successor Anthony Greenwood, apparently heedless of the government's prevarication over the improvement of road communications and of the uncertainty caused by his own ministry's brake on development. In 1968 Greenwood determined to 'strengthen' the corporation by appointing a new and 'very energetic' chairman,[50] Sir Frank Price.[51] Internal changes followed, and ministry pressure was kept up with a target building rate of two thousand houses a year being represented to the corporation as essential to secure the town's future. Woodside estate was accordingly built west of Madeley at an earlier stage (1968–73) and on a larger scale than had been planned, and the old centre of Madeley was replanned and altered very rapidly. The people of Dawley felt that the heart of the new town was being neglected and denied much-needed capital investment.[52] Moreover land reclamation in the old Dawley area, where dereliction was worst, was put off, with deleterious consequences for Telford development

[41] *Shropshire Jnl.* 16 Sept. 1966; cf. below, Madeley, Public Services.   [42] *Shropshire Star*, 18 Mar. 1967.
[43] Inf. from T.D.C.; Thomas, 'Telford', 25 sqq. Cf. Fenter, 'Bldg. Development in Telford'.
[44] Invented 1964, abolished 1969: *The Times*, 6 and 17 Oct. 1969; *Sunday Times*, 18 Oct. 1970; H. Wilson, *The Labour Govt. 1964–70* (1971), 3–4.
[45] For the regions see Brian C. Smith, *Regionalism in Eng.* (Acton Soc. Trust, 1964–5), i. 15–19, 64–5, 72–3, 92; ii. 19–20; iii. 17–22, 42–3; Wilson, op. cit. 64.
[46] Dept. of Econ. Affairs, *W. Midlands regional study*, 62, 67 sqq., 76; M. Aldridge, *Brit. New Towns: Programme*

without Policy (1979), 133–4.
[47] R. Crossman, *Diaries of a Cabinet Minister*, i (1975), 306–8. Cf. for Sharp's influence ibid. 127, 130, 272–3, 463–4, 505, 554, 581, 616–18.
[48] Thomas, 'Telford', 22 sqq.; Cullingworth, *New Towns Policy*, 259, 261–2.
[49] Cullingworth, op. cit. 258, 263–4.
[50] Ibid. 265; private inf.; *Town Planning Rev.* xliii. 348–9; Tolley, 'Post-War Changes in E. Salop.' 195, 205.
[51] See below.
[52] Private inf.; local inf.; [U. Rayska], *Redevelopment of Madeley* (T.D.C. 1979), 8 sqq.

corporation's plans to build around the town centre in the 1980s.[53] The repercussions of Crossman's visit thus had enduring effects upon the town's growth.[54]

Repercussions were felt in the economic as well as the planning sphere. In the later 1960s, while the government considered proposals for the new town's enlargement, developments were delayed not only in the old Dawley area but also in Wellington and Oakengates.[55] The delays occurred at a damaging time, for locally, as nationally, economic growth was slowing down. That had not been foreseen. The planning of Dawley in the early 1960s had assumed the continuance of virtually full male employment and considerable local rises in female employment and, especially in the new town centre, service employment. It also assumed that manufacturing firms from expanding and mobile sectors of the regional economy would be attracted: added to the area's more basic heavy industry they would help to create an industrially balanced new town.[56] The assumptions allowed for Dawley's disadvantages: communications were poor, and local heavy industries dependent on iron, coal, and clay were in decline and were leaving behind them a ruined landscape unattractive to new industry. Nevertheless in spite of high unemployment in the 1930s the east Shropshire (Coalbrookdale) coalfield had prospered in the 1940s and 1950s. Employment in the vehicle components industry, in the manufacture of engineering and electrical goods, and in metal and clothing manufactures had increased. That was due partly to the prosperity of the British car industry[57] and partly to the fact that firms had moved into the area: six in Dawley new town, employing 1,287 people in 1964, had come to Dawley or Madeley between 1941 and 1960. The new jobs, amounting to 28 per cent of the new town's 4,563 industrial jobs in 1964, were mainly women's; and it is noteworthy that the large pool of female labour available in the area, the result of the long preponderance of heavy industry, probably continued to help the new town to attract firms from the conurbation.[58] Even coalmining, which had been expected to lose much of its labour force, had done well: collieries decreased from five in 1947 to one by the end of 1967, but production and productivity increased over the same period and there was no loss of jobs.[59] Post-war prosperity had increased even more markedly in the Wellington–Oakengates area immediately north of Dawley;[60] there were 15,045 industrial jobs there in 1964, when almost half of the new town's labour force (4,449) commuted north to work. The new town depended on its northern neighbours, especially Wellington, for services and service employment and was economically united with them. The Dawley plan had aimed to make the new town economically independent,[61] but it had seemed that while independence was being achieved the northern area's continued prosperity would provide a reliable source of employment for Dawley.

In the 1960s and 1970s, however, the established industries of the Telford area began to fail. Its last two collieries closed in 1967 and 1979.[62] The post-war growth in the local manufacture of vehicle components had been almost entirely due to Sankey's Hadley works, by far the area's greatest manufacturing employer in 1964;[63] falling demand, however, destroyed very many jobs there from the late 1970s. At Priorslee

[53] *Town Planning Rev.* xliii. 354–5; below.
[54] Thomas, 'Telford', 23 sqq.
[55] Cullingworth, *New Towns Policy*, 259–62.
[56] Madin, *Dawley Rep. No. 2: Interim Proposals*, paras. 2:56–7, 6:17–20, 27–38, 46–59; ibid. diagrams 15a–16; R. S. Tolley, 'Changing Ind. Geog. of E. Salop.' *W. Midlands Studies*, v. 2–3; idem, 'Female employment and ind. dev.: Coalbrookdale coalfield', *N. Staffs. Jnl. Field Studies*, xiii. 78.
[57] *W. Midlands Studies*, v. 5–7; Tolley, 'Post-War Changes in E. Salop.' 23–8, 101–58, 200–6.
[58] Madin, *Dawley Rep. No. 2: Interim Proposals*, paras.

6:19–21; *N. Staffs. Jnl. Field Studies*, xiii. 67–82.
[59] *W. Midlands Studies*, v. 2–3, 6.
[60] Ibid. 4–8.
[61] Madin, *Dawley Rep. No. 2: Interim Proposals*, paras. 2:107, 6:12–16, 23–6; ibid. cap. 6, sect. 1, app.; ibid. maps 5–6.
[62] Ibid. paras. 6:17–18; below, Lilleshall, Econ. Hist. (Mines, Quarries, and Sandpits); Madeley, Econ. Hist. (Coal and Ironstone).
[63] Madin, op. cit. para. 6:13; ibid. cap. 6, sect. 1, app.; ibid. map 14; *W. Midlands Studies*, v. 4, 6–7.

Shropshire's last blast furnace was blown out in 1959 and its last rolling mill closed in 1982. The Lilleshall Co., which had owned both,[64] became a steel stockholding, engineering, and property company.[65] Off the coalfield Wellington was losing manufacturing jobs in the 1960s and becoming more dependent on services.[66] The annual rate of creation of manufacturing jobs in new plants in the Telford area declined by 20 per cent between 1949–60 and 1960–8, and between 1971 and 1983 the number of jobs in Telford's indigenous industries fell from 17,500 to a little over 10,000.[67]

As economic growth slowed, ambivalent policies at the Ministry of Housing and Local Government contributed to the evaporation of Birmingham's interest in the new town. As has been seen, the city's initial enthusiasm for Dawley had coincided with what seemed to be the final defeat of the ruling Labour group's plans for peripheral expansion. Even, however, as his ministry was insisting on Dawley's expansion as part of the *Regional Study*'s strategy,[68] Richard Crossman, following his own instincts[69] rather than Dame Evelyn Sharp's policies, was furthering developments incompatible with the *Study*: the resumption of Birmingham's peripheral expansion. He authorized building at Water Orton (Warws.) in 1964, and in 1966, alleging the *Study*'s failure to plan adequate provision of housing land in the early 1970s, he approved studies for the city's further expansion into north Worcestershire. The basis was thus laid for Birmingham's spectacular house-building programme of the later 1960s,[70] overshadowing those of all the city's overspill schemes put together, including the region's two new towns.[71] Although a Birmingham alderman was deputy chairman of Dawley development corporation 1963–8 and another chaired Telford development corporation 1968–71, Birmingham showed little practical interest in the new town.[72] W.T. Bowen, the Dawley deputy chairman,[73] and Sir Frank Price, the Telford chairman,[74] advocated dispersal of population from the city[75] but the Labour group, of which they were leading members, lost influence and cohesion after the Conservatives took control of Birmingham in 1966.[76] It became clear that overspill population and industry were coming to Telford primarily from the Black Country and not from Birmingham.[77] By 1968, moreover, industry was not coming at a satisfactory rate: there were many empty houses, and the prospect of hundreds more presaged a severe crisis.[78]

The crisis in industry and employment notwithstanding, indeed as perhaps the only conceivable way of retrieving the situation in the long term, the government expanded the new town's area in December 1968 to include Wellington and Oakengates.[79] Anthony Greenwood renamed it Telford[80] in honour of the great civil engineer[81] who, from 1788 to 1834, had been Shropshire's first county surveyor.[82] Telford, double the size of Dawley, was to take a further 50,000 people from the conurbation, and the population projected for the early 1990s was 220,000, almost treble that of the original Dawley plan.[83]

[64] Below, Hadley, Econ. Hist. (Engineering); Wombridge, Econ. Hist. (Iron and Steel).

[65] Local inf.

[66] *W. Midlands Studies*, v. 4, 6, 8.

[67] Ibid. 6, 10 n. 13; *The Times*, 24 Nov. 1983.

[68] Above.

[69] Oddly, they favoured the Conservatives' 1952 Act: Crossman, *Diaries*, i. 307.

[70] Incl. the Chelmsley Wood est. at Water Orton.

[71] Sutcliffe and Smith, *Birm. 1939–70*, 150–2, 231–3, and pl. facing p. 65.

[72] Private inf.

[73] And chmn. of a Birm. overspill subcttee.: Sutcliffe and Smith, op. cit. 136, 141; inf. from T.D.C.

[74] Sutcliffe and Smith, op. cit. 103, and pl. facing p. 209; *Who's Who* (1983), 1813.

[75] Sutcliffe and Smith, op. cit. 71, 151–2.

[76] Ibid. 87, 108.   [77] Private inf.

[78] Cullingworth, *New Towns Policy*, 264–5.

[79] Under the New Towns Act, 1965, c. 59: *Dawley New Town (Designation) Amendment (Telford) Order 1968* (Stat. Instr. 1968, no. 1912); cf. Cullingworth, op. cit. 262–3.

[80] Thomas, 'Telford', 29; *S.C.C. Mins.* 1968–9, 223; cf. Crossman, *Diaries*, i. 307.

[81] *D.N.B.*

[82] *V.C.H. Salop.* iii, frontispiece, 127–8, 361.

[83] Ibid. 220; Cullingworth, *New Towns Policy*, 173, 258 sqq.

Between Telford's designation and the publication of its Basic Plan in 1971[84] the industrial crisis became more acute.[85] While the falling rate of job creation in the new town in the 1960s[86] coincided with the beginning of a decline in the national economic growth rate, the new town suffered also from uncertainties caused by successive planning reappraisals and from the government's failure to honour its pledges to improve road communications with the conurbation. Nevertheless much the weightiest influence on the new town's economy was the inflexible regional policy of the Board of Trade (from 1970 the Department of Trade and Industry) in issuing industrial development certificates (I.D.C.s) for new premises for manufacturing industry.[87] The Board had opposed Dawley's designation, and almost continuously from 1963 to 1979 the Board and the Department restricted the new town's industrial recruitment area to the Birmingham conurbation: in effect, as Birmingham's interest was slight, to the Black Country. Even there I.D.C. policy gave recruiting priority to the assisted areas, and grants were available to induce firms to move to them in preference to the new towns. Between 1945 and 1963, however, the conurbation had exported 120,000 jobs, 100,000 of them outside the region, and by the later 1960s, contrary to the assumptions made during the planning of the new town, there was not enough mobile industry to fulfil plans for the new towns in addition to those for the assisted areas. As the national recession worsened, moreover, Black Country towns were increasingly anxious, and in terms of zoned industrial land increasingly able, to keep their industries. In the opinion of many the Department of Trade and Industry's policy made Telford the most disadvantaged new town. The new towns in Wales and the north of England were in assisted areas; on the other side of the conurbation Redditch's designation had had the Board of Trade's blessing from the outset while Milton Keynes (designated 1967), Peterborough (1967), and Northampton (1968), though not in the West Midlands region, were allowed to recruit industry from the whole of it. With the sole exception of Telford, the new towns outside the assisted areas lay east or south of Birmingham and benefited from proximity to, or easy communications with, London.[88]

During the crisis of the late 1960s an unprecedented application for intermediate assisted area status for Telford failed,[89] as did another in 1981.[90] Nevertheless the severity of Telford's employment crisis in 1968 persuaded the Board of Trade temporarily to relax its I.D.C. policy. Anthony Greenwood, with the corporation's chairman (Price) and officials, met Gwyneth Dunwoody, parliamentary secretary to the Board: Telford was agreed to be 'on the sick list', and an unofficial 'concordat' allowed Telford to recruit industry throughout the West Midlands region; it lasted into the early 1970s, just long enough to bring some large employers to Halesfield, the corporation's largest industrial estate, begun in 1967. Other large estates followed at Stafford Park (from 1973) and Hortonwood (from 1979), and half a million square metres of factory space were provided between 1968 and 1983, almost entirely on land made available by the corporation. A few firms built factories on ground leased from the corporation, but generally the corporation built standard factories for letting. Within the limits of I.D.C. policy, reimposed in the mid 1970s, the corporation marketed these speculative properties vigorously, and as the decade passed they began

[84] For the Plan see below.
[85] Private inf.   [86] Above.
[87] F. Schaffer, *The New Town Story* (1970), 105–8; *Town Planning Rev.* xliii. 351, 353–5, 357–9; *N. Staffs. Jnl. Field Studies*, xiii. 78; *Reorganisation of Central Govt.* [Cmnd. 4506], pp. 7 sqq., H.C. (1970–1), xx.
[88] Private inf.; Schaffer, op. cit. 112–13; Cullingworth,

New Towns Policy, 170–3; Tolley, 'Post-War Changes in E. Salop.' 195–204; Aldridge, *Brit. New Towns*, 2, 137 sqq., 149; Hall, *Containment of Urban Eng.* ii. 334, 336; *Town Planning Rev.* xliii. 351, 357.
[89] *Town Planning Rev.* xliii. 348; *S.C.C. Mins.* 1967–8, 324.
[90] *Reps. of Dev. Corporations 31 Mar. 1982*, H.C. 508, p. 339 (1981–2).

to outlast the ten years of I.D.C. control.[91] In 1979 moreover Telford was at last allowed to recruit manufacturing industry from virtually the whole West Midlands region.[92] Meanwhile in 1976, though the Department of Trade and Industry at first disapproved, Telford had begun to recruit industry from the U.S.A., Europe, and Japan. The foreign firms required larger factories, and they began to be built at Stafford Park, each one having to be fought for in the Department of Trade and Industry's regional office in Birmingham.[93] By 1983 over 2,000 jobs in Telford were provided by c. 40 foreign companies,[94] preponderantly American and many of them involved in high-technology industries rather than the metal-finishing industries characteristic of the Black Country.[95] The new arrivals included the American industrial robot manufacturer Unimation[96] and three firms from Japan: Nikon U.K. Ltd. (Instruments Division) opened a warehouse at Halesfield in 1983;[97] a factory near Apley Castle was built for Hitachi Maxell, video tape manufacturers, in 1983;[98] and that year Ricoh, office equipment manufacturers, took a 22-a. site for a factory at Priorslee adjoining the newly opened M 54, the first in Telford's new enterprise zone.[99]

Thus from the later 1970s, as it escaped I.D.C. controls, Telford began to attract high-technology firms and to diversify its industry. Service employment, outside I.D.C. controls, also increased. While they lasted the controls had confined the town's industrial recruitment to the Black Country and its typical metal trades, thus hindering realization of the changes to the area's industrial character proposed in 1964 by the ministry's planning consultants for Dawley: the establishment of modern industry alongside the old heavy manufactures. The consultants had then expected, as one of the most important concomitants of the 'steepening rate of technical advance', the 'spread of middle-class standards throughout the population'.[1] As the development corporation's recruitment task eased, however, a deepening national recession meant that, despite the creation of new jobs, there were net job losses from 1979 (Table I). Unemployment grew from 3.4 per cent in 1969 and 1970 to over 8 per cent in 1972 and 22.3 per cent (10,060 people) in 1983; long-term unemployment rose even faster, making forecasts of social change such as those of 1964 seem speculative; and attendant social stress was especially prominent in Woodside and a few other areas of both old and new housing. Nevertheless the rate of increase in unemployment was slowing down by 1983 and was making some progress against national and regional trends.[2]

Telford grew rapidly during the 1970s. Its population increased by 25,800, the number of jobs by 8,537 (7,166 of them on corporation industrial estates).[3] Three of the planned eight district centres—at Madeley, Stirchley, and Dawley—and eight housing estates served by them were completed. A ninth estate, Hollinswood, was built near Telford town centre, and much of the town centre itself was built during the decade on reclaimed land at Malinslee. From 1975[4] work on housing estates in

---

[91] Private inf.; Thomas, 'Telford', 36–7; Fenter, 'Bldg. Development in Telford'; *Reps. of Dev. Corporations 31 Mar. 1969*, H.C. 398, pp. 469–70 (1968–9), xliii; *31 Mar. 1983*, H.C. 81, p. 317 (1982–3); *Town Planning Rev.* xliii. 360 n. 52.

[92] Excl. Oswestry intermediate assisted area (designated 1971, abolished 1982: 815 *H.C. Deb.* 5th ser. 22; 970 *H.C. Deb.* 5th ser. 1302 sqq., *493–4*; 26 *H.C. Deb.* 6th ser. 611) and Birm. inner city partnership area (designated 1980: *Municipal Jnl.* 28 Mar. 1980): *Reps. of Dev. Corporations 31 Mar. 1979*, H.C. 289, pp. 456–7 (1979–80).

[93] Private inf.; below, plate 1.

[94] *The Times*, 24 Nov. 1983 (p. 22).

[95] Private inf.; *Reps. of Dev. Corporations 31 Mar. 1983*, 309.

[96] T.D.C. *Telford Ind. Dir.* [c. 1979], 28.

[97] Inf. from T.D.C.

[98] *Shropshire Star*, 12 Nov. 1983 (p. 3).

[99] Ibid. 24 Oct. 1983 (pp. 1, 6). For the zone see ibid. 16 Nov. 1982; 2 Dec. 1983 (p. 16).

[1] Madin, *Dawley Rep. No. 2: Interim Proposals*, para. 6:59.

[2] *N. Staffs. Jnl. Field Studies*, xiii. 78; *Telford Development Strategy: 6th Monitoring Rep.* (T.D.C. 1983), 8–12, 22–8; B. Trinder, *Hist. Salop.* (1983), 121; *Shropshire Star*, 10 Mar. 1982.

[3] Table I. For the ind. estates see above, for the rest of this para. see below.

[4] *Telford Observer*, 1 Nov. 1972.

north Telford began, and bypasses or ring roads were made at Oakengates, Hadley, and Wellington so that, as in the other district centres, old streets could be pedestrianized. From sewage works built at Gitchfield (commissioned 1970) and Rushmoor (1975) two main drainage systems were constructed during the decade to

TABLE I

TELFORD: POPULATION AND EMPLOYMENT 1968–83

Date	Population	Total jobs	Jobs on T.D.C. estates (with % of total)	
Dec. 1968	74,750	35,671	496	(1.4)
Sept. 1969	76,200	35,710	878	(2.4)
" 1970	78,200	35,948	1,835	(5.1)
" 1971	80,800	36,191	2,605	(7.2)
" 1972	84,200	36,743	3,411	(9.3)
" 1973	87,100	39,861	4,550	(11.4)
" 1974	89,000	40,928	5,404	(13.2)
" 1975	90,000	40,986	5,039	(12.3)
" 1976	93,980	42,036	6,259	(14.9)
" 1977	97,900	43,637	6,716	(15.4)
" 1978	100,300	44,681	7,500	(16.8)
" 1979	102,000	44,247	8,044	(18.2)
" 1980	104,200	42,397	7,773	(18.3)
" 1981	104,200	39,414	6,625	(16.8)
" 1982	106,600	38,852	7,051	(18.2)
" 1983	107,700	39,037	7,764	(19.9)

Sources: Telford Development Strategy: 1st Monitoring Rep.–7th Monitoring Rep. (T.D.C. 1978–84); (for no. of jobs on T.D.C. estates in 1978) T.D.C. Employment in Telford 1979 (1980), 20; no. of jobs on T.D.C. estates 1979–82 supplied or confirmed from T.D.C. bd. mtg. agenda 10 Nov. 1983 (management accts. 1983–4, physical projections, p. 12).

serve south and north Telford respectively, the scale of engineering work under Hill's Lane estate, Madeley, being comparable to that on a section of London's underground railway.[5] Other services—water, gas, electricity, and the telephone—were also reorganized,[6] and the construction of a new road system, designed to knit the town together, was undertaken.

While that growth was being achieved changes in government and regional planning policies continued to beset the new town. Even as the Dawley plan was being expanded into a plan for Telford in the late 1960s the strategy of the 1965 Regional Study, justifying that expansion, was being abandoned. In the 1950s and early 1960s industry and commerce, growing naturally within the conurbation, had resisted dispersal,[7] and the Study had not dealt in detail with the provision of employment in the overspill areas.[8] In 1967 'senior government officials' asked the West Midlands

[5] i.e. to London Transport's Victoria line, built at the same time: private inf.
[6] Private inf.; Reps. of Dev. Corporations 31 Mar. 1969, 471.
[7] Hall, Containment of Urban Eng. i. 532–4.
[8] Sutcliffe and Smith, Birm. 1939–70, 151.

planning authorities to produce a planning study for the conurbation and 'a wide surrounding area'. The result, published in 1971 and accepted for the new[9] Department of the Environment by Geoffrey Rippon in 1974, was a 'preferred strategy' of growth south and east of Birmingham, in an arc stretching from Droitwich in the south to Tamworth in the north and including Redditch new town and outliers at Bedworth (near the M 6) and Daventry (near the M 1);[10] the arc coincided with the route planned for the M 42 motorway,[11] whose first section was completed in 1976.[12] Growth, assisted by improved commuter rail services, was thus planned to occur in Birmingham's satellite towns in a way that (as the 1965 *Study* had reluctantly recognized) least disrupted people's lives or the region's economic efficiency.[13] Birmingham's peripheral expansion was readily absorbed into the altered regional planning strategy accepted in 1974. On the other hand, though the commitment to develop Telford remained, the strategy was unfavourable to Telford,[14] on the far side of the conurbation and still without the long-promised improvement in road communications, defined in 1969 as a motorway link to the M 6.[15]

The 1965 *Regional Study* had foreseen a Telford population of 280,000 by 1981, a forecast lowered in 1971 to 153,100 and lowered further in 1973.[16] In 1975 the population target was fixed at *c.* 150,000 by 1986.[17] The deepening national recession and the implications of a sharply declining national birth rate were the main influences on the downward revision of the town's population target but they were not the only ones. The development corporation had always set its face against 'high rise' building, and internal studies in the 1970s showed that high density development, characteristic of the second-generation new towns, was implied in the population projections of the late 1960s;[18] low density development suggested to the corporation a town with an 'eventual' capacity of the order of 180,000.[19] In the mid 1970s, as the implications of those studies were becoming apparent, Telford, in common with the other new towns, was overtaken by a new set of national planning priorities formulated by the Labour government as concern increased for the physical and social problems accumulating in the centres of old towns and cities.[20] In 1977 Peter Shore, secretary of state for the Environment, announced winding-up dates for new town corporations and lowered the population targets for their towns. Telford development corporation was to be wound up in 1986, when the town's population should have reached 130,000 with an increase to 150,000 foreseen for the following ten years.[21] That autumn, in accordance with Shore's requirements, the corporation produced a ten-year Development Strategy to carry the town through its final phase of induced growth and beyond.[22] Compared with the Basic Plan of 1971 it represented a 'drawing back from the edges'.[23]

The Basic Plan[24] had assigned areas of agricultural or derelict land around

[9] *Public Administration*, lix. 135–7.
[10] W. Midland Regional Study, *A Developing Strategy for the W. Midlands* (1971), pp. 75 sqq., and fig. 18; 'A Developing Strategy for the W. Midlands': *Rep. of W. Midlands Planning Authorities' Conf.* (1974).
[11] Hall, *Containment of Urban Eng.* i. 506.
[12] *Policy for Roads: Eng. 1978* [Cmnd. 7132], p. 38, H.C. (1977–8), iv.
[13] *Developing Strategy* (1971), pp. 75 sqq.; Dept. of Econ. Affairs, *W. Midlands regional study*, 64, 66.
[14] 'Developing Strategy': *Rep.* (1974), pp. 14–17, and fig. 27; Thomas, 'Telford', 26, 39–40.
[15] *Town Planning Rev.* xliii. 353. Part was opened in 1975 (*Shropshire Star*, 10 Dec. 1975), the rest in 1983 (below).
[16] Dept. of Econ. Affairs, *W. Midlands regional study*, 73; *Developing Strategy* (1971), p. 92; 'Developing Strategy': *Rep.* (1974), pp. 15–16.

[17] *The Guardian*, 20 Aug. 1975.
[18] e.g. Madin's *Dawley: Wellington: Oakengates* (1966).
[19] Private inf.; cf. Thomas, 'Telford', 17–18.
[20] *Policy for the Inner Cities* [Cmnd. 6845], H.C. (1976–7), xliv; Aldridge, *Brit. New Towns*, 150 sqq.
[21] T.D.C., Constitutional Doc. viii; 929 *H.C. Deb.* 5th ser. 1112.
[22] T.D.C. *Telford Development Strategy* (1977).
[23] Inf. (1977) from Mr. J. F. Boyce, then dep. gen. manager T.D.C.
[24] Thomas, 'Telford', 29–36, 41. Para. based on T.D.C. *Telford Basic Plan Proposals* (1970); T.D.C. *Telford Basic Plan* [map 1970]; T.D.C. *Telford Development Strategy* (1977); *Telford Development Strategy: 1st–7th Monitoring Rep.* (T.D.C. 1978–84); T.D.C. *Telford in the 1980's* [1980]; T.D.C. *Telford Street Plan* (1981); S.C.C. *Mins.* 1982–3, 275–6; inf. from T.D.C. and from S.C.C. Planning Dept.

Wellington and Admaston, north of Hadley, and north and east of Oakengates and St. George's, for housing in five northern residential districts and for industry; it had shifted the new town centre north-west from the area around Stone Row to that around Malinslee Hall; and it had extended Dawley's horseshoe loop of primary roads into a 15-km. ring road bisected by the motorway link (M 54) to the M 6 and flanked by a subsidiary box of roads to the north-east. The Plan had been modified in the early 1970s when plans to locate industry at Leegomery and housing at Hortonwood were transposed; at the same time an industrial area planned for Lightmoor had been dropped owing to the cost of providing main drainage there. Shore's reductions of the population target modified the Plan further, and the 1977 Development Strategy eliminated house building during the development corporation's life from several areas around the town's northern and eastern edges: between Wrockwardine Bank and Admaston; at Bratton; at Donnington Wood, where the corporation's land reclamation in the early 1980s ended at Lodge Road, the area to the south being left to the district council; at Priorslee, where a proposed district centre was deferred indefinitely; and at Nedge Hill.

A transportation study, prepared in the mid 1970s, had also to be accommodated to the Development Strategy. A revision of it assessed the reduction in traffic resulting from the modifications to the Basic Plan. Dawley, designated in the year that saw the Beeching Report and *Traffic in Towns* published, had been conceived around a system and hierarchy of roads connected to the main national routes. Not surprisingly therefore one of the revised transportation study's main effects was to reduce the town's planned road network: the western part of the primary ring road was abandoned, though some sections were built to reduced specifications as local roads. The planned ring road thus became a cross formed by the eastern primary road and the M 54 intersecting near the town centre. Local public transport was to consist of bus services run by the Midland Red Omnibus Co. Throughout the new town's existence, however, the private car had everywhere been undermining the economy of public transport,[25] and over the 78 square kilometres of scattered settlement in Telford bus services were unlikely to run profitably or with full efficiency before the town reached its planned population.[26] Meanwhile, in the early 1980s, expressions of dissatisfaction with the services[27] pointed to the relative impoverishment of those without private transport in a town formed from widely scattered settlements and at a time when car ownership remained as universal an aspiration as ever and as potent an influence on urban planning.[28] The railway's rôle in Telford had greatly diminished. Much of the area's network of old branch lines had closed even before the Beeching Report appeared,[29] and in 1967 the Paddington–Birkenhead line was downgraded;[30] few but local services (between Wolverhampton, Shrewsbury, and Chester) ran through Telford thereafter. Nevertheless Shrewsbury–Euston intercity passenger services were introduced, picking up at Wellington, and the construction of a Telford central station remained an important part of the town centre plan to be achieved during the corporation's existence.[31]

In 1981 Shore's Conservative successor as secretary of state for the Environment,

[25] C. Buchanan & Partners, *Telford Transportation Study: Summary Rep. and Basic Plan* (T.D.C. May 1977); idem, *Telford Transportation Study: Review* (T.D.C. Oct. 1977); inf. from T.D.C.; Thomas, 'Telford', 19–20, 30; cf. Aldridge, *Brit. New Towns*, 126.

[26] Buchanan, *Transportation Study: Rev.*; private inf.; *Shropshire Star*, 17 Apr. 1979.

[27] Local inf.; cf. *Redditch Indicator*, 8 Aug. 1975.

[28] Cf. Buchanan, *Transportation Study: Rev.*; Sir C. D.

Buchanan in *The Times*, 23 Nov. 1983 (p. 10); Aldridge, *Brit. New Towns*, 127–8.

[29] Brit. Rlys. Bd. *Reshaping of Brit. Rlys. Pt. I: Rep.* (1963), 130–3; F. J. Osborn and A. Whittick, *New Towns: Their Origins, Achievements and Progress* (1977), 345.

[30] R. Christiansen, *W. Midlands* (Regional Hist. of Rlys. of Gt. Brit. vii, 1973), 260.

[31] Local inf.; T.D.C. *Telford in the 1980's*, 9; *Shropshire Star*, 12 Jan. 1984 (p. 17).

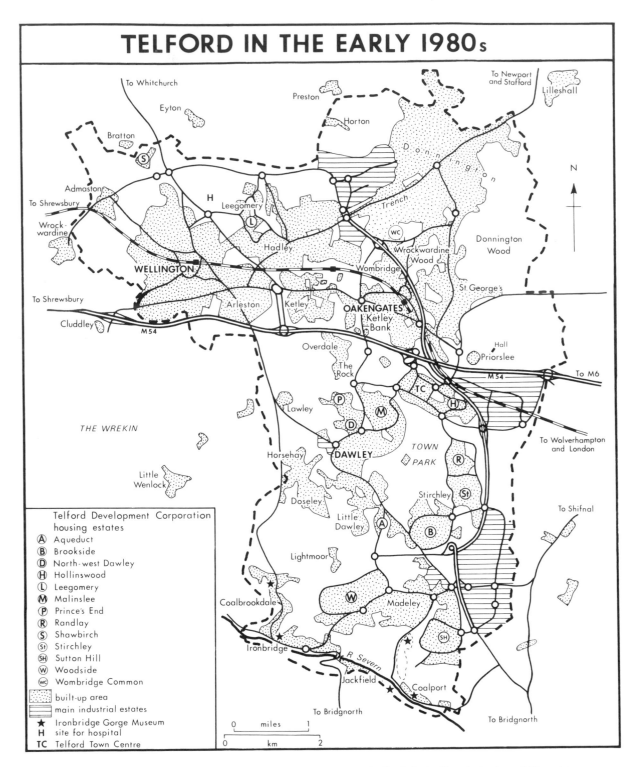

TELFORD IN THE EARLY 1980s

Telford Development Corporation housing estates

Ⓐ Aqueduct
Ⓑ Brookside
Ⓓ North-west Dawley
Ⓗ Hollinswood
Ⓛ Leegomery
Ⓜ Malinslee
Ⓟ Prince's End
Ⓡ Randlay
Ⓢ Shawbirch
Ⓢ̲ᵗ Stirchley
Ⓢ̲ᴴ Sutton Hill
Ⓦ Woodside
ⓌC Wombridge Common

built-up area
main industrial estates
★ Ironbridge Gorge Museum
H site for hospital
TC Telford Town Centre

The industrial estates shown are Halesfield, Heath Hill, Hortonwood, Stafford Park, Trench Lock, and Tweedale.

Michael Heseltine, confirmed what had already become clear, that the development corporation's life was to be prolonged to 'the late 1980s' and that Telford's population target should no longer be a target: population growth was to depend essentially on demand for private housing.[32] The significance of the statement should not be obscured by the fact that the corporation had fostered private house building in the 1970s to achieve a long-term balance in the town between public rented housing and owner-occupation nor by the government-stimulated sale of corporation houses to tenants, which would also contribute to the desired balance.[33] The statement marked the virtual end of building public housing for rent, and it restricted further public investment to the minimum needed to support further growth. In north Telford, developed from 1975, rented corporation housing was much less significant than in the south; the corporation's only considerable housing schemes in the northern area were those at Wombridge Common (165 dwellings 1975–8), Leegomery (1,059 dwellings 1978–c. 1981), and Shawbirch (178 dwellings completed by 1982). Together the northern estates amounted to little more than the corporation's first one at Sutton Hill, and Shawbirch was regarded in 1982 as the corporation's last foreseeable major scheme.[34]

In the early 1980s the most serious effects of the reductions defined by Shore and Heseltine were felt in the central areas of Telford, where the lack of building west and north of the town centre marked a break in the town's physical cohesion. The knitting together of north and south was seen as one of the corporation's most urgent remaining tasks; building at Old Park, the Rock, Lawley, and also at Priorslee was the principal means of fulfilling it; and the commitment of resources to induce growth to 130,000 and to plan for a mature town of 150,000 was the essential precondition. Those aspirations suffered a setback after the abolition of a population target and the cessation of building houses for rent in 1981.[35] Certainly by 1983 it was widely accepted that Telford's population might not reach 120,000 before its corporation was wound up,[36] a state of affairs not primarily due to the ministerial statements of 1977 and 1981. Nor was building at Old Park, which would have had the additional advantage of completing the town centre's urban surroundings, or the Rock immediately feasible: land reclamation there, having been delayed by the suspension of the Dawley plan after 1965, was too recent in 1983 to allow large-scale building for some years to come.[37]

By 1981 the government had caused the new town's plan to be suspended or fundamentally changed four times in sixteen years. During that time the primary objective of the new town changed from taking conurbation overspill to becoming a regional economic 'growth point'. Its secondary purpose was emphasized even more. The reclamation and rehabilitation of a derelict and depressed area was essential to promote new growth;[38] and it harmonized with the government's concern for reversing the decay of old areas. Not surprisingly the causes and logic of the changes were not always apparent to outside observers. Telford's purpose and identity seemed difficult to perceive, and for some the town's lineaments were blurred by the fact that designs and plans incorporated in its early phases were later modified.[39] Sutton Hill, Woodside, and most of Brookside for instance were laid out with separate

[32] 998 *H.C. Deb.* 5th ser. 291; private inf.
[33] Private inf.
[34] Below, Hadley, intro.; Wellington, Growth of Settlement; Wombridge, Growth of Settlement.
[35] *Telford in the 1980's*, 5, 18; T.D.C. bd. mtg. agenda 10 Nov. 1983 (management accts. 1983–4, physical projections, p. 1); cf. map on facing p.
[36] Private inf.
[37] *Town Planning Rev.* xliii. 354–5; inf. from S.C.C. Planning Dept. Cf. below, plate 32.   [38] Private inf.
[39] See e.g. Thomas, 'Telford', 18, 28–9, 34, 37–8; T.D.C. *Telford in the 1980's*, 1–3, 23; Trinder, *Hist. Salop.* 121.

pedestrian and vehicle routes,[40] but from 1974, despite initial opposition from the county surveyor,[41] the Radburn principle[42] was modified to produce a less conventional design for Brookside's fourth phase.[43] The change was incorporated in the design of Stirchley and Randlay estates, even though they were confined by the perimeter roads that had been put out to contract as a whole in the difficult period after 1965, when the new town's future had seemed uncertain. On Hollinswood and later estates[44] cul-de-sacs off sinuous 'spinal' roads served people and vehicles well and made better use of land. It was also at Brookside, Stirchley, Hollinswood, and Randlay that the philosophy of the Plowden Report, favouring two tiers of primary education, determined the county council's school building in the 1970s.[45]

Local diversity persisted, but the town acquired its own character and was enriched by successful experiments. On the corporation's estates around Madeley for instance the churches' work was furthered by pastoral centres, and that at Brookside, like Stirchley new church, was a particularly successful example of interdenominational co-operation, the good Anglican–Methodist relations at Brookside recalling an intrinsic theme of Madeley's history.[46] The corporation's links with the churches were maintained by its social development department,[47] which helped them to plan their strategies within the new town. In 1970 the Methodist church reorganized its old circuits to make two new ones called Telford South and Telford North; Telford South circuit later concluded a £100,000 deal with the corporation to rid itself of eight old churches and achieve a new 'strategic presence' for Methodists in the town.[48] The dioceses of Lichfield and Hereford had originally agreed that the whole of Dawley new town should be in Hereford; though the plan was dropped after the new town's enlargement was proposed[49] the dioceses nevertheless co-operated within Telford: in 1971 and 1972 they created rural deaneries named Telford and Telford Severn Gorge respectively,[50] and in Telford deanery a new parish of Central Telford was made in 1975.[51] Many ventures fostered by the social development department[52] brought the name Telford into wider currency: societies and voluntary organizations, notably the town's leading football club in 1969,[53] incorporated it in their titles, and from 1974 the Wrekin and Telford Festival became an important event for a wide surrounding area.[54] Also with encouragement from the corporation the Dawley and Oakengates chambers of commerce combined in 1970 to form the Telford chamber; the Wellington chamber's decision to remain separate indicated continued dissatisfaction with the supersession of Wellington's proposed central redevelopment by Telford town centre.[55]

Whatever headway the name Telford made in general and ecclesiastical use, for secular administrative purposes official usage restricted it to the new town; it did not figure on the local-government map. At designation Dawley new town had included Dawley urban district, a small part of Oakengates U.D., and parts of Shifnal and Wellington rural districts and of the municipal borough of Wenlock.[56] Dawley new

[40] Fenter, 'Bldg. Development in Telford'.
[41] *Shropshire Star*, 27 Feb. 1975.
[42] Ministry of Transport, *Traffic in Towns* (1963), 222; *D.N.B.* 1922–30, s.v. Howard, Sir Ebenezer.
[43] T.D.C. *Roads in Urban Areas: Brookside 4* (1974).
[44] Notably Malinslee and Leegomery: private inf.
[45] Cf. Central Advisory Council for Educ., Eng., *Children and their Primary Schs.* (1967); below, Dawley, Educ.; Madeley, Educ.; Stirchley, Educ.
[46] Below, Madeley, Churches; Prot. Nonconf.; Stirchley, Churches; Nonconf.; cf. below, Madeley, Educ., for John Fletcher (Controlled) Jnr. Sch.
[47] Inf. from T.D.C.
[48] Cf. S.R.O. 4286/6/4; /12/1; *Shropshire Star*, 25 July

1970; *Methodist Recorder*, 2 Aug. 1979.
[49] S.R.O. 3937/9/1–2.
[50] Inf. from Preb. C. Hill, dean of both since 1980.
[51] Below, Dawley, Churches.
[52] For the dept.'s work see e.g. G. Brooke Taylor, 'Telford's social relations dept.' *Town and Country Planning*, xxxvii. 17–22; *Telford Social Trends*, i, ed. J. MacGuire (T.D.C. 1980).
[53] Below, Wellington, Social and Cultural Activities.
[54] Below, Wombridge, Social and Cultural Activities.
[55] *Telford Observer*, 25 Feb. 1970; *Shropshire Star*, 7 May, 30 Oct. 1975.
[56] *Dawley New Town (Designation) Order 1963*, and accompanying map (copy in S.R.O. 2981, parcel VI).

town was wholly in Dawley U.D. 1966–8, but when Telford was created Oakengates U.D., most of Wellington U.D., and wide areas of Wellington R.D. were also included in the new town.[57] The area's urban and rural districts[58] and the whole of the new town were included in a new district from 1974, but that extended north as far as Newport and Chetwynd and was called the Wrekin,[59] the name used since 1918 for the county's eastern parliamentary constituency.[60] Even when a new parliamentary borough constituency virtually conterminous with Telford was recommended in 1979, the name proposed for it was still the Wrekin;[61] and when, between 1978 and 1982, Wrekin district council worked out a scheme for new and altered civil parishes, the name Telford was not proposed for any of them.[62]

Despite the apparently indefinite postponement of Telford's physical unity and of the maturing of its frequently modified plan, and despite the incompleteness of its institutional identity, the vast changes wrought in the area had gone far enough by 1984 to fix the plan's physical lineaments and so to indicate the ways in which it would eventually be completed. In particular three features seemed to unite Telford and establish its identity: the high quality of the corporation's landscape improvements, enhanced by the beauty of Telford's natural setting; the town centre; and the town's road system.

Extensive industrial dereliction within the new town sullied the splendour of a natural setting dominated by the Wrekin and opening out into awesome prospects along the Severn Gorge. So great were the problems of reclamation that, uniquely among new towns Dawley, later Telford, had a landscape structure plan ranking equally with its basic development plan.[63] By 1983, mainly in the 1970s and early 1980s,[64] 1,231 ha. of derelict land had been reclaimed and 1,295 mine shafts had been treated, almost entirely by the development corporation. Much remained to be done: another 900 ha. of derelict land for reclamation and over 1,600 mine shafts for treatment.[65] Much of the reclaimed land was destined for housing, industry, and roads, but a second objective was to penetrate the town with areas of semi-wild, wooded landscape, crossed by footpaths and cheap to maintain.[66] The centrepiece of the plan was Telford town park laid out in the mid 1970s. Extending over 182 ha. between Dawley, Stirchley, and the town centre[67] the park recalled, albeit on the larger scale typical of second- and third-generation new towns, the central feature of Ebenezer Howard's original conception of the 'social city'.[68] Southwards from the park the Silkin Way footpath, opened in 1977,[69] led to extensive areas of open space for recreation. In those parts the natural beauty and historic remains of Coalbrookdale and the Severn Gorge were protected and conserved and, emphasizing the area's historic significance, the internationally celebrated Ironbridge Gorge Museum of industrial archaeology was built up from 1967. In Coalbrookdale the museum combined with the University of Birmingham to create the Institute of Industrial

[57] V.C.H. Salop. ii. 235–7; iii. 168–9, 220; Dawley New Town (Designation) Amendment (Telford) Order 1968, map accompanying Explanatory Note.

[58] All of which had discussed amalgamation at various times in the post-war yrs.: Wellington Jnl. 8 May 1948; Shrews. Chron. 26 Jan. 1950; 6 Jan., 28 Sept. 1956; S.R.O., DA 6/119/1, pp. 20–1, 26.

[59] Sources cited in V.C.H. Salop. iii. 169 n. 29.

[60] V.C.H. Salop. iii. 344, 354.

[61] The eventual Wrekin boro. constituency incl. Newport and more of the rural parts of Wrekin dist.: cf. S.C.C. Mins. 1979–80, 18–20; Parl. Constituencies (Eng.) Order 1983 (Stat. Instr. 1983, no. 417).

[62] Dist. of Wrekin Council, Parish Review (June 1982).

[63] I. J. Brown, 'Mineral Working and Land Reclamation in the Coalbrookdale Coalfield' (Leicester Univ. Ph.D. thesis, 1975); M. Whitcut, 'Derelict Land and Reclamation Problems in Telford', Chartered Land and Minerals Surveyor, iii (2), 3–26; Town Planning Rev. xliii. 347; Thomas, 'Telford', 30–3.

[64] Town Planning Rev. xliii. 354–5.

[65] S.C.C. Mins. 1982–3, 275–6; T.D.C. Derelict Land and Reclamation Problems in Telford New Town: Outline, Origins and Solution (1978).

[66] Telford in the 1980's, 15–16.

[67] Telford Observer, 11 Oct., 1 Nov. 1972; map on p. 14.

[68] Hall, Containment of Urban Eng. ii. 337–8; Aldridge, Brit. New Towns, pl. 1–2.

[69] Shropshire Star, 1 Apr. 1977; Telford and Wrekin News, June 1977.

Archaeology, a collaboration which in 1984, when an M.A. course was offered, seemed to renew the town's earlier aspirations to be a seat of higher education.[70]

By 1983 Telford's ten-year-old town centre was helping greatly to crystallize the town's identity and to establish its future rôle in the region and the county. The first phase, two large supermarkets and 23 other shops, opened in 1973.[71] Expansion continued and the second phase was opened by Elizabeth II in 1981.[72] Plans for later phases then included the building of smaller shops with offices over them for specialized and professional services.[73] By 1983, besides a wide range of shops in covered malls easily accessible from nearby car parks, the centre also included offices and leisure facilities. Wrekin district council established its headquarters in the first office block, Malinslee House, opened in 1976.[74] Other offices followed, and in 1981–2 the national computer centre of the Inland Revenue P.A.Y.E. branch was built there;[75] the speed with which it was authorized and built[76] indicated the corporation's determination to miss no chance of stimulating Telford's growth as a service centre and of demonstrating its suitability as a town for high-technology operations. In 1984 new police headquarters and magistrates' courts were being built on the west towards the ridge that concealed the empty site of Old Park beyond. The corporation aimed also to concentrate the main indoor leisure facilities at the town centre and so make it the focus of Telford's social life.[77] Other authorities, however, had plans or existing facilities that modified corporation policy in that respect. In the late 1970s Wrekin district council intended the phased construction of a combined sports, arts, and community centre in Wellington, the fruit of which was a new swimming pool, opened in 1981.[78] Nor had the corporation any real option but to recognize that enlargement of Oakengates town hall, which was begun with corporation help in 1983,[79] was the only practicable way of providing a large auditorium in Telford.[80] Other social and recreational facilities did, however, begin to rise in Telford town centre. The corporation built the West Midlands Tennis and Racquet Centre there, opened in 1983 and immediately the scene of major events. An ice-skating rink was being built in 1984; unlike the tennis centre, which was let to a commercial concern, the rink was to be run by Wrekin district council.[81] Corporation and county council plans for a town centre library were at last approved in 1984;[82] the library was to be included in a building planned as Meeting Point House, which would also contain meeting rooms and conference facilities.[83]

Telford's road system and motorway link had always been central to the town's design and to the plans for its growth. The new roads linked old and new settlements and, by separating through and local traffic, greatly reduced the time taken to travel about the town. Local bitterness at the very long delay in completing the M 54 gave way to optimism about its effects on the town when, late in 1983, Telford was finally provided with its most important missing feature and the essential means of promoting its economic growth.[84]

---

[70] Inf. from I.G.M.T.; below, Madeley, intro.; Social and Cultural Activities. For the proposed univ. (soon abandoned following a change of govt. policy: cf. *Wellington Jnl.* 12 Feb. 1965; *Birm. Post,* 29 June 1968) see above.

[71] Below, Dawley, Econ. Hist.

[72] *Telford Jnl.* 30 Oct., 13 Nov. 1981; *Shropshire Star,* 13–14 Nov. 1981.

[73] *Telford Jnl.* 30 Oct. 1981.

[74] Below, Dawley, Econ. Hist. (Telford town centre); *Estates Gaz.* 6 Dec. 1975 (p. 714); below, plate 2.

[75] *Shropshire Star,* 26 Aug. 1981.   [76] Private inf.

[77] *Telford in the 1980's,* 7–11.

[78] Below, Wellington, Social and Cultural Activities; cf.

Shropshire Star, 1 July 1977.

[79] *Telford Jnl.* 19 Oct. 1979; 11 Sept. 1981; local inf.

[80] *Telford in the 1980's,* 14, 22; cf. below, Wombridge Social and Cultural Activities.

[81] *Telford Jnl.* 11 Sept. 1981; *Shropshire Star,* 21 Dec. 1983; inf. from T.D.C.

[82] S.R.O., S.C.C. Leisure Activities Cttee. mins. 17 June, 7 Oct. 1983; *Shropshire Star,* 19 Jan. 1984; *S.C.C. Mins.* 1983–4, 181–2.

[83] *Telford in the 1980's,* 10–11, 21; inf. from T.D.C.

[84] *The Times,* 24 Nov. 1983; *Shropshire Star,* 25 Nov. 1983; cf. T.D.C. *Telford Development Strategy* (1977), p. 18; Thomas, 'Telford', 9–10, 29; *Telford in the 1980's,* 2, 9.

TELFORD

At the beginning of 1984 the development corporation completed 21 years of existence. It had inherited an area grievously blighted by over two and a half centuries of mining and heavy industry. It had removed the worst of the dereliction, but as it did so the coal and iron industries collapsed, leaving a new legacy of very high unemployment; hopes that it would not become chronic were founded on the importation to the area of modern industry based on advanced technology. In little over fifteen years changes had been made on a scale and at a speed greater than the coalfield had ever previously known and, united for the first time as one town, the area was given the opportunity to discover a new identity while cultivating pride in the traditions of its industrial past.

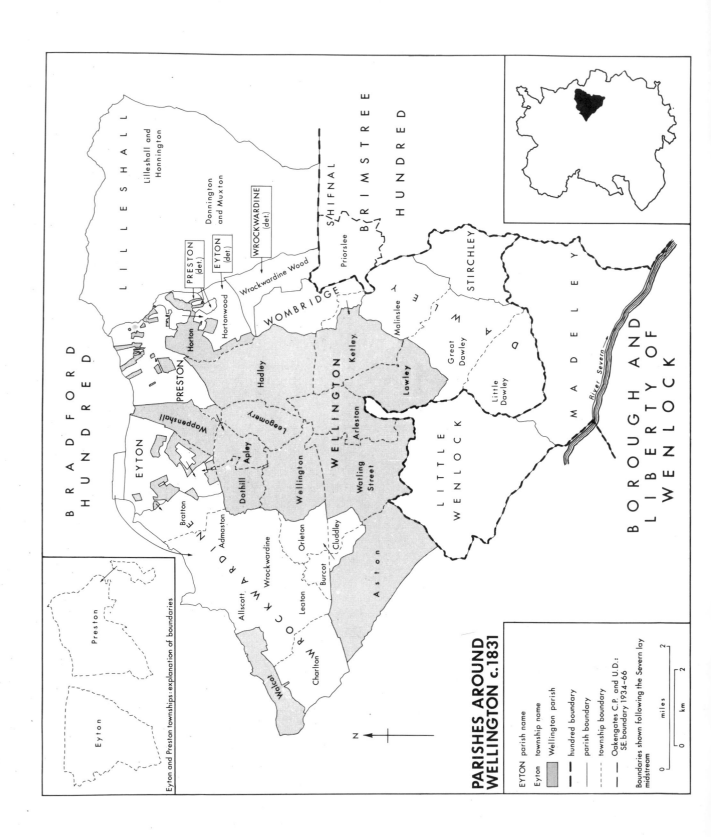

PARISHES AROUND WELLINGTON c.1831

LILLESHALL

Lilleshall and Honnington

Donnington and Muxton

PRESTON (det.)

EYTON (det.)

WROCKWARDINE (det.)

SHIFNAL

B R I M S T R E E   H U N D R E D

Priorslee

Wrockwardine Wood

WOMBRIDGE

Hortonwood

Horton

Malinslee

STIRCHLEY

Hadley

Ketley

Great Dawley

B R A D F O R D   H U N D R E D

PRESTON

Leegomery

Wappenshall

WELLINGTON

Lawley

Little Dawley

M A D E L E Y

River Severn

EYTON

Apley

Dothill

Wellington

Arleston

Watling Street

Aston

LITTLE WENLOCK

Bratton

Admaston

Wrockwardine

Orleton

Cluddley

Burcot

W R O C K W A R D I N E

Allscott

Leaton

B O R O U G H   A N D   L I B E R T Y   O F   W E N L O C K

Walcot

Charlton

N

Preston

Eyton

Eyton and Preston townships: explanation of boundaries

EYTON   parish name

Eyton   township name

Wellington parish

— · — ·   hundred boundary

————   parish boundary

- - - - -   township boundary

— · · —   Oakengates C.P. and U.D.:
SE boundary 1934–66

Boundaries shown following the Severn lay midstream

0   miles   2

0   km   2

THE LIBERTY AND BOROUGH OF WENLOCK

(part)

THE HISTORIES given below of Madeley and Little Wenlock conclude the topographical account of the liberty and borough of Wenlock. The two parishes, lying north of the river Severn, formed part of the municipal borough until 1966. Histories of the other parishes which once formed part of the liberty and borough, with a general account of the liberty and of the borough's government, will be found in Volume X.

MADELEY
INCLUDING COALBROOKDALE, COALPORT, AND IRONBRIDGE

Communications, p. 23. Growth of Settlement, p. 27. Social and Cultural Activities, p. 32. Manor and Other Estates, p. 35. Economic History, p. 40. Local Government, p. 56. Public Services, p. 58. Churches, p. 59. Roman Catholicism, p. 66. Protestant Nonconformity, p. 67. Education, p. 72. Charities for the Poor, p. 76.

THE POPULOUS parish of Madeley was an area of old industry and extensive farm land. It was largely built over in the 1960s and 1970s after the inclusion of most of it in 1963 within Dawley (from 1968 Telford) new town. The ancient parish contained 2,841 a.[1] (1,151 ha.) and extended just over 6 km. from west to east. It was wedge-shaped, wider in the eastern half which contained the original settlement. Madeley town lay 1 km. west of the crossing of the roads from Worcester (and Bridgnorth) to Wellington and from Shifnal to Much Wenlock, equidistant (8½ km.) from Wellington to the north-west and Much Wenlock to the south-west. Until 1966, when it was absorbed into Dawley urban district and civil parish, the whole parish formed part of the borough of Wenlock and its boundaries remained those of the ancient parish, the area here treated.

The parish was bounded on the south for just over 6 km. by the Severn, flowing for most of that distance through the Severn Gorge. Much of the northern boundary (with Dawley) was formed by the Loamhole and Lightmoor brooks, much of

the eastern boundary (with Kemberton and Sutton Maddock) by the Mad brook and a stream draining into the Severn at Coalport. The western boundary was marked in part by the Birches brook and a sunken lane,[2] but in the 13th century additional definition there had been provided by linear clearings through the woodland extending into Little Wenlock.[3]

The central part of the parish is a plateau defined by the deeply incised Coalbrookdale (valley of the Caldebrook)[4] on the west, Lightmoor dingle on the north, and Washbrook valley on the east. The land rises to over 152 m. above the steep slopes of the Severn Gorge and then slopes gently down to the north. West of Coalbrookdale the land is hilly. From Blists Hill, east of the Washbrook valley, the land falls steeply southwards but more gently northwards to the Mad brook.

Productive Middle and Lower Coal Measures underlie most of the parish. They dip towards the east and are exposed in the Severn Gorge. Thinning beds of Upper Coal Measures siltstones (Coalport Formation) and marl (Hadley Formation), with sandstones, occur at Coalport, in the

---

[1] O.S. *Area Bk.* (1883). This art. was written 1980–2 and revised 1983. Mr. J. B. Lawson and Dr. M. D. G. Wanklyn are thanked for drawing attention to some sources cited below, Communications; Econ. Hist. Help and advice was also given by the Revd. A. G. Kinch (Prot. Nonconf.), the Revd. A. J. Nicholson (Rom. Cath.), and the Revd. V. J. Price and the Revd. W. A. Zwalf (Churches).

[2] For this and the next para. see O.S. Map 1/25,000, 33/70

(1951 edn.), SJ 60 (1957 edn.). For the brooks and their names see S.P.L., Deeds 8201; D. H. Robinson, *The Wandering Worfe* (1980), 78; M. E. R. Jackson, 'Notes on Hist. of Madeley' (microfilm in S.P.L.), bk. 2A, p. 117; S.R.O. 690/13.

[3] Below, Econ. Hist. (Agric.).

[4] E. Ekwall, *Concise Oxf. Dict. Eng. Place-Names* (4th edn.), 114.

21

Washbrook valley, north of Park Lane and Park Street, and around the western edge of the productive coalfield in a crescent from Woodside to Madeley Wood. The drift cover is mainly boulder clay, but sands and gravels occur around Cuckoo Oak, Hills Lane, and Blists Hill in the east and near Lodge and Strethill farms in the west. There are alluvial deposits in the lower part of Coalbrookdale and westwards along the Severn. Lincoln Hill on the east side of Coalbrookdale is a spectacular outcrop of Silurian limestone.[5] The steep slopes of the Severn Gorge and of Coalbrookdale are geologically unstable and landslips are common; mining subsidence also affects the area.[6]

Suggestions of prehistoric or Roman roads through the parish[7] seem to be based on no strong evidence:[8] a flint arrowhead and a find of four Roman coins of the 3rd–4th centuries[9] seem insufficient to set aside the likelihood that Madeley was first settled in cleared woodland[10] some time before the mid 8th century.[11] Madeley acquired a market and fair in the later 13th century and a 'new town' was laid out east of the original settlement. Coal was being mined by 1322, ironstone by 1540.

A hoard of early 17th-century coins was found in Madeley Wood in 1839, and the area was of some strategic importance during the Civil War.[12] There was a royalist garrison in Madeley in February 1645 but it was abandoned after the fall of Shrewsbury later that month.[13] Two months later the parish church was garrisoned by a Parliamentarian troop.[14] In 1648 the county committee was alerted to prevent the occupation of Madeley Court by royalist conspirators.[15] After the battle of Worcester in 1651 Charles II passed a night and a day (4–5 September) in Francis Wolfe's barn at Upper House.[16]

A Rogationtide procession, presumably to beat the bounds, was still observed, with ale and 'a collation' in the late 17th and early 18th century.[17]

Though its minerals were exploited on an increasingly large scale from the earlier 17th century, the parish remained predominantly agricultural in the later 17th century with, in 1660, a range of trades appropriate to a small market town: mercer, tailors, glover, butchers, carpenters, coopers, bowyer, and smiths. In the late 17th century some of the tradesmen began to specialize in work for the mines and the river trade. There were also several gentlemen and clergymen, others of no stated occupation, and numbers of servants.[18]

The industrial population c. 1660 was small, perhaps not exceeding three dozen, consisting chiefly of colliers and trowmen with a few skilled workers and probably some labourers.[19] By the early 18th century, however, the growing number of industrial workers was becoming an increasingly distinct component of the population: the furnace men were the only parishioners to work on Sundays,[20] and in the church a miners' gallery was built. J. W. Fletcher, vicar 1760–85, deplored the spiritual consequences of industrial work,[21] and in times of distress riot and disorder were feared, sometimes with good reason.[22] As the manorial estate was broken up from 1705 cottage properties on long lease and small freeholds multiplied, so that the industrial settlements sprawling through Madeley Wood and into Coalbrookdale attracted the interest of politicians seeking votes. A tradition of political radicalism was established.[23]

In the 18th century the Darbys of Coalbrookdale made historic contributions to the technology of the iron industry and erected in 1779–80 the world's first large iron bridge,[24] across the Severn from Madeley Wood to Benthall. The bridge stimulated the growth of the new town of Ironbridge and, as one of the wonders of the age, drew countless travellers[25] to be equally gratified by the neighbourhood's spectacular blast furnaces, coking hearths, limestone mines and kilns, tunnels, and inclined planes.[26]

By the end of the 19th century Madeley's landscape was less scarred by industry than Dawley's, and there was a wider range of social class among its population.[27] Madeley and Coalbrookdale retained substantial numbers of middle-class residents. Nevertheless a century of economic stagnation was blighting all parts of the parish by the 1950s: the old furnace at Coalbrookdale was

[5] Inst. Geol. Sciences Map 1/25,000, *Telford* (1978 edn.).

[6] T.D.C. *Severn Gorge* ([1975] copy in S.P.L.), 3–13; J. Randall, *Hist. Madeley* (Madeley, 1880), 174; S.R.O. 4044/93, p. 79 (no. 1443); I. J. Brown, 'Mineral Working and Land Reclamation in the Coalbrookdale Coalfield' (Leicester Univ. Ph.D. thesis, 1975), 194–526.

[7] O.S. Map *Roman Brit.* (2nd edn. 1928), S. sheet; *T.S.A.S.* xlix. 25.

[8] O.S. Map *Roman Brit.* (4th edn. 1978), but cf. O.S. Map *Brit. in Dark Ages* (2nd edn. corr. reprint 1971).

[9] SA 659, 663; *T.S.A.S.* liv, p. xiii. For a spurious antiquity found at Madeley Wood see *Antiquaries Jnl.* xi. 165; xx. 288–9.

[10] *Eng. P.N. Elements* (E.P.N.S.), ii. 18–20; *N. & Q.* 9th ser. ii. 144, 256. Cf. M. Gelling, *Signposts to the Past* (1978), 126–8; Ekwall, *Concise Oxf. Dict. Eng. P.N.* 310–11.

[11] H. P. R. Finberg, *Early Charters of W. Midlands* (1961), pp. 148, 203, 206, 212.

[12] *Salopian Jnl.* 18 Dec. 1839; *V.C.H. Salop.* i. 454.

[13] *Cal. S.P. Dom.* 1644–5, 283, 298; *T.S.A.S.* 4th ser. ii. 16–17.

[14] S.R.O. 2280/Rg/1, 14 Apr. 1645.

[15] *T.S.A.S.* 3rd ser. x. 89 n., 94–5; 4th ser. ii. 294. For the co. cttee. see *V.C.H. Salop.* iii. 359.

[16] *Chas. II's Escape from Worcester: Narratives Assembled by S. Pepys*, ed. W. Matthews (1967), 17, 44–8, 81, 90–1, 94, 112, 118; *T.S.A.S.* 3rd ser. vii. 184, 192; xlix. 15; Randall,

Madeley, 45–54, 219, 332, 334, App. pp. I–VII.

[17] S.R.O. 2280/6/1, 1682 and 1709 accts.

[18] P.R.O., E 179/168/219, mm. 16–17; M. D. G. Wanklyn, 'Ind. Development in Ironbridge Gorge before Abraham Darby', *W. Midland Studies*, xv. 4–5.

[19] P.R.O., E179/168/219, mm. 16–17.

[20] H.W.R.O.(H.), Heref. dioc. rec., reply to visit. arts. 1716.

[21] Trinder, *Ind. Rev. Salop.* (1981), 158.

[22] Ibid. 227 sqq.; *Salopian Shreds & Patches*, i. 91; *T.S.A.S.* iv. 421; lv. 11–12; *Popular Protest and Public Order . . . 1790–1920*, ed. R. Quinault and J. Stevenson (1974), 36, 46.

[23] *V.C.H. Salop.* iii. 261 n. 31, 340, 342; S.R.O. 516/12; 2280/2/8, s.a. 1709, J. K[ynaston] to vicar; Randall, *Madeley*, 197–200; 2836/1; Trinder, *Ind. Rev. Salop.* (1981), 231, 234–6; below, Local Govt.

[24] Cf. *E.H.R.* xcv. 703; *Local Historian*, xiv. 426–7.

[25] N. Cossons and B. Trinder, *The Iron Bridge: Symbol of Ind. Rev.* (1979), 53 sqq.

[26] Ibid. 63; 'The Most Extraordinary District in the World': *Ironbridge and Coalbrookdale*, ed. B. Trinder (1977); Pool Hill Girls' Sch. log bk. 1863–87, 16 Aug. 1864 (extract supplied by Mrs. J. McFall); S.R.O. 4624/2/2, 25 June 1879.

[27] e.g. *Shropshire Mag.* Feb. 1967, 30; below, maps on pp. 24 and 108; J. McFall, 'Educ. in Madeley Union of Salop. in 19th Cent.' (Keele Univ. M.A.(Educ.) thesis, 1973), 46–9.

'shockingly sordid' before its restoration in 1959,[28] while Ironbridge and some of the industrial hamlets were shabby and derelict. Dawley (later Telford) development corporation's first housing and industrial estates were built in the parish in the 1960s and 1970s, extensive areas were developed for open-air recreation, and agriculture came to an end. Development was controlled in the historically important areas of Coalbrookdale and the Severn Gorge: those parts of the parish became the new town's showpiece,[29] justifying its claim to be the 'Birthplace of Industry'.[30] The Ironbridge Gorge Museum Trust, created (in 1967) and fostered by the development corporation, realized inchoate local aspirations[31] to make an open-air[32] museum of industrial archaeology. Its achievements[33] focused international attention on the area in 1978 when it won the European Museum of the Year award. In 1979, during celebrations of the Iron Bridge's bicentenary, the prince of Wales visited the area and later became the museum's patron.[34]

Notable persons connected with the parish, apart from the Darby family and three lords of the manor, include J. W. Fletcher (1729–85), vicar from 1760,[35] James Glazebrook (1744–1803), a miner native to the parish and converted by Fletcher,[36] and George Pattrick (1746–1800), a popular London preacher who preached at Madeley on notable occasions, laid the new church's foundation stone in 1794, and died and was buried in the parish.[37] John Randall (1810–1910),[38] artist[39] and writer on local history,[40] topography, and geology, lived most of his life in Madeley.[41] Sir Wyke Bayliss (1835–1906), artist and writer on art, was a native of the parish[42] as was the lawyer and administrator Lord Moulton (1844–1921).[43] John Russell, the South Wales coal owner,[44] and Thomas Parker (1843–1915), electrical engineer and inventor of smokeless fuel,[45] grew up in Coalbrookdale; the fact that their successful careers were made elsewhere perhaps symbolized the emigration of entrepreneurial talent as the area's economic importance declined from the mid 19th century.[46] The channel swimmer Capt. Matthew Webb (1848–83) also spent his youth in the parish and learnt to swim in the Severn.[47] The writer Edith Pargeter (born 1913), alias Ellis Peters, lived in Madeley from 1956.[48] W. A. Wright, the professional footballer who captained Wolverhampton Wanderers and England, was born in Ironbridge in 1924.[49]

COMMUNICATIONS. The Severn was early the county's main artery of trade,[50] on which barges and the larger trows were in use by the early 15th century.[51] By the earlier 17th century there was a community of barge and trow men settled in the Severn Gorge[52] whence, from riverside wharves,[53] coal became the staple trade up to Shrewsbury and down to Bristol.[54] In 1772, partly to put an end to the degrading work of the gangs of bow-haulers, Richard Reynolds began to urge the making of a horse tow path. There was one from Coalbrookdale to Bewdley by c. 1800; William Reynolds made the stretch through his father's property in Madeley Wood and the Lloyds. A horse path up river to Shrewsbury was made in 1809.[55]

The Coalbrookdale Co. owned a small river fleet briefly c. 1800, but other industrialists never tried to integrate river transport into their operations. Further improvement of the river in the 19th century was resisted by barge owners supported by W. R. Anstice and many of the parish's industrialists. Nevertheless competition from the railways, in which the Coalbrookdale Co. was also involved, caused the river trade to decline sharply in the mid 19th century, and it was virtually extinct by the 1880s.[56]

Before 1780 the Severn was not bridged be-

[28] Pevsner, Shropshire, 156; A. Raistrick, 'Old Furnace at Coalbrookdale', Ind. Arch. Rev. iv. 123 sqq.

[29] T.D.C. Telford: Basic Plan Proposals (1970), 25–6, 34; T.D.C. Telford in the 1980's [1980], 2.

[30] Legend on roadside name signs.

[31] Origins of Ironbridge Gorge Mus.: Rep. of Hon. Sec. I.G.M.T. (1982; copy in S.R.O. 4390); Salop. News Letter, xxix. 3; local inf.

[32] K. Hudson, Social Hist. of Museums (1975), 92–3.

[33] B. Trinder, 'Ironbridge Gorge Mus.' Local Historian, ix. 289–93; N. Cossons, 'Ironbridge—The First Ten Yrs.' Ind. Arch. Rev. iii. 179–86.

[34] The Times, 15 Feb. 1978; Shropshire Star, 14 Feb. 1978; 5–6 July 1979; inf. from I.G.M.T.   [35] D.N.B.

[36] D.N.B.; L. Tyerman, Wesley's Designated Successor (1882), 122–5, 132.

[37] D.N.B.; V.C.H. Essex, viii. 14; S.R.O. 1681, box 229, marr. settlement (1789), probate papers, etc.; 2280/Rg/6, memo. at front by Sam. Walter; /BRg/1, f. 52; /MRg/5, p. 16.

[38] W. Mate & Sons Ltd. Shropshire: Historical, Descriptive, Biographical (1906), pt. 2, p. 174; B. Trinder, intro. to reprint (Salop. Co. Libr. 1975) of Randall, Madeley.

[39] Below, Econ. Hist. (Clay and Ceramic Ind.).

[40] Aged 91, he contributed to V.C.H. Salop. i. 415–81 (corr. ibid. ii. 316–19; iii. 398); S.R.O. 3763/2/1, Randall to H.A. Doubleday, 6 Feb. 1901, 16 Sept. 1902.

[41] Tablet in St. Mic.'s unveiled 1912: St. Mic.'s, Madeley, Par. Mag. Oct. 1912; S.R.O. 2280/1/39.

[42] Who Was Who, 1897–1916, 48; Jackson, 'Madeley', bk. 1, p. 79.

[43] D.N.B. 1912–21; Complete Peerage, xiii. 168.

[44] Trinder, Ind. Rev. Salop. (1981), 155.

[45] Tit-Bits, 18 Feb. 1905; Proc. Inst. Mech. Engineers, Jan.

1916, 128–9; The Times, 15 Jan. 1936, p. 14a; V.C.H. Staffs. ii. 155–6; Birm. Post Midland Mag. 27 Apr. 1968; tablet in Holy Trin. Coalbrookdale.

[46] Trinder, op. cit. 154–5; Church Soc. Essentials, v, [p. 2] (copy in S.R.O. 3937/9/2).

[47] D.N.B.; M.A. Jarvis, Capt. Webb and 100 yrs. of Channel Swimming (1975); tablet in Holy Trin. Coalbrookdale.

[48] Who's Who (1982), 1688; Jackson, 'Madeley', bk. 1A, p. 237; Shropshire Mag. Nov. 1953, 17–18; Oct. 1967, 22; S.R.O. 725/4, p. 124; 803/1, p. 126.

[49] Who's Who (1982), 2440.

[50] T. S. Willan, 'Trade of Severn Valley, 1600–1750', Econ. H.R. viii. 68–9.

[51] S.P.L., Haughmond Cart. f. 168; S.R.O. 4001/J/5, leet bk. 1434–1563, pp. 62–3, 144–5; Hist. MSS. Com. 13, 10th Rep. App. IV, Gatacre, 443–4. Cf. Trinder, Ind. Rev. Salop. 105–6; V.C.H. Salop. i. 426 n.2.

[52] Trinder, op. cit. 109; P.R.O., E 179/168/219, m. 16d. (10 trowmen 1660). Probate and other records yield inf. from the 1630s: inf. from Dr. B. S. Trinder.

[53] For those at the termini of early rlys., etc., see below.

[54] See e.g. Randall, Madeley, 256–7, 333; V.C.H. Salop. i. 454; Cal. S.P. Dom. 1677–8, 136; J. Plymley, Gen. View of Agric. of Salop. (1803), 83; Trinder, op. cit. 104, 106; Econ. H.R. viii. 69, 71, 77–8. Cf. two pamphs., cited ibid. 72 n. 5, 78 n. 3, and probably dating from 1661, in B.L. 816. m.8(50–1); Reasons Wherefore making Stower and Saltwerp Navigable will advantage Co. of Salop (copy in Staffs. R.O., D.(W.) 1788, P59, B3).

[55] Trinder, op. cit. 108–9, 117; Plymley, op. cit. 289, 314.

[56] A. Raistrick, Dynasty of Iron Founders (1970), 231, 261; Trinder, op. cit. 116–17, 259–60; Randall, Madeley, 259–61, 334; below.

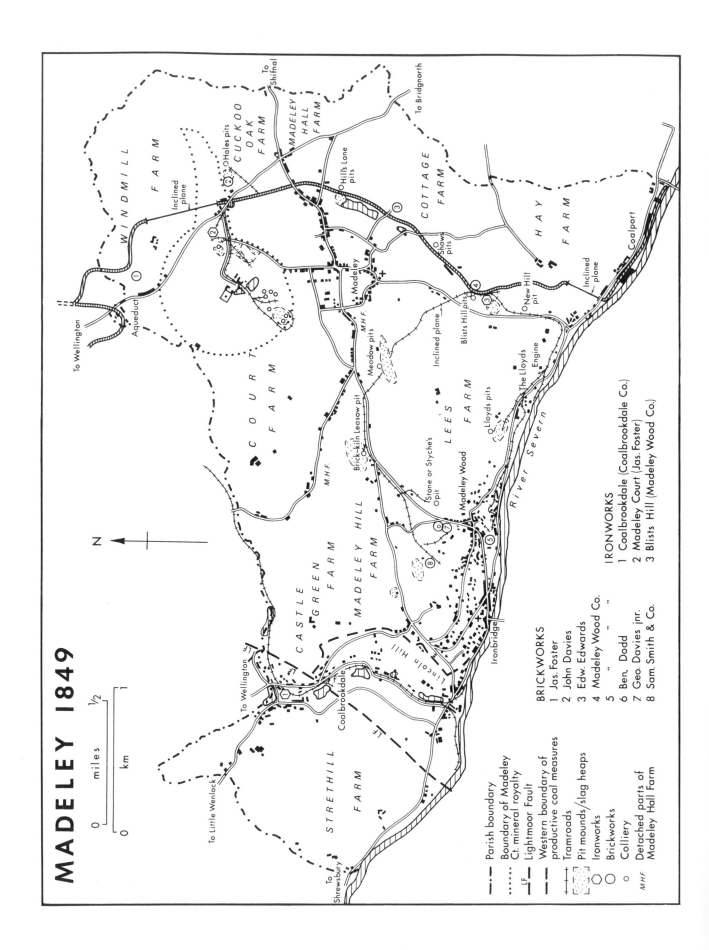

MADELEY 1849

N

miles 0 ½ 1
km 0 1

Legend:
- Parish boundary
- Boundary of Madeley Ct. mineral royalty
- LF Lightmoor Fault
- Western boundary of productive coal measures
- Tramroads
- Pit mounds/slag heaps
- Ironworks
- Brickworks
- Colliery
- M.H.F. Detached parts of Madeley Hall Farm

BRICKWORKS
1 Jas. Foster
2 John Davies
3 Edw. Edwards
4 Madeley Wood Co.
5 " "
6 Ben. Dodd
7 Geo. Davies jnr.
8 Sam. Smith & Co.

IRONWORKS
1 Coalbrookdale (Coalbrookdale Co.)
2 Madeley Court (Jas. Foster)
3 Blists Hill (Madeley Wood Co.)

To Shifnal
To Bridgnorth
Hales pits
Hill's Lane pits
Shows pits
New Hill pit
Inclined plane
Coalport
Blists Hill pits
Inclined plane
Engine
The Lloyds
Lloyds pits
River Severn
Stone or Styche's Opit
Madeley Wood
Brick-kiln Leasow pit
Meadow pits
M.H.F.
Madeley
Inclined plane
Aqueduct
To Wellington
Ironbridge
Lincoln Hill
Coalbrookdale
To Wellington
To Little Wenlock
To Shrewsbury

WINDMILL FARM
CUCKOO OAK FARM
MADELEY HALL FARM
COTTAGE FARM
HAY FARM
COURT FARM
LEE'S FARM
MADELEY HILL FARM
CASTLE GREEN FARM
STRETHILL FARM

tween Buildwas and Bridgnorth, coracles and ferries serving instead. The making and use of coracles in Madeley, continuing in the early 1980s, was probably of long standing[57] when observed in the mid 17th century.[58] About 1780 there were several regular ferries in the Severn Gorge.[59]

Two principal roads crossed the parish from early times and were turnpiked under an Act of 1764.[60] The road from Worcester via Bridgnorth to Wellington, bypassing Madeley to the east, was unimportant for communications within the parish. The Shifnal to Much Wenlock road, however, crossed the parish from east to west and lanes led out of it. Presumably one ran south to the Green and Madeley Wood.[61] From the two southward loops forming the streets of Madeley town[62] lanes went south to the Lloyds (Dabley Lane)[63] and, from near Cottage Farm, past Bowdler's mill to the farm's land, the Hay, and Sutton wood.[64] On the north were lanes giving access to parts of the open fields adjoining the manorial demesne and leading to Madeley Court,[65] and Park Lane led around Rough Park to Lightmoor.

Though there was apparently no public road along Coalbrookdale until the later 18th century, when one was made beside the railway, from the 17th century the ironworks used the dale as a route to the Wharfage at Loadcroft. The earliest route between Madeley and Coalbrookdale was a bridle road (probably the later Church Road) over Lincoln Hill,[66] probably adopted by the parish c. 1854.[67] The later Station Road, along the western slopes of the dale to Sunniside, was still private in 1849[68] and the later Coach Road, leading out of it north to Upper furnace pool,[69] was presumably built alongside the railway in 1864.[70]

In 1724 the parish roads were said to be 'in indifferent repair'.[71] The terrain limited improvement, and the turnpike road up Lincoln Hill was notoriously steep.[72] In the later 18th century byroads were often impassable, especially in bad weather.[73]

Two Severn toll-bridges, opened 1780–1, modi-

fied the parish's road communications;[74] both were financed by local industrialists, especially the ironmasters.[75] The wooden Preen's Eddy (later Coalport) bridge was opened between Sutton Maddock and Broseley parishes in 1780, its proprietors having power to build connecting roads.[76] One from the Wenlock turnpike in Broseley was completed to the Worcester–Wellington road[77] soon after the failure of a Madeley road Bill[78] in 1797.[79] Though the bridge and the new road lay just outside the parish, both were important for William Reynolds's development of Coalport in the 1790s;[80] Reynolds was probably the moving spirit behind the building of the road.[81] Coalport bridge was rebuilt in iron in 1799 and 1818[82] and became a county bridge in 1922.[83] The Coalport–Ironbridge road through the Lloyds was private property in 1849[84] and at least part remained unadopted in 1909[85] and later.[86] In 1909 the ferro-concrete Haynes Memorial (or Free) bridge was built across the Severn near the Lloyds Gate.[87] In 1922 a war-memorial footbridge was built from Coalport to the Tuckies, replacing Coalport ferry closed in 1912.[88]

The building of the Iron Bridge 1777–80 caused the Madeley turnpike trustees to provide a route to it from near the top of Lincoln Hill, first by improvement of an existing lane (the later Ironbridge High Street) then by a sharp turn uphill into a 'new road' (the later Church Hill). From 1782 the owners of Loadcroft wharf allowed the use of the Wharfage as a road to the bridge from the bottom of Lincoln Hill. Better connexions between the bridge and the turnpike were made under an Act of 1806 renewing the Madeley trust for the second time: the Wharfage was turnpiked, though wharfingers kept their right to stack on it, and by 1810 the road eventually known as Madeley Hill had been constructed from Ironbridge High Street to the turnpike road near Hill Top. The Iron Bridge was closed to traffic in 1934, and in 1950 the proprietors conveyed it to the county council.[89]

The road from the Shifnal to Much Wenlock

[57] V.C.H. Salop. i. 200; ii. 202; The Observer, 22 Feb. 1976; U. Rayska, Victorian and Edwardian Salop. from Old Photos. (1977), pl. 144; Ironbridge Quarterly, 1982.4, 4–6.
[58] Diary of Marches of Royal Army (Camd. Soc. [1st ser.] lxxiv), 251.
[59] Cossons and Trinder, Iron Bridge, 27; Eng. Topog. (Gent. Mag. Libr.), x. 86.
[60] 4 Geo. III, c. 81; Trinder, Ind. Rev. Salop. 143–5.
[61] S.R.O. 2280/6/95, 6 Dec. 1797. Cf. /2/45, no. 1883.
[62] Below, Growth of Settlement.
[63] Jackson, 'Madeley', bk. 1A, p. 6; S.R.O. 2280/2/45; /48, p. 110 (no. 922); /6/95, 6 Dec. 1797.
[64] S.R.O. 2280/2/45; /48, pp. 8, 24–5, 110 (esp. nos. 1101–2, 1108, 1121).
[65] Below, Growth of Settlement; deed and plan of 1837 (in possession of Mr. S. B. Smith) referring to N. boundary of S.R.O. 2280/2/45, nos.561–2, as the bridle rd. from Park La. to Madeley Ct.
[66] Randall, Madeley, 291; S.R.O. 4406/1, p. 94; Tyerman, Wesley's Designated Successor, 363.
[67] S.R.O. 2280/6/102, 30 Mar. 1854.
[68] Nos. 3266, 3270, 3432 in S.R.O. 2280/2/45; /48 (pp. 16, 26); S.R.O. 1987/30/3–4; W.B.R. Madeley dist. cttee. min. bk. 1919–26, pp. 66–7 (adoption, 1920).
[69] O.S. Map 6", Salop. XLIII. SW. (1884 edn.); T.D.C. Telford Street Plan (1980).
[70] Below.
[71] T.S.A.S. lvi. 318–19.
[72] Orders of Q. Sess. iii. 22; Q. Sess. Rolls, 1696–1820, 87.
[73] Randall, Madeley, 290–1; F. W. Macdonald, Fletcher of

Madeley (1885), 61; S.R.O. 2280/6/95, 6 Dec. 1797.
[74] Trinder, Ind. Rev. Salop. 146; Cossons and Trinder, Iron Bridge, 37 sqq., 79.
[75] Cossons and Trinder, op. cit. 17, 19–22, 24–5, 35–6, 79–82; L. S. Pressnell, Country Banking in the Ind. Rev. (1956), 375, 382.
[76] Cossons and Trinder, op. cit. 79–81.
[77] Trinder, Ind. Rev. Salop. 145–6.
[78] S.R.O. 1104, parcel 33, Thos. Barnfield's letter bk. 1795–1806, corresp. re new rd. 1795–7 (ref. from Brig. C. Goulburn); 1681, box 196, Madeley turnpike trust min. bk. 1792–1818, 9 Sept. 1795, sqq.
[79] C.J. lii. 106, 187–8, 398, 409–10, 416.
[80] Below, Growth of Settlement.
[81] R. S. Edmundson, 'Coalport China Wks.' Ind. Arch. Rev. iii. 126.
[82] B. Trinder, 'Coalport Bridge', Ind. Arch. Rev. iii. 153–7.
[83] Cossons and Trinder, Iron Bridge, 83.
[84] S.R.O. 2280/2/45–6; /48, pp. 25 (no. 1274), 69–70 (nos. 1157, 1275), 74 (no. 1312), 88 (no. 1312a).
[85] W.B.R. Madeley dist. cttee. min. bk. 1906–13, pp. 197, 201, 207; cf. ibid. pp. 42, 185, 200, 228, 442.
[86] Perhaps until 1926: ibid. 1919–26, pp. 91–2, 327, 375, 380–1, 387.
[87] Cossons and Trinder, Iron Bridge, 46; Shropshire Mag. Dec. 1959, 17, 19.
[88] Kelly's Dir. Salop. (1926), 149; W.B.R. Madeley dist. cttee. min. bk. 1906–13, pp. 404, 409–12.
[89] Cossons and Trinder, op. cit. 35, 37–8, 43–7; Trinder, Ind. Rev. Salop. 146.

road at Dale End up Coalbrookdale to Wellington was turnpiked *c.* 1817.[90]

The new town development corporation greatly modified the road pattern by building three large housing estates 1966–75, each with a perimeter road. Woodside estate cut Park Lane, and its perimeter road became the Madeley–Lightmoor route. Central Madeley was bypassed to the north by Parkway (built 1967–8) and to the east by a link road (opened 1979) from Madeley roundabout to Coalport Road at Blists Hill.[91] In the 1970s the Madeley section of the Bridgnorth–Wellington road lost importance to two new roads. Brockton Way, opened 1971, connected Queensway (the new town's 'eastern primary road') to the old Bridgnorth–Wellington road in Sutton Maddock parish. Castlefields Way, opened 1978, ran north from Parkway to Southall, in Dawley. In 1980 the two roads were connected by the new town's 'southern district road', a new Dawley–Bridgnorth link across the north-east part of Madeley parish; Bridgnorth Road then became a cul-de-sac.[92]

Despite some road improvements in the Severn Gorge by the early 1980s traffic there was becoming heavier and more congested[93] and there were plans[94] for a new relief road.

The earliest rail or waggon ways in the parish led out of the coalmine adits in Madeley Wood down to the Severn.[95] One, almost a mile long, was laid from the Lane pit in 1692. Another, from a pit in Lloyds dingle or 'gutter', had a 'wind' and chain to let coal and ironstone waggons down the steep hillside; tenants of mines north of the Wenlock road were allowed to use it in 1706.[96] The Coalbrookdale Co. built a railway at Lake Head in 1748, and by 1758 three railways from coal and ironstone pits converged on the Madeley Wood ironworks.[97] Tramways were laid in a sandstone adit mine at Madeley Wood and an early 19th-century ironstone mine in Ironbridge; from the latter an inclined plane ran down to the Severn.[98] In 1786 William Reynolds began a technically more ambitious route in the riverside meadows soon to be developed as Coalport: the Tar Tunnel, said to have been projected as an underground canal, was driven *c.* 1,000 yards into the side of the Severn Gorge to reach pits at Blists Hill *c.* 150 ft. below ground. In the event rails were laid to bring out the coal. Employed for mine drainage and ventilation, the tunnel was used in connexion with local mines until the

1930s.[99] A tunnel built in Ironbridge in 1800, probably another of Reynolds's, carried a tramway from Lincoln Hill limeworks to Bedlam furnaces.[1]

Until the 1850s exports from the coalfield were routed south through Madeley parish to the Severn. Early wharves, served by wooden railways, were in the western part of the parish between Strethill Farm and Dale End. The railways were important to the Coalbrookdale Co. and from 1767 Richard Reynolds introduced iron rails, the first in the country; by 1785 the company had over 20 miles of iron railways. In the 1790s a new canal shifted through traffic to Coalport in the eastern part of the parish.[2]

In 1728 William Forester and William Hayward had a railway built from Little Wenlock to take their coal and ironstone to Meadow wharf;[3] by 1732 they had had a 'wind' built, and the lessee had to keep it and the railway bridges in repair.[4] In 1750 the Coalbrookdale Co. laid a two-mile line from Forester's mines at Coalmoor to their Coalbrookdale furnaces,[5] a new or additional line perhaps being laid *c.* 1776.[6] Probably in the 1750s rails down the dale gave access to the Severn.[7] In 1755 a new company line from Horsehay probably joined the line of 1750 near Stoney Hill; connexions from Horsehay were made to Lawley, Ketley, and (by 1788) Donnington Wood. From 1794, however, Horsehay–Coalbrookdale traffic was by canal from Horsehay to Brierly Hill; thence, from the foot of an inclined plane, a new railway ran along Lincoln Hill and down to the Severn by an inclined plane near Lower forge. In the 1820s the railway was replaced by a third Horsehay–Coalbrookdale line which ran down Lightmoor dingle.[8]

A branch of the Shropshire Canal built through the eastern part of the parish 1789–92, with inclined planes at Windmill farm and the Hay, connected most parts of the coalfield to the Severn, and it survived the competition of a private railway (*c.* 1799–1815) to the east.[9] Tramways converged on the canal at Blists Hill: one from Bedlam furnaces and the Lloyds pit, another from Meadow pit[10] via an inclined plane (replaced by a bridge *c.* 1861) north of Lee dingle. There was a short spur to the Shaws pits. Further north tramways were built from Madeley Court pits and ironworks to the Tweedale basin near the bottom of the Windmill farm incline, and from the Hales pits.[11] The canal was taken over by the L.N.W.R.

[90] Below, Wellington, Communications.
[91] T.D.C *Telford Street Plan* (1980); below, Growth of Settlement; *Shropshire Star*, 19 Oct. 1979 (p. 21).
[92] T.D.C. *Telford Street Plan and Guide* (1976); T.D.C. *Telford Street Plan* (1980); *Shropshire Star*, 29 May, 3 June 1980; *Telford Jnl.* 30 May 1980.
[93] Cossons and Trinder, *Iron Bridge*, 47; S.C.C. Planning Dept. *Severn Gorge Dist. Plan: Written Statement* (1980), 20–7.
[94] Treated urgently from 1982: *Shropshire Star*, 7–8 July 1982, and local press thereafter.
[95] Raistrick, *Iron Founders*, 173–4. Cf. M. J. T. Lewis, *Early Wooden Rlys.* (1970), 276.
[96] Lewis, op. cit. 237; Apley Estate Office, Bridgnorth, vol. of Madeley Ct. misc. papers 1544–1837, copy lease of 1706.
[97] Lewis, op. cit. 239.
[98] I. J. Brown, 'Underground in Ironbridge Gorge', *Ind. Arch. Rev.* iii. 159 fig. 2, 163–5; S.R.O. 2280/2/46, nos. 1677, 2562 (entrances).
[99] Trinder, *Ind. Rev. Salop.* 126–7; I. Brown and B.

Trinder, *The Tar Tunnel* (I.G.M.T. 1979).
[1] *Ind. Arch. Rev.* iii. 159 fig. 2, 162.
[2] Trinder, op. cit. 122–3, 136 sqq.; Raistrick, *Iron Founders*, 176–81. Cf. Lewis, *Early Wooden Rlys.* 238.
[3] S.R.O. 1224, box 256, deed of 1728.
[4] Ibid. box 227, deed of 1732. Cf. Lewis, op. cit. 240, 258. One such 'wind' is illustr. in S. Smith, *View from the Iron Bridge* (I.G.M.T. 1979), p. 13.
[5] S.R.O. 1224, box 259, deed and plan of 1750.
[6] Ibid. parcel 315, rental Mich. 1776, f. 6v.
[7] Trinder, *Ind. Rev. Salop.* 122; cf. Lewis, *Early Wooden Rlys.* 241; S.R.O. 1681, box 179, G. Young, 'Plan of part of Coalbrookdale', 1786.
[8] Trinder, op. cit. 122, 135–6; below, Dawley, Communications. [9] Trinder, op. cit. 128–30, 132–3, 136–40.
[10] Probably also from brickwks. and pits farther E. and N.
[11] S.R.O. 2280/2/45–6; B. Baxter, *Stone Blocks and Iron Rails* (1966), 188–9. For Lee dingle bridge (presumably built when the Coalport Branch Rly. was made) see N. Cossons and H. Sowden, *Ironbridge: Landscape of Industry* (1977), 144–5.

in 1857 and closed north of Tweedale basin in 1858. It served mines and works in the parish but fell into disuse after 1894, closed in 1907,[12] and remained an unsightly nuisance until filled c. 1944.[13]

The Madeley branch of the G.W.R., opened in 1854, had a station near Madeley Court and terminated at Lightmoor.[14] About 1858 the Coalbrookdale Co.'s Wellington & Severn Junction Railway, later part of the G.W.R., reached Lightmoor from the north; only in 1864, however, did the G.W.R.'s Wenlock Railway, crossing the Severn by the Albert Edward bridge,[15] make the long-planned extension through Coalbrookdale, where there was a station, to Lightmoor Junction, whose passenger service then ceased. The sparse passenger services on the Madeley branch ceased in 1915.[16] From 1964, save for a temporary revival of passenger traffic for the Iron Bridge bicentenary in the summer of 1979,[17] the Madeley branch and the line of 1864 linking it south to Buildwas were used only by coal trains to Ironbridge 'B' power station. Halts at Lightmoor, opened as Lightmoor Platform 1907, and Coalbrookdale had lost their passenger services in 1962.

The Coalport Branch Railway, later part of the L.N.W.R., opened through the eastern part of the parish in 1860, had a station called Madeley Market in the low town, and terminated at Coalport East station. Both stations closed for passengers in 1952 and entirely in 1960.[18]

The Severn Valley Railway, later part of the G.W.R., opened in 1862 and, though not entering the parish, served it with two stations, one called Ironbridge and Broseley, in Benthall, and one called Coalport West, in Broseley. Both stations closed in 1963 and the line in 1970.[19]

GROWTH OF SETTLEMENT. There were 6 villeins, 4 bordars, and 4 serfs in the manor in 1086,[20] and 11 inhabitants paid the 1327 subsidy.[21] In 1642 the adult population was 330 or more,[22] in 1660 poll tax was paid by 340, and in 1672 tax was paid on 174 hearths in 61 houses;[23] the adult population was 451 in 1676[24] and little more 35 years later.[25]

In the 18th century population grew rapidly as industry expanded. There were perhaps c. 340

families by 1753,[26] half or more in Madeley Wood and possibly a fifth in Coalbrookdale.[27] Marriages increased in the late 1750s and early 1760s[28] when baptisms also greatly outstripped burials.[29] By 1782 estimated population was 2,690: 560 families in 440 houses. By 1793 it was 3,677 (851 families in 754 houses), and in 1801 it was 4,758 (942 families in 921 houses).[30]

Population grew steadily 1801–61, stabilized in the 1860s at a peak of c. 9,470, then, owing to the area's economic decline, fell for half a century reaching 7,398 in 1921. Over the next forty years, perhaps as a result of wartime increases, the censal population averaged 7,687. The civil parish was abolished in 1966,[31] when its redevelopment by Madeley district committee and the new town development corporation[32] was beginning to produce a vast increase trebling the population to some 20,800 by 1981.[33]

The open fields of the original settlement at Madeley were accessible from two southward loops (the later Church Street and Station Road) out of the Wenlock–Shifnal road; the church and probably the early farmsteads stood by the loops.[34] Cottage Farm, Station Road, belonging to generations of Bowdlers, was probably the last such farmstead: its c. 70 a., sold for building in 1965, lay south-east of the town and ran up to the Sutton Maddock boundary.[35] The Little Hay, or Webb's tenement, a timber-framed house at the eastern end of Church Street near Market Place, was sold with 47 a. in 1705;[36] its wide main range contains a central cruck truss perhaps formerly spanning an open hall, and there is a cross wing with jettied gables. Other substantial houses were later built in the area. On the western arm of Church Street the 17th-century Upper House, mostly of stone but with some timber framing, was tenanted by the Wolfes until 1690 and owned by their heirs the Heatherleys 1705–65;[37] in the 18th century it was extended by wings at right angles to each end, and it was further enlarged and much refitted in the earlier 19th century. Opposite Upper House, Madeley Hall was built for the Ashwoods in the early 18th century.[38]

Northward growth was confined by the manorial demesne, though on the north back lanes led to parts of the open fields: Shooting Butts Lane

[12] B. Trinder, *The Hay Inclined Plane* (I.G.M.T. 1978).
[13] W.B.R. Madeley dist. cttee. min. bk. 1906–13, p. 333; 1919–26, p. 180; 1937–43, pp. 85–6; S.P.L., Caradoc news cuttings, xix, p. 77; L.M.S. Rly. Act, 1944, 8 & 9 Geo. VI, c. 2 (Local).
[14] Para. based on Trinder, *Ind. Rev. Salop.* 257; R. Christiansen, *W. Midlands* (Regional Hist. of Rlys. of Gt. Brit. vii, 1973), 154, 156–7; *Railway Mag.* xci (1965), 378, 444; C. R. Clinker, *Clinker's Reg. of Closed Stations 1830–1977* (Bristol, 1978), 31, 75, 91, 159, 166, 168; S.R.O. 1888/21; W.B.R. Madeley dist. cttee. min. bk. 1906–13, p. 34; 1919–26, p. 333.
[15] *Kelly's Dir. Salop.* (1885), 835.
[16] Though revived from July to Sept. 1925.
[17] *Railway Mag.* cxxv (1979), 371.
[18] Trinder, *Ind. Rev. Salop.* (1981), 153; Christiansen, *W. Midlands*, 157–8; *Clinker's Reg.* 31, 68.
[19] Sir G. Nabarro, *Severn Valley Steam* (1971), 1, 7; *Clinker's Reg.* 31, 68, 164.   [20] *V.C.H. Salop.* i. 312.
[21] *T.S.A.S.* 2nd ser. iv. 335.
[22] Ho. of Lords papers 1641–2, Protestations Oxon. and Salop. ff. 194–5, mentioning no Rom. Cath.
[23] P.R.O., E 179/168/219, mm. 16–17; *Hearth Tax 1672* (Salop. Arch. Soc.), 35–6, 41.
[24] W.S.L., S. MS. 33; R. F. Skinner, *Nonconf. in Salop.* (Shrews. 1964), pl. III.

[25] S.R.O. 2280/2/9, s.a. 1711, suggests an adult pop. of c. 471. But see *W. Midland Studies*, xv. 4.
[26] S.R.O. 2280/2/10, pp. 1–30 (at end).
[27] Below.
[28] S.R.O. 2280/MRg/2, note on fly-leaf.
[29] Cf. ibid./Rg/5; /BRg/1.
[30] Plymley, *Agric. of Salop.* 344 and n. There were also 22 empty hos. in 1801.
[31] *V.C.H. Salop.* ii. 224, 229, 237; *Census*, 1961; I. Gregory, 'The E. Salop. Coalfield and the "Gt. Depression" 1873–96' (Univ. of Keele M.A. thesis, 1978), 3–6, 184–9.
[32] Below.
[33] 1981 census figs. compiled in S.C.C. Planning Dept.; cf. *Telford Social Trends*, i, ed. J. MacGuire (T.D.C. 1980), 24. The SE. side of Sutton Hill est. (formerly in Sutton Maddock par.) probably had an additional pop. of c. 950.
[34] See map.
[35] S.R.O. 1987/19/3; 2280/2/45, 48 (p. 8); T.D.C. deed pkt. 72.
[36] Deed in possession of Mr. A. M. Jeffrey.
[37] G. Allen-Woolfe and R. Rathbone, *Story of a Royal Tankard (1661–1702)* (1975), 9–11, 23–4; S.R.O. 210/1; 516/11; 1681, box 31, copy deed of 1705; q. sess. rec. parcel 282, reg. of papist deeds 1717–90, pp. 131–4.
[38] Below, Man. and Other Est.

(later Bridle Road and Victoria Road)[39] on the west and a lane between Burnt Hill and Little field on the east; the latter met a lane running north from the Wenlock-Shifnal road (there called High Street). A house on the corner of the lane and High Street incorporates a small timber-framed, late medieval open hall with a two-storeyed south end. At its north end is a later cross wing; the south end was extended in brick in the early 19th century and behind it cottages were added later in the century and subsequently incorporated into the house.[40] Between Shooting Butts Lane and the main road the Villa was built c. 1820 with a main front of three bays; it incorporates older materials and cellar walls.[41]

The grant of a weekly market in 1269[42] stimulated the growth of a new town east of Madeley, along the road to Shifnal: burgage tenements ran off what became the lower part of High Street, Bridge Street, and Prince Street.[43] In the 1320s 25 tenants held some 52 burgages by charter in 'the town of the new market of Madeley'; another 7 burgages, in the lord's demesne, were held by 4 life tenants.[44] The new town did not expand much thereafter.[45] In 1677, however, the unlicensed building of three cottages in the new town was presented at the manor court.[46]

Squatter cottages were built along the roads from Madeley to Lincoln Hill[47] and to Lightmoor[48] and there were a few more distant ones, such as that beside the Bridgnorth–Wellington road near the Sutton Maddock boundary.[49]

The second settlement in the parish, just over two kilometres west of Madeley, was in Coalbrookdale, where assarting was in progress in the earlier 13th century.[50] Inhabitants are mentioned in 1274 and 1327 and perhaps a separate field of Caldebrook, with those of Madeley, in 1322.[51] One of the two manorial reeves elected in 1380 was for Caldebrook.[52]

There was a bloomsmithy in Coalbrookdale by 1536[53] but in 1700 the 'whole village' comprised no more than a furnace, five houses, and a forge or two.[54] Most of the houses may have been near Upper furnace but one, White End, was lower down the dale near the Great forge.[55] There was at least one farmstead[56] in the valley some way below Upper forge pool: the substantial timber-framed house of 1636,[57] divided into cottages by 1786,[58]

was known as Rose Cottage in 1980, when it was partly a workshop. It had been much altered internally; a substantial central brick chimney stack, its hearth lintel bearing monograms similar to those on the Old furnace, was probably an early 18th-century insertion.[59] The timber-framed Yew Tree Cottage, Dale End, is much restored.[60]

Before Abraham Darby's arrival in 1708 Coalbrookdale's environs were 'very barren' with 'little money stirring'. By the 1750s the quickening of the Coalbrookdale Co.'s enterprises had filled the valley bottom with works, railways, and houses comprising a settlement perhaps approaching 400 inhabitants.[61] The Darbys had built themselves houses in the upper dale and, from the 1740s, a random scatter of workers' cottages appeared along the valley, some in terraces like Tea Kettle Row,[62] others in converted farm buildings.[63] Severn House, Dale End, was built c. 1757 by George Goodwin, master collier and partner in the Madeley Wood Co.[64] Next to it Eastfield House existed by c. 1815.[65] By the early 19th century houses and gardens spread out at either end of Upper furnace pool: westwards where imposing houses were built near the Darbys' along what became Darby Road, and eastwards at Woodside and up Lightmoor dingle. Among the cottages on the eastern side of the upper dale were 34 in five rows built by the Coalbrookdale Co. in the 1780s and early 1790s: less spacious than Tea Kettle Row, they had, like it, brewhouses. Lower down were more cottages and gardens around Upper forge and Boring mill pools; some of the dwellings there in 1827 were in former industrial buildings.[66] Many buildings in Coalbrookdale from the 1770s incorporated cast-iron features, including window frames and chimney pots.[67]

Madeley Wood, on the southern edge of the parish sloping down to the Severn, remained largely woodland and common pasture until the 18th century,[68] though there was mining in the area by the early 14th century[69] and cottages were proliferating in the 17th and 18th centuries. The master grubbers who worked for Sir Basil Brooke in the earlier 17th century lived in Madeley Wood[70] near his pits;[71] so probably did their workmen. Of eight cottages built unlicensed 1674–7 three or four were in Madeley Wood. The builders were apparently fined c. £10 a year until

[39] Jackson, 'Madeley', bk. 1A, p. 142.
[40] 61–65 High St. Cf. *Shropshire Star*, 14 Feb. 1973.
[41] See R. Baugh, *Map of Salop.* (1808).
[42] *Cal. Chart. R.* 1257–1300, 123.
[43] Cf. T. Rowley, *Salop. Landscape* (1972), 179.
[44] S.R.O. 1224/2/10.
[45] S.R.O. 2280/2/45, suggests that not many more than 60 burgage plots were ever built on.
[46] Ibid. /14/2, nos. 45–6.
[47] e.g. ibid. /2/45, nos. 603–11, 613–14, 2719–21; /14/2, no. 38.
[48] e.g. ibid. /2/45, nos. 230a, 252, 252a, 254, 279.
[49] Ibid. no. 1011.   [50] Eyton, iii. 241.
[51] Ibid. 320–1; *T.S.A.S.* 2nd ser. iv. 335.
[52] S.R.O. 1224/2/4.
[53] *L. & P. Hen. VIII*, xix (1), p. 635; *V.C.H. Salop.* i. 460.
[54] Trinder, 'Most Extraordinary Dist.' 18.
[55] Below, Man. and Other Est.
[56] Possibly that of the Stanleys' Cawbrook fm.: ibid.
[57] Date on dormer; W. G. Muter, *The Bldgs. of an Ind. Community: Coalbrookdale and Ironbridge* (1979), 25 and pl. 36.
[58] S.R.O. 1681, box 179, G. Young, 'Plan of part of

Coalbrookdale, 1786'; E. Mercer, *Eng. Vernacular Hos.* (1975), 76, 196.
[59] Muter, op. cit. 55; cf. below, Econ. Hist. (Iron and Steel).
[60] Muter, op. cit. 46; *Salop. News Letter*, xxxiii. 7.
[61] S.R.O. 2280/2/10, pp. 23 sqq. (at end), suggests that c. a fifth of c. 340 fams. in the par. lived in Coalbrookdale in 1753; cf. Trinder, *Ind. Rev. Salop.* 25; Raistrick, *Iron Founders*, 38–9, 70–2, 74 and facing pl.
[62] Trinder, 'Most Extraordinary Dist.' 18–19 and pl. 4–5; Muter, *Coalbrookdale and Ironbridge*, 27, 36–7.
[63] Like the later Rose Cottage: see above.
[64] S.R.O. 2287/1–15; Trinder, *Ind. Rev. Salop.* 403; Muter, op. cit. 26, 61.
[65] B.L. Maps, O.S.D. 208; S.R.O. 2280/2/46 no 3405; /48, p. 33 (no. 3405).
[66] *T.S.A.S.* lviii. 250–4; Muter, op. cit. 25, 32–4, 37–45, 47, 54–6; Raistrick, *Iron Founders*, 250–2.
[67] Muter, op. cit. 48, 52–3, 56.
[68] Below, Econ. Hist. (Agric.).
[69] *V.C.H. Salop.* i. 416, 460.
[70] P.R.O., SP 23/105, pp. 225–9.
[71] Below, Econ. Hist. (Coal and Ironstone).

presentment,[72] an arrangement probably guaranteeing what was in effect prompt registration and thereafter tenure for a small rent. Madeley Wood was the manor's last extensive common waste and thus the probable location of most, if not all, of the 16 cottages presented in 1715 as built without licence on the waste; 9 of them also involved illegal inclosure. Next year 12 cases were presented, 2 aggravated by inclosure.[73] By 1711 about half of the parish's population lived in Madeley Wood; they were mainly cottagers, most households with servants being in Madeley and Coalbrookdale.[74]

After the break-up of the manorial estate in 1705 increasing numbers of cottages in Madeley Wood were occupied by freeholders or on long leases. John Pitt and John Ashwood, steward and bailiff of the manor, bought 70 or more cottage properties in 1705[75] probably as a joint speculation;[76] at least two thirds, probably more, seem to have been in Madeley Wood. By the earlier 1730s the lords of the manor were granting 99-year leases of cottages or of land for cottages, and Richard Reynolds evidently continued the practice in the 1780s; there were forty such leaseholds by 1774, many, perhaps most, in Madeley Wood.[77] Cottages were divided or extended for new generations; new ones were often built in the corners of the irregular plots, which were themselves divided into separate gardens with minutely defined rights of way. Brewhouses were sometimes common to the dwellings multiplied on one plot.[78]

Two main concentrations of cottages had formed in Madeley Wood by the mid 18th century. One was around the Green,[79] 2 km. southwest of Madeley town: there the Golden Ball was licensed in 1728[80] and J. W. Fletcher's first Methodist meetings were held in 1762.[81] The name Madeley Wood later clung to that locality.[82] Settlement probably straggled west along the road to Lincoln Hill (later Belmont Road and Hodgebower), where 17th- and early 18th-century cottages remained in 1974.[83] There were cottages near the Brockholes and the Foxholes c. 1710.[84] Belmont House, a fashionable villa of 1753,[85] was built where the cottages began to thin out in the west. South-east of the Green lanes led downhill to Bedlam Hall, a brick Jacobean building, and the Lloyds, a large timber-framed house dated 1621.[86] Bedlam was the name of the riverside jumble of cottages built near the Madeley Wood Co.'s furnaces from 1758;[87] public houses opened in 1763 and 1780.[88] The Lloyds, so called in 1726,[89] or Lloyds coppice, was a wide tract of wood and waste, originally the eastern part of Madeley Wood, extending from the Green and Bedlam to the Washbrook. It remained largely unbuilt[90] but there were coalpits there by the earlier 18th century.[91] Before the end of the century there was probably a small riverside settlement at the Lower Lloyds.[92] New Buildings, an L-shaped terrace of 16 cottages, with outside privies,[93] was erected there in the earlier 19th century.[94] Madeley Wood Hall was built nearby in the early 19th century for the Anstice family, previously of Bedlam Hall.[95]

The other main settlement in the early 18th century was at the west end of Madeley Wood. It ran from Dale End along the Wharfage, a riverside lane[96] 'leading into Madeley Wood',[97] to the ferry where the Iron Bridge was built 1777–80.[98] Its growth conformed to the haphazard development of the whole Madeley Wood area. Robert Phillips (d. 1771)[99] left his children four freeholds there (presumably produced by subdivision), the leasehold tenement he lived in, and a garden which he had inclosed and held under the lords of the manor.[1] The Phillipses were ground colliers. Their properties were bounded by houses described as new in 1745 and 1760.[2] From the ferry a track (later called High Street, where a cruck was uncovered in 1969)[3] started uphill and perhaps went as far as the Green.[4] Other early houses were obliterated by the development of a small town[5] between the two earlier settlements during the sixty years after the Iron Bridge opened in 1780.[6]

[72] S.R.O. 2280/14/2, nos. 15, 42–44.
[73] S.R.O. 1681, box 130, ct. r. 1715–16. Twenty-three inclosures of commons were also presented 1715–17: ibid. ct. r. 1715–17.
[74] S.R.O. 2280/2/9, s.a. 1711.
[75] S.R.O. 1987/19/3. For their offices see S.R.O. 1681, box 130, ct. and suit r. 1715–21, 1723; Lincs. Archives Office, 2 Haw. 1/G/44; 3 Haw. 3/E/8.
[76] For their sales 1705–6 see e.g. S.R.O. 1681, box 148, sale to Eleanor Boden; box 149, sale to Thos. Hodgkiss; S.R.O., list of deeds of Stone Head Ho. or Rock Church, sale to John Cox, jnr. Ashwood's heir evidently had no such property by 1771: Wrekin Dist. Council, Madeley Hall deeds, abstr. of title of 1848 (abstr. deed of 1771).
[77] Cf. tenants' names (S.R.O. 1681, box 133, conveyance of ½ man. to Abr. Darby 1774; 1987/19/3) with inhs.' names (S.R.O. 2280/2/8–9, arranged topographically); Plymley, Agric. of Salop. 344.
[78] Ind. Heritage: Trans. 3rd International Conf. on Conservation of Ind. Monuments, iii, ed. M. Nisser (Stockholm, 1981), 375–6.
[79] Raistrick, Iron Founders, pl. facing p. 112. Notes on this drawing (printed in Smith, View from the Iron Bridge, p. 33) seem misleading: the hos. on the right are evidently those straggling west from the Green towards Lincoln Hill.
[80] Co. of Salop, Reg. of Public Hos. 1901 (copy in S.P.L., accession 6117), 337.
[81] Muter, Coalbrookdale and Ironbridge, 14 and pl. 11; S.R.O., list of deeds of Stone Head Ho. or Rock Church; S.R.O. 2280/2/46, nos. 1704–5; below, Prot. Nonconf.

[82] See e.g. Muter, op. cit. 4 fig. 1, 7 fig. 3, 13 fig. 6.
[83] Ibid. 26, 28–30, 46–8, 55–6, 59–60, 69 n. 96, and pl. 55
[84] 3rd Rep. Com. Char. H.C. 5, p. 306 (1820), iv.
[85] Muter, op. cit. 26, 50, 54–5, and pl. 39, 63.
[86] S.R.O. 2280/2/46; H. E. Forrest, Old Hos. of Wenlock (Shrews. 1914), 100, and pl. facing p. 97; Jackson, 'Madeley', bk. 3A, p. 71.
[87] S.R.O. 2280/2/46; Trinder, Ind. Rev. Salop. 39.
[88] Reg. of Public Hos. 1901, 332, 340.
[89] S.R.O. 2280/3/9.
[90] Ibid. /2/45–6; O.S. Map 6″, SJ 60 SE. (1954 edn.).
[91] Trinder, Ind. Rev. Salop. 160; V.C.H. Salop. i. 464.
[92] 'Lower Lloyds' on Raistrick, Iron Founders, pl. facing p. 112.
[93] S.R.O. 2280/2/45, nos. 1420–1, 1423–36; inf. from Mr. J. L. McFall.
[94] Not on B.L. Maps, O.S.D. 213.
[95] Trinder, Ind. Rev. Salop. 219; Jackson, 'Madeley', bk. 1A, pp. 1, 6; bk. 3A, p. 364; Randall, Madeley, 174.
[96] J. Rocque, Map of Salop. (1752).
[97] T.D.C., deed bdle. 1129/A/1–2.
[98] Cossons and Trinder, Iron Bridge, 25, 27–8, 35.
[99] S.R.O. 2280/BRg/1, f. 29v.
[1] T.D.C. deed bdle. 1129/A/7.
[2] Ibid. /A/3–6.
[3] Muter, Coalbrookdale and Ironbridge, 46.
[4] Cf. above, Communications.
[5] Randall, Madeley, 347.
[6] Cossons and Trinder, Iron Bridge, 43; below, plate 14.

Heart of the new town, and earliest laid out, was the area at the end of the bridge, where the Tontine inn was built in the 1780s and a market place provided. Away from the bridge growth was haphazard,[7] probably along existing hillside tracks.[8] The Reynoldses, lords of the manor, owned the area; they sold or leased land but took little initiative in its development.[9] Used as an address,[10] the bridge soon gave the growing town its name. By the 1830s Ironbridge was a busy port. Focus of the area's 'professional and commercial pursuits' in 1837 and with a population of c. 3,000 in 1841,[11] it yet never became a self-sufficient town: municipal, social, cultural, and educational institutions were shared with Coalbrookdale, Madeley, and Much Wenlock,[12] and from the mid 19th century a hundred years of economic stagnation blighted it. Away from the few fashionable residential areas such as Church Hill and Hodgebower[13] unhealthy 'back-to-earth' houses spread over the hillside[14] and by 1912 'tiers of dirty cottages' above riverside tips of industrial refuse formed a dull and squalid town whose deterioration was not halted before the 1960s. Madeley district committee attempted modest improvements in the town centre in the late 1950s[16] but a more ambitious scheme, after the committee acquired the Square and market in 1961, was deferred when Dawley new town proposals became known later that year.[17]

The growth of new industrial settlements, notably Coalport and Aqueduct, was stimulated by the building of the Shropshire Canal's Coalport branch through the east end of the parish in 1789–92.[18] Richard Reynolds bought c. 20 a. of riverside near Preen's Eddy bridge 1787–8. A canal terminus opened there in 1792, and the name Coalport was in use by 1794. The owners also improved road communications. From 1793 William Reynolds (d. 1803) controlled development, and between 1797 and 1800 several factories and 30 houses were built. By 1797 Coalport was Shropshire's most important river port, promising to rival Stourport.[19] By 1851 it had a population of 343. The main employers were the china manufacturers, with an élite work force which included many single women.[20] North of

Coalport in the 1830s the Madeley Wood Co. built canalside terraces for the workers in its new Blists Hill ironworks.[21]

At Aqueduct, named from the canal crossing of the Bridgnorth–Wellington road near the parish's northern boundary, there was little housing or industry, except Gilbert Gilpin's chain works, before 1840, when James Foster began to mine his Madeley Court estate. He brought workers from Wombridge and built terraces in Foster's Row along the turnpike road. By 1857 there was a population of 393, mostly depending on the nearby mines and ironworks.[22]

Like Ironbridge, the settlements at Madeley Wood, the Lloyds, Coalport, and Blists Hill all stagnated between the mid 19th and mid 20th century. Even in Madeley and Coalbrookdale old industrial premises were converted to housing;[23] those places, however, fared better than the riverside, offered better housing sites, and were consequently the scene of the district committee's first housing schemes. It built 44 council houses 1925–30 at the west end of Madeley in a triangle between Park Lane, Ironbridge Road, and West View Terrace; 46 more were built in Coalbrookdale 1929–31: 20 in Paradise, 22 in Dale Road, and 4 at Woodside.[24] Another 16, the first part of Beech Road, were built along the road from Madeley to Lincoln Hill.[25]

The pace of building quickened from 1933 as slums and overcrowding were tackled.[26] Ironbridge and Coalbrookdale were dealt with first by building 82 houses at Wrekin View 1935–7.[27] North and east of Madeley, 82 houses in Coronation Crescent were built 1936–40 and 48 in Tweedale Crescent 1939–40.[28]

After the war building was resumed, to clear slums and relieve the housing shortage. Progress was at first slow and concentrated in Madeley. In 1946 and 1947 27 prefabricated bungalows were put up in Victoria and Station roads,[29] pre-war schemes were completed by 6 houses in Tweedale Crescent and 2 at Wrekin View,[30] and the Rookery estate (20 houses) was built in the grounds of Tinsley House,[31] a building of c. 1883.[32] In the 1950s a major slum clearance programme for Coalbrookdale and Ironbridge was made possible

[7] Muter, *Coalbrookdale and Ironbridge*, 3, 5, 15–18, pl. 16, 24; below, plate 20.

[8] S.R.O. 2280/2/46; below, plate 31.

[9] Cf. S.R.O. 2280/2/45–6, 48 (pp. 69–89) for what remained to them in 1849.

[10] e.g. S.P.L., Deeds 13279 (1805).

[11] Muter, *Coalbrookdale and Ironbridge*, 8, giving too high a fig. for the town's pop. c. 1840; P.R.O., HO 107/928/12–15, giving c. 3,600 for Ironbridge, Madeley Wood, Bedlam, the Lloyds, Lincoln Hill, etc.

[12] Below, Social and Cultural Activities; Local Govt.; Public Services; Educ.; cf. Trinder, *Ind. Rev. Salop.* 328.

[13] Muter, op. cit. 8.

[14] Ibid. 48, 69 n. 94.

[15] *Murray's Handbk. for Salop. and Ches.* (1879), 31; J. E. Auden, *Shropshire* (Little Guides, 1912), 138.

[16] S.R.O., DA 6/119/1, pp. 16, 21–2, 58, 69, 85–6, 103, 150, 169, 186, 210, 210a, 212–13, 220, 235, 247, 259, 299–300, 305–6, 375–6.

[17] Ibid. pp. 227, 234, 244, 277–8, 309, 318, 386, 411, 436–7, 450–2, 461–2, 473.

[18] Above, Communications.

[19] Plymley, *Agric. of Salop.* 84, 289, 297, 315; R. S. Edmundson, 'Coalport China Wks.' *Ind. Arch. Rev.* iii. 123 fig. 3, 125–6; above, Communications.

[20] S.R.O. 2979/3, Coalport; Randall, *Madeley*, 197–200, 284–5.

[21] Trinder, *Ind. Rev. Salop.* 236, 323.

[22] *Salop. News Letter*, xxxix. [1–5]; xl. 16–22; xli. 21; S.R.O. 2598/1.

[23] Muter, *Coalbrookdale and Ironbridge*, 17, 52–3, and pls. 22, 72; Jackson, 'Madeley', bk. 1A, p. 245.

[24] W.B.R. Madeley dist. cttee. min. bk. 1919–26, pp. 302, 348; 1926–32, pp. 13, 68, 100, 134–5, 162–3, 183, 185, 213, 239, 252, 260, 266, 295, 307, 318–19, 384–5, 405.

[25] Ibid. 1926–32, pp. 318–19, 331, 335, 405.

[26] Under Greenwood's Housing Act, 1930, 20 & 21 Geo. V, c. 39, etc. Cf. ibid. 1926–32, pp. 371–2, 397–8, 404; 1932–7, pp. 4–5, 54, 70–1, 112–13, 279–80, 289, 327.

[27] Ibid. 1932–7, pp. 135–6, 140–1, 150–1, 243, 339, 353, 360, 457; S.R.O. 2879/1, p. 175.

[28] Madeley dist. cttee. min. bk. 1932–7, pp. 353–4, 457; 1937–43, pp. 123, 130, 143, 197, 206, 252, 267.

[29] Ibid. 1943–6, pp. 182–3, 206, 245–7, 284, 300; cf. Coalbrookdale Friends' meeting min. bk. 1858–1951 (in possession of Mr. A. E. Morris, Lilleshall), pp. 146–8.

[30] Madeley dist. cttee. min. bk. 1943–6, pp. 11, 207, 215, 241, 256, 292. [31] Ibid. pp. 267–8, 286, 292.

[32] Cf. O.S. Map 6″, Salop. XLIII. SE. (1888 edn.); *Kelly's Dir. Salop.* (1885), 887.

by the extension of Beech Road and the building of Roberts and School roads. There, on the high land above Madeley Wood, 100 houses were built 1951–4 and another 16 in 1956 and 1959–60.[33] At the same time a large estate was begun off Church Street, Madeley, comprising Anstice Road, South Drive, and Upper Road, with 68 houses 1951–4 and 80 more in the later 1950s.[34] In the 1960s slum clearance was furthered by new building in Coalport at Riverside Avenue in 1961[35] and in Coalbrookdale with 58 houses at Sunniside and 10 more for sale, 1962–3,[36] and 12 bungalows were added at Wrekin View in 1961.[37] Much the biggest housing programme ever carried out by the district committee, however, was achieved at Madeley in the years 1962–6: Joseph Rich Avenue (24 dwellings) and Meadcroft (20 old people's bungalows, one of them the ward's thousandth council house, and a warden's house) were built between Victoria Road and Park Street,[38] while east of the town, either side of Queen Street, Cuckoo Oak and Hills Lane estates provided 485 dwellings and 14 shops.[39] Most housing was for local people but some miners' families, moved from north-east England at the National Coal Board's request, were settled at Hills Lane.[40]

Between 1966 and 1974 Dawley U.D.C. started eight housing schemes (208 dwellings) in the old Madeley ward. Three were modest additions to the district committee estates but four others developed areas off New Road (32 dwellings) and Bridle Road (106). Slums had been largely cleared by the end of 1973[41] when houses near the Brewery inn, Coalport, were demolished.[42] The Bridle Road scheme included 30 old people's sheltered dwellings. There were 163 such dwellings in Madeley by 1979: 61 built by Telford development corporation on its estates, 52 by private trusts, and 50 by the local authority, which was then providing 34 more at Madeley Hall.[43] Two dozen more off Church Street, Madeley, were completed by the development corporation in 1981.[44]

The development corporation's first housing estates were built around Madeley:[45] Sutton Hill (1,233 houses partly in Sutton Maddock ancient parish) in 1966–9, Woodside (2,420 houses)

1968–73,[46] and Brookside (1,792 houses partly in Stirchley ancient parish) 1971–5.[47] The planned increase of population in Madeley's immediate neighbourhood necessitated the redevelopment of its centre. Parkway, a bypass, was built 1967–8, and between 1968 and 1970 new shops and flats were built round two pedestrian squares obliterating the west end of Park Avenue.[48] The rest of central Madeley was included in a conservation area in 1980.[49]

Speculative building played little part in the growth of 20th-century Madeley before the 1960s.[50] Bennett Road (c. 1960), off Queen Street,[51] and Bostock Crescent (c. 1962), Aqueduct,[52] were private. Later the new town corporation encouraged private housing,[53] and estates were built around Glendinning Way, around St. Michael's church and in Station Road, Madeley, to the south of Sutton Hill estate, and at Madeley Wood.

At Madeley Wood in 1976 the development corporation and a private builder began to restore old cottages and build new houses on Jockey Bank[54] as part of the planned regeneration of the Severn Gorge. The scenery of the Gorge and Coalbrookdale and the area's historic importance and dereliction led to the designation of a conservation area,[55] covering Ironbridge and Coalbrookdale in 1971 and extended in 1974 and 1980 along the riverside from Madeley Wood to Coalport and up the Washbrook valley to include Lee dingle, Blists Hill, and the centre of Madeley outside the redevelopment of 1968–70.[56] In the later 1970s the corporation restored many buildings in the centre of Ironbridge,[57] notably on the Wharfage and in High Street, effecting improvements deferred since 1961;[58] Wrekin district council assisted in improving the Square.[59] Meanwhile by 1979 the achievements of Ironbridge Gorge Museum and the bicentenary of the Iron Bridge had focussed national and international attention on the area.[60] New residents were attracted, property values rose, and the gentrification of Ironbridge was noted as an inevitable result of the cultivated growth of prosperity. The decay that had earlier seemed squalid began to seem romantic.[61]

[33] S.R.O., DA 6/112/7; /119/1, pp. 148–9, 157, 186–7, 306, 319–20.
[34] Ibid. /112/7; Jackson, 'Madeley', bk. 2A, pp. 189–90.
[35] S.R.O., DA 6/119/1, pp. 324, 390, 431, 440–1.
[36] Ibid. pp. 484, 522, 532, 562–3, 565, 585; Jackson, op. cit. bk. 3A, p. 89.
[37] S.R.O., DA 6/119/1, pp. 324, 390, 431, 440–1.
[38] S.R.O., DA 6/135, file on grouped dwellings; Wellington Jnl. 7 Aug. 1964.
[39] S.R.O., DA 6/135, files on Cuckoo Oak and Hills La. housing.   [40] Local inf.
[41] Dawley U.D.C., A Story 1966–1974, s.v. Housing (copy in S.R.O., DA 8/294); cf. Dawley U.D.C. Ann. Rep. of M.O.H. 1968, 14–15 (copy in S.R.O., DA 8/880).
[42] Inf. from Mr. J. L. McFall.
[43] T.D.C. Exec. Management Cttee. agendas 15 Jan. (rep. 5) and 19 Feb. (rep. 5) 1980.
[44] Inf. from the director of housing, T.D.C.
[45] Above, Telford.
[46] [U. Rayska], Redevelopment of Madeley (T.D.C. 1979), 5–8; inf. from the archivist T.D.C.; below, plates 45–6.
[47] Below, Stirchley, Growth of Settlement.
[48] Rayska, op. cit. 8–16 and endpaper maps.
[49] Inf. from S.C.C. Planning Dept.
[50] S.R.O., DA 6/119/1, p. 410.
[51] Ibid. pp. 94, 377, 407–8, 416.
[52] Ibid. pp. 431–2; ibid. /112/10, dist. cttee. min. 14 Feb. 1963.
[53] Rayska, Madeley, 17.
[54] Inf. from the archivist, T.D.C.; cf. Architects' Jnl. 8 Aug. 1979, 285–6, 293.
[55] Recognized by Dept. of Environment as of outstanding national importance: S.C.C. Planning Dept. Severn Gorge Dist. Plan: Written Statement (1980), 4, 30.
[56] T.D.C. Severn Gorge [1975], esp. map on p. 40; T.D.C. Ironbridge '75 [1975]; Cossons and Sowden, Ironbridge, 16–17, 62, 84–5, 94, 102, 134; inf. from S.C.C. Planning Dept.
[57] Inf. from the archivist, T.D.C.
[58] Above.
[59] Local inf.
[60] Above, intro.
[61] Architects' Jnl. 8 Aug. 1979, 284; cf. e.g. Telford Jnl. 4 July 1975 (letter from N. Cossons); 26 Oct. 1979 (letter from the Revd. W. A. Zwalf and the Revd. C. F. Carter); Cossons and Sowden, Ironbridge, 7, 10, 18–20, 58, 60, 84, 103.

SOCIAL AND CULTURAL ACTIVITIES. Early records of secular social activities in the parish are those of perennial efforts to suppress tippling, gaming, and desecration of the Lord's Day.[62] In the 1660s and 1670s there were 15 or more alesellers,[63] many of them probably carrying on other occupations too.[64] About 1762 there were perhaps 20 or 30 'tippling houses' and the vicar, J. W. Fletcher, visited them to attempt the conversion of their habitués. In the late 18th and early 19th century the parish, led at first by Abraham Darby (III) and Richard Reynolds, concerted measures with the Wenlock magistrates to reduce the number of alehouses and to limit their social use. About 1783 there were 18 public houses. One licensee was induced to do away with a fives court c. 1811.[65]

By 1847 there were 52 public houses.[66] They had multiplied most where the miners, ironworkers, and bargemen were. Of thirteen 18th-century licences surviving in 1901, eleven were in the Ironbridge and Madeley Wood area; one was for the parish's oldest public house, the Golden Ball (licensed 1728) at Madeley Wood. Before the 1820s Madeley had only the Three Horse Shoes (1749) but in the mid 19th century numbers in and around the town increased greatly; one of the earliest licences was that for the Royal Oak in 1831.[67] The Earl Grey beerhouse, Coalbrookdale, was bought by Francis Darby in 1839.[68] Later in the century there were only two or three public houses in the dale, one of them, the Commercial (1839; renamed the Grove c. 1956), eventually acquired by the Coalbrookdale Co.[69]

The Tontine, built opposite the Iron Bridge in the earlier 1780s, was soon the parish's most imposing inn, widely advertised as a good staging inn and with an assembly room.[70] In 1851 three of the parish's four posting inns were near the Iron Bridge,[71] the other on the turnpike road through Coalbrookdale to Wellington.[72] Some public houses were meeting places for friendly societies[73] and sporting clubs or teams;[74] some had clubrooms. In the late 19th century four of the five pubs with the worst police records were in the Ironbridge and Madeley Wood area, though the worst was the Three Furnaces, opened near Madeley Court in 1841. Most pubs had only works, mining, or roadside trade;[75] in 1901 the impressive, early 19th-century frontage of the Crown, Hodgebower, distinguished the only inn besides the Tontine with any superior custom.[76]

The closure of eight pubs 1911–21 (four in Ironbridge) and two others in 1926 and 1933 (in Madeley) brought numbers from 50 in 1909 to 40 in 1937. By 1980, though new pubs had opened on the new housing estates in the 1960s and 1970s, there were only 31 in the ancient parish area.[77] Many of them had bowling greens, social clubs, and regularly organized games, and some raised charitable funds.[78]

Increasing trade and population bred violence. In Ironbridge colliers and bargemen fought on market day, and by the 1760s the parish wake, held after Michaelmas, was notorious for the drunkenness caused by its shows and bull-baiting. J. W. Fletcher, vicar 1760–85, and Richard Reynolds, lord of the manor, opposed baiting. Reynolds's predecessors had required some of their cottage tenants to keep a dog or fighting cock for them, but Reynolds laid out walks through his woods to provide more civilized recreation for all classes. In 1788 the vestry resolved to withhold poor relief from any who kept a dog or fighting cock.[79] In 1810 most of the parish's employers announced that they would try to prevent those concerned in a bull-baiting at the recent wake from getting work.[80] Badgers[81] and bulls were baited at Ironbridge wake, but bull-baiting there was finally put down by the curate and others c. 1825.[82] A Primitive Methodist protracted meeting in Ironbridge the week before the 1858 wake[83] may have been intended to stiffen resistance to the wake's allurements, which by then were probably few. So were, by 1869, those of the annual pleasure fair held at Ironbridge on 29 May.[84] Other events replaced them. An annual Ironbridge fête, started in 1864, included sports, a high-wire act, and fireworks in 1875.[85] Regular visits by circuses[86] and fun fairs[87] began and, stemming from the

[62] T.S.A.S. xi. 70; S.R.O. 2280/6/103, copy of notice 17 May 1812.
[63] See e.g. S.R.O. 1224/2/371, 389.
[64] As c. 1650: P.R.O., SP 23/105, p. 193 (blacksmith, 'lime man', tailor).
[65] L. Tyerman, Wesley's Designated Successor (1882), 168, 525; H. M. Rathbone, Letters of Ric. Reynolds (1852), 47; S.R.O. 2280/6/95, 1 Oct. 1781; /6/96 (at end), petition of 1807; /6/103, letters of 25 Sept. 1811, 12 Oct. 1812.
[66] S.R.O. 2280/2/48, omitting mention (s.v. Wright, Ben., no. 3199) of the Commercial, Coalbrookdale.
[67] Co. of Salop, Reg. of Public Hos. 1901 (copy in S.P.L., accession 6117), 332–65, modifying Randall, Madeley, 369–72; U. Rayska and A. Carr, Telford Past and Present (1978), 63.
[68] S.R.O. 1987/4/12–13.
[69] The others were the Coalbrookdale (1843), and the Post Office (1868). See Reg. of Public Hos. 1901, 333, 356, 360; S. Bagshaw, Dir. Salop. (1851), 579; Trinder, Ind. Rev. Salop. 332; cf. S.R.O. 725/4, p. 10; 803/1, p. 102.
[70] S.R.O. 245/6; Muter, Coalbrookdale and Ironbridge, 17–18; below, plate 20.
[71] The Tontine, Three Tuns (1790), and White Hart (1805): S. Bagshaw, Dir. Salop. (1851), 578.
[72] The Commercial: ibid. 579.
[73] e.g. the Three Tuns, Ironbridge: Orders of Q. Sess. iii. 256; S.R.O. 3217/50.
[74] Madeley Town F.C. was formed at the All Nations:

Eddowes's Jnl. 23 Sept. 1885.
[75] Reg. of Public Hos. 1901, 332–65; Trinder, Ind. Rev. Salop. 332.
[76] Reg. of Public Hos. 1901, 335; Muter, Coalbrookdale and Ironbridge, 18.
[77] Kelly's Dir. Salop. (1909), 78, 117–18, 144–5; (1937), 81, 123, 151–2; Wenlock div. J.P.s' licensing regs. 1911–28, 1929–38, 1957– (in use) (in possession of magistrates' clk.).
[78] Jackson, 'Madeley', bk. 1A, pp. 233–4; 2A, pp. 202, 222–3; Rest Room Rev. l. 33–4.
[79] Salopian Shreds & Patches, vii. 116; Tyerman, Wesley's Designated Successor, 66–7; V.C.H. Salop. ii. 191; S.R.O. 1681, box 130, cottage lease; Skinner, Nonconf. in Salop. 39; Trinder, Ind. Rev. Salop. 279, 366.
[80] S.R.O. 2280/6/103, copy of circular notice 8 Oct. 1810.
[81] Randall, Madeley, 348.
[82] And possibly at Madeley a yr. or two earlier: V.C.H. Salop. ii. 192; Jackson, 'Madeley', bk. 1A, p. 135.
[83] S.R.O. 2533/130, 14 June 1858.
[84] P.O. Dir. Salop. (1856), 75; Eddowes's Jnl. 2 June 1869. The fair was still recorded over 70 yrs. later: Kelly's Dir. Salop. (1941), 121.
[85] V.C.H. Salop. ii. 202; Boro. of Wenlock Express, 14 Aug. 1875 (ref. to 11th ann. fête).
[86] Jackson, 'Madeley', bk. 1A, p. 223; bk. 2A, p. 119.
[87] Ibid. bk. 1A, pp. 211, 223; Rayska, Victorian and Edwardian Salop. from Old Photos. pl. 32.

celebration of royal events, summer carnivals began to be held at Madeley[88] and Ironbridge,[89] and later at Coalport,[90] where Jackfield wake was held in the late 19th century.[91]

A friendly society existed by 1794,[92] and others were later formed at Coalbrookdale,[93] Ironbridge,[94] Madeley Wood,[95] and Park Lane.[96] Some met at public houses,[97] others had temperance links. Works and chapels had provident societies, and the Coalbrookdale Co. employees' subscriptions contributed also to their sons' education. Lodges of Odd Fellows, Foresters, freemasons, and others were established during the 19th century, and there was a branch of the Shropshire Provident Society 1853–1945. About 1880 some 3,000 members, subscribing £2,380 a year, were claimed for the parish's provident societies.[98] The freemasons' lodge was meeting in Wellington by 1969.[99]

As public houses increased from the 1830s temperance societies opened branches throughout the parish, and there was a 'British Workman' at Ironbridge from c. 1880 to c. 1905, at Coalbrookdale in the 1880s, and at Madeley in 1895.[1] Libraries were founded from the 1830s, when two church Sunday schools had lending libraries attached.[2] Reading rooms were opened and literary societies founded.[3] By 1864 the vicar of Madeley was patron of a working man's subscription library which had 200 members in 1903.[4] The Ironbridge Reading, Lecture and Billiard Rooms at the Wharfage were recorded from 1885 to 1941;[5] they were probably the assembly rooms mentioned in 1885 and 1892.[6] About that time there were also assembly rooms in St. Luke's Road, Ironbridge, sold in 1906 as a Volunteers' armoury.[7] The Ironbridge parish room, opened c. 1909 in the old infant school, contained a reading room and library.[8]

The Ironbridge Mechanics' Institution flourished 1840–c. 1852. Alfred Darby (d. 1852) arranged to buy its library for the Coalbrookdale Literary and Scientific Institution, formed in 1853; its officers were largely the Coalbrookdale Co.'s owners and senior staff; there were middle-class and working-class subscriptions. The library opened in the company's boys' school in 1853, a reading room in the girls' church school in 1855. A building (with a librarian's house) was opened in 1859, the Tudor Gothic design by the company manager Charles Crookes being realized in the company's own blue and white brick. Newspapers and periodicals were taken and the library grew to over 3,000 books by 1890. There was an annual lecture programme and, from 1856, a popular day excursion, usually in August. By the 1890s, however, the institution was suffering from the growing popularity of outdoor pursuits with the young. A room was devoted to recreational uses, and the Coalbrookdale Social Club was formed in the institution in 1898. Institution membership was then only 46, and in 1899 it amalgamated with the Club.[9]

Similar bodies were founded elsewhere. A literary and artistic institute at Coalport, in existence by 1856,[10] gave way in 1892 to a temperance coffee house, which was associated with the china works and included a newspaper reading room and a small library; it closed soon after 1917.[11] At Madeley the Anstice Memorial Institute and Workmen's Club was opened in 1869. The Italianate building included a reading room, library, and large lecture hall. Altered over the years, the institute was much used for plays, dances, and many other social gatherings; the library closed in 1942.[12]

The county library had book centres in the parish from the late 1920s; that at Madeley became a branch in the 1950s. There were branches at Ironbridge 1958–71 and Sutton Hill 1968–81, and a local-history reference library in the Coalbrookdale Institution annexe was open in 1966 and 1967.[13]

The *Ironbridge Weekly Journal and Borough of Wenlock Advertiser*, started in 1868, was sold by the Ironbridge postmaster Joseph Slater in 1874[14] to local Conservatives who, stimulated to strengthen their position in the borough that year, formed a company to publish it.[15] It was retitled the *Borough of Wenlock Express and General*

[88] Jackson, op. cit. bk. 1A, pp. 192–3, 219, 245.

[89] *Telford Jnl.* 4 Mar. 1977 (photo. of 1936 carnival).

[90] *Dawley Observer*, 21 Aug. 1968. Cf. I.G.M.T. Libr., diaries, etc., of C. F. Peskin (1862–1949), an invaluable source for the par.'s social life.

[91] *Shropshire Jnl.* 21 Aug. 1970.

[92] S.R.O., q. sess. order bk. 1789–96, f. 262v.; cf. *Orders of Q. Sess.* iii. 70, 173, 199.

[93] *Orders of Q. Sess.* iii. 132, 171; iv. 12, 50.

[94] Ibid. iii. 191, 256.

[95] Ibid. iv. 24, 26, 43.   [96] Ibid. iii. 97.

[97] Ibid. 256; S.R.O. 3217/50.

[98] Randall, *Madeley*, 199, 354–8; S.R.O. 436/6720, p. 75; /6733, pp. 64, 75; /6749, p. 9; 2280/16/185, pp. 21–3; below, Educ.; A. Graham, *Hist. of Freemasonry in Salop.* (Shrews. 1892), 84; Jackson, 'Madeley', bk. 1, p. 89; bk. 1A, pp. 139, 247; *Eddowes's Jnl.* 28 June 1854; *Rep. Registrar Friendly Socs. 1871*, H.C. 394, p. 108 (1872), liv; *1872*, H.C. 323, pp. 132–3 (1873), lxi.

[99] H. Temperton, *Hist. of Craft Freemasonry in Salop. 1732–1982* [1982], 38–9, 81, 108.

[1] Randall, op. cit. 302, 354; *Kelly's Dir. Salop.* (1885), 835, 866; (1895), 133; (1905), 113.

[2] *Educ. Enq. Abstract*, H.C. 62, p. 778 (1835), xlii.

[3] Randall, op. cit. 172; cf. *Eddowes's Jnl.* 3 Feb., 8 Dec. 1869 (reps. of Ironbridge Reading and Mutual Improvement Soc.).

[4] S.R.O. 2280/6/114; /13/14.

[5] *Kelly's Dir. Salop.* (1885), 866; (1941), 121–2.

[6] As venue of Bapt., Cong., and freemasons' mtgs.: below, Prot. Nonconf.; Graham, *Freemasonry*, 49.

[7] Bought as a Volunteers' armoury 1906: T.D.C., Old Armoury deeds.

[8] *Kelly's Dir. Salop.* (1909), 116–17; (1917), 109–10; (1922), 116–17; (1941), 121–2.

[9] S. Bagshaw, *Dir. Salop.* (1851), 569, 576; T. Kelly, *Geo. Birkbeck: Pioneer of Adult Educ.* (1957), 316; S.P.L., MS. 6785, ann. rep. 1854; McFall, 'Educ. in Madeley Union', 61–2; Muter, *Coalbrookdale and Ironbridge*, 21–2 and pl. 29; Randall, *Madeley*, 301–2.

[10] *P.O. Dir. Salop.* (1856), 78.

[11] *Kelly's Dir. Salop.* (1885), 887–8; (1891), 356–7; (1917), 136; S.R.O. 1681, box 13, prospectus, corresp., and rep. of 1892; Rayska, *Victorian and Edwardian Salop.* pl. 35.

[12] *Eddowes's Jnl.* 22 Sept. 1869; Randall, *Madeley*, 175 n., 177–8; Pevsner, *Shropshire*, 193; Jackson, 'Madeley' *passim* (esp. bk. 2A, pp. 74–5, 96).

[13] Jackson, op. cit. bk. 2A, pp. 75, 96; R. C. Elliott, 'Development of Public Libraries in Salop.' (Loughborough Univ. M.A. thesis, 1970; copy in co. libr.), 99–100, 104–5, 112–14, 125–7; inf. from co. libr.

[14] *Ironbridge Weekly Jnl.* 20 June 1874; 2 Jan. 1875; E. Cassey & Co. *Dir. Salop.* (1871), 185–7.

[15] P.R.O., BT 31/2076/9218; *V.C.H. Salop.* iii. 342.

Advertiser in 1875 and the *Wenlock and Ludlow Express and Shropshire Advertiser* in 1877.[16] The paper probably ceased in 1882.[17] The *Shropshire Examiner and All Round the Wrekin Advertiser*, started in 1873, proclaimed itself the organ of mining and other industrial interests.[18] Its owner, the Liberal John Randall, sold it in 1874 to a Wolverhampton man who began to publish it from Wellington.[19] In 1879 Randall, who had meanwhile brought out a monthly magazine,[20] started the *Wrekin Echo* as the 'only recognized organ' of Liberals and nonconformists in mid and south Shropshire. In 1881, the year in which Lord Granville obtained the Madeley postmastership for Randall, the *Echo* was merged with the new *Shropshire Guardian*, the Liberals' main county paper.[21] The *Telford Times*, a monthly, later three-weekly, free newspaper started in 1982, was published in Ironbridge.[22]

Movies reached Madeley *c.* 1903 and there was a cinema in the former Bethesda chapel 1910–58; there were others at Ironbridge *c.* 1916–1966 and Dale End *c.* 1933–1959.[23] A casual mention of an Ironbridge theatre may refer to one of the touring companies which visited the parish at the turn of the 19th and 20th centuries; one such used to pitch along Waterloo Street near the old Bedlam furnaces.[24] Plays were also staged at the Anstice Memorial hall.[25]

From 1979 to 1983 WSM, a community radio station in Woodside controlled by a board of householders, regularly transmitted music, local news, and other matters of community interest for *c.* 8 hours daily by cable to Woodside, Sutton Hill, and Madeley.[26]

As in most 20th-century towns, social life in Madeley was centred on sport and pubs. Nevertheless clubs and societies for other,[27] more specialized[28] interests proliferated; those common in mining communities[29]—choral societies,[30] brass and silver bands,[31] and homing-pigeon clubs[32]—showed particular vitality. St. John Ambulance Brigade, with a unit in the parish from *c.* 1900,

had its own premises, the Lowe Memorial Hall, Park Lane, in the 1950s.[33] Units of the usual uniformed youth organizations were formed in the 20th century, and there were five youth clubs in 1980.[34]

Madeley Rest Room, a meeting place for old people, developed out of R. N. Moore's religious and social work in the 1920s. Meetings were weekly in the Anstice Memorial Institute 1929–34 but thereafter every weekday in a new room in Park Avenue and, from 1968, its successor in Church Street.[35] The Rest Room published a *Review* from 1930[36] and was the precursor of others in Dawley, Oakengates, and Hadley.[37] The Ironbridge Fellowship Club, formed in the 1950s, had its own premises, and other clubs, including some for old people, met in community centres and similar buildings, which numbered 26 in 1980, half of them publicly provided.[38]

In 1860 Ironbridge supplied the headquarters, and soon after the designation, of a volunteer rifle corps formed for the borough of Wenlock and represented, from 1888 to 1967, by a company of the Volunteer (from 1908 Territorial) battalion, K.S.L.I.[39] It had an armoury in St. Luke's Road 1906–26[40] and a drill hall in Waterloo Street from the First World War until it was absorbed in 1947 in the Wellington company, which used the T.A. centre at Hill Top in Madeley 1952–67.[41]

Recreational use of the Severn increased as its commercial traffic declined. Matthew Webb learnt to swim in it,[42] and a floating bath was in use by 1879. The Ironbridge Rowing Club was formed *c.* 1870 and held open regattas 1883–91 (usually combined with other sports) and from 1950.[43] River excursions became popular from the mid 19th century.[44] Fishing was very popular in the mid 20th century, not only on the Severn but elsewhere, as at Upper furnace pool, New pool, and Madeley Court pool, the last-named stocked by an angling club *c.* 1958.[45]

About 1896 the vicar of Madeley counted the main obstacles to his work as indifference, drink,

---

[16] Issues of 29 May 1875 and 17 Feb. 1877. The masthead claimed circulation in increasing nos. of towns: cf. ibid. 29 May, 25 Dec. 1875; 10 Feb. 1877.
[17] Issue of 4 Mar. 1882 is last in B.L. Cf. P.R.O., BT 31/2076/9218. [18] *Examiner*, 2 May 1874.
[19] Ibid. 19 and 26 Dec. 1874. For Randall's politics see *Wellington Jnl.* 4 Sept. 1909; 3 Sept. 1910.
[20] *Salopian and W. Midland Monthly Illustr. Jnl.* 1875–80 (set in S.P.L.).
[21] *Wellington Jnl.* 4 Sept. 1909; 3 Sept. 1910; S.P.L., accession 1161, p. 19; *V.C.H. Salop.* iii. 313, 345.
[22] Inf. from the publisher.
[23] S.R.O. 4044/94, p. 140; S.R.O., DA 34 (S.R.O. 3279/1), Central file, copy letter 13 Apr. 1966; ibid. Plaza files of 1951–6 (memo. 30 Aug. 1951), 1956–9 (letter 27 May 1959); Jackson, 'Madeley', bk. 1A, pp. 138–9, 222; bk. 2A, p. 174; bk. 3A, p. 87; *Kelly's Dir. Salop.* (1917), 110; (1934), 82; T.D.C. Central Cinema deeds. The Picture Ho., Ironbridge (1912), was short-lived: F. J. Brown, 'Cinemas of Telford 1910–83' (TS. lent by Mr. Brown).
[24] S.R.O. 3673/1, pp. 16–17; *Shropshire Mag.* Dec. 1959, 17.
[25] *Kelly's Dir. Salop.* (1909), 143; (1913), 146; Jackson, op. cit. bk. 2A, p. 174. [26] Local inf.; S.R.O. 4591.
[27] See Jackson, op. cit. bk. 1A, pp. 216–17; bk. 2A, pp. 82–5, 222–4; bk. 3A, pp. 49–90, 155–62, 166–81, 196–204, 327.
[28] Dramatic socs. were perh. short-lived: *Shrews. Chron.* 1 May 1953 (p. 9). But cf. Jackson, op. cit. bk. 2A, pp. 98–100.
[29] J. Benson, *Brit. Coalminers in the 19th Cent.: a Social Hist.* (1980), 158, 162.

[30] Jackson, op. cit. bk. 1A, p. 256; bk. 2A, pp. 73, 84; bk. 3A, p. 83; *Rest Room Rev.* 1. 34.
[31] Jackson, op. cit. bk. 2A, pp. 116, 163; cf. ibid. p. 245; *Eddowes's Jnl.* 16 Sept. 1868 (ref. to Coalbrookdale brass band at Ironbridge fête); Rayska, *Victorian and Edwardian Salop.* pl. facing p. v.
[32] Jackson, op. cit. bk. 2A, p. 83.
[33] *Kelly's Dir. Salop.* (1900), 109 (1st mention of Ironbridge corps); Jackson, op. cit. bk. 1A, p. 188; 2A, p. 224.
[34] Scouts (from *c.* 1912), guides (from 1931), cadets, etc.: Jackson, op. cit. bk. 2A, pp. 167–70, 185; Hist. Note in *Freedom of Wenlock to K.S.L.I.* (1965; pamph. in possession of Mr. G. Archer Parfitt); *Telford Social Trends*, i. 210–13. Cf. *St. Mic.'s, Madeley, Par. Mag.* July 1912.
[35] *Rest Room Rev.* 1; Rayska, *Redevelopment of Madeley*, 11.
[36] Set in possession of Mr. G. R. Moore, Madeley.
[37] *Rest Rm. Rev.* 1. 26.
[38] Local inf.; *Telford Social Trends*, i. 206–9; cf. Rayska, *Madeley*, 5.
[39] G. A. Parfitt, *Salop. Militia and Volunteers* (Hist. of Corps of King's Salop. Light Inf. iv [1970]), 253; Hist. Note in *Freedom of Wenlock to K.S.L.I.* (1965); inf. from Mr. Parfitt.
[40] T.D.C. deeds.
[41] Inf. from Mr. Parfitt; Jackson, 'Madeley', bk. 2A, pp. 183–4.
[42] *D.N.B.*
[43] *V.C.H. Salop.* ii. 202–3.
[44] Jackson, 'Madeley', bk. 1A, p. 247; 2A, p. 119.
[45] *Telford Social Trends*, i. 228; Jackson, op. cit. bk. 1A, p. 72.

and 'the passion for amusement, especially football'.[46] Madeley Town F.C. had been formed at the All Nations in 1885[47] and Ironbridge United was one of the county's stronger clubs in the 1890s and 1900s.[48] Regular cricket had been established by 1855, and by the 1890s there were clubs at Coalbrookdale (formed 1882) and Madeley, the latter one of the area's two leading ones. Club cricket and football offered temptations to rowdyism and even corruption in the late 19th and early 20th century, but the clubs were on the whole respectably led. W. G. Dyas captained Ironbridge F.C., was a leading Madeley C.C. player, and advised on the latter club's purchase of its ground in 1925. Despite protests from the clergy Madeley C.C. introduced Sunday cricket to the area in 1940, and a Sunday football league based on Ironbridge was founded in 1973.[49] By 1980 the only league football played by teams from the area of the ancient parish was in the local Sunday leagues.[50] Madeley C.C. played league cricket 1948–50 and from 1979. Coalbrookdale C.C. played in the Shropshire Cricket League from its first season in 1949 but in 1959 the club was merged in the Coalbrookdale works sports and social club and the team ceased playing in 1962. Madeley Miners' C.C. ceased in the late 1960s when the Miners' Welfare ground (purchased in 1923 and laid out as sports grounds) was acquired for the Madeley Education and Recreation Centre.[51]

Few outdoor recreational facilities in the parish were publicly provided before the 1950s. Earlier there had been private efforts on behalf of children's playing fields[52] but the first in Madeley to be equipped by the local authority was Trevor's Field, Park Street, in 1953;[53] another was opened at Hill Top c. 1960.[54] By 1980 there were public football pitches at the Alexander Fleming and Abraham Darby schools, at the Regatta Field recreation ground, Dale End, and at Sunniside.[55] Madeley Education and Recreation Centre, opened to the public in 1971 on 56 a. between Madeley and Woodside, was created by Telford development corporation and the county and district councils; it had outdoor and indoor sports facilities, a swimming pool, and a theatre and cinema.[56] Great Hay golf course opened in 1976[57] and became private when the Telford Hotel, in-

cluding a golf and country club, opened in 1981.[58]

From 1976 Telford development corporation made 200 a. of under-used, industrially derelict land north and west of Woodside into a public recreation area known as Rough Park.[59] Twenty acres developed by 1980 included $3\frac{1}{2}$ a. of allotments, formed 1976–8, between Beech Road and Woodside Way and an area for children's unsupervised play west of Castlefields Way. A riding school at Rough Park Farm stables continued to use land there. By 1980 the whole area south of the Lightmoor valley and east of Dale Coppice had been reclaimed and seeded as grassland, and there were plans to create woodland, other amenities, and footpaths linking Rough Park via the Silkin Way to Telford town park[60] and the Severn Gorge.

MANOR AND OTHER ESTATES. In the earlier 8th century Sigward, a follower (*comes*) of King Ethelbald of Mercia, is said to have held 3 hides of land at *MADELEY* by charter. Between 727 and 736 he sold his estate for a large sum of money to Milburga, daughter of a sub-king of the Magonsæte.[61] Madeley then remained a possession of the church of Wenlock, which St. Milburga had ruled as abbess, until the dissolution of Wenlock priory in 1540 when it passed to the Crown.[62] Wenlock held Madeley, like its other possessions, of the Crown except between c. 1074 and 1102 when the priory held its estates of the earls of Shrewsbury.[63]

In 1544 Robert Brooke bought the manor from the Crown; it was to be held as $\frac{1}{20}$ knight's fee.[64] Brooke (kt. 1555), a zealous papist who was elected speaker of the Commons in April 1554, was chief justice of Common Pleas from October 1554. On his death in 1558 the manor passed to his widow Dorothy, and c. 1572 it came to his eldest son John (d. 1598).[65] John was succeeded by his son Basil (kt. 1604),[66] a leading Roman Catholic and a prominent industrialist, courtier, and Civil War conspirator.[67] Sir Basil died in 1646,[68] and in 1652 his son Thomas forfeited his estates for treason against parliament.[69] Soon afterwards Thomas recovered the manor through Maj. John Wildman, the speculator in royalists'

[46] E. J. Sturdee, *Visit to the 'Mecca of Methodism'* (Annals of Church Pastoral-Aid Work, v [c. 1896]), 18 (copy in S.R.O. 2280/16/103).

[47] *Eddowes's Jnl.* 23 Sept. 1885.

[48] G. Riley, *Salop. F.A. 1877–1977*, list of Salop. F.A. cup winners; *V.C.H. Salop.* ii. 199–200.

[49] *Madeley (Salop) Cricket Club 1855–1980* [1980], 4–11, 15, 34 (copy in S.P.L.); Riley, op. cit.; Jackson, 'Madeley', bk. 3A, p. 81. For Dyas see Jackson, op. cit. bk. 1, p. 91; W. Mate & Sons Ltd. *Shropshire: Historical, Descriptive, Biographical* (1906), pt. 2, p. 189.

[50] Football reps. in Wed. edns. of *Shropshire Star* 1980–1 season.

[51] *Madeley (Salop) C.C.* 15, 17, 19–21, 23–4, 28; Jackson, 'Madeley', bk. 1A, p. 250; 2A, pp. 124–6; 3A, pp. 82, 175; inf. from Mr. K. F. Green, Hadley.

[52] *Rest Rm. Rev.* 1. 23.

[53] Jackson, 'Madeley', bk. 2A, pp. 202, 226.

[54] Ibid. p. 149. [55] *Telford Social Trends*, i. 226–7.

[56] *Shropshire Mag.* Feb. 1972, 20–1; Rayska, *Redevelopment of Madeley*, 17; *Telford Social Trends*, i. 213.

[57] *Telford Social Trends*, i. 224.

[58] Inf. from T.D.C.; *Shropshire Star*, 1 Sept. 1981.

[59] Para. based on T.D.C., New Towns Act, 1965, Section

6 (1) Submission no. 114; ibid. Exec. Management Cttee. suppl. agenda 16 Dec. 1980.

[60] Cf. Rayska, *Madeley*, 10. For the town pk. see below, Dawley, Social and Cultural Activities.

[61] *V.C.H. Salop.* ii. 38–9; H. P. R. Finberg *Early Charters of W. Midlands* (1961), pp. 148, 203, 206, 212.

[62] *V.C.H. Salop.* ii. 45–7; P.R.O., SC 6/Hen. VIII/3021, mm. 4d.–5d.

[63] *V.C.H. Salop.* i. 291; iii. 7, 10.

[64] *L. & P. Hen. VIII*, xix (1), p. 635; J. Randall, *Old Court House, (or Manor House,) Madeley* (Madeley, 1883), 26–8. A rent reserved to the Crown was extinguished in 1549: S.R.O. 245/2.

[65] *D.N.B.* s.v. Broke, Sir Rob.; Emden, *Biog. Reg. Univ. Oxf. 1501 to 1540* (1974), 73; *Hist. Parl., Commons, 1509–58*, i. 174–5, 503–6; 1558–1603, i. 488.

[66] P.R.O., C 142/256, no. 9; *D.N.B.* s.v. Brook, Sir Basil.

[67] C. V. Wedgwood, *King's War, 1641–1647* (1958), 284–6; J. Bossy, *Eng. Cath. Community 1570–1850* (1975), 56–7, 103; J. C. H. Aveling, *The Handle and The Axe: Cath. Recusants in Eng. from Reformation to Emancipation* (1976), 151–2, 167; P.R.O., CP 43/213, rot. 93.

[68] B.L. Add. MS. 21237, f. 15.

[69] *Acts & Ords. of Interr.* ed. Firth & Rait, ii. 592.

and papists' lands.[70] Thomas Brooke died at the Hay in 1675, when his grandson Basil, a minor,[71] may already have had an interest in the estate.[72] Basil died without issue in 1699 leaving Madeley to his cousin Comberford Brooke, of Comberford (Staffs.). Comberford Brooke died abroad in 1710[73] and Madeley descended to his son Basil, who died a minor in 1727.[74] The manor was then divided between Basil's sisters Catherine, who married J. U. Smitheman of Little Wenlock, and Rose, who in 1733 married John Giffard, a London merchant and younger brother of the owner of Chillington (Staffs.).[75]

Catherine Smitheman died in 1737, and her half of the manor passed to her husband. When he died in 1744 it descended to their son John, a minor.[76] John Smitheman and his wife sold it in 1774 to Abraham Darby (III),[77] and in 1781 Darby and his wife sold it to Darby's former brother-in-law Richard Reynolds.[78]

Rose Giffard died a widow in 1763.[79] Her four daughters inherited equal shares of her half of the manor. In 1765 one of them, Rose, married Peter Parry, of Tywysog (Denb.),[80] and in 1766 the Parrys sold their eighth to Rose's unmarried sisters Anne and Mary.[81] In 1774 Anne and Mary Giffard agreed to sell their three eighths of the manor to Abraham Darby (III),[82] but the agreement never took effect and in 1780 the sisters' three eighths were sold to Richard Reynolds.[83] In 1775 the remaining Giffard sister Barbara, widow of Thomas Slaughter, sold her eighth of the manor to William and Edward Elwell, two West Bromwich ironfounders, and their brother John, a Westminster ironmonger.[84] Abraham Darby (III) bought the Elwells' eighth in 1778,[85] and he and his wife sold it to Richard Reynolds in 1781.[86]

Reynolds thus reunited the whole manor in his own hands in 1780–1.[87] Eminent as Quaker philanthropist and ironmaster, Reynolds died in 1816.[88] His real property then descended to his

son Joseph and his daughter Hannah Mary Rathbone. In 1824, on the partition of the inheritance, Madeley came to Joseph[89] who conveyed it to his three sons in 1853: a seventh to Thomas Reynolds, three sevenths to Joseph Gulson Reynolds, and three sevenths to Dr. William Reynolds. Thomas (d. 1854) left his seventh to his two brothers.

Between 1871 and 1889 the manor passed by various means[90] to the Ball family, descendants of Joseph Reynolds's daughter Rebecca and her husband (and second cousin)[91] Joseph Ball. In 1891 eleven members of the family settled their shares or interests in the manor on trustees, the leading trustee being the Revd. C. R. Ball, locally reputed lord of the manor.[92] The manor remained in the hands of the Ball trustees for the rest of its existence, probably until c. 1940; it became the custom to appoint two trustees from the Revd. A. W. Ball's descendants, two from those of his brother Canon C. R. Ball.[93] Canon Ball died in 1918,[94] the leading trustee thereafter apparently being his nephew E. A. R. Ball (d. 1928).[95]

By 1641 the manor was encumbered with debts, reckoned at £10,000 in 1651.[96] Thomas Brooke had to repurchase it in the 1650s, and by the 1690s, when it was probably worth c. £1,000 a year,[97] his grandson Basil's estate was further encumbered by the costs of his industrial enterprises. Accordingly in 1695 the manor was settled on trustees empowered to sell land but charged with the continuance of the coal and iron works.[98] Until the 18th century it consisted of the whole parish[99] except for the vicar's glebe and for some land in Coalbrookdale which had been sold in 1540;[1] it also included c. 2 a. in Benthall parish, the Bower yard and weir.[2] The manor was valued for sale in 1702. Sales began soon after, some to sitting tenants, but the mineral rights were reserved.[3] Coppice land in Madeley Wood (the Lloyds) and Coalbrookdale (with Cawbrook or

[70] *Cal. Cttee. for Compounding*, v. 3298; G. F Hammersley, 'Hist. of Iron Ind. in Forest of Dean Region, 1562–1660' (London Univ. Ph.D. thesis, 1972), 253 n., 476. For Wildman see *D.N.B.*; M. Ashley, *John Wildman* (1947), 71–2.
[71] S.P.L., MS. 2790, p. 385; 4645, p. 242; S.R.O. 2280/Rg/1, bur. 23 Oct. 1658; /2, bur. 20 Feb. 1675.
[72] H.W.R.O.(H.), Heref. dioc. rec., visit. bk. 23 (referring to Basil as patron of the living before his grandfr.'s death).
[73] Staffs. R.O., D. 661/6/1/24, abstr. of title to Madeley Ct. est. 1827; S.R.O. 1681, box 130, copy will; Randall, *Old Ct. Ho.* 50.
[74] S.P.L., MS. 4645, p. 242; S.R.O. 2280/BRg/1, 24 Apr. 1727.
[75] Randall, op. cit. 60–1, 88; S.R.O. 1681, box 134, marr. settlement 20 June 1733; S.P.L., MS. 4082, pp. 3198–9.
[76] Randall, *Old Ct. Ho.* 1, 63–5; S.R.O. 1681, box 131, deed of 21 Oct. 1728; S.P.L., MS. 2790, p. 387.
[77] S.R.O. 1681, box 133, deed of 1–2 Sept. 1774.
[78] Ibid. deed of 18–19 June 1781.
[79] Ibid. box 136, copy will, 7 Nov. 1761; Skinner, *Nonconf. in Salop.* 32 n. 39.
[80] S.P.L., MS. 4082, p. 3199.
[81] S.R.O. 1681, box 130, abstr. of title to ⅜ of Madeley man. 1695–1769.
[82] S.R.O., q. sess. rec. parcel 282, reg. of papist deeds 1717–90, pp. 161–2.
[83] S.R.O. 1681, box 134, deed of 18 Dec. 1780.
[84] Ibid. box 135, deeds of June–July 1775; cf. C. J. L. Elwell, *The Iron Elwells* (Ilfracombe, 1964), 38–43, 46–51, 53–55.
[85] Negotiated 1776. See S.R.O. 1681, box 135, deed of 26–7 May 1778; box 139, draft arts. of agreement 1776; *The Blackcountryman*, xii (4), 66; Raistrick, *Iron Founders*, 88,

[98] *T.S.A.S.* lviii. 255 n. 56.
[86] S.R.O. 1681, box 135, deed of 18–19 June 1781.
[87] *Reynolds-Rathbone Diaries and Letters 1753–1839*, ed. Mrs. Eustace Greg (priv. print. 1905), 173; Raistrick, *Iron Founders*, 88–9, 247.
[88] *D.N.B.*; below, plate 21.
[89] For this para. and the next see S.R.O. 1681, box 145, abstr. of title of the Revd. C. R. Ball to land at Madeley Wood, 1893.
[90] Principally the wills of J. G. (d. 1871) and Dr. Wm. (d. 1877) Reynolds and their unm. sis. Jane (d. 1879). Cf. ibid. box 141, Madeley man. memo. as to shares, 1883.
[91] *Reynolds–Rathbone Diaries*, 204.
[92] *Kelly's Dir. Salop.* (1891: 1917). Some of the intricate early Ball–Reynolds relationships are set out in H. S. Torrens, 'Reynolds–Anstice geol. coll. 1776–1981', *Archives of Nat. Hist.* x. 431–3.
[93] W.B.R. Madeley dist. cttee. min. bk. 1937–43, pp. 22, 29, 250; S.R.O. 1681, box 141, Edith M. Ball to G. P. Hyslop, 20 May 1929.
[94] *Who Was Who, 1916–28*, 46; *Alum. Cantab. 1752–1900*, i. 135.
[95] See e.g. S.R.O. 1681, box 146, conveyances.
[96] *Cal. Cttee. for Compounding*, iii. 2232.
[97] S.R.O. 210/1.
[98] P.R.O., C 5/180/133; Madeley Manor Act, 7 & 8 Wm. III, c.4 (Priv. Act).
[99] P.R.O., E 315/111, f. 29; below, Econ. Hist. (Agric.).
[1] *L. & P. Hen. VIII*, xv, pp. 468–9; xvii, p. 212; P.R.O., C 1/1184/47–9.
[2] S.R.O. 1681, box 132, arts. of agreement *re* Bower yd. 1704.
[3] S.R.O. 210/1; 516/11; 1987/19/3.

Stanley's farm) was bought back into the manor in the 18th century.[4] By 1849 the lord of the manor owned only 291 a. of land[5] and in 1910 *c.* 126 a. (mainly Lees farm and land at Lincoln Hill).[6] Most of the land, including Madeley Wood Hall with almost 97 a.,[7] was sold piecemeal in the earlier 1920s.[8] The mineral rights, long the manor's most valuable constituent, were sold (except the beds of Broseley tile clay leased to Geo. Legge & Son) to the lessee, the Madeley Wood Co. Ltd., in 1929.[9]

The Coalbrookdale property separated from the manor in 1540.[10] descended in the Lokier and Sprott families, with the Marsh (in Barrow) from (Staffs.). The estate, consisting of Court and Windmill farms,[12] was bought in 1828 by James Foster, the Stourbridge ironmaster (d. 1853) and the largest landowner in the parish in 1849.[13] The Fosters sold the house and Court farm to the tenant Joseph Barnett, part in 1919 and the rest in 1936. In 1964 Dawley development corporation bought the house and most of the land, *c.* 172 a., from Barnett's son.[14]

Madeley Court is an L-shaped building.[15] Two ranges of fine locally quarried ashlar form the north and east sides of a forecourt; in their angle is a porch with a side entrance. On the south side of the forecourt is a gatehouse.

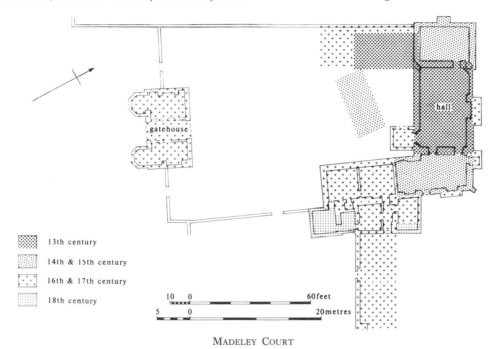

13th century

14th & 15th century

16th & 17th century

18th century

10   0   60 feet
5   0   20 metres

MADELEY COURT

the later 16th century to the 18th: suit was made for it at Marsh manor court in the 18th century. It seems to have consisted of two farms: Strethill farm, probably including the later Meadow farm and mostly sold to Mary Rathbone and her sister-in-law Rebecca Darby in 1805; and Caldebrook or Cawbrook farm, apparently acquired by the Stanleys who *c.* 1705 purchased land which they held of the manor.[11]

In 1705 Madeley Court and almost 520 a. of demesne was bought by Matthias Astley of Tamhorn (Staffs.). His granddaughter Mary Astley (d. 1826) carried the property to her husband (and cousin) Richard Dyott, of Freeford

The earliest building is probably the 13th-century hall block, forming the north side of the forecourt and originally free standing. It had only a single room at the level of the ground to the south, where it was entered at the east end; on the north ground level there was an undercroft. Not much later another, almost free-standing, building touched the hall at its south-west corner, and by the end of the Middle Ages wings running south on slightly diverging axes abutted the hall's east and west gables. Between them another building orientated east-west may have been a chapel. A lease of 1498 mentioned a chapel chamber, tower, hall, parlour, and outhouses.[16] About

[4] Below, Econ. Hist. (Agric.). For the Stanleys see *Salop. N. & Q.* 12 Oct. 1900.
[5] S.R.O. 2280/2/48, p. 87.
[6] S.R.O. 4044/93-4.
[7] S.R.O. 1681, box 146, copy conveyance of 24 July 1925.
[8] Ibid. conveyances.
[9] Below, Econ. Hist. (Iron and Steel, and sources there cited; Clay and Ceramic Industries).
[10] Above.
[11] *Cal. Pat.* 1560-3, 87; S.P.L., Deeds 1501, 1509, 1541, 1557; Skinner, *Nonconf. in Salop.* 30; S.R.O. 210/1; 1224/2/479-508; 1681, box 132, agreement to sell timber, etc., endorsement *re* conveyance to Stanley; 1987/3/1, 3-7, 13-14, 16-17, 24; /15/1-9; /30/2.
[12] Apley Est. Office, Bridgnorth, vol. of Madeley Ct. Misc.

Papers 1544-1837, copy agreement (incomplete); S.R.O. 1359, box 55, corresp. *re* sale, 1827; Staffs. R.O., D. 661/6/1/24, abstr. of title, 1827; S. Shaw, *Hist. Staffs.* i (1798), 362, 378.
[13] Randall, *Old Ct. Ho.* 52; S.R.O. 2280/2/48, pp. 41-4. Cf. plate 23; Burke, *Land Gent.* (1937), 812.
[14] T.D.C. Madeley Ct. fm. deeds; *Kelly's Dir. Salop.* (1909), 144; (1937), 151.
[15] Thanks are offered to Mr. R. A. Meeson for inf. based on excavations which he directed at Madeley Ct. 1978-9. See also Pevsner, *Shropshire*, 29-30, 193-4, and pl. 43b; *Salop. News Sheet*, viii. 3; H. Avray Tipping, *Eng. Homes, Period III*, i (1929), 154-60; below, plate 4. The following descr. assumes the hall to be N. (rather than NNE.) of the courtyd.
[16] P.R.O., E 315/94, ff. 12v.-13.

1508 the buildings were in decay. In the later 1530s the manorial bailiff John Wylcocks lived in the house, and after 1540 Hugh Leighton of Rodenhurst, lessee of the manor since 1534, allowed John Bayley, last prior of Wenlock, and his servants to lodge in the house;[17] Bayley died there in 1553.[18]

It was presumably for John Brooke (succ. c. 1572, d. 1598) that both wings were partly rebuilt and extended, the east-west building between them probably being demolished. The forecourt was formalized and the line of the wings extended by enclosing walls. The two-storeyed gatehouse with three-storeyed flanking turrets was built in the centre of the south side of the court, the porch in front of the hall doorway being built about the same time. Details of the gatehouse link it with Condover,[19] where Walter Hancock worked in the 1590s.[20]

By the earlier 17th century an upper floor had been added above the hall; it had a gallery and two chambers, both having garderobes beside the hall chimney stack. Another range, late 16th- or early 17th-century, projected east from the centre of the east wing and there may also have been a range continuing west on the line of the hall. A large formal garden west of the house was enclosed with red brick walls in the 17th century; an elaborate sundial[21] and 'astronomical toy' stands on 15-in. stone pillars in the centre.

The house was perhaps occupied by royalists and by the county committee in the 1640s.[22] The last lord of the manor to live there was Basil Brooke (d. 1699).[23] Thereafter the house's status gradually declined. The west wing was probably demolished in the 18th century. The east range was shortened at the same time but a two-roomed, two-storeyed block was added to the south-east corner of the east wing. Abraham Darby (I) was renting part of the house at his death in 1717. Later in the 18th century gentlemen farmers lived there, giving way to yeomen in the 19th century.[24] After 1840, when James Foster was mining under his property, the house declined rapidly: spoil heaps isolated it and covered the old fish or mill ponds.[25] C. W. Pearce, W. O. Foster's manager, lived in part of it until c. 1909 but in spite of his solicitude the house was already 'far gone to

decay' by 1883 and seemed likely soon to disappear.[26] Some repairs were made in 1904[27] but seventy years later, despite scheduling as an ancient monument, the hall range (long a farm store) and garden walls were ruinous and the gatehouse (formerly divided into cottages) had begun to crack apart. None of the buildings was inhabited after 1977.[28] In 1973 Telford development corporation marked the new town's tenth anniversary by announcing that the house would be restored. The building was made structurally sound and weatherproof 1976–9, and later the gatehouse was partly dismantled and rebuilt.[29]

The rectory, appropriated to Wenlock priory in 1344, was worth £8 in 1346[30] and 1370, perhaps £5 net in the 1370s.[31] In 1535 it was let for a reserved rent of £2 to Richard Charlton, still tenant in 1544 when the Crown sold the impropriate tithes to Robert Brooke.[32] The rectory descended with the manor until the early 18th century.[33] In the sales of manorial lands begun in 1705 the rectorial tithes due from, and eventually merged with, the Court demesnes and the Hay farm were sold with them.[34] By 1713 the remaining great tithes were the property of John Ashwood,[35] who built Madeley Hall and was apparently Comberford Brooke's executor and Basil Brooke's guardian.[36] By then Ashwood, a purchaser of small properties in the sales of 1705,[37] also owned 111 a. which his father had held as tenant in 1702 besides half of 'Fosbrooke's tenement' (54½ a.).[38] John's son William (d. 1739) and William's son John bought more land in Madeley and it was thus a considerable estate which, with the impropriate tithes, John's daughter Dorothy (d. 1783) brought in marriage in 1770 to Henry Hawley (cr. bt. 1795).[39] The Hawley family broke up the estate in the earlier 19th century. Their agent and tenant Timothy Yate, of Madeley Hall, was exchanging land with them by 1810,[40] and sales[41] seem to have begun before 1849 when Sir J. H. Hawley, Dorothy Ashwood's grandson,[42] owned some 333 a.[43] Most of that was sold in 1848: Madeley Hall, with 183 a., to Joseph Yate (d. 1893);[44] Castle Green farm to Francis and John Yates;[45] and the Lodge farm, with some 36 a., to Francis Darby.[46] By 1849 great tithes from some 1,284 a. in the parish had been merged with the land, mainly the

---

[17] P.R.O., E 315/108, ff. 32–53; E 321/1/21 and 51. Cf. P.R.O., LR 2/184, ff. 106, 120v.

[18] T.S.A.S. vi. 121; lx. 99.

[19] Tipping, Eng. Homes, Period III, i. 164–6.

[20] For him cf. Montg. Coll. lix. 138–40; M. Airs, Bldgs. of Brit.: Tudor and Jacobean (1982), 25–6; Arch. Jnl. cxxxviii. 34–5.   [21] Arch. Jnl. xi. 413.

[22] T.S.A.S. 3rd ser. x. 89n., 94–5; 4th ser. ii. 16–17, 294. For the cttee. see V.C.H. Salop. iii. 359.

[23] Randall, Old Ct. Ho. 48–9.

[24] Ibid. 81–2, 87; Randall, Madeley, 41; T.S.A.S. lix. 124; S.P.L., MS. 4360, p. 360; S.R.O. 2280/2/9, s.a. 1711.

[25] Below, Econ. Hist. (Coal and Ironstone). For the ponds see S.R.O. 2280/2/45, nos. 194, 325.

[26] Kelly's Dir. Salop. (1909), 144; Randall, Madeley, 41–2, 331; idem, Old Ct. Ho. 5, 8, 87; Salop. News Letter, xl. 19–20.

[27] T.S.A.S. 3rd ser. iv, p. xxi.

[28] T.D.C. Sec.'s files P/9/3 and P/9/3A–C; T.D.C. Madeley Ct. fm. deeds; inf. from T.D.C.; T.S.A.S. liv. 156; S.P.L., Deeds 18476.

[29] Shropshire Star, 17 Jan. 1973; T.D.C. Sec.'s file P/9/3B; inf. from T.D.C.

[30] B.L. Add. MS. 50121, pp. 2–10, 14–16; Reg. Trillek (C.S.), 288.

[31] Eyton, iii. 323; B.L. Add. MS. 6164, ff. 195, 207; Dugdale, Mon. v. 78.

[32] Valor Eccl. (Rec. Com.), iii. 216; P.R.O., SC 6/Hen. VIII/3021, m. 5d.; L. & P. Hen. VIII, xix (1), p. 635.

[33] P.R.O., C 142/256/9; CP 43/213, rot. 93; S.R.O. 2280/2/36.

[34] S.R.O. 2280/2/36; T.D.C. Hay fm. deeds; below.

[35] S.R.O. 516/11; 2280/2/36; cf. S.P.L., MS. 4645, p. 181.

[36] Jackson, 'Madeley', bk. 1, p. 88; S.R.O. 2280/3/6.

[37] S.R.O. 1987/19/3.   [38] S.R.O. 210/1; 516/11.

[39] Lincs. Archives Office, 2 Haw. 1/G/45–51, 55–62; S.R.O. 1681, box 178, abstr. of title of Sir J. Hawley; S.P.L., MS. 4645, p. 181; G.E.C. Baronetage, v. 300.

[40] Lincs. Archives Office, 2 Haw. 1/G/63–4.

[41] e.g. the c. 100 a. with gt. tithes merged, belonging in 1847 to J. Bartlett and T. L. Beddoes: cf. field names in S.R.O. 2280/2/48, pp. 7, 10; Wrekin Dist. Council, Madeley Hall deeds, abstr. of title of Sir J. H. Hawley, 1848.

[42] Burke, Peerage (1949), 974; D.N.B.

[43] Rest of para. based on S.R.O. 2280/2/48.

[44] Wrekin Dist. Council, Madeley Hall deeds.

[45] T.D.C. deeds of land at Woodside (incl. Cas. Green fm.), covenant to produce deeds, 1848.

[46] S.R.O. 1681, box 178, deed of 1848; 1987/19/37.

former Court demesnes (634 a.), the Hay farm, and land which the Hawleys then, or had formerly, owned. The remaining impropriate tithes were commuted to £115 10s. that year and sold in 1858.[47]

The Yate family owned the Hall from 1848 to 1946.[48] In 1914 Joseph Yate's unmarried daughter Louisa Ann conveyed it, with a reduced and mortgaged estate, to her cousin Col. Charles E. Yate (cr. bt. 1921, d. 1940)[49] and in 1946 Sir Charles's nephew, Lt.-Col. V. A. C. Yate, sold the house and its contents, with surrounding land and outbuildings, to Wenlock corporation.

Madeley Hall, built of brick on a moulded stone plinth in the early 18th century, has a principal front, to the east, of 5 bays and a west front with a recessed centre. The house was extended north and west in 1921. In the early 1980s it was converted to flats by the Wrekin district council. Extensive internal alterations before that had left some original oak panelling. A terrace along the east front led south to a two-storeyed gazebo of the late 18th century. The outbuildings include a detached 18th-century brick barn, two timber-framed farm buildings with a wheel house attached to one of them, and a long range of stone-fronted stables heightened and enlarged in brick in the 19th century.

The Lodge, former farmhouse of the Lodge farm, was made into three separate dwellings. The southern, stone, block is 17th-century[50] but the north range, converted to cottages in the 19th century, incorporates features that may survive from earlier.

Abraham Darby and his descendants, often several households of them at a time, lived in the parish for two and a quarter centuries,[51] eventually owning much land there. About 1709 Abraham (I) occupied a timber-framed house, formerly Lawrence Wellington's, near the Great forge in Coalbrookdale. Later known as White End, it was demolished in 1939.[52] John and Ann Darby moved into it c. 1711 when their son Abraham (I) took part of Madeley Court,[53] later (c. 1715) beginning a new brick house for himself at the top of Coalbrookdale; that was either the present Dale House or the Grange, family tradition favouring the former. The house was not quite finished at his death in 1717, and his widow was denied the use of it by her brother-in-law Thomas Baylies. Soon afterwards, however, Thomas Goldney and Darby's son-in-law Richard Ford, the new managers of the Coalbrookdale works, obtained possession. Abraham (II) was brought up there[54] but little remains of the early 18th-century house.

Originally of two storeys with attic dormers and a symmetrical main front of five bays, it seems to have been remodelled in the early 19th century, when the attics were incorporated into an extra storey and some of the rooms reconstructed. Edmund Darby's widow Lucy rented it from the Coalbrookdale Co. in 1849,[55] and in the later 19th century the company's general manager, W. G. Norris (d. 1911), lived there.[56] Earlier 20th-century alterations included the addition of an iron balcony across the main front; converted into flats, the house was internally replanned in 1952–3 when all except the sash windows of the main elevation were replaced by iron casements and the pitched roof by a lead flat. Glynwed Foundries Ltd. sold it to Telford development corporation in 1980.[57]

About 1750 Abraham Darby (II) built Sunniside above Loamhole dingle.[58] In 1758 he bought half of the Hay, a 266-a. farm which had belonged to the Purcells 1705–55. Abraham (III) bought the rest of Hay farm in 1771,[59] and c. 1775, while attempting to acquire all the shares of the manor, he left Coalbrookdale for the Hay at the opposite end of the parish. He lived there in style, dying in 1789. His son Francis, then a minor, lived there 1803–7. Later tenants included Robert Ferriday (d. 1842), the purchaser of Upper House c. 1830, and the brothers John (d. 1841) and Thomas (d. 1843) Rose, managers of the nearby Coalport porcelain works.[60]

The Hay Farm is a red brick house of various dates. Although ostensibly 18th-century, it may be of earlier origin. The principal, east, front has a recessed centre of three bays flanked by two unequal short wings. The central range has a plan which may be 17th-century, but its walls appear contemporary with the early 18th-century north wing. A south wing and additional service room on the north-west were added later in the 18th century, probably by Abraham Darby (III). In the 19th century the house was partly rendered, the interior was extensively replanned, and a conservatory was built between the wings on the east front. The farm buildings were altered and partly demolished during the Hay's conversion to a hotel and golf and country club, opened in 1981.[61] Largely 18th-century and of brick, they incorporated the stone walls of an earlier barn.

Francis Darby moved back to Coalbrookdale in 1807. Other members of the family lived there in the earlier 19th century in large detached residences of the 18th or early 19th century.[62] Besides Dale House, Sunniside,[63] and the White House,[64] there were the Grange, a symmetrically fronted

[47] Church Com. deeds of 1858.

[48] Para. based on Wrekin Dist. Council, Madeley Hall deeds.

[49] D.N.B. 1931–40.

[50] Randall, Madeley, 326–31, supposes a romantic medieval hist. See below, pl. 31.

[51] B. Trinder, Darbys of Coalbrookdale (1978), 66; Raistrick, Iron Founders, 3, 274.

[52] Trinder, op. cit. 23, 66, correcting Raistrick, op. cit. 47 n. 2; S.R.O. 2280/2/8, s.a. 1709, 1710. For Wellington see below, Econ. Hist. (Iron and Steel).

[53] S.R.O. 2280/2/9, s.a. 1711–15; T.S.A.S. lix. 124.

[54] Trinder, op. cit. 23, 66; Raistrick, op. cit. 43–4, 47; P.R.O., PROB 5/22/1–4.

[55] S.R.O. 2280/2/48, p. 22 (no. 3313).

[56] S.R.O. 4044/94, p. 120 (nos. 2222–3); Wellington Jnl. 9 and 16 Dec. 1911.

[57] Local inf.

[58] Trinder, Darbys, 66.

[59] S.R.O. 749/1–2, 4–8, 13–19, 22–8.

[60] Trinder, Darbys, 48; U. Rayska, The Hay: Brief Hist. (T.D.C. 1979; copy in S.P.L.), 5, 7–9; S.R.O. 1359, box 52, lease of 1810; 2448/1, pp. 32–3, 56; T.D.C., deed pkt. 187, Rob. Ferriday's will.

[61] Shropshire Star, 1 Sept. 1981.

[62] Trinder, op. cit. 64, 66; Muter, Coalbrookdale and Ironbridge, 25.

[63] Above.

[64] Later Sunniside: below.

house of five bays belonging *c.* 1850 to Richard Darby, retired ironmaster;[65] Mount Pleasant, probably the new house started in 1803 by Edmund Darby[66] on the site of Abraham (II)'s summer house;[67] and the Chesnuts, where Abraham (IV) lived *c.* 1850.[68] The unusual plan of the Chesnuts, with entrance in each end elevation, strengthens the likelihood that Sarah Darby (d. 1821) reconstructed it from an unequal pair of older houses bought from Edward Cranage in 1809.[69] Interior fittings are also of several styles: some panelling and doors seem to be later 18th-century, other doors and the main staircase could be *c.* 1820 and many doorcases *c.* 1840. By 1849 the house was Abraham Darby (IV)'s[70] and from *c.* 1853 to *c.* 1901 it was Coalbrookdale vicarage.[71] In 1980 the house was two dwellings; the larger, called the Chesnuts, had been restored in the 1970s when some new fittings, matching the original ones, had been introduced.

By 1849 Francis Darby (d. 1850) was the second largest landowner in the parish with 437 a.,[72] over half of it inherited;[73] the rest included his extensive purchases[74] around Sunniside[75] and on the opposite side of Coalbrookdale,[76] with the sporting rights over his property.[77] In 1851 all his real estate was settled on his younger daughter Adelaide Anna,[78] then living at the White House.[79] She and her husband Henry Whitmore sold the Hay farm in 1853 to Joseph Reynolds, whose legatee sold it in 1909.[80] When Sunniside was demolished *c.* 1856 the Whitmores adopted its name for the White House.[81] In 1879 Whitmore's widow added Greenbank farm, Little Dawley,[82] to the Sunniside estate, which she left to her elder sister Matilda Frances, Abraham (IV)'s widow. During the sisters' time a deer herd was maintained in Sunniside's grounds. Mrs. Darby died in 1902 leaving the estate to her kinsman A. E. W. Darby, of Adcote;[83] in his hands it was united with other Darby property to the south formerly enjoyed by his uncle Abraham (IV),[84] the owner

of 161 a. in the parish in 1849.[85] In 1910 A. E. W. Darby owned 401 a. in Coalbrookdale and to the west, including 87 a. in Little Dawley.[86] On his death in 1925 the estate passed to his daughter Mrs. F. M. Cope-Darby (d. 1935), of Sunniside. Her trustees dispersed the estate by sale in the 1950s and 1960s. Sunniside was demolished in 1960.[87]

John Bartlett, incumbent of Buildwas 1822–61,[88] was living at Upper House in 1824.[89] By *c.* 1830 he was living in the extreme west of the parish near the Buildwas boundary, at Marnwood House[90] which he had probably built[91] on property acquired from Joseph Reynolds and Abraham Darby (IV).[92] In 1849 he owned 122 a. in the parish,[93] much of it formerly owned by the Hawleys.[94] Bartlett, married to William Reynolds's daughter,[95] took much interest in Madeley affairs[96] and after his death in 1861 was commemorated by an obelisk erected in Market Square, Ironbridge.[97]

By 1849 the Coalbrookdale and Madeley Wood companies were among the parish's principal landowners with 107 a. and 70 a. respectively.[98] The Madeley Wood Co. Ltd. owned the former manorial mineral rights from 1929[99] until Nationalization in 1947, but its landed property, with that of the Anstices, had been sold in 1926.[1] The Coalbrookdale Co. and its successors[2] continued to own much property in Coalbrookdale and Ironbridge.[3] In the 1930s W. J. Legge and his nephew W. G. Dyas, of the Villa, were said to be the chief landowners in the parish.[4]

ECONOMIC HISTORY. AGRICULTURE. In 1086 there was woodland for fattening 400 swine, one of the largest tracts in the county.[5] In the 12th century the men of Madeley enjoyed pannage with other common rights, defined in 1190 and surrendered in 1234, in the Wrekin woods.[6] The manor lay in the royal forest of Mount Gilbert

[65] Muter, *Coalbrookdale and Ironbridge*, 25, and pl. 37; Trinder, *Darbys*, 64.

[66] S.R.O. 245/14; 2280/2/47 (no. 3293); /48, p. 36 (no. 3293).

[67] Inf. from Lady Labouchere. Cf. Smith, *View from the Iron Bridge*, pp. 14–15.

[68] Trinder, *Darbys*, 64.

[69] Sarah Darby's will, proved 1822 (extract in I.G.M.T. Libr., 1978/181).

[70] Ibid.; S.R.O. 2280/2/48, p. 34 (no. 3280).

[71] Below, Churches.

[72] S.R.O. 2280/2/45–8.

[73] Mostly from his father, viz. Hay fm., Sunniside, White Ho., etc.

[74] Mainly 1837–41: S.R.O. 1681, box 180, abstr. of purchases, 1851.

[75] Mainly Furnace Bank fm. and pt. of Stanley's (Cawbrook) fm.: S.R.O. 1987/19/33–4; /30/3–4.

[76] *c.* 31 a.: ibid. /11/2; /21/2.

[77] Bought 1848 after purchase of Lodge fm.; S.R.O. 6181, box 180, abstr. of purchases; above, p. 38.

[78] T.D.C. Hay fm. deeds.   [79] Trinder, *Darbys*, 64.

[80] T.D.C. Hay fm. deeds.

[81] Trinder, op. cit. 66; inf. from Lady Labouchere.

[82] S.R.O. 1987/28/22–6.

[83] Burke, *Land Gent.* (1914), 494; wills of Adelaide Anna Whitmore (pr. 1899) and Matilda Frances Darby (pr. 1903).

[84] Under wills of Mary Rathbone (pr. 1807: S.R.O. 1987/32/3–4) and Sarah Darby (pr. 1822: I.G.M.T. Libr., 1978/181).

[85] S.R.O. 2280/2/48, p. 35.

[86] T.D.C. deed pkt. 103 (with plan); S.R.O. 4044/77, pp.

89–91; /94, pp. 116–20, 123, 128.

[87] T.D.C. deeds (e.g. pkts. 89, 103); inf. from Lady Labouchere; Raistrick, *Iron Founders*, 274; Jackson, 'Madeley', bk. 3A, p. 89; S.R.O., DA 6/119/1, pp. 291–2, 298, 335.

[88] *Alum. Cantab. 1752–1900*, i. 174; *V.C.H. Bucks*. iii. 379.

[89] T. Gregory, *Salop. Gaz.* (1824), 284.

[90] T.D.C. deed pkt. 187, Rob. Ferriday's will; Pigot, *Nat. Com. Dir.* (1835), 350.

[91] Traditions of an earlier ho. there seem to derive from cellars extending beyond the ho.: inf. from Maj. H. H. M. Milnes.

[92] S.R.O. 1987/32.

[93] S.R.O. 2280/2/48, pp. 10–11.

[94] i.e. the *c.* 95 a., with gt. tithes merged, pt. of Madeley Hill fm., 1847: cf. field names in S.R.O. 2280/2/48, p. 10; Wrekin Dist. Council, Madeley Hall deeds, abstr. of title of Sir J. H. Hawley, 1848.

[95] Clwyd R.O., Hawarden, D/DM/391/1, Reynolds pedigree; Greg, *Reynolds–Rathbone Diaries*, app. VI; cf. will of Susanna Ball Bartlett, pr. 1873.

[96] Below, Churches; Educ.

[97] T. Cassey & Co. *Dir. Salop.* (1871), 185.

[98] S.R.O. 2280/2/48, pp. 15–22, 60–2.

[99] Above.   [1] T.D.C. deed pkt. 261, sale partics.

[2] Cf. below, Lawley, Man. and Other Est.

[3] Deeds in possession of Thorn-Pudsey & Derry, Ironbridge; T.D.C. deeds (e.g. pkt. 1372); local inf.

[4] *Kelly's Dir. Salop.* (1934), 150; (1937), 150; Jackson, 'Madeley', bk. 1, pp. 90–2.

[5] *V.C.H. Salop.* i. 312, 483.

[6] *Cart. Shrews.* ed. U. Rees (1975), ii, pp. 353–4.

until 1301.[7] In 1283 Wenlock priory was allowed to inclose its wood of Madeley with a small dike and a low hedge (*haia*) and make a park there; Hay farm and the demesne park[8] may date from then. By 1322 the Hay was given over to pasture and tillage[9] and in 1379 the park had herbage worth 40*d*. a year but no underwood.[10]

The main wooded areas were in the west and south. Woodland survived along the boundaries with Buildwas[11] and Little Wenlock.[12] In 1232 trenches, or cleared strips marking the boundary with Little Wenlock, were renewed[13] through what was known by 1379 as Timber wood. Payment of pannage for 126 swine in Timber wood and 99 in the park in 1379[14] may indicate that mature trees abounded over the high land west of the wooded slopes of Coalbrookdale and in the park. The former area may gradually have been converted to coppice[15] whose clearance for pasture and meadow was completed in the 18th century.[16] Pannage for 58 pigs in the lord's wood was paid in 1431, and for 94 pigs in 1449.[17] The southern edge of the parish long contained the main area of woodland, Madeley wood, sloping steeply down into the Severn Gorge[18] and used as common[19] as late as the end of the 17th century.[20] The lack of pannage there in 1379 may indicate that it was already largely coppiced.[21] Madeley woods were described as inclosed grounds in the 1650s,[22] and inclosure of woodland may have allowed commoning to persist.

Lessees of the manor in 1498 were forbidden to cut oak, ash, and crab; from the park and the outwoods they were allowed wood for repairs, but building timber could be taken only under the bailiff's supervision.[23] Coppice land, sometimes let,[24] was increasingly useful for local industry. Timber too was required.[25] In 1702 the manorial estate contained 3,369 trees (including 131 ashes) and 160 cords of wood, worth £1,548 or about 9 per cent of the value of the land. In 1705 Coal-brookdale timber and coppice wood worth £600 was sold to the lessees of the Madeley Wood coal mines. Madeley Wood (including Lloyds coppice) was apparently excluded from the valuation, and most coppice land remained with the manor,[26] or was reunited to it,[27] in the 18th century. About 1720 the vicar claimed tithe wood from coppices.[28] By 1785 twenty-one years' growth was worth £15 or £16 an acre; barked oak poles were sold for use in the coal pits and the young bark fetched £1 a ton more than old bark. Timber was taken from Lloyds coppice for the pits in the 1790s.[29]

Coppice management in Coalbrookdale was practised in the 1840s, though the woods were then partly used for recreation,[30] an increasingly important use of local woodland in the next century. By 1981 much regard was had to the woods in Coalbrookdale[31] and Lloyd's coppice and around Blists Hill as important parts of Telford's landscape; they were mostly derelict coppice-with-standards, with much dead elm.[32]

In 1086 the estate was rated at 4 hides, 3 of them geldable. Its value in 1066 had been £4; by 1086 it was worth only 50*s*. There were 2 plough-teams in demesne in 1086 and 4 held by 6 villeins and 4 bordars; there was room for 6 more. The bordars' share probably implies continued expansion of cultivation.[33] Open fields were extended into wooded margins: the 'new land' (so called in 1321) of Meriotesbache and that next to Botshawe[34] perhaps represented such additions to Mill field in the mid 13th century.[35] Later, however, arable farming contracted. In 1291 there were 5 carucates, each worth 18*s*. a year.[36] By the 1370s there were only 3; a third of the arable then lay fallow and common, each of the two sown parts being worth 30*s*. a year.[37]

The open fields lay around Madeley town. South-east and south lay Mill field by 1381.[38] Westwards lay West field by the later 16th century,[39] perhaps 'le Schanofeld' of 1381.[40] To

[7] Ibid. p. 249; *V.C.H. Salop.* i. 488; Eyton, iii. 319.
[8] Eyton, iii. 320; *Cal. Pat. 1281–92*, 90–1; Randall, *Madeley*, 8, 332.
[9] Eyton, iii. 321.
[10] Dugdale, *Mon.* v. 77.
[11] J. Rocque, *Map of Salop.* (1752); C. and J. Greenwood, *Map of Salop.* (1827).
[12] i.e. in Loamhole dingle: Greenwood, op. cit; R. Baugh, *Map of Salop.* (1808).
[13] *Cal. Close*, 1231–4, 94. For trenches see O. Rackham, *Ancient Woodland* (1980), 155.
[14] S.R.O. 1224/2/4. For Timber wood cf. below, L. Wenlock.
[15] See ref. to Timber coppice *c.* 1705: *T.S.A.S.* lviii. 162.
[16] Pt. of Davis's coppice was 'plain ground' by 1702: S.R.O. 210/1, s.v. Thos. Stanley; 2280/2/45, esp. nos. 3439–40; /48, p. 30 (nos. 3439–40).
[17] S.R.O. 1224/2/8–9.
[18] Rocque, *Map of Salop.*; Greenwood, *Map of Salop.*; Randall, *Madeley*, 325–6; S.C.C. Planning Dept. *Severn Gorge Dist. Plan: Written Statement* (1980), 2, diagram after p. 56.
[19] P.R.O., E 315/132, ff. 128–30.
[20] When it was driven for strays: below, Local Govt.; cf. S.R.O. 2280/14/2, nos. 9, 20.
[21] Cf. Rackham, *Ancient Woodland*, 120.
[22] P.R.O., C 6/10/60.
[23] P.R.O., E 315/94, f. 12v. For uses, etc., of oak, ash, and crab see Rackham, op. cit. 162–6, 206, 300, 355–6.
[24] S.R.O. 2280/14/1.
[25] P.R.O., SP 23/105, pp. 199, 207, 213, 230, for the coaling of 96 cords in 1645; ibid. pp. 180, 217, 223, 225, 228, 230, for the timber stock and requirements of Madeley Wood iron and coal wks.
[26] S.R.O. 210/1; 1681, box 132, agreement of 1705; 2280/2/36, 45–6, 48 (esp. pp. 70, 72, 74–5). Some may have been sold with Hay fm.: cf. S.R.O. 210/1; 271/1, pp. 241–2 (refs. to Sheepwash coppice).
[27] e.g. the Lloyds, Captain's coppice, etc. (pt. of the Stanleys' Cawbrook fm.), in 1740 and 1788: S.R.O. 1681, box 130, abstr. of title; box 131, deed of 1740; 1987/30/2.
[28] S.R.O. 2280/2/36–41.
[29] E. J. Howell, *Shropshire* (Land of Britain, lxvi), 284. Cf. S.R.O. 271/1, pp. 188, 206 and *passim*.
[30] S.R.O. 1681, box 153, abstr. of lease.
[31] Dedicated under the 1947 and 1967 (s.5) Forestry Acts: T.D.C. deed pkt. 103.
[32] Inf. from Mr. R. Tobin. Cf. S.C.C. Planning Dept. *Severn Gorge Dist. Plan: Written Statement* (1980), 28.
[33] *V.C.H. Salop.* i. 312; cf. S. P. J. Harvey, 'Evidence for Settlement Study: Domesday Bk.' *Medieval Settlement*, ed. P. H. Sawyer (1976), 197–9; R. Lennard, *Rural Eng. 1086–1135* (1959), 356.
[34] S.R.O. 1037/19/1; cf. Merrington's Patch and the Shaws (1849): S.R.O. 2280/2/45, nos. 898, 1038, 1040–1; /48, pp. 60 (nos. 1038, 1040–1), 100 (no. 898).
[35] *Cal. Chart. R. 1327–41*, 488 (Morettesbech, 1262).
[36] *Tax. Eccl.* (Rec. Com.), 164.
[37] B.L. Add. MS. 6164, f. 193v.; 6165, f. 51r.–v.
[38] *Cat. Anct. D.* iii, D 553; S.R.O. 2280/2/45, nos. 927–8, 1028, 1030; /48, pp. 8 (nos. 1028, 1030), 13 (no. 928), 66 (no. 927).
[39] H.W.R.O.(H.), Heref. dioc. rec., glebe terrier *temp.* John Brooke (d. 1598); S.R.O. 2280/2/45, nos. 618–19, 622–3; /48, pp. 6 (nos. 622–3), 61 (nos. 618–19).
[40] *Cat. Anct. D.* iii, D 553.

the north a small area of open field was confined by Shooting Butts Lane and the demesne around the Court.[41] To the north-east what may have been a large area of open field was known by several names, perhaps as a result of reorganization and fragmentation: nearest to Madeley was Cradeley (in 1381)[42] or Little or Town (c. 1540)[43] field; further north-east was Downall field or Downfield (by the later 16th century), part of which, called the Hales, was pasture by the earlier 17th century;[44] further north still the name Old field[45] probably indicates a part of the open fields absorbed into the demesne as the arable shrank.

By the 1320s inhabitants of Coalbrookdale apparently held land in the fields of Madeley. There is, however, a hint that in 1322 Coalbrookdale had a field of its own perhaps lying south of the later Castle Green farm, for field land between the way from Coalbrookdale to Madeley and the highway over Marlehull was mentioned that year.[46] In the later 16th century holdings lay scattered in Mill, West, Little, and Downall fields, but in the mid or later 17th century the destruction of the open fields was evidently completed by consolidation of holdings.[47]

The medieval park and demesne were restocked with deer of the king's gift in the 1290s.[48] Besides deer closes the park and demesne included horse pasture, a rabbit warren, a dovecot,[49] fishponds, and an eyrie of swans.[50] There was another warren in sandy slopes near Strethill, a farm separated from the manor in 1540.[51] In the manor the lord's monopoly of free warren and sporting rights[52] was breached only in 1848.[53] The fishponds, damaged by the escheator c. 1260, included a nursery by 1498. They and the swans' eyrie were still valued as sources of food for the priory in 1498,[54] and the manor had perhaps long included the Bower weir, on the Benthall bank of the Severn.[55] The weir may have been identical with the fishery belonging to Much Wenlock manor in 1086[56] and reserved to the priory when Benthall was subinfeudated.[57] In the early 16th century tenants of the Bower weir paid part of their rent to the

priory in fish. The weir was destroyed c. 1534[58] but evidently rebuilt in the later 16th century for by 1575 John Brooke owned one there and another at the Hay;[59] both probably disappeared in the 17th century.[60] Fishing the Severn and the stocking of private pools retained some economic importance in the 18th and 19th centuries,[61] but in the 20th century they were more significant for recreation.[62]

The imparking of part of the demesne and the contraction of woodland and arable suggest an increase in pastoral farming from the 13th century or earlier. In the 14th century Madeley park was one of two which were important in the wider pastoral economy of Wenlock priory's estates: the monks grew no grain for sale, they and their livestock consuming all the demesne corn and corn rents. In 1390 the park and meadows in Madeley barely sufficed to keep the priory's livestock. Sheep farming, significant for the priory's economy in the 13th century,[63] was long important in Madeley. In 1334 tenants in the new town were forbidden to wash diseased sheep in the Washbrook ford.[64] Personal[65] and place[66] names reinforce the sparse evidence. Lack of sheep was alleged as a cause of poverty in 1341.[67] Foreign sheep were pastured in the manor in the 14th[68] and 17th–18th centuries.[69] In the mid 17th century there were sheep walks on the demesne and a shepherd was employed.[70] Later flocks were few and small (averaging seven), kept by a few farmers and tradesmen, but in Coalbrookdale flocks of 82 (on Strethill farm) and 52 were recorded in 1673 and 1710.[71]

Animal husbandry was important in the later 17th century. In 1677 owners of swine and cattle were presented for nuisances in the highways and lanes and for trespasses, pound breach, and oppression of the commons.[72] In 1678 and 1690 stray sheep were rounded up in Coalbrookdale and Madeley Wood for the lord of Bourton hundred.[73] In fact, however, mixed farming was general: most farmers[74] who owned cattle also owned ploughs, muck, and grain, though cattle

[41] i.e. the Twenty Butts: H.W.R.O.(H.), Heref. dioc. rec., glebe terriers; S.R.O. 2280/2/45, nos. 512–13; /48, p. 63 (nos. 512–13).
[42] Cat. Anct. D. iii, D. 553; cf. S.R.O. 2280/2/45, no. 45; /48, p. 7 (no. 45).
[43] P.R.O., LR 2/184, f. 118v.; cf. S.R.O. 2280/2/45, nos. 361–2, 364, 425; /48, p. 6 (nos. 361–2, 364, 425).
[44] H.W.R.O.(H.), Heref. dioc. rec., glebe terriers temp. John (c. 1572–1598) and Sir Basil Brooke (1604–46). Cf. (for Halesfield) S.R.O. 2280/2/45, nos. 59, 62–3, 71; /48, p. 63 (nos. 59, 62–3, 71).
[45] S.R.O. 2280/2/45, nos. 96, 101–2; /48, p. 41 (nos. 96, 101–2); ridge and furrow visible 1946: R.A.F. aerial photo. 106G/UK/1698, no. 4106.
[46] Eyton, iii. 321; S.R.O. 1037/19/1.
[47] H.W.R.O.(H.), Heref. dioc. rec., glebe terriers.
[48] Cal. Close, 1288–96, 184, 364.
[49] S.R.O. 2280/2/45, nos. 146–50, 183, 209–13, 321; /48, pp. 42–4 (nos. 146–50, 183, 209–13, 321). Dairy ho. meadow is probably the earlier dove ho. meadow: cf. S.R.O. 210/1.
[50] P.R.O., E 315/94, ff. 12v.–13.
[51] S.R.O. 2280/2/45, nos. 3467, 3478; /48, p. 35 (nos. 3467, 3478); above, Man. and Other Est.
[52] Reserved e.g. in S.R.O. 1681, box 153, lease of coppices, 1840; 1987/19/2, 37.
[53] S.R.O. 1987/10/1 (earliest sale noticed).
[54] Rot. Hund. (Rec. Com.), ii. 111; P.R.O., E 315/94, ff. 12v.–13.
[55] P.R.O., E 315/132, ff. 127–34.
[56] D. J. Pannett, 'Fish Weirs of Severn', Evolution of

Marshland Landscapes (Oxf. Univ. Dept. for External Studies, 1981), 144; cf. V.C.H. Salop. i. 312.
[57] Eyton, iii. 223–4, 273 sqq.
[58] P.R.O., E 315/132, ff. 127–34.
[59] Hist. MSS. Com. 13, 10th Rep. IV, Gatacre, p. 443; Salop. News Letter, xliv. 29–30.
[60] Marshland Landscapes, 147, 150, 155.
[61] Randall, Madeley, 262–71; Orders of Q. Sess. iv. 57; S.R.O. 1681, box 32, (Wm. Ferriday's?) notebk.
[62] Above, Social and Cultural Activities.
[63] V.C.H. Salop. ii. 42–3.
[64] S.R.O. 566/1.
[65] i.e. bercarius, bercator in 1322 and 1334: S.R.O. 566/1; 1037/19/1; Eyton, iii. 321.
[66] i.e. Sheepwash leasow, Sheep leasows, Sheep Hill: S.R.O. 210/1.
[67] Inq. Non. (Rec. Com.), 187.
[68] S.R.O. 1224/2/1.
[69] S.R.O. 2280/2/4, 25 Mar. 1684; /8, 25 and 27 Mar. 1710; /9, 24–5 Mar. 1720.
[70] Ibid. /2/45, no. 107; /48, p. 41 (no. 107); P.R.O., SP 23/105, p. 193.
[71] H.W.R.O.(H.), Heref. dioc. rec., prob. invs. of John Hagar, trowman, 1673; Jas Colley, 1710.
[72] S.R.O. 2280/2/14/2 (nos. 2–4, 9, 12, 18, 20).
[73] S.R.O. 1224/2/510, ff. [13v., 41, 49].
[74] H.W.R.O.(H.), Heref. dioc. rec., prob. invs. of Rog. Evans and Fra. Rushon, 1665; Humph. Bowdler and Thos. Bowen, 1666; Wm. Shrig(s)ley, 1669; Frances Turner, 1671; John Hagar (trowman) and Thos. Stanley, 1672; John Fors-

were often their most valuable possessions. Corn crops included wheat, rye, hard corn (mixed wheat and rye),[75] barley, and oats; peas (probably sometimes with oats),[76] and vetches were also sown. Crops were probably rotated: in 1718–19 peas followed barley and barley followed peas and oats in different parts of the vicar's glebe.[77] Spring-sown crops, or lent tilling,[78] were less valuable than winter corn.[79] Farmers' herds, the largest recorded amounting to thirty,[80] averaged eleven. The vicar, without meadow or common but with tithe hay,[81] kept cattle.[82] Oxen and bullocks figured in the larger herds. Horses were plentiful but cattle too were evidently still used as draught animals.[83] Small herds (three to fourteen, averaging six) were kept by some tradesmen,[84] trowmen,[85] and widows;[86] occasionally a labourer or collier managed to keep a single cow.[87] The parish lay beyond the southern limit of the Cheshire cheese country[88] and little cheese seems to have been made commercially. Few cattle owners had more cheese than was needed for domestic consumption, and then only modest quantities.[89] A collier who died in 1711 owning £10 worth of butter and cheese, but no cattle, may have traded in dairy products.[90]

Apples were cropped[91] and bees kept.[92] All classes kept poultry[93] and pigs, though not in large numbers; one farmer had eleven pigs,[94] but three was an average number owned. Hemp and flax were widely grown; small crops or the residues of larger crops were dressed and worked into yarn and cloth at home,[95] but considerable quantities were occasionally grown:[96] 7 a. of flax were mentioned in 1718.[97] Hops were grown in the 17th century.[98] Such ancillary crops may have been more important than most surviving records suggest: Henry Bowdler (fl. 1650) kept his orchard and hopyard after making his holding over to his son-in-law.[99]

There seem to have been substantial tenants in the manor in the 13th century: one claimed a carucate in 1271.[1] As in its other manors Wenlock priory exacted 'terciary', a third of a deceased tenant's goods.[2] Heriot was still due from lease-holders in 1702.[3] In the 14th century servile tenants needed the lord's permission to marry,[4] and until at least 1380 a *curia bondorum* was held for tenants outside the new town.[5]

In the 1320s tenure was for life or lives,[6] and in the early 15th century a surrender fine called 'varneth' was still payable.[7] A buoyant demand for land brought in some £5 in fines from the Madeley tenants in 1321–2.[8] By 1341, however, tenants were scarce.[9] Copyholding largely gave way to leaseholding in the later Middle Ages. By 1540 Wenlock priory owned all the land in the manor except the vicar's glebe and a few burgages[10] with their gardens.[11] In the later 16th century over 70 per cent of the lord's rent came from leaseholders, barely a quarter from copyholders.[12]

In 1702 about a third in extent and value of the manor's 2,074 a. of agricultural land[13] was leased for lives or (in one case) a term of years. Each of the five leaseholders owed a small reserved rent, a couple of capons, and a few shillings in lieu of heriot. Four of the leaseholders were among the six largest tenants, who held over 100 a. each and altogether over two fifths of the agricultural acreage: the lessees of Hay farm and Upper House held 256 a. and 150 a., the other four large tenants an average of 113 a. each. The demesne around the Court (c. 540 a.) was about a quarter of the manor's agricultural acreage; it was perhaps then kept in hand, and the rest of the manor was probably let for economic rents. Eleven tenants holding between 25 a. and 100 a. (one leasing 47 a.) occupied another quarter, and nine tenants of under 25 a. (the smallest with only 4 a.) occupied almost a twentieth.

Hay farm seems to have remained the largest farm in the 19th and 20th centuries. In 1849, with 195 a., it was one of four of 150 a. or more; there were two of 100–149 a. and four with 50–99 a.

brooke, snr., 1676; David Price *alias* Trickels, 1680; Jane Forsbrooke, 1681; Ric. Twyford, 1682; John Cope, 1683; Hen. Cope, 1685; Tim. Turner, 1691; John Blest, 1694; Thos. Birch, 1699; John Roberts, 1701; Hen. Taylor, 1705; Jas. Colley, 1710; Luke Twyford, 1712; John Hutchinson and Wm. Roe, 1714; Audley Bowdler, 1715; Geo. Deuksell, 1717; Rog. Roe, 1718; John Brook, 1721; Edw. Herbage, 1725; John Goodman, 1734; John Harper, 1749; and John Wheeler, 1750. Dr. B. S. Trinder is thanked for the loan of transcripts of c. 150 prob. invs. from the 1660s to the 1750s; this and the next para. are based on them.

[75] Cf. *Yeomen and Colliers in Telford*, ed. B. Trinder and J. Cox (1980), 84.

[76] Often listed together: invs. of Frances (1671) and Tim (1691) Turner; John Blest, 1694. Cf. *V.C.H. Staffs.* xvii. 28.

[77] S.R.O. 2280/2/9, notes for 1718–19; cf. ibid. notes for 1714.   [78] Inv. of Geo. Deuksell, of Furnace Bank, 1717.

[79] Trinder and Cox, *Yeomen and Colliers*, 84.

[80] Inv. of Wm. Roe, 1714.

[81] H.W.R.O.(H.) Heref. dioc. rec., glebe terrier *temp.* John Brooke (c. 1572–1598).

[82] Invs. of Mic. Richards, 1671; Benj. Taylor, 1705.

[83] Invs. of Audley Bowdler, 1715 (an ox harrow); Rog. Roe (of Lodge fm.: S.R.O. 516/11), 1718 (2 ox chains).

[84] Invs. of John Cowper, ? weaver, 1681; Wm. Ashwood, 1682; Wm. Ashwood, 1697.

[85] Invs. of Ric. Brooke, 1670; John Hagar 1672.

[86] Invs. of Armilla Aston, 1662; Alice Hutchinson, 1664.

[87] Invs. of Edw. Boden, 1691; John Stockton, 1701.

[88] Trinder and Cox, *Yeomen and Colliers*, 77–80.

[89] Eight out of 44 cattle-owners owned over £1 worth of cheese but none owned over £5 worth.

[90] Inv. of Mic. Hotchkiss (appraised 1711).

[91] S.R.O. 2280/2/8–9.

[92] Ibid.; invs. of John Blest, 1694; Geo. Deuksell, 1717.

[93] Inv. of Rog. Roe, 1718, lists them in unusual detail. Cf. Trinder and Cox, *Yeomen and Colliers*, 83.

[94] Inv. of Thos. Bowen, 1666.

[95] Invs. of Rog. Evans, 1665; John Goodman, 1734; Dorothy Starkey, 1668; John Hagar, 1672; Rog. Downes, 1720.

[96] Invs. of Benj. Taylor (vicar), 1705 (£5 worth of hemp and flax); Edw. Herbage, snr., 1725 (a hemp rick).

[97] S.R.O. 2280/2/9, 27 June 1718.

[98] Inv. of Humph. Bowdler, 1666.

[99] P.R.O., SP 23/105, pp. 191, 195.

[1] Eyton, iii. 320.

[2] *T.S.A.S.* lviii. 74–6; cf. *V.C.H. Salop.* ii. 43.

[3] S.R.O. 210/1; 2280/14/2, no. 30; cf. below, L. Wenlock, Econ. Hist. (Agric.).

[4] S.R.O. 1037/19/1; 1224/2/1.

[5] Below, Local Govt.

[6] S.R.O. 1037/19/1.

[7] S.R.O. 1224/2/6–7.

[8] S.R.O. 1037/19/1.

[9] *Inq. Non.* (Rec. Com.), 187.

[10] Probably those belonging to Our Lady's guild: P.R.O., E 36/258, f. 3; *Cal. Pat.* 1548–9, 317–18.

[11] P.R.O., E 315/111, f. 29.

[12] P.R.O., SC 6/Hen. VIII/3021, mm. 4d.–5d.; S.R.O. 2280/14/1, counting doubtful life tenants as copyholders, tenants of cottages and Stringer's land as tenants at will.

[13] i.e. 673 a. valued at £358 p.a. out of 2,074 a. valued at £1,022. This para. is based on S.R.O. 210/1.

The ten farms[14] probably accounted for some 70 per cent of the parish's agricultural land.[15] Of the ten largest farms in 1849 all but Strethill and Madeley Hall[16] were let. Not all the tenants were farmers. Lees farm was let to William Anstice, managing partner in the Madeley Wood Co., the Cottage farm to Charles Dyas, licensee of the Royal Oak.[17] Francis and John Yates, barge owners, coal merchants, and maltsters, held the Court farm in partnership with William Dyas, a butcher, maltster, and grocer,[18] who also held 22 a. nearby on his own account.[19] Some smaller mid 19th-century tenants probably had other occupations, as did Peter Hopley, charter master and joint tenant of 39 a. near Madeley Court.[20] Tenants who were not farmers evidently employed farmers or bailiffs.[21]

About 95 per cent of farm land in the parish was rented in 1891, only 77 per cent by 1938.[22] Hay farm was bought by a farmer in 1909.[23] Some farmers acquired more than one farm: H. P. Price of Castle Green farm bought Hill Top (later Grange) farm (112 a.) in 1948 and Roughpark farm (81 a.) in 1952.[24] Owner occupation tended to increase. Court farm was bought by the tenant.[25] Of three farms sold in 1926, the Cottage farm was bought by the tenants, Cuckoo Oak farm was resold to the tenant next year, and Springhill farm was bought by a Shifnal farmer whose widow sold it to the tenant in 1954.[26]

Few farms crossed the parish boundary, though in the west most of the former Furnace Bank farm was farmed with Greenbank farm in Little Dawley in 1849.[27] Not all farms were compact in 1849, particularly holdings under 50 a. The break-up of the manorial estate from 1705 had fixed even the larger farms. In 1702 and 1849 Hay farm included 20 a. of meadow near Madeley Court. In 1849 Madeley Hall's farm was the most dispersed, with 23 a. near the hall, 25 a. off Park Lane, and 65 a. near the eastern parish boundary.[28]

Mining and industry contributed to destroy some farms[29] and made inroads into others, like Lodge farm (109 a. in 1732 and probably larger earlier) where sand was dug for Coalbrookdale Co. castings. Some farms lost only peripheral land.[30] Most of the larger mid 19th-century farms survived more or less intact until the 1960s,[31] though Sunniside (otherwise Westminster or the Moors)[32] farm in Coalbrookdale eventually separated from Strethill farm.[33] There were more

changes in the Park Lane area, and in the eastern part of the parish Madeley Hall's land formed Springhill farm c. 1880.[34] Small holdings also survived into the 20th century.[35] One at Hill's Lane, of 8 a. in 1926, formed the nucleus of a 51-a. farm by 1958; the farm, about a third of it rough grazing over old pitmounds and sand pits, was partly owner occupied but mostly rented from three or four owners.[36] By 1981 only two areas of agricultural land remained. That west of

TABLE II

MADELEY: LAND USE, LIVESTOCK, AND CROPS

	1867	1891	1938	1965
Percentage of grassland	44	56	78	53
arable	56	44	22	47
Percentage of cattle	11	27	35	38
sheep	52	57	55	48
pigs	37	16	9	14
Percentage of wheat	63	56	57	20
barley	25	29	17	77
oats	12	13	24	3
mixed corn & rye	0	2	1	0
Percentage of agricultural land growing roots and vegetables	13	12	4	2

Sources: P.R.O., MAF 68/143, no. 15; /1340, no. 6; /3880, Salop. no. 264; /4945, no. 264.

Coalbrookdale was outside Telford and unlikely to be affected by development, but that around Lees farm was planned for future housing;[37] it was mainly rough, and in places wet, pasture.

By the mid 20th century farm buildings varied greatly. At Madeley Court, the Hay, and the Lodge 17th-century (and perhaps earlier) buildings remained in use alongside later ones.[38] Other farms, such as Hill Top and Springhill, had been built in modern times;[39] Edward Foster, later a leading Shropshire farmer (kt. 1950), had farmed

[14] Named on the map on p. 24. Para. based on S.R.O. 2280/2/45–8. For Hay fm. see also T.D.C. deed pkt. 129.
[15] Cf. P.R.O., MAF 68/143, no. 15.
[16] S.R.O. 2280/2/48, pp. 29–30, 34–5, 104–5.
[17] Ibid. pp. 8, 71–2; Randall, Madeley, 173–4, 176, 370.
[18] S. Bagshaw, Dir. Salop. (1851), 575, 577–8; P.O. Dir. Salop. (1856), 77.
[19] S.R.O. 2280/2/48, pp. 6, 108.
[20] Ibid. p. 42; S. Bagshaw, Dir. Salop. (1851), 575.
[21] e.g. S.R.O. 2280/2/48, p. 72 (no. 1486); P.R.O., HO 107/1989, f. 262.
[22] P.R.O., MAF 68/1340, no. 6; MAF 68/3880, Salop. no. 264.
[23] Above, Man. and Other Est.
[24] T.D.C. deed pkt. 18, abstrs. of title; Jackson, 'Madeley', bk. 2A, pp. 141–2.
[25] Above, Man. and Other Est.
[26] T.D.C. deed pkts. 72, 116, 261; Kelly's Dir. Salop. (1926), 150; (1929), 147.
[27] S.R.O. 2280/2/48, p. 29 (s.v. Edw. Edwards); 1987, box 19, map. Cuckoo Oak fm. incl. land in Kemberton in the 20th

cent.: T.D.C. deed pkt. 261.
[28] S.R.O. 210/1; 2280/2/45–8; map on p. 24.
[29] e.g. Cawbrook fm., Coalbrookdale.
[30] Lincs. Archives Office, 2 Haw. 1/G/47–8; S.R.O. 210/1; 1681, box 178, deed of 1848; 1987/19/37; 2280/2/45–8 (esp. /48, pp. 28–9); S. Bagshaw, Dir. Salop. (1851), 568.
[31] S.R.O. 2280/2/45–8; Kelly's Dir. Salop. (1885–1941); T.D.C. deed pkts.
[32] Jackson, 'Madeley', bk. 2A, p. 141.
[33] Kelly's Dir. Salop. (1885–1941).
[34] Cf. ibid. (1891), 356; S.R.O. 2280/2/48, pp. 104–5; O.S. Map 1/2,500, Salop. XLIII. 15 (1883 edn.).
[35] Jackson, 'Madeley', bk. 2A, pp. 141–2.
[36] Ibid. p. 141; T.D.C. deed pkt. 261, sale partics. of 1926.
[37] T.D.C. Telford Development Strategy, map (Feb. 1979).
[38] Below, Man. and Other Est. For the jumble of old and new bldgs. at the Ct. see T.D.C., Sec.'s Dept. file P/9/3A, plan and rep. 1967.
[39] Both 1849 × 1882: cf. S.R.O. 2280/2/45; O.S. Maps 1/2,500, Salop. XLIII. 14–15 (1883 edn.).

at Hill Top before 1914.[40] Cuckoo Oak farm buildings provided ample accommodation for the land but had not been well maintained;[41] those at Castle Green farm were excellent.[42]

In 1801 wheat occupied 46 per cent of recorded cereal acreage, oats 31 per cent, and barley 23 per cent. Peas, potatoes, and turnips were grown.[43] Farming was mixed in 1849 but little more than one acre in three on the ten largest farms was meadow or pasture, though meadow predominated in the centre of the parish north and west of Madeley. In the later 19th and earlier 20th century the area of agricultural land averaged 1,700 a. Industrial decline may have increased it slightly. Farmers turned from arable to livestock, especially cattle; sheep maintained their position; pigs declined,[44] though there was some interest in intensive pig and poultry breeding in the mid 1930s.[45] Arable farming recovered in the mid 20th century just before the loss of almost all agricultural land.

MILLS. Wenlock priory owned a mill in Madeley in 1291.[46] Perhaps a second one was given to the priory in 1363.[47] One mill mentioned in the 1370s was let for 10s. a year.[48] Mills and millers were mentioned in the 14th and 15th centuries[49] and in a survey of c. 1540.[50] A mill on the manorial estate was mentioned in 1593[51] and one was repaired in 1649 or 1650.[52]

There were three mills near Madeley town: one near Madeley Court and, lower down the same stream, the Clock mill and Washbrook mill.[53] The Court mill, an early 17th-century brick building with stone dressings, a stone gable and adjoining stone wall, and heavy internal timber framing,[54] was ruinous in 1980. It had ceased working between the 1820s and 1847;[55] the wheel had gone by 1880 and the pool was covered by industrial spoil.[56] Between at least the 1440s and the 1540s the Cook or Coke family seem to have held one, or perhaps both, of the mills lower down the stream.[57] The upper one was probably the Clock mill held by Thomas Roberts in 1702 and bought from the manor by John Ashwood in 1705; in

1847 there was no mill but the pool survived[58] and the Madeley Wood Co. built a cement mill there beside the Shropshire Canal; it worked until c. 1914.[59] With what was later known as the Cottage farm, Washbrook mill was bought from the manor by Audley Bowdler in 1705; it remained with his heirs in 1847 but, probably soon after, was acquired by the Madeley Wood Co. It ceased working in the early 1900s, and its overshot wheel was broken up during the Second World War.[60]

There was a windmill north-east of Madeley Court by 1702;[61] the ruined brick tower, but none of the machinery, remained in 1981.[62] A supposed windmill on top of the Whales Back above Coalbrookdale was probably a folly or prospect tower.[63]

The Caldebrook was beginning to be used for industrial power by the early 16th century, and the bloomsmithy in existence by 1536[64] probably stood where the Lower forge, Dale End, was later located.[65] By 1520 there was also a mill higher up Coalbrookdale. Tenanted by the Warhams in the 16th century,[66] it probably formed part of the property bought from the Crown by William Sprott in 1540[67] and may have stood in the lower half of the dale; it was later sold and may have been the corn mill sold again in 1602.[68] In 1753 a pair of mills (perhaps the former Middle forge) occupied the future site of the Boring mill, built in 1780.[69] By or during the 18th century the Caldebrook's power was given wholly to industry and the stream was ponded in five places: at the Upper (Old) furnace, the Lower furnace, the Upper forge, the Boring mill, and the Lower forge. The New pool in Lightmoor dingle had probably been made c. 1698.[70]

Abraham Darby (III) provided a corn mill in Coalbrookdale for his workers, probably that worked in 1801 by the injection water from the nearby *Resolution* steam engine. The mill, probably rebuilt c. 1821,[71] evidently ceased working in the 1870s.[72]

COAL AND IRONSTONE. Coalbrookdale, though giving its name to the east Shropshire coalfield,[73]

[40] Jackson, 'Madeley', bk. 2A, p. 142; *Kelly's Dir. Salop.* (1913), 148.

[41] T.D.C. deed pkt. 261, valuation of 1954.

[42] T.D.C. deed pkt. for Duroclay Ltd., sale partics. of 1952.

[43] P.R.O., HO 67/12/155.

[44] S.R.O. 2280/2/45–8; Table II, and sources thereto.

[45] W.B.R. Madeley dist. cttee. min. bk. 1932–7, pp. 248–9.

[46] *Tax. Eccl.* (Rec. Com.), 164.

[47] Eyton, iii. 270; *Cal. Pat. 1361–4*, 393.

[48] B.L. Add. MSS. 6164, f. 193v.; 6165, f. 51.

[49] e.g. S.R.O. 566/1; 1224/2/4, 9; P.R.O., E 315/94, f. 12v.

[50] P.R.O., LR 2/184, ff. 79, 106v., 118v.; SC 6/Hen. VIII/3021, m. 5; cf. S.R.O. 1224, box 342, Prior Gosnell's reg. f. 32.

[51] S.R.O. 2280/14/1.

[52] P.R.O., SP 23/105, p. 221.

[53] O.S. Nat. Grid SJ 6956 0507, 6990 0391.

[54] SA 15276; inf. from Mr. R. A. Meeson, who surveyed the bldg. for T.D.C. 1979–80; Randall, *Madeley*, 332.

[55] Randall, *Old Ct. Ho.* 82; S.R.O. 2280/Rg/7, p. 192 (nos. 1531–4); /2/45, no. 189; /48, p. 43 (no. 189).

[56] Randall, *Madeley*, 332; O.S. Map 6", Salop. XLIII. SE. (1888 edn.).

[57] S.R.O. 1224/2/9; P.R.O., LR 2/184, ff. 79, 106v., 118v.; SC 6/Hen. VIII/3021, m. 5.

[58] S.R.O. 210/1; 1987/19/3; 2280/2/45, nos. 834–5, 838a; /48, pp. 8 (no. 835), 36 (no. 834), 104 (no. 838a).

[59] *Salop. News Letter*, xxxvii. 40.

[60] S.R.O. 1987/19/3; 2280/2/45, nos. 831, 931; /48, p. 8 (nos. 831, 931); *Salop. News Letter*, xxxvii. 39; Jackson, 'Madeley', bk. 1A, p. 248.

[61] At O.S. Nat. Grid SJ 6972 0528: S.R.O. 210/1.

[62] Inf. from Miss U. B. M. Rayska.

[63] Smith, *View from Iron Bridge*, pp. 14–16; S.R.O. 2280/2/45, no. 3274; /48, p. 30 (no. 3274).

[64] P.R.O., LR 2/184, ff. 107, 117; SC 6/Hen. VIII/3021, m. 5d.

[65] Below, Iron and Steel.

[66] P.R.O., LR 2/184, ff. 107, 120v.; SC 6/Hen. VIII/3021, m. 5d.; cf. S.R.O. 1987/30/2; 2280/2/45, nos. 3376–9; /48, pp. 22 (nos. 3376–8), 35 (no. 3379); /14/1, showing 'mill hill' held of the man. by Wm. Warham, 1593.

[67] *L. & P. Hen. VIII*, xv, pp. 468–9; xvii, p. 212; P.R.O., C 1/1184/47–9; above, Man. and Other Est.

[68] S.P.L., Deeds 1541, 1557, 10125; *Cal. Pat. 1560–3*, 87.

[69] Raistrick, *Iron Founders*, 74 (no. 39); below, Iron and Steel.

[70] Map on p. 49; below, Iron and Steel.

[71] *T.S.A.S.* lviii. 254; Trinder, *Darbys*, 69; idem, *Ind. Rev. Salop.* 234, 329.

[72] S.R.O. 2280/2/45, no. 3182; /48, p. 22 (no. 3182); S. Bagshaw, *Dir. Salop.* (1851), 578; E. Cassey & Co. *Dir. Salop.* (1874), 129 (mentioned); *P.O. Dir. Salop.* (1879), 307 (not mentioned).

[73] *V.C.H. Salop.* i. 32.

is barren of productive measures.[74] Its beds of Silurian limestone and Wenlock shales[75] were recognized as the western boundary of the coalfield in Madeley parish.[76] Eastwards the whole parish overlies the Middle and Lower Coal Measures and workable seams of coal and ironstone were generally available. The most accessible outcroppings, and scene of the earliest mining, lay in Madeley Wood, the north-east side of the Severn Gorge, where the river has cut through the coal measures. The coal seams dip eastwards, and only in the 19th century, as the older mines were worked out, did mining operations shift to the deeper seams in the east of the parish.[77]

Sea coals were being dug in the Brockholes by 1322.[78] The coal mines were farmed out in 1390,[79] and c. 1540 an ironstone mine near Coalbrookdale was let for £5 a year.[80]

John Brooke, who owned the manor from c. 1572, seems to have been employing colliers in 1579.[81] The beginnings of large-scale mining in Madeley, like the great expansion of the east Shropshire coalfield generally,[82] probably coincided with the growth of the down-river coal trade in the late 16th century, when Madeley coals were among the first shipped to Worcester,[83] and with the development of local iron and steel works by Sir Basil Brooke, lord of the manor 1598–1646.[84]

Brooke worked four coal mines in Madeley though, perhaps as a result of his involvements elsewhere,[85] with insufficient capital[86] to deal with the serious drainage problems.[87] After 1645 the county committee's annual lettings discouraged tenants (the first of whom was Richard Foley) from investing in the mines.[88] In 1649, however, the committee let the manor to Edward Cludde of Orleton, a relative of the Brookes. He managed the mines closely, eliminating, for example, the frauds arising when bargemen worked also as colliers. He invested some £2,000 so that by 1651, when he bid for a 7-year lease,[89] the coal works were said to be in a better state than in Brooke's time: two mines had been saved and the whole coal works made safe for twenty years. The mines consisted of four 'insets' driven horizontally into the Madeley Wood hillside; each was worked by master grubbers (normally two partners) and their ground colliers. Two of the main ways were

1,000 yards long, the other two 700 and 500 yards; for half or more of those distances water had to be forced out by engines. The seams of coal varied in thickness from eighteen inches to a yard.[90]

In 1651, the year of his death, Cludde passed his tenancy of the manor to Francis Wolfe (I), formerly clerk of the works. Wolfe soon began to raise capital, doubtless to continue the works,[91] and his son Francis (II) was probably still running them in 1669.[92] Later the young Basil Brooke, lord of the manor, began to spend great sums of money 'in digging and winning coal'.[93] For over a century longer his successors as lords continued to be actively and directly involved—as owners, capitalists, or industrial entrepreneurs—in the exploitation of their mines, though from time to time areas of coal and ironstone were leased out. In the later 18th century the mines were concentrated in the hands of an industrial partnership which included the lord of the manor until 1794.[94]

The mid 17th-century method of working the Madeley Wood mines, from levels driven into the hill, remained largely unchanged in 1711.[95] By then, however, mining was being extended north of the Shifnal to Much Wenlock road. In 1650 a few insubstantial tenants had failed in their bid to lease the manor and its coal and iron works,[96] but by the early 1690s some of the capital involved in this northward expansion was evidently provided by parishioners, including farmers and men like Lawrence Wellington (I),[97] the Coalbrookdale forgemaster.[98] Others involved probably contributed mining skills.[99] A lease of some northern mines was granted to two Londoners in 1692; they were permitted to lay 1,500 yards of wooden rails from the Lane pit to the Severn. In 1706 all coal and ironstone north of the road was leased to William Phillips for 31 years with licence to prospect for new mines. Phillips was also allowed to make new waggonways and Severn wharves and to use existing railways to the south, specifically that from the pit in Lloyds dingle with its 'wind' and chain down to the Severn.[1]

In the early 18th century the lord of the manor was encouraging individual master miners to open up new pits in the older mining area, Madeley

[74] S.R.O. 3763/2/1, J. Randall to [H.A. Doubleday], 9 Jan. 1901.

[75] Inst. Geol. Sciences Map 1/25,000, *Telford* (1978 edn.).

[76] *V.C.H. Salop.* i. 458; cf. e.g. S.R.O. 1681, box 184, lease of 1858, referring to mines, etc., 'eastward of the chasm in Lincoln Hill'.

[77] I. J. Brown, 'Mineral Wealth of Coalbrookdale, Pt. I', *Bull. Peak Dist. Mines Hist. Soc.* ii. 255–9; *V.C.H. Salop.* i. 471–2.

[78] S.R.O. 1037/19/1; cf. W. F. Mumford, *Wenlock in the Middle Ages* (Shrews. 1977), 151.

[79] S.R.O. 1224, box 342, Prior Gosnell's reg. f. 35v.

[80] P.R.O., LR 2/184, ff. 107, 120v.

[81] H.W.R.O.(W.), ref. 008.7 BA 3585/67a (inv.).

[82] J. U. Nef, *Rise of Brit. Coal Ind.* (1932), i. 65.

[83] A. D. Dyer, *City of Worcester in 16th cent.* (1973), 55–6, 62–4.

[84] Below, Iron and Steel.   [85] Ibid.

[86] Cf. P.R.O., C 6/10/60; G. F. Hammersley, 'Hist. of Iron Ind. in Forest of Dean Region, 1562–1660' (London Univ. Ph.D. thesis, 1972), 172.

[87] What follows is based on P.R.O., SP 23/105, pp. 177–203.

[88] Ibid. pp. 199, 201, 209, 211, 213, 225–9.

[89] Ibid. pp. 179–80, 187, 191–3, 217; cf. S.P.L., MS. 2790, p. 385; 2793, p. 219.

[90] P.R.O., SP 23/105, pp. 180, 217, 225–9; *W. Midland Studies*, xv. 5.

[91] S.P.L., MS. 2793, p. 219; *T.S.A.S.* lvi. 71, 85; P.R.O., C 3/467/11; SP 23/105, pp. 177, 219.

[92] Below, Iron and Steel.

[93] P.R.O., C 5/180/133.

[94] When Wm. Reynolds & Co. replaced Ric. Reynolds & Co.: below.

[95] *V.C.H. Salop.* i. 465.

[96] *Salop. News Letter*, xliv. 4–6.

[97] Apley Estate Office, Bridgnorth, vol. of Madeley Ct. Misc. Papers 1544–1837, copy lease of 1706. For the farmers see H.W.R.O.(H.), Heref. dioc. rec., prob. invs. of John Blest, 1694; Thos. Stanley, 1672; Luke Twyford, 1712; and Rog. Roe, 1718; S.R.O. 210/1; 516/11.

[98] Below, Iron and Steel.

[99] Rec. of the 1703 lease of Madeley Wood mines (below) illustrate the different involvements of capitalists and master colliers: cf. S.R.O. 1224, box 64, Harrison fam. deeds 1703–9; 2280/3/6.

[1] S.R.O. 2280/3/7; Apley Estate Office, vol. of Madeley Ct. Misc. Papers 1544–1837, copy lease of 1706.

Wood, and the manorial bailiff John Ashwood was buying timber for their works.[2] In 1703, however, to assure the jointure of Basil Brooke's widow Winifred[3] and so permit the sale of manorial lands on behalf of his creditors and heirs,[4] a large 21-year mining leasehold was created, though with protection for existing interests. Its 600–700 a. centred on the vicar's New leasow, the nearest pits to which were the Lane pit, not included in the lease, and Holland's pit, perhaps the later (Craw) Stone, or Styches pit. Its tenants were evidently to receive the rent and royalties from the northern leasehold of 1692, and their own holding apparently included all coal and ironstone workings south of the road. They took John Ashwood as their clerk. If possible they were to employ Madeley colliers, three of whom were to be permitted to carry on their new workings in the Double and Flint coal. At the Lloyds in 1719 the lessees erected a steam pumping engine, the earliest known in Shropshire,[5] to reduce drainage costs.

The break-up of the manorial estate from 1705[6] left the coal and iron works intact. The minerals 500 yards around Madeley Court were sold[7] but not exploited until 1840.[8] About 1721 the vicar established his right to royalties from mining under his glebe.[9]

The lease of 1703 ended in 1724,[10] Winifred Brooke having died.[11] The lords of the manor seem to have resumed the Madeley Wood mines.[12] In the 1730s J. U. Smitheman, lord of half the manor, worked them, buying large numbers of iron wheels for railway waggons from the Coalbrookdale Co. and installing a steam pumping engine there shortly before his death in 1744.[13] The mines north of the Shifnal to Much Wenlock road, comprising the Lane and Paddock pits, seem still to have been worked separately in 1741, a royalty being paid to Smitheman and John Giffard.[14]

Smitheman's son John eventually became active in the coal trade and, in 1756, principal founding partner in the Madeley Wood Co. The partners included several master colliers who held leases of pits and foot roads. The company held manorial coal and ironstone on lease and became

an iron-making concern too. Its works were bought by Abraham Darby (III) in 1776 when he was buying up shares in the manor,[15] ultimately to engross its minerals. His capital, however, was insufficient[16] and the manor passed to Richard Reynolds in 1780 and 1781.[17] In the 1790s the Coalbrookdale Co. and the Reynoldses, concentrating mining operations in their own hands, equipped their pits with new, locally made winding engines; new pits were opened at Blists Hill and Rough Park.[18] When the Darby and Reynolds interests were finally disentangled in 1797 the Madeley Wood enterprises and coal mining were taken over by William Reynolds & Co., who had succeeded Richard Reynolds & Co. in 1794.[19] After William Reynolds's death in 1803 they passed under the Anstices' control.[20]

In the earlier 19th century, and evidently in the late 19th century, coal and ironstone mining was the most profitable activity of the Anstices' Madeley Wood Co.[21] Outside the Madeley Court area the company had the lease of all the coal and ironstone in the manor. Its successor the Madeley Wood Co. Ltd., formed in 1918[22] and acquired from the Anstices by their managers the Cadmans in the 1920s,[23] bought the manorial mines in 1929[24] and owned them until Nationalization in 1947.[25]

Though it reduced wages in 1821[26] the Madeley Wood Co. was a reasonably good, even paternal, employer by 19th-century standards.[27] It eschewed tommy shops[28] and c. 1841 tried, within the limits set by subcontracting to charter masters, to eliminate infant labour from its mines.[29] Boys over six years old worked in the coal seams, though fewer were employed in the thicker ironstone seams.[30] Labour relations worsened in the 1900s when the Anstices brought professional managers in, and a strike c. 1912 contributed to the closure of all but three of the company's mines.[31]

At the beginning of the 19th century, as the older mines were becoming exhausted, mining operations began to shift east and north.[32] The Hills Lane, Meadow, Hales, Blists Hill, and Shaws pits had been sunk by the early 1840s. There were new sinkings at Halesfield c. 1870.[33]

[2] Para. based on S.R.O. 1224, box 64, lease of 1703.
[3] Cf. S.R.O. 1681, box 132, deed of 1705 conveying Madeley Ct. (reciting 1683 marr. settlement); 2280/3/6.
[4] P.R.O., C 5/180/133; Randall, Old Ct. Ho. 50.
[5] S.R.O. 2280/2/45, nos. 1797, 1809; /3/6–7, 9, 13; Trinder, Ind. Rev. Salop. (1981), 94, mislocating the engine.
[6] Above, Man. and Other Est.
[7] Apley Estate Office, vol. of Madeley Ct. Misc. Papers 1544–1837, agreement of 4 Oct. 1703; above, Man. and Other Est. [8] Below.
[9] S.R.O. 2280/2/10–11; /3/3–6, 8–10, 13–15, 37–43.
[10] Ibid. /3/6.
[11] In 1716: V.C.H. Oxon. xi. 10.
[12] S.R.O. 2280/3/9–10.
[13] Above, Man. and Other Est.; Trinder, Ind. Rev. Salop. (1981), 72, 95; V.C.H. Salop. i. 464.
[14] S.R.O. 2280/3/11.
[15] Trinder, op. cit. 26, 42, 55, 271; S.R.O. 1681, box 132, lease and arts. of partnership, 1765; box 133, deed of 1–2 Sept. 1774; 1987, box 20, purchase papers, 1776; V.C.H. Salop. i. 464 (corr. below, Corrigenda); above, Man. and Other Est.; below, Iron and Steel.
[16] Raistrick, Iron Founders, 13, 88–9, 98–9, 208.
[17] Above, Man. and Other Est.
[18] Raistrick, op. cit. 211; Trinder, Ind. Rev. Salop. (1981), 101; S.R.O. 271/1, pp. 188–9, 192.
[19] Raistrick, op. cit. 212–19; Shrews. Chron. 14 May 1794.

[20] Trinder, Ind. Rev. Salop. (1981), 139, 142.
[21] Though pig-iron production was maintained: ibid. 139, 142, 144; Gregory, 'E. Salop. Coalfield', 76–86.
[22] T.D.C. deed pkt. 439, deed of 1918 (Anstices to Madeley Wood Co. Ltd.).
[23] Jackson, 'Madeley', bk. 1A, pp. 3, 23, 27; S.R.O. 1324/4; V.C.H. Salop. i. 472; Shropshire Mag. Feb. 1967, 30; Wellington Jnl. 3 June 1939 (p. 14). For the Cadmans see Burke, Peerage (1959), 368.
[24] S.R.O. 1681, box 141, request to sell (30 May 1929) and completion statement (18 Nov. 1929); box 184, corresp., draft conveyances, etc., 1929.
[25] Staffs. R.O., D. 570/27; D. 1055/1–37.
[26] Trinder, Ind. Rev. Salop. (1981), 233.
[27] 1st Rep. Com. Child. Emp. App. Pt. I [381], p. 40, H.C. (1842), xvi; Randall, Madeley, 176–8; Gregory, 'E. Salop. Coalfield', 76–86.
[28] 1st Rep. Com. Child. Emp. App. Pt. I, 80.
[29] Not always successfully: ibid. 33–4, T.S.A.S. liii. 12.
[30] 1st Rep. Com. Child. Emp. App. Pt. I, 30–2, 41, 79–80; T.S.A.S. liii. 14–15.
[31] Shropshire Mag. Feb. 1967, 31; below.
[32] Randall, Madeley, 174, 176.
[33] Ibid. 174; I. J. Brown, Coalbrookdale Coalfield: Cat. of Mines and Mining Bibliog. (Salop. Co. Libr. 1968), 14–15. For the co.'s shaft sinking dept. cf. S.P.L., Watton press cuttings, iv. 432; S.R.O. 2280/BRg/4, p. 169.

The 19th-century sinkings were exhausted in their turn. For some years after 1912 the Meadow pit, and evidently the Shawfield pit (working 1917), were the only productive pits open in the parish; the Meadow pit ceased production in 1920. Woodside mine worked from 1927 to 1947[34] but the life of Madeley's mining community was prolonged until 1967 as a result of the company's earlier extension of its mining interests east of the parish boundary.[35] The Madeley Wood pit in Kemberton, sunk in 1864 c. 1,200 yards north-east of Halesfield, was by 1934 one of only three significant collieries in Shropshire: it then produced c. 110,000 tons of coal a year, almost 17 per cent of the county's total. The colliery was re-equipped and reconstructed in the late 1930s (when the Halesfield shafts began to be used for its ventilation) and by the National Coal Board in the late 1940s and early 1950s.[36] The closure of the colliery in 1967[37] marked the end of underground mining. In the 1960s, however, Duroclay Ltd. got coal on the former Castle Green farm as part of its opencast clay extraction there.[38]

Madeley Court mines were worked for some seventy years from 1840, when James Foster[39] began to exploit the coal and ironstone of his royalty,[40] letting it to charter masters.[41] Mining began on the southern edge of the royalty where there were several pits in 1849.[42] By 1881 the spoil heaps there had been planted with trees and other shafts had been sunk, perhaps in the early 1870s, to the north-east.[43] The Fosters' royalty did not coincide exactly with the circle defined in 1703 but had been adjusted to conform with their surface ownership: a segment south of Gypsy Lane had been exchanged[44] for an area north of Halesfield where F. Guest chartered two pits.[45]

All the spoil heaps south of the Court had been planted by 1901[46] and mining in the Court royalty ended over the next few years. Production ceased in 1910 and 15 of the 17 pits were officially abandoned in 1911. Guest's pits, the subject of a drainage agreement in 1893, ceased production

c.1903 and were leased for Halesfield drainage to the Madeley Wood Co., which mined the Flint coal there briefly in 1916.[47]

IRON AND STEEL. Earliest evidence of iron making in the parish is the leasing of 'le Newhouse and Calbroke smithy' in 1536 to Hugh Morrall for 63 years.[48] Morrall also held an ironstone mine nearby. The water-powered[49] smithy, presumably a bloomery forge, stood near Dale End[50] and so can almost certainly be identified with the Lower forge,[51] where hearth plates dating from 1602 were found.[52] The contemporary existence of the Michell alias Smitheman family[53] indicates some turning of an established copyholding family to the new trade.

Early in the 17th century Sir Basil Brooke, lord of the manor 1598–1646, began to involve himself in iron making in the forest of Dean, where he became an overseer (1615–19), later a lessee (1628–35), of the Crown's ironworks.[54] About 1615 he acquired an interest in a steel cementation patent, and it seems to have been in Madeley that he made steel, importing Dean iron for the purpose.[55] His steel works, said to be in Madeley Wood in 1645[56] but probably in the lower part of Coalbrookdale,[57] evidently operated until c. 1680[58] and may have stimulated coal production in his nearby mines.[59] Brooke also made iron in Shropshire,[60] notably in Madeley where he built or rebuilt[61] a blast furnace at the head of Coal-brookdale, probably in 1638, the date on a monogrammed iron lintel over the tapping hearth of the Old, or Upper, furnace.[62]

Brooke's iron and steel works, like his coal mines, fell to the Parliamentarians in 1645 and were later let to Richard Foley and then to Edward Cludde. Cludde put them in order[63] and workmen from other parts of the country may have been brought to Madeley.[64] Francis Wolfe (I), Cludde's clerk of the coal and iron works,[65] acquired Cludde's tenancy of the manor in 1651.[66] His son Francis (II), who was supplying blooms

[34] Brown, op. cit. 14–15; Jackson, 'Madeley', bk. 1A, p. 23; W. Howard Williams, 'Dawley New Town Hist. Survey: Industries' (TS. 1964), addns. p. 6 (copy in S.P.L., accession 5202).
[35] T.D.C. deed pkt. 439, deed of 1918 (plan 2).
[36] Shropshire Star, 16 Dec. 1964; Staffs. R.O., D. 570/27; Shropshire Mag. Feb. 1967, 30–2; Mar. 1967, 29.
[37] Shropshire Mag. Feb. 1967, 29; Mar. 1967, 29.
[38] T.D.C. unnumbered deed pkt. for former Duroclay Ltd. property; Williams, 'Dawley Hist. Survey: Inds.' addns. p. 6; O.S. Map 1/2,500, SJ 6704 (1963 edn.); below, plate 31.
[39] Above, Man. and Other Est.
[40] Salop. News Letter, xl. 19–20.
[41] Ibid. xxxviii. 6.
[42] S.R.O. 2280/2/45.
[43] O.S. Map 1/2,500, Salop. XLIII. 11 (1883 edn.); Salop. News Letter, xxxviii. 5. For the nearby ironwks. see below, Iron and Steel.
[44] T.D.C. deed pkt. 439, deed of 1918 (plan 2).
[45] Salop. News Letter, xxxviii. 6–8.
[46] O.S. Map 1/2,500, Salop. XLIII. 11 (1902 edn.).
[47] Salop. News Letter, xxxviii. 5, 8; Shropshire Mag. Mar. 1967, 29.
[48] P.R.O., SC 6/Hen. VIII/3021, m. 5d.
[49] P.R.O., LR 2/184, ff. 107, 117, 118v., 120v.
[50] Nr. two pastures called Bulmers Grene (ibid. f. 118v.; SC 6/Hen. VIII/3021, m. 5), later Bullesmores, etc. (S.R.O. 210/2; 1987/30/2).

[51] S.R.O. 2280/2/46, no. 2865.
[52] Randall, Old Ct. Ho. 56–7.
[53] P.R.O., LR 2/184, ff. 106, 117. Cf. S.R.O. 1224/2/9.
[54] Above, Man. and Other est.; Hammersley, 'Iron Ind. in Dean Region', 149, 151–4, 158–63, 171, 496–7; V.C.H. Glos. ii. 225.
[55] Hammersley, op. cit. 152–3.
[56] P.R.O., SP 23/105, pp. 199, 201.
[57] i.e. the steelho. converted to a malt ho. in the 18th cent.: Raistrick, Iron Founders, 74, 228, 251–2, 286; T.S.A.S. lvi. 71.
[58] W. Midland Studies, xv. 5.
[59] Steel cementation used coal: R. Plot, Nat. Hist. of Staffs. (1686), 373–5.
[60] For his forge at Montford c. 1610 see Salop. News Letter, xliv. 7.
[61] It has been suggested (ibid. 6) that 'Reking' (? Wrekin) ironwks., mentioned in 1635 (P.R.O., SP 16/321, f. 80), was in Coalbrookdale. Hammersley (op. cit. 152–3) suggests that Brooke's iron making in Madeley antedated 1638.
[62] Raistrick, Iron Founders, 30; cf. Ind. Arch. Rev. iv. 117–34; Trinder, Darbys, frontispiece; Ironbridge Quarterly, 1982.3, 3.
[63] P.R.O., SP 23/105, pp. 187, 191, 199, 201, 207, 209, 211, 213, 223; above, Coal and Ironstone.
[64] T.S.A.S. lvi. 201, n. 11; cf. Raistrick, Iron Founders, 42.
[65] P.R.O., SP 23/105, p. 219.
[66] Above, Coal and Ironstone.

to the Foleys in 1669,[67] was having to buy cord-wood from as far away as Caus in 1680,[68] local coppices being apparently earmarked for other nearby furnaces.[69] By 1685 the furnace may have been taking ironstone from Lawley.[70]

Lawrence Wellington (I), of Coalbrookdale, was apparently operating the furnace in 1688 and supplying pig to Wytheford forge, but whether as

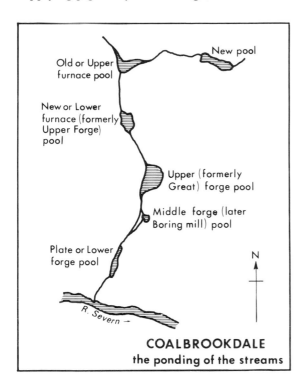

COALBROOKDALE
the ponding of the streams

a tenant or as manager for Basil Brooke is uncertain; he was certainly one of Brooke's creditors. Brooke's industrial operations incurred great losses and the manor was vested in trustees in 1695. Next year the ironworks in Coalbrookdale were let to Shadrach Fox of Malinslee: he immediately sublet to Wellington the Great and the Plate forges, with charcoal houses, a steelhouse, a

smith's shop lately worked by Cornelius Hallen, and other buildings.[71] Fox probably made the New pool in Lightmoor dingle c. 1698 as a reserve for his Coalbrookdale furnace.[72]

After an explosion at the furnace Fox absconded c. 1705[73] and his lease of the Coalbrookdale works was evidently acquired by Richard Corfield (d. by 1715) and Thomas Dorset. The furnace was still damaged when it was sublet in 1708[74] to Abraham Darby (I),[75] a Bristol brass and iron founder and ironmonger. Besides being well acquainted with the properties of coke,[76] Darby was interested in smelting iron (for founding) without the use of charcoal[77] and so was probably undeterred by the difficulties of obtaining wood in the area.[78] He rebuilt the furnace and in 1709 introduced coke as a smelting fuel;[79] by c. 1713 he evidently regarded the results as satisfactory.[80]

Darby's innovation was not widely imitated,[81] nor did its full significance[82] begin to be appreciated, for forty years or more. It was his son Abraham (II) who then improved the technique to produce pig suitable for making wrought bar in the forges.[83] Meanwhile in 1715 the concern started by Abraham (I), the Coalbrookdale Co.,[84] had become principal lessee (with an undertenant at the Lower forge) of the Coalbrookdale works,[85] which it continued to lease from the lords of the manor[86] until it bought them in 1845.[87] At first the mainstay of its business was a wide range of fine castings and hollow ware.[88] Nevertheless from 1718, when the Old forge was restored, it began to produce wrought iron in a small way and to take over the Coalbrookdale forges.[89]

Five forges are known to have used the Caldebrook's power at various times in the 17th and early 18th centuries; outside the dale, and probably at that period, there was a forge in Park Lane, but its approximate site[90] is all that is known of it. In 1696 Shadrach Fox had sublet the Great and Plate forges in the dale to Lawrence Wellington (I)[91] who was importing Dean pig 1696–1704.[92] In 1714 four Dale forges were listed, the small[93] Upper and Middle forges in addition to those mentioned in 1696.[94] A fifth, the Old forge near

[67] *Sel. Rec. of Phil. Foley's Stour Valley Iron Wks. 1668–74,* i (Worcs. Hist. Soc. N.S. ix), 58, 64, 77, 107, 109–10; *T.S.A.S.* lvi. 85.   [68] *V.C.H. Salop.* viii. 297.

[69] Trinder, *Ind. Rev. Salop.* (1981), 15; inf. from Mr. J. B. Lawson, based on Thynne papers, vols. xxi–xxiii, at Longleat.

[70] Raistrick, *Iron Founders,* 30.

[71] S.R.O. 625, box 15, copy of Mr. Wm. Woodhouse's forge acct. 1687–8; 4406/1, pp. 94–5; P.R.O., C 5/180/133.

[72] S.P.L., Deeds 8201. It encroached on the Wellingtons' property at the Ridges, L. Dawley: cf. ibid. 8201, 8207; *T.S.A.S.* lvi. 85, whose suggestion about New furnace (for which see below) is here discarded.

[73] Raistrick, *Iron Founders,* 30; *T.S.A.S.* lvi. 85; *Orders of Q. Sess.* i. 219, 221.

[74] *T.S.A.S.* lvi. 71, 85–6; Raistrick, op. cit. 30–7.

[75] *D.N.B.* contains a short erroneous notice.

[76] Raistrick, op. cit. 19 sqq.; Joan Day, *Bristol Brass* (1973), 32–40, 205; Trinder, *Ind. Rev. Salop.* (1981), 13–15; *T.S.A.S.* lvi. 86.

[77] As late as July 1712 he may have considered peat smelting at Furness as an alternative to his Coalbrookdale experiment: M. W. Flinn, 'Abr. Darby and the Coke-smelting Process', *Economica,* N.S. xxvi. 57–8.

[78] Above; above, Agric.

[79] Raistrick, *Iron Founders,* 30–7; T. S. Ashton, *Iron and Steel in the Ind. Rev.* (1951), 26–38, 249–50; Trinder, *Ind. Rev. Salop.* (1981), 13–14. Cf. *Ind. Arch. Rev.* iv. 127, for the

possibility that he used a hot blast.

[80] In 1714 he negotiated a new lease (in S.R.O. 1681, box 139) of the wks. to begin in 1717. Early accts. of Darby's work are reviewed in *T.S.A.S.* lviii. 153–66.

[81] B. L. C. Johnson, 'Midland Iron Ind. in early 18th Cent.' *Business Hist.* ii. 74; Trinder, op. cit. 16; *W. Midland Studies,* xv. 5–6.

[82] *Business Hist.* ii. 74; 'Blast Furnaces Since Darby's Day', *Engineering,* clxxxviii. 248; Hammersley, 'Iron Ind. in Dean Region', 26–7, 490–2.

[83] Trinder, op. cit. 21–3.

[84] Name formally adopted 1790: Raistrick, *Iron Founders,* 4–5.

[85] *T.S.A.S.* lvi. 87.

[86] Ibid.; Raistrick, op. cit. 58, 88–9, 247–51, 286; S.R.O. 1681, box 138, leases of 1805, 1838; box 139, leases of 1714, 1774, 1781; Trinder, *Ind. Rev. Salop.* (1981), 23.

[87] S.R.O. 1681, box 138, copy deed.

[88] Raistrick, op. cit. 37, 39, 45–6; *Business Hist.* ii. 71–2, 74.

[89] Raistrick, op. cit. 53–4; below.

[90] O.S. Nat. Grid SJ 681 048: S.R.O. 2280/2/45, nos. 246–50, 2732; /48, pp. 40, 59 (nos. 246–50, 2732).

[91] S.R.O. 4406/1, pp. 94–5.

[92] *T.S.A.S.* lvi. 71.

[93] Ibid. 72, 85, confounding Middle and Gt. forges.

[94] S.R.O. 1681, box 139, lease of 1714.

the Old furnace, was probably then disused.[95] Until his death in 1708 Wellington lived in White End[96] near the Great forge. In 1715 Fox's successors, the Corfields, assigned all their Coalbrookdale interests, including the five forges, to Darby.[97] He was a founder, not a forgemaster,[98] and that year he built his New or Lower furnace,[99] probably using the Upper forge pool.[1] The Upper forge is not known to have worked thereafter and eventually ceased to exist, perhaps in the 1740s,[2] its name being applied logically to the Great forge.[3] In 1718, the year after Darby's death, the Coalbrookdale Co. began to take an interest in the forges, and the Old forge was restored to working order.[4] Probably then[5] the Great forge[6] was sublet to Capt. Thomas Stanley, but the company took it back in 1720.[7] The Middle forge, perhaps located where the Boring mill was built in 1780, on the next pond above the Lower forge,[8] may have been converted to non-industrial use after 1722.[9] By 1708 the Plate or Lower forge had long been sublet to Cornelius Hallen; he may have made frying pans there.[10] The Hallens continued at the forge as the Coalbrookdale Co.'s undertenants, and as suppliers of the Coalbrookdale and other works, until the 1730s.[11]

From the 1730s to the 1790s the Coalbrookdale Co. expanded greatly,[12] capital and financial management being contributed by two Bristol mercantile families, the Goldneys (1718–c. 1770) and the Reynoldses (from c. 1780); policy and management of the works remained mostly with the Darbys. From the 1750s the company integrated its operations, acquiring mines and blast furnaces, including the Bedlam furnaces in Madeley Wood and mines and mineral rights belonging to Madeley manor. In Coalbrookdale three generations of Abraham Darby (I)'s descendants contributed notably to the development of the iron industry, and senior workmen like George and Thomas Cranage were also tackling outstanding technological problems. Two contributions in particular go far to explain the area's 20th-century claim to be the 'Birthplace of Industry'. The first of them was Abraham (II)'s successful use of coke c. 1750 to make pig suitable for conversion to malleable bar. The company exploited his discovery in its new ironworks at Horsehay, thereby freeing the Old furnace, Coalbrookdale, for its second great contribution to industrial development, the precise casting of steam-engine parts. The firm's success in that sphere led eventually to

the visit of Richard Trevithick to Coalbrookdale and the manufacture of the first steam locomotive there in 1802.

Apart from those notable historic contributions the company's prestige and profits were increased by a vast range of manufactures including architectural ironwork and eventually large civil engineering projects like the Iron Bridge (1777–80) and some of its successors at home and abroad. If the bridge was not in the forefront of design and had little influence on later bridge designs, it nevertheless greatly stimulated the use of iron and increased the company's fame.[13]

By 1790 the Coalbrookdale partners owned one of the largest iron-making concerns in the country. In 1797, however, the Darby and Reynolds interests were separated. The Darbys continued to trade as the Coalbrookdale Co., but in the early 19th century their Coalbrookdale works became less important than their operations elsewhere: the furnaces shut down in 1818 and closure of the works was considered in the 1820s. From the 1830s the manufacture of art castings stimulated recovery, and in 1851 the Coalbrookdale foundry was claimed as the world's biggest. After 1886[14] the company once more had no ironworks outside Coalbrookdale. The Darbys had relinquished management in 1849, but during the chairmanship (1886–1925) of A. E. W. Darby, the last Darby connected with the firm, new foundries and workshops were built at Dale End (1901) and over the Lower furnace pool, filled in 1903. In 1930 new works, erected over the filled Upper forge pool, replaced the Upper Works erected around and over the Old furnace during the 19th century. By then the company was newly incorporated in Allied Ironfounders Ltd., itself absorbed into Glynwed Foundries Ltd. in 1969. Mainstays of production after 1945 were new types of fire grate and the 'Rayburn' cooker. In 1978 the works became Glynwed's automobile and engineering division.[15]

In the 19th century the Madeley Wood Co. and the Fosters made pig iron from coal and ironstone raised in the parish. The Madeley Wood Co. emerged in the early 19th century after William Reynolds's interests in Madeley Wood had passed to the Anstices.[16] From 1832 its blast furnaces, erected at Bedlam in 1757–8 by the earlier Madeley Wood Co.,[17] were shifted eastwards with the company's mining operations to a canalside site on Blists Hill, where the company built three

[95] Raistrick, *Iron Founders*, 45, 52, 283.
[96] Taken by Darby at Mich. 1708. See *T.S.A.S.* lvi. 85; S.P.L., MS. 328, f. [36] 7 Jan. 1709/10.
[97] *T.S.A.S.* lvi. 87.
[98] Raistrick, *Iron Founders*, 53.
[99] Ibid. 6, 43–4, 50, 52, 103 sqq.; *T.S.A.S.* lvi. 85, 88.
[1] i.e. the next pond below Old or Upper furnace. See *T.S.A.S.* lvi. 88; lviii. 165, n.9; Trinder, *Ind. Rev. Salop.* (1981), 16; idem, *Darbys*, 67.
[2] Raistrick, op. cit. 52, 74, 279, 286.
[3] Called Upper forge in 1753: ibid. 74; but cf. S.R.O. 1681, box 139, lease of 1774.
[4] Raistrick, op. cit. 53–4.
[5] S.P.L., MS. 330, p. 275. The suggestion that Stanley occupied it by 1715 (*T.S.A.S.* lvi. 86–7) seems unjustified.
[6] Not Middle forge as stated in *T.S.A.S.* lvi. 72, 85–7; Raistrick, op. cit. 53. [7] S.P.L., MS. 330, p. 275.
[8] Trinder, *Darbys*, 67. For Boring mill see Raistrick, op.

cit. 152, 251 (no. 67); *T.S.A.S.* lviii. 245–6.
[9] Raistrick, op. cit. 54 n. 1, 286 (not mentioned 1734).
[10] Above; S.R.O. 4406/1, pp. 94–5; *T.S.A.S.* lvi. 85–6; Raistrick, op. cit. 251 (no. 70). Refs. to the Hallens at Upper forge (ibid. 54; *T.S.A.S.* lvi. 72) are mistaken: cf. S.R.O. 1224/2/392–3.
[11] *T.S.A.S.* lvi. 85, 90; Raistrick, op. cit. 54, 115; Trinder, *Ind. Rev. Salop.* (1981), 32.
[12] Next three paras. based on Raistrick, op. cit.; *Coalbrookdale Ironworks: A short hist.* (I.G.M.T. 1975).
[13] Ted Ruddock, *Arch Bridges and their Builders, 1735–1835* (1979), 132 sqq., 138–41, 149–51, 158, 160, 226 n. 7, 236; *Ind. Arch. Rev.* vi. 45, 50.
[14] Below, Dawley, Econ. Hist. (Iron), for Horsehay wks.
[15] Inf. from Mr. J. Bernstein, managing director, Glynwed Foundries Ltd.; below, plate 26.
[16] Trinder, *Ind. Rev. Salop.* (1981), 44.
[17] Ibid. 26.

new blast furnaces in 1832, 1840, and 1844.[18] With limestone from Lincoln Hill and local coal and ores the company produced first class grey forge iron and melters. Its technology was old fashioned but its cold-blast pig was widely considered the best for hollow-ware manufacture, and the company survived the late 19th-century depression by concentrating on that manufacture. Profits, however, came from coalmining rather than iron making. Two of the furnaces were blown out shortly after 1908, the third in 1912 after a strike;[19] thereafter the company became simply colliery proprietors.[20]

In 1845–6 James Foster built three blast furnaces near the newly opened mines on his Madeley Court estate. They replaced his Wombridge furnaces, and Foster moved workmen and plant from Wombridge to create a modern ironworks. For most of their life only two of the three furnaces were in blast together. All the Madeley Court pig was sent to the Fosters' ironworks in Staffordshire and Worcestershire to be blended with other types for the manufacture of high-quality bar. The ironworks ceased in 1902[21] but in 1912 were taken over by Thomas Parker (d. 1915), an electrical engineer.[22] He and his son C. H. Parker established Court Works Ltd., a foundry firm which, seventy years later, had long specialized in iron castings for the electrical industry.[23]

OTHER METAL AND ENGINEERING TRADES. Smiths are recorded in the parish in the 14th and 17th centuries.[24] By the late 17th century there were smiths, nailers, two platers (at least one of them perhaps making frying pans),[25] a pot founder, a brass founder, and a gunsmith. Some of those involved in the small metal trades were beginning to specialize in work for the mines and ironworks. Such occupations continued and multiplied in the 18th century.[26] Clockmakers were mentioned in the 18th century.[27]

Lead ore, brought by river, was smelted near Dale End in the mid 18th century and near the Lloyds and at Coalport in the late 18th and early 19th century.[28]

Many iron-using and engineering enterprises, one or two of them originating in the late 18th century, flourished in the 19th and 20th centuries; notable among them was the manufacture of chains. The foundries, forges, and engineering shops were small in comparison with the Coalbrookdale, Madeley Wood, and Madeley Court works. From the late 1960s, however, some large new factories, along with many smaller ones, were opened on new industrial estates for concerns in the engineering and metal trades.

At the turn of the 18th and 19th centuries William Horton and Benjamin Edge opened chain manufactories at Coalport. Edge, apparently a Norfolk Quaker, established his in William Reynolds's former rope factory, which his father may have managed. There was a good trade with local colliery firms, and Gilbert Gilpin of Dawley took over Horton's factory. About 1819, however, Gilpin established a new chain works at Aqueduct. His executors were running it in 1827, and in the early 1850s it survived as Charles Clayton's foundry, producing rollers, hurdles, and gates: later it seems to have been a nail factory. The Edges took Gilpin's Coalport works and were still making chains in Coalport in 1863.[29] By 1870 they had moved and had chain, wire rope, and engineering works at the canalside Madeley foundry and at Upton (in Shifnal).[30] The firm concentrated in Shifnal c. 1880 leaving chain making in Madeley to William Walton,[31] also a general smith.[32] Walton finished soon after 1905,[33] his works near the canal bridge being taken by G. J. Muirhead Ltd., bankrupt by 1910.[34]

The Waltons, established in the parish from 1773, were general smiths and engineers; by 1905 their engineering works in Church Hill, Ironbridge, was let to Beddoes & Green who ran it until c. 1912. Thomas Dorsett set up as ironfounder and implement maker in 1837, and c. 1905 his son was making agricultural implements in Park Street[35] where the family had a business as late as 1941.[36]

Several metal and light engineering firms came to the parish in the 1940s, converting vacant industrial and other buildings, though not always successfully. The Ironbridge Metal Co. opened works at Madeley Wood and Dale End in the 1940s to recover aluminium from aluminium foil, but in 1950 the unsuitability of the Madeley Wood works, a century-old malthouse, was partly responsible for an explosion which closed both

[18] Ibid. 139; *Salop. News Letter*, xxxvii. 40; above, Coal and Ironstone; below, plates 27–8.
[19] Gregory, 'E. Salop. Coalfield', 13–14, 76–86; *Resources and Ind. Hist. of Birm. and Midland Hardware Dist.* ed. S. Timmins (Brit. Assoc. 1866), 107; *Salop. News Letter*, xxxvii. 40.
[20] Above, Coal and Ironstone.
[21] *Salop. News Letter*, xl. 19–20; *Griffiths' Guide to Iron Trade of Gt. Brit.* (1873), 101; N. Mutton, 'The Foster Fam.: Study of a Midlands Industrial Dynasty 1786–1899' (London Univ. Ph.D. thesis, 1974), 113–14, 118–19; *V.C.H. Salop.* i. 455–6; *V.C.H. Staffs.* ii. 127.
[22] *St. Mic.'s, Madeley, Par. Mag.* June 1912; Jackson, 'Madeley', bk. 1, pp. 86–7; bk. 1A, p. 108; draft will of Thos. Parker, 1915 (copy in S.P.L.). For Parker see above, intro.
[23] T.D.C. *Telford Ind. Dir.* (1982).
[24] S.R.O. 566/1; P.R.O., SP 23/105, pp. 193, 203.
[25] Above, Iron and Steel.
[26] e.g. *W. Midland Studies*, xv. 4–6, H.W.R.O.(H.), Heref. dioc. rec., prob. invs. of Wm. Ashwood snr., 1667; Ben. Cox, 1720; Rog. Downes, 1720; Thos. Glasebrook, 1695; Cornelius Hallen, 1746; Thos. Rowley, 1755; Jas. Smitheman, 1710; P.R.O., E 134/27 Geo. II Hil./8, mm. 7,

10; E 179/168/219, mm. 16–17.
[27] *Orders of Q. Sess.* ii. 191–2; *Bye-Gones, 1930–1*, 165; Raistrick, *Iron Founders*, 228.
[28] Prob. inv. of Chris. Pritchard, 1753; *W. Midland Studies*, xv. 4; Trinder, *Ind. Rev. Salop.* (1981), 10, 131.
[29] *V.C.H. Salop.* i. 479–81; Trinder, *Ind. Rev. Salop.* (1981), 129, 131–2; *Salop. News Letter*, xxxvii. 40–1; xl. 17–18; Williams, 'Dawley Hist. Survey: Inds.' pp. 25–7; *P.O. Dir. Salop.* (1856), 78; S.R.O. 2280/2/45, nos. 1288, 1291–2; /48, pp. 28 (no. 1292), 74 (nos. 1288, 1291).
[30] *P.O. Dir. Salop.* (1870), 86, 127, 211.
[31] Cf. ibid. (1879), 354, 396; *Kelly's Dir. Salop.* (1885), 888, 935; *Salop. News Letter*, xxxvii. 41.
[32] *P.O. Dir. Salop.* (1870), 87.
[33] *Kelly's Dir. Salop.* (1905), 141 (last mention).
[34] S.R.O. 4044/93, p. 38 (no. 713); *V.C.H. Salop.* i. 472; *Salop. News Letter*, xxxvii. 41.
[35] *V.C.H. Salop.* i. 472; S.R.O. 2280/2/45, no. 536; /48, p. 31 (no. 536); 4044/93, pp. 18 (no. 312), 99 (no. 1816); S.R.O. 2079/XLIII. 14. SE. and 15. NW., nos. 312, 1816; *Kelly's Dir. Salop.* (1905), 113, 141; (1913), not mentioning Beddoes & Green.
[36] Descr. as ironmongers: *Kelly's Dir. Salop.* (1905–41).

works.[37] Coventry Tool & Gauge Co. Ltd. established a branch works in the barn and outbuildings of Upper House in 1941,[38] and the same year, moving from London, Chillcotts Ltd., sheet metal workers and manufacturers of gaskets, washers, silencers, etc., took part of the old china works at Coalport. Another part was later taken by the Coalport Metalware Co. Ltd., makers of fancy goods, formed in 1946 by partners from Birmingham. By 1963 there were half a dozen other firms in the metal finishing, pressing, welding, and steel fabrications trades; one of them used the old Madeley market buildings as the Arcade Press Works.[39]

QUARRIES AND SANDPITS. Stone was being mined and quarried by the mid 17th century, notably at Lincoln (perhaps once Limekiln)[40] Hill, the outcrop of Silurian limestone east of Coalbrookdale.[41] Three men were killed at the limekilns there in 1647,[42] and limeworks were mentioned in 1651 and 1694.[43] The hill was gradually hollowed out[44] by centuries of quarrying and by adit and shaft mining. By 1758 it was split by a 'vast pit' a quarter of a mile long and 52 yards wide, perhaps the result of a collapse. The view down into the chasm in 1801 revealed 'prodigious caverns' and 'stupendous' supporting pillars; on the hillside was a deep quarry with other pillared caverns and limekilns at the bottom.[45]

Some Lincoln Hill stone was evidently being sold to local ironworks in the early 19th century though not all the beds were rich in suitable fluxing stone;[46] for a century or more the ironworks had also drawn on sources across the river.[47] Stone seems, however, to have been got for agricultural dressing.[48] The Lincoln Hill workings were acquired by Richard Reynolds in 1795 and later passed to the Madeley Wood Co.[49] In the 1840s, however, the company assigned its interests in the limeworks and kilns, then scattered around the north-east and eastern flanks of the hill and at its southern tip, to Edward Smith of the Lloyds, an ale and porter merchant, maltster, and limeburner. Large-scale extraction had ceased by c. 1850 and the workings may have closed for a time in the later 19th century. By 1892 they were

being run by the Madeley Wood Co. again but output was small, only three men being employed. John Hill took the mine in 1902 and worked it with one other man until 1907 when it finally closed.[50]

Building stone was being exported from the parish by 1588 when 80 tons were sent down river for Sir Edward Pytts's house at Kyre Park (Worcs.).[51] That may have been the Carboniferous sandstone,[52] evidence of whose working abounds near Bedlam and Jockey Bank.[53]

Before the brick-building of the late 18th and early 19th century local stone was widely used: the old and the new St. Michael's,[54] Madeley Court and its gatehouse, the Lodge,[55] and many cottages and roadside walls were evidently built of materials quarried nearby.

The Washbrook valley and part of the Court demesne overlie Upper Coal Measures siltstones[56] and there is evidence of quarrying on Hay farm[57] and the Court demesne.[58] 'Black Rock'[59] was apparently quarried in Lightmoor dingle in the early 1860s.[60]

Deposits of sand and gravel were worked, notably on Lodge farm[61] and near Hill's Lane coal pits.[62] The fine sand of Lodge farm (on land bought by Francis Darby in 1848)[63] was long used by the Coalbrookdale Co. for casting.[64] In 1849 there were sandholes near Strethill Farm[65] and old gravel pits near the Prince Street canal bridge and on Cuckoo Oak farm.[66]

CLAY AND CERAMIC INDUSTRIES. Red and white clays occurring in the parish were used for making bricks and tiles on a considerable scale from the 18th century to the 20th. The red clays were found on the sloping surface of the Severn Gorge, spread over the denuded edges of the coal measures; the white clays were bedded between the coal seams. The purer white clays were suitable for refractory and pottery ware. Most of the 19th- and 20th-century brickworks stood beside a clay mine, and the parish's last such mine (Blists Hill) closed in 1933.[67] Fine porcelain and some earthenware was made for 130 years after 1796, West Country clays being imported at first by water and later by rail.[68] The last clay manufacture in the

[37] Shrews. Chron. 19 May 1950; 18 July 1952; Express & Star, 15 May, 5–6 July 1950.
[38] Williams, 'Dawley Hist. Survey: Inds.' p. 37; T.D.C. deed pkt. 187.
[39] Williams, op. cit. pp. 36–7.
[40] Jackson, 'Madeley', bk. 3A, p. 363.
[41] Inst. Geol. Sciences Map 1/25,000, Telford (1978 edn.).
[42] Ind. Arch. Rev. iii. 160.
[43] P.R.O., SP 23/105, pp. 183, 192–3, 203; Randall, Madeley, 57. Cf. W. Midland Studies, xv. 4; J. Hill, 'A premature Welfare State?', Local Historian, xiv (1), 15.
[44] For technical, etc., details see I. J. Brown, Hist. of Limestone Mining in Salop. (Salop. Mining Club Acct. vi, 1967), 17–21; idem, Interim Rep. on the Lincoln Hill Limestone Mines (Salop. Caving and Mining Club Acct. xiii, 1981).
[45] Trinder, Ind. Rev. Salop. (1981), 59; T.S.A.S. lviii. 255.
[46] Ind. Arch. Rev. iii. 160.
[47] Trinder, op. cit. 15; 1st Rep. Com. Child. Emp. App. Pt. I [381], p. 43, H.C. (1842), xvi.
[48] Ind. Arch. Rev. iii. 160. Silurian limestone was unimportant as a bldg. stone: A. Clifton-Taylor, Pattern of Eng. Bldg. (1972), 99.
[49] Ind. Arch. Rev. iii. 160; Raistrick, Iron Founders, 212.
[50] Brown, Interim Rep.; S.R.O. 1681, box 173, lease of 1848; box 184, lease of 1836 and assignment of 1841; 2280/2/45, no. 2766; /46, nos. 2767, 2825; /48, pp. 84 (nos. 2549, 2825), 107 (nos. 2766–7); S. Bagshaw, Dir. Salop. (1851),

575; Trinder, op. cit. 59, 147.
[51] A. D. Dyer, City of Worcester in 16th cent. (1973), 63.
[52] The late 16th-cent. wk. at Kyre is in sandstone: V.C.H. Worcs. iv. 279–80.
[53] Ind. Arch. Rev. iii. 165.
[54] S.R.O. 2280/6/1, accts. for 1683; /6/95, 14 Apr. 1794.
[55] Randall, Madeley, 44–5, 331.
[56] Inst. Geol. Sciences Map 1/25,000, Telford (1978 edn.).
[57] S.R.O. 271/1, p. 192; 2280/2/45, no. 1268.
[58] S.R.O. 2280/2/45, no. 319; /48, p. 42 (no. 319).
[59] Presumably L. Wenlock basalt: below, Dawley, Econ. Hist. (Quarries).
[60] Randall, Madeley, 307.
[61] S.R.O. 2280/2/45, nos. 2683, 2685–8, 2692, 2696; /48, pp. 28–9 (nos. 2683, 2685–8, 2692, 2696).
[62] Ibid. /45, no. 945; /48, p. 60 (no. 945); Bull. Peak Dist. Mines Hist. Soc. ii. 355.
[63] S.R.O. 1987/19/37.
[64] S. Bagshaw, Dir. Salop. (1851), 568.
[65] S.R.O. 2280/2/45, nos. 3476–7, 3479, 3494; /48, pp. 34–5 (nos. 3476–7, 3479, 3494).
[66] At O.S. Nat. Grid SJ 702 047 and 708 048: ibid. /45, nos. 41, 372; /48, pp. 7 (no. 41), 30 (no. 372).
[67] V.C.H. Salop. i. 442; Bull. Peak Dist. Mines Hist. Soc. ii. 339–42.
[68] Trinder, Ind. Rev. Salop. (1981), 127; R. S. Edmundson, 'Coalport China Wks.' Ind. Arch. Rev. iii. 128, 135.

parish, that of sanitary pipes, ceased in the 1950s but there was opencast mining of fireclay in the Woodside area until the mid 1960s.[69]

Before the late 18th century bricks were probably made in temporary clamps near a source of clay or a building site. Field names[70] perhaps indicate such burnings. In the late 18th century the coal and iron industries needed great quantities of bricks and there were kilns among the Madeley coalpits, at the Lloyds and Blists Hill.[71] In 1793 the Madeley coal works paid Joseph Dodd for building an oven to burn bricks for a new mine,[72] and Joseph Davies was making bricks regularly in the 1790s, probably wholly or mainly for the Madeley mines.[73] In July 1795 John Davis made 6,425 bricks for the Rough Park mines. Whether such brickmakers were the coal masters' employees or worked as contractors to the mines is uncertain, but the coal masters evidently provided enough of the demand to give them effective control of the brickmakers' prices and operations.[74]

The growth of Ironbridge and Coalport enlarged the brickmakers' market and the names Dodd and Davies occur among the independent brickmakers of the mid 19th century.[75] Other works were founded. In the 1790s William Reynolds started one at Coalport to make common bricks; it closed shortly after 1810.[76] In the early 19th century Roger Cock made white bricks near Bedlam[77] at a works later taken over by the Madeley Wood Co.[78]

Largest of the mid 19th-century works, to judge from the supply of bricks for St. Luke's, Ironbridge (1835–6), was the Woodlands, said to have been started in 1780, which supplied over 61 per cent of the 321,000 bricks needed; Roger Cock supplied another 17 per cent.[79] By 1849 there were eight brickworks in the parish. Three were run by ironmasters: James Foster had one near Windmill Farm, the Madeley Wood Co. others at Bedlam and Blists Hill. John Davies's works at Halesfield is probably to be identified with the Tweedale Patent Drain Tile & Brick Works in existence by 1843. Another Davies ran one of the two works at Madeley Hill in 1849 and 1874. The Woodlands works belonged to Samuel Smith & Co. in 1849[80] but probably by 1870 it was operated by George Legge & Son.[81] In the 1870s Legges evidently also acquired the Madeley Hill works.[82]

Legges eventually became the only brick and tile makers in the parish. By the mid 1880s, however, the Madeley Wood Co. was advertising a wide range of Broseley bricks and tiles; the company's manufacture, previously divided between the white brick works at Bedlam and the red brick works at Blists Hill, was concentrated at Blists Hill in the 1880s.[83] Legges had other late 19th-century competitors in the parish, the short-lived Old Court Tile and Ceramic Art Works of W. J. Jeffrey & Son c. 1891[84] and the Fosters' Madeley Court Co. with a works just north of the Halesfield colliery,[85] which was perhaps the 'clay works' at Madeley Court mentioned in 1880.[86] Neither of those existed in 1912 when Legges took over the Blists Hill Brickworks,[87] larger than their own Woodlands works;[88] they seem to have bought the Blists Hill works a few years later.[89] In 1915, when the Madeley Wood Co. negotiated a new lease of the manorial coal and ironstone, the beds of Broseley tile clay were left out, and George Legge & Son simultaneously took a large area of them. The Legge leasehold centred on the Blists Hill works either side of the canal,[90] and there the Legges concentrated their manufacture; the Madeley Hill brickworks had already closed[91] and the Woodlands may have closed then or soon after.[92]

Legges were liquidated in 1938 after a protracted dispute and litigation with Wenlock borough over the culverting of the Washbrook under Blists Hill pit mound; brick making ceased, though tile making continued. Sanitary pipes were made after the Second World War but another bankruptcy in 1956 closed the works finally.[93]

Mention was made of a Madeley potter in 1761,[94] but the earliest certainly known works in the parish[95] was the porcelain manufactory built at Coalport in 1795–6 for Edward Blakeway and John and Richard Rose; it stood between the road

[69] Bull. Peak Dist. Mines Hist. Soc. ii. 344; T.D.C. unnumbered deed pkt. for former Duroclay Ltd. property; O.S. Map 1/2,500, SJ 6704 (1963 edn.).

[70] Brick-kiln leasow, Brick-kiln fields: S.R.O. 2280/2/48, pp. 25 (nos. 1122, 1124), 61 (no. 1844), 106–7 (nos. 2740–1).

[71] Trinder, Ind. Rev. Salop. (1981), 60; S.R.O. 271/1, p. 188.

[72] S.R.O. 271/1, f. 82.   [73] Ibid. passim.

[74] Ibid. f. 161; Raistrick, Iron Founders, 211.

[75] Below.

[76] Trinder, Ind. Rev. Salop. (1981), 129.

[77] Tibnam & Co. Salop. Dir. (1828), 25. Pigot, Nat. Com. Dir. (1835), 350, locates him at Hodgebower, perh. his dwelling. There was a brickyd. there in 1849: S.R.O. 2280/2/48, p. 94 (no. 2030).

[78] V.C.H. Salop. i. 442–3.

[79] Ibid. 444; Shrews. Chron. 15 Oct. 1937 (p. 13).

[80] S.R.O. 2280/2/48, pp. 36–7 (nos. 67, 936, 938), 42 (no. 111), 61 (nos. 1080, 1087), 66 (nos. 1902–3), 75 (no. 1676), 93 (nos. 2700–1, 2706); Williams, 'Dawley Hist. Survey: Inds.' p. 8; E. Cassey & Co. Dir. Salop. (1874), 186. For earlier brickwks. of the Davies fam. in Madeley Wood and Jackfield see above; V.C.H. Salop. i. 443–4.

[81] P.O. Dir. Salop. (1870), 207.

[82] Ibid. (1879), 335, 354; Cassey, Dir. Salop. (1874), 186. Legges' acquisitions of the Smith and the Davies wks. seem to be confounded in V.C.H. Salop. i. 444.

[83] Randall, Madeley, 367; Williams, 'Dawley Hist. Survey: Inds.' pp. 4, 7; Kelly's Dir. Salop. (1891), 334, 357, advts. p. 42; (1905), 114, 141, advts. p. 15.

[84] Williams, op. cit. pp. 7–8.

[85] At O.S. Nat. Grid SJ 705 053: ibid. p. 8; O.S. Map 6", Salop. XLIII. SE. (1888 edn.).

[86] Randall, Madeley, 367.

[87] St. Mic.'s, Madeley, Par. Mag. June 1912.

[88] Cf. S.R.O. 4044/93, pp. 58 (nos. 1045–6), 91 (no. 1667).

[89] S.P.L., L.F. Chitty colln. 240/25; S.R.O. 1681, box 99, sched. of deeds of Madeley Wood Co. to Geo. Legge & Son, 1920.

[90] S.R.O. 1681, box 145, leases of 1915; Williams, 'Dawley Hist. Survey: Inds.' p. 7.

[91] Williams, op. cit. p. 5; S.R.O. 4044/93, p. 82 (no. 1487).

[92] Kelly's Dir. Salop. (1922), 143, evidently refers to the Blists Hill wks. only. Cf. Williams, op. cit. p. 4.

[93] W.B.R. Madeley dist. cttee. min. bks. 1932–7, 1937–43; Jackson, 'Madeley', bk. 1A, pp. 252–5, 257; Williams, op. cit. pp. 7, 11–12.

[94] Wellington par. reg. marr. 19 Jan. 1761 (transcript in S.P.L.).

[95] V.C.H. Salop. i. 437 (citing no source), alleges that a pottery belonging to a Mr. Young, of Shrews., preceded Rose, Blakeway & Co. on the same site.

and the canal.[96] John Rose had worked at Caughley for Thomas Turner, probably from 1784 (beginning as an apprentice) until 1793 when he became Blakeway's partner in a pottery at Jackfield (in Broseley). Rose, Blakeway & Co. left the Jackfield works when they opened the Coalport works.

The firm prospered and in 1799 took over Turner's Caughley works. In 1803 it became bankrupt, but new owners immediately reconstituted it as John Rose & Co., keeping Rose as managing partner. In 1814 the company took over the adjacent porcelain works of Anstice, Horton & Rose, founded as an earthenware manufactory by Walter Bradley in 1796 and taken over in 1800 by William Reynolds, William Horton, and John Rose's brother Thomas. Rose, Blakeway & Co. probably demolished the Caughley works soon after to concentrate production at Coalport; it was then the county's only porcelain works.

During its 130 years (1796–1926) at Coalport the concern founded by John Rose, and connected with his family until 1875,[97] made a great range of richly decorated, flower-encrusted porcelains and plainer tea and table wares.[98] In the 19th and early 20th century four hundred or more workers seem to have been employed.[99] Difficult trading conditions and a strike in 1923 caused the sale of the business to Cauldon Potteries Ltd.; the works closed in 1926 and the business moved to Stoke-on-Trent, some of the artists and workers migrating with it.[1]

There may have been a small china decorating works in Madeley in the 1790s,[2] and c. 1826 T. M. Randall, a former apprentice of John Rose, established a small porcelain works at the lower end of Madeley,[3] perhaps near the junction of Hill's Lane and Prince Street.[4] There he succeeded in producing ware closely resembling old Sèvres. He also redecorated Sèvres ware and applied Sèvres decoration to ware made by others; his artists included his nephew John Randall.[5] T. M. Randall closed his works in 1840[6] and moved to Shelton in the Potteries.

OTHER INDUSTRIES AND INDUSTRIAL ESTATES. Sir Basil Brooke may have been making soap in Madeley for a short time in the 1630s. A mid 19th-century soap works at Aqueduct perhaps belonged to Charles Clayton. Candle making was important to the mines in the 17th century[8] and a candle factory worked in Madeley town in the early 20th century.[9]

Oil and natural gas have been prospected for, or encountered, at various times in the parish[10] but, unlike natural bitumen, never commercially exploited. Bitumen was extracted in some quantity from the Tar Tunnel at Coalport in the 1790s; some was sold but the rest was used by William Reynolds within his own concerns. Near the tunnel mouth it was boiled to make pitch. Small amounts were extracted for forty years after Reynolds's death in 1803. Tar works had been carried on by the Madeley Wood Co. at the time of its acquisition by Abraham Darby (III) in the 1770s.[11]

The Phoenix Chemical Works, Mawkins Lane, was established c. 1850 by Jesse Fisher, inventor of a commercial process for making carbon bisulphide, an ingredient of the firm's artificial manure. 'Fisher's stinkhouse' was continued by Rowland Fisher until c. 1879.[12]

The malthouse established by Abraham Darby (I)[13] was profitable to his descendants well into the 19th century,[14] and malting remained a significant local industry in the 19th century as public houses increased[15] and local brewing persisted; some pubs had malthouses.[16] There were usually about half a dozen malthouses[17] but in the 1920s and 1930s the industry ceased in the parish.[18]

Ropes were in demand by the collieries until the invention of improved chains, and in the 1790s William Reynolds, perhaps in partnership with William Horton, tenant of a rope walk there, had a hemp rope factory near the Coalport china works; in 1798 it became a chain works.[19] Rope making, however, continued at Coalport until the 1840s.[20] At some time there was a rope walk at the other end of the parish in Loamhole dingle.[21] Timber was also in local demand and there were timber

[96] Two paras. based on G. A. Godden, *Coalport and Coalbrookdale Porcelains* (1970), 1–66, 94–5; R. S. Edmundson, 'Coalport China Wks.' *Ind. Arch. Rev.* iii. 122–33; idem, 'Bradley & Co., Coalport Pottery 1796–1800', *Northern Ceramic Soc. Jnl.* iv. 127–55. Those accts. supersede *V.C.H. Salop.* i. 436–7 (corr. ibid. ii. 318).

[97] For the firm's hist. after 1814 see *V.C.H. Salop.* i. 437–9 (corr. ibid. ii. 318); C. Mackenzie, *Ho. of Coalport 1750–1950* (2nd edn. 1953); *Ind. Arch. Rev.* iii. 132 sqq. See below, plate 12.

[98] W. Mankowitz and R. G. Haggar, *Concise Encyclopedia of Eng. Pottery and Porcelain* (1957), 57; M. Messenger, *Caughley and Coalport Porcelain in Clive Ho., Shrews.: Cat.* (1976); *Coalport China Wks. Mus.* (I.G.M.T. 1978), 5, 11; G. A. Godden, *Brit. Porcelain: Illustr. Guide* (1974), 149–76.

[99] *Ind. Arch. Rev.* iii. 135, 145 n. 6; Godden, *Coalport and Coalbrookdale Porcelains*, 147–51. Cf. *Shropshire Mag.* Jan. 1955, 21–2.

[1] *Ind. Arch. Rev.* iii. 141; Mackenzie, *Ho. of Coalport*, 86, 94, 98, 110 sqq.; *Coalport China Wks. Mus.* 11–12.

[2] Godden, *Coalport and Coalbrookdale Porcelains*, 16.

[3] Para. based on W. Turner, 'Madeley Porcelain', *The Connoisseur*, xxx. 153–60, 248–54; *V.C.H. Salop.* i. 439–40; Randall, *Madeley*, 205–10.

[4] At O.S. Nat. Grid SJ 7011 0450, where wasters were found by Mr. A. McCall in 1979: inf. from Mr. R. S. Edmundson. Randall's yd. was nearby: S.R.O. 2280/2/45, no. 387; /48, p. 56 (no. 387). Excavation (1965) on the traditional site, further E., revealed nothing: *Salop. News Letter*, xxix. 3.

[5] F. A. Barrett, *Caughley and Coalport Porcelain* (Leigh on Sea, 1951), 55, 71–3.

[6] Ibid. 71.

[7] *V.C.H. Salop.* i. 440.

[8] *W. Midland Studies*, xv. 4; Williams, 'Dawley Hist. Survey: Inds.' p. 35; *Salop. News Letter*, xl. 18 (corr. ibid. xli. 21).

[9] Re-erected at Blists Hill by I.G.M.T.

[10] *Bull. Peak Dist. Mines Hist. Soc.* ii. 348; *Shropshire Star*, 2 Feb. 1980 (p. 3). For Ironbridge and Madeley gas wks. see below, Public Services.

[11] I. Brown and B. Trinder, *The Tar Tunnel* (I.G.M.T. 1979); Plymley, *Agric. of Salop.* 70–1; S.R.O. 1987, box 20, Madeley Wood Co. purchase papers.

[12] Williams, 'Dawley Hist. Survey: Inds.' p. 35; *Ind. Chemistry*, ed. B. H. Paul (1878), 139.

[13] Raistrick, *Iron Founders*, 228, 286; *T.S.A.S.* lvi. 71.

[14] Raistrick, op. cit. 12, 248, 278.

[15] Above, Social and Cultural Activities.

[16] Raistrick, op. cit. 228–9; S.R.O. 2280/2/48, pp. 37 (no. 2427), 50 (no. 3025), 59–60 (nos. 416, 2526, 2732), 66 (no. 1578), 95 (no. 2077).

[17] See e.g. S.R.O. 2280/2/48, pp. 35 (no. 3422), 45 (no. 868), 67 (no. 632), 98 (no. 2524), 104 (no. 3199), 106 (no. 2308), 109 (no. 2517); *P.O. Dir. Salop.* (1856), 195–6; *Kelly's Dir. Salop.* (1885), 1073; (1900), 390–1.

[18] *Kelly's Dir. Salop.* (1917–41).

[19] *Salop. News Letter*, xxxvii. 40; Plymley, *Agric. of Salop.* 341 n.; *Ind. Arch. Rev.* iii. 131.

[20] Tibnam & Co. *Salop. Dir.* (1828), 31; H. Green, 'Linen Ind. of Salop.' *Ind. Arch. Rev.* v. 118–19.

[21] S.R.O. 2280/2/45, no. 3244; /48, p. 29 (no. 3244).

merchants and timber yards in the parish in the 18th, 19th, and 20th centuries; one at Coalport from *c.* 1874 to *c.* 1930, was also a boat builder.[22]

Printing and publishing were established in Madeley by 1791 when John Edmunds, bookseller and printer, had premises in High Street. Edward Dyas, probably one of his employees, invented the composition of which printers' inking rollers were later made.[23] Edmunds's son Daniel had the business as late as 1817[24] and it may later have been carried on by the Walter family. They printed for the Whigs in 1832, William Smith for the Tories.[25] Smith had a press at Ironbridge from *c.* 1807 to *c.* 1842,[26] and from the mid 19th century Joseph Slater's press at Ironbridge and John Randall's at Madeley produced newspapers, magazines, almanacks, and books.[27] Slater and Randall had successors until *c.* 1909 and *c.* 1917 respectively.[28]

In 1920 the Madeley Wood Co.'s pit heaps were taken over by the Madeley Wood Cold Blast Slag Co., run by Thomas Jones.[29] The company crushed the slag at a works in the Lloyds[30] and between the wars[31] sold it for road metal.

Labour surpluses and vacant buildings attracted several firms to the parish, notably from London and the Midlands, before and after the Second World War.[32] In 1927 part of the recently closed Coalport china works was occupied by Nuway Manufacturing Co. Ltd. of Birmingham, who made rubber-link matting from old car tyres. Production was suspended 1942–5 but grew thereafter, and *c.* 1979 an associated company was manufacturing steel supported staircases at Halesfield.[33] Merrythought Ltd., soft toy makers,[34] was founded in 1930 by a former employee of the Chad Valley Co. Ltd. and took over the old Severn foundry, Dale End.[35] Clifford Williams & Son Ltd., of Birmingham, joined by two other partners to become Pyjamas Ltd., took over the drill hall and assembly rooms, Ironbridge, in 1951 and 1953 respectively for garment making. In 1962 production was transferred to a new factory in Queen Street and it was expected that the 100-strong labour force would be doubled.[36] By *c.* 1979 the parent firm also had premises at Halesfield.[37]

In the early 1960s the district committee tried to promote industrial developments in the area around Cuckoo Oak, Queen Street, and Hill's Lane, and efforts were made to attract Birmingham industrialists.[38] The committee assisted the move of Pyjamas Ltd. in 1962 to a new factory in Queen Street for a larger labour force.[39] Nevertheless further industrial developments, with associated housing and road works, were halted in 1962 by the maturing of government plans to include Madeley in Dawley new town.[40]

By the late 1970s manufacturing industry, with the notable exception of Glynwed Foundries in Coalbrookdale,[41] was largely concentrated in areas east and north-east of the centre of Madeley: on Telford development corporation's industrial estates at Tweedale (with the old-established Court works as a northern outlier) and Halesfield, and in the adjacent Prince and Queen streets.[42] Coventry Tool & Gauge Ltd., however, remained on its original site until 1980,[43] one of two engineering firms in central Madeley. Tweedale was developed from 1966 as the new town's first industrial estate. Halesfield, its largest, was developed from 1967 mainly on former agricultural land but including the site of the Madeley Wood colliery in Kemberton; the area had been taken into Dawley U.D. in 1966 from Kemberton, Shifnal, and Sutton Maddock parishes.[44]

MARKETS AND FAIRS. In 1269 the prior of Wenlock was granted an annual fair on 20–22 September and a Tuesday market in Madeley;[45] the market stimulated the development of a new town.[46] By 1802 the fair was held on 20 October; it was mainly a pleasure fair by the 1880s, as was an Ironbridge fair on 29 May.[47]

Madeley market house was burnt in the 17th century and the market ceased.[48] After its revival by John Edmunds in 1763[49] the market was held in the open at Cross Hill and in a wooden building near Upper House. Thereafter the market was moved, first to Madeley Wood and then, probably in the 1780s, to Ironbridge.[50] Residents of Madeley had no market nearer than Ironbridge or Dawley until 1869–70 when the lords of the manor agreed to the revival of a market there,[51]

[22] S.P.L., Deeds 553; S.R.O. 2280/2/45–8; 2640/1–24; Jackson, 'Madeley', bk. 2, p. 95.
[23] *T.S.A.S.* xlviii. 71, 87–8, 103–5, 110–12.
[24] Ibid. 112; S.R.O. 1048/176.
[25] *T.S.A.S.* xlviii. 103, 186; Pigot, *Nat. Com. Dir.* (1835), 350; (1842), 8; S.R.O. 1922/1–2, 4–6.
[26] *Orders of Q. Sess.* iii. 135; Pigot, *Nat. Com. Dir.* (1842), 8.
[27] S. Bagshaw, *Dir. Salop.* (1851), 577; above, Social and Cultural Activities.
[28] *Kelly's Dir. Salop.* (1909), 117–18; (1917), 110.
[29] S.P.L., L.F. Chitty colln. 240/25; Williams, 'Dawley Hist. Survey: Inds.' p. 43.
[30] See e.g. W.B.R. Madeley dist. cttee. min. bk. 1919–26, p. 252; 1926–32, pp. 74, 97–8.
[31] Still mentioned in *Kelly's Dir. Salop.* (1941), 150.
[32] Cf. above, Telford; above, Other Metal and Engineering Trades.
[33] Williams, 'Dawley Hist. Survey: Inds.' p. 45; T.D.C. *Telford Ind. Dir.* [*c.* 1979], 18; cf. S.R.O. 2280/7/66.
[34] T.D.C. *Telford Ind. Dir.* (1982), 40.
[35] Williams, op. cit. p. 38.   [36] Ibid. pp. 35–6.
[37] T.D.C. *Telford Ind. Dir.* [*c.* 1979], 29.
[38] S.R.O., DA 6/119/1, pp. 261, 265, 417, 421.
[39] Ibid. pp. 279–80, 292–3, 310, 319–20, 333, 336–8.

[40] Ibid. pp. 397, 405, 421, 423, 430, 506–7, 522, 537, 543, 556–8, 583, 587.
[41] Above, Iron and Steel.
[42] Para. based on T.D.C. *Telford Ind. Dir.* [*c.* 1979], 1–30; (1982), 9–68; T.D.C. *Telford Development Strategy* (map, 1979).
[43] When it closed: local inf.; cf. above.
[44] Above, Telford; *V.C.H. Salop.* ii. 235–7.
[45] *Cal. Chart. R.* 1257–1300, 123; Eyton, iii. 320.
[46] Above, Growth of Settlement.
[47] J. Plymley, *Gen. View of Agric. of Salop.* (1803), 336; Randall, *Madeley*, 325; *Rep. R. Com. Mkt. Rights*, i [C. 5550], p. 197, H.C. (1888), liii; xiii (2) [C. 6268–VIa], p. 423, H.C. (1890–1), xl; above, Social and Cultural Activities. S. Bagshaw, *Dir. Salop.* (1851), 567, lists a fair on 26 Jan. as well as the Oct. and May fairs.
[48] Camden, *Brit.* (1806), iii. 28; *Univ. Brit. Dir.* iii (1794), 867 (attributing the destruction to the Civil War).
[49] *Univ. Brit. Dir.* iii (1794), 867; cf. *T.S.A.S.* xlviii. 110–12.
[50] Randall, *Madeley*, 219; *Univ. Brit. Dir.* iii (1794), 867. Cf. Plymley, *Agric. of Salop.* 334, where 'Coalbrookdale' evidently means 'Ironbridge'.
[51] Randall, op. cit. 219–20; *Eddowes's Jnl.* 24 Nov., 8 and 15 Dec. 1869.

and a hall and arcade were built at the west end of High Street.[52] Market day was Saturday and trade was mainly in vegetables, meat, and hardware.[53] The market was not held after 1903[54] until c. 1980, when Wrekin district council revived it on Saturdays in Russell Square.[55]

The opening of the Iron Bridge in 1780 led to the erection of impressive market buildings around a square on half an acre near the bridge end,[56] and a Friday market was established there by 1802.[57] The market building, of two floors and an attic storey, was originally over an open arcade[58] but by 1847 the arcade was filled with shops. East of Market Square stood a market hall[59] and a butter market whose open arcaded ground floor was also eventually filled by a shop;[60] farther east was the open potato market.[61] In 1927 covered and open markets occupied 2,000 sq. yd. each and a Saturday market had been added since 1888[62] but was later discontinued.[63] In 1922 the lords of the manor sold the market rights with the hall and the old butter market to Mrs. A. J. Jarvis, whose heirs sold them to D. H. J. Pool in 1954. In 1961 Pool sold them to the borough of Wenlock[64] which bought Market Square about the same time.[65] The hall was demolished shortly afterwards.[66]

LOCAL GOVERNMENT. As a member of the liberty of Wenlock priory the manor was subject to the twice yearly leet of Bourton hundred[67] which, in the 1660s, 1670s, and earlier 1680s, regularly fined Madeley offenders against the assize of bread and of ale.[68] Other offences fined in the 1670s included assault, receiving strangers,[69] and keeping swine unyoked and unringed.[70] Bourton's jurisdiction over strays was maintained[71] as late as 1690[72] but by the early 18th century the only fines imposed seem to have been those for default of suit.[73] Exaction of suit ceased in 1735.[74]

Manor court records survive for 1334, 1344, 1379–80, 1403, 1411, 1420, 1431, 1449, 1677, 1715–23, 1816, 1839–44, 1846, and 1852.[75] The court leet[76] originated in the twice yearly great tourns or hundreds held for Madeley new town by 1320; there were also three-weekly 'little hundreds' for the new town. In the 14th century a court for unfree tenants (curia bondorum) was held, often on the same days as the new town courts. By 1411, possibly in 1380,[77] the curia bondorum and the new town's little court seem to have merged; the great hundred was still said to be held for the new town in 1411 but simply for Madeley by 1420. Meetings of the little courts on other than great court days were not recorded after 1379. Distinct meetings of the little court, or court baron, appear to have ceased by 1677 and may have ceased much earlier. Recorded meetings of the great court were in April, May, or June and October, November or December in the 14th, 15th, 17th,[78] 18th, and 19th centuries. By 1715 meetings seem to have been only annual,[79] and they evidently ceased in the 1870s.[80]

Division of work between the courts in the 14th and 15th centuries[81] was rough, depending probably on the status of persons. The curia bondorum, later the little court, seems to have been the main forum for agricultural and tenurial regulation, and the woodwards invariably presented there. Aletasters were probably chosen in the little court in 1380 and 1411[82] but infractions of the assize of ale were presented in all three courts. Only in the new town great hundred were more serious offences[83] presented.

In the late 17th and early 18th century the court laid pains for a wide range of nuisances, encroachments, trespasses, trading and other petty offences, receiving inmates, breaches of the peace, and fornication (lairwite); in 1677 a felony (sheep stealing) was presented and there were several presentments for resorting to litigation before recourse to the churchwardens and constable.[84]

Suit of court was reserved when the manorial estate was broken up in the early 18th century.[85] By the 19th century, however, particular nuisances came before the court only occasionally. Fines levied on traders with deficient weights in 1816 were given to the poor in bread, but almost all recorded 19th-century presentments were formal and general: those of common victuallers, butchers, bakers, and defaulting suitors.[86]

[52] E. Cassey & Co. Dir. Salop. (1871), 220; cf. S.R.O. 4044/93, p. 21 (no. 378).

[53] Rep. R. Com. Mkt. Rights, xiii (2), 419, 424–6.

[54] S.R.O. 1681, box 144, acct. bk. 1900–6.

[55] Local inf.

[56] Cf. above, Growth of Settlement; Randall, Madeley, 219, 325; below, plate 20.

[57] Plymley, Agric. of Salop. 334.

[58] Muter, Coalbrookdale and Ironbridge, 15, 16 fig. 7, pl. 16.

[59] S.R.O. 2280/2/46, nos. 2399–2401, 2414–18; /48, p. 83 (nos. 2399–2401, 2414–18); S.R.O. 2079/XLIII. 14.SE. nos. 1858, 1882; S.R.O. 4044/93, p. 101 (no. 1858); /94, p. 102 (nos. 1882 sqq.).

[60] Wrekin Dist. Council, conveyance to Wenlock boro. 1961.

[61] Randall, Madeley, 237; S.R.O. 1681, box 146, draft lease, corresp., etc., 1912.

[62] Min. of Ag. and Fish. Rep. on Mkts. and Fairs in Eng. and Wales, ii (H.M.S.O. 1927), 134.   [63] Local inf.

[64] S.R.O. 1681, box 146, copy deed of 1922; Wrekin Dist. Council, deeds.

[65] S.R.O., DA 6/119/1, pp. 234, 244, 278, 309, 318. Cf. S.R.O. 1681, box 146, copy deeds, etc., of 1923 and 1924 (sale of Mkt. Sq., except war memorial, to Lloyds Bank Ltd.).

[66] S.R.O., DA 6/119/1, pp. 411, 436.

[67] S.R.O. 1224/2/510, f. [23]; V.C.H. Salop. iii. 49–50.

[68] S.R.O. 1224/2/370–1, 374, 376–81, 383–4, 386–7, 389, 511. The assize of bread was mentioned as late as 1675 but the offenders were alesellers.

[69] Ibid. /387.   [70] Ibid. /377.

[71] Ibid. /510, ff. [41, 47, and 3v., 8v. from end].

[72] Ibid. ff. [49 and 13v. from end].

[73] Ibid. /390–4.

[74] Cf. ibid. /395–432, 500, 515–27.

[75] S.R.O. 566/1; 1190, box 23, ct. r.; 1224/2/1, 4–9; 1681, box 130, ct. rec.; 2280/14/2; Lincs. Archives Office, 2 Haw. 3/E/1–14.

[76] Randall, Madeley, 240   [77] Below, n. 82.

[78] S.R.O. 1224/2/1, 4–10; 2280/14/2.

[79] S.R.O. 1681, box 130, ct. rec., estreats 1816, 1839–44, 1846; Lincs. Archives Office, 2 Haw. 3/E/1–14.

[80] E. Cassey & Co. Dir. Salop. (1871), 220; Randall, Old Ct. Ho. 70.

[81] Para. based on S.R.O. 1224/2/1, 4–9.

[82] Ibid. /4, 6. The first, called simply curia, is assumed to be the little ct.; it had possibly absorbed the curia bondorum, last recorded 9 Nov. 1379.

[83] See ibid. /1, 23 Nov. 1344.

[84] Lincs. Archives Office, 2 Haw. 3/E/1–14; S.R.O. 1681, box 130, ct. rec. 1715–23; 2280/14/2, esp. nos. 1, 31–4, [49].

[85] e.g. S.R.O. 1987/19/1, 3.

[86] S.R.O. 1681, box 130, estreats, 1816, 1839–44, 1846, ct. r. 1852.

The court evidently met in a public house in Madeley town in the early 18th century[87] but later at Madeley Wood[88] or Ironbridge, in the Tontine inn by 1839.[89] W. R. Anstice, agent and kinsman of the lords of the manor, was the last steward, occurring from 1846, and in his time the court finally became merely 'an excuse for guzzling and dissipation'.[90]

There were other manorial officers besides the constables, aletasters, and woodwards already mentioned. By 1320 burgage tenants in the new town were obliged to serve as reeve or beadle to keep the market and fairs.[91] Two reeves were elected at a court in 1380, one of them for Coalbrookdale.[92] A constable of the lower town (i.e. the new town) was chosen and sworn in court in the late 17th and early 18th century[93] but the constables of the upper and lower towns were then paid from the parish rates.[94]

The lower town's inhabitants were presented at the manor court in 1677 for not providing stocks, pillory, 'tumble stool', and shooting butts.[95] By 1783, however, the vestry was ordering the repair of stocks,[96] evidently at Madeley Wood.[97] In 1847 the manorial pound was on the south side of Park Street, east of its junction with Park Lane. In 1935 it was said to be productive of 'nuisances'.[98]

The vestry's importance grew from the mid 17th century when it was levying rates. The early rates were for specific purposes: such as the £8 collected c. 1661 for the 'setting forth' of a child left on the parish. A poor rate was levied regularly in the later 17th century, and the two overseers merged some small charity incomes with it. Relief was mainly in pensions and sick and clothing grants. The poor were being badged by 1705[99] and put to work with hemp by 1718.[1]

The vicar was distributing the charities by 1759,[2] and in 1766 the poor were being farmed, those receiving indoor relief housed at Madeley Wood by the contractor; pauper children aged seven or more were to be apprenticed at parish expense.[3] Local distress was experienced in the 1770s and 1780s,[4] and from 1783 the vestry was nominating parishioners to take apprentices.[5] In 1781–2, 1784–5, and finally in 1787 the parish resumed direct responsibility for all the poor. By 1784 there was a workhouse where able-bodied paupers were put to work; from 1787 it was governed by a salaried overseer under the direction of two senior overseers.[6] A new house of industry was built at the Brockholes c. 1796.[7]

Between 1816 and 1817 the poor rate levied by the parish doubled[8] and expenditure trebled, post-war distress reaching a peak in 1818.[9] All 'the poor' were out of work in 1817, when men were mending roads to keep them from 'idleness'.[10] By 1828 relief was administered by a select vestry; there were overseers for Madeley, Madeley Wood, and Coalbrookdale, and by 1834 the vestry clerk acted as assistant overseer. Richard Darby and his relatives were prominent as select vestrymen[11] and after 1836 as guardians of the Madeley union, in which the parish was included 1836–1930.[12] The union used the parish house of industry[13] until a union workhouse was built near Lincoln Hill in 1874.[14]

There were two highway surveyors from the later 17th century,[15] and by 1836 the vestry was employing a salaried surveyor who also collected the highway rate. The vestry ceased to concern itself with roads in 1880 when the parish became an urban sanitary district,[16] to whose board parish gas-lighting inspectors' powers also passed.[17] Madeley urban sanitary district was superseded by one covering the borough of Wenlock in 1889.[18]

From 1782 Madeley was in the jurisdiction of Broseley court of requests.[19] The court was superseded in 1847 by Madeley county court,[20] held at first in a court house adjoining the Royal Oak, from 1858 in a new building in High Street.[21] The court had bankruptcy jurisdiction from 1870[22] but was abolished in 1950.[23]

Edward IV's charter of 1468 to Wenlock

[87] At Mic. Bayley's ho. 1715–20: ibid. suit r. Mic. Bayley snr. lived on the Madeley, rather than the Madeley Wood, side of the par. 1711–15: S.R.O. 2280/2/9. John Bayley, aleseller, occ. 1685: S.R.O. 1224/2/511.

[88] In 1816 at John Mantle's ho.: S.R.O. 1681, box 130, estreats 1816, recording him as a common victualler.

[89] S.R.O. 1681, box 130, estreats 1839.

[90] Ibid. estreats 1846; Randall, Old Ct. Ho. 70; Eddowes's Jnl. 3 Aug. 1881 (obit.).

[91] S.R.O. 1224/2/10.

[92] Ibid. /2/4.

[93] S.R.O. 1681, box 130, ct. r. 1715–21; 2280/14/2.

[94] S.R.O. 2280/6/1a.

[95] Ibid. /14/2, no. 23.

[96] Ibid. /6/95, 17 Mar. 1783.

[97] Ibid. 1 Nov. 1790.

[98] Ibid. /2/45, no. 599; /48, p. 69 (no. 599); W.B.R. Madeley dist. cttee. min. bk. 1932–7, p. 259.

[99] S.R.O. 2280/6/1a, overseers' accts.

[1] H.W.R.O.(H.), Heref. dioc. rec., prob. inv. of Rog. Roe, 1718.

[2] S.R.O. 210/2.   [3] S.R.O. 2280/6/95.

[4] Randall, Madeley, 74–5.

[5] S.R.O. 2280/6/95, 21 Apr. 1783.

[6] Ibid. 11 June 1781 to 23 Apr. 1787.

[7] Ibid. 14 Apr. 1794; 3rd Rep. Com. Char. H.C. 5, pp. 306–7 (1820), iv.

[8] Some Facts, shewing the Vast Burthen of The Poor's Rate in a particular District . . ., by a member of the Salop. Co. Cttee. for the employment of the poor destitute of work (Holborn, 1817), 6–7 (copy in S.P.L.).

[9] Rep. Sel. Cttee. Poor Rate 1816–21, H.C. 556, suppl. appx., p. 144 (1822), v.

[10] Skinner, Nonconf. in Salop. 97.

[11] S.R.O. 2280/6/102.

[12] V. J. Walsh, 'Admin. of Poor Laws in Salop. 1820–55' (Pennsylvania Univ. Ph.D. thesis, 1970), 148–50, 329, 331, 335–6; V.C.H. Salop. iii. 173 n. 75; Kelly's Dir. Salop. (1929), 147. Cf. J. M. Noble, 'New Poor Law in Madeley Union, 1843–51' (Wolverhampton Coll. for Day Students, Hist. Principal Course Special Study, 1971–4; copy in S.R.O. 3730/1).

[13] Walsh, op. cit. 206 sqq., 217–21; Randall, Madeley, 241.

[14] S.R.O. 134/7, p. 103; P.O. Dir. Salop. (1879), 353; Randall, op. cit. 245–9.

[15] S.R.O. 2280/6/1a; T.S.A.S. lvi. 316.

[16] S.R.O. 2280/6/102; 10th Ann. Rep. Local Govt. Bd. [C. 2982], p. 494, H.C. (1881), xlvi. Cf. V.C.H. Salop. iii. 178.

[17] S.R.O. 1491/15, 5 Apr. 1850; 2280/L/1; W.B.R. Madeley local bd. min. bk. 1880–9, p. 101; Public Health Act, 1875, 38 & 39 Vic. c. 55, s. 163.

[18] Local Govt. Bd.'s Prov. Order Conf. (No. 4) Act, 1889, 52 & 53 Vic. c. 22 (Local).

[19] Broseley Small Debts Act, 1782, 22 Geo. III, c. 37.

[20] Created by the Co. Cts. Act, 1846, 9 & 10 Vic. c. 95: Lond. Gaz. 9 Mar. 1847, p. 1010.

[21] P.O. Dir. Salop. (1856), 75; Randall, Madeley, 239; T.D.C. St. Mic.'s church hall deeds.

[22] Under the Bankruptcy Act, 1869, 32 & 33 Vic. c. 71, s. 79: Lond. Gaz. 1 Jan. 1870, p. 4.

[23] Co. Ct. Dists. (Misc.) Order, 1950 (Stat. Instr. 1950, no. 391).

priory's town of Wenlock had included the whole of the priory liberty within a borough, and Madeley remained in the borough until 1966.[24] From 1889 the civil parish became one of the municipal borough's four wards and sanitary divisions, with its own district committee consisting of the nine Wenlock borough councillors elected for the ward and the aldermen living in it.[25] The committee appointed subcommittees[26] and acted as the local authority in the district until 1966. It was virtually autonomous, wielding the powers of a district council, notably with regard to public health and housing, and eventually coming to misconceive itself as one.[27] By the 1940s Labour councillors were prominent on the committee,[28] which, from the late 1950s, was beginning to feel that socially and politically Madeley ward had more in common with Dawley urban district to the north than with the other wards of Wenlock borough.[29] In 1963 all the parish except the western extremity beyond Coalbrookdale and Sunniside was included in the designated area of Dawley (from 1968 Telford) new town.[30] On the dissolution of Wenlock M.B. in 1966 Madeley C.P. was included in Dawley C.P. and U.D.,[31] merged in the district of the Wrekin in 1974.[32]

Wenlock municipal offices were gradually concentrated in Ironbridge. The old dispensary at the corner of Church Hill and High Street was known as the Municipal Buildings by c. 1900.[33] In course of time the rates, borough surveyor's, and housing offices were accommodated there.[34] The district committee met in the workhouse board room from 1889 but the committee and its subcommittees used Ironbridge police court room and Madeley Hall barn in the 1950s. From 1957 the committee used Southside, Church Hill,[35] where offices were provided for Wenlock's town clerk, borough surveyor (moving from the Municipal Buildings), and public health inspector (moving from Broseley). In 1966 Southside passed to Dawley U.D.C. and accommodated its clerk, public health inspector, and housing department until new municipal offices were opened in Dawley in 1968.[36]

PUBLIC SERVICES. Unwholesome water supplies and the drinking of polluted Severn water contributed to the virulence of the 1832 cholera epidemic in Ironbridge and Madeley Wood.[37] The poorer classes' houses long remained without good water[38] and c. 1880 water from the Severn, into which sewage discharged, was still being hawked around Madeley Wood and Lincoln Hill.[39] Ironbridge was partly supplied by iron mains from a spring at Sutton Hill in the earlier 1890s.[40] Otherwise the parish drew from local wells and springs until, c. 1902, the Madeley & Broseley Water Works Co. began to supply all parts from a well at Harrington, a reservoir being built on the disused Meadow pit mound.[41]

Sewage disposal was haphazard until the later 1930s and unsatisfactory for thirty years more. In the 19th century, as Madeley Wood and Ironbridge were developed, increasing amounts of sewage were discharged into large brick culverts originally built to carry storm water downhill to the Severn.[42] Mortality rates were high in the parish in the mid 1860s,[43] and Ironbridge, Madeley Wood, and Madeley low town became notorious for fever.[44] Other areas too were affected: in 1856 fever carried off five of the vicar of Madeley's children in ten days.[45] Measures against diphtheria epidemics[46] were necessary until the 1940s,[47] when cases of scarlet fever and paratyphoid were still occasionally reported.[48] By 1879 nuisances and 'abominations' from night-soil accumulation were frequent in the parish's densely inhabited districts.[49] In the 1880s, after the formation of an urban sanitary district, scavenging became more systematic[50] and at first boys, probably the scavenger's, were used to clean the culverts[51] which were still partly uncovered in the early 20th century.[52] Madeley's pollution of the Severn was regarded as 'most serious' in 1911[53] but the district committee, disagreeing, refused to prepare a sewerage scheme, alleging that its cost would complete the parish's 'ruin'.[54] Minor streams also were increasingly polluted as housing extended. In 1929 the Coalbrookdale Co.'s alarm at the district committee's plan to put sewage into the brook caused the committee to redirect the

[24] V.C.H. Salop. ii. 237; iii. 50, 247.
[25] 52 & 53 Vic. c. 22 (Local); W.B.R. Madeley dist. cttee. min. bk. 1889–99; Jackson, 'Madeley', bk. 2A, pp. 153–4.
[26] See e.g. W.B.R. Madeley dist. cttee. min. bk. 1919–26, pp. 57–9.
[27] e.g. ibid. p. 308; Shrews. Chron. 5 and 12 Dec. 1947; Wellington Jnl. 6 and 13 Dec. 1947.
[28] W.B.R. Madeley dist. cttee. min. bks.; local press reps.
[29] S.R.O., DA 6/119/1, pp. 20–1, 26, 91, 524, 533, 557, 567–8, 577–8, 592, 595.
[30] Dawley New Town (Designation) Order, 1963 (Stat. Instr. 1963, no. 64) and map; Dawley New Town (Designation) Amendment (Telford) Order, 1968 (Stat. Instr. 1968, no. 1912) and map.
[31] V.C.H. Salop. ii. 237.
[32] Sources cited ibid. iii. 169 n. 29.
[33] S.R.O. 1681, box 126, Ironbridge dispensary papers.
[34] Ibid.; inf. from Mr. J. L. McFall; W.B.R. Madeley dist. cttee. min. bk. 1943–6, pp. 145–6, 155, 163–4.
[35] W.B.R. Madeley dist. cttee. min. bks. 1889–1946; S.R.O., DA 6/112/7, 9–11; /119/1, esp. pp. 49, 56.
[36] Inf. from Mr. McFall; S.R.O., DA 6/119/1, pp. 26, 578, 592, 595; below, Dawley, Local Govt.
[37] Randall, Madeley, 249–54.
[38] The Builder, 4 Mar. 1865, p. 159.
[39] Randall, op. cit. 358.

[40] Kelly's Dir. Salop. (1895), 105 (1st mention).
[41] Ibid. (1900), 71, 109, 136; (1905), 74, 112, 139, 262; S.R.O. 1681, box 187, deed and corresp. 1900–2. Cf. O.S. Map 6″ Salop. XLIII. SE. (1903 and 1928 edns.); A. H. S. Waters, Rep. on Water Supply (S.C.C. 1946), 16–18, 91.
[42] S.R.O. 119/82, Wenlock town clk. to Local Govt. Bd. 11 Nov. 1909.
[43] The Builder, 4 Mar. 1865, 159.
[44] J. Randall, Shall We Have a Local Board? (1879; copy in S.R.O. 1438/9).
[45] Randall, Madeley, 215–16; Wellington Jnl. 11 Dec. 1875 (J. H. A. Phillips's obit.).
[46] McFall, 'Educ. in Madeley Union', 102.
[47] W.B.R. Madeley dist. cttee. min. bk. 1937–43, pp. 102, 182, 295, 300, 306, 312, 321.
[48] Ibid. pp. 102, 274, 280.
[49] Randall, Shall We Have a Local Bd?
[50] S.R.O. 119/82, Wenlock town clk. to Local Govt. Bd. 11 Nov. 1909.
[51] W.B.R. Madeley U.S.D. min. bk. 1880–9, pp. 134, 287–8.
[52] S.R.O. 119/82, Wenlock town clk. to Local Govt. Bd. 11 Nov. 1909.
[53] Ibid. S.C.C. clk. to Wenlock town clk. 22 May 1911.
[54] Ibid. Wenlock town clk. to Local Govt. Bd. (3 July 1912) and S.C.C. clk. (27 Nov. 1913).

sewerage for its Coalbrookdale housing to the river.[55] At the other end of the parish the Washbrook had become a sewer by the early 1930s.[56] Disposal works in the Washbrook valley near Station Road and an outfall above Brockholes were built to serve Madeley town and the council housing around Hill Top in the years 1935–7, when government grants became available.[57] A scheme to serve Aqueduct and the eastern side of the parish, however, was deferred in 1939 and realized only in 1961[58] with completion of the Cuckoo Oak works, soon extended for the first stage of Dawley new town's development. Ironbridge and Coalport were not served by any works, and Coalbrookdale had a small works adequate only for Sunniside. Pollution of the Severn with inadequately treated or raw sewage continued during the 1970s. Telford development corporation's disposal works at Gitchfield (in Broseley) became operational in 1970 but the drainage of Ironbridge and Coalbrookdale was completed by trunk sewers only c. 1980.[59]

Ironbridge dispensary opened in 1828. In its first half century c. 1,100 cases a year were dealt with. A building, erected on land acquired by the Wenlock Franchise Savings Bank trustees in 1829, ceased to be used as a savings bank before 1870 and as the dispensary in the earlier 1880s. Thereafter the thousand or so patients attended practitioners' surgeries instead, and the building was sold in 1906.[60] A child-welfare centre was opened in Ironbridge by voluntary effort in 1918,[61] others in Madeley, Sutton Hill, and Woodside by the county council in 1956, 1968, and 1969.[62] In 1932 the Ironbridge public-assistance institution (the former union workhouse), claimed as one of the three best in the county, was designated as suitable for chronic sick and epileptics.[63] By 1939 three quarters of its inmates were in sick wards.[64] Known as the Beeches Hospital from c. 1948,[65] it became a long-stay hospital under the Birmingham Regional Hospital Board.[66]

In 1801 the vestry decided to acquire a hearse and resolved that poor parishioners have the use of it free.[67] The district committee laid out a public cemetery near Castle Green 1942–3.[68]

Ironbridge and Coalbrookdale were supplied with gas from the Ironbridge Gas Light Co.'s works, built in 1839 near the Madeley Wood Co.'s coke hearth.[69] Madeley gas works, Hill's Lane, was built in 1852 by a company of local shareholders formed the previous year. The Ironbridge company acquired the Madeley company in 1923, and gas was still made at Ironbridge in 1939; the works closed in 1958.[70] Electricity became available from 1931 and was used for public lighting from 1934.[71]

There was a post office at Ironbridge by 1828, one at Madeley by 1842, others in Coalbrookdale and Coalport by 1856.[72] John Randall, Madeley's postmaster 1881–1910, was followed by his daughters 1910–39;[73] his son was postmaster at Ironbridge c. 1900–1912.[74]

A lock-up in Market Place, Ironbridge,[75] was built probably in 1842.[76] It was replaced by a police station, with court room and cells, built in Waterloo Street in 1862;[77] that closed in turn to be replaced by one in Dale End (formerly Eastfield) House, which closed c. 1975; c. 1980 there were sub-stations in Brookside, Ironbridge, Madeley, and Woodside.[78]

The need of a fire engine in Ironbridge was felt in 1869,[79] and a twelve-strong volunteer brigade was formed in 1886. The fire station was in Waterloo Street[80] until the 1940s[81] when it moved to Dale End;[82] the Dale End station closed in 1980, when Telford central fire station opened at Stafford Park.[83] A new fire and ambulance station at Cuckoo Oak opened in 1972.[84]

CHURCHES. Parts of Madeley old church may have been 12th-century,[85] and its dedication to St. Michael, recorded c. 1740,[86] may suggest an early centre of worship.[87]

[55] W.B.R. Madeley dist. cttee. min. bk. 1926–32, p. 169–70, 210.

[56] Geo. Legge & Son Ltd. v. Wenlock Corporation: *The Times*, 23 Dec. 1937; *Shrews. Chron.* 24 Dec. 1937.

[57] W.B.R., Madeley dist. cttee. min. bk. 1932–7, pp. 136, 141, 189–90, 271, 329–30, 352, 391, 407, 452, 465, 472, 481; 1937–43, pp. 8, 78; cf. *V.C.H. Salop.* iii. 208.

[58] Madeley dist. cttee. min. bk. 1937–43, pp. 56, 64–5, 79, 88–9, 136, 198, 215–16, 253; S.R.O., DA 6/119/1, p. 467; 6/135, file on Aqueduct sewage disp.

[59] S.R.O., DA 6/119/1, pp. 375–6, 392, 445; Rayska, *Redevelopment of Madeley*, 2–4; J. H. D. Madin & Partners, *Dawley New Town Survey and Analysis: Rep. No. 1* (May 1964), para. 8:2 and map 13; inf. from T.D.C.; *Reps. of Dev. Corporations 31 Mar. 1971*, H.C. 550, p. 533 (1970–1), xli; *Telford Jnl.* 16 Nov. 1979; above, Telford.

[60] S.R.O. 1681, box 126, dispensary papers; Randall, *Madeley*, 240–1, 353–4. Cf. *Kelly's Dir. Salop.* (1885), 865; (1941), 121.

[61] *V.C.H. Salop.* iii. 209 n. 15.

[62] Jackson, 'Madeley', bk. 2A, pp. 199–200; inf. from Salop Area Health Auth.

[63] S.R.O. 1211/2.

[64] *S.C.C. Mins.* 1939–40, table facing p. 409.

[65] When conditions were bad: *V.C.H. Salop.* iii. 217–18.

[66] Birm. Regional Hosp. Bd., *Birm. Regional Hosp. Bd. 1947–66* (1966), 210.

[67] S.R.O. 2280/6/95, 9 Oct. 1801.

[68] W.B.R. Madeley dist. cttee. min. bk. 1937–43, pp. 78, 348, 354, 368, 421, 469, 475–6, 483–4; 1943–6, pp. 5–6. Cf. S.R.O., DA 6/200/2.

[69] S.R.O. 1491/15.

[70] *P.O. Dir. Salop.* (1879), 353; *Kelly's Dir. Salop.* (1891), 355; *Wellington Jnl.* 3 June 1939; local inf.

[71] W.B.R. Madeley dist. cttee. min. bk. 1926–32, pp. 176–7, 183–4, 186, 344, 347–8, 350, 362, 372, 387; 1932–7, pp. 81, 156–7, 168–9, 181–2, 190–1.

[72] Tibnam & Co. *Salop. Dir.* (1828), 22–3; Pigot, *Nat. Com. Dir.* (1842), 8; *P.O. Dir. Salop.* (1856), 76–8; cf. S.R.O. 4548/1.

[73] *Wellington Jnl.* 3 Sept. 1910; *Shropshire Mag.* Aug. 1962, 19–20; Jackson, 'Madeley', bk. 1A, p. 236.

[74] *Kelly's Dir. Salop.* (1900), 109; *St. Mic.'s, Madeley, Par. Mag.* Oct. 1912; *Shrews. Chron.* 20 Sept. 1912 (obit.).

[75] *P.O. Dir. Salop.* (1856), 77.

[76] S.R.O. 2924/82; Co. of Salop. *Acct. of Receipts & Expenditure of Public Stock, 1842*.

[77] *P.O. Dir. Salop.* (1879), 334; Randall, *Madeley*, 236–7.

[78] Local inf.; T.D.C. deed pkt. 1317.

[79] *Eddowes's Jnl.* 27 Jan. 1869.

[80] *Kelly's Dir. Salop.* (1895), 105; (1937), 123.

[81] Ibid. (1941), 121, gives the stn.'s address as the Wharfage.

[82] Inf. from Mr. H. D. G. Foxall.

[83] Inf. from S.C.C. Fire Service. Cf. *Shrews. Chron.* 4 May 1979; *Shropshire Star*, 31 Oct. 1980.

[84] *S.C.C. Mins.* 1971–2, 465; 1972–3, 25.

[85] Cranage, iii. 205.

[86] B.L. Add. MS. 30316, ff. 5, 29v.

[87] F. Arnold-Forster, *Studies in Ch. Dedications* (1899), i. 38; F. Bond, *Dedications & Patron Saints of Eng. Churches* (1914), 39.

The living, recorded *c.* 1218, was a rectory[88] in the patronage of the alien priory of Wenlock.[89] When it was appropriated to the priory in 1344, the priory became patron of the vicarage but the Crown exercised the priory's patronage, presumably until its denization in 1395;[90] in the early 16th century the priory was conveying turns.[91] The advowson passed to the Crown in 1540. Robert Brooke bought it in 1544,[92] and the Brookes, lords of the manor and Roman Catholics, presented in 1569 (probably the first opportunity)[93] and through nominees or trustees probably in 1645[94] and certainly in 1672 (when the trustees too were Roman Catholics).[95] Sir Basil Brooke apparently conveyed turns in 1607 and 1626.[96] Comberford Brooke presented in 1706[97] and sold the advowson in 1707 to a former vicar's widow Margaret Taylor (d. 1720),[98] who presented her son Jeremiah in 1709. Jeremiah (d. 1728),[99] patron before his mother's death,[1] later sold the advowson to John Kynaston of Hardwick.[2] It descended in the Kynastons[3] until 1847, turns exercised in 1831 and 1841 having been bought from them.[4] In 1847 Sir J. R. Kynaston sold the advowson to the vicar, J. H. A. Gwyther, and in 1849 Gwyther sold it to the Revd. W. F. Cobb. Cobb sold it in 1858 to the Revd. John Bartlett (d. 1861),[5] whose widow left it to the Revd. C. F. Cobb (d. 1896).[6] In 1897 Cobb's heirs sold it to the Church Pastoral Aid Society, the patron in 1980.

The rectory was worth £8 in 1291.[7] At appropriation the vicar had the former rectory house and the lesser tithes and mortuaries, though mortuary beasts and the tithes of arable crofts were reserved to the priory; the vicar was to pay the precentor of Wenlock 2*s*. 6*d*. a year for the lesser tithes of the new town and was to bear all charges on the church except certain clerical taxes.[8] The vicarage was worth £3 6*s*. 8*d*. in 1379[9] and £5 5*s*. in 1535, when there was glebe,[10] probably 20 a. or more mostly in the open fields but with three pastures for summering three cows. The vicar had no meadow or common but tithed hay throughout the parish.[11] In the earlier 17th century the lord of the manor paid him 8*s*. a year in lieu of offerings and tithes, but tenants of the manorial demesne and park paid vicarial tithes, including hay, in the normal way. By the 1660s the lord's 8*s*. was claimed as a modus in lieu of all vicarial tithes from the Court demesne, and a similar proffer of 25*s*. a year was being made for the Hay farm. The vicar went to law but the payment of 8*s*., though agitating a later vicar in 1726, persisted as a modus for the Court demesne.[12]

The 18th-century vicars tithed a wide range of produce, including that of corn mills, in kind and money. Easter offerings of 3*d*. a man and 2*d*. a woman, with smoke penny, garden penny, and an egg for each hen, were due from all households, even Madeley Court;[13] the Quaker Darbys, however, refused to render them.[14] On the ground of receiving smoke penny at Easter Jeremiah Taylor claimed tithe wood, but by 1847 woodlands (200 a.) and gardens were tithe-free.[15] About 1720 Taylor established his right to the minerals under his glebe, in 1722 receiving compensation and royalty of £240 for *c.* 3,270 tons got under the New Leasow during his incumbency. Royalties came in only occasionally and by 1775 were at a lower rate than those paid to the lords of the manor.[16] In 1859 the mineral royalties were adjudged to belong to the benefice rather than the incumbent and were used to create a fund for the improvement of the vicarage house.[17]

The vicarage, of three bays in the later 16th century and two in 1699,[18] was rebuilt by Taylor *c.* 1716.[19] 'Much better' in 1781 than the average country parsonage,[20] it is of red brick with stone dressings and has a compact plan with an entrance front of five unequal bays and secondary fronts of three bays. Considerable alterations took place in the mid 19th century when a new drawing room was added on the east and a bay window on the south. Most of the windows on the entrance front were then blocked and the principal rooms refitted. The coach house and stables are mid 19th-century. The gate piers are contemporary with the house but the iron gates were hung in 1979. The house was sold in 1976,[21] a house on the opposite side of the churchyard, once a curate's residence, having been bought in 1972 and rebuilt as the vicarage.[22]

[88] Eyton, viii. 47; cf. *Cal. Pat.* 1266–72, 113.
[89] Only collations by lapse and exchanges are recorded: *Reg. Swinfield* (C.S.), 531; *Reg. Orleton* (C.S.), 54, 229–31, 248–9, 267, 385, 388.
[90] B.L. Add. MS. 50121, pp. 2–10, 14–16; *Cal. Pat.* 1343–5, 198; 1345–8, 162; 1348–50, 553; 1391–6, 276; *V.C.H. Salop.* ii. 42.
[91] *Reg. Bothe* (C.S.), 382; Heref. Dioc. Regy., reg. 1539–52, f. 86.
[92] *V.C.H. Salop.* ii. 45; *L. & P. Hen. VIII*, xix (1), p. 635.
[93] H.W.R.O.(H.), Heref. dioc. rec. visit. bk. 1, f. [6 from end]; below.
[94] S.R.O. 2280/8/1–2.
[95] Cf. *T.S.A.S.* 3rd ser. v. 375; *V.C.H. Oxon.* xi. 16. For the trustees, Basil Fitzherbert and John Purcell, cf. P.R.O., E 13/664, m. 19; Burke, *Peerage* (105th edn. 1978), 2509; *T.S.A.S.* ix. 60; *V.C.H. Staffs.* iii. 100; below, Rom. Cath.
[96] H.W.R.O.(H.), Heref. dioc. rec. visit bk. 6, f. [6v.]; bk. 14, p. 6.
[97] Heref. Dioc. Regy., reg. 1683–1709, f. 180v.
[98] P.R.O., CP 43/495, rot. 14; S.P.L., MS. 4081, p. 2417; *S.P.R. Heref.* xvi (3), pp. vi, 11.
[99] *Dioc. of Heref. Institutions (1539–1900)*, ed. A. T. Bannister (Heref. 1923), 61, 73.
[1] S.R.O. 2280/3/6.
[2] For what follows see advowson deeds in possession of Bridges, Sawtell & Adams, Warwick Ct., High Holborn; *Heref. Dioc. Yr. Bk. 1980–81*, 49.

[3] For them see *T.S.A.S.* 2nd ser. vi. 216–17, 219–21.
[4] Bannister, *Heref. Institutions*, 150, 158; S.R.O. 2280/2/43.
[5] *Alum. Cantab. 1752–1900*, i. 174; *V.C.H. Bucks.* iii. 379.
[6] *Alum. Cantab. 1752–1900*, ii. 76.
[7] *Tax. Eccl.* (Rec. Com.), 167.
[8] *Cal. Pat.* 1340–3, 473; *Cal. Papal Reg.* iii. 168; *Cal. Papal Pets.* i. 81; B.L. Add. MS. 50121, pp. 2–10, 14–16; Heref. Dioc. Regy., reg. 1682–1709, ff. [1a]–2.
[9] Dugdale, *Mon.* v. 78.
[10] *Valor Eccl.* (Rec. Com.), iii. 210.
[11] H.W.R.O.(H.), Heref. dioc. rec. 16th- and 17th-cent. terriers.
[12] S.R.O. 2280/2/42, 48; P.R.O., E 13/664, mm. 19–20.
[13] S.R.O. 2280/2/10–11; /3/2.
[14] Randall, *Madeley*, 294–5. Cf. Tyerman, *Wesley's Designated Successor*, 424.
[15] Randall, op. cit. 33–4; S.R.O. 2280/2/36–41, 48.
[16] S.R.O. 2280/2/10–11; /3/3–6, 8–10, 13–15.
[17] Ibid. /3/37–43; advowson deeds, papers in Bartlett v. Yate (in Chancery).
[18] H.W.R.O.(H.), Heref. dioc. rec. terriers; ibid. inv. of Benj. Taylor, 1705 (listing rms.).
[19] S.P.L., MS. 4081, p. 2417.
[20] Tyerman, *Designated Successor*, 489; below, plate 19.
[21] Inf. from Mr. D. G. Wassell.
[22] Inf. from the vicar; Heref. Dioc. Regy., reg. 1969– (in use), pp. 119–21; S.R.O. 2280/4/1 sqq.

The benefice was worth £34 a year c. 1708,[23] c. £85 a year by the later 1750s,[24] and less than £100 a year 1760–85.[25] The reputed value in 1819 was £290.[26] The vicarial tithes were commuted to £226 a year in 1847[27] when the living was worth c. £300.[28] Almost 18 a. of glebe produced £63 rent in 1887.[29] There were small augmentations in 1871 and 1920.[30]

Master Philip, a physician, was rector c. 1220.[31] Richard of Châtillon, rector 1267,[32] and Otes of Arbois, 1299–1317,[33] were, like the contemporary priors of Wenlock,[34] foreigners. Two later rectors, William Hodnet (1320–2)[35] and James Giffard (1322–3),[36] and the first vicar John of Bridgnorth (1344–6) bore local names.[37] The last rector John Aaron, 1323–44, evidently enjoyed the patron's confidence[38] and became also rector of Broseley chapel, another priory living. In 1344 he was assisted by John of Stirchley, the parochial chaplain, and Roger of Kemberton, chaplain of St. Mary's service.[39]

By 1547 there was a stock of £6 for a stipendiary, perhaps a parochial chaplain.[40] The origins of Our Lady's service are unknown, but in the 1540s it was also known as St. Mary's guild and its property was held by two wardens who were also the churchwardens. In 1547 its chaplain had 52s. a year to celebrate at Our Lady's altar. The endowment, including copyhold worth 7s. 6d. a year, consisted mainly of houses, cottages, and c. 9 burgages in the new town; property seems also to have been rented from the lord of the manor by the chaplain or wardens. Robert Brooke bought the guild property from the Crown in 1549.[41]

The mid 16th-century vicars were local men: William Warham, occurring 1535, d. c. 1538, and William Buckenall, 1539–53 or later,[42] came from established local families,[43] and Buckenall's immediate successor, possibly William Parkinson, 1562–9, was presented by the owners of a turn bought by local men in 1539.[44] No vicar before 1645 is known to have been at university though Buckenall, as guild chaplain, presumably taught

the grammar school[45] and Thomas Lawe, 1569–1607 had had some schooling. Lawe was probably the first vicar presented by the Brookes, and the patron may have wanted him as a man ordained before the Reformation.[46] He was old by the 1580s and had a curate. His successor William Clemson, 1607–26, was 'not a preacher'.[47] Michael Richards, 1645–71, a graduate, was presented after the parishioners had testified to his 'painful and industrious' pastorate in supplying the late vicar's place. A good preacher,[48] Richards was a Presbyterian.[49] His living was augmented by £30 from the sequestrated rectory, but from 1650 he found it difficult to get from the lessee.[50] For almost three centuries Richards's successors were university men. For 90 years most were local men, some of them pluralists.[51]

In 1757 Rowland Chambre[52] made the Swiss J. W. Fletcher (de la Fléchère) his curate,[53] probably to entitle him to holy orders. Tutor to Thomas Hill's sons at Tern and one of the century's most extraordinary religious figures, Fletcher was converted in 1755 and became a Methodist. He was doing duty in Madeley by 1759 but his preaching antagonized local clergymen. The embarrassed Hill[54] offered him a Cheshire living,[55] refused as too rich and easy. Chambre, however, took it, and in 1760 Hill's nephew Edward Kynaston put Fletcher into Madeley. The parish did not confine Fletcher's ministry: he founded Methodist societies round about and in the mid 1760s was active throughout the coalfield. From 1770, however, as the leading anti-Calvinist Evangelical after John Wesley,[56] he was preoccupied with controversy. His pastoral work in the early 1770s was concentrated on Madeley but from 1776, broken in health, he spent much time away. In 1782 he returned newly married but with just over three years to live.

Fletcher's incumbency began an eighty years' exposure of Madeley to intense Evangelical and Methodist influences, more generally potent after his death. John Smitheman, lord of the manor,

[23] Heref. Dioc. Regy., reg 1683–1709, f. 188v.
[24] S.R.O. 2280/2/10.
[25] Randall, Madeley, 148. Cf. S.R.O. 2280/2/11.
[26] H.W.R.O.(H.), Heref. dioc. admin. rec. (clergy and benefices), diocese bks., vol. marked 'Notitia', p. 41.
[27] S.R.O. 2280/2/48.
[28] S. Bagshaw, Dir. Salop. (1851), 568.
[29] Return of Glebe Land, 1887, H.C. 307, p. 60 (1887), lxiv.
[30] Heref. Dioc. Regy., reg. 1869–83, p. 141; 1919–26, p. 146.
[31] Eyton, viii. 47, 61; T.S.A.S. 2nd ser. x. 189; S.R.O. 327, box 9, deeds of Ellis de Say.
[32] Cal. Pat. 1266–72, 113.
[33] Reg. Swinfield, 531; Reg. Orleton, 54, 385.
[34] V.C.H. Salop. ii. 40, 46; T.S.A.S. lx. 98, 100, 105.
[35] Reg. Orleton, 229–31, 248–9; S.P.L., MS. 2789, p. 318.
[36] Reg. Orleton, 248–9, 267, 388; L.J.R.O., B/A/1/2, f. 202; /1/3, f. 4.
[37] Cal. Pat. 1343–5, 198; 1345–8, 162.
[38] Reg. Orleton, 267; B.L. Add. MS. 50121, pp. 8 10; Cal. Pat. 1327–30, 271, 413.
[39] B.L. Add. MS. 50121, p. 15; Eyton, ii. 33–5.
[40] T.S.A.S. 3rd ser. x. 382.
[41] Ibid. 364–5; P.R.O., SC 6/Hen. VIII/3021, m. 4d.; LR 2/184, ff. 106v.–107v., 119v.–120; S.R.O. 245/2.
[42] Valor Eccl. iii. 210; Reg. Bothe, 382; T.S.A.S. 2nd ser. xii. 95, 314.
[43] Visit. Salop. 1623, ii. 311, 487–8; T.S.A.S. vii. 222; Reg. Bothe, 311; Cat. Anct. D. iii, D 553; S.R.O. 1142/1.
[44] T.S.A.S. 4th ser. xi. 186–7, 201; Heref. Dioc. Regy., reg.

1539–52, f. 86 (purchasers incl. a Charlton and a Lawley).
[45] P.R.O., LR 2/184, ff. 106v., 120; below, Educ.
[46] By Abbot Smart of Wigmore, bp. of Paneas: T.S.A.S. xlvi. 43; H.W.R.O.(H.), Heref. dioc. rec. visit. bk. 1, f. [6 from end]; bk. 6, f. [6v.]. Cf. C. Haigh, 'Continuity of Catholicism in Eng. Reformation', Past & Present, xciii. 40–1.
[47] Heref. dioc. rec., visit. bk. 2, f. [15]; bk. 5, f. [24]; bk. 11, f. [7v.]; bk. 14, p. 6; T.S.A.S. 3rd ser. viii. 43, 50.
[48] Alum. Oxon. 1500–1714, iii. 1252; S.R.O. 2280/Rg/1; /8/1–4, 8–9, 11.
[49] T.S.A.S. 3rd ser. vii. 272.
[50] S.R.O. 2280/2/28; Cal. Cttee. for Compounding, iii. 2232.
[51] For the Taylors 1672–1704, 1709–28, see Alum. Oxon. 1500–1714, iv. 1458–9; S.P.R. Heref. xvi (3), pp. vi, xii, 8; Heref. Dioc. Regy., reg 1672–82, f. 79; S.R.O. 2280/Rg/13, bur. 17 Apr. 1728; for Ric. Cooper 1706–9, Bannister, Heref. Institutions, 59, 61; Alum. Oxon. 1500–1714, i. 325: for John Jandrell 1728–52, Alum. Cantab. to 1751, ii. 462; T.S.A.S. 4th ser. ii. 99, 106–7.
[52] Alum. Cantab. to 1751, i. 316; T.S.A.S. 4th ser. ii. 106; S.P.L., MS. 4077, p. 302.
[53] This and the next para. based on Tyerman, Wesley's Designated Successor; Macdonald, Fletcher of Madeley; D.N.B; Trinder, Ind. Rev. Salop. caps. 14, 19.
[54] Perh. concerned about the approaching gen. electn.: V.C.H. Salop. iii. 268–9.
[55] Thornton-le-Moors: G. Ormerod, Hist. of Co. of Chester (1882), ii. 20, 22.
[56] R. A. Knox, Enthusiasm, 484.

opposed his institution and soon left the parish.[57] In 1768 Fletcher counted no farmer in the parish as God-fearing and met hostility or indifference from his churchwardens and neighbouring clergy. His theology was disputed by the Quakers, led by the Darbys, and by his own prominent convert Richard Hill of Hawkstone,[58] who published an attack on him in 1773 and had it hawked round Madeley. Fletcher reciprocated Roman Catholic hostility by opposing the opening of a mass house in 1769.

Though there were rich converts and believers, Fletcher hoped that the poor, with fewer worldly ties, would be more susceptible to religion than their betters.[59] His chief concern was for their conversion.[60] Though privately relieving poverty, he was no social or political reformer[61] but staunchly conservative, cursed by the colliers for helping to crush the food riots of 1782.[62] Believing the millenium imminent, he exhorted the iron-workers to seek providential or spiritual promptings in their working routine and daily round. His fervent piety lacked the check of common sense.[63] Uncomprising with ordinary worldliness,[64] he not only strove against his parishioners' brutalizing recreations[65] and drunkenness[66] but criticized even mild diversions and children's play. Not surprisingly he was prey to a sense of failure and his epitaph ends with Isaiah's complaint against 'a disobedient and gain-saying people'.[67]

Fletcher's wholehearted disciples were a select congregation, governed and separated by the discipline of church Methodism persisting until the 1830s in Madeley, long after it had ceased elsewhere. After 1785 the living had passed to more conventional clergymen,[68] but Fletcher's work had been continued by his widow Mary (d. 1815)[69] and her adopted daughter Mary Tooth (d. 1843).[70] They lived in the vicarage[71] and Mary Fletcher chose the Evangelical curates, Melville Horne, 1786–92, and Samuel Walter, 1792–1815. Isolated from the robust growth of denominational differences, the Madeley church Methodists living under this régime became an introspective, unworldly, and timorous group, harbouring Fletcher's millenarian expectations and living on memories of him nourished by dreams and vis-

ions. A cult of medieval intensity grew up: relics and pictures were treasured and displayed, the church and vicarage became places of pilgrimage, and posthumous appearances of Fletcher were recorded in the Evangelical magazines.

From 1815 Methodists and church people grew apart. Both claimed the succession to Fletcher's labours though there was no open conflict. A generation after his death Fletcher was a less contentious and apparently more powerful influence on the parish than during his life. The parish church remained strongly Evangelical and, like the Wesleyan chapels, well attended.[72] Even later it was to Fletcher's influence that observers ascribed a high degree of civilization among the Madeley working classes and an unusual standard of cleanliness and comfort in the miners' cottages.[73]

As denominational separation of Madeley Methodists and church people was completed in the early 1830s[74] there was a sustained growth of church activity. Day schools and (at Ironbridge and Coalbrookdale) new churches were founded. Local industrialists helped to start services at Coalport and Aqueduct. Near Coalport a school-room in a Madeley Wood Co. warehouse was licensed for worship in 1842.[75] and from 1909 or earlier until 1946 services were held in the Coffee Room, owned by the church 1935–c. 1948. In 1934, besides occasional meetings, there was monthly communion and a 40-strong Sunday school. House services seem to have begun in 1946 and after the Coffee Room's closure there was monthly communion in the Coronation Hall.[76] James Foster built St. Paul's mission church, Aqueduct (opened 1851 and enlarged to hold 200 in 1864), for his Madeley Court workers. The Fosters paid for its renovation in 1909, when a silver communion service was acquired,[77] gave the building to the church in 1951, and were still contributing to running costs in the 1950s.[78]

The Evangelical tradition produced an austerity of worship apt for the new parish church opened in 1797.[79] The parish clerk evidently led the singing,[80] and the singers in the gallery had to keep to plain tunes.[81] In the 1820s, however, the singers were encouraged to instruct children and others, and the parish began to buy instruments

[57] Skinner, Nonconf. in Salop. 60, 94; S.R.O. 1224, box 258, lease of L. Wenlock property, 1762; 2089, lease of W. Coppice, 1764.

[58] Cf. V.C.H. Salop. ii. 13, 183, 192; iii. 130, 262–3; D.N.B.

[59] More central to his concerns than social problems as such: Tyerman, Designated Successor, 56–9; but cf. Trinder, Ind. Rev. Salop. 268.

[60] i.e. rather than their temporal welfare: e.g. Tyerman, op. cit. 270–3, 539.

[61] Unlike Evangelical leaders of a later generation: Oxf. Dict. Christian Church (1974), 486.

[62] Trinder, Ind. Rev. Salop. 379.

[63] To some extent John Wesley's view: Macdonald, Fletcher, 80 n. 1.

[64] S.R.O. 2280/3/14.

[65] Esp. when they profaned the Lord's day: cf. V.C.H. Salop. ii. 191.

[66] But he was not an abstainer.

[67] S.R.O. 2280/3/14; Tyerman, Designated Successor, 106; Randall, Madeley, 156; Rom. 10:21 (cf. Isa. 65:2).

[68] The patron's son Edw. Kynaston (1785–6; 2nd bt. 1822) and kinsman Hen. Burton (1786–1831, absentee): S.P.L., MS. 2789, p. 407; 2790, p. 501; H. Owen and J. B. Blakeway, Hist. Shrews. (1825), ii. 150; Burke, Land. Gent. (1914), 281; S.P.R. Lich. xiv (2), pp. xi, xiii; Admissions to St. John's Coll.,

Cambridge, iv (ed. Sir R. F. Scott), 169.

[69] H. Moore, Life of Mrs. Mary Fletcher (1818); V.C.H. Essex, vi. 190, 224, 228.

[70] Trinder, Ind. Rev. Salop. 271, 274–5.

[71] Rest of para. based on ibid. 270–7, 280–1, 285; Randall, Madeley, 164; Wesley, Letters, ed. J. Telford, vii. 294, 324; Moore, Mary Fletcher (14th edn. 1856), 212, 228–9, 254–5, 273–4, 286–7, 299–300, 366.

[72] Trinder, op. cit. 274–6.

[73] J. M'Owan, A Man of God: Memoir of the Rev. Peter M'Owan, ed. G. Osborn (1873), 209; E. J. Sturdee, Visit to the 'Mecca of Methodism' (Annals of Ch. Pastoral-Aid Wk. v [c. 1896]), 17 (copy in S.R.O. 2280/16/103).

[74] Trinder, op. cit. 274–5.

[75] Heref. Dioc. Regy., reg. 1822–42, p. 650.

[76] St. Mic.'s, Madeley, Par. Mag. Nov. 1909; S.R.O. 2280/SRgC/1; /7/30, 34–140; local inf.

[77] S.R.O. 2280/7/1; Randall, Madeley, 167–8; Par. Mag. May, Aug., Oct. 1909; D. L. Arkwright and B. W. Bourne, Ch. Plate Archd. Ludlow (Shrews. 1961), 4.

[78] Salop. News Letter, xl. 21; S.R.O. 2280/7/3–4, 22–3.

[79] Trinder, Ind. Rev. Salop. 271, rightly calls it a 'meeting ho.'

[80] S.R.O. 2280/6/96, 26 Sept. 1833.

[81] Ibid. /6/95, 15 Mar. 1797.

for them.[82] An organ was given in 1839.[83] Joseph Reynolds gave a silver communion service in 1825[84] and a silver paten was made from two chalices used until then.[85] The plate had included a silver chalice and a paten parcel gilt in 1552–3, but in 1664 and 1687 only a carved silver bowl and two pewter flagons and a plate were mentioned.[86] In the 18th and 19th centuries communion was monthly.[87] Ringing on 5 November had continued after the six bells of 1726–7[88] were rehung in 1798, and the custom was kept up in the early 20th century, when royal birthdays were similarly celebrated.

There was great emphasis on preaching: by the mid 19th century there were two or three Sunday sermons and a Wednesday evening one.[89] J. H. A. Gwyther (from 1857 Phillips),[90] vicar 1841–59, and G. E. Yate, 1859–1908, taught Fletcher's doctrines and worked on his 'theological lines'.[91] Yate's relations owned Madeley Hall, and family ties[92] connected him to clergymen who had officiated under John and Mary Fletcher.[93] Services were attended by up to 800 c. 1880. Many lay people continued to be involved in church work and, as well as the services at Coalport, there were regular church meetings at Lower Madeley, Blists Hill, and the Lloyds;[94] the Lloyds mission still existed in the mid 1920s.[95] Towards the end of his long incumbency Yate had a curate, and there was a lay reader paid for by the patron. There were 43 Sunday school teachers, 27 district visitors, temperance and other societies, and an adult bible class of 70–80. There were probably c. 150 regular monthly communicants. Weekly communion was introduced by the energetic E. B. Pryce, 1909–24.[96]

The 20th-century vicars normally had a curate,[97] sometimes two,[98] and lay readers and district visitors were active in Pryce's time. Pryce began the parish magazine in 1909 and was responsible for the Laudian alterations of 1909–10[99] which focussed attention on the communion table rather than the pulpit. At the same time a new organ was installed[1] and Pryce made the services more musical and introduced a surpliced choir.[2] The six bells of 1726–7 were recast c. 1944 when two more were given.[3] Pew payments were discontinued in 1948.[4] A parish hall was acquired in 1952 but was sold in 1968, the former Church Street infant school having been used as a hall since 1965.[5]

Of Pryce's successors only Alexander Lord, 1955–69, stayed ten years or more. The building of new estates at Sutton Hill, Woodside, and Brookside 1966–75 greatly increased the population, and in 1968 a pastoral centre owned by the church was opened at Sutton Hill, where the curate lived in the late 1970s, looking after a local congregation. Woodside and Brookside church people had the use of Baptist and Methodist pastoral centres. Brookside was transferred to Central Telford parish in 1980, St. Paul's, Aqueduct, closing at the same time.[6]

The former church of *ST. MICHAEL* consisted of nave, chancel, and north tower near the east end of the nave; east and west of the tower were a north chancel and a north aisle. Perhaps by the 1640s there was a clock on the north side of the tower.[7] The lower part of the tower may have been 12th-century. A cottage-like building[8] north of the tower was evidently the 'cross-aisle' mentioned in 1717; it had a west door.[9] North and east windows in the north chancel and north aisle may have been 13th- or 14th-century,[10] as may a window near the west end of the chancel's south wall; other windows in the nave's south wall and at the chancel's east end were probably 17th- and 18th-century. Blocking of windows, and perhaps of a door, in the chancel's south wall may have been done in the late 17th century when private pews were erected. A south porch was built in 1661,[11] a small north porch at a date unknown.

The north chancel was called the Lady chancel in 1659[12] and may have originated as a chapel for St. Mary's guild. Later it was known as the Lord's chancel.[13] It contained Brooke family monuments,[14] and in the 18th century members of the families who succeeded them at Madeley

[82] Ibid. /6/96, 29 Dec. 1824; 27 Dec. 1827.

[83] Ibid. 20 June 1839.

[84] Ibid. 2 Sept., 29 Dec. 1825; 31 May 1832.

[85] Arkwright and Bourne, *Ch. Plate Archd. Ludlow*, 43.

[86] *T.S.A.S.* 2nd ser. xii. 95, 314, 326; S.R.O. 2280/6/1, invs. of 1664 and 1687.

[87] S.R.O. 2280/1/45–6; /6/114–16; Randall, *Madeley*, 284.

[88] Replacing the 3 or 4 16th- and 17th-cent. ones: *T.S.A.S.* 2nd ser. xii. 95, 314; S.R.O. 2280/6/1, *s.a.* 1657 and invs. of 1664 and 1687; /6/95, 14 June 1798; H. B. Walters, *Ch. Bells of Salop.* (Oswestry, 1915), 67–9, 80, 441, 454.

[89] S.R.O. 2280/SRg/1.

[90] *Alum. Cantab. 1752–1900*, iii. 182.

[91] Trinder, *Ind. Rev. Salop.* 275–6; Sturdee, 'Mecca of Methodism', 3, 7.

[92] *Alum. Cantab. 1752–1900*, vi. 610; Burke, *Peerage* (1939), 2633; above, Man. and Other Est. (rectory). For his grandmother Anne Yate (*née* Gilbert) see Moore, *Mary Fletcher* (14th edn. 1856), 306, 312, 346–9.

[93] Nat. Gilbert (his gt. uncle) and Melville Horne (a relative of the Gilberts): Jackson, 'Madeley', bk. 1, p. 97; E. C. Peele and R. S. Clease, *Salop. Par. Doc.* (Shrews. [1903]), 220; Tyerman, *Wesley's Designated Successor*, 36–7, 513–16; *Alum. Cantab. 1752–1900*; iii. 47; Sturdee, 'Mecca of Methodism', 7.

[94] Trinder, *Ind. Rev. Salop.* 275–6; Randall, *Madeley*, 167; Sturdee, op. cit. 18.   [95] *Par. Mag.*

[96] S.R.O. 2280/SRg/4–5; 2280/6/114–16; *Par. Mag.* Nov. 1909.

[97] Licences in Heref. Dioc. Regy., regs.

[98] e. g. 1912–13, when the patron contributed to a second: *Par. Mag.* July 1912, Oct.–Nov. 1913; S.R.O. 2280/6/96, 8 Apr. 1912.

[99] Bound set of *Par. Mag.* 1909–24, in the vicar's possession; *Par. Mag.* May 1909.

[1] *Par. Mag.* Nov. 1909.

[2] Ibid. May 1909; *Shrews. Chron.* 6 May 1910.

[3] Heref. Dioc. Regy., reg. 1938–53, p. 232 (fac. 1 Sept. 1944).

[4] S.R.O. 2280/6/65–6.

[5] T.D.C. St. Mic.'s ch. hall deeds; Church Soc. *Essentials*, v (Nov. 1965), [p. 2] (copy in S.R.O. 3937/9/2). Cf. Sturdee 'Mecca of Methodism', 7–8 (mentioning par. rm. *c.* 1896); S.R.O. 2280/6/96, 17 Apr. 1911; /13/21–32.

[6] Inf. from the vicar; *Wrekin Light*, July 1968 (copy in S.R.O. 2732); *Essentials*, v, [p. 2].

[7] S.P.L., MS. 372, vol. i, p. 80; T. Gregory, *Salop. Gaz.* (1824), pl. facing p. 284; B.L. Add. MSS. 21181, f. 10; 21237, f. 21v. (for dimensions); S.R.O. 2280/6/1a, *s.a.* 1642.

[8] Cranage, iii. 205.

[9] T. Gregory, *Salop. Gaz.* (1824), pl. facing p. 284; Heref. Dioc. Regy., reg. 1710–23, f. 58 (mention of *insula transversa*).

[10] B.L. Add. MS. 21181, f. 10.

[11] S.P.L., MS. 372, vol. i, p. 80; below.

[12] S.R.O. 2280/6/1a, *s.a.* 1659.

[13] Ibid. /2/11, *s.a.* 1774. Cf. 2280/BRg/1, 16 May 1774 (Wm. Purton).

[14] *Bye-Gones, 1911–12*, 78; B.L. Add. MS. 21237, ff. 15, 19.

Court[15] and Hay farm[16] were buried there.

By the late 17th century the impropriator had a pew on the north side of the chancel;[17] it is unlikely to have been used by him save between c. 1713 and 1770.[18] In 1683 other family pews were built in the chancel;[19] with other pews built elsewhere in the church, they descended with houses in the parish. Private pews were erected under the tower in 1712 and in the cross aisle in 1717. In 1722 a gallery for the iron and coal miners was built over the north aisle; it may have extended into the west end of the nave, a gallery there, with that over the north aisle, being enlarged 1749–50. By 1786 the front of the west gallery was reserved for the parish singers.[20]

In 1788 the vestry had the tower taken down.[21] The building of a new church was soon mooted but only in 1794 did a vestry committee approve a revised plan by Thomas Telford[22] for a building to provide 600 sittings for some £1,600. The old church, then ruinous, was demolished, and for two and a half years Sunday morning services were held in the vicarage barn, afternoon services (including baptisms and celebrations of holy communion) in Coalbrookdale and Madeley Wood schoolrooms. The new church was opened in 1797.

Externally Telford's church,[23] not orientated, was an octagon lit by two tiers of iron-framed windows,[24] with a square north tower. Even before the alterations of 1909–10 a more conventional internal arrangment of rectangular 'nave' leading to a narrower southern 'chancel' was defined by the rectangular plan of west, north, and east galleries and by corner vestries squaring off the south end. Until 1909 the pulpit, a three-decker until 1904, stood before the communion table; behind it the clear-glazed south window was curtained.[25] Outside the upper windows either side of the chancel are the weathered effigies of John and Sir Basil Brooke and their wives, saved from the old church. Other memorials were saved but some furnishings passed into private hands.[26]

The sale of c. 96 pews in 1795–7 raised £1,018 towards building costs;[27] the pews descended with houses in the parish.[28] The west and east galleries were extended over the vestries in 1846 to provide more free places, and c. 1880 the church held 1,000.[29]

In 1909–10 a chancel was built and the church was receiled, repaved, reseated except for the galleries, and reglazed[30] with cathedral glass.[31] The pulpit was moved to the west side of the chancel[32] and the communion table was elevated on steps. An oak reredos was erected in 1914[33] and in 1920 a low open screen, a war memorial, was placed between the choir and nave seats; it was later moved to the back of the nave. E. B. Pryce, the vicar who wrought the changes, later had pictures hung in the church.[34]

The registers begin in 1645, the earlier ones[35] having perhaps been destroyed when the church was occupied by troops that year.[36] Apart from gaps 1667–8, 1676–95, and 1719–26, they are complete.[37] Marriages were solemnized in Dawley church 1794–7.[38]

The churchyard was enlarged when the church was rebuilt 1794–7.[39] Some 1½ a. was added in 1842, 1½ a. more in 1875.[40] A churchyard renovation fund was established c. 1923, and some mounds were levelled and stones removed in 1957 and 1980.[41] By 1979 burials were restricted to interments in family graves.[42]

The church of *ST. LUKE*, Ironbridge, was built 1835–6 by subscription and with the aid of grants. Prominent subscribers included the Madeley Wood Co. and the Revd. John Bartlett. The church, accommodating 1,062, and its small graveyard were consecrated in 1837,[43] when James Thompson of the Lightmoor works, gave a silver communion service.[44]

In 1845 St. Luke's was assigned a parish comprising Ironbridge, Coalbrookdale, and the westernmost parts of the ancient parish. The creation of Coalbrookdale parish in 1851 reduced St. Luke's to little more than Ironbridge, but it was

[15] The Astleys (B.L. Add. MS. 21237, f. 21 and v.) and Purtons (S.R.O. 2280/2/11, s.a. 1774).

[16] The Purcells: B.L. Add. MS. 21237, f. 21 and v.

[17] Heref. Dioc. Regy., reg. 1683–1709, f. 3.

[18] Above, Man. and Other Est.

[19] Heref. Dioc. Regy., reg. 1683–1709, ff. 2–3v., 9, 15 and v.

[20] Ibid. f. 15 and v.; 1710–23, ff. 13v.–14, 58, 105; 1723–54, f. 119 (fac. 5 Dec. 1749); 1772–1802, ff. 149, 168. Cf. S.R.O. 1987/4/2–3.

[21] Para. based on S.R.O., QR 159/3; S.R.O. 1066/16, 17 Apr. 1793; 2280/Rg/6, memo. at front by Sam. Walter; /6/95 (esp., at back, Bp. Butler's letter, 28 Mar. 1797); Orders of Q. Sess. iii. 34; Salopian Jnl. 7 May, 17 Sept., 1 Oct. 1794; Heref. Dioc. Regy., reg. 1772–1802, f. 201.

[22] Slightly changed from that in Edinb. Encyclopaedia (1830), vi (2), pl. CLXXVI: cf. ibid. 643–4.

[23] For what follows see Pevsner, Shropshire, 192; below, plate 19.

[24] Bought in Birm.: S.R.O. 2280/6/95, 17 May 1796.

[25] Ibid. /6/57; /6/96, 13 Aug. 1811; Heref. Dioc. Regy., reg. 1902–19, p. 114; vicar's vestry, photos. of 1903 and 1904.

[26] S.R.O. 2280/6/95, 7 Dec. 1795; Randall, Madeley, 211–15, 373; Bye-Gones, 1886–7, 41, 89; 1911–12, 78, 183; Salop. N. & Q. i–ii. 158.

[27] S.R.O. 2280/6/57–9.

[28] Ibid. /6/59–60, 63–4.

[29] Ibid. /6/96, 6 Aug., 17 Dec. 1846; Randall, Madeley, 167.

[30] Heref. Dioc. Regy., 1902–19, pp. 357–9, 395; S.R.O. 2280/6/70–3; /6/96, 28 Mar. 1910.

[31] Par. Mag. May 1909.

[32] Cf. S.R.O. 2280/6/96, 26 July 1855.

[33] Ibid. 17 Apr. 1911, 13 Apr. 1914; Heref. Dioc. Regy., reg. 1902–19, p. 563; Par. Mag. Feb. 1913, July–Aug. 1914.

[34] Par. Mag. Oct. 1913, July 1920; Heref. Dioc. Regy., reg. 1919–26, p. 60.

[35] T.S.A.S. vi. 98.

[36] Peele and Clease, Salop. Par. Doc. 219; Cranage, iii. 206.

[37] S.R.O. 2280/Rg/1–2, 4–7, 9–16; /BRg/1–10; /MRg/1–3, 5–18; inf. from the vicar. Cf. H.W.R.O.(H.), Heref. doc. rec. Madeley transcripts for 1638, 1661–75, 1678, and 1684–1750.

[38] S.R.O. 2280/Rg/6, memo. at front by Sam. Walter.

[39] Ibid. /6/95, 22 Oct., 13 Nov., 11 Dec. 1793, and Bp. Butler's letter 28 Mar. 1797.

[40] Ibid. /6/96, 14 Apr. 1842, 10 Aug. 1874; S.R.O. 1681, box 152, petition to consecr. [1842]; Heref. Dioc. Regy., reg. 1842–6, pp. 8–10; 1869–83, pp. 307, 311.

[41] S.R.O. 2280/6/96, 1 Apr. 1923, 21 Apr. 1924; Heref. Dioc. Regy., reg. 1953–68, p. 223.

[42] Inf. from the vicar. Cf. S.R.O. 2280/5/2–11; /6/102, 5 June 1856.

[43] Ironbridge par. rec. bk. of subscriptons 1834–9; new ch. cttee., pewholders', etc., min. bk. 1834–43; S.R.O. 2280/7/143; plaque in vestry; Heref. Dioc. Regy., reg. 1822–42, pp. 345–57.

[44] Arkwright and Bourne, Ch. Plate Archd. Ludlow, 35; S.R.O. 1922/12–18.

enlarged north-eastwards in 1975.[45]

The vicar of Madeley was patron,[46] and in 1978 he was included in the patronage board of a new united benefice of Coalbrookdale, Ironbridge, and Little Wenlock.[47] Incumbents of Ironbridge were at first known as perpetual curates[48] but soon after 1858 as rectors.[49]

Pew rents, paid for over a century,[50] were at first almost the whole endowment of the living. In 1851 the incumbent received £90 from pew rents, £5 in fees.[51] Augmentations subscribed in 1848 and 1855, however, were met by grants from Queen Anne's Bounty,[52] whose governors bought the impropriate tithe rent charge on the ancient parish for the living from Sir J. H. Hawley in 1858.[53] Augmented in 1859 and 1866,[54] the living was worth £196 by 1865, £250 by c. 1880;[55] there were further augmentations in 1909 and the 1920s.[56]

In 1956 the Rectory, built on land in Hodgebower bought in 1834, was exchanged for Mount Pleasant, also in Hodgebower.[57] That was given up c. 1976 when the last resident rector died.[58] The former Madeley Wood Methodist manse, bought in 1978, became a curate's house.[59]

On Census Sunday 1851 500 adults and 80 children attended in the morning, 700 worshippers in the evening; attendance at the afternoon Sunday school was said to average 160 and upwards.[60] George Wintour, rector 1867–98, and his predecessors were normally assisted by a curate,[61] but c. 1880 the church was not well attended.[62] A lay reader was appointed in 1898.[63] Under Wintour's successor there seems to have been a rapid improvement, for in 1899 there were more applications for rented pews than could be met.[64] A new organ was installed in 1900,[65] a parish magazine existed by 1908,[66] and from c. 1912 the former parochial infant school was used as a parish room.[67]

In 1937 the church had a sizeable working-class congregation 'loyal in their financial support'. Singing was hearty, there was a 40-strong choir, and special musical services were frequent.[68] The

church's tradition had been Evangelical but Edward Roberts, rector 1916–50, introduced Anglo-Catholic forms of worship.[69] His long incumbency, one of only three to last ten years or more,[70] ensured the permanency of his changes, but the patron was the nominee of an Evangelical society and in 1956 the bishop collated after lapse.[71]

The church, by Thomas Smith of Madeley, is Commissioners' Gothic in pale brick, comprising shallow sanctuary, nave with galleries on three sides, and embattled tower.[72] Orientation is reversed to provide a foundation for the tower.[73] The tower contains one large (1838) and two small bells clocked for striking hours and quarters; a customary tolling was practised in the early 20th century. Eight tubular bells were hung in 1920 as a war memorial.[74] An oak reredos and brass altar cross were provided in 1922. The church's renovation 1933–4 included the oak-panelling of the sanctuary[75] and probably the repewing of the nave. The nave is lit by pairs of lancets cut across by the galleries; aisle-like areas under the galleries were furnished as a children's corner (south) c. 1933[76] and a Lady chapel (north) in 1952.[77] The nave was redecorated in 1954, when the tower clock was given two illuminated faces as a war memorial,[78] and in 1979 when a pair of bronze gilt candlesticks set with amethysts once Abraham Darby (III)'s was given for the high altar by Lady Labouchere.[79]

The registers, beginning in 1837 (baptisms), 1838 (marriages), and 1846 (burials), are complete. The graveyard, last used for a burial in 1903,[80] was slightly enlarged in 1909.[81]

A schoolroom in Coalbrookdale was used for Sunday afternoon services and the administration of sacraments while Madeley church was rebuilt 1794–7. It was probably in the Coalbrookdale Co.'s boys' school, whose new building of 1840 was licensed for worship in 1850. By then the recently baptized Abraham Darby (IV) had undertaken to endow a new benefice with £100 a year. On Census Sunday 1851 morning service was attended by 80 adults and 50 children, after-

[45] Heref. Dioc. Regy., reg. 1842–6, pp. 272–3; 1969– (in use), p. 193 and facing plan.

[46] Ibid. 1842–6, p. 289; 1938–53, p. 481.

[47] Ibid. 1969– (in use), pp. 308–9.

[48] Ibid. 1842–1919, admissions and resignations 1845–1916.

[49] Ironbridge par. rec. bur. reg. signature 1 Dec. 1869; cf. Heref. Dioc. Regy., reg. 1938–53, pp. 471, 481; below.

[50] Ironbridge par. rec. pew-rent acct. bks. 1843–57, 1857–91, 1927–56.

[51] P.R.O., HO 129/358, no. 42.

[52] C. Hodgson, Q. Anne's Bounty (2nd edn.), suppl. pp. xvi, xxxii, lxvi.

[53] Church Com. deeds.

[54] Heref. Dioc. Regy., reg. 1857–69, pp. 93, 509; Lond. Gaz. 3 July 1866, p. 3795.

[55] Clergy List (1865); Randall, Madeley, 168.

[56] Heref. Dioc. Regy., reg. 1902–19, pp. 325–6; 1919–26, pp. 146, 344; 1926–38, p. 228.

[57] Ironbridge par. rec. ch. bldg. papers, Jos. Reynolds to Revd. Geo. Edmonds, 27 Aug. 1834; S.R.O. 657/2, pp. 108, 110; 803/1, p. 108; 2280/2/46, no. 2644; /48, p. 110 (no. 2644); O.S. Map 1/2,500, Salop. XLIII. 14 (1927 edn.); Heref. Dioc. Regy., reg. 1953–68, p. 143.

[58] S.R.O. 3658/1, 1CD, p. 2; inf. from the Revd. W. A. L. Zwalf.

[59] Heref. Dioc. Regy., reg. 1969– (in use), pp. 287–8, 301–3; inf. from the Revd. C. F. Carter.

[60] P.R.O., HO 129/358, no. 42.

[61] Heref. Dioc. Regy., regs. 1842–1901, curates' licences

1846–95.

[62] Randall, Madeley, 168.

[63] Heref. Dioc. Regy., reg. 1883–1901, p. 644.

[64] Ironbridge par. rec. corresp. betw. T. D. Thomas and dioc. registrar, 1899; cf. Eccl. Com. instr. (with plan) 24 Mar. 1887.

[65] Heref. Dioc. Regy., reg. 1883–1901, p. 696.

[66] Ironbridge par. rec. heating and ventilating cttee. min. bk. 1901–9, 23 July 1908.

[67] Perh. replacing rm. in Waterloo St.: S.R.O. 4044/93, p. 74 (no. 1350); cf. S.R.O. 2079/XLIII. 14. SE.; below, Educ.

[68] Shrews. Chron. 22 Oct. 1937.

[69] Inf. from Mr. Carter.

[70] Heref. Dioc. Regy., regs.

[71] Ibid. 1953–68, p. 144.

[72] Pevsner, Shropshire, 43, 157; Cranage, iii. 200.

[73] Inf. from Mr. Carter; below, plate 20.

[74] Walters, Ch. Bells of Salop. 66; Heref. Dioc. Regy., reg. 1919–26, p. 83.

[75] Heref. Dioc. Regy., reg. 1919–26, p. 228; 1926–38, pp. 381–2, 429; Shrews. Chron. 22 Oct. 1937.

[76] Shrews. Chron. 22 Oct. 1937.

[77] Heref. Dioc. Regy., reg. 1938–53, p. 545; 1953–68, p. 28.

[78] Ibid. reg. 1953–68, p. 61.

[79] Ibid. 1969– (in use), p. 329; inf. from Mr. Zwalf.

[80] Ironbridge par. rec. bur. reg. 1846–1903; cf. ibid. copy of Order in Council 21 Oct. 1890.

[81] Heref. Dioc. Regy., reg. 1902–19, p. 374.

noon service by 100 adults and 60 children.[82] Later that year Darby gave £6,000, his sister-in-law Adelaide Anna Darby gave the church site, and *HOLY TRINITY* church was built 1851–4.[83]

In 1851 a new parish was formed from Ironbridge and Little Dawley and patronage of the new living was conferred on Abraham Darby (IV). He died in 1878 and his widow became patron.[84] After her death in 1902 the patronage descended with the Sunniside estate until 1959 when Lady Labouchere and her fellow trustee conveyed it to the bishop of Hereford who, in 1978, was included in the patronage board of the new united benefice of Coalbrookdale, Ironbridge, and Little Wenlock.[85]

In 1856 pew rents of £62 13s. were assigned to the vicar, and the living was worth £250 in 1865;[86] ½ a. of glebe produced £12 rent in 1887.[87] There were augmentations in 1926 and 1955[88] and in 1929 the living was worth more than the older churches of Ironbridge and Madeley.[89]

Abraham Darby (IV) gave the Chesnuts, Darby Road, as a vicarage house c. 1852.[90] About 1901 a large new vicarage was built in Paradise, on land near the church provided by the patron. It was sold c. 1970.[91] A third benefice house built nearby was used for the livings united in 1978.[92]

Six of the eight vicars between 1851 and 1967 were graduates; one remained thirty years, two for over twenty.[93] Coalbrookdale was held in plurality with Little Wenlock and Buildwas 1968–77.[94]

The church has an exceptionally large collection of Victorian and modern silver. Mrs. Alfred Darby, the founder's sister-in-law, gave a silver-gilt chalice (Augsburg c. 1700) formerly belonging to the Swabian charterhouse of Buxheim; there is a German cruet tray of the same date and a paten (London 1849) made to match the chalice.[95]

About 1880 the church, accommodating 850, was said to be generally well filled. Communion was monthly, with c. 60 communicants, and on the 'usual' festivals.[96] In 1871 Edward Edwards left £50 a year towards the expenses of public worship after any necessary repairs to his tombstone; the legacy was conditional on the restoration of the parish clerk to his position in the church and its services,[97] and a clerk was still being appointed at the end of the century.[98] The pew renters met briefly before the annual vestry to authorize the spending of Edwards's legacy.[99] A church hall was built at Dale End in 1901.[1]

The church, built of local stone in the Decorated style to a design of Reeves & Voysey, consists of chancel and nave of eight bays, north and south aisles, west porch, and embattled west tower;[2] it is orientated south-east.[3] Corbel heads in the nave arcading are said to represent members of the Darby family. A south aisle window contains a 16th-century Flemish depiction of the Last Supper, the gift of Mrs. Henry Whitmore (*née* Darby). The centre-aisle ends of the low box pews are finished with high poppy heads, perhaps late 19th-century. One of the county's principal rings, of eight bells (1852), was given to the church by Abraham Darby (IV); in 1925 two trebles were added in memory of Maurice Darby, killed in action in 1915.[4] In 1931 the sanctuary and chancel were refurnished and decorated in his memory to designs by H. S. Goodhart-Rendel, restored in 1971. The south aisle's east end, formerly a Lady chapel, contained the organ 1906–31 and became a choir vestry in 1950.[5] Memorials include tablets to members of the Fox family, including A. C. Fox-Davies.[6]

The registers begin in 1851 (baptisms) and 1854 (marriages and burials) and are complete. The churchyard was enlarged in 1923 and 1931.[7]

ROMAN CATHOLICISM. Madeley was prominent among the centres of Shropshire recusancy[8] because the lords of the manor from the 16th to the 18th centuries[9] persisted in the old faith. Other names which figure in the parish's history, however, are encountered: a Charlton in the late 16th century,[10] Glazebrooks, Webbs, and Wolfes in the later 17th century.[11] Mass may have been celebrated at Upper House, home of the Wolfes,

[82] S.R.O. 2280/Rg/6, memo. at front by Sam. Walter; below, Educ.; S. Bagshaw, *Dir. Salop.* (1851), 569; P.R.O., HO 129/358, no. 41.

[83] Heref. Dioc. Regy., reg. 1847–56, pp. 322–3, 505–7; S.R.O. 1681, box 179, plan of land; Coalbrookdale par. rec. flower festival souvenir programme, 1972.

[84] Heref. Dioc. Regy., reg. 1847–56, pp. 321–4; 1869–83, pp. 518, 716; 1883–1901, p. 646; Coalbrookdale par. reg. bur. 4 Dec. 1878.

[85] *Kelly's Dir. Salop.* (1905), 74; (1922), 78; Heref. Dioc. Regy., reg. 1926–38, p. 152; 1938–53, pp. 416, 438; 1953–68, pp. 222, 297, 590; 1969– (in use), pp. 290, 306, 308–9; above, Man. and Other Est.

[86] Heref. Dioc. Regy., reg. 1847–56, pp. 684–5; *Clergy List* (1865).

[87] *Return of Glebe Land, 1887*, 58.

[88] Heref. Dioc. Regy., reg. 1926–38, p. 14; 1953–68, p. 125.

[89] *Kelly's Dir. Salop* (1929), 81, 120, 146.

[90] S.R.O. 1681, box 179, draft conveyances, corresp., etc., 1852; I.G.M.T. Libr. 1980/976.2.

[91] Heref. Dioc. Regy., reg. 1902–19, pp. 14, 82; arms and patron's initials on bldg.; inf. from Mr. J. G. Lees.

[92] Heref. Dioc. Regy., reg. 1969– (in use), pp. 20, 25–6, 308–9.

[93] Ibid. regs. *passim*.

[94] Ibid. 1953–68, pp. 590–1; *Crockford* (1977–9), s.v. Kirby, J.P.

[95] Inf. from Mr. Zwalf; Arkwright and Bourne, *Ch. Plate*

Archd. Ludlow, intro., 23–4.

[96] Randall, *Madeley*, 169.

[97] Coalbrookdale par. rec. vestry min. bk. 1854–1928, 9 Apr. 1871; tablet in ch.; *P.O. Dir. Salop.* (1870), 43. Cf. Heref. Dioc. Regy., reg. 1847–56, pp. 684–5.

[98] Coalbrookdale par. rec. Revd. C. B. Crowe to B. Fletcher, 25 Feb. 1899 (offer of clkship. and descr. of duties).

[99] Ibid. vestry min. bk. 1854–1928, 19 Apr. 1892 sqq. For the renters cf. pew-rent acct. bks. 1891–1906, 1908–21.

[1] Foundation stone.

[2] Pevsner, *Shropshire*, 156; Cranage, iii. 190.

[3] S.R.O. 1681, box 179, plotting 17 Aug. 1850.

[4] Inf. from Mr. Zwalf; Walters, *Ch. Bells of Salop.* 66, 446, 459; Heref. Dioc. Regy., reg. 1919–26, p. 405; tablet in base of tower.

[5] Coalbrookdale par. rec. flower festival souvenir programme, 1972; ibid. copy of 'Coalbrookdale Par. Ch.' (TS. c. 1971); Heref. Dioc. Regy., reg. 1902–19, p. 172; 1938–53, p. 457.

[6] Heref. Dioc. Regy., reg. 1953–68, p. 38; *Who Was Who, 1916–28*, 375.

[7] Heref. Dioc. Regy., reg. 1919–26, p. 305; 1926–38, p. 311.

[8] *S.P.R. Rom. Cath.* p. xv.

[9] Above, Man. and Other Est.

[10] *Recusant R. 1592–3* (Cath. Rec. Soc. xviii), p. 270.

[11] H.W.R.O.(H.), Heref. dioc. visit. rec., chwdns.' presentments 1664, 1669, 1672, 1680, 1681; *Salop. N. & Q.* i & ii. 31; iii. 10.

in the 17th century,[12] and Madeley Court was used as a mass centre c. 1695[13] and presumably at least until Basil Brooke's death in 1699.[14] In 1676 there were 51 adult papists in Madeley, the largest Catholic population in Shropshire and perhaps an indication that an eighth or more of the population was Catholic.[15] In 1664 and 1681 John Beddoe kept an unlicensed school, evidently for Catholic children. There were twelve Catholic families in the parish in 1716.[16]

The numerous families in Madeley suspected of disaffection to the Crown in 1691 and 1715 included Catholic families of some standing. Several Catholics registered their ownership of landed property in 1717. Most substantial were the Purcells, armigerous minor gentry, six of whom had refused the oath of allegiance in 1715.[17] Others were John Heatherley or Hatherley, son-in-law of Francis Wolfe (II);[18] Richard Blest and the Goodmans, modestly endowed yeomen; and two owners of cottages.[19] The Purcells' estates were sold in 1755,[20] the Heatherleys' in 1765,[21] and by 1767 few of the 72 Catholics recorded seem to have been of substance: many heads of families were colliers or blacksmiths. Nevertheless they included Thomas Slaughter, evidently steward of the manor and related to the lords, an innkeeper, and an engineer. A priest officiated every third Sunday.[22]

The Madeley Catholics remained numerous and evidently self-confident. A Catholic, one Haughton, led a demonstration against the vicar, J. W. Fletcher, in 1762. Fletcher tried to present him at the visitation but was thwarted by his churchwardens.[23] In 1769 Fletcher, provoked by the conversion of two parishioners, opposed the opening of a mass house[24] incorporated in the rear part of a newly built presbytery in High Street. Apparently replacing an earlier one, the mass house opened in 1770; it was built on land given by the Giffards,[25] presumably Rose Giffard's daughters who owned shares of the manor.[26] Fletcher's widow Mary maintained friendly relations with the Catholic priest John Reeve (occ. 1804–12) and he attempted her conversion.[27]

Catholics were said to be few c. 1804[28] but were perhaps under-estimated. The chapel is said to have accommodated c. 200, though by 1851 there were 400 sittings.[29] In 1824 the priest also served Middleton Priors[30] and in the earlier 19th century other Shropshire missions, such as Wellington occasionally from 1834–5.[31]

In 1851 Sunday morning attendances at Madeley were said to average 300 adults and 100 children; evening services were attended by 100.[32] In 1852–3 a new church was built,[33] and a graveyard provided, next to the old chapel and presbytery. St. Mary's, with accommodation for c. 500, is in the Early English style to a design of J. A. Hansom.[34] The church, renovated in 1961–2, was served from Shifnal by 1891, when the former chapel and presbytery, known as Arundel House, housed a boarding school. Madeley, separated from a large parish extending from Wigwig to Sheriffhales, acquired a resident priest again in 1970. From 1978, when Much Wenlock and Broseley were separated, St. Mary's parish approximated to the ancient parish and had a Catholic population of some 900.

PROTESTANT NONCONFORMITY. There were no protestant dissenters in the parish in 1676[35] and probably none before the Quakers arrived. Their small meeting, started c. 1717, provided the only sustained protestant dissent from the church in the 18th century, for local Methodists did not separate from it until the 19th century, and the Baptists seem not to have been permanently established until 1857. Congregational worship began only in 1872.

In later 19th-century Madeley denominational loyalties did not divide the nonconformists.[36] Primitive Methodists might happily attend a Baptist tea meeting[37] or Independent and Wesleyan ministers a Baptist minister's lecture.[38] In 1885 Wesleyans lent their chapel to Baptist 'friends' when Spurgeon came to preach.[39] Shared social conditions did more than sectarian theologies to form local nonconformist culture,[40] and even distinctions between church and chapel were blurred

[12] Randall, *Madeley*, 166; S.P.L., Deeds 15437.
[13] W.S.L., H.M. 36 s.v. Dawley (shorthand transcribed by Mr. N. W. Tildesley).
[14] Above, Man. and Other Est.
[15] W.S.L., S. MS. 33; Skinner, *Nonconf. in Salop.* pl. III. There were 400 conformists and no prot. nonconformists.
[16] H.W.R.O.(H.), Heref. dioc. rec., chwdns.' presentments 1664, 1681; reply to visit. arts. 1716.
[17] Randall, *Madeley*, 56; *T.S.A.S.* vii. 181; 2nd ser. i. 90; S.R.O., q. sess. rec. parcel 281, reg. of papist deeds 1717–88, pp. 6–7, 11, 33–4, 46–7.
[18] S.R.O., q. sess. rec. parcel 281, reg. of papist deeds 1717–88, pp. 66–7; G. Allen-Woolfe and R. Rathbone, *The Story of a Royal Tankard (1661–1702)* (1975), 23–4. The Wolfes too were armigerous: *T.S.A.S.* vii. 232.
[19] S.R.O., q. sess. rec. parcel 281, reg. of papist deeds 1717–88, pp. 33, 68–70. Some papist owners of Madeley property lived elsewhere: ibid. pp. 67–8, 147.
[20] S.R.O. 749/4–8; deed of 1755 conveying Webb's tenement, etc., in possession of Mr. A. M. Jeffrey, Madeley.
[21] S.R.O., q. sess. rec. parcel 282, reg. of papist deeds 1717–90, pp. 131–4.
[22] H.W.R.O.(H.), Heref. dioc. rec., return of papists 1767. For Slaughter cf. S.R.O. 2280/MRg/2, p. 50 (no. 37); above, Man. and Other Est.
[23] Tyerman, *Wesley's Designated Successor*, 77–8; Trinder, *Ind. Rev. Salop.* 269.

[24] Tyerman, op. cit. 156–8.
[25] Ibid. 59, 168; Jackson, 'Madeley', bk. 1A, p. 212; *Shrews. Chron.* 14 Jan. 1955; Randall, *Madeley*, 166.
[26] Above, Man. and Other Est. Cf. S.R.O., q. sess. rec. parcel 282, reg. of papist deeds 1717–90, pp. 161–2.
[27] Trinder, *Ind. Rev. Salop.* 304; H. Moore, *Life of Mrs. Mary Fletcher* (14th edn. 1856), 419–20, 423–6; S.R.O. 2266/1.
[28] J. Benson, *Life of Rev. J. W. de la Flechere* (1805), 140.
[29] Jackson, 'Madeley', bk. 1A, p. 212; P.R.O., HO 129/358/47.
[30] T. Gregory, *Salop. Gaz.* (1824), 284–5.
[31] *S.P.R. Rom. Cath.* p. xv; Jackson, 'Madeley', bk. 1A, p. 213; Trinder, *Ind. Rev. Salop.* 304.
[32] P.R.O., HO 129/358/47.
[33] What follows is based on *S.P.R. Rom. Cath.* p. xv; Jackson, 'Madeley', bk. 1A, pp. 212–13; P.O. Dir. Salop. (1870), 85; inf. from the Revd. A. J. Nicholson, par. priest.
[34] *D.N.B.*
[35] Skinner, *Nonconf. in Salop.* pl. III.
[36] e.g. B. Trinder, *Meth. New Connexion in Dawley and Madeley* (Wesley Hist. Soc., W. Midlands Branch, Occ. Publn. i [1968]), 11–12.
[37] S.R.O. 2533/130, 14 Dec. 1857.
[38] S.P.L., Watton press cuttings, x. 49–50.
[39] S.R.O. 2533/95, 19 June 1885.
[40] Trinder, *Ind. Rev. Salop.* 285, 291–2, 306.

by the Methodist and Evangelical traditions of Madeley parish church.[41]

Unsectarian prayer meetings held at Ironbridge *c.* 1880[42] may be the Baptist and Congregational meetings, probably joint, held in Ironbridge assembly rooms, probably at the Wharfage, from *c.* 1885 to *c.* 1922;[43] the Congregationalists who helped to begin the meetings may have done so after a short-lived attempt to found a chapel in Ironbridge.[44] In 1883 the Gospel Army Mission began to use the Malthouse in Park Street, Madeley, but soon ceased to do so.[45] About 1895 there was a mission hall in Waterloo Street, Ironbridge.[46] The Central Cinema, Waterloo Street, was sometimes called the Central Hall, and Wesleyan-sponsored recitals were occasionally given there.[47] The Salvation Army used Ironbridge assembly rooms from 1894 to *c.* 1903.[48] It had premises in Park Street, Madeley, in 1909[49] and in 1910 occupied the former Zion chapel, Ironbridge,[50] which it used during the First World War.[51] In 1935 the Army opened a hall in Waterloo Street, Ironbridge,[52] but it soon closed.[53] Jehovah's Witnesses used the former Central Cinema in Waterloo Street, Ironbridge, 1972–80; in 1980 they opened a newly built Kingdom Hall in Queen Street, Madeley.[54]

FRIENDS. Abraham Darby (I) was involved in the affairs of the Broseley Quaker meeting by 1706.[55] There were eight Quaker families in Madeley parish in 1716 but no meeting[56] until 1717 when Darby's new house in Coalbrookdale was licensed for meetings.[57] There were *c.* 20 Quakers in the parish in 1719,[58] and meetings in Coalbrookdale, attended by 'persons of account', continued after Darby's death. After Abraham (II) built a meeting house in 1741 the Broseley and Coalbrookdale meetings merged.[59] By the late 1740s there were Sunday and Wednesday meetings in the meeting house, Friday meetings at Sunniside, and other meetings, perhaps occasional, at the works.[60] In 1763 Abraham (II) left provision for the enlargement of the meeting

house and the enclosure of a burial ground. His own burial was the first,[61] and by 1770 the meeting house had been enlarged.[62]

The Coalbrookdale meeting was probably always small. In the late 18th century it evidently consisted of the Darbys, the Reynoldses, their households, and some of their senior employees,[63] men like the Luckocks.[64] There were 66 members in 1798,[65] when Elizabeth Gurney (later Fry), the future prison reformer,[66] stayed in Coalbrookdale and decided to become a Quaker.[67]

By 1808 the meeting house by Tea Kettle Row[68] had become 'inconvenient', and Richard Reynolds paid for a new one on a better site[69] acquired from Francis Darby.[70] Numbers probably declined when the Reynoldses left the area in the early 19th century and some of the Darbys joined the established church in the late 1840s. Newdale meeting united with Coalbrookdale in 1843,[71] but on Census Sunday 1851, in a meeting house accommodating 260, only 25 attended in the morning, 16 in the afternoon.[72]

Informal links between the Coalbrookdale meeting, the Darbys, and the Coalbrookdale Co. persisted. Mrs. Adelaide Anna Whitmore (*née* Darby) gave land to enlarge the burial ground in 1851.[73] W. G. Norris (d. 1911), whose mother was a Luckock and who was a leading member of the meeting, was also managing partner in the works.[74] Later the Simpsons, who ran the Horsehay works (at first for the Coalbrookdale Co.), attended the meeting. By 1860, when membership of the Shropshire monthly meeting was 23, Coalbrookdale was the only particular meeting in the county, and so it remained until 1931. By 1940 only two families attended the meeting which, in its last years, 1940–*c.* 1947, was held in a private house at Woodside.[75] The meeting house, closed in 1940,[76] was demolished in 1961, but the burial ground was maintained by the Ironbridge Gorge Museum Trust from 1975.[77]

METHODISTS. Methodism in Madeley began when J. W. Fletcher came as vicar in 1760.[78] In

---

[41] Above, Churches. [42] Randall, *Madeley*, 172.

[43] *Kelly's Dir. Salop.* (1885), 866; (1891), 333; (1922), 116; cf. above, Social and Cultural Activities.

[44] Trinder, *New Connexion*, 12.

[45] G.R.O., Worship Reg. no. 27429 (cancelled 1896 on revision of list).

[46] *Kelly's Dir. Salop.* (1895), 106.

[47] S.R.O. 2533/40, 27 June 1918; T.D.C. Central Cinema deeds; *Kelly's Dir. Salop.* (1917), 110.

[48] G.R.O., Worship Reg. no. 34531.

[49] *Kelly's Dir. Salop.* (1909), 144.

[50] S.R.O. 4044/94, [p. 141].

[51] Trinder, *New Connexion*, 19.

[52] G.R.O., Worship Reg. no. 56391 (cancelled 1954 on revision of list).

[53] Not in *Kelly's Dir. Salop.* (1937, 1941).

[54] G.R.O., Worship Reg. no. 72890; T.D.C. Central Cinema deeds; inf. from T.D.C.

[55] *T.S.A.S.* lix. 124.

[56] H.W.R.O.(H.), Heref. dioc. rec., Wenlock deanery bdle. of replies to visit. articles, 1716.

[57] *T.S.A.S.* lix. 124; *Orders of Q. Sess.* ii. 28.

[58] Skinner, *Nonconf. in Salop.* 84.

[59] Ibid. 31; *T.S.A.S.* lix. 126; *Orders of Q. Sess.* ii. 107; P.R.O., RG 31/7, Salop. no. 96.

[60] Skinner, op. cit. 31, 37; *Orders of Q. Sess.* ii. 117, 142, 184; P.R.O., RG 31/7, Salop. nos. 99, 110, 133.

[61] S.R.O. 1987/25/8; /34/1; *Quaker Burial Grounds* (I.G.M.T. Inf. Sheet no. 3).

[62] Trinder, *Ind. Rev. Salop.* 304; *V.C.H. Salop.* ii. 12.

[63] Trinder, op. cit. 304–6. Cf. S.P.L., Deeds 10682.

[64] Randall, *Madeley*, 284 sqq.

[65] Skinner, *Nonconf. in Salop.* 37.

[66] *D.N.B.* For prison visiting by Coalbrookdale Friends in the later 18th cent. see Skinner, op. cit. 31, 38.

[67] Raistrick, *Iron Founders*, 222–4.

[68] See Randall, *Madeley*, 289. The schoolrm. or mtg. ho. mentioned 1847 (S.R.O. 2280/2/47, no. 3327; /48, p. 71 (no. 3327)) seems too far from the Row to be the 1741 Quaker mtg. ho.

[69] *Quaker Burial Grounds*.

[70] S.R.O. 1987/31/6; 2280/2/47, no. 3279; /48, p. 26 (no. 3279). It was presumably the mtg. ho. reg. in 1814: *Orders of Q. Sess.* iii. 191; P.R.O., RG 31/7, Salop. no. 337.

[71] *V.C.H. Salop.* ii. 12.

[72] P.R.O., HO 129/358, no. 43.

[73] *Quaker Burial Grounds*.

[74] Randall, *Madeley*, 285; *T.S.A.S.* lix. 125; P.R.O., HO 129/358, no. 43; *Wellington Jnl.* 9 Dec. 1911 (obit.).

[75] A. H. Simpson, *Brief Notes concerning Coalbrookdale Friends' Mtg. and Horsehay Wks.* (1975; copy in S.P.L.); Coalbrookdale mtg. min. bk. 1858–1947 (in possession of Mr. A. E. Morris, Lilleshall). The mtg. was formally recorded until 1954: *V.C.H. Salop.* ii. 12.

[76] G.R.O., Worship Reg. no. 4773; Simpson, op. cit.

[77] Jackson, 'Madeley', bk. 3A, p. 177; *Quaker Burial Grounds*; inf. from I.G.M.T.

[78] *V.C.H. Salop.* ii. 13; above, Churches.

1761 he fostered societies at Madeley Wood and Coalbrookdale, each about twenty strong.[79] He and his curate served them on alternate Sundays. From 1765 John Wesley's preachers from the Shrewsbury circuit also served them.[80] By 1762 the Madeley Wood Methodists met at the 'Rock church', a widow's house near Madeley Green,[81] and in 1764 the Coalbrookdale society met at the Bank.[82] In 1776 Fletcher undertook the building of a meeting house near the Rock church, eventually completed only at great expense to him. It was to be used to teach children reading and writing during the day and for worship and the religious instruction of adults in the evening.[83] A second meeting house in the parish was built in Coalbrookdale in 1785; it was enlarged in 1789 and rebuilt 1828.[84]

John Wesley made the first of many visits[85] to Madeley in 1764, but the parish church could not contain his hearers and a window near the pulpit had to be taken out for the sake of those in the churchyard.[86] That happened again in 1771.[87] In 1773 and 1774 Wesley preached in the open air at Madeley Wood to many colliers. In 1779, when he used the new Madeley Wood meeting house, he found that Methodist discipline had broken down during Fletcher's absence abroad, and in 1782 he helped the Fletchers to revive the local societies and classes.[88]

After her husband's death in 1785 Mary Fletcher remained in the vicarage and fitted up its barn as a preaching house. Wesley used it in 1789.[89] In 1800 her adopted daughter Sarah Lawrance opened a meeting house at Coalport. For most of Samuel Walter's curacy (1792–1815) there were thus four Methodist meetings, in the vicarage barn and in the Madeley Wood, Coalbrookdale, and Coalport meeting houses.[90] Others may have been short-lived. Mary Fletcher was intent on reviving one in the low town in 1790,[91] and by 1811 there was a house meeting in Madeley Lane,[92] perhaps the same as her Rough Park meeting.[93]

For its first half-century Madeley Methodism was bound to the parish church by strong ties of conviction and loyalty. The Fletchers never contemplated schism. Methodist meetings were timed not to conflict with church services,[94] and Mary Fletcher chose the curates 1785–1815.[95] The Cranages, especially William (d. 1823 aged 63),

long represented Wesleyans 'of the true type', worshipping regularly in chapel but always taking communion in church on sacrament Sundays.[96]

When Mary Fletcher died in 1815 the situation began to change, albeit slowly. Her adopted daughter Mary Tooth left the vicarage but was allowed to continue her meetings in the barn, and in 1816 the Wesleyans decided not to build a chapel in Madeley.[97] Madeley, however, became the centre of a large Wesleyan circuit (at first known as Broseley circuit) which included places where relations with the church were bad.[98] In the 1820s moreover Revivalist missionaries arrived:[99] less solicitous for the church than the Wesleyans, they were nevertheless welcomed by many Wesleyans, and their acceptance as an established sect (from 1829 the New Connexion)[1] developed denominational awareness among the Methodists. In 1831 the vicarage barn was demolished, and in 1833 the Wesleyans opened a chapel in Madeley.[2] Mary Tooth's Madeley class and Coalport society seemed increasingly anomalous: the rump of Mary Fletcher's unofficial sub-circuit,[3] the two groups of 'old believers' continued strong in numbers[4] but their relations with the Wesleyan circuit were uneasy. The Wesleyan ministry barely accepted Coalport as a Wesleyan chapel[5] and regarded the Madeley church Methodists as only 'half and half'.[6] Until Mary Tooth's death in 1843 the Madeley class met at her house, in an upper room fondly remembered by one former member but recalled by a Wesleyan minister as 'an old ricketty garret'.[7]

The mid 19th century was a time of prosperity for the Madeley Wesleyans, largely unaffected by controversies which split Wesleyans in the northern coalfield parishes.[8] In 1837–8 they built a large new chapel at Madeley Wood to replace Fletcher's old meeting house, which had been enlarged in 1821;[9] in Madeley the imposing chapel in Court Street was built 1841–2[10] to replace the modest one of 1833;[11] and in 1849 a new chapel was opened on the Wharfage at Ironbridge. The three new buildings provided c. 1,610 sittings (900 free) besides those in the older buildings at Coalbrookdale and Coalport. In 1851 Sunday morning or afternoon attendance at the three chapels was said to average 600 adults and over 480 children. Madeley Wood chapel, with places for 800 (450 free), drew as many adults and

[79] Tyerman, *Wesley's Designated Successor*, 64.
[80] Randall, *Madeley*, 169–70; Skinner, *Nonconf. in Salop.* 71.
[81] Randall, op. cit. 127, 132; Trinder, *Ind. Rev. Salop.* 269; Tyerman, op. cit. 76–7, 79.
[82] Randall, *Madeley*, 169; cf. S.R.O. 2280/16/185, p. 3.
[83] Randall, op. cit. 132–4; Trinder op. cit. 270.
[84] S.R.O. 1681, box 144, deed of 29 Sept. 1862; 2280/16/185, pp. 4–7, 10–11, 27, 29–30.
[85] Others were in 1768, 1771, 1773, 1774, 1779, 1782, 1788, and 1789; J. Wesley, *Wks.* (1872), iii. 338, 440, 502; iv. 24, 145–6, 222, 448; J. Wesley, *Letters*, ed. J. Telford, vi. 75; vii. 114; viii. 49. Cf. Jackson, 'Madeley', bk. 1A, p. 183.
[86] Wesley, *Wks.* iii. 190–1.
[87] Ibid. 440.
[88] Ibid. 502; iv. 24, 145–6, 222.
[89] Ibid. iv. 448; Trinder, *Ind. Rev. Salop.* 270.
[90] Trinder, op. cit. 271; S.R.O. 4035/4–5.
[91] Skinner, *Nonconf. in Salop.* 94; H. Moore, *Life of Mrs. Mary Fletcher* (14th edn. 1856), 275–6.
[92] *Orders of Q. Sess.* iii. 173; S.R.O., q. sess. file 10/391.
[93] Randall, *Madeley*, 159; S.P.L., C. 98.7 v.f. (copy

Shrews. Circuit plan, 1813).
[94] Trinder, *Ind. Rev. Salop.* 272–4.
[95] Above, Churches.
[96] Randall, *Madeley*, 284.
[97] Trinder, *Ind. Rev. Salop.* 274.
[98] Ibid. 274, 285; *V.C.H. Salop.* ii. 13.
[99] Below.
[1] Trinder, *Ind. Rev. Salop.* 287, 295–6, 306; idem, *New Connexion*, 5–6, 11.
[2] Trinder, *Ind. Rev. Salop.* 275.
[3] Cf. ibid. 271.
[4] Ibid. 275; S.R.O. 2533/1.
[5] Trinder, *Ind. Rev. Salop.* 274–5.
[6] Wesley Hist. Soc., Salop. Branch, *Bulletin*, i (12) (Mar. 1979; copy in S.R.O. 3543/13).
[7] Trinder, op. cit. 274–5, 278; R. Plummer, *Successful Class-Leader exemplified in a Memorial of Ben. Pollard* (1861), 74; Jackson, 'Madeley', bk. 1A, p. 205.
[8] Trinder, op. cit. 296.
[9] S.R.O. 2280/16/183; 2533/40, 42.
[10] S.R.O. 2533/103; Pevsner, *Shropshire*, 193.
[11] Wesley Hist. Soc., Salop. Branch, *Bull.* i (12).

69

children as the other two together and its evening congregation averaged 550–600.[12]

The Madeley Wesleyans, like Methodists throughout the coalfield, thrived on revival, but the last great revival in the coalfield was in 1862.[13] Thereafter membership declined: in 1865 there were 401 members of the five Wesleyan chapels in the parish, in 1880 only 230.[14] Nevertheless congregations remained large, perhaps totalling 1,500 c. 1880,[15] and there were Wesleyan day schools.[16] There was a small-scale Methodist revival throughout east Shropshire in the early 1880s,[17] and in Madeley a new Wesleyan society of six members began in Park Lane in 1881[18] and the old chapel[19] in Coalbrookdale was ambitiously rebuilt in an Italianate style in 1885.[20] Membership, however, continued to fall. The Wharfage chapel closed in 1889. The Park Lane society ceased in 1890. By 1905 the four chapels had only 142 members.[21] The Coalport chapel had 10 members in 1907; its lease had run out, the landlord was unsympathetic, and so it closed.[22] It had long been clear that Madeley had failed to keep the position Fletcher had given it as a Methodist 'stronghold'.[23] Madeley Wesleyan circuit was abolished in 1908, its Madeley chapels going to Wellington circuit.[24]

New Connexion Methodists arrived in the parish in the 1820s, Primitive Methodists in the 1840s. By the 1840s Wesleyans and the New Connexion, though not the Primitives, were probably just past the zenith of their fortunes. Nevertheless the Methodists may have remained the largest group of Christians in the parish in 1851,[25] and common traditions fostered good relations.[26] Doctrinal lectures by a New Connexion minister c. 1830 were well attended by other denominations.[27] In 1859 a New Connexion chapel was opened to 'assist' rather than 'rob' the other churches, and by the end of the 19th century Methodist local preachers took appointments regardless of denomination.[28] Declining membership, common to all, doubtless helped to produce such effects. Hardest hit was the New Connexion.

In 1822 meetings began in a cordwainer's house in Madeley Lane and a moulder's house at Madeley Green. They were probably the first fruits in Madeley of the great revival which followed the Cinderhill riots of 1821. In 1823 two Revivalist preachers, Winfieldite missionaries, began to use a room in Hodgebower. The meeting was included in a Revivalist circuit formed in Dawley, and in 1827 the congregation opened Zion chapel[29] near Madeley Green;[30] all 80 sittings were free. When the Revivalists joined the New Connexion in 1829 Zion was included in the new Dawley Green circuit. In 1851 attendances were said to average 80 adults and 30 children in the morning, 30 adults and 35 children in the afternoon, and 120 adults in the evening, and there was a Sunday school.[31]

Dawley Green circuit had a resident minister. The first, William Cooke, was to be one of the New Connexion's most distinguished leaders and theologians. He started a cottage meeting in Coalbrookdale which flourished, with another in Park Lane, Madeley, in the 1830s. Later, in the 1860s, Aqueduct was one of the connexion's most solidly established cottage meetings. Cooke's successors, however, were often inexperienced young ministers, and the prominent laymen who were influential preferred organs, choirs, and new chapel building to revival. The opening of Bethesda, Park Lane, in 1860 was the fruit of such a policy. Built to accommodate c. 200 by a society formed in 1855, Bethesda, despite the éclat of its opening, eventually weakened the connexion in the area: in the later 19th century, when Madeley's population was declining, it failed to compete with the town's other churches and diverted New Connexion resources from Zion. About the time it was rebuilt, in 1876, Zion opened a branch chapel at the Lloyds which lasted a dozen or more years.[32] The rebuilding, however, introduced pew rents, and after 1870 decline was swift. Bethesda was 'dirty and dilapidated' in the mid 1870s, and c. 1880 attendance at Zion averaged 70, fewer than in 1851; attendance at Bethesda averaged 60, and the two memberships totalled only 38. Both chapels closed c. 1901. Bethesda reopened c. 1902 but closed again in 1906 or 1907.

Primitive Methodist meetings in Madeley date from the 1840s. For twenty or more years after the great revival of 1821 the area had been left to the New Connexion,[33] but by 1851 there were three Primitive meetings in the parish. A schoolroom in Ironbridge accommodating 85 was used from c. 1846 and a 'preaching room' in Madeley High Street, with 70 sittings, probably from about then; Aqueduct chapel was registered in 1850. On Census Sunday 1851 the Ironbridge and Madeley evening services were attended by 23 (about half the average) and 65 respectively.[34]

The Primitives, expanding more cautiously than the New Connexion, fared better in the later

[12] P.R.O., HO 129/358, nos. 45, 48, 50. There are no returns for Coalbrookdale and Coalport: Trinder, *Ind. Rev. Salop.* 284.
[13] Trinder, op. cit. 291, 294.
[14] S.R.O. 2533/4, June 1865, June 1880.
[15] Randall, *Madeley*, 170, whose membership figs. (300), however, seem too high.
[16] See below, Educ.
[17] Trinder, *New Connexion*, 16.
[18] S.R.O. 2533/4, Dec. 1881.
[19] *P.O. Dir. Salop.* (1856), 75; Skinner, *Nonconf. in Salop.* pl. XI.
[20] G.R.O., Worship Reg. nos. 1741, 29125; Pevsner, *Shropshire*, 156; Cossons and Sowden, *Ironbridge*, 55.
[21] S.R.O. 2533/5, Mar. 1889, Mar. 1890; /6, June 1905.
[22] Ibid. /6, June 1907; /117–18; Randall, *Madeley*, 159 (inaccurate in some respects).
[23] E. Elliot, *Hist. Congregationalism in Salop.* [1898], 306.
[24] *V.C.H. Salop.* ii. 14; *Kelly's Dir. Salop.* (1909), 144.
[25] Trinder, *New Connexion*, 9–10, table B; idem, *Ind. Rev.*

Salop. 284–5, 409.
[26] *Shropshire Jnl.* 19 Mar. 1965 (cutting in S.R.O. 2533/140); Trinder, *New Connexion*, 15 (Connexion's display of Fletcher relics at a bazaar); *Shrews. Chron.* 29 Oct. 1937; S.R.O. 2533/102, p. 48.
[27] Also by deists and sceptics: Trinder, op. cit. 6.
[28] Ibid. 13; Trinder, *Ind. Rev. Salop.* 306.
[29] *Orders of Q. Sess.* iii. 227, 236, 266; P.R.O., RG 31/7, Salop. nos. 387, 389, 408, 459; Trinder, *Ind. Rev. Salop.* 286–7, 289; *V.C.H. Salop.* ii. 14, 16.
[30] S.R.O. 2280/2/46, no. 2203; /48, p. 109 (no. 2203).
[31] P.R.O., HO 129/358, no. 46; Trinder, *New Connexion*, 6.
[32] Closed 1887 × 1900. This para. is based on Trinder, *New Connexion*; Randall, *Madeley*, 171–2. For Cooke see F. Boase, *Modern Eng. Biog.* i. 703; Wesley Hist. Soc., Salop Branch, *Bull.* i (13).
[33] Trinder, *New Connexion*, 4–5, 7–8.
[34] P.R.O., HO 129/358, nos. 49, 51; Heref. Dioc. Regy., reg. 1847–56, p. 300. There is no return for Aqueduct.

19th century.[35] They worked hard throughout the parish,[36] trying repeatedly in the 1850s and 1860s to establish cottage or schoolroom meetings at the Lloyds and Blists Hill and in Coalbrookdale.[37] The room in Madeley High Street was replaced by a small chapel in Prince Street, that in turn by Mount Zion, a larger building of 1865 on the corner of High Street and Station Road.[38] Mount Zion and a chapel opened in Ironbridge in 1860[39] flourished in the 1880s. Their membership was 90 c. 1880, over twice that of the New Connexion chapels. Since 1851 moreover attendance at the two Primitive chapels had quadrupled while attendances at Zion (New Connexion) had fallen.[40] The Ironbridge Primitive chapel was rebuilt, as Providence, in 1883.[41] Madeley Primitive circuit existed from 1881 to 1906 when the Madeley chapels were reunited to the Dawley (thenceforth Dawley and Madeley) circuit.[42]

Aqueduct chapel closed in 1917 when there were only three members.[43] Mount Zion was in financial difficulty at the turn of the century, by which time there were pew rents. The chapel debt, however, was paid off in 1903 by the sale of a house,[44] and in 1932 the Primitives were able to contribute two of their three chapels in Madeley to the reunited Methodist church. Three of the Fletchers' four Wesleyan chapels had also survived, and for almost a decade there were five Methodist chapels in the parish, with seating for 1,860: two in Madeley and others at Madeley Wood, Ironbridge, and Coalbrookdale.[45] Providence closed in 1941,[46] and in 1951 the four other chapels, which had remained in their old circuits (connexionally separate before 1932),[47] were placed in one circuit;[48] the change facilitated closures resulting from declining membership in the late 1960s. Coalbrookdale chapel closed in 1970, Mount Zion in 1977.[49]

In the 1970s one minister[50] was responsible for the two surviving chapels and, with the clergy of Central Telford parish, for a congregation worshipping at the Methodist-owned Brookside pastoral centre, opened in 1972 and shared with the Anglicans from 1974;[51] the Brookside congregation, whose members, 69 in 1980, enjoyed local reciprocal membership of the Anglican and Methodist churches, was the most ecumenically advanced in the ancient parish. Methodist membership at Madeley Wood was small, average congregations were even smaller; membership declined in the 1970s.[52] At Madeley, however, membership almost doubled,[53] and in 1974–5 the former day school buildings were linked to the chapel and vestry to provide a minister's office, with a kitchen, coffee bar, and other rooms.

BAPTISTS. In 1748 and 1773 a collier's house in Coalbrookdale[54] and a clockmaker's in Madeley[55] were licensed for dissenting worship, perhaps for Baptist worship since, except for Quakers and Methodists, the only protestant dissenters' meeting recorded in 18th-century Madeley was a Baptist one mentioned in 1760.[56] From 1818 a former club room on Lincoln Hill was used by a congregation which was probably an offshoot of the Broseley Old Baptists.[57] Almost forty years later thirteen founding members formed the Particular Baptist church in Madeley.[58] A room in Park Lane and the old court room were used for worship 1857–8. In 1858 Ænon chapel, High Street, was opened with accommodation for 250. A Sunday school was formed in the mid 1870s, and c. 1880 there were 30 church members and congregations averaged 100. The church did not always have a pastor and during the longest such period (1878–1900), and later, there were pastoral links with Broseley chapel; a united pastorate with Donnington and Shifnal was tried in 1885. During the longest pastorate (1929–38) membership grew, and in 1931 the Sunday school was provided with its own building next to the chapel. R. N. Moore (1880–1953), a leading member of the church throughout the earlier 20th century, was widely known and much loved for his work for old people.[59]

A Baptist pastoral centre built on Woodside estate 1968–9 was at first the responsibility of the Ænon pastor. In the later 1970s, however, Ænon and Woodside had no pastor, and in 1980 the thriving Bridgnorth Baptist church appointed a full-time pastoral worker to take charge of Woodside.[60]

CONGREGATIONALISTS. Services began early in 1872. At first they were in private houses but in

[35] Trinder, *New Connexion*, 12, 15, 20.

[36] With camp and missionary mtgs., open-air preachings, protracted and revival services: S.R.O. 2533/130.

[37] Ibid. Park La. and Coalport are also mentioned: ibid. 17 Dec. 1855, 16 Mar. 1863.

[38] *Shropshire Jnl.* 19 Mar. 1965; name and date on bldg.

[39] S.R.O. 2533/130, 14 May 1860; G.R.O., Worship Reg. no. 13250.

[40] Randall, *Madeley*, 171–2.

[41] *Kelly's Dir. Salop.* (1900), 109; G.R.O., Worship Reg. no. 27711; S.P.L., Deeds 19293; S.R.O. 2079/XLIII. 14. NE.; 4044/94, [p. 141].

[42] *Prim. Meth. Min.* (1881), 29; (1906), 42.

[43] *Salop. News Letter*, xl. 19; S.R.O. 1936/3–6; 2533/131, 4 Sept. 1920.   [44] S.R.O. 2533/140.

[45] Meth. Dept. for Chapel Affairs, *Meth. Church Bldgs.: Statistical Returns* (1940), 269–70.

[46] S.R.O. 2533/138, incl. loose 'application for auth. to sell [the chap.]', 14 Mar. 1941; S.R.O., DA 6/112/7, Publ. Health Subcttee. mins. 31 May 1954.

[47] S.R.O. 1936/63–118; *Kelly's Dir. Salop.* (1934), 123, 150; (1941), 122, 149.

[48] Madeley and Dawley 1951–70, Telford South from 1970: cf. S.R.O. 4286/6/4; /12/1; *Shropshire Star*, 25 July 1970.

[49] Inf. from the Revd. A. G. Kinch; G.R.O., Worship Reg. no. 29125 (de-reg. 1970).

[50] Para. based on inf. from Mr. Kinch, minister from 1970.

[51] G.R.O., Worship Reg. no. 73276 (reg. 5 Jan. 1973); Lich. Dioc. Regy., bps.' reg. Y, p. 185.

[52] From 39 (1971) to 20 (1980).

[53] From 54 (1970) to 95 (1980).

[54] S.R.O., q. sess. order bk. 1741–57, f. 89v.; cf. S.R.O. 1987/26/5–6.

[55] P.R.O., RG 31/7, Salop. no. 154; cf. *Orders of Q. Sess.* ii. 191–2; D. J. Elliott, *Salop. Clock and Watchmakers* (1979), 82.

[56] Tyerman, *Wesley's Designated Successor*, 59, 168.

[57] *Orders of Q. Sess.* iii. 210; P.R.O., RG 31/7, Salop. no. 370; cf. J. Randall, *Broseley and Its Surroundings* (Madeley, 1879), 225.

[58] Rest of para. based on G.R.O., Worship Reg. nos. 7769, 8899; Randall, *Madeley*, 172; *Shropshire Mag.* Sept. 1958, 13; date on Sun. sch.; ch. rec. in possession of Mr. G. R. Moore, esp. min. bk. 1856–90; G.L. Tubbs, 'Until He Come . . .' (TS. 1976).

[59] *Rest Rm. Rev.* l; *Lond. Gaz.* 1 Jan. 1953, p. 19.

[60] *Wrekin Light*, Nov. 1968, p. 4 (copy in S.R.O. 2732); local inf.; inf. from the Revd. B. Thompson, Bridgnorth.

November, when a church was formed, a room in Park Lane was provided. A church, designed to hold *c.* 300, and Sunday school were built 1874–5 at the corner of Park and Church streets.[61] Congregations averaged 50 in the morning and 100 in the evening *c.* 1880, and there was an 80-strong Sunday school.[62] By 1980 there were 21 members but apparently no Sunday school.[63]

EDUCATION. The priest of St. Mary's guild, suppressed in 1547, kept a grammar school.[64] There were two schoolmasters in 1671, at least one unlicensed. The vicar was probably teaching boys 1672–80,[65] but there was no free or 'charity' school.[66] There are references to teachers, writing masters, and schools in 18th- and early 19th-century Coalbrookdale and Madeley Wood.[67] A schoolroom near Sunniside was mentioned in Abraham Darby (II)'s will of 1763,[68] and succeeding managers of the Coalbrookdale Co. provided schools and Sunday schools.[69] The company's British day school was by 1818 the largest in the parish, but a free school was then greatly needed.[70]

The Coalbrookdale Co.'s school was exceptional. Almost all the early sustained provision of elementary education was in the Sunday schools. In 1818 some 750 children attended four Sunday schools while twelve unendowed day schools (including the Coalbrookdale Co.'s school) had only 523 pupils, 173 of whom, at the eight principal ones (excluding the company's school), paid 3*d.*–6*d.* a week. From 1813, according to regulations of the parish church's newly founded Sunday school society, the Sunday schools sat 9 a.m.–noon and 1.30–4.00 p.m.; primers, catechisms, testaments, religious tracts, slates, and copy books were used. The principal Sunday school, evidently that at Madeley Wood, had *c.* 150 pupils in 1818.[71] It owed its existence to J. W. Fletcher who intended the meeting house which he built there *c.* 1777 to be used also as an elementary day school.[72] How long a day school was carried on is uncertain,[73] but Abiah Darby prompted Fletcher to found Sunday schools at Madeley Wood, Coalbrookdale, and Madeley in 1784 and 1785.[74] A fourth Sunday school was founded at Coalport before 1810.[75]

In 1818 two of the four Sunday schools evidently met in the Madeley Wood and Coalport Wesleyan chapels, though they were carried on by the parish Sunday school society which, in 1814, built a room in the churchyard for Madeley Sunday school.[76] Coalbrookdale Sunday school parted from the society in 1816, as Wesleyans and church people began to separate. A separate church Sunday school began in the Madeley Wood house of industry in 1821, when afternoon services began in the Wesleyan chapel: and early next year the Madeley Wood Wesleyans reorganized their Sunday school, which then included an adult school. Another church Sunday school began in the Ironbridge dispensary *c.* 1830.[77] In 1838 the Madeley Wood Wesleyans founded a Sunday school society to teach poor children of all denominations to read the Scriptures 'and to understand and practise every moral virtue'.[78]

By 1833 free elementary education was being provided by six Sunday schools, three Wesleyan[79] with 261 girls and 230 boys, and three church schools[80] with 225 girls and 165 boys. There were also eighteen day schools (615 pupils), where fees were paid, but in one (founded 1829) the patron and proprietor and two or three local subscribers made up deficiencies;[81] it was probably John Bartlett's school near Marnwood Hall gate.[82] By 1824 Bartlett (incumbent of Buildwas 1822–61)[83] was a prominent member of the parish Sunday school society; through it he pressed for a central parish school and succeeded in founding parochial infant schools at Madeley and Ironbridge in 1829 and 1831.[84]

By 1871 there were church schools serving all parts of the parish, Wesleyan schools in Madeley and Madeley Wood (widely supported in the coalfield parishes by subscribers and fund-raising efforts),[85] and the undenominational company school in Coalbrookdale. The voluntary schools sufficed to avoid the compulsory establishment of a school board, though fear of a board prompted the rector of Ironbridge to retain management of his infant school until 1885 and inspired the managers of the Coalbrookdale schools to appeal for subscriptions and propose voluntary rates. Only poor children's education was a charge on the rates before 1903. A few indoor pauper children were taught, badly, at the Madeley union

[61] Elliot, *Hist. Congregationalism in Salop.* 306–8; Wrekin District Council, Madeley Hall deeds, letter of C. E. Yate, 6 Nov. 1914.

[62] Randall, *Madeley*, 172.

[63] *Utd. Ref. Ch. Yr. Bk. 1980*, 72.

[64] *T.S.A.S.* 3rd ser. x. 365.

[65] H.W.R.O.(H.), Heref. dioc. rec., visit. bk. 22, [f. 4v.]; bk. 23, *s.a.* 1674, 1677, 1680. For the unlicensed John Beddoe cf. above, Rom. Cath.

[66] H.W.R.O.(H.), Heref. dioc. rec., Wenlock deanery bdle. of replies to visit. articles, 1716.

[67] Raistrick, *Iron Founders*, 30; P.R.O., E 134/27 Geo. II Hil./8, m. 10; Randall, *Madeley*, 293–4; S.R.O. 245/17; 1681, box 152, lease of 1792 (Ric. Reynolds to Geo. Hotchkiss); *T.S.A.S.* lviii. 253.   [68] S.R.O. 1987/34/1.

[69] Raistrick, op. cit. 90. Cf. McFall, 'Educ. in Madeley Union', 37.

[70] *Digest Educ. Poor*, H.C. 224, pp. 755, 768 (1819), ix (2); Randall, *Madeley*, 293.

[71] S.R.O. 2280/11/2, 15; *Digest Educ. Poor*, ii. 755, 768; *1st Rep. Com. Child. Emp. App. Pt. I*, 33, 78–9, 87.

[72] Above, Prot. Nonconf.

[73] McFall, 'Educ. in Madeley Union', 54; Tyerman, *Wesley's Designated Successor*, 527.

[74] Trinder, *Ind. Rev. Salop.* 370–2; 'Subscribers Donations for Bldg. a Mtg. Ho. and Sunday Sch., Coalbrookdale, Feb. 9, 1785' (TS.; copy in S.P.L., class M 55 v.f.); S.R.O. 2280/6/95, 14 Feb. 1785; Randall, *Madeley*, 134–5. Cf. Tyerman, op. cit. 526–8 (giving too early a date for Fletcher's Sun. schs.).

[75] McFall, op. cit. 42.

[76] S.R.O. 2280/11/15–56; /16/180.

[77] Ibid. /11/15; /16/182. A Wesleyan sch. rm. was built at Madeley Wood *c.* 1823: S.R.O. 2533/42, 4 Oct. 1823.

[78] S.R.O. 2280/16/184; cf. 2533/40, 17 Apr. 1837.

[79] Madeley Wood, Coalbrookdale, and Coalport. The last may have separated from the ch. soc. in or after 1821: cf. S.R.O. 2280/11/12–13.

[80] Madeley, Madeley Wood, and Ironbridge.

[81] *Educ. Enq. Abstract*, H.C. 62, pp. 777–8 (1835), xlii.

[82] S.R.O. 2280/2/45, no. 3455; /48, p. 10 (no. 3455).

[83] *S.P.R. Lich.* xiv (3), p. viii.

[84] S.R.O. 2280/11/15.

[85] McFall, 'Educ. in Madeley Union', 53.

school in Broseley until 1851 when the union joined the South East Shropshire District School at Quatt. By the 1860s workhouse children were sent to the Blue Schools in Ironbridge. When the guardians were empowered to pay school fees, few parents applied, preferring to keep their children away.[86]

There was no public provision in 19th-century Madeley for schooling beyond the elementary stage, though by the 1840s and 1850s some children were continuing their education as half-timers at school, others at night schools. School managers sometimes stopped their employees from teaching a night school, considering it detrimental to the day school; at other times they encouraged night schools and took on part-time or temporary teachers to help in them. By 1859 a winter night school at Madeley Wood Wesleyan School was held thrice weekly for pupils aged 11–18.[87] A school of art founded for Wenlock borough in 1856 gradually centred in the Coalbrookdale institution.[88] In the 1890s the influence of the art school and the institution helped to bring the county council's organization of technical instruction to a high degree of perfection.[89] The school had branches throughout the borough and in Dawley, and c. 1906 an art library was provided at the institution. In 1949–50 there were very many well attended evening-institute classes in Coalbrookdale and Madeley.[90]

In the 19th century there were many private schools, most of them ephemeral.[91] In the earlier 1840s the artist J. C. Bayliss kept one, probably in Park Hall,[92] which was used as a private school later in the century.[93] By 1851 William Evans, secretary of the Ironbridge Mechanics' Institution, kept another in Ironbridge. There were then three boarding schools in the parish, two of them for girls;[94] those at Brockholes and Dale Coppice lasted many years. The rector of Ironbridge took boarding pupils in the 1870s.[95] The school near Marnwood Hall evidently became a private school for young middle-class children in the later 19th century.[96] In the 1890s boys from the private Ironbridge High School were gaining county-council scholarships,[97] and in 1906 a girls' high school in Ironbridge was mentioned; it was possibly the private school, for girls only from c. 1909, in St. Luke's Road between 1891 and 1937.[98] In the Baptist schoolroom in High Street, Madeley, there was another girls' private school from 1886 to c. 1922[99] and a boarding school in Arundel House (the Roman Catholic presbytery) in the 1890s.[1]

The borough of Wenlock succeeded Madeley school attendance committee as local education authority for the parish in 1903, and in 1912 the county council took over.[2] One of the eight elementary schools in the parish became a council school in 1916 and closed 1938, one closed in 1926, five became controlled 1946–52, one remained aided. Secondary education was first publicly provided in 1911 when the county council opened Coalbrookdale Secondary (later High) School.[3] In 1937 Madeley Senior School opened to complement the high school. Some reorganization of schools was being planned before Dawley new town's designation,[4] and from the mid 1960s secondary schools became comprehensive and many new schools were built.[5]

Madeley Wood Methodist (formerly Wesleyan) School originated in the day school planned by Fletcher for his first meeting house and the Sunday school which he later established there. After the opening of the new Wesleyan chapel at Madeley Wood in 1838[6] Fletcher's old building was used only by the Sunday school. In 1853, however, it was fitted up as a day school, to be supported largely by fees of 3d. a week, deficiencies being supplied by subscriptions and collections. With government grants a new infant schoolroom in Fletcher's memory and a teacher's house were built 1858–9 and another schoolroom in 1864, by which time the school had 280 places. Later in the 19th century the infant department was merged with the mixed school whenever an infants' mistress could not be afforded.[7] In 1903–4 the school had 168 boys and girls and 122 infants,[8] but by 1928 there were only 122 boys and girls and 69 infants.[9] The school became a junior

[86] Ibid. 50, 52, 121–2; Mins. of Educ. Cttee. of Council: Schs. of Parochial Unions, 1850–2 [1532], pp. 300, 315, H.C. (1852), xxxix; Ironbridge C.E. Boys' Sch. log bk. (in possession of Mr. A. Rigby, Oakengates) 27 Aug., 19 Nov. 1866; 19 Aug. 1869; 22 Apr. 1872; 6 Oct. 1879. The union sch. is reserved for treatment under Broseley.

[87] McFall, op. cit. 57–9; 1st Rep. Com. Child Emp. App. Pt. I, 33, 79; Mins. of Educ. Cttee. of Council, 1857–8 [2380], p. 427, H.C. (1857–8), xlv.

[88] V.C.H. Salop. i. 424, 434. For the inst. see above, Social and Cultural Activities.

[89] S.C.C. Mins. Intermediate Educ. Cttee. rep. 22 July 1893, 31; McFall, 'Educ. in Madeley Union', 59–60.

[90] Kelly's Dir. Salop. (1905), 74; (1913), 80; S.C.C. Mins. (Educ.) 1906–7, 94; 1950–1, 102.

[91] e.g. advts. in Shrews. Chron. 10 Jan. 1806, 10 July 1807 (Miss Bray's); 20 Jan. 1809, 12 Jan. 1810 (Brockholes Ho.); 20 July 1810 (Lincoln Hill). Dr. R. Hume is thanked for these refs.

[92] Jackson, 'Madeley', bk. 1, pp. 79–80; bk. 1A, p. 243.

[93] Ibid. bk. 1A, p. 242; Salopian and W. Midland Monthly Illustr. Jnl. Jan. 1880 (advt.); Kelly's Dir. Salop. (1885), 1087; girls' sch., Pk. La., mentioned in P.O. Dir. Salop. (1870), 258; E. Cassey & Co. Dir. Salop. (1871), 221.

[94] S. Bagshaw, Dir. Salop. (1851), 576; cf. S.R.O. 2280/2/46, no. 2300; /48, p. 65 (no. 2300).

[95] Kelly's Dir. Salop. (1885), 835, 1087 (s.v. Timmis);

(1895), 106, 382 (s.v. Johnston); Ironbridge C. E. Boys' Sch. log bk. 27 Mar. 1871, 26 Apr. 1872, 26 Apr. 1873.

[96] McFall, 'Educ. in Madeley Union', 64.

[97] Ibid. 63; cf. Kelly's Dir. Salop. (1895), 106, 382; (1905), 114, 424.

[98] Kelly's Dir. Salop. (1891), 334, 577; (1909), 117, 425; (1937), 123, 477; S.C.C. Mins. (Educ.) 1906–7, 86; Cossons and Sowden, Ironbridge, 88–9; S.R.O. 4044/93, p. 98 (no. 1802).

[99] Baptist ch. min. bk. 1856–90 (in possession of Mr. G. R. Moore), 30 Sept. 1886 sqq.; Kelly's Dir. Salop. (1891), 356, 577; (1922), 143, 436.

[1] Kelley's Dir. Salop. (1891), 356, 577; Jackson, 'Madeley', bk. 1A, p. 243.

[2] Lond. Gaz. 30 Aug. 1878, p. 4934; S.R.O. 2699/7, p. 273. Cf. V.C.H. Salop. iii. 177 (corr. below, Corrigenda).

[3] McFall, 'Educ. in Madeley Union', 64; S.R.O. 2699/7, p. 273.

[4] Jackson, 'Madeley', bk. 1A, p. 244.

[5] Below; cf. V.C.H. Salop. iii. 200, 220.

[6] Above; above, Prot. Nonconf.

[7] P.R.O., ED 7/103, ff. 172–5; S.P.L., Watton press cuttings, x. 25; McFall, 'Educ. in Madeley Union', 54, 145; inscr. on bldg.

[8] Public Elem. Schs. 1906 [Cd. 3182], p. 543, H.C. (1906), lxxxvi.

[9] S.C.C. Mins. (Educ.) 1928–9, 68.

mixed and infant school in 1937,[10] when Madeley Senior School opened, and became controlled in 1952.[11] It closed in 1969, the 129 children[12] thereafter attending Woodside schools.[13]

Coalbrookdale Boys' School was established before 1816, probably by the early 1790s, in premises belonging to the Coalbrookdale Co. It was conducted on the Lancasterian or British system under the company's direction and in 1818 was the largest day school in the parish with 123 pupils.[14] In 1840 a new two-storeyed building was erected below Woodside. Later in the century the school lost its primacy in numbers and by 1857 there were only 73 pupils.[15] Attendance averaged 126 in 1903–4, and there were 87 boys by 1928.[16] From 1916, when the county council bought the school from the company, it was known as Coalbrookdale Boys' Council School.[17] It closed in 1938, the year after Madeley Senior School opened; the pupils then transferred to the church school.[18]

Madeley Parochial Infant School, founded in 1829, was held in the Sunday school room in the churchyard until 1844 when it moved to the ground floor of the new National school.[19] In 1853 the infants moved to the former Wesleyan chapel, Church Street.[20] There were 120 pupils in 1903–4, 149 in 1928.[21] The school became controlled in 1948 and closed in 1965, over half of its 97 pupils transferring to the junior (former National) school.[22]

Ironbridge Parochial Infant School for the 'poorer classes' was built at the bottom of Madeley Hill in 1831. In 1833 it and the Madeley infant school together, maintained by fees, accommodated 147 children in roughly equal numbers. In 1858, financed largely by voluntary contributions and church collections, it was attended by 60 infants and c. 30 girls. The mistress had furnished lodgings rent-free.[23] The school first received a National Society grant in 1875, and in 1885 it was managed with the adjacent mixed Blue Schools.[24] Then or soon afterwards the infants moved into the Blue Schools, for by 1895 the old infant school housed Ironbridge High School.[25] In 1903–4 attendance averaged 79 infants. There were 64 pupils in 1928,[26] when the school became the mixed school's infant department.[27]

Coalbrookdale C.E. (Aided) School (known as Coalbrookdale Church School from 1854) for girls and infants was founded by Mrs. Abraham Darby in 1831. In 1840 it moved to new buildings in Wellington Road near the works; a school house was provided. There were 100 pupils in 1855. Connexions with the Darbys and the Coalbrookdale Co. persisted, and at the end of the 19th century the school was managed by company officials and maintained by subscriptions and voluntary rates.[28] In 1903–4 attendance averaged 94 girls and 78 infants, and by 1928 there were 149 pupils. In 1938 Coalbrookdale Boys' Council School closed and the boys joined the girls and infants in the church school,[29] which then became a junior mixed and infant school.[30] In 1971 the school moved to the former Coalbrookdale High School premises at Dale End where, having absorbed Ironbridge C.E. (Controlled) School, it became Coalbrookdale and Ironbridge C.E. (Aided) Primary School.[31] There were 150 pupils in 1980.[32]

Madeley National (later C.E.) School was built, with government and National Society grants, opposite the vicarage in 1844[33] on a small piece of glebe without room for a playground; it opened in 1845 and was supported by local industrialists.[34] The two-storeyed school was built in the Tudor style then becoming popular in the county and later employed for other schools in the parish.[35] There were 'neat' children of the 'right spirit' but at first teaching was inefficient. Boys and girls occupied the upper floor, infants the room below, and attendance averaged 213 by 1850, 270 by 1851. Conditions improved after the infants moved out in 1853. Boys and girls were separated, and a playground, walled off from the churchyard, was provided c. 1854.[36] Attendance averaged 146 boys and 138 girls in 1903–4,[37] 141 boys and 110 girls in 1928.[38] Eleven-year-olds went to the new senior school in 1937.[39] The junior school became controlled in 1948, took 52 infants when their nearby school closed in 1965, and closed in 1967, when there were 188 pupils.[40]

[10] S.R.O. 2533/80, p. 24.
[11] S.R.O. 4025/7, pp. 198, 205; S.C.C. Mins. (Educ.) 1952–3, 43.
[12] Ibid. 1967–8, 306; 1969–70, 118; S.R.O. 3346/3/8.
[13] S.C.C. Mins. (Educ.) 1969–70, 205.
[14] Digest Educ. Poor, 755, 768; cf. above, Churches.
[15] P.R.O., ED 7/103, ff. 153–4; McFall, 'Educ. in Madeley Union', 55; Muter, Coalbrookdale and Ironbridge, 20 and pl. 26.
[16] Public Elem. Schs. 1906, 543; S.C.C. Mins. (Educ.) 1928–9, 68.
[17] S.C.C. Mins. (Educ.) 1915–16, 25.
[18] Ibid. 1938–9, 132; below.
[19] S.R.O. 2280/11/15, 4 Nov. 1828 sqq.; cf. e.g. ibid. /11/56, refs. to day sch. 1843–6.
[20] Mins. of Educ. Cttee. of Council, 1853–4, ii [1788], p. 549, H.C. (1854), lii; S.R.O. 2280/6/96, 20 Aug. 1851, 8 Dec. 1852; inscr. on bldg.
[21] Public Elem. Schs. 1906, 543; S.C.C. Mins. (Educ.) 1928–9, 68.
[22] S.R.O. 2782/43–4; 3346/3/4; 4189/4, p. 113.
[23] S.R.O. 2280/7/141–2; /11/15, 29 May 1830 sqq.; inscr. on bldg.; P.R.O., ED 7/103, ff. 159–60; Educ. Enq. Abstract, 777–8.
[24] McFall, 'Educ. in Madeley Union', 50, 76.
[25] Kelly's Dir. Salop. (1895), 106, 382; inf. from Mr. F. W. Lloyd.

[26] Public Elem. Schs. 1906, 543; S.C.C. Mins. (Educ.) 1928–9, 68.
[27] S.R.O. 2879/1, pp. 11, 14, 37–8.
[28] McFall, 'Educ. in Madeley Union', 52, illustr. betw. pp. 147–8; Clwyd R.O., Hawarden, D/DM/391/1, 29 June 1831; I.G.M.T. Libr. 1980/976.2–3; P.R.O., ED 7/103, ff. 155–6.
[29] Public Elem. Schs. 1906, 543; S.C.C. Mins. (Educ.) 1928–9, 68; above.
[30] See e.g. S.R.O. 2782/38.
[31] S.C.C. Mins. (Educ.) 1967–8, 306; 1968–9, 246, 256–7; 1970–1, 278, 390; S.C.C. Educ. Cttee. Sch. List. (1969–70).
[32] S.C.C. Educ. Cttee. Educ. Dir. (1980), 9.
[33] Date on bldg.; see below, plate 19.
[34] McFall, 'Educ. in Madeley Union', 46–8.
[35] Pevsner, Shropshire, 43, 193, 242; Muter, Coalbrookdale and Ironbridge, 20–1.
[36] Mins. of Educ. Cttee. of Council, 1848–50 [1215], pp. ccxxviii, 363, H.C. (1850), xliii; 1850–1, ii [1358], p. 511, H.C. (1851), xliv; 1851–2, ii [1480], p. 419, H.C. (1852), xl; 1852–3, ii [1624], p. 499, H.C. (1852–3), lxxx; S.R.O. 2280/6/96, 26 July 1855; above.
[37] Public Elem. Schs. 1906, 543; cf. S.R.O. 2280/6/114–16.
[38] S.C.C. Mins. (Educ.) 1928–9, 68.
[39] e.g. S.R.O. 2699/51, p. 81; 2782/13, p. 34.
[40] S.R.O. 2782/43–4; 3346/3/6; 4189/4, pp. 113, 121; S.C.C. Mins. (Educ.) 1947–8, 143.

Ironbridge Ragged School, Milner's Lane, was opened by Quakers and local industrialists in the 1840s[41] in an upper storey provided by the Maws. In 1854, when there were 60 pupils, the government inspector called it 'missionary in character', praising its appropriateness to the district.[42] The withdrawal of ragged school grants caused it to close in 1870, but from 1871 to 1874 it continued under the Maws' patronage as Severnside Undenominational School, qualified for grants and with an average attendance of over 50. After 1874 it lasted for a time as a Sunday school.[43]

The Lloyds Parochial (later Church) School was established c. 1852 by the Madeley Wood Co. in a former warehouse. In 1862, with the vicar's concurrence, it was managed by John Anstice, a partner in the company. School pence from some 60 mixed pupils then produced c. £12, the deficiency in cost being made up by the company's partners.[44] In 1903–4 there were 68 boys and girls and 49 infants. The school closed in 1926.[45]

Ironbridge Parochial School, from 1946 Ironbridge C.E. (Controlled) School, was the only large church school in the parish founded without government or National Society grants. Built 1859–60 in St. Luke's Road, it became known from the colour of its brick as the Blue Schools. There were houses for the master and mistress at the east end. Financed largely by voluntary contributions and school pence, the school was attended by 80 girls and 60 boys in 1860.[46] After 1885 it evidently took the girls from the adjoining parochial infant school which then came under the same management and then or soon afterwards moved into the same building.[47] In 1903–4 attendance averaged 125 mixed pupils. In 1928 there were 88 mixed pupils,[48] and in that year the infant school became the infant department of the school. From 1937, when 11-year-olds went to the new senior school, the school became a junior mixed and infant school with 118 pupils.[49] In September 1939 St. Alban's R.C. School was evacuated from Liverpool to share the school's buildings, a shift system being introduced: local children used the school in the mornings, St. Alban's children and teachers in the afternoons; children under 6 were excluded. Evacuee numbers soon dropped but in 1941 another evacuation of Liverpool children raised St. Alban's numbers to 97 and the church school's to 131. In 1943 St.

Alban's was merged in the church school[50] which became controlled in 1946. In 1969, after the playground subsided, the school, with 66 pupils, moved to the former Coalbrookdale High School premises at Dale End where, in 1971, it was merged in the newly formed Coalbrookdale and Ironbridge C.E. (Aided) Primary School.[51]

Madeley Wesleyan (later Methodist) School, established in 1871, opened in Sunday school buildings erected in 1853 behind the Fletcher Memorial Chapel, Court Street. Attendance at first averaged 52 mixed pupils.[52] In 1903–4 it averaged 154 mixed pupils and 70 infants, and in 1928 there were 187 pupils.[53] The school became a junior mixed and infant school in 1937, when the senior school opened, and was controlled from 1947.[54] It closed in 1967, when there were 107 pupils.[55]

Coalbrookdale County High School (originally Secondary School), Dale End, opened by the county council in 1911 for 75 boys and 75 girls, at first had only 46 boys and 24 girls. The first headmaster, Maurice Jones, had formerly run the private Ironbridge High School and latterly (c. 1909) a fee-paying class in Trinity Hall, Dale End. Though small, the school drew pupils from a wide surrounding area, at times from as far away as Cound and Presthope. The foundation was a dual one, the boys' and girls' schools being separate until 1932 when the girls' headmistress retired and the schools were united. In 1965 the school amalgamated with the modern school at Hill Top to form the Abraham Darby Comprehensive School. The Dale End premises were at first used by the new school's first- and second-year pupils[56] but in 1968, after extensions to the former modern school's premises, the comprehensive school was concentrated at Hill Top.[57]

Madeley Senior Council School, Hill Top, opened in 1937 with 400 mixed places.[58] Known as Madeley Modern School from 1944,[59] it was enlarged 1958–9 and had 619 pupils by the end of 1959. It amalgamated with Coalbrookdale High School in 1965 to form the Abraham Darby Comprehensive School.[60]

Madeley Nursery School, Victoria Road, opened in 1946 in the prefabricated premises of a war-time nursery.[61] It moved to a new building in Bridle Road in 1976.[62] There were 60 pupils in 1980.[63]

[41] McFall, 'Educ. in Madeley Union', 53.
[42] Ibid. 50 n.2, 53; S. Bagshaw, Dir. Salop. (1851), 569, 576.
[43] P. A. James, 'Evolution of Educ. in Ironbridge Gorge, 1780–1880' (Birm. Univ. M.Ed. dissertation, 1981), 40.
[44] P.R.O., ED 7/103, ff. 170–1; S.R.O. 2280/2/45, no. 1397; /48, p. 75 (no. 1397).
[45] Public Elem. Schs. 1906, 543; S.C.C. Mins. (Educ.) 1919–20, 110; 1922–3, 44; 1923–4, 14, 37; 1926–7, 34.
[46] McFall, 'Educ. in Madeley Union', 50; Muter, Coalbrookdale and Ironbridge, 19 (fig. 8), 21, and pl. 28; P.R.O., ED 7/103, ff. 157–8.
[47] Above.
[48] Public Elem. Schs. 1906, 543; S.C.C. Mins. (Educ.) 1928–9, 68.
[49] Above; S.R.O. 2879/1, pp. 159, 161–2.
[50] S.R.O. 2879/1, pp. 202, 207–8, 228–9, 269; /5.
[51] S.C.C. Mins. (Educ.) 1946–7, 23; 1967–8, 306; 1969–70, 30, 118–19; 1970–1, 178; S.C.C. Educ. Cttee. Sch. List (1969), 6; (1972), 10.

[52] P.R.O., ED 7/103, ff. 167–9; O.S. Map 6″, Salop. XLIII. SE. (1903 edn.).
[53] Public Elem. Schs. 1906, 543; S.C.C. Mins. (Educ.) 1928–9, 68.
[54] S.R.O. 2782/14, p. 63; S.C.C. Mins. (Educ.) 1947–8, 21.
[55] S.R.O. 2782/14, pp. 237–8; 3346/3/6.
[56] Shropshire Mag. Jan. 1972, 18; Mar. 1972, 35; Apr. 1972, 28; Kelly's Dir. Salop. (1895–1913); S.R.O. 1681, box 82, agreement, copy deeds, etc., 1908–9; S.C.C. Mins. (Educ.) 1908–9, 152; 1911–12, 44; inf. from Mr. F. W. Lloyd; below.
[57] S.C.C. Mins. (Educ.) 1967–8, 306.
[58] Ibid. 1937–8, 52.
[59] Cf. S.R.O. 2782/39–40; 3346/3/4.
[60] Jackson, 'Madeley', bk. 2A, pp. 210, 212; below.
[61] S.C.C. Mins. (Educ.) 1945–6, 97, 137, 156, 173, 182; 1946–7, 8; Jackson, 'Madeley', bk. 1A, p. 243; inf. from S.C.C.
[62] S.C.C. Mins. (Educ.) 1972–3, 345; S.C.C. Educ. Cttee. Sch. List (1976), 3. [63] Educ. Dir. (1980), 3.

Madeley County Infant School, Upper Road, opened in 1952[64] and had 161 pupils in 1980.[65]

Abraham Darby Comprehensive School, formed in 1965 by amalgamation of Coalbrookdale High School and Madeley Modern School,[66] was concentrated on the latter's site in 1968.[67] There were 1,244 pupils in 1980.[68]

Madeley (Controlled) Junior School, Upper Road, opened next to Madeley County Infant School in 1967.[69] Long-planned, it was a joint C.E. and Methodist school to replace the church school closed in 1967 and the Methodist school closed in 1969; within a few weeks it was named John Fletcher (Controlled) Junior School.[70] There were 291 pupils in 1980.[71]

Alexander Fleming County Infant School, Southgate, Sutton Hill, opened in 1968 and had 150 pupils in 1980.[72]

Alexander Fleming County Junior School, Southgate, Sutton Hill, opened in 1968 and had 303 pupils in 1980.

St. Mary's R.C. (Aided) Primary School, Coronation Crescent, Madeley, opened in 1969 and had 284 pupils in 1980.

Woodside County Junior School, Wensley Green, opened in 1969 and had 284 pupils in 1980.

Woodside County Infant School, Wensley Green, opened in 1969 and had 154 pupils in 1980.

Hills Lane County Primary School opened in 1970. In 1976, when an infant school opened alongside, it became John Randall County Junior School.[73] In 1980 there were 254 pupils.

Madeley Court Comprehensive School, Court Street, opened in 1971 and had 979 pupils in 1980.[74]

Thomas Parker Special School, Brookside, opened in 1971 and had 59 pupils in 1980.[75]

William Reynolds County Junior School, Westbourne, Woodside, opened in 1972 and had 280 pupils in 1980.

William Reynolds County Infant School, Westbourne, Woodside, opened in 1972 and had 169 pupils in 1980.[76]

Holmer Lake County First School, Brookside, opened in 1974 and had 277 pupils in 1980.[77]

Brindleyford County First School, Brookside, opened in 1974 and had 313 pupils in 1980.[78]

John Randall County Infant School, Hills Lane, opened in 1976 and took the infants of the adjacent primary school, which then became a junior school. In 1980 there were 134 pupils.[79]

CHARITIES FOR THE POOR. In 1661 Michael Richards, the vicar, provided for a 5s. rent charge to be paid to five of the poorest people in the parish. Nothing more is known of the charity.[80] By 1674 five charitable sums given for the poor amounted to £22 and produced £1 6s. 5d. in 1674–5. By 1686 the capital was £34 9s. The parish appointed new trustees, among them Basil Brooke, in 1688 and regulated investment of the stock in 1695. The overseers seem to have used the charity money indiscriminately with the poor rate, a fact which may explain the statement in 1716 that the parish had no charities.[81]

The 17th-century charities probably account for at least one of two sums of £30[82] added to a £40 legacy of Basil Brooke (d. 1699) for the parish poor. In 1706 and 1713 cottages, gardens, and other land in Madeley Wood were bought. In the later 18th century the income was distributed in sums of 5s. or less to widows and other poor. About 1796 a house of industry was built on the charity property, and in 1797 the property was in effect exchanged for rent charges of £18 4s. 6d. One Johnson, fl. before 1786, left a 5s. rent charge for five poor widows. By 1820 it had been commuted for £5 which, with £1 arrears, had been banked by the parish charity estate trustees. In the early 19th century the 5s. was distributed with the £18 4s. 6d. as clothing tickets. For over forty years in the mid 19th century, save in the cholera years, the charity income was accumulated as a reserve fund for times of exceptional distress. When the house of industry was sold c. 1878, £750 was added to the charity capital. Distribution resumed in 1879 and the charity was given away as blankets for many years thereafter.[83] Known from 1912 as Madeley United Charities, the income, c. £52 in 1975, was applied for the general benefit of the poor.[84]

James Embery (d. 1827) of Ironbridge left the interest on £50 for the relief of widows.[85] Nothing more is known of the bequest.

In 1839 Mrs. Cotton left the interest on £200 to buy bread for the poor.[86] The income was £5 in 1908, £14 in 1975.

---

[64] Inf. from S.C.C. Educ. Dept.; cf. S.C.C. Mins. (Educ.) 1959–60, 200.

[65] Educ. Dir. (1980), 10.

[66] S.C.C. Mins. (Educ.) 1963–4, 7; S.C.C. Mins. 1964–5, 89, 313.

[67] S.C.C. Mins. (Educ.) 1967–8, 306.

[68] Educ. Dir. (1980), 2.

[69] Inf. from S.C.C. Educ. Dept.

[70] S.R.O. 3346/3/7; S.C.C. Mins. (Educ.) 1959–60, 200; inf. from the Revd. A. G. Kinch.

[71] Educ. Dir. (1980), 10.

[72] This and the next 5 paras. based on ibid. 10–11; inf. from S.C.C. Educ. Dept.

[73] Inf. from the headmaster (1977). Cf. S.C.C. Mins. (Educ.) 1974–5, 184–5.

[74] Inf. from S.C.C. Educ. Dept.; Educ. Dir. (1980), 2.

[75] S.C.C. Mins. (Educ.) 1971–2, 279; 1972–3, 137; Sch. List (1971), 11; Educ. Dir. (1980), 11.

[76] Inf. from S.C.C. Educ. Dept.; Educ. Dir. (1980), 10.

[77] S.C.C. Mins. (Educ.) 1971–2, 279; Sch. List (1974), 10; Educ. Dir. (1980), 9.

[78] S.C.C. Mins. (Educ.) 1970–1, 295; 1971–2, 277; 1972–3, 248; 1973–4, 120; Educ. Dir. (1980), 9.

[79] Inf. from S.C.C. Educ. Dept.; Educ. Dir. (1980), 10.

[80] S.R.O. 2280/8/10. The settlement was revocable.

[81] Ibid. /6/1a, overseers' accts. 1673–1713; H.W.R.O. (H.), Heref. dioc. rec., reply to visit. articles, 1716.

[82] S.R.O. 2280/6/1a, note c. 1686 betw. overseers' accts. for 1683 and 1684, accts. for 1693.

[83] Char. Don. 1786–8, ii, H.C. 511–II, pp. 1040–1 (1816), xvi (2); 3rd Rep. Com. Char. H.C. 5, pp. 306–7 (1820), iv; Randall, Madeley, 217, 242–5; S.R.O. 210/2; 1681, copy lease and deeds of 1797 (boxes 143, 152) and deeds of 1805 (boxes 149, 152); 2280/6/103, inv. of char. deeds; /10/1–4, 7, 10–29, 117–18; Madeley ch. benefaction bd.

[84] S.C.C. chars. index; Review of Local Chars. (S.C.C. 1975), 65.

[85] Madeley ch. benefaction bd.; S.R.O. 2280/BRg/3, p. 185; /10/31.

[86] Rest of section based on Madeley ch. benefaction bd.; S.R.O. 2280/10/32–6, 47–119; 2280/Cha/1; S.C.C. chars. index; Review of Local Chars. 65.

The Bartlett Memorial Charity was founded in 1863 when land was conveyed in trust to be let to the deserving poor of Madeley parish as allotment gardens.[87] In 1975 income from land and stock was £9, surplus funds being used for the benefit of the poor.

The Wilcox Charity, founded by will proved 1865, was to be distributed to twenty or thirty widows of the Madeley Wood area. In 1975 income was £12.

James Mellor's charity, founded in 1870, was endowed with £36 12s. 5d.; half of the interest was to be used for twenty widows aged over sixty.

In the 1880s and 1890s some 10s. a year was so distributed. By 1963 the charity formed part of Madeley United Charities.

By will proved 1871 Edward Edwards left stock for gifts of bread, coal, or clothing, to Church of England widows of Coalbrookdale parish. In 1975 the income of his charity, which included a bequest of Elizabeth Edwards, was £10.

Mrs. Elizabeth Morgan's charity, established 1886, was endowed with £50. Around the turn of the century the annual income of c. £2 10s. was distributed to numerous widows. In 1975 income was £7.

LITTLE WENLOCK

LITTLE Wenlock village lies 4½ km. south of Wellington and 3½ km. west of Dawley.[88] The civil parish, lying immediately west of Dawley (later Telford) new town, was greatly extended in 1966; until then it had formed part of the borough of Wenlock and its boundaries had remained those of the ancient parish, the area here treated.

The ancient boundaries rarely followed watercourses or roads, for in early times Little Wenlock was separated from its neighbours by woodlands in which boundaries seem to have been defined in the 13th century by man-made clearings.[89] At the southernmost tip the boundary followed Birches brook and a tributary. Except for a narrow arm of territory extending northwards from the northeast corner, the ancient parish was compact in shape. It covered 2,764 a.[90] (1,119 ha.). The parish's western edge lies on the flank of the Wrekin, at a height of c. 245 metres above O.D. A small valley along the base of the slope separates the Wrekin from an eastern outlier, called Darrow Hill in 1839,[91] which occupies the north-west quarter of the parish and rises to 258 metres above O.D., the parish's highest point. The ground descends gradually from it southwards and eastwards to the parish boundaries. The ancient parish's northern edge lay along an east–west watershed at c. 235 metres above O.D., a long eastern spur of Maddock's Hill (in Wellington parish). Streams from the sides of Darrow Hill and the spur, flowing through valleys southwards and eastwards, drain almost all the parish, several of them converging on Lyde brook. The undulating landscape was always predominantly agricultural, but before the 19th century the eastern half was marked by many small coalpits and in 1980 by post-war opencast workings. The high terrain, well wooded in parts and without main roads or large settlements, gave most of the parish a character of quiet seclusion in the late 20th

century, especially by contrast with its neighbour Telford.

The presence of early man is suggested by two hoards of Bronze Age weapons found in the parish's north-west corner, at Willowmoor, c. 1790 and in 1834.[92] A nearby group of mounds, however, may be of natural origin.[93] A burial place below the Wrekin was noted in 975,[94] apparently where Little Wenlock and Wroxeter parishes met Aston township.[95] The parish probably took the Celtic main component of its name from Much Wenlock,[96] a few kilometres away, and the presence of Celtic speakers at Little Wenlock cannot be inferred from it.

In 1727 there were three principal roads out of the parish, beginning at Little Wenlock or Huntington; the short Huntington Lane[97] linked the two places.[98] Of the three the only one still used as a highway in 1980, Spout Lane, ran west from Little Wenlock to Shrewsbury; it formed the parish boundary south of Wrekin wood and was mentioned in 1232.[99] By the 1320s another of the three ran south from Little Wenlock to Buildwas bridge[1] and thence to Much Wenlock; known as Buildwas Lane in 1980, it was then only a track. The third road ran north-west from Huntington to Wellington, by way of the Hatch. It was superseded in the 19th century[2] by the road from Little Wenlock to Wellington, which in 1727 had been only a cartway as it left the parish.

Another cartway, from Huntington to Arleston, had been a highway (alta via) in 1301[3] and formed the western boundary of the parish's northern arm. The growth of a mining settlement later revived its importance, as New Works Lane. Cartways from Little Wenlock to Coalbrookdale and Horsehay assumed importance only in the later 18th century as settlements there developed; minerals were usually taken by waggonway.[4]

The Wellington–Coalbrookdale turnpike road

[87] O.S. Nat. Grid SJ 698 040.
[88] This art. was written 1980 and revised 1982–3. Thanks are due to Mr. N. J. Clarke for his comments on it in draft.
[89] Below, Econ. Hist.
[90] Census, 1951, Co. Rep. Herefs. and Salop. 8.
[91] S.R.O. 2142/1, 3.
[92] SA 1779–80.
[93] SA 1781.
[94] Cart. Sax. ed. Birch, iii, no. 1315.
[95] O.S. Nat. Grid SJ 629 077. But cf. T.S.A.S. lvi. 32–3.

[96] E. Ekwall, Concise Oxf. Dict. Eng. P.N. (4th edn.), 506.
[97] So called by 1982: local inf.
[98] In this section details of rds. in 1727 are based on S.R.O. 1224/1/59.
[99] Cal. Close, 1231–4, 94.   [1] S.R.O. 1224/2/10.
[2] The Huntington–Wellington route is the only one marked in R. Baugh, Map of Salop. (1808).
[3] Cartulary of Shrews. Abbey, ed. U. Rees (1975), ii, p. 247.
[4] Below, Econ. Hist.

authorized in 1817[5] crossed the parish's northern extremity and its eastern edge. It was the parish's only classified road in 1980. The principal unclassified roads were those from Little Wenlock to Wellington and Horsehay.[6]

There were six alesellers in the late 1780s,[7] and in the earlier 19th century many public houses. In 1839 Little Wenlock had five, Coalmoor three, Horsehay two, and Huntington and Smalleyhill one each.[8] By 1881[9] there remained only the Swan (closed by 1901)[10] and the Spread Eagles (closed 1958)[11] at Little Wenlock, and the All Labour in Vain, Horsehay (still open in 1980). The Huntsman opened in Little Wenlock c. 1964.[12]

In 1803 there were six friendly societies, with 246 members.[13] By 1812–13 membership had fallen to 140, but it rose to 162 in 1814–15.[14] The societies included one formed at Little Wenlock in 1791, another formed at Coalmoor in 1801, and a Union Society formed in 1812, which met at Smalleyhill. A Beneficial Society, formed in 1845, met at the Spread Eagles.[15]

There was a church room belonging to Lord Forester[16] opposite the church by 1895. The vestry[17] and the parochial church council[18] met there, and in 1898 it was open for recreation on Saturdays.[19] Social gatherings were held in the school until 1934 when a new village hall opened south-east of the village.[20] A local committee raised the money[21] and Lord Forester contributed the proceeds from the sale of the church room.[22] The National Coal Board provided a large hall near the village centre in 1963 and demolished the old one in advance of opencast working.[23] A youth club formed in 1942[24] later lapsed; in 1980 it had recently been revived, the number of young people having increased.[25]

GROWTH OF SETTLEMENT. In the Middle Ages the only centres of population were Little Wenlock, the manorial and ecclesiastical centre, and Huntington, always a smaller place. Eight inhabitants were recorded in 1086.[26] By the 1320s there were 42 tenants[27] but in 1540 only 24;[28] in both periods undertenants seem to have gone unrecorded. In 1642 the protestation was taken by all 82 men in the parish who were over 18. In 1660

there were 147 poll-tax payers, 31 of them at Huntington,[29] and 174 adult inhabitants were returned in 1676.[30] In the 18th century workers' cottages were built in brick in the industrial parts of the parish. The population, 980 in 1801, fell to 941 by 1811,[31] perhaps because of a reduction of coalmining in the parish.[32] The opening of the Lawley ironworks in 1822[33] and the expansion of coalmining in neighbouring parishes[34] caused Little Wenlock's population to rise to 1,091 by 1841, when there were 202 inhabited houses.[35] There was a gradual decline 1841–61. A sharp drop (988 to 783) 1861–71 was probably due to the closure of Lawley ironworks.[36] Further industrial closures in neighbouring parishes[37] and agricultural depression combined to cause large-scale emigration from the parish between 1871 and 1891, when the population fell to 420. It remained at that level for sixty years or more.[38] The number of houses halved 1841–91.[39] The unemployed who remained suffered severe privation.[40] From the 1960s, however, with the development of Dawley (later Telford) new town on its boundaries, the parish became an attractive rural home for middle-class newcomers, whose influence on the character of its buildings, though not on the size of its settlements, was marked.

Little Wenlock village occupies a south-east spur of what was called Darrow Hill (c. 220 metres above O.D.) in the centre of the parish, with extensive views south, east, and west. By 1727, and probably much earlier, its houses and farms lay close together along the arms of a T formed by the junction of the roads to Shrewsbury (west), Much Wenlock (south), and Wellington via Huntington (east). The church, rectory, and Old Hall (the former manor house) lay at the end of the southern arm, on which stood also the capital messuages of the Smitheman and Warham estates. It therefore seems likely that the village had grown from that single street. By the later Middle Ages the outer ends of the eastern and southern arms were linked by a curving lane, called the Alley, along which by 1727 stood more houses,[41] including a cruck-framed cottage (standing in 1983).

By 1980 the early 18th-century pattern had hardly changed, though since the Second World

[5] Below, Wellington, Communications.

[6] O.S. Map 1/50,000, sheet 127 (1977 edn.).

[7] S.R.O. 1224, box 206, man. ct. presentments of 1787, 1789.   [8] S.R.O. 2142/1.

[9] O.S. Map 6″, Salop. XLIII. NW. (1889 edn.).

[10] Ibid. (1903 edn.).

[11] M. E. R. Jackson, 'Notes on Hist. of Madeley' (microfilm in S.P.L.), bk. 3A, p. 91.

[12] S.R.O. 1490/1, p. 126.

[13] Abstr. Rel. to Poor, H.C. 175, p. 423 (1803–4), xiii.

[14] Abstr. Rel to Poor, H.C. 82, p. 377 (1818), xix.

[15] S.R.O., q. sess. rec. parcel 285, friendly socs. reg., s.vv. Coalmoor and Wenlock, L.; Registrar of Friendly Socs. List of Friendly Socs. in Co. of Salop, 1793–1855 (H.M.S.O. 1857), pp. 9, 39 (copy in S.R.O.).

[16] Par. rec., vestry min. bk. 1818–1958, 17 Apr. 1935.

[17] Ibid. passim.

[18] Par. rec., P.C.C. min. bk. 1929–44, passim.

[19] L. Wenlock Par. Mag. Jan. 1898 (copy in par. rec.).

[20] Local inf.

[21] Shrews. Chron. 26 Oct. 1934.

[22] Par. rec., vestry min. bk. 1818–1958, 17 Apr. 1935.

[23] Local inf.

[24] Par. rec., youth club min. bk. 1942–4.

[25] Local inf.

[26] V.C.H. Salop. i. 312.

[27] S.R.O. 1224/2/10. For the date see below, Econ. Hist. (Agric.).

[28] P.R.O., SC 6/Hen. VIII/3021, mm. 10d–11d.

[29] Ho. of Lords papers 1641–2, Protestations Oxon. and Salop. f. 200; P.R.O., E 179/168/219, mm. 17d.–18.

[30] T.S.A.S. 2nd ser. i. 91.

[31] V.C.H. Salop. ii. 229.

[32] Below, Econ. Hist.

[33] Ibid.

[34] V.C.H. Salop. ii. 230.

[35] S. Bagshaw, Dir. Salop. (1851), 566.

[36] V.C.H. Salop. ii. 229, 233; below, Econ. Hist.

[37] Above, Madeley, Econ. Hist.; below, Dawley and Wellington, Econ. Hist.

[38] V.C.H. Salop. ii. 229. There are no separate figs. for the ancient par. after 1951.

[39] Census, 1891, Area, Hos., and Pop. i. 302.

[40] I. Gregory, 'E. Salop. Coalfield and the "Gt. Depression" 1873–96' (Keele Univ. M.A. thesis, 1978), 177.

[41] S.R.O. 1224/1/59; below, plate 56.

War there had been much in-filling with private houses, and some of the old ones had been lavishly improved. Private houses of good quality had been built on the west, along Spout Lane,

ground (*c.* 220 metres above O.D.) in the north on the upper Lyde brook. In 1727 it consisted of four farms and some cottages,[43] about the same number of dwellings as were there in the early 14th[44]

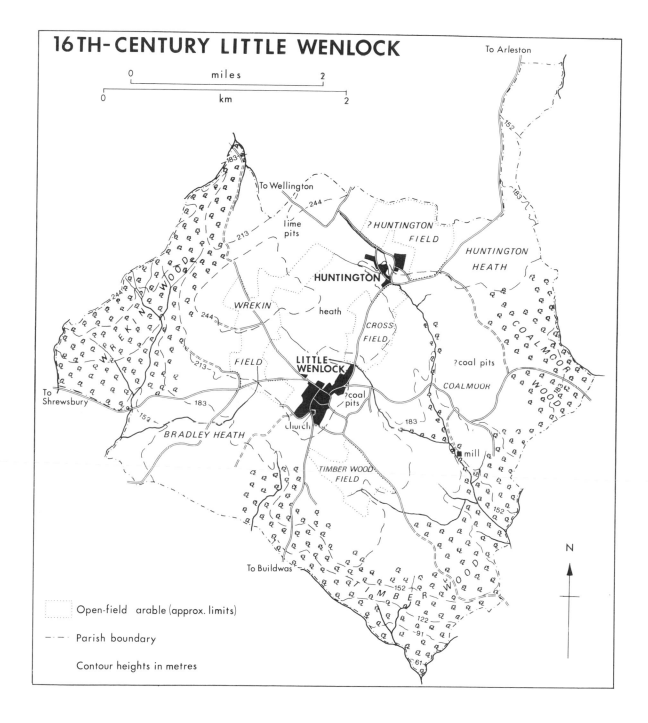

16TH-CENTURY LITTLE WENLOCK

To Arleston

miles

km

To Wellington

HUNTINGTON

lime pits

?HUNTINGTON FIELD

HUNTINGTON HEATH

WREKIN

heath

CROSS FIELD

COALMOOR

WOOD

FIELD

LITTLE WENLOCK

?coal pits

?coal pits

COALMOOR

To Shrewsbury

church

To Buildwas

BRADLEY HEATH

TIMBER WOOD FIELD

mill

TIMBER WOOD

N

Open-field arable (approx. limits)

Parish boundary

Contour heights in metres

and on the south, off Witchwell Lane. There was a block of three council houses, and a group of old people's bungalows had been provided.

Huntington, existing by 1190,[42] stands on high

and early 16th[45] centuries. They were linked by an irregular triangle of lanes,[46] through which the brook ran. By 1839 a few houses had been added southwards in Huntington Lane,[47] and by 1980

[42] *Cart. Shrews.* ii, p. 354.
[43] S.R.O. 1224/1/59.
[44] Ibid. /2/10.

[45] S.R.O. 1224, box 342, Prior Gosnell's reg., f. 38.
[46] S.R.O. 1224/1/59.
[47] S.R.O. 2142/3.

the buildings in that part included two modern private houses. Huntington nevertheless remained a loosely knit hamlet rather than a village.

Of the small groups of workmen's and miners' cottages that had been built by 1839 in the eastern half of the parish, as at Coalmoor, Huntington heath, Little Worth, Lawley Furnaces, and Smalleyhill,[48] the most populous was probably New Works, which had attained its full extent by 1798.[49] The cottages straggled along both sides of the southern end of the lane to Arleston, where it formed the western boundary of the parish's northern arm. They included at least two brick rows by 1798, which survived in 1980 though thoroughly modernized. New Works changed little in the 19th and earlier 20th century,[50] but by 1980 there had been much recent modernization and in-filling with small private houses and bungalows.

MANOR AND OTHER ESTATES. In 1066 *LITTLE WENLOCK* belonged to the church of Wenlock[51] and it remained with Wenlock priory until the Dissolution.[52] Wenlock held the manor of the Crown except during the years between c. 1074 and 1102 when it held its estates of the earls of Shrewsbury.[53]

In 1545 Anthony Foster bought the manor from the Crown[54] on behalf of James Leveson of Lilleshall.[55] It descended with Lilleshall manor until 1590 when it was bought by Sir Rowland Hayward,[56] a former lord mayor of London.[57] After his death in 1593[58] it passed successively to his widow Catherine[59] (d. by 1608),[60] their son George (kt. 1604, d. 1615), and Sir George's brother John[61] (kt. 1619),[62] who in 1623 sold it to Francis Forester[63] (d. 1637) of Watling Street, already a freeholder in the parish.[64] From Francis it descended through his son Francis[65] (bur. 1665)[66] to his grandson, also Francis Forester[67] (d. 1692),[68] who agreed in 1684 to sell it next year to his son William[69] (kt. 1689; d. 1718).[70] It sub-

sequently passed in the direct male line, to William's son William (d. 1758),[71] grandson Brooke (d. 1774), who had been allotted part of the estate from 1735,[72] and great-grandson George[73] (d.s.p 1811).[74] George left the manor and estate to his cousin Cecil Forester of Rossall,[75] who then adopted the additional surname of Weld. He was created Baron Forester in 1821 and died in 1828.[76] Thereafter the manor descended with the peerage. In 1917 both passed to the 6th baron,[77] who in 1918 sold all the manorial estate, partly to the sitting tenants and partly by auction.[78] In 1981 the ownership of any manorial rights was unknown.[79]

A manor house existed by the 1320s,[80] probably on the site of the Old Hall, capital messuage of the Hayward estate by the later 17th century.[81]

In 1309 John of Charlton sued the prior of Wenlock for 4½ virgates at Huntington,[82] and a few small freeholds existed in the earlier 14th century.[83]

In 1544 the Crown sold a large part of the parish to Thomas Sheldon and Lawrence Poyner, acting for John Forester the younger, of Watling Street.[84] At Forester's death in 1591 his heir was his grandson Francis Forester,[85] who bought the manorial estate in 1623.

In 1623 Sir John Hayward, before selling the manor to Forester, conveyed two (or possibly three) portions of the manorial estate to other purchasers. One was sold to his cousins[86] George and William, sons of William Hayward.[87] By 1666 it had passed to William Hayward 'the younger'[88] (d. 1708).[89] It afterwards descended to his son William[90] (d. 1727) and then to his son William (d. 1763), a serjeant at law.[91] Though he owned some property in the parish in 1763,[92] he had sold most of his estate there to William Forester,[93] apparently in 1754.[94]

The Haywards' capital messuage, called the Old Hall by 1980, stands east of the church.[95] Part of a small medieval stone house may remain in the north-west corner of the building, much of which consists of part of a 16th- or early 17th-century

48 Ibid. /2–3; P.R.O., RG 10/2753, ff. 6–7, 9 and v., 18 and v., 21, 23v.–24v.
49 S.R.O. 1224, box 259, deed (with annexed map).
50 S.R.O. 2142/2; O.S. Map 6″, Salop. XLIII. NW. (1889, 1903, and 1928 edns.).
51 V.C.H. Salop. i. 312. Arguments for Wenlock's ownership in 975 appear in T.S.A.S. lvi. 32.
52 V.C.H. Salop. ii. 45.   53 Ibid. i. 291; iii. 7, 10.
54 L. & P. Hen. VIII, xx (1), p. 424.
55 Ibid. (2), p. 546.
56 S.P.L., MS. 4646, p. 133.
57 T.S.A.S. 4th ser. v. 53.
58 P.R.O., C 142/241, no. 125.   59 Ibid. /363, no. 194.
60 B.L. Add. Ch. 5437.
61 P.R.O., C 142/363, no. 194.
62 T.S.A.S. 4th ser. v. 53.
63 S.R.O. 1224, box 224, deed of 1651.
64 Ibid. box 264, deed of 1622.
65 P.R.O., C 142/483, no. 46.
66 T.S.A.S. 2nd ser. iii. 166.
67 In possession by 1673: S.R.O. 1224, box 208, deed.
68 S.P.L., MS. 2790, p. 277.
69 S.R.O. 1224, box 264, deed of 1684.
70 W. A. Shaw, Kts. of Eng. (1906), ii. 265; T.S.A.S. 2nd ser. iii. 168–70.
71 T.S.A.S. 2nd ser. iii. 172; S.R.O. 1224, box 268, deed of 1714.
72 S.R.O. 1224, box 270, deed of 1735; box 274, deed of 1741; Burke, Peerage (1938), 1035.
73 S.R.O. 1224, box 270, deed of 1735.
74 T.S.A.S. 2nd ser. iii. 174.
75 S.R.O. 1224, box 272, will of 1805. In possession 1811: ibid. box 206, man. ct. presentments.
76 T.S.A.S. 2nd ser. iii. 177.
77 S.R.O. 1224, box 272, Geo. Forester's will, 1805; box 291, wills of 1st and 2nd barons, 1821 and 1872; 1681, box 36, abstr. of title of 1918.
78 S.R.O. 1681, box 44, sale plans; parcel 46, sale partic. Conveyance of the auctioned lots was to be effected in 1919.
79 Inf. from Ld. Forester.   80 S.R.O. 1224/2/10.
81 Below.
82 Pedigrees from the Plea Rolls, ed. G. Wrottesley (1905), 547.
83 Cal. Pat. 1327–30, 473–4; 1345–8, 452.
84 L. & P. Hen. VIII, xix (2), pp. 187, 197.
85 P.R.O., C 142/228, no. 85.
86 S.P.L., MS. 4646, p. 133.
87 S.R.O. 1224, box 224, deed of 1651. A Wm. Hayward, with a son Geo., d. as patron of the living 1640: P.R.O., C 142/499, no. 32.
88 S.R.O. 1339/7.
89 S.P.L., MS. 4646, p. 133.
90 In possession 1722: S.R.O. 516/12. The est.'s extent in 1727 is shown on S.R.O. 1224/1/59 (map).
91 S.P.L., MS. 4646, p. 133.
92 S.R.O. 1224, box 258, deed.
93 Ibid. box 314, Lady Day rental of 1769.
94 Ibid. box 257, deed of 1754; box 259, Wm. Ferriday to —, 4 Jan. 1755.
95 S.R.O. 1224/1/59.

two-storeyed stone house, to which were added, about the mid 17th century, symmetrical canted bays east and west. A fire destroyed the east end of the house in the early 18th century.[96] Between 1708 and 1727[97] the remaining parts were extended east and north in brick.

In 1623 Sir John Hayward sold another portion, comprising 34 a. of arable and 40 a. of pasture, with meadow and woodland, to William Warham of the Birches.[98] In 1678 William's third son,[99] William Warham of Whittimere, sold it to his nephew[1] William Whitmore (d. 1700) of Shipley.[2] By 1714 the estate belonged to the lord of the manor.[3] The Warhams' capital messuage was probably the house known in 1980 as the Stone House,[4] near the north end of Little Wenlock's main street. Built in 1661,[5] it has a front of three bays, with end stacks and a gabled rear elevation.

A third estate, perhaps bought by John Smitheman (d. 1667) in 1623,[6] certainly belonged to his son John by 1669.[7] On John Smitheman's death in 1689[8] the estate presumably passed to his son John (d. 1709) and thence to his son John (d. 1733) and to his son John Unett (d. 1744),[9] who left it to his son John Smitheman (d. 1809) of West Coppice. He left it to his grandson J. T. Smitheman Edwardes, who sold the estate, c. 152 a., to Lord Forester in 1825.[10] The Smithemans' capital messuage, called the Manor House in 1980, stands in the middle of Little Wenlock village.[11] It is a late 17th-century two-storeyed brick building,[12] formerly a wing added to a timber-framed two-storeyed house[13] that was demolished between 1918 and 1925.[14] In 1689 the Smitheman house had a parlour and 'dwelling house' downstairs and three rooms above.[15]

ECONOMIC HISTORY. AGRICULTURE. It seems likely that in the Anglo-Saxon period the manor was predominantly wooded with few inhabitants, their economy based in great part on pig rearing. In 1086 the estate was rated at 3 hides. Its value fell from 70s. in 1066 to 40s. in 1086. There was only one ploughteam in demesne with three more between four villeins and two bordars. There was, however, woodland for fattening 300 swine,[16] a large number by Shropshire standards.[17] The woods against the Wrekin were intensively used for pasture and pannage, to which pigs were sometimes brought from distant estates. Wenlock priory's rights to pannage in the Wrekin woods were defined in 1190[18] but only in 1234 were Little Wenlock's common rights in the woods delimited from its neighbours':[19] linear clearings (trencheas)[20] were then renewed in the woods bordering Buildwas, Madeley, Dawley, and Wellington, and in the Wrekin wood above the road from Little Wenlock to Shrewsbury.[21]

The manor was in the royal forest of Mount Gilbert until 1301[22] but under a charter of Richard I it was held to be exempt from waste and the regard of the forest.[23] Parts of the manor were reserved for hunting in the 11th century and Huntington may have been the huntsmen's tun.[24] In 1086 the manor's wood included two hays and a hawk's nest.[25] The presence of Domesday bordars with a share in the ploughteams, however, suggests that assarting was in progress,[26] and there seems to have been much assarting in the later 12th century.[27]

In the 1320s the manor's customary holdings, probably open-field arable, consisted of 15 half-virgates, 17 quarter-virgates (called nooks), and 2 half-nooks.[28] One tenant held 2 half-virgates, two others a half-virgate and a nook each, two 2 nooks, and the rest one tenement each.[29] Until recently each half-virgate had owed the same labour services: 'pool work' at Martinmas, three days' ploughing a year, a day's mowing, four days' reaping, carriage with one beast to the priory from Little Wenlock and Sutton (near Shrewsbury), and haulage of timber from Timber wood towards the priory as far as Buildwas bridge. The holding also rendered fixed quantities of corn, oats, geese, and hens. Nooks and half-nooks owed proportionate fractions. Each tenant owed suit of court and paid tallage, and on his death a heriot was due, with a third of his movables, called terciary, an exaction usual on the priory's estates.[30] The labour services were given a money value but in 1291 commutation was unusual.

[96] Local inf.
[97] The arms of Hayward impaling Bailey are in plaster at the head of the stairs. Wm. Hayward (d. 1727) inherited his father's est. 1708, having married Mary Bailey by 1699: S.P.L., MS. 4646, p. 133.
[98] S.R.O. 1224, boxes 224 and 227, deeds.
[99] S.P.L., MS. 2795, p. 253.
[1] S.P.L., MS. 4645, pp. 168–9.
[2] S.R.O. 1224, box 227, deed.
[3] Ibid. box 274, deed.
[4] H. E. Forrest, Old Hos. of Wenlock (Shrews. 1914), 110; S.P.L., accession 6634 (Hayward scrapbk.), p. 3.
[5] Date formerly on chimney stack: S.P.L., accession 6634, p. 3; local inf.
[6] H.W.R.O.(H.), Heref. dioc. rec., par. reg. transcript of 1667–8.
[7] S.R.O. 1224, box 227, deed.
[8] H.W.R.O.(H.), Heref. dioc. rec., inv. of John Smitheman, 1689.
[9] S.P.L., MS. 2790, p. 387. The est.'s extent in 1727 is shown on S.R.O. 1224/1/59 (map).
[10] S.R.O. 1224, box 225, abstr. of title and deed.
[11] S.R.O. 1224/1/59.
[12] SA 12824. John Smitheman had 5,000 bricks when he d. in 1689: H.W.R.O.(H.), Heref. dioc. rec., inv. of John Smitheman, 1689.
[13] Forrest, Old Hos. of Wenlock, 107, and photo. facing p. 112.

[14] S.R.O. 1681, parcel 46, sale partic. p. 41; O.S. Map 1/2,500, Salop. XLIII. 5 (1927 edn.).
[15] H.W.R.O.(H.), Heref. dioc. rec., inv. of John Smitheman, 1689.
[16] V.C.H. Salop. i. 312.
[17] Ibid. 483.
[18] Cart. Shrews. ii, p. 354.
[19] Ibid. p. 353.
[20] See O. Rackham, Ancient Woodland (1980), 155.
[21] Close R. 1231–4, 94.
[22] Cart. Shrews. ii, p. 249.
[23] Eyton. ix. 145; V.C.H. Salop. i. 488; ii. 40.
[24] Ekwall, Concise Oxf. Dict. Eng. P.N. 258.
[25] V.C.H. Salop. i. 312.
[26] S. P. J. Harvey, 'Evidence for Settlement Study: Domesday Bk.' Medieval Settlement, ed. P. H. Sawyer (1976), 197–9.
[27] Eyton, iii. 324.
[28] The following acct. of the man. in the 1320s is based on S.R.O. 1224/2/10. Its date is between 1321, when Hen. of Caerwent received his cottage (S.R.O. 1037/19/1), and 1330, when Ric. Dod had ceased to be rector (Eyton, iii. 328). The one illegible entry is assumed from its position to refer to a ½-virgate.
[29] The customary holdings totalled 12 virgates, or 3 hides, the man.'s 1086 assessment.
[30] V.C.H. Salop. ii. 43. For the Eng. form of Lat. terciaria see S.R.O. 1224, box 256, deed of 1669.

About 1300 the priory ceased to cultivate the demesne and let it in small lots to the customary tenants. It was never resumed thereafter. As labour services were thus superfluous the customary holdings were converted to leaseholds (for some of the larger ones) and copyholds. The labour services were commuted to cash but the other renders and dues continued. In the mid 15th century the copyholder had also to pay a 2s. surrender fine called 'varneth'.[31] In the 1320s each tenancy was for the lives of the tenant, his wife, and their eldest child.

As well as the customary holding the tenant sometimes rented additional land, as 'acres' (perhaps in separate plots) from the demesne or elsewhere and as acres of 'new' land, probably on former wastes. One piece of 'new' land was at Coalmoor gate, probably where open fields had bordered the waste.

There were two large free tenants in the 1320s. The rector held a lease of the manor house and 30 a. (probably of the demesne) for 20s. rent and terciary. Thomas Foreman, besides a half-virgate and a large portion of demesne, held a house and land by 'perpetual charter' for 8s. rent, grain renders, suit of Bourton 'hundred', and terciary. There remained three tenants who held only 'new' land: one of them 19 a. Six others held only cottages, sometimes with a few acres of land.

As a result of the recent changes about £19 was paid in cash rents in the 1320s, against less than £2 in 1291.[32]

The end of demesne cultivation probably denoted serious agricultural difficulties. Moreover by 1341 the corn had been destroyed by storms, there were no sheep, and much arable lay fallow.[33] In 1370 cash rents totalled little more than £4.[34] By 1390, however, they were over £12.[35] An improvement during the 15th century gave rents (including small annual supplements in lieu of terciary) totalling just under £15 in 1510–11.[36]

In the later Middle Ages arable occupied only a small proportion of the parish, about a fifth in 1623.[37] There were said to be three fields in 1589:[38] Wrekin field north-west of the village (mentioned in the 1320s),[39] Cross (or Lyde) field north-east (mentioned 1540),[40] and probably Timber Wood field south-east (mentioned 1604).[41] Quarry field existed in 1604,[42] perhaps as a fragment of Timber Wood field.[43] Huntington field in 1607 seems to have been the same as Wrekin field.[44] Field-names north of Huntington in 1727[45] nevertheless suggest the former presence of some arable (not necessarily open) occupied exclusively by inhabitants of Huntington.

Inclosure of the open-field arable was probably piecemeal. In 1322 a tenant was licensed to inclose one selion.[46] The process, however, was still incomplete in 1727, when 12 a. of Wrekin field and three small fragments of Cross field remained open.[47]

In 1291 only one acre of demesne meadow was recorded.[48] In the 1320s there were some meadows held in severalty, but apparently no common meadows.[49] In 1607 the glebe included two pieces of meadow inclosed out of Wrekin and Timber Wood fields,[50] and most of the streams had meadows by them in the early 18th century, in scattered parcels. On the Forester estate they totalled over 170 a.[51]

Between and beyond the arable fields in the later Middle Ages lay common wastes and common woodlands, together covering about two thirds of the parish. Neglect of the dead hedges separating open fields and waste was frequently punished in the 14th and 15th centuries.[52] There were four main areas of waste. One lay south-west of Little Wenlock, where Bradley heath, Hither lea, and Marlemore[53] were mentioned as commons.[54] Coalmoor, east of Little Wenlock, was another, to judge by its name. A large heath lay north of the village, west of Huntington Lane, and north-east of Huntington lay Huntington heath, with Wildermoore nearby.[55]

Inclosure of the heaths, mostly for pasture, was in progress by 1380 when a hay in Marlemore was mentioned.[56] There were several hays in the earlier 16th century.[57] Some commonable wastes remained in 1551 but tenants had to pay to use them,[58] and in 1589 the rector had no common for cattle or sheep outside the open fields.[59]

Beyond the fields and heaths and stretching to the manorial boundaries were three uninclosed woods in the later Middle Ages: Wrekin wood on the west (estimated at 220 a. in 1545), Coalmoor wood on the east (180 a.), and Timber wood on the south (200 a.).[60] The manorial tenants kept many pigs. In 1379 23 tenants rented pannage for 200 swine and in the 15th century herds tended to become larger and fewer.[61] Large numbers were still being kept in 1541.[62] Individual herds varied greatly in size; the largest in 1449 contained 37 animals.[63]

[31] S.R.O. 1224/2/8–9.
[32] *Tax. Eccl.* (Rec. Com.), 164.
[33] *Inq. Non.* (Rec. Com.), 187.
[34] B.L. Add. MS. 6165, f. 51v.
[35] S.R.O. 1224, box 342, Prior Gosnell's reg., f. 35v.
[36] Ibid. f. 38.
[37] S.R.O. 1224, box 224, deed of 1650.
[38] H.W.R.O.(H.), Heref. dioc. rec., glebe terrier.
[39] S.R.O. 1224/2/10.
[40] P.R.O., SC 6/Hen. VIII/3021, m. 10d.; LR 2/184, f. 157.
[41] H.W.R.O.(H.), Heref. dioc. rec., glebe terrier.
[42] Ibid.
[43] A field named Quarry lay S. of the village in 1727: S.R.O. 1224/1/59.
[44] H.W.R.O.(H.), Heref. dioc. rec., glebe terrier.
[45] S.R.O. 1224/1/59.
[46] S.R.O. 1037/19/1.
[47] S.R.O. 1224/1/59; 1224, box 295, L. Wenlock survey.
[48] *Tax. Eccl.* (Rec. Com.), 164.
[49] S.R.O. 1224/2/10.
[50] H.W.R.O.(H.), Heref. dioc. rec., glebe terrier.
[51] S.R.O. 1224/1/59; 1224, box 295, L. Wenlock survey.
[52] S.R.O. 1224/2/1, 4, 6–9.
[53] Called Marlmers in 1833: O.S. Map 1″, sheet 61 NE. (1833 edn.).
[54] S.R.O. 1224/2/4; P.R.O., LR 2/184, ff. 104 and v., 157–158v.; SC 6/Hen. VIII/3021, m. 10d. See S.R.O. 1224/1/59 for locations.
[55] S.R.O. 1224/1/59.
[56] Ibid. /2/4.
[57] Ibid. /1/59; T. F. Dukes, *Antiquities of Salop.* (1844), 95–6; P.R.O., SC 6/Hen. VIII/3021, m. 11.
[58] P.R.O., LR 2/184, f. 104 and v.
[59] H.W.R.O.(H.), Heref. dioc. rec., glebe terrier.
[60] P.R.O., E 318/875, m. 2.
[61] S.R.O. 1190, box 23, ct. r.; 1224/2/4, 8–9.
[62] S.R.O. 1224/2/14, m. 4.
[63] Ibid. /2/9.

In the 13th century only Timber wood, as its name suggests, was regularly exploited for building material. It was the manor's nearest woodland to Wenlock priory, and tenants owed haulage of timber from it to the priory.[64] The tenants' common rights prevented woodland management in most of the woods. In 1545 nearly half the estimated 600 a. were 'waste' or 'destroyed'. Another tenth, reserved to the commoners, had no usable timber. The rest had timber of 60–100 years' growth but the commoners had consumed most new growth.[65] Sir Walter Leveson inclosed all the woodland,[66] presumably between 1573[67] and 1590, thus curtailing the commoners' rights.

Between the earlier 14th century and the earlier 16th tenures changed. The demesne lands had been reunited under a single lessee by 1520. In 1540, as in the 1320s, some tenants were leaseholders and the rest copyholders.[68] By 1540, however, the leases were for terms of 50–81 years. Most copyholds were still for lives, but a few were also for long terms of years. There were only two tenures at will, both insignificant.

In 1540 there were 21 farms, a few with cottages attached: 7 were leaseholds paying rents just over 20s., 13 were small copyholds with rents averaging c. 12s. 6d., and one was a large copyhold paying 31s. 4d. There were 2 separate cottage holdings. Terciary had been commuted and included in rents; annual 'wood silver' of 4d. or 8d. was also included.[69]

By the later 17th century rents had increased greatly. In 1688 c. 30 of the 45 holdings paid rents averaging less than 30s. and were evidently cottages and smallholdings. The larger farm rents averaged £16 10s. The highest for one holding was £30. Most tenants had a single holding, but one paid £30 for a large farm with two smaller holdings, and another held two large farms for £28.[70] Leases were usually for 99 years terminable on three or fewer lives. Heriot was still payable.[71] By the end of the 17th century clearance and inclosure had broken down the three blocks of woodland into several separate woods.[72] In the earlier 18th century they were exploited for charcoal and mining timber.[73]

By 1727 half the agricultural holdings on the Forester estate (excluding the diminutive remnants of open fields) were cottages averaging less

than ¼ a., and were clearly distinct from the next largest group, 18 holdings averaging 39 a. Above them, and less clearly distinct, were 7 holdings averaging 131 a.[74] All the biggest farms and most of the smaller ones were run from houses in Little Wenlock or Huntington, and each was fragmented owing to the accidents of piecemeal inclosure and partial consolidation. Nevertheless seven of the smaller farms, totalling c. 260 a., lay in discrete blocks near the edges of the parish, their houses set amid their fields. They included the Wrekin, Willowmoor, and Leasows farms,[75] evidently the newest and created in single operations out of woodland or waste.

In the later 17th and earlier 18th centuries the farmers practised a mixed economy of dairying, sheep, and cereals[76] as in neighbouring parishes.[77] The substantial farmers included a few tradesmen. Herds of cattle averaged about 10 animals, and the largest recorded had 28. Herds consisted mostly of oxen, used as draught animals,[78] and cows, heifers, and immature beasts. Bullocks too were kept, but not necessarily for beef.[79] Some of the larger farmers made cheese in commercial quantities. Less substantial people often had one or two domestic cows. Sheep flocks averaged about 15 animals, rather fewer than in some nearby parishes. Several large farmers had no sheep, and the largest recorded flock had only 38. Horses, however, were kept by rather more of the people than in some neighbouring parishes, and one farmer had eight. Substantial farms, and a few of the smaller holdings, usually had pigs. The average was about 3 animals, and 9 was the most recorded except for the 15 that belonged to a butcher in 1745.

Wheat, barley, and oats were the usual cereals, and mixed grains were equally used, especially hard corn, a mixture of wheat and rye.[80] Peas were common and clover was first mentioned in the 1720s, as elsewhere.[81] Most farmers also had hay, and in 1727 the Forester estate had at least 16 hemp butts.[82]

By 1727 convertible husbandry was general on the farms of the Forester estate,[83] and 18th-century leases, standardized by 1757,[84] required crops to be sown 'in course and not out of turn'. A maximum of four (sometimes three) successive crops was stipulated and clover had to be sown

[64] Ibid. /2/10.   [65] P.R.O., E 318/875, m. 2.
[66] H.W.R.O. (H.). Heref. dioc. rec., glebe terrier of 1607.
[67] When he was due to come into possession: below, Lilleshall, Man. and Other Est.
[68] The following acct. of the man. in 1540 is based on P.R.O., SC 6/Hen. VIII/3021, mm. 10d.–11d.
[69] S.R.O. 1224, box 242, Prior Gosnell's reg. f. 38; P.R.O., E 318/996, m. 11; LR 2/184, ff. 104v.–105, 156–158v. 'Wood silver' was perhaps in lieu of timber haulage: see J. L. Fisher, *Medieval Farming Glossary* (1968), 41.
[70] S.R.O. 1224, box 296, Lady Day rental of 1688, pp. 6–9.
[71] Ibid. box 256, deeds of 1654, 1669, 1684–96.
[72] S.R.O. 1224/1/59.
[73] S.R.O. 1224, box 255, deed of 1720.
[74] Ibid. box 295, L. Wenlock survey, ff. 31–53. This survey (and the present acct.) omits two farms (104 a. altogether) held by Wm. Ferriday that lay partly in Wellington par. and included the N. arm of L. Wenlock par.: see ibid. survey of Watling Street Demesne, etc., f. 18.
[75] S.R.O. 1224/1/59.
[76] The following 2 paras. are based on H.W.R.O.(H.), Heref. dioc. rec., invs. of Ric. Wood, 1666; Geo. Grice, 1667;

Wm. Greene, 1668; Ric. Parton, 1671; Fra. Woosely, 1673; John Swyfte, 1682; Thos. Briscoe, 1685; John Smitheman, 1689; Edw. Burgwyn, 1691; Geo. Buttery, 1691; Wm. Parton, 1691; Wm. Sherrington, 1699; Wm. Boycott, 1709; Ric. Wheelwright, 1709; Wm. Whyston, 1713; Geo. Wheelwright, 1714; John Fletcher, 1715; Ric. Jervis, 1715; John Simmonds, 1715; Wm. Wheelwright, 1715; Wm. Wheelwright, 1717; Sam Green, 1719; Wm. Wright, 1720; Margery Swift, 1727; Fra. Parton, 1729; Rob. Dorral, 1730; Geo. Fletcher, 1730; Edm. Gray, 1730; John Owsley, 1731; Fra. Evans, 1736; Ric. Guist, 1737; Dan. Rogers, 1739; Rog. Thresslecock, 1742; Ric. Taylor, 1745; John Rogers, 1754; Eliz. Owsley, 1755; Thos. Cartledge, 1760; Rob. Taylor, 1760.
[77] *Yeomen and Colliers in Telford*, ed. B. Trinder and J. Cox (1980), 72–90; above, Madeley, Econ. Hist.
[78] Trinder and Cox, op. cit. 88–9.
[79] Ibid. 76, 88.
[80] Ibid. 84.
[81] Ibid. 86.
[82] S.R.O. 1224/1/59.
[83] Ibid. cultivation symbols.
[84] S.R.O. 1224, box 258, agreement of 1757.

with the last of the cycle.[85] The use of rotation turnips was negligible; peas, with 48 a. in 1801, were more common.[86] Woodlands were carefully exploited.[87] Where a coppice was included in a farm, the tenant had the use of it for pasture; immediately before felling, however, and for as long as it contained very young growth, the lord could exclude animals, and he then allowed a rent reduction.[88]

Ninety-nine-year farm leases, terminable on three or fewer lives, lasted into the later 18th century.[89] Sometimes, as in the 1760s, they were renewed for nominal rents and large fines.[90] Mid 18th-century leases required carriage services for minerals.[91] Farm rents rose little in the earlier 18th century, but later in the century were raised sharply whenever old leases fell in.[92] Around the end of the century annual tenancies began to be introduced[93] and rents could be increased generally, in step with prices, as in 1793, 1804, and 1808. In the 80 years after 1714 average farm rents had increased less than 50 per cent; in the 16 years from 1793 the average increase was over 90 per cent.

About 1800 the larger farms were virtually the same size as in the 1720s, and there remained many smallholders.[94] Part of Wrekin field was still open in 1762,[95] and in the 1770s common grazing was still available in the lanes.[96] During the earlier 19th century the larger farms remained constant in number, but increased their average size by about half at the expense of the smallholdings, whose number fell. There were more cottages, which may also have taken land from smallholdings.[97] Consolidation of scattered farms, still only partly achieved by the 1820s[98] (when some of the old leases were still in force),[99] was virtually complete by the 1840s.[1] In the later 19th and early 20th century the number and average size of larger farms changed little but the smallholdings dwindled to a handful.[2]

During the earlier 19th century corn was probably the major cash crop, the proportion of arable to permanent grass being about 2 to 1 in 1839, though a few farms on the edges of the parish were almost wholly pastoral.[3] On the mixed farms about a fifth of the arable was in long leys, and over the other four fifths cereals predominated, with small acreages of peas, potatoes, turnips, and clover.[4] By 1816 the tenants were usually required to follow a four-course rotation: a cereal followed by a fallow or turnips, then another cereal undersown with a mixture of clover and rye-grass. Turnips were compulsory after wheat sown after

clover, and each farmer had to sow a minimum annual acreage of turnips.[5] By the 1840s those requirements had generally produced the 'Norfolk' rotation of wheat–turnips–barley–clover, usually with long leys between rotations. Many variations were nevertheless possible, and small acreages of vetches, peas, beans, and mangolds were grown.[6]

TABLE III

LITTLE WENLOCK: LAND USE, LIVESTOCK, AND CROPS

	1867	1891	1938	1965
Percentage of grassland	26	70	91	71
arable	74	30	9	29
Percentage of cattle	12	23	35	28
sheep	71	40	57	47
pigs	17	37	8	25
Percentage of wheat	55	38	70	55
barley	37	33	1	35
oats	8	29	29	9
mixed corn & rye	0	0	0	1
Percentage of agricultural land growing roots and vegetables	10	5	2	4

Sources: P.R.O., MAF 68/143, no. 15; /1340, no. 11; /3880, Salop. no. 263; /4945, no. 263.

In the late 19th and early 20th century farmers turned over almost completely from arable to livestock, especially cattle. There was a revival of arable cultivation in the mid 20th century, especially for barley, but pasture still predominated and pig farming increased.[7]

Woodlands, all kept in hand by the lord until 1918,[8] remained at a fairly constant acreage in the 19th and 20th centuries.[9] During 1831 sales of timber, cordwood, and bark were expected to realize over £400.[10]

MILLS. By 1330 there were two water mills: one at Little Wenlock, another, not recorded later, at

---

[85] Ibid. box 257, deeds of 1745; box 258, deeds of 1757, 1761, 1762.

[86] P.R.O., HO 67/12, no. 143.

[87] e.g. S.R.O. 1224, box 255, deed of 1732.

[88] Ibid. box 258, deed of 1761.

[89] e.g. ibid. deeds of 1775, 1798.

[90] e.g. ibid. deeds of 1762.

[91] Ibid. deeds of 1761, 1762; box 257, deeds of 1741, 1745.

[92] Para. based on S.R.O. 1224, parcels 311–18, rentals of 1714–1813.

[93] Such tenancies may be inferred from L. Wenlock rentals of the 1790s onwards, though the earliest known L. Wenlock example dates from 1804 (mentioned ibid. box 295, survey of 1808, ff. 5v.–6).

[94] Ibid. survey of 1808.

[95] Ibid. box 258, deed of 25 Feb.

[96] Ibid. box 204, estreats of fines of 1775, 1777.

[97] S.R.O. 2142/1.

[98] S.R.O. 1224/1/60.

[99] S.R.O. 1224, box 295, valuation of Mrs. Davies's farm, 1828; ibid. partic. of rent alterations 7 July 1826.

[1] S.R.O. 2443/1.

[2] S.R.O. 1681, parcel 46, sale partic. pp. 3–5; P.R.O., MAF 68/3880, Salop. no. 263.

[3] S.R.O. 1224, box 295, survey of 1808; 2142/1.

[4] P.R.O., HO 67/12, no. 143; S.R.O. 1224, box 295, survey of 1808.

[5] S.R.O. 1224, box 258, printed agreements of 1816–24.

[6] S.R.O. 2443/1.

[7] See Table III.

[8] S.R.O. 2142/1; 1681, parcel 46, sale partic. p. 6.

[9] S.R.O. 2142/2–3; O.S. Maps 6", SJ 60 NE. (1966 edn.), NW. (1954 edn.).

[10] S.R.O. 1224, box 295, estimate of wood sales.

'Haliwelle' (perhaps near Holloway hays[11] in the north of the parish).[12] In 1727 a mill lay on Lyde brook.[13]

In the 17th and 18th centuries the Roberts family were millers as undertenants or assigns of absentee lessees.[14] The Coalbrookdale Co. was lessee c. 1808[15] but twenty years later the mill had gone, its place taken by a new steam corn mill at Horsehay.[16] John Clark held that mill in 1872[17] but by 1882 it had apparently closed.[18]

COAL, IRONSTONE, AND FIRECLAY. About half of the parish, east of the Little Wenlock fault, had abundant coal near the surface.[19] Coalmoor was so called by the early 14th century[20] and an Adam Collier was mentioned in 1344.[21] In 1540 there were two mines, one leased to Edmund Brydge-wode and Thomas Boswell, another formerly leased to John Forester but then derelict.[22]

In the 17th century the pits lay in three main groups: one immediately east and south of Little Wenlock village, another farther east at Coal-moor, and a third (extending into Wellington parish) near the heath, north-east of Huntington, at least part of which was known by the early 18th century as the New Works.[23] In 1611 Sir George Hayward was employing labourers to mine on his Little Wenlock estate,[24] and in the 1680s Francis and William Forester mined the coal and iron-stone on their own estate and on those of the Haywards and Smithemans, who received royal-ties. The Foresters' annual production in Little Wenlock parish averaged c. 2,700 stacks.[25] Francis Forester's pits also yielded about 150 dozens[26] of ironstone a year, most of it bought by William Stanier and some by Lawrence Wellington.[27]

Although the Foresters disposed of some of their Little Wenlock coal by Severn sale and landsale, and used a little for lime burning, they sold most of it to a Mr. Corfield (until 1686), a Mr. Lacon (probably John Lacon of West Cop-pice, d. 1716),[28] and (from 1686) to Samuel Bowdler of Arlescott.[29] In 1705 Sir William Fores-ter contracted to supply Bowdler's successor,[30] Thomas Sprott of the Marsh, with 4,000 stacks a year for 21 years for Severn sale. On Sir William's death in 1718 his heir leased his coal in Little Wenlock parish, with the unexpired period of the Sprott contract, to Richard Hartshorne of Ketley for 21 years on a royalty basis.

By then William Hayward and John Smithe-man were working their own minerals.[31] Where

the Forester and Hayward estates were intermin-gled disputes and inefficiency resulted, and in 1727–8, after William Hayward's death, his son co-operated with William Forester in making joint arrangements with Hartshorne, intended to cover the next 21 years. Forester and Hayward let all their coal works in the parish (except Hayward's Coalmoor works) to Hartshorne, who agreed to extract 5,600 stacks a year (4,000 from Forester's land and 1,600 from Hayward's) for a reserved rent, and any quantity over that on a royalty basis, with liberty to make coke at the Huntington pits. The Sprott contract had expired and Forester and Hayward leased a Severn wharf at Strethill from Thomas Sprott's son Henry. They built a wag-gonway to it from near Little Wenlock village, which they let to Hartshorne in return for rent plus a royalty of every stack carried down the rails (a miniumum of 4,000 stacks). Forester and Hayward were to have use of the tracks to carry ironstone from Little Wenlock to the Severn.[32] By 1732 Hartshorne claimed that the demand for coals 'by water carriage' was not enough, so Forester and Hayward reduced the rent and allowed him to make up the 4,000 stacks by landsale.[33] The following year Hartshorne died[34] and the Foresters probably then resumed direct working of their mines.

Hayward's works at Coalmoor produced Clod coals particularly suited to the needs of the Coal-brookdale ironworks, and until 1740 were those works' principal suppliers. At first Hayward's father (d. 1727) worked the Coalmoor works him-self, but in 1726 he leased them for 21 years to Richard Ford (d. 1745)[35] of Coalbrookdale,[36] who supplied their whole output to the Coalbrookdale works. The pits yielded annually about 1,240 stacks of 'big' coals and (at least until 1732) about 700 stacks of coke made at the pits, but they were abandoned in 1742 or 1743 because of increasing drainage difficulties.[37]

In 1740, when the Hayward mines faltered, William Forester and his son Brooke contracted to sell the Coalbrookdale Co. all the Clod coals from pits in the Huntington heath and Smalleyhill area (extending into Wellington parish) and the comp-any agreed to use no other supplier except Hayward.[38] In 1750 the company was permitted to lay a railway for Clod coals from the Forester pits to Coalbrookdale; the Foresters were allowed to carry other coals (at least 1,500 stacks a year) on it for Severn sale.[39] In 1755 the Foresters' Severn

[11] 'Hallywell Hayes' in 1540: P.R.O., SC 6/Hen. VIII/3021, m. 11.
[12] S.R.O. 1224/2/10.
[13] Ibid. /1/59.
[14] S.R.O. 1224, box 206, suit r. of 1757; box 257, deed of 1733; box 295, survey of 1727, f. 47; 1987/35/9; 3331/1, f. 2.
[15] S.R.O. 1224, box 295, survey, f. 59.
[16] S.R.O. 2142/1, 3.
[17] Par. rec., ch. rate bk. 1857–72.
[18] O.S. Map 1/2,500, Salop. XLIII. 6 (1882 edn.).
[19] Inst. Geol. Sciences Map 1/25,000, Telford (1978 edn.).
[20] In 'Colmor[e]syate': S.R.O. 1224/2/10.
[21] Ibid. /2/1.
[22] P.R.O., SC 6/Hen. VIII/3021, m. 11.
[23] S.R.O. 1224, parcel 298, lime acct. bk. 27 Oct. 1716.
[24] S.R.O. 2374, box 1, deed.
[25] S.R.O. 1224, box 296, coal acct. bks. 1681–9; coal accts. 1689–91. A stack (10 horseloads) for Severn sale occupied 117,649 cu. in. or weighed 32, 36, or 42 cwt. (according to

type), and of Clod coal was 35 cwt.: ibid. box 256, deeds of 1718, 1728; box 260, deeds of 1740, 1750.
[26] A dozen of ironstone (11 strikes) was 44 cwt. (ibid. box 259, deeds of 1756, 1798) or occupied 72,960 cu. in. (Trinder, Ind. Rev. Salop. 52).
[27] S.R.O. 1224, box 296, 'Old master's work' acct. bk.; 'Coalmeadow' acct. bk., pp. 10, 35, 45, 53.
[28] S.P.R. Lich. xiv (3), p. v.
[29] S.R.O. 1224, box 296, coal acct. bks. 1681–9.
[30] S.R.O. 1242, box 5, abstr. of title c. 1842.
[31] S.R.O. 1224, box 256, deed of 1718.
[32] Ibid. deeds of 1728.
[33] Ibid. box 227, deed.
[34] Trinder, Ind. Rev. Salop. 197.
[35] Ibid. 29.
[36] S.R.O. 1224, box 260, deed of 1740.
[37] P.R.O., E 134/27 Geo. II Hil./8.
[38] S.R.O. 1224, box 260, deed.
[39] Ibid. box 259, deed of 1750, plan c. 1750.

coal was selling well[40] and in that year the Coalbrookdale Co. contracted to buy annually 2,000 wagons of Double and Flint coals from the Forester pits (the New Works) for Severn sale.[41] The contract of 1740 was renewed in 1756, the Foresters agreeing for 21 years to supply annually from the New Works 4,000 stacks of Clod coal and 400 dozens of ironstone.[42] Ironstone was also sent to the Leighton furnace.[43]

About 1776 a new railway was built for the Coalbrookdale Co. through Coalmoor to Horsehay[44] and in 1777 the Foresters withdrew from direct involvement in coalmining in the parish when George Forester leased his Little Wenlock coal mines to Abraham Darby (III).[45] The lease was renewed for 21 years in 1798 in favour of the Coalbrookdale Co. on a royalty basis, a minimum royalty being guaranteed. Limits were placed on opening new pits near Little Wenlock village,[46] and in practice mining was concentrated in the New Works area,[47] though in 1808 there were also pits at Coalmoor and Little Worth.[48] In 1798–9 the New Works (partly in Wellington) produced over 10,000 tons of coal for iron making.[49] The minerals, as in 1777,[50] were destined for Coalbrookdale, Ketley, and Horsehay, except for certain coals leased in 1798 to the tenants of the limeworks.[51]

By 1833 mining had contracted to the New Works area[52] as more productive deposits in adjacent parishes were worked.[53] The Coalbrookdale Co. took 21-year leases of the coal and ironstone mines in 1847[54] and 1868.[55] By 1882, however, the only active pit in Little Wenlock was immediately south of the road from New Works to Lawley, and it too had closed by 1901. By then there had been a revival of small-scale mining nearby. The Buckatree and the New Works collieries opened between 1882 and 1901.[56] A colliery near Lawley Furnaces, extending into Wellington parish, opened in the same period.[57] The Buckatree colliery closed in 1902[58] and the New Works colliery was disused by 1925,[59] but shafts remained open at the Lawley Furnaces colliery,[60] one of them until at least 1937.[61] Meanwhile in 1908 Lord Forester leased the coal and fireclay of 42 a. at Coalmoor to the Coalmoor Sanitary Pipe Co., which bought them outright in 1919.[62] New shafts were sunk at Coalmoor[63] and in the 1930s other sites in the south-east were worked.[64]

During and after the Second World War opencast working was begun at several sites, some of which had not been exploited for over a century. In 1943 land on Upper Huntington farm was among the first areas in Shropshire to be requisitioned for opencast mining,[65] and by 1949 there were also workings at Huntington heath, Little Worth, Lawley Furnaces, and immediately south of Little Wenlock village.[66] By 1980 coalmining had ceased and most of the old sites had been returned to agriculture or taken over for fireclay extraction. A large opencast site at New Works had become a refuse tip.

LIMESTONE. Carboniferous limestone occurred abundantly at the surface in a band that ran north-westwards from Little Wenlock village, to curve north-eastwards and to cross the northern parish boundary towards Steeraway.[67]

In 1619–20 a Lilleshall churchwarden bought 4 strikes of lime from Huntington[68] and at the beginning of the next century the Foresters had two commercial limeworks in the parish, at Wenlock field, north-west of the village, and at the Hatch, north-west of Huntington. The Hatch works was the larger, sending lime as far north as Market Drayton, and west as far as Atcham and Haughmond. In 1716 over 1,000 loads of lime were produced, two thirds of them at the Hatch.[69]

In 1728 the two works, together with the Foresters' nearby Steeraway works, in Wellington parish, were leased to Richard Hartshorne the elder and John Southall, a Wellington mercer, whose partnership that year was joined by Robert Peach, a Northamptonshire tanner; the partners took a new lease that year.[70] In 1734 Hartshorne's death caused the lease to be surrendered[71] and for the next fifty years the Foresters seem to have kept their works in hand.[72] By the 1770s their sales of lime from Little Wenlock and Steeraway totalled c. £3,000 a year.[73] There seem to have been no commercial limestone workings on the Hayward or Smitheman estates, and in 1728 William Hayward agreed to lease to William Forester any limeworks that should be opened on Hayward's land near Forester's Wenlock field site.[74]

In 1784 George Forester leased all the works to John Colley and a Mr. (probably Henry) Cart-

[40] Ibid. Wm. Ferriday to [Wm. Forester], 11 Jan. 1755.
[41] Ibid. box 260, deed defining a wagon of such coals as 52½ cwt. [42] Ibid. deed.
[43] Ibid. box 259, Wm. Ferriday to —, 4 Jan. 1755.
[44] Ibid. parcel 315, Mich. rental of 1776, f. 6v.
[45] Ibid. Lady Day 'roll at large' of 1777, f. 6v. The lease was presumably for 21 yrs., and thus the one that expired 1 Jan. 1798: I.G.M.T. Libr., acc. no. 1978–279, p. 22.
[46] S.R.O. 1224, box 259, deed.
[47] Ibid. box 295, valuation of Dothill est. 1809, ff. 23v.–4.
[48] R. Baugh, Map of Salop. (1808).
[49] I.G.M.T. Libr., Coalbrookdale Co. settling jnl. 1798–1808, pp. 11–27.
[50] I.G.M.T. Libr., acc. no. 1978–279, p. 22.
[51] S.R.O. 1224, box 255, deed; box 259, deed.
[52] O.S. Map 1", sheet 61 NE. (1833 edn.).
[53] S. Bagshaw, Dir. Salop. (1851), 565–6.
[54] S.R.O. 604 (uncat.), R. Garbitt to G. Potts, 8 May 1847.
[55] S.R.O. 1681, box 42, deed.
[56] O.S. Map 1/2,500, Salop. XLIII. 2 (1882 and 1902 edns.).
[57] Ibid. XXXVI. 14 (1882 and 1902 edns.).
[58] I. J. Brown, Coalbrookdale Coalfield (Shropshire Co.

Libr. 1968), 18.
[59] O.S. Map 1/2,500, Salop. XLIII. 2 (1927 edn.).
[60] O.S. Map 6", Salop. XXXVI. SW. (1929 edn.).
[61] O.S. Map 1/2,500, Salop. XXXVI. 14 (1937 edn.).
[62] S.R.O. 1681, box 41, deed; box 44, deed. On the co.'s hist. see below, Dawley, Econ. Hist.
[63] O.S. Map 6", Salop. XLIII. NW. (1928 edn.).
[64] Brown, Coalbrookdale Coalfield, 19.
[65] Jackson, 'Madeley', bk. 3A, p. 91.
[66] O.S. Map 1/25,000, SJ 60 (1957 edn.).
[67] Inst. Geol. Sciences Map 1/25,000, Telford (1978 edn.).
[68] S.R.O. 4462/CW/1/7. A strike of lime was defined in 1728 as 2,186.55 cu. in. (roughly 1 imperial bushel) and consisted of 1½ 'pieces': S.R.O. 1224, box 227, deed 27 Sept. 1728.
[69] S.R.O. 1224, parcel 298, lime acct. bk. 1715–17. A load of lime was defined in 1728 as 20 strikes: box 227, deed 27 Sept. 1728. In the 1680s it had been called a score, 6 scores making a 'hundred': box 296, coal and lime acct. bk. 1681–9.
[70] Ibid. box 257, deed.
[71] Ibid. deed.
[72] Ibid. box 299, acct. bk. 1737–8.
[73] e.g. ibid. parcel 315, Mich. rental of 1776, f. 19v.
[74] Ibid. box 227, deed.

wright at £525 a year.[75] When the lease expired in 1798 a new one, including mines of coal for lime burning, was granted to Richard Emery of Watling Street at a rent of £1,000,[76] increased to £1,300 in 1819[77] and £1,600 in 1828.[78] By 1814 the parish had limeworks at the Hatch, Old field (the former Wenlock field), and Cross field, east of Huntington Lane.[79] All three were working in 1824[80] but the Cross field site had closed by 1833[81] and the Old field site closed between 1833 and 1839.[82] By 1833 the limestone workings at the Hatch were connected by tramway to the Horsehay ironworks.[83] The Emery lease was due to expire in 1840, and about that time a new lease was granted to the Lilleshall Co. It expired in 1849[84] and Lord Forester kept his works in hand until 1854, when he let them to a partnership of Richard and Thomas Groom and William and John Ison; as the Steeraway Lime Co.[85] they and their successors continued to hold them until at least 1916.[86]

The Hatch workings, apparently after a period of disuse, reopened 1874–82. At that period 3,000–6,000 tons a year were extracted,[87] mostly for the Steeraway kilns, though there were kilns at the Hatch.[88] These had closed by 1901,[89] when the workings again reopened. After 1901 fewer than 8 men were usually employed and the site finally closed in 1918.[90]

OTHER INDUSTRIES. An iron forge belonged to Richard the clerk at Little Wenlock c. 1180.[91] Large-scale iron making began in 1822 when the Lawley furnace was blown in near the New Works. Its first tenants were the company formed in 1818 to lease the Ketley furnaces; by 1829, as the Lawley Co., its leading partners were Henry Williams and William Hombersley.[92] In 1830 over 3,000 tons of pig were made.[93] In 1847 the works was leased to the Coalbrookdale Co.,[94] which held it until c. 1870[95] when it closed.[96]

In the 18th century the Fletcher family were ropers.[97]

Potters were living in the parish by the 1730s,

including the interrelated Deakin and Cartlidge families[98] at Coalmoor.[99] In 1767 Thomas Cartlidge was renting clay pits, pot houses, and kilns from John Smitheman at a site at Coalmoor,[1] called Potter's meadow in 1817.[2] In 1767 Andrew Bradley became lessee of the works[3] and by 1775, as Andrew Bradley & Co., was supplying fire bricks and ground clay to the Horsehay works.[4] By 1780 Richard Reynolds & Co. had apparently taken over, and in July supplied 10,000 bricks from Coalmoor to Horsehay[5] but by 1796 Horsehay also had its own brick and pot works.[6] In the early 19th century Thomas Machin ran a pot works at the Coalmoor site[7] but by 1839 it had closed.[8] In 1839 there was a brick kiln at Smalleyhill,[9] gone by 1881.[10]

Basalt outcrops in several parts of the parish.[11] Commercial extraction began when the Coalmoor Basalt Co. was formed in 1930, with a works on the Horsehay road. In the 1930s the rock was crushed to make roadstone, and the works also produced concrete goods.[12] In 1982 its main product was building blocks[13] but in 1983 the site was occupied by waste-disposal contractors.

Three malthouses were standing in 1808 and 1839,[14] and in 1851 there were five maltsters, three of them also farmers.[15] Benjamin Dawes of Huntington was making malt until the 1870s[16] but seems to have had no successor in the parish.

LOCAL GOVERNMENT AND PUBLIC SERVICES. As a member of the extensive liberty of Wenlock priory the manor was subject to the twice-yearly tourns of Bourton 'hundred' and probably to its lesser court,[17] but by 1674 it had ceased to owe suit.[18]

Manor court rolls survive for 1334, 1344, 1379–80, 1403, 1411–12, 1420, 1431–2, and 1449–50,[19] a fine roll for 1321,[20] and other records for the 18th and 19th centuries.[21] In the 14th and 15th centuries there was a three-weekly court.[22] It was then mainly concerned with agricultural regula-

[75] Ibid. parcel 316, Lady Day rental of 1783, f. 19v.; parcel 317, Mich. rental of 1785, f. 16v.
[76] Ibid. box 255, deeds of 1797–8. [77] Ibid. deeds.
[78] Ibid. box 162, rental of 1828, ff. 62v.–63.
[79] B.L. Maps, O.S.D. 208.
[80] S.R.O. 1224, box 295, damages estimate.
[81] O.S. Map 1″, sheet 61 NE. (1833 edn.).
[82] S.R.O. 2142/1–3.
[83] O.S. Map 1″, sheet 61 NE. (1833 edn.).
[84] S.R.O. 604 (uncat.), R. Garbitt to G. Potts 8 May 1847.
[85] V.C.H. Salop. i. 449.
[86] I. J. Brown, Hist. of Limestone Mining in Salop. (Salop. Mining Club Acct. vi, 1967), 15.
[87] Ibid. 13–14.
[88] O.S. Map 6″, Salop. XLIII. NW. (1889 edn.).
[89] Ibid. (1903 edn.).
[90] Brown, Hist. Limestone Mining, 14–16.
[91] P.R.O., E 32/143.
[92] Trinder, Ind. Rev. Salop. 235; S.R.O. 1224, parcel 191, Mich. gathering roll of 1829, s.v. Mines and Minerals.
[93] Trinder, op. cit. 235.
[94] S.R.O. 604 (uncat.), R. Garbitt to Coalbrookdale Co. 21 Apr. 1847.
[95] P.O. Dir. Salop. (1870), 156.
[96] V.C.H. Salop. ii. 233.
[97] H.W.R.O.(H.), Heref. dioc. rec., inv. of Geo. Fletcher, 1730; par. reg. bur. 13 Jan. 1749/50; 18 Sept. 1757; 4 Feb. 1759; marr. 7 Nov. 1757 (transcript in S.P.L.); S.R.O. 1224, parcel 317, Mich. rental of 1792, f. 9v.
[98] Par. reg. marr. 25 Dec. 1731; bur. 26 Nov. 1736; 31

Mar. 1747; 5 Jan. 1747/8; 1 May 1760; bap. 29 Apr. 1749; 1 Sept. 1751 (transcript in S.P.L.); S.R.O. 1224, box 206, suit r.; H.W.R.O.(H.), Heref. dioc. rec., inv. of Thos. Cartledge, 1760.
[99] H.W.R.O.(H.), Heref. dioc. rec., inv. of Sam. Deakin, 1729.
[1] S.R.O. 1224, box 225, deed.
[2] Ibid. box 258, deed. [3] Ibid. box 225, deed.
[4] S.R.O. 245/144, pp. 56, 74.
[5] Ibid. p. 390.
[6] S.R.O. 245/145, passim.
[7] S.R.O. 1224, box 258, deed of 1817; box 295, survey of 1808, ff. 4v.–5; ibid. valuation of Smitheman est. of 1825.
[8] S.R.O. 2142/1. [9] Ibid. /1–2.
[10] O.S. Map 6″, Salop. XLIII. NW. (1889 edn.).
[11] Inst. Geol. Sciences Map 1/25,000, Telford (1978 edn.).
[12] Wellington Jnl. 1 July 1939.
[13] T.D.C. Telford Ind. Dir. (1982), 18.
[14] S.R.O. 1224, box 295, survey of 1808, ff. 2v., 21, 33v.–34, 35v.; 2142/1.
[15] S. Bagshaw, Dir. Salop. (1851), 566.
[16] P.O. Dir. Salop. (1870), 163; par. rec., ch. rate bk. 1857–72.
[17] S.R.O. 1224/2/10. See V.C.H. Salop. iii. 49–50.
[18] S.R.O. 1224/2/510, ff. [21–3].
[19] Ibid. /2/1, 4–9; 566/1; 1190, box 23.
[20] S.R.O. 1037/19/1.
[21] In S.R.O. 1224, boxes 204, 206–7.
[22] The following acct. of manorial admin. is based on the rec. listed above.

tion, copyhold conveyances, and breaches of the assize of ale. Pleas of debt were also heard. Manorial officers included woodwards, aletasters, two reeves, and two constables. By the 1730s there were stocks and a pound.[23] In the later 18th and earlier 19th century the 'court leet and court baron' met yearly to deal with a dwindling list of routine presentments: of defaults of suit, of butchers, bakers (until 1817), and alesellers, and of neglect of hedges and ditches next to highways (until c. 1780) and trespass thereon by animals (until c. 1828). It was still appointing constables and aletasters in 1840.

In the earlier 18th century a parish meeting determined who should receive weekly poor relief[24] and audited the accounts.[25] By 1748 the parish rented a poorhouse,[26] and was still renting one in 1813.[27] The number of adults receiving weekly relief rose from 52 in 1802–3 to 92 in 1812–13.[28] A parochial workhouse[29] was opened at Little Worth,[30] apparently in 1814, and 16 adults were admitted in 1814–15.[31] The elected overseers administered relief until 1823. Thereafter the workhouse was run by an assistant overseer, and outdoor relief was gradually withdrawn by the elected overseers.[32] The workhouse closed in 1836[33] and Little Wenlock was in Madeley poor-law union 1836–1930.[34]

Little Wenlock was within the jurisdiction of the Broseley court of requests from 1782[35] until its abolition under the County Courts Act, 1846.[36]

Edward IV's 1468 charter to Wenlock priory's town of Wenlock included in a borough the whole of the priory liberty, and Little Wenlock remained in the borough until 1966.[37] The parish was in Madeley rural sanitary district 1872–89 and in the Barrow sanitary division and ward of Wenlock borough 1889–1966.[38] It was not assigned to a highway district under the Highway Act, 1862,[39] and remained a highway authority until the formation of Wenlock urban sanitary authority in 1889.[40] On the dissolution of Wenlock municipal borough in 1966 a very small area at the tip of the parish's northern arm was transferred to Dawley civil parish and U.D. The rest

of Little Wenlock C.P. was extended northwards to take in a large part of Wellington Rural C.P. and was transferred to Wellington rural district.[41] In 1974 Little Wenlock C.P. and the former Dawley U.D. were assigned to the district of the Wrekin.[42] In 1963 the part later in Dawley U.D. was included in the designated area of Dawley new town[43] and in 1968 in that of Telford.[44]

A post office had opened at Horsehay, within the parish, by 1856[45] and in 1880 a sub-postmaster was appointed at Little Wenlock.[46] Both offices were open in 1980. In the early 20th century a private water supply was piped to Little Wenlock village from a source in Spout Lane, and it was the parish's only piped supply until after the Second World War.[47] In 1934 Little Wenlock was one of the first Shropshire villages to have mains electricity.[48]

CHURCH. There was a church probably by the 12th century.[49] The living, a rectory when mentioned in the mid 13th century, remained so in 1978 when it was united to two neighbouring livings.

In the later 13th century both the bishop of Hereford and Wenlock priory claimed the advowson. Peter of Langogne was collated before 1268 by his fellow Burgundian, Bishop Peter d'Aigueblanche.[50] The priory presented its own candidate c. 1278 but Bishop Cantilupe would not admit him.[51] In 1300, however, Peter of Langogne's successor was instituted on Wenlock's presentation.[52] The advowson remained with the priory until 1540.[53] and descended with the manor until 1590 or later.[54] The Crown presented in 1381 because Wenlock was an alien priory[55] and in 1571,[56] presumably because Walter Leveson was a minor. By 1608 the patrons were William Hayward and Maurice Wright, perhaps trustees, who then granted the advowson to Sir George Hayward[57] (d. 1615).[58] Sir George's widow was patron[59] but his brother Sir John held the advowson by 1623 and did not sell it with the manor.[60] He died without issue in 1636[61] and William

[23] S.R.O. 3331, ff. 47v., 49.
[24] Ibid. f. 59.   [25] Ibid. f. 43.
[26] Ibid. f. 55v.
[27] S.R.O. 1224, box 314, Lady Day rental of 1769, pp. 11–12; parcel 318, rental of 1813, ff. 17v.–18.
[28] Abstr. Rel. to Poor, H.C. 175, p. 423 (1803–4), xiii; Abstr. Rel. to Poor, H.C. 82, p. 377 (1818), xix.
[29] Par. rec., overseers' acct. bk. 1818 37, 1 Apr. 1828.
[30] Local inf.
[31] Abstr. Rel. to Poor, H.C. 82, p. 377 (1818), xix; par. reg. bur. 16 Dec. 1814 (first ref. to bur. of an inmate).
[32] Par. rec., overseers' acct. bk. 1818–37.
[33] Ibid. 30 Oct. 1836.
[34] V. J. Walsh, 'Admin. of Poor Laws in Salop. 1820–55' (Pennsylvania Univ. Ph.D. thesis, 1970), 150 (copy in S.R.O.); V.C.H. Salop. iii. 170; Kelly's Dir. Salop. (1929), 301.
[35] Broseley, etc., Small Debts Act, 1782, 22 Geo. III, c. 37.
[36] 9 & 10 Vic. c. 95.
[37] V.C.H. Salop. ii. 211, 236–7; iii. 247.
[38] Ibid. ii. 204 (and Act cited ibid. n. 10), 215–16. Cf. ibid. iii. 177–8; Public Health Act, 1872, 35 & 36 Vic. c. 79, s. 4.
[39] 25 & 26 Vic. c. 61. Cf. V.C.H. Salop. iii. 178.
[40] No successor was elected when the highway surveyor retired in 1890: par. rec., vestry min. bk. 1818–1958, 24 Mar. 1890.
[41] V.C.H. Salop. ii. 236–7.
[42] Sources cited ibid. iii. 169, n. 29.

[43] Dawley New Town (Designation) Order 1963 (Stat. Instr. 1963, no. 64), accompanying map (copy in S.R.O. 2981, parcel VI).
[44] Dawley New Town (Designation) Amendment (Telford) Order 1968 (Stat. Instr. 1968, no. 1912), map accompanying Explanatory Note.
[45] P.O. Dir. Salop. (1856), 43.
[46] Jackson, 'Madeley', bk. 3A, p. 91.
[47] S.R.O. 1681, box 44, plan no. 1; parcel 46, sale partic. p. 33; A. H. S. Waters, Rep. on Water Supplies (S.C.C. 1946), p. 16.
[48] Jackson, 'Madeley', bk. 3A, p. 91.
[49] Below.
[50] Reg. Swinfield (C.S.), 71.
[51] Reg. Cantilupe (C.S.), 185–6.
[52] Eyton, iii. 328.
[53] Ibid.; Reg. Trefnant (C.S.), 185; Reg. Spofford (C.S.), 361.
[54] L. & P. Hen. VIII, xx (1), p. 424; xx (2), p. 546; P.R.O., CP 25(2)/202/32 Eliz. I Trin. [no. 7].
[55] Cal. Pat. 1377–81, 607.
[56] Ibid. 1569–72, p. 187.
[57] B.L. Add. Ch. 5437.
[58] P.R.O., C 142/363, no. 194.
[59] Heref. Dioc. Regy., reg. 1609–26, p. 297 (n.d. but betw. entries of 1621).
[60] S.R.O. 1224, box 224, deed of 1651.
[61] T.S.A.S. 4th ser. v. 53.

Hayward (d. 1640), a cousin,[62] was afterwards patron, succeeded by his son George.[63] By 1663 William Hayward (d. 1708) was patron.[64] The advowson descended thereafter with the Haywards' Little Wenlock estate[65] and was bought by William Forester (d. 1758).[66]

It again descended with the manor until 1930 when Lord Forester gave a third turn to the vicar of Much Wenlock in exchange for a third turn in the patronage of Broseley with Benthall.[67] From 1968 the rector also held Coalbrookdale vicarage[68] and in 1978 both livings were united with Ironbridge, with Lord Forester and the vicar of Much Wenlock among the joint patrons.[69]

In 1291 the rectory was valued at £4 6s. 8d.[70] The great tithes were allegedly worth 32s. in 1341, with a high proportion of the rector's income attributed to glebe, small tithes, and oblations.[71] By 1331,[72] and until 1608 or later,[73] the rector owed an annual pension of 20s. to the patron. At first, therefore, the priory seems to have enjoyed much of the rectorial income, without the burden of collection that would have followed appropriation. In 1379 the rectory was worth £5[74] and in 1425 less than £6 13s. 4d.[75] Throughout the 15th century the living was often exempted, on grounds of poverty, from clerical taxes.[76]

Later the value of the tithes was put higher and was the rector's greatest source of income. The living was reckoned over £50 c. 1708.[77] In 1819 the tithes alone were worth £505.[78] In 1632 all were paid in kind except for calves, cows, and lambs.[79] In 1838 the only tithes not payable in kind were those of hay in Huntington field, customarily commuted;[80] in 1607 Huntington's inhabitants had yielded the hay of their Tithe meadow in lieu of hay tithes.[81] In 1722 the rector leased the tithes of wood, bark, and faggots to William Forester.[82] In 1838 all the tithes were commuted to a rent charge of £551 13s.[83] The living's value was £550 in 1865.[84] In 1865 £6 a year from the tithes were intended to be paid to the incumbent of the new

Lawley chapel, and in 1867 the parish's north-eastern part was taken into Lawley consolidated chapelry (Lichfield diocese).[85] In 1932 the rector's income was £530.[86]

By the 17th century the glebe contributed only a slight proportion of the living's value. In addition to the parsonage house it comprised c. 11 a. by 1632.[87] It was 11 a. in 1818[88] but by 1839 was just over 8 a.,[89] of which nearly 5 a. had not been glebe in 1727;[90] there had been a considerable exchange in 1833.[91] There were still 8 a. in 1887[92] but only 1½ a. by 1929.[93]

In the 1320s the rector was renting the manor house[94] but by 1589 there was a parsonage house,[95] which in 1716 was 'old but well covered'.[96] In 1713 it had a hall, parlour, kitchen, back kitchen, and buttery on the ground floor, and two rooms above.[97] In 1980 the Old Rectory, by then a private residence, included a 17th-century hall with a north kitchen and an early 18th-century south parlour.[98] There were brick additions of 1856[99] and later. A new rectory house, completed c. 1958[1] just south of the old house,[2] was sold c. 1973 when the rector moved to Coalbrookdale.[3]

No pre-Reformation rector is known to have been a graduate, though Thomas Seman received a seven-year licence to study c. 1300.[4] Richard Fenemor, rector in 1552–3,[5] was a former monk of Wenlock. By 1555 he was curate of Acton Round.[6] John Singar, rector,[7] was living at Bushey (Herts.) c. 1567.[8] From the late 16th century until the late 19th, as the living became richer, incumbents usually held it until death and there were some long incumbencies.

George Baxter, instituted in 1608, was a graduate and licensed preacher[9] and a friend of Richard Baxter,[10] whose convictions he shared. In 1643 the royalist governor of Shrewsbury ordered his arrest[11] but by 1647 he was Presbyterian minister at Little Wenlock[12] and was allowed to remain until his death c. 1663.[13] William Whiston, rector 1690–1713,[14] was resident at his death[15] but Thomas Jordan, rector 1713–35,[16] was believed to be

[62] S.P.L., MS. 4646, p. 133.
[63] P.R.O., C 142/499, no. 32.
[64] T.S.A.S. 3rd ser. v. 376.
[65] Ibid. 4th ser. ii. 68, 77, 95; Dioc. of Heref. Institutions (1539–1900), ed. A. T. Bannister (Heref. 1923), 64.
[66] S.R.O 1224, box 270, will.
[67] Lond. Gaz. 28 Feb. 1930, pp. 1286–7.
[68] Crockford (1980), 573.
[69] Ibid. 1308; Heref. Dioc. Regy., reg. 1969– (in use), pp. 306, 308–9.
[70] Tax. Eccl. (Rec. Com.), 167.
[71] Inq. Non. (Rec. Com.), 187.
[72] Cal. Pat. 1348–50, 188–9.
[73] Valor Eccl. (Rec. Com.), iii. 209; B.L. Add. Ch. 5437.
[74] B.L. Add. MS. 6164, f. 195.
[75] Reg. Spofford, 89.
[76] Ibid. 137, 195, 265; Reg. Myllyng (C.S.), 75, 151.
[77] Heref. Dioc. Regy., reg. 1683–1709, ff. 188–9.
[78] S.R.O. 515/10, p. 280.
[79] H.W.R.O.(H.), Heref. dioc. rec., glebe terrier.
[80] S.R.O. 2142/1.
[81] H.W.R.O.(H.), Heref. dioc. rec., glebe terrier.
[82] S.R.O. 1224, box 256, deed.
[83] S.R.O. 2142/1.
[84] Clergy List (1865), benefice list, 242.
[85] Below, Lawley, Church.
[86] Crockford (1932), 645.
[87] H.W.R.O.(H.), Heref. dioc. rec., glebe terrier.
[88] S.R.O. 515/10, p. 253.   [89] S.R.O. 2142/1.
[90] S.R.O. 1224/1/59.
[91] S.R.O. 604 (uncat.), [W.] Wyley to [Revd. T. Forester],

12 Oct. 1832.
[92] Return of Glebe Land, 1887, H.C. 307, p. 62 (1887), lxiv.
[93] Kelly's Dir. Salop. (1929), 301.
[94] S.R.O. 1224/2/10.
[95] H.W.R.O.(H.), Heref. dioc. rec., glebe terrier.
[96] Ibid. visit. return.
[97] Ibid. inv. of Wm. Whyston, 1713.
[98] A crude sketch of the ho. in 1727 exists: S.R.O. 1224/1/59.
[99] Local inf.
[1] S.R.O. 888/1, p. 120; 949/1, pp. 119–20.
[2] Local inf.
[3] S.R.O. 2688/3, p. 493; 2893/4, pp. 53, 498–500.
[4] Eyton, iii. 328.
[5] T.S.A.S. 2nd ser. xii. 97, 312.
[6] T.S.A.S. lx. 102.
[7] Ibid. 4th ser. xi. 201.
[8] Ibid. 186.
[9] H.W.R.O.(H.), Heref. dioc. rec., visit. bk. 14, p. 11.
[10] T.S.A.S. 4th ser. x. 139–40.
[11] S.P.L., Deeds 13306.
[12] W. A. Shaw, Hist. Eng. Church 1640–60, ii. 409; Calamy Revised, ed. A. G. Matthews, 556.
[13] H.W.R.O.(H.), Heref. dioc. rec., visit. bk. 23, s.v. Wenlock deanery.
[14] T.S.A.S. 4th ser. ii. 77; par. reg. bur. 23 May 1713 (transcript in S.P.L.).
[15] H.W.R.O.(H.), Heref. dioc. rec., inv. of Wm. Whyston, 1713.
[16] Bannister, Heref. Institutions, 64; par. reg. bur. 19 Jan. 1734/5 (transcript in S.P.L.).

living in Oxford in 1716; he had an assistant curate. There were then two Sunday services, with one sermon in winter and two in summer; communion was held four times a year.[17] Jordan was succeeded by John Hayward, the patron's brother.[18] He was perpetual curate of Quatford from c. 1763[19] and was buried there in 1786.[20] An assistant curate was licensed in 1757[21] and others were continuously employed thereafter until 1841.[22] Michael Pye Stephens, rector 1786–1817,[23] was also rector of Hughley 1777–1803[24] and of Sheinton 1803–17.[25] Related to the Foresters,[26] he was convivial and fond of field sports.[27] In 1799 he

From 1841 to c. 1973 the rectors were resident. George Edmonds, instituted 1841,[41] had an assistant curate 1846–7[42] and for a few months before his death in 1889.[43] Edmonds was a rich bachelor.[44] Partly at his own expense he founded the village school[45] and restored the church.[46] On Census Sunday 1851 there were 118 adult attenders at the morning service and 67 in the afternoon.[47] In extreme old age Edmonds was deaf and eccentric and the parish was neglected.[48] T. A. Nash, rector 1889–98,[49] an Evangelical of saintly reputation, restored the parish's religious life. He became fatally ill, however, and from 1897 to 1898

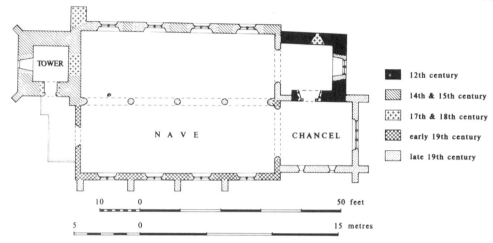

Key:
- 12th century
- 14th & 15th century
- 17th & 18th century
- early 19th century
- late 19th century

TOWER — NAVE — CHANCEL

10   0   50 feet
5   0   15 metres

THE CHURCH OF ST. LAWRENCE

was living at Barrow.[28] His curate at Little Wenlock throughout was John Turner.[29] Turner and his successors lived at the parsonage house.[30] Dr. Townshend Forester, rector 1818–41,[31] was presented by his brother.[32] He was perpetual curate of Benthall 1796–1841,[33] vicar of St. John in Bedwardine (Worcs.) 1818–41,[34] and in 1839 lived at Broseley[35] where he was rector 1799–1841.[36] Forester's assistant curates at Little Wenlock included G. L. Yate (1818–24),[37] an Evangelical whose uncle Nathaniel Gilbert had assisted Fletcher at Madeley,[38] and the antiquary C. H. Hartshorne[39] (1826–36).[40]

employed as assistant curate D. H. S. Cranage,[50] the antiquary and later dean of Norwich.[51] J. W. Johnson, rector 1898–1922,[52] rejected all ritual and, apparently believing in predestination, took little interest in pastoral work.[53]

In 1980 there was a service every Sunday, alternately in the morning and evening.[54] Average attendance on ordinary Sundays was c. 20.[55]

The church of *ST. LAWRENCE*, so named by 1817,[56] is built of ashlar, rubble, and red brick and has a chancel with north vestry, nave with north aisle and glazed west porch, and a tower at the west end of the aisle.

[17] H.W.R.O.(H.), Heref. dioc. rec., visit. return.
[18] S.P.L., MS. 4646, p. 133.
[19] S.R.O. 4236/Rg/2, predecessor bur. 5 Apr. 1763.
[20] Ibid. /3, bur. 14 Mar. 1786.
[21] Heref. Dioc. Regy., reg. 1755–71, f. 26v.
[22] Ibid, 1772–1802, ff. 109, 146; 1791–1821, f. 118v.; 1822–42, pp. 45, 97, 237, 290; par. reg. s.a. 1758–1812 (transcript in S.P.L.); par. rec., bap. reg. 1813–58; ibid. bur. reg. 1813–98; ibid. marr. reg. 1813–37; T.S.A.S. 4th ser. vi. 320.
[23] T.S.A.S. 4th ser. vi. 320; Bannister, *Heref. Institutions*, 142.   [24] Bannister, op. cit. 108, 131.
[25] T.S.A.S. 4th ser. vii. 166; S.R.O. 2660/Rg/2; /MRg/1–2 (he signs until 1817).
[26] S.R.O. 3916/1/1, p. 20.
[27] J. Randall, *Severn Valley* (1882), 339–43.
[28] S.R.O. 3916/1/1, p. 20.
[29] Heref. Dioc. Regy., reg. 1772–1802, f. 146; par. reg. bap. 8 Nov. 1818.
[30] Heref. Dioc. Regy., reg. 1791–1821, f. 118v.; 1822–42, pp. 45, 97, 237, 290.
[31] Bannister, *Heref. Institutions*, 142, 158.
[32] Burke, *Peerage* (1949), 782.
[33] Bannister, op. cit. 125, 158.
[34] T.S.A.S. 2nd ser. iii. 175.
[35] Heref. Dioc. Regy., reg. 1822–42, p. 463.

[36] Bannister, *Heref. Institutions*, 127, 158.
[37] Par. reg. bap. 8 Nov., 27 Dec. 1818; bur. 29 Aug., 10 Sept. 1824.
[38] Above, Madeley, Churches.
[39] D.N.B.
[40] Par. reg. marr. 8 May 1828; bap. 21 Feb. 1836.
[41] And previously vicar of Madeley: Bannister, *Heref. Institutions*, 150, 158.
[42] Par. reg. bap. 21 June 1846; 17 Jan. 1847.
[43] Ibid. bur. 27 Apr., 11 July 1889.
[44] D. H. S. Cranage, *Not Only a Dean* (1952), 63.
[45] Below, Educ.
[46] *Salopian Shreds & Patches*, ii. 94.
[47] P.R.O., HO 129/358, no. 39.
[48] Cranage, *Not Only a Dean*, 63.
[49] Heref. Dioc. Regy., reg. 1883–1901, pp. 232, 646.
[50] Cranage, op. cit. 62–7.
[51] D.N.B. 1951–60.
[52] Heref. Dioc. Regy., reg. 1883–1901, p. 646; 1919–26, p. 228. He had been vicar of Benthall 1892–8: Bannister, *Heref. Institutions*, 207, 214.
[53] Cranage, *Not Only a Dean*, 66–7.
[54] *Newsletter for Pars. of Coalbrookdale, Ironbridge, and L. Wenlock*, July 1980, 3.
[55] Inf. from the rector.
[56] B.L. Add. MS. 21181, f. 63.

The vestry (formerly the chancel), which is exceptionally small internally and has thick walls, has a small blocked window, probably of the 12th century, in the north wall. In the late Middle Ages the chancel's north and south walls were heightened,[57] its east end was rebuilt, and it received a new roof. The lower part of the north wall of the aisle (formerly the nave) is medieval and has part of a blocked doorway towards its west end. The surviving arch-braced roof of the former nave and most of the windows, which have been replaced, were probably made in the 15th century. The western buttresses of the tower are also of medieval origin but the tower was reconstructed in 1667, when a large buttress was added on the north. In the 18th century a new window was put into the east wall of the chancel and another into the south,[58] and a west gallery may have been built.[59] In 1822 a south aisle of brick was added to the nave.[60] In the period 1875–6 new windows, buttresses, and a porch (extended 1892)[61] were added to the aisle, and a new brick chancel was built at its east end. The aisle then became the nave, separated from the north aisle by a new arcade of four bays. The old chancel was converted to a baptistery and vestry, connected to the new chancel by making its south window into a doorway, and was provided with a new east window. The north wall of the old nave was rebuilt, with windows to match those on the south.[62]

The furniture, fittings, and glass date almost entirely from 1876 or later.[63] A cast-iron grave slab dated 1611, one of the earliest known,[64] is set in the floor of the old chancel. In 1915 there were five bells, all of 1704 (two recast 1892).[65] There is a chest dated 1733. In 1961 the communion plate consisted of a silver flagon, chalice, and two patens, all of 1742.[66] An 18th-century oval stone font[67] stands in the aisle. The arms of George IV, formerly in the aisle, were stored in the vestry in 1982.

The graveyard, formerly semicircular,[68] was extended northwards in 1851; it contains several iron slabs of the 18th and early 19th century. In 1944 an additional graveyard off Witchwell Lane was consecrated.[69]

The registers begin in 1689[70] and are complete thereafter.

NONCONFORMITY. No dissenters or Roman Catholics were reported in 1676[71] or 1716,[72] and in the later 18th century Methodism was resisted by the farmers. When John Fletcher tried to preach in the parish a noisy disturbance took place.[73] Wesleyans from Lawley Bank preached in the coalmining area c. 1799.[74] In 1813 Wesleyans had weekly preaching at their 'Horsehay and Little Wenlock' station.[75] By 1816, and until the 1840s or later, there were also meetings at Coalmoor and Huntington.[76] In the 1870s there were weekly Wesleyan services at Lawley Furnaces.[77] A house was licensed for meetings in 1825,[78] perhaps for the Revivalist Methodists. In 1839 members of the New Connexion met weekly at New Works, Huntington, Coalmoor, and Little Wenlock.[79] Meetings were still taking place in 1860.[80] In the 1850s Primitive Methodists met at Coalmoor, New Works (by 1837),[81] and Little Wenlock[82] but the Coalmoor society met from 1858 at the Moreton's Coppice chapel, in Dawley parish.[83] By 1890 the only meeting was at New Works,[84] where the society (inactive from 1927) expired in 1930.[85] In the early 1930s rallies organized by Dawley and Madeley Methodist circuit were held at New Buildings Farm[86] and the village hall.[87]

EDUCATION. William Poole was a schoolmaster at Little Wenlock in 1671[88] and there was a schoolhouse, apparently at the rectory, in 1713.[89] There was more than one school in 1716 but no free or charity school.[90] William Hazlehurst (d. 1766)[91] was tenant of a schoolhouse.[92] In 1818 the parish had only a Sunday school but in 1819 a room was being repaired for a day school to be

57 Former S. wall plate and rafter ends temporarily exposed in 1982.

58 S.P.L., MS. 372, vol. i, p. 19; S.P.L., J. H. Smith colln., no. 210; date on tower parapet.

59 A skylight existed at the W. end of the nave roof: S.P.L., J. H. Smith colln., no. 210.

60 S. Bagshaw, Dir. Salop. (1851), 566; P.O. Dir. Salop. (1856), 141.

61 Cranage, iii. 214.

62 Salopian Shreds & Patches, ii. 94–5. Cranage wrongly dated the work 1865: op. cit. 214. The correct date is confirmed by par. rec., vestry min. bk. 1818–1958, 6 May 1875; plaque in new chancel.

63 Salopian Shreds & Patches, ii. 94–5; Heref. Dioc. Regy., reg. 1883–1901, pp. 670–1; 1919–26, p. 350; 1926–38, p. 445.

64 Inf. from I.G.M.T.

65 H. B. Walters, Ch. Bells of Salop. (Oswestry, 1915), 69–70,

66 D. L. Arkwright and B. W. Bourne, Ch. Plate Archd. Ludlow (Shrews. 1961), 38.

67 Present by 1817: B.L. Add. MS. 21181, f. 63.

68 S.R.O. 1224/1/59.

69 Heref. Dioc. Regy., reg. 1847–56, pp. 324–5; 1938–53, pp. 239–41.

70 H.W.R.O.(H.), Heref. dioc. rec., include L. Wenlock transcripts 1660–76, 1678, and 1680 on.

71 T.S.A.S. 2nd ser. i. 91.

72 H.W.R.O.(H.), Heref. dioc. rec., visit. return.

73 R. F. Skinner, Nonconformity in Salop. (Shrews. 1964), 72.

74 S.R.O. 2280/16/185, p. 13; Trinder, Ind. Rev. Salop. 197.

75 S.P.L., C 98.7 v.f., Shrews. circuit plan.

76 Shrews. Sch. libr., Broseley circuit bk. 1815–41.

77 S.P.L., L 98.7 v.f. Wellington circuit plan of 1878.

78 P.R.O., RG 31/2, Lich., no. 1109. The signatories were from Madeley. One had been a Wesleyan minister in 1800: B. Trinder, Meth. New Connexion in Dawley and Madeley (Wesley Hist. Soc., W. Midlands Branch, Occ. Publ. i [1968]), 2.

79 S.R.O. 3677/1.

80 Trinder, Meth. New Connexion, 14.

81 S.R.O. 3605/2.

82 S.R.O. 2533/130, passim.

83 Ibid. 21 Apr. 1856.

84 S.R.O. 1936/2.

85 Ibid. /44, 53–4.

86 Ibid. /67.

87 Ibid. /73–4.

88 H.W.R.O.(H.), Heref. dioc. rec., visit. bk. 22, f. [4v.].

89 Ibid. inv. of Wm. Whyston, 1713.

90 Ibid. visit. return.

91 Par. reg. (transcript in S.P.L.).

92 S.R.O. 1224, box 314, Lady Day rental of 1769, p. 11.

opened in 1820.[93] The only schools in 1833, however, were three private ones.[94]

Little Wenlock parochial school, founded in 1842 by the rector George Edmonds, was held in a building in the grounds of the Old Hall.[95] In 1867 he paid for a new building adjoining the churchyard and it was vested in Lord Forester. The school was in association with the National Society by 1869, when attendance averaged 65. A certificated mistress was first appointed in 1877.[96] Lord Forester sold the premises to the county council in 1921.[97] As Little Wenlock County School it closed in 1958, when there were only 17 pupils.[98] Afterwards most of the younger children were taken daily to Dawley.[99]

CHARITIES FOR THE POOR. In the period 1667–76 an endowment left by George Baxter, rector (d. c. 1663),[1] yielded £1 a year, distributed in cash.[2] By the 1780s, however, the charity was forgotten.[3] By 1672[4] Mrs. Alice Green had left 10s. a year out of land in Brierley (Staffs.)[5] to be

distributed in cash.[6] The income was lost after 1897.[7] Maurice Hayward (d. 1760) left the interest on £10 for bread.[8] In the early 1870s the income, then 10s., ceased.

Mrs. Mary Tipton left £50 in 1844, most of the interest to be distributed to the poor. The income in 1897 was £1 7s. 8d. In 1845 Mrs. Hannah Shepherd left the interest on £100 to be distributed as clothing. In 1897 the income was £2 15s. 4d. Margaret Poole left the interest on £19 19s. in 1874, to be distributed in bread or flannel. The income was 12s. 9d. in 1875. In 1889 George Edmonds, rector, bequeathed the interest on £400, most of it to be given in cash to the poor within Little Wenlock ecclesiastical parish.[9] In 1897 the income was £11 6s. 4d. In 1914 George Thorneycroft gave £23 6s. 8d., the interest to be given in cash.

By 1925 the surviving charities were usually distributed in coal. In 1970 they were formally amalgamated as the Little Wenlock United Charities, and in 1975 the income was £17, from stock.[10]

[93] *Digest Educ. Poor*, H.C. 224, pp. 763, 770 (1819), ix (2); p. 1475 (1819), ix (3).
[94] *Educ. Enq. Abstract*, H.C. 62, p. 786 (1835), xlii.
[95] D. R. Dishington, 'Hist. of L. Wenlock' (1970; MS. in par. rec.), p. 6.
[96] P.R.O., ED 7/103, ff. 162–165v.; S.R.O. 1681, box 29, sch. acct. bk., front endpaper.
[97] *S.C.C. Mins. (Educ.)* 1921–2, 55.
[98] Ibid. 1957–8, 134; 1958–9, 103.
[99] Local inf.   [1] Above, Church.
[2] S.R.O. 3331/1, ff. 3, 4, 6v., 10v.

[3] *Char. Don. 1786–8*, ii, H.C. 511–II, pp. 1040–1 (1816), xvi (2).
[4] S.R.O. 3331/1, f. 6 and v.
[5] *3rd Rep. Com. Char.* H.C. 5, p. 308 (1820), iv.
[6] *Char. Don. 1786–8*, ii. 1040.
[7] Par. rec., vestry min. bk. 1818–1958. What follows is based on that and a board in the ch.
[8] *3rd Rep. Com. Char.* 308.
[9] S.R.O. 1681, box 29, Char. Com. to —, 13 Nov. 1889 (copy).
[10] *Review of Local Chars.* (S.C.C. 1975), 66.

BRADFORD HUNDRED

BRADFORD, the 'broad ford' (mentioned in the 1140s) from which Shropshire's most extensive hundred took its name,[1] lies within the manor and parish of Ercall Magna where the road from High Ercall to Shrewsbury crosses the river Roden.[2] Bradford bridge apparently remained the meeting place of the hundred court until the early 17th century.[3]

Bradford hundred was formed by an amalgamation of the Domesday hundreds of Hodnet and Wrockwardine, respectively the north and north-western and the south and south-eastern parts of the resulting hundred.[4] The suggestion that Wrockwardine hundred was conterminous with an ancient British area called Ercall[5] must contend with the likelihood that the hundred boundaries of Domesday Shropshire were little more than a century old.[6] The estates forming Wrockwardine hundred amounted to $173\frac{5}{12}$ hides in 1086, those forming Hodnet amounted to $96\frac{7}{8}$. In 1086 the *caput* of each hundred was the manor after which it was named. Before the Conquest both manors had been held by King Edward the Confessor; in Wrockwardine, and doubtless in Hodnet too, Earl Edwin had received the 'third penny' from the hundred profits. By 1086 both manors, with all the hundred profits, belonged to Roger, earl of Shrewsbury, and they escheated to the Crown in 1102 after the rebellion of his son Earl Robert.[7]

Hodnet and Wrockwardine hundreds were amalgamated in the mid or later 12th century, for Wrockwardine still existed c. 1140[8] but Bradford hundred had been created by 1203.[9] The reason for the union is not clear, for even before it took place Wrockwardine was the county's largest hundred.[10] The change may, however, have served the convenience of the great feudatories with lands and fees in both hundreds, pre-eminent among whom were the Pantulfs of Wem (whose barony lay almost wholly within the two hundreds)[11] and the FitzAlans of Oswestry.[12] The FitzAlans' quasi-hereditary shrievalty[13] was certainly used to reinforce the family's power elsewhere in Shropshire by modifying the county's administrative geography.[14] Between 1180 and 1201 the brothers-in-law[15] Hugh Pantulf and William FitzAlan (II) were successive sheriffs,[16] and they may have caused the hundreds to be amalgamated during that period. More precisely, the choice of Bradford as the new hundred meeting place may suggest the year 1190–1 when William of Ercall (*alias* of Hadley), lord (if the elder of that name) of the manor of Ercall Magna, was William FitzAlan (II)'s under-sheriff;[17]

[1] O. S. Anderson, *Eng. Hundred Names* (Lund, 1934), 153; Eyton, ix. 65–6.
[2] At O.S. Nat. Grid SJ 587 166: S.R.O. 2258/1 (nos. 397–400, 453–4, 467).
[3] P.R.O., SC 2/197/96; Staffs. R.O., D. 593/J/10, ct. r.; Barnard MSS., Raby Castle, box 7, bdle. 22, no. 8.
[4] *V.C.H. Salop.* iii. 8, 40.
[5] G. Jones, 'Continuity Despite Calamity: The Heritage of Celtic Territorial Organization in Eng.' *Jnl. Celtic Studies*, iii. 27; E. Ekwall, *Concise Oxf. Dict. Eng. P.N.* (4th edn.), 167–8.
[6] *V.C.H. Salop.* iii. 6.
[7] Ibid. i. 283, 293, 315; iii. 9, 42.
[8] Ibid. iii. 11 (corr. below, Corrigenda).

[9] *Pleas bef. King or his Justices, 1198–1212*, iii (Selden Soc. lxxxiii), pp. 81–3.
[10] Eyton, vii. 197.
[11] *V.C.H. Salop.* i. 297–8; iii. 51.
[12] As successors of the sheriff Reynold of Bailleul and of Turold of Vesly: ibid. i. 296, 298, 319–21; Eyton, vii. 198–203; ix. 152–5.
[13] *V.C.H. Salop.* iii. 10–12.
[14] Ibid. 35–6.
[15] Eyton, vii. 239; ix. 167.
[16] Ibid. iii. 67–9; ix. 165; *V.C.H. Salop.* iii. 12.
[17] *V.C.H. Salop.* iii. 12 (corr. below, Corrigenda); Eyton, ix. 80.

THE HUNDRED OF BRADFORD c.1831

Ercall was probably[18] a second cousin of FitzAlan's half-sister,[19] the wife of Hugh Pantulf.[20]

The composition of Bradford hundred never differed greatly from that of the hundreds combined to produce it,[21] but there were peripheral gains and losses. The transfer of Sheriffhales from Staffordshire may have been initiated by Earl Roger or by one of his sons in the late 11th century.[22] In the event, however, only part of the manor was transferred, with resulting administrative anomalies over the centuries.[23] Sheriffhales seems to have been taxed with Cuttlestone hundred (Staffs.) in 1327,[24] 1332,[25] and 1381,[26] but by the later 17th century the Shropshire and Staffordshire parts were being taxed with Bradford and Cuttlestone hundreds respectively.[27] Tyrley's transfer to Pirehill hundred (Staffs.) may have taken place early in the 12th century and for the Pantulfs' convenience.[28] Cheswardine was probably gained from Pirehill hundred when Henry I acquired that manor from Robert of Stafford.[29]

Buildwas, exempted from Condover hundred in the late 12th century when Richard I granted Buildwas abbey quittance of suit at the hundred court,[30] was treated as in Bradford hundred in 1236.[31] Emstrey (including Cronkhill and Chilton) was accounted part of Condover hundred until 1672 or later; by 1788, however, it was apparently being rated with the rest of Atcham parish in Bradford hundred.[32]

Albrightlee and Longner were in Wrockwardine hundred in 1086.[33] Longner became part of the 'old liberties' of Shrewsbury[34] presumably at an early date. Pimley, in Bradford hundred by 1255,[35] seems to have been incorporated within the borough liberties in 1495,[36] and Albrightlee, probably in Bradford hundred c. 1285,[37] may also have been incorporated in the liberties in 1495.[38] Nevertheless Albrightlee may have been taxed with the liberties of Shrewsbury in 1327,[39] and it and Pimley were also said to be in Bradford hundred in 1515. The hundred and the borough liberties seem then to have overlapped.[40]

Although in the Domesday hundred of Baschurch (later Pimhill), Crudgington[41] and Moreton Corbet[42] were taxed with Bradford hundred in 1327;[43] Crudgington was probably,[44] and Moreton Corbet was certainly, in Bradford hundred by 1255.[45] Preston Brockhurst in Baschurch hundred was a divided manor in 1086;[46] the greater part became a member of Moreton Corbet[47] and, probably in the 14th century, was

[18] i.e. if Wm. FitzAlan (I)'s 1st wife was Wm. and Hamon Peverel's niece. See *T.S.A.S.* liii. 122–3; Eyton, ix. 68–9, 78–9.

[19] Rather than (as suggested in *V.C.H. Salop.* iii. 12) FitzAlan's own cousin. Eyton (ix. 80) assumed Wm. of Ercall (II), fl. 1190s – 1220s (ibid. 80–2), to have been the under-sheriff, though he is referred to as *juvenis* and *minor* during his fr.'s life in the 1190s (ibid. ii. 133 n. 98, 282; ix. 80–1).

[20] Eyton, vii. 239; ix. 167.

[21] Cf. *V.C.H. Salop.* ii. 207; iii. 8, 40; *Feud. Aids,* iv. 226–8; *T.S.A.S.* 2nd ser. i. 133–200; B.L. Add. MS. 50121, p. 32; Staffs. R.O., D. 593/J/10, subsidy assessment, 1524; *Hearth Tax 1672* (Salop. Arch. Soc.), 44–103. *V.C.H. Salop.* iii. 8, generally accords with Eyton's suggestions where Dom. Bk.'s hund. rubrics are doubtful (see *V.C.H. Salop.* iii. 2 n. 18; cf. Eyton, vii–x, esp. vii. 197–202, and ix. 150–6), but for Crudgington see below.

[22] Cf. *V.C.H. Salop.* iii. 43; Eyton, ii. 258–9, 261–2; *T.S.A.S.* lvii. 157.

[23] *V.C.H. Staffs.* iv. 61; *Orders of Q. Sess.* i, orders 1638–60, 3; i. 38.

[24] *S.H.C.* vii (1), 245–6. Cf. *T.S.A.S.* 3rd ser. vii. 375–8 (not mentioned).

[25] *S.H.C.* x (1), 124.

[26] *S.H.C.* xvii. 199–200.

[27] *V.C.H. Staffs.* iv. 61; *Hearth Tax 1672,* 93.

[28] Eyton, ix. 192; *S.H.C.* 1945–6, 24–6; *V.C.H. Staffs.* iv. 2.

[29] *V.C.H. Salop.* iii. 49 n. 13.   [30] Ibid. viii. 1.

[31] P.R.O., JUST 1/1589. L. Buildwas, as a member of Wroxeter presumably in Wrockwardine hund. 1086, was in Bradford hund. 1255: Eyton, vii. 320, 322.

[32] *V.C.H. Salop.* ii. 207; viii. 2; S.R.O., q. sess. order bk. 1783–9, f. 254v.

[33] *V.C.H. Salop.* i. 311, 314.

[34] H. Owen and J. B. Blakeway, *Hist. Shrews.* (1825), i. 86 n. 2.

[35] *Rot. Hund.* (Rec. Com.), ii. 57.

[36] Owen and Blakeway, op. cit. i. 268.

[37] Eyton, viii. 249–50; *Collect. Topog. et Geneal.* i. 113. Cf. P.R.O., JUST 1/1589.

[38] *T.S.A.S.* 2nd ser. ii. 72–4; 3rd ser. i. 180–1.

[39] Ibid. 3rd ser. vii. 361–2, 364–5.

[40] Ibid. 2nd ser. ii. 72–5.

[41] *V.C.H. Salop.* i. 327; iii. 8. 'Crugetone', implausibly suggested (Eyton, x. 308) as a lost man. nr. Stanwardine in the Fields, was a berewick of Ercall Magna in 1066 (ibid. ix. 63), Rob. the butler's estate by 1086 and forfeited c. 1102 (*V.C.H. Salop.* i. 298, 327), and given to Shrews. abbey by Hamon Peverel in the later 1130s (Eyton, viii. 127–9, 152–3; ix. 64, 102).

[42] Eyton, x. 39–40.

[43] *T.S.A.S.* 2nd ser. i. 158–9, 184.

[44] Eyton, ix. 102.

[45] Ibid. x. 187.

[46] Ibid. x. 178, 180; *V.C.H. Salop.* i. 335, 339–40.

[47] Eyton, x. 180–1.

attracted into Bradford hundred.[48] Charlton (in Shawbury)[49] also passed from Baschurch to Bradford. Acton Reynald, Besford, and parts of Preston Brockhurst[50] were the only parts of Shawbury parish never in Bradford hundred.[51]

Bradford hundred comprised a third of the area of the medieval county and it was assessed to the 1381 poll tax in at least two divisions, the northern one[52] closely resembling the permanent division fixed two centuries later.[53] By 1590 the hundred contained 20 of the 100 allotments into which the county was divided for militia and rating; in 1638 Bradford's rating was increased to $23\frac{1}{8}$ of the county's 100 allotments.[54] Bradford hundred was said in 1575 to be 'as large as any two within the shire',[55] and divisions for magistrates' and other administrative business were accordingly necessary at a comparatively early date.[56] At first the divisions were temporary or *ad hoc*. The hundred was, for example, divided into halves for the militia musters of 1539 but not for those of 1542. By 1590, however, North and South divisions had been fixed, and they were not seriously modified before 1836.[57] The North division was used for tax assessment and collection in the earlier 17th century,[58] and after the establishment of a Presbyterian ecclesiastical system it was adopted as the area of the fourth classis with a meeting place at Whitchurch.[59]

In the 1630s the county magistrates used the North and South divisions and even subdivided the North division into two: one half, closely resembling the later Drayton division, comprised the five eastern allotments of Hodnet, Moreton Say, Stoke and (Child's) Ercall, Drayton, and Cheswardine.[60] North and South seem to have been permanently subdivided by the mid 18th century. By 1788, and probably earlier, the North was divided into Drayton and Whitchurch divisions, the South into Newport and Wellington divisions, for collection of the county rate.[61] In Bradford North the magistrates used the Drayton and Whitchurch divisions for their Michaelmas licensing sessions between 1759 and 1768 and again in the early 19th century; in Bradford South separate licensing sessions were held for the Newport and Wellington divisions from c. 1805.[62] The four magistrates' divisions were increased to five in 1836 when Wem division was formed from the Whitchurch division and detached parts of Pimhill hundred.[63] The hundred name remained in use in association with the five petty-sessional divisions until the 1860s;[64] the divisions themselves lasted until 1954.[65] The coroner's district called Bradford North was absorbed in one called North Shropshire in 1972[66] and that called Bradford South and Brimstree (Shifnal) was renamed East Shropshire in 1974.[67]

Bradford hundred seems to have been worth 20 and 30 marks a year in the 13th and

[48] i.e. 1327 × 1414: *T.S.A.S.* 3rd ser. v. 58–9; P.R.O., JUST 1/753, rott. 11 (2), 13 (1). Cf. Eyton, x. 40; *V.C.H. Salop.* ii. 207, 209. *V.C.H. Salop.* iii. 40, is thus wrong in showing the whole of Preston in Pimhill c. 1500.

[49] Eyton (viii. 250), probably correct in disbelieving Dom. Bk.'s rubric Culvestan hund., suggested Baschurch or Wrockwardine hund., opting for the latter, *V.C.H. Salop.* iii. 8, opts for the former.

[50] Eyton, x. 38–41, 61–5, 173–81.

[51] *V.C.H. Salop.* ii. 207, 209, 211.

[52] P.R.O., E 179/242/34; cf. E 179/240/308(7).

[53] Below. The div. in 1381 incl. a few extra townships mainly in Gt. Bolas, Chetwynd, Edgmond, Ercall Magna, and Waters Upton pars.

[54] S.R.O., q. sess. order bk. 1, schedule 14 July 1638. Cf. *V.C.H. Salop.* iii. 85–6, 102.

[55] B.L. Harl. MS. 539, f. 168.

[56] Cf. *V.C.H. Mdx.* vi. 4–5.

[57] *V.C.H. Salop.* ii. 207; iii. 74, 106; *T.S.A.S.* 3rd ser. viii. 248–51, 255–75, and pl. facing p. 245; *L. & P. Hen. VIII*, xvii,

pp. 507–8; S.R.O. 999/Ss 67; S.P.L., MS. 4071, pp. 222–4.

[58] Glamorgan Archive Service, CL/Deeds I/Salop. 1642, June 5; S.R.O. 999 /Ss 67; 1378/22 (incomplete).

[59] W. A. Shaw, *Hist. Eng. Church 1640–60*, ii. 31, 412; *T.S.A.S.* 4th ser. ii. 297. Cf. ibid. xlvii. 1–14 (where the E. part of the N. div. has been incl. in the S. div., almost certainly in error).

[60] An area crossed by an important vagrant route (*V.C.H. Salop.* iii. 101). See *Cal. S.P. Dom.* 1631–3, esp. pp. 11, 69, 80, 256; 1633–4; 1634–5; 1636–7; 1637; Addenda 1625–49.

[61] Cf. S.R.O., q. sess. order bk. 1783–9, ff. 254v.–255.

[62] S.R.O., q. sess. rec. parcels 255–9, regs. of alesellers' recognizances 1753–1828.

[63] *V.C.H. Salop.* ii. 207 (corr. ibid. iii. 398).

[64] S.R.O. 119/33, bridge list of 1862.

[65] *S.C.C. Mins.* 1953–4, 62–3; S.R.O. 900/1, p. 39. Cf. *V.C.H. Salop.* iii. 227.

[66] *S.C.C. Mins.* 1972–3, 190.

[67] Inf. from the coroner; cf *S.C.C. Yr. Bk. 1972–3*, 20; *1974–5*, 18.

14th centuries.[68] The Barons' War may temporarily have reduced its worth to only £5 a year, the value ascertained in 1264, and after the Black Death its value fell to under £8.[69] In the 15th century the value evidently fell: it was leased for £6 a year in 1435 and was said to be worth only 4 marks a year net in 1498.[70] In 1543 the lord of the hundred was said to be entitled to the forfeited chattels of felons, fugitives, warrantors, and outlaws.[71]

In 1267 the Crown granted the hundred for life to Walter of Pedwardine[72] (kt. c. 1270),[73] a minor landowner[74] of some service to the royalists during the civil war[75] and to the FitzAlans.[76] Pedwardine (d. 1297) was to render 8 marks a year at the Exchequer. In 1292 he was temporarily deprived of the hundred, which he had made over to the bailiff for 36 marks a year 'to the injury of all the freeholders'; the bailiff, William Cressett, was then under indictment for murder.[77] In Edward I's last years the hundred was held by Walter de Kyngeshemede during pleasure, and in 1309 Edward II granted it to John de Vaux for life.[78] In 1310 Vaux exchanged it with the king's cook Richard of Cleobury for the keeping of Kinver forest and manor (Staffs.). Cleobury, like Vaux, was to hold the hundred for life; perhaps for non-payment of the farm, however,[79] he was deprived, and in the 1320s the hundred was committed to the sheriff or other accountants during pleasure.[80] In 1327 it was granted for life to Queen Isabel in augmentation of her dower by 24 marks a year.[81]

The queen was deprived of her property after the earl of March's downfall in 1330,[82] and in 1331 Edward III granted the hundred in tail male to Sir John de Neville of Hornby (Lancs.), who had helped to arrest March. On Neville's death without male issue in 1335 the hundred escheated to the Crown and was evidently restored to Richard of Cleobury, who had been pardoned his arrears in 1327.[83]

In 1338 Edward III granted the hundred in tail male to his chamberlain Lord Ferrers of Groby[84] and it remained in private hands almost continuously thereafter. It descended with the barony of Ferrers of Groby until 1445[85] and thereafter with the manor of Tettenhall Regis (Staffs.).[86] In 1601–2 Francis Newport (kt. 1603), one of the county's leading magistrates and probably its richest gentleman,[87] bought the hundred from Sir Humphrey Ferrers; at the same time he also acquired the Crown's reversionary rights on any failure of the heirs male of the 1338 grantee.[88] Sir Francis died seised in fee in 1623[89] and the hundred then passed to his son Sir Richard, cr. Baron Newport 1642. On his death in 1651 the hundred evidently passed to his son and heir Francis,[90] but the story is confused. In 1653 it was surveyed as part of Charles

[68] Eyton, ix. 155–6; *Cal. Close*, 1268–72, 437; 1369–74, 356; *Cal. Fine R.* 1319–27, 180, 263; *Abbrev. Rot. Orig.* (Rec. Com.), i. 277; *Cal. Chart. R.* 1327–41, 230–1; P.R.O., E 163/4/23, mm. 1–3; E 199/38/75(2); E 372/173, Salopia; SC 5/8/6, m. 3.

[69] *Cal. Inq. Misc.* i, pp. 96–7.

[70] Barnard MSS., Raby Castle, box 7, loose deed; *Cal. Inq. p.m. Hen. VII*, ii, p. 159.

[71] P.R.O., E 370/11/3.

[72] *Cal. Pat.* 1266–72, 79; *Cal. Inq. p.m.* ix, p. 434.

[73] Eyton, vii. 345; xi. 199, 239, 304.

[74] Ibid. iv. 190, 367; v. 78; xi. 328, 337–8.

[75] Ibid. iv. 276; viii. 31–2; xi. 330–1.

[76] Ibid. x. 340; xi. 239.

[77] Ibid. ix. 156.

[78] *Cal. Pat.* 1307–13, 201.

[79] Ibid.; 1327–30, 159; *Cal. Close*, 1307–13, 411; *Cal. Fine R.* 1307–19, 75, 80; *Cal. Chanc. R. Var.* 103; *Abbrev. Rot. Orig.* (Rec. Com.), i. 174–6; *Rot. Parl.* (Rec. Com.), i. 435–6; *V.C.H. Staffs.* ii. 344; xx. 129, 131.

[80] *Cal. Fine R.* 1319–27, 110, 180, 263; *Abbrev. Rot. Orig.* i. 265, 277; *Cal. Mem. R.* 1326–7, pp. xxvii, 5, 9; P.R.O., E 372/173, Salopia.

[81] *Cal. Pat.* 1327–30, 68; *Cal. Close*, 1330–3, 20.

[82] *D.N.B.* s.v. Isabella.

[83] *V.C.H. Salop.* iii. 44; *V.C.H. Lancs.* viii. 193; *Cal. Close*, 1333–7, 121, 174, 207; *Cal. Pat.* 1327–30, 159; *Cal. Fine R.* 1327–37, 469.

[84] *Cal. Pat.* 1338–40, 5; *Cal. Close* 1337–9, 352; 1346–9, 319; *Cal. Inq. p.m.* viii, p. 319; ix. p. 434; T. F. Tout, *Chapters in Admin. Hist.* vi (1933), 46.

[85] *Cal. Close* 1369–74, 355–6; 1392–6, 303; *Cal. Inq. p.m.* ix, p. 434; xiii, p. 67; xvi, p. 212; *Cal. Inq. p.m.* (Rec. Com.), iii. 93, 115, 174; iv. 224. Cf. *Complete Peerage*, v. 356.

[86] *Cal. Inq. p.m.* (Rec. Com.), iv. 284; *Cal. Inq. p.m. Hen. VII*, ii, p. 159; P.R.O., C 2/Eliz. I/F 3/32; /F 9/19; E 370/11/3; B.L. Add. MS. 30325, ff. 12, 15. Cf. *V.C.H. Staffs.* xx. 16.

[87] W. A. Shaw, *Kts. of Eng.* (1906), ii. 101; *V.C.H. Salop.* iii. 66, 95, 238; *Hist. Parl., Commons*, 1558–1603, iii. 131.

[88] Barnard MSS., Raby Castle, box 7, bdle. 22, nos. 2–7, 10; B.L. Add. MS. 15553, ff. 105–7; P.R.O., C 54/1722, mm. 5d.–6d.; CP 25(2)/203/44 Eliz. I Hil. no. 1.

[89] P.R.O., C 142/402, no. 146.

[90] Barnard MSS., Raby Castle, box 7, bdle. 22, no. 11; P.R.O., CP 25(2)/528/18 Chas. I East [no. 13]; *D.N.B.*

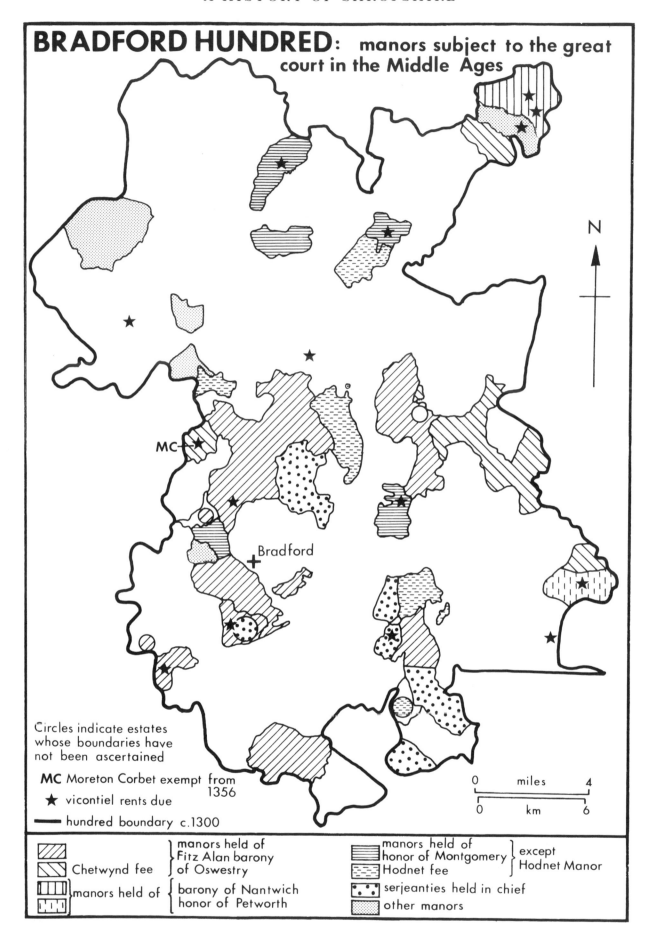

BRADFORD HUNDRED: manors subject to the great court in the Middle Ages

N

MC

Bradford

Circles indicate estates
whose boundaries have
not been ascertained

MC Moreton Corbet exempt from
1356
★ vicontiel rents due
— hundred boundary c.1300

0 miles 4
0 km 6

	manors held of Fitz Alan barony of Oswestry		manors held of honor of Montgomery	except Hodnet Manor
Chetwynd fee			Hodnet fee	
manors held of	barony of Nantwich honor of Petworth		serjeanties held in chief	
			other manors	

I's former possessions, then settled on the Commonwealth trustees; at the same time the profits of courts and all the royalties were said to belong to the inheritance of Francis Newport, then known as 'Mr.' Newport, of Eyton on Severn.[91] In 1661 Charles II leased the hundred, with three others (Condover, Pimhill, and Stottesdon) then remaining in the Crown, to Richard Salter the younger for 31 years. Later all four hundreds were included in Queen Catherine's jointure.[92] In 1672, however, the Crown granted and confirmed all four hundreds, with return of writs, to Francis, Lord Newport,[93] and he was created Viscount Newport of Bradford in 1675 and earl of Bradford in 1694.[94] After 1672 Bradford hundred evidently descended with the Newports' peerage dignities until 1734 when it passed away from the 3rd earl of Bradford's legitimate heirs, descending with the manor of Harley.[95] Although they did not own the hundred, the Newports' legitimate heirs, the Bridgemans, were later created Baron (1794), and earl of (1815), Bradford.[96] In 1805 the hundred belonged to the earl of Darlington,[97] cr. marquess (1827) and duke (1833) of Cleveland.[98] On his death in 1842 it passed to his son Henry, the 2nd duke (d. 1864), during whose time the hundred court ceased to function.[99]

Twice-yearly (eventually annual) great courts and three-weekly small courts for the hundred were held throughout the Middle Ages and beyond.[1] In almost exactly half of the manors in the hundred, however, the jurisdiction of the great court was curtailed during the 13th century by courts leet that exempted them from the sheriff's tourn in the great hundred.[2] The exempt manors were the more extensive ones, accounting perhaps for some two thirds of the hundred's area. In nearly every instance, whether a manor became exempt depended on the ease with which leet jurisdiction alternative to the hundred's could be provided and so on the manorial lord's status and position in the landowning and feudal hierarchies. Almost invariably the hundred's greater landowners and tenants in chief secured leet jurisdiction for the courts of their demesne manors. Contrariwise minor tenants in chief and (with a notable group of exceptions)[3] lords of subinfeudated manors were generally held to suit at the hundred court: indeed the chief or the mesne lord of a place might, at subinfeudation, pass down to its terre tenant the specific duty, *inter alia*, of suit to the hundred.[4] Between the end of the 13th century and the end of the 16th very few manors became exempt from the hundred or lost their exemption.

Almost half of the manors exempt from suit to the hundred were in ecclesiastical ownership: properties of the see of Coventry and Lichfield[5] and of the abbeys of Shrewsbury,[6] Lilleshall,[7] Haughmond,[8] Combermere (Ches.),[9] and Buildwas.[10] Some

[91] P.R.O., E 317/Salop./1; cf. CP 25(2)/590/1653 Trin. [no. 23]. See also *D.N.B.*, and (for the disregard of his peerage dignity) cf. S.R.O. 999/Oo 4.

[92] S.R.O. 171, box 1, lease of 1661; P.R.O., E 156/16, m. 40.

[93] *V.C.H. Salop.* iii. 45; *Cal. S.P. Dom.* 1671, 586; 1671–2, 420; P.R.O., C 66/3134, no. 19.

[94] *Complete Peerage*, ii. 274; Eyton, vii. 202.

[95] *V.C.H. Salop.* iii. 45, 254–5; viii. 75, 88; P.R.O., CP 25(2)/714/32 & 33 Chas. II Hil. [no. 10]; Barnard MSS. Raby Castle, box 7, bdle. 22, no. 12; S.R.O., q. sess. rec. box 260, reg. of gamekeepers 1742–79, 1 Dec. 1743; 18 Oct. 1764; 1 Oct. 1766; S.R.O. 659/1.

[96] *V.C.H. Salop.* iii. 254, 295.

[97] S.R.O. 659/1; P.R.O., CP 43/889, rot. 466.

[98] *Complete Peerage*, iii. 284.

[99] Ibid. 285; below.

[1] *Rot. Hund.* ii. 55–8; *Cal. Inq. p.m.* xv, p. 185; *T.S.A.S.* xi. 338; P.R.O., SC 2/197/96; Staffs. R.O., D. 593/J/10, ct. r.; S.R.O. 2842/1; 2919/1/1, m. 11d.; 4406/1, pp. 8–9, 136–7; below.

[2] This and the next four paras. based on *V.C.H. Salop.* iii. 47–8, 50–2; *Rot. Hund.* ii. 55–9, 65, 94–6; *Plac. de Quo Warr.* (Rec. Com.), 675–80, 684, 687, 708–9, 720; P.R.O., SC 2/197/96; Staffs. R.O., D. 593/J/10, ct. r.; Eyton, vii–x.

[3] Those in Wem barony.

[4] As seems to have happened at Gravenhunger (*Coll. Topog. et Geneal.* i. 118, here interpreted otherwise than in Eyton, ix. 377) and Withington (*Cal. Inq. p.m.* iv, p. 125).

[5] Prees.

[6] Betton in Hales, Eyton on Severn (incl. Aston and Booley), Pimley, Sleap (incl. Buttery, Crudgington, and Kynnersley), and Wollerton. Cf. *V.C.H. Salop.*

[7] Atcham, Cold Hatton (after the abbey acquired it 1260 × 1265: cf. ibid. iii. 53 and n. 70), Lilleshall, Longdon upon Tern, Tern (but see below), and Uckington. Cf. *V.C.H. Salop.* ii. 73, 78.

[8] Nagington (but see below), Uffington (incl. Haughmond), and Walcot. Cf. *V.C.H. Salop.* ii. 68.

[9] Chesthill (but see below), Dodecote, and Drayton. Cf. *V.C.H. Ches.* iii. 151.

[10] Buildwas and Stirchley. Cf. *V.C.H. Salop.* ii. 52–3.

abbeys realized their privileges only gradually: Lilleshall, Haughmond, and Combermere each owned an estate that owed or did suit to the hundred in 1255, though none of them is known to have done suit after the 13th century;[11] another Haughmond property, however, never achieved exemption.[12] Also privileged were four large manors of former royal demesne[13] and the demesne estates of the FitzAlans, barons of Oswestry,[14] the Dunstanvilles, barons of Castle Combe (Wilts.),[15] and the Warennes, cadets and tenants in serjeanty of the earls of Surrey.[16] The Audleys and the Erdingtons[17] acquired manors in the hundred[18] that were already,[19] or soon became, privileged liberties. Marchamley for example, unlike the other subinfeudated manors of the FitzAlan fee, became exempt from suit to the hundred; it did so almost certainly because the Audleys held it in demesne,[20] whereas their manors of Whixall, Gravenhunger, and Woore were subinfeudated and continued to owe suit. The barons of Wem were in fact alone in securing immunity not only for their demesne manors[21] but also for the barony's extensive subinfeudated estates, virtually all of which were attracted to the leet courts (Hinstock[22] being the main one) of an unusually compact and highly organized fee.

Manors that were held to suit to the hundred comprised virtually all the subinfeudated estates of the FitzAlan fee[23] including virtually all the manors, whether held in demesne or subinfeudated, of the Chetwynds,[24] the FitzAlans' tenants in fee.[25] Three other manors,[26] though not part of the Chetwynd fee, were held of families who elsewhere held of the Chetwynds and did hundred suit.[27] Suit also continued to be owed by three manors held in chief as serjeanties.[28] Hodnet, held in chief by the Hodnets as a serjeanty of the honor of Montgomery,[29] was said to owe suit in 1255, and all the rest of the Hodnet fee continued to do suit.[30] So too did Poynton, another member of the honor,[31] and the four manors in the hundred held for castle guard at Montgomery.[32] Three subinfeudated manors held of baronies whose *capita* lay in other counties[33] also did suit.

Although all the Hodnet fee was said to do suit in 1255, Sir Otes of Hodnet's position seems to have been anomalous: the hundred jurors included him among the

[11] Tern, Nagington, and Chesthill.

[12] ½ Haughton (held of the barony of Pulverbatch).

[13] Cheswardine, Edgmond (incl. Newport), Wellington, and Wrockwardine.

[14] Upton Magna and Wroxeter (incl. Norton).

[15] Adderley (incl. Calverhall, Shavington, and Spoonley). Cf. Eyton, ii. 268 sqq.; Sanders, *Eng. Baronies*, 28; and, for the barony's admin., *V.C.H. Wilts.* v. 48, 64, 70.

[16] Whitchurch.

[17] *V.C.H. Salop.* iii. 13–14.

[18] Edgmond (incl. Newport), Marchamley, Shawbury (incl. ½ L. Wytheford), Wellington, and Weston-under-Redcastle (incl. Wixhill).

[19] On the privileged position of royal manors (e.g. Edgmond and Wellington) see *V.C.H. Salop.* iii. 49.

[20] For the Audleys' privileges cf. *Cal. Chart. R.* 1226–57, 35.

[21] Wem, Dodington, and Hinstock.

[22] To which Dawley, Eyton upon the Weald Moors (incl. Bratton and Horton), ½ Lawley, Tibberton, and Waters Upton owed suit.

[23] Berwick Maviston, Eaton Constantine, Child's Ercall (incl. Hungryhatton and the Lees), Hadley, High Hatton, ½ Haughton, Hopton and Espley, Leighton (incl. Garmston), Preston Boats, Rodington (incl. Somerwood), Stanton upon Hine Heath (incl. Roden and Rodenhurst), Sugdon, ½ Withington, Gt. Wytheford (incl. Edgebolton and Muckleton), and ½ L. Wytheford.

[24] Chetwynd (incl. Bearstone), Howle, Moreton Corbet, Puleston, Sambrook (incl. Ellerton), Stockton, and until some time between 1255 and 1285 ½ Lawley.

[25] *V.C.H. Salop.* i. 298. For the fam. cf. H. E. Chetwynd-Stapylton, *The Chetwynds of Ingestre* (1892), cap. 1.

[26] Dorrington, Lee Brockhurst, and Soulton.

[27] Respectively the Willeys (cf. Eyton, ii. 48 sqq.), the Pitchfords (cf. ibid. vi. 271–2, 288), and the Corbets of Moreton Corbet. The Willeys' tenants at Dorrington were Chetwynd cadets.

[28] Leegomery (incl. L. Dawley, Ketley, Malinslee, and Wappenshall), Rowton (incl. Ellerdine), and ½ Withington.

[29] The honor was evidently treated as an escheat by the Crown after c. 1215: *V.C.H. Salop.* iii. 38. Eyton's theory that it did not escheat (Eyton, xi. 145–7) is inconsistent with much evidence he adduces elsewhere and is partly based on misapprehensions concerning Bulwick (Northants.) and Upminster (Essex): cf. Sanders, *Eng. Baronies*, 22 n. 7; *V.C.H. Essex*, vii. 149.

[30] ½ Lawley (part of the Chetwynd fee until some time between 1255 and 1285), Longford, Peplow (incl. L. Bolas), and Preston upon the Weald Moors; Cotton and Moston, held of the barony of Pulverbatch. Cotton, however, was absorbed in Hodnet, later exempt (see below).

[31] It did suit c. 1590 but had not done suit in 1255.

[32] Cherrington, Ightfield, Longslow, and Sandford (incl. Aychley). All were Tournai escheats (*V.C.H. Salop.* i. 298, 339) whose services had been due at Shrawardine castle until the 1220s (cf. Eyton, xi. 136).

[33] Gravenhunger and Woore (in the Audleys' share of the barony of Nantwich: cf. G. Ormerod, *Hist. of Co. of Chester* (1882), iii. 390–1, 422–4) and Woodcote incl. Lynn (honor of Petworth, Suss.: cf. Eyton, iii. 1–2).

lords who exercised jurisdiction in respect of the assize of bread and of ale; all the other lords so listed[34] had leet courts in manors exempt from the great hundred. In 1292, though he had no charter therefor, William of Hodnet was probably allowed the jurisdiction and it seems evident that a court leet, thus developed, allowed Hodnet manor to escape the great hundred's jurisdiction. The Hodnets' concern to establish the liberty was evidently limited to the central part of their fee for its outlying members continued to owe suit to the great hundred. In 1592 the heir of John Vernon (d. 1591)[35] of Hodnet owed personal suit at the great hundred, but probably only for the render of his 2s. vicontiel rent.[36]

A few other manors of the types that seem normally to have owed suit in fact escaped the duty: two serjeanties and a knight's fee, all held in chief,[37] and three subinfeudated manors. Two of the three[38] last mentioned manors, Moreton Say and Stoke upon Tern, were members of the barony of Weobley (Herefs.). In 1243 Hugh de Say (d. c. 1249), member of a family[39] who were probably cadets of the 12th-century barons of Clun, withdrew his manor of Moreton Say from suit of the hundred. His brother Walter's manor of Stoke upon Tern, however, continued to do suit. Later Hugh's son Robert held Moreton under his older brother Hugh, to whom their uncle Walter's manors passed. Shortly before 1255 Hugh exchanged his Shropshire estates with John de Verdun for Irish lands. Verdun was coheir of the barony of Weobley[40] and the terre tenancy of Stoke thus passed to one of its overlords, who soon afterwards[41] withdrew the manor from suit to the great hundred. The changes may have affected Bletchley and other subinfeudated members of Moreton and Stoke. Bletchley did suit to the hundred in 1255 but is not known to have done so thereafter. In the earlier 14th century the manor seems to have had only a court baron[42] but between 1376 and 1390 the Corbets of Moreton Corbet evidently held a court leet there.[43] By c. 1400, however, both Bletchley and Moreton Say were within the leet jurisdiction of Stoke.[44]

The personal status of the great landowners, and the imperceptible ways in which it was used to secure privilege, gradually ceased to suffice for the creation of liberties. Privileges arrogated by or granted to such men and their heirs in the 13th century became attached to their estates and were allowed to their successors in the 14th, but by then royal charters were necessary for the acquisition of new franchises. Between the 1250s and the 1350s the Corbets of Moreton Corbet added several manors to their inheritance, including (in Bradford hundred) Bletchley, the half of Lawley in the barony of Wem, and Shawbury. Moreton Corbet, part of the Chetwynd fee, was perhaps their only manor held to suit to the great hundred,[45] and in 1356 Robert Corbet (II) obtained a charter granting him a court leet ('view of frankpledge');[46] thereafter the manor was exempt. Richard Corbet of Moreton owed personal suit in 1592 but probably only for the render of his 2s. vicontiel rent.[47]

Until the earlier 17th century it was probably normal for the hundred to be leased.[48]

---

[34] The bp. of Coventry and Lich., the abbots of Combermere, Lilleshall, and Shrews., Jas. of Audley, Ralph le Botiler (baron of Wem), Wal. de Dunstanville, Giles of Erdington, John FitzAlan, Hamon le Strange (of Wrockwardine), John le Strange (III) (of Cheswardine), and Wm. de Warenne.

[35] Cf S.P.R. Lich. xi (2), 3.

[36] For the rent see P.R.O., E 317/Salop./1; Barnard MSS., Raby Castle, box 7, bdle. 22, no. 12.

[37] Gt. Bolas (incl. Isombridge), Longford, and Uppington.

[38] The third man. was Ercall Magna.

[39] For geneal., etc., details cf. Eyton, v. 30 sqq.

[40] Ibid. viii. 62–3; Sanders, Eng. Baronies, 95.

[41] He withdrew Stokesay from Munslow hund. 1255 ×

1274: Eyton, v. 34–6.

[42] Cts. not descr. as gt. or small: S.R.O. 2919/1/1, mm. 1–2.   [43] Ibid. mm. 4, 12; /1/2.

[44] S.R.O. 327, box 7, damaged Stoke ct. r. c. 1400 (datable by mention of Thos. [Corbet], vicar of Ercall Magna: cf. Eyton, viii. 71; ix. 112).

[45] But little is known of Bletchley's status 1255–1376.

[46] Cal. Chart. R. 1341–1417, 148; cf. V.C.H. Salop. iii. 53.

[47] For the rent see P.R.O., E 317/Salop./1; E 370/11/3, m. 1; Barnard MSS., Raby Castle, box 7, bdle. 22, no. 12.

[48] Barnard MSS., Raby Castle, box 7, loose deed (lease of 1435); box 12, bdle. 24, leases of 1602; P.R.O., C 2/Eliz. I/F 3/32.

William Greene bought a lease from Sir Humphrey Ferrers in 1590 and held the courts as steward. Immediately he tried to enforce neglected suit to the hundred leet from Chetwynd and other manors but was resisted by 'divers persons of great worship and wealth'.[49] His efforts were continued by a new steward,[50] but it is evident that similar difficulties over the enforcement of suit and the liability of various manors to render vicontiel rents recurred throughout the 17th century and in the early 18th century.[51] Persistently defaulting manors like Chetwynd may eventually have succeeded in permanently evading the jurisdiction of the hundred leet[52] by holding leet courts of their own. Hadley apparently had a court leet by 1667.[53] Some manors, however, were still being constrained to make suit to the hundred leet in the mid 18th century,[54] and c. 1840 an annual leet was still being held for the appointment of constables in those townships for which no manorial leet was held.[55]

About 1590 presentments to the hundred leet included the common round of petty offences: affrays (some involving bloodshed), theft, forestalling, pound breach and rescue of distraints, and infractions of the assize of bread and of ale. Nuisances obstructing roads and watercourses were presented, as were those arising from the neglect or breach of hedges and gates, the failure to ring swine, and the oppression of commons. The court laid pains against the non-provision of pounds and the statutory offences of failing to provide stocks and pillories; other statutory offences dealt with included the illegal use of guns, illegal games-playing (chiefly at cards and bowls), the failure to take oaths, and the neglect of statute labour on the roads.[56]

In 1592 William Greene despaired of realizing any profit from the leet and, surrendering his lease of the hundred, negotiated a new one of the stewardship, issues, and profits of the small courts only.[57] A court roll of 1359 records 52 cases before one session of the small court, mainly pleas of debt and trespass.[58] Such cases were evidently brought to the court from manors subject to the leet and from those that were exempt.[59] The civil jurisdiction of the hundred court was vigorously maintained until the 1840s. Confirmation of the hundred to Lord Newport in 1672 included the right to hold a court of record for the recovery of debts under £20;[60] it was referred to as the king's court of record and sometimes (from the 1680s) simply as 'Wellington court', for at some time between 1602 and 1682 the court had moved from Bradford bridge to Wellington, probably to the 'town hall'.[61] Court rules, probably dating from the 1680s, and a contemporary list of fees refer to a steward, his clerk (normally an attorney), a deputy steward, a sergeant or sergeants to execute process, and a gaoler. Attorneys' attendance on court days was to be in person 'or by their menial clerks and not by any solicitor or others'. Jury days were kept every quarter day following the county quarter sessions of the peace, and oftener if necessary. All 'practice and proceedings' were to accord as nearly as possible with the 'law and practice of other courts of law'. Officers in breach of court rules were to be suspended by the steward until Viscount Newport's pleasure was known.[62]

In the later 1830s, when its business was increasing, the court sat fortnightly for the

[49] P.R.O., C 2/Eliz I/F 3/32; /F 9/19; SC 2/197/96.
[50] Staffs. R.O., D. 593/J/10, ct. r.
[51] Barnard MSS., Raby Castle, box 7, bdle. 22, nos. 12–13. For the vicontiel rents cf. P.R.O., E 317/Salop./1; E 370/11/3.
[52] P.R.O., C 2/Eliz. I/F 9/19.
[53] Below, Hadley, Local Govt. and Public Services.
[54] e.g. L. Dawley: S.R.O. 2374, box 4, papers in Corbet and D'Avenant v. Slaney, W. Gibbons to R. Slaney, 7 Mar. 1781.
[55] Return of Cts. of Requests, H.C. 619, pp. 132–3 (1840), xli; cf. S.R.O. 231/18.
[56] P.R.O., SC 2/197/96; Staffs. R.O., D. 593/J/10, ct. r.

[57] P.R.O., C 2/Eliz. I/F 3/32.
[58] S.R.O. 2919/1/1, m. 11d.
[59] e.g. abbot of Lilleshall v. Thos. Hochekyns of Wroxeter: ibid.
[60] S.P.L., MS. 4071, pp. 204–6.
[61] i.e. the mkt. hall, where Wellington man. ct. met by 1687: S.R.O. 327, box 5, precept to witness, 1732; below, Wellington, Econ. Hist., Local Govt. For Bradford bridge as the mtg. place in 1602 see Barnard MSS., Raby Castle, box 7, bdle. 22, no. 8.
[62] S.R.O. 327, box 5, ct. rules and list of fees, both endorsed 'Wellington Ct.'; 4406/1, pp. 8–9.

preliminary stages of civil actions and twice a year for their trial; one of the two courts for trial was generally on the same day as the annual court leet.[63] Practice in the court probably declined after the introduction of new county courts in 1847 and its jurisdiction was in any case abolished (with all other such) in 1867.[64]

In 1806 the debtors' gaol in Wellington consisted of five filthy and unkempt rooms, three of them wholly dark, in the gaoler's house. A visit in November 1802 revealed no prisoners,[65] but a prisoner died in the gaol in 1829.[66] The previous year Robert Garbett had been appointed gaoler by the duke of Cleveland, and in the early 1830s between 6 and 19 debtors a year, averaging just over 11, were confined in Garbett's house in Walker Street. Garbett received fees on each prisoner's discharge, payable by the county quarter sessions since 1815; they averaged 6 guineas a year over the 1830s but about twice that in the late 1830s. Quarter sessions granted him a salary of £8 in 1840.[67] The gaol closed in 1844 soon after a final delivery by the steward, Uvedale Corbett,[68] under the Execution Act, 1844, which abolished imprisonment for debts under £20.[69]

A seal in use in 1732 was circular, 28 mm. in diameter; beneath a coronet it displayed the Newports' crest (a unicorn's head) with the legend, roman: HVNDRE[DVM] . DE . BRADFORD.[70]

The hundred stretched c. 40 km. north from Little Buildwas to Whitchurch and Woore and extended c. 20 km. west from the Staffordshire border to Shrewsbury, Wem, and the Welsh border, thus comprising the eastern part of the north Shropshire plain. Most of the area, apart from its south-eastern fringe, consists of Triassic formations: Bunter Pebble Beds and Red Sandstones and Keuper Marls. Around Prees, however, and stretching almost 13 km. north-east of the village, is an area of Jurassic rocks. Glacial drift, increasing in depth towards the west, covers virtually the whole area. At Hawkstone and Weston-under-Redcastle the Triassic sandstone is exposed in dramatic ridges[71] exploited at Bury Walls for defensive purposes in the Iron Age[72] and incorporated in a great 18th-century park whose cliffs thrilled Dr. Johnson by their suggestion of 'the sublime, the dreadful, and the vast'.[73]

The Hawkstone hills are uncharacteristic of the gently rolling country on which they intrude and which owes its form to the drift cover. Hamlets, villages, and small towns are generally sited little above their lowland surroundings; more rarely they are in valleys. Very few villages stand out prominently on high ground,[74] Prees and Wrockwardine, both on unusual geological formations, being notable exceptions.[75] The landscape generally resembles the undulating Cheshire plain into which it merges almost imperceptibly, even where the Ellesmere moraine forms a watershed between the two counties.[76] A small part of the northern area of the hundred drains northwards by the river Weaver through Cheshire to the Mersey, but the rest drains southwards by the Roden, the Tern, and their tributaries into the Severn at Atcham. In many places the drift cover, or perhaps the collapse of saliferous formations in the Keuper,

[63] S. and B. Webb, *Manor and Borough*, i (1908), 56 n. 3; *Return of Cts. of Requests*, 132–3; S.R.O., q. sess. Auditing and Finance Cttees. rep. bk. 1837–43, p. 96. Cf. Pigot, *Nat. Com. Dir.* (1835), 380; (1842), 44.

[64] *V.C.H. Salop.* iii. 165.

[65] *Salopian Shreds & Patches*, iii. 115.

[66] *Abstr. of Q. Sess. Rolls 1820–30*, ed. M. C. Hill (S.C.C. 1974), 321/112.

[67] *Executions for Debt: Returns*, H.C. 199, pp. 213–14 (1835), xliv; S.R.O., q. sess. Auditing and Finance Cttees. rep. bk. 1837–43, pp. 89–90, 96; S.R.O. 14, Wellington tithe appt. and map (no. 423).

[68] Later a co.-ct. judge: *V.C.H. Salop.* iii. 167.

[69] 7 & 8 Vic. c. 96, s. 57; *Shropshire Conservative*, 24 Aug. 1844.

[70] S.R.O. 327, box 5, precept to witness, 1732.

[71] *V.C.H. Salop.* i. 37–46, 56, 59–60, and maps facing pp. 1, 23; R. W. Pocock and D. A. Wray, *Geol. of Country around Wem* (Geol. Surv. Memoir, 1925).

[72] *V.C.H. Salop.* i. 352, 357–8; SA 1139.

[73] *Country Life*, 3 and 10 July 1958, 18–21, 72–5.

[74] D. Sylvester, *Rural Landscape of the Welsh Borderland* (1969), 301–2.

[75] For Prees see *V.C.H. Salop.* i. 40, 59; *T.S.A.S.* 4th ser. xi. 243–5. For Wrockwardine see below.

[76] Sylvester, op. cit. 271, 293–4.

has blocked natural drainage, sometimes over considerable areas like the Weald Moors north of Wellington and Whixall Moss on the Welsh border.[77] There is a great variety of soils[78] giving rise to grade 2 and grade 3 agricultural land, the former preponderant in the south, the latter in the north.[79]

By 1086 woodland was recorded in almost half of the estates in Hodnet hundred, but the heathlands that extended into Wrockwardine hundred were virtually woodless. In Wrockwardine hundred two thirds of the Domesday estates recorded no woodland.[80] Nevertheless a great tract of countryside in the south part of Wrockwardine hundred was included by the Norman kings in their forest of Mount Gilbert (or the Wrekin).[81] Outside the nucleated villages and hamlets settlement was widely dispersed, as in other areas with wood–pasture economies.[82] At the same time the ill-drained mosses, the extensive heathlands across the centre of Bradford hundred, and the surviving woods were all exploited as common pasture or meadow and for fuel.[83] Parishes containing several townships dependent on a central village or small market town are more typical of the area than single-township parishes.[84] Market Drayton, Newport, Wellington, Wem, and Whitchurch developed into market towns in the Middle Ages.

Increasingly from the 17th century the area shared the predominantly pastoral and dairy economy of Cheshire.[85] Between the 16th and the 19th centuries artificial drainage reclaimed the Weald Moors.[86] Around Whixall Moss and in many smaller such areas, however, despite reclamation over a long period, there remains abundant evidence of their peculiar economies and distinctive ecological characteristics.[87] Much of the former mosses and heaths has become grade 4 agricultural land.[88]

Along the south-east fringe of the hundred, where it bordered the borough of Wenlock and Brimstree hundred, an area of higher land coincides with the northern part of the east Shropshire coalfield. With two adjacent parishes formerly in Wenlock borough, that high land forms the southern half of the area treated in the present volume. To the south-west the productive Coal Measures run up against the hilly area around the Wrekin. Scenically that does not resemble north Shropshire, and its Pre-Cambrian, Cambrian, and Silurian rocks, with northern outliers in Wrockwardine and Lilleshall, link it to Shropshire south of the Severn.[89]

[77] V.C.H. Salop. i. 42–3, 46, 56, 59–60; Proc. of Meres and Mires Conference at Attingham Pk. Dec. 1965, ed. P. Oswald and A. Herbert (Natural Environment Research Council: Nature Conservancy [1966]), 14–22 (copy in S.P.L.).

[78] E. Shaw, 'Farming in Salop.' Jnl. R. Agric. Soc. of Eng. cxxxii. 50–1; C. P. Burnham and D. Mackney, 'Soils of Salop.' Field Studies, ii (1), 83–113 and map.

[79] Min. of Ag., Fish and Food, Agric. Land Classificn. Map 1″, sheets 118–19 (1970–1 edn.),

[80] Eyton, vii. 198–201; ix. 152–5; Domesday Geog. of Midland Eng. ed. H. C. Darby and I. B. Terrett (1971), 136–41, 437–9. Cf. O. Rackham, Ancient Woodland (1980), 112, 116, 125–6; Sylvester, Welsh Borderland, 94, 102, 296–7.

[81] V.C.H. Salop. i. 485–6 (corr. ibid. ii. 319).

[82] Sylvester, op. cit. 40, 191, 196, 200–1, 300–1.

[83] Ibid. 293–4, 301–5; Proc. Meres and Mires Conf. 32–4;

cf. P. R. Edwards, 'Farming Econ. of NE. Salop. in 17th Cent.' (Oxf. Univ. D.Phil. thesis, 1976), 8.

[84] Sylvester, op. cit. 203–4, 211, 301.

[85] Edwards, op. cit. esp. caps. 2–3; Jnl. R. Agric. Soc. of Eng. cxxxii. 51–3; T. Rowley, Salop. Landscape (1972), 21–2, 163, 171.   [86] T.S.A.S. lxiii. 1–10; V.C.H. Salop. i. 46.

[87] Proc. Meres and Mires Conf. 33; C. A. Sinker, 'N. Salop. Meres and Mosses: a Background for Ecologists', Field Studies, i (4), 101–38, esp. (for Whixall Moss) 121–6.

[88] Agric. Land Classificn. Map 1″, sheets 118–19 (1970–1 edn.).

[89] V.C.H. Salop. i. 3 sqq. and map facing p. 1; above, p. 1 and maps on pp. 3, 20; T.S.A.S. x. 386–7; Inst. Geol. Sciences Map 1/25,000, Telford (1978 edn.); D. L. Dineley, 'Salop. Geology: an Outline of the Tectonic Hist.' Field Studies, i (2), 88, 95.

DAWLEY

THE INDUSTRIAL parish of Dawley in the heart of the east Shropshire coalfield became an urban district in the 19th century and the centre of a new town in the 20th. The ancient parish contained 2,790 a. (1,123 ha.) in three townships: Malinslee (862 a.) in the north-east, Great Dawley (997 a.) in the centre, and Little Dawley (931 a.) in the south-west.[1] The urban district was enlarged to 3,259 a. (1,319 ha.) in 1934 by the addition of parts of Priorslee, Stirchley, and Wellington Rural civil parishes.[2] In 1966 Dawley U.D. was extended to 9,461 a. (3,829 ha.) to coincide approximately with the area that had been designated as Dawley new town in 1963. Madeley,[3] the remainder of Stirchley, and parts of Benthall, Broseley, Kemberton, Oakengates, Priorslee, Shifnal, Sutton Maddock, Little Wenlock, and Wellington Rural C.P.s were added to Dawley, and 12 a. (5 ha.) at Hollinswood were transferred to Oakengates U.D.[4] This article treats the history of the ancient parish of Dawley only.

Dawley was a compact area c. 5 km. in length from north-east to south-west and c. 2 km. wide, on the central plateau of the coalfield. The highest land was along the parish's north-western edge, where the ground rises to 208 metres above O.D. near Dawley Bank. The land falls gently to the south-east in Malinslee and Great Dawley townships, but in Little Dawley relief is more marked. Horsehay dingle bisects the township, and the parish's southern boundary followed Loamhole and Lightmoor brooks, which flow through deeply incised valleys to converge at the head of Coalbrookdale. Elsewhere the parish boundary did not follow marked physical features, but Dawley was contained on the north-west by a watershed that separated streams draining to the Severn and the Weald Moors, and on the north-east by the Randlay valley.

Most of the parish was underlain by the Coal Measures. Only in the Horsehay and Little Dawley areas, where Lower Carboniferous sandstones and Little Wenlock basalt outcrop, was there a lack of workable seams of coal and ironstone. Productive Middle Coal Measures lay near the surface along the north-west edge of the parish from Old Park to Heath Hill, and in the south at Lightmoor. East of the Lightmoor fault in Malinslee and Great Dawley the seams lay deeper, under siltstones and sandstones of the Upper Coal Measures. The drift cover is mainly boulder clay, but glacial sands and gravels occur around Moor Farm in the south of the parish.[5]

The small hamlets and scattered farms of a wood–pasture economy were transformed from the 16th century by the haphazard growth of industrial workers' cottages as mining and, later, iron making engulfed the parish. In Great Dawley, probably always the most populous township, the centre of settlement had shifted by the late 18th century from the hamlet by the church to the straggling industrial settlements of Dawley Green and Dawley Bank. By the mid 19th century High Street, as Dawley Green came to be known, had gained most of the features of a small town, to which the outlying industrial communities at Horsehay, Dawley Bank, Old Park, Dark Lane, and Hinkshay looked. Most land in Great Dawley and Malinslee was scarred by the extractive industries; only in the western half of Little Dawley did a predominantly agricultural landscape survive. When the pits and ironworks closed in the later 19th century Dawley began to stagnate and decline. Until after the Second World War the parish suffered unemployment and the industrial legacies of sub-standard housing and landscape dereliction. Dawley underwent a transformation, social, economic, and environmental, from 1963 when it was included in the designated area of Dawley (from 1968 Telford) new town.

The community of industrial workers that grew in Dawley during the Industrial Revolution had many characteristics typical of mining areas of the day. The Dawley cottagers' 'irregularity and disorderly behaviour' were noted in the mid 18th century.[6] The miners were at the mercy of the coal masters and the notorious sub-contractors called charter masters,[7] and rising food prices in the late 18th and early 19th century led to a succession of riots.[8] The most serious in Dawley were the Cinderhill riots triggered by a reduction in wages in 1821, when 3,000 colliers confronted troops on a slag mound near Old Park. Two rioters were killed when troops opened fire and one of the leaders was later executed.[9]

Notable natives included Samuel Peploe (1668–1752), the son of a Little Dawley farmer and bishop of Chester from 1726;[10] Capt. Matthew Webb (1848–83), the son of a Dawley physician and the first man to swim the English Channel (in 1875);[11] Albert Stanley (1862–1915), born at Dark Lane, the son of a Primitive Methodist miner and eventually leader of the Cannock miners and M.P. for North-West Staffordshire;[12] and Edith Pargeter (b. 1913), the novelist, who also published under the name of Ellis Peters.[13] A monument to Webb, in the form of a drinking fountain, was placed in High Street in 1910;[14] it was moved in 1956[15] but returned to near its original position in 1980. Among characters of

[1] O.S. Map 6", Salop. XLIII. NW. (1903 edn.); L.J.R.O., B/A/15, Dawley Magna; S.R.O. 1560/1. This art. was written 1980. Dr. B. S. Trinder kindly commented on a draft.

[2] V.C.H. Salop. ii. 222n.; Census, 1951, Co. Rep. Herefs. and Salop. 7.

[3] Whose westernmost pt. was excl. from the new town 1963.

[4] V.C.H. Salop. ii. 235–7; Census, 1971, Co. Rep. Salop. i. 8.

[5] Inst. Geol. Sciences Map 1/25,000, Telford (1978 edn.).

[6] S.R.O. 2374, box 4, case papers of 1808.

[7] Trinder, Ind. Rev. Salop. 343–7.

[8] Ibid. 376–82. [9] Ibid. 384–5; Salopian Jnl. 7 Feb. 1821.

[10] D.N.B. [11] D.N.B.

[12] Dict. Labour Biog. i, ed. J. M. Bellamy and J. Saville (1972), 308–11.

[13] Shrews. Chron. 20 Nov. 1964; M.E.R. Jackson, 'Notes on Hist. of Madeley' (microfilm in S.P.L.), bk. 1A, p. 237.

[14] Kelly's Dir. Salop. (1926), 87.

[15] S.R.O., DA 8/100/6, p. 1272.

local note was William Ball (1795–1852), the 'Shropshire giant', a 40-stone shingler at Horsehay ironworks.[16]

COMMUNICATIONS. Great Dawley was crossed from north-west to south-east by the main Wellington–Worcester (and Bridgnorth) road, turnpiked 1764.[17] In 1752 the road entered the parish at Dawley Bank and ran by Dawley Green Lane (later Bank Road and King Street), Dun Cow Bank (New Street), and Finger Lane to Southall.[18] By the early 19th century it had been diverted from Lawley by Ball's Hill, near Heath Hill, to Dawley Green.[19] The parish's commercial centre grew up at the junction between the old and new routes at Dawley Green, the road through the settlement being known at High Street by 1851.[20] A second major route was the Wellington–Coalbrookdale turnpike, opened c. 1817.[21] Across the south-west corner of the parish it was made by improving a road that followed parts of the former Horsehay–Coalbrookdale waggonway.[22] The stretch along Loamhole dingle was known as Jigger's Bank, at the foot of which was a tollhouse.[23] The Wellington–Worcester turnpike was diverted to follow the new road, a new section being built c. 1827 from the older route at Ball's Hill to the new road at Lawley.[24]

Brandlee Lane, the road from Dawley Green to Horsehay, was described in 1780 as the road to Much Wenlock.[25] It seems to have been taken over as a private toll road by the Coalbrookdale Co., who put up a turnpike gate at Horsehay, but it was transferred to the parish in 1840.[26] The scattered nature of both early agricultural settlement and 18th- and 19th-century industry gave rise to a complex network of minor lanes, tracks, and footpaths by the early 19th century.[27]

From 1970 the road pattern underwent major changes. The centre of Dawley was bypassed in 1976 by the new Spring Hill Road skirting from Heath Hill to Portley, and in 1980 High Street was pedestrianized. New major roads in the Old Park and Dawley Bank areas linked the Wellington–Bridgnorth route to Telford town centre and the new housing estates in Malinslee.

The growth of industry in the late 18th and early 19th century superimposed a new network of communications on the existing road pattern. The earliest industrial routes were the wooden railways built c. 1755–6 to link the Coalbrookdale Co.'s new Horsehay furnaces to their mines in Ketley and Lawley and to Coalbrookdale itself.

That from Ketley and Lawley was 16 ft. wide and entered the parish at Dawley Bank; it ran north-west of Dawley Green to Horsehay.[28] That from Horsehay to Coalbrookdale ran a short distance through Little Wenlock parish before re-entering Dawley and running down Jigger's Bank to Coalbrookdale.[29] Both had rails of oak or ash in the 1760s, replaced by iron rails from the 1770s.[30]

In 1788–9 the Hollinswood–Southall length of the Shropshire Canal was built down the eastern edge of the parish, a branch from Southall by the head of Horsehay dingle to Brierly Hill, at the head of Coalbrookdale, being opened c. 1792.[31] Building capital was raised principally from the local coal and iron masters, over 30 per cent being subscribed by the Coalbrookdale Co. partners. The canal became the main artery for the coal and iron industries, linking Coalbrookdale and Horsehay to Old Park, Ketley, and Donnington. At the Brierly Hill canal terminus two shafts were sunk 120 ft., down which iron crates were lowered to a tramway driven into the hill at the head of Coalbrookdale. The disadvantages of transhipment at Brierly Hill led first to the replacement of the shafts by an inclined plane in 1794 and, c. 1801, to the construction of a railway along the towpath from Brierly Hill to Horsehay. Thereafter the canal south-west of Horsehay fell into disuse.

Further railways were built from mines and ironworks in Dawley to wharves on the canal. The longest were the Coalbrookdale Co.'s waggonway from Brandlee to Dawley Castle wharf, with feeders from Portley and Deepfield collieries, built by 1817;[32] that from Old Park ironworks to the canal at Hinkshay, probably built by 1812;[33] and that from Coalbrookdale by the Lightmoor valley to the canal near Dawley Castle, built in 1810–11.[34]

The canal remained the central line of freight transport until standard gauge railways reached the area in the 1850s. The Madeley branch of the Shrewsbury & Birmingham Railway (later G.W.R.), opened in 1854, cut across the southern edge of the parish at Lightmoor.[35] The Wellington & Severn Junction Railway, in which the Coalbrookdale Co. held about three quarters of the shares, was laid from Ketley Junction to Horsehay in 1857 and thence to Lightmoor c. 1858. An extension to Coalbrookdale opened in 1864. There was a station at Horsehay with 10 sidings serving the area's ironworks and other industries, and halts at Lightmoor (from 1907), Doseley (from 1932), and Green Bank (from 1934).[36] The line closed to passengers in 1962 and to goods in 1964,[37] but the section from Horsehay to Light-

[16] Life of Mr. Wm. Ball (copy in I.G.M.T. Libr. 1979/ 1075).   [17] 4 Geo. III, c. 81.
[18] J. Rocque, Map of Salop. (1752).
[19] R. Baugh, Map of Salop. (1808).
[20] S. Bagshaw, Dir. Salop. (1851), 376–7.
[21] 57 Geo. III, c. 12 (Local and Personal); B.L. Maps, O.S.D. 208.
[22] Cf. S.R.O. 1224, box 259, plan c. 1750, deed of 1750; box 260, deed of 1755; Baugh, Map of Salop.; B.L. Maps, O.S.D. 208; Trinder, Ind. Rev. Salop. (1981), 82.
[23] S.R.O. 1560/1.   [24] S.R.O., dep. plan 219.
[25] S.R.O. 327, box 5, ct. r.
[26] S.R.O. 1560/5, May 1840.
[27] B.L. Maps, O.S.D. 208; O.S. Map 1″, sheet 61 NE. (1833 edn.).   [28] S.R.O. 2374, box 1, deed of 1756.
[29] S.R.O. 1224, box 259, plan c. 1750, deed of 1750; box 260, deed of 1755; M. J. T. Lewis, Early Wooden Rlys.

(1970), 259, 271–2, pl. 60; Trinder, Ind. Rev. Salop. (1981), 82.
[30] S.P.L., MS. 332, pp. 172, 217, 242; Trinder, Ind. Rev. Salop. 123.
[31] For this para. see C. Hadfield, Canals of W. Midlands (1969), 153, 157, 159; Trinder, op. cit. 128–36.
[32] S.R.O. 2224/1.
[33] S.R.O. 2374, box 3, rental of 1812; O.S. Map 1″, sheet 61 NE. (1833 edn.).
[34] I.G.M.T. Libr. 1978/169.
[35] R. Christiansen, W. Midlands (Regional Hist. of Rlys. of Gt. Brit. vii, 1973), 270.
[36] Ibid. 156–7; 271; cf. S.R.O., dep. plan 350; J. M. Tolson, 'In the Tracks of the Iron Masters', Railway Mag. xci. 373–8.
[37] C. R. Clinker, Clinker's Reg. of Closed Stations 1830–1977 (Bristol, 1978), 65, 75.

moor was reopened for freight in 1965.[38] The Coalport Branch Railway (later L.N.W.R.), built along the line of the canal down the eastern edge of the parish, opened in 1860.[39] Dawley was served by Malinslee station, at Dark Lane, and Stirchley (from 1923 Dawley and Stirchley) station, in Stirchley. The line closed to passengers in 1952 and entirely in 1964.[40] Between 1908 and 1959 the G.W.R. had a goods line, originally called the Old Park line, between Hollinswood and Stirchley.[41]

GROWTH OF SETTLEMENT. In 1086 there were 7 villeins in Great Dawley, and only a serf, a villein, and two bordars in Little Dawley.[42] Sixteen inhabitants of the parish were assessed to the subsidy in 1327.[43] By the later 17th century Great Dawley was considerably more populous than either of the other townships: 25 householders there paid hearth tax in 1672, compared with c. 15 householders each in Little Dawley and Malinslee.[44] By 1801 the parish had 3,869 inhabitants, and population rose to a peak of 11,254 in 1871, the largest increases occurring in the 1820s, 1830s, and 1850s. The more heavily industrialized townships of Great Dawley and Malinslee grew faster than Little Dawley: between 1811 and 1831 Little Dawley accounted for only 277 of the parish's increase of 3,813 inhabitants.[45] The closure of mines and ironworks in the late 19th century led to great poverty[46] and an exodus in search of work elsewhere.[47] A drop in population of over 4,000 occurred between 1871 and 1891.[48] Emigration overseas accounted for part of the reduction:[49] families were leaving Malinslee for Australia in 1878[50] and there was an emigration agent at Dawley Bank in the late 1880s.[51] Despite a slight increase at the turn of the century, the parish contained only 7,359 inhabitants in 1931, the last censal year before boundary changes occurred.[52] The population housed in the area of the ancient parish was growing rapidly in the 1970s[53] following the designation of Dawley (from 1968 Telford) new town in 1963.

The pre-industrial settlement pattern appears to have been one of small hamlets and outlying farmsteads. In Great Dawley a cluster of dwellings probably lay around the church, parsonage, and castle in the Middle Ages. Outlying farms,

recorded from the later 16th century, were established at 'Charles Hall' (probably near Dawley Bank), Hinkshay, and Horsehay,[54] where the surviving farmhouse is partly timber-framed. In Little Dawley there were 8 tenements, a capital messuage called the Ridges (near Lightmoor), and a cottage c. 1580.[55] Settlement was concentrated in the southern half of the township in the later 18th century.[56] The nucleus of dwellings lay in Little Dawley village, where several cased timber-framed houses, including one with cruck trusses, survived in 1980.[57] The scatter of houses across the south-west of the township included Wynne's Coppice, another timber-framed house.[58] Much woodland survived in the north-west of the township in 1772, but a new farmstead, Woodlands Farm, had been built there by c. 1815.[59] Malinslee contained six messuages and four cottages in 1406 but may previously have been more extensive: in 1363 seven cottages and a house were said to be in decay.[60] The pre-industrial settlement pattern may have consisted of scattered dwellings: farms at Dark Lane, Hinkshay, 'Park House', and 'Coppy House', probably individual dwellings, are recorded from the later 17th century.[61]

Between the 16th and the 19th centuries numerous cottages were built in Dawley as the population of miners and ironworkers grew. Most were built by the labourers themselves along roadsides and on pieces of waste, their tenure ratified by payment of rent to the lord of the manor.[62] The proliferation of cottages reached its peak in the late 18th and early 19th century, the period of most rapid industrial growth. In 1799 Dawley was described as 'formerly a small village, but . . . now full of cottages from one end to the other'.[63] Those built at that time were typically of brick and tile, although sandstone raised from the mines was also used. Many had one storey and a half, sometimes with a hipped roof.[64]

In Great Dawley manor there were 7 cottages in 1567, of which 4 had recently been built;[65] there were 3 more by 1569, another one by 1572.[66] The number rose to 56 by 1753, 93 by 1781,[67] and 'at least 150' by 1812.[68] The heaviest concentration of cottages was in the northern half of Great Dawley township, where the shallow seams north-west of the Lightmoor fault were mined at an early date around Dawley Bank, Heath Hill, and

[38] Christiansen, W. Midlands, 157.
[39] Ibid. 158; cf. S.R.O., dep. plan 367; Trinder, Ind. Rev. Salop. (1981), 153.
[40] Clinker's Reg. 37, 91; Shropshire Star, 26 Sept. 1979.
[41] Christiansen, W. Midlands, 157.
[42] V.C.H. Salop. i. 317, 321.
[43] T.S.A.S. 2nd ser. i. 169.
[44] Hearth Tax 1672 (Salop. Arch. Soc.), 92–3.
[45] V.C.H. Salop. ii. 222.
[46] R. Woods to J. Crump, 4 Nov. 1878 (letter in possession of Mr. R. Evans, Cleobury Mortimer).
[47] S.R.O. 4139 (Pool Hill Boys' Sch. log bk. extracts), 15 Oct. 1886.
[48] V.C.H. Salop. ii. 222.
[49] S.R.O. 1987, box 20, W. G. Norris to M. Darby, May 1893 (copy).
[50] Woods to Crump, 4 Nov. 1878.
[51] Kelly's Dir. Salop. (1885), 841; (1891), 307.
[52] V.C.H. Salop. ii. 222
[53] When the pop. of the U.D. (incl. Madeley and Stirchley from 1966) almost doubled: cf. Census 1971; 1981 census figs. compiled in S.C.C. Planning Dept.

[54] S.P.L., Deeds 8384; S.R.O. 2374, box 1, deeds of 1578, 1611, and 1613. There were fields called Charles hay nr. Dawley Bank in 1843: L.J.R.O., B/A/15, Dawley Magna.
[55] Staffs. R.O., D. 593/B/2/5/4/2, rental.
[56] S.P.L., MS. 2481, Map XIII.
[57] SA 12705 (Ivy Fm.), 12706 (11 Holly Rd.), 12022 (15–15A Holly Rd.).
[58] Salop. News Letter, xxxiii. 7.
[59] S.P.L., MS. 2481, Map XIII; B.L. Maps, O.S.D. 208.
[60] S.R.O. 513, box 1, ct. r.
[61] Ibid. box 9, deed of 1674; S.R.O. 665/1/279.
[62] S.P.L., Deeds 8201; S.R.O. 2374, box 4, case papers of 1780, 1808.
[63] S.R.O. 3916/1/1.
[64] e.g. that at Pool Hill (O.S. Nat. Grid SJ 6796 0698); cf. B. Trinder, Blists Hill Open Air Museum (I.G.M.T. 1978), 16.
[65] S.P.L., Deeds 8384.
[66] S.R.O. 567, box 30, ministers' acct. 1567–72; S.P.L., Deeds 8403, lists 11 cottages.
[67] S.R.O. 2374, box 1, rentals.
[68] Ibid. box 3, survey.

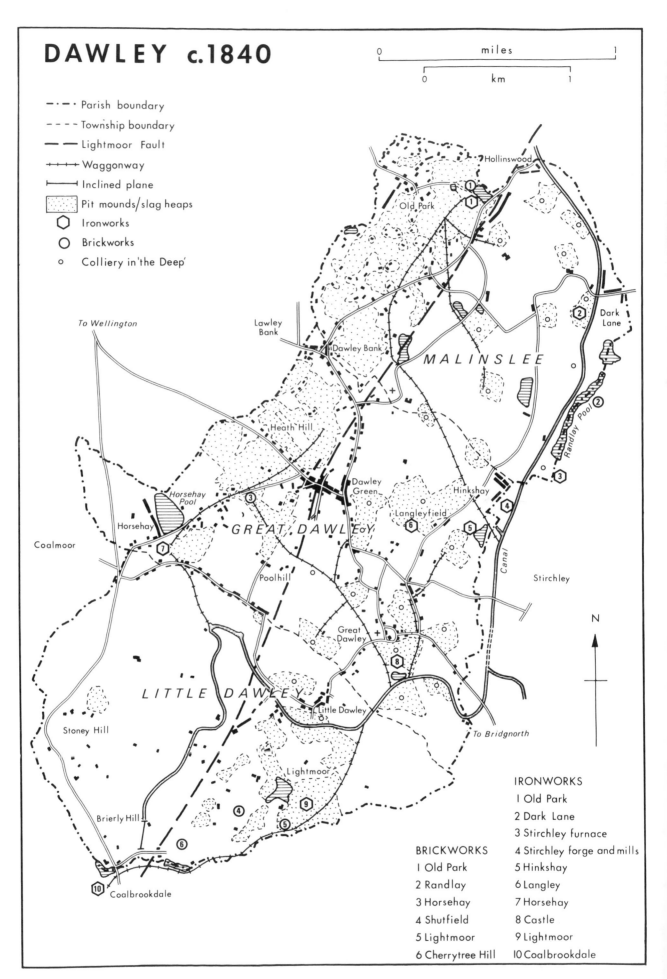

DAWLEY c.1840

miles
0 ——————————————— 1

km
0 ——————————————— 1

- —·—·— Parish boundary
- ———— Township boundary
- —— — Lightmoor Fault
- +++++ Waggonway
- |——| Inclined plane
- Pit mounds/slag heaps
- ⬡ Ironworks
- ◯ Brickworks
- ○ Colliery in 'the Deep'

To Wellington

Hollinswood

Old Park

Lawley Bank

Dawley Bank

MALINSLEE

Dark Lane

Heath Hill

Randlay Pool

Horsehay Pool

Dawley Green

Hinkshay

Horsehay

Langleyfield

GREAT DAWLEY

Coalmoor

Poolhill

Stirchley

Canal

LITTLE DAWLEY

Great Dawley

Stoney Hill

Little Dawley

To Bridgnorth

Lightmoor

N

Brierly Hill

Coalbrookdale

IRONWORKS
1 Old Park
2 Dark Lane
3 Stirchley furnace
4 Stirchley forge and mills
5 Hinkshay
6 Langley
7 Horsehay
8 Castle
9 Lightmoor
10 Coalbrookdale

BRICKWORKS
1 Old Park
2 Randlay
3 Horsehay
4 Shutfield
5 Lightmoor
6 Cherrytree Hill

108

Dawley Green. At Dawley Green, a piece of waste at a road junction on the crest of a ridge, cottages were being built by the early 17th century. In 1611 a cottage there was leased to a joiner and a piece of ground was leased to a miner as the site for a timber-framed cottage.[69] Waste land survived there and at Dawley Bank in the mid 18th century, but by the early 19th century c. 60 more cottages had been built, strung out along Dawley Green Lane (later King Street and Bank Road) and the road that later became High Street, the town's commercial centre; little waste remained.[70]

In Little Dawley the illegal building of a cottage was presented in 1592[71] and new cottages were being erected on patches of waste by the earlier 18th century.[72] The township contained 98 cottages in 1838 and 120 in 1851;[73] they were scattered among the pit mounds and slag heaps of the Lightmoor area and along roadsides, notably along Holywell Lane and Woodhouse Lane.[74]

In Malinslee there were 7 cottages in 1607[75] and 10 by 1700;[76] they probably represented the beginnings of the large but haphazard scatter of cottages that had grown up by c. 1815 in Old Park, the area of early mining north-west of the Lightmoor fault.[77]

A contrasting element in the industrial settlement pattern was formed by the rows of cottages put up by the coal and iron masters on their own property. The earliest were at Horsehay and Old Park. Old Row, Horsehay, was a terrace of twenty-five 1½-storeyed brick houses[78] built in three stages by the Coalbrookdale Co., probably soon after the Horsehay furnaces were built in 1754 and certainly by 1796.[79] At Old Park 58 cottages were built between c. 1790 and 1797 by I. H. Browne for workmen in the Old Park ironworks and mines;[80] twenty-four of them, built on the site of Park Farm (demolished c. 1796),[81] were probably the long terrace near the ironworks, later known as Forge Row.[82] Further terraces, built between c. 1815 and 1833,[83] included those on the Botfield freeholds at Hinkshay (a 'double row' of 48 back-to-back cottages, a 'single row' of 21 houses, and the later 'new row' or Ladies' Row of 10 more spacious cottages)[84] and Dark Lane (over 60 cottages in three long terraces);[85] and the isolated terrace of Stone Row (6 cottages built of massive sandstone blocks).[86] Of slightly later date were the Coalbrookdale Co.'s terraces: New Row, at Horsehay,[87] and Sandy Bank (or Dill Doll) Row, built c. 1840.[88]

The rapidly increasing demand for housing led to the conversion of former industrial buildings. As early as 1791 a pattern maker's shop at Old Park ironworks was converted into two cottages,[89] and at Horsehay the former potteries had been divided by 1843 into 24 separate dwellings,[90] including the Round House, a converted kiln inhabited until c. 1960.[91]

Cottages frequently had little land attached to them and by the mid 19th century there were extensive areas of garden allotments at Horsehay, Dawley Green, Great Dawley, and Hinkshay, in which cottagers rented unfenced plots.[92] Many cottages also had separate pigsties and brew houses, making home-cured bacon and home-brewed ale notable components of working-class diet in the 19th century.[93]

In the isolated industrial communities, scattered throughout the parish by the mid 19th century, shops were rare. Dawley Green, where there were several alehouses[94] and shops[95] along the Wellington–Bridgnorth road by c. 1800, had become the parish's commercial centre by the mid 19th century.[96] Most of the buildings fronting High Street were rebuilt during the early and mid 19th century, and the groups of cottages strung out along the highway coalesced into a continuous street frontage. The development of Chapel Street and Meadow Road, running back from High Street, accompanied the commercial growth of the town at that time.[97] The town's mid 19th-century prosperity is reflected in several moderately large detached houses, notably in King Street.

The rate of settlement growth slowed down in the mid 19th century. The main areas of new housing were Langley Terrace (later Crown Street), Langleyfield, built in the 1850s; New Town, off King Street, and St. Luke's Road, Doseley, dating from the 1860s;[98] and along Wellington Road, Horsehay, developed in the 1870s.[99] Stagnation followed when the iron and coal industries declined in the 1870s and 1880s. Except for two short terraces, Wilmot Road, Old Park, and Myford Cottages, near Horsehay, both

[69] Ibid. box 1, leases.
[70] Ibid. box 4, case papers of 1780, 1808; S.R.O. 2224/1.
[71] Staffs. R.O., D. 593/J/10, Bradford hund. ct. r.
[72] S.P.L., Deeds 7686–7704; Craven estate rec. at St. John's Coll., Oxf., L. Dawley surveys.
[73] S.P.L., MSS. 2507–8.
[74] M. W. Hunt, 'Squatter Settlements in the Coalbrookdale Area' (Liverpool Polytechnic Dept. Architecture dissertation for R.I.B.A. 1974), 4 (copy in I.G.M.T. Libr.); B. Trinder, 'Open Village in Ind. Brit.' Ind. Heritage: Trans. 3rd International Conf. on Conservation of Ind. Monuments, iii, ed. M. Nisser (Stockholm, 1981), 373–4.
[75] P.R.O., C 142/292, no. 192.
[76] S.R.O. 513, box 9, deed.
[77] B.L. Maps, O.S.D. 208.
[78] S.R.O. 2224/1.
[79] Inf. from Dr. B. S. Trinder. Cf. S.R.O. 245/145, refs. to company hos., Horsehay wks. accts. 1796–8.
[80] S.R.O. 1150/898.
[81] i.e. on death of A. Davies, tenant there: ibid.; S.P.R. Lich. xviii (1), 344.
[82] O.S. Map 6", Salop. XXXVI. SE. (1889 edn.).
[83] B.L. Maps, O.S.D. 208; O.S. Map 1", sheet 61 NE.

(1833 edn.).
[84] Salop. News Letter, xxxiii. 2–6; xliv. 23–4; S.R.O. 4044/77, pp. 72–3; below, plate 42.
[85] Salop. News Letter, xli. 12–16.
[86] N.M.R., Photos. AA 63/6563–4 (copies in S.P.L.).
[87] Built c. 1830 × 1843: O.S. Map 1", sheet 61 NE. (1833 edn.); L.J.R.O., B/A/15, Dawley Magna.
[88] S.R.O. 245/140, p. 60; 1857/1.
[89] M.U.L., Botfield papers, Old Pk. memo. bk. 1788–91.
[90] L.J.R.O., B/A/15, Dawley Magna.
[91] Local inf.; below, plate 41.
[92] L.J.R.O., B/A/15, Dawley Magna.
[93] e.g. at Horsehay, Frame Lane, Hollinswood, and Hinkshay in the 1850s: S.R.O., dep. plans 350, 367. Cf. Salop. News Letter, xxxiv. 15.
[94] Below, Social and Cultural Activities.
[95] S.R.O. 2374, box 4, case papers of 1808; 2224/1.
[96] I. Slater, Dir. Salop. (1844), 8–11.
[97] S.R.O. 1560/8; 2224/1; O.S. Maps 1/2,500, Salop. XLIII. 6–7 (1882 edn.); L.J.R.O., B/A/15, Dawley Magna.
[98] P.R.O., HO 107/1988; RG 9/1855; RG 10/2749.
[99] O.S. Map 6", Salop. XLIII. NW. (1889 edn.).

built c. 1903,[1] there was hardly any new building between 1880 and 1926.[2] Indeed the drop in population led to the abandonment of some cottages and in 1891 over 18 per cent of the parish's dwellings were unoccupied. The number of houses in the parish fell from 2,255 in 1871 to 1,859 in 1891.[3] The most notable building dating from the late 19th-century depression was Horsehay Cottage, the home of H. C. Simpson, managing partner of the Horsehay Co., who enlarged an existing cottage into a large villa c. 1896;[4] a handsome coach house and stable block south of the Cottage was added in the early 20th century.

After the First World War the urban district council tried to tackle the insanitary and overcrowded conditions that characterized a high proportion of Dawley's housing. In 1920 it was estimated that Dawley needed over 240 new houses to alleviate those conditions,[5] but a major programme of local-authority house building began only in 1927. Between then and 1939 370 houses were built at five sites in the centre of the parish between St. Leonard's church and New Road: 60 in the angle between Finger Road and New Road 1927–30 and 1935–6, 26 at Portley Road 1931–2, 64 at Alma Avenue and Rhodes Avenue[6] 1933–4, 112 at Ardern Avenue 1936–9, and 48 at Attwood Terrace[7] 1937–8.[8] Most were two-storeyed houses in pairs or blocks of four, built to standard government-approved designs in locally produced brick and tile.[9] Individual houses and small groups of cottages throughout the parish were designated slum-clearance areas under the 1930 Housing Act, their inhabitants moving to the new houses.[10] In 1936, however, 106 houses in the urban district were still classified as overcrowded.[11]

Environmental improvements were carried out. The large pit mounds of the Paddock, Portley, and Parish collieries in the centre of the parish were planted with conifers by the U.D.C. from 1928 to c. 1934 and from 1949 to c. 1960.[12]

Slum clearance and house building resumed after the Second World War and resulted in a major expansion of the central built-up area between Dawley Bank and Little Dawley by 1962. Housing conditions remained poor in many parts of the parish, notably Dawley Bank, Hinkshay, and Crown Street.[13] Buses were converted as

dwellings in the early 1950s,[14] and after the 1954 Housing Act, under which nearly 500 houses were classified as sub-standard,[15] the U.D.C. made numerous small clearance and demolition orders.[16]

The earliest post-war council housing extended existing estates near St. Leonard's church: 40 houses were built at St. Leonard's Place 1946–7,[17] 50 in Eyton Road and Moor Road 1948–9.[18] Later council housing was concentrated in two large areas: the 61-a. Manor Farm estate, south-west of New Road, on which c. 350 houses and flats were built 1950–5;[19] and the Langley Farm estate, east of King Street, on which over 350 houses were built 1957–66.[20] Smaller projects included the Ley, a pioneering arrangement of 20 old people's bungalows with common room and warden's quarters, built 1956–7.[21] Although the work was primarily to rehouse local people, the council provided 100 dwellings between 1958 and 1961 for Birmingham overspill population.[22] Planning permissions for industrial and other developments were held up from 1961, and the U.D.C.'s building programme was curtailed in 1962 until the decision to designate the area part of a new town had been taken.[23]

Speculative building was negligible until the late 1950s, but by 1963 over 500 houses had been built on private estates, notably either side of Holly Road, north-east of Little Dawley, and on the Wallows Farm estate north of Stirchley Lane.[24]

Between 1966 and 1974 the U.D.C. started or planned eight more housing schemes (437 dwellings) between Dawley Bank and Trinity Road, Dawley; the biggest of them, 180 dwellings built for Wrekin district council 1975–7, was an extension of the Langley Farm estate eastwards to Malinslee County Primary School. Clearance of older housing continued and was largely completed by the mid 1970s.[25] Many of the early 19th-century terraces were demolished: Stone Row in 1963,[26] the Hinkshay rows c. 1968,[27] Crown Street c. 1970,[28] Dark Lane rows in 1971,[29] and Sandy Bank Row in 1976.[30] Many scattered cottages at Old Park were cleared when the derelict pit mounds there were reclaimed after opencast mining in the 1970s.

As a result of the designation of Dawley new

[1] Reg. of Persons Entitled to Vote: Mid or Wellington Div. of Co. of Salop (1904).

[2] O.S. Maps 6", Salop. XXXVI. SE., XLIII (edns. of 1884–9, 1903, and 1928–9).

[3] Census, 1881, 1891.

[4] Date on porch; A. H. Simpson, Some Brief Notes Concerning Coalbrookdale Friends' Mtg. and the Horsehay Wks. (copy in S.P.L.).

[5] Wellington Jnl. 30 Oct. 1920.

[6] Named after Ric. Alma Rhodes, chmn. of the U.D.C. from 1934.

[7] Named after Ernest Attwood, chmn. of the U.D.C. Estates Cttee.

[8] S.R.O., DA 8/100/2–4, passim.

[9] Ibid. /100/2, p. 254; /100/3, pp. 77, 364.

[10] e.g. ibid. /100/3, pp. 24, 317–18.

[11] Ibid. /100/4, p. 230.

[12] Ibid. /100/2, pp. 189, 201; /100/3, pp. 147, 311, 361; /100/6, ff. 567, 572v., pp. 653, 1155.

[13] Ibid. /100/5, f. 344.

[14] Ibid. /100/6, f. 600v., p. 1041.

[15] Ibid. p. 1179.

[16] Ibid. /100/6–7, passim.

[17] Ibid. /100/5, ff. 405v., 449v., 453.

[18] Ibid. /100/6, ff. 522, 541, 571, 597, 656

[19] Ibid. f. 479v.–p. 1189, passim.

[20] Ibid. pp. 1152–1567, passim; Dawley U.D.C.: A Story, 1966–74 (copy in S.R.O., DA 8/294); below, plate 44.

[21] S.R.O., DA 8/100/6, pp. 1235–1503, passim; ibid. /100/7, p. 2253.

[22] Under the Town Development Act, 1952, 15 & 16 Geo. VI & 1 Eliz. II, c. 54: ibid. /100/6, pp. 1301–2, 1503, 1569; /100/7, pp. 1919, 2010; Express & Star, 23 Oct. 1958; inf. from S.C.C. Planning Dept.

[23] S.R.O., DA 8/100/7, pp. 2012, 2095.

[24] Ibid. /100/6, p. 1414; /100/7, pp. 1625–1924 (passim), 2487.

[25] Wrekin District Council, Tech. Resources file H.8/1 (1974–83) and completion bks.; Dawley U.D.C.: A Story, 1966–74.

[26] S.R.O., DA 8/100/7, p. 2466.

[27] S.R.O. 1969/4; 2128/4.

[28] O.S. aerial photos., film 71.193, frame 383 (copy in S.P.L.).

[29] Salop. News Letter, xli. 12–16.

[30] Inf. from the archivist, T.D.C.

town in 1963 further extensive building took place, particularly in the northern half of the parish. Three housing estates were built by Telford development corporation: Hollinswood, straddling the former boundary with Shifnal parish, containing 1,178 dwellings and completed 1975–7; north-west Dawley, completed in 1977 with 239 dwellings; the Malinslee estate, north-east of St. Leonard's church, where schemes comprising 1,127 dwellings were completed 1977–c. 1980; and the Aqueduct estate, a scheme for 247 dwellings begun in 1977. The corporation remodelled and partly rebuilt the centre of Dawley, around High Street, in the later 1970s, and the northern half of Malinslee township was chosen as the site for Telford's town centre: the first shops opened in 1973.[31]

SOCIAL AND CULTURAL ACTIVITIES. There were at least three alehouses in 1543 and from 1590, when they harboured illegal gaming and card playing, to 1619.[32] By 1753 there were 10 licensed premises and the number fluctuated between 7 and 11 throughout the late 18th and early 19th century.[33] Among the alehouses that existed by the later 18th century were the Wicket near the parish church (later the Old Wicket as distinct from the New Wicket near St. Leonard's church), the Dun Cow at Dawley Green, and the Finger on the Wellington–Worcester turnpike. Most early 19th-century alehouses lay along the major roads in the populous central part of the parish. There were three at Dawley Bank and at least four at Dawley Green in 1817.[34] After the relaxation of licensing laws the number of taverns increased and many beerhouses were opened throughout the parish. In 1851 there were 22 taverns and 15 beerhouses and by 1879, although the number of public houses remained stable, the number of beer retailers had increased to 28. Seventeen public houses and all but two of the beer retailers were in Great Dawley; Malinslee had one beerhouse only. By the late 1970s there were 18 pubs, inns, or licensed hotels in the area of the ancient parish, about half of them in and around central Dawley. The Ironmaster was opened in Telford town centre c. 1980.[35]

Controlling drink and drunkenness was difficult. In the 1790s there were unlicensed alesellers in Dawley,[36] and in 1820 the parish meeting circulated handbills, stating the laws against drunkenness, and appointed someone to superintend the conduct of alehouse keepers and their customers.[37] The strength of Methodism in the area was associated with the growth of a temperance movement in the late 19th century[38] and there was an Anglican mission to combat drunkenness in the Dawley Bank area in 1882.[39]

Dawley's wake was held on All Saints' Day in the early 18th century.[40] The wakes were last recorded in 1873, when they were held at the end of September.[41] There was a bull ring at Dawley Bank in the early 19th century[42] and cock fighting is said to have lingered on in Dawley until the 20th century.[43] Both horse and foot racing took place at Dawley Green in 1843.[44] By 1863 the annual livestock fair, held in June at Dawley Green, had become an important social event. The 'pleasure fair', as it came to be known, was recorded until 1895, and was followed by sports and games in 1876. Circuses regularly visited Dawley Green in the later 19th century.[45]

The Dawley Sunday Schools' Demonstration, held on August bank holiday Monday, began in 1876[46] and was a notable annual event for nearly a century. Pupils and teachers from Sunday schools throughout Dawley walked in procession carrying banners, to converge on a field at the corner of King Street and Meadow Road, where an open-air service was held. The groups then returned to their own chapels for tea and sports.[47] The form of the demonstration probably derived from Primitive Methodist processions to preaching places, recorded in the area in the 1850s,[48] and from annual Sunday school treats, which included processions in 1875.[49] In 1878 c. 2,500 children and c. 300 teachers from 15 nonconformist Sunday schools took part.[50] Later Anglican Sunday schools also participated. By the 1930s a flower show was held in the town park on the same day. After the Second World War the processions met on the playing fields at Doseley Road.[51] The demonstration declined in size in the 1960s as several Methodist chapels closed, and it last took place c. 1974.[52]

Numerous friendly and provident societies were recorded in Dawley after registration was introduced in 1794.[53] Many met in alehouses[54] but some sectarian societies met in chapels.[55] Some ironmasters encouraged the societies: in the early 19th century I. H. Browne and the Botfield

[31] Ibid.; *Telford and Wrekin News*, May 1979, p. 4; D. G. Fenter, 'Bldg. Development carried out in Telford by the Development Corp.' (TS. in S.R.O. 3763); below, Econ. Hist.

[32] S.R.O. 327, boxes 4–5, ct. r. of 1543–1609; S.R.O., q. sess. rec. parcel 254.

[33] S.R.O., q. sess. rec. parcels 255–9, regs. of alesellers' recognizances 1753–1828.

[34] Ibid.; S.R.O. 2224/1.

[35] S. Bagshaw, *Dir. Salop.* (1851), 377–8; *P.O. Dir. Salop.* (1879), 312–13, 355; *P.O. Telephone Dir.* (1976), sect. 303 (YP), 144–51, 186–7; local inf.

[36] *Q. Sess. Rolls*, 121, 128, 130.

[37] S.R.O. 1560/5, 24 July 1820.

[38] S.R.O. 3038/11/1; 3298/17–18; 3840/13.

[39] Below, Churches.

[40] B.L. Add. MS. 30316, f. 6.

[41] S.R.O. 4139, 29 Sept. 1873.

[42] S. Mostyn Jones, *Baptist Church, Dawley* (Wellington, 1946), [5].

[43] *V.C.H. Salop.* ii. 191–2.

[44] *Shrews. News and Cambrian Reporter*, 16 Sept. 1843.

[45] S.R.O. 4139, *passim*.

[46] *Wellington Jnl.* 12 Aug. 1876.

[47] Ibid.; local inf. (in possession of the archivist, T.D.C.); J. McFall, 'Educ. in Madeley Union of Salop. in 19th Cent.' (Keele Univ. M.A. (Educ.) thesis, 1973), 25 and n. 1.

[48] S.R.O. 2533/130, 14 Dec. 1857, 25 Apr. 1859.

[49] *Wellington Jnl.* 7 Aug. 1875.

[50] Ibid. 10 Aug. 1878.

[51] Local inf.; S.R.O. 2732, Demonstration programme, 1964.

[52] Inf. from Mr. J. Cadwallader, Ketley Bank.

[53] Friendly Socs. Act, 33 Geo. III, c. 54, s. 2. Twenty-two socs. were reg. in Dawley 1794–1841: S.R.O., q. sess. rec. parcel 285, friendly socs. reg.

[54] Registrar of Friendly Socs. *List of Friendly Socs. in Co. of Salop, 1793–1855* (H.M.S.O. 1857; copy in S.R.O.).

[55] e.g. Prim. Meth. friendly soc., meeting in chap. at Lightmoor: S.R.O. 2533/130, 8 Dec. 1862.

brothers contributed to Malinslee Club,[56] possibly the friendly society formed in 1797 and held at Old Park Office[57] or that which met in 1835 at Lawley Bank.[58] The Coalbrookdale Co. established a medical and educational fund, to which its employees contributed, in the earlier 19th century.[59] A lodge of the Independent Order of Odd Fellows (Manchester Unity), formed in 1856, survived in 1937.[60] There was a branch of the Shropshire Provident Society 1853–1945.[61]

A library and reading room in High Street, recorded from 1856, was known by 1870 as the Literary Institute.[62] It was managed by a committee, whose secretary was latterly the headmaster of Langley Board School, and it contained c. 3,000 volumes by 1900. It seems to have closed c. 1907.[63] A second reading room, on Bank Road, known as the Dawley Bank Institute, was recorded from 1909 to 1917.[64] Dawley was the only urban district to be served by the county library service established in 1925. The county opened a local library centre in the town c. 1927.[65] A full-time, professionally staffed branch library, the first in the county service, was opened at Dawley in 1949.[66] The original premises, the former Congregational chapel off High Street,[67] were replaced by a prefabricated building in King Street in 1973.[68]

A public park and recreation ground was opened in 1901 on a 2-a. site between Dawley National School and George Street, given to the town by W. S. Kenyon-Slaney and H. C. Simpson.[69] Tennis courts and a bowling green were made there in 1922.[70] Part of the site had previously been a cricket ground, apparently given to the parish in the mid 19th century. In 1886 R. C. Wanstall, vicar of Dawley Magna, proposed, apparently in vain, that it be levelled and converted into a recreation ground by the unemployed.[71] Similar schemes to provide recreation grounds by using the unemployed were put into effect between the World Wars. Part of Horse Leasow, a site levelled in 1927, was used as a children's playground,[72] and a pit mound at Dawley Bank was levelled and converted into a playing field c. 1930 under the direction of Edward Parry, vicar of Malinslee.[73]

The first hall for social purposes was the Town Hall in New Street, built as a temperance hall in 1873.[74] It passed to the urban district council and was let for public meetings, concerts, and dances in the 1920s.[75] After the Second World War users included Roman Catholic and nonconformist groups.[76] After the First World War the Memorial Recreation Hall in King Street was built.[77] In 1928, when the building was used by the Dawley Child Welfare Society and as a school clinic, management passed from the War Memorial Committee to the U.D.C.[78] In 1980 the premises were used by Dawley Social Club. The former Congregational chapel off High Street was used as an assembly room in the early 20th century.[79]

In 1913 the Town Hall was occupied by the Royal Windsor Variety and Picture Palace.[80] It did not survive the First World War. The first purpose-built cinema was the Cosy cinema in Burton Street, which opened c. 1921[81] and closed in 1956.[82] The Royal cinema, King Street, opened c. 1938[83] and closed as a cinema in 1961,[84] but bingo was played there nightly in 1980. A playhouse in New Street, recorded in 1929,[85] was evidently short-lived.

The only newspaper produced exclusively for the Dawley area was the *Dawley Observer* (from 1968 the *Telford Observer*), founded by a young journalist on the designation of the new town in 1963. Published from a terraced house in Chapel Street, it appeared weekly until 1972.[86]

A strip of open land, centring on the Randlay valley along the ancient boundary between Dawley and Stirchley, was designated as a central town park for the new town in 1971; by 1980 it included a sports complex, exhibition area, open-air theatre, and tram line.[87] At Hinkshay, at the southern end of the park, a field-study area was opened in 1970.[88] Telford Horsehay Steam Trust was founded in 1975 to preserve steam locomotives. It rapidly acquired several.[89]

MANORS AND OTHER ESTATES. The manor of *GREAT DAWLEY*, sometimes styled Dawley Pantulf,[90] was considered a member of Wellington manor and was held by Grim at some time before 1086. In 1086 Roger of Montgomery, earl of Shrewsbury by 1074, held it in chief and

[56] M.U.L., Botfield papers, cash bks. 1804–15, *passim*.
[57] *List of Friendly Socs. in Co. Salop* (1857).
[58] Below, Lawley, intro.
[59] Below, Educ.
[60] *List of Friendly Socs. in Co. Salop* (1857); J. Jones & Son, *Dir. of Wellington & Dist.* (1937), 142.
[61] S.R.O. 436/6720, p. 66; /6733, p. 31.
[62] *P.O. Dir. Salop.* (1856), 43; (1870), 47.
[63] Ibid. (1870), 47; (1879), 312; *Kelly's Dir. Salop.* (1885–1909).
[64] *Kelly's Dir. Salop.* (1909–17); S.R.O. 4044/77, p. 36.
[65] S.C.C. *Salop. Co. Library: 1st Ann. Rep.* (1927; copy in S.R.O.); S.R.O., DA 8/100/2, p. 165.
[66] R. C. Elliott, 'Development of Public Libraries in Salop.' (Loughborough Univ. M.A. thesis, 1970), 94–6 (copy in Salop. Librs.).
[67] *Wrekin Light*, June 1968, 3 (file 1967–9 in S.R.O. 2732/PM/352–70).
[68] Inf. from Salop. Librs.
[69] *Kelly's Dir. Salop.* (1905), 80; O.S. Map 1/2,500, Salop. XLIII. 6 (1927 edn.).
[70] S.R.O., DA 8/100/1, pp. 301–2.
[71] S.R.O. 1952/114–15.
[72] S.R.O., DA 8/100/2, p. 66.
[73] S.R.O. 2732/PF/1–74.

[74] Date stone; A. Lester, *Fifty Years* (1896), 16 (copy in S.P.L.).
[75] *Kelly's Dir. Salop.* (1905), 80; S.R.O., DA 8/100/1, pp. 9–10, 382.
[76] Below, Rom. Cath.; inf. from Mr. D. Bickerton, pastor, Telford Full Gospel Ch.
[77] *Kelly's Dir. Salop.* (1922), 84.
[78] S.R.O., DA 8/100/2, pp. 143–4.
[79] S.R.O. 4044/77, p. 21; inscr. over doorway.
[80] *Kelly's Dir. Salop.* (1913), 87.
[81] Ibid. (1922), 84; S.R.O., DA 8/100/1, p. 92.
[82] S.R.O., DA 8/100/6, p. 843; /100/7, p. 1962; DA 34 (S.R.O. 3279/I), Cosy file, letter 25 June 1956.
[83] S.R.O., DA 8/100/4, pp. 293, 301, 312; *Kelly's Dir. Salop.* (1941), 87.
[84] S.R.O., DA 8/100/7, pp. 1991, 2433; DA 34 (S.R.O. 3279/I), Royal file of 1956–61, letter 18 Dec. 1961.
[85] *Kelly's Dir. Salop.* (1929), 88.
[86] Copies in S.P.L., I.G.M.T. Libr., and Madeley branch libr. Cf. *Shropshire Jnl.* 29 Dec. 1972.
[87] Inf. from the archivist, T.D.C.
[88] *Dawley U.D.C.: A Story, 1966–1974*, [14].
[89] *Shropshire Star*, 24 Mar. 1983; B. Duckett, *Telford Tour by Rail* (n.d.; copy in S.P.L.).
[90] Eyton, viii. 45.

William Pantulf held it under him.[91] The tenancy in chief was evidently forfeited after 1102 and, with the other estates held by William in 1086, Great Dawley became a member of the Pantulfs' barony of Wem; the township's constable continued to attend the court at Hinstock until 1851 or later.[92]

Great Dawley was held of the barons of Wem by a younger branch of the Pantulfs descended from Ralph Pantulf, who was recorded c. 1170–c. 1192. His son William, who had succeeded by 1199, was dead by 1203 and Dawley passed to William's son or brother, Alan. Alan's heir, Adam Pantulf, was a minor in 1218 and was dead by 1240, when Great Dawley was held by his heirs.[93] In 1255 there were four coparceners: William of Caverswall, Richard Irish, Michael of Morton, and Christine of Dawley, wife of John of Charnes.[94] In 1304 they were said to be descendants of the four sisters and coheiresses of Hugh, son of John 'de Pauncefot' (recte Pantulf?).[95] William of Caverswall conveyed his share to his coparcener Michael of Morton c. 1258 but reserved an annual rent of £3 13s. 4d. as mesne lord. Richard Irish's portion descended to Richard Irish of Dawley, who settled his estates on his son William and his heirs in 1292;[96] Richard Irish owned it in 1304[97] but it has not been traced beyond that date. Michael of Morton's moiety had passed to his son Michael by c. 1285[98] and descended to William of Morton, clerk, by 1316.[99] The Charnes' quarter had descended by c. 1285 to Reynold of Charnes,[1] still the owner in 1310.[2]

The descent of the manor in the earlier 14th century is obscure, but by 1346[3] the Morton moiety had passed to Richard, earl of Arundel, and the Charnes portion to Roger of Oakley, husband of Isabel, daughter and coheir of William of Charnes.[4] Arundel's interest in the manor was recorded from 1345[5] and he consolidated his tenure in 1354 when Roger and Isabel sold him their quarter of the manor.[6] Thereafter until 1560 the manor descended with the earldom of Arundel, except for the period of its annexation to Richard II's principality of Chester (1397–1400)[7] and a life grant to Sir Roland Lenthall's wife Margaret (d. 1423).[8] In 1560 Earl Henry sold Great Dawley to Rowland Hayward (kt. 1570), lord mayor of London 1570[9] and the purchaser of Little Dawley in 1590.[10] On Hayward's death in 1593 both manors passed successively to his sons

George (kt. 1604, d. 1615) and John (kt. 1619).[11] In 1623 Sir John sold Great Dawley, except for a 72-a. estate, to Fulke Crompton.[12] By his will dated 1642 Crompton settled the manor on his wife Mary for her life, with reversion to their children Fulke and Frances.[13] Mary Crompton, a royalist, was in possession by 1645 and continued to take the profits until 1652, when Eyton Crompton, a Parliamentarian, claimed the manor, and the estate was sequestrated for Mary's delinquency.[14] In 1655, however, the manor was settled under the terms of Fulke Crompton's will on Frances Crompton on her marriage with Clement Throckmorton of Haseley (Warws.). In 1672 she sold Great Dawley to Robert Slaney (d. 1706) of Hatton Grange,[15] with whose descendants it remained until 1900.

In 1696 Slaney settled the estate on his second son Robert in tail male. On the younger Robert's death without male issue in 1728 the manor passed to his elder brother's son Robert Aglionby Slaney (d. 1757).[16] Thereafter the estate passed from father to son, the following being lords: Plowden (d. 1788), Robert (d. 1834), and Robert Aglionby. On R. A. Slaney's death in 1862[17] his estates were divided between his daughters, Great Dawley passing to Frances Catherine (d. 1896), wife of William Kenyon, who assumed the additional name and arms of Slaney in 1862. Their son Col. W. S. Kenyon-Slaney, M.P. for Newport, succeeded to the property, and sold the remaining manorial estate at Dawley (c. 300 a.) in 1900.[18]

Dawley Castle, the medieval manor house of Great Dawley, lay c. 250 metres south of the church.[19] William of Morton was licensed to fortify the house in 1316.[20] In the First Civil War the house was held by royalist forces until captured for Parliament in 1645. After an abortive attempt to plant a royalist garrison there in 1648 an order was made for the house's demolition.[21] By 1762 the site had become a farmstead,[22] and buildings, surrounded by remains of the water-filled moat, survived in 1817.[23] All trace of the former house was obliterated in the early 19th century by slag heaps from the adjacent Castle furnaces.[24]

The manor of LITTLE DAWLEY was held of Reynold the sheriff by Benet in 1086. T.R.E. it had been held by Sistain.[25] From the 13th to the 16th century it was considered to be merely a member of Leegomery manor but from 1590 it was again styled an independent manor. Little

[91] V.C.H. Salop. i. 317; iii. 7.
[92] Bk. of Fees, ii. 964; V.C.H. Salop. iii. 10, 51–2; P.R.O., C 139/5, no. 35; S.R.O. 327, boxes 4–5, ct. leet verdicts, 1478–1851.   [93] Eyton, viii. 42–3.
[94] Rot. Hund. (Rec. Com.), ii. 56, 58.
[95] P.R.O., CP 40/149, m. 73d.
[96] Eyton, viii. 43, 45.
[97] P.R.O., CP 40/149, m. 73d.
[98] Collect. Topog. et Geneal. i. 115.
[99] Cal. Pat. 1313–17, 566.
[1] Collect. Topog. et Geneal. i. 115.
[2] Rot. Chart. (Rec. Com.), 299; P.R.O., C 143/82, no. 20.
[3] Feud. Aids, iv. 237.   [4] S.H.C. 1914, 26–7.
[5] Cal. Pat. 1343–5, 488.
[6] P.R.O., CP 25(1)/195/15, no. 55.
[7] 21 Ric. II, c. 9, repealed by 1 Hen. IV, c. 3; Cal. Fine R. 1391–9, 253; Camden, Brit. ed. Gibson (1753), ii. 654. For the background see V.C.H. Ches. ii. 11, and sources there cited.
[8] Cal. Inq. Misc. vi, p. 114; Cal. Fine R. 1422–30, 210;

P.R.O., C 139/5, no. 35; Feud. Aids, iv. 249, 270.
[9] Cal. Pat. 1558–60, 368; P.R.O., CP 25(2)/200/2 Eliz. I East. [no. 13].
[10] Below.
[11] P.R.O., C 142/363, no. 194.
[12] S.R.O. 1268/128.
[13] S.R.O. 1952/10.
[14] Cal. Cttee. for Money, iii. 1453; T.S.A.S. 3rd ser. x. 94 n.
[15] S.R.O. 1268/128.
[16] S.R.O. 1952/28; Burke; Land. Gent. (1952), 2327.
[17] D.N.B.
[18] Burke, Land. Gent. (1952), 2327–8; S.R.O. 1268/1.
[19] At O.S. Nat. Grid SJ 688 062: S.R.O. 2224/1; O.S. Map 6″, Salop. XLIII. NE. (1889 edn.).
[20] Cal. Pat. 1313–17, 566.
[21] T.S.A.S. 3rd ser. x. 94 n, 96; 4th ser. ii. 293–4.
[22] S.R.O. 1952/44, abstr. of lease, 24 June 1762.
[23] S.R.O. 2224/1.
[24] L.J.R.O., B/A/15, Dawley Magna (plan, 1843).
[25] V.C.H. Salop. i. 321.

Dawley was recorded as a member of Leegomery by 1285[26] but the connexion between the two places probably originated in the 12th century: Alfred de Cumbray, lord of Leegomery, was fined for a forest offence in Dawley c. 1180.[27] No medieval undertenants of Little Dawley are known; demesne lordship was presumably retained by the lords of Leegomery.[28]

In 1590 Sir Walter Leveson sold Little Dawley, thenceforth described as a manor, to Sir Rowland Hayward,[29] the owner of Great Dawley. Both manors passed to Sir John Hayward,[30] who sold Little Dawley to William Craven (cr. Baron Craven 1627, earl of Craven 1665) in 1624–5.[31] On Craven's death in 1697 the lordship passed to his kinsman William, 2nd Baron Craven, and descended with the barony (from 1801 the re-created earldom) until 1941 or later,[32] although a large part of the estate was divided and sold in 1854.[33]

A medieval stone building in Little Dawley, demolished in 1911,[34] was then known as the 'old manor house'.[35] No other evidence for the existence of a manor house has been found.

Like Little Dawley, *MALINSLEE* was a member of Leegomery manor during the Middle Ages. It was not mentioned by name in Domesday Book and was described as a separate manor only from the 16th century. Its position as a member of Leegomery was stated explicitly in 1284 or 1285[36] and was recorded until 1613.[37] From 1334 or earlier Malinslee was held of the lords of Leegomery by the Eytons of Eyton upon the Weald Moors.[38] It descended with the manor of Eyton until 1701[39] when Soudley Eyton (d. 1701) sold Malinslee to Isaac Hawkins of Burton-upon-Trent.[40] From 1655 to the end of the 17th century Malinslee was held in trust, its profits being used to create a stock for the younger children of Sir Thomas Eyton (d. 1659).[41]

Under Isaac Hawkins's will, proved 1713,[42] the manor passed to his daughter Rebecca Walthall (d. 1756) for her life and then to his grandson Isaac Hawkins Browne, the poet.[43] On his death in 1760 it descended to his son Isaac Hawkins Browne (d. 1818), the M.P. and essayist, who acquired the neighbouring manor of Stirchley in

1777.[44] He left the estate to his wife Elizabeth (d. 1839) for her life with reversion to his kinsman Robert Cheney (d. 1820).[45] By Cheney's will interest in the manor was divided between his children but all shares descended, after his son Edward's death in 1884, to his grandson Alfred Capel Cure of Badger Hall.[46] Cure sold the Malinslee and Stirchley estates in 1886 to the Haybridge Iron Co.[47] Most of the Malinslee estate was divided and sold in 1904.[48]

No evidence has been found for the existence of a manor house. Malinslee Hall was built, probably in the 1790s, by Thomas Botfield (d. 1801), the lessee of much of the manorial estate.[49] It was a brick house with a principal front of three storeys and three bays, capped by a stone cornice. The central entrance, beneath a wide, segmental-headed arch, was decorated with Ionic pilasters. It was occupied by William Botfield in the early 19th century,[50] and after his death in 1840 it was lived in by the ironworks managers and housed the offices of the Old Park Iron Co.[51] The house was demolished c. 1971 when Telford town centre was laid out.[52]

The rectory, consisting of parsonage, tithe barn, c. 25 a. of glebe, and tithes,[53] was appropriated to Battlefield college in 1410.[54] After the college's dissolution in 1548 the estate was leased out by the Crown; William Charlton of Wombridge held it in the mid 16th century[55] and other lessees in Elizabeth I's reign.[56] The freehold seems to have been acquired by John Watson (d. 1606) of Church Aston.[57] The estate descended to his granddaughter Muriel and thereafter, with the advowson of Stirchley, to the Phillips family of Shifnal, the owners in the mid 19th century.[58] Revell Phillips owned Dawley rectory in 1854[59] but the property had been sold and divided by c. 1910.[60]

Little Lee, an estate that Reynold of Charnes held of Peter of Eyton and Hugh de Say under Thomas Tuchet, lord of Leegomery, in 1310,[61] probably lay in Malinslee, perhaps near its boundary with Stirchley.[62] About 1320 Peter of Eyton, whose descendants held Malinslee, and Walter grandson of Leonard of Lee, owner of Leonard's Lee, an estate in Shifnal,[63] were described as

[26] *Feud. Aids*, iv. 219.
[27] Eyton, vii. 340–1.
[28] Below, Wellington, Man. and Other Est.
[29] P.R.O., CP 25(2)/202/32 Eliz. I Trin. [no. 2].
[30] Above.
[31] P.R.O., CP 25(2)/311/22 Jas. I Hil. [no. 2].
[32] Burke, *Peerage* (1970); S.P.L., MSS. 2481, 2507–9; leases in S.P.L., Deeds, *passim*; *Kelly's Dir. Salop.* (1885–1941).
[33] S.R.O. 407/8–9.
[34] Below, Churches.
[35] S.R.O. 2732, corresp. *re* Malinslee chap. 1910.
[36] *Feud. Aids*, iv. 219; Eyton, vii. 348.
[37] P.R.O., C 142/332, no. 148.
[38] S.R.O. 513, box 1, ct. r.
[39] Below, Eyton, Man. and Other Est., and sources there cited. Thos. of Eyton who (with his wife Cath.) was ld. of Malinslee 1406 (S.R.O. 513, box 1, ct. r.) may be the Thos. who held Eyton in 1420.
[40] S.R.O. 513, box 10, deed.
[41] Ibid. box 8, deed of 1655; box 9, deeds of 1669, 1674.
[42] Ibid. box 36, will.   [43] *D.N.B.*
[44] Below, Stirchley, Man. and Other Est.
[45] S.R.O. 1265/218. For pedigree of Browne and Cheney see S.P.L., MS. 4645, p. 264.
[46] S.R.O. 1265/219, 289.
[47] T.DC., Grange farm, Stirchley, deeds.
[48] S.R.O. 1268/3.
[49] S. Bagshaw, *Dir. Salop.* (1851), 376. Descr. based on N.M.R., Photos. AA 63/6568–71 (copies in S.P.L.).
[50] *Eng. Topog.* (Gent. Mag. Libr.), x. 7.
[51] S. Bagshaw, *Dir. Salop.* (1851), 376–7; *P.O. Dir. Salop.* (1870), 87–8.
[52] Inf. from the archivist, T.D.C.
[53] L.J.R.O., B/V/6, Dawley 1612–1767.
[54] *V.C.H. Salop.* ii. 129–30.
[55] S.R.O. 513, box 8, deeds of 1563–4.
[56] P.R.O., C 66/1144, mm. 14–16.
[57] P.R.O., C 142/291, no. 92; /381, no. 148; CP 25(2)/477/9 Chas. I Mich. [no. 19].
[58] Below, Stirchley, Churches.
[59] S.R.O. 1560/8.
[60] S.R.O. 4044/77, *passim*.
[61] Eyton, viii. 44; *Cal. Pat.* 1307–13, 350.
[62] In the 1220s land in Stirchley adjoined a meadow belonging to Ric. s. of Ralph, of L. Lee: Eyton, ii. 315; viii. 116–17; *T.S.A.S.* xi. 334.
[63] Eyton treats L. Lee and Leonard's Lee together, but they were tenurially distinct, the latter being a member of Shifnal man.: Eyton, ii. 314–16; *Cartulary of Shrews. Abbey*, ed. U. Rees (1975), ii. pp. 342–3.

coparceners in 'Lee'.[64] Their ancestors' interest in Little Lee was recorded in 1240 and 1256, when William of Eyton's wife Maud and her sister Nichole released land there to Leonard's son Henry.[65] The estate has not been traced after the early 14th century.

Until the 19th century the three manorial estates accounted for most land in the parish. Only in Great Dawley were there other freeholds of long standing. There the manorial estate covered 720 a. of the township's 997 a. in 1812.[66] Among the other freeholds was one held by the Burtons of Longner in the 18th and early 19th century. The property, covering 106 a. in 1853,[67] is probably to be identified with land in Dawley held in the 16th century by the Corbets of Moreton Corbet, lords of Lawley manor.[68] The estate appears to have descended with Lawley[69] until 1853 when most of it was sold by Robert Burton to the Coalbrookdale Co.[70] Other freeholds included that belonging to Thomas Dodd of Great Dawley in 1679, which was absorbed into the manorial estate in 1749;[71] that at Langleyfield held by the Clowes family of Stirchley Hall and their descendants in the mid 18th century;[72] and those of the industrialists John Gibbons, John Onions, and Adam Wright, recorded in 1817.[73]

During the earlier 19th century the Coalbrookdale Co. and the Botfield family, the major coal and iron masters in Dawley, acquired extensive estates in the parish. The Horsehay estate (121 a.), bought from Robert Slaney c. 1815,[74] and 96 a. bought from Robert Burton in 1853,[75] formed the core of the Coalbrookdale Co.'s property in Great Dawley, which contained 284 a. when it was divided and sold in 1910.[76] In 1824 Thomas and William Botfield bought Moor farm (42 a.) in Great Dawley, formerly part of the Clowes' freehold,[77] and Hinkshay farm (51 a.), which had been separated from Slaney's manorial estate in 1814.[78] The following year they acquired Dark Lane (74 a.) in Malinslee, which had been separated from the manorial estate in 1701.[79] Their nephew and heir, Beriah Botfield, bought Langleyfield (31 a.), formerly another part of the Clowes' freehold, in 1857.[80] All Beriah Botfield's

property in Dawley was sold by his trustees in 1873 to the Haybridge Iron Co.[81]

ECONOMIC HISTORY. AGRICULTURE. The element *leah*, in the township names Dawley and Malinslee and in the minor names Brandlee, Doseley, Langley, and Portley, suggests that the early medieval landscape consisted of clearings in an area of late-surviving woodland.[82] In Little Dawley the existence of two Domesday bordars with a share in $\frac{1}{2}$ ploughteam[83] suggests woodland clearance and the continued expansion of cultivation.[84] Dawley was within the forest of Mount Gilbert until disafforested in 1301.[85] Assarting continued in the late 13th century[86] and in Malinslee in the mid 14th century.[87] Small enclosures continued to be carved out of woodland and waste in Great Dawley in the mid 16th century.[88]

The largest wooded area, probably the Dawley wood mentioned in 1535,[89] was in Little Dawley, where there was a league of wood in 1086.[90] On the evidence of later field names, woodland may have covered most of the township west of Horsehay dingle in the Middle Ages.[91] The name Pawn Hatchett, near Doseley,[92] probably records a 'hatch-gate' leading into woodland,[93] possibly into Frame wood (or Frame rough), a wood near Horsehay in Great Dawley, recorded in 1573 and grubbed up c. 1755.[94] In 1772 there were still c. 130 a. of woodland in Little Dawley.[95] In Malinslee the lord's wood, probably 'Lywode' mentioned in 1420, was subject to frequent encroachments, including the felling of much oak timber, in the mid 14th century.[96] Only a small block of woodland, in the vicinity of the later Wood colliery, remained in the township in 1808.[97] In the 18th and early 19th century much of the parish's woodland was coppiced to provide charcoal and pit-props for local industry.[98]

In Great Dawley there were at least two areas of open field. The larger, known simply as 'the common field' in 1612,[99] lay along the boundary with Little Dawley. That part north-west of the road since called Holly Road was later called Pool Hill field, that part to the south-east of the road

[64] Eyton, ii. 317; *T.S.A.S.* xi. 327–8.
[65] Eyton, ii. 315–16.
[66] S.R.O. 2374, box 3, survey.
[67] S.R.O. 1681, box 122, partic. of Burton est.
[68] Rog. Corbet held land in Dawley, 1535 (*Valor Eccl.* (Rec. Com.), iii. 103); Sir And. Corbet's wood in Dawley occ. 1566 (S.P.L., Deeds 8384).
[69] Cf. below, Lawley, Man. and Other Est.
[70] S.R.O. 1681, box 122, deed.
[71] S.R.O. 2374, box 2, deeds of 1679–1749.
[72] S.R.O. 1265/1–14.
[73] S.R.O. 2224/1.
[74] Ibid.
[75] S.R.O. 1681, box 122, deed.
[76] S.R.O. 1857/1.
[77] S.R.O. 1265/1–14, 51–2.
[78] Ibid. /152–3, 159–60.
[79] Ibid. /217, 221.
[80] Ibid. /11–12, 70–1, 127.
[81] Ibid. /261. For the Botfields see B. Botfield, *Stemmata Botevilliana: Memorials of the Fams. of De Boteville, Thynne, and Botfield, in the Cos. of Salop and Wilts.* (Westminster, 1858).
[82] *Eng. P.N. Elements* (E.P.N.S.), ii. 18–20.

[83] *V.C.H. Salop.* i. 321.
[84] S. P. J. Harvey, 'Evidence for Settlement Study: Domesday Bk.' *Medieval Settlement*, ed. P. H. Sawyer (1976), 197–9; R. Lennard, *Rural Eng. 1086–1135* (1959), 356.
[85] *V.C.H. Salop.* i. 486; *Cart. Shrews.* ii, p. 249.
[86] P.R.O., E 32/145, m. 6d.; /147, m. 6.
[87] In 1347 four tenants there took land 'newly measured' in 'le Hawkesherd': S.R.O. 513, box 1, ct. r.
[88] S.P.L., Deeds 8384.
[89] Staffs. R.O., D. 593/B/2/5/2/3.
[90] *V.C.H. Salop.* i. 321.
[91] Map on p. 116.
[92] At O.S. Nat. Grid SJ 677 066: S.P.L., MS. 2481, Map XIII.
[93] *Eng. P.N. Elements* (E.P.N.S.), i. 213–14.
[94] S.P.L., Deeds 8403; MS. 332, p. 8; S.R.O. 2374, box 4, case papers of 1781. Cf. Frame Lane, which forms the boundary between Gt. and L. Dawley tns.
[95] S.P.L., MS. 2481, Map XIII.
[96] S.R.O. 513, box 1, ct. r. of 1334–72, 1420.
[97] R. Baugh, *Map of Salop.* (1808).
[98] S.P.L., MSS. 332–3 (*passim*), 2507–8; S.R.O. 4406/1 pp. 160–2; M.U.L., Botfield papers, acct. bks. 1795–1815.
[99] L.J.R.O., B/V/6, Dawley, 1612.

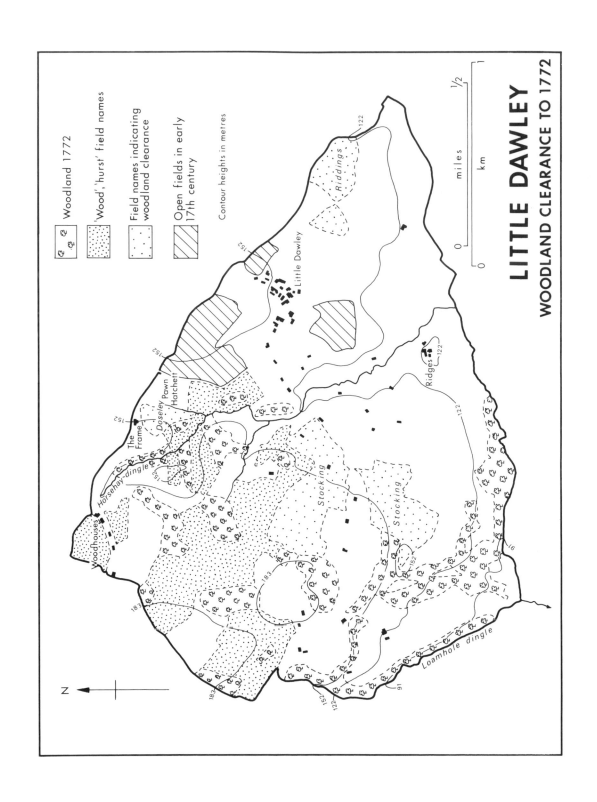

LITTLE DAWLEY
WOODLAND CLEARANCE TO 1772

Woodland 1772

'Wood', 'hurst' field names

Field names indicating
woodland clearance

Open fields in early
17th century

Contour heights in metres

Little Dawley

Riddings

Ridges

Doseley Pawn
Hatchett

The Frame

Horsehay-dingle

Woodhouses

Stocking

Stocking

Loamhole dingle

Rednall field and Castle field.[1] Coppy Greave field lay north of Great Dawley village, near the later Portley colliery. Land in Rednall and Coppy Greave fields was inclosed after 1632 and before 1718;[2] Pool Hill field was inclosed in stages in the early 18th century; a part remaining open c. 1750 had been inclosed by 1767.[3] The open fields accounted for only a small proportion of the township, a larger acreage probably being held in severalty. On the periphery of the township were a number of hays, large enclosures probably for stock. Horsehay, Smeeth hay, Dawley hay, and Charles hay lay along the north-western edge and Hinkshay in the eastern corner.[4] By the late 16th century farmsteads had been built at Horsehay, Hinkshay, and possibly Charles hay.[5] Common waste survived in the mid 18th century on the high land between Dawley Bank and Heath Hill[6] and may also have survived late near Hinkshay where 'moor' field names were recorded in the 19th century.[7]

Little Dawley had three open fields in 1616:[8] Pool Hill and Rednall fields were contiguous to the fields so named in Great Dawley.[9] Bandrich field probably lay immediately south of Little Dawley village, extending west to Holywell Lane; the field was described as 'over Madeley way' in 1631.[10] Piecemeal inclosure, sometimes stated to be for pasture, was in progress before 1631.[11] Part of Pool Hill field, along the township boundary north of the village, remained open in 1772[12] but had been inclosed by 1825.[13] By the mid 18th century the rest of the township was held in severalty in small, irregular enclosures. Waste may have survived late on the glacial sands and gravels in the south and east of the township where 'moor' names are recorded.[14]

In Malinslee the field name 'Goldiforlong', recorded in 1340, and reference to land in selions in 1345 imply the existence of an open field there in the mid 14th century. There was also a hay called Lyehay, recorded from 1347, and a park recorded from 1506; Old Park, the mining district in the north-west of the township, was named from the latter.[15]

The small extent of known open arable fields and the late survival of woodland and waste suggest that the parish economy was largely pastoral. Horsehay and Hinkshay ('stallion-

enclosure'),[16] perhaps significantly situated on opposite sides of the parish, probably record early-medieval horse rearing. In the mid 14th century horses, goats, pigs, and especially cattle frequently damaged crops in Malinslee,[17] and the demesne farm of Great Dawley had 20 oxen and 3 cows in 1349.[18] In the late 17th and early 18th century dairying and cattle rearing seem to have been important; relatively little corn was grown and sheep were less important than in adjacent parishes to the north. Hemp butts, a 'peas croft' (then pasture), and orchards were mentioned in 1631 and later.[19]

In 1086 there were 7 villeins holding one plough, and another plough in demesne at Great Dawley.[20] In 1528–9 and 1570–3 there were 9 landed holdings in the manor in addition to the demesne (described as Dawley Castle and two parcels of meadow in 1567)[21] and cottages. The tenants, called copyholders in 1569, held their farms for life and their tenures were normally renewed. In the 1570s each, except the tenant of Horsehay, held a piece of (often newly inclosed) waste ground at the lord's will.[22] Hinkshay farm, formerly part of the Stirchley Hall estate, was separated and let on long lease in 1578. Sir George and Sir John Hayward granted further leases for lives between 1611 and 1621.[23] Plowden Slaney let farms in Great Dawley on 21-year leases in the 1760s.[24]

In Little Dawley a villein and 2 bordars held ½ plough in 1086, when another ½ plough, a serf, and the woodland were held in demesne.[25] By c. 1580 all the holdings were let on leases, 7 on leases for lives, 2 for terms of years.[26] In 1631 there were 7 farms varying in size from 71½ a. to 133 a. and occupying altogether 706 a.; 6 were leased for lives, one for 80 years. There were also 4 small tenancies, 2 of them leased for lives, one at will. The relative size of the holdings did not vary greatly during the 17th and 18th centuries but in the 1630s and 1640s each increased by almost a quarter in size. Leasing for lives and heriots continued in 1730.[27] but by 1838 all farms in the manor were held on rack rents.[28]

Part of Malinslee's demesne was leased in 1340, and by 1406 all the manor's demesne was shared between the 6 landed holdings at a total rental of 43s. 2d.[29] Mid 14th-century tenancies were for life

[1] Ibid. 1632, 1718; S.R.O. 2374, box 1, deed of 1656.
[2] L.J.R.O., B/V/6, Dawley, 1612–1718.
[3] Ibid. 1718–67; S.R.O. 2374, box 2, map of c. 1750.
[4] S.R.O. 2224/1; L.J.R.O., B/A/15, Dawley Magna.
[5] Above, Growth of Settlement.
[6] S.R.O. 2374, box 4, case papers of 1781.
[7] At O.S. Nat. Grid SJ 695 076: S.R.O. 2224/1; L.J.R.O., B/A/15, Dawley Magna.
[8] S.P.L., Deeds 8439.
[9] There is no indication whether they were common fields shared by the two tns.
[10] Craven estate rec. at St. John's Coll., Oxf., L. Dawley survey of 1631; Proc. of Seminar on Local Hist. in Telford (Telford Hist. and Arch. Soc. Occ. Paper, i), 3–4 and pl. I. Cf. Bandridge meadow at O.S. Nat. Grid SJ 681 056: S.R.O. 1560/1.
[11] Craven estate rec. at St. John's Coll., Oxf., L. Dawley survey of 1631.
[12] S.P.L., MS. 2481, Map XIII.
[13] I.G.M.T. Libr., map of Dawley Parva, 1825.
[14] e.g. Lightmoor, Green moor, the Moor: S.P.L., MS. 2481, Map XIII.
[15] S.R.O. 513, box 1, ct. r.

[16] Eng. P.N. Elements (E.P.N.S.), i. 243.
[17] S.R.O. 513, box 1, ct. r. of 1334–72.
[18] S.R.O. 1093, box 1, ministers' acct.
[19] Yeomen and Colliers in Telford, ed. B. Trinder and J. Cox (1980), pp. 72–9, 81, 84; Craven estate rec. at St. John's Coll., Oxf., L. Dawley surveys.
[20] V.C.H. Salop. i. 317.
[21] S.P.L., Deeds 8384; S.R.O. 567, box 30, ministers' acct. 1528–9.
[22] S.P.L., Deeds 8403; S.R.O. 567, box 30, ministers' acct. 1567–72.
[23] S.R.O. 2374, box 1, leases.
[24] S.R.O. 1952/44.
[25] V.C.H. Salop. i. 321.
[26] Staffs. R.O., D. 593/B/2/5/4/2, rental.
[27] S.P.L., Deeds 8432–6, 8438–9, 8587–8602, 8612–19, 9857, 10434, 10439, 10557, 10891–2, 10900, 12755, 12758, 12768, 12777, 12981, 13014–15, 13080, 13086, 13092, 13099, 13100; Craven estate rec. at St. John's Coll., Oxf., 17th- and 18th-cent. L. Dawley surveys.
[28] S.P.L., MS. 2507.
[29] S.R.O. 513, box 1, ct. r.

on payment of a heriot and entry fine. Labour services included harrowing and reaping, bringing in the lord's hay, and collecting nuts.[30] By 1406 there were 4 cottagers and 6 landed tenants, 4 of whom held ½ virgates, 1 held one virgate, and 1 held a messuage called Sayslonde. All except the last, which was held by lease (*per cartam*), were held by money rent, suit of court, heriot, and 'farfee' — a dropping fine recorded in Malinslee from 1336.[31] Long leases were granted in the early 17th century,[32] and by *c.* 1680 most tenancies had been converted to leaseholds.[33]

From the later 18th century the growth of mining and the iron industry removed a large acreage from agricultural use. Farming provided employment for a decreasing proportion of the population, and surviving farms geared their production to the needs of the industrial community. By 1905 only 1,547 a. (55 per cent of the parish) were classed as agricultural land,[34] but as early as 1831 only 29 families (2 per cent of Dawley households) were employed chiefly in farming.[35]

The demand for horses as draught animals in the collieries and ironworks led to specialization in horse rearing. The Coalbrookdale Co.'s tenant at Horsehay farm in 1759 worked a team of horses as a haulier for the company.[36] By 1796 the farm was managed by the company, the main crops being oats, hay, and vetches, grown as horse fodder,[37] and in the mid 19th century the farm supported 30–40 draught horses for the Horsehay ironworks.[38] Likewise the Botfields' works farm at Malinslee provided fodder and grazing for the collieries' stock, and farm horses were used for hauling iron.[39] Grassland predominated: in 1801 only 601 a. (21 per cent of the parish) were cultivated, mainly for oats and wheat.[40] Between 1867 and 1965 the proportion of agricultural land under grass rose from under half to over four fifths; cattle were increasingly kept in preference to sheep or pigs. Of the cereals grown wheat remained the most popular. The amount of vegetables and root crops grown steadily declined. By 1980 virtually all land in Malinslee and Great Dawley was put to non-agricultural uses, and farmland survived only in Little Dawley.

Most holdings remained small, several 19th-century farms being no more than smallholdings. The largest farms were in Little Dawley where there were 7 holdings, each containing between 80 a. and 179 a., in 1772.[41] As the extractive industries spread holdings became smaller: in 1871 there were 8 farming households in the township occupying from 7½ a. to 105 a. One man held 10 a. on which he kept three cows.[42] On the Slaney estate in Great Dawley the largest holding (other than those of the iron-making partnerships) was of 103 a. in 1812, and only 6 of the 18 landed tenants held more than 30 a.[43] Three householders in the Old Park area of Malinslee described themselves as farmers in 1871, although none held more than 17 a.[44]

MILLS. A mill at Malinslee was recorded in 1334 and 1347[45] but not thereafter. In the early 17th century farmers in Malinslee took their corn to Eyton upon the Weald Moors mill.[46] A water corn mill on Horsehay brook, at Horsehay, was recorded from 1573,[47] and at Ridges, near Lightmoor, a bloom smithy and water mill were recorded in 1631, the mill in 1698 and 1715.[48] The pools at both places were converted to provide a head of water for the iron furnaces built at those sites in the 1750s.[49]

There may have been a windmill in the southeast corner of Great Dawley township near a field named Windmill hill, recorded in 1718,[50] and a 19th-century colliery known as Mill pit.[51]

There were steam flour mills at Pool Hill and beside the canal near Botany Bay colliery in 1843.[52] The latter was in existence by 1833.[53] That at Pool Hill was probably operated in 1852 by

TABLE IV

DAWLEY: LAND USE, LIVESTOCK, AND CROPS

	1867	1891	1938	1965
Percentage of grassland	45	61	89	86
arable	55	39	11	14
Percentage of cattle	12	29	45	62
sheep	53	42	36	25
pigs	35	29	19	13
Percentage of wheat	71	53	63	60
barley	18	26	0	21
oats	11	20	37	15
mixed corn				
& rye	0	1	0	4
Percentage of agricultural land growing roots and vegetables	15	11	3	2

Sources: P.R.O., MAF 68/143, no. 14; /1340, no. 6; /3880, Salop. no. 228; /4945, no. 228.

---

[30] Ibid. ct. r. of 1334–7, 1338–49.
[31] Ibid. 1336, 1406.
[32] S.R.O. 513, box 8, deeds of 1601–26.
[33] S.R.O. 665/1/279.
[34] Salop. Agric. Returns, 1905.
[35] *Census*, 1831.
[36] S.P.L., MS. 332, pp. 108, 150.
[37] S.R.O. 245/145, *passim*.
[38] Ibid. /140, p. 58.
[39] M.U.L., Botfield papers, works farm acct. bk. 1844–60.
[40] P.R.O., HO 67/14/84.
[41] S.P.L., MS. 2481, Map XIII.
[42] P.R.O., RG 10/2752.

[43] S.R.O. 2374, box 3, survey.
[44] P.R.O., RG 10/2751.
[45] S.R.O. 513, box 1, ct. r.
[46] Ibid. box 8, deeds of 1616–26.
[47] S.P.L., Deeds 8403; S.R.O. 2374, box 1, deed of 1613.
[48] Craven estate rec. at St. John's Coll., Oxf., L. Dawley survey of 1631; cf. S.P.L., Deeds 8201, 8207; S.P.L., MS. 2481, Map XIII.
[49] Trinder, *Ind. Rev. Salop.* 34; S.P.L., Deeds 12777.
[50] L.J.R.O., B/V/6, Dawley, 1718.
[51] S.R.O. 1268/4.
[52] L.J.R.O., B/A/15, Dawley Magna (nos. 258, 1830).
[53] O.S. Map 1", sheet 61 NE. (1833 edn.).

Henry Cooke,[54] recorded as a miller from 1840 to 1868.[55] A steam mill in Chapel Street, operated by Thomas Jones, was recorded from 1885 to 1905.[56]

COAL AND IRONSTONE. Nearly the whole parish overlies the Lower and Middle Coal Measures, which contained workable seams of coal and ironstone. The minerals lay near the surface on the high ground along the north-west edge of the parish, west of the Lightmoor fault, and in the south around Lightmoor where the land drops away towards Coalbrookdale. East of the Lightmoor fault in Malinslee and Great Dawley the top of the productive seams lay c. 400 ft. (120 metres) below ground.[57] Mining was recorded in Dawley from the 16th century but large-scale extraction took place only after the establishment of ironworks in the parish in the 1750s; the deep seams east of the Lightmoor fault were mined only after c. 1800. By 1831 the collieries and ironworks employed 1,379 men and supported over 90 per cent of the parish's families.[58] Most mines had closed by 1900 but a few small collieries continued to work in the earlier 20th century. Since the Second World War the shallow seams on the west side of the parish have been stripped by opencast methods.

In the 16th century ironstone appears to have been more highly prized than coal. The first evidence of mining was in 1526–9, when Robert Moreton was obtaining ironstone at 'Wodds copy' in Great Dawley,[59] and in 1569 the ironstone in Great Dawley was farmed out at will for £14 compared with only 20s. for the coal mines, then held by John Boycott under a 21-year lease of 1555–6.[60] In the early 17th century Sir George Hayward, lord of Great and Little Dawley and Little Wenlock, worked ironstone and coal in his three manors, employing day or weekly labourers in his mines.[61] There was an ironstone mine on Ridges farm, near Lightmoor, in 1631. By 1666 Richard Walker had taken a lease of the mines in Little Dawley.[62] In Malinslee the Eytons appear to have exploited the minerals in the early 17th century.[63] In 1655 Sir Thomas Eyton settled Malinslee on trustees, who were to mine coal and quarry ironstone and use the profits for his younger children.[64] By c. 1680 the annual value of the mines there was put at c. £200.[65] After buying the manor in 1701 Isaac Hawkins worked the mines there himself.[66]

In the early 18th century control of mining in Great and Little Dawley passed to industrialists with interests elsewhere in the coalfield. Richard Hartshorne of Ketley, the leading east Shropshire coal master of the period,[67] and George Benbow of Malinslee leased the mines in Great Dawley from Robert Slaney in 1710. They agreed to supply coal and ironstone to Slaney's ironworks at Kemberton.[68] Hartshorne had also rented coal mines in Little Dawley by 1728[69] and he renewed the lease of the Great Dawley mines in 1731.[70] On his death in 1733 the Little Dawley coalworks, valued at £130 a year in 1730, were leased for 99 years to Thomas Barker,[71] chief North Wales agent to the London Lead Co., which had established a smeltery at Benthall in 1731.[72]

Early mining was confined to those areas where productive measures lay near the surface and could be worked from open pits or adits. Nevertheless vertical shafts for raising minerals by gins appear to have been in use by 1710.[73] One of the earliest areas of coalmining may have been at Coalpit Bank on the high ground between Dawley Bank and Heath Hill,[74] recorded from 1615.[75] Nearby at Brandlee there were at least five gin-pits, apparently operated by charter masters, in 1737.[76] There were clusters of pits in those places and at Old Park in 1752[77] and further pits on the valley sides near Lightmoor by 1772.[78] Coking took place at the pit head in Great Dawley in the early 18th century.[79] The small shallow workings in the areas of early mining produced a landscape of confused spoil heaps and almost lunar dereliction, which survived until the 1970s.

The beginning of large-scale mining coincided with the construction of iron furnaces at Horsehay in 1754 and Lightmoor in 1758 and the rise of industrial partnerships that integrated the extraction of coal, ironstone, and clay with the manufacture of iron, bricks, and tiles. Industrial activity in the late 18th and early 19th century was closely related to the pattern of landownership, mineral rights in the three manors being acquired by separate companies. In Great Dawley, after Hartshorne's lease had expired, the mines under Slaney's estate were leased in 1754 for 21 years to Abraham Darby (II).[80] By extending that lease[81] and by purchase[82] the Coalbrookdale Co. retained control over most minerals in Great Dawley throughout the late 18th and 19th century. A separate small royalty in the north-east corner of

---

[54] S.R.O. 1560/8, p. 18.

[55] W. Robson, Dir. Salop. (1840), 47; I. Slater, Dir. Salop. (1849), 11; (1868), 30; P.O. Dir. Salop. (1856), 43, 196; (1863), 844.

[56] Kelly's Dir. Salop. (1885–1905).

[57] Inst. Geol. Sciences Map 1/25,000, Telford (1978 edn.); J. Prestwich, 'On the Geology of Coalbrook Dale', Trans. Geol. Soc. London, 2nd ser. v. 413–95.

[58] Census, 1831.

[59] S.P.L., Deeds 7180; S.R.O. 567, box 30, ministers' acct. 1528–9, m. 2 and d.

[60] S.P.L., Deeds 8403. In 1567 the Gt. Dawley coal mines were let to Ric. Boycot at the same rent: ibid. 8384; S.R.O. 567, box 30, ministers' accts. 1567–9, 1570–2.

[61] P.R.O., WARD 2/87/3; S.R.O. 2374, box 1, deed of 1611.

[62] Craven estate rec. at St. John's Coll., Oxf., L. Dawley survey of 1631; S.P.L., Deeds 9816.

[63] Mining clauses in leases of 1616–27: S.R.O. 513, box 8.

[64] Ibid. deed of 1655.

[65] S.R.O. 665/1/279.

[66] S.R.O. 513, box 10, deed of 1705.

[67] Trinder, Ind. Rev. Salop. 197.

[68] S.R.O. 796/192.

[69] S.R.O. 407/12.

[70] S.R.O. 2374, box 1, deed.

[71] S.R.O. 1681, box 183, deed; Craven estate rec. at St. John's Coll., Oxf., L. Dawley survey of 1730.

[72] Salop. News Letter, xli. 16–18.

[73] S.R.O. 796/192.

[74] Cf. 'Coalpit Bank green' (S.R.O. 2374, box 1, deed of 1756), which lay between 'M. Nock's yard' (at Dawley Bank: ibid. box 4, case papers of 1780) and 'Dawley hay' (nr. Heath Hill: S.R.O. 2224/1).

[75] S.P.L., Deeds 8438.

[76] Trinder and Cox, Yeomen and Colliers, pp. 383–4.

[77] J. Rocque, Map of Salop. (1752); cf. S.R.O. 2374, box 4, case papers of 1780–1, witnesses' depositions.

[78] S.P.L., MS. 2481, Map XIII.

[79] S.R.O. 796/192; 2374, box 1, deed of 1733.

[80] S.R.O. 2374, box 1, deed.

[81] S.R.O. 1681, box 118, deed of 1779; box 119, deed of 1877; S.R.O. 2224/1.

[82] Above, Man. and Other Est.

Great Dawley was acquired in 1826 by the Langley Field Co., in which George Bishton of Neachley and Adam Wright, the Pool Hill ironmaster, were partners.[83] The collieries, ironworks, and brick yards established there by Bishton and Wright were bought by Beriah Botfield in 1856.[84]

In Little Dawley Thomas Barker, lessee of the minerals, entered into a partnership with William Ferriday, the mining agent,[85] in 1733.[86] By 1793 the lease was vested in Ferriday's nephew William and others,[87] but the mines were worked by undertenants from the 1750s. In 1753 Ferriday and Barker's brother John leased the minerals to a group of local charter masters: Beriah Botfield, William Gibbons, and Richard Bayley, all of Dawley, and William Baugh of Madeley.[88] The operations were taken over in 1758 by the Lightmoor Coalworks partnership, of which William Ferriday, William Goodwin of Madeley, and Thomas Botfield were the principal shareholders in 1791.[89] In 1793 the partners sublet the Lightmoor mines to Francis Homfray and John Addenbrooke, lessees of the Lightmoor ironworks since 1787, who continued to operate the Little Dawley mines until 1822 or later.[90] On the expiry of the original lease to Barker in 1832 Addenbrooke and his partners renewed the lease for 21 years,[91] but the Coalbrookdale Co. took a 40-year lease of the Lightmoor works and mineral rights throughout the manor from 1839.[92]

In Malinslee the mines were operated by the owner, I. H. Browne,[93] until Thomas Botfield established the Old Park ironworks in 1790, when Browne agreed to supply coal and ironstone to the new works.[94] In 1797 Botfield took a 21-year renewable lease of the minerals in Malinslee[95] and, after his death in 1801, the mines there were operated by his sons Thomas (d. 1843), William (d. 1840), and Beriah (d. 1813), and grandson Beriah (d. 1863) until 1856. On Beriah Botfield's failure to agree terms with the lords of the manor the mines were leased in 1856 to the Old Park Iron Co.,[96] which was wound up in 1871,[97] and in 1874 to the Wellington Iron & Coal Co.,[98] which failed in 1877.[99] In 1893 the Haybridge Iron Co., which had bought the manor in 1886, leased the mines to Alfred Seymour Jones of Wrexham.[1]

Mineral production increased rapidly in the later 18th and early 19th century. The annual quantity of coal raised in Little Dawley increased from 4,338 stacks (7,592 tons)[2] of top and bottom coal and 123 dozens of 'lump' coal, in 1753–4,[3] to 4,018 stacks (7,032 tons) of furnace coal, 5,733 tons of coal for the Severn trade, and landsale coal to the value of £620 in 1779–80. By 1837–8 the mines there produced 24,695 tons of furnace coal and 6,815 tons of slack. Ironstone production there rose from an annual average of 1,138 dozens (2,504 tons) in the years 1774–80 to 18,069 tons in 1837–8.[4]

The increase was achieved by the sinking of larger, deeper pits and the use of more sophisticated mining techniques. By 1754 a steam engine was draining the Lightmoor pits, and coal was raised from the shafts by horse-gin.[5] By the end of the century pits had been sunk to 208 ft. (63 metres) at Old Park,[6] 463 ft. (141 metres) at Lightmoor, and 348 ft. (106 metres) at Great Dawley.[7] In 1797 the Old Park collieries consisted of 34 pits, each named after the charter master who operated it. Only two pits had steam engines to raise coals, most possessing a gin or even only a 'turn barrel' or windlass.[8] Although several such small pits continued to operate in Malinslee until the 1890s[9] the early 19th century saw the opening of large collieries to exploit the deep seams southeast of the Lightmoor fault. The Coalbrookdale Co. was involved in 'deep work' in Dawley by 1794[10] and the earliest known pits 'in the deep' were those at Langley Farm, recorded c. 1800,[11] and at Langleyfield, recorded from 1803.[12] The cluster of mines in the south-east corner of Great Dawley were sunk c. 1810 to obtain Clod coal for the Coalbrookdale Co.'s new furnaces at the Castle ironworks.[13] By 1817 the Botany Bay, Mill, Castle Yard, Barker's Yard, Yew Tree, Deepfield, and Portley pits had been sunk.[14] In Malinslee expansion across the fault probably took place in the 1820s and early 1830s,[15] when 11 collieries were opened between Hollinswood and Hinkshay. By 1841 a seam was being worked 754 ft. (230 metres) below the surface at Puddley Hill colliery.[16]

Those large deep mines rapidly exploited the minerals east of the fault: on the Coalbrookdale Co.'s mines in Great Dawley the Clod coal, the most suitable for use in blast furnaces,[17] had been exhausted by 1850 and the Double coal by c.

[83] S.R.O. 1265/70–1, 74.
[84] Ibid. /119.
[85] Trinder, Ind. Rev. Salop. 38–40.
[86] S.R.O. 1681, box 183, deed; V.C.H. Salop. i. 463–4.
[87] S.R.O. 1681, box 183, deed of 1793.
[88] Ibid. deed of 1754.
[89] Ibid. deeds of 1758, 1791.
[90] M.U.L., Botfield papers, Lightmoor acct. bk.
[91] S.P.L., Deeds 13082.
[92] S.R.O. 1224, box 228, deed of 1840; 1987/35/12.
[93] S.R.O., q. sess. order bk. 1757–72, f. 91v.
[94] S.R.O. 1150/897.
[95] Ibid. /898.
[96] S.R.O. 14/3/8.
[97] S.R.O. 1265/280.
[98] Ibid. /285.
[99] Ibid. /287.
[1] Ibid. /269.
[2] Conversion of figures from stacks to tons based on sources cited above, p. 85 n. 25.
[3] M.U.L., Botfield papers, Lightmoor acct. bk.
[4] S.P.L., Deeds 7730; S.P.L., MS. 2507.

[5] M.U.L., Botfield papers, Lightmoor acct. bk.; S.R.O. 1681, box 183, deed of 1754.
[6] M.U.L., Botfield papers, Old Pk. memo. bk. 1788–91.
[7] J. Plymley, Gen. View of Agric. of Salop. (1803), 53–5, 58–9.
[8] S.R.O. 1150/898.
[9] Johnson, Poole, & Bloomer, mining agents, Brierley Hill, plans E 86/5962, A–H.
[10] I.G.M.T. Libr. 1978/279.
[11] S.R.O. 1190, bundle 120, map of c. 1800.
[12] W. Howard Williams, 'Dawley New Town Hist. Survey: Industries' (TS. 1964), p. 54 (copy in S.P.L., accession 5202).
[13] I.G.M.T. Libr. 1978/169.
[14] B.L. Maps, O.S.D. 208; S.R.O. 2224/1.
[15] i.e. c. 1815 × 1833: B.L. Maps, O.S.D. 208; O.S. Map 1″, sheet 61 NE. (1833 edn.). L. Eyton pit was sunk 1828, Puddley Hill 1829, Malinslee 1831: S.R.O. 1011, box 425, R. Garbitt to E. Bloxam, 20 Dec. 1861.
[16] S.R.O. 14/3/10.
[17] M. W. T. Scott, 'On the "Symon Fault" in the Coalbrookdale Coalfield', Quart. Jnl. Geol. Soc. London, xvii. 458.

1867.[18] Annual production in the company's Little Dawley mines in 1861–2 was only 7,574 tons of coal and 4,463 tons of ironstone,[19] less than a quarter of annual production in the 1830s. The closure of local ironworks between 1876 and 1886 led to the closure of almost all the parish's pits. Moor Farm, Wallows, Little Eyton, Portley, Parish, Southall, and Mill collieries had closed by 1882,[20] and by 1901 Lawn colliery, Malinslee, was the only shaft east of the fault remaining open.[21] It closed in 1908.[22]

The continuing demand for fireclay in the 20th century led to further mining in the shallow seams on the western side of the parish. A drift mine at Coalmoor, near Stoney Hill, opened by 1901 and operated in 1908 by the Coalmoor Sanitary Pipe Co. for coal and fireclay, had closed by 1925.[23] There were several short-lived mines in the Stoney Hill, Lightmoor, Doseley, Pool Hill, and Old Park areas between the World Wars.[24] One of the longer-lived was at Brandlee, where a colliery mining coal and fireclay in 1908[25] remained open in 1957; it continued as a small private mine after nationalization.[26]

The coal and fireclay seams in the Lower Coal Measures capping the high ground at Coalmoor and Stoney Hill were stripped by opencast mining in the 1950s,[27] and unworked coal in the disturbed area of early small-scale workings at Old Park was similarly stripped in the 1970s.[28]

IRON. A forge operated by Richard of Dawley was recorded c. 1180.[29] There was a bloom smithy at the Ridges, near Lightmoor, c. 1580,[30] and in 1631 Ridges farm, the second largest in Little Dawley, included a 'smithy coppice' as well as the bloom smithy and an ironstone mine.[31]

The Horsehay ironworks was built in 1754 by the Coalbrookdale Co. on the site of a water mill.[32] Their construction coincided with the company's lease of mines in Great Dawley and Ketley. The first furnace was blown in in 1755, a second in 1757. Pig-iron production averaged c. 90 tons a month in the period 1767–73, but output increased dramatically when the second furnace was rebuilt in 1799 and a third one was brought into blast in 1805. A forge was built at Horsehay c. 1781 and wrought iron was produced by the Wright & Jesson process. In 1817 the works

comprised three furnaces, two forges, two rolling mills, and a slitting mill.[33] The principal customers for both pig and bar iron from Horsehay in the late 18th and early 19th century were the forge-owners and merchants of the Black Country.[34] After a period of slack management in the early 19th century, production was raised and consumption of raw materials reduced when, from 1830, Alfred and Abraham Darby (IV) took an active interest in the works. Pig production rose to 65 tons weekly from each blast furnace.[35] A wide variety of iron ware was made in the mid 19th century: the plates for S.S. Great Britain (launched 1843) were rolled at Horsehay[36] and the Albert Edward Bridge (built across the Severn near Buildwas in 1863) was made there. In 1873 the works was said to produce all kinds of iron 'from a rail bar to a wire rod'.[37] Annual production of finished bar and plates was c. 15,000 tons in 1870.[38] In the early 1860s the Horsehay furnaces were blown out, the forges and rolling mills thereafter relying on supplies of pig from the Coalbrookdale Co.'s surviving furnaces at Lightmoor and Dawley Castle. The depression in the iron trade in the 1870s and 1880s eventually led to the closure of the forges and mills at Horsehay in 1886. The works was taken over by the Simpsons, who developed the heavy engineering side of the business.[39]

The first furnace at Lightmoor was built in 1758 by the Lightmoor Furnace Co., whose principal partners were Richard Syer of Norton, William Ferriday, and the group of charter masters who operated the Lightmoor coalworks.[40] Initially the main customers were the Knight family's forges in the Stour Valley,[41] and in 1787 the furnace was leased by the Lightmoor Co. to Francis Homfray and John Homfray (later Addenbrooke), who also had business connexions in the Stour Valley. By the end of the century there were three blast furnaces and a forge at Lightmoor.[42] The works was taken over in 1839 by the Coalbrookdale Co., which kept two furnaces in blast producing pig for sale and for forging at Horsehay.[43] The furnaces were blown out in 1883[44] and the buildings taken down in the early 1890s.[45]

The Old Park ironworks was built in 1790 by Thomas Botfield on land leased from I. H.

[18] S.R.O. 1681, box 121, rep. on Dawley mines, 1892.
[19] S.P.L., MS. 2509; below, plate 25.
[20] O.S. Maps 6", Salop. XXXVI. SE., XLIII (1884–9 edn.).
[21] Ibid. (1903 edn.). Puddley Hill colliery remained open as a pumping pit only: Williams, 'Dawley Hist. Survey: Inds.' p. 48.
[22] Rep. Insp. Mines, Stafford Dist. (No. 9), 1908 [Cd. 4672–viii], p. 216, H.C. (1909), xxxiii. There were no working mines in Malinslee c. 1910: S.R.O. 4044/78.
[23] Rep. Insp. Mines, Stafford Dist. (No. 9), 1908, 216; O.S. Map 6", Salop. XLIII. NW. (1903 and 1928 edns.).
[24] I. J. Brown, Coalbrookdale Coalfield: Cat. of Mines (Salop. Co. Libr. 1968), 15–18.
[25] Rep. Insp. Mines, Stafford Dist. (No. 9), 1908, 215.
[26] Kelly's Dir. Salop. (1917, 1922); S.R.O. 1324/1; 2361/1–2.
[27] Shrews. Chron. 15 Jan. 1954; O.S. Map 6", sheet SJ 60 NE. (1966 edn.).
[28] I. J. Brown, 'Mineral Working and Land Reclamation in the Coalbrookdale Coalfield' (Leicester Univ. Ph.D. thesis, 1975), 347, 377.
[29] P.R.O., E 32/143.
[30] Staffs. R.O., D. 593/B/2/5/4/2, rental of c. 1580.
[31] Craven estate rec. at St. John's Coll., Oxf., L. Dawley survey of 1631.
[32] For this para. see A. Raistrick, Dynasty of Iron Founders (1970), 115–25; Trinder, Ind. Rev. Salop. 34–5, 56–7, 66–7, and sources there cited.
[33] S.R.O. 2224/1.
[34] Trinder, op. cit. 81–4.
[35] Ibid. 238.
[36] Barclay Fox's Jnl. ed. R. L. Brett (1979), 148; E. Corlett, The Iron Ship (1975), 24.
[37] Trinder, Ind. Rev. Salop. 257–8; S. Griffiths, Griffiths' Guide to the Iron Trade of Gt. Brit. (1873), 100.
[38] P.O. Dir. Salop. (1870), 47.
[39] Trinder, op. cit. 396–7. For the later hist. of Horsehay wks. see below.
[40] S.R.O. 1681, box 183, deeds of 1758; S.P.L., Deeds 12777.
[41] Inf. from Dr. B. S. Trinder.
[42] M.U.L., Botfield papers, Lightmoor acct. bk.; Trinder, Ind. Rev. Salop. 70–1.
[43] S.R.O. 1560/8, p. 100; P.O. Dir. Salop. (1856), 42; (1870), 47; Griffiths, Iron Trade of Gt. Brit. 257; Raistrick, Iron Founders, 243–4.
[44] Trinder, op. cit. 396.
[45] S.R.O. 1207/12.

Browne. Forges, mills, and a third blast furnace were soon added to the two original furnaces.[46] By 1806 it was the largest ironworks in Shropshire and the second largest in Britain,[47] probably partly as a result of the vigorous management of Gilbert Gilpin, works manager from 1799[48] to 1813.[49] While there he perfected improvements in chain making that led to the widespread adoption of chains in industry.[50] After leaving Old Park he started his own chain works at Coalport.[51] As at Horsehay, Old Park's principal markets for pig were the Black Country, Severn Valley, and Lancashire forges.[52] In 1812 the Botfields' main customers were John Knight of Stourbridge and Daniels & Co.[53] The Old Park works passed, with the mines in Malinslee, to the Old Park Iron Co. in 1856 and to the Wellington Iron & Coal Co. in 1874.[54] In the early 1870s the works had four furnaces (two in blast) and three mills and forges.[55] The works closed in 1877 when the Wellington Iron & Coal Co. failed.[56]

Two furnaces built on the site of Dawley Castle were brought into blast by the Coalbrookdale Co. in 1810. Like those at Lightmoor, they produced pig for the company's forges at Horsehay and Coalbrookdale.[57] By the early 1870s,[58] and possibly by 1852,[59] only one was in blast, and iron production ceased in 1883.[60]

More furnaces were built in the 1820s, a period of prosperity in the iron trade.[61] Langley furnaces, near the site later occupied by Langley Board School, were blown in in 1824 and 1825 by George Bishton and Adam Wright, partners in the Langley Field Co.[62] The history of the works is not clear: it seems to have been untenanted in 1843;[63] in 1852 Garbett, Clemson & Co. occupied the works and one furnace appears to have been in blast.[64] By 1856 Thomas C. Hinde & Co., ironmasters of Pain's Lane, operated the works;[65] Hinde sold the estate and works to Beriah Botfield the following year.[66] The furnaces seem to have been blown out by the early 1870s[67] and no trace of the ironworks survived in 1882.[68]

The Botfield brothers built further pairs of blast furnaces on their freehold property at Hinkshay c. 1826 and at Dark Lane in the early 1830s,[69]

to supply pig to their Old Park and Stirchley forges. After Beriah Botfield's death in 1863 iron making was carried on at Hinkshay and Dark Lane by his trustees, Leighton & Grenfell,[70] until 1873 when the works were sold to the Haybridge Iron Co.[71] In the early 1870s three of the four furnaces remained in blast[72] but both pairs of furnaces were disused by 1881, although a foundry survived at Dark Lane until c. 1894.[73]

Several small iron-using industries grew up in Dawley in the mid 19th century. Spade and shovel makers and a chain factory were recorded in the 1850s. James Poole, publican of the New Wicket inn, Malinslee, in the 1850s, made boilers, chains, and nails, and other members of the Poole family were recorded as boiler makers at Malinslee in the 1870s. Those small concerns disappeared on the closure of local ironworks in the late 19th century.[74]

The Horsehay works was bought in 1886 by the Horsehay Co., a partnership between H. C. Simpson, formerly of Rotherham (Yorks. W.R.), and his brother. The Simpsons expanded the heavy engineering side of the works, concentrating on the manufacture of bridges, roofs, and girders. They employed c. 500 men at the works c. 1900.[75] The 'Sentinel' steam waggon was developed at Horsehay c. 1900–1903.[76] By 1913 the Horsehay Co. Ltd. also specialized in making gas plant.[77] After the Second World War the company was taken over by the Adamson Alliance Co. Ltd. and in 1948 the works was rebuilt to manufacture heavy cranes.[78] In 1980 Adamson–Butterley Ltd. made many types of heavy machinery, including travelling cranes, bridges, and mining equipment, at Horsehay.[79]

In 1947 J. C. Hulse & Co. Ltd. established an iron foundry on the site of the former Langleyfield brickworks, for the production of manhole covers, gully gratings, cisterns, and other grey iron castings.[80] The foundry was extended in 1963[81] but closed c. 1976.[82] From c. 1961 the former Shutfield brickworks at Lightmoor was used by Intermetric Processes Ltd. (later Pressmoor Ltd.), an engineering firm specializing in small steel fabrications.[83]

---

[46] S.R.O. 1150/897; M.U.L., Botfield papers, Old Pk. memo. bk. 1789–91.
[47] Trinder, *Ind. Rev. Salop.* 73–4.   [48] Ibid. 207.
[49] M.U.L., Botfield papers, acct. bk. 1810–15. Cf. S.R.O. 4455.
[50] *V.C.H. Salop.* i. 479, where Gilpin is wrongly stated to have been working at Stirchley furnaces.
[51] Ibid. 480.
[52] Trinder, *Ind. Rev. Salop.* 83.
[53] M.U.L., Botfield papers, iron sale acct. bk. 1812–14.
[54] Above.
[55] Griffiths, *Iron Trade of Gt. Brit.* 257, 277.
[56] Trinder, *Ind. Rev. Salop.* 396.
[57] Ibid. 237–8; Raistrick, *Iron Founders*, 255.
[58] Griffiths, *Iron Trade of Gt. Brit.* 257.
[59] When blast furnaces there rated at £15 15s. Cf. Lightmoor and Horsehay wks. (each with 2 in blast), where furnaces rated at £31 10s.: S.R.O. 1560/8, pp. 1–2, 100.
[60] Trinder, *Ind. Rev. Salop.* 396.
[61] Ibid. 385.
[62] Williams, 'Dawley Hist. Survey: Inds.' p. 21; S.R.O. 1265/70–1, 74.
[63] L.J.R.O., B/A/15, Dawley Magna.
[64] Langleyfield furnaces rated at £15 15s.: S.R.O. 1560/8, p. 82.
[65] *P.O. Dir. Salop.* (1856), 43; S.R.O. 1011, box 425, lawyer's bill.

[66] S.R.O. 1265/127.
[67] Griffiths, *Iron Trade of Gt. Brit.* 257.
[68] O.S. Map 6", Salop. XLIII. NE. (1889 edn.).
[69] Trinder, *Ind. Rev. Salop.* 241.
[70] *P.O. Dir. Salop.* (1870), 47.
[71] Griffiths, *Iron Trade of Gt. Brit.* 101.
[72] Ibid. 257.
[73] O.S. Map 6", Salop. XLIII. NE. (1889 edn.); Williams, 'Dawley Hist. Survey: Inds.' p. 21.
[74] S. Bagshaw, *Dir. Salop.* (1851), 377; S.R.O. 1560/8, p. 75; *P.O. Dir. Salop.* (1856, 1870, 1879).
[75] Trinder, *Ind. Rev. Salop.* 397; *Kelly's Dir. Salop.* (1891), 307; *V.C.H. Salop.* i. 479; A. H. Simpson, *Brief Notes concerning Coalbrookdale Friends' Mtg. and Horsehay Wks.* (1975; copy in S.P.L.).
[76] W. J. Hughes and J. L. Thomas, 'The Sentinel': a hist. of *Alley & MacLallan and the Sentinel Waggon Wks.* i (1973), 56–8, 65.
[77] *Kelly's Dir. Salop.* (1913), 88.
[78] Williams, 'Dawley Hist. Survey: Inds.' p. 32; Ed. J. Burrow & Co. Ltd. *Wellington R.D. Official Guide* [1967], 27.
[79] T.D.C. *Telford Ind. Dir.* [c. 1979].
[80] Williams, op. cit. p. 33.
[81] S.R.O., DA 8/100/7, p. 2464.
[82] *P.O. Telephone Dir.* (1975, 1978), sect. 303.
[83] T.D.C. *Telford Ind. Dir.* [c. 1979]; G.P.O. *Telephone Dir.* (1960, 1962), sect. 72.

CLAY INDUSTRIES. The drift cover of glacial boulder clay and sand was probably used for brick making in many small brick yards before the 19th century. Mid 18th-century cottages at Dawley Green and Dawley Bank were built of bricks made from sand and clay dug near Heath Hill[84] and by 1754 the Lightmoor Coal Co. had a brickworks, possibly in Brick Kiln leasow near Lightmoor, where there was a brick kiln in 1788.[85] The clay industries grew in scale in the late 18th and early 19th century as the coal and iron masters built brick, tile, and pottery kilns to use the red clays of the Coalport Beds and the white fireclays of the Middle Coal Measures, which could be raised from their mines.[86] Small brickworks proliferated: there were two kilns in Little Dawley in 1793[87] and three brick yards on the Coalbrookdale Co.'s land around Dawley Green in 1817.[88] By the mid 19th century, however, the clay industries were concentrated in several large brick and tile works. The industry weathered the late 19th-century industrial depression, specializing in the manufacture of sanitary pipes and fire bricks in the early 20th century.

The Coalbrookdale Co.'s brick and pot works near Horsehay,[89] primarily making refractory clay vessels for the Wright & Jesson process,[90] existed by 1796 when new round-ware and dish-moulding houses were added.[91] By 1801 the pottery was held by Edward Thursfield.[92] It was recorded in 1817 but had closed by 1843.[93] Fire bricks were also made at Horsehay in the 1790s[94] and the works making white bricks east of the pottery continued in operation until after 1882.[95] The brickworks was taken over c. 1900 by Days' Automatic Waste Water Closet & Sanitary Pipe Syndicate Co. Ltd., a Wolverhampton firm, which made drainpipes, sinks, cattle troughs, and fire bricks from local fireclay.[96] The works closed c. 1915.[97]

A group of large brickworks was established in the Lightmoor area in the early 19th century. Shutfield and Cherrytree Hill brickworks had been built by 1825.[98] From 1838, or earlier, to the 1850s they were operated by successive tenants of Woodlands farm[99] but were later leased to the Coalbrookdale Co., which also had a works making red bricks at Lightmoor, recorded from 1852.[1] In 1894 all three works concentrated on tile production, using red clay from the Coalport beds, mined locally, and fireclay from mines in Great Dawley.[2] Clay mining continued at Lightmoor until the 1930s.[3] The Cherrytree Hill brickworks closed in the early 20th century[4] but the other works remained open for some time. The Lightmoor works was taken over by Coalmoor Refractories Ltd. c. 1951, the Shutfield works by an engineering firm c. 1961.[5]

The Botfields were making bricks at Old Park by 1809,[6] possibly in the brickworks by the Old Park ironworks, in which fire bricks were made in 1874.[7] A works making white bricks at Langleyfield colliery opened between 1844 and 1852 and closed between 1901 and 1925.[8] In the 1870s a brickworks was opened beside the Coalport branch railway, north of Dark Lane.[9] It was reputedly operated c. 1910 by the Randlay Brick & Tile Co., whose main works was in Stirchley,[10] and it closed c. 1940.[11]

In the 20th century production of common bricks and tiles ceased but several specialist works were established. The Coalmoor Sanitary Pipe Co. Ltd. (later the New Coalmoor Sanitary Pipe Co. Ltd.) made sanitary pipes and fire bricks near Woodlands Farm from 1908 to c. 1948 using fireclay mined nearby.[12] The company was bought c. 1948 by Coalmoor Refractories Ltd., makers of refractory bricks for the steel industry, for which local fireclays were particularly well suited. In 1951 they acquired the Lightmoor brickworks and transferred their brick-making operations there. In 1980 the company employed c. 150 in both the clay-quarrying and brick-making sides of its activities.[13] In 1928 the Doseley Brick Co. Ltd. (later Doseley Pipe Co. Ltd.), one of the Johnston group of companies, started to make common bricks at Doseley from the clay overburden in the basalt quarry there. The works changed to making salt-glazed stoneware pipes in 1932 and continued to manufacture vitrified clay pipes until c. 1975.[14] Sommerfeld Flexboard Ltd., formerly of Trench, occupied the premises from c. 1979.[15]

QUARRIES. Limestone quarries and limekilns in Little Dawley were recorded from 1653 to 1728.[16] Glacial sands were quarried near Moor Farm, Little Dawley, and in Horsehay dingle in the 19th

[84] S.R.O. 2374, box 4, case papers of 1781.
[85] M.U.L., Botfield papers, Lightmoor acct. bk.; S.P.L., MS. 2481, Map XIII.
[86] Brown, 'Mineral Working in Coalbrookdale Coalfield', 120.
[87] S.P.L., Deeds 9864A.
[88] S.R.O. 2224/1.
[89] At O.S. Nat. Grid SJ 677 073: ibid.
[90] Inf. from Dr. B. S. Trinder.
[91] S.R.O. 245/145, passim.
[92] I.G.M.T. Libr. 1978/169.
[93] S.R.O. 2224/1; L.J.R.O., B/A/15, Dawley Magna.
[94] S.P.L., MS. 334, passim.
[95] S.R.O. 1560/8, pp. 1–2; 2224/1; L.J.R.O., B/A/15, Dawley Magna; O.S. Map 6", Salop. XLIII. NW. (1889 edn.).
[96] V.C.H. Salop. i. 434–5; Kelly's Dir. Salop. (1900–13).
[97] Kelly's Dir. Salop. (1913), 88; (1917), no mention.
[98] I.G.M.T. Libr., map of Dawley Parva, 1825.
[99] S.P.L., MS. 2507; S.R.O. 1560/1; /8, p. 113; P.O. Dir. Salop. (1856), 43.
[1] S.R.O. 1560/8, p. 100.
[2] S.R.O. 1207/12.
[3] Brown, Cat. of Mines, 15–18.

[4] It was open in 1901 but disused by 1925 (O.S. Map 6", Salop. XLIII. SW. (1903 and 1928 edns.)) and prob. by 1910 (S.R.O. 4044/77, p. 79, giving ann. value as £32 only).
[5] Above; Williams, 'Dawley Hist. Survey: Inds.' pp. 5–6.
[6] M.U.L., Botfield papers, cash acct. bk. 1804–10.
[7] S.R.O. 1265/285.
[8] L.J.R.O., B/A/15, Dawley Magna; S.R.O. 1560/8, p. 82; O.S. Map 6", Salop. XLIII. NE. (1903 and 1929 edns.).
[9] At O.S. Nat. Grid SJ 703 092. The wks. was built 1874 × 82: S.R.O. 1265/285; O.S. Map 6", Salop XLIII. NE. (1889 edn.).
[10] S.R.O. 4044/78, p. 126; below, Stirchley, Econ. Hist.
[11] Inf. from Miss Joan Nickless.
[12] S.R.O. 1681, box 41, deed of 1908; Kelly's Dir. Salop. (1909–41); S.R.O., DA 8/100/6, f. 513.
[13] Inf. from Mr. E. A. Taylor, Coalmoor Refractories Ltd.
[14] Kelly's Dir. Salop. (1909–41); Burrow, Wellington R.D. Official Guide [1967], 29; inf. from Mr. S. G. Darrell, Johnston Bros. Ltd.
[15] Below, Hadley, Econ. Hist. (Engineering); Brit. Telecom, Telephone Dir. (1983), sect. 303 (Alpha), p. 456.
[16] S.P.L., Deeds 13092, 13100; S.R.O. 407/12; Craven estate rec. at St. John's Coll., Oxf., L. Dawley surveys.

century. Both pits appear to have been deserted by 1900.[17]

The Upper Coal Measures sandstone was quarried for building stone in Malinslee. Buildings at Old Park furnaces were of stone from a quarry on Spout House farm in 1791,[18] and the early 19th-century cottages at Stone Row were built of large sandstone blocks, probably from the nearby quarry recorded in 1856.[19] Holy Trinity church, Great Dawley, built in 1845 was said in 1851 to be of local sandstone.[20]

The Little Wenlock basalt, outcropping at Horsehay, was quarried on a larger scale. The 'Black Rock' or 'Dhu Stone' at Doseley in Horsehay dingle, a tourist attraction in the late 18th century on account of its columnar structure,[21] was worked for roadstone by the Coalbrookdale Co. by 1894,[22] in a quarry that appears to have been opened by 1817.[23] The quarry was leased to the Pyx Granite Co. Ltd. of Malvern (Worcs.) in 1912[24] and was acquired c. 1920 by Basalts Ltd., one of the Johnston Bros. group, which had opened another, short-lived, basalt quarry (now called Simpson's Pool) west of Horsehay Cottage in 1919. In 1926 Johnston Bros. opened a concrete plant at Doseley, using the basalt as aggregate. Basalt quarrying at Doseley ceased in 1961 when reserves were exhausted. At about the same date the concrete plant was reorganized to make concrete pipes using aggregate from the company's quarries at Leaton (in Wrockwardine). In 1980 Johnston Pipes Ltd. employed c. 100 people at Doseley.[25]

OTHER INDUSTRIES. In the early 20th century the large slag heaps at Horsehay ironworks were removed by the G.W.R. as hardcore for an Oxfordshire railway opened in 1910.[26] In the 1920s there was a short-lived revival of activity at the disused ironworks when slag was removed for road metal. In 1920 Dawley urban district council took a lease of the Castle slag mound and installed a slag crusher.[27] The council continued to sell slag from there in 1931.[28] Tarmac Ltd. acquired the neighbouring Botany Bay slag mound in 1922,[29] and Waymack Ltd., another tarmacadam manufacturer, was working the slag mound at Old Park in 1927 and 1929.[30] The industry seems to have come to an end in the early 1930s.

The void left by the closure of mines and ironworks in the late 19th century was not filled until after the Second World War when several new factories, drawing on local labour but not on local raw materials, were opened. The largest were J. A. Harris & Sons (Old Park) Ltd., an engineering works (employing c. 120 in 1980) at Old Park, opened in 1948; Pyjamas Ltd. (later Clifford Williams & Co. Ltd.), a clothing factory opened in 1953 in the former Malinslee C.E. School buildings, employing c. 200 in 1980 in adjacent new premises on Cemetery Road; Ever-Ready Co. (G.B.) Ltd., a dry cell battery factory employing c. 2,000 in 1980, which opened at Hinkshay in 1956;[31] and Cuxson Gerrard & Co. Ltd., manufacturers of medical and hygienic supplies at Dawley Bank in the 1960s.[32] In 1977 Telford development corporation built a small industrial estate at Heath Hill. By 1980 it contained 42 workshops housing manufacturing, warehousing, and haulage businesses, including a number of light engineering concerns.[33]

Other manufacturing industries in Dawley have included Walter Simmonds's football factory in Chapel Street, recorded from 1905 to 1937,[34] and Mor-Isis Products, an ice-cream factory at Blews Hill from 1953 to c. 1974.[35]

MARKET. Population increase in the late 18th and early 19th century, and the accompanying growth of Dawley Green (later High Street) as the parish's commercial centre resulted in the establishment of a weekly market and annual cattle fair. A market house had been built at the west end of High Street by 1836,[36] and in 1844 the Saturday market was said to be well attended.[37] Nevertheless Wellington market continued to attract many inhabitants of Dawley in the 1860s.[38] A new market hall with an arcaded façade surmounted by a clock was built opposite the earlier one in 1867.[39] It was managed by the Market Hall Co. Ltd. and traded principally in foodstuffs.[40]

The market declined and the hall was sold to Lloyds Bank in 1958.[41] From 1977 an open-air market was held on Fridays in High Street.[42]

TELFORD TOWN CENTRE. Dawley new town's draft master plan of 1964 recommended that the town's commercial and retailing centre should be

[17] S.R.O. 1207/12; O.S. Map 6", Salop. XLIII. SW. (1888 and 1903 edns.); Inst. Geol. Sciences Map 1/25,000, Telford (1978 edn.).
[18] M.U.L., Botfield papers, Old Pk. memo. bk. 1788–91.
[19] Brown, 'Mineral Working in Coalbrookdale Coalfield', 178; S.R.O., dep. plan 367, Dawley par. no. 59.
[20] S. Bagshaw, Dir. Salop. (1851), 374.
[21] 'The Most Extraordinary District in the World': Ironbridge and Coalbrookdale, ed. B. Trinder (1977), 49.
[22] S.R.O. 1207/12.
[23] S.R.O. 2224/1, sched. B, no. 41.
[24] S.R.O. 2273/7.
[25] Kelly's Dir. Salop. (1917–41); A. G. Sheppard Fidler, Rep. on Dawley (1962), mineral valuer's rep. (Sept. 1960), p. 2; inf. from Mr. Darrell.
[26] Inf. from Dr. Trinder.
[27] S.R.O., DA 8/100/1, pp. 8, 287–8. V.C.H. Salop. iii. 194, notes the co. council's 'huge' programme of main-rd. reconstruction in the later 1920s.
[28] S.R.O., DA 8/100/3, p. 65.
[29] Inf. from Mr. C.C. Wallis, Tarmac Roadstone Holdings Ltd.
[30] S.R.O., DA 8/100/2, pp. 6, 171; Kelly's Dir. Salop. (1929), 149.
[31] Williams, 'Dawley Hist. Survey: Inds.' pp. 36, 38, 39; S.R.O., DA 8/100/6, pp. 1163, 1294, 1325; inf. from Messrs. J. A. Harris & Sons, Clifford Williams & Co., and Ever-Ready Co.
[32] Williams, op. cit. p. 38; G.P.O. Telephone Dir. (1966), sect. 72, p. 2047.
[33] T.D.C. Telford Ind. Dir. [c. 1979], passim; inf. from the archivist, T.D.C.
[34] Kelly's Dir. Salop. (1905–37).
[35] Williams, 'Dawley Hist. Survey: Inds.' p. 40; S.R.O., DA 8/100/6, p. 955; P.O. Telephone Dir. (1973–5), sect. 303.
[36] S.R.O. 1560/5, 9 Mar. 1836; L.J.R.O., B/A/15, Dawley Magna.
[37] I. Slater, Dir. Salop. (1844), 8.
[38] S.R.O. 4139.
[39] P.O. Dir. Salop. (1870), 47.
[40] Rep. R. Com. Mkt. Rights, xiii (2) [C. 6268–VIa], pp. 416–18, H.C. (1890–1), xl.
[41] S.R.O., DA 8/100/6, pp. 1428, 1452, 1580.
[42] Shropshire Star, 9 July, 15 Nov. 1977.

on the eastern side of Dawley ancient parish,[43] but the first phase of Telford town centre was opened farther north in 1973 on the site of Malinslee Hall and the ruined chapel. It contained two large supermarkets and 23 other shops, mainly branches of national retailing chains. By 1979 the shopping centre provided employment for 1,200 people. A second phase, intended to provide another 1,000 jobs, was under construction in 1980. The development corporation built three office blocks in the town centre: Malinslee House, St. Leonard's (from 1979 Walker) House, and Darby House. The largest, Malinslee House, was opened in 1976 and contained offices of Wrekin district council (whose headquarters it became), the local police, and the development corporation.[44]

LOCAL GOVERNMENT. Great Dawley owed suit from 1310 or earlier[45] to the leet court of Wem barony, held at Hinstock. The vill's presentments there were recorded from 1478 until 1851.[46] Little Dawley and Malinslee made suit to Bradford hundred court in 1592,[47] the obligation originating in their membership of Leegomery manor, which made suit to that court in 1255.[48] Little Dawley continued to make suit to the hundred court, at Wellington, until the 18th century.[49]

Courts baron for Great Dawley were held only occasionally in the 16th century.[50] One, in April 1569, was apparently the occasion of a court dinner. Another court, probably the next, was held in September 1571.[51] Profits were small,[52] though the manorial bailiff accounted for a felon's goods c. 1569.[53] No courts had been held there within memory in 1780, when the lords of Hinstock manor held a court in Dawley in an unsuccessful attempt to claim manorial rights in the township.[54]

Profits of Little Dawley court baron were said to be worth 20s. a year in 1653. Records of the court, held annually in October from the late 18th century, survive from 1698 to 1810.[55]

At Malinslee the Eytons held courts in the 14th and 15th centuries. Matters dealt with were mainly agricultural, but a presentment for fornication was made in 1372. A constable's appointment was recorded in 1406. In the 16th century Malinslee matters were dealt with at the Eytons' court at Eyton upon the Weald Moors.[56]

A pinfold was in need of repair in 1721.[57]

Dawley was within the jurisdiction of the Broseley court of requests from 1782[58] until its abolition under the County Courts Act, 1846.[59]

Records of the parish meeting, from 1820 a select vestry of 20 members, survive from 1806.[60] Separate overseers were appointed for each of the three townships by 1807. There was a salaried assistant overseer by 1813, when a paid treasurer was also appointed to enable the assistant overseer to concentrate on relieving the poor. Levy of the poor rate from Dawley's large, scattered labouring population proved difficult. In 1807 the parish meeting ordered that every householder who kept a dog was liable to pay the rate, presumably in an attempt to levy rates from the parish's numerous cottagers. By 1813, however, many ratepayers were in arrears and the accounts showed a 'considerable' deficit.[61] Annual expenditure on the poor rose to £590 in 1816–17 (c. 2s. 4d. a head of population) but fell to £119 (9d. a head) in 1819–20.[62] After the death of Richard Lewis, the assistant overseer, in 1828[63] relief was administered by a vestry committee, meeting every three weeks at the poorhouse.[64] In 1831 a total of 96 paupers, mainly widows, received weekly pay.[65] In 1836 Dawley became part of Madeley poor-law union, despite requests by the vestry that it should either unite with Wellington union or remain independent.[66]

The parish rented a cottage as a poorhouse c. 1784.[67] It was probably that in Dawley Green Lane (later Bank Road)[68] which the overseers bought and enlarged in 1813.[69] In the summer of that year, before being extended, the poorhouse contained c. 50 inmates.[70] After Dawley joined the Madeley union the building became redundant and was leased in 1838,[71] although a room was rented back in 1847 as a refuge for the destitute.[72] In 1852–3 the property was sold and the proceeds used to buy the site of the tithe barn in the south-west corner of Holy Trinity churchyard, on which a building for vestry meetings and a Sunday school was erected.[73]

In the mid 19th century various methods of organizing the maintenance of parish roads were tried. In 1837 there were separate salaried surveyors for Great and Little Dawley townships. A highways board of 20 members, responsible for the whole parish, was created in 1839, but in 1843 the parish reverted to the appointment of salaried

[43] J. H. D. Madin & Partners, *Dawley New Town: Short Memo. on Draft Master Plan* (Oct. 1964), map 7 (copy in S.R.O. 3937/6).
[44] *The Times*, 3 May 1978, suppl. p. III; *Telford and Wrekin News*, May 1979, 4; local inf.; below, plate 2.
[45] Eyton, viii. 44; *V.C.H. Salop.* iii. 51–2.
[46] S.R.O. 327, boxes 4–5, ct. r.
[47] Staffs. R.O., D. 593/J/10, ct. r.
[48] *Rot. Hund.* (Rec. Com.), ii. 57.
[49] S.R.O. 2374, box 4, papers in Corbet and D'Avenant v. Slaney, W. Gibbons to R. Slaney, 7 Mar. 1781.
[50] There were none 1528–9: S.R.O. 567, box 30, ministers' acct. 1528–9, m. 2.
[51] Ibid. ministers' accts. 1567–9 (m. 1 and d.), 1570–2 (m. 1 and d.); S.P.L., Deeds 9721.
[52] Only 11s. 2d. in 1569, 4s. in 1571: S.R.O. 567, box 30, ministers' acct. 1570–2, m. 1d.
[53] Ibid. ministers' acct. 1567–9, m. 1.
[54] Case papers of 1780–1, in S.R.O. 327, box 6, and S.R.O. 2374, box 4.
[55] S.P.L., Deeds 7685–7724, 8201–15; Craven estate rec. at

St. John's Coll., Oxf., L. Dawley survey of 1653.
[56] Ct. r. for Eyton and Malinslee survive for 1334–49, 1355–9, 1369–72, and 5 dates 1406–1587: S.R.O. 513, box 1.
[57] S.R.O. 327, box 4, ct. r.
[58] Broseley, etc., Small Debts Act, 1782, 22 Geo. III, c. 37.
[59] 9 & 10 Vic. c. 95.
[60] S.R.O. 1560/5.
[61] Ibid. 30 Mar. 1807, 30 Aug. 1813.
[62] S.R.O., DA 8/951/1.
[63] S.R.O. 4084/Rg/10, p. 194.
[64] S.R.O. 1560/5, 2 July 1829 – 7 Dec. 1832.
[65] S.R.O., DA 8/951/2.
[66] *V.C.H. Salop.* iii. 169–70; S.R.O. 1560/5, 3 Mar., 12 May 1836.
[67] S.R.O. 2374, box 1, rental of 1781–8.
[68] At O.S. Nat. Grid SJ 6860 0810: S.R.O. 2224/1.
[69] S.R.O. 1560/5, 30 Aug., 27 Sept. 1813; 4084/P/1.
[70] S.R.O., DA 8/951/1.
[71] S.R.O. 1560/5, 17 Oct. 1838; 4084/P/2.
[72] S.R.O. 1560/7, 25 Mar. 1847.
[73] Ibid. 4 June 1852 – 28 June 1855.

surveyors. A second highways board, of 13 members, was created in 1850 but separate surveyors were again appointed from 1855. In 1860 a board was appointed with responsibility for Great Dawley township only. A successful solution was reached in 1865 when another board, covering the whole parish, was created. It had 20 members, 12 for Great Dawley, 4 for Little Dawley, and 4 for Malinslee.[74]

A board of health was created at the time of the 1831–2 cholera epidemic;[75] it was probably short-lived. In 1876 Dawley became an urban sanitary district with a board of 12 members.[76] The board became an urban district council in 1894.[77] The U.D.C. employed only one full-time chief officer, a combined sanitary inspector and surveyor, until 1943.[78] Its offices were in the market hall[79] until a house in King Street was bought as council offices in 1935.[80] In 1966, when Madeley was merged with Dawley urban district, the enlarged U.D. was divided into six wards and a council of 24 members formed.[81] New offices, built on derelict land east of High Street and known as the Civic Centre, were opened in 1968.[82] The U.D. was abolished in 1974; thereafter the area, not assigned to any civil parish, coincided with eleven urban wards of the district of the Wrekin.[83]

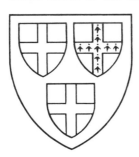

DAWLEY URBAN DISTRICT. *Gules, three escutcheons argent, the first charged with a cross of the field, the second with a cross erminois, the third with a cross vert*

[Granted 1956]

The U.D.C.'s common seal was circular, 35 mm. in diameter, inscribed (roman) URBAN DISTRICT COUNCIL OF DAWLEY at the circumference and 1894 across the face.[84] Ever-Ready Ltd. secured a grant of arms for the U.D.C. in 1956.[85] The shield's three escutcheons and the motto *Trinis catenis vinctus* alluded to the parishes of St. Luke, St. Leonard, and the Holy Trinity, and the crest (on a wreath of the colours a demi triton winding a conch horn and crowned with an

antique crown all or) to Capt. Webb.[86]

In 1963 the whole ancient parish, except a few acres on the northern boundary near Hollinswood, was designated part of Dawley new town.[87] The parts excluded were, however, embraced in the designated area of Telford new town in 1968.[88]

PUBLIC SERVICES. The Dawley Gas Co., formed in 1848,[89] built a works at the southern end of Chapel Street.[90] It supplied street lighting in the central built-up area around Dawley Green, the capital cost having been raised by subscription among the ratepayers in 1849.[91] In Old Park, Dark Lane, and Hinkshay, which were not served by gas mains, the streets were lit by oil lamps from c. 1922.[92] Mains electricity reached Dawley c. 1934[93] and electric street lamps replaced the gas ones in 1951.[94]

In the later 18th century street soil in Great Dawley was taken away by a contractor for use as manure on his land.[95] The rapid and haphazard growth of housing in the early 19th century resulted in poor sanitary conditions, which in 1865 were said to be worse than those of Madeley.[96] In the 1890s sewerage was rare and watercourses were often polluted. In 1896 c. 40 per cent of the population obtained water from public wells, often far from their homes. The rest drew water from wells or pumps on their premises, supplies that were liable to contamination. The urban district council considered that a piped supply from outside the parish would be prohibitively expensive.[97] A scheme sanctioned in 1904, to supply Dawley with water from a well in the Weald Moors near Buttery Farm (in Edgmond), appears to have come to nothing.[98] In 1909 the U.D.C. arranged for a supply from the Madeley & Broseley Water Co. Water was piped from Madeley to Little Dawley and pumped thence to two reservoirs at Dawley Bank and Lawley Bank, from which it was distributed by gravity to most of the parish.[99] Nevertheless 48 per cent of all houses in the urban district were without a private piped supply in 1951.[1] By 1961 the number of such households had dropped to 10 per cent.[2]

In 1930 the U.D.C. drew up a sewage disposal scheme, and by 1934 sewers led from the central built-up area to lagoons at Castle Fields and Stirchley pools, where the effluent was clarified.[3]

[74] S.R.O. 62/1; 1560/5–7, passim.
[75] S.R.O. 1560/5, 24 Aug. 1832; cf. S. and B. Webb, Stat. Authorities for Special Purposes (1922), 463–4.
[76] Under the Public Health Act, 1875, 38 & 39 Vic. c. 55: S.R.O. 1560/7, 16 Mar. 1876; Kelly's Dir. Salop. (1891), 306.
[77] Local Govt. Act, 1894, 56 & 57 Vic. c. 73, s. 21; Kelly's Dir. Salop. (1900), 77.
[78] S.R.O., DA 8/100/5, pp. 308, 314.
[79] S.R.O. 3673/1, p. 10; Dawley Observer, 4 Mar. 1966.
[80] S.R.O., DA 8/100/4, pp. 58, 62, 126.
[81] Shropshire Star, 18 Feb. 1966; Dawley Observer, 28 Jan. 1966. [82] Dawley U.D.C.: A Story, 1966–74.
[83] Inf. from Wrekin District Council.
[84] Impression in S.R.O. 4084/Ve/5 (deed of 1897).
[85] S.R.O., DA 8/100/6, pp. 1132, 1325.
[86] S.R.O., DA 8/295.
[87] Dawley New Town (Designation) Order 1963 (Stat. Instr. 1963, no. 64), accompanying map (copy in S.R.O. 2981, parcel VI).
[88] Dawley New Town (Designation) Amendment (Telford) Order 1968 (Stat. Instr. 1968, no. 1912), map accompanying Explanatory Note.

[89] S.R.O. 2070/2.
[90] P.O. Dir. Salop. (1856), 43; P.R.O., HO 107/1988, f. 155 (mention of gas man in Chap. La.).
[91] S.R.O. 1560/7, 28 Dec. 1849.
[92] S.R.O., DA 8/100/1, p. 406; /100/3, p. 224.
[93] Ibid. /100/3, p. 430; /100/4, p. 147.
[94] Ibid. /100/6, p. 741.
[95] S.R.O. 2374, box 4, papers in Corbet and D'Avenant v. Slaney, examination of A. Jones (folded in letter of 7 Mar. 1781).
[96] The Builder, 4 Mar. 1865, p. 159.
[97] S.R.O. 119/10, M.O.H. Rep., Dawley U.S.D., 1896; cf. S.R.O. 1242, box 2, corresp. re pollution of Horse Leasow pond.
[98] Oakengates and Dawley Joint Water Bd. Act, 1904, 4 Edw. VII, c. 238 (Local); cf. S.R.O. 3129/16/1, plans of proposed supply (copies).
[99] Kelly's Dir. Salop. (1909), 83; A. H. S. Waters, Rep. on Water Supplies (S.C.C. 1946), 20.
[1] Census, 1951, Co. Rep. Herefs. and Salop. 65.
[2] Census, 1961, Co. Rep. Salop. 62.
[3] S.R.O., DA 8/100/2, p. 382; /100/3, p. 428.

A more comprehensive scheme was introduced when a sewage works was opened near Moor Farm in the south-east corner of the parish in 1950. Initially it served only the central urban area but in 1955 sewerage was extended to drain the Horsehay and Doseley areas.[4] As a result the number of houses in the U.D. without exclusive use of a water closet dropped from over 53 per cent in 1951 to 23 per cent in 1961.[5]

There was a post office in High Street by 1840,[6] and by 1856 sub-offices had opened at Dawley Bank, Horsehay (across the boundary in Little Wenlock), and Little Dawley.[7] Further sub-post offices were opened at Dark Lane in the 1890s and at Old Park c. 1903.[8]

There was a lock-up at Dawley Green by 1843[9] and a police station in the parish by 1856.[10] The lock-up was sold in 1872.[11] Dawley had one constable in 1840.[12] A police sub-divisional H.Q., within the Wellington division, was established in Malinslee House (opened in 1976).[13]

CHURCHES. There were medieval chapels at Great Dawley and Malinslee and perhaps at Little Dawley. Only the first, which had come to be considered a parish church by the 16th century, was recorded in documentary sources. New churches were built at Malinslee and Little Dawley to cater for the rapid population growth of the early 19th century, and the ancient parish was consequently divided into three ecclesiastical districts in the 1840s. In 1975 the three parishes were combined with Stirchley and Lawley to form the new parish of Central Telford.

Architectural evidence and reference to a priest of Dawley in 1186–7 suggest that there was a chapel at Great Dawley before the end of the 12th century. The lords of Great Dawley manor presented to the living as to a parish church in the mid 13th century, but the advowson of Dawley 'chapel' was confirmed by them to Walter of Dunstanville, patron of the mother church of Shifnal, in 1256.[14] Thereafter until the 16th century it was considered to be a chapel in Shifnal parish[15] and, as such, was appropriated to Battlefield college in 1410.[16] The connexion with

Shifnal ceased after 1563 when the rectory and church of Dawley were leased from the Crown.[17] The living was a curacy, from 1792 called perpetual,[18] until it became a vicarage in 1866.[19]

After the dissolution of Battlefield college in 1548 Dawley was a royal donative.[20] The rectory was acquired by John Watson (d. 1606) and thereafter the impropriator seems to have been responsible for providing a minister.[21] In 1655 William Pierrepont and Sir John Corbet, both staunch Parliamentarians,[22] were named as patrons,[23] the rectory having been sequestrated.[24] After the Restoration patronage was again exercised by the impropriators, who also held the advowson of Stirchley. From 1715 curates were normally licensed to the cure but there was no formal presentation and institution until the living became a vicarage.[25] In 1878 Andrew Phillips conveyed the advowson of Dawley to the bishop of Lichfield,[26] who held it until the living was absorbed into Central Telford parish in 1975.[27]

The living was a poor one until augmented in the late 18th and early 19th century. In 1639 the impropriator paid the curate a stipend of 20 marks (£13 6s. 8d.)[28] and by the early 18th century the curate was said to have c. £12 yearly,[29] made up of a modus of £6 6s. 8d. for tithes in Malinslee, a payment of £4 10s. from the impropriator in lieu of the tithe of hay in Great and Little Dawley, and small tithes valued at c. £1.[30] The impropriator John Revell (d. 1729) left the curate an additional £5 yearly, charged on land at Hadley.[31] In 1756 the living was further augmented by Rebecca Walthall's legacy towards obtaining Queen Anne's Bounty.[32] By 1832 the living was worth £154 16s. 8d., of which £104 came from interest on augmentations from Queen Anne's Bounty and parliamentary grants made between 1779 and 1825.[33] Further augmentations between 1837 and 1878[34] increased the living's gross annual value to £302 in 1903.[35]

The great tithes, a tithe barn on the south side of the churchyard,[36] and c. 25 a. of glebe scattered in Great Dawley township belonged to the impropriator.[37] So did the parsonage to the east of the churchyard, which was described in 1851 as an old timber-framed building fit for demolition.[38]

[4] Ibid. /100/6, f. 494v.–p. 1153.
[5] Census, 1951, Co. Rep. Herefs. and Salop. 65; 1961, Co. Rep. Salop. 62.
[6] W. Robson, Dir. Salop. (1840), 47; S. Bagshaw, Dir. Salop. (1851), 376.
[7] P.O. Dir. Salop. (1856), 43.
[8] Kelly's Dir. Salop. (1891–1905).
[9] At O.S. Nat. Grid SJ 6852 0745: L.J.R.O., B/A/15, Dawley Magna, no. 914. Cf. S.R.O., q. sess. Const. Cttee. rep. bk. 1839–53, p. 440; 1854–65, pp. 19, 22.
[10] P.O. Dir. Salop. (1856), 43; Kelly's Dir. Salop. (1941), 86.
[11] Orders of Q. Sess. iv. 203.
[12] S.R.O., q. sess. Const. Cttee. rep. bk. 1839–53, p. 76.
[13] Inf. from W. Mercia Constabulary; above, Econ. Hist. (Telford Town Centre).
[14] Eyton, viii. 45; P.R.O., CP 40/149, m. 73d.
[15] Cal. Close, 1441–7, 371; Valor Eccl. (Rec. Com.), iii. 195.
[16] V.C.H. Salop. ii. 129.
[17] S.R.O. 513, box 8, deed of 1563.
[18] L.J.R.O., B/A/1/26, p. 24.
[19] Lich. Dioc. Regy., bps.' reg. R, p. 125.
[20] V.C.H. Salop. ii. 130; L.J.R.O., B/V/1/2, 5; S.R.O. 924/389.

[21] Above, Man. and Other Est.; L.J.R.O., B/V/1/55, p. 130.
[22] V.C.H. Salop. iii. 91.
[23] T.S.A.S. xlvii. 9.
[24] W. A. Shaw, Hist. Eng. Church 1640–60, ii. 492.
[25] L.J.R.O., B/A/1/19, f. 182; Lich Dioc. Regy., episc. reg. 31, pp. 221–2; benefice and inst. bk. 1868–1900, p. 11.
[26] Lich. Dioc. Regy., bps.' reg. S, p. 392.
[27] Ibid. R (Orders in Council), p. 350.
[28] L.J.R.O., B/V/1/65.
[29] Ibid. B/V/6, Dawley, 1705.
[30] W.S.L., H.M. 36 (shorthand transcribed by Mr. N. W. Tildesley); cf. L.J.R.O., B/V/6, Dawley, 1612–1726.
[31] L.J.R.O., B/V/6, Dawley, 1733–1853.
[32] B.L. Add. Ch. 44253.
[33] S.R.O. 3916/1/3; C. Hodgson, Q. Anne's Bounty (2nd edn.), pp. clxxix, ccxciv.
[34] Hodgson, op. cit. p. ccxxiii; Lich. Dioc. Regy., bps.' reg. R, p. 673; S, p. 248; L.J.R.O., B/V/6, Dawley, 1853.
[35] Crockford (1903).
[36] L.J.R.O., B/V/6, Dawley, 1612; B/A/15, Dawley Magna; S.R.O. 1560/7, 29 July 1853.
[37] L.J.R.O., B/V/6, Dawley, 1612, 1632, 1718; above, Man. and Other Est.
[38] S. Bagshaw, Dir. Salop. (1851), 375.

There was no curate's residence until 1838 when a house was built at Brandlee.[39]

The names of two mid 13th-century incumbents are known. One of them, Peter of Radnor, archdeacon of Salop, was said to have been parson until his death c. 1279.[40] The late 16th and early 17th century was marked by short incumbencies,[41] often those of young men who left for more lucrative livings.[42] Complaints of laxity were made against Thomas Patmore, recorded as curate 1635–9.[43] The living was temporarily made more attractive in 1647 when Francis Watson, the impropriator, gave the church an annuity of £56 in settlement of his fine for delinquency.[44] From c. 1665 Dawley was generally served by the rectors of Stirchley,[45] who often employed assistant curates at Dawley. Robert Bromhall, an elderly man, was licensed as deacon there in 1697 and also served Wombridge.[46] Edward Fosbrooke, recorded as curate 1730–63,[47] was rector of Stirchley 1758–75. John Rogers, curate 1772 (or earlier) to 1792, also held Shifnal and Stirchley livings. He employed an assistant curate, who lived at Stirchley and did duty there and at Dawley. In 1772 there was one Sunday service, with additional prayers in Lent and on some holy days, and communion, taken by 20–30, four times a year.[48] Dawley was held with Stirchley until 1832.

By the late 18th century the increased population had far outgrown the capacity of the old church: it was noted in 1799 that many parishioners went to church at Wellington or Madeley.[49] In 1805 St. Leonard's, a new church with 795 sittings, was built on the borders of Malinslee and Great Dawley townships, a site more convenient than that of the old church for the growing industrial population of Old Park, Dawley Bank, and Dawley Green. The old church was closed except for burials, and the intention was that St. Leonard's would thenceforth be the sole parish church.[50] Pressure from some parishioners for the reopening of the old church was felt by 1810[51] and services were resumed there c. 1818, St. Leonard's becoming merely a chapel of ease until it was assigned a district chapelry in 1843.[52] Assistant curates, who lived in the parish, were employed in the 1820s and 1830s, and the number of Sunday services at Great Dawley increased from one in 1824 to two in the 1830s, and three in

1843. Communion was given seven times a year by 1832.[53]

After the separation of Malinslee chapelry in 1843 and Little Dawley parish in 1844[54] the old church was rebuilt, and the new church, dedicated to the Holy Trinity, served the central built-up area of Great Dawley township.[55] On Census Sunday 1851 morning service there was attended by 160 adults, that in the afternoon by 80, and evening service by 370.[56]

In 1872, during the incumbency of R. C. Wanstall (1870–88), an Evangelical who was concerned to reach his parish's large labouring population,[57] a small brick mission chapel was opened at Hinkshay.[58] It closed c. 1969[59] and the building was used in 1980 as a social club for the adjacent Ever-Ready factory.

The ancient parish church, whose dedication has not been traced,[60] stood a little south-east of the church of the *HOLY TRINITY*, which replaced it. Only the 12th-century font and several 18th-century monumental inscriptions survive from the former building.[61] The old church[62] was a small stone building consisting of chancel, nave with south porch, and west tower. Nave and chancel were probably 12th-century. In the early 14th century a doorway and window were inserted into the south wall of the chancel. The tower was added, and windows inserted in the south wall of the nave, in the late 14th and 15th century. In 1716 five new bells were acquired,[63] and a west gallery was inserted in 1720, perhaps when the brick porch was added. The church suffered badly from mining subsidence in the late 18th and early 19th century, and massive brick buttresses were built to support it after 1786 and before 1824, probably in 1819 when the church was repaired after being reopened.[64] In 1826 the parish meeting rejected the possibility of replacing the church by a new building on a site that would be free from subsidence.[65] A new south gallery was built and a small vestry added in 1838.

Holy Trinity church, designed by Harvey Eginton of Worcester,[66] replaced the old church in 1845.[67] It is of sandstone, in the Perpendicular style, and consists of a chancel with north vestry, aisled nave with west gallery, west tower, and south porch, which was converted into a baptistery in 1883.[68]

[39] S.R.O. 4084/Pge/1; S.R.O. 3916/1/3.
[40] P.R.O., CP 40/149, m. 73d. For his career see A. B. Emden, *Biog. Reg. Univ. Oxf. to 1500*, iii. 1541; *V.C.H. Staffs.* iii. 14, 31, 33.
[41] 14 curates occ. 1558–1639: L.J.R.O., B/V/1/2–62; B/V/6, Dawley, 1612.
[42] e.g. Rob. Bell (occ. 1570–3), Ric. Felton (1581–4), John Davies (1612), Thos. Wilkes (1614). For their careers see sources in previous n.; below, Eyton; Stirchley; *T.S.A.S.* 3rd ser. viii. 44–5.
[43] L.J.R.O., B/V/1/55, p. 130.
[44] Shaw, *Hist. Eng. Church 1640–60*, ii. 492.
[45] *S.P.R. Lich.* xviii (1), pp. vii–viii; below, Stirchley, Churches.
[46] W.S.L., H.M. 36; L.J.R.O., B/A/1/18, f. 30v.
[47] *S.P.R. Lich.* xviii (1), 75; L.J.R.O., B/V/6, Dawley, 1730–63.
[48] L.J.R.O., B/V/5, visit. return of 1772.
[49] S.R.O. 3916/1/1.
[50] Ibid. /1/3; L.J.R.O., B/A/2(i)/E, pp. 235–9.
[51] S.R.O. 1560/5, 1 Jan. 1810.   [52] Below.
[53] S.R.O. 3916/1/3.
[54] Lich. Dioc. Regy., bps.' reg. M, p. 620; P & QA (Orders

in Council), pp. 54–5, 56–7 (1st nos.).
[55] The benefice continued to be known as Dawley Magna in dioc. rec.
[56] P.R.O., HO 129/358, no. 26.
[57] S.R.O. 4084/SRg/1, letter of 26 Sept. 1870 (on endpaper).
[58] Ibid. /SRg/1, 5 Apr. 1872; /Mi/1.
[59] Ibid. /Mi/3–4.
[60] The holding of Dawley wake on All Saints' Day c. 1740 (B.L. Add. MS. 30316, f. 6) perhaps suggests the dedication.
[61] Cf. Cranage, vii. 567–8; B.L. Add. MS. 21237, ff. 24–5.
[62] Descr. based on Bodl. MS. Top. Salop. c. 2, ff. 201–2; S.P.L., MS. 372, vol. i, p. 20; J. H. Smith colln., no. 64; S.R.O. 3916/1/3.
[63] H. B. Walters, *Ch. Bells of Salop.* (Oswestry, 1915), 288–9.
[64] S.R.O. 1560/5, 12 Aug. 1819; below, plate 34.
[65] Ibid. 14 Aug. 1826.
[66] L.J.R.O., B/C/5, Dawley faculty 1844; D. Ware, *Short Dict. Brit. Architects* (1967), 88.
[67] Lich. Dioc. Regy., bps.' reg. N, pp. 320–4; S.R.O. 4084/Ch/11.
[68] *Salopian Shreds & Patches*, v. 161.

Among the fittings, most of which were moved to St. Leonard's *c.* 1805 but later returned to Great Dawley,[69] were the bells, a medieval silver paten remodelled *c.* 1582, and a chalice of 1746.[70]

The registers begin in 1666 and are complete, except for baptisms 1840–2 and burials 1835–42, which were entered in volumes later used by St. Leonard's church, Malinslee.[71]

The churchyard, confined on the south and east by the roads to Little Dawley and Dawley Green, had become crowded with graves by 1824, despite the provision of extra land for burials at St. Leonard's church in 1805.[72] The consecrated area was extended by a total of over 2 a. in 1834,[73] *c.* 1843,[74] 1890,[75] 1940,[76] and 1954.[77]

Malinslee had a separate chapel in the 12th century and was then presumably in Shifnal parish,[78] but Malinslee was subsequently considered part of Dawley parish and was served by the incumbents of Dawley until St. Leonard's, built in 1805, was allotted a district chapelry in 1843. The medieval chapel, an isolated building a little east of Spout House,[79] was a small sandstone structure *c.* 15 metres long, consisting of chancel and nave divided by a stone screen; it has been dated to *c.* 1150.[80] In 1909 the ruin was bought by Edward Parry, vicar of Malinslee, who proposed to restore it as a place of worship to designs by W. A. Webb.[81] The scheme came to nothing and the chapel was taken down to make way for Telford town centre, and the stones stored, by Telford development corporation in 1971.[82]

In 1805 the church of *ST. LEONARD* was built on the south-west edge of Malinslee township by I. H. Browne, owner of Malinslee, and Thomas Gisborne, with money left for charitable purposes by Browne's great-grandfather Isaac Hawkins.[83] Although intended to replace Dawley old church, St. Leonard's remained a chapel of ease until 1843 when it was assigned a district chapelry covering Malinslee township and Dawley Bank.[84] The benefice was in the gift of the vicar of Dawley Magna. The living was abolished in 1975 when Malinslee became part of the new parish of Central Telford.[85]

In the 1830s the income of the assistant curate who served St. Leonard's was *c.* £105, of which £50 came from pew rents and £55 from the subscriptions of the major landowners and industrialists.[86] After becoming a separate benefice the living was augmented by grants from Queen Anne's Bounty in 1845–6 and 1855[87] and other grants in 1867 and 1879.[88] By 1884 those augmentations produced £243 16s. 10d. yearly, while pew rents and fees were worth only £15.[89] In 1897 and 1903 the annual income was further increased by *c.* £25 by the purchase of a glebe cottage and *c.* 2½ a. of land.[90] The cottage was sold in 1961.[91]

A vicarage immediately north of the church was provided in the 1840s;[92] it was demolished in 1975.[93]

St. Leonard's served as the parish church from 1805, but the old church was reopened *c.* 1818 and St. Leonard's became a chapel of ease for the northern parts of the parish. In 1824 there was one Sunday service at St. Leonard's. By 1829 most of the duty was done by an assistant curate who lived at Dawley Green and there were two services with sermons each Sunday. Communion services increased from five a year in 1824 to seven in the 1830s.[94] After Malinslee became a separate benefice the church's activity increased. The new parish's population was large and scattered and the vicars of Malinslee frequently employed curates in the late 19th and early 20th century.[95] In 1851 a mission room in a building at Old Park was licensed.[96] It may have been the forerunner of Malinslee Institute, built 1859,[97] in which week-day services were held in the 1880s.[98] The Institute was converted into an infant school in 1898.[99] A second mission room, on the south side of the churchyard, was built in 1883 as a result of a mission to combat drunkenness in the Dawley Bank area, led by the Revd. Gilbert James of Burton-upon-Trent in 1882. The room later served as a church hall until it was demolished in 1974.[1] The parish's longest-serving vicar was Edward Parry (1895–1935), a forceful character who influenced many aspects of parish life. In the 1890s he was the moving force behind the foundation of Malinslee Institute infant school and in the 1920s attempted the reclamation of pit mounds for playing fields and gardens and built several houses using unemployed labour.[2]

St. Leonard's church is an octagonal building of local sandstone with a west tower.[3] It closely resembles Thomas Telford's Madeley church

[69] S.R.O. 3916/1/3.

[70] S. A. Jeavons, *Ch. Plate Archd. Salop* (Shrews. 1964), p. 31.

[71] S.R.O. 4084/Rg/1–27; *S.P.R. Lich.* xviii (1). Madeley marriages were solemnized at Dawley 1794–7: above, Madeley, Churches.

[72] S.R.O. 3916/1/3.

[73] Lich. Dioc. Regy., bps.' reg. K, pp. 286–9.

[74] L.J.R.O., B/A/15, Dawley Magna (nos. 311–13).

[75] Lich. Dioc. Regy., bps.' reg. T, pp. 323, 344–5.

[76] Ibid. W, pp. 695, 698–9.

[77] S.R.O. 4084/Chy/40.

[78] Eyton, vii. 348–9.

[79] At O.S. Nat. Grid SJ 699 088. Descr. of remains based on Cranage, vii. 606–7; S.P.L., MS. 372, vol. i, pp. 21–2; N.M.R., Photos. BB 71/1757–75 (copies in S.P.L.); *Salop. News Letter*, xli. 12.

[80] On archit. and arch. grounds (in the absence of contemporary documentary evidence).

[81] S.R.O. 2732, papers *re* Malinslee chap. 1909–33.

[82] Local inf.

[83] By will proved 1713: L.J.R.O., B/C/5, Dawley new church faculty of 1804; B/A/2(i)/E, pp. 235–9.

[84] Above; Lich. Dioc. Regy., bps.' reg. M, p. 620.

[85] Lich. Dioc. Regy., episc. reg. 31, p. 88; bps.' reg. R (Orders in Council), p. 350.

[86] S.R.O. 3916/1/3.

[87] Hodgson, *Q. Anne's Bounty* (2nd edn.), suppl. pp. xi, xii, lxvii, lxxxvii.

[88] Lich. Dioc. Regy., bps.' reg. R, p. 162; S, p. 291.

[89] S.R.O. 3916/1/29.

[90] S.R.O. 2732/Li/12; inv. of ch. goods [*c.* 1934].

[91] Ibid. corresp. of 1961.

[92] P.R.O., HO 107/1988, f. 300.

[93] Inf. from the Revd. R. A. J. Hill.

[94] S.R.O. 3916/1/3.

[95] S.R.O. 2732, curates' licences.

[96] Ibid. /ChR/1.

[97] P.R.O., ED 7/102, f. 234v.

[98] *Malinslee Par. Mag.* 1883–5 (copies in S.R.O. 2732).

[99] Below, Educ.

[1] S.R.O. 2732/PM/1 (Mar.–Sept. 1883); R. Hill, *A Telford Church: St. Leonard's Malinslee* (Malinslee, 1980), [5–6] (copy in S.R.O. 4107/1).

[2] *Shropshire Mag.* May 1963, pp. 27–8; S.R.O. 2732, *passim*.

[3] L.J.R.O., B/C/5, Dawley faculty of 1804. Descr. based on S.P.L., MS. 372, vol. iii, p. 105; Cranage, vii. 608.

(1794) in design[4] and was built in 1805 by John Simpson, who did much local work for Telford;[5] it is not, however, certain whether Telford was directly involved in scaling down his Madeley design for Malinslee.[6] Internally the church was galleried and originally had nearly 800 sittings. An extra 200 seats were provided by extending the galleries in the 1830s.[7] and further internal modifications were made in 1901.[8] In 1975–6 a major internal reorganization took place to enable the church to be used for social purposes; a kitchen and lavatories were provided and the galleries made into separate rooms by the erection of glass screens.[9]

Bells, plate, and registers were removed from Dawley old church to St. Leonard's but were returned when the old church reopened c. 1818. William Botfield gave a new set of plate to St. Leonard's in 1833[10] and four bells in 1839;[11] the latter were replaced by a set of six bells in 1887.[12] The registers, which begin in 1835, are complete. They contain baptisms and burials for the whole of Dawley parish until 1843.[13]

An early 18th-century tradition that there was formerly a chapel at Little Dawley,[14] and mention of a house there called the 'old chapel' in 1631,[15] suggest that there was an early chapel in the township. It may have been a medieval stone building demolished in 1911,[16] which was then known as the 'old manor house'.[17] In 1844 Little Dawley township and the Horsehay area were constituted a separate parish,[18] and the church of ST. LUKE was built at Doseley next year.[19] The living, in the gift of the Crown and the bishop of Lichfield alternately, was endowed with £150 a year by the Ecclesiastical Commissioners on its creation.[20] It was augmented four times between 1889 and 1913.[21] A parsonage was built north-west of the church in 1845 and enlarged in 1899;[22] it was sold in 1974.[23]

St. Luke's was designed by R. Griffiths of Broseley.[24] It is of red and pale grey brick with sandstone dressings and consists of apsidal sanctuary with north vestry, nave with south porch of timber and brick, and a western bell turret of stone, containing one bell. Architectural details are Norman in style.[25] A Sunday school was built

between the church and vicarage in 1912; a timber lych-gate to the churchyard was built in 1920; and the graveyard was extended north-east of the church in 1932.[26] The registers begin in 1845 and are complete.[27] On the creation of Central Telford parish in 1975 St. Luke's was made redundant; it was sold in 1980.

Patronage of the three Dawley livings was suspended when they fell vacant in 1964–5[28] and in 1975 they were combined with Lawley and Stirchley to form the new parish of Central Telford, served by a team ministry. The right to present the team rector was vested in a patronage board, which presented every first, second, and fourth turn, the Crown presenting at the third turn.[29] The three 19th-century vicarages in Dawley were replaced by a rectory, containing a small meeting room, at the new Hollinswood housing estate in 1976,[30] and by new vicarages at Chiltern Gardens, Dawley, c. 1977, and adjacent to St. Leonard's church, Malinslee, in 1980.[31] The parish was divided into four pastoral districts, centred on churches at Dawley (Holy Trinity), Stirchley (All Saints), town centre (St. Leonard), and Lawley (St. John). Each member of the team ministry, consisting of the rector and three vicars, was responsible for a district.[32]

ROMAN CATHOLICISM. Papist families were recorded between 1639 and 1767[33] but there is no evidence of a Roman Catholic community of any size in Dawley until the 20th century. In 1958 the Town Hall was used for Roman Catholic services: until then local Catholics had had to travel to Madeley or Wellington to church.[34] In the same year the church began negotiations to buy land on Paddock Mound[35] and in 1964 a church hall was opened there, behind the Dun Cow inn. Weekly mass, celebrated by the Shifnal parish priest, was then attended by c. 100.[36] Dawley was created a separate parish in 1978[37] and by 1980 the hall had been dedicated to St. Paul. From 1979 the Anglican St. Leonard's, Malinslee, was used by Roman Catholics for mass on Saturday evenings, and in 1980 Sunday mass was also said in the Hollinswood community centre.[38]

[4] Edinburgh Encyclopaedia (1830), vi (2), 644; above, Madeley, Churches.
[5] M.U.L., Botfield papers, acct. bk. 1804–10; H. Colvin, Biog. Dict. Brit. Architects 1600–1840 (1978), 738.
[6] Cf. Ted Ruddock, Arch Bridges and their Builders 1735–1835 (1979), 148, 225 n. 10; Hill, A Telford Church, [2–3]; J. B. Lawson, 'Thos. Telford in Shrews.' Thos. Telford: Engineer, ed. A. Penfold (1980), 10.
[7] S.R.O. 3916/1/3.
[8] S.R.O. 2732, faculty of 1901.
[9] Hill, A Telford Church, [6].
[10] Jeavons, Ch. Plate Archd. Salop, pp. 79–80.
[11] S.R.O. 3916/1/3.
[12] Walters, Ch. Bells of Salop. 291–2.
[13] S.R.O. 2732/Rg/1–16; 3916/1/40.
[14] B.L. Add. MS. 30316, f. 6.
[15] Craven estate rec. at St. John's Coll., Oxf., L. Dawley survey of 1631; cf. S.P.L., Deeds 8594, 8599.
[16] T.S.A.S. 4th ser. ii, pp. i–ii; photo. in S.P.L.
[17] Above, Man. and Other Est.
[18] Lich. Dioc. Regy., bps.' reg. P & QA (Orders in Council), pp. 54–5 and map between pp. 56–7 (1st nos)
[19] Ibid. bps.' reg. N, pp. 334–9.
[20] Bps.' reg. P & QA (Orders in Council), p. 55 (1st nos).

[21] Bps.' reg. T, p. 256; U, p. 363; V, pp. 149, 394.
[22] J. Picken, Dawley Parva: the formation of the parish and the erection of St. Luke's church (Shrews. 1945), 20, 22 (copy in S.R.O. 2732), Kelly's Dir. Salop. (1905), 81.
[23] Inf. from the Revd. R. A. J. Hill.
[24] Picken, op. cit. 12–19.
[25] Cranage, vii. 569.
[26] Picken, op. cit. 12–19.
[27] S.R.O. 4063/Rg/1–16.
[28] Lich. Dioc. Regy., benefice and inst. bk. 1952–68, pp. 119, 124, 132.
[29] Ibid. bps.' reg. R (Orders in Council), p. 350.
[30] Ibid. Y, pp. 224–5.
[31] Inf. from the Revd. C. Hill, Churches Planning Officer, Telford Area Interdenominational Cttee.
[32] Inf. from Revd. Preb. D. H. R. Jones, rector.
[33] L.J.R.O., B/V/1/65, 72; B/A/11, return of papists of 1706; /12(i), f. 88; T.S.A.S 2nd ser. i. 84.
[34] S.R.O., DA 8/100/6, p. 1472.
[35] Ibid. p. 1555.
[36] Express & Star, 10 Aug. 1964.
[37] Shropshire Star, 15 Dec. 1979.
[38] Shrews. Dioc. Yr. Bk. (1980), 57; Hill, A Telford Church, [6]; Shrews. Dioc. Catholic Voice, Apr. 1981, 11.

PROTESTANT NONCONFORMITY. William Hayward, curate of Dawley in 1651 and ejected at the Restoration,[39] seems to have left no following: no nonconformists were recorded in 1676,[40] though in 1716 a man was accused at the county assizes of slandering the church and the sacrament.[41]

Under John Fletcher's influence Methodism spread from Madeley in the later 18th century and by 1824 half of Dawley's population was said to be dissenting.[42] On Census Sunday 1851 nonconformist worshippers, though not fully recorded, far outnumbered those in the three Anglican churches at morning services.[43] By 1870 a Baptist chapel, 12 Methodist chapels, and a Congregational mission station had been built in Dawley. The nonconformist congregations remained strong during the depressed years of the early 20th century. They included many shopkeepers and small businessmen, from whose ranks were drawn several urban district councillors.[44] In 1933 the vicar of Malinslee noted that most of the real estate in his parish was in dissenters' hands.[45] The national decline in church membership in the mid 20th century was accentuated in Dawley by the break-up of old industrial communities due to new town development. By 1980 only 4 Methodist chapels and the Baptist church remained open.

Other protestant groups, not long-lived or numerous locally, met in Dawley intermittently from the late 19th century.

BAPTISTS. A congregation of Particular Baptists was formed at Dawley Bank in 1817. At first services were held in cottages, and the first baptism was conducted in a pool among the pit mounds.[46] In 1846, when church membership stood at 13, a small chapel seating 200 was opened at Dawley Bank on the site of the former bull ring. A minister's house was built nearby at the same time[47] and on Census Sunday 1851 the chapel was attended by 60 adults in the morning, 110 in the afternoon, and 180 in the evening.[48] At that time the chapel served worshippers from Hadley, Ketley Bank, and Newdale, as well as from the various settlements in Dawley.[49] Galleries were inserted in 1851 but accommodation remained inadequate and in 1860 a new chapel was built on the same site. A large galleried building with an imposing blue-brick façade, it seated 600. A

projecting porch added in 1893 was raised in 1906 to include stairs and an organ loft. In 1871 a cemetery was opened across the parish boundary at Lawley Bank.[50] Congregations remained large until slum clearance and rebuilding in the 1960s scattered the community in and around Dawley Bank. The congregation had 57 adult church members in 1978 and consisted largely of older people.[51]

METHODISTS. *Wesleyan Methodism.* John Fletcher, vicar of Madeley 1760–85, had founded a Methodist society at Dawley Bank by 1765:[52] it was probably for that group that a house near Dawley Bank was registered for worship in 1773.[53] The group thrived: in 1799 the meeting was well attended and a fifth of the parish was said to 'follow the Methodists' either there or at Madeley.[54] The 1799–1801 Methodist revival in Coalbrookdale resulted in the foundation of a society at Little Dawley, where Coalbrookdale men preached and led a small class from 1799.[55] By 1813 weekly services were held for the societies at Dawley Bank (then known as the Lawley Bank society), Little Dawley, and Dawley Green; a society at Horsehay and Little Wenlock had preaching fortnightly.[56] Those and other societies in Dawley were placed in the Madeley circuit on its creation in 1835 and passed to the newly created Dawley circuit in 1870.[57]

A chapel at Little Dawley, probably that which stood west of Ivy Farm in 1825,[58] was registered in 1805.[59] It was eventually replaced in 1837 by a larger building, known as the 'Big Penny',[60] in the centre of the village.[61] The congregation consisted largely of industrial workers: 13 of the new chapel's 18 trustees were miners.[62] In 1851 Census Sunday afternoon worship was attended by 138 adults,[63] but membership of the society declined from 146 in 1838 to 64 in 1869.[64] The chapel remained open in 1980. Other Wesleyan societies west and south-west of Dawley were at Horsehay, which built a chapel just inside Wellington parish at Spring Village c. 1816,[65] and at Stoney Hill, which had 22 members in 1838 but only 9 in 1869 and had ceased to meet by 1880.[66]

In 1819 a chapel was built at Dawley Green on the corner of the roads later known as High Street and Chapel Street.[67] The plain octagonal building[68] was replaced in 1860 by an imposing

[39] *Walker Revised*, ed. A. G. Matthews, 305.
[40] *T.S.A.S.* 2nd ser. i. 84.
[41] S.R.O. 4406/1, pp. 80–90.
[42] S.R.O. 3916/1/3.
[43] P.R.O., HO 129/358, nos. 26–38. Returns record 682 adults at nonconf. chapels and meetings; 240 adults at Anglican chs. No return was made for St. Leonard's, Malinslee.
[44] e.g. R. A. Rhodes (d. 1941), Prim. Meth. lay preacher, chmn. of U.D.C. and of Madeley guardians, co. councillor and alderman (S.R.O. 1936/70; *V.C.H. Salop.* iii. 173 and n.); Edw. Fellows (d. 1945), Prim. Meth. lay preacher, U.D.C. member, and J.P. (S.R.O. 1936/3–116; S.R.O., DA 8/100/1).
[45] S.R.O. 3916/1/29.
[46] Trinder, *Ind. Rev. Salop.* 302.
[47] Date stone (reset in present chap.); S. Bagshaw, *Dir. Salop.* (1851), 375; S. Mostyn Jones, *Baptist Church, Dawley* (Wellington, 1946), [5].
[48] P.R.O., HO 129/358, no. 31.
[49] Dawley Bank Baptist Ch. min. bk. 1848–84, baptismal roll (in possession of ch. sec.).
[50] Ibid.; G.R.O., Worship Reg. no. 9556; Jones, *Bapt. Ch. Dawley*, 8–11.

[51] *Baptist Union Dir. 1978–9*, 119; inf. from Mr. J. Cadwallader, ch. sec.
[52] L. Tyerman, *Wesley's Designated Successor* (1882), 99 and n. 2.
[53] P.R.O., RG 31/7, Salop. no. 155.
[54] S.R.O. 3916/1/1, f. 61 and v.
[55] Trinder, *Ind. Rev. Salop.* 286; S.R.O. 2280/16/185, p. 12–13.
[56] S.P.L., C 98.7 v.f., Shrews. circuit plan.
[57] *V.C.H. Salop.* ii. 13–14; S.R.O. 2533/1–4.
[58] At O.S. Nat. Grid SJ 6815 0608: I.G.M.T. Libr., map of Dawley Parva, 1825.
[59] P.R.O., RG 31/7, Salop. no. 232.
[60] *Wrekin Light*, Dec. 1967, 12.
[61] Date stone. The Springwell mount may have encroached on the first chap., a nearby barn then being used: inf. from Mrs. E. Williams per Mr. K. B. Jones.
[62] Trinder, *Ind. Rev. Salop.* 306.
[63] P.R.O., HO 129/358, no. 35.   [64] S.R.O. 2533/1–4.
[65] Below, Lawley, Nonconf.
[66] S.R.O. 1936/1; 2533/1–4.
[67] S.R.O. 2533/7.
[68] S. Bagshaw, *Dir. Salop.* (1851), 375.

chapel in polychrome brick with a tower.[69] Membership grew from 79 in 1838 to 121 in 1869; there were 150 evening worshippers on Census Sunday 1851.[70] After 1960 several smaller Methodist societies merged with the High Street church. In 1960 the former Primitive society at Bank Road united with it and the High Street chapel was known thereafter as the Central Methodist Church.[71] Lawley Bank society joined in 1968,[72] Hill Top society, Old Park, c. 1973, and some members of Finger Road church in 1976.[73] The Central Church became the focus for Methodist activity in the Dawley area of the new town in the mid 1960s. In 1967 its ground floor was converted into an interdenominational pastoral centre[74] and in 1977–8 the church was taken down and replaced by a modern, brick-faced church and pastoral centre on the same site. In 1980 morning and evening services there were attended by c. 30 and c. 50 adults.[75]

A Wesleyan chapel built c. 1818 just outside the parish boundary at Lawley Bank[76] was replaced by a large brick chapel built at Dawley Bank in 1840.[77] In 1851 Census Sunday services were attended by 235 adults in the morning and 375 in the afternoon.[78] Membership fell, however, from 132 in 1838 to 83 in 1869.[79] By 1957 the chapel was not used for worship, services being held in the adjacent Sunday school[80] built in 1907.[81] Membership of the Lawley Bank society fell to 38 in 1960 and the society united with that of Dawley Central Methodist Church in 1968.[82] The Dawley Bank chapel, used as a factory in 1963,[83] was demolished in 1976.[84]

Unable to buy land in Stirchley,[85] the Wesleyan group there built a brick chapel on Stirchley Lane, just inside Dawley parish, in 1841.[86] A decade later on Census Sunday 35 adults attended the morning service and 70 that in the evening.[87] Membership was small in the mid 19th century[88] but the church remained open in 1980, with a congregation of c. 20 at morning services and c. 40 in the evenings.[89]

By 1885 the resident minister of the Dawley circuit lived in a manse in Chapel Street, known from c. 1910 as Wesley House. It was a manse until 1958 or later.[90]

Wesleyan societies in the northern end of the parish were placed in the Ketley Bank and Shifnal circuit on its creation in 1869.[91] At Old Park a chapel, known later as Hill Top church, had been built in 1853.[92] There were also cottage meetings at Hinkshay, recorded from 1874 to 1908,[93] and at Malinslee Lodge, where services were discontinued in 1884.[94] Hill Top church remained open until c. 1973[95] when the congregation, with 31 members, united with the Central Methodist Church.[96]

New Connexion Methodism. The religious revival that followed the failure of the Cinderhill riots in January 1821 brought a mission of Revivalist Methodists to Dawley that year.[97] They were supported by Benjamin Tranter, Wesleyan agent of the Coalbrookdale Co., and built a large chapel at Brandlee in 1822. Despite its Revivalist origins the chapel (New Connexion from 1829) had a strong musical tradition, fostered by a choral society founded in 1845 by Tranter's son William. The chapel had a congregation of 200 on Census Sunday evening 1851.[98] It closed and was demolished in 1937.

The connexion had cottage meetings at Hinkshay and Stoney Hill in the mid 19th century, and in 1865 a second chapel, a small brick building, was built in an isolated position at Lightmoor, where a New Connexion society had met since 1849. It was known popularly as 'Fat Bacon' because members kept pigs to raise money for the building.[99] The chapel closed c. 1938,[1] the congregation joining the former Wesleyan society at Little Dawley.[2]

Resident New Connexion ministers in Dawley were recorded from 1879 to 1905[3] but no manse seems to have been provided.

Primitive Methodism. Primitive Methodism reached the northern part of the coalfield during the revival of 1821–2 but did not spread into Dawley until a further revival in the late 1830s.[4] In 1841 the Primitives built a chapel in Dawley Green Lane (later Bank Road).[5] Evening service there was attended by 146 adults on Census Sunday 1851.[6] In 1927 the Bank Road society had 42 members.[7] The chapel, a large stuccoed brick building, closed in 1960, its congregation uniting with the former Wesleyan church in High Street.[8]

By the 1850s the Primitives had established

[69] G.R.O., Worship Reg. no. 9708; N.M.R., Photo. AA 63/6546 (copy in S.P.L.); below, plate 39.
[70] S.R.O. 2533/1–4; P.R.O., HO 129/358, no. 34.
[71] S.R.O. 4113/5/1, 5 Apr. 1960.
[72] S.R.O. 3840/1/1–2.
[73] Inf. from Mr. A. G. Duckett, L. Wenlock.
[74] *Wrekin Light*, June 1967, 1; S.R.O. 4113/5/1, 21 Nov. 1966; 11 Apr. 1967.
[75] Inf. from Mr. Duckett.
[76] Below, Lawley, Nonconf.
[77] S.R.O. 2533/7. S. Bagshaw, *Dir. Salop.* (1851), 375, dates the new chap. 1846.
[78] P.R.O., HO 129/358, no. 30.
[79] S.R.O. 2533/1–4.
[80] S.R.O. 3840/2, 28 Jan. 1957.
[81] Date stone.
[82] S.R.O. 3840/1/1–2; 3840/2, 18 July 1960.
[83] S.R.O. 3914/7; below, plate 38.
[84] *Shropshire Star*, 8 Oct. 1976.
[85] Below, Stirchley, Nonconf.
[86] S.R.O. 2533/7. The date 1840, however, is painted above the entrance.
[87] P.R.O., HO 129/358, no. 29.
[88] S.R.O. 2533/1–4.
[89] Local inf.

[90] *Kelly's Dir. Salop.* (1885–1941); S.R.O. 3802/1.
[91] S.R.O. 3027/1/190; *V.C.H. Salop.* ii. 14.
[92] Date stone.
[93] S.R.O. 3027/1/7, 195, 205.
[94] Ibid. /1/195, *passim*.
[95] S.R.O. 4113/3/2, 5.
[96] Inf. from Mr. Duckett.
[97] For this para. see B. Trinder, *Meth. New Connexion in Dawley and Madeley* (Wesley Hist. Soc., W. Midlands Branch, Occ. Publ. i [1968]); *V.C.H. Salop.* ii. 16; *Meth. New Connexion Mag.* 3rd ser. vi. 44–5.
[98] P.R.O., HO 129/358, no. 33.
[99] Trinder, op. cit. 10, 13–14.
[1] S.R.O. 4113/6/1.
[2] Trinder, op. cit. 19.
[3] *P.O. Dir. Salop.* (1879), 312; *Kelly's Dir. Salop.* (1885–1909).
[4] Wesley Hist. Soc., Salop. Branch, *Bulletin*, i (7) (copy in S.R.O. 3543/9).
[5] Date stone: photo. in S.P.L.
[6] P.R.O., HO 129/358, no. 32.
[7] S.R.O. 1936/42.
[8] S.R.O. 4113/5/1, 5 Apr. 1960; G.R.O., Worship Reg. no. 48555.

numerous small cottage meetings in Dawley. In the period 1854–64 the newly formed Dawley Green circuit included societies at Woodhouse Lane, Frame Lane, Stoney Hill, Holywell Lane, and Burroughs Bank (all in Little Dawley), and at Horsehay Potteries, Finger Lane, Langley Square, and Hinkshay (in Great Dawley).[9] At the northern end of the parish there were three cottage meetings, at Old Park, Dark Lane, and Park Forge Row, attended by between 49 and 137 people on Census Sunday evening 1851.[10] They remained in Oakengates (from 1865 Oakengates and Wellington) circuit.[11]

The Primitives' success in Dawley in the mid 19th century led to the erection of several chapels to serve the small groups in outlying industrial settlements in the late 1850s and early 1860s. Membership of the church slumped, however, towards the end of the century and the Primitive connexion even had to consider withdrawing from Dawley.[12]

At the northern end of the parish in 1857 the Old Park society built Bethesda, a small brick chapel,[13] whose congregation consisted largely of miners and ironworkers from the immediate vicinity in the later 19th century.[14] If a second Old Park registration[15] referred to another chapel, it must have been short-lived. The Dark Lane society built a chapel just inside Shifnal parish in 1865.[16] Cottage meetings continued at Park Forge Row until c. 1890,[17] and at Old Park until 1913.[18] The latter society, in Dawley (from 1906 Dawley and Madeley) circuit, struggled on with very few members until 1930.[19] Bethesda closed in 1963, its congregation uniting with the former Wesleyan church nearby at Hill Top.[20]

A chapel of blue and yellow brick was built in 1858 at Moreton's Coppice, Horsehay,[21] to serve the Primitive groups at Horsehay Potteries, Woodhouse Lane, Stoney Hill, and Coalmoor (in Little Wenlock).[22] There was also a mission room at Horsehay in the late 1880s, possibly the building registered for worship in 1875.[23] The Horsehay society had 45 members in 1927.[24] The congregation was joined by that of the former Wesleyan chapel at Spring Village in 1968[25] and Moreton's Coppice chapel remained open in 1980.

At Gravel Leasowes, near Lightmoor, a small chapel called Jubilee chapel, but popularly known as the 'Pop Bottle',[26] was opened in 1861 to serve the societies at Burroughs Bank, Holywell Lane, and Frame Lane.[27] It was enlarged in 1864[28] but closed in 1901.[29]

In 1863 a small brick chapel was opened at Finger Lane (later Finger Road).[30] The society there had 33 members in 1927.[31] The chapel closed in 1976 and was demolished for road widening.[32]

A preacher's house was built by the trustees of Dawley Green Lane chapel c. 1859.[33] It was probably the manse in King Street, known as Rock Villa, recorded from 1890 until at least 1958.[34]

OTHERS. A Congregational mission station was built in High Street c. 1866.[35] There were resident ministers in the town in the 1870s[36] but the chapel closed as such during the 1880s:[37] it survived in the 1890s as an undenominational mission.[38]

Other places of worship were a Gospel Army Mission room in King Street, registered 1883, closed by 1896;[39] a Salvation Army barracks in King Street, opened by 1885, closed c. 1902;[40] and a Spiritualist church in the former Primitive Methodist chapel, Bank Road, recorded 1963–80.[41]

A congregation of the Assemblies of God was founded in Dawley in 1963 and opened a temporary church in Chapel Street the following year.[42] It had ceased to meet by 1970 when Bridgnorth Full Gospel Church, a member of the Assemblies of God movement, moved to Dawley. After meeting in rented premises the Telford Full Gospel Church (as it had come to be called) acquired the former Wesleyan Methodist Sunday school building at Dawley Bank in 1971. There was a congregation of c. 70 in 1980.[43]

Telford meeting of the Society of Friends met in the Central Methodist Church in the late 1960s and in the church offices at Telford town centre from 1974.[44]

EDUCATION. Richard Wilding, curate of Daw-

[9] S.R.O. 2533/130.
[10] P.R.O., HO 129/358, nos. 36–8.
[11] S.R.O. 3038/1/1; V.C.H. Salop. ii. 15.
[12] S.R.O. 1936/68.
[13] Date stone; G.R.O., Worship Reg. no. 8423; P.M. Mag. 1866, 358; Wellington Jnl. 4 July 1857.
[14] S.R.O. 4113/2/1.
[15] In 1861: G.R.O., Worship Reg. no. 14083.
[16] O.S. Map 6″, Salop. XLIII. NE. (1889 edn.); photo. in S.P.L.; Shropshire Star, 23 June 1970.
[17] S.R.O. 3038/1/1–3, passim.
[18] Ibid. /1/12, 7 June 1913.
[19] S.R.O. 1936/3–118.
[20] S.R.O. 3027/1/181, 29 Nov. 1963.
[21] Date stone; Wellington Jnl. 23 Aug. 1857.
[22] S.R.O. 2533/130, 21 Apr. 1856.
[23] Kelly's Dir. Salop. (1885), 840; (1891), 306; G.R.O., Worship Reg. no. 22537.
[24] S.R.O. 1936/42.
[25] Wrekin Light, Oct. 1968, 4.
[26] Ibid. Dec. 1967, 12.
[27] S.R.O. 2533/130, 10 June 1861; G.R.O., Worship Reg. no. 14967.
[28] S.R.O. 2533/130, 28 Sept. 1863; 20 June 1864.

[29] Inf. from Mr. S. Thomas through Mr. K. B. Jones; cf. O.S. Map 6″, Salop. XLIII. SW. (1884 and 1903 edns.).
[30] Date stone: photo. in S.P.L.
[31] S.R.O. 1936/42.
[32] S.R.O. 4113/4/1–2; G.R.O., Worship Reg. no. 47999.
[33] S.R.O. 2533/130, 29 Apr. 1858; 13 Jan. 1859.
[34] S.R.O. 1936/2–118; 3802/1; Kelly's Dir. Salop. (1900–41).
[35] At O.S. Nat. Grid SJ 6852 0737: O.S. Map 1/2,500, Salop. XLIII. 6 (1882 edn.). Dr. B. S. Trinder gives date of chap. as 1867 (Wrekin Light, June 1968, 3), but there was a Cong. Sunday sch. in Dawley from 1866 (Wellington Jnl. 10 Aug. 1878).
[36] E. Elliot, Hist. of Congregationalism in Salop. [1898], 186, 273, 306.
[37] Ibid. 10; Wrekin Light, June 1968, 3.
[38] Local inf. in possession of Dr. B. S. Trinder.
[39] G.R.O., Worship Reg. no. 27039.
[40] Ibid. no. 32369; Kelly's Dir. Salop. (1885–1905).
[41] S.R.O., DA 8/100/7, p. 2528; T.D.C. Telford Street Plan (1980).
[42] S.R.O., DA 8/100/7, p. 2731; Dawley Observer, 14 Feb. 1964.
[43] Inf. from Mr. D. Bickerton, pastor.
[44] Inf. from Mr. A. E. Morris, Lilleshall.

ley in 1605, and William Banks, rector of Stirchley 1715–58, probably held schools in Dawley[45] and Richard Poyner was recorded as a schoolmaster there 1718–22.[46] By 1772 I. H. Browne, owner of Malinslee, was paying for the schooling of 15 children, probably in the Sunday school that he and his tenants, the Botfields, continued to support in 1799.[47] By 1833 there were 8 Sunday schools, two run by the established church and supported by subscription and six provided by nonconformists. There were several private schools for young children but no public day school, despite the rapidly increasing population.[48] The earliest nonconformist Sunday school in the area was probably the Wesleyan school at Lawley Bank, opened 1806.[49] Other Wesleyan schools were opened at Little Dawley in 1813 and Horsehay in 1819; the Revivalist Methodists opened a school at Brandlee in 1822.[50] In 1833 one of the nonconformist Sunday schools had a lending library attached.[51]

Public day schools were founded from 1832. In 1875 a school board for the parish was formed compulsorily. It was chaired by W. G. Norris, a Quaker and manager of the Coalbrookdale Co., the first vice-chairman, and from 1894 the clerk to the board, being Charles Buckworth-Herne-Soame (9th bt. 1888; d. 1906), an Anglican and physician.[52] A board school was opened at Langley in 1878 and the board took over the management of the Pool Hill schools in 1887. The standard of elementary education in Dawley was high in the later 19th century, particularly at Pool Hill and Langley schools.[53] A notable feature of the curriculum was the regular instruction in art and drawing that, from the 1860s, visiting masters gave to both boys and girls at Pool Hill, Langley, and Dawley Bank schools.[54] Evening schools were held at the National schools from the 1860s[55] and were started at Pool Hill under the county council's guidance in 1893.[56] In the later 19th and earlier 20th century children were often absent from school in September when they accompanied their parents to pick fruit in Gloucestershire.[57]

The paucity of private schools in later 19th-century Dawley probably reflects the small middle-class population of the area. Only Mrs. E. M. Smith's school for girls in King Street, recorded from 1879 to 1900, lasted for more than a few years.[58]

After the Second World War some 19th-century schools, whose buildings needed replacing, were closed, and new schools were opened for Dawley's expanding population. Dawley was one of the last places in Shropshire to be provided with secondary education, a modern school opening only in 1956. In the provision of nursery education, however, government aid put it ahead of other parts of the county, nursery classes being opened in primary schools under the government's urban aid programme in the early 1970s.[59]

Malinslee Church of England School opened in 1832 as a day school for the Malinslee area. Pupils paid 2d. weekly, remaining costs being met by the Botfields.[60] In 1844 the school moved into buildings at Dawley Bank, converted from cottages. R. H. Cheney and Beriah Botfield, owner and lessee of Malinslee respectively, were the managers in 1855, when the school contained 80 boys and 50 girls.[61] The school was known as Malinslee National School from c. 1857. An infant department for 80 was opened in new buildings in 1855[62] and the school premises were further enlarged in 1885 and 1895.[63] The school established at Malinslee Institute in 1895 became a second infant department. In 1906 there were places for 204 older children and 120 infants at Dawley Bank and 94 infants at the Institute. The school was closed in 1950 when juniors were transferred to Langley County School and children over 13 to Pool Hill School.[64]

Dawley Church of England (Aided) School, united to the National Society, was opened in 1841 in new premises near the parsonage at Brandlee, on land given by R. A. Slaney.[65] In 1863 there were 59 boys and 56 girls, paying from 1d. to 4d. weekly according to their parents' means; deficiencies in the school's finance were made up by Beriah Botfield.[66] The buildings were enlarged in 1892[67] and 1899,[68] and by 1903–4 average attendance was 174 in the mixed and 118 in the infant departments.[69] The school became Aided in 1952[70] and from 1956 it became a contributory primary school to the newly opened Dawley Modern School. A nursery class was added in 1974, and the school contained 166 pupils in 1980.[71]

Captain Webb County School, formerly Pool Hill School, originated in a British boys' school opened by the Coalbrookdale Co. in a room over the stables at Horsehay Farm in 1843. The school moved to Pool Hill c. 1846 and a girls' department opened in 1849. The new schoolrooms, put up 1845–7, were heated by under-floor hot water pipes. The schools were financed primarily by funds for medical and educational purposes contributed by the company's employees. Their child-

[45] L.J.R.O., B/V/1/24; B/V/3, list of schmasters, 1726.
[46] Ibid. B/V/4, 28 June 1718; 30 May 1722 (refs. owed to Dr. R. Hume).
[47] Ibid. B/V/5, visit. return of 1772; S.R.O. 3916/1/1.
[48] Educ. Enq. Abstract, H.C. 62, p. 773 (1835), xlii.
[49] Wellington Jnl. 10 Aug. 1878.
[50] J. McFall, 'Educ. in Madeley Union of Salop. in 19th Cent.' (Keele Univ. M.A. (Educ.) thesis, 1973), 43–4.
[51] Educ. Enq. Abstract, 773.
[52] List. of Sch. Boards, 1902 [Cd. 1038], p. 75, H.C. (1902), lxxix; S.R.O. 559/XXIV/7/2–4.
[53] Inf. from Mrs. J. McFall (evid. of inspectors' ann. reps.).
[54] McFall, 'Educ. in Madeley Union', 115–16.
[55] Ibid. 113.
[56] S.R.O. 559/XXIV/7/3, pp. 120–1; V.C.H. Salop. iii. 198.
[57] McFall, op. cit. 16, 249–50.
[58] P.O. Dir. Salop. (1879), 526; Kelly's Dir. Salop. (1885–

1900).
[59] S.C.C. Mins. (Educ.) 1971–2, 63, 65.
[60] S.R.O. 3916/1/3.
[61] P.R.O., ED 7/102, ff. 238–9.
[62] Ibid. ff. 236–7.
[63] S.R.O. 2732/PM/2 (Sept. 1885); McFall, 'Educ. in Madeley Union', 45.
[64] S.C.C. Mins. (Educ.) 1905–6, 114; 1950–1, 142.
[65] S.R.O. 2374, box 3, papers re sch.; 4084/S/1.
[66] P.R.O., ED 7/102, f. 240.
[67] Date stone.
[68] S.R.O. 4084/Ve/1, Apr. 1899–Apr. 1900.
[69] Public Elem. Schs. 1906 [Cd. 3182], p. 536, H.C. (1906), lxxxvi.
[70] S.C.C. Mins. (Educ.) 1952–3, 44.
[71] Ibid. 1974–5, 13; S.C.C. Educ. Cttee. Sch. List (1975), 4; S.C.C. Educ. Cttee. Educ. Dir. (1980), 3, 9.

ren were educated free; others paid school pence of 3d. or 6d. weekly. In 1855 there were 134 boys and 136 girls, and only 7 children paid school pence.[72] Because of the trade depression of the mid 1880s the company discontinued its support of the schools and management passed to the school board in 1887. The board formed one mixed department but continued the separate infant department.[73] Although there was accommodation for 725 pupils in 1906, average attendance in 1903–4 was only 297 in the mixed and infant departments.[74] Its ample space and central position led to its choice as a secondary school after the Second World War. In 1955 it was an all-age school receiving senior pupils from 5 other primary schools.[75] After the construction of the secondary modern school nearby the following year, Pool Hill School became a primary school. In 1966 it became a junior school when an infant school was opened in adjacent new buildings; a nursery class was added to the infant school in 1971.[76] The junior school was rebuilt after the original buildings were destroyed by fire in 1977 and the two schools were united in 1980 to form a primary school, renamed the Captain Webb County School.[77] It had 481 pupils that year.[78]

Hinkshay Mission School for infants was opened in 1873, with a National Society grant, at the Church of England mission chapel at Hinkshay. The school struggled on, short of funds, until at least 1876[79] and probably closed when Langley Board School opened nearby in 1878.

Langley County Junior (formerly Board) School was opened by the school board in 1878 in new buildings on the edge of a spoil mound south of Langleyfield colliery. Average attendance in the first term was 81 boys, 76 girls, and 80 infants.[80] After Dawley Modern School opened in 1956, Langley became a contributory junior school. In 1976 it moved from the original premises to new buildings in Spout Lane, next to St. Leonard's infant school.[81] There were 398 pupils at Langley New School in 1980.[82]

Malinslee Institute National Infants' School originated in 1898 as a second infant department of Malinslee National School. It was founded to serve children in the Old Park area and was housed in buildings put up in 1859 and previously used as a mechanics' institute.[83] The school owed its existence to Edward Parry, vicar of Malinslee, who met, and overcame, determined opposition

from nonconformist school board members.[84] He bought the building himself in 1897 and vested it in the Lichfield Diocesan Trust in 1913.[85] In 1920, after the addition of a new classroom, the school could accommodate 113 children.[86] It closed in 1956 when its pupils were transferred to St. Leonard's County Infants' School.[87]

St. Leonard's County Infants' School opened in 1951 on the edge of new housing estates around St. Leonard's church.[88] A nursery class was added in 1971, and in 1980 the school contained 234 pupils.[89]

Dawley Modern School was opened at Pool Hill in 1956 to take children over 11 from four contributory primary schools.[90] There were c. 500 pupils on the roll until 1965 when comprehensive secondary education was introduced and the school was renamed the Phoenix School.[91] The number of pupils had risen to 1,159 by 1980.[92]

Two 'special' schools were opened: Southall (in Rowan Avenue) in 1973 and Hinkshay (in the former Langley school building) in 1976.[93]

The Ladygrove (formerly North West Dawley) County School was opened in 1979, and Malinslee County Primary School in 1980,[94] as primary schools serving the new housing estates in Dawley Bank and Malinslee; they had 158 and 175 pupils respectively in 1980.[95] Another new estate was served by Hollinswood County First School, opened 1976, and Hollinswood County Middle School, opened 1980; in 1980 they had 442 and 191 pupils respectively.[96]

CHARITIES FOR THE POOR. Richard Hodden, by will dated 1684, left £7 a year charged on land to the poor of Dawley.[97] In the early 19th century it was distributed, sometimes with the poor's stock, in small doles mainly to widows.[98] In 1860 Hodden's charity was apportioned between the parishes of Dawley Magna, Malinslee, and Little Dawley,[99] and from 1912 was administered through the consolidated charities of the three parishes.[1]

By will proved 1756 Rebecca Walthall, owner of Malinslee, left the interest on £40 to be distributed in Malinslee.[2] In 1820 the yearly interest, 40s., was distributed in small sums by William Botfield.[3] By 1912 the stock had increased to £44 18s. 2d. and Walthall's charity became part of the Malinslee Consolidated Charities.[4]

[72] P.R.O., ED 7/103, f. 151; S.R.O. 245/140, p. 77.
[73] S.R.O. 559/XXIV/7/2, pp. 324–5; S.R.O. 4139, s.a. 1884–7. [74] Public Elem. Schs. 1906, 536.
[75] S.C.C. Mins. (Educ.) 1954–5, 132.
[76] Ibid. 1971–2, 65–6; Sch. List (1966), 8; (1972), 4.
[77] Sch. List (1979), 9; Educ. Dir. (1980), 9.
[78] Educ. Dir. (1980), 3, 9.
[79] Inf. (from Nat. Soc. rec.) in possession of Mrs. McFall.
[80] P.R.O., ED 7/102, f. 232; S.R.O. 559/XXIV/7/2, passim.
[81] S.C.C. Mins. (Educ.) 1974–5, 337.
[82] Educ. Dir. (1980), 9.
[83] P.R.O., ED 7/102, ff. 234–5; O.S. Map 6″, Salop. XLIII. NE. (1889 and 1903 edns.).
[84] S.R.O. 559/XXIV/7/3, p. 324; McFall, 'Educ. in Madeley Union', 45.
[85] S.R.O. 2732/Sc/17.
[86] S.C.C. Mins. (Educ.) 1919–20, 92.
[87] Ibid. 1955–6, 279; S.R.O. 2732/Sc/57–94. The bldgs. were later demolished.

[88] S.C.C. Mins. (Educ.) 1950–1, 142.
[89] Ibid. 1971–2, 63–4; Educ. Dir. (1980), 3, 9.
[90] S.C.C. Mins. (Educ.) 1955–6, 279.
[91] S.R.O. 2782/5; S.C.C. Mins. 1964–5, 89–90; S.C.C. Mins. (Educ.) 1965–6, 65.
[92] Educ. Dir. (1980), 2.
[93] Sch. List (1973), 11; (1976), 11.
[94] Ibid. (1979), 9; Educ. Dir. (1980), 10.
[95] Educ. Dir. (1980), 9; inf. from S.C.C. Educ. Dept.
[96] S.C.C. Mins. (Educ.) 1974–5, 121; Sch. List (1976), 10; Educ. Dir. (1980), 3, 10; inf. from S.C.C. Educ. Dept.
[97] S.R.O. 4084/Cy/1.
[98] 3rd Rep. Com. Char. H.C. 5, p. 244 (1820), iv; S.R.O. 1560/5, 6 May 1829.
[99] S.R.O. 4084/Cy/5.
[1] S.R.O. 2732/Cy/37; Review of Local Chars. (S.C.C. 1975), 65.
[2] B.L. Add. Ch. 44253; S.P.L., MS. 4645, p. 264.
[3] 3rd Rep. Com. Char. 244.
[4] S.R.O. 2732/Cy/37.

Enoch Cooper, by will dated 1721, left the interest on £20 to the poor of Dawley. The capital sum became the core of a poor's stock of £33 that was lent to George Yorke of Madeley Wood in the mid 18th century.[5] Payment of interest and distribution of the charity were last recorded in 1829, when it was known as 'York's legacy'.[6]

Alfred Purcell left the interest on £100 to the poor of Malinslee by will proved 1872.[7] The interest amounted to £2 13s. 4d. in 1912, when Purcell's charity became part of the Malinslee Consolidated Charities.[8]

By will proved 1887 William Slaney Lewis left the interest on £200 to be distributed in blankets and clothing to widows in Dawley,[9] and William Greenhalgh's will, proved 1892, left the interest on £100 to be apportioned equally between the parishes of Dawley Magna, Malinslee, and Little Dawley.[10] Both charities were included in the scheme that consolidated the charities of the three parishes in 1912.

In 1975 annual income from endowments comprised in the Malinslee, Little Dawley, and Dawley Magna Consolidated Charities was £14.[11]

EYTON UPON THE WEALD MOORS

EYTON upon the Weald Moors lies 4 km. north of Wellington, 1 km. east of the Wellington–Crudgington road. The civil parish contains 578 ha. (1,428 a.)[12] but its compact shape by no means corresponds to that of the ancient parish which contained 1,232 a. (499 ha.) in two townships 4 km. apart: 782 a. in the township of Eyton, where land in Eyton and Wellington parishes lay intermixed, and 450 a. in two detached portions known as the Hoo (81 a.) and Hortonwood (369 a.), which together constituted Hortonwood township.[13] This article treats the history of the parish, manor, and township of Eyton and the pre-industrial history of Hortonwood township. Aspects of the later history of Hortonwood are covered under Wrockwardine Wood.[14]

In 1882 Eyton township was a compact block of land containing 1,059 a. (429 ha.)[15] on the southern edge of the formerly fen-like Weald Moors. It was defined on the west by field boundaries, on the south by the ancient Newport–Shrewsbury road, and on the east by a watercourse running down to the Weald Moors. The northern boundary followed ditches laid out on the inclosure and drainage of the Weald Moors in the early 19th century. Before inclosure, boundaries in the Moors were complicated by the existence of areas intercommoned by a number of adjacent communities, and clear-cut boundaries between townships probably crystallized at a late date. The boundaries between Eyton and neighbouring estates required clarification in the 1230s, and disputes over common rights in that part of the Weald Moors continued into the late 16th and early 17th century.[16]

By the late 18th century the township was divided in a pattern of great complexity[17] between the ancient parishes of Eyton (782 a.) and Wellington (277 a.).[18] It is not clear when the territorial division occurred: in 1635 Sir Philip Eyton, owner of the whole township, paid two thirds of his tithe to Eyton and one third to Wellington but that need not imply that the township was so divided on the ground.[19] By 1769 the territory of each parish could be mapped and was settled in that year by the erection of merestones where land in one parish lay open to that in the other.[20] Some boundaries however followed the Shrewsbury Canal, a fact suggesting that boundaries were altered after it crossed the township in 1794.[21] The pattern was simplified in 1883–4 when the detached portions of Wellington and Eyton parishes were absorbed into surrounding or adjoining parishes.[22] Nevertheless substantial portions in the south-east part of the township remained in Wellington parish (from 1894 Wellington Rural civil parish, from 1898 Hadley C.P.) until they were transferred, together with land formerly in Wappenshall township, to Eyton C.P. in 1905.[23] The civil parish had been further enlarged in 1884 by the transfer of Wrockwardine moor from Wrockwardine parish,[24] and in 1934 Eyton C.P. received part of Dothill township from Hadley and Wellington Rural C.P.s.[25]

Eyton township lies on glacial deposits overlying the Upper Coal Measures and Triassic sandstone on the northern edge of the east Shropshire coalfield. The village lies at the junction between areas of contrasting drift material, free-drained fluvio-glacial sands and gravels forming the higher land in the south and west of the township, and wetter lake clay giving way to the

[5] 3rd Rep. Com. Char. 244–5.
[6] S.R.O. 1560/5, 27 Feb., 6 May 1829.
[7] S.R.O. 1206/32, pp. 640–1.
[8] S.R.O. 2732/Cy/37.
[9] S.R.O. 4084/Cy/17.
[10] Ibid. /Cy/23.
[11] Review of Local Chars. 65.
[12] Census, 1971, Co. Rep. Salop. 7. This art. was written 1979. Thanks are offered to the Revd. J. C. Duxbury, Mrs. P. A. Green, and Mrs. T. H. Udale for their help.
[13] O.S. Map 1/2,500, Salop. XXXVI. 1 (1882 edn.); O.S. Area Bk. (1882).
[14] Below.
[15] O.S. Maps 1/2,500, Salop. XXXVI. 1, 5 (1902 edn.); O.S. Area Bks. Eyton (1882); Wellington (1882; not counting detachment no. 3, believed to have been in Bratton tns.: below, Wellington, intro.)

[16] Close R. 1227–31, 588; 1237–42, 147; T.S.A.S. liv. 282–7.
[17] S.R.O. 665/1/284.
[18] O.S. Map 1/2,500, Salop. XXXVI. 1, 5 (1902 edns.); O.S. Area Bks. Eyton (1882); Wellington (1882).
[19] L.J.R.O., B/V/6, Eyton, 1635.
[20] S.R.O. 665/1/281; below, plate 57.
[21] Below; below, Wellington, Communications.
[22] Divided Parishes and Poor Law Amendment Act, 1882, 45 & 46 Vic. c. 58; 14th Ann. Rep. Local Govt. Bd. [C. 4515], pp. xlvii, 191, 204, H.C. (1884–5), xxxii; O.S. Area Bk. (1882, with emendation slip); O.S. Maps 6", Salop. XXXVI. NE., NW. (1890 edn.).
[23] Below, Hadley, Local Govt. and Public Services.
[24] Below, Wrockwardine, Local Govt. and Public Services.
[25] Below, Wellington, intro.; Hadley, Local Govt. and Public Services.

peat-filled Weald Moors in the north.[26] Before the drainage of the Weald Moors in the early 19th century the distinction was reflected in contrasting patterns of land use, cultivated land being restricted to the drier ground south and west of the village. The position of the village on the edge of the higher land gives it the island-like appearance recorded in its name.[27]

The community at Eyton has never been large. In 1086 there were 4 oxherds on the demesne, 2 villeins, and 1 bordar;[31] in 1563 there were 6 households[32] and in 1587 a total of 11 tenants in the township.[33] In 1672 *c.* 23 householders paid hearth tax[34] and in 1776 the township contained 18 tenements.[35] In 1841 the whole township contained 120 inhabitants in 25 households[36] and by

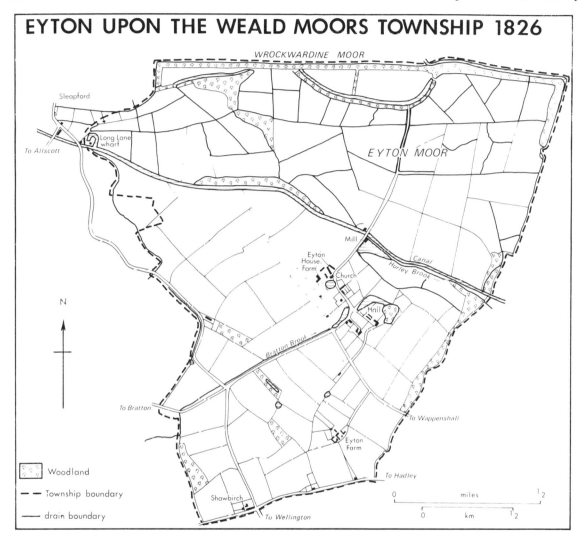

EYTON UPON THE WEALD MOORS TOWNSHIP 1826

WROCKWARDINE MOOR

Sleapford

To Allscott

Long Lane
wharf

EYTON MOOR

N

Mill

Eyton
House.
Farm

Church

Hall

Canal

Hurley Brook

Bratton Brook

To Bratton

Eyton
Farm

To Wappenshall

To Hadley

Woodland

Township boundary

drain boundary

Shawbirch

To Wellington

miles   0   1   2

km   0   1   2

Eyton village consists of a scatter of houses along the road between the church and Eyton Hall. The number of dwellings appears to have dwindled since the mid 18th century.[28] Most of the present buildings are of brick and date from the late 18th or the 19th century, although 17th-century timber-framed construction survives in the School House. The township contains two outlying farmsteads: Shawbirch, which is recorded from *c.* 1680,[29] and Eyton Farm, the home farm of the Eyton Hall estate, built between *c.* 1785 and *c.* 1805.[30]

1861 the population had risen to 165, of which the Eyton Hall household accounted for 34.[37] The civil parish of Eyton (enlarged in 1905) contained 184 inhabitants in 1911; thereafter the population declined to 92 in 1971.[38]

The township was bounded on the south, and in part on the west, by major roads that were turnpiked in 1726.[39] Two lanes formerly led into the village: one, known as Bratton Way in 1769, left the Wellington–Crudgington road near Wheelwright Cottage (now Denwood), the other left the old Newport–Shrewsbury road near

[26] Inst. Geol. Sciences Map 1/25,000, *Telford* (1978 edn.).
[27] E. Ekwall, *Concise Oxf. Dict. Eng. P.N.* (4th edn.), 172.
[28] S.R.O. 665/1/280, compared with O.S. Map 6″, Salop. XXXVI. NW. (1890 and later edns.).
[29] S.R.O. 665/1/279.   [30] Ibid. /1/283–4.
[31] *V.C.H. Salop.* i. 332.
[32] B.L. Harl. MS. 594, f. 160.
[33] S.R.O. 513, box 1, ct. r.
[34] *Hearth Tax 1672* (Salop. Arch. Soc.), 87.
[35] S.R.O. 665/1/11.
[36] P.R.O., HO 107/905.
[37] P.R.O., RG 9/1900.
[38] *V.C.H. Salop.* ii. 223; *Census, 1971, Co. Rep. Salop.* 7.
[39] 12 Geo. I, c. 9.

Shawbirch to enter the village at its southern end.[40] In 1807 both lanes were closed and the present road to the village, following the line of Bratton brook, was built.[41] The Shrewsbury Canal was built across the township in 1794 between Wappenshall junction and Long Lane wharf.[42] A lock-keeper's cottage was built near Eyton mill, where the occupation road from the village to the Weald Moors crossed the canal.

The ready supply of coal afforded by the canal led one of the 19th-century squires, probably T. C. Eyton (d. 1880), to build a gas plant near Eyton mill to provide domestic lighting for the village. The works was operating by 1871 but ceased to function during the 1880s.[43] For water supply the village relied on private boreholes until a piped supply was provided c. 1960.[44]

In the 19th century the township's social life was dominated by the Eyton family. A cricket club, one of the earliest in the county, flourished at Eyton from c. 1839 to 1853 under the patronage of Thomas Eyton, the 'father of Shropshire cricket'.[45] He and his son, T. C. Eyton, were moving forces in the short-lived Wrockwardine and Eyton Benefit Society, which was founded in 1840 but had ceased by 1842.[46] A lodge of Odd Fellows (Manchester Unity) in 1871–2 probably had Bratton members too.[47] In 1898 the village had a clothing club, and a reading room was open two evenings a week in winter.[48] During the 1950s Eyton Hall, then uninhabited, was used for village gatherings, but in 1967 the cedar-clad village hall was built on land given to the village by Capt. A. C. Eyton (d. 1954).[49]

Hortonwood township consisted of two blocks of land containing in all 450 a., lying 4 km. east of Eyton township between Preston upon the Weald Moors and Wrockwardine Wood. The larger portion (369 a.) contained part of the straggling roadside settlement of Trench and lay north of the Wellington–Newport road, which formed its southern boundary. The smaller portion, an irregularly shaped block of 81 a. known as the Hoo, lay to the north.[50]

The definition of what were probably parts of the Domesday manor of Horton as the township of Hortonwood in Eyton parish may have been a long-drawn-out process, perhaps affected to some degree by the connexions between Eyton and Horton manors.[51] Part of the lordship of Horton, near the Hoo, was certainly in Eyton parish by 1499.[52] In 1620 Sir Philip Eyton extended his ownership of land in Horton and Horton's wood (*alias* the Trench)[53] and by 1635, after some years' woodland clearance in the area,[54] he claimed Horton's wood and its tithes as belonging to Eyton parish. That year Francis Charlton, laying the ground for litigation, gathered part of the tithes to make 'a title thereunto for the parish of Wellington'.[55] Nevertheless Hortonwood was firmly reckoned part of Eyton parish during the 18th and earlier 19th centuries, though in the 1820s some inhabitants of Trench Lane were uncertain whether they belonged to the manor of Horton or that of Wrockwardine.[56] In 1859 Hortonwood was included in the new ecclesiastical parish of Wrockwardine Wood.[57] In 1884 the Hoo was absorbed into Wellington (from 1894 Wellington Rural, from 1898 Hadley) C.P. and Hortonwood was transferred to Wrockwardine Wood C.P.[58]

The township lies on boulder clay and fluvio-glacial sands and gravels overlying the Upper Coal Measures and Triassic sandstone,[59] the land rising towards the south. Its name, consistently given as Horton's wood from the 17th to the 19th century,[60] suggests that it was an area of late settlement resulting from woodland clearance, and wooded areas survived in the early 17th century.[61]

Settlement in Hortonwood township consisted c. 1930 of a small agricultural hamlet at Hortonwood, single farmsteads at Trench Farm and Trench Lodge (a new farmstead site occupied c. 1825),[62] and the ribbon of 19th- and early 20th-century housing, in-filling between earlier small farms and cottages, along the southern boundary at Trench. During the mid 20th century the farming landscape north of the railway was replaced by a new industrial landscape; in 1979 large acreages were occupied by Trench Farm sewage works (built 1904–5),[63] the Central Ordnance Depot (begun 1938),[64] and Hortonwood industrial estate (under construction).

In 1086 Horton (which probably included the area later known as Hortonwood) was waste and no population was recorded.[65] By 1587 there were 18 tenants on the Eyton family's estate in 'Hor-

[40] S.R.O. 665/1/280.
[41] S.R.O., QR 231/70–2.
[42] Trinder, *Ind. Rev. Salop.* (1981), 85.
[43] S.R.O. 2009/1; P.R.O., RG 10/2808; O.S. Map 6″, Salop XXXVI. NW. (1890 and 1902 edns.).
[44] A. H. S. Waters, *Rep. on Water Supplies* (S.C.C. 1946), 95; local inf.   [45] *V.C.H. Salop.* ii. 195–6.
[46] S.R.O. 436/6720.
[47] *Rep. Registrar Friendly Socs. 1871*, H.C. 394, p. 108 (1872), liv; *1872*, H.C. 323, p. 133 (1873), lxi.
[48] Hobson & Co. *Wellington Dir., Almanack, & Diary* (1898), 51.
[49] Inf. from Mr. R. A. Nunn, Community Council of Salop.
[50] O.S. *Area Bk.* (1882).
[51] Both, as parts of Wem barony, owed suit to Hinstock leet; at least part of Horton was subject to Eyton ct. baron by 1359 and in the 16th cent., when the Eyton fam. may have owned the ¼ of Horton man. that belonged to them in 1616. See below, Local Govt.; below, Hadley, Man. and Other Est.
[52] S.P.L., Deeds 18633.
[53] In exchange for ¼ Preston man. with Fra. Charlton: below, Preston, Man. By 1631 Eyton claimed to be sole ld. of

Horton: below, Hadley, Man. and Other Est.
[54] Below, Econ. Hist.
[55] L.J.R.O., B/V/6, Eyton, 1635. For Charlton's interest in Wellington rectorial tithes see below, Wellington, Man. and Other Est.
[56] S.R.O. 327, box 5, notices to quit, 17 Sept. 1828; Wm. Tayler to — Bratton, 19 Apr. 1829.
[57] Eyton par. rec., overseers' acct. bks., rate bks.; Lich. Dioc. Regy., bps.' reg. P & QA (Orders in Council), p. 117 (2nd nos.).
[58] Below, Wellington, Local Govt.; Wrockwardine Wood, Local Govt.
[59] Inst. Geol. Sciences Map 1/25,000, *Telford* (1978 edn.).
[60] S.R.O. 665/1/257; Staffs. R.O., D. 1287/13, *passim*; par. rec., rate bk. 1845–8.
[61] S.R.O. 665/1/256.
[62] B.L. Maps, O.S.D. 208; O.S. Map 1″, sheet 61 NE. (1833 edn.).
[63] S.R.O., DA 12/100/2, p. 234; /100/3, p. 129; /100/4, p. 156.
[64] Programme of T.D.C. visit to C.O.D. Donnington 26 Feb. 1976 (copy in possession of the archivist, T.D.C.).
[65] *V.C.H. Salop.* i. 332.

ton', but it is not known how many lived in Horton's wood and how many in Horton (in Wellington).[66] There were 15 cottagers and smallholders in Horton's wood in 1635.[67] The population of Hortonwood township had risen to 266 by 1841 and continued to grow, reaching 352 in 1891.[68]

Most of the 19th-century population lived along Trench Lane, the Wellington–Newport road that formed the township's southern boundary. A few dwellings had been built along the north side of Trench Lane by c. 1630[69] and by 1772 the steadings of seven farms and smallholdings lay strung out along the highway.[70] The growth of industry during the 19th century resulted in a proliferation of workers' cottages. In 1841 there were 44 households containing 211 inhabitants along the north side of Trench Lane[71] and, with the mid-century expansion of the iron industry in Donnington and Oakengates, the population of Trench continued to grow: the north side of the road contained 309 inhabitants in 1871.[72] In the rest of the township, where settlement was scattered, the hamlet of Hortonwood and cottages near the Hoo and Horton contained only 55 inhabitants in 1841.[73]

The Wellington–Newport road, where it bounded the township on the south, was known c. 1630 as Trench Way and in the 18th century as Trench Lane.[74] It was turnpiked in 1763.[75] The Shropshire Union Railway was driven through the southern part of the township in 1849[76] with a station at Trench Crossing. The line was closed to passengers in 1964[77] although the section through Trench remained in use to serve private sidings in Donnington.[78]

An aleseller was licensed in Eyton parish in 1614[79] although it is not known whether he lived in Eyton or Hortonwood. There is no later evidence of licensed premises in Eyton township except the record of an innkeeper living at Shawbirch in 1851.[80] Three alesellers were licensed at Trench in the later 18th century but it is not certain whether their premises lay in Hortonwood or Wrockwardine Wood. The Duke of York, Trench, so known by 1823, was probably licensed by 1800.[81] It was one of three public houses on the north side of Trench Road (formerly Trench Lane) in 1979. In 1871–2 there were two lodges of Odd Fellows (Manchester Unity) in Trench:

'Miners' Glory' with 21 members, 'Marquis of Stafford' with 270. Trench Bowling Club had a green near the western end of the former township in 1979, and at the eastern end there was a T.A.V.R. Centre, opened in 1964.[82]

MANOR AND OTHER ESTATES. In 1066 Wighe and Ouiet held *EYTON* as two manors. In 1086 Eyton was one of the numerous manors held of Roger, earl of Shrewsbury, by William Pantulf.[83] By 1242 it was described as a member of the barony of Wem, which Pantulf's heirs had held in chief since the early 12th century.[84] The overlordship of Eyton remained with the barons of Wem, the feudal tie being recorded in 1582;[85] Eyton manor still owed suit to the leet court of Hinstock in 1851.[86]

Warin, the undertenant of Eyton in 1086, was possibly a cadet of the Pantulf family and probably the ancestor of the Eyton family that held the manor until 1954.[87] The earliest known members of the family were Robert of Eyton, who granted land at Buttery (in Edgmond) to Shrewsbury abbey during Henry II's reign,[88] and Peter of Eyton, who witnessed charters to Wombridge priory between 1180 and 1194.[89] Peter's son, Peter of Eyton (II), who was referred to between c. 1220 and 1238, is known to have held land in Eyton.[90]

Peter (II) was dead by 1242 when William of Eyton, presumed to be his son, held 1 knight's fee in Eyton.[91] By 1255 William had been succeeded by his son Peter (III), a minor in ward to Peter Peverel.[92] Peter of Eyton (III) was of age in 1272[93] and lived until at least 1301 when he was returned as a knight of the shire.[94] He was succeeded by his son Peter (IV), who was in possession of the manor in 1311 and lived until at least 1324.[95]

John Eyton, whose relationship to Peter (IV) is not known, had probably succeeded to the manor by 1327[96] and held it until 1346 or later.[97] He appears to have been followed by Peter Eyton (V), who is generally accepted to have been his son and occurred between 1354 and 1384.[98] He held the manor by 1366.[99] Peter (V) is thought to have been succeeded by John Eyton, presumably his son, who was sheriff in 1394[1] and appears to

[66] S.R.O. 513, box 1, ct. r.
[67] L.J.R.O., B/V/6, Eyton, 1635.
[68] P.R.O., HO 107/905; *V.C.H. Salop.* ii. 223 n.
[69] S.R.O. 38/4, 11.
[70] Staffs. R.O., D. 1287/13/1/1.
[71] P.R.O., HO 107/905.
[72] *V.C.H. Salop.* ii. 232; P.R.O., RG 10/2810.
[73] P.R.O., HO 107/905.
[74] S.R.O. 38/4, 11; Eyton par. rec. *passim*.
[75] Below, Wellington, Communications.
[76] Trinder, *Ind. Rev. Salop.* 225–6.
[77] C. R. Clinker, *Clinker's Reg. of Closed Stations 1830–1977* (Bristol, 1978), 137.
[78] Below, Lilleshall, Communications; Wellington, Communications.
[79] S.R.O., q. sess. rec. parcel 254, badgers', drovers', and alesellers' licensing bk.
[80] P.R.O., HO 107/1997.
[81] S.R.O., q. sess. rec. parcels 255–9, regs. of alesellers' recognizances, 1753–1828; *P.O. Dir. Salop.* (1856; 1870); *Kelly's Dir. Salop.* (1891; 1941).
[82] For the opening of Territorial Ho. see *Shrews. Chron.* 31

July 1964 (p. 11); for the Odd Fellows *Rep. Registrar Friendly Socs. 1871*, p. 108; *1872*, H.C. 323, p. 134 (1873), lxi.
[83] *V.C.H. Salop.* i. 332.
[84] *Bk. of Fees*, ii. 964, 972; Eyton, ix. 161.
[85] S.R.O. 513, box 8, inq. p.m. of Thos. Eyton (copy).
[86] P.R.O., C 142/332, no. 148; S.R.O. 327, boxes 4–6, suit r. and verdicts.
[87] Eyton, viii. 27.
[88] *Cartulary of Shrews. Abbey*, ed. U. Rees (1975), i, p. 29.
[89] Eyton, viii. 28.
[90] Ibid. 28–30; *Close R.* 1227–31, 588; 1237–42, 147.
[91] *Bk. of Fees*, ii. 964, 972; Eyton, viii. 30.
[92] *Rot. Hund.* (Rec. Com.), ii. 58.
[93] Eyton, viii. 33.
[94] Ibid.; *Cart. Shrews.* ii, p. 246.
[95] Eyton, viii. 34.
[96] *T.S.A.S.* 2nd ser. i. 181.
[97] *Cal. Pat.* 1345–8, 181; *Feud. Aids*, iv. 237.
[98] Eyton, viii. 34; *Sir Chris. Hatton's Bk. of Seals*, ed. L. C. Loyd and D. M. Stenton (1950), p. 148.
[99] *S.H.C.* N.S. x (2), 198.
[1] Eyton, viii. 35.

have died without issue.[2] The descent of the manor during the 15th century is not clear. Thomas Eyton, a tax collector in Shropshire in 1414 and 1415,[3] was lord between 1420 and 1431[4] but his relationship to his 14th-century predecessors and to the 16th-century lords of Eyton is uncertain.[5]

Lewis Eyton, referred to from 1491,[6] was in possession of the manor by 1506.[7] He was dead by 1514[8] and was succeeded by his son Henry, who was lord in 1529 and died in 1537.[9] The manor passed to Henry's grandson and heir Thomas Eyton, who held it until his death in 1582, when his son Robert obtained livery.[10] Robert died in 1604 having devised his estates to his son Richard Eyton for life.[11] On Richard's death without issue the manor passed to his uncle William Eyton (d. 1612);[12] William was succeeded by his nephew Philip Eyton (kt. 1619), who obtained general livery in 1614.[13] On Sir Philip's death in 1636 Eyton passed to his son Thomas (kt. 1642), a royalist whose estates were sequestrated in 1647; he compounded in 1650 and died in 1659.[14] The estate then passed to his son Philip (d. 1672), who conveyed Eyton Hall and demesne to his mother Margaret (d. 1679) for her life.[15] Eyton passed successively to Philip's sons Philip (d. 1689) and Soudley (d. 1701).[16] On Soudley's death without issue the estate passed to his uncle, the Revd. John Eyton of Wellington (d. 1709),[17] who was succeeded by his son Soudley, a minor.[18]

On Soudley Eyton's death without issue in 1719[19] the manor passed to his brother Thomas and thereafter until 1904 Eyton passed from father to son,[20] the following being lords: Thomas (d. 1776); Thomas (d. 1816), banker and receiver-general of the county;[21] Thomas (d. 1855); Thomas Campbell (d. 1880), a distinguished naturalist;[22] Thomas Slaney (d. 1899); and Ralph Aglionby Slaney (d. 1904). On R. A. S. Eyton's death the estates at Eyton and Bratton passed to his mother Isabel Sarah Dashwood Eyton (née Ruxton), who married her first husband's cousin, Archibald Cumberland Eyton, in 1907. Mrs. Eyton remained lady of the manor until her death in 1941 and Eyton then passed to her widower, who died without issue in 1954. He was succeeded

by his kinsman, Charles Llewellyn Grant Morris-Eyton, great-grandson of Isabel by her first marriage.[23]

The estate remained intact until 1963 when Eyton Hall and Eyton farm were sold to R. G. Murphy of Shifnal, chairman of the Wrekin Brewery Co.[24] Eyton House farm and other property in the parish were purchased from the trustees of the Eyton estate by T. H. Udale & Sons, who later bought Eyton farm from Murphy's son, R. G. R. Murphy of Eyton Hall.[25]

No trace of the medieval manor house survives. It is thought to have stood at the north end of the village near the church,[26] its existence being recorded in the name of Eyton House Farm, the house described in 1776 as 'the capital messuage called Eyton Hall'.[27] Thomas Eyton (d. 1776) had moved his seat to Wellington by 1757[28] and the old hall at Eyton had become ruinous by 1763.[29] The family remained in Wellington until 1816 when, after his father's suicide, Thomas Eyton (d. 1855) returned to live in Eyton.[30] By 1825 he had built the central five-bayed portion of the present Hall by enlarging an 18th-century farmhouse of three bays.[31] The north and south wings were added later in the century,[32] probably by T. C. Eyton (d. 1880), who also built a galleried museum wing on the west and imparked c. 70 a. south-east of Eyton Hall and stocked it with fallow deer. A half-mile drive, lined by a walnut avenue, led to the house through the park from the south.[33] After 1963 the avenue was felled and the house reduced in size.

The Eytons' interest in the manor of Horton, more especially in those parts (the Hoo and Horton's wood) that became the township of Hortonwood in Eyton parish, is substantiated by their grants of land and easements in the vicinity of Humber brook at Lubstree moor from c. 1200 to the later 16th century.[34] Peter of Eyton owned wood in Horton in 1271,[35] and in 1620 the family consolidated its landed property in Horton's wood. The Eytons are not, however, known to have owned land in Horton's wood after the 17th century. Hoo Hall in Preston parish and 24 tenements in Preston, Horton's wood, and the Hoo were sold in 1659 by Sir Thomas Eyton's widow, Margaret, and son, Philip, to Edmund

[2] S.P.L., MS. 2788, p. 276.
[3] *Cal. Fine R.* 1413–22, 85, 120.
[4] S.R.O. 972, box 225, deed of 1420; *Feud. Aids*, iv. 248, 270.
[5] Thos. is not named in *Visit. Salop 1623*, i (Harl. Soc. xxviii), 180–2, or Burke, *Land. Gent.* (18th edn.), iii. 308–10. In those sources the 16th-cent. lds. are said to descend from Humph. Eyton, bro. of John (II). Thos. is tentatively placed as a s. of Humph. in S.P.L., MS. 2788, p. 284.
[6] S.P.L., MS. 2788, p. 284.
[7] S.R.O. 513, box 1, ct. r.
[8] Deed recited in S.R.O. 513, box 8, deed of 1529.
[9] Ibid.; Eyton, viii. 36; P.R.O., E 150/858, no. 2.
[10] S.R.O. 513, box 8, inq. p.m. of 1582 (copy).
[11] P.R.O., C 142/292, no. 192.   [12] Ibid. /332, no. 148.
[13] S.R.O. 513, box 8, deed.
[14] *T.S.A.S.* 3rd ser. viii. 339, 345, 350–60.
[15] S.R.O. 513, box 8, deed of 1659.
[16] S.R.O. 665/1/2, 5.
[17] S.P.L., MS. 289, ff. 27–33.
[18] S.R.O. 327, box 6, Hinstock man. suit r. 1705–25.
[19] S.P.L., MS. 2788, p. 287.
[20] Burke, *Land. Gent.* (18th edn.), iii. 308–9.
[21] W. R. Ward, *Eng. Land Tax in 18th Cent.* (1953), 165; L. S. Pressnell, *Country Banking in the Ind. Rev.* (1956), 394;

Shrews. Chron. 26 Jan. 1816.
[22] D.N.B.
[23] Burke, *Land. Gent.* (18th edn.), iii. 308–9.
[24] *Daily Telegraph*, 26 June 1963, 22; *Shropshire Mag.* July 1963, 54.
[25] Inf. from Mrs. T. H. Udale.
[26] *T.S.A.S.* 3rd ser. viii. 348; *Shropshire Mag.* Jan. 1953, 19.
[27] S.R.O. 665/1/11, where Ric. Bellis is given as tenant. Identification with Eyton Ho. farm is suggested ibid. /1/284, 286.
[28] S.R.O., q. sess. rec. box 260, regs. of gamekeepers 1711–79, 1788–98; ibid. parcel 261, reg. of gamekeepers 1799–1807.
[29] S.R.O. 665/1/5850.
[30] Ibid. /1/6018; W. Hughes, *Sheriffs of Salop. 1831–86* (Shrews. 1886), 25.
[31] S.R.O. 665/1/286; C. & J. Greenwood, *Map of Salop.* (1827).
[32] S.P.L., J. H. Smith colln. no. 283.
[33] S. Bagshaw, *Dir. Salop.* (1851), 393; O.S. Map 6", Salop. XXXVI. NW. (1890 edn.); F. Leach, *County Seats of Salop.* (Shrews. 1891), 275.
[34] Eyton, viii. 29; S.P.L., Deeds 18633; S.R.O. 38/96.
[35] P.R.O., E 32/147, m. 6.

Waring,[36] the Anabaptist sheriff of Shropshire.[37] On Waring's death in 1682 the property was divided equally between his daughters, Hannah, who that year married George Ashby of Quenby (Leics.), and Elizabeth, wife of William Colemore. Hannah's share was sold in 1719 to Richard Higgins of Wappenshall, from whom it was purchased by the trustees of Preston hospital in 1731. At the same date the trustees also acquired Elizabeth's moiety.[38] The hospital enlarged its holding in the township in 1750 by buying two tenements, former Eyton family property, from Humphrey Pitt of Shifnal.[39]

By 1772 the trustees owned the whole of Hortonwood township except c. 30 a. near Hortonwood Farm.[40] The hospital remained the principal landowner until the mid 20th century; c. 1937 and in 1942 extensive areas were bought by the War Department for the construction of the Central Ordnance Depot, Donnington, and a further 7 holdings totalling 301 a. in Hortonwood and Preston were sold by the trustees c. 1953.[41] Between 1973 and 1978 much land in the township was purchased by Telford development corporation for Hortonwood industrial estate.[42]

ECONOMIC HISTORY. In 1086 Eyton township was assessed at 3 hides, the main feature then, as later, being the high proportion of the land that was in demesne. There were 2 ploughteams on the demesne while the 2 villeins and 1 bordar who were mentioned held only ½ team. The estate's value had dropped from 33s. in 1066 to 20s. at the time of the Domesday survey, and there was potential for a further 1½ team to be employed.[43]

Before the 19th century the pattern of land use was dominated by the division between the higher, better drained ground in the south and west of the township, where the community's arable land was concentrated, and the wet, low-lying Weald Moors in the north, which provided extensive reserves of pasture and meadow. In the late 16th and the early 17th century the arable area was organized as three open fields, the area under crop in any one year being divided between the winter field, ploughed at Michaelmas, and the Lent field, ploughed at the feast of St. Chad (2 March).[44] In the 17th century the three fields were known as Holt field, north-west of the village, Little field, south-west of the village beside Bratton brook, and Dossett field, south-east of the village in the area of the later Eyton Hall deer park. The fields still lay open in 1635 but had been inclosed by 1694.[45] There was more arable in Mill field, on the edge of the Weald Moors, where ploughed out ridge and furrow was visible in 1975.[46]

Concern over the boundaries between Eyton

and neighbouring estates in the Weald Moors in 1231[47] perhaps suggests that pressure on the reserves of pasture and meadow was beginning to be felt. In the early 15th century the lord of Eyton appears to have encouraged clearance and improvement in the area by granting land in the Weald Moors on long lease, rent free for the first eight years while the tenants cleared scrubland.[48] By the late 16th century a band of 'pastures several' in Eyton township flanked the still unimproved part of the Weald Moors known as Rough moor, on which common rights were claimed by Wrockwardine, Eyton, Kynnersley, Wappenshall, and Preston.[49] In 1650 the inhabitants of

TABLE V

EYTON UPON THE WEALD MOORS: LAND USE,
LIVESTOCK, AND CROPS

	1867	1891	1938	1965
Percentage of grassland	52	75	83	34
arable	48	25	17	66
Percentage of cattle	18	28	32	21
sheep	68	62	52	44
pigs	14	10	16	35
Percentage of wheat	54	39	58	66
barley	43	47	15	33
oats	3	10	27	1
mixed corn & rye	0	4	0	0
Percentage of agricultural land growing roots and vegetables	15	8	8	23

Sources: P.R.O., MAF 68/143, no. 14; /1340, no. 10; /3880, Salop. no. 231; /4945, no. 231.

Eyton and Bratton were said to have encroached 300 a. in the Weald Moors.[50] The inclosure of Eyton moor and adjacent areas was completed in the 19th century under the Wildmoors Inclosure and Drainage Act of 1801.[51] Most of the land north of the canal remained under grass until further drainage after the Second World War enabled it to be converted to arable.[52] Conversion to arable at that period, notable in other parts of the parish, reversed a trend of the later 19th and earlier 20th century whereby grassland and cattle farming had increased considerably at the expense of arable. Sugar beet became an important crop[53] after the Allscott factory opened in 1927.

[36] Staffs. R.O., D. 1287/13/11/1.
[37] V.C.H. Salop. iii. 109, 253; S.P.R. Lich. iii (3), p. iii.
[38] Staffs. R.O., D. 1287/13/11/1.
[39] Ibid. /13/3/8; /13/11/2.
[40] Ibid. /13/1/1, 5.
[41] T.D.C., deed pkts. 907, 1104.
[42] T.D.C., Hortonwood farm, Orchard farm, Trench farm, and Hoo Hall deeds.
[43] V.C.H. Salop. i. 332.
[44] S.R.O. 513, box 1, ct. r. 1587; S.R.O. 665/1/260.
[45] L.J.R.O., B/V/6, Eyton, 1635, 1694; cf. S.R.O. 665/1/

280, 286.
[46] L.J.R.O., B/V/6, Eyton, 1635, 1694; Potato Mktg. Bd. photos. (1975), nos. 3604, 3606 (copies in S.P.L.).
[47] Close R. 1227–31, 588–9.
[48] S.R.O. 972, box 225, deed of 1420.
[49] S.R.O. 38/1, 8, 9; T.S.A.S. liv. 255–326.
[50] T.S.A.S. lxiii. 8.
[51] 41 Geo. III, c. 77 (Local and Personal); S.R.O. 3121/1; O.S. Area Bk. (1882), Eyton.
[52] Inf. from T. H. Udale & Sons Ltd., Eyton Ho. Farm.
[53] P.R.O., MAF 68/3880, Salop. no. 231; /4945, no. 231.

Woodland survived in the south-west corner of the township at Shawbirch in 1626.[54] That may have been the wood of Eyton mentioned in 1235.[55] Little woodland remained in Eyton by the late 18th century[56] but between *c.* 1805 and 1825 a number of plantations were made, mainly with a mixture of oak and ash but with some larch; most of them survived in 1979 as scrubby woodland.[57]

A high proportion of the township remained in demesne in the early 17th century. In 1635 there was only one ploughteam in the parish and that belonged to the lord of the manor, Sir Philip Eyton;[58] in 1646 the demesne was valued at £160 while the rental value of the remainder of the township, divided into several small tenements, was only £38 6s. 11d.[59]

By *c.* 1680 the estate, including the demesne, was let as 13 holdings, of which 7 were held on leases for lives,[60] but some land in Eyton was farmed by the lord in 1709.[61] By 1776 the whole estate consisted of 11 landed tenements and 7 cottages.[62] The pattern of land holding underwent considerable change during the late 18th and the early 19th century, particularly after 1816 when Thomas Eyton went to live in Eyton. The acreage held in hand by the lords of the manor rose from 92 a. *c.* 1785 to 250 a. in 1816, 397 a. in 1818, and 409 a. in 1829.[63] Most of it (337 a. in 1829) was farmed from the home farm, Eyton Farm, where a courtyard of buildings had been built *c.* 1800.[64] It was managed by a bailiff during the 1840s and 1850s[65] but had been leased out by 1871.[66]

By 1840 the remaining land in the township had been consolidated into five farms: Eyton House farm (264 a.), Shawbirch farm (120 a.), and three smaller holdings in Eyton village of 87 a., 30 a., and 15 a.[67] Further consolidation took place during the 20th century and by *c.* 1965 most land in the township belonged to two large holdings, Eyton House farm, which had absorbed the land of the smaller holdings in the village, and Eyton farm, to which the land of Shawbirch farm had been added before 1929. In 1979 both Eyton farm and Eyton House farm were run by T. H. Udale & Sons Ltd.[68]

Eyton mill, first recorded in 1506,[69] stood north-east of the village on Hurley brook. The brook was supplemented by water from a branch of Bratton brook that had been diverted to feed the mill by 1769.[70] In 1659 there were said to be 4 water corn mills under one roof in Eyton[71] and 3 mills were mentioned in 1744 and 1776.[72] During the early 19th century the mill was let with a farm of over 80 a.[73] but in the 1850s and from *c.* 1890 until *c.* 1907, when grain ceased to be ground, it was run by the tenant of Eyton farm.[74]

Farming was always the main activity in the township and the high proportion of agricultural labourers in the village in the 19th century reflected the concentration of land into large holdings. Eleven of the 25 heads of household in the township in 1861 were hired farm workers.[75] Most other inhabitants of the village between 1841 and 1871 worked at the various ancillary occupations associated with an agricultural community.[76]

Hortonwood's name suggests that the township originated as woodland belonging to the vill of Horton. It is probably to be identified with the ½ league of woodland and a hay that were recorded in Horton in 1086.[77] The boundaries of the detached parts of Eyton upon the Weald Moors, Preston upon the Weald Moors, and Wrockwardine in that area required clarification in 1238.[78] Assarting in the wood of Horton is recorded in 1271.[79] Woodland containing oak, ash, crab, and yew survived in 1616, carefully preserved by the Eytons within fences and quickset hedges; its major economic value was as pasture for tenants on the Eyton family's estate, and there was 'great store' of timber.[80] The wooded area may then have been concentrated in the east of the township where there was a demesne wood called the 'Hakles' in 1587.[81] In 1616 Horton's wood contained a number of cottages old and new, some of which had been erected during Robert Eyton's lordship (1582–1604).[82] By 1635 eleven cottages in Horton's wood had each had 4 a. allotted to them, a fact that may indicate a period of active woodland clearance in the early 17th century.[83]

The pattern of small farms, which survived into the 19th century appears to have been established by 1659. The land in Horton's wood and Preston, sold by the Eyton family in that year, consisted of 24 small tenements, mostly let on rack rents at an average rent of £4 16s. 4d., in addition to the 'Hakelyes' let for £25 a year, and the demesnes of Hoo Hall.[84] In 1772 the township contained 12 holdings, of which 7 were farms of 30–70 a. and 5 were smallholdings under 15 a.[85] Despite the growth of industrial settlement at Trench in the 19th century the farming pattern remained substantially unchanged. None of the 9 farmers in the township in 1871 occupied more than 70 a.,[86] and

[54] S.R.O. 1224/1/1.
[55] Eyton, ix. 145.
[56] S.R.O. 665/1/283.
[57] Ibid. /1/284, 286, 335.
[58] L.J.R.O., B/V/6, Eyton, 1635.
[59] *T.S.A.S.* 3rd ser. viii. 350–1.
[60] S.R.O. 665/1/279.
[61] *Yeomen and Colliers in Telford*, ed. B. Trinder and J. Cox (1980), p. 336.
[62] S.R.O. 665/1/11.
[63] Ibid. /1/283–4; S.P.L., MS. 6756.
[64] S.R.O. 665/1/283–4, 286.
[65] P.R.O., HO 107/1997; *P.O. Dir. Salop.* (1856), 53.
[66] S.R.O. 2600/1.
[67] S.P.L., MS. 6756, p. 236.
[68] *Kelly's Dir. Salop.* (1929), 104; inf. from Mrs. T. H. Udale.
[69] S.R.O. 513, box 1, ct. r.
[70] S.R.O. 665/1/280, 307.

[71] S.R.O. 513, box 8, deed.
[72] S.R.O. 665/1/8, 11.
[73] S.P.L., MS. 6756, pp. 226–7, 233, 236.
[74] *P.O. Dir. Salop.* (1856); *Kelly's Dir. Salop.* (1891; 1905; 1909).
[75] P.R.O., RG 9/1900. The Eyton Hall household is excluded from the calculation.
[76] Ibid.; RG 10/2810; HO 107/905, 1997.
[77] *V.C.H. Salop.* i. 332.
[78] *Close R.* 1237–42, 147.
[79] P.R.O., E 32/147, m. 6.
[80] S.R.O. 665/1/256.
[81] S.R.O. 513, box 1, ct. r. The wood is identified from the name 'Hackles Yate' *c.* 1630: S.R.O. 38/11.
[82] S.R.O. 665/1/256.
[83] L.J.R.O., B/V/6, Eyton, 1635.
[84] Staffs. R.O., D. 1287/13/11/1.
[85] Ibid. /13/1/1, 5.
[86] P.R.O., RG 10/2810.

the holdings remained small on the break-up of the Preston hospital estate in 1953.[87]

The only commercial activity in the township, before the construction of the industrial estate (opened 1979),[88] was concentrated at Trench, the roadside settlement that straddled the boundary between Hortonwood and Wrockwardine Wood townships.[89]

LOCAL GOVERNMENT. As a member of the barony of Wem, Eyton owed suit, probably from *c.* 1245, to the leet court of the barony held at Hinstock. In the late 15th century the townships of Eyton, Horton, and Bratton made presentments together at the Hinstock leet but by 1540 separate presentments were made for each township. The constables of Eyton and Horton continued to appear at Hinstock as late as 1851.[90]

Rolls of the court baron of Eyton survive for 1359, 1360, 1362, 1422, and 1587. In the 14th century the court's jurisdiction covered Bratton (in Wrockwardine) and at least part of Horton in addition to Eyton; by 1506 Malinslee (in Dawley), for which separate courts had been held in the 14th century, was also included. The court's work mostly concerned agricultural matters, the roll for 1587 recording detailed pains governing husbandry in each of the four townships. Admissions to copyhold land in Horton were enrolled in 1359 and 1422. There were no references to the appointment of manorial officers, except for the election of separate constables for the townships of Bratton, Eyton, and Horton in 1506. The 1506 court, however, was unusual in being a leet held for Eyton.[91]

The appointment of an overseer of the poor in Eyton parish is recorded from 1724[92] and two overseers were appointed annually by 1809.[93] The appointment of a churchwarden is recorded from 1764 to 1884, two wardens being appointed from 1885. In the later 18th century the office of churchwarden was served alternately by parishioners living in Eyton and Hortonwood townships.[94]

In addition to weekly cash payments to the poor, the parish occasionally provided clothing and footwear, house repairs, and medical treatment during the 18th century. Communion money and the church offertory were also distributed, in small amounts, mainly to widows, in the late 18th and the mid 19th century.[95] The parish poor appear to have been concentrated in the industrial settlement at Trench Lane: in 1742 the overseer had to make five journeys to Trench to order the poor there to bring in their certificates.[96]

The parish was in Wellington poor-law union 1836–1930.[97]

Eyton civil parish and the Hoo, the detached portion of the parish transferred to Wellington in 1884, became part of Wrekin highway district in 1863 and were part of Wellington rural district from 1894 until 1974. Hortonwood, which had been transferred to Wrockwardine Wood C.P. in 1884, became part of Oakengates urban district on its creation in 1898. Both parts of the ancient parish were included from 1974 within the district of the Wrekin. Shawbirch, in Eyton C.P., Hortonwood, and the Hoo were included in 1968 in the designated area of Telford new town.[98]

CHURCH. Eyton church was recorded in 1336 when William of Kynardeseye was instituted on the death of the previous rector.[99] Its description as a chapel in the mid 16th century[1] suggests that its parochial status remained uncertain; it had perhaps originated as a manorial chapel founded by the lords of Eyton. The parishioners of Eyton were buried at Wellington until the mid 19th century,[2] a fact that suggests that the parish originated as a chapelry in Wellington parish. Nevertheless incumbents of Eyton were consistently described as rectors from 1336 and the independent parochial status of the church is not in question after the mid 16th century. John Eyton, lord of Eyton, presented to the living in 1336[3] and the advowson descended with the manor until the living was united with the vicarage of Wellington, of which the Eyton family were also patrons, in 1767.[4]

A proportion of the greater tithes in Eyton township was appropriated to the owners of Wellington rectorial tithes.[5] In 1635 Sir Philip Eyton paid two thirds of the tithe of his estate at Eyton (the whole township) to the rector of Eyton, the other third being paid to Wellington 'parish'.[6] As late as 1736 the rector of Eyton collected tithes from the whole of Eyton township and made an annual payment of £5 14s. to St. John Charlton in lieu of 'the tithes of Eyton which are in the parish of Wellington'.[7] Tithes were paid in kind except for the tithe hay of the part of the Weald Moors in Eyton township, for which a modus of 7s. 6d. was paid from at least 1698.[8]

The glebe, which in 1635 consisted of a croft, a piece of meadow, and a number of small parcels of arable scattered in the open fields, had been consolidated by 1694 into two contiguous closes totalling 13½ a. In addition the rector held a number of cottages in Eyton township, given as 5 in 1635 and as 3 from 1694. During the in-

[87] T.D.C., Trench farm and Hortonwood farm deeds.
[88] Below, Hadley, Econ. Hist.
[89] Trinder, *Ind. Rev. Salop.* (1981), 198; above, intro.
[90] S.R.O. 327, boxes 4–5, ct. verdicts, 1478, 1484, 1540–5, 1590–1600, 1708–1851; *V.C.H. Salop.* iii. 51–2.
[91] S.R.O. 513, box 1, ct. r.
[92] Par. rec., overseers' acct. bk. 1724–52.
[93] Ibid. poor rate bks. 1809–13, 1845–8, 1859–64, 1864–8.
[94] Ibid. chwdns.' acct. bks. 1766–1806, 1869–1960.
[95] Ibid. overseers' accts. 1778–90; collections acct. bk. 1838–54.
[96] Ibid. overseers' acct. bk. 1724–52.
[97] V. J. Walsh, 'Admin. of Poor Laws in Salop. 1820–55' (Pennsylvania Univ. Ph.D. thesis, 1970), 150 (copy in S.R.O.); *Kelly's Dir. Salop.* (1929), 103.

[98] S.R.O., q. sess. order bk. 1861–9, p. 127; *V.C.H. Salop.* ii. 217, 223, 225, 228; sources cited ibid. iii. 169 n. 29; *Dawley New Town (Designation) Amendment (Telford) Order 1968* (Stat. Instr. 1968, no. 1912), map accompanying Explanatory Note.
[99] L.J.R.O., B/A/1/2, f. 214v.
[1] Ibid. B/V/1/2, 3, 7.
[2] Ibid. B/A/2(i)/A–D, f. 90 and v.
[3] Ibid. B/A/1/2, f. 214v.
[4] Ibid. B/A/2(i)/A–D, ff. 90v.–91v.
[5] Below, Wellington, Churches; Man. and Other Est.; S.R.O. 625, box 10, deeds of 1628, 1665.
[6] L.J.R.O., B/V/6, Eyton, 1635.
[7] Ibid. 1736.
[8] Ibid. 1698.

cumbency of John Manning, mentioned 1597–1605, the glebe and tithes were farmed to David Roe of Eyton for £7 13s. 4d. a year.[9] In 1807 the glebe was given to Thomas Eyton, lord of the manor, in exchange for property in Wellington.[10] In 1635 there was no parsonage house at Eyton, nor had there been one in living memory.[11]

The living was valued at £2 4s. 8d. in 1535;[12] at £26 in 1655;[13] and at 'near' £40 c. 1693.[14] It was reputed to be worth between £40 and £50 on the eve of the union with Wellington in 1767.[15]

Most of those pre-Reformation rectors whose names are recorded were probably Shropshire men[16] and few seem to have been graduates.[17] After the Reformation the living was sometimes held in plurality, intermittently being held with Wellington and thus effecting an unofficial union of the livings before they were legally united in 1767. Such a union was mooted in 1655[18] but almost a century earlier John Gryce, mentioned as rector 1553–84,[19] was also vicar of Wellington 1562–81 or later.[20] John Manning and his successor Richard Felton, rector 1606–20 or later,[21] both employed curates.[22] The few post-Reformation rectors unbeneficed elsewhere did not stay long. The exception was Richard Lane, 1635–65 or later.[23] He was succeeded by a series of pluralists. John Eyton, rector 1675–1709 and lord of the manor from 1701, was vicar of Wellington from 1689.[24] He lived at Wellington but officiated in both churches, although Eyton church was also served during his incumbency by Samuel Pritchard, rector of Preston upon the Weald Moors.[25] He was succeeded as rector by his cousin's son, Robert Eyton (1709–18), later archdeacon of Ely, who likewise held the living of Wellington from 1713.[26]

Vincent Corbet, rector 1720–50,[27] was also rector of Moreton Corbet[28] and employed curates at Eyton during his long incumbency. Richard Tourneor, mentioned as curate 1725–39,[29] was a graduate and son of a rector of Waters Upton,[30] while Richard Smith, mentioned as curate 1747–51,[31] another young graduate, became vicar of

Wellington in 1751, rector of Eyton in 1760, and first incumbent of the united living of Wellington with Eyton until his death in 1773.[32] Corbet's successor, John Fieldhouse, 1750–60,[33] also employed curates at Eyton, among them another future incumbent of the combined living.[34]

As well as burying at Wellington the inhabitants of Horton's wood also christened there in the early 17th century.[35] During the late 18th century one service was held at Eyton each Sunday[36] and in 1799 additional services were held on Christmas Day and Good Friday and communion, taken by 16 communicants, was given four times a year.[37] Use of the church increased temporarily between 1787 and 1790 when weddings for Wellington parish were held at Eyton during the demolition and rebuilding of Wellington church.[38] The frequency of services remained the same in 1824 and 1843 as in the previous century.[39] In 1871 evening services were held fortnightly in addition to the weekly Sunday morning service, and in 1888 the vestry resolved that a regular Sunday afternoon service should be instituted.[40] After the Second World War services were held once each Sunday with communion once a month given to 10–20 communicants. Preachers regularly included lay readers in addition to the rector or curate.[41]

The church of ST. CATHERINE,[42] replacing one that was so called in 1366,[43] is built of red brick with sandstone dressings and has an apsidal chancel with north vestry, nave, and west tower. Of the earlier church, demolished c. 1743, little is known except that it was notably small.[44] Some window glass, however, including an early 16th-century depiction of St. Catherine, was reset in the later church and survives. The church of 1743,[45] also small and plain, consisted only of the nave and tower. Contemporary with it are a small west gallery, a pulpit whose sounding board is now the vestry table, and the font and font cover. The nave benches were cut down from the 18th-century oak box pews in 1902.[46] The apse and, probably, the vestry were added in 1850 and the

[9] Ibid. 1635, 1694. For Manning's dates see L.J.R.O., B/V/1/23–4.

[10] L.J.R.O., B/A/2(i)/F, pp. 19–30.

[11] Ibid. B/V/6, Eyton, 1635.

[12] Valor Eccl. (Rec. Com.), iii. 186.

[13] T.S.A.S. xlvii. 10–11.

[14] W.S.L., H.M. 36 (shorthand transcribed by Mr. N. W. Tildesley).

[15] L.J.R.O., B/A/2(i)/A–D, f. 90 and v.

[16] e.g. Wm. de Kynardeseye (1336) and Thos. Patiton of Wenlock (1341): ibid. B/A/1/2, ff. 214v., 218.

[17] A poss. exception was Thos. Newport, rector 1389 and 1391 (S.R.O. 972, box 225, deed of 1389; Cal. Pat. 1388–92, 244, 448), perh. the graduate rector of Pulverbatch 1394–1413 (V.C.H. Salop. viii. 139).

[18] T.S.A.S. xlvii. 10.

[19] Ibid. 2nd ser. xii. 322; L.J.R.O., B/V/1/2–3, 5, 7, 8, 11, 15.

[20] L.J.R.O., B/A/1/15, f. 40; B/V/1/13; T.S.A.S. 3rd ser. i. 260.

[21] T.S.A.S. 3rd ser. v. 349; L.J.R.O., B/V/1/28, 32, 37.

[22] L.J.R.O., B/V/1/23, 25, 32.

[23] T.S.A.S. 3rd ser. v. 355; 4th ser. iv. 180; Wellington par. reg. bur. 28 Oct. 1675 (transcript in S.P.L.).

[24] T.S.A.S. 3rd ser. v. 370; 4th ser. iv. 189–90.

[25] W.S.L., H.M. 36.

[26] S.P.L., MS. 2788, p. 287; T.S.A.S. 4th ser. v. 188–9.

[27] T.S.A.S. 4th ser. v. 192; L.J.R.O., B/A/1/21, p. 9.

[28] T.S.A.S. 4th ser. v. 192.

[29] Par. rec., overseers' acct. bk. 1724–52; L.J.R.O., B/V/6,

Eyton, 1730, 1736, 1739.

[30] Alum. Oxon. 1715–1886, iv. 1429; T.S.A.S. 4th ser. v. 191.

[31] Parrec., overseers' acct. bk. 1724–52; L.J.R.O., B/V/6, Eyton, 1748; B/A/4A/33.

[32] Alum. Oxon. 1715–1886, iv. 1318; T.S.A.S. 4th ser. v. 202, 204, 208.

[33] L.J.R.O., B/A/1/21, p. 9; T.S.A.S. 4th ser. v. 204.

[34] Steph. Panting, curate 1759 (L.J.R.O., B/V/6, Eyton), inst. 1778 (T.S.A.S. 4th ser. vi. 296).

[35] L.J.R.O., B/V/6, Eyton, 1635.

[36] Ibid. B/V/5, visit. return of 1772; B/A/2(i)/A–D, f. 90 and v.

[37] S.R.O. 3916/1/1.

[38] S.P.L., Eyton par. reg. transcript 1698–1812, iii, note facing p. 47.

[39] S.R.O. 3916/1/3, 6.

[40] Par. rec., visit. return of 1871; vestry min. bk. 1883– (in use), s.a. 1888.

[41] S.R.O. 3916/1/33; par. rec., services regs. 1944–62, 1962–79.

[42] Descr. based on S.P.L., MS. 372, vol. ii, p. 76; S.P.L., MS. 3065, no. 68; J. H. Smith colln., no. 82; Cranage, vii. 588–9; Pevsner, Shropshire, 129–30.

[43] S.H.C. N.S. x (2), 198.

[44] S.R.O. 2009/4.

[45] Date stone (restored). In 1796 date stone was on E. wall of ch.: B.L. Add. MS. 21236, f. 370b. A certif. for a rebuilding brief was issued in 1734: Orders of Q. Sess. ii. 84.

[46] Par. rec., acct. for ch. restoration, 1902.

nave roof was renewed without a ceiling in the late 19th century. The tower contains three bells of 1732[47] and an 18th-century clock, probably that mentioned in 1770.[48]

Apart from a silver-gilt paten of c. 1340, the plate consists of 17th- and 18th-century pieces, some pewter; an almsdish bears the arms of Eyton.[49]

The church had a very small graveyard, used only from 1860,[50] until the apex of land between the road and the drive to Eyton House Farm was consecrated in 1873.[51] It was extended by the consecration of a detached plot in 1951.[52]

The register of baptisms and marriages begins in 1698. Burials are registered from 1860.[53]

NONCONFORMITY. A Wesleyan society met at Hortonwood in 1824.[54] There was a Primitive Methodist society in the Oakengates and Wellington circuit at Eyton in 1865, when the steward was a shepherd.[55] The group ceased in 1870.[56]

EDUCATION. Eyton Council School originated as an unendowed day school supported by the lords of the manor. It was mentioned in 1818[57] and had been founded by Thomas Eyton (d. 1816), probably after 1799.[58] There were 20 boys and girls in 1833[59] and 27 in 1859.[60] Pupils paid

1d. to 3d. a week, according to their place of residence and parental circumstances; remaining costs were met by the Eyton family.[61] Control of the school passed to Wellington school board in 1894. Between 1894 and 1907 numbers on the register fluctuated between 35 and 50[62] but had dropped to 20 by 1946, when seniors transferred to Wellington Modern School.[63] In 1958 the school closed, the 10 pupils transferring to other schools.[64]

The school served a wider area than the parish: it had been founded for the children of cottage tenants on the Eyton estate[65] and in the later 19th century contained pupils from the hamlets of Bratton and Long Lane (in Wrockwardine) and Wappenshall (in Wellington).[66] Its character seems to have changed little by 1956, when 16 of the 19 children on the roll came from hamlets on the Eyton estate and the high proportion of farm labourers' children in the school resulted in a quick turnover of pupils.[67]

In 1838 the school was housed in a small cottage, since demolished, west of the village.[68] In 1859 it moved to a timber-framed house, formerly a farm, on the village street;[69] a new classroom was added in 1898.[70] After closure the building became two private dwellings.

CHARITIES FOR THE POOR. None known.

LILLESHALL

LILLESHALL village lies 4 km. south-west of Newport, with the Newport–Wellington road bypassing the village to the west.[71] The ancient parish boundaries are marked on the north and west by Headford and Humber brooks, which drain on the north-west into the Weald Moors, an area where the manorial boundaries (conterminous with those of the parish) required definition in the 13th and 16th centuries.[72] The southern boundary is marked by Watling Street, and a lane thence to the Woodhouse farm runs north for a short distance along the southernmost stretch of the eastern boundary.

Unaltered until 1898 the parish boundary enclosed a compact area of 6,175 a.[73] (2,499 ha.)

extending north from Watling Street to the Weald Moors. The land falls gradually from south-east to north-west, dropping c. 120 metres and then levelling out. Streams watering the centres of settlement flow north-west across the parish to drain into the Weald Moors at the boundary. There are two greatly contrasting areas. The larger is the agricultural north and east, centring on Lilleshall village. The south-west was densely occupied by coal mines and ironworks in the earlier 19th century, and a century later they were mostly derelict, leaving much of that area as an unsightly waste. In the south-west a small part of the parish was taken into Oakengates in 1898, and from 1968 Telford new town included the whole

[47] H. B. Walters, Ch. Bells of Salop. (Oswestry, 1915), 328.
[48] Par. rec., chwdns.' acct. bk. 1764–1806.
[49] S. A. Jeavons, Ch. Plate Archd. Salop (Shrews. 1964), pp. 27, 35, 45, 69, 71.
[50] Par. rec., bur. reg. 1860– (in use).
[51] Lich. Dioc. Regy., bps.' reg. R, p. 620.
[52] Par. rec., vestry min. bk. 1883– (in use), Apr. 1951.
[53] Par. rec., regs.; L.J.R.O., B/V/7, Eyton.
[54] S.R.O. 3767/XVII/A, E; 1824 circuit plan (copy in Hanley Ref. Libr., Stoke-on-Trent). Refs. kindly supplied by Mr. J. H. Lenton.
[55] S.R.O. 3038/1/1, pp. 6, 9; P.R.O., RG 9/1900.
[56] S.R.O. 3038/1/1, 15 June 1868; June 1870.
[57] Digest Educ. Poor, H.C. 224, p. 767 (1819), ix (2).
[58] P.R.O., ED 7/102, f. 295. No sch. was mentioned in 1799: S.R.O. 3916/1/1.

[59] Educ. Enq. Abstract, H.C. 62, p. 774 (1835), xlii.
[60] P.R.O., ED 7/102, f. 291.
[61] Ibid. ff. 291, 295.
[62] S.R.O. 559/XXIV/19/2; 665/1/5834.
[63] S.R.O. 916/9, p. 5.
[64] Ibid. p. 85; S.C.C. Mins. (Educ.) 1958–9, 45, 102.
[65] P.O. Dir. Salop. (1856), 53.
[66] P.R.O., ED 7/102, f. 291; S.R.O. 665/1/5834.
[67] S.R.O. 916/9.
[68] S.R.O. 746/4; 2009/1. The bldg. stood at O.S. Nat. Grid SJ 6505 1473.
[69] P.R.O., ED 7/102, f. 291.
[70] S.R.O. 665/1/5834.
[71] This art. was written 1979–80 and revised 1983.
[72] Below, Econ. Hist. (Agric.).
[73] O.S. Area Bk. (1882).

industrial area, with a view to its redevelopment. By 1983 the waste areas had been greatly improved by landscaping.

A small 1st-century Roman military installation, apparently surrounded by a later civil settlement, stood at Redhill in the south-east corner of the parish, where Watling Street crossed the summit of the hill.[74] It was probably Uxacona, named in the Antonine Itinerary.[75] Nearby are indications of both Iron Age and Roman occupation.[76] There is no evidence that Redhill was occupied beyond the Roman period.

In the early Middle Ages the sandstone slopes in the south probably supported unbroken woodland, the only remnant of which is Abbey wood. The extreme north was a waterlogged waste, though later reclaimed. From the early Middle Ages until the late 18th century the population therefore mostly lived and worked within a central drift-covered belt stretching from north-east to south-west between the less attractive areas[77] and including the villages of Lilleshall, Honnington, Muxton, and Donnington. Within the central belt, at its north-eastern end, a long outcrop of bare volcanic rock, Lilleshall Hill (132 metres above O.D.), rises dramatically some 60 metres above the surrounding fields.

The obelisk on Lilleshall Hill, designed by G. E. Hamilton, was begun in 1833 in memory of the 1st duke of Sutherland.[78] Its inscription was composed by the Revd. J. J. Blunt,[79] the vicar's son, later Lady Margaret professor of divinity at Cambridge.[80]

The remains of Lilleshall abbey were garrisoned for the Crown in the First Civil War and fell to Parliament in 1645 after long resistance.[81] A long depression north of the abbey is supposed to indicate the position of the attackers' siegeworks.[82] Already in 1598, however, the field where it lies was called the Knole,[83] a name suggesting surface irregularities.[84] A hoard of 522 coins, buried c. 1643, was found at Donnington in 1938.[85]

Annual Rogationtide perambulations, by the vicar and parishioners, of the township boundaries of Lilleshall and of Muxton and Donnington, were recorded from the 17th century,[86] when they were claimed as an ancient custom.[87] The proceedings, called 'bannering', usually lasted three days.[88] They were last recorded in 1797.[89]

Robin's (or Our Lady's) well, a 'pin' well near Lilleshall Grange, was restored c. 1909.[90]

Notable people connected with the parish, besides the lords of the manor, include the 15th-century religious writer John Mirk, canon of Lilleshall,[91] and Sir Gordon Richards, the champion jockey, born at Donnington Wood in 1904.[92]

COMMUNICATIONS. Two important thoroughfares served the parish from an early period. Watling Street formed its southern boundary, and in 1398 the canons of Lilleshall claimed that hospitality to travellers along it was a serious drain on their income.[93] The Lilleshall section was part of the length from Shrewsbury to Crackleybank that was, in 1726, among the first Shropshire roads to be turnpiked.[94] By 1808 there was a tollgate at Redhill.[95] The Lilleshall part was disturnpiked in 1875[96] and became a main road in 1878.[97] In 1931 the part then in St. George's civil parish was superseded as a main road by the St. George's bypass.[98] In 1983 the rest was part of the trunk road from the first part of the M 54[99] to the M 6.

The Wellington–Newport road crossed from south-west to north-east. It was evidently in use by 963 when, at a place called 'eotan ford', it crossed Headford brook, which formed the parish boundary in the north-east.[1] In the later Middle Ages the ford gave its name to one of Lilleshall's open fields. The road linked the parish's principal medieval settlements. Near the western parish boundary it was called Trench Way in 1288[2] and Trench Lane in 1717.[3] It was turnpiked in 1763.[4] By 1804 there were tollgates north and south of Lilleshall village, at the junction with the Edgmond road and at Haybrook bridge.[5]

Until the early 19th century a road from the southern end of Lilleshall village street led south-east, passing north of the grange house and the abbey, to Hilton (Staffs.), in Sheriffhales, where it joined the road from Shifnal to the London–Chester road. In 1717 it was called Manor Lane.[6] Between 1804 and 1813 the Lilleshall part was re-aligned to begin on the Wellington–Newport road at Honnington and run south of the Grange and abbey to Hilton.[7] It was turnpiked in 1823[8] and disturnpiked in 1867.[9] Called Lilyhurst Road

[74] T.S.A.S. lvii. 132–3; SA 1113.
[75] A. L. F. Rivet and C. Smith, Place-Names of Roman Brit. (1979), 482.
[76] At O.S. Nat. Grid SJ 7234 1105: SA 734.
[77] Geol. Surv. Map 1″, drift, sheet 153 (1929 edn.); Inst. Geol. Sciences Map 1/25,000 Telford (1978 edn.).
[78] Gent. Mag. ciii (2), 459; H. Colvin, Biog. Dict. Brit. Architects, 1600–1840 (1978), 383.
[79] T.S.A.S. i. 148.   [80] D.N.B.
[81] T.S.A.S. l. 166–8.
[82] SA 1112.
[83] Staffs. R.O., D. 593/H/14/1/1; S.R.O. 38/13.
[84] Eng. P.N. Elements (E.P.N.S.), i. 103.
[85] D.F. Allen, 'Wellington, Salop. 1938', Brit. Numismatic Jnl. xxvi. 92.
[86] S.R.O. 4462/CW/2, s.a. 1676–7, 1677–8, 1685–6, and passim.
[87] Ibid. s.a. 1687–8.
[88] Ibid. s.a. 1677–8, 1695–6; S.R.O. 4462/CW/3, pp. 5, 81.
[89] S.R.O. 4462/CW/3, p. 125.
[90] At O.S. Nat. Grid SJ 7294 1473: SA 739.
[91] D.N.B.

[92] G. Richards, My Story (1955), 10; Reg. of Persons Entitled to Vote: Mid or Wellington Div. of Co. of Salop (1904), p. 148, s.v. Richards, Nathan.
[93] Hist. MSS. Com. 4, 5th Rep., Sutherland, p. 450.
[94] 12 Geo. I, c. 9.
[95] R. Baugh, Map of Salop. (1808).
[96] Ann. Turnpike Acts Continuance Act, 1875, 38 & 39 Vic. c. 194 (Local).
[97] Highways and Locomotives (Amendment) Act, 1878, 41 & 42 Vic. c. 77.
[98] Below, Wombridge, Communications.
[99] Below, Wellington, Communications.
[1] Cart. Sax. ed. Birch, iii, no. 1119; T.S.A.S. lvi. 29.
[2] S.R.O. 972, box 220, deed.
[3] Ibid. parcel 234, middle map of Lilleshall.
[4] Below, Wellington, Communications.
[5] S.R.O. 38/15.
[6] S.R.O. 972, parcel 234, middle map of Lilleshall.
[7] Ibid. parcel 238, map of 1813; 38/15.
[8] 4 Geo. IV, c. 47 (Local and Personal).
[9] Ann. Turnpike Acts Continuance Act, 1867, 30 & 31 Vic. c. 121.

in 1949,[10] it was a minor road in 1983.

The road west from Lilleshall past Lubstree park to Preston upon the Weald Moors was probably the 'Lubbesty' mentioned in 1283[11] and the *via de Lubsty* of 1428–9.[12] The last element of the name is likely to be OE. *stig*, 'a path, a narrow road';[13] if so the road may be pre-Conquest. It seems to have existed by the early 13th century, when 'Hundefordehull' existed where the road crossed Humber brook,[14] presumably by a ford. The road was mapped *c.* 1580 as the way from Lilleshall to Wrockwardine.[15] In 1717 it was called Preston Way near Lilleshall and Kingstreet Way west of Donnington.[16] By 1817 that western part was called Humber Lane.[17]

Another road, in use by 1717,[18] ran NNW. from the north end of Lilleshall to Brockton and Edgmond. Willmore Lane, so called by 1717,[19] ran east from Lilleshall past Willmore Grange to Little Hales and Chetwynd Aston. It was in use to Little Hales by 1594.[20] In the 19th century, however, the part east of Willmore pool seems to have fallen into disuse.[21]

A lane north-west from Lilleshall, called Moor Lane by 1596,[22] ended in 1649 at Moor green on the edge of the Weald Moors.[23] About 1810 it was extended across the moors to Kynnersley,[24] and the new length was known by 1881 as Kynnersley Drive.[25]

The Donnington Wood Canal, the first in Shropshire, was built between *c.* 1765 and 1767 for Earl Gower & Co. It ran north-east from the Donnington Wood mines to the London–Chester road at Pave Lane (in Edgmond), where a coal wharf was built.[26] At the same time a branch was cut from Hugh's Bridge, on the main line, to Collier's End, at the Lilleshall limeworks. At Willmore bridge, on the branch, another branch was made northwards to limeworks at Pitchcroft (in Edgmond). The Pitchcroft branch itself had two short branches north-west to other parts of the Lilleshall limeworks.[27] Coal could travel from Donnington Wood via the branches to the lime-kilns, and lime and limestone to Donnington Wood or Pave Lane. After the Donnington Wood furn-aces opened in 1785 limestone could travel directly to them, and when the Old Lodge furnaces opened in 1825 a short connecting arm was cut to the main canal.[28] At Hugh's Bridge the limeworks branch, which was at a lower level than the main line, at first terminated in a tunnel, in which goods were raised and lowered between the levels through vertical shafts. By 1797 that arrangement had been superseded by an inclined plane.

The Donnington Wood end was joined *c.* 1788 to the Wombridge Canal, which provided a link with coal and ironstone workings at Wombridge, and from *c.* 1790 with the new Shropshire Canal. From 1794 the junction also gave indirect access to the new Shrewsbury Canal.[29]

The limeworks branch and its incline were last used in the 1870s.[30] Thereafter the main canal was little used north of Muxton Bridge,[31] and most of it closed in 1882.[32] South of Muxton Bridge the canal was redundant by 1904.[33]

The Humber Arm, an offshoot of the Newport branch of the Birmingham & Liverpool Junction Canal (part of the Shropshire Union Canal from 1846), lay wholly within the parish, beginning in the north-west corner and ending at the duke of Sutherland's Lubstree wharf on Humber Lane, which opened in 1844. The arm gave the Lil-leshall Co. a more direct outlet to the national canal network than before, and it carried out quantities of coal, pig iron, and fluxing limestone before the local railways opened. Tramways link-ed the wharf to the company's various works.[34] In 1870 the Shropshire Union Railways & Canal Co., anxious to divert traffic from its Trench incline, agreed to lease the wharf from the 3rd duke, and brought a revived traffic to the Humber Arm. The Lilleshall Co. then built a standard-gauge railway to replace the tramways. The 5th duke closed Lubstree wharf in 1922 when the S.U.R.C.C. was absorbed by the L.M.S.R., and the Humber Arm was formally abandoned in 1944.[35] In its last years Lubstree wharf was used for bringing in cheese from Cheshire and taking out coal, a traffic called the 'Cheshire run'.[36]

The S.U.R.C.C.'s Wellington–Stafford rail-way line passed through the parish. Its station at Donnington, opened in 1849,[37] was closed for passengers in 1964, and for freight in 1965.[38] Be-tween Donnington and Newport, however, the line was used for freight until 1969, and the Wellington–Donnington section afterwards re-mained open for the use of the Central Ordnance Depot and the Midland Iron Works, which had private sidings.[39]

GROWTH OF SETTLEMENT. Until the late 18th century the population was concentrated in the villages of Lilleshall, Honnington, Muxton,

[10] O.S. Map 1/25,000, SJ 71 (1951 edn.).
[11] P.R.O., C 143/6, no. 14.
[12] L.J.R.O., B/C/5, Lilleshall abbey acct. r. of 1428–9.
[13] *Eng. P.N. Elements* (E.P.N.S.), ii. 152.
[14] Eyton, viii. 258.
[15] *T.S.A.S.* liv, pl. facing p. 258.
[16] S.R.O. 972, parcel 234, N. and middle maps of Lil-leshall.
[17] B.L. Maps, O.S.D. 208.
[18] S.R.O. 972, parcel 234, N. map of Lilleshall.
[19] Ibid. middle map of Lilleshall.
[20] S.R.O. 38/104.
[21] C. & J. Greenwood, *Map of Salop.* (1827); O.S. Map 6", Salop. XXXI. SW. (1887 edn.).
[22] S.R.O. 38/109.   [23] S.R.O. 1910/486.
[24] S.R.O. 38/15; 972, parcel 233, Lilleshall map of 1816.
[25] O.S. Map 6", Salop. XXX. SE. (1886 edn.).
[26] Trinder, *Ind. Rev. Salop.* 126.

[27] Ibid.; S.R.O. 38/15; /17, f. 65.
[28] *Shropshire Mag.* May 1954, 21.
[29] C. Hadfield, *Canals of W. Midlands* (1969), 41; Trinder, op. cit. 126–7, 132, 138, 140–1.
[30] Hadfield, op. cit. 238; D. R. Adams and J. Hazeley, *Survey of the Church Aston – Lilleshall Mining Area* (Salop. Mining Club Acct. vii, 1970), 51.
[31] *Shropshire Mag.* May 1954, 21.
[32] Trinder, *Ind. Rev. Salop.* 260.
[33] *Shropshire Mag.* May 1954, 21.
[34] Trinder, op. cit. 253, 255–6.
[35] Hadfield, *Canals of W. Midlands*, 239, 242, 250–1.
[36] Inf. from the late Mr. R. W. Ward.
[37] R. Christiansen, *W. Midlands* (Regional Hist. of Rlys. of Gt. Brit. vii, 1973), 270.
[38] C. R. Clinker, *Clinker's Reg. of Closed Stations 1830–1977* (Bristol, 1978), 39.
[39] Ibid.; Christiansen, op. cit. 159, 271; local inf.

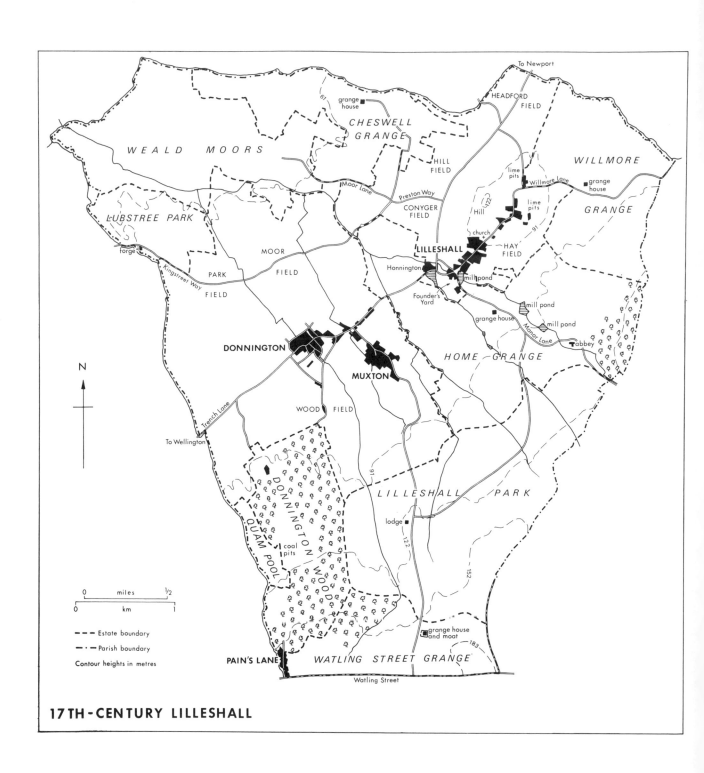

17TH-CENTURY LILLESHALL

and Donnington. There were 22 recorded inhabitants in 1086.[40] By the early 14th century growth had been considerable. There were c. 145 free tenants c. 1337 as well as neifs and the landless. Donnington had 33 per cent of the free tenants, Lilleshall 27 per cent, Honnington 22 per cent, and Muxton 18 per cent.[41] Population collapsed at the Black Death[42] and had not fully recovered by 1563, when there were 84 households.[43] Industrialization, mainly at Donnington Wood, caused the population to rise. In 1676 the Compton census recorded 428 adults.[44] There were c. 200 houses by 1772,[45] 2,060 inhabitants in 1801, and 3,987 by 1851. Thereafter there was little growth until the mid 20th century when Donnington was deliberately transformed by housing development. The population of Lilleshall civil parish rose from 2,611 in 1931 to 8,005 in 1951.[46] From the 1960s Muxton, Donnington, and Donnington Wood, as parts of Telford new town, expanded further, but more gradually. Lilleshall C.P. had 10,900 inhabitants in 1971, but by 1981 only 10,470 people lived within the 1971 boundary.[47]

The earliest surviving domestic buildings in the four ancient villages are nearly all timber-framed, but in the late 18th century timber gave way to brick or, in a few surviving examples, stone. A certain uniformity is apparent in the well built farms and Leveson-Gower estate cottages erected in the north and east parts of the parish in the 18th and 19th centuries. Many industrial houses, including several large blocks or 'barracks', were built in the south-west in the later 18th and earlier 19th century by Earl Gower & Co. and its successors. Less spacious and substantial than the estate cottages, few of them were fit for habitation in the 20th century, when nearly all were replaced by council houses. After the demolition of the Old Lodge in the 19th century, the parish possessed no house of notable size or distinction.

The neighbourhood of Lilleshall Hill, the hill from which the parish took its name,[48] was settled by 963, when Headford brook was the boundary between Church Aston and the 'lil sæte'.[49] By the 16th century the church and most of the village's houses lay along a street (called Church Road by 1959)[50] below the hill's south-eastern flank. The street is linked at each end to the Wellington–Newport road. In 1585 a fire, which began at the south end, destroyed 14 houses, then the greater part of the village, and reached at least as far as the church.[51] In 1983 several houses seemed to date from the rebuilding after the fire.[52] Until the 19th century the street ended at the south in a triangular space whence two short lanes led west

to Newport and Muxton via the Wellington–Newport road, and another ran south-eastwards to the abbey. In 1717 a water mill lay on the triangle's east side and houses on the other sides.[53] About 1810 the roads out of that space were closed: that leading to the abbey was taken farther south, and the village street was extended southwards to join it east of Honnington pool. The former open space and mill pond were then mostly absorbed into the grounds of the Hall.[54]

Few houses lay immediately north of the church in 1717, but farther north, in the southern half of Limekiln Lane (which continued the village street northwards), there were houses associated with the limeworks. They did not reach as far north as the junction with Willmore Lane,[55] but by 1804 houses had been built from that junction northwards along Limekiln Lane, to within about 250 metres of its junction with the Newport–Wellington road.[56] The new houses are likely to have been associated with an expansion of limeworking. Lilleshall Barracks were built c. 1810 on the western edge of the Collier's Side limestone quarry, and linked to the Wellington–Newport road by a new lane[57] (called Barracks Lane by 1959).[58] The barracks formed a row of 12 single-storeyed brick houses, with a wash house at each end and in the centre. The last occupant left in 1947[59] and the buildings were demolished c. 1965.[60] A smaller block farther along the lane, called the Nook, was built by 1813.[61] By 1979 it had been converted into one house.[62]

By 1804 the base of Lilleshall Hill was ringed by some 15 houses, all built since 1717 on the waste.[63] By 1841 there were over 20, occupied by agricultural labourers, miners, and people in other humble occupations.[64]

The settlement pattern at Lilleshall was little changed after the early 1800s. In the 1850s eight stone houses called Limeworks (or Stone) Row were built near the limeworks;[65] they were still occupied in 1980. By 1851, however, the works was employing fewer men, and employed gradually fewer until it closed.[66] There was hardly any more building on new sites until 1922, when six council houses were completed in Limekiln Lane.[67] The Woodlands council estate (18 houses) was completed in 1949 in Barracks Lane,[68] and another called Rock Acres (20 houses) in 1955 south-west of the church.[69] In 1965 more council houses were begun in Limekiln Lane,[70] and by 1980 some small private housing schemes had been carried out, mostly in and next to Limekiln Lane, but one (Church Meadow) immediately north-east of the church.

[40] V.C.H. Salop. i. 314.
[41] S.P.L., Deeds 16329.
[42] Below, Econ. Hist. (Agric.).
[43] B.L. Harl. MS. 594, f. 161v.
[44] T.S.A.S. 2nd ser. i. 84.
[45] L.J.R.O., B/V/5, visit. return of 1772.
[46] V.C.H. Salop. ii. 224.
[47] Figs. compiled in S.C.C. Planning Dept.
[48] E. Ekwall, Concise Oxf. Dict. Eng. P.N. (4th edn.), 298.
[49] Cart. Sax. ed. Birch, iii, no. 1119; T.S.A.S. lvi. 29.
[50] O.S. Map 6", SJ 71 SW. (1967 edn.).
[51] T.S.A.S. iii. 301; Salopian Shreds & Patches, iv. 37.
[52] Dept. of Environment, List of Bldgs.: Dist. of Wrekin (1983), pp. 145–7 (copy in S.C.C. Planning Dept.).
[53] S.R.O. 38/15; 972, parcel 234, middle map of Lilleshall.
[54] S.R.O. 38/15; 972, parcel 238, map of 1813.

[55] S.R.O. 972, parcel 234, middle map of Lilleshall.
[56] S.R.O. 38/15.
[57] Ibid.; 972, parcel 238, map of 1813.
[58] O.S. Map 6", SJ 71 NW. (1968 edn.).
[59] Adams and Hazeley, Survey, 38.
[60] Shropshire Mag. Apr. 1965, 40.
[61] S.R.O. 972, parcel 238, map of 1813.
[62] Adams and Hazeley, Survey, 38.
[63] S.R.O. 38/15; 972, parcel 234, middle map of Lilleshall.
[64] S.P.L., abstr. of census, 1841 (TS. [1975]).
[65] Ibid. 1851, 1861 (TSS. [1975]).
[66] Ibid. 1841–71 (TSS. [1975]).
[67] S.R.O., DA 23/114/1, pp. 136, 174.
[68] S.R.O., DA 26/114/4, p. 888.
[69] Ibid. /114/6, p. 1747.
[70] Adams and Hazeley, Survey, 35–6.

Honnington lies on the Wellington–Newport road where the lanes from the south end of Lilleshall formerly joined the road. The settlement existed by the 1270s,[71] and by 1404 was sometimes accounted a separate township.[72] In 1539 Honnington had more cottage holdings than any other township, and they formed a higher proportion of all its holdings than in any other township.[73] It therefore seems likely that most of the inhabitants lived by working part-time on the nearby home grange. Honnington declined between 1539 and 1717, perhaps because of the trend away from arable towards livestock;[74] the home grange needed fewer workers. By 1717 Honnington comprised merely one large farm and a few cottages.[75]

Muxton existed by 1186.[76] In 1717 it lay almost wholly in two neighbouring settlements.[77] The main group of houses extended c. 200 metres along Muxton Lane, which ran south-eastwards from the Wellington–Newport road. A few houses lay along a small western fork off the street (called Laneside by 1959).[78] The other settlement stretched some 250 metres along the main road either side of its junction with Muxton Lane. Westwards the houses reached nearly to Donnington. Eastwards the main-road settlement had been extended towards Honnington by 1804,[79] and by 1881 had reached the Haybrook.[80] In the 1950s new private houses along the road to Wellington extended far enough west to connect Muxton and Donnington.[81] There was otherwise little building on new sites before the 1960s, except as in-filling. By 1975, as part of Telford's development, a great many houses were built south of the main road on vacant land flanking the north end of Muxton Lane, both east (Sutherland Drive and its branches) and west (Fieldhouse Drive and its branches). Near the lane's southern end Granville Drive was added on the east.[82]

Donnington was mentioned c. 1180[83] and by 1539 was the most populous township, having 14 'able' men for the militia, against 11 in Lilleshall and 8 in Muxton.[84] In 1717 many of the houses stood close together along the Wellington–Newport road, from near Donnington Farm westwards to the junction with what was later School Road. Just as many houses stood in winding back lanes close to the main street.[85] Until the 1930s the pattern did not change.[86]

From 1931 to 1937 an estate of 118 council houses (named Jubilee Avenue in 1935)[87] was completed at Donnington on the south side of the Wellington–Newport road, west of the old village.[88] All but the first 10 were built for people from unfit dwellings in Donnington Wood and Lilleshall.[89] In 1939 council housing at Donnington for local people was postponed to meet the needs of incoming civilian employees at the Central Ordnance Depot, newly established there. Between 1940[90] and 1944[91] the council completed 844 houses for them[92] on land south of the Wellington–Newport road, from Jubilee Avenue westwards to the parish boundary. The development was first called New Donnington[93] but later simply Donnington.[94] From 1951 to 1954 a further 258 council houses were added to the part of New Donnington east of Wrekin Drive.[95] Development went as far east as the site of the former Donnington Barracks[96] (renamed School Road in 1951)[97] and as far south as the eastern part (named Queen Street in 1952, and later Queen's Road) of Oakengates Road, where unfit houses were cleared away. A few of the houses were reserved for incoming skilled workers, but most were allocated to local people. All but the first 36, in School Road, were prefabricated. Having thus reached the northern margin of the Donnington Wood area, where derelict workings made building difficult, New Donnington ceased to expand so easily and attention was turned to its internal development.[98] In the late 1960s, however, the estate began to grow southwards as part of Telford.[99]

After the Second World War the War Department created an estate for army personnel north-east of the Central Ordnance Depot.[1] In 1951 there were 2,137 such people living at Donnington.[2]

Until the late 18th century Donnington wood remained a large block of ancient woodland south-west of Donnington, with some small and dispersed settlements on its western side.[3] One of them, Quam Pool (mentioned in 1345),[4] lay partly in Wrockwardine Wood.[5] From the late 18th century to the early 19th Earl Gower & Co. and its successors converted the woodland piecemeal

[71] S.R.O. 972, box 220, deed of 1270 × 1275.
[72] S.P.L., MS. 4426.
[73] P.R.O., LR 2/184, ff. 4–13v.
[74] Below, Econ. Hist. (Agric.).
[75] S.R.O. 38/15; 972, parcel 234, middle map of Lilleshall; O.S. Map 6″, Salop. XXXVI. NE. (1928 edn.).
[76] Eyton, viii. 232.
[77] S.R.O. 972, parcel 234, middle map of Lilleshall.
[78] Names recorded on O.S. Map 6″, SJ 71 SW. (1967 edn.).
[79] S.R.O. 38/15.
[80] O.S. Map 6″, Salop. XXXVI. NE. (1890 edn.).
[81] O.S. Maps 1/25,000, SJ 71 (1951 edn.); 6″, SJ 71 SW. (1967 edn.).
[82] T.D.C. Telford Street Plan and Guide (1975).
[83] Eyton, viii. 229.
[84] L. & P. Hen. VIII, xiv (1), p. 288. The Lilleshall fig. presumably included Honnington.
[85] S.R.O. 972, parcel 234, middle map of Lilleshall.
[86] S.R.O. 38/15; O.S. Map 6″, Salop. XXXVI. NE. (1890, 1903, and 1928 edns.).
[87] S.R.O., DA 23/114/3, p. 102.
[88] Ibid. /114/2, pp. 176, 226; /114/3, pp. 64, 91, 101, 106; DA 26/100/7, p. 312.

[89] S.R.O., DA 23/114/3, pp. 68, 72; DA 26/100/7, p. 220.
[90] A. H. Fernyhough, Hist. of Royal Army Ordnance Corps 1920–1945 (R.A.O.C. [1967]), 409, 411.
[91] S.R.O., DA 26/114/2, p. 344.
[92] V. Shore, 'Survey of Donnington' (TS. 1962), p. 2 (copy in S.P.L.).
[93] O.S. Map 1/25,000, SJ 71 (1951 edn.).
[94] O.S. Map 6″, SJ 71 SW. (1967 edn.).
[95] S.R.O., DA 26/114/5, pp. 1172, 1316, 1404, 1559.
[96] Ibid. /114/4, p. 978.
[97] Ibid. p. 1164.
[98] Ibid. /114/5, pp. 1222, 1367, 1417, 1535–6, 1546–7, 1557, 1570–2.
[99] O.S. Map 6″, SJ 71 SW. (1967 edn.); T.D.C. Telford Street Plan and Guide (1975).
[1] O.S. Maps 1/25,000, SJ 71 (1951 edn.); 6″, SJ 71 SW. (1967 edn.).
[2] K. C. Riley, 'Changes in Population in the Wellington–Oakengates Conurbation 1801–1951' (London Univ. M.A. thesis, 1958), 175.
[3] S.R.O. 972, parcel 234, middle map of Lilleshall.
[4] Ibid. box 225, deed.
[5] Below, Wrockwardine Wood, intro.

to pits and works. Company housing was put up next to the scattered undertakings[6] and Donnington Wood (as the whole development was known) therefore had no natural focus. Its only coherence was in its inhabitants' dependence on the company. Workers' barrack blocks were nevertheless sometimes large enough to foster distinct communities. The biggest were Waxhill Barracks (built by 1804),[7] with 27 dwellings,[8] and Donnington Barracks, with some 67[9] (mostly built c. 1810).[10] Both communities formed dissenting congregations[11] and Donnington Barracks proved to be a centre of industrial unrest in 1842.[12] Granville Buildings, built in the mid 19th century, consisted of 40 dwellings.[13]

When Donnington Wood's industries declined in the later 19th century, new houses were not built and many existing ones became unfit. Most of Waxhill Barracks was demolished between 1880 and 1901[14] and the rest of it in the 1930s, when Donnington Barracks and other unfit houses were also cleared.[15] Redevelopment was deterred by the terrain of derelict mines but by 1983 the waste areas had been improved by landscaping.

Pain's Lane, represented in 1980 by Duke Street, St. George's, was mentioned in 1592.[16] It lay in the south-west corner of the parish, and ran NNE. for some 225 metres from Watling Street to the edge of Donnington wood.[17] Cottages existed there by 1650,[18] and in 1717 it was flanked by houses and yards.[19] In 1816 the settlement on Pain's Lane had kept the character of a village street[20] but later in the century it developed outside Lilleshall parish to become the industrial hamlet of St. George's.[21]

SOCIAL AND CULTURAL ACTIVITIES. Two licensed alesellers traded in Lilleshall in the period 1615–19,[22] and in the mid 18th century there were two public houses.[23] One, known as the Red Lion by 1794,[24] stood on the west side of the street, south of the church.[25] It probably closed in

the 1840s.[26] The Red House, so called by 1822, stood north of the village on the Wellington–Newport road, and in 1979 was still the only public house conveniently placed for the villagers; the 3rd duke of Sutherland (1861–92) had allowed no other to open.[27]

There was a licensed aleseller in Muxton 1618–19.[28] By the mid 18th century there were two public houses. That on the south side of the Wellington–Newport road in 1783[29] apparently closed c. 1807. The other, on the north side in 1804, moved c. 1806 to an adjacent site,[30] which was occupied in 1979 by the Sutherland Arms, known before 1856[31] as the Bush (1822) or Holly Bush (1851).[32]

Donnington had three licensed alesellers in 1619.[33] In 1775 there was one, evidently near what was later School Road;[34] known as the Field by 1822, the house seems to have closed in the 1830s.[35] Another, east of the corner of School Road and Queen's Road in 1979, was first licensed between 1828 and 1839[36] and known as the Bell by 1856.[37] The Boot (closed 1878) and the Flag stood nearby in the 19th century.[38] The White House, formerly part of Donnington Farm, opened during the Second World War,[39] and the Champion Jockey, Wrekin Drive, c. 1954.[40]

From the late 18th century friendly societies were formed in the parish. One, at the Red Lion, was formed in 1786 and still existed in 1844.[41] A Donnington Wood club lent £100 in 1792–3 towards the restoration of the parish church and was still active in 1808–9.[42] A friendly society or 'dividend club' was meeting at John Pearce's public house (later the Bush) by 1800[43] and existed in 1841.[44] In 1802–3 there were said to be two friendly societies in the parish, with 331 members,[45] and some 560 people were said to be members of friendly societies meeting in the parish 1812–15.[46] The Lilleshall Co.'s employees had a miners' sick fund, formed in 1802, and a club for the relief of colliers and miners, formed in 1823 and active until the passing of the Work-

---

[6] S.R.O. 972, parcel 233, Lilleshall map of 1816.
[7] S.R.O. 38/15.
[8] Trinder, *Ind. Rev. Salop.* 316.
[9] S.R.O., DA 26/100/7, p. 220.
[10] S.R.O. 38/15; 972, parcel 238, map of 1813.
[11] Below, Prot. Nonconf.
[12] Trinder, *Ind. Rev. Salop.* 390.
[13] W. Howard Williams, 'Lilleshall Co. Hist. 1802–1966' (TS. [c. 1966]), p. 7 (copy in S.R.O. 3072/1).
[14] O.S. Map 6", Salop. XXXVI. NE. (1890 and 1903 edns.).
[15] S.R.O., DA 23/114/3, p. 72; DA 26/100/7, pp. 217, 220; /114/2, p. 27.   [16] S.R.O. 38/101.
[17] S.R.O. 972 parcel 234, map of Lilleshall pk. etc.; parcel 242, map of c. 1642.
[18] P. R. Edwards, 'Farming Econ. of NE. Salop. in 17th Cent.' (Oxf. Univ. D.Phil. thesis, 1976), 267.
[19] S.R.O. 972, parcel 234, map of Lilleshall pk. etc.
[20] Ibid. parcel 233, Lilleshall map.
[21] Below, Wombridge; Wrockwardine Wood.
[22] S.R.O., q. sess. rec. parcel 254, badgers', drovers', and alesellers' licensing bk.
[23] Except where otherwise stated, inf. on public hos. in the 18th and early 19th cent. is ibid. parcels 255–9, regs. of alesellers' recognizances 1753–1828.
[24] Ibid. parcel 285, friendly socs. reg.
[25] S.R.O. 972, box 41, survey of 1813; parcel 238, map of 1813.
[26] S.R.O. 38/18, f. 113; S. Bagshaw, *Dir. Salop.* (1851), 397.

[27] Geof. K. Smith, *St. Mic. and All Angels, Lilleshall* (2nd edn.; Lilleshall, 1976), 8.
[28] S.R.O., q. sess. rec. parcel 254, badgers', etc. licensing bk.
[29] S.R.O. 972, parcel 234, middle map of Lilleshall; box 41, survey of 1775 × 1783, p. 42.
[30] S.R.O. 38/15; /17, ff. 20 (no. 288), 43 (no. 289), 49; /18, f. 24; 972, box 41, survey of 1808, ff. 13, 27, 42.
[31] *P.O. Dir. Salop.* (1856), 66.
[32] S. Bagshaw, *Dir. Salop.* (1851), 399.
[33] S.R.O., q. sess. rec. parcel 254, badgers', etc. licensing bk.
[34] S.R.O. 38/15; 17, f. 70 (no. 94).
[35] S.R.O. 673/2/20, no. 129; /2/24.
[36] S.R.O. 38/18, f. 53.
[37] *P.O. Dir. Salop.* (1856), 66.
[38] A. J. Frost, *Story of Donnington* (Donnington [1979]), 17–18.
[39] Ibid. 26.
[40] S.R.O., DA 26/114/5, p. 1572.
[41] S.R.O., q. sess. rec. parcel 285, friendly soc. reg.; S.R.O. 673/1/7, 20 Nov. 1839; /1/16, 20 Nov. 1844.
[42] S.R.O. 4462/CW/3, pp. 107–65.
[43] S.R.O., q. sess. rec. parcel 285, friendly socs. reg.
[44] S.R.O., q. sess. order bk. 1796–1808, p. 591; Registrar of Friendly Socs. *List of Friendly Socs. in Co. of Salop, 1793–1855* (H.M.S.O. 1857), p. 24 (copy in S.R.O.); S.R.O. 673/1/7, 20 Nov. 1829; /1/16, 20 Nov. 1841.
[45] *Abstr. Rel. to Poor*, H.C. 98, p. 415 (1803–4), xiii.
[46] *Abstr. Rel. to Poor*, H.C. 82, p. 369 (1818), xix.

men's Compensation Act, 1907.[47] Other societies and lodges occurred in the mid 19th century: Donnington Amicable Society, meeting at the Field 1834–52,[48] the 'Marquis of Stafford' lodge of the Independent Order of Odd Fellows (Manchester Unity) meeting at Muxton from 1845,[49] and the Donnington Friendly Society 1847–52.[50] The Shropshire Provident Society's Lilleshall branch, formed 1853,[51] was dissolved with the parent body in the 1940s.[52]

Another form of providence was encouraged by the Lilleshall Savings Bank, opened in 1818[53] at the instance of James Loch,[54] following the exceptional pauperism of 1817. The marquess of Stafford was its patron.[55] Intended for small savings of the 'industrious classes',[56] the bank proved popular and successful. It closed in 1892.[57] Smaller savings were encouraged by the Lilleshall Sunday School Savings Fund (or Lilleshall Penny Savings Bank)[58] and the Donnington Wood Penny Bank.[59]

More specialized in their benefits were the Lilleshall Children's Clothing Club,[60] the Lilleshall Female Clothing Club,[61] the Duchess of Sutherland's Lilleshall Penny Club,[62] (merged c. 1863 with another club to form the Lilleshall and Sheriffhales Clothing Club),[63] the Donnington Wood Female Clothing Club,[64] and the Donnington Wood School Clothing Club.[65]

Nineteenth-century societies with social and cultural aims included the Lilleshall Church Missionary Association,[66] the Lilleshall Young Men's Improvement Society,[67] the Lilleshall Temperance Savings Society,[68] the Lilleshall Temperance Deposit Club,[69] and the Lilleshall Musical Society.[70] The local temperance movement was led in the 19th century by Miss E. D. H. Battersby[71] and resulted in the opening of an iron coffee tavern and refreshment room in Wellington Road, Donnington, converted by 1980 into a house and shop.[72]

The Donnington Wood Mechanics' Institution was established in 1851, many books being given by the 2nd duke of Sutherland. Lectures on popular subjects were planned.[73] In 1867 a mechanics' institute was founded at Donnington, mainly at the expense of the 3rd duke and C. C. Walker.[74]

It stood in Wellington Road, opposite the Midland Iron Works, and in 1891 had a library (c. 1,500 volumes), reading room, and recreation room, and over 700 members. It was demolished c. 1950. In 1891 science and art classes were held in the works dining hall.[75] By 1875 St. George's Reading Room and Institute had been established[76] and in 1876 it was amalgamated with St. George's Granville Literary Institute, for which the Lilleshall Co. provided accommodation at the Granville Hospital (in Wrockwardine Wood township).[77] In 1899 a new St. George's Literary Institute and Library was erected near the church, on a site given by the 4th duke. It included a billiard room.[78] From 1927 the county council rented its reading room as a cookery classroom for schools. A smaller reading room was created on the first floor[79] and was used by the county library as a local centre until 1956.[80] In 1980 billiards was still played at the institute, and the Good Neighbours, an old people's club serving St. George's and Priorslee, also met there.[81] The county council's Donnington branch library opened in 1960.[82]

In 1891 the 500-seat dining hall at the Midland Iron Works was used for concerts and entertainments,[83] and many functions were held at Donnington Wood vicarage until the Donnington Wood Institute opened in 1901[84] near St. Matthew's church. From about 1934 the institute was used only for church purposes.[85] In 1963 it was greatly enlarged,[86] and in 1980, as St. Matthew's Hall, was still used. The James Memorial Hall, Lilleshall, administered by the parochial church council, was built c. 1937.[87] By 1947 Lilleshall Men's Institute had its own premises,[88] a converted building in Limekiln Lane, but by 1967 it was little used[89] and the trustees agreed to lease it to the Lilleshall youth club.[90] In 1980 weekly bingo was played there, but the youth club had recently closed.[91] The Turreff Hall, Donnington, was built during the Second World War by the American army[92] and later adopted by the county council.[93] In 1962 it was the only undenominational hall in Donnington.[94] By 1979, however, it had become a county library store. There was

[47] W. K. V. Gale and C. R. Nicholls, *The Lilleshall Co. Ltd.: a Hist. 1764–1964* (1979), 38, 77.
[48] S.R.O. 673/1/3, p. 231; /1/17, 17 Jan. 1852.
[49] Ibid. /1/17, 23 Aug. 1845, 6 July 1850.
[50] Ibid. 17 Apr. 1847, 17 Jan. 1852.
[51] S.R.O. 436/6720, pp. 67–8.
[52] Ibid. /6903, 7142.
[53] S.R.O. 673/1/1, p. 22.
[54] J. R. Wordie, 'A Great Landed Estate in the 18th Cent.' (Reading Univ. Ph.D. thesis, 1967), 128.
[55] S.R.O. 673/1/1, p. 7.
[56] Ibid. p. 10.
[57] S.R.O. 673/1/2, 14 Jan. 1893.
[58] Ibid. /1/5, 20 Nov. 1877; /1/17, 1 May 1858.
[59] Ibid. /1/5, 20 Nov. 1876; /1/31, 9 July 1892.
[60] Ibid. /1/6, 29 Jan. 1820; /1/31, 20 Feb. 1892.
[61] Ibid. /1/3, p. 198; /1/31, 5 Nov. 1892.
[62] Ibid. /1/16, 20 Nov. 1840.
[63] Ibid. /1/25, 8 Nov. 1862, 20 June 1863; S.R.O. 972, parcel 168, subscription bk. 1909–17.
[64] S.R.O. 673/1/17, 15 Nov. 1845, 10 Mar. 1855.
[65] Ibid. 7 Jan. 1846, 14 Jan. 1854.
[66] Ibid. 673/1/5, 20 Nov. 1880; /1/16, 20 Nov. 1842.
[67] Ibid. /1/17, 10 Dec. 1859.
[68] Ibid. /1/25, 5 Nov. 1864; /1/31, 3 Sept. 1892.
[69] Ibid. /1/5, 20 Nov. 1880; /1/25, 25 Mar. 1865.

[70] S.R.O. 4462/Soc/1/1.
[71] Smith, *St. Mic.* 8; local inf.
[72] *Shrews. Chron.* 4 Feb. 1897; local inf.
[73] S. Bagshaw, *Dir. Salop.* (1851), 398.
[74] *P.O. Dir. Salop.* (1879), 341.
[75] *Kelly's Dir. Salop.* (1891), 340; local inf.
[76] *Wellington Jnl.* 20 Mar. 1875.
[77] Ibid. 26 Feb. 1876.
[78] *Kelly's Dir. Salop.* (1900), 191.
[79] *S.C.C. Mins. (Educ.)* 1927–8, 13; 1933–4, 32; S.R.O. 1563/22.
[80] *S.C.C. Mins. (Educ.)* 1955–6, 173.
[81] Local inf.
[82] *S.C.C. Mins. (Educ.)* 1960–1, 126.
[83] *Kelly's Dir. Salop.* (1891), 340.
[84] Frost, *Story of Donnington*, 31.
[85] S.R.O., DA 23/100/8, p. 132.
[86] Plaques on bldg.
[87] Par. rec., deed of 1937.
[88] S.R.O. 4462/Soc/2/1, 9 Jan. 1947.
[89] Ibid. 12 July 1967.
[90] Ibid. 9 Nov. 1967.
[91] Notices on bldg.
[92] Frost, *Story of Donnington*, 26.
[93] *S.C.C. Mins. (Educ.)* 1950–1, 90.
[94] Shore, 'Survey of Donnington', p. 3.

then a shortage of public meeting places in Donnington,[95] despite the opening of a community centre by Lilleshall parish council in 1975;[96] many organizations had been formed at Donnington since 1939 as a result of the C.O.D. development. Among those with their own premises were the Silver Threads Club (for old people), the Coddon Sports and Social Club, the Sea Cadet Corps, and the British Legion.[97] By 1975 Donnington Wood Working Men's Club also had its own premises.[98]

Lilleshall park was created for deer hunting, presumably in the Middle Ages. Deer remained there in the early 18th century,[99] and in 1780 foxes were hunted in Donnington wood.[1] Sports other than hunting claimed adherents, and a narrow field north-east of the abbey was known, perhaps facetiously, as the bowling alley in 1598.[2] Lilleshall cricket ground was opened c. 1890,[3] and in 1980 was controlled by Lilleshall Cricket Club. In 1980 Lilleshall Tennis Club had courts next to the cricket field. At St. George's there was a recreation ground by 1883, when annual athletic sports were first held there.[4] A public recreation ground near St. George's church, on a site provided by the Lilleshall Co.,[5] was opened in 1918;[6] it soon had the best athletics track in the county.[7] St. George's had one of the county's leading football clubs. It was formed by 1877,[8] and by 1921 was based at St. George's recreation ground.[9] In 1980 the ground also provided for bowls, tennis, and hockey, but no longer had a running track. Donnington Wood recreation ground was established c. 1934 by the Miners' Welfare Fund[10] and acquired for public use by Wellington rural district council in 1957.[11] Tennis, bowls, and football were played there[12] and swimming pools and a games hall were added later.[13]

The Globe cinema, Donnington, opened for C.O.D. personnel during the Second World War.[14] It was open to the public in 1962[15] but by 1979 had become a bingo hall.[16] The Little Theatre was opened in 1954 by the Donnington Garrison Operatic and Dramatic Society which still flourished there in 1979.[17] An annual fun fair (previously at Oakengates) began nearby c. 1980.[18]

MANOR AND OTHER ESTATES. Before 1066 LILLESHALL was among twelve prebendal estates held by the collegiate church of St. Alkmund, Shrewsbury.[19] It was said in the 12th century that St. Alkmund's had been founded and endowed by Æthelflæd, lady of the Mercians (d. 918), and that ten prebends had been created for the college by King Edgar (d. 975).[20] In 1086 Lilleshall was held of the college by Godebold the priest,[21] probably as a prebend. He was a clerk of Roger of Montgomery, earl of Shrewsbury,[22] and it seems possible that the college held the manor of Earl Roger[23] (d. 1094). If the earl and the two sons who succeeded him were the tenants in chief, St. Alkmund's presumably held in chief after Earl Robert's forfeiture in 1102.[24] Godebold was succeeded as lord by his son Robert. Another clerk of the earls of Shrewsbury, Richard of Beaumais (bishop of London from 1108, d. 1127), was Robert's successor and apparently held the manor of Henry I in chief, which suggests that St. Alkmund's was then under Richard's rule. In 1128 the king granted the manor to Richard's nephew, Richard of Beaumais (II).[25] About 1145, as dean of St. Alkmund's, he conveyed the manor, with royal consent, to Arrouaisian canons from Dorchester (Oxon.) for a new abbey, which they established at Lilleshall by 1148.[26] It was many years before the canons could establish full possession, for some land and rights had been alienated since 1086.[27]

The manor was held in demesne by the abbey until surrendered to the Crown in 1538.[28] In 1543 James Leveson (d. 1547)[29] of Wolverhampton, a merchant of the staple, bought the manor from the Crown.[30] His son and heir Richard (kt. 1553) died in 1560, leaving the manor to his executors for thirteen years and thereafter to his son and heir Walter[31] (born 1550, kt. 1587).[32] At Sir Walter's death in 1602[33] the manor passed to his son and heir Sir Richard,[34] who became vice-admiral of England in 1604.[35]

Dying in 1605 without lawful issue[36] Sir Richard left the manor to trustees for the payment of legacies and debts and thereafter to his third cousin,[37] Richard Leveson of Halling (Kent).[38] The younger Richard's father, Sir John (d. 1615),

[95] S.R.O., S.C.C. Leisure Activities Cttee. mins. 5 Oct. 1979, pp. 8–9.
[96] Frost, Story of Donnington, 26.
[97] Shore, 'Survey of Donnington', pp. 4–5.
[98] P.O. Telephone Dir. (1975), sect. 303, p. 81.
[99] Hist. MSS. Com. 4, 5th Rep., Sutherland, p. 208.
[1] V.C.H. Salop. ii. 167.
[2] Staffs. R.O., D. 593/H/14/1/1.
[3] O.S. Map 6", Salop. XXXVI. NE. (1890 and 1903 edns.).
[4] Wellington Jnl. 11 and 25 Aug. 1883.
[5] O.S. Map 6", Salop. XXXVI. SE. (1929 edn.); Gale and Nicholls, Lilleshall Co. 95.
[6] G. M. James, 'Here be Dragons': Brief Glimpse into Hist. of St. Geo.'s, Telford [1982], 24 (corrected copy in S.P.L.).
[7] V.C.H. Salop. ii. 194.
[8] Ibid. 199–200.
[9] G. Riley, Salop. F.A. 1877–1977 (Shrews. [1977]), [8].
[10] Frost, Story of Donnington, 25; S.R.O., DA 23/100/8, p. 121.
[11] S.R.O., DA 26/110/5, p. 1436.
[12] Ibid. /100/12, p. 76.
[13] Frost, Story of Donnington, 25.
[14] Ibid. 26.
[15] Shore, 'Survey of Donnington', p. 5.

[16] Frost, op. cit. 26.
[17] Shropshire Star, 17 Sept. 1979.
[18] Inf. from Wrekin District Council.
[19] V.C.H. Salop. i. 314–15, 336, 348.
[20] Dugdale, Mon. vi (2), 750.
[21] V.C.H. Salop. i. 314.
[22] T.S.A.S. lvi. 253.
[23] V.C.H. Salop. i. 291, assumes it to be so.
[24] Ibid. iii. 10.
[25] Dugdale, Mon. vi (1), 262.
[26] V.C.H. Salop. ii. 70–1.
[27] Eyton, viii. 29, 232. Cf. V.C.H. Salop. ii. 72.
[28] L. & P. Hen. VIII, xiii (2), p. 243.
[29] P.R.O., C 142/85, no. 58.
[30] L. & P. Hen. VIII, xviii (1), p. 535.
[31] P.R.O., C 142/131, no. 186; Staffs. R.O., D. 593/C/5, Sir Ric. Leveson's will.
[32] T.S.A.S. 4th ser. v. 328.
[33] P.R.O., C 142/283, no. 90.
[34] Staffs. R.O., D. 593/C/9/2, deed of 1603.
[35] D.N.B.
[36] P.R.O., C 142/312, no. 158.
[37] S. Shaw, Hist. Staffs. ii (1801), 169.
[38] Staffs. R.O., D. 593/C/9/2, two deeds 23 Mar. 1604/5 and Sir Ric. Leveson's will.

became sole trustee by 1609[39] and left the trust to his widow and executrix, Christian, reserving Lilleshall manor to her as long as she should choose to live there.[40] In 1616 Lilleshall was seized by the Crown for a debt of Sir Richard's still owing to it; in 1617, however, Christian bought a Crown lease of the manor to trustees to the uses of Sir John's will.[41] In 1622–3 the Crown debt was paid off and in 1623 Christian discharged her last functions as Sir John's executrix.[42] By the end of 1623 her son Richard (kt. 1626)[43] was in possession.[44]

At Sir Richard's death without lawful issue in 1661 the manor passed under his will[45] to his widow Katherine (d. 1674)[46] for life, and thereafter to his grandnephew William Leveson-Gower (formerly Gower) of Stittenham (Yorks. N.R.). William (4th bt. 1689) died in 1691[47] and Lilleshall descended from father to son until 1823, the following[48] being lords: Sir John (cr. Baron Gower 1703, d. 1709); John, 2nd baron (cr. Earl Gower 1746, d. 1754);[49] Granville, 2nd earl (cr. marquess of Stafford 1786, d. 1803);[50] George Granville, 2nd marquess (cr. duke of Sutherland 1833, d. 1833).[51] In 1823 the marquess settled the manor for life on his son George Granville, Earl Gower[52] (2nd duke 1833). After the 2nd duke's death in 1861 the manor continued to descend with the dukedom.[53] Most of the manorial estate, except in Donnington Wood, was sold by the 5th duke (d. 1963) in separate lots in 1914 and 1917.[54] The manorial rights were not sold but by 1919 their nature and value were unknown.[55] They were settled on the 5th duke for life in 1927.[56]

The Levesons' first house in the parish seems to have been the hunting lodge in the deer park. In 1604 it was occupied by Sir Richard Leveson (d. 1605). There were then two storeys: above the hall and offices were a great chamber and several other chambers including Sir Robert Harley's.[57] Harley (1579–1656)[58] was Sir Richard's cousin[59] and presumably lived at the lodge. The building was improved c. 1615.[60] In 1645 Sir Richard Leveson was living at the lodge while the abbey

buildings were garrisoned.[61] The Levesons were never continuously in residence, and Sir Richard (d. 1661) was the only head of the family to be buried in the parish. In the late 17th century day-to-day custody of the buildings was in the hands of the resident keeper of the deer park.[62] In 1679 the lodge's most prominent feature was a deep balcony supported on an open arcade and with a balustraded parapet; the balcony faced east over the open part of the park. In 1774 the lodge's ground plan was roughly rectangular, with the longer sides facing east and west.[63] About 1800 the house appeared from the west as a mainly timber-framed building with much decorative studding, on stone foundations and with parts wholly of stone.[64] In the later 18th century the lodge's surroundings became increasingly unattractive. Lord Gower had left it for good probably by 1774, by which time the deer park had been split up,[65] and certainly by 1783.[66] Part at least was inhabited in 1796[67] but the house was gradually taken down and the remains were demolished c. 1818.[68]

The Hall (later the Old Hall), the Leveson-Gowers' Shropshire seat after they left the lodge, is said to have been built in the late 1750s[69] but it incorporates a timber-framed farmhouse, probably of the 17th century. In the 1820s it was considered too modest for Lord Gower, the new lord of the manor,[70] and it ceased to be the family's Shropshire seat when the new Lilleshall Hall (in Sheriffhales) was completed for him in 1830.[71] In 1839 the 2nd duke kept the Old Hall in hand,[72] possibly as a dower house.[73] It was later let[74] and in 1917 the 5th duke sold it to C. & W. Walker Ltd.[75] In 1930 the firm sold it to the National Federation of Retail Newsagents, Booksellers, and Stationers[76] as a convalescent home for members.[77] The home closed c. 1972, and the house was vacant until 1977 when, with the assistance of Wrekin district council, Old Ben Homes reopened it as retirement flats for newsvendors and others.[78]

After its appropriation to Lilleshall abbey the rectory descended with the manor, except that in

[39] S.R.O. 38/166.
[40] Staffs. R.O., D. 593/C/10/1, Sir John Leveson's will.
[41] Ibid. /C/10/3, deeds 14 Feb., 15 May 1617.
[42] Ibid. /P/6/7, accts. of 1622–3.
[43] T.S.A.S. 4th ser. xi. 167.
[44] Staffs. R.O., D. 593/C/10/3, deed 19 Feb. 1622/3; /C/14/1, deeds 21 and 28 Nov. 1623.
[45] Ibid. /C/14/4, Sir Ric. Leveson's will.
[46] T.S.A.S. i. 139.   [47] Burke, Peerage (1949), 1942.
[48] For dates and titles see Complete Peerage, s.vv. Gower; Stafford; Sutherland.
[49] In possession by 1712: S.R.O. 1238/31, m. 2.
[50] Ibid.; below, plate 22.
[51] S.R.O. 1238/31, mm. 9–14. In possession by 1804: S.R.O., q. sess. rec. parcel 261, reg. of gamekeepers, ff. 105v.–6.
[52] S.R.O. 972, box 152, deed (draft); 1238/31, mm. 15–17.
[53] S.R.O. 972, box 208, abstr. of title, mm. 6–14. In possession by 1893: ibid. m. 15.
[54] S.R.O. 972, parcels 205, 207, sale partic. of 1914, 1917; Wellington Jnl. 28 July 1917.
[55] S.R.O. 972, parcel 211, jnl. note 25 Feb. 1919.
[56] Deed of 14 Jan. 1927: inf. from Dr. J. D. P. McCallum.
[57] Staffs. R.O., D 593/C/9/2, inv.   [58] D.N.B.
[59] Visit. Salop. 1623, i (Harl. Soc. xxviii), 137, 215.
[60] Hist. MSS. Com. 4, 5th Rep., Sutherland, p. 140.
[61] Diary of Marches of Royal Army (Camd. Soc. [1st ser.], lxxiv), 172.

[62] S.R.O. 4462/Rg/1, bap. 3 Apr. 1658, 27 Feb. 1661/2; bur. 15 Sept. 1667, 1 Dec. 1676; /2, bur. 25 Mar. 1706; Cal. S.P. Dom. July–Sept. 1683, 266; Hist. MSS. Com. 4, 5th Rep., Sutherland, p. 208.
[63] S.R.O. 972, parcel 233, maps of 1679, 1774.
[64] [F. Stackhouse Acton], Castles and Old Mansions of Salop. (Shrews. 1868), betw. pp. 32 and 33; below, plate 6.
[65] S.R.O. 972, parcel 233, map of 1774.
[66] Ibid. box 41, survey of 1775 × 1783, f. 13.
[67] S.R.O. 4462/Rg/4, 12 Oct. 1796.
[68] J. Loch, Acct. of Improvements on Est. of Marquess of Stafford (1820), app. p. 83; [Stackhouse Acton], Castles and Old Mansions of Salop. 33.
[69] Shropshire Mag. Aug. 1958, 16.
[70] E. Richards, '"Leviathan of Wealth", W. Midland Agric. 1800–50', Ag. H.R. xxii. 103.
[71] H. Colvin, Biog. Dict. Brit. Architects, 1600–1840 (1978), 963.
[72] S.R.O. 38/18, f. 2.
[73] Local inf.
[74] S. Bagshaw, Dir. Salop. (1851), 397; P.O. Dir. Salop. (1856 and later edns.); Kelly's Dir. Salop. (1891 and later edns.).
[75] S.R.O. 972, parcel 207, sale partic. of 1917; parcel 210, list of purchasers.
[76] S.C.C. Mins. (Educ.) 1930–1, 94.
[77] Shropshire Mag. May 1952, 31–2.
[78] Shropshire Star, 21 Jan. 1978.

1543 Sir Edward Aston bought the rectory from the Crown[79] and sold it to James Leveson.[80] The rectorial tithes (which excluded the great tithes of 'Shelton's old farm' and of the vicarial glebe)[81] were commuted in 1845 to an annual rent charge of £772 17s. 6d., of which the £770 due from the manorial estate was extinguished and merged with the freehold by 1849.[82]

By 1404 there was only one other freehold within the manor, at Muxton, held of the canons by a chief rent of 4s.[83] The holder in 1539 was Robert Hakyn.[84] About 1780 Isaac Hawkins Browne, presumably a descendant, was said to have recently sold the land (c. 50 a.) in three lots, none of it to Earl Gower.[85] By 1851, however, all except 6 a. belonged to the 2nd duke of Sutherland,[86] and by 1879 those 6 a. too had been absorbed into the manorial estate.[87]

ECONOMIC HISTORY. AGRICULTURE.

The manor was worth £6 in 1066, £4 in 1086. The estate was taxed at 10 hides. There were two ploughteams on the demesne and eight among the tenants, but there was room for nine more. A league of woodland covered the high ground in the south,[88] and the north-west lay within the Weald Moors.

Some reclamation of woods and marshes had probably taken place by 1086. The five bordars[89] almost certainly occupied assarts outside the open fields.[90] It was presumably the Domesday lord of the manor, Godebold the priest, who inclosed a large area of rising ground on the edge of the Weald Moors; called the 'Haye Gubald' by 1224[91] and Lubstree park by 1283, it was said to be over a league in circumference 'by the perch of the forest'.[92] In 1277 Adam and Ralph of Preston and Robert of Ford acknowledged the abbot's right to improve (expedire) it by further inclosure[93] and that improvement, and the abbot's right to hunt deer there, received royal sanction in 1283.[94]

The park was described in 1199–1200 as an old purpresture,[95] for until 1301 the whole manor lay within the forest jurisdiction of Mount Gilbert.[96] The abbot was amerced c. 1180 for bringing 7½ a. of wheat and 7 a. of oats under cultivation, and some of his tenants were amerced for similar encroachments. At the same time another man was amerced for a purpresture at Donnington.[97] In 1184–5 three men had recently been amerced for assarting.[98] By 1198–9 the canons were paying

20s. a year for licence to cultivate 5 a. of moor near the abbey.[99]

By 1221 occupation of the Weald Moors had so proceeded that the abbots of Shrewsbury and Lilleshall had to settle a boundary between their moors of Kynnersley and Donnington.[1] By 1291 the rest of Lilleshall's northern boundary, that with Longford manor, was agreed as a brook in the Weald Moors,[2] presumably that forming the ancient parish boundary and called the Abbot's brook by 1682.[3] Woodland clearance proceeded at the same time. In 1250 the canons were allowed to keep an unauthorized assart of 23 a. in Lilleshall wood on payment of an annual rent to the Crown.[4]

In improving their wastes the canons negotiated agreements with holders of existing grazing or other rights. In 1277, for example, Adam and Ralph of Preston and Robert of Ford relinquished their common of pasture in all lands so far asserted or inclosed by the abbot within the manor, and they and Peter of Eyton (III) acknowledged the abbot's right to inclose and reclaim (approare) thirty 'great royal' acres of his wood within a line from Waxhillgate across the wood to the 'Qualmesmytthe' (presumably near Quam Pool)[5] and beyond, thence south along the boundary of the king's wood (i.e. the parish boundary) to Watling Street, east along the road to 'Elfeþeston' (possibly the Allot stone standing c. 1642 at the south-east corner of the parish),[6] and so north to Willmore grange.[7] That boundary included nearly all the ancient woodland in the parish, and a large proportion of it was afterwards imparked,[8] presumably by the canons. The assart was licensed by the king in 1280.[9]

Other negotiations about that time were probably also connected with the canons' schemes for agricultural improvement. Walter de Dunstanville (d. 1270), lord of Shifnal, quitclaimed to them woodland on the Lilleshall side of Watling Street, but kept his right to common of herbage there and was granted pannage for 60 swine in the abbot's foreign wood there (perhaps Donnington wood) in return for a grant of common of pasture in his wood at Lizard.[10] In 1275 John, lord of Grindle, quitclaimed to the canons his common rights in their wood on the Lilleshall side of Watling Street. In 1279 Hugh of Haughton quitclaimed to the canons his pasture rights in any part of their Lilleshall lands that had been or would be improved, and next year the canons sold him com-

[79] L. & P. Hen. VIII, xviii (1), p. 201.
[80] Staffs. R.O., D. 593/B/2/7/8, deed.
[81] Below, Churches.
[82] S.R.O. 4462/T/3; L.J.R.O., B/A/15, Lilleshall.
[83] S.P.L., MS. 4426.
[84] P.R.O., LR 2/184, f. 8.
[85] S.R.O. 972, box 41, survey of 1775 × 1783.
[86] S. Bagshaw, Dir. Salop. (1851), 394.
[87] P.O. Dir. Salop. (1879), 341.
[88] V.C.H. Salop. i. 314.   [89] Ibid.
[90] S. P. J. Harvey, 'Evidence for Settlement Study: Domesday Bk.' Medieval Settlement, ed. P. H. Sawyer (1976), 197–9.
[91] Eyton, viii. 258.
[92] P.R.O., C 143/6, no. 14.
[93] S.R.O. 972, box 220, deeds.
[94] P.R.O., C 143/6, no. 14; T. F. Dukes, Antiquities of Salop. (1844), 170.

[95] Pipe R. 1200 (P.R.S. N.S. xii), 253.
[96] Cartulary of Shrews. Abbey, ed. U. Rees (1975), ii, p. 249.
[97] P.R.O., E 32/143.
[98] Pipe R. 1185 (P.R.S. xxxiv), 129.
[99] Pipe R. 1199 (P.R.S. N.S. x), 76. Still being paid in 1211–12: ibid. 1212 (P.R.S. N.S. xxx), 90.
[1] Cart. Shrews. ii, pp. 268–9.
[2] S.R.O. 972, box 225, deed of 1284 × 1291.
[3] S.R.O. 81/559.
[4] Cal. Pat. 1247–58, 61.
[5] Map on p. 000. The pool was mentioned as 'Qualmpole' in 1345: S.R.O. 972, box 225, deed.
[6] S.R.O. 972, parcel 242, map.
[7] Ibid. box 220, deeds; S.P.L., Deeds 16317.
[8] Map on p. 148.
[9] Cal. Pat. 1272–81, 364–5.
[10] Eyton, viii. 230.

mon of pasture (except for goats and horses) in their foreign wood in Lilleshall manor (saving the abbot's right to make improvements) and pannage for 29 pigs and a boar between Michaelmas and Martinmas.[11]

The abbey's demesne arable consisted in 1330 of 10 carucates attached to four granges.[12] The home grange was administered from a building between the abbey and Lilleshall village; the grange house was mentioned in 1536–7[13] and stood on the site of the present Lilleshall Grange.[14] The other three granges were probably established by reclamation of marsh and wood. Willmore grange (in existence by 1277)[15] and Cheswell grange (by 1301)[16] lay on the edge of the Weald Moors.[17] The former's buildings were demolished in the 19th century.[18] Watling Street grange (in existence by 1301)[19] lay near the manor's southern edge, its moated[20] house characteristic of late woodland colonization.[21] In 1330 the granges' arable was managed in a three-year rotation; the two parts under cultivation were worth £15 while the third lay fallow and in common. The canons also had 40 a. of meadow, worth 40s. a year, their park, a foreign wood (mentioned before 1270)[22] in which common of pasture existed, and a separate pasture.

The abbey had two broad classes of tenants outside the granges. The free tenants, probably occupiers of reclaimed land outside the open fields,[23] paid cash rents totalling £26 18s., but the neifs, probably including occupiers of the ancient[24] open fields of Lilleshall, Muxton, and Donnington, yielded only £4 0s. 4d. in cash and presumably owed labour services. In 1281 they had been amerced for neglecting to bring in the lord's hay at the proper time.[25] Cash yielded by neifs in Lilleshall, Honnington, and Muxton c. 1337 was 14 per cent of that rendered by free tenants there, but in Donnington was 36 per cent.[26]

In the 1330s and 1340s Lilleshall's arable and pasture was becoming less profitable. In 1336 the abbot stated that cattle disease and other adversities had forced him to lease out some of his demesnes because he could no longer cultivate them,[27] presumably for lack of plough beasts; the affected demesnes probably included Lilleshall, where a 'great murrain' of sheep was suffered in 1341.[28] Increase of the manor's population had necessitated a new aisle in the parish church,[29] and some unwanted open-field arable seems to have been inclosed for crofts to settle otherwise landless families. In 1345 the canons secured a

tenant's consent to their inclosure of twelve open (campestrales) acres in the fields of Lilleshall, Muxton, and Donnington, on which to build messuages and cottages. The tenant was allowed to inclose a selion at Muxton and build two cottages on it.[30]

In 1330 the manor was valued at £58 18s. 8d., in 1353, after the Black Death, at only £34 18s. 10d. Some indication of population loss is the fall in annual income from pleas and perquisites of the manor courts, from 6s. 8d. in 1330 to 12d. in 1353. The demesne arable was worth only £10 in 1353, against £15 in 1330. By 1353 the underwood in the abbot's park was worth nothing because there were no purchasers; the underwood of the foreign wood, which had been worth 3s. 4d. 'before the pestilence',[31] was worth only 12d. The demesne meadow was reduced from 40 a. to 24 a. Cash rents came to only £22 but represented two thirds of the manor's value, as against a half in 1330;[32] labour services were probably difficult to exact.

By 1375 the manor's value had dropped further, and it was worth only £12 13s. 4d. to the abbey.[33] The granges' arable had been reduced to 9 carucates, and was worth only £4. Cash rents had fallen to a mere £4, or a third of the manor's value. A corresponding increase of labour services need not, however, be inferred, for stock rearing, which needed fewer men than tillage, seems to have assumed more importance; the demesne meadow, for example, remained at 24 a. and kept its 1330 value per acre.

By 1404 there had been a general recovery.[34] The manor, not counting land kept in hand and tithes, yielded a gross annual income of about £70. At the beginning of the 15th century the granges, except part of Willmore grange, were kept in hand. Each was run by a bailiff, who received a nominal salary but lived, except at the home grange, by farming the milk, paying half-yearly milk rents to the canons. The granges were worked at least partly by paid labourers. In 1405–6 the home grange employed at least a dozen, including two beadles, a carter and his son, a shepherd, and two dairymaids. Some were paid only seasonally. The wages, too small to provide a living, were presumably supplemented in most cases by a cottage holding. The canons employed additional wage-labour on the granges at the busier times of year for ditching, road-mending (paviamentum), weeding, haymaking, and reaping. Corn and oats were being grown.

Holdings outside the granges (excluding mills)

[11] S.R.O. 972, box 220, deed.
[12] Details of the man. in 1330 are from B.L. Add. MS. 6165, f. 37.
[13] P.R.O., E 315/400, f. 2.
[14] S.R.O. 38/13, map of 1634.
[15] S.R.O. 972, box 220, deeds.
[16] Cart. Shrews. ii, p. 249.
[17] Map on p. 148.
[18] S.R.O. 972, parcel 233, Lilleshall map of 1816; O.S. Map 6", Salop. XXXI. SW. (1887 edn.).
[19] Cart. Shrews. ii, p. 249.
[20] The ho. stood c. 1642 in Mott meadow (S.R.O. 972, parcel 242, map), presumably the same as the Moote croft of 1547 (S.R.O. 38/162). The site was cursorily excavated in 1958 before being levelled: T.S.A.S. lvi. 21–5.
[21] H. E. J. Le Patourel and B. K. Roberts, 'The Significance of Moated Sites', Medieval Moated Sites, ed. F.

A. Aberg (C.B.A. Res. Rep. xvii, 1978), 49–50.
[22] Eyton, viii. 230.
[23] As, e.g., John of Ingestre, who held a virgate and 5 assarts in 1327: S.R.O. 972, box 225, deed.
[24] So called in 1345: ibid. deed.
[25] S.P.L., Deeds 19398.
[26] Ibid. 16329.
[27] Cal. Pat. 1334–8, 248.
[28] Inq. Non. (Rec. Com.), 185.
[29] Below, Churches.
[30] S.R.O. 972, box 225, deed.
[31] B.L. Add. MS. 50121, p. 152. Ibid. 6165, f. 41, gives 4s. 4d.
[32] Details of the man. in 1353 are ibid. 6165, f. 41.
[33] Details of the man. in 1375 are ibid. f. 49.
[34] Details of the man. in 1404 and 1405–6 are from S.P.L., MS. 4426.

1.   Stafford Park industrial estate in 1983, from the east: Telford development corporation factories of the early 1980s south of the M54; Telford town centre is in the middle distance; the Wrekin is beyond

2.   Town centre in 1983, from the north-west over the Forge interchange on the M54

TELFORD

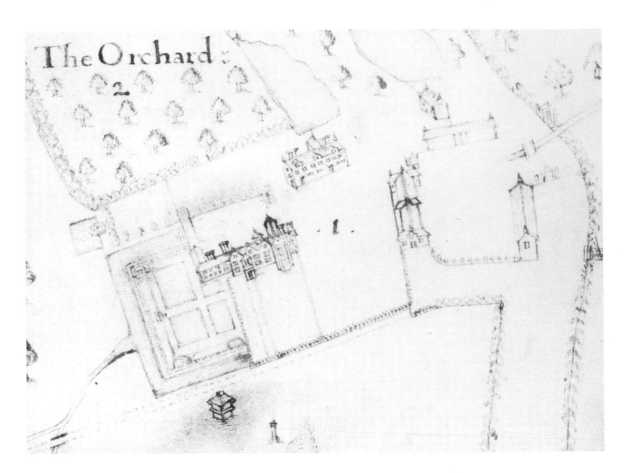

3. DOTHILL HOUSE from the east in 1626: the formal garden incorporates a medieval moat

4. MADELEY COURT in the earlier 20th century: beyond the gatehouse is the 16th-century entrance porch between the north and east wings, which are both medieval but were remodelled in the 16th and 17th centuries

5. ORLETON: the hall, remodelled *c.* 1830, and the 16th-century gatehouse; the bridge over the moat may be medieval

6. LILLESHALL: the Old Lodge from the west, demolished *c.* 1818

7. BURCOT: toll house, built 1835 on the Holyhead road

8. WOMBRIDGE: Trench inclined plane, built 1794 on the Shrewsbury Canal

9. WELLINGTON: the newly built railway station in 1849

10. WROCKWARDINE WOOD: the Lilleshall Co.'s New Yard works built in the early 1860s

11. HADLEY: the Castle Car Works *c*. 1900: the Shropshire Union Canal is on the right

12. COALPORT: the china works in the early 20th century; the Shropshire Canal (closed 1907) ran between the kilns and the foreground; the Severn is beyond

13. WALCOT BRIDGE, built 1782

14. THE IRON BRIDGE, built 1777–80: view of *c.* 1900 from the west

15. The Green, northward view from the churchyard in 1983; the open space is probably what remained of the town's earliest market place, the buildings to the east representing encroachments upon it

16. New Street from the south-east in 1983; building began in the 13th centry; façades are mostly of the 19th century and often hide earlier buildings

WELLINGTON

17. OAKENGATES: view west along Market Street, the town's main street, built up in the 1830s and 1840s

18. HADLEY: an early 20th-century carnival passing Castle Houses, Castle Street, built *c.* 1900 by G.F. Milnes & Co. for workers at their Castle Car Works

19. MADELEY *c*. 1850: the vicarage of *c*. 1716, Telford's church of 1794–7, and the National school of 1844

20. IRONBRIDGE: view from the bridge in the 1920s; the Tontine inn was built in the 1780s; the market building of *c*. 1790, beyond Market Square, formerly surmounted an open arcade

21. Richard Reynolds (d. 1816) manager of the Coalbrookdale
Co. 1763–8, partner in the Ketley works till 1794

22. Granville Leveson-Gower, Earl Gower (later
marquess of Stafford), K.G. (d. 1803), founding partner in Earl Gower & Co. 1764

23. James Foster (d. 1853), builder of ironworks at Wombridge and Madeley Court

24. Charles Clement Walker (d. 1897), director of
C. & W. Walker Ltd. 1857–97

INDUSTRIALISTS

25. MINING AT LIGHTMOOR *c.* 1860

26. COALBROOKDALE FROM THE SOUTH IN THE 1920S

28. Coking at Blists Hill c. 1890

30. Running iron into the pig beds at Priorslee in 1959

27. Blists Hill blast furnaces in the 1890s

29. Charging the furnace at Priorslee in 1959

IRON MAKING

32. HOLLINSWOOD AND OLD PARK IN 1950, from the north-east across Priorslee furnaces; the derelict mining area is bounded by fields in Ketley and Lawley townships

31. IRONBRIDGE IN 1963, from the south-west; the Lodge is just above the centre of the picture, opencast fireclay mining at Woodside top left, Lightmoor brickworks top centre

33. Wellington: All Saints', demolished 1787

34. Dawley: the old church, demolished c. 1845

35. Wrockwardine: St. Peter's in 1790

36. Wombridge: St. Mary and St. Leonard's, built 1757

CHURCHES AND CHAPELS (I)

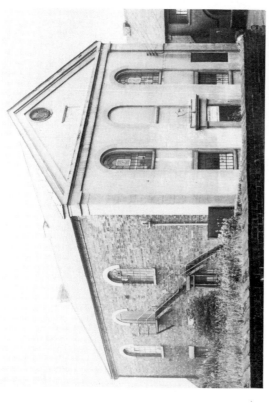

38. Dawley Bank: the former Wesleyan Methodist chapel, Bank Road, built 1840

37. Wellington: Baptist chapel, King Street, built 1828; enlargement in 1897 altered its appearance

39. Dawley: Wesleyan chapel, High Street, built 1860, demolished 1977

40. Blists Hill: St. Chad's mission church (opened near Granville colliery, 1888) re-erected at Blists Hill 1977

CHURCHES AND CHAPELS (II)

42. Hinkshay Row: early 19th-century back-to-back cottages

43. Urban Terrace, Regent Street, Wellington: built by the urban district council 1902

41. The Round House, Horsehay: a converted pottery kiln

HOUSING (I)

44. Lancaster Avenue, Langley estate, Dawley: built by the urban district council 1958–61

45. Sutton Hill, Madeley: the new town's first estate (1966–9); pedestrians and motor traffic were separated

46. Woodside, Madeley, from the north-west: the new town's largest estate (1968–73), with Rough Park Farm near the perimeter road; Madeley is top left

47. Acacia Drive, Leegomery: built by Telford development corporation c. 1981

HOUSING (II)

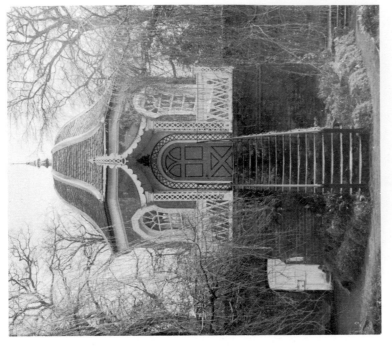

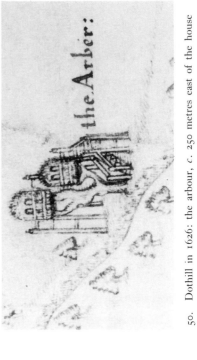

49. Orleton: mid 18th-century gazebo

50. Dothill in 1626: the arbour, c. 250 metres east of the house

48. Dothill in 1734: the house (7), court (S), and Little Canal (Y: an arm of the medieval moat) are bottom left; most of the gardens extend west to the Pool (A) and the Long Canal (B), with the 'Wood with Vistoes' (F) beyond

GARDENS

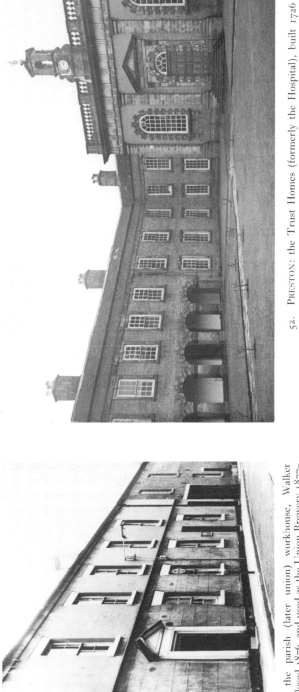

51. WELLINGTON: the parish (later union) workhouse, Walker Street, built 1797, closed 1876, and used as the Union Brewery 1877–c. 1920

52. PRESTON: the Trust Homes (formerly the Hospital), built 1726

53. WELLINGTON: Wrekin Hospital, the former union workhouse opened 1876

54. WROCKWARDINE: Cludde's Almshouses. built 1841

55. Aston: north of the hamlet lies Overley Hill, crowned by Cox's chemical works (top left) with an abandoned length of Watling Street visible as a dark line running east from it across two fields whose northern boundaries mark the 'king's boundary' with Wrockwardine; ploughed-out open-field strips surround the hamlet; Rockway Lane runs south-east (the picture's right) and Aston Hall is at bottom centre

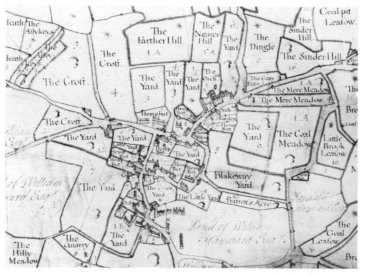

56. Little Wenlock in 1727: showing the church at the south end of the main street (bottom centre), the rectory across the street from it, and the hall east of the church

57. Eyton township: merestone of (?) 1769 at O.S. Nat. Grid SJ 648 139 between Wellington and Eyton parishes

THE RURAL LANDSCAPE

yielded cash rents of £37 6s. 6½d. in 1404. Virtually all were from Donnington (46 per cent), Honnington (20 per cent), Muxton (17 per cent), and Lilleshall (16 per cent). Quam Pool accounted for 1 per cent.[35] Collecting the corn tithes at Donnington cost 8s. in 1405–6, but only 2s. each in Lilleshall and Muxton. In 1422 tenants kept c. 400 pigs in the lord's park and wood, in 73 herds of up to 18 animals.[36]

By 1429 Willmoor, Watling Street, and Cheswell granges had been farmed out.[37] Otherwise there was little change. Ordinary wages at the home grange were about the same as in 1405–6, and were paid to about the same numbers. The respective cash rents from Donnington, Honnington, Muxton, and Lilleshall townships remained virtually the same as in 1405–6. By 1437 the only change seems to have been that ordinary wages at the home grange were paid to fewer people.

In the 16th century the manor's economy continued to be based on the four granges and on the land of tenants in the four townships.[38] There were also clear signs of a continuing movement from tillage to livestock.

Throughout the century the home grange remained the only grange in hand and was mainly devoted to livestock. In 1536–7 it comprised 157 a.[39] of arable, but 331½ a. of pasture and 35 a. of meadow. In October 1538 there were 18 oxen, 15 milch cows and a bull, 20 young steers and heifers, 8 weaning calves, 40 sheep and lambs, and 35 hogs. There were only 54 qr. of unsold grain: 1 of wheat, 13 of rye, 20 of barley, 10 of oats, and 10 of dredge. At Lubstree park, which had recently been let on a 41-year lease, the canons had 10 cows and a bull.[40] In 1598 the demesne comprised not only the home grange but also the 'new' park and the 'rough and plain' of Lubstree park (in which a few parcels had nevertheless been let).

The other three granges were let by 1539 on long leases, but by 1598 Willmore grange had been broken into several holdings of pasture and meadow which were mostly let to holders of farms in the Lilleshall–Honnington open fields. Cheswell grange was by then leased for three lives, and the greater part of it was devoted to livestock. It had 50 strikes' seedness (c. 33 a.) of arable, but 32½ beasts' gate (c. 43 a.) of pasture,[41] and 22 days' math of meadow.

Outside the demesne and granges lived the great majority of the manor's tenants, their houses lying in the villages of Lilleshall and Honnington, Muxton and Donnington, each pair of villages being surrounded by a set of open fields. Two thirds of the manor's open-field arable lay in the Donnington–Muxton set, where three fields were mentioned in 1652:[42] Moor field, Park field (so called in 1625),[43] and Wood field. The other third lay in the Lilleshall–Honnington set, where four fields were mentioned in the 16th century: Hay field, Conyger field, Hill field (so called in 1345),[44] and Headford field (so called in 1409).[45]

In the earlier 16th century there was in the open fields a marked tenurial distinction between holdings with arable and those without. Over four fifths of the former were held at will (the rest by lease or copy), but less than half the latter (nearly all the rest being leaseholds). The contrast may reflect conditions in the early Middle Ages, when the makers of inclosures outside the ancient areas of tillage may have been rewarded with more desirable tenures. By 1598, however, holdings with open-field arable had become predominantly leaseholds, the few copyholds had been extinguished, and two thirds of the surviving tenancies at will were mere cottage holdings.

The change to leasehold tenure for the larger holdings within the open fields began in 1577. Sir Walter Leveson, lord of the manor during the change, suffered severe financial difficulties in later life and died in the Fleet,[46] and it therefore seems likely that he started selling leases to his tenants in order to raise money. The length of his leases, however, was carefully restricted. In 1538–9 the leases in force were nearly all for terms of years; for larger holdings the canons had granted terms between 41 and 81 years. Sir Walter's open-field leases were mostly for three lives, with an average duration of not more than c. 25 years.[47] Of 59 leases in force in 1598, 39 were for lives (usually three); of the 20 for terms of years 11 were dated in 1577 or before, and only 5 were for longer than 21 years.

At least quarter of the arable in the open fields in 1598 was described as inclosed (probably after consolidation of holdings), and such inclosed arable, when converted to permanent pasture, caused loss of commonable land. In 1589 some Muxton pasture had recently been inclosed out of the open fields, and in 1593 pastures had been lately inclosed out of the Lilleshall–Honnington open fields. There nevertheless remained large amounts of uninclosed arable, and holdings could still lie scattered throughout the open fields; a 1597 lease included 8 strikes' seedness of arable 'in every of the leet or common fields of Lilleshall'.[48] Moreover 16th-century leases of common of pasture in the open fields, and 17th-century regulations for stinting in them,[49] imply the continued

[35] Accounted for under Donnington in 1538–9: P.R.O., LR 2/184, f. 12v.

[36] S.P.L., Deeds 16330.

[37] The following details of the man. in 1428–9 and 1436–7 are based on L.J.R.O., B/C/5, Lilleshall abbey acct. r.

[38] The following acct. of 16th cent. agric. is based on surveys and accts. of 1536–7 (P.R.O., E 315/400, f. 2 and v.), 1538–9 (P.R.O., SC 6/Hen. VIII/3009, mm. 16d.–20), 1539 (P.R.O., LR 2/184, ff 4–13v.), and 1598 (Staffs. R.O., D. 593/H/14/1/1, s.v. Lilleshall, etc.).

[39] Such 'acres' were larger than those assumed on the est. in 1598, and both kinds were probably larger than statute acres.

[40] M. E. C. Walcott, 'Inventories and Valuations of Religious Hos.', Archaeologia, xliii (1), 209.

[41] In 1598 a strike's seedness (presumably the area sown

with a strike of seed) was c. ⅔ 'acre' on Lilleshall man. and a beast's gate c. 1⅓ 'acre': Staffs. R.O., D. 593/H/14/1/1, giving some equivalents.

[42] S.R.O. 38/153.

[43] Staffs. R.O., D. 593/J/13/2/1, 13 Oct. 1625.

[44] S.R.O. 972, box 225, deed.

[45] Staffs. R.O., D. 593/J/1/1, 10 Aug. 1409.

[46] Wordie, 'Gt. Landed Estate', 29.

[47] In the late 18th cent. the actual term of a lease for 3 lives on the Leveson Gower Salop. estates averaged c. 23 yrs.: J. R. Wordie, 'Rent Movements and the Eng. Tenant Farmer, 1700–1839', Research in Econ. Hist. vi. 207. Dr. Wordie kindly provided a copy of his paper in advance of publication.

[48] S.R.O. 38/108.

[49] Edwards, 'Farming Econ.' 134.

existence of arable holdings open to common grazing at the prescribed seasons.

During the 16th century the average size of the larger open-field arable holdings diminished as their number increased. In 1538–9 nearly all the arable in the Donnington–Muxton open fields was held by ten large tenants at Donnington and three at Muxton; by 1598, however, the larger holdings were in the hands of fifteen Donnington and seven Muxton tenants.[50] In the Lilleshall–Honnington open fields nearly all the arable was held by five tenants at Lilleshall and one at Honnington in 1538–9, but by 1598 the larger holdings were in the hands of twelve tenants. Such a development was perhaps a result of population growth. Over the same period, however, the cottage holdings, which usually had a croft but little or no open-field arable, seem not to have become more numerous.

During the century there was a tendency, more marked on the Lilleshall–Honnington side of the manor, for holdings of all sizes to include more pasture. In 1538–9 all the larger arable holdings in the Lilleshall–Honnington fields had meadow, but only some had permanent pasture; by 1598, however, all had permanent pasture (up to 22 beasts' gate) as well as meadow (up to 12 days' math). Eight small tenants, most of them at Honnington, held the rest of the Lilleshall–Honnington open-field arable in the 16th century; they had a little meadow but, in 1538–9, no permanent pasture; by 1598, however, some had up to 4 beasts' gate. By 1598 the larger arable holdings in the Donnington–Muxton fields all had permanent pasture (up to 11 beasts' gate) and meadow (up to 8 days' math). Most of the five or so small Muxton tenants who held the rest of the Donnington–Muxton open-field arable had a little meadow (up to 3 days' math) in 1598, but none had any permanent pasture.

In the earlier 16th century a number of substantial holdings in the open fields consisted of meadows or pastures without arable. In 1538–9 there were about twenty such holdings, nearly all of them at Donnington and Honnington. By 1598, however, there were only about five (two at Donnington). The rest had presumably been absorbed into farms that had arable.

On the Lilleshall–Honnington side of the manor there were about fifteen cottage holdings in the 16th century (two thirds of them at Honnington in 1538–9), with usually a small croft and sometimes some meadow, permanent pasture, or garden. There were a few on the Donnington–Muxton side (two thirds of them at Muxton) with usually a small croft or garden, sometimes some meadow (as in 1538–9) but never any permanent pasture. The large number and high proportion of Honnington's cottagers suggests that many of them were employees of the nearby home grange.

By the end of the century the amount of pasture available within the open fields seems to have become inadequate to the demand, perhaps as a result of population growth and inclosure of commonable land. In 1598 the area of permanent pasture in proportion to arable in the Lilleshall–Honnington fields was 1:2, and in the Donnington–Muxton fields only 1:5. By then, however, steps had been taken to provide additional pastures outside the open fields by improving marsh and woodland and by letting off parcels of Willmore grange.

The Weald Moors, in which Lilleshall and other manors had common rights, offered a large tract of grazing. During the later 16th century increased use of the moors, and attempts to improve them by draining, led to conflict between adjoining manors and a need to define their respective rights more precisely.[51] In 1574 Walter Leveson and the lord of Kynnersley agreed a boundary between their manors,[52] which also became the parish boundary. In 1582 the earl of Shrewsbury, lord of Wrockwardine, a manor that claimed common rights throughout the Weald Moors, granted his interest in the moor to Leveson for a perpetual rent.[53] Leveson, having thus established exclusive rights for his Lilleshall tenants south of the 1574 boundary, was able to inclose and improve the moor and to let off separate holdings. Of the 21 such holdings listed in 1598 at least 14 had been let in or after 1592. All but one were let as pasture, in lots from 2 twinters' gate to 6 beasts' gate, and usually for three lives. Sixteen of the tenants also held land in one of the sets of open fields. In Weald Moor leases of 1594 or later the tenant was normally allowed to clear the land and required to maintain its watercourses, bridges, and roads.[54]

In 1592 Leveson promoted a reclamation of part of Donnington wood. On 24 April he granted 13 leases of inclosed areas of the wood, totalling 46½ beasts' gate. Twelve of them, unlike his leases in the open fields, were short term (21-year) 'improving' leases. The tenant could clear the land for pasture while Leveson, in partnership with his brother-in-law[55] Vincent Corbet of Poynton, reserved the timber, underwood, and minerals.[56] All the new leaseholders were also tenants in the Donnington–Muxton fields.

The manorial tenants in 1598 did not necessarily depend solely on agriculture. Humphrey Smythe of Muxton, who held 46 strikes' seedness of arable and 6 beasts' gate of pasture, was also a 'clocksmith'.[57] Edward Shelton of Donnington, who held 16 strikes' seedness of arable and 5 beasts' gate of pasture, was a wheelwright.[58] William Wynshurste of Donnington, with 6 beasts' gate of pasture and 5 days' math of meadow, was a weaver.[59] Robert Dawe, tenant of 11 beasts' gate of pasture, was a finer of iron.[60] John Morte of Lilleshall, holder of arable and meadow and of 4 beasts' gate of pasture on Willmore grange, was a tailor.[61] So was Richard Rowley of Donnington,[62] who had 3 beasts' gate of pasture and 6 days' math

[50] The sources used in this art. do not mention whether any of the recorded tenants sublet their holdings.
[51] *T.S.A.S.* lxiii. 1–10.
[52] S.R.O. 1910/477.
[53] *T.S.A.S.* 4th ser. v. 246.
[54] S.R.O. 38/165, 174, 177–8, 180–5.
[55] *Visit. Salop. 1623*, i. 137.

[56] S.R.O. 38/101, 132–42.
[57] Ibid. /101.
[58] Ibid. /137.
[59] Ibid. /143.
[60] Ibid. /158.
[61] Ibid. /102.
[62] Ibid. /149.

of meadow. One of the biggest agricultural tenants, Barnaby Careswell of Lilleshall, was a surgeon.[63]

During the 17th century the movement towards consolidation and inclosure of open-field arable holdings was taken further, so that by 1717 only two furlongs, in Moor field, remained divided into separately held strips.[64] In the 1670s, however, the movement still had some way to go. In Lilleshall and Honnington, in addition to the four open fields named in 16th-century records, there were by 1625 open fields called Small field and Limecroft field;[65] they may have been areas detached from the original fields by consolidation and inclosure.[66] It was possible in 1674 for a holding to include strips in all six fields.[67] The inconvenience of such an arrangement soon afterwards formed the subject of a petition by some small tenants to William Leveson-Gower, the new lord of the manor. They advocated further inclosure, to be preceded by consolidation of holdings, and Leveson-Gower encouraged the process.[68]

The reduction of common of pasture by inclosure of the open-field arable and of the Weald Moors created difficulties for the smaller livestock farmers, which probably contributed to their eventual demise.[69] In 1617 a stint over the open fields of 8 beasts and 60 sheep for every ploughland was established, but in 1652 a reduction of 10 sheep for every ploughland was ordered, and cottagers were to be allowed only one beast. Increased competition for holdings is suggested by the large increase of entry fines and rents that occurred over the century.[70] More land, however, became available for rent in 1650, when nearly all the remaining demesne lands were let.[71] They were provided in 1653 with a new grange house, a long stone building of two and a half storeys, later much altered, and divided by 1980 into three dwellings. Sir Richard Leveson's arms and initials and the date are set in the centre of the north front. The deer park was kept in hand. By 1679 the part west of, and including, the lodge had been inclosed, but the greater part remained open.[72] About 1720 starving deer, which had to compete with cattle and horses for grazing inside the park, were escaping and causing damage outside.[73] The open part of the park was divided up c. 1774 and the whole let off.[74]

In the later 17th and earlier 18th century most farmers had both livestock and cereals. Herds of cattle averaged 15, rather more than in some neighbouring parishes, and cheese was widely made, sometimes on a large scale. Farmers kept sheep less often than in some nearby parishes, but their flocks were of comparable size, averaging 30.[75] Horse dealing formed part of the economy of

several local families during the 17th century. They traded at fairs at Derby, Stafford, and Penkridge (Staffs.), as well as at Shrewsbury and Bridgnorth.[76] There were at least four hemp butts and a hemp yard in 1598[77] and in 1717 there were about 15 hemp yards.[78] The parish was noted for hemp in 1784[79] but in 1804 there were only five small hemp butts.[80]

From the 1680s to 1720, while the Revd. George Plaxton was chief agent for the Leveson-Gower estates, expiring leaseholds were turned into tenancies at will, and by 1720 few leaseholds remained. In the 1720s the rents were racked, and during the agricultural depression of the 1730s and 1740s increases continued though more moderately. Lilleshall escaped the worst effects of the depression because its farms did not rely mainly on cereals.[81]

In 1755 the advantage that had accrued to the landlord by rack renting was suddenly abandoned. To pay for election expenses Lord Gower offered every tenant on his Lilleshall estates a 99-year lease terminable on three lives, at the 1755 rent and for an entry fine of only one year's rent. Most accepted and until the 1790s, when a good proportion of the leases was beginning to fall in, the landlord lacked an incentive to improve his estate. Rack rents replaced the 1755 leases as they expired.[82]

As the leases fell in the marquess of Stafford appointed the first of a succession of energetic chief land agents. Using the latest techniques of estate management to extract the maximum sustained return compatible with the tenants' ability to pay, the agents, inaugurated a thorough policy of raising rents and improving holdings. The most celebrated was James Loch, from 1812 to 1855. When prices fell after the Napoleonic wars the landlord made further improvements to enable tenants to pay the rent increases he still demanded of them. Rent reduction was considered a last resort, but in 1821 Loch conceded a new renting system, in which half of a tenant's rent was reducible as the price of wheat fell. The total rent nevertheless rose between 1816 and 1833 despite a considerable fall in prices.[83] Moreover after 1825 Loch advised the landlord against investing in further estate improvements.[84]

By the 1850s rents had been increased further, but Loch's improvements had placed the tenants in a favourable position to weather price depressions, and their rents were then considered low in relation to the value of their farms. By then there had been a shift of emphasis at Lilleshall from landlord investment and control to tenant enterprise.[85]

Throughout the 18th and early 19th century,

[63] Ibid. /106, 112.
[64] S.R.O. 972, parcel 234, N. map of Lilleshall.
[65] Staffs. R.O., D. 593/J/13/2/1, 26 Apr. 1625.
[66] Edwards, 'Farming Econ.' 230.
[67] S.R.O. 38/121.
[68] Edwards, op. cit. 230.
[69] Below.
[70] Edwards, op. cit. 33–4, 134, 272; Wordie, 'Gt. Landed Estate', graph following p. 34.
[71] S.R.O. 1910/480.
[72] S.R.O. 972, parcel 233, map of Lilleshall pk. 1679; parcel 234, map of Lilleshall pk. etc.
[73] Staffs. R.O., D. 593/P/16/1/26.

[74] S.R.O. 972, parcel 233, map of Lilleshall pk. 1774.
[75] Yeomen and Colliers in Telford, ed. B. Trinder and J. Cox (1980), pp. 72–83.
[76] Edwards, 'Farming Econ.' 170–1, 173, 178–9.
[77] Staffs. R.O., D. 593/H/14/1/1.
[78] S.R.O. 972, parcel 234, Lilleshall maps.
[79] V.C.H. Salop. i. 422.
[80] S.R.O. 38/17.
[81] Research in Econ. Hist. vi. 197, 202–4.
[82] Ibid. 206–7.
[83] Ibid. 208–10, 212, 217.
[84] Ag. H.R. xxii. 104.
[85] Ibid. 105, 116.

and without the direct intervention of the land-lord, the larger farmers were able gradually to increase their holdings at the expense of those with medium-sized farms.[86] In 1804, apart from 1,163 a. held by the Lilleshall Co., the manor had 25 farms over 50 a. and averaging 160 a.[87] By 1839, again excluding the Lilleshall Co.'s land, there were only 18 farms over 50 a. and they averaged 228 a.[88] While large farms were becoming larger, population growth caused an increase in the number of cottage holdings and a reduction in their average size; population growth eventually led also to an increase, in the early 19th century, in the area of the estate occupied by cottages, again at the expense of medium-sized farms. Thus by the 1830s the economic and social distinction between farmer and cottager had become absolute.[89]

In 1810 some of the farms remained fragmented, but by 1820 Loch had achieved a complete reorganization and consolidation. Field boundaries were rationalized, access roads were built or realigned, and drainage was greatly improved, especially in the north. Unsuitable farm buildings were replaced by model farms such as the Lilleshall Hill, Woodhouse, Muxton Hill, Honnington Grange, Hincks, and Donnington farms.[90]

In 1801 the main crops at Lilleshall were wheat (690 a.), oats (384 a.), and barley (325 a.). Rye, turnips, rape, potatoes, beans, and peas were also grown.[91] In 1820 the tenants were said to be excellent livestock farmers. They were also good cultivators of the lighter soils, but had been less successful on the stiffer ones. Most tenants on the heavier land, however, had begun to plough with only two horses abreast, a Norfolk practice advocated by Loch. On some of the farms with heavier soil Loch encouraged the tenants to put more down to grass.[92] In the 1840s the farmers were required to follow a five-course rotation on their arable, and could be fined for ploughing up permanent pasture.[93]

In the later 19th and early 20th century livestock farming, especially of cattle, became predominant. Sheep farming declined[94] but not so much as in the Wellington area.[95] Farmers were able to weather the agricultural depression and were helped by individual rent reductions. In the 1890s, dissatisfied with livestock prices at local markets, they held auctions on their own farms, attracting buyers from Herefordshire, Staffordshire, and Warwickshire.[96] In the mid 20th century arable farming resumed its earlier supremacy, but barley did not predominate over wheat[97] as it did around Wellington.[98] There was also more diversification. In 1979 potatoes and daffodils were grown on a large scale at Honnington

Grange and fruit at Lubstree Park.[99] The tradition of efficient farming established under the Leveson-Gowers was maintained in the 20th century.[1] For example in 1979 Donnington farm and Honnington Grange were being worked as a single unit (c. 735 a.), from whose arable parts hedges and isolated trees had been removed.

On the eve of the 5th duke's sales in 1914 and 1917 there were 17 farms over 50 a. Excluding two farms that extended into an adjoining parish, the average size was 247 a. The largest was Lubstree Park. Its tenant, T. H. Ward, also held

TABLE VI

LILLESHALL: LAND USE, LIVESTOCK AND CROPS

	1867	1891	1938	1965
Percentage of grassland	54	65	71	32
arable	46	35	29	68
Percentage of cattle	16	23	28	30
sheep	74	49	59	49
pigs	10	8	13	21
Percentage of wheat	60	49	72	59
barley	27	33	8	40
oats	13	17	19	1
mixed corn & rye	0	1	1	0
Percentage of agricultural land growing roots and vegetables	11	11	11	13

Sources: P.R.O., MAF 68/143, no. 1; /1340, no. 10; /3880, Salop. no. 127; /4945, no. 127.

Donnington Wood farm.[2] Ward was progressive and successful, and his family was to include a number of notable agriculturists.[3] In 1914 he bought Donnington Wood farm and the Hincks, and his son T. C. Ward bought Lubstree Park.[4] T. C. Ward owned some 1,100 a. in the parish at his death in 1956.[5] In 1979 T. H. Ward's descendants owned or farmed Lubstree Park, Watling Street Grange, Woodhouse, Honnington Grange, and Donnington farms. Some farmland in the parish, however, had recently been bought by an insurance company.[6]

MILLS. There was a mill in 1086 worth

[86] J. R. Wordie, 'Social Change on the Leveson Gower Estates, 1714–1832', *Ec. H.R.* 2nd ser. xxvii. 593–609.
[87] S.R.O. 38/17.
[88] Ibid. /18.
[89] *Ec. H.R.* 2nd ser. xxvii. 593–609.
[90] Loch, *Acct. of Improvements.* Detailed descrs. of 17 large Lilleshall farms are given in the app. pp. 83–92, 113–14.
[91] P.R.O., HO 67/14/161.
[92] Loch, op. cit.
[93] R. Perren, 'Effects of Agric. Depression on Eng. Estates of Dukes of Sutherland, 1870–1900' (Nottingham Univ. Ph.D. thesis, 1967), 158–9.

[94] See Table VI.
[95] Below, Wellington, Econ. Hist. (Agric.).
[96] Perren, 'Agric. Depression', 329–32, 415–17.
[97] See Table VI.
[98] Below, Wellington, Econ. Hist. (Agric.).
[99] Inf. from the late Mr. R. W. Ward.
[1] E. J. Howell, *Shropshire* (Land of Britain, lxvi), 274.
[2] S.R.O. 972, parcels 205, 207, sale partic. of 1914, 1917.
[3] *Shropshire Mag.* July 1954, 22–5.
[4] S.R.O. 972, parcel 206, list of purchasers.
[5] *Shrews. Chron.* 10 Feb. 1956.
[6] Local inf.

nothing.[7] The abbot was amerced *c.* 1180 for having a mill within the royal forest,[8] perhaps on Lilleshall manor, and *c.* 1200 for making a mill and a pond in the forest.[9] The latter was probably at Lubstree park, where the lords of Preston and Eyton manors at about that time permitted the abbot to make a mill and pond (Lubstree pool) on Humber brook.[10] The pond lay immediately upstream of the crossing of the brook by the Lilleshall–Preston road in 1580. By then the mill had been replaced by a water-powered forge.[11]

In 1330 the abbot had two water mills on his demesne, one of them within the abbey precincts ('infra abbatiam') worth 26*s.* 8*d.* a year, the other outside and worth 40*s.* a year.[12] In 1353 their value was 12*s.* and 10*s.*[13] There was only one water mill on the demesne in 1375, but it was worth 53*s.* 4*d.*[14] By 1404 John the miller rented a mill or mills at Honnington.[15] In 1428–9 and 1436–7 Thomas Millward was renting a mill or mills at Lilleshall outside the demesne.[16] In 1536–7 one water mill was recorded on the demesne.[17] In 1538–9 there were two mills at Honnington, let together, and another 'within Lilleshall park'; all three were rented by Thomas Fletcher in 1538.[18] John Jenckes, 'the miller', occurred in 1637–8.[19]

In 1634 there were three mill sites on the stream between Lilleshall abbey and the village, all on the demesne. The first, a wheat mill, lay north-west of the abbey ruins. Another, an old malt mill, stood some 200–300 metres downstream. At the third site, by the pond 'at Lilleshall town's end', stood mills of unspecified number.[20] In 1717 each of the first two ponds had a building, presumably a mill, on its downstream side, and a mill was recorded next to the town's end pond.[21] That mill remained in 1805,[22] but the others had apparently gone by 1804.[23]

Between 1775 and 1804 a windmill was built on the west side of Lilleshall village street.[24] It was rented in 1804 by Joseph Boycot,[25] who, as a miller, had been tenant of the three mill ponds *c.* 1780.[26] The building was called the Old Windmill in 1880[27] and had disappeared by 1901.[28] The large pond immediately south of the Wellington–Newport road at Honnington existed by 1717[29] and may previously have been a mill pond. Between 1817 and 1819 Honnington Grange farm was provided with its own corn mill[30] driven by water

from the pond. Later a turbine replaced the mill.[31]

It is likely that the Lilleshall mills were less used after *c.* 1820 when the Donnington Wood corn mills (in Wrockwardine Wood) came into operation.[32]

MINES, QUARRIES, AND SANDPITS. The parish formerly had valuable minerals, especially coal and ironstone at Donnington Wood and limestone at Lilleshall village.

The Coal Measures are near the surface on the west side of Donnington Wood, but dip towards the east, especially beyond the Lightmoor fault.[33] The earlier pits were therefore on the extreme west of the parish. Mining did not progress northwards beyond the Boundary fault, just south of Donnington village.

The manor had a coal mine worth 20*s.* a year in 1330,[34] but it was not mentioned in 1353 or 1375.[35] The road name Coalpit Way occurred at Donnington wood in 1592.[36] In April 1592 Sir Walter Leveson, in partnership with his brother-in-law[37] Vincent Corbet of Poynton, let several parcels at Donnington wood, reserving any coal there; the tenants were expected to clear the surface.[38] In 1717 a field called Bradshaw Leasow coalpits lay on the western edge of the wood.[39] Outside the Donnington wood area two fields on either side of the Muxton–Honnington road, which both acquired the name Pit leasow in the 18th century,[40] may have been associated with coalpits that, according to local tradition, lay nearby.[41]

Limestone was being extracted in the parish by the early 17th century and limekilns existed there in 1625,[42] though lime was brought in from Huntington, in Little Wenlock, *c.* 1620.[43] Lilleshall lime was used in the 1650s in building Audlem grammar school (Ches.).[44] Drainage, however, seems already to have been a problem; in 1655 a bather drowned in the Lilleshall lime pits.[45]

In 1674 the new landlord, William Leveson-Gower, leased all the minerals in the manor (except in Lilleshall park) to Francis Charlton of Apley for 21 years. By the time the lease expired the surface coal at Donnington wood was exhausted, and the deeper coal could not be mined until proper drainage had been devised. At the limestone workings satisfactory drainage had re-

---

[7] *V.C.H. Salop.* i. 314.

[8] Ibid. 486.

[9] *Pipe R.* 1200 (P.R.S. N.S. xii), 253.

[10] Eyton, viii. 28–9, 258.

[11] *T.S.A.S.* liv, pl. facing p. 258 (on date see ibid. lxiii. 3).

[12] B.L. Add. MS. 6165, f. 37.

[13] Ibid. 50121, p. 152.

[14] Ibid. 6165, f. 49.

[15] S.P.L., MS. 4426.

[16] L.J.R.O., B/C/5, Lilleshall abbey acct. r.

[17] P.R.O., E 315/400, f. 2.

[18] P.R.O., LR 2/184, f. 7v.; P.R.O., SC 6/Hen. VIII/3009, m. 17.

[19] S.R.O. 4462/Con/7.

[20] S.R.O. 38/13.

[21] S.R.O. 972, parcel 234, middle map of Lilleshall.

[22] S.R.O. 4462/Gl/1.

[23] S.R.O. 38/15, 17.

[24] Ibid. /15; S.R.O. 972, box 41, survey of 1775 × 1783, f. 8.

[25] S.R.O. 38/17, f. 31.

[26] S.R.O. 972, box 41, survey of 1775 × 1783, f. 8.

[27] O.S. Map 6", Salop. XXXVI. NE. (1890 edn.).

[28] Ibid. (1903 edn.).

[29] S.R.O. 972, parcel 234, middle map of Lilleshall.

[30] Loch, *Acct. of Improvements*, app. p. 114 and pl. 32.

[31] Inf. from the late Mr. Ward.

[32] Below, Wrockwardine Wood, Econ. Hist. (Mill).

[33] Inst. Geol. Sciences Map 1/25,000, *Telford* (1978 edn.).

[34] B.L. Add. MS. 6165, f. 37.

[35] Ibid. ff. 41, 49.

[36] S.R.O. 38/132.

[37] *Visit. Salop. 1623*, i. 137.

[38] S.R.O. 38/101, 132–42; Staffs. R.O., D. 593/H/14/1/1.

[39] S.R.O. 972, parcel 234, map of Lilleshall pk. etc. No other name on the map appears to refer to active coal workings.

[40] Ibid. middle map of Lilleshall; S.R.O. 38/15; /17, ff. 19, 25.

[41] T. H. Whitehead and others, *Country between Wolverhampton and Oakengates* (Geol. Surv. Memoir, 1928), 76.

[42] Staffs. R.O., D. 593/J/13/2/1, 13 Oct. 1625.

[43] Above, L. Wenlock, Econ. Hist. (Limestone).

[44] *Chester Arch. Soc. Jnl.* li. 44.

[45] S.R.O. 4462/Rg/1, bur. 23 June 1655.

cently been effected, but they could not be exploited without coal for the kilns. Sir John Leveson-Gower was advised not to lease the minerals again, because of the tenant's inclination to exhaust them before his lease expired, and they remained in hand 1695–1715. Between 1715 and 1764 they were leased to a succession of tenants, all of whom failed to make them pay,[46] although some iron ore from Donnington Wood was being used from 1755 at the Horsehay ironworks in Dawley. Much greater investment in drainage and equipment was needed.[47]

To that end a partnership was formed in 1764 between Earl Gower and the brothers John and Thomas Gilbert, the earl having a half share. Earl Gower & Co. (from 1786 the Marquis of Stafford & Co.) continued in existence until 1802, and its main concern was to rent and develop the coal and limestone industries on the earl's Shropshire estates.[48] The company's period of greatest investment was between 1764 and 1773.[49] Other lessees, the Donnington Wood Co., held the Donnington Wood ironstone workings,[50] and by 1788 coal and ironstone mines covered the western side of Donnington Wood.[51] The Donnington Wood Co. made an underground level to drain its workings.[52] Individual coalpits were managed by charter masters, contractors to the company who had a share of the profits.[53] The system survived at one pit until 1913.[54]

In 1802 the Marquis of Stafford & Co. was dissolved, to be replaced by the Lilleshall Co., a new partnership between the marquess's second son, Lord Granville Leveson-Gower (cr. Viscount Granville 1815, Earl Granville 1833), John Bishton the elder, James Birch, John Onions, and William Phillips. The last four were already lessees of the Donnington Wood ironworks and ironstone mines, and thus brought the parish's iron-making resources into direct combination with the former company's coal and limestone enterprises.[55] From 1802 all extraction of ironstone and limestone in the parish and of coal (until coal nationalization in 1947) was carried out by the Lilleshall Co. During January 1805 the Donnington Wood pits produced 6,750 tons of coal and 1,300 tons of ironstone,[56] and there was further expansion until the middle of the century, especially into the deeper seams that lay on the east side of the wood. The company sank its first deep mine, at Waxhill Barracks, in 1818,[57] and another, the Freehold pit, at about the same

period.[58] The Muxton Bridge pit was opened by 1840.[59] There were over 400 a. of coalpits and waste tips in the parish in the 1840s,[60] and their production was running at some 100,000 tons of coal a year, with 50,000 tons of iron ore.[61] By 1860 the Granville pit had been sunk[62] and sinking of the Grange (originally the Albert and Alexandra) pit[63] began in 1864.[64]

From the late 19th century coalmining in the parish gradually declined. The Waxhill Barracks colliery ceased production c. 1900,[65] and that at Muxton Bridge soon afterwards.[66] The Freehold colliery closed in 1928[67] and only the Grange and Granville collieries survived until nationalization.[68] In 1951 the two were connected underground, and from 1952 the Grange served merely to ventilate the Granville.[69] In 1979 the Granville colliery, then employing some 560 men, was closed. It was the last coal mine in Shropshire. Increasing geological difficulties had contributed to falling production and several years of heavy losses.[70]

In the later 18th century the Lilleshall limestone workings assumed their greatest extent as opencast quarries. There were two main quarries. The larger, Collier's Side, lay immediately northeast of Limekiln Lane. The smaller lay on the west side of the lane. From the quarries underground workings are believed to have begun in the late 18th century, and it was from the underground workings that most of the limestone was thenceforth extracted, while kilns stood on the old quarry floors.[71] Output of limestone at Lilleshall during January 1805 was 7,400 tons.[72] The white stone was favoured as a flux for iron making, while the grey made an excellent hydraulic cement[73] and was so used by 1767.[74] By 1846 the fluxing limestone was exhausted.[75] About 1856 the annual output of limestone from all the Lilleshall Co.'s workings was 26,000 tons, a high proportion of which was from Lilleshall.[76] About 1858 the Willmore limestone mine was begun, east of the old quarries, and before it closed in 1882 it had yielded an estimated 175,000 tons.[77] From c. 1860 the company began to move its limestone mining activity to Presthope, in Much Wenlock, and later to Nantmawr, in Oswestry. Drainage difficulties made the main Lilleshall workings unprofitable.[78] By the 1870s large-scale production had ceased[79] but small amounts of agricultural lime probably continued to be made.[80]

A disused sandstone quarry, said to have sup-

[46] Wordie, 'Gt. Landed Estate', 162–6.
[47] Trinder, *Ind. Rev. Salop.* 42.
[48] Ibid.; Wordie, op. cit. 192–4; above, plate 22.
[49] Wordie, op. cit. 201, 225.
[50] Gale and Nicholls, *Lilleshall Co.* 16; Trinder, op. cit. 72; *Salop. News Sheet*, xvii. 7.
[51] S.R.O. 691/1.
[52] *Salop. News Sheet*, xvii. 7–8.
[53] Trinder, *Ind. Rev. Salop.* 343–4.
[54] I. J. Brown, *Mines of Salop.* (Buxton, 1976), 34.
[55] Trinder, op. cit. 72–3.
[56] Wordie, 'Gt. Landed Estate', 229.
[57] Gale and Nicholls, *Lilleshall Co.* 28.
[58] Brown, *Mines of Salop.* 41.
[59] Gale and Nicholls, op. cit. 29.
[60] Trinder, *Ind. Rev. Salop.* 320.
[61] Frost, *Story of Donnington*, 12.
[62] Brown, *Mines of Salop.* 34.
[63] Whitehead and others, *Country between Wolverhampton and Oakengates*, 63 n.

[64] Brown, op. cit. 39.
[65] Ibid. 41.
[66] *V.C.H. Salop.* i. 456; S.R.O., DA 26/114/5, p. 1385.
[67] Brown, op. cit. 42.
[68] Gale and Nicholls, *Lilleshall Co.* 99.
[69] Brown, op. cit. 39.
[70] *Shropshire Star*, 2 Nov. 1977; 11 Aug. 1978.
[71] I. J. Brown, *Hist. of Limestone Mining in Salop.* (Salop. Mining Club Acct. vi, 1967), 5; Adams and Hazeley, *Survey*, pp. 29–36 and fig. 7.
[72] Wordie, 'Gt. Landed Estate', 229.
[73] Whitehead and others, *Country between Wolverhampton and Oakengates*, 35.
[74] Trinder, *Ind. Rev. Salop.* 97.
[75] Ibid. 249.
[76] Adams and Hazeley, *Survey*, 43.
[77] Ibid. 47–50.
[78] *V.C.H. Salop.* i. 449; Gale and Nicholls, *Lilleshall Co.* 40.
[79] Hadfield, *Canals of W. Midlands*, 238; Adams and Hazeley, *Survey*, 2, 51.
[80] Adams and Hazeley, *Survey*, 44.

plied stone for St. George's church,[81] adjoined Watling Street in 1882,[82] and nearby on the north-east the name 'quarell fylde' occurred in 1547.[83] Another disused sandstone quarry occurred in 1881 north-east of the Old Lodge site.[84] By 1839 igneous rock was being quarried from Lilleshall Hill for road making,[85] and quarrying was recorded there in 1900.[86] Excellent foundry sands were dug at Donnington Wood[87] until the early 20th century.[88]

IRON AND ENGINEERING. The parish's abundance of suitable materials favoured the early development of ironworking. In some form it was being carried on at Donnington wood by 1277, when the 'qualmesmytthe' (probably the 'smithy of the spring')[89] lay isolated in the wood between Waxhillgate and the manor's western boundary.[90] The smithy was near Quam Pool and by 1804 the area was occupied by ironworks and mines.[91]

Between the late 16th and late 18th century there was commercial iron making in the parish on a small scale. By 1580 Walter Leveson owned water-driven hammers on Humber brook at Lubstree pool,[92] where the abbot's mill had stood.[93] It was alleged in 1583 that the pond had been brought back into use only in recent years.[94] Robert Dawe of Lubstree, described in 1595 as a finer,[95] rented a cottage at Lubstree park and pasture on both sides of the brook[96] and may be assumed to have worked the Lubstree forge or 'hammer smithies' (so called in 1600).[97] A successor, Thomas Dawes the 'hammersman', occurred 1658–61 as tenant of the pasture, but the hammer house was rented by William Whitmore the lodge keeper.[98] The neighbourhood was known as the Hammers by 1678[99] and thence by 1881 as the Humbers.[1] By 1585 a bloom forge was working in Lilleshall village at the 'Pool'. Since it was from that forge that a fire spread through the village,[2] the pool was probably the mill pond taken into the Hall grounds c. 1810.[3] In 1591 Sir Walter Leveson leased his Shropshire ironworks, furnaces, forges, and hammers to his brothers-in-law,[4] Richard Corbet of Moreton and Vincent Corbet of Poynton, for 10 years.[5] The Lilleshall furnace,

one of the earliest blast furnaces in the west Midlands,[6] may have stood at Donnington wood, where by the following year Vincent Corbet had rights in the ironstone and in the wood (for charcoal burning).[7]

In the later 17th century ironworks on the manor seem to have been carried on, like the mines, by lessees, and associated trades, founding and nail making, developed. Thomas Fox of Muxton was an ironmaster in 1666–7,[8] and in the period 1686–9 John Charlton and his father[9] Francis, of Apley Castle, occurred as lessees of ironworks in Lilleshall manor[10] as well as of all the mines. Small amounts of charcoal slag occur beside the stream from one of the former mill ponds[11] to a point north of Lilleshall Grange.[12] Nail making was carried on at Pain's Lane in the late 17th century.[13] Before 1717 iron was being cast immediately upstream of the supposed mill pond at Honnington, on the right bank of the stream. The place was called Founders yard in 1717 and was rented by John James.[14] In 1804 the same field was called Furnace meadow and rented by the Lilleshall Co.[15]

Large-scale iron making in the parish began in 1785, when a furnace came into blast at Donnington Wood. The works was started by William Reynolds and Joseph Rathbone on 36 a. leased from Earl Gower, adjoining the north side of the Donnington Wood Canal on the western edge of the parish. Gower contributed £2,000 to the enterprise. In 1796 John Bishton and his partners bought the works and in 1797 became lessees of the site too. In 1802 the works passed to the Lilleshall Co., which owned it thereafter. By 1802 there were two furnaces, and a third was added in that year.[16] The pig iron was of high quality and in 1810 was being used at the Soho Foundry, Smethwick.[17] In spite of a stoppage in 1817 caused by the general depression,[18] and another in 1821 caused by colliers who were protesting against wage reductions, all the furnaces remained active until 1846 when one was blown out. The other two were blown out c. 1859.[19] Associated with the Donnington Wood furnaces was the nearby Yard, comprising a foundry and small engineering shop.

[81] James, 'Here be Dragons', 7.
[82] O.S. Map 6″, Salop. XXXVI. SE. (1889 edn.); Whitehead and others, Country between Wolverhampton and Oakengates, 91.
[83] S.R.O. 38/162; 972, parcel 242, map of c. 1642.
[84] O.S. Map 6″, Salop. XXXVI. NE. (1890 edn.); Whitehead and others, op. cit. 91.
[85] Adams and Hazeley, Survey, 40.
[86] O.S. Map 6″, Salop. XXXVI. NE. (1903 edn.).
[87] K. C. Riley, 'Changes in Population in the Wellington–Oakengates Conurbation 1801–1951' (London Univ. M.A. thesis, 1958), 8.
[88] O.S. Map 1/2,500, Salop. XXXVI. 11 (1902 edn.).
[89] Thanks are due to Dr. M. Gelling for this translation.
[90] Sd.O. 972, box 220, deed.   [91] S.R.O. 38/15, 17.
[92] T.S.A.S. liv, pl. facing p. 258 (on the date see ibid. lxiii. 3); Staffs R.O., D. 593/B/2/7/5.
[93] Above (Mills).
[94] Staffs. R.O., D. 593/B/2/7/5, Rob. Eyton's deposition.
[95] S.R.O. 38/158.
[96] Ibid.; Staffs. R.O., D. 593/H/14/1/1.
[97] Staffs. R.O., D. 593/I/1/15/1, deed.
[98] S.R.O. 1910/491.
[99] S.R.O. 4462/Rg/1, bur. 24 Sept. 1678; /2, bap. 17 May 1754.

[1] O.S Map 6″, Salop. XXXVI. NE. (1890 edn.).
[2] T.S.A.S. iii. 301; Salopian Shreds & Patches, iv. 37.
[3] S.R.O. 38/15; 972, parcel 238, map of 1813.
[4] Visit. Salop. 1623, i. 136–7.
[5] Staffs. R.O., D. 593/C/8/2, deed.
[6] H. R. Schubert, Hist. of Brit. Iron and Steel Ind. (1957), 380. Cf. T.S.A.S. lvi. 70–1; V.C.H. Staffs. xvii. 38.
[7] S.R.O. 38/101, 132–42.
[8] B.L. Add. MS. 21236, f. 271v.
[9] S.P.L., MS. 2789, p. 199.
[10] Staffs. R.O., D. 593/C/16/3, accts.
[11] At O.S. Nat. Grid SJ 732 145.
[12] Inf. from Dr. B. S. Trinder.
[13] S.R.O. 4462/CW/2, s.a. 1674–6, 1695–6. Thos. Allcock (mentioned therein) was living at Pain's La. 1693 (P.R.O., RG 31/7, Salop. no. 35) and fields there were named after the fam. by 1717 (S.R.O. 972, parcel 234, map of Lilleshall pk. etc.).
[14] S.R.O. 972, parcel 234, middle map of Lilleshall.
[15] S.R.O. 38/15; /17, f. 7.
[16] Trinder, Ind. Rev. Salop. 67, 69, 72–3, 408.
[17] Gale and Nicholls, Lilleshall Co. 24.
[18] E. Richards, 'Industrial Face of a Gt. Estate', Ec. H.R. xxvii. 422.
[19] Trinder, Ind. Rev. Salop. 240, 384.

It closed in 1861[20] when the New Yard engineering works opened in Wrockwardine Wood township.[21]

In 1825 the company brought into blast two new furnaces near the site of the Old Lodge. In 1830 the Donnington Wood and Old Lodge ironworks together produced 15,110 tons. A third furnace was added at the Old Lodge in 1846 and two more c. 1859.[22] The Old Lodge furnaces produced cold-blast pig iron of the finest quality, but eventually it could not compete with cheaper iron made elsewhere or with Bessemer steel, and in 1888 the last of the Old Lodge furnaces was blown out. Thereafter the company concentrated all its iron and steel making at Priorslee.[23]

In 1857 Charles Walker & Sons of Clerkenwell, engineers, moved to a railside site at Donnington and changed the firm's name to C. & W. Walker.[24] The works, known by 1880 as the Midland Iron Works,[25] was directed, from 1857 until his death in 1897, by C. C. Walker.[26] The firm specialized in making gas-purification plant and gas holders. At first the works employed 30–40 men, but it soon became one of the world's leading suppliers of gas equipment. There were 200–300 employees by 1870,[27] 400–500 by 1879,[28] and 700–800 by 1891,[29] and in 1899 the firm became a limited company.[30] In 1948 the works covered nearly 18 a. but the workforce had fallen to c. 400.[31] From the 1960s, when coal gas was superseded by natural gas, the firm specialized in containers for other gases, chemicals, and grain. In 1979 it still employed over 300 people but had recently sold part of the site for occupation by smaller firms.[32]

BRICKS AND TILES. Before the late 18th century bricks were made in several parts of the parish, and sometimes on a commercial scale. A Brick furlong occurred south of Lilleshall Grange in 1598.[33] In the later 17th century the Broadhurst and Barber families were supplying the parish officers with bricks and tiles,[34] presumably made in the parish.[35] A Brick Kiln close occurred at Lubstree park in 1717,[36] and a Brick Kiln piece north of Watling Street Grange in 1774.[37] In 1804 there was a Brick Kiln leasow south-west of Cheswell Grange and a Brick Kiln piece south of New Lodge.[38]

In the late 18th and early 19th century large-scale brick and tile making catered for industrial and housing development at Donnington Wood[39] and agricultural improvements, which demanded bricks, roof tiles, and drainage pipes. From 1761 to 1780 Joseph Taylor occurred as tenant of a large brick and tile works on the northern edge of Donnington wood;[40] the works, called the Woodfield (or Waxhill) brick yard,[41] remained active until the beginning of the 20th century.[42] In 1804, after the Lilleshall Co. had assumed control of the industry, there was a Wood Brick Kiln piece north-east of Pain's Lane,[43] and a brick yard was still working there in 1850. There was a brick yard at the White colliery near the canal at Donnington Wood in 1839;[44] it closed between 1880 and 1901[45] as did a small yard west of the Old Lodge site.[46] Brick and tile making in the parish became concentrated at the mechanized Donnington Wood brickworks[47] that opened in 1876 near the old Pain's Lane works.[48] About 1908 it was producing 3–4 million bricks a year.[49] The bricks were of high quality but proved expensive after the Second World War,[50] and the works closed in 1972.[51]

CENTRAL ORDNANCE DEPOT. Donnington was chosen in 1936 as the site of a depot to replace the Royal Arsenal, Woolwich.[52] The site was not ideal, considered strategically, but was designed to provide employment in a depressed area.[53] In addition to a loss of mining and iron-making jobs since the 19th century, the parish had suffered heavy redundancies in 1931 when the New Yard works at St. George's closed.[54] Construction of the depot, adjoining the north side of the railway, began in 1938. The first stores were brought from Woolwich in 1939,[55] six hundred civilians were transferred thence in 1940, and the depot was completed in 1943. By 1962, with its associated units, it was the biggest employer of civilian labour in the parish.[56] In 1976 nearly 4,000 civilians worked there.

LOCAL GOVERNMENT. In 1255 the abbot's manor of Lilleshall did no suit to the shire or the hundred, and in 1292 the abbot claimed to hold two great courts a year with all the pleas of the sheriff's tourn.[57] Court rolls or drafts survive for

[20] V.C.H. Salop. i. 471; Gale and Nicholls, Lilleshall Co. 46.
[21] Below, Wrockwardine Wood, Econ. Hist. (Iron and Steel).
[22] Trinder, op. cit. 239–40.
[23] V.C.H. Salop. i. 470; below, Wombridge, Econ. Hist. (Iron and Steel).
[24] Para. based on C. & W. Walker Ltd. The Progress of C. & W. Walker Ltd. [1948] (copy in S.P.L.).
[25] O.S. Map 6″, Salop. XXXVI. NE. (1890 edn.).
[26] Shrews. Chron. 4 Feb. 1897; above, plate 24.
[27] P.O. Dir. Salop. (1870), 74.   [28] Ibid. (1879), 341.
[29] Kelly's Dir. Salop. (1891), 340.
[30] Frost, Story of Donnington, 16.
[31] Riley, 'Population in Wellington–Oakengates', 173.
[32] Frost, op. cit. 23.
[33] Staffs. R.O., D. 593/H/14/1/1; S.R.O. 38/13.
[34] S.R.O. 4462/P/1/3, s.a. 1685–6; /CW/2, s.a. 1695–7.
[35] The fams. were local: S.R.O. 972, parcel 234, N. and middle maps of Lilleshall.   [36] Ibid. N. map of Lilleshall.
[37] S.R.O. 972, parcel 233, Lilleshall pk. map.
[38] S.R.O. 38/15; /17, ff. 40, 48.
[39] e.g. Trinder, Ind. Rev. Salop. 99.
[40] Wordie, 'Gt. Landed Estate', 192; S.R.O. 4462/CW/3, pp. 1, 49, 65.
[41] W. Howard Williams, 'Lilleshall Co. Hist. 1802–1966' (TS. [c .1966]), p. 7 (copy in S.R.O. 3072/1).
[42] O.S. Map 6″, Salop. XXXVI. NE. (1903 and 1928 edns.).
[43] S.R.O. 38/15; /17, f. 10.
[44] Williams, 'Lilleshall Co. Hist.' pp. 1, 7.
[45] O.S. Map 6″, Salop. XXXVI. NE. (1890 and 1903 edns.).   [46] Ibid. SE. (1889 and 1903 edns.).
[47] V.C.H. Salop. i. 444.
[48] Williams, 'Lilleshall Co. Hist.' p. 7.
[49] V.C.H. Salop. i. 444.
[50] Gale and Nicholls, Lilleshall Co. 111.
[51] Williams, 'Lilleshall Co. Hist.' p. 7.
[52] Para. based on programme of T.D.C. visit to C.O.D. 26 Feb. 1976 (copy in possession of the archivist, T.D.C.).
[53] Fernyhough, Hist. R.A.O.C. 1920–45, 442.
[54] Gale and Nicholls, Lilleshall Co. 89–90.
[55] Fernyhough, op. cit. 409.
[56] Shore, 'Survey of Donnington', p. 6.
[57] Eyton, viii. 230; Plac. de Quo Warr. (Rec. Com.), 679.

1281, 1359, 1408–9, 1422–3, 1592, 1625–55 (intermittently), and 1812, and other records for dates between 1624 and 1817.[58] In 1281 the great court was held on the same day as one of the little courts.[59] In the early 15th century the manor's little court was apparently held every four weeks and heard separate groups of presentments for Lilleshall, Honnington, Muxton, and Donnington. The manorial officers included two constables, two aletasters, and a bailiff, parker, and woodward.[60] At that period, however, the great and little courts were held on different days.[61]

By 1592 the 'view of frankpledge and little court' were held as one session, and their jurisdiction included Longdon upon Tern manor. In 1592 Lilleshall manor had two constables and two aletasters; one of each was assigned to Lilleshall (presumably including Honnington) and one to Muxton and Donnington jointly.[62] The two manorial divisions persisted into the 19th century. By the 17th century the court was called a 'view of frankpledge with great and baron court' or 'court leet and court baron'. The officers included, for each division, a constable, an aletaster, a 'keeper of the field' (increased by 1655 to two 'overseers for the fields and field hedges') as well as a hayward, and two 'overseers of the watercourses and ditches' (also called 'overseers of the moor ditches'[63] and, by 1812, 'brooklookers').[64] Each division had a pinfold and stocks in the 17th century.[65] In 1717 a Pinfold yard occurred at Lilleshall on the west side of the later Limekiln Lane,[66] and in 1813 a Pinfold croft lay at Donnington on the west side of the lane from the village to Donnington wood.[67] By 1812 the court was concerned only with regulating agriculture, but continued to appoint two constables.[68]

By the 1630s the manorial divisions were used for parish government; there was a churchwarden and overseer for each by the 1650s.[69] A highway surveyor occurred in 1678–9.[70] By the later 17th century the parish rates were regulated, and the accounts audited, by a body of 'lewners', usually eight, drawn from the two divisions.[71] They were sometimes augmented by other parishioners,[72]

thus forming, presumably, the vestry meeting, so called by 1792 (when some 15 people were present).[73] By the later 18th century there were usually no more than four lewners, and from the 1820s they normally included the vicar.[74]

In the 17th century poor rates and charitable bequests were supplemented by 'charity money' or 'communion money', collected at communion services.[75] By 1803 the poor were farmed. There was no workhouse,[76] but by 1804 one had opened at Lilleshall.[77] About 1810 it was transferred to Donnington.[78] There were usually 8–10 inmates 1812–15[79] but by April 1817 there were 49;[80] the house was accordingly enlarged[81] but numbers never reached that level again.[82] In 1813 the inmates were employed in flax spinning[83] and in 1820 a steam engine was installed.[84] By 1812, and until 1837, a salaried workhouse keeper[85] administered the parish's indoor and outdoor relief.[86] The overseers passed all the rate income to him and he accounted to the parish for its use.[87] In the later 19th century poor-relief was supplemented both by endowed charities and by the dukes' *ex gratia* benefactions.[88]

A Lilleshall board of health was formed, apparently at the time of the national cholera outbreak of 1831–2,[89] but was probably short-lived.[90]

The parish was included in Newport poor-law union 1836–1930[91] In 1863 it was put in Newport highway district[92] and in 1872 in Newport rural sanitary district. In 1894 it was placed in Newport rural district,[93] which was absorbed by Wellington R.D. in 1936.[94] In 1898 the extreme south-west corner of the ancient parish was assigned to the new St. George's civil parish in the new Oakengates urban district. In 1934 St. George's C.P. was absorbed by the new Oakengates C.P.[95] In 1968 the Muxton, Donnington, Donnington Wood, and St. George's areas were included in the designated area of Telford new town.[96] In 1973–4 the part of Shifnal C.P. and R.D. in Telford (224 ha.) was added to Lilleshall C.P. and the areas of Lilleshall and Oakengates C.P.s were included in Wrekin district.[97] In 1982

[58] Staffs. R.O., D. 593/J/1/1, 3, 4; /J/13/1, 2; S.R.O. 1910/484–8; S.P.L., Deeds 16330, 19398–9.
[59] S.P.L., Deeds 19398.
[60] Staffs. R.O., D. 593/J/1/1; S.P.L., Deeds 16330. Aletasters were mentioned 1359: S.P.L., Deeds 19399.
[61] S.P.L., Deeds 16330; MS. 4426; L.J.R.O., B/C/5, Lilleshall abbey acct. r. of 1428–9 and 1436–7.
[62] Staffs. R.O., D. 593/J/1/3, ct. r.
[63] Ibid. /J/13/2/1, ct. r. of 1625–6; S.R.O. 1910/484–8.
[64] Staffs. R.O., D. 593/J/1/4, ct. r.
[65] Ibid. /J/13/2/1, ct. r. of 1625–6; S.R.O. 4462/Con/7.
[66] S.R.O. 972, parcel 234, middle map of Lilleshall.
[67] Ibid. parcel 238, map.
[68] Staffs. R.O., D. 593/J/1/4, ct. r.
[69] S.R.O. 4462/P/1/1; /CW/1/12.
[70] Ibid. /P/1/2.
[71] Ibid. /P/1/1, s.a. 1651–2, 1656–7, 1659–60; /P/1/2–3, passim; /CW/2, passim.
[72] Ibid. /CW/2, s.a. 1683–4.
[73] Ibid. /CW/3, p. 538.
[74] Ibid. passim.
[75] S.R.O. 4462/CW/1/4; /P/1/1–3, passim.
[76] Abstr. Rel. to Poor, H.C. 98, p. 414 (1803–4), xiii.
[77] S.R.O. 38/15; /17, f. 67.
[78] S.R.O. 972, box 41, survey of 1808, f. 56, no. 34; box 41, survey of 1813, f. 44; parcel 238, map of 1813.
[79] Abstr. Rel. to Poor, H.C. 82, p. 369 (1818), xix.
[80] S.R.O. 4462/P/1/5, at end.

[81] Ibid. general accts. 10 Feb., 20 Apr., 23 July 1818.
[82] S.R.O. 4462/P/1/5–7, weekly pay lists.
[83] Ibid. /P/1/5, general accts. 30 July 1813.
[84] Ibid. 15 Nov. 1820.
[85] S.R.O., QR 297/125.
[86] S.R.O. 4462/P/1/5–7, passim.
[87] Ibid. /P/1/4.
[88] S.R.O. 972, box 169, lists of recipients.
[89] S.R.O. 4462/Misc/7. At least 6 of the 8 named therein were local surgeons in 1835: Pigot, Nat. Com. Dir. (1835), 365, 382.
[90] S. and B. Webb, Stat. Authorities for Special Purposes (1922), 463–4.
[91] V. J. Walsh, 'Admin. of Poor Laws in Salop. 1820–55' (Pennsylvania Univ. Ph.D. thesis, 1970), 150 (copy in S.R.O.); Kelly's Dir. Salop. (1929), 4.
[92] S.R.O., q. sess. order bk. 1861–9, p. 127.
[93] V.C.H. Salop. ii. 216.
[94] Salop Review Order, 1936 (Min. of Health order no. 80345). The date 1934 is wrongly given in V.C.H. Salop. ii. 216–17.
[95] V.C.H. Salop. ii. 224–5.
[96] Dawley New Town (Designation) Amendment (Telford) Order 1968 (Stat. Instr. 1968, no. 1912), map accompanying Explanatory Note.
[97] New Parishes Order 1973 (Stat. Instr. 1973, no. 688); Census, 1971, Rep. for Co. of Salop as constituted on 1st Apr. 1974, 2.

Lilleshall C.P. was renamed Lilleshall and Donnington C.P.[98]

PUBLIC SERVICES. Donnington had a post office by 1851[99] and another opened at Lilleshall c. 1880.[1] A third, at Donnington Wood, opened c. 1910.[2]

Gas was supplied to Lilleshall Old Hall and Donnington by 1870 from the Midland Iron Works.[3] By 1879 the works was connected to Lilleshall village[4] and by 1909, as the Lilleshall Gas Co., to Donnington Wood.[5] The gas company was taken over by the Wellington (Salop) Gas Co. in 1939.[6] Electricity was available to Lilleshall and Donnington Wood by 1941.[7]

An isolation hospital was built near the canal at Donnington Wood c. 1878 by Wellington rural sanitary authority.[8] It was last used c. 1884 and replaced c. 1902 by another nearby,[9] which was redundant by 1905.[10]

In 1899 standpipes throughout Donnington Wood were being supplied with water pumped from the Granville colliery. Mains were first laid at Lilleshall, Muxton, and Donnington in 1906 from the duke of Sutherland's new works at Lilleshall (with a reservoir at Lilleshall Hill).[11] Mains at Donnington Wood were laid in the period 1908–9 from the duke's new works at Hilton in Sheriffhales parish (with a reservoir at Redhill).[12]

Sewerage of some sort was laid at Donnington Wood in 1905 by the Lilleshall Co.[13] In 1939 main sewerage was provided at Muxton and Donnington, with a new sewage works at Donnington.[14] Lilleshall village was first connected to that system in the 1960s,[15] having previously had small disposal works serving council estates and a few other properties.[16] Donnington sewage works was later superseded by the Rushmoor works (in Wrockwardine) opened 1975.[17]

Part of Donnington Wood Farm was converted into a fire station in 1941.[18] In 1945 Wellington rural district council opened its ambulance station there;[19] it was run by a joint committee of the R.D.C. and Dawley and Oakengates urban dis-

trict councils from 1946[20] to 1948, when it passed to the county council.[21] In 1980 the site was occupied by a recently built health centre and new ambulance station.[22]

A police sub-station opened in Wellington Road, Donnington, in 1943.[23]

CHURCHES. It was believed in the early 14th century that an ancient church at Lilleshall was the first resting place of the remains of St. Alkmund (d. c. 800) before their translation to Derby.[24] The font, presumed to have been made for Lilleshall, seems to indicate that a church existed by the early 12th century, and the dedication to St. Michael, though not traced in medieval records, may denote an early religious site.[25]

Between 1161 and c. 1170 the canons of Lilleshall received episcopal licence to appropriate the church's revenues,[26] and the benefice was a vicarage by 1238.[27] The earliest recorded presentation of a vicar by the canons occurred in 1314.[28] In 1369 and 1519, during abbatial vacancies, the patronage was exercised by the Crown.[29] In 1538 the canons surrendered the advowson to the Crown,[30] which sold it in 1543 to Sir Edward Aston of Tixall (Staffs.),[31] who immediately conveyed it to James Leveson, lord of the manor.[32] Except during the period 1823–33, when it was kept by the 2nd marquess of Stafford[33] (cr. duke of Sutherland 1833), the advowson was held by the lords of the manor until c. 1920, when the 5th duke sold it to Sir John Leigh of Lilleshall Hall, Sheriffhales.[34] It passed from him c. 1924 to H. B. Rudolph of Manor Farm, Sheriffhales,[35] and in 1945 from him to the bishop of Lichfield,[36] the patron in 1979.[37]

At first the vicars seem to have had no glebe. Before 1286 William of Preston (vicar by 1275)[38] paid the abbot for a lifetime lease of a plot of land between the 'Weald Moor field' (perhaps the later Moor field) and Lilleshall village, 6 a. of adjacent land, and an arable assart[39] with adjacent meadow; he was to pay rent and tithe.[40] Those holdings, at least in part, eventually became the glebe.[41] In

[98] Inf. from S.C.C. Sec.'s Dept.
[99] S. Bagshaw, *Dir. Salop.* (1851), 398; *P.O. Dir. Salop.* (1856) 66.
[1] *P.O. Dir. Salop.* (1879), 341; *Kelly's Dir. Salop.* (1885), 873.   [2] *Kelly's Dir. Salop.* (1909), 88; (1913), 90.
[3] *P.O. Dir. Salop.* (1870), 74.
[4] Ibid. (1879), 341.
[5] *Kelly's Dir. Salop.* (1909), 126.
[6] Below, Wellington, Local Govt., Public Services.
[7] *Kelly's Dir. Salop.* (1941), 90, 131.
[8] S.R.O., *S.C.C. Mins.* (R. G. Venables's copy), 1902–3, Sanitary Cttee. rep. 31 Jan. 1903, newscutting facing p. 85.
[9] O.S. Map 6", Salop. XXXVI. NE. (1903 edn.); S.R.O., DA 23/100/2, p. 141.
[10] Frost, *Story of Donnington*, 31.
[11] *S.C.C. Mins.* Sanitary Cttee rep. 28 Oct. 1899, 59–61; S.C.C. *Rep. by County M.O.H.* 1906, 81.
[12] S.C.C. *Rep. by County M.O.H. 1908*, 94; *1909*, 104; S.R.O. 972, box 180, R. C. Frain to F. Todd, 29 Aug. 1918.
[13] S.C.C. *Rep. by County M.O.H. 1905*, 66.
[14] S.R.O., DA 26/112/1, p. 97.
[15] Ibid. /112/6, p. 1926.
[16] Ibid. /112/5, p. 1540.
[17] *Telford Jnl.* 7 Aug. 1975.
[18] S.R.O., DA 26/111, 'various' sect. p. 63.
[19] Ibid. /112/2, p. 513.
[20] Ibid. p. 521; DA 26/134 (S.R.O. 3070/12/7), file 222, deed (copy).

[21] Under the National Health Service Act, 1946, 9 & 10 Geo. VI, c. 81: S.C.C. *Proposals for an Ambulance Service* (1947), 4, 13 (copy in S.R.O., DA 26/134 (S.R.O. 3070/15/5), file 221); *S.C.C. Mins.* 1947–8, 15.
[22] Frost, *Story of Donnington*, 26; local inf.
[23] S.R.O., Standing Joint Cttee. min. bk. 1936–46, p. 382.
[24] P. Grosjean, 'Codicis Gothani Appendix', *Analecta Bollandiana*, lviii. 182.
[25] F. Arnold Forster, *Studies in Ch. Dedications* (1899), i. 38; F. Bond, *Dedications and Patron Saints of Eng. Chs.* (1914), 39.
[26] B.L. Add. MS. 50121, p. 47. By c. 1170 Wm., dean of Lichfield, a witness, had ceased to hold office: *V.C.H. Staffs.* iii. 197. Another lic. was issued 1188 × 1194: Eyton, viii. 227.
[27] Eyton, viii. 228.
[28] L.J.R.O., B/A/1/1, f. 67v.
[29] *Cal. Pat.* 1367–70, 290; *L. & P. Hen. VIII*, iii (1), p. 33.
[30] *L. & P. Hen. VIII*, xiii (2), p. 243.
[31] Ibid. xviii (1), p. 200.
[32] Staffs. R.O., D. 593/B/2/7/8, deed.
[33] S.R.O. 972, box 152, deed of 1823 (draft).
[34] *Kelly's Dir. Salop.* (1922), 125.
[35] Ibid. (1926), 213.
[36] *Lond. Gaz.* 10 Aug. 1945, p. 4082.
[37] *Lich. Dioc. Dir.* (1979), 123.
[38] S.R.O. 972, box 220, deed of 1270 × 1275.
[39] Ibid. deed of 1288.   [40] Ibid. deed n.d.
[41] S.R.O. 972, parcel 234, N. map of Lilleshall.

1286 the bishop assigned to the vicar a house, a garden, and an assarted croft with a meadow at the end, all formerly William of Preston's; accustomed rights of common; the small tithes, the tithes of all gardens and crofts cultivated by hand, the tithes of pannage, and the hay tithes of Donnington, Lilleshall, and Honnington; and all oblations, altar dues, and mortuaries.[42] Two years later the abbot conceded to the vicar haybote, housebote, and firebote from Lilleshall wood, the corn tithes of the vicar's assart, and herbage for his horse in a plot of land.[43]

In 1291 the church was valued at £4 13s. 4d. a year;[44] the small tithes were said in 1341 to make up £4 and glebe, oblations, and other payments 13s. 4d.[45] In 1535 the vicarage's gross annual value was put at £7.[46] By 1538 the abbot had leased the rectorial tithes to the vicar.[47] In 1646 Sir Richard Leveson had to settle £80 a year on the incumbent, out of rectorial tithes,[48] but that arrangement did not outlast the Interregnum. The annual value of the living was £25 in 1665[49] and £40 c. 1693.[50]

The glebe (c. 11 a.) was not increased until 1748, but the vicars held a greater area as tenants.[51] In 1748 Earl Gower gave c. 30 a.,[52] which was matched in 1750 by £200 from Queen Anne's Bounty.[53] The annual value in 1772 was c. £60.[54] In 1789 some 8 a. in Edgmond parish were bought for the living by Queen Anne's Bounty,[55] and in 1799 the vicar's income was £180 a year.[56] In 1818 some 28 a. of glebe were exchanged with the marquess of Stafford for an equal area in the parish,[57] so that the glebe (49 a.) was 'much improved'. In addition by 1805[58] the vicar had the great tithes of 'Shelton's old farm'[59] (106 a.)[60] and surplice fees of £12 a year. The gross annual value was c. £340.[61] By 1845 for several years the 'Shelton' tithes had been commuted by agreement to an annual rent charge of £25, and the small tithes (except of the vicarial glebe) had been leased to the duke at £239 a year.[62] In 1845 the small tithes (except of the vicarial glebe) were commuted to £254 14s. 10d. Those of that pro-

portion of the vicarial glebe not kept in hand were commuted by 1849 to a corresponding proportion of £6 7s. 6d., and the great tithes of the vicarial glebe had been merged in the vicar's freehold.[63] The Edgmond land was sold c. 1849.[64] In 1884 the gross annual income was c. £391. Rent from the glebe yielded £69. Gross tithe rent charge remained as in 1849, but £9 of it went to the vicar of Donnington Wood. The income from Queen Anne's Bounty was £25. Offerings, surplice fees, and mortuary fees brought in c. £10.[65] Nearly all the glebe was sold in 1915,[66] the tithe rent charge on that part having been merged that year in the freehold.[67] Small parcels of glebe were sold in 1946 and 1954.[68]

The vicarage house, south of the church, was burnt in the fire of 1585.[69] Described as 'small and ancient' in 1799,[70] the house was of three bays, timber-framed and tiled.[71] About 1817[72] the vicar added two 'good parlours' (with bedrooms over), and a new barn, stable, and cow house.[73] The house was demolished in 1967[74] and a new vicarage was completed on the site in 1968.[75]

No pre-Reformation vicar is known to have been at either university. Richard Nonyley, instituted 1413,[76] had a grown-up son in 1422.[77] John Longdon's incumbency, 1427–80, was exceptionally long.[78] William Jackson served 1535–58.[79] Thomas Millington[80] was in 1603 among the minority of the archdeaconry's clergy licensed to preach.[81] In 1614 he was accused of misconduct with three women.[82] In the years 1606–47 communion was given at Easter, Whitsun, All Saints, and Christmas.[83] In 1653, after the death of William Peake,[84] the parishioners tried to get Henry Oasland, the noted preacher,[85] as their minister,[86] but received instead Joseph Fisher, 'presented' by Humphrey Mackworth, governor of Shrewsbury.[87] Fisher was ordained priest by the bishop of Whithorn in 1661–2,[88] but remained only until 1663.[89] Henry Haughton, vicar 1663–1710,[90] was noted by his bishop c. 1693 as an 'idle tippling man'; the archdeacon knew nothing of him except 'that he shits'.[91] Throughout the

[42] B.L. Add. MS. 50121, p. 158 (confirmed 1315: L.J.R.O., B/A/1/1, f. 17v.).
[43] S.R.O. 972, box 220, deed of 1288.
[44] Tax. Eccl. (Rec. Com.), 248.
[45] Inq. Non. (Rec. Com.), 185.
[46] Valor Eccl. (Rec. Com.), iii. 186.
[47] P.R.O., SC 6/Hen.VIII/3009, m. 17.
[48] W. A. Shaw, Hist. Eng. Church 1640–60, ii. 481; Cal. Cttee. for Compounding, ii. 990.
[49] L.J.R.O., B/V/1/67, s.a. 1665, f. 9v.
[50] W.S.L., H.M. 36 (shorthand transcribed by Mr. N. W. Tildesley).
[51] S.R.O. 972, parcel 234, Lilleshall maps.
[52] S.R.O. 4462/Be/3.
[53] C. Hodgson, Q. Anne's Bounty (2nd edn.), p. ccxciv.
[54] L.J.R.O., B/V/5, visit. return of 1772.
[55] S.R.O. 4462/Gl/4.
[56] S.R.O. 3916/1/1, p. 69.
[57] L.J.R.O., B/A/2(i)/F, pp. 474–5.
[58] S.R.O. 4462/Gl/1.   [59] Ibid. /T/2.
[60] L.J.R.O., B/A/15, Lilleshall.
[61] S.R.O. 3916/1/3, no. 20.
[62] S.R.O. 4462/Gl/4.
[63] Ibid. /T/3; L.J.R.O., B/A/15, Lilleshall.
[64] S.R.O. 4462/Gl/5.
[65] S.R.O. 3916/1/26/25.
[66] S.R.O. 4462/Gl/6–7.

[67] Ibid. /T/4.
[68] Ibid. /Gl/10–12.
[69] Salopian Shreds & Patches, iv. 37.
[70] S.R.O. 3916/1/1, p. 69.
[71] S.R.O. 4462/Gl/1, 8.
[72] L.J.R.O., B/A/2(i)/F, pp. 384–7, 408–9.
[73] S.R.O. 3916/1/3, no. 20.
[74] Par. rec., photo. of 1967.
[75] Inf. from the vicar.
[76] L.J.R.O., B/A/1/7, f. 118v.
[77] S.P.L., Deeds 16330.
[78] L.J.R.O., B/A/1/9, f. 99; /1/12, f. 90v.
[79] Valor Eccl. (Rec. Com.), iii. 186; L.J.R.O., B/V/1/2, p. 33.
[80] L.J.R.O., B/V/1/23; B/A/1/16, f. 56.
[81] T.S.A.S. 2nd ser. v. 260.
[82] L.J.R.O., B/V/1/29.
[83] S.R.O. 4462/CW/1/4–11.
[84] S.R.O. 1910/487.
[85] D.N.B.
[86] T.S.A.S. 3rd ser. vii. 283; S.R.O. 4462/CW/1/12.
[87] T.S.A.S. iv. 88; S.R.O. 4462/Rg/1, s.a. 1653.
[88] L.J.R.O., B/V/1/67, s.a. 1662, f. 9v.
[89] S.R.O. 4462/Rg/1, 4 Aug. 1663.
[90] Ibid. /Rg/2, bur. 12 Oct. 1710; L.J.R.O., B/A/1/17, f. 37.
[91] W.S.L., H.M. 36.

period 1672–98 communion was given five times a year, Palm Sunday and Good Friday having been substituted for All Saints.[92]

In 1772 Richard Ogle, vicar 1772–85,[93] was non-resident; he had an assistant curate with £30 a year and surplice fees,[94] and a curate was mentioned 1778–85.[95] In 1772 there were two Sunday services, one with a sermon, and prayers on feast days and in Lent. There were four communions a year, with 40–50 communicants.[96] J. C. Woodhouse, vicar 1785–1814[97] and a noted pluralist,[98] was also non-resident. He lived in Donington parish in 1799,[99] where he was rector 1773–1833,[1] and became dean of Lichfield in 1807.[2] By 1787 Woodhouse had an assistant cur-

During the three incumbencies 1814–47 an assistant curate was employed only 1816–17 and 1835–43.[9] John Blunt (vicar 1815–43)[10] was by 1831 perpetual curate of Blurton (in Trentham, Staffs.)[11] but did not reside there. He was reported in 1824 to act at Lilleshall 'with great credit'.[12] Despite the existence of St. George's, the number of communicants at St. Michael's in 1824 and 1843 kept its 1799 level, though in 1824 there was communion only five times a year. Six times was usual again by 1843. By 1824 there was a sermon at both Sunday services.[13]

The opening of St. Matthew's, Donnington Wood, reduced the number of communicants at St. Michael's to an average of twenty by 1847,

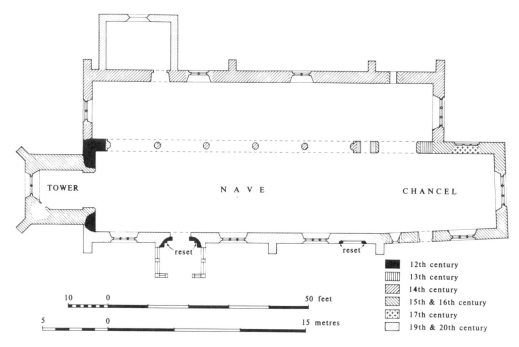

TOWER   N A V E   C H A N C E L

reset   reset

10   0   50 feet

5   0   15 metres

- 12th century
- 13th century
- 14th century
- 15th & 16th century
- 17th century
- 19th & 20th century

THE CHURCH OF ST. MICHAEL AND ALL ANGELS

ate, and he continued to employ one.[3] In the late 1790s the curate lived in the vicarage.[4] The parish church was extensively repaired in Woodhouse's early years and he helped to promote the building of St. George's chapel, Pain's Lane. His curates included Thomas Moss (1791–3),[5] a minor author,[6] and Stephen Hartley (1794–1814).[7] By 1799 there was communion six times a year, with an average of 50 communicants; there were prayers every Sunday morning (with a sermon) and afternoon, and on festivals, on Wednesdays and Fridays in Lent, and every day in Holy Week.[8]

when there was communion four times a year.[14] One of the difficulties at St. Michael's was an insufficiency of free sittings; these were 'much wanted' by working people but in 1824 were confined to the north aisle.[15] In 1843 there was no accommodation for the poor.[16] St. Matthew's presumably satisfied some of the demand and at St. Michael's in 1851 the paucity of free seats (72) was blamed for reduced attendances. Average adult attendance on Sunday was then 170 in the morning, 110 in the afternoon.[17] In the 1860s the aisle was exclusively occupied by working-class families.[18]

[92] S.R.O. 4462/CW/2.
[93] T.S.A.S. 4th ser. v. 207; L.J.R.O., B/A/1/24, p. 171.
[94] L.J.R.O., B/V/5, visit. return of 1772.
[95] T.S.A.S. i. 151.
[96] L.J.R.O., B/V/5, visit. return of 1772.
[97] Ibid. /B/A/1/24, p. 171; /1/28, p. 203.
[98] V.C.H. Staffs. iii. 69, 185.
[99] S.R.O. 3916/1/1, p. 69.
[1] T.S.A.S. 4th ser. v. 208; S.P.R. Lich. iii (3), 106.
[2] V.C.H. Staffs. iii. 197.   [3] T.S.A.S. i. 151.
[4] Shrews. Chron. 9 Dec. 1796 (p. 3); S.R.O. 3916/1/1, p. 69.
[5] S.R.O. 4462/MRg/1, 5 Feb. 1791, 6 May 1793.
[6] S. Shaw, Hist. Staffs. ii (1801), 237–8; D.N.B.

[7] T.S.A.S. i. 151.
[8] S.R.O. 3916/1/1, p. 69.
[9] S.R.O. 4462/BRg/1; T.S.A.S. i. 151.
[10] L.J.R.O., B/A/1/28, p. 225; Lich. Dioc. Regy., episc. reg. 31, p. 1.
[11] Rep. Com. Eccl. Revenues [67], p. 487, H.C. (1835), xxii.
[12] S.R.O. 3916/1/3, no. 20.
[13] Ibid.; /1/6, no. 21.
[14] Ibid. /1/18.
[15] Ibid. /1/3, no. 20.
[16] Ibid. /1/6, no. 21.
[17] P.R.O., HO 129/366, no. 13.
[18] T.S.A.S. i. 145.

The vicar 1847–69 was H. G. de Bunsen,[19] son of Baron Bunsen.[20] He employed an assistant curate throughout[21] but did some of the duty himself.[22] By 1851 Bunsen lived at the Old Hall and his curate at the vicarage.[23] S. E. Marsden, curate 1858–61,[24] was bishop of Bathurst (Australia) 1869–85.[25] In Bunsen's time the ecclesiastical parish was reduced by the creation of Donnington Wood and St. George's parishes, and later vicars acted without assistant clergy.[26]

An iron mission church dedicated to St. Chad was opened in 1888 near the Granville colliery. In 1977 it was re-erected at the Ironbridge Gorge Museum, Blists Hill,[27] after several years' disuse.[28] Another, St. John the Evangelist's, was built at Muxton in 1894[29] at the duke of Sutherland's expense[30] and was still in use in 1980.[31] A brick garrison church, built by prisoners of war, opened at Donnington in 1948. It was independent of the parish and diocese, being under the archbishop of Canterbury's ordinary jurisdiction. The registers begin in 1948 and are complete.[32]

The parish church of *ST. MICHAEL AND ALL ANGELS* consists of a chancel, nave with north aisle (with projecting north vestry) and south porch, and west tower, all of sandstone. There is no chancel arch. The dedication to St. Michael was recorded in 1807[33] but in 1856 was given as St. Michael and All Angels.[34]

The earliest datable structural feature is the late 12th-century south doorway of the nave.[35] Probably contemporary was a round-headed window found in 1856 in the north wall of the nave near its west end and afterwards removed.[36] A doorway, blocked by 1787, near the east end of the south wall of the nave, may be of the same period.[37] The chancel was probably rebuilt in the 13th century, its surviving features of that period being a single lancet and, possibly, the priest's doorway, both in the south wall. Perhaps contemporary was a lancet, since destroyed, in the south wall of the nave, west of the south doorway. The aisle was added in the early 14th century and was joined to the nave by an arcade of four bays cut through the north wall of the nave. The trussed-rafter roof of the aisle, although much restored, may be original. A square-headed lowside window near the east end of the north wall of the aisle probably dates

from the 15th century. A large east window and square-headed north and south windows were put into the chancel in the 15th or earlier 16th century. Indeed the whole chancel seems to have been rebuilt at that period. The roof, continuous over chancel and nave, is believed to be 15th-century. The west tower of three stages was almost certainly completed between 1538 and 1553. One of two stone shields set in its south wall is charged with a goat's head erased, the crest of the Levesons of Lilleshall.[38] Two 13th-century capitals are re-used high up on its outside west wall. The tower was presumably completed by 1553 when the church had three 'great' bells.[39] The band of quatrefoils below the tower parapet is characteristic of local late-medieval west towers.[40]

Several improvements were carried out in the later 17th century. An east-facing gallery was built over the west end of the aisle in 1657 at Sir Richard Leveson's expense. His widow Katherine beautified the chancel, adorned the pulpit and communion table, and gave £100 towards further improvements.[41] They may have included two large dormers in the south side of the nave roof; one of them was dated 1667.[42]

In the early 1790s, mostly in 1792–3,[43] several alterations were made, presumably according to the plan drawn up in 1791–2 by a Mr. Bishop.[44] Two triangular buttresses were built to support the outward-leaning south wall of the nave and the porch was replaced. A gallery was built at the west end of the nave and was lit by a small south dormer; by 1838 the gallery was used by children. The space beneath was lightened by replacing the lancet at the west end of the south wall of the nave with a square-headed window. In 1794–5 the owners of the three small freeholds[45] entitled to seats in the aisle gallery were bought out by the parish[46] and it was turned over to the use of the psalm singers,[47] formed by 1791.[48] Several medieval windows were fitted with casements, their mullions having been removed. The roof was coved in, and the church was repaved with bricks and repewed, except that a few ancient benches were spared at the west end of the nave. In 1792–3[49] the ancient font was removed, and in 1795 stood under a nearby farmyard pump.[50]

[19] Lich. Dioc. Regy., episc. reg. 31, p. 119; benefice and inst. bk. 1868–1900, p. 5.
[20] *Salopian Shreds & Patches*, viii. 32.
[21] *T.S.A.S.* i. 151–2.
[22] S.R.O. 3916/1/10.
[23] S. Bagshaw, *Dir. Salop.* (1851), 397.
[24] *T.S.A.S.* i. 152.
[25] *Australian Dict. of Biog.* v. 212.
[26] *P.O. Dir. Salop.* (1870 and later edns.); *Kelly's Dir. Salop.* (1895 and later edns.); *Lich. Dioc. Dir.* (1941–2 and later edns.).
[27] B. Trinder, *Blists Hill Open Air Museum* (I.G.M.T. 1978), 14; above, plate 40.
[28] Geof. K. Smith, *St. Mic. and All Angels, Lilleshall* (2nd edn.; Lilleshall, 1976), 36.
[29] *Kelly's Dir. Salop.* (1895), 114.
[30] Smith, *St. Mic.* 36.
[31] Local inf.
[32] Inf. from the chaplain.
[33] B.L. Add. MS. 21012, p. 72.
[34] Plaque in ch.
[35] Descr. based on Bodl. MS. Top. Salop. c. 2, f. 337; B.L. Add. MS. 21012, p. 72; S.P.L., MS. 372, vol. i, p. 40; ibid. 6742, pp. 15–18; S.P.L., J. H. Smith colln., no. 126; S.R.O. 3916/1/1, p. 69; /1/3, no. 20; *T.S.A.S.* i. 135–47; Cranage, vii.

598–602; Pevsner, *Shropshire*, 165–6; Smith, *St. Mic.*
[36] It may be the blocked round headed opening visible in the N. chancel wall by 1905: Cranage, vii. 597.
[37] Blocked doorways similarly positioned occur at Cardington and Clunbury: Pevsner, *Shropshire*, 18 n., 93, 109.
[38] Burke, *Gen. Armory* (1884), 604.
[39] *T.S.A.S.* 2nd ser. xii. 320.
[40] For NE. Salop. examples see Cranage, vii. 577, 628, 660; viii. 672, 698, 723; x. 844. Nearby towers at Gnosall and Haughton (both Staffs.) have similar decoration.
[41] Smith, *St. Mic.* 27.
[42] Much work was done on a dormer in 1674–5: S.R.O. 4462/CW/2.
[43] Ibid. /CW/3, pp. 104–7, 538.   [44] Ibid. p. 103.
[45] S.R.O. 972, box 41, survey of 1775 × 1783.
[46] S.R.O. 4462/CW/3, p. 112.
[47] The singers' gallery mentioned 1812 (ibid. p. 165) and 1838 (S.R.O. 3916/1/3, no. 20).
[48] S.R.O. 4462/CW/3, pp. 101 (first pmnt. to singing master 1790–1), 117 (first pmnt. for psalm singing 1795–6), and annual pmnts. to singers thereafter.
[49] Ibid. pp. 105, 538.
[50] B.L. Add. MS. 21236, f. 273. Cf. S. Bagshaw, *Dir. Salop.* (1851), 394, locating the pump at the Old Hall.

In 1856 the church was restored under John Norton's direction. The south wall of the nave was rebuilt, windows were inserted there and in the chancel and aisle, and a new south porch was provided. The church was repaved throughout. The galleries were taken down. The roof timbers were exposed and the dormers removed. A fifth arch was opened in the north wall of the nave, west of the medieval arcade. In 1897 a vestry was built, projecting north from the aisle and entered from it by the medieval north doorway. Until then, and since at least 1824, the west end of the aisle, formerly underneath the gallery, had been the vestry, and in 1824 it was also a schoolroom. After the First World War a memorial window was inserted in the north wall of the aisle, immediately east of the vestry.

The richly ornamented font is 12th-century. It was restored to the west end of the church in 1826 and furnished with a new pedestal,[51] so replacing an 'elegant marble vase' of 1799–1800[52] that had stood within the communion rail. In 1856 the font was placed on a square platform set with medieval tiles from the chancel floor. A large monument to Sir Richard and Katherine Leveson stands against the north wall of the chancel. Probably the work of Edward and Joshua Marshall,[53] it was set up at the cost of Francis Leveson-Fowler (d. 1667) and both effigies were made before 1669.[54] James I's arms, set up in 1605–6,[55] were displaced by those of the Commonwealth in 1652–3.[56] Charles II's arms, painted on wood, were formerly fixed above a tiebeam in the chancel roof, but in 1856 were placed in front of the tower arch.

The stained glass, including work by Michael & Arthur O'Connor and John Hardman & Co., and most of the furniture and fittings date from 1856 or later. The five benefaction boards (one dated 1676) were in the church by 1795,[57] and the stone tables of Commandments flanked the east window by 1824. The east window glass in the aisle, the 'working men's window',[58] was inserted in 1860 at the expense of local working men. It is obstructed by the organ (1891) given by the marchioness of Stafford. When, in 1970, the aisle became St. Chad's chapel, it was furnished with an altar table (c. 1900) from a West Bromwich church[59] and a communion rail (1940) from Donnington Roman Catholic church.

There was a tower clock by 1638[60] and the present mechanism dates from 1966. A sundial at the east end of the chancel wall was in situ by 1787.

In 1553 the church had a silver chalice and paten, parcel gilt.[61] In 1964 the plate consisted of a pair of silver chalices and patens of 1661, a silver paten of 1700, and a silver flagon of 1871.[62] The registers begin in 1653[63] and are complete thereafter. In 1553 there were three great bells, of 'one accord', and a sanctus bell.[64] The six bells present in 1979 dated from 1825[65] and had been recast in 1963.[66] The ancient churchyard is roughly square. An additional graveyard on the opposite side of the village street was consecrated in 1908.[67]

A chapel of ease dedicated to ST. GEORGE was consecrated in 1806 on land at Pain's Lane provided by the marquess of Stafford.[68] The cost of erection was met by the Lilleshall Co., by John Bishton and partners (lessees of mines and works at Snedshill), who gave £200, and by trustees of the late Isaac Hawkins of Burton-upon-Trent, who gave £800. The vicar of Lilleshall, J. C. Woodhouse, a partner in the Lilleshall Co. by 1807,[69] 'contributed handsomely' and actively promoted the new foundation, which was intended to serve the workpeople of the neighbouring industrial district.[70] In 1806 the chapel was licensed for baptisms and burials[71] and in 1837 for marriages.[72]

In 1807 the curacy was filled on the nomination of the vicar of Lilleshall[73] but in 1815 the patronage was vested in the marquess of Stafford.[74] It descended thereafter with the patronage of Lilleshall church[75] until c. 1920, when the 5th duke of Sutherland sold it to Sir John Leigh.[76] By 1925 it had passed to Sir Offley Wakeman, who then conveyed it to the bishop of Lichfield,[77] the patron in 1979.[78] By 1831 the living was a perpetual curacy.[79] In 1861 Pain's Lane, comprising parts of Lilleshall, Shifnal, and Wrockwardine Wood ecclesiastical parishes, became a consolidated chapelry.[80] The incumbents were titular vicars from 1868.[81] The ecclesiastical parish was sometimes officially known as Pain's Lane until 1915 or later,[82] but by then the name St. George's was more current, even in official usage,[83] and had long been preferred locally.[84] In 1982 the living was united with that of Priorslee, with the vicar of Shifnal and the bishop as joint patrons.[85]

In 1806 the curacy was endowed by the mar-

[51] S.R.O. 4462/CW/3, p. 227.
[52] Ibid. p. 131.
[53] M. Whinney, *Sculpture in Britain 1530 to 1830* (1964), 241.
[54] S.R.O. 4462/Cy/4/1.
[55] Ibid. /CW/1/3.
[56] Ibid. /1/12.
[57] B.L. Add. MS. 21236, f. 271v.
[58] S.R.O. 673/1/17, 5 Mar. 1859.
[59] The Good Shepherd, Spon Lane. See *V.C.H. Staffs.* xvii. 59.
[60] S.R.O. 4462/CW/1/10.
[61] *T.S.A.S.* 2nd ser. xii. 333.
[62] S. A. Jeavons, *Ch. Plate Archd. Salop* (Shrews. 1964), pp. 41, 47, 95.
[63] E. C. Peele and R. S. Clease, *Salop. Par. Doc.* (Shrews. [1903]), 203.
[64] *T.S.A.S.* 2nd ser. xii. 320, 333.
[65] S.R.O. 4462/CW/3, p. 221.
[66] Geof. K. Smith, 'St. Mic. and All Angels, Lilleshall', *Ringing World*, lxvi. 410.
[67] Lich. Dioc. regy., bps.' reg. V, pp. 157–8.

[68] L.J.R.O., B/A/2(i)/E, pp. 284–9.
[69] Wordie, 'Gt. Landed Estate', 232.
[70] S.R.O. 3916/1/13, no. 11.
[71] L.J.R.O., B/A/2(i)/E, p. 288.
[72] Lich. Dioc. Regy., bps.' reg. K, pp. 724–5.
[73] L.J.R.O., B/A/1/28, p. 87.
[74] Staffs. R.O., D. 593/B/3/6/6.
[75] S.R.O. 972, box 152, deed of 1823 (draft).
[76] *Kelly's Dir. Salop.* (1922), 199.
[77] *Lond. Gaz.* 28 July 1925, pp. 5034–5.
[78] *Lich. Dioc. Dir.* (1979), 131.
[79] Lich. Dioc. Regy., episc. reg. 29, p. 252.
[80] Ibid. bps.' reg. Q (Orders in Council), p. 26.
[81] *P.O. Dir. Salop.* (1870), 122.
[82] Lich. Dioc. Regy., bps.' reg. V, p. 510.
[83] Ibid. benefice and inst. bk. 1900–29, p. 11.
[84] The name St. George's, for the township, was approved by a public meeting c. 1865, and afterwards by the Post Office: *Souvenir of Bazaar and Garden Fete, July 17th, 18th, and 19th, 1912, in aid of St. George's Tower Fund*, [25] (copy in S.P.L.).
[85] Below, Wombridge, Churches.

quess of Stafford with 1¼ a. of land in Steelhouse Lane, Wolverhampton; all tithes, offerings, and fees were reserved to the vicar and parish officers of Lilleshall.[86] The curacy was augmented by Queen Anne's Bounty in 1808, 1809, and 1810, each time with £200. In 1815 the marquess gave an augmentation of £200, matched by £300 from Queen Anne's Bounty, from which another £200 was received in 1816.[87] By 1824 the curate was also receiving £100 a year from the estate of John Bishton (d. 1809), who had stipulated that it should be paid as long as any of his descendants was associated with the Lilleshall Co.'s coal and iron works. In 1824 the curate's gross income, including £5 from the Wolverhampton land, was about £120.[88] From 1843 he had the marriage fees.[89] The Bishton stipend was still being paid in 1843 when the living was worth £147 a year gross,[90] but by 1851 it had ceased and the curate was reduced to £37 a year from Queen Anne's Bounty, £3 from fees, and £5 from 1 a. of glebe,[91] presumably the Wolverhampton land.

In 1855 several new endowments were made: £200 each from the Lilleshall Co. and the Diocesan Society, £240 from private donations, land worth £315 from the 2nd duke of Sutherland, and £200 from Queen Anne's Bounty.[92] The glebe was enlarged in 1862 by 1¼ a. next to the parsonage[93] and in 1870 amounted to some 3 a.[94] By 1884 the vicar's gross annual income, some £136, included £48 4s. 4d. from the Ecclesiastical Commissioners, £39 7s. 4d. from Queen Anne's Bounty, c. £24 from pew rents, and c. £15 from surplice fees;[95] in addition the glebe was worth an estimated £10 a year.[96] Benefactions of 1885–6 added over £28 a year to the vicar's income[97] and by 1891 it had reached some £220 net.[98]

Until the 1850s the perpetual curate or, when he was non-resident, the assistant curate lived in a house at Snedshill, in Shifnal parish. It was not held as glebe.[99] A new house was completed c. 1858[1] just north of Watling Street, within Lilleshall parish. The large three-storeyed brick building, plain but with Gothic details, remained the vicarage until the living was united with Priorslee in 1982.[2]

The first curate, C. R. Cameron (1807–31),[3] was also perpetual curate of Wombridge 1808–

56.[4] He was an Evangelical[5] and his wife wrote religious tales for children and moral tracts for working people.[6] By 1824 there were two Sunday services, each with a sermon, and communion four times a year attended by about thirty. There were 400 seats, 350 of them free.[7] From 1831 to 1836 Cameron was assistant curate at St. George's to his successor,[8] his son-in-law[9] J. H. C. Moor.[10] In 1843 Moor was living in Warwickshire, employing as assistant curate Robert Coalbank.[11] Coalbank eventually succeeded Moor and remained until 1858.[12] A strong Calvinist and 'right worthily beloved', Coalbank gathered a number of 'attached workers' in the choir and Sunday school.[13] In 1843 he was holding additional Wednesday evening services and celebrating communion monthly. Communicants had increased to forty or fifty.[14] By 1851 average Sunday morning attendance was c. 200; on Sunday evenings it was as many as 400–500.[15] In 1862 the new church was designed to provide 700 sittings, 500 of them free.[16] Until at least 1903 Coalbank's successors were assisted by a curate,[17] and one was licensed in 1934.[18] In 1918 the services were 'very musical' and the congregation was 'accustomed to ritual'. It was admitted, however, that nonconformity in the parish was stronger than the church.[19]

The first chapel was a plain brick building in the form of an equal-armed cross, and had simple pointed windows with Y tracery.[20] A narrow tower of three stages projected west from the west end of the nave and served as a porch with vestry above. The badly constructed building was quickly attacked by damp and mining subsidence. Costly repairs were carried out[21] but eventually, when the new parish was created, it seemed best to build a new church on the site. Consecrated in 1862 as a memorial to the 2nd duke,[22] the new church cost some £4,000, almost all of it privately donated.[23]

Designed by G. E. Street, the second church consists of a tunnel-vaulted chancel with north vestry, aisled and clerestoried nave of four bays, and a south porch under a tower. The style is late 13th-century and its handling, and the use of contrasted brick and grey and red stone are held to place the building among Street's most original early works.[24] The tower was completed only in 1929: designed by Bertram Butler,[25] it had a

[86] L.J.R.O., B/A/2(i)/E, pp. 286–7, 289.
[87] Hodgson, *Q. Anne's Bounty* (2nd edn.), pp. cxc, ccxciv.
[88] S.R.O. 3916/1/3, no. 11.
[89] Lich. Dioc. Regy., bps.' reg. K, pp. 724–5 (Blunt, vicar of Lilleshall, d. 1843: ibid. episc. reg. 31, p. 1).
[90] S.R.O. 3916/1/6, no. 11.
[91] P.R.O., HO 129/366, no. 14.
[92] Hodgson, *Q. Anne's Bounty* (2nd edn.), suppl. pp. xxxiii, lxvii.
[93] Lich. Dioc. Regy., bps.' reg. Q, p. 583.
[94] *P.O. Dir. Salop.* (1870), 122. [95] S.R.O. 3916/1/29.
[96] *Return of Glebe Land, 1887*, H.C. 307, p. 64 (1887), lxiv.
[97] Lich. Dioc. Regy., bps.' reg. S, p. 738; T, pp. 32, 54.
[98] *Kelly's Dir. Salop.* (1891), 402.
[99] S.R.O. 3916/1/3, no. 11; /1/6, no. 11; S. Bagshaw, *Dir. Salop.* (1851), 483.
[1] *Souvenir of Bazaar, 1912* [15].
[2] Inf. from the Revd. Preb. C. Hill.
[3] L.J.R.O., B/A/1/28, p. 87; Lich. Dioc. Regy., episc. reg. 29, p. 252.
[4] L.J.R.O., B/A/1/28, p. 105; Lich. Dioc. Regy., episc. reg. 32, p. 107.
[5] Trinder, *Ind. Rev. Salop.* 387.

[6] Ibid. 278, 340–2, 354, 372–3, 381–2; *D.N.B.* s.v. Cameron, Lucy Lyttelton.
[7] S.R.O. 3916/1/3, no. 11.
[8] *D.N.B.* s.v. Cameron, Lucy Lyttelton.
[9] M.I. of Mary Anne Moor in ch.
[10] Lich. Dioc. Regy., episc. reg. 29, p. 256.
[11] S.R.O. 3916/1/6, no. 11.
[12] Lich. Dioc. Regy., episc. reg. 32, p. 149.
[13] *Souvenir of Bazaar, 1912*, [21].
[14] S.R.O. 3916/1/6, no. 11.
[15] P.R.O., HO 129/366, no. 14.
[16] Lich. Dioc. Regy., bps.' reg. Q, pp. 562–7.
[17] *Souvenir of Bazaar, 1912*, facing p. [40].
[18] S.R.O. 4428/Cl/3.
[19] S.R.O. 972, parcel 211, jnl. note 25 Mar. 1918.
[20] Descr. based on S.P.L., MS. 372, vol. iii, p. 104; S.P.L., J. H. Smith colln., no. 189; S.R.O. 3916/1/3, no. 11.
[21] S.R.O., q. sess. order bk. 1819–27, f. 235; W. A. Bewes, *Ch. Briefs* (1896), 360.
[22] *P.O. Dir. Salop.* (1870), 122.
[23] Lich. Dioc. Regy., bps.' reg. Q, pp. 562–7.
[24] Cranage, vii. 620; Pevsner, *Shropshire*, 44, 239.
[25] James, *'Here be Dragons'*, 10.

pyramidal roof instead of the stone spire intended by Street.[26] A carillon was installed in it in 1929.[27] In 1964 the communion plate consisted of a modern silver chalice and some Victorian plated pieces.[28] The registers begin in 1806[29] and are complete.

A chapel of ease at Donnington Wood, dedicated to *ST. MATTHEW* and intended to serve the surrounding colliery district,[30] was licensed in 1845.[31] The site was provided by the 2nd duke of Sutherland, who also met the cost of erection and furnishing, some £1,700. The church was consecrated in 1850[32] and was designed to provide 500 seats, all free.[33] There were baptisms there from 1845, burials from 1850, and marriages from 1851.[34] In 1845 the chapel was intended to be served by the vicar of Lilleshall or his curate[35] but in 1850 it was assigned a district within Lilleshall ecclesiastical parish.[36] In 1850 patronage of the living, a perpetual curacy[37] until 1868 when it became a titular vicarage,[38] was vested in the 2nd duke.[39] The advowson descended with Lilleshall manor until c. 1920 and was then acquired by Sir John Leigh.[40] By 1925 Sir Offley Wakeman was patron; he then conveyed it to the bishop of Lichfield,[41] still the patron in 1979.[42]

In 1850 the 2nd duke endowed the living with £1,000,[43] and in 1851 the fees arising at the chapel, until then reserved to the vicar of Lilleshall,[44] became payable to the perpetual curate of Donnington Wood.[45] In 1851 the incumbent's annual income was £45 from endowment, £1 10s. in fees, and £50 from unspecified sources.[46] A further endowment of £600 was given in 1853,[47] and in 1860 endowments of £400 by the duke of Sutherland and £200 by the Diocesan Society were made, matched by £200 from Queen Anne's Bounty.[48] By 1870 the annual value of the living was £218.[49] In 1884 the vicar was receiving £171 10s. net, and £9 out of the tithe rent charge of Lilleshall parish; there was no glebe, and no fees were taken for churchings, marriages, or funerals.[50] Until 1917 the dukes of Sutherland contributed £20 to the vicar's stipend but, with the sale of most of the 5th duke's Lilleshall

property, it was decided in 1918 to reconsider the payment annually.[51]

The vicarage, an ancient timber-framed house, stood outside Donnington Wood ecclesiastical parish, on the north side of the Newport–Wellington road. It was not held as glebe but belonged to the successive patrons.[52] In 1983 a new vicarage was under construction in St. George's Road.[53]

In 1851 average Sunday attendance was sixty in the morning, three hundred in the evening.[54] The first incumbent, Thomas O'Regan, held the living until 1900.[55] Well respected, he influenced striking miners to return to work and to improve their conditions at home and at the pit.[56] He began to employ an assistant curate in the 1890s[57] and later went to live in Surrey.[58] None of his successors had an assistant curate, except in the years 1953–5 and 1961–5.[59] By 1953 weekday services were being held in a Lady chapel made in 1950 in the south transept.[60] In 1962 the church sustained a Sunday school, a youth club (ceased by 1979),[61] scouting groups, and a Mother's Union branch.[62]

The church, designed in the Early English style by George Gilbert Scott, consisted of chancel, transepts, and nave with west gallery, south porch, and west bellcot.[63] A north choir vestry and west baptistery were added c. 1965[64] in the Grinshill sandstone of the original building. In 1964 the plate consisted of a silver chalice and paten of 1851, a silver gilt chalice and paten of 1960, and several pieces of modern silver.[65] The single bell (1953) replaced an earlier one. The registers begin in 1845 and are complete.[66]

ROMAN CATHOLICISM. Sir Walter Leveson (d. 1602) and his daughter Elizabeth are claimed to have been papists.[67] There were four (in one family) in 1626,[68] two or three between 1662 and 1706,[69] and none in 1772.[70] After the Central Ordnance Depot opened in 1939 a Roman Catholic church was founded at Donnington on the north side of the Wellington–Newport road.[71] It was replaced in 1949 by a temporary church in Winifred's Drive,[72] dedicated to Our Lady of the

[26] *Kelly's Dir. Salop.* (1934), 210.
[27] Ibid.
[28] Jeavons, *Ch. Plate Archd. Salop*, pp. 91, 124.
[29] Peele and Clease, *Salop. Par. Doc.* 288.
[30] S.R.O. 3916/1/6, no. 21.
[31] Lich. Dioc. Regy., episc. reg. 31, p. 105.
[32] Ibid. bps.' reg. O, pp. 423–4, 427–8. Elsewhere the cost is put at £1,875: P.R.O., HO 129/366, no. 15.
[33] S.R.O. 3916/1/6, no. 21.
[34] Peele and Clease, *Salop. Par. Doc.* 154.
[35] Lich. Dioc. Regy., episc. reg. 31, p. 105.
[36] *Lich. Dioc. Dir.* 1948–9, 133. Dist. boundary defined 1851: Lich. Dioc. Regy., bps.' reg. OA, pp. 463–5.
[37] S. Bagshaw, *Dir. Salop.* (1851), 398.
[38] *P.O. Dir. Salop.* (1870), 74.
[39] *Return of Pars. Divided and Dists. Assigned to Churches*, H.C. 557, p. 48 (1861), xlviii.
[40] Lich. Dioc. Regy., benefice and inst. bk. 1900–29, p. 62.
[41] *Lond. Gaz.* 28 July 1925, pp. 5034–5.
[42] *Lich. Dioc. Dir.* 1979, 115.
[43] Lich. Dioc. Regy., bps.' reg. O, p. 426.
[44] Ibid. p. 428.   [45] Ibid. reg. OA, p. 466.
[46] P.R.O., HO 129/366, no. 15.
[47] Hodgson, *Q. Anne's Bounty* (2nd edn.), suppl. p. lxxxvii.
[48] Ibid. suppl. pp. lxvi–lxvii.
[49] *P.O. Dir. Salop.* (1870), 74.

[50] S.R.O. 3916/1/26/12, 25.
[51] S.R.O. 972, parcel 211, jnl. note 29 July 1918.
[52] Frost, *Story of Donnington*, 40.
[53] Inf. from the vicar.
[54] P.R.O., HO 129/366, no. 15.
[55] Lich. Dioc. Regy., benefice and inst. bk. 1900–29, p. 2.
[56] Frost, *Story of Donnington*, 34.
[57] *Kelly's Dir. Salop.* (1895), 78.
[58] Ibid. (1900), 81.
[59] *Crockford* (1975–6), 86, 140.
[60] S.R.O. 3916/1/26/14; Frost, *Story of Donnington*, 33.
[61] Frost, op. cit. 35.
[62] Shore, 'Survey of Donnington', p. 3.
[63] Descr. based on Cranage, vii. 570; Pevsner, *Shropshire*, 122; Frost, op. cit. 32–40.
[64] Foundation stones of 1965.
[65] Jeavons, *Ch. Plate Archd. Salop*, pp. 87, 110, 122, 124, 126.
[66] Peele and Clease, *Salop. Par. Doc.* 154.
[67] *T.S.A.S.* vii. 339.
[68] L.J.R.O., B/V/1/48.
[69] Ibid. B/V/1/72, 74, 81; B/A/11, 1706, Lilleshall; *T.S.A.S.* 2nd ser. i. 84.
[70] L.J.R.O., B/V/5, visit. return of 1772.
[71] Frost, *Story of Donnington*, 31.
[72] *Shrews. Chron.* 14 Jan. 1955.

Rosary.[73] In 1962 its parish included Trench and Hadley.[74] A church designed in a modern style opened c. 1967 and the adjacent former church became the church hall and social club.[75]

PROTESTANT NONCONFORMITY.

Dissent accompanied the development of the parish's industries. No dissenters were recorded in 1676[76] but in 1693 Thomas Allcock's house at Pain's Lane was licensed for meetings.[77] There was said to be no dissent in 1772.[78] In 1799 the vicar claimed that there were very few nonconformists but noted that they had increased with the population,[79] and his encouragement of St. George's chapel at Pain's Lane suggests that he recognized an incipient challenge from dissent.

The Particular Baptists seem to have made the first notable gains.[80] At Donnington William Snow's house was licensed in 1811 and that of Richard Pickering, engineer, in 1813. The house of John Barnett, labourer, at Donnington Wood was licensed in 1814.[81] In 1820 a chapel was built in what was later Queen's Road, Donnington Wood;[82] there were 43 members in 1824.[83] In 1851 the chapel had 204 seats (100 free) and standing room for 55. On Census Sunday 1851 fifty people attended in the morning, a hundred in the afternoon, and two hundred in the evening.[84] In 1968 a new chapel opened in Queen's Road, a little west of the old one, which was then sold.[85]

For the Wesleyan Methodists there was fortnightly preaching at the 'Newport and Lilleshall' station in 1813.[86] A house in Lilleshall was licensed in 1815[87] as was a schoolroom there in 1816.[88] Some Methodists, probably Wesleyans, were attending Lilleshall church in 1824,[89] when there was also weekly preaching at the 'Aston and Lilleshall' station.[90] A Lilleshall society was recorded 1840–61[91] and about a dozen Wesleyans met in the later 19th century[92] in the quarry west of Limekiln Lane.[93] There was fortnightly preaching at Waxhill Barracks in 1813[94] and a

society was also meeting at Donnington 1816–36.[95] There was weekly preaching at the 'Rookery and Redhill' station in 1824.[96]

In 1821 Primitive Methodism took hold in east Shropshire,[97] and for twenty years it divided the territory with the New Connexion; the Primitives kept north of Watling Street, the New Connexion south.[98] Primitive Methodist meetings at two houses in Donnington Wood were registered in 1821 and 1822.[99] A camp meeting, attended by some 4,000, was held in 1839 near the Donnington Wood furnaces and began a local revival.[1] In 1851 there were at least three congregations, all in private houses. One at Waxhill Barracks had 25 attenders on Census Sunday evening.[2] The same evening others at Muxton and in Lilleshall village each had 20 attenders.[3] A brick chapel opened in Wellington Road, Donnington, in 1866.[4] It had 200 seats in 1940,[5] but by 1962 only thirty adult worshippers.[6] In 1967, when the Wrekin Drive church opened,[7] the old building closed for Methodist worship[8] and was sold to the Serbian Orthodox church.[9]

The New Connexion opened a brick chapel at Donnington Barracks (later School Road) in 1846.[10] It had 140 seats in 1940,[11] but by 1967, when the chapel closed,[12] only 17 members.[13] The congregation moved to the Wrekin Drive church and the old building was demolished.[14]

The United Methodist Free Churches had a chapel at Waxhill Barracks from 1862 to c. 1890 and a 'sanctuary' at Donnington Barracks that was registered for a few months in 1866.[15]

A new Methodist hall opened in Wrekin Drive, Donnington, in 1948[16] to replace St. John's chapel, Trench.[17] In 1967 the congregation, joined by the Wellington Road and School Road congregations, moved into a new church next to the hall.[18]

In 1906 an Independent church, its members having seceded in 1905 from the Primitive Methodist congregation at Wrockwardine Wood,[19] registered the disused isolation hospital at Don-

[73] G.R.O., Worship Reg. no. 65093.

[74] Shore, 'Survey of Donnington', p. 3.

[75] Frost, Story of Donnington, 31; G.R.O., Worship Reg. nos. 65093, 70813.

[76] T.S.A.S. 2nd ser. i. 84.

[77] P.R.O., RG 31/7, Salop. no. 35.

[78] L.J.R.O., B/V/5, visit. return of 1772.

[79] S.R.O. 3916/1/1, p. 69.

[80] See V.C.H. Salop. ii. 11.

[81] P.R.O., RG 31/7, Salop. nos. 283, 315, 331.

[82] Kelly's Dir. Salop. (1905), 84.

[83] Shropshire Circular Letter, 1824, 10 (copy in S.P.L., class C 98.6 v.f.).

[84] P.R.O., HO 129/366, no. 19.

[85] Frost, Story of Donnington, 31; G.R.O., Worship Reg. nos. 61335, 72079.

[86] S.P.L., C 98.7 v.f., Shrews. circuit plan.

[87] L.J.R.O., B/A/2(i)/F, p. 231. Cf. P.R.O., RG 31/2, Lich. no. 479; S.H.C. 4th ser. iii. 34.

[88] L.J.R.O., B/A/2(i)/F, p. 364. Cf. P.R.O., RG 31/2, Lich. no. 541; Wesley Hist. Soc. Proc. xxiv. 108.

[89] S.R.O. 3916/1/3, no. 20.

[90] S.P.L., L 98.7 v.f., Wellington circuit plan.

[91] S.R.O. 3767/XVII/A.

[92] S.R.O. 3027/1/1–3.

[93] Adams and Hazeley, Survey, 35.

[94] S.P.L., C 98.7 v.f., Shrews. circuit plan.

[95] Shrews. Sch. libr., Broseley circuit bk. 1815–41.

[96] S.P.L., L 98.7 v.f., Wellington circuit plan.

[97] V.C.H. Salop. ii. 14.

[98] B. Trinder, Meth. New Connexion in Dawley and Madeley (Wesley Hist. Soc., W. Midlands Branch, Occ. Publ. i [1968]), 7.

[99] P.R.O., RG 31/7, Salop. nos. 382, 391.

[1] T.S.A.S. lviii. 178.

[2] P.R.O., HO 129/366, no. 18.

[3] Ibid. nos. 16–17.

[4] Kelly's Dir. Salop. (1885), 872.

[5] Meth. Church Bldgs.: Statistical Returns (1940), 268.

[6] Shore, 'Survey of Donnington', p. 3.

[7] Below.

[8] G.R.O., Worship Reg. no. 46107.

[9] S.R.O. 3767/XXIII/C, K. H. Capsey to Revd. P. H. W. de Visme 19 Sept. 1967; — to K. H. Capsey 25 Sept. 1967.

[10] Kelly's Dir. Salop. (1885), 843.

[11] Meth. Church Bldgs.: Statistical Returns (1940), 268.

[12] G.R.O., Worship Reg. no. 61360.

[13] S.R.O. 3767/XV/G, closure application 1 Aug. 1967.

[14] Ibid. Wellington R.D.C. to Revd. P. H. W. de Visme 25 July 1967; Littlewood, Peace, & Lanyon to Revd. R. Hallam 12 Feb. 1969.

[15] G.R.O., Worship Reg. nos. 15070 (cancelled 1896), 17254 (cancelled Dec. 1866); O.S. Map 6", Salop. XXXVI. NE. (1890 edn.).

[16] G.R.O., Worship Reg. no. 62658; S.R.O. 3767/XXIII/A, programme 30 Oct. 1948.

[17] Below, Wrockwardine Wood, Prot. Nonconf.

[18] G.R.O., Worship Reg. no. 70873.

[19] S.R.O. 1861/102–3; below, Wrockwardine Wood, Prot. Nonconf.

nington Wood as a Central Hall; they remained there in 1980 as an Independent Evangelical church.[20]

A group of Quakers from Horsehay, Dawley, Edgmond, and Lilleshall began meeting monthly at a house in Lilleshall in the winter of 1964–5. The meeting later moved to Wellington.[21]

SERBIAN ORTHODOXY. A church dedicated to St. Nicholas opened *c.* 1949 in the former Roman Catholic church at Donnington.[22] In 1968 some members, having seceded for reasons of Yugoslav politics,[23] registered another church in the former Wellington Road Methodist church.[24] In the 1970s services at the latter, also dedicated to St. Nicholas, were held monthly and attracted a large congregation. At Easter some of the worshippers would attend in national costume.[25]

EDUCATION. Roger Schoolmaster lived in the manor 1408–9.[26] By 1437 there may have been a school in Lilleshall abbey, and in 1538 it may have had gentlemen's sons as pupils.[27]

By 1674 a schoolhouse[28] was repaired and heated by the parish.[29] William Penson, clerk, occurred as schoolmaster from 1694[30] to 1722;[31] not paid by the parish, he took fees from the pupils, paupers' fees being paid by the overseers.[32] In 1680 the parish bought a dictionary for the parishioners' children.[33] In 1772 two charity schools were recorded: one for 12 boys, the other for 10 girls. The pupils learned to read English. Lord Gower gave £4 a year to the master and £3 to the mistress.[34] Repairs and heating were, as before, charged to the parish.[35] In 1815 the schools were a 'Latin free grammar school' and an 'English school' and still received £7 a year.[36] They remained until 1818 when a National school, opened at Snedshill Coppice (in Shifnal), began to provide for Lilleshall parish.[37]

Private schools were mentioned in 1786 and 1796.[38] In 1818 three dame schools had 47 pupils,[39]

and in 1833 three schools had 67: one for girls, founded in 1832 and supported by the duchess of Sutherland, and two mixed, one of them founded in 1829. There was a fee-paying evening school, attended by 12 men and 8 women.[40] In 1843 one dame school of 40 pupils was recorded,[41] and in 1871 there was a private school with 21 pupils.[42]

Lilleshall County Primary School was founded as a National school in 1844[43] in an outbuilding of the Old Hall.[44] In 1852 each pupil was paying 2d. a week[45] but the school was otherwise supported by the 2nd duke of Sutherland.[46] In the early 1850s there was only one long, poorly lit room. There were about a hundred pupils, in five mixed classes, under a certificated master and a boy pupil-teacher. The school's character was 'agricultural'. The older boys worked for an hour each afternoon on allotments in the school garden, while the girls were taught needlework by the master's wife. The appointment of a trained mistress *c.* 1853 was expected to improve domestic instruction, and about then the 'animated' master began a class in geometry.[47]

In 1869–70 an average of 195 pupils attended during the day and 25 in the evenings.[48] A master's house was provided by 1861.[49] An infant department was created *c.* 1895.[50] Average attendance 1903–4 was 135 mixed pupils and 43 infants.[51] The 5th duke sold the school in 1922 to C. & W. Walker Ltd., who then leased it to the county council. It was reconstituted as Lilleshall Council School in 1923 for 160 mixed pupils and 45 infants.[52] Thereafter the freehold passed with that of the Old Hall.[53] The departments were amalgamated in 1934[54] and the recognized accommodation was reduced to 182.[55] In 1966 there were 103 pupils, but by 1969 there were 166 and a new school was proposed.[56] In 1972 new buildings were opened in Limekiln Lane.[57] In 1978 there were 274 pupils in separate junior and infant departments.[58] The juniors remained in the Old Hall premises in 1979.[59]

Donnington Wood C.E. (Controlled) School opened as a National school in 1847 in a new brick

[20] G.R.O., Worship Reg. no. 41639; Frost, *Story of Donnington*, 31; *Telford Social Trends*, i, ed. J. MacGuire (T.D.C. 1980), 218.
[21] Inf. from Mr. A. E. Morris.
[22] Frost, op. cit. 31 (giving 1945 as the opening date).
[23] Local inf.   [24] G.R.O., Worship Reg. no. 71344.
[25] Inf. from Mrs. R. M. Davies.
[26] Staffs. R.O., D. 593/J/1/1.   [27] *V.C.H. Salop.* ii. 77.
[28] S.R.O. 4462/CW/2, *s.a.* 1674–5, 1679–80, 1690–1, 1697–8.
[29] Ibid. *passim*. A sch. rm. at the end of the N. aisle of the ch. was built by Sir Ric. Leveson in 1657, according to Birm. Univ. Libr., Mytton Papers, iv. 815. Cf. above, pp. 169–70.
[30] S.R.O. 4462/P/1/3.   [31] Ibid. /Rg/2, bur. 30 June 1722.
[32] Ibid. /P/1/3, *s.a.* 1693–4.
[33] Ibid. /CW/2, *s.a.* 1680–1.
[34] L.J.R.O., B/V/5, visit. return of 1772.
[35] S.R.O. 4462/CW/3, *passim*.
[36] *Abstr. Rel. to Poor*, H.C. 82, p. 369 (1818), xix.
[37] S.R.O. 4462/Sch/1, 5 June 1818; *Digest Educ. Poor*, H.C. 224, pp. 755, 767 (1819), ix (2); below, Wombridge, Educ. *Shrews. Chron.* 17 June 1786 (p. 3); 9 Dec. 1796 (p. 3). Refs. kindly supplied by Dr. R. Hume.
[38]
[39] *Digest Educ. Poor*, 755, 767.
[40] *Educ. Enq. Abstr.* H.C. 62, p. 776 (1835), xlii.
[41] S.R.O. 3916/1/8, no. 21.
[42] *Return Elem. Educ.* H.C. 201, pp. 338–9 (1871), lv.

[43] P.R.O., ED 7/102, f. 367; S. Bagshaw, *Dir. Salop.* (1851), 395.
[44] Staffs. R.O., D. 593/N/3/7/1, Old Hall insurance, 1843 (ref. supplied by Mr. M. Rhodes).
[45] *Mins. of Educ. Cttee. of Council, 1852–3*, ii [1624], p. 500, H.C. (1852–3), lxxx.
[46] S. Bagshaw, *Dir. Salop.* 395.
[47] *Mins. of Educ. Cttee. of Council, 1850–1*, ii [1358], p. 511, H.C. (1851), xliv; *1851–2*, ii [1480], p. 420, H.C. (1852), xl; *1852–3*, ii. 463, 500; *1853–4*, ii [1788], pp. 514, 549, H.C. (1854), lii.
[48] *Rep. of Educ. Cttee. of Council* [C. 165], p. 635, H.C. (1870), xxii.
[49] S.P.L., abstr. of census, 1861 (TS. [1975]).
[50] *Return of Schs. 1893* [C. 7529], p. 506, H.C. (1894), lxv; *1899* [Cd. 315], p. 686, H.C. (1900), lxv (2).
[51] *Public Elem. Schs. 1906* [Cd. 3182], p. 537, H.C. (1906), lxxxvi.
[52] *S.C.C. Mins. (Educ.)* 1922–3, 44–5; 1924–5, 10, 71; 1930–1, 94.
[53] Ibid. 1930–1, 94; local inf.; above, Man. and Other Est.
[54] S.R.O. 2699/11, p. 162.
[55] *S.C.C. Mins. (Educ.)* 1934–5, 74.
[56] Ibid. 1969–70, 136.
[57] S.C.C. Educ. Cttee. *Sch. List* (1972), 7.
[58] Ibid. (1978), 6.
[59] Local inf.

building[60] in Church Road, provided by the 2nd duke of Sutherland.[61] There was a certificated master in 1850 with some 160 mixed pupils.[62] An infant department opened in a new wing in 1851[63] under a former pupil,[64] and 34 infants were attending in 1852.[65] By 1852 allotments, like those at Lilleshall, had been started.[66] In 1854 separate boys' and girls' departments were created.[67] A master's house was provided c. 1851.[68] The girls' room was enlarged at the 3rd duke's expense in 1868.[69] A new infant department was formed in 1893.[70] In 1903–4 average attendance was 141 boys, 110 girls, and 93 infants.[71] The girls' and infant departments were amalgamated in 1933.[72] In 1935 the 5th duke sold the school to the Salop Archidiaconal Board of Education.[73] In 1939 senior pupils moved to Wrockwardine Wood Senior (Mixed) Council School (in Wombridge) and the departments were amalgamated.[74] In 1949 the school acquired controlled status[75] and the infants moved to the council infant school in Baldwin Webb Avenue. In 1955 the junior school, which had become overcrowded, acquired the former Donnington Wood nursery school as an annexe.[76] The number of pupils continued to grow,[77] and in 1965 new premises in Leonard Close opened, with the old buildings as their annexe.[78] In 1978 there were 415 pupils.[79] From 1965 to 1975 the former nursery school housed a special unit for handicapped children.[80]

Donnington Wood County School, for infants, opened in 1949 in new buildings in Baldwin Webb Avenue.[81] In 1952 it began to use the former Donnington Wood nursery school (a wartime nursery adopted by the county council in 1947)[82] as an annexe.[83] In 1955 there were 100 pupils there and 240 in the main buildings. The total included a class of juniors temporarily displaced from the overcrowded junior school in Church Road. By then, however, the number of infants had fallen enough for the annexe to be transferred to the junior school.[84] In 1975 it was decided to add a nursery class of 50 places to the infant school,[85] and the annexe, again vacant, was used to house it.[86] In 1978 there were 269 pupils altogether.[87]

St. Matthew's C.E. (Aided) School, for juniors and infants opened in 1971 in new buildings in Church Road, Donnington Wood.[88] There were 249 pupils in 1978.[89]

CHARITIES FOR THE POOR. Sir Richard Leveson (d. 1661) left a £5 rent charge for annual doles.[90] In the mid 19th century it became customary to distribute most of it in Donnington Wood and the rest in St. George's.[91] In 1919 the income was merged with that of the Lilleshall share of the Foxley Charity.[92]

Sir Richard Leveson's widow Katherine (d. 1674) left £120 a year out of Foxley manor (Northants.) to provide twelve life pensions for widows, three of whom were to be Lilleshall parishioners. Each was to wear a gown with the initials K L on the breast; by 1821 that was no longer done in Lilleshall. Katherine also left £100 a year out of Foxley for apprenticing ten boys annually, two of them to be sons of Lilleshall parishioners. In 1876 the widows' pensions were raised to £20 and eligibility was extended, failing suitable widows, to other poor. The apprenticeships were raised to £30 and the Foxley Charity's objects were extended to include scholarships and grants to school leavers.[93] Lilleshall's annual share was £102 in 1975.

Katherine Leveson's will provided for the foundation of a hospital for 20 women at Temple Balsall (Warws.). If there were any vacancies after Balsall's needs were met, they were to be filled from other named places, among them Lilleshall parish.[94] In 1861 Lilleshall's contingent benefit became a permanent one of four weekly pensions of 8s. for female parishioners.[95] In 1975 Lilleshall's annual share was £21.

Mrs. Rebecca Walthall, by will proved 1756, left the interest on £10 to be distributed in Muxton. In the 1780s the annual interest was 10s.[96] By 1884 the annual interest, 5s. 6d., was divided between two Muxton widows.[97] The income was £2 in 1975.

A charity was established in 1888 under the will of William Slaney Lewis, who left £200 stock to provide blankets and clothing for widows in St. George's ecclesiastical district. In 1975 the income was £5.

By will proved 1894 St. John Tipton left £200 stock, the income to be distributed in St. George's parish in clothing or other necessaries.[98] The income in 1975 was £5.

C. C. Walker, by will proved 1897, gave £500 stock for the sick poor of Lilleshall civil parish.[99]

[60] P.R.O., ED 7/102, ff. 368v.–369.

[61] S. Bagshaw, *Dir. Salop.* (1851), 398.

[62] *Mins. of Educ. Cttee. of Council, 1850–1,* ii. 511.

[63] P.R.O., ED 7/102, f. 370v.

[64] *Mins. of Educ. Cttee. of Council, 1851–2,* ii. 419.

[65] Ibid. *1852–3,* ii. 510.   [66] Ibid. 462, 511.

[67] Frost, *Story of Donnington,* 28.

[68] P.R.O., ED 7/102, f. 368v.; *Kelly's Dir. Salop.* (1885), 843.

[69] *P.O. Dir. Salop.* (1870), 74.

[70] Frost, *Story of Donnington,* 28.

[71] *Public Elem. Schs. 1906,* 537.

[72] S.R.O. 2699/11, pp. 91–2.

[73] S.C.C. Mins. (Educ.) 1935–6, 73.

[74] Ibid. 1939–40, 86; S.R.O. 2699/13, p. 63.

[75] S.R.O. 3387/16, pp. 95, 134.

[76] S.C.C. Mins. (Educ.) 1955–6, 62; S.R.O. 3387/17, pp. 411–12.

[77] Ibid. 1957–8, 34.

[78] Frost, *Story of Donnington,* 28–9.

[79] *Sch. List* (1978), 10.

[80] Frost, op. cit. 28.

[81] S.R.O. 3387/16, p. 161.

[82] Ibid. /15, pp. 160, 191.

[83] Ibid. /16, p. 582.

[84] Ibid. /17, pp. 356, 411–12.

[85] S.C.C. Mins. (Educ.) 1974–5, 261.

[86] Frost, *Story of Donnington,* 28.

[87] *Sch. List* (1978), 10.   [88] Frost, op. cit. 29.

[89] *Sch. List* (1978), 10.

[90] Following paras. based on *5th Rep. Com. Char.* H.C. 159, pp. 408–9 (1821), xii; *Review of Local Chars.* (S.C.C. 1975), 66–7.

[91] S.R.O. 4462/Cy/2/4.

[92] S.R.O. 972, parcel 211, jnl. note, 3 Feb. 1919; Char. Com. scheme, 30 Sept. 1919.

[93] Char. Com. scheme, 24 Nov. 1876.

[94] *V.C.H. Warws.* iv. 88, 91.

[95] Temple Balsall Hospital Act, 1861, 24 & 25 Vic. c. 24.

[96] *Char. Don. 1786–8,* ii, H.C. 511–II, p. 1015 (1816), xvi (2).

[97] S.R.O. 3916/1/26/25.

[98] S.C.C. chars. index; *Kelly's Dir. Salop.* (1900), 191.

[99] S.R.O. 4462/Cy/1/1, 7.

The income was £11 a year in 1975.

By will proved 1944 Mrs. Edith Emily Todd left stock for pensions in certain parishes, among them Lilleshall ecclesiastical parish. In 1947 the Lilleshall share was vested in the Todd Trust (Lilleshall) Ltd., which in 1969–70 paid 25 pensions of 10s. a week.[1] The annual income in 1975 was £1,024.

By 1634 sums were occasionally contributed to the parochial poor's stock, which amounted to £57 by 1726. By 1757 only two sums remained: £15 producing 12s. a year then but nothing after 1800, and a £20 legacy of Thomas Winshurst (will proved 1673), producing 16s. a year then[2] but nothing after 1788. Both were lost by 1821.

PRESTON UPON THE WEALD MOORS

THE MANOR and township of Preston upon the Weald Moors lies 5 km. north-east of Wellington. It was originally subject to Wellington church but became a separate parish in the 13th century.[3]

Parts of the township's southern boundary are marked by the road from Preston to Hurleybrook, in existence by 1283,[4] and by Hurley brook. Ditches across the Weald Moors mark its boundaries on the west, north, and east. The eastern boundary partly coincides with the course of Humber brook and may have done so wholly until the 13th century.[5] As in Eyton and the other Weald Moors parishes some boundaries impinging on the moor may have been formally

ing 84 a. in the south-eastern detachment. By 1842 fields amounting to 139 a., scattered mainly across the north and east of the township and mostly formerly owned by the Charltons of Apley,[11] were counted as part of Wellington parish. By then the south-eastern detachment too was fragmented by 11 a. of closes belonging to Wellington parish.[12] The complex parish boundaries thus produced may have been no older than the later 18th century.[13] They were rationalized 1883–4 when the parts of Wellington parish in Preston township were added to Preston civil parish and Preston parish's fragments of the south-eastern detachment were assigned to Wellington and

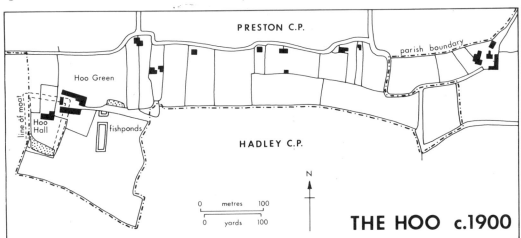

THE HOO c.1900

defined only at a relatively late date.[6] Disputes over rights on the Weald Moors in the 16th and 17th centuries, however, did not directly concern Preston, and maps drawn up for claimants c. 1580 showed the township's boundaries as well defined, with the possible exception of those on the northwest.[7] Preston township also included a detached part (probably the manor's original woodland)[8] to the south-east; its boundaries required elucidation in 1238.[9] Preston was in the forest of Mount Gilbert until 1301.[10]

The area of the ancient township (the subject of the present article) was 1,074 a. (424 ha.) includ-

Wrockwardine Wood C.P.s. Preston thus became a civil parish of 990 a. (401 ha.).[14]

Preston township lies on glacial deposits overlying Permian breccia and sandstone and Triassic Bunter Pebble Beds on the northern edge of the east Shropshire coalfield. Both Preston village, in the centre of the township, and the Hoo hamlet to the south-east and near the boundary, lie on red marl and sand, with some sand and gravel to the east and west. North and south is boulder clay, giving way to peat and alluvium on the Weald Moors.[15] Preston village is an agglomeration of 19th-century brick farms, with scattered 18th-

---

[1] Ibid. /PCC/4.

[2] Char. Don. 1786–8, ii. 1014–15.

[3] Below, Church; Wellington, Churches. This art. was written 1981.   [4] Above, Lilleshall, Communications.

[5] Eyton, viii. 258; S.R.O. 972, box 220, deed of 1277.

[6] Above, Eyton; T.S.A.S. lxiii. 1–10.

[7] S.R.O. 38/1.   [8] Below, Econ. Hist.

[9] Close R. 1237–42, 147.

[10] Eyton, viii. 259; Cartulary of Shrews. Abbey, ed. U. Rees (1975), ii, p. 249.

[11] Staffs. R.O., D. 1287/13/4/1.

[12] S.R.O. 3129/16/17; 3882/6/2; O.S. Area Bks. (1882), Preston; Wellington.

[13] Below, Church; Wellington, Man. and Other Est.

[14] Divided Parishes and Poor Law Amendment Act, 1882, 45 & 46 Vic. c. 58; 14th Ann. Rep. Local Govt. Bd. [C. 4515], pp. 191, 204, H.C. (1884–5), xxxii; Census, 1971.

[15] V.C.H. Salop. i, map facing p. 1; Geol. Surv. Map 1″, drift, sheet 153 (1929 edn.); Inst. Geol. Sciences Map 1/25,000, Telford (1978 edn.).

century and later houses, grouped around a square of streets, within which is the churchyard. At the west end of the village are the Preston Trust Homes (Preston hospital until 1946), alms-houses founded in the early 18th century.[16] About 1953 a small group of council houses was built south of the village.[17] Kinley farm, 1 km. west of the village, may have been the focus of a small medieval hamlet, 'houses' being noted there in 1650.[18] To the south-east lies Hoo Hall. Property boundaries east of it suggest that there was formerly a linear hamlet there, largely depopulated by 1842. Hoo Green lay between hall and hamlet.[19]

Roads run from the village in three directions: north-west through the Weald Moors to Kynnersley; south-west to Wappenshall; and south to join a road from Lilleshall to Hurleybrook, from which lanes lead off to the Hoo and Horton. The last named road, in part coinciding with Preston's boundary, existed by 1283.[20]

In 1833 a hoard of five middle Bronze Age axeheads was found east of Kinley Farm,[21] and a burnt hearth was noted on the Weald Moors in 1922.[22]

In 1086 there were 2 oxherds on the demesne and 3 villeins;[23] 8 householders paid the 1327 subsidy,[24] and 25 paid hearth tax in 1672.[25] In 1799 Preston was described as a 'very small village' of 170 persons.[26] By 1841 there were 247 inhabitants,[27] including 42 in the hospital.[28] Although by 1851 there were 63[29] hospital residents, the parish population had fallen slightly. The 1883–4 boundary changes had little effect on population, which remained at the mid 19th-century level until after the First World War. Thereafter, owing to agricultural mechanization,[30] population gradually fell, although it rose again in the 1960s, to 226 by 1981.[31]

The first part of the Shrewsbury Canal, opened in 1794,[32] cut the south-west corner of the parish, and the Birmingham & Liverpool Junction Canal's Newport branch, built in 1835, bisected the township from west to east, following the edge of the Weald Moors.[33] The building of a bridge over the latter canal probably provided the occasion for the straightening and realignment of the road to Kynnersley;[34] there were two other bridges, both near Kinley. Immediately west of the village bridge was a canal keeper's cottage, to the east a winding pool and boathouse.[35] The canal was last used in the 1940s and partly filled c. 1970.[36] In the

later 18th century one, or occasionally two, alesellers were licensed.[37] No later licensed premises are known.

MANOR. Before the Conquest Burrer held PRESTON. In 1086 Ralph de Mortimer held it of Roger, earl of Shrewsbury, the tenant in chief.[38] Mortimer soon lost it, possibly by forfeiture for rebellion in 1088.[39] Earl Roger's son, Robert of Bellême, forfeited the family interest by rebellion in 1102. Probably from c. 1100 or soon after, Preston formed part of the fee of Hodnet, under which it was listed in 1284 (or 1285) and 1292.[40] The Ludlow family acquired Hodnet in the early 14th century, and in 1381 and 1391 Preston was listed as one of their manors. The Vernons succeeded the Ludlows at Hodnet[41] and in the early 18th century a chief rent of 6d. was paid for Kinley to 'Madam' Vernon.[42] From c. 1884 to c. 1903 Algernon Heber-Percy of Hodnet attempted, unsuccessfully, to reintroduce lapsed manorial rights.[43]

Pain of Preston was lord in the period 1187–9. In the early 13th century the manor passed to his four coheirs: Agnes, wife of William of Preston and later of Roger of Preston;[44] Sabin, wife of William of Horton, who, like her sister, was also later married to a Roger of Preston; Margery, wife of Thomas Rabas; and Sibyl of Preston.

By 1256 Henry and Sibyl of Lee had acquired Thomas Rabas's quarter from him; that year Robert of Ford sued them for it. In 1258 Thomas Rabas was allowed to retain possession of the quarter for life but with remainder to Robert and his heirs. Robert was lord in 1277. In 1292 Richard of Ford, presumably Robert's heir, was one of the four coparceners, with Pain of Preston (fl. 1296–1320), William of Preston (fl. 1304), and William of Horton. The last named was presumably a descendant of the early 13th-century William of Horton, and the recurrence of the surname Preston makes it possible that the other two quarters also remained in the same families between the early 13th century and 1292: Adam and Ralph of Preston probably held quarters in 1277. In 1336 the coparceners of the manor — to judge from their exercise of the patronage of the church[45] — were Richard of Preston, Richard of Horton (presumably William of Horton's heir), Thomas Steventon, and Hugh of the Heath[46] in right of his wife.[47]

[16] Inf. from Bradford Estate Office; below, Chars.

[17] S.C.C. Planning Dept., planning permission no. 7648, 4 Aug. 1953.

[18] S.R.O. 1011/233, f. 8.

[19] S.R.O. 1263/1; the Hoo hamlet is shown on O.S. aerial photo., film 71.071, frame 356 (copy in S.P.L.).

[20] Above, Lilleshall, Communications.

[21] T.S.A.S. liv. 240–54.

[22] SA 786.

[23] V.C.H. Salop. i. 331.

[24] T.S.A.S. 2nd ser. i. 156.

[25] Hearth Tax 1672 (Salop. Arch. Soc.), 88.

[26] S.R.O. 3916/1/1, p. 63.

[27] V.C.H. Salop. ii. 226.

[28] Ibid. 231.

[29] Ibid. 232.

[30] St. Lawrence's C.E. Primary Sch. log bk. (at the sch.) rep. 1959.

[31] 1981 census figs. compiled in S.C.C. Planning Dept.

[32] Trinder, Ind. Rev. Salop. (1981), 85.

[33] C. Hadfield, Canals of W. Midlands (1969), 150, 160.

[34] Cf. S.R.O., dep. plan 306; 1263/1.

[35] O.S. Map 6″, Salop. XXXVI. NW. (1887 edn.).

[36] Inf. from Mr. W. T. Winnall.

[37] S.R.O., q. sess. rec. parcels 255–7, regs. of alesellers' recognizances, 1753–1801.

[38] V.C.H. Salop. i. 331; iii. 10.

[39] Eyton, viii. 255, 257.

[40] Feud. Aids, iv. 221; Eyton, viii. 260.

[41] Eyton, ix. 333; Cal. Inq. p.m. xv, pp. 135–6; xvi, pp. 407–8; Cal. Close, 1389–92, 238; S.P.R. Lich. xi (2), p. iv.

[42] S.R.O. 625, box 11, acct. of charges on est. of St. John Charlton.

[43] S.R.O. 3887, box 60, letters to G. G. Warren.

[44] Rog. was possibly the younger bro. of Baldwin of Hodnet (d. 1224). For this para. see Eyton, viii. 39, 258.

[45] The exercise of patronage has been used to elucidate the following manorial descent.

[46] Eyton, ii. 316–17; viii. 259–61; S.R.O. 972, box 220, deed of 1277.

[47] K. C Newton, Medieval Local Records (Hist. Assoc. 1971), 14–15.

Richard of Horton's quarter of the manor was held by him or another of the same name in 1336, 1345, 1350, 1369, and 1370. Philip of Horton had succeeded by 1382 and Richard Horton by 1402;[48] Philip, and after him Richard, are very probably to be identified with the contemporary owners of Dothill.[49] The subsequent succession is uncertain, but it appears that by 1481 the quarter was divided between Joan (*née* Horton), the wife of Reynold Sowdeley, her nephew William Titley, and her grandnephew William Steventon (II); all were descended from the Richard of Horton seised in Edward III's reign. By 1554 two separate thirds of this quarter were in the hands of Richard Sowdeley and William Charlton; the remaining third had evidently been subdivided between John Steventon and Francis Charlton, owners of quarters of the manor. The quarter was perhaps reunited in the Sowdeleys' hands later in the 16th century when it seems to have belonged to a John Sowdeley.[50] Its further descent is again uncertain but in 1614 it was in the hands of Sir Vincent Corbet,[51] who sold it in 1620 to Sir Philip Eyton.[52] Sir Philip thus probably became lord of a moiety of the manor,[53] though only briefly: later that year he exchanged the newly acquired quarter with Francis Charlton for property in Horton's wood.[54] Thereafter, presumably, it descended with another quarter that Charlton already held.

In 1336 Thomas Steventon held a quarter. Walter Steventon held it in 1345 and 1370. In 1382 Richard of Wrenbury was holding it, but from 1402 it was again held by the Steventons. Walter Steventon was lord in 1402 and 1428[55] and William Steventon (II) was lord of the quarter in 1481, when he also held a third share in another quarter;[56] he was alive in 1507. The quarter then seems to have descended with Dothill until 1659,[57] for Richard Steventon, who died that year, left it to his cousin Thomas Newport[58] (cr. Baron Torrington 1716, d. 1719),[59] who in turn left his property in Preston to Preston hospital.[60] In the 1660s Preston Hall was the capital messuage of the quarter. Standing close to the church the Hall was rebuilt in brick in the 18th century.[61]

The quarter of the manor held in 1336 by Hugh of the Heath was still in his possession in 1353, when he and his daughter Gillian sold the reversion to Sir Alan of Charlton[62] (d. 1360).[63] Thereafter the quarter descended with Apley.[64] Its capital messuage, in Kinley, was mentioned in 1381.[65] In 1676 Kinley Hall farm consisted of a house of 3

bays, barning of 3 little bays, and 78 a. of land. Mention of the moat yard, apparently next to the house, suggests that the medieval messuage had been moated.[66] The modern Kinley Farm was built on the site *c.* 1820 and the farm was bought *c.* 1927 by the tenant Harry Sankey.[67]

Richard of Preston and his wife Margaret had acquired their quarter of the manor from Richard's father William of Preston in 1332.[68] Richard of Preston died between 1345 and 1350, when his widow Margaret held it. The quarter eventually passed to the Eytons of Eyton upon the Weald Moors who owned a quarter in 1659. William Cotton, who acted as a joint patron of the living in 1382 and 1402 probably then had an interest in the quarter.[69] In 1659, soon after the death of Sir Thomas Eyton, his widow Margaret and their son Philip sold it to Edmund Waring of Humphreston, the sheriff, who in 1674 settled it on his son Richard at his marriage. On Richard's death the quarter was apparently divided between his sisters Elizabeth Colemore and Hannah, wife of George Ashby, who sold his property in Preston to Richard Higgins of Wappenshall in 1719. In 1731 Elizabeth Colemore and Richard Higgins sold their property to Preston hospital.[70] The hospital sold Hoo Hall farm *c.* 1953 and it was later bought by Telford development corporation.[71]

The capital messuage of the quarter is identifiable from 1612, when it was called 'le Howghe Hall'.[72] In the Middle Ages it was probably moated, and had two fishponds to the east. In 1981 Hoo Hall had a late 16th-century hall range, running east-west, with a cross wing projecting northwards beyond its east end. The hall range, of three bays in 1981, formerly extended farther west beyond a closed truss and is unequally divided by a large brick chimney stack, probably late 17th-century and contemporary with the first stage of replacing the timber walls by brickwork. The cross wing retains exposed timber framing in its upper storey. The rest of its walls and those of the south side of the hall were renewed in, or encased by, brick in the 19th century. The interior contains late 16th- or early 17th-century panelling, not all *in situ*; some late 16th-century plasterwork in the main upper room of the cross wing; a rearranged late 17th-century staircase with turned balusters; and two moulded stone fireplaces, one surmounted by the arms of Eyton quartering Pantulf in plaster. A farm range lay to the north-east.

[48] Eyton, viii. 261; L.J.R.O., B/A/1/9, f. 99v.
[49] Below, Wellington, Man. and Other Est.
[50] *Pedigrees from the Plea Rolls*, ed. G. Wrottesley (1905), 456–7; S.R.O. 665/1/257; L.J.R.O., B/A/1/15, f. 6v.
[51] S.R.O. 322, box 2, survey of Salop. est. of Sir V. Corbet.
[52] P.R.O., CP 25(2)/344/18 Jas. I Hil. [no. 7].
[53] Below.
[54] S.R.O. 665/1/257–8; below, Hadley, Man. and Other Est.
[55] Eyton, viii. 261; *Salop. Peace Roll, 1400–14*, ed. E. G. Kimball (1959), pp. 110, 114; L.J.R.O., B/A/1/9, f. 99v.
[56] Wrottesley, *Pedigrees from the Plea Rolls*, 456–7.
[57] Below, Wellington, Man. and Other Est.
[58] S.P.L., Deeds 5658.
[59] *Hist. Parl., Commons*, 1715–54, ii. 294.
[60] *9th Rep. Com. Char.* H.C. 258, p. 360 (1823), ix.
[61] Barnard MSS., Raby Castle, box 12, bdle. 21, deeds 21 Aug. 1662, 12 Apr. 1664.

[62] P.R.O., CP 25(1)/195/15, no. 2; Newton, *Medieval Local Records*, 14–15.   [63] *T.S.A.S.* liii. 258.
[64] *Cal. Inq. p.m.* xv, p. 136; P.R.O., C 137/67, no. 149; *Sir Chris. Hatton's Bk. of Seals*, ed. L. C. Loyd and D. M. Stenton (1950), p. 148; *Cal. Pat.* 1391–6, 23–4; L.J.R.O., B/A/1/9, f. 99v.; below, Wellington, Man. and Other Est. (Apley).
[65] *Cal. Inq. p.m.* xv, p. 136.
[66] S.P.L., MS. 2340, f. 18.
[67] Inf. from Mr. J. H. Sankey. An acct. for the rebldg. of Kinley farmho. *c.* 1754 is in S.R.O. 676/21.
[68] P.R.O., CP 25(1)/194/11, no. 49.
[69] Eyton, viii. 260–1.
[70] Staffs. R.O., D. 1287/13/11/1; *V.C.H. Salop.* iii. 114.
[71] T.D.C., deed pkt. 907.
[72] P.R.O., C 142/332, no. 148. It was probably the 'Hoyall' mentioned in 1481: Wrottesley, *Pedigrees from the Plea Rolls*, 456.

ECONOMIC HISTORY. In 1086 the manor of Preston contained a demesne ploughteam and two oxherds, and three villeins with a ploughteam; it was assessed at 1 hide. Its value had fallen from 40s. in 1066 to 20s. in 1086, and there was land available for two more ploughteams.[73]

In the Middle Ages there was open-field land, as suggested by the mention of the 'field of Preston' in 1412.[74] 'Preston fields' lay north of the

moning. Some internal divisions already existed. Wappenshall may have had some detached moorland in Preston township,[80] possibly the irregular area called Shut moor in 1842.[81] Part of Hawksmoor was the only part of Preston's moorland available to Preston commoners in 1724.[82]

By 1724[83] the whole parish was divided into farms and smallholdings. The largest was the 193-a. Hall farm, Rowley's farm having 141 a. and

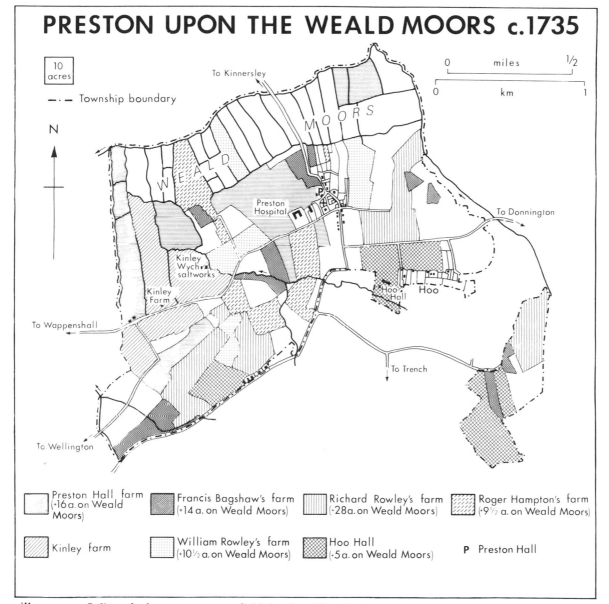

PRESTON UPON THE WEALD MOORS c.1735

10 acres

—·— Township boundary

N

0 miles ½
0 km 1

To Kinnersley

WEALD MOORS

Preston Hospital

To Donnington

Kinley Wych saltworks

Kinley Farm

Hoo Hall   Hoo

To Wappenshall

To Trench

To Wellington

Preston Hall farm (+16 a. on Weald Moors)	Francis Bagshaw's farm (+14 a. on Weald Moors)
Kinley farm	William Rowley's farm (+10½ a. on Weald Moors)

Richard Rowley's farm (+28 a. on Weald Moors)

Hoo Hall (+5 a. on Weald Moors)

Roger Hampton's farm (+9½ a. on Weald Moors)

P Preston Hall

village c. 1580[75] and there was open-field land there in the late 17th and early 18th century.[76] Hoo Hall was sold in 1659 with 'all the field land lying in four fields'.[77] Some 19th-century field boundaries clearly perpetuated strip divisions[78] and broad curving ridge and furrow survives north of the village,[79] but the extent of the field land is unknown.

By 1580 most of Preston's Weald Moor boundaries were well defined and there was no intercom-

Hoo Hall 110 a. Another five farms had 50–100 a., eleven smaller holdings averaging 17 a. each. The regular size and shape of the closes and the division of the farms' lands indicate that a comprehensive inclosure and apportionment of lands had been made. Only Kinley farm was consolidated, its land running down the western edge of the parish. Otherwise the farms had compact groups of closes in three or four areas of the parish: on the central higher ground, in the

[73] V.C.H. Salop. i. 331.
[74] Salop. Peace Roll, 1400–14, pp. 110, 114.
[75] S.R.O. 38/1.
[76] S.P.L., MS. 2340, survey of c. 1676; S.R.O. 4309, box 2, survey of 1724.
[77] Staffs. R.O., D. 1287/13/11/1.

[78] S.R.O. 1263/1; dep. plan 306.
[79] At O.S. Nat. Grid SJ 681 157.
[80] S.R.O. 38/1.
[81] S.R.O. 1263/1.
[82] S.R.O. 4309, box 2, survey of 1724.
[83] Ibid.

'wastes' of the south-west corner of the township, on the Weald Moors, and in the south-east detachment. The preponderance of field names indicating grassland[84] suggests that pastoral farming predominated at the time of inclosure. Nevertheless in 1682 a farm had *c.* 10 a. under corn, 17 cattle, and a few pigs and horses, with flax being woven and cheese manufactured in the farmhouse.[85]

In 1842, apart from one small arable parcel, the Weald Moors were given over to meadow and pasture in about equal proportions. Most of the township south of the moors was arable. The farms were largely those of 1724, although there had been some changes producing rather larger and more compact farms, with fewer of them divided between three or four distinct parts of the parish.[86]

In 1867 there was still slightly more arable than pasture.[87] By 1891, however, when sheep and

TABLE VII

PRESTON UPON THE WEALD MOORS: LAND USE, LIVESTOCK, AND CROPS

	1867	1891	1938	1965
Percentage of grassland	47	66	83	63
arable	53	34	17	37
Percentage of cattle	25	29	36	75
sheep	59	61	49	0
pigs	16	10	15	25
Percentage of wheat	61	59	74	32
barley	32	33	17	68
oats	7	8	9	0
mixed corn & rye	0	0	0	0
Percentage of agricultural land growing roots and vegetables	23	12	17	18

Sources: P.R.O., MAF 68/143, no. 1; /1340, no. 10; /3880, Salop. no. 130; /4945, no. 130.

cattle were increasing, there was approximately twice as much pasture as arable,[88] by 1938 five times as much.[89] After the Second World War the trend reversed, and in 1981 areas of the Weald Moors were being ploughed.

Domesday records ½ league of woodland.[90] It is likely that it was the detached portion of the township, where nearly all the field names indicate woodland;[91] that portion adjoined the similar woodland detachments of Eyton at Hortonwood and Wrockwardine at Wrockwardine Wood.[92] In 1616 certain estates in Preston, including Kinley, had pannage rights in the detachment.[93] By 1724 the detachment had been cleared of woodland and divided into closes.[94] Kinley farm had no land there, perhaps an indication that the township's inclosure and apportionment took place between those dates.

In 1676 a windmill stood *c.* 1 km. west of the village, in or near open-field land.[95]

Salt was produced by two adjacent works at Kingley Wych east of Kinley Farm, exploiting the brine springs, which *c.* 1800 produced 4–5,000 gallons of brine every 24 hours.[96] One of the works was owned by the Charltons, the other, the Charity Salt Works, by Preston hospital. Both were first mentioned in 1707, when the latter was owned by Thomas Newport. Little more is known of the Charity works, which probably closed soon after 1736: a very small amount of coal was bought for them that year[97] but hospital accounts from 1734 included the saltworks without showing any income.[98]

In 1721 Samuel Stringer surrendered his lease of the Charlton saltworks, and between then and 1730[99] they were leased to local mining interests. They were afterwards administered directly by the estate until 1739 when Francis Dorsett began to operate them on his own account, which he did until at least 1760. In 1763 the saltworks were leased to John Briscoe of Wellington, lessee of Kinley farm, and William Ball, described as a salt proprietor of Middlewich (Ches.). The works were redundant by 1799 but a building remained on the site until *c.* 1960; the brine well was finally filled *c.* 1970.[1]

The brine was extracted from a pit, probably by a horse-powered pump; it was stored in cisterns and then boiled in iron pans. Two pans operated in 1721[2] using cheap coal from the Wombridge mines. Blood was added to speed evaporation. The salt was moulded and sold retail or wholesale; tolls on the Watling Street turnpike were compounded. In the half year to March 1731, 3,312 bushels of salt were sold, 522 remained in stock.[3]

Common red bricks were manufactured on the township's southern boundary: a brickworks was noted in 1724.[4] In 1831 it produced 60,000 bricks and 17,000 tiles, used in the new hospital lodges;[5] it was reputedly the source of the bricks used in the 1827 additions. The brickworks went out of use in the late 19th century but in 1919 a small

[84] S.R.O. 1263/1.
[85] *Yeomen and Colliers in Telford*, ed. B. Trinder and J. Cox (1980), pp. 268–9.
[86] S.R.O. 3882/6/2.
[87] P.R.O., MAF 68/143, no. 1.
[88] Ibid. /1340, no. 10.
[89] Ibid. /3880, Salop. no. 130.
[90] *V.C.H. Salop.* i. 331.
[91] S.R.O. 1263/1.
[92] Above, Eyton, Econ. Hist.; below, Wrockwardine Wood, Econ. Hist.
[93] S.R.O. 665/1/256.

[94] S.R.O. 4309, box 2, survey of 1724.
[95] S.P.L., MS. 2340, ff. 39–40.
[96] Acct. of the saltwks. based on Trinder, *Ind. Rev. Salop.* (1981), 31–2.
[97] S.R.O. 625, bdle. 22, coal accts., Mich. 1736.
[98] Staffs. R.O., D. 1287/13/2, receiver's bk. 1734–69.
[99] For this para. cf. S.R.O. 625, box 10; 676, accts. various.
[1] Inf. from Mr. Sankey.
[2] S.R.O. 625, box 10, lease.
[3] S.R.O. 676/24.
[4] S.R.O. 4309, box 2, survey of 1724, p. 57.
[5] Staffs. R.O., D. 1287/13/1/3, receipt.

beehive kiln remained on the site.[6]

Sand was extracted north-west of the village before 1887.[7]

LOCAL GOVERNMENT. No evidence of a manorial court has been found. There were Preston presentments to the Bradford hundred court in 1590 and 1592.[8]

Records of the appointment of an overseer of the poor survive from 1727, two overseers being appointed annually from 1739. In 1763 the system changed and £10 was paid to Richard Mansel for keeping the poor, although some payments were also made directly to individuals. During the 18th century money was disbursed on clothing, house repairs, and pensions, the amount fluctuating between c. £4 and £15.[9] There was no poorhouse. Preston was in the Wellington poor-law union 1836–1930.[10]

There was apparently only one churchwarden being appointed for much of the 18th century.[11] Records of the parish surveyor of highways survive from 1791 to 1827. They show money raised by levies being spent on labour and materials for raising and draining the parish roads.[12] Preston became part of Wrekin highway district in 1863,[13] and was part of Wellington rural district from its inception until 1974[14] when it became part of Wrekin district.[15] Part of the south-east of the parish was included in 1968 in the designated area of Telford new town.[16]

CHURCH. The name Preston, the priests' *tun*,[17] may indicate ecclesiastical ownership of the vill before 1066. About 1280 Thomas Lyart was vicar of Wellington and rector of Preston chapel.[18] By 1336, whence institutions were regularly recorded, the independent status of Preston church was established.[19]

The advowson apparently descended with the manor, whose partition caused uncertainty over the exercise of turns.[20] From the earlier 18th century the right of presentation was held by Preston hospital and the Charltons. The Charlton family presented for one turn in three, last doing

so in 1940.[21] When the rectory was united with the benefices of Kynnersley and Tibberton in 1978, patronage of the united benefice was vested in the patrons of the three former livings jointly.[22]

A proportion of the great tithes in Preston township was paid to the Wellington tithe owners. The amount due to St. John Charlton in respect of the rectorial tithes of Wellington was questioned in 1743.[23] A territorial apportionment was later made, possibly in the later 18th century.[24] In 1838 the township's tithes were commuted to £235 a year: the great tithes to £199 shared equally between St. John Chiverton Charlton and the rector; the small tithes to £36, those in Preston parish producing £23 for the rector, those in Wellington parish £13 for the vicar of Wellington.[25]

There were 24 a. of glebe in 1724,[26] 23 a. and a cottage in 1884, three cottages and some land having recently been sold.[27] In 1942 the War Department compulsorily purchased 16 a.,[28] c. 9 a. remaining in 1981 as glebe.[29]

In 1743 the parsonage, a 'very poor' house, was let for £2.[30] Described in 1799 as a small thatched cottage,[31] it was a two-roomed baffle-entry farmhouse of two storeys with some internal subdivision, c. 10.36 × 5.79 metres overall. Outside was a four-bayed barn. In 1827 the parsonage was extended and modernized by W. T. Birds, apparently the first resident rector for over a century. The old house was encased within a new brick rectory, which had over twice the floor space of the old, the rooms including two parlours downstairs and four bedrooms upstairs.[32] The rectory was sold in 1954 and became a private house. During the Second World War its cellars were designated the village's air-raid shelter.[33]

The living was valued at 60s. in 1535,[34] £24 in 1665,[35] £70 in 1799,[36] £198 in 1828–31 and 1871, and £231 in 1932. From 1900 or earlier the rector was usually chaplain of the hospital, with a stipend of £40 in 1917.[37]

Two medieval incumbents surnamed Preston may have been members of the family holding part of the manor.[38] Only one pre-Reformation rector is known to have been a graduate, the pluralist William Grinshill, 1422–8.[39] There was

[6] T. H. Whitehead and others, *Country between Wolverhampton and Oakengates* (Geol. Surv. Memoir, 1928), 202.

[7] O.S. Map 6″, Salop. XXXVI. NW. (1887 edn.).

[8] P.R.O., SC 2/197/96; Staffs. R.O., D. 593/J/10, ct. r. m. 1d.

[9] S.R.O. 4608/P/1.

[10] V. J. Walsh, 'Admin. of Poor Laws in Salop. 1820–55' (Pennsylvania Univ. Ph.D. thesis, 1970), 148–50 (copy in S.R.O.); *Kelly's Dir. Salop.* (1929), 196.

[11] S.R.O. 4608/CW/1–2; /P/1.

[12] S.R.O. 4608/H/1.

[13] S.R.O., q. sess. order bk. 1861–9, p. 127.

[14] *V.C.H. Salop.* ii. 217.

[15] Sources cited ibid. iii. 169, n. 29.

[16] *Dawley New Town (Designation) Amendment (Telford) Order 1968* (Stat. Instr. 1968, no. 1912).

[17] E. Ekwall, *Concise Oxf. Dict. Eng. P.N.* (4th edn.), 374.

[18] Eyton, viii. 40, 261.

[19] L.J.R.O., B/A/1/2, f. 214v.

[20] See e.g. ibid. /1/15, f. 6v.; S.R.O. 625, box 19, abstr. of title [1666 × 1698]; ibid. corresp. betw. T. Dorsett and J. Shirke, 28 Feb. 1743/4; S.R.O. 1005/169.

[21] Lich. Dioc. Regy., benefice and inst. bk. 1929–52, p. 73.

[22] Church Com. scheme, 14 July 1978 (confirmed 25 July 1978: *Lond. Gaz.* 28 July 1978, p. 9086).

[23] S.R.O. 4309, box 3, T. Dorsett to J. Shirke, 1 Feb. 1743/4. For Charlton see below, Wellington, Man. and Other Est.

[24] On the analogy of Eyton: above; cf. O.S. *Area Bks.* (1882), Preston; Wellington; S.R.O. 3129/16/17.

[25] L.J.R.O., B/A/15, Preston. The rector's commuted small tithes included a sum for Easter dues and offerings.

[26] S.R.O. 4309, box 2, survey of 1724.

[27] S.R.O. 3916/1/26/39.

[28] S.R.O. 4309, box VI, Preston; 4608/Gl/6–7.

[29] Inf. from Mr. Winnall.

[30] S.R.O. 4309, box 3, T. Dorsett to J. Shirke, 1 Feb. 1743/4.

[31] S.R.O. 3916/1/1, p. 63.

[32] S.R.O. 2222/8.

[33] Inf. from Mrs. J. A. Matkin.

[34] *Valor Eccl.* (Rec. Com.), iii. 187.

[35] L.J.R.O., B/V/1/67, f. 10 (2nd nos.).

[36] S.R.O. 3916/1/1, p. 63.

[37] *Rep. Com. Eccl. Revenues* [67], pp. 494–5, H.C. (1835), xxii; *Kelly's Dir. Salop.* (1871), 283; (1900), 183; (1917), 184; *Crockford* (1932), 509.

[38] John, 1363–?9 (*S.H.C.* N.S. x (2), 196, 200); Ric., 1370–82 (or –83) (ibid. 203, 214).

[39] A. B. Emden, *Biog. Reg. Univ. Oxf. to 1500*, ii. 835; below, Wellington, Churches.

no pulpit in the church in 1576.[40] From the later 17th century, or earlier, the living was generally held in plurality. Samuel Pritchard, 1678–1714,[41] also held Eyton upon the Weald Moors.[42] William Sockett, 1714–?32,[43] also served the chapel at Wombridge although it was not a dependent chapelry of Preston.[44] Wombridge did not have rights of marriage until 1760 and largely relied on Preston and its incumbents until c. 1805.[45] Henry Wood, c. 1743–1795,[46] a pioneer of steam power, also held High Ercall and Kynnersley,[47] the latter living also being held by his curate[48] and successor at Preston, Richard Spearman,[49] 1795–1826.[50] In 1799 there was one service on Sundays, alternating mornings and evenings with Kynnersley; communion was celebrated quarterly and there were 20 communicants.[51]

W. T. Birds, 1826–61,[52] was also perpetual curate of Penley (Flints.).[53] In 1843 he instituted an additional service at the hospital for residents.[54] William Houghton, 1861–95,[55] wrote several books, mainly on natural history,[56] and was an authority on eastern languages, for which he was granted a civil list pension.[57] Between the 1890s and 1930s there were usually two Sunday services, although in the period 1910–17 three or four were normal.[58] In the early 20th century Preston was served by elderly rectors whose incumbencies were brief; some also held Kynnersley. In 1933 it was revealed that no churchwardens had been appointed for a number of years.[59] H. J. Moreton, 1947–74, held the living with that of Hadley.[60] In 1981 the weekly Sunday morning service at Preston had a congregation of c. 20.[61]

The church of ST. LAWRENCE, so called in 1871,[62] is of red brick with stone dressings, and consists of a chancel with north vestry, nave, and west tower. It replaced a church which was said c. 1736 to be beyond repair and so small that it would not contain more than half the inhabitants of Preston,[63] the population having recently increased with the opening of the hospital. Little is known of the earlier church except that it had a bell tower (perhaps built after 1553) and clock and was built at least partly of stone. In 1553

there were two small bells, a silver chalice, and a gilt paten.[64] The new church was built between 1739 and 1742, the nave and lower stages of the tower being of that date.[65] The keystone of the west doorway is inscribed 'T.H. 1739', Thomas Higgins being the churchwarden whose name appeared on the list of petitioners for a brief.[66] The tower contains two bells, one of 1715.[67] The plate is 18th-century and later.[68] The chancel and vestry were added in 1853; Preston hospital bore the expense of the chancel and of new pews at the east end of the nave for its widows and children.[69] The top stage of the tower may also be of that date. There was a west gallery containing a barrel organ and, in 1843, 30 seats for the poor.[70] The gallery was removed in a major restoration of 1905 when the pews and pulpit were rebuilt, incorporating much 18th-century panelling, and a new font was installed.[71]

The registers begin in 1693 and are complete thereafter.[72]

NONCONFORMITY. A meeting house was registered at Preston in 1803.[73] In 1846 there was a Primitive Methodist mission at Kinley, connected with Leegomery and included in the Wrockwardine Wood circuit;[74] it was evidently short-lived.[75]

EDUCATION. In 1799 a governess taught 13 girls boarded in Preston hospital;[76] in 1818 and 1851 there were 20 girls taught by the master or matron in the hospital hall.[77] A boarding school established in 1830 had 6 boys in 1833.[78] By 1843 there was a Sunday school with c. 50 pupils and a dame school with c. 17, held in a 'close and dirty room'.[79]

In 1846 a National school with 45 places was built at the expense of the Revd. S. H. Macaulay and his wife, with the aid of a small government grant. Attendance averaged 25 in 1849.[80] The income in 1873 consisted of £27 in contributions and £7 8s. 6d. in 2d. fees from 33 pupils; a disproportionately small number of infants, seven, was probably due to the village's remoteness. The uncertificated mistress received £14 a

[40] L.J.R.O., B/V/1/10.
[41] Ibid. /1/19, f. 170; T.S.A.S. 3rd ser. v. 372.
[42] W.S.L., H.M. 36 (shorthand transcribed by Mr. N. W. Tildesley).
[43] L.J.R.O., B/A/1/19, f. 170; Wellington par. reg. bur. 23 July 1732 (transcript in S.P.L.).
[44] Trinder and Cox, Yeomen and Colliers, p. 43. For his probate inv. see ibid. pp. 376–7.
[45] J. E. G. Cartlidge, The Vale and Gates of Usc-con (Congleton, [1935]), 66–7; below, Wombridge, Churches.
[46] S.R.O. 4608; L.J.R.O., B/A/1/26, pp. 101–2.
[47] The Engineer, 13 Aug. 1948.
[48] S.R.O. 4608.
[49] S.R.O. 3916/1/1, p. 63.
[50] L.J.R.O., B/A/1/26, pp. 101–2; Lich. Dioc. Regy., episc. reg. 29, p. 114.
[51] S.R.O. 3916/1/1, p. 53.
[52] Lich. Dioc. Regy., episc. reg. 29, p. 114; 32, p. 215.
[53] Alum. Cantab. 1752–1900, ii. 270.
[54] S.R.O. 3916/1/6.
[55] Lich. Dioc. Regy., episc. reg. 32, p. 215; benefice and inst. bk. 1868–1900, p. 101.
[56] Including Brit. Fresh-water Fishes (2 vols. folio, 1879).
[57] Shrews. Chron. 13 Sept. 1895, p. 5 (obit.).
[58] S.R.O. 4608/SRg/1–2.   [59] S.R.O. 3916/1/26/41.
[60] Crockford (1975–6), 681.
[61] Inf. from the Revd. J. J. Davies.

[62] E. Cassey & Co. Dir. Salop. (1871), 283.
[63] S.R.O., q. sess. files, 1/73.
[64] Ibid. /74; S.R.O. 4608/P/1, s.a. 1733, 1735; T.S.A.S. 2nd ser. xii. 320, 332.
[65] Descr. based on Cranage, vii. 617; Pevsner, Shropshire, 232.
[66] S.R.O., q. sess. files, 1/73.
[67] H. B. Walters, Ch. Bells of Salop (Oswestry, 1915), 281.
[68] S. A. Jeavons, Ch. Plate Archd. Salop (Shrews. 1964), pp. 61, 105, 120.
[69] S.R.O. 4608/CW/2, s.a. 1853.
[70] S.R.O. 3916/1/6.
[71] Ibid. /1/34; S.R.O. 4608/ChF/3.
[72] S.R.O. 4608. Bps.' transcripts (L.J.R.O., B/V/7, Preston) begin in 1668.
[73] P.R.O., RG 31/7, Salop. no. 221.
[74] S.R.O. 3605/1, pp. 158–9; above, Hadley, Nonconf.
[75] Not mentioned in P.R.O., HO 129.
[76] S.R.O. 3916/1/1, p. 63.
[77] Ibid. /1/3, p. 72; Digest Educ. Poor, H.C. 224, p. 768 (1819), ix (2); S. Bagshaw, Dir. Salop. (1851), 416; inf. from the warden, Preston Trust Homes.
[78] Educ. Enq. Abstract, H.C. 62, p. 781 (1835), xlii.
[79] S.R.O. 3916/1/8, no. 26.
[80] S.R.O. 3887, box 60, details of trust deed; Mins. of Educ. Cttee. of Council, 1849–50 [1215], p. ccxxviii, H.C. (1850), xliii.

year and a house rent free. Attendance averaged 18 in 1873,[81] 22 in 1895.[82] A replacement school built on a site given by the hospital trustees opened in 1898;[83] it had 90 places in 1912.[84] Girls from the hospital probably began to attend the new school, for attendance averaged 68 in 1905,[85] c. 50 between 1914 and 1933,[86] c. 67 in 1936, and c. 76 in 1943.[87] Evacuees from Smethwick (Staffs.)[88] and Harrow (Mdx.)[89] were admitted in 1939 and 1940.[90] Senior pupils transferred to Wellington Modern School from 1946;[91] the parish population fell during the 1950s;[92] no girls boarded in the hospital after 1952;[93] and the school had only 28 pupils in 1959.[94] Known as St. Lawrence's C.E. Primary School by 1957, it then became controlled[95] and was soon greatly improved.[96] A demountable classroom was added in 1966 and 15 pupils from the closed Kynnersley C.E. School were admitted, numbers rising to 52.[97] In 1981 there were 47 pupils.[98]

CHARITIES FOR THE POOR. Preston hospital was founded under the will, proved 1716, of Catherine, Lady Herbert, daughter of the 1st earl of Bradford, the bequest being a thanksgiving for her rescue when lost on the Alps. She left £6,000 to her brother Lord Torrington and other trustees to build and endow almshouses in Shropshire for 12 women and 12 girls.[99] The numbers of widows and girls were each soon increased to 20. In 1719 Torrington's estate was added to her legacy, with an additional £1,000 to build a hall in the middle of the almshouses. The money was largely invested in South Sea annuities, sold in 1730 to buy an estate mainly in Preston, to which land in Hortonwood was added in 1750. In 1802 Lord Mountrath, whose mother was a Newport, left £4,000 with the intention of increasing each widow's pension to £30 a year. From 1827 the number of widows was increased to 26 and in 1830 each received £18 a year, 2 tons of coal, and bedding and furniture, with £5 allowed for funeral expenses. Twenty of the widows also received £4 half-yearly from Lord Mountrath's gift. The widows, selected by trustees nominated by the Bridgemans, were women formerly of good station but in reduced circumstances. Each usually occupied a linked parlour-bedroom in the west wing and had her own small garden.

Girls were lodged in dormitories in the east wing, clothed, and educated from the ages of 7 to 14, the older girls being taught dairying, with the expectation of going into service.[1] By 1880 the ages had risen to 10 and 16. No girls boarded in the hospital after 1952.[2]

The original building, by an unknown architect but in the style of Gibbs, faces south forming three sides of a quadrangle, with a hall in the centre of the north wing. It was apparently complete by c. 1726,[3] and is of red brick with stone dressings. The hall, formerly used as a schoolroom and for Sunday services, has giant pilasters, two large arched windows, and a grand doorway facing the courtyard. It is outset from, and taller than, the two bays between it and the angles of the wings. The first three bays of each wing are closed, the remaining nine bays being open on the ground floor in loggias with elliptical arches.

The building was designed to house 20 widows and 20 girls but in 1799, when there were 20 widows, only 13 girls were resident.[4] In 1807 plans were put forward not only to subdivide the hall, and to provide a sick room by division of the steward's room, but also to provide places for eight more girls.[5] In 1809 temporary places were being provided for them at Lady Bradford's instigation but some of the girls already slept three to a bed, which was thought 'not wholesome'.[6] In 1827 the two side wings were carried forward to a design by J. H. Haycock[7] of outward-curving quadrants of three bays, originally of one storey only, later raised to two, and two storeyed pavilions. The additions provided eight apartments for eight more widows, although by 1830 only six more were resident.

Two lodges were built south of the hospital in 1831, one to house the first resident male servant, a gardener, felt to be necessary because a night emergency would oblige one of the girls to walk a considerable distance to get help. There were also fears of robbery, especially when the widows had been paid their pensions.[8] In the same year 58 cwt. of iron railings were bought from the Coalbrookdale Co.[9] Separating the main building from the avenue of trees that approaches from the lodges are fine wrought-iron gates by Robert Bakewell (fl. 1707–55).[10] An infirmary block built in 1893 was the last major alteration.[11]

Preston shared in a charity established by will of Andrew Charlton of Apley, proved 1617.[12]

[81] P.R.O., ED 7/102, ff. 559, 561.
[82] Kelly's Dir. Salop. (1895), 176.
[83] Ibid. (1900), 183, stating that it had 69 places.
[84] Log bk. (at the sch.), p. 1.
[85] Kelly's Dir. Salop. (1905), 189.
[86] Log bk.
[87] Ibid. reps. 1936, 1943.
[88] i.e. from St. Phil. Neri's R.C. Primary Sch. Cf. V.C.H. Staffs. xvii. 138–9.
[89] i.e. from the Waifs and Strays home.
[90] Log bk. 1 Sept., 13 Oct. 1939; 4 June 1940. They boarded at the hosp.
[91] Ibid. 4 Sept. 1946. Some went to High Ercall Mod. Sch. 1957–62: ibid. 3 Sept. 1957; 20 Sept. 1958; 27 July 1962.
[92] V.C.H. Salop. ii. 226.
[93] Inf. from the warden.
[94] Log bk. rep. 1959.
[95] Ibid.
[96] Ibid. 22 Feb. 1960.
[97] Ibid. rep. 1966.
[98] S.C.C. Educ. Cttee. Educ. Dir. (1981), 7.

[99] This acct. based on 24th Rep. Com. Char. H.C. 231, pp. 360–7 (1831), xi; J. Cornforth, 'Charity on a Noble Scale', Country Life, 16 Apr. 1964, 902–5; Pevsner, Shropshire, 232; Ed. J. Burrow & Co. Ltd. Wellington R.D. Official Guide [1962], 19.
[1] Staffs. R.O., D. 1287/13/1, rental July 1753.
[2] Inf. from the warden; M. McCrea, 'A Pair of Shoes: An Acct. of the Lives and Time of Jessie and Norah Shoebotham' (TS.; copy in S.P.L.).
[3] The rainwater heads are dated 1726. See above, plate 52.
[4] S.R.O. 3916/1/1, p. 63.
[5] Staffs. R.O., D. 1287/13/3; ibid. /13/4/1; ibid. /13/11/4.
[6] Ibid. /13/4/1, H. Bowman to C. Ware, 21 Jan. 1809.
[7] H. Colvin, Biog. Dict. Brit. Architects, 1600–1840 (1978), 408.
[8] Staffs. R.O., D. 1287/13/4/1, P. Potter to C. Ware, 28 Dec. 1830.
[9] A. Raistrick, Dynasty of Iron Founders (1970), 57.
[10] Country Life, 11 Mar. 1982, 673.
[11] S.R.O. 818/82–95.
[12] Below, Wellington, Chars.

STIRCHLEY

STIRCHLEY was formerly a farming parish with an industrial belt along the north-west edge, but in the 1970s it was transformed by the building of houses as part of Telford new town. It lies on the edge of the east Shropshire coalfield, 2 km. north of Madeley and 5 km. west of Shifnal. The ancient parish and township were conterminous, forming a compact block of 840 a. (340 ha.) until 1934, when the transfer of the north-west side of the parish to Dawley urban district reduced its size to 568 a. (230 ha.).[13] Stirchley ceased to be a separate administrative unit on the absorption of the parish into Dawley U.D. in 1966.[14]

Lying in gently rolling terrain, the parish was roughly triangular in shape. Its boundaries bore little relationship to landform except in the north-east, where Edge brook formed part of the boundary with Shifnal, and in the north-west, where the boundary with Dawley followed the incised Randlay valley. The parish was bisected by the Mad brook valley, to the north-east of which a rounded hill, rising to 158 metres, formed the highest point in the parish. Stirchley is underlain by the Coalport Beds of the Upper Coal Measures, on which the extensive drift cover of boulder clay gives rise to a heavy soil, which favoured a pastoral economy and the retention of much permanent grassland until the 19th century.[15] After 1800 the productive Middle Coal Measures beneath the Coalport Beds were mined from shafts in the west half of the parish and clay was quarried for brick making.

The growth of industry in the 19th century resulted in only minor changes to the settlement pattern and until the 1970s the parish contained little more than the small cluster of houses near the church west of the Mad brook valley and a scatter of outlying farms in the east. The landscape underwent a dramatic transformation during the 1970s as extensive housing estates were built over much of the south and east as part of Telford new town development programme.

Stirchley village lay at the hub of a radial pattern of roads, lanes, and paths, linking the outlying farms to the village or giving access to distant fields. Only the Dawley–Shifnal road, which crossed the parish from west to east, appears to have been of more than local importance. The ancient road pattern survived the changes of 19th-century industrialization but was modified substantially during the 1970s.[16] Queensway, Telford's 'eastern primary road' link-ing the new residential and industrial areas between Oakengates and Madeley and providing a through route to Bridgnorth, was built down the eastern edge of the parish 1969–71, with a network of minor roads running from it to the perimeters of the new housing estates in Stirchley.[17]

The Coalport branch of the Shropshire Canal was built along the western edge of the parish in 1788–9, the branch to Coalbrookdale leaving the canal where it emerged from Southall Bank tunnel in the south-west corner.[18] The tramway from Hollinswood to the Severn at Sutton wharf, built c. 1798 following disputes between the canal company and coal owners, crossed Stirchley, entering the parish at the north end and passing by the Mad brook valley to Holmer in the south-east corner. Opened in 1799, the tramway closed in 1815.[19] In 1860 the Coalport Branch Railway (later L.N.W.R.) was built on the line of the canal with a station where the Stirchley–Dawley road crossed the line.[20] The station was closed to passengers in 1952 and the line closed completely in 1964.[21] In 1854 the Madeley branch of the G.W.R. cut the south-east corner of the parish near Holmer.[22] The G.W.R. also laid the Old Park mineral line from Hollinswood to the Randlay valley in 1908 to serve the industries in Stirchley.[23]

Public services came to Stirchley comparatively early for such a small village. Mains electricity was provided c. 1933[24] and the village pump and private wells were replaced by a piped water supply c. 1947.[25]

The only building for social activities in the old village was the parish room, opened in 1922 and enlarged in 1928 perhaps to house the county library book centre which opened in Stirchley in 1928. The building was burnt down and replaced in 1935 by the brick church hall south of the rectory.[26] From 1970 social facilities were provided in the district and local centres of the Stirchley and Randlay housing estates. They included a youth club and sports complex at Stirchley centre and a community centre at Randlay housed in the former Mount Pleasant farm buildings.[27] There was a county branch library from 1975 in Stirchley Upper School.[28]

GROWTH OF SETTLEMENT. Stirchley remained a very small agricultural community until

[13] O.S. Map 6", Salop. XLIII. NE. (1903 edn.); V.C.H. Salop. ii. 227 n.; Kelly's Dir. Salop. (1941), 261. This art. was written 1979–80.   [14] V.C.H. Salop. ii. 236.

[15] Inst. Geol. Sciences Map 1/25,000, Telford (1978 edn.).

[16] R. Baugh, Map of Salop. (1808); O.S. Maps 1", sheet 61 NE. (1833 edn.); 6", Salop. XLIII. NE (1889 and later edns.); 1/50,000, sheet 127 (1977 edn.).

[17] U. Rayska, Development of Stirchley (T.D.C. 1980).

[18] V.C.H. Salop. i. 427.

[19] Trinder, Ind. Rev. Salop. 139–40; Baugh, Map of Salop.; Salopian and W. Midland Monthly Illustr. Jnl. Dec. 1877, 60 (copy in S.P.L.).

[20] Trinder, Ind. Rev. Salop. (1981), 153.

[21] C. R. Clinker, Clinker's Reg. of Closed Stations 1830–1977 (Bristol, 1978), 37.

[22] Trinder, Ind. Rev. Salop. 258.

[23] S.R.O. 1404/1; O.S. Map 6", Salop. XLIII. NE. (1889 and later edns.); R. Christiansen, W. Midlands (Regional Hist. of Rlys. of Gt. Brit. vii, 1973), 157; below, Wombridge, Communications.

[24] S.R.O. 1345/62.

[25] A. H. S. Waters, Rep. on Water Supplies (S.C.C. 1946), 90; S.R.O. 1034/6, pp. 144, 156, 160.

[26] S.R.O. 1345/34, 62; R. C. Elliott, 'Development of Public Libraries in Salop.' (Loughborough Univ. M.A. thesis, 1970), app. II (copy in Salop. Librs.).

[27] S.C.C. Mins. (Educ.) 1972–3, 347; T.D.C. Leisure & Recreation in the Wrekin (1978); Telford and Wrekin News, May 1979, 4.

[28] Inf. from Salop. Librs.

the 19th century. The parish contained 7 households in 1563[29] and only 3 farms and 5 cottages in 1612.[30] In 1672 hearth tax was paid by 11 inhabitants[31] and the parish was said to contain c. 10 houses a century later.[32] As industry spread into the parish in the early 19th century, population rose from 143 in 1801 to a peak of 333 in 1871. The largest decennial increase, almost 100, was in the 1820s when new collieries and ironworks were opened. In the late 19th and early 20th century, as the coal and iron industries failed, the population declined steadily, dropping to 166 in 1931, the last date for which census figures for the ancient parish are available.[33] Stirchley was included within the designated area of Dawley new town in 1963 and by 1979 the population housed in the area of the ancient parish had risen to c. 7,000.[34]

In the later 13th century the parish contained at least two settlements: Stirchley, presumably near the church, and 'Oulmeyre', probably near the later Holmer Farm.[35] Grange Farm, a third medieval settlement, originated as Buildwas abbey's grange and was probably established after the abbey acquired the manor in the mid 13th century.

The Brands (later Upper Brands) was built c. 1660[36] and from then until the 19th century the parish contained only four principal farmsteads (Stirchley Hall, near the church, and the outlying farmsteads of Grange farm, Holmer, and Brands) and a cluster of cottages and smallholdings around the church.

The increase in population in the early 19th century resulted in small but significant changes to the settlement pattern. Two houses in Stirchley, leased by the Botfields, the Dawley ironmasters, were converted into 15 cottages for industrial workers in 1803,[37] and at Mount Pleasant 5 houses, inhabited by labouring families in the mid 19th century, had been built before c. 1815.[38] Six houses were under construction in the parish in 1821.[39] As industrial activity continued during the mid 19th century more groups of houses were built for workers in the collieries and ironworks. Northwood Terrace, a row of 4 brick houses, was built in the 1840s to house the ironworks managers and was consequently known as Clerks Row,[40] and nearer the ironworks the Furnace Houses (later demolished) were built for foundry workers c. 1858.[41] The population increase at the time coincided with the first appearance of a licensed alehouse, the Rose and Crown, converted from an existing house in the 1840s.[42] There was shop in the village by 1841.[43]

The mid 19th century also saw the division of Brands farm into three smaller holdings, which resulted in the construction of Holmer House c. 1835[44] and Lower Brands in the 1860s.[45] Thereafter, apart from a group of council houses built near Grange Farm c. 1950,[46] there was little development until 1970.

After Dawley (later Telford) development corporation acquired almost all the parish, between 1964 and 1969,[47] the landscape changed dramatically. The farmsteads of Upper and Lower Brands, Holmer House, and Holmer were demolished as new housing estates were built over much of the south and east parts of the parish. In the Brookside estate, straddling the boundary between Stirchley and Madeley ancient parishes, 1,792 corporation houses were built between 1971 and 1975,[48] and 500 private houses were built from 1972 on parts of the former Stirchley Hall farm south and south-east of the old village.[49] In Stirchley residential district schemes comprising 948 corporation dwellings were completed between 1975 and 1977 on the former Lower Brands and Holmer House farms; the district was focused on a centre, east of Mad brook, containing health, sports, and social facilities, schools, and a new church. At Randlay, in the north-east, schemes comprising 507 corporation dwellings were completed between 1977 and 1978 and private houses were under construction in 1979. By then most of the surviving open land had been converted to ancillary 'urban' uses. The derelict industrial land in the north-west had been designated for recreational use as part of Telford's town park, while the western side of the Mad brook valley below Grange Farm was occupied by playing fields. Mad brook was dammed in the south-east corner of the parish in 1968–70 to create a balancing reservoir known as Holmer Lake.[50]

MANOR AND OTHER ESTATES. It is possible that 'Styrcleage', left by Wulfric Spot to Burton abbey in his will of c. 1003, is to be identified with Stirchley, particularly as Longford, with which Stirchley was connected in the 12th century, was also included in Wulfric's gift.[51] No later connexion with Burton has been found. *STIRCHLEY* is not mentioned by name in

[29] B.L. Harl. MS. 594, f. 161v.
[30] L.J.R.O., B/V/6, Stirchley, 1612.
[31] *Hearth Tax 1672* (Salop. Arch. Soc.), 87.
[32] L.J.R.O., B/V/5, visit. return of 1772.
[33] *V.C.H. Salop.* ii. 227, 231.
[34] Inf. from the archivist, T.D.C.
[35] Buildwas abbey's est. was described c. 1284 as 'the vills of Sturcheley and Culmeyre [*recte* Oulmeyre?]': S.P.L., Deeds 2651; cf. *Cartulary of Shrews. Abbey*, ed. U. Rees (1975), ii, p. 249. Rog. of Hulemor occ. 1271 (P.R.O., E 32/147), Ric. of Oulemor 1327 (*T.S.A.S.* 2nd ser. i. 187), both in Stirchley contexts.   [36] *S.P.R. Lich.* v (3), 4, 14.
[37] S.R.O. 513, box 17, deed of 1813 reciting lease of 1803; M.U.L., Botfield papers, cash acct. bk. 1795–1804.
[38] B.L. Maps, O.S.D. 208; P.R.O., HO 107/906; /1998.
[39] S.R.O. 1345/58.
[40] P.R.O., HO 107/906; /1998; RG 10/2752.
[41] P.R.O., RG 9/1856, using place and date of birth of

children as evid. for removal of fam. to Stirchley and, by implication, date of construction of hos.
[42] P.R.O., HO 107/906; /1998.
[43] P.R.O., HO 107/906.
[44] O.S. Map 1″, sheet 61 NE. (1833 edn.); S.R.O. 1268, tithe map.
[45] P.R.O., RG 9/1856; RG 10/2752.
[46] *Reg. of Electors, Wrekin Co. Const.* 1949–51.
[47] T.D.C., Stirchley deeds (various properties).
[48] Rayska, *Dev. of Stirchley.*
[49] *Telford and Wrekin News*, May 1979, p. 4; T.D.C., Stirchley Hall deeds.
[50] *Telford and Wrekin News*, May 1979, p. 4; Rayska, op. cit.; D. G. Fenter, 'Bldg. Development carried out in Telford by the Development Corp.' (TS. in S.R.O. 3763).
[51] H. P. R. Finberg, *Early Charters of W. Midlands* (1961), p. 149; *Charters of Burton Abbey*, ed. P. H. Sawyer (1979), p. xxix.

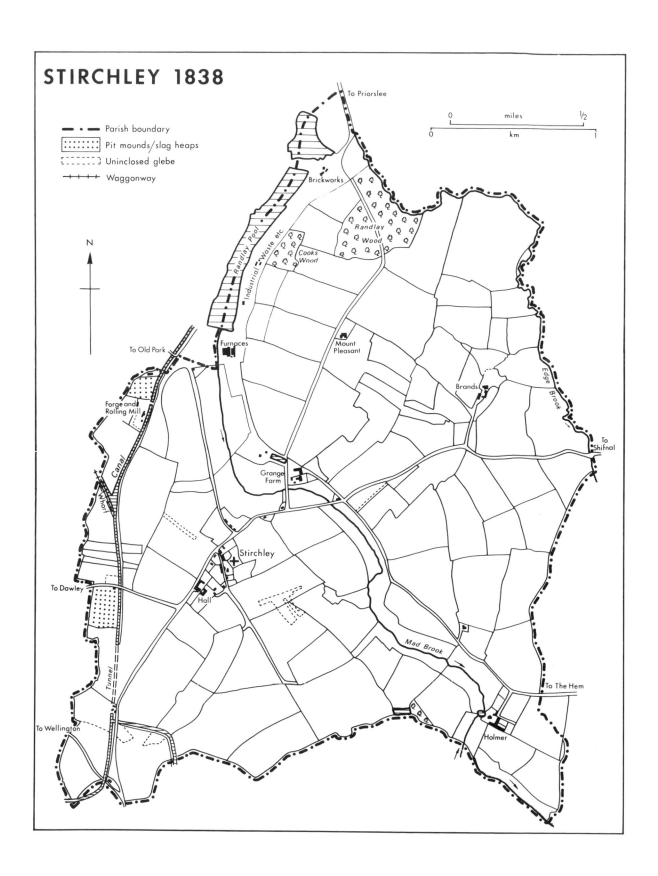

STIRCHLEY 1838

— · — Parish boundary
Pit mounds/slag heaps
Uninclosed glebe
Waggonway

N

To Priorslee

Brickworks

Randlay Wood

Cooks Wood

Randlay Pool

Industrial Waste etc.

To Old Park

Furnaces

Mount Pleasant

Brands

Edge Brook

To Shifnal

Forge and Rolling Mill

Canal

Wharf

Grange Farm

Stirchley

To Dawley

Hall

Mad Brook

To The Hem

Tunnel

To Wellington

Holmer

Domesday Book but the later descent of the overlordship of the manor suggests that it was one of the four unnamed berewicks of Longford recorded in 1086.[52] The Brimpton family, lords of Longford, were recorded as overlords of Stirchley from 1185 to c. 1285[53] but no later evidence of the connexion with Longford has been found. By 1375 the overlordship of Stirchley had passed to Richard, earl of Arundel and Surrey, with whose son, Earl Richard (d. 1397), it remained in 1382.[54]

In the late 12th century Stirchley was held of Robert of Brimpton's widow Eve by Bartholomew son of Peter FitzToret.[55] The mesne lordship passed, presumably by Bartholomew's daughter Joan, wife of Richard Corbet (II) (fl. 1195–1217),[56] successively to the Corbet and Burgh families of Wattlesborough. It descended with Wattlesborough[57] until the partition of Sir John Burgh's estates in 1501, when Stirchley was assigned to his daughter Isabel, wife of Sir John Lingen. A few days later, however, their son John and his cousins John Newport and Thomas Mytton conveyed (inter alia) interest in the wood of Stirchley to their cousin Sir Thomas Leighton of Wattlesborough.[58]

The undertenant of Stirchley between 1167 and 1180 was Osbert of Stirchley.[59] He was probably succeeded by Richard of Stirchley, who was recorded from 1203 to 1207[60] but was presumably dead by 1208 when the manor was disputed between Osbert, son of William, and Walter of Stirchley. In settlement Stirchley was assigned to Walter for his life with reversion to Osbert and his heirs. It was agreed in 1227 that ½ virgate of land, an assart, and a croft were to pass to Walter's heirs, who would pay a token rent to Osbert in lieu of all services.[61] Walter died in 1232 and the manor reverted to Osbert (sometimes styled Osbert of Stirchley or parson of Diddlebury).[62] Osbert granted a plot of land in Stirchley to Wombridge priory,[63] ½d. rent in the vill to Lilleshall abbey,[64] and by two separate grants of c. 1243 and 1247 he released the whole manor to Buildwas abbey,[65] which may have had land at Holmer since the 1220s.[66] Buildwas continued to hold the manor until its dissolution in 1536.[67]

By the end of the 15th century most land in Stirchley was in three large holdings, which descended as separate freehold estates after the Dissolution, Grange farm and Holmer farm being the abbey's granges and Stirchley Hall farm being held freely of the abbey. In the 16th and early 17th centuries both the Grange[68] and the Stirchley Hall estate[69] were described as manors; the descent of each is treated separately below. Between 1747 and the 1890s the properties were united in the same hands and their owners were styled lords of the manor of Stirchley.[70] In 1964–5 all three ancient estates were purchased by Dawley development corporation, which thus became owner of almost the entire ancient parish.

STIRCHLEY GRANGE contained 285 a. in the 18th century[71] but was more extensive before the separation of Brands farm in the mid 17th century.[72] In 1537 the freehold of the estate was bought, with most of Buildwas abbey's other property, by Edward, Lord Grey of Powis.[73] Grey settled parts of his estate, including Stirchley Grange, on his illegitimate son Edward Grey of Buildwas, who conveyed them c. 1576 to Sir John Throckmorton, on whose death in 1580 they passed to his son Francis, the Catholic conspirator.[74] Francis's estates reverted to the Crown on his execution in 1584 and Stirchley Grange was acquired from the Crown c. 1587 by Daniel Rogers, the diplomatist,[75] on whose death in 1591 they passed to his widow Susan.[76] Their son, Francis, who held the estate by 1610,[77] sold it in 1620 to John Careswell of Shifnal.[78]

The estate had been let on long lease by Buildwas abbey before 1500; in 1534 it was leased in reversion to Richard Cleobury for 95 years.[79] Cleobury's lease passed to his daughter Margaret, wife of Richard Spenser, and was bought in 1556 by John Forster of Sutton Maddock. The Grange remained in the hands of the Forsters until 1611 or later, despite protracted lawsuits by which the freeholders attempted to gain possession.[80]

In 1621 John Careswell sold the estate to William Cookes of Snitterfield (Warws.),[81] with whose descendants it remained until Richard Cookes gave it by his will dated 1725 to his godson the Revd. Richard Phillips.[82] Phillips sold Grange farm in 1747 to Thomas Clowes, owner of Stirchley Hall, on whose death next year the combined estate passed to his sister Elizabeth, wife of Thomas Hodgetts of Ashwood Lodge (Staffs.). In 1763 Hodgetts devised the estates that his wife had owned to his nephew, the Revd. Samuel

[52] Eyton, viii. 114.

[53] Ibid. 115, 120; Collect. Topog. et Geneal. i. 118; Feud. Aids, iv. 222.

[54] Cal. Inq. p.m. xiv, p. 110; xv, p. 296.

[55] Eyton, viii. 114–15.

[56] Ibid. x. 186–7.

[57] Cal. Inq. p.m. xiv, p. 110; xv, p. 296; Cal. Close, 1381–5, 171; P.R.O., C 139/49, no. 32; /50, no. 47; S.P.L., Deeds 6173. Cf. V.C.H. Salop. viii. 196–7.

[58] T.S.A.S. 4th ser. v. 215–16, 219.

[59] Pipe R. 1167 (P.R.S. xi), 60; Eyton, viii. 115.

[60] Eyton, viii. 115–16.

[61] T.S.A.S. 2nd ser. x. 326; 3rd ser. vii. 388.

[62] Eyton, viii. 117.

[63] T.S.A.S. xi. 334–5.

[64] Staffs. R.O., D. 593/A/1/19/13.

[65] Dugdale, Mon. v. 357 (date suggested by Eyton, viii. 117); T.S.A.S. 4th ser. vi. 189–90; cf. Rot. Hund. (Rec. Com.), ii. 57.

[66] Eyton, ix. 182. Cf. ibid. ii. 134; viii. 117.

[67] P.R.O., SC 6/Hen. VIII/3006, mm. 8, 14. In 1423 the man. was said to be a member of Dawley: P.R.O., C 139/5,

no. 35.

[68] P.R.O., E 134/34 Eliz. I East./14; E 178/1888, mm. 2–4; SC 6/Hen. VIII/3006, m. 8; S.R.O. 513, box 17, deed of 1621.

[69] L. & P. Hen. VIII, xx (2), p. 414; S.R.O. 513, box 13, deeds of 1560, 1611; P.R.O., C 142/241, no. 125; E 134/7 Jas. I Hil./19.

[70] S.R.O. 513, box 15, deed of 1760; box 16, deed of 1777; S.R.O. 1265/289; P.O. Dir. Salop. (1856), 127; (1870), 147; Kelly's Dir. Salop. (1885), 963; (1891), 446.

[71] S.R.O. 513, box 16, deed of 1777.

[72] S.P.R. Lich. v (3), 4; N.L.W., Ottley papers 1308.

[73] L. & P. Hen. VIII, xii (2), p. 166.

[74] P.R.O., E. 178/1888; D.N.B.

[75] Acts of P.C. 1587–8, 423; D.N.B..

[76] P.R.O., E 134/34 Eliz. I East./14.

[77] Ibid. /7 Jas. I Hil./19.

[78] P.R.O., CP 43/152, rot. 45.

[79] S.R.O. 513, box 13, deed.

[80] Ibid. deed of 1611; P.R.O., E 134/34 Eliz. I East./14.

[81] S.R.O. 513, box 17, deed.

[82] Ibid. will (copy).

Nott, who sold the Stirchley properties to Isaac Hawkins Browne of Foston (Derb.) in 1777.[83] Browne, M.P. and essayist, died in 1818[84] having left the estate to his wife Elizabeth (d. 1839) for her life with reversion to his kinsman Robert Cheney (d. 1820).[85] By Cheney's will the manor was divided between his children but all shares descended, after the death of his son Edward in 1884, to his grandson Alfred Capel Cure of Badger Hall.[86] Cure sold the Stirchley estate in 1886 to the Haybridge Iron Co., which later sold Grange farm and Stirchley Hall separately. Grange farm was bought by William Wall in 1896 and changed hands three times between then and its purchase by Dawley development corporation in 1965.[87]

No remains of the medieval grange buildings survive. Grange farmhouse contains a 17th-century brick wing with vestiges of stone mullioned windows, to which a cross wing of brick with sandstone quoins was added in the 18th century.

STIRCHLEY HALL farm, a holding of 208 a. in the 18th century,[88] can be identified with the estate held of Buildwas abbey in the early 15th century by the earl of Arundel and considered in the late 15th and the 16th century to be a member of the Arundels' manor of Dawley. It is not clear how the family came to hold the estate, but it appears to have been acquired by Earl Richard (1330–76), who was overlord of the chief manor.[89] It is conceivable that the estate represented the holding of 3 messuages and $1\frac{1}{2}$ carucate of land that Walter, son and heir of Walter of Stirchley (life tenant of the manor in the early 13th century), recovered in 1288.[90] Stirchley Hall descended with the earldom of Arundel until 1560 when it was purchased by Rowland Hayward (kt. 1570).[91] After his death in 1593 it passed successively to his sons George (kt. 1604, d. 1615) and John (kt. 1619).[92] Sir John sold the property in 1621 to John Forster of Sutton Maddock, former lessee of Stirchley Grange, and his son Francis. Francis Forster was succeeded by his nephew Francis Forster, who sold Stirchley Hall to Robert Clowes in 1683.[93] By his will dated 1704 Clowes left the estate to his cousin Thomas Clowes, on whose death in 1740 it descended to his son Thomas,[94] who purchased Grange farm in 1747 and died without issue in 1748.[95] Thereafter the estate descended with Grange farm until both properties

were bought by the Haybridge Iron Co. in 1886. By 1894 Stirchley Hall had been sold to I. J. Fletcher. He sold it in 1909, and in 1920 it was purchased by J. J. Ward, who sold it to Dawley development corporation in 1964.[96]

A 'hall of Stirchley' may have existed in the mid 14th century.[97] The centre of Stirchley Hall's south front represents the 17th-century stone house, which was built or remodelled for M. Forster in 1653[98] and then had a three-roomed plan with two storeys, attics, and cellars. It incorporates part of an earlier house, from which the hall ceiling and chimney stack survive. The initials R P on the central boss of the ceiling have been attributed to Roger Poyner, tenant of the house in 1567.[99] The stack was repaired in 1721[1] and the brick western cross wing may have been added about then. Later in the 18th century and early in the 19th century additions were made to the north and at the east end.

HOLMER farm, which included 90 a. in Stirchley parish in the early 19th century,[2] had been let on long lease by the end of the 15th century[3] and was bought with Buildwas abbey's other possessions by Edward, Lord Grey of Powis, in 1537. Grey's natural son, Edward Grey, sold it to Francis Newport of High Ercall between 1577 and 1590[4] and the property descended with the Newport estates in Shropshire during the 17th and 18th centuries, passing to the earl of Darlington (cr. duke of Cleveland 1833) on the division of the estates in 1808.[5] It descended to the duke's heirs and was sold by Lord Barnard in 1920. In 1964 the estate was purchased by Dawley development corporation,[6] and the farmstead was demolished to make way for housing development in the 1970s.

Only two of the late 13th-century undertenancies[7] in Stirchley manor seem to have been sizeable estates. That of Walter of Stirchley's son and heir Walter, possibly representing the later Stirchley Hall, has already been referred to. The estate of the Perton family, of Perton (Staffs.),[8] was recorded from c. 1240.[9] On William of Perton's death c. 1280 it was variously estimated as 59 a. or 1 carucate.[10] The Pertons were connected with Stirchley as late as 1393[11] but definite evidence of their undertenancy there has not been found after the 13th century. Fields named Perton Wood were part of Grange farm in the 18th century,[12] which perhaps implies that the

[83] S.R.O. 513, box 15, wills of 1748, 1763; box 16, deed of 1777.   [84] D.N.B.
[85] S.R.O. 1265/218. For pedigree of Browne and Cheney see S.P.L., MS. 4645, p. 264.
[86] S.R.O. 1265/219, 289.
[87] T.D.C., Grange farm deeds.
[88] S.R.O. 513, box 16, deed of 1777.
[89] Ibid. box 13, inq. p.m. of 1423; Cal. Fine R. 1422–30, 210; L. & P. Hen. VIII, xx (2), p. 414.
[90] Eyton, viii. 116, 122.
[91] S.R.O. 513, box 13, deed; W. A. Shaw, Kts. of Eng. (1906), ii. 75.
[92] T.S.A.S. li. 128, 130; P.R.O., E 134/7 Jas. I Hil./19. For pedigree of Hayward see S.P.L., MS. 4645, p. 375.
[93] S.R.O. 513, box 13, deeds.
[94] Ibid. box 15, will (adm. granted 1740); S.P.R. Lich. xviii (1), 103.
[95] S.R.O. 513, box 15, deed of 1747; S.P.R. Lich. v (3), 18.
[96] T.D.C., Stirchley Hall deeds.
[97] Adam 'de aula de Stircheleye' occ. 1337, 1341: S.R.O.

513, box 1, Malinslee ct. r.
[98] Date stone.
[99] S.P.L., Deeds 8384. His widow was tenant in 1572: ibid. 8403.
[1] Date stone.
[2] S.R.O. 248/10.
[3] P.R.O., SC 6/Hen. VIII/3006, m. 14.
[4] Barnard MSS., Raby Castle, box 2, bdle. 7, deed of 1590; box 12, bdle. 25, deed of 1577.
[5] Ibid. box 12, bdle. 21, deed of 1696; bdle. 25, deed of 1695; cf. V.C.H. Salop. iii. 254–5.
[6] T.D.C., Holmer farm, Grange farm deeds.
[7] Eyton, viii. 121–3; Dugdale, Mon. v. 357.
[8] S.H.C. 1913, 28, 326; E. A. Hardwicke, Connected Annals of the family of Perton of Perton, Co. Stafford (Calcutta, 1897).
[9] P.R.O., E 210/6683.
[10] Cal. Inq. p.m. ii, pp. 200, 299.
[11] S.H.C. xv. 59.
[12] S.R.O. 513, box 16, deed of 1777.

estate later reverted to Buildwas abbey and was absorbed into its grange.

ECONOMIC HISTORY. AGRICULTURE.

Stirchley was within the royal forest of Mount Gilbert until 1301[13] and probably contained uncleared woodland well into the medieval period. The wood of Stirchley, which survived in the early and mid 13th century, lay in the north-east along the boundary with Shifnal.[14] In the late 12th and mid 13th century the inhabitants cleared woodland to bring new land into cultivation,[15] and the names Brands ('land cleared by burning') and, near Holmer, Stockings ('a clearing with stumps') probably record this process.[16] A major reduction of the wooded area occurred after 1277 when the monks of Buildwas were licensed to assart 60 a. in Stirchley, probably when establishing their granges.[17] Timber and coaling wood were supplied from the parish for the Old Park ironworks (in Dawley) in 1789–90[18] but by the 19th century little woodland remained: in 1811 there were 42 a. of coppice in the parish[19] and by 1838 only 23 a. of wood survived, mostly in Randlay wood in the north.[20]

Stirchley's open fields do not seem to have been extensive in the 16th and 17th centuries. Most open arable land lay in the west, between Mad brook and the road to Dawley, in a field known in the 17th century as the common field towards Dawley, but there were other small areas of open cultivation in Cross furlong, immediately south of the village, and in the Lower field, east of Mad brook beside the road to Shifnal. Inclosure occurred by exchanges of strips between the owners of Stirchley Hall and Grange farm in 1611, 1695, and 1716,[21] but unfenced strips of glebe survived into the 19th century.[22]

Most land in the parish was held as inclosed permanent grassland from the 16th century, or earlier, until the 19th century. The pastures in the south belonging to Stirchley Hall had been inclosed by c. 1540,[23] and most of the glebe consisted of similar 'several' leasows in the 17th century.[24] Most of the field pattern that survived into the 20th century had probably been established by the end of the Middle Ages.

The name Stirchley ('pasture for young bullocks'),[25] the numerous 'leasow' field names,[26] and the lack of evidence for extensive open fields all suggest that livestock farming played an important part in the parish economy. In the later 16th century the value of Grange farm was given by stating that it supported a herd of 80 cows, an expression suggesting that it was a dairy farm.[27] In

the early 19th century the acreage under crops increased from only 221 a. (26 per cent of the parish) in 1801[28] to 542 a. (65 per cent) by 1839.[29]

Between 1867 and 1938 the percentage of agricultural land in Stirchley under grass rose from under half to 90 per cent. By 1965 it had declined back to its 1867 level. Between 1867 and 1965 the number of cattle kept rose markedly; sheep declined proportionately. Pigs retained their popularity. Wheat usually accounted for two thirds of the cereal acreage, barley and oats being the other cereals usually grown. Between 1867 and 1965 the amount of vegetables and roots grown commercially declined to an insignificant level.[30]

TABLE VIII

STIRCHLEY: LAND USE, LIVESTOCK, AND CROPS

	1867	1891	1938	1965
Percentage of grassland	44	58	90	45
arable	56	42	10	55
Percentage of cattle	8	27	45	60
sheep	64	47	42	6
pigs	28	26	13	34
Percentage of wheat	61	49	70	63
barley	21	25	0	34
oats	18	26	30	2
mixed corn & rye	0	0	0	1
Percentage of agricultural land growing roots & vegetables	12	13	2	3

Sources: P.R.O., MAF 68/143, no. 14; /1340, no. 6; /3880, Salop. no. 236; /4945, no. 236.

From the 15th century or earlier until the 19th century most land in the parish was in a few large holdings. In 1341 Buildwas abbey kept a third of the parish in hand,[31] presumably as its two granges, both of which, with the cottages in the village that belonged to them, had been let on long leases by 1500.[32] In the 17th and 18th centuries there were four large farms in the parish: Stirchley Hall (208 a. in 1777),[33] to which most of the glebe was also let in the late 18th century,[34] Grange farm (285 a. in 1777),[35] Holmer (c. 97 a. in 1826),[36] and Brands (c. 123 a. in 1832),[37] which was separated from the Grange

[13] *Cart. Shrews.* ii, p. 249.
[14] *T.S.A.S.* xi. 335, 337; Eyton, ix. 145; P.R.O., E 32/147, m. 6.
[15] P.R.O., E 32/143; /145, m. 6d.; /147, m. 6.
[16] S.R.O. 1268/6; *Eng. P.N. Elements* (E.P.N.S.), i. 47; ii. 156–7.
[17] *Cal. Pat.* 1272–81, 227, 242.
[18] M. U. L., Botfield papers, Old Pk. memo. bk. 1788–91.
[19] S.R.O. 513, box 4, deed of 1811.
[20] S.R.O. 1268/6.
[21] L.J.R.O., B/V/6, Stirchley, 1612; S.R.O. 513, box 13, deeds of 1611, 1668, 1687, 1695; box 17, deed of 1716.
[22] S.R.O. 1268/6.
[23] P.R.O., E 134/7 Jas. I Hil./19, m. 5.
[24] L.J.R.O., B/V/6, Stirchley, 1612.

[25] E. Ekwall, *Concise Oxf. Dict. Eng. P.N.* (4th edn.), 443.
[26] S.R.O. 1268/6.
[27] P.R.O., E 134/34 Eliz. I East./14, m. 6.
[28] P.R.O., HO 67/14/246.
[29] S.R.O. 1268/6.
[30] See Table VIII.
[31] *Inq. Non.* (Rec. Com.), 193.
[32] P.R.O., SC 6/Hen.VIII/3006, mm. 8, 14.
[33] S.R.O. 513, box 16, deed.
[34] S.R.O. 1345/48.
[35] S.R.O. 513, box 16, deed.
[36] i.e. Holmer farm in 1828 and 8 a. sold in 1826: S.R.O. 248/10; 1150/889a.
[37] i.e. Brands farm in 1838 and 15 a. sold in 1832: S.R.O. 1268/6; T.D.C., Holmer House deeds.

estate *c.* 1660.[38] Another smaller farm was amalgamated with Stirchley Hall in 1801.[39]

During the 19th century the Brands estate was fragmented into three holdings: Holmer House farm, a smallholding of 17 a. established in the 1830s;[40] Lower Brands farm (54 a.), which was separated in the 1860s;[41] and the remaining 53 a. farmed from the original farmstead, subsequently known as Upper Brands farm.[42] By 1907 83 a. of the Grange estate was farmed as a separate holding, from the farmstead at Mount Pleasant.[43]

After the purchase of almost all the parish by the new town development corporation during the 1960s little land remained in agricultural use. By 1979 no farms survived in the area of the ancient parish, almost the only productive land being Telford development corporation's central nursery at Grange Farm, where from 1971 an 8-a. site produced plants for landscaping purposes.[44]

MILLS. There was a mill 'below the garden' in Stirchley *c.* 1240[45] and two mills were mentioned when the vill was granted to Buildwas abbey in 1247.[46] One mill was recorded on the abbey's property in Stirchley in 1291.[47] One of the mills probably stood immediately south of Mount Pleasant, where a field named Mill hill or Windmill field was recorded in post-medieval sources.[48] Remains of pools and floodgates that survived at Holmer in the 19th century suggest that there may have been a mill on Mad brook at that point.[49]

INDUSTRIES. Stirchley remained an agricultural community until the beginning of the 19th century when coal and ironstone mining, iron founding, and brick making were started in the northwest quarter of the parish within reach of the Shropshire Canal. Industry came to Stirchley as a result of a partnership between I. H. Browne, owner of most of the parish, and the Botfield family, the Dawley ironmasters who had established collieries and ironworks on Browne's Old Park estate in Dawley in the late 18th century. William Botfield had rented 20 a. on the western edge of Stirchley by 1800,[50] and he and his brothers Thomas and Beriah took leases of cottages in the parish for their workmen from 1803.[51]

In 1811 they took a lease of 487 a. of the combined Stirchley Hall and Grange estate from Browne,[52] thus gaining access to the minerals under most of the north and west half of the parish. Between then and *c.* 1840 they established collieries, ironworks, and a brickworks on their Stirchley royalties. Beriah Botfield, who succeeded his father Beriah and uncles, did not renew the lease in 1856 and the land, mineral rights, and plant were leased to the Old Park Iron Co.,[53] which continued the industrial operations in Stirchley until it was wound up in 1871.[54] By 1900 mining and ironworking had ceased. A chemical works, occupying one of the former ironworks, flourished until 1932 and brick making and the crushing of furnace slag for road metal continued until the 1960s. The following account treats each industry separately.

The top of the productive Middle Coal Measures lay *c.* 143 metres below ground level in Stirchley.[55] The earliest mining recorded in the parish was the sinking of a shaft by William Botfield early in 1811 in the west,[56] probably at the location known as Stirchley New Work *c.* 1815 and Stirchley pits in 1840.[57] By 1815 the damaged land around the colliery and coke hearths extended to 4 a.[58] The Botfields consolidated the area under which they could mine by taking a lease of mineral rights under 17 a. of glebe in 1814[59] and buying some scattered fields from Lord Darlington in 1826.[60] By 1822 four pits appear to have been in production,[61] and by 1840[62] there were five collieries in the parish: Randlay pits, sunk in 1820;[63] Cuxey's Wood pits, sunk 1834–5;[64] Forge pits, sunk 1825–6;[65] Grange colliery, probably opened by 1833;[66] and the original shaft at Stirchley pits. The extent of seams that could be worked was restricted by the Limestone fault, east of which the coal lay deeper: in 1843 an attempt to mine coal near Mount Pleasant was abandoned on encountering the fault.[67] After the Old Park Iron Co. was wound up in 1871 the mines were leased to the Wellington Iron & Coal Co. Ltd. in 1874[68] but by 1879 had reverted to the landowners, the Cheney family.[69] By 1881 all the pits except Grange colliery had been closed.[70] Despite the lease of mineral rights to Alfred Seymour Jones of

[38] *S.P.R. Lich.* v (3), 4, 14.
[39] S.R.O. 513, box 14, deed; cf. S.R.O. 1345/48.
[40] T.D.C., Holmer House deeds; S.R.O. 1268/6; cf. P.R.O., HO 107/1998.
[41] T.D.C., Lower Brands deeds; S.R.O. 1150/842.
[42] S.R.O. 1150/858; P.R.O., RG 10/2752.
[43] T.D.C., Mount Pleasant deeds.
[44] Inf. from the archivist, T.D.C.
[45] P.R.O., E 210/6683.
[46] *T.S.A.S.* 4th ser. vi. 190.
[47] *Tax. Eccl.* (Rec. Com.), 260.
[48] S.R.O. 513, box 13, deed of 1687; box 17, deed of 1716; S.R.O. 1268/6.
[49] *Salopian and W. Midland Monthly Illustr. Jnl.* Dec. 1877, 60.
[50] M.U.L., Botfield papers, cash acct. bk. 1795–1804; cf. S.R.O. 513, box 4, deed of 1811.
[51] S.R.O. 513, box 17, deed of 1813 reciting lease of 1803.
[52] Ibid. box 4, deed.
[53] S.R.O. 14/3/8.
[54] S.R.O. 1265/280.
[55] Inf. from Dr. I. J. Brown; cf. Inst. Geol. Sciences Map 1/25,000, *Telford* (1978 edn.).

[56] M.U.L., Botfield papers, cash acct. bk. 1810–15; cf. S.R.O. 513, box 4, deed of 1811, locating pit in Far Randle Pool, a field at O.S. Nat. Grid SJ 694 065: S.R.O. 1268/6.
[57] B.L. Maps, O.S.D. 208; S.R.O. 1816/26.
[58] M.U.L., Botfield papers, cash acct. bk. 1810–15.
[59] S.R.O. 1265/216.   [60] S.R.O. 1150/889.
[61] The Botfields' mines were assessed for the par. rate at £134 6s. 8d., at £33 6s. 8d. for each pit: S.R.O. 1345/60.
[62] S.R.O. 1816/26.
[63] At O.S. Nat. Grid SJ 705 081: inf. from Dr. Brown.
[64] At SJ 701 077: W. Howard Williams, 'Dawley New Town Hist. Survey: Industries' (TS. 1964), addns. and corr. (1965), p. 6 (copy in S.P.L., accession 5202).
[65] At SJ 696 071: S.R.O. 1011, box 425, R. Garbitt to E. Bloxam, 20 Dec. 1861.
[66] At SJ 701 071: O.S. Map 1″, sheet 61 NE. (1833 edn.).
[67] Inst. Geol. Sciences Map 1/25,000, *Telford* (1978 edn.); M. W. T. Scott, 'On the "Symon Fault" in the Coalbrookdale Coalfield', *Quart. Jnl. Geol. Soc. London*, xvii. 458.
[68] S.R.O. 1265/285.
[69] *P.O. Dir. Salop.* (1879), 417; *Kelly's Dir. Salop.* (1885), 963.
[70] O.S. Map 6″, Salop. XLIII. NE. (1889 edn.).

Wrexham in 1893, Grange colliery was closed in 1894.[71]

Coal and ironstone were not afterwards mined from shafts in the parish but the deep seams under Lower Brands and Holmer House farms south-east of the Limestone fault were mined from Kemberton colliery in the early 20th century.[72]

Ironworking was started in the parish c. 1826 by the Botfield brothers. Blast furnaces were built at the south end of Randlay reservoir (or Randay pool)[73] and a forge and rolling mill were opened probably c. 1828, west of the Shropshire Canal on land purchased from Lord Darlington in 1826.[74] The blast furnaces were leased with the mining royalties to the Old Park Iron Co. after Botfield's lease expired in 1856.[75] After the company was wound up in 1871 the furnaces were leased in 1874 to the Wellington Iron & Coal Co., which failed in 1877.[76] The furnaces passed back to the owner of the site, Edward Cheney, who kept them in blast for a few years, but they were shut down by 1885.[77] The forge and rolling mills, which were Botfield's freehold property, were sold by Beriah Botfield's trustees in 1873 to the Haybridge Iron Co.,[78] which rebuilt the works in 1876 and established a nail factory on the site in 1874 or 1875.[79] The nail factory was sold to John Maddock in 1876;[80] he moved his operations to Oakengates two years later[81] but nails continued to be made at Stirchley for a few years under different proprietors.[82] The factory had closed by 1885[83] but the adjacent forge and rolling mills continued to be operated by the Haybridge Co., the rolling mill closing finally c. 1900.[84]

The use of the drift burden of boulder clay and the marls of the Upper Coal Measures for brick and tile making coincided with the exploitation of other mineral resources by the Botfields. The brothers were manufacturing bricks in Stirchley in 1808–9,[85] possibly in a field south of Stirchley village, later called Brick Kiln leasow, where disused clay pits were still visible in 1980 and where there appear to have been buildings c. 1815.[86] There was a second Brick Kiln leasow north of Upper Brands.[87] Randlay brickworks in

the north, which continued to manufacture bricks until 1964 or later, had been established by the Botfields by 1838.[88] In 1893 the Haybridge Iron Co. leased the works to George Wilkinson, who formed, with Adam Boulton, the Randlay Brick & Tile Co. (from 1939 A. Boulton & Co.). The partners bought the works and c. 40 a. of surrounding land in 1898.[89] Clay was obtained on site from an extensive pit, which was enlarged after the purchase of more land in 1905 and used until 1969.[90] In 1964 the brickworks employed 91[91] and the three kilns produced c. 300,000 bricks a week.[92]

The site of the former furnaces was leased in 1886 to Thomas Groom, the Wellington timber merchant, who transferred his Wrekin Chemical Works to Stirchley on obtaining the lease. The chemical works extracted wood naphtha and tar from timber supplied by the Grooms' yard at Wellington and converted the residue into charcoal. Acetate of lime and sulphur were also manufactured.[93] Groom's successor, George Wilkinson, bought the site in 1904[94] and the works closed in 1932.[95]

The extensive slag mounds that surrounded the former furnaces were exploited as a source of aggregate for road building and concrete manufacture from the 1890s. The mounds south-west of the Wrekin Chemical Works were leased in 1893, and purchased in 1907, by H. C. Johnson, a Wrexham quarry owner, who had built a slag crusher on the site by 1901.[96] The industry expanded during the 1920s when most of the slag mounds in the parish were acquired by Tarslag (1923) Ltd. and the Bilston Slag Co. (1924) Ltd.[97] By 1925 there were four slag-crushing plants in the parish,[98] the largest being Tarslag's works, employing up to c. 130 men, which both crushed the slag and coated it with tar and bitumen. Tarmac Ltd., which succeeded the Bilston company, also manufactured 'Vinculum' concrete walling blocks at Stirchley from c. 1925 to c. 1935, and Tarslag operated a short-lived concrete plant there as well. Impurities and the variable quality of the slag led to the closure of the works.[99] By the Second World War most of the slag mounds had

[71] S.R.O. 1265/269; 1345/62.
[72] S.R.O. 1681, box 90, corresp. of 1909–15; box 184, deed of 1916.
[73] At O.S. Nat. Grid SJ 700 074: Trinder, *Ind. Rev. Salop.* 241; O.S. Map 1″, sheet 61 NE. (1833 edn.). Called 'Old Park Iron Works' on O.S. Map 6″, Salop. XLIII. NE. (1889 edn.).
[74] At SJ 696 072: S.R.O. 1265/261; O.S. Map 1″, sheet 61 NE. (1833 edn.); S.R.O. 1011, box 425, W. Botfield to E. Browne, 14 Aug. 1827. Chain making at Old Park (above, Dawley, Econ. Hist.) is wrongly located in *V.C.H. Salop.* i. 479 at Stirchley furnaces.
[75] S.R.O. 14/3/8; 1265/279.   [76] S.R.O. 1265/285, 287.
[77] *P.O. Dir. Salop.* (1879), 417; cf. *Kelly's Dir. Salop.* (1885), 963.
[78] S.R.O. 1265/261.
[79] Ibid. /263; *Salopian and W. Midland Monthly Illustr. Jnl.* Apr. 1875; Nov. 1876 (copies in S.P.L.).
[80] S.R.O. 1265/264.
[81] S.R.O. 1404/1.
[82] *P.O. Dir. Salop.* (1879), 417.
[83] S.R.O. 1345/62.
[84] S.R.O. 1404/1; Williams, 'Dawley Hist. Survey: Inds.' addns. and corr. (1965), p. 5.
[85] M.U.L., Botfield papers, cash acct. bk. 1804–10.
[86] At O.S. Nat. Grid SJ 702 063: S.R.O. 1268, tithe appt. and map; B.L. Maps, O.S.D. 208.
[87] S.R.O. 1268/6.
[88] At O.S. Nat. Grid SJ 703 080: ibid. /6a; Williams, 'Dawley Hist. Survey: Inds.' p. 10.
[89] T.D.C., Randlay brickworks deeds.
[90] Ibid.; O.S. Map 6″, Salop. XLIII. NE. (1889, 1903, and 1929 edns.); inf. from Dr. Brown.
[91] J. H. D. Madin & Partners, *Dawley New Town Rep. No. 2: Interim Proposals* (Sept. 1964), map 14 and cap. 6, sect. 1, app.
[92] *Dawley Observer*, 4 Feb. 1966.
[93] S.R.O. 1404/1; *V.C.H. Salop.* i. 479 n.
[94] Williams, 'Dawley Hist. Survey: Inds.' addns. and corr. (1965), p. 4; cf. S.R.O. 1268/3, sale partic. of 1904.
[95] Williams, 'Dawley Hist. Survey: Inds.' p. 39.
[96] S.R.O. 1268/3, sale partic. of 1904; O.S. Map 6″, Salop. XLIII. NE. (1903 edn.); T.D.C., Stirchley deeds (Tarmac property).
[97] T.D.C., Stirchley deeds (Tarmac property); J. B. F. Earle, *A Century of Road Materials* (1971), 19.
[98] O.S. Map 6″, Salop. XLIII. NE. (1929 edn.).
[99] Inf. from Mr. S. J. Insull, Dudley.

been exhausted and Tarslag's crushing and coating plant closed in 1941. Tarmac continued to remove slag from Stirchley for processing elsewhere until c. 1964.[1]

The new town development corporation bought the derelict industrial land on the west side of the parish in 1967 and 1969.[2] Ten years later few buildings remained there except the chimney at the site of Stirchley furnaces, built in 1873[3] and preserved as an industrial monument in part of Telford's town park.

LOCAL GOVERNMENT. In 1284 or 1285 the abbot of Buildwas claimed the right to hold courts at Stirchley.[4] The pleas and perquisites of the abbot's court there were valued at 6s. 8d. in 1291[5] but no court records survive. No courts were held at the time of the Dissolution.[6] Buildwas abbey withdrew Stirchley's suit from Bradford hundred court on acquiring the manor c. 1243[7] but by 1590 Stirchley was again making suit to the hundred court. In that year it was presented for not using the pillory and for having no lock on the pound or stocks.[8] In 1612 the tenant of Stirchley Hall, considered in the 15th and 16th centuries to be a member of Dawley manor, owed suit to the manor court of Great Dawley when he was summoned.[9]

The parish had two churchwardens in 1612 but only one in the later 18th century.[10] The appointment of an overseer was recorded from 1766. In the 19th century the number of unpaid parish officials increased, two overseers being appointed annually from 1837 and a road surveyor from 1839. The offices were filled largely by the small group of tenant farmers on whom the bulk of the rates were levied. For most of the 19th century the day-to-day administration of parish affairs fell to a salaried official. From 1814 to 1823 Edward Blocksidge of Dawley held the combined posts of overseer, churchwarden, and surveyor at an annual salary of £14. Blocksidge's appointment ended in 1823; in 1838 a new salaried post of assistant overseer was created.[11]

Only a small number of poor families were supported by the parish during the late 18th century, no more than four paupers receiving a full year's weekly pay in any one year between 1766 and 1800. The overseers also bought clothes, medical treatment, and fuel for the poor and assisted towards their payment of rent, and the

poor rate was occasionally used towards the upkeep of the parish roads. In 1785 a family of children from Stirchley was lodged in Dawley poorhouse.[12]

Stirchley was in Madeley poor-law union 1836–1930.[13] The parish was a member of Wrekin highway district 1863–81 but reverted to maintaining its own roads between 1881 and 1895 when it was placed in Shifnal rural district.[14] In 1934 the north-west side of the parish was transferred to Dawley urban district, to which the rest of the parish was added in 1966.[15] Stirchley was within the designated area of Dawley (from 1968 Telford) new town from 1963 and the district of the Wrekin from 1974.

CHURCHES. Stirchley church, not recorded until 1238,[16] had been built, as architectural evidence shows, by the 12th century. It is possible that, like those of Great Dawley, Malinslee, and Priorslee, the church was originally a chapel of ease in Shifnal parish.[17] The living was a rectory from 1238, or earlier,[18] until 1975 when it was abolished and Stirchley became part of the new parish of Central Telford.[19]

Wenlock priory had obtained the patronage by 1238 when Osbert, lord of Stirchley, released all his interest in the advowson to the prior.[20] The priory owned the advowson until the Dissolution, although the Crown exercised the priory's patronage, presumably until its denization in 1395.[21] In 1520 and 1535 the priory conveyed turns to others. Robert Brooke of Madeley presented in 1554[22] but the patronage had reverted to the Crown by 1565.[23] In 1569 it was leased for 21 years to Francis Barneham, a London alderman.[24] Sir Rowland Hayward bought the advowson from London speculators in 1582 and sold it again to Richard Halywell of Stirchley in 1585. George Halywell sold it to Richard Dod and Roger Banes in 1613 and Banes conveyed his moiety to Dod in 1622.[25] Francis Gibbons and George Browne presented in 1623 but whether as patrons in full right or as purchasers of a turn is not known.[26] By 1655 the advowson had passed to Muriel, daughter of Francis Watson of Church Aston, later wife of Robert Leicester.[27] The Leicesters sold it in 1669 to Rosamund Revell (d. 1690) of Shifnal,[28] in whose family it remained until the late 19th century. In 1687 she leased it to William Banks, of Dawley, for the life of John Revell (d. 1729).[29] On

---

[1] Williams, 'Dawley Hist. Survey: Inds.' p. 43; inf. from Mr. Insull, and from Mr. C. C. Wallis, Tarmac Roadstone Holdings Ltd.

[2] T.D.C., Stirchley deeds (Randlay brickworks, Tarmac property, Grange farm).   [3] Date stone.

[4] Eyton, viii. 120; cf. Collect. Topog. et Geneal. i. 118.

[5] Tax. Eccl. (Rec. Com.), 260.

[6] P.R.O., SC 6/Hen.VIII/3006, m. 8.

[7] Rot. Hund. (Rec. Com.), ii. 57.

[8] P.R.O., SC 22/197/96; Staffs. R.O., D. 593/J/10, ct. r.

[9] S.R.O. 513, box 13, deed of 1612.

[10] L.J.R.O., B/V/6, Stirchley, 1612–1708; S.R.O. 1345/1.

[11] S.R.O. 1345/48, 60, 62.

[12] Ibid. /48.

[13] V.C.H. Salop. iii. 169–70; Kelly's Dir. Salop. (1929), 4.

[14] S.R.O., q. sess. order bk. 1861–9, p. 127; Orders of Q. Sess. iv. 252; S.R.O. 1345/60, 62; V.C.H. Salop. ii. 217.

[15] V.C.H. Salop. ii. 217, 227 n.

[16] T.S.A.S. 4th ser. iv. 173.

[17] Eyton, viii. 123.

[18] T.S.A.S. 4th ser. iv. 173.

[19] Lich. Dioc. Regy., bps.' reg. R (Orders in Council), p. 350.

[20] T.S.A.S. 4th ser. iv. 173.

[21] Cal. Pat. 1348–50, 338, 466; 1367–70, 327, 334, 460; 1377–81, 98, 148, 626; 1381–5, 168–9; cf. V.C.H. Salop. ii. 42.

[22] S.R.O. 1224, box 342, Prior Gosnell's reg., f. 19v.; L.J.R.O., B/A/1/15, ff. A, 7.

[23] Cal. Pat. 1563–6, 295.

[24] Ibid. 1566–9, 438.

[25] Soc. Antiquaries, MS. 640.

[26] L.J.R.O., B/A/1/16, f. 33.

[27] T.S.A.S. xlvii. 10; cf. W.S.L., H.M. 36 (shorthand transcribed by Mr. N. W. Tildesley); Burke, Ext. & Dorm. Baronetcies (1844), 307.

[28] S.R.O. 924/389; cf. W.S.L., H.M. 36. For her death see S.R.O. 1335/1/1.

[29] S.P.L., Deeds 10190, p. 27.

John's death it was divided between his daughters Sarah (d. 1757), wife of Robert Moreton, and Anne (d. 1746), wife of Revell Phillips. In the later 18th century a turn (exercised 1792) was conveyed to others,[30] but both moieties eventually descended to Anne's grandson, Revell Phillips (d. 1816).[31] His sons Revell and Hugo Moreton Phillips held the advowson in 1827[32] and their brother Andrew was a patron in 1876.[33] By 1878 it had passed to the Jones family of Wombourne (Staffs.).[34] J. W. Jones presented between 1879 and 1917[35] and Mrs. Ellen Dinsdale of Illinois, who had an interest in the advowson from 1891 or earlier,[36] presented in 1930[37] and sold the patronage in 1933 to the Church Association Trust (from 1951 the Church Society Trust), with whom it remained until 1975.[38] On the creation of Central Telford parish in that year the trust was included in the patronage board of the new parish.[39]

The annual value of the living was placed at £2 13s. 4d. in 1291,[40] at £5 in 1380,[41] and at £6 5s. 8d. net in 1535.[42] It was said to be worth £26 in 1639,[43] £30 in 1705,[44] and c. £50 in 1772.[45] In the 18th century the rector received all tithes in kind except those of calves and milk, for which an ancient modus was paid.[46] The tithes were commuted in 1839 to an annual rent charge of £200.[47] The living had 45½ a. of glebe, a large endowment in relation to the size of the parish.[48] From 1766 to 1812 the glebe was let to the tenant of Stirchley Hall farm[49] but in the mid 19th century all but a few acres were farmed by H. M. Phillips during his long incumbency.[50] In 1862 the rector exchanged 11 a. of glebe scattered in small parcels for an 8-a. field near the church,[51] and in 1920 all the glebe, except the rectory and adjacent yards, was sold to the owner of Stirchley Hall.[52]

The rectory and its farm buildings lay immediately south of St. James's churchyard. The house was rebuilt in 1783 because the earlier parsonage, recorded from 1612 and described in 1698 as a two-bay house with a separate kitchen, had fallen out of repair.[53] By 1817 the condition of the new parsonage had deteriorated and the rector was granted leave to live elsewhere.[54] It was enlarged during the 1830s[55] and modernized in 1894;[56] the farm buildings were rebuilt c. 1878.[57] The house was sold c. 1961.[58]

Among the medieval rectors were two men with local connexions: Walter Perton (1309–49),[59] a member of the family that held an estate in the parish in the late 13th century,[60] and Philip of Harley (1362–9),[61] who from c. 1344 was steward to Wenlock priory, the patron.[62] In the later 14th century the living changed hands frequently[63] but Richard Withgys (1416–74)[64] was the first of five rectors between the 15th and 19th centuries to hold the living for more than 40 years.[65] An ample glebe and small parish may have made the living attractive. George Arden (c. 1655–1715), the longest serving rector and a graduate,[66] was described as 'an ordinary man; no preacher'.[67] He conformed in 1662[68] and lived in Stirchley until his death. In 1655 it was suggested that the parish could be united with Dawley[69] and an unofficial union had begun by 1655 when Arden occured as incumbent of Dawley. Thereafter until 1831 the two parishes, both in the patronage of the Revell family and their descendants, were often served by the same priests.[70]

Arden's successors in the 18th century were almost all graduates with local connexions: William Banks (1715–58), born in Dawley, was presented by his father;[71] John Rogers (1775–92), one of the family of the Home (in Wentnor) and son of a rector of Myndtown, held Stirchley in plurality with Shifnal;[72] and Roger Clayton (1792–1827), of the Wroxeter family, had been curate of Stirchley during his predecessor's incumbency.[73] During the late 18th and early 19th century one service was held at Stirchley each Sunday, alternating mornings and evenings with Dawley. Part of the duty was regularly done by

[30] T.S.A.S. 4th ser. v. 301.
[31] S.P.L., Deeds 10188, 10190. For pedigree of Revell, Moreton, and Phillips see S.P.L., MSS. 4079, pp. 1358–9; 4645, p. 441.
[32] Lich. Dioc. Regy., episc. reg. 29, p. 131; cf. S.R.O. 3916/1/3.
[33] Clergy List (1876).
[34] Lich. Dioc. Regy., benefice and inst. bk. 1868–1900, p. 46.
[35] Ibid. 1868–1900, p. 97; 1900–29, pp. 30, 50.
[36] Crockford (1891).
[37] Lich. Dioc. Regy., benefice and inst. bk. 1929–52, p. 5.
[38] Ibid. 1929–52, pp. 82, 139; S.R.O. 1345/62.
[39] Lich. Dioc. Regy., bps.' reg. R (Orders in Council), p. 350.
[40] Tax. Eccl. (Rec. Com.), 245.
[41] Dugdale, Mon. v. 78.
[42] Valor Eccl. (Rec. Com.), iii. 187.
[43] L.J.R.O., B/V/1/65.   [44] B/V/6, Stirchley, 1705.
[45] B/V/5, visit. return of 1772.
[46] S.P.R. Lich. v (3), 13.
[47] S.R.O. 1268/6.
[48] Ibid.; cf. S.P.R. Lich. v (3), 12–14; L.J.R.O., B/V/6, Stirchley, 1612–1857.
[49] Poor rate on glebe pd. by Wm. Nicholls (S.R.O. 1345/48), tenant of Stirchley Hall (S.R.O. 513, box 16, deed of 1777).
[50] S.R.O. 1268/6; Salopian and W. Midland Monthly Illustr. Jnl. Dec. 1877, 61–2.
[51] L.J.R.O., B/V/6, Stirchley, 1869.

[52] T.D.C., Stirchley Hall deeds.
[53] L.J.R.O., B/V/6, Stirchley, 1612–1783.
[54] S.R.O. 1345/37.
[55] S.R.O. 3916/1/3.
[56] S.R.O. 2337/6.
[57] S.R.O. 3916/1/29.
[58] Inf. from the Revd. C. Hill, Churches Planning Officer, Telford Area Interdenominational Cttee.
[59] L.J.R.O., B/A/1/1, f. 65; /1/2, f. 222.
[60] Cal. Inq. p.m. ii, p. 39.
[61] S.H.C. N.S. x (2), 194, 202.
[62] T.S.A.S. lx. 110.
[63] There were 5 rectors 1362–83: S.H.C. N.S. x (2), 194, 202–3, 208, 213–14.
[64] L.J.R.O., B/A/1/8, f. 15v.; /1/12, f. 89.
[65] The others were Rob. Bell (1576–1623), Geo. Arden (c. 1655–1715), Wm. Banks (1715–58), and H. M. Phillips (1827–77).
[66] Alum. Oxon. 1500–1714, i. 30.
[67] W.S.L., II.M. 36.
[68] L.J.R.O., B/V/1/67, f. 10; R. F. Skinner, Nonconformity in Salop. (Shrews. 1964), 101.
[69] T.S.A.S. xlvii. 9.
[70] S.P.R. Lich. xviii (1), pp. vii–viii.
[71] Ibid. p. 10; Alum. Cantab. to 1750, i. 81; T.S.A.S. 4th ser. v. 190.
[72] S.P.R. Lich. xviii (1), p. viii; Alum. Oxon. 1715–1886, iii. 1220.
[73] Alum. Cantab. 1752–1900, ii. 63; L.J.R.O., B/V/6, Stirchley, 1779, 1783; S.R.O. 3916/1/1.

curates.[74] Communion was received four times a year by 10–20 parishioners.[75] Hugo Moreton Phillips (1827–77), a member of the Shifnal family and joint owner of the advowson,[76] was a genial and popular rector.[77] Later incumbencies were short and included those of three elderly men.[78] The frequency of services increased during the 19th century, two full services being held each Sunday by 1843[79] and communion being celebrated at least once a month by the end of the century. A Wednesday evening service was also held from 1894 to 1908.[80] A choir accompanied by a bass viol led the singing in 1827; a harmonium bought in 1865 was replaced by an organ in 1919.[81]

Doubt over Stirchley's future independence had arisen by 1949 when the parish meeting resolved that, if independent status could not be maintained, the parish should be annexed to Shifnal.[82] In that year J. W. M. Finney, vicar of Shifnal, was instituted as rector and until 1972 Stirchley fell within the care of the vicars of Shifnal. Presentation was suspended on Finney's death in 1959, his successor being licensed as priest-in-charge.[83] During Finney's incumbency Stirchley was served by a succession of curates, who lived in the rectory.[84] Between 1972 and the creation of Central Telford parish in 1975 the parish was served by a priest-in-charge, who lived in the new Brookside housing estate.[85]

The ancient parish church of *ST. JAMES*[86] has a stone chancel and a brick nave with north aisle and west tower.[87] The later 12th-century chancel arch, of three carved orders, is set in the filling of a larger arch. The latter and the surviving original windows in the chancel walls are also of the mid to late 12th century. Old masonry, similar to that of the chancel, on the inner face of the nave and tower walls may also be 12th-century. A new window was put into the south wall of the chancel in the 14th century but the church was not enlarged in the later medieval period.

About 1740[88] the nave was cased and remodelled in red brick with dressings of sandstone and given a new roof above a flat plaster ceiling. The tower was similarly treated and was heightened by one stage; the bell frame is dated 1748. About that time the nave was refitted, with box pews and a new pulpit and reading desk. Early in the 19th century the lower of the two original east windows was replaced by one of larger size. It was in turn replaced later in the century by a small one similar to the original chancel windows. In 1838 Thomas, William, and Beriah Botfield provided *c.* 120 new sittings by constructing a north aisle incorporating a gallery for their workmen;[89] the gallery extended into the nave, cutting into, and partly obscuring, the chancel arch. The nave ceiling, which had become unsafe, was removed in 1877,[90] and in 1919 the front of the gallery was set back into the aisle.[91] In 1979, during a general restoration, the plaster was removed from the east wall of the nave, and some small areas of later medieval wall painting were there exposed.

The fittings included a 17th-century communion table; three bells, of *c.* 1410, 1594, and 1664;[92] and an Elizabethan chalice.[93] The registers begin in 1658 and are complete.[94]

On the creation of Central Telford parish in 1975 St. James's church became redundant,[95] and it was sold in 1978 to Telford development corporation,[96] which restored it in 1979–80 for use as a museum. Thereafter the increased population in the area of the former parish of Stirchley was served by a team vicar responsible for the Stirchley district of Central Telford parish. The vicar officiated both at the Methodist-owned Brookside pastoral centre and at the new church of *ALL SAINTS* in Stirchley district centre.[97] All Saints is a flat-roofed brick building with adjacent rooms for social use. From the sanctuary four concrete posts rise through the roof to form an open 'spire' in which a three-dimensional cross is suspended. The building was licensed for worship in 1975.[98] In 1976 it was agreed that the building should be shared by the Anglican and Roman Catholic congregations in Stirchley.[99] By 1981 occasional joint services were held and the church acted as a community centre as well as a place of worship.[1]

NONCONFORMITY. There were individual Roman Catholics in the parish at various dates between 1614 and 1772 but there is no evidence of a long-standing recusant family or community; the rector claimed in 1772 that no one had been 'perverted' recently.[2]

Humphrey Chambers, a Presbyterian minister

[74] L.J.R.O., B/V/5, visit. return of 1772; S.R.O. 1345/40; 3916/1/3.

[75] S.R.O. 3916/1/1, 3.

[76] Lich. Dioc. Regy., episc. reg. 29, p. 131.

[77] *Salopian and W. Midland Monthly Illustr. Jnl.* Dec. 1877, 61–2.

[78] W. H. Painter (1894–1910), J. J. Evans (1910–17), H. Penkivil (1917–29): *Crockford* (1910, 1932).

[79] S.R.O. 3916/1/3, 8.

[80] S.R.O. 1345/29.   [81] Ibid. /48, 60, 62.

[82] Ibid. box 17, min. of par. mtg. 29 Mar. 1949.

[83] Lich. Dioc. Regy., benefice and inst. bk. 1929–52, p. 139; 1952–68, p. 59.

[84] S.R.O. 1345/32; *Crockford* (1957–8); *Reg. of Electors, Wrekin Co. Const.* 1950–60.

[85] Lich. Dioc. Regy., benefice and inst. bk. 1968– (in use), pp. 28, 48; *Crockford* (1973–4).

[86] Dedication first recorded *c.* 1740: B.L. Add. MS. 30316, f. 28v.

[87] Acct. based on Pevsner, *Shropshire*, 293–4; Cranage, vii. 621–2; S.P.L., MS. 372, vol. i, p. 81; S.P.L., J. H. Smith colln., no. 194; R. A. Meeson, 'The enigmatic Norman

chancel of the Church of St. James, Stirchley' (forthcoming in *T.S.A.S.* lxiv).

[88] W. A. Bewes, *Ch. Briefs* (1896), 320; *T.S.A.S.* 4th ser. x. 220.

[89] S.R.O. 3916/1/3; inscr. on gallery.

[90] S.R.O. 1345/60; *Salopian and W. Midland Monthly Illustr. Jnl.* Dec. 1877, 60–1.

[91] S.R.O. 1345, box 15, bills and receipts of 1919.

[92] H. B. Walters, *Ch. Bells of Salop.* (Oswestry, 1915), 295.

[93] S. A. Jeavons, *Ch. Plate Archd. Salop* (Shrews. 1964), pp. 32, 99.

[94] S.R.O. 1345/1–11; *S.P.R. Lich.* v (3).

[95] Lich. Dioc. Regy., bps.' reg. R (Orders in Council), p. 350.

[96] Inf. from the archivist, T.D.C.

[97] Inf. from the Revd. C. Hill.

[98] Lich. Dioc. Regy., episc. reg. 43, p. 163.

[99] Ibid. bps.' reg. Y, pp. 218–19.

[1] Inf. from the Revd. C. Hill; *Shrews. Dioc. Catholic Voice,* Apr. 1981, 8.

[2] L.J.R.O., B/A/12(i), f. 93; B/V/1/29; B/V/5, visit. return of 1772; W.S.L., H.M. 36.

who had been a schoolmaster in Wellington in the 1630s,[3] was living in Stirchley in 1648.[4] George Arden, rector c. 1655–1715, conformed in 1662 and kept his living but may nevertheless have been sympathetic to the nonconformist cause, for he received and helped Jonathan Lovel, the ejected curate of Alveley, in 1667.[5] There were no dissenters in the parish in 1676 and c. 1695,[6] nor were any recorded in the 18th century.[7]

In 1811 a house in Stirchley was registered for worship by Methodists,[8] and by 1813 the Wesleyan group at Kemberton and Stirchley had weekly preaching on the Shrewsbury circuit.[9] In the earlier 19th century the group met at Holmer Farm, 'where they preached in the granary from a cornbin, with a side saddle for a pulpit cushion'.[10] Unable to buy land for a chapel in Stirchley, they acquired a plot just outside the parish on the road to Dawley; Stirchley Wesleyan Chapel was built there and was registered for worship in 1854.[11] There was a Primitive Methodist class meeting in Stirchley in the early 1860s.[12]

In 1972 a Methodist-owned pastoral centre was opened in the Brookside housing estate and in 1980 it was used jointly by Methodists and Anglicans, services being taken by clergy of each denomination alternately.[13] In 1976 provision was made for the new All Saints' church at Stirchley district centre to be shared by the Anglican and Roman Catholic congregations.[14]

In 1980 the former parish rooms adjoining the Old Rectory were used by the Telford 1st Christian Spiritualist Church, which had acquired the premises the previous year.[15]

EDUCATION. Before the construction of the new town housing estates Stirchley was served by one village school but in the 1970s new schools were built to serve the enlarged population.

William Banks, rector 1715–58, was listed as a schoolmaster in 1726.[16]

Stirchley County Primary School originated as an unendowed day school founded between 1818 and 1833[17] and supported by the Botfield family and the rector.[18] It contained only 12 children in 1833,[19] and the parish clerk acted as schoolmaster during the 1850s.[20] By 1861 the school, a parish day school, was taught by a mistress in a building that was apparently near the rectory.[21]

In 1879 control passed to the new Stirchley school board[22] and in 1880 a new school for 80 pupils was built at the north end of the village on land bought from the lords of the manor; it opened in 1881.[23] There were 86 children on the register in 1902 and overcrowding remained a problem throughout the first decade of the century.[24] By 1948 children over 11 went to Madeley Secondary Modern School, Pool Hill County School, or Coalbrookdale High School, and numbers on the roll dropped from 67 in 1946 to 43 in 1951.[25] There were only 30 pupils on the register in 1973 and the school closed at the end of that year, children being transferred to the new schools at Brookside.[26]

A three-tier system of education was introduced on the construction of the Brookside, Stirchley, and Randlay housing estates in the 1970s. 'First' schools were opened at Brookside in 1974.[27] Brookside County Middle School, at Brookside local centre, was opened in 1974, Stirchley County First School at Calcott centre in 1975, Stirchley Middle and Upper schools at Stirchley district centre in 1975; there were 436, 410, 619, and 565 pupils in 1979. Randlay County First School opened in 1980.[28]

'Special' education was provided by the Thomas Parker Special School from 1971[29] and by Telford Education Guidance Unit, housed in the former Stirchley primary school building, from c. 1975;[30] the former had 59 pupils in 1980.[31]

CHARITIES FOR THE POOR. By will dated 1725 Richard Cookes, owner of Stirchley Grange, gave 17s. rent.[32] Known in the late 18th and early 19th century as Darrall's Money, from the name of the person then paying the rent, the charity was distributed to widows.[33] In the mid and late 19th century the annual distribution of Cookes's charity was supplemented by Clowes's and Smith's charities.[34] In 1975 the annual income of Cookes's charity was £1.[35]

Thomas Clowes, by will proved 1749, left 20s. yearly.[36] In the early 19th century it was paid by the Stirchley Hall tenant without reference to

[3] L.J.R.O., B/V/1/57, 62.
[4] Calamy Revised, ed. A. G. Matthews, 556.
[5] Ibid. 328.
[6] T.S.A.S. 2nd ser. i. 85; W.S.L., H.M. 36.
[7] L.J.R.O., B/V/5, visit. return of 1772; S.R.O. 3916/1/1.
[8] P.R.O., RG 31/7, Salop. no. 287; Orders of Q. Sess. iii. 172.
[9] S.P.L., C 98.7 v.f., Shrews. circuit plan.
[10] Salopian and W. Midland Monthly Illustr. Jnl. Dec. 1877, 62.
[11] G.R.O., Worship Reg. no. 1739.
[12] S.R.O. 2533/130, 9 June 1862; 14 Mar. 1864.
[13] G.R.O., Worship Reg. no. 73276; Lich. Dioc. Regy., bps.' reg. Y, p. 185; Rayska, Dev. of Stirchley; inf. from the Revd. C. Hill.
[14] Lich. Dioc. Regy., episc. reg. 43, p. 163; bps.' reg. Y, pp. 218–19.
[15] Inf. from the Revd. C. Hill.
[16] L.J.R.O., B/V/3, list of schmasters, 1726.
[17] Digest Educ. Poor, H.C. 224, p. 769 (1819), ix (2); Educ. Enq. Abstr. H.C. 62, p. 784 (1835), xliii.
[18] S. Bagshaw, Dir. Salop. (1851), 418.
[19] Educ. Enq. Abstr. 784.

[20] S. Bagshaw, Dir. Salop. (1851), 418; P.O. Dir. Salop. (1856), 127.
[21] P.R.O., RG 9/1856.
[22] S.R.O. 1345/60.
[23] P.R.O., ED 7/103, f. 77; S.R.O. 559/XXIV/16, treas. acct. bk.; 1265/291.
[24] S.R.O. 1034/6, pp. 1, 41.
[25] Ibid. pp. 157, 160, 163, 175.
[26] S.C.C. Mins. (Educ.) 1972–3, 248.
[27] Above, Madeley, Educ.
[28] S.C.C. Mins. (Educ.) 1971–2, 277; 1972–3, 248, 347; 1973–4, 140; 1974–5, 274, 359; S.C.C. Educ. Cttee. Sch. List (1979), 2–3, 10.
[29] S.C.C. Mins. (Educ.) 1970–1, 210; Sch. List (1971), 11.
[30] S.C.C. Mins. (Educ.) 1973–4, 144.
[31] S.C.C. Educ. Cttee. Educ. Dir. (1980), 11.
[32] S.R.O. 513, box 17, will (copy).
[33] S.R.O. 1345/48, 60; Char. Don. 1786–8, ii, H.C. 511–II, pp. 1016–17 (1816), xvi (2); 3rd Rep. Com. Char. H.C. 5, p. 6 (1820), iv.
[34] S.R.O. 1345/60, 62.
[35] Review of Local Chars. (S.C.C. 1975), 65.
[36] S.R.O. 513, box 15, will of 1748.

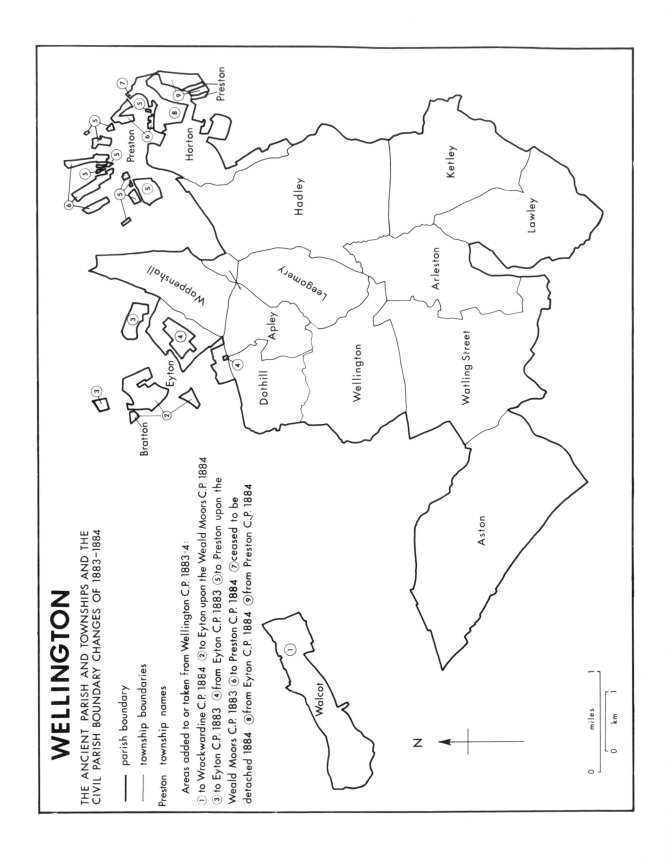

WELLINGTON

THE ANCIENT PARISH AND TOWNSHIPS AND THE
CIVIL PARISH BOUNDARY CHANGES OF 1883–1884

——— parish boundary

——— township boundaries

Preston township names

Areas added to or taken from Wellington C.P. 1883-4:
① to Wrockwardine C.P. 1884 ② to Eyton upon the Weald Moors C.P. 1884
③ to Eyton C.P. 1883 ④ from Eyton C.P. 1883 ⑤ to Preston upon the
Weald Moors C.P. 1883 ⑥ to Preston C.P. 1884 ⑦ceased to be
detached 1884 ⑧ from Eyton C.P. 1884 ⑨ from Preston C.P. 1884

parish officials.[37] It was distributed with Cookes's charity 1830–76 but not paid at all thereafter, the Stirchley Hall tenant disputing the obligation.[38]

Between 1878 and 1887 Cookes's charity was supplemented by a payment of £1 7s., the yearly interest on £27 devised by one Smith.[39]

WELLINGTON

Communications, p. 198. Growth of Settlement, p. 204. Social and Cultural Activities, p. 210. Manors and Other Estates, p. 215. Economic History, p. 222. Local Government, p. 232. Public Services, p. 236. Churches, p. 238. Roman Catholicism, p. 242. Protestant Nonconformity, p. 243. Islam, p. 245. Education, p. 245. Charities for the Poor, p. 251. Hadley and Horton, p. 253. Ketley, p. 267. Lawley, p. 276.

THE OLD market town of Wellington lies just north of Watling Street 16 km. east of Shrewsbury. By the beginning of the 19th century it was second only to the county town in size and importance, a position that it maintained in the 20th century. In 1968 it was included in Telford new town. Wellington was the centre of a large and varied parish: the easternmost townships lay on the east Shropshire coalfield and developed as loose-knit mining and industrial areas. During the 20th century housing and, in a smaller degree, industry expanded into the parish's rural areas, a movement stimulated by Telford development corporation from the 1970s. Nevertheless parts of the ancient parish remained completely rural in 1983.[40]

The ancient parish comprised 9,243 a.[41] (3,740 ha.) and contained twelve whole townships (Apley, Arleston, Aston, Dothill, Hadley, Horton, Lawley, Leegomery, Walcot (detached), Wappenshall, Watling Street, and Wellington) and most of Ketley township, and had small parts (mostly detached) in Bratton,[42] Eyton upon the Weald Moors, and Preston upon the Weald Moors townships. Without the detached parts it was roughly square, with Aston, Horton, and Wappenshall as excrescences. Its boundaries, and those of the townships, often followed water-courses or roads.[43]

The ancient and civil parishes were conterminous until 1883. In 1883–4 the detached areas (with one small exception) were transferred to other C.P.s: 130 a. to Eyton upon the Weald Moors, 139 a. to Preston upon the Weald Moors, and 414 a. (Walcot township) to Wrockwardine. At the same time Wellington C.P. took in three detached parts (129 a.) of Eyton C.P. (including

the Hoo, whose absorption connected a ¼-a. detached part of Wellington to the rest of the parish) and two detached parts (42 a.) of Preston C.P.[44]

In 1894 Wellington C.P. was divided into Wellington Urban and Wellington Rural C.P.s;[45] Wellington Urban was, and remained, conterminous with Wellington urban district.[46] The U.D. and Urban C.P., enlarged by territory from the Rural C.P. in 1903[47] and 1934 and from Wrockwardine C.P. in 1934,[48] were abolished in 1974;[49] thereafter their area, not assigned to any C.P., coincided with six wards of the district of the Wrekin, except that the south-western part of the former U.D. was included (with adjoining C.P.s) in Wrockwardine ward.[50]

In 1898 the north-eastern part of Wellington Rural C.P. was created Hadley C.P.[51] Thereafter Wellington Rural C.P. gradually lost more territory to the adjacent C.P.s: to Wellington Urban in 1903[52] and 1934, to Eyton, Hadley, Oakengates, and Wrockwardine in 1934, to Dawley in 1934[53] and 1966, and to Little Wenlock in 1966;[54] it gained a small area from Hadley C.P. in 1934.[55] In 1976 what remained of Wellington Rural C.P. was renamed Ketley.[56]

The present article treats the whole ancient parish except for the small parts in Bratton, Eyton, and Preston townships;[57] within it, however, the coalfield townships of Hadley (with Horton), Ketley, and Lawley receive, as far as possible, separate treatment.[58]

Outside the coalfield townships the only part of the ancient parish included in Dawley new town in 1963 was a small area of Arleston township.[59] From 1968, however, the designated area of Telford new town covered all but the northern, southern, and western extremities of the ancient

[37] 3rd Rep. Com. Char. 6.
[38] S.R.O. 1345/60; 3916/1/29.   [39] S.R.O. 1345/60, 62.
[40] This art. was written 1981–3.   [41] O.S. Area Bk. (1882).
[42] S.R.O. 560/419, presumably referring to detached area no. 3 (6.7 a.) in O.S. Map 1/2,500, Salop. XXXVI. 1 (1882 edn.).
[43] L.J.R.O., B/A/15, Eyton upon the Weald Moors; Preston upon the Weald Moors; S.R.O. 14, tithe maps; 1856/1–7.
[44] Divided Parishes and Poor Law Amendment Act, 1882, 45 & 46 Vic. c. 58; 14th Ann. Rep. Local Govt. Bd. [C. 4515], pp. xlvii, 204, H.C. (1884–5), xxxii; O.S. Area Bk. (1885); O.S. Maps 6″, Salop. XXX. SW.; XXXV. NE., SE., SW.; XXXVI. NE., NW. (1887–90 edn.).
[45] 24th Ann. Rep. Local Govt. Bd. [C. 7867], p. 274, H.C. (1895), l; ibid. Suppl. [C. 7905], p. 13, H.C. (1895), li.
[46] O.S. Map 6″, Salop. XXXVI. SW. (1903 edn.); 32nd Ann. Rep. Local Govt. Bd. [Cd. 1700], p. 341, H.C. (1903), xxiv; Salop Review Order, 1934 (Min. of Health order no. 77933).
[47] 32nd Ann. Rep. Local Govt. Bd. p. 341; O.S. Map 6″, Salop. XXXVI. SW. (1929 edn.).
[48] Salop Review Order, 1934; O.S. Maps 6″, SJ 60 NE.,

NW.; SJ 61 SE., SW. (1954 edn.).
[49] Below, Local Govt.
[50] Inf. from Wrekin District Council.
[51] 28th Ann. Rep. Local Govt. Bd. [C. 9444], p. 318, H.C. (1899), xxxvii; O.S. Maps 6″, Salop. XXXVI. NW. (1902 edn.), NE., SE., SW. (1903 edns.). For the hist. of Hadley C.P. see below, Hadley, Local Govt. and Public Services.
[52] 32nd Ann. Rep. Local Govt. Bd. p. 341; O.S. Map 6″, Salop. XXXVI. SW. (1929 edn.).
[53] Salop Review Order, 1934; O.S. Maps 6″, SJ 60 NE., NW.; 61 SE., SW. (1954 edn.).
[54] Salop Order 1966 (Min. of Housing and Local Govt. order no. 22958).
[55] Salop Review Order, 1934; O.S. Map 6″, SJ 61 SE. (1954 edn.).
[56] S.C.C., Planning Dept. file no. 051001, Wrekin District Council sec. to co. sec. 15 July 1976.
[57] Treated above: see Eyton; Preston.
[58] Treated below: see Hadley; Ketley; Lawley.
[59] Dawley New Town (Designation) Order 1963 (Stat. Instr. 1963, no. 64), accompanying map (copy in S.R.O. 2981, parcel VI).

parish. The excluded areas were still rural in character: in the north they comprised most of Wappenshall township, small parts of Apley and Hadley townships, the former Wellington part of Bratton township, and almost all the former Wellington parts of Eyton and Preston townships; in the south and west they comprised Aston and Walcot townships, most of Watling Street township, a large part of Arleston township, and a small part of Wellington township.[60]

The southern part of the parish is dominated by the Wrekin, a celebrated Midland landmark.[61] It is composed mainly of volcanic rocks and its summit (407 metres above O.D.) lies in Aston township. Its slopes and those of its northern foothills, Maddock's Hill (280 metres), the Ercall (265 metres), and Lawrence's Hill (c. 215 metres), descend steeply northwards and westwards over the southern half of the parish to c. 100 metres above O.D., and thence level off gradually towards the Weald Moors reaching c. 50 metres at the northern limit of Wappenshall township. The centre of Wellington town (c. 95 metres above O.D.) is on sand and gravel, which extends immediately westwards, but the surrounding land consists predominantly of boulder clay. Farther north and east, in Apley, Dothill, and Leegomery townships, sand and gravel again predominate, and lake clay and peat cover most of the northern part of Wappenshall township. Most of the parish drains north towards the Weald Moors. Parts of Aston, however, drain south-westwards by Bell brook to the Severn at Wroxeter, and Walcot is drained by the Tern.

The summit of the Wrekin, frequented in the Bronze Age,[62] was occupied by a large hill fort in the Iron Age,[63] presumably the pre-Roman capital of the Cornovii.[64] Crop marks on the lower slopes perhaps represent other Bronze Age, Iron Age, and Roman sites.[65] Wooden buildings inside the fort were apparently burnt,[66] possibly by Roman forces. In the 7th century the fort may have served as a British refuge.[67] A hermitage on the Wrekin, recorded in 1267 and 1500,[68] was perhaps associated with a holy well.[69] The suggestion that a beacon was formerly maintained on the summit[70]

may be supported by the field name Bonfire Stock in Aston township.[71]

At the northern edge of Leegomery township, near Black butts,[72] was a multi-ditched rectangular enclosure, probably used in the Iron Age and Roman periods.[73]

Two healing wells are known. One on the Wrekin was dedicated to St. 'Hawthorn', perhaps the Welsh St. Arfan.[74] It was probably the 'fair fountain' recorded near the summit c. 1540[75] and was still visited in the later 19th century.[76] St. Margaret's well, recorded in 1723, was in Leegomery township.[77] It was visited annually on Good Friday but destroyed in the mid 19th century. Local customs included 'clipping' All Saints' church on Shrove Tuesday; the children joined hands round the building while the boys gave a blast on toy trumpets. It was also customary to watch the sunrise from the top of the Wrekin on Easter Day.[78]

Charles I and his forces stopped at Wellington 19–20 September 1642 on the way from Nottingham to Shrewsbury.[79] Apley Castle, garrisoned for the king, was taken in March 1644 by Parliamentarian forces, who garrisoned Wellington church at the same time, but Apley and Wellington were recaptured by royalists a few days later.[80] Part of Prince Maurice's army was quartered at Wellington in February 1645.[81]

Distinguished natives[82] included William Withering (1742–99),[83] physician, botanist, and mineralogist; H. J. Gauntlett (1805–76), the composer; R. W. Eyton (1815–81), the historian; Sarah Smith (1832–1911), the writer better known as 'Hesba Stretton';[84] C. G. Lawson (1851–82), the landscape painter; and D. H. S. Cranage (1866–1957), antiquary and dean of Norwich.[85] Sir George Downing (c. 1684–1749), founder of Downing College, Cambridge, lived at Dothill in his youth.

COMMUNICATIONS. The Roman Watling Street crossed the parish[86] and bounded several townships.[87] In 1301 it crossed 'Clerkenebrugge' near the parish's western edge.[88] From Oakengates

[60] Dawley New Town (Designation) Amendment (Telford) Order 1968 (Stat. Instr. 1968, no. 1912), map accompanying Explanatory Note.
[61] V.C.H. Salop. i, frontispiece. Para. based on O.S. Maps 1/25,000, SJ 60; SJ 61 (1957–8 edn.); Inst. Geol. Sciences Map 1/25,000, Telford (1978 edn.).
[62] SA 1782–3, 2812; Trans. Caradoc & Severn Valley Field Club, xv. 74; R. E. Davies, Handbk. to the Wrekin (1895), 11 (copy in S.P.L.); V.C.H. Salop. i. 370, 412.
[63] SA 1069; A. H. A. Hogg, Hill Forts of Brit. (1975), 295–6; V.C.H. Salop. i. 369–70; K. M. Kenyon, 'Excavations on the Wrekin, 1939', Arch. Jnl. xcix. 99–109; idem, 'The Wrekin', ibid. cxiii. 208–9; W. Midlands Arch. News Sheet, xvi. 9–10.
[64] V.C.H. Salop. i. 216; Arch. Jnl. cxiii. 208–9.
[65] SA 1786, 2317, 2356.
[66] W. Midlands Arch. News Sheet, xvi. 9–10; G. Webster, The Cornovii (1975), 10, 26.
[67] G. Jones, 'Continuity Despite Calamity: The Heritage of Celtic Territorial Organization in Eng.' Jnl. Celtic Studies, iii. 23–9.
[68] V.C.H. Salop. ii. 23.
[69] Below.
[70] C. S. Burne, Salop. Folk-Lore (1883), 364.
[71] Barnard MSS., Raby Castle, box 12, bdle. 11, deed of 1653.
[72] So called in 1723: S.R.O. 972, parcel 236, Leegomery and Wappenshall map.
[73] SA 2000.
[74] St. Arfan (known only from place names) may have been Arthen, a son of the legendary Brychan: F. Arnold Forster, Studies in Ch. Dedications (1899), ii. 240. For other Arthens see Early Welsh Genealogical Tracts, ed. P. C. Bartrum, 170, and refs. there given.
[75] Leland, Itin. ed. Toulmin Smith, ii. 83.
[76] Burne, Salop. Folk Lore, 420.
[77] c. O.S. Nat. Grid SJ 655 122: S.R.O. 972, parcel 236, Leegomery and Wappenshall map.
[78] Burne, op. cit. 322, 333, 335, 433.
[79] T.S.A.S. li. 28.
[80] Ibid. l. 159–63.
[81] Cal. S.P. Dom. 1644–5, 297–8.
[82] Para. based on D.N.B. unless otherwise stated.
[83] For the yr. of his birth, par. reg. bap. 13 Apr. 1742 (transcript in S.P.L.).
[84] D.N.B. 1901–11.
[85] P.R.O., RG 10/2806, f. 60v.; Who Was Who, 1951–60, 252–3.
[86] I. D. Margary, Roman Roads in Brit. (1973), p. 292 (no. 1h); above, plate 55.
[87] T.S.A.S. lvi. 32; O.S. Map 1", Index to Tithe Survey [c. 1851], sheet 61 NE.
[88] Cartulary of Shrews. Abbey, ed. U. Rees (1975), ii, p. 247.

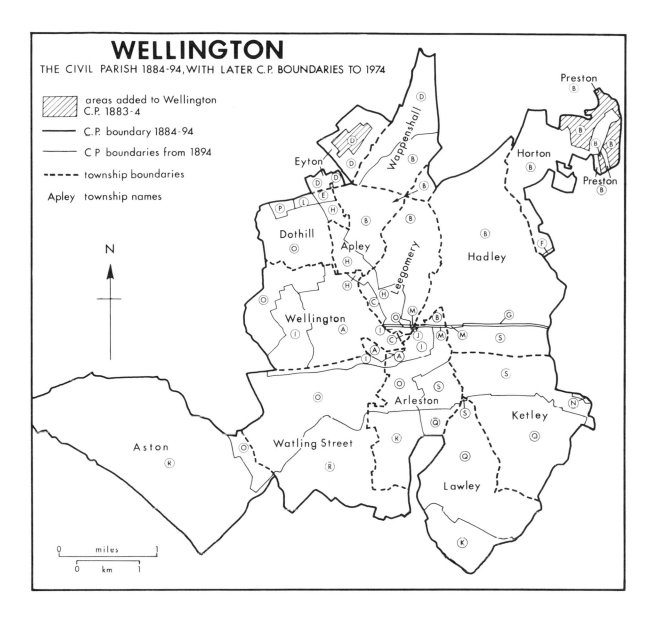

WELLINGTON
THE CIVIL PARISH 1884-94, WITH LATER C.P. BOUNDARIES TO 1974

areas added to Wellington C.P. 1883-4

C.P. boundary 1884-94

C P boundaries from 1894

township boundaries

Apley township names

N

Preston

Horton

Wappenshall

Eyton

Dothill

Apley

Leegomery

Hadley

Wellington

Arleston

Ketley

Aston

Watling Street

Lawley

0 miles 1

0 km 1

KEY TO CIVIL PARISHES FROM 1894 TO 1974

A   Wellington Urban
B   Wellington Rural 1894–8, Hadley from 1898
C   Wellington Rural 1894–8, Hadley 1898–1903, Wellington Urban from 1903
D   Wellington Rural 1894–8, Hadley 1898–1905, Eyton upon the Weald Moors from 1905
E   Wellington Rural 1894–8, Hadley 1898–1934, Eyton from 1934
F   Wellington Rural 1894–8, Hadley 1898–1934, Oakengates from 1934
G   Wellington Rural 1894–8, Hadley 1898–1934, Wellington Rural from 1934
H   Wellington Rural 1894–8, Hadley 1898–1934, Wellington Urban from 1934
I   Wellington Rural 1894–1903, Wellington Urban from 1903
J   Wellington Rural 1894–1903, Wellington Urban 1903–34, Hadley from 1934
K   Wellington Rural 1894–1934, Dawley from 1934
L   Wellington Rural 1894–1934, Eyton from 1934
M   Wellington Rural 1894–1934, Hadley from 1934
N   Wellington Rural 1894–1934, Oakengates from 1934
O   Wellington Rural 1894–1934, Wellington Urban from 1934
P   Wellington Rural 1894–1934, Wrockwardine from 1934
Q   Wellington Rural 1894–1966, Dawley from 1966
R   Wellington Rural 1894–1966, Little Wenlock from 1966
S   Wellington Rural

Parts of C.P.s beyond the Wellington C.P. boundary of 1884–94 are not shown.

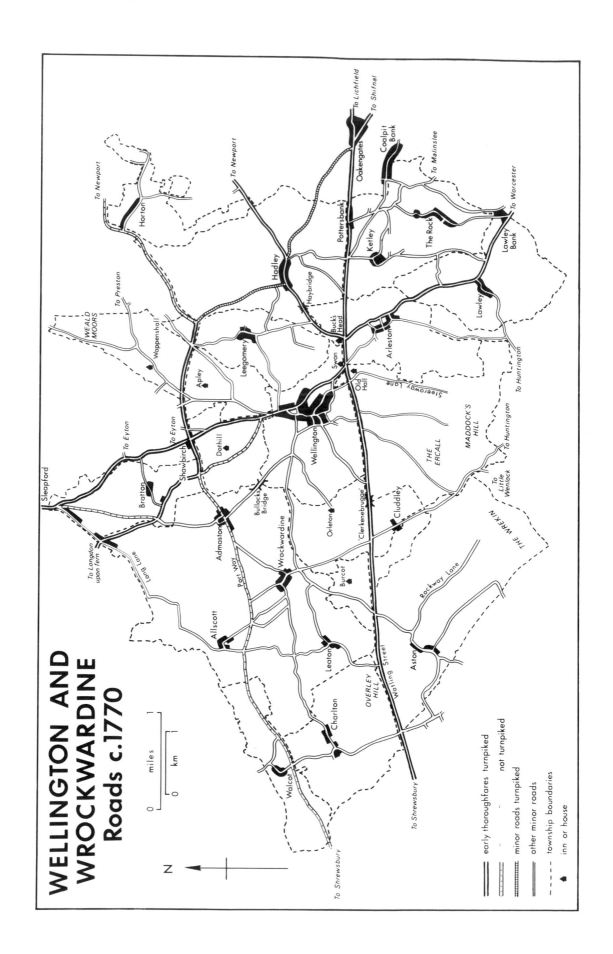

WELLINGTON AND
WROCKWARDINE
Roads c.1770

N

0 ——— miles 1

0 ——— km

early thoroughfares turnpiked
not turnpiked
minor roads turnpiked
other minor roads
township boundaries
inn or house

To Shrewsbury
To Newport
To Preston
To Eyton
To Eyton
To London upon Tern
Long Lane
To Shrewsbury
To Lichfield
To Shifnal
To Mainslee
To Worcester
To Huntington
To Huntington
To Little Wenlock

Sleapford
Horton
WEALD MOORS
Wappenshall
Apley
Leegomery
Hadley
Haybridge
Pottersbank
Oakengates
Coalpit Bank
Ketley
The Rock
Lawley Bank
Buck's Head
Swan
Arleston
Old Hall
Lawley
Steerawoy Lane
MADDOCK'S HILL
THE ERCALL
Bratton
Shawbirch
Dothill
Wellington
Cluddley
'Clerkenebrugge'
Orleton
Admaston
Bullock's Bridge
Wrockwardine
Port Way
Burcot
Rockway Lane
THE WREKIN
Allscott
Leaton
OVERLEY HILL
Watling Street
Aston
Charlton
Walcot

200

(in Wombridge) a south-easterly branch via Shifnal existed by 1335, when two men were granted tolls on the Wellington–Shifnal road for making a causeway on it,[89] and that was the usual Wellington–London route in 1695.[90] Watling Street and its Shifnal branch were turnpiked in 1726[91] and from the late 18th century the former also carried much traffic to the Staffordshire & Worcestershire Canal at Gailey (Staffs.).[92]

After the union of the Irish and British parliaments (1801) the route along Watling Street and through Shifnal was improved as part of the Holyhead–London road. Local traffic to Wolverhampton and Birmingham benefited.[93] From c. 1817 a new road from Pottersbank via Snedshill to Shifnal bypassed Oakengates to the south-west.[94] Detours on Watling Street were opened c. 1822 at Ketleybrook[95] and in 1835 at Overley Hill.[96] Watling Street west of Pottersbank and the Pottersbank–Shifnal road were disturnpiked in Wellington parish in 1866.[97] In 1879 that route was designated a main road[98] and remained so throughout Wellington parish until 1975, when it was bypassed by the first part of the M 54.[99] In 1981 it was still a main road between Ketleybrook and Beveley roundabouts, but only as part of Telford's internal road system.[1]

A westward continuation of the medieval Trench Way[2] entered the parish from the north-east, reached Hadley, and continued via Haybridge[3] to the Buck's Head on Watling Street (in Arleston township).[4] Turnpiked to Newport in 1763,[5] it was disturnpiked in 1867[6] and designated a main road in 1879.[7] In 1983 the Haybridge–Ketleybrook part of Telford's 'north-west district road' was under construction and was intended to supersede the section of the old road from Haybridge to the Buck's Head.

Opposite the Buck's Head a road running south-eastwards via Dawley Bank[8] was in the 18th century the main road from Wellington to Worcester, Gloucester, Bath, and Bristol.[9] Bridgnorth was reached that way via the Shifnal–Bridgnorth road.[10] In 1764 the road was turnpiked from the Buck's Head to Sutton Maddock

and thence towards Dudley as far as the New Inn,[11] Rudge Heath.[12] In Wellington parish its line was superseded by a new road, authorized in 1827, south-eastwards from the new Wellington–Coalbrookdale turnpike road at Lawley to Ball's Hill in Dawley.[13] The new length and its continuation to the New Inn were disturnpiked in 1867[14] and in 1879 were designated a main road only as far as Sutton Maddock,[15] whence the main road from Shifnal took Wellington traffic to Bridgnorth. The Wellington–Bridgnorth route remained a main road in 1983.

An early road crossed the parish in the north, bounding several townships.[16] Presumably a westward continuation of the medieval 'Lubbesty',[17] it was mapped c. 1580 as the way from Lilleshall to Wrockwardine[18] and in 1626 as the Newport–Shrewsbury highway.[19]

Those early thoroughfares were not aligned on Wellington, though Watling Street and its branches were accessible from the town via Shrewsbury Way[20] (later Haygate Road)[21] and Mill Bank. Early roads to the north and north-west, however, left the town centre directly.

In the 16th century the usual northward route from Wellington crossed Dothill township and the Newport–Shrewsbury road, which there delimited Dothill and Wrockwardine parish. Northbound travellers then skirted Bratton village and turned into a road from Admaston to Sleapford (near Crudgington, in Ercall Magna); those travelling north-west, went on to Longdon upon Tern.[22]

By 1726 the route across Dothill township had lost its importance. Travellers north and north-west from Wellington then used an old road that bounded Apley and Dothill townships[23] and crossed the Newport–Shrewsbury road at Shawbirch. Thence northbound traffic went on to Sleapford[24] and travellers to the north-west went west along the Newport–Shrewsbury road to pick up the old route to Longdon. The Wellington–Shawbirch–Crudgington road, with a continuation south via Back Lane and Mill Bank to the Swan on Watling Street, was turnpiked in 1726,[25] disturnpiked in

[89] Cal. Pat. 1334–8, 188.
[90] R. Morden, Map of Salop. [1695].
[91] 12 Geo. I, c. 9.
[92] Trinder, Ind. Rev. Salop. (1981), 91; V.C.H. Staffs. ii. 288; v. 105.
[93] Trinder, op. cit. 148–9.
[94] B.L. Maps, O.S.D. 208 (noting Feb. 1817 that construction was imminent); 6th Rep. Sel. Cttee. Holyhead Rd. H.C. 549, p. 419 (1819), v.
[95] 4th Rep. Sel. Cttee. Holyhead Rd. H.C. 343, pp. 77–8 F2121822), vi; 1st Rep. R. Com. Holyhead Rd. H.C. 305, p. 24 (1824), ix.
[96] 13th Rep. R. Com. Holyhead Rd. H.C. 437, p. 8 (1836), xxxvi.
[97] Ann. Turnpike Acts Continuance Act, 1865, 28 & 29 Vic. c. 107.
[98] Under the Highways and Locomotives (Amendment) Act, 1878, 41 & 42 Vic. c. 77: S.R.O. 560/744.
[99] Below.
[1] T.D.C. Telford Street Plan (1981).
[2] Above, Lilleshall, Communications.
[3] Mentioned 1635: S.R.O. 1224, box 250, deed.
[4] A 'great road' on B. Wood, Map of Salop. [c. 1710].
[5] 3 Geo. III, c. 59.
[6] Ann. Turnpike Acts Continuance Act, 1867, 30 & 31 Vic. c. 121.
[7] Under 41 & 42 Vic. c. 77: S.R.O. 560/744.

[8] Below, Lawley, intro.
[9] J. Rocque, Map of Salop. (1752); 4 Geo. III, c. 81.
[10] Rocque, op. cit.; R. Baugh, Map of Salop. (1808).
[11] 4 Geo. III, c. 81; Baugh, op. cit.; Trinder, Ind. Rev. Salop. (1981), 88.
[12] S.R.O. 1847/18, Claverley tithe map.
[13] S.R.O., dep. plan 219; 7 & 8 Geo. IV, c. 15 (Local and Personal).
[14] 30 & 31 Vic. c. 121.
[15] Under 41 & 42 Vic. c. 77: S.R.O. 560/744.
[16] O.S. Map 1", Index to Tithe Survey [c. 1851], sheet 61 NE.
[17] Above, Lilleshall, Communications.
[18] T.S.A.S. liv, pl. facing p. 258.
[19] S.R.O. 1224/1/1.
[20] Mentioned c. 1676: S.P.L., MS. 2340, f. 47.
[21] The rd. from Haygate to Wellington town mentioned 1681: Barnard MSS., Raby Castle, box 9, abstr. of title, f. 187.
[22] T.S.A.S. liv, pl. facing p. 258; S.R.O. 1224/1/1. The N. portion of the Admaston–Sleapford rd. was indicated by field boundaries in 1839: L.J.R.O., B/A/15, Wrockwardine.
[23] O.S. Map 1", Index to Tithe Survey [c. 1851], sheet 61 NE.
[24] 12 Geo. I, c. 9. Route mapped N. to Shawbirch crossroads in 1626: S.R.O. 1224/1/1.
[25] 12 Geo. I, c. 9; R. Baugh, Map of Salop. (1808).

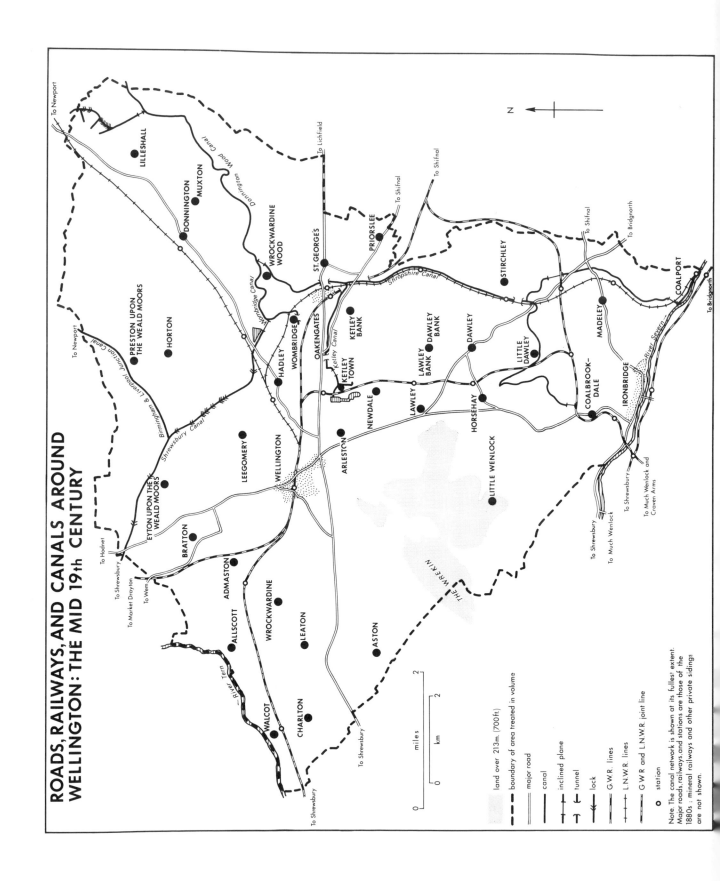

ROADS, RAILWAYS, AND CANALS AROUND WELLINGTON: THE MID 19th CENTURY

To Newport

LILLESHALL

MUXTON

DONNINGTON

Donnington Wood Canal

To Lichfield

WROCKWARDINE WOOD

ST. GEORGE'S

PRIORSLEE

To Shifnal

To Shifnal

To Bridgnorth

STIRCHLEY

To Shifnal

Wombridge Canal

Shropshire Canal

MADELEY

COALPORT

PRESTON UPON THE WEALD MOORS

HORTON

To Newport

Birmingham & Liverpool Junction Canal

Shrewsbury Canal

WOMBRIDGE

OAKENGATES

HADLEY

KETLEY BANK

Ketley Canal

KETLEY TOWN

DAWLEY BANK

DAWLEY

LITTLE DAWLEY

COALBROOK-DALE

IRONBRIDGE

River Severn

To Bridgnorth

LEEGOMERY

NEWDALE

LAWLEY BANK

LAWLEY

HORSEHAY

EYTON UPON THE WEALD MOORS

WELLINGTON

ARLESTON

LITTLE WENLOCK

To Shrewsbury

To Much Wenlock

To Much Wenlock and Craven Arms

To Hodnet

BRATTON

To Shrewsbury

To Market Drayton

To Wem

ADMASTON

WROCKWARDINE

LEATON

ASTON

THE WREKIN

ALLSCOTT

River Tern

WALCOT

CHARLTON

To Shrewsbury

N

miles
2

km
2

0

land over 213m. (700ft.)

boundary of area treated in volume

major road

canal

inclined plane

tunnel

lock

G.W.R. lines

L.N.W.R. lines

G.W.R. and L.N.W.R. joint line

station

Note: The canal network is shown at its fullest extent. Major roads, railways, and stations are those of the 1880s; mineral railways and other private sidings are not shown.

1866,[26] and designated a main road in 1879,[27] which it remained in 1983. Between Watling Street and Shawbirch it was expected to be superseded by Telford's 'north-west district road', then under construction. The route from Wellington via Shawbirch to Longdon and Cotwall (in Ercall Magna) was also turnpiked in 1726; east and south-east of Shawbirch it continued via the Newport–Shrewsbury road and the lane (later called Hadley Park Road) to Hadley, and thence by Hadley Lane (later Hadley Road) to Oakengates.[28] Coalbrookdale castings for Liverpool went in 1816 to the Ellesmere Canal at Edstaston (in Wem),[29] probably through Cotwall. The Cotwall–Oakengates route was disturnpiked in 1865.[30] Its Cotwall–Shawbirch section was designated a main road in 1879[31] and ranked as a secondary road by 1983; by then the rest consisted only of minor roads.

In 1817 a new turnpike road was authorized, to be built southwards from the Swan, on Watling Street, to Coalbrookdale;[32] south of Horsehay it followed an existing route.[33] Disturnpiked in 1875,[34] it became a main road in 1878[35] and so remained in 1983.

Early minor roads led to outlying resources. One ran north from Wappenshall to the Weald Moors.[36] Steeraway Lane[37] (later Limekiln Lane) ascended from Watling Street Hall (later the Old Hall) to the woods and limestone quarries. Rockway Lane[38] led to the Wrekin woods and pastures from Aston. In Walcot a hollow-way[39] descended from the Newport–Shrewsbury road to the mill, where in 1782 subscribers built an elegant stone bridge over the Tern, designed by William Hayward.[40]

Other minor roads linked Wellington with nearby settlements.[41] Wrockwardine Way[42] (later Wrockwardine Road), described in 1691 as the king's highway,[43] led west from the north end of Church Street, with a northward branch across Bullocks bridge[44] called Admaston Way (later Admaston Road) and a southward called Orleton Way[45] (later Orleton Lane). Branches from the Wellington–Shawbirch road served Leegomery, Apley, Wappenshall, and Eyton.[46]

The main roads were much improved from the 1970s under Telford development corporation, with broad new internal roads to link them. The

principal linking road in Wellington parish was the 'north-west district road' from Watling Street (at Ketleybrook), which passed east of Wellington to Shawbirch; it was under construction in 1983. It continued a new road built south from Ketleybrook to the M 54 motorway.[47] The motorway's first completed part (opened 1975)[48] created a southern bypass for Wellington. Work to extend that short length to the M 6 at Essington (Staffs.) was completed in 1983. One purpose of the new roads was to keep through traffic away from Wellington town.

The Shrewsbury Canal, from Wombridge, opened as far as Long Lane (in Wrockwardine) in 1794, having crossed Wappenshall township, and it reached Shrewsbury in 1797.[49] In 1835 it was joined at Wappenshall by the Newport branch of the Birmingham & Liverpool Junction Canal, which thus connected the coalfield canals to the national system.[50] Until the arrival of railways most coalfield companies used Wappenshall as the national outlet for their coal and iron. Rather than negotiate the coalfield canals, however, the producer normally carried goods to Wappenshall by road, there to load them on his own narrowboats. Likewise a wide variety of incoming goods was unloaded at Wappenshall for road distribution in the coalfield.[51] A large warehouse was built there.[52] A major import was fluxing limestone from north Wales; in the 1830s and 1840s thousands of tons reached the coalfield annually through Wappenshall.[53]

From 1849 railways superseded the Wappenhall route except for some local traffic.[54] The Trench–Wappenshall section of the Shrewsbury Canal was disused from 1921. Goods towards Shrewsbury, mostly coal from the Newport branch, used the junction until the Second World War but did not go beyond Longdon upon Tern after 1936. The canals through Wappenshall were formally abandoned in 1944.[55]

In 1849 the Shrewsbury–Wellington line was opened jointly by the Shrewsbury & Birmingham Railway Co. (later G.W.R.) and the Shropshire Union Railways & Canal Co. (later L.N.W.R.), with a station at Wellington, whence in the same year the S.B.R.C. opened a line to Wolverhampton and the S.U.R.C.C. one to Stafford.[56] The latter closed to passengers in 1964[57] but was open

[26] 28 & 29 Vic. c. 107.
[27] Under 41 & 42 Vic. c. 77: S.R.O. 560/744.
[28] 12 Geo. I, c. 9; Baugh, *Map of Salop.*
[29] Trinder, *Ind. Rev. Salop.* (1981), 91.
[30] 28 & 29 Vic. c. 107.
[31] Under 41 & 42 Vic. c. 77: S.R.O. 560/744.
[32] 57 Geo. III, c. 12 (Local and Personal).
[33] Above, Dawley, Communications.
[34] Ann. Turnpike Acts Continuance Act, 1873, 36 & 37 Vic. c. 90.
[35] 41 & 42 Vic. c. 77.
[36] Mapped *c.* 1580: *T.S.A.S.* liv. 298 and pls. facing pp. 258, 274.
[37] Mentioned 1667: S.R.O. 1224, box 250, deed.
[38] Mapped 1817: B.L. Maps, O.S.D. 208. Name deduced from adjoining Rocky Lane leasow (no. 215) and Rockway furlong (nos. 222–3) in S.R.O. 14, tithe appt.; 1856/6.
[39] Mentioned 1583: S.R.O. 112, box 90, ct. r.
[40] Date stone (describing it as Hayward's last work); above, plate 13.
[41] B.L. Maps, O.S.D. 208.
[42] Mentioned 1605: S.R.O. 999/Tt 2.

[43] S.R.O. 1224, parcel 205, ct. bk. 23 Oct. 1691. It then adjoined Honeywall leasow, located from S.R.O. 14, tithe appt. and map (no. 124).
[44] O.S. Nat. Grid SJ 639 124. Mapped 1626: S.R.O. 1224/1/1.
[45] Both mentioned *c.* 1676: S.P.L., MS. 2340, ff. 50, 51.
[46] S.R.O. 665/280; 972, parcel 236, Leegomery and Wappenshall map; 1224/1/1; q. sess. r. 210/85.
[47] T.D.C. *Telford Street Plan and Guide* (1975).
[48] *Shropshire Star*, 11 Dec. 1975.
[49] Trinder, *Ind. Rev. Salop.* (1981), 85.
[50] C. Hadfield, *Canals of W. Midlands* (1969), 164.
[51] Trinder, op. cit. 150–2.
[52] R. Russell, *Lost Canals of Eng. and Wales* (1971), 153; F. Brook, *W. Midlands* (Ind. Arch. of Brit. Isles, i, 1977), 94.
[53] Trinder, op. cit. 147, 150.
[54] Ibid. 152.
[55] Hadfield, *Canals of W. Midlands*, 250–1, 321.
[56] E. T. MacDermot, *Hist. of G.W.R.* ed. C. R. Clinker, i (1964), 181–2; above, plate 9.
[57] R. Christiansen, *W. Midlands* (Regional Hist. of Rlys. of Gt. Brit. vii, 1973), 271.

to goods as far as Stafford until 1966; thereafter it ran only to private sidings at Donnington.[58]

By 1867 branch lines in the coalfield townships afforded direct rail services to Coalbrookdale, Coalport, Craven Arms, and Much Wenlock.[59]

In Wellington township the Wellington & Drayton Railway Co. (later G.W.R.) opened a branch in 1867 from the Shrewsbury–Wellington line to Market Drayton.[60] It closed to passengers in 1963[61] and to all traffic in 1967.[62]

GROWTH OF SETTLEMENT. No archaeological evidence has been found for continuity of settlement sites between the Romano-British and Anglo-Saxon periods, but the possibility of administrative continuity within Wrockwardine hundred has been argued.[63] The name Walcot may have denoted a settlement of Celtic people who remained beyond c. 700,[64] and outside the coalfield there are few names with *leah* to suggest that the Anglo-Saxons found unoccupied land to reclaim.[65]

Wellington, from which the parish took its name, may have been the chief settlement well before 1066. It then had five dependent berewicks.[66] The name may be derived from an unattested personal name *Weola* or possibly from *weoleah* ('sacred grove with a heathen temple').[67] If there was a pre-Christian religious site it may have been where the parish church was built, on a slight knoll.

There is reason to believe that the church, rather than any defensive site or conjunction of early routes, was Wellington's original focus. The only early highways into the town, those from the north and north-west that united on its outskirts,[68] were aligned on and terminated in the Green, a triangular space of c. ⅛ ha., whose south side adjoined the medieval churchyard.[69] That the Green was the original, probably Anglo-Saxon, market place, situated where visitors to the church naturally congregated, is suggested not only by its shape and site[70] but also by its use for cattle fairs in more recent times.[71] Wellington's earliest dwellings were presumably built on its east and west sides. The town seems to have had originally no major road through it, and travellers who did not wish to enter the Green probably bypassed it along Back Lane (later King Street).[72]

In 1086 the inhabitants of the emergent town were few. The recorded population of the whole

manor, including the berewicks, was only 33 including a priest.[73] Nevertheless the town probably grew considerably in the 12th and 13th centuries.[74] Before 1309, probably when the market was granted in 1244,[75] Wellington seems to have been deliberately enlarged on lower ground south of the churchyard, about a new square market place of c. ¼ ha. that was joined to the

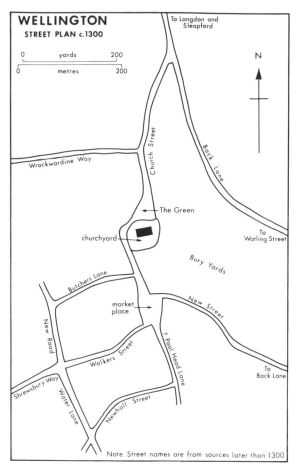

WELLINGTON
STREET PLAN c.1300

Note. Street names are from sources later than 1300

Green by a southern continuation of Church Street.[76] New Street[77] was laid out south-eastwards from the new market place and joined it to Back Lane and thus to Watling Street and the south-east.[78] West of the new market place, not necessarily at the same period, a grid of streets seems to have been laid out, eventually known as Butchers Lane (later Market Street),[79] Walkers

[58] Ibid. 159; C. R. Clinker, *Suppl. to Clinker's Reg. of Closed Stations 1830–1977*, ii (1981), 2; above, Lilleshall, Communications.
[59] Below, Hadley, intro.
[60] Christiansen op. cit. 162.
[61] C. R. Clinker, *Clinker's Reg. of Closed Stations 1830–1977* (Bristol, 1978), 93.
[62] Christiansen, op. cit. 165.
[63] *Jnl. Celtic Studies*, iii. 22–30.
[64] K. Cameron, 'The Meaning and Significance of OE. *walh* in Eng. Place Names', *E.P.N.S. Jnl.* xii. 19–20, 31.
[65] Map on p. 3.   [66] *V.C.H. Salop.* i. 317.
[67] M. Gelling and others, *Names of Towns and Cities in Brit.* (1970), 190.
[68] Above, Communications.
[69] S.R.O. 1931/3.
[70] Cf. H. M. Colvin, 'Domestic Architecture and Town Planning', *Medieval Eng.* ed. A. L. Poole (1958), i. 56–7; M.

Aston and J. Bond, *Landscape of Towns* (1976), 74–5; C. Platt, *Eng. Medieval Town* (1979), 35; above, plate 15.
[71] Below, Econ. Hist. (Mkts. and Fairs).
[72] Mentioned 1661: S.R.O. 1224, box 250, deed. Located from S.R.O. 1931/3.
[73] *V.C.H. Salop.* i. 317.
[74] The reported statement of a 1284 jury that Wellington had only 14 hearths in 1212 (Eyton, ix. 45) is suspect in the light of Domesday.
[75] Below, Econ. Hist.
[76] The High St. mentioned in or near the mkt. pl. in 1601 (S.R.O. 999/Tt 1) may have been that continuation.
[77] Mentioned 1309: *T.S.A.S.* 2nd ser. x. 189. See above, plate 16.
[78] New St. was considered a highway (*via regalis*) in 1349: *T.S.A.S.* 2nd ser. x. 190.
[79] Mentioned 1605: S.R.O. 999/Tt 2. Located from S.R.O. 746/5.

(later Walker) Street,[80] and Newhall Street (later Foundry Road),[81] linked by Tan Bank,[82] Water Lane, and New Road.[83] Walker Street, which led directly from the new market place, had a westward continuation to Watling Street at Haygate and thus to Shrewsbury.[84]

In 1327 Wellington, with Apley, Arleston, Aston, and Dothill, had 29 taxpayers,[85] far fewer than Shrewsbury, Bridgnorth, or Ludlow, and was comparable in size to Market Drayton, Newport, Much Wenlock, and Whitchurch.[86] In 1563 the parish had 219 households,[87] of which Wellington town, with Apley, Arleston, and Dothill, probably had c. 130.[88] The total population apparently doubled in the next hundred years. In 1676 the parish returned 1,544 adults at the Compton census.[89] The town probably accounted for c. 725 of them.[90] Nevertheless Wellington's relative size among Shropshire towns was similar to what it had been in the 14th century.[91] In the 18th century, however, its population grew threefold and in 1801,[92] with c. 4,000 inhabitants,[93] the town was, with Bridgnorth, second only to Shrewsbury.[94]

Expansion before the 19th century hardly transgressed the medieval street plan. The part of New Street nearest the new market place had burgage plots by 1309.[95] Behind them, on the north,[96] lay inclosures called the Bury Yards.[97] By 1800 the street was built up as far as the junction with Back Lane. Other medieval burgage plots apparently fronted the Green (east and west sides), Church Street, the new market place (east side), and Walker Street. No evidence of medieval burgages occurred in other parts of the western grid c. 1800, and occupation of the grid had perhaps never been completed; by 1800 only Walker Street and Tan Bank were fully built up.[98] Some marketing probably took place at an early period at the south end of Church Street, where it entered the new market place.[99] By c. 1600[1] the market place was occupied by two parallel north–south rows of permanent shops, which divided it into Dun Cow Lane (later Duke Street),[2] Crown

Street,[3] and Pig Market (later Bell) Street,[4] and the south end of Church Street became the market place.[5] Most buildings in Wellington earlier than the 18th century were timber-framed, but in the early 19th many were rebuilt or cased in brick.

On the fringes of the town there were small separate settlements by the late 17th century on Back Lane[6] (the central part)[7] and Street Lane[8] (i.e. the Watling Street from Haygate to Wrekin Road).[9] By the 1750s another settlement, called Watling Street,[10] lay at the junction of Mill Bank and the Watling Street.[11] A small settlement called the New Town, on the way from Wellington to Haygate, had been formed by 1739[12] but was never more than a few cottages.[13]

By the early 19th century the most handsome streets were Church Street (with the Green and the Market Place) and Walker Street. New Street, with Nailors Row and Chapel Lane leading off,[14] was the most populous and had many small tradesmen[15] but was poorly built except near the Market Place. Wellington's best houses were detached brick mansions built west and north of the town in the 18th and early 19th century. On the Haygate road was the Mount and on the Wrockwardine road (called Mansion House Lane) where it entered the town[16] lay the Vineyard (built c. 1721)[17] and Parville House. Other detached houses lay at the town's northern extremity near the edge of the Apley demesne.[18]

The town's population continued to grow vigorously in the earlier 19th century, especially in the 1820s and 1830s, and reached 6,084 in 1841.[19] The undeveloped parts of the western grid began to fill, especially with commercial and industrial premises.[20] Walker Street, having the workhouse and parish offices, became the town's administrative focus, in which other offices opened later in the century and in the next.[21] The greatest early 19th-century growth, however, consisted of workmen's housing on the south-east side of the town. New Street was already built up and between 1800 and 1840 more rows were built off

[80] Mentioned 1680: S.R.O. 1224, box 204, ct. r.
[81] Located from (and first mentioned in) S.R.O. 746/5.
[82] Mentioned 1769: S.R.O. 1224, box 253, deed. Probably the former Pool Head La.: below, Public Services.
[83] Located from (and first mentioned in) S.R.O. 746/5. Water La. was later reckoned part of Bridge Rd., New Rd. part of Wrekin Rd.: O.S. Map 1/500, Salop. XXXVI. 9. 18 (1882 edn.).
[84] Above, Communications.
[85] T.S.A.S. 2nd ser. i. 174.
[86] Ibid. 137–8, 149, 173; 2nd ser. iv. 290–1, 325; 3rd ser. vii. 362–4, 370–1.
[87] B.L. Harl. MS. 594, f. 161.
[88] Estimate based on those tns.' proportion of the par.'s 'able' men in 1542: L. & P. Hen. VIII, xvii, pp. 507–8.
[89] T.S.A.S. 2nd ser. i. 85.
[90] Estimate based on the town's proportion of the par.'s households in 1672: Hearth Tax 1672 (Salop. Arch. Soc.), 84–9.
[91] Ibid. 28–30, 52–4, 71–2, 82–4, 162–7, 220–4, 251–3.
[92] V.C.H. Salop. ii. 228.
[93] Estimate based on the town's proportion (with Apley and Dothill) of the par.'s pop. in 1841: ibid.
[94] Ibid. 220, 227.
[95] T.S.A.S. 2nd ser. x. 189.
[96] S.R.O. 14, tithe appt. and map (nos. 693, 861, 870).
[97] Mentioned 1349: T.S.A.S. 2nd ser. x. 190.
[98] S.R.O. 1931/3.
[99] Hence its wide splay, shown on the earliest known street plan (1793): S.R.O. 1224/1/6.
[1] The White Lion, Crown St., has early 17th cent. decoration.
[2] Mentioned 1787: S.R.O. 1224, box 204, ct. r. Located from S.R.O. 1931/3.
[3] Mentioned 1806: S.R.O. 1931/3. Perhaps the former Middle St., mentioned 1710: S.R.O. 999/W 5–6.
[4] Mentioned 1702: S.R.O. 1224, parcel 205, ct. bk. Located (as Swine Mkt.) from S.R.O. 746/5.
[5] Called Market Pl. by 1806: S.R.O. 1931/3. There were 'standings' in front of the Talbot (opposite Butchers La.: S.R.O. 746/5) in 1727 (S.R.O. 1224, box 251, deed).
[6] Inhabited by 1667: par. reg. bur. 2 Apr. (transcript in S.P.L.).
[7] S.R.O. 1931/3.
[8] Inhabited by 1696: S.R.O. 1224, box 250, deed.
[9] S.R.O. 1931/3.
[10] Eng. Topog. (Gent. Mag. Libr.), x. 154.
[11] S.R.O. 1931/3.
[12] S.R.O. 1224, box 251, deed.
[13] e.g. S.R.O. 1931/3.
[14] Ibid.
[15] S.R.O. 3129/5/5.
[16] S.R.O. 1931/3. Later Vineyard Rd.
[17] T.S.A.S. liii. 283.
[18] S.R.O. 1931/3.
[19] V.C.H. Salop. i. 228.
[20] S.R.O. 14, tithe appt. and map.
[21] Below, Local Govt.; Public Services.

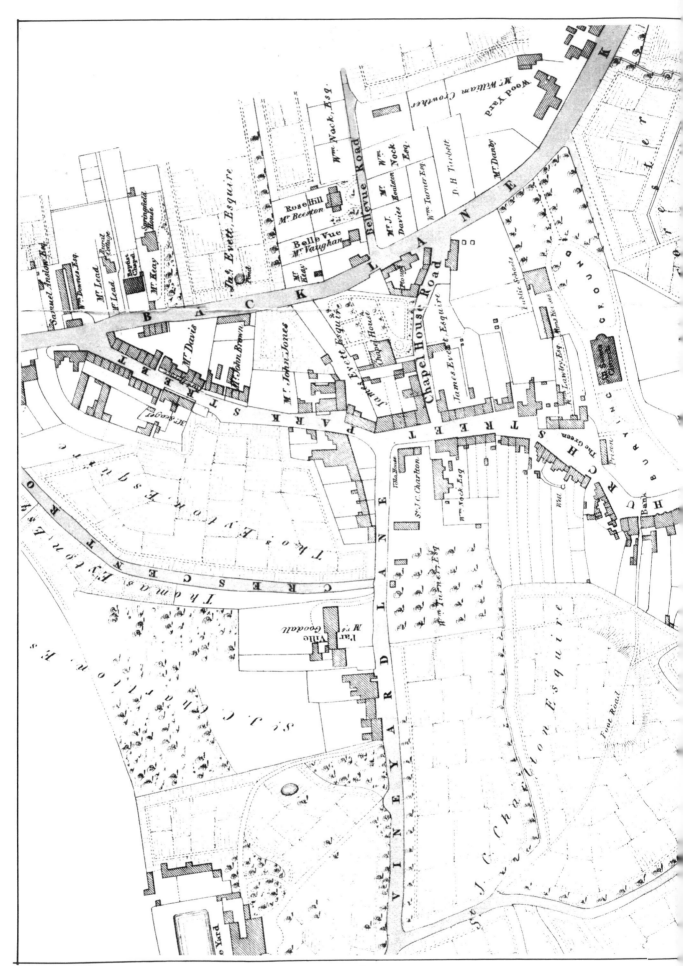

WELLINGTON *c.* 1838 (scale 27 in. to 1 mile). North is at the top.

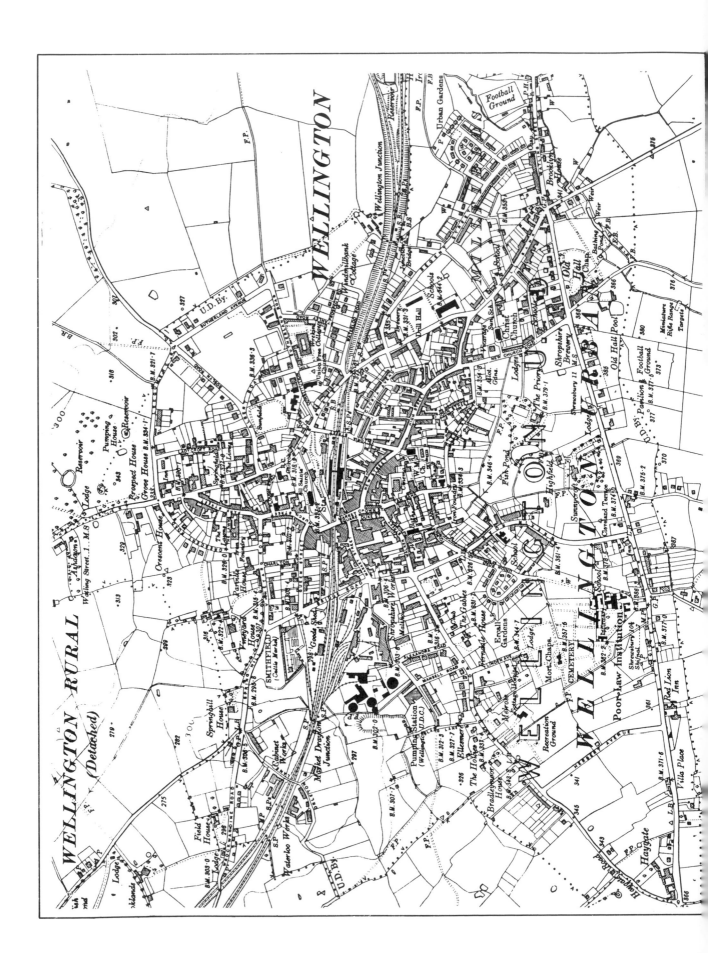

it: for example Burnett's Yard, Jackson's Yard, Brown's Yard, and Corbett's Yard;[22] at the same time Nailors Row and Chapel Lane were extended. In Jarratt's Lane (later Glebe Street), a south-east continuation of Tan Bank, a small group of cottages[23] expanded northwards as Parton (later New) Square and southwards[24] as Bladen's Court.[25]

Wellington's population growth slowed in the mid and late 19th century, with only a short-lived acceleration after the introduction of railways in 1849.[26] In the 1880s the population of the urban sanitary district was falling[27] and in 1898 a local society existed to assist emigrants.[28] The town nevertheless spread markedly from the 1840s,[29] with both new detached middle-class houses at its edges and working-class dwellings of improved design indicating dissatisfaction with the density of occupation that had prevailed until then. In 1897 Lord Forester projected a spacious estate of middle- and working-class houses extending for two miles along the south side of Watling Street,[30] though it was never built.

In the 1890s many of the 18th- and early 19th-century cottages, especially in and around New Street, were fit only for demolition.[31] Replacement became urgent, but speculative developers had little interest in providing the cheap housing needed by people displaced from premises condemned by the urban district council, such as the 40 houses demolished in Nailors Row in 1897.[32] In 1900 the urban district's population was increasing again[33] and the Wellington Workmen's Dwellings Society petitioned the U.D.C. to provide council houses.[34] The council estimated that at least fifty were urgently needed[35] but it decided to build by instalments.[36] The first sixteen, Urban Terrace, designed by T. H. Fleeming, were completed in 1902[37] in Regent Street. No more were built until the period 1920–5, when another 96 were completed nearby.[38] On the west side of the town the council completed Ercall Gardens (40 houses) off Union Road in 1924;[39] 12 were for sale.[40] Notable increases of population in

the 1930s and 1940s, when that of the U.D. (including the area added in 1934) rose by a third, and in the 1950s and 1960s, when it rose by a half,[41] were paralleled by those of the council's housing stock.

The U.D.C. built 213 houses near Orleton Lane in the period 1928–35,[42] including 68 to complement slum clearance.[43] It then turned to land south of Watling Street, mostly in Arleston township. The first 70 council houses there were finished in 1939[44] and a further 578 dwellings (including 36 flats) were built 1947–54.[45] Thereafter the council concentrated on sites on the north-west side of the town and on cleared sites near the centre. Its Park Walls estate (310 houses, 6 of them for sale) was completed 1955–7[46] and the first phase (296 flats, maisonettes, and houses) of the Dothill estate in 1963.[47] The first town-centre council housing, 27 flats (School Court) off King Street, was completed in 1959.[48] By 1963, when the 2,000th council dwelling was opened,[49] the U.D.'s need for council housing had virtually been met[50] and by 1972 only 95 such dwellings had been added.[51] The council's building land was in any case almost exhausted, for further expansion at Dothill was impossible before the Rushmoor sewage works opened[52] in 1975.[53]

From the 1920s private developers provided houses for sale. At first the south and south-west sides of the town were especially favoured,[54] but in 1958 planning consent was given for the largest single private development to date, the Brooklands estate (376 houses) on the north-west.[55] Private development was also encouraged by the U.D.C. at Dothill.[56]

By the mid 20th century Wellington's commercial centre was badly congested. In 1946 the U.D.C. commissioned a redevelopment plan from G. A. Jellicoe[57] but it was not executed.[58] In 1963 the council, in collaboration with property developers,[59] prepared an ambitious plan for a large pedestrian shopping centre, with offices and an inner ring road.[60] It was postponed in 1965 when proposals to extend Dawley new town were

[22] S.R.O. 14, tithe appt. and map. Names are those of O.S. Map 1/500, Salop. XXXVI. 9. 19 (1882 edn.).
[23] S.R.O. 1931/3.
[24] S.R.O. 746/5.
[25] The name in O.S. Map 1/500, Salop. XXXVI. 9. 24 (1882 edn.).
[26] Above, Communications.
[27] V.C.H. Salop. ii. 228.
[28] Hobson & Co. Wellington Dir., Almanack, & Diary (1898), 15.
[29] S.R.O. 14, tithe map; O.S. Map 1/2,500, Salop. XXXVI. 9 (1882 edn.).
[30] Estates Gaz. 6 Feb. 1897; S.R.O. 1681, box 45, plans.
[31] Wellington Jnl. 24 Dec. 1898; 22 July 1899.
[32] Ibid. 24 Mar. 1900.
[33] V.C.H. Salop. ii. 228.
[34] Under the Housing of the Working Classes Act, 1890, 53 & 54 Vic. c. 70: Wellington Jnl. 24 Feb. 1900.
[35] Wellington Jnl. 21 Apr., 8 Dec. 1900.
[36] Ibid. 12 Jan. 1901.
[37] S.R.O., DA 13/100/4, p. 378; /100/5, p. 60; above, plate 43.
[38] DA 13/100/8, pp. 421, 430; /100/10, pp. 16, 82; /100/12, p. 139; O.S. Map 1/2,500, Salop. XXXVI. 9 (1902 and 1927 edns.).
[39] S.R.O., DA 13/100/10, pp. 17, 25; O.S. Map 1/2,500, Salop. XXXVI. 9 (1927 edn.).
[40] S.R.O., DA 13/100/10, p. 54.

[41] V.C.H. Salop. ii. 228; Census, 1971.
[42] S.R.O., DA 13/100/10, p. 420; /100/11, p. 122; /100/12, pp. 75, 139, 342.
[43] Under the Housing Act, 1930, 20 & 21 Geo. V, c. 39.
[44] S.R.O., DA 13/100/14, p. 16.
[45] Ibid. /100/16, 23 Apr. 1947; 3 May 1948; 3 Jan. 1949; /100/17–18, Ho. Cttee. mins. 30 May, 31 Oct. 1949; 30 Jan., 1 May, 3 July 1950; /100/19, p. 11; /100/20, p. 334; /100/21, pp. 52, 200, 307.
[46] Ibid. /100/21, p. 226; 100/22, p. 368; /100/23, pp. 342–3.
[47] Wellington Jnl. 27 Apr. 1963.
[48] S.R.O., DA 13/100/26, p. 425; /100/27, p. 107.
[49] Wellington Jnl. 27 Apr. 1963.
[50] Shrews. Chron. 13 Dec. 1963.
[51] Ed. J. Burrow & Co. Ltd. Wellington Official Guide [1972], 21.
[52] Shropshire Star, 2 Jan. 1973.
[53] Telford Jnl. 7 Aug. 1975.
[54] O.S. Maps 1/2,500, Salop. XXXVI. 9, 13 (1927 and 1939 edns.); SJ 61 SE., SW. (1954 edn.).
[55] S.R.O., DA 13/100/25, p. 421.
[56] Ibid. /100/29, p. 300; /100/30, Gen. Purposes Cttee. rep. 23 Apr. 1963; /100/31, p. 31.
[57] C. H. Simmons, 'Civic Centre in Glebe St., Wellington', Architects' Jnl. cxx. 492–4.
[58] Pevsner, Shropshire, 308.
[59] Wellington Jnl. 3 Aug. 1963.
[60] Ibid. 27 July 1963.

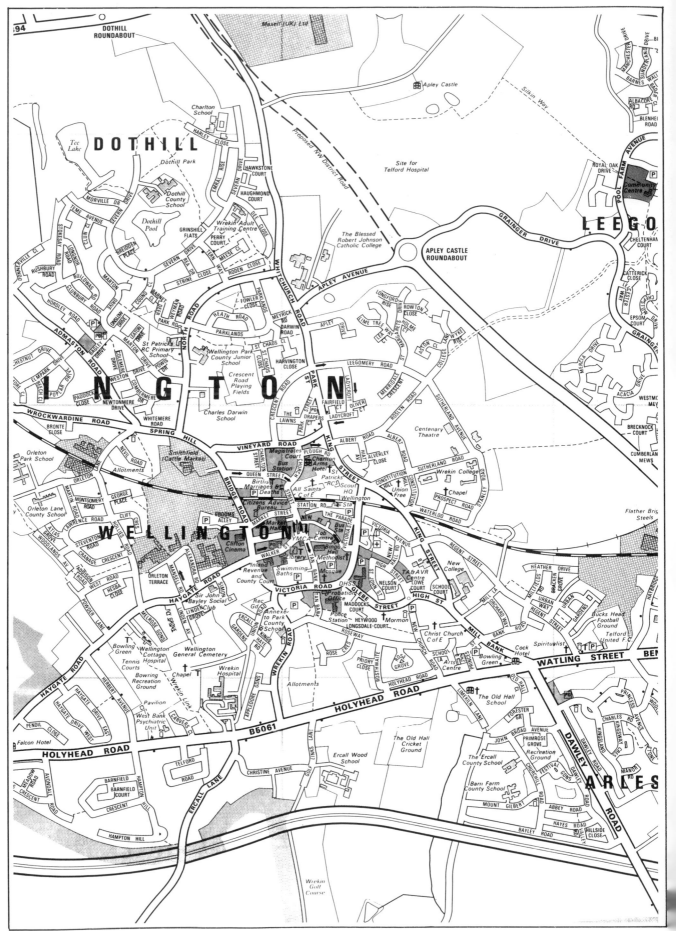

WELLINGTON *c.* 1983

mooted,[61] and then lapsed. In 1969, after Telford new town had been designated and planned, a more conservative scheme was substituted, to preserve and improve existing streets and to pedestrianize them by building the ring road.[62] The road was completed in 1979.[63]

Telford's designation in 1968 did not result in a rapid extension of housing near Wellington. In fact the U.D.'s population fell by nearly a tenth in the 1970s; town-centre redevelopment and a decline of manufacturing may have been causes. In 1981 the former U.D. had 15,691 inhabitants.[64] The development corporation's Leegomery scheme, an extension of Hadley, did not reach completion of its first phase until 1978.[65] Only in 1982 did the corporation complete the first phase (178 dwellings in Eyton C.P.) of its Shawbirch scheme,[66] part of which was planned to be in Dothill township.[67] By then the corporation had a surplus of houses to rent[68] and regarded Shawbirch as its last scheme.[69] There was, however, a demand for private houses.[70] The Shawbirch scheme included private estates,[71] and 128 houses[72] were also provided c. 1980[73] on the north-east side of the town, partly in Apley township.[74]

By the 11th century there were a number of settlements outside Wellington itself but in the later Middle Ages most of them shrank and some virtually disappeared. Apley, Arleston, Aston, Dothill, and Walcot were presumably Wellington manor's five Domesday berewicks. At Apley 12 tenants were named in 1384[75] but the settlement afterwards shrank. No record of its open fields is known and in 1672 only the big house paid hearth tax.[76] At Dothill there was some 13th-century occupation east of the capital messuage[77] and the presence of open fields in the later Middle Ages[78] suggests that there was more than one household. By 1626, however, only the big house remained.[79] Aston and Walcot each had several households in 1672 and each was a small group of farms and cottages in 1983;[80] there had been no significant growth or contraction since the 17th century.

Arleston was said in 1284 to have had 24 hearths in 1212.[81] In 1672 thirteen households paid hearth tax.[82] In 1841, after growth presumably stimulated by mining,[83] there were c. 25 houses, mostly on the inner west side of the

northern square of a two-squared grid of lanes bounded east by Arleston Lane, with Arleston House in the southern square. The unoccupied parts of the grid may have been abandoned medieval house sites. By then the township also had workmen's cottages at New Works (partly in Little Wenlock)[84] and on Watling Street from the Swan eastwards to Ketleysands.[85] Wellington's district under the Improvement Act of 1854 included the settlement round the Swan; in 1903 the U.D. absorbed Bennetts Bank farther east, and in 1934 the rest of Arleston's Watling Street houses.[86] Between 1939 and 1954 the area between Watling Street and Arleston village was filled with council housing and thus absorbed by Wellington town.[87]

Leegomery was *caput* of an extensive manor in 1086.[88] By 1723 it was a nucleated hamlet of four large houses and a few cottages. A field then called the Old Town c. 400 metres SSE. of Leegomery House, may have been the site of houses abandoned in the later Middle Ages.[89] Three farms were amalgamated in 1734[90] and by 1842 there remained only Leegomery House and some cottages.[91] By 1901 Wellington town was beginning to impinge on the township's south-western edge,[92] which was added to the U.D. in 1903.[93] In the late 1970s Telford development corporation's Leegomery housing estate began to cover the township's eastern side, absorbing the old hamlet.[94]

Wappenshall (mentioned 1228)[95] consisted by 1723 of Wappenshall Farm and c. 3 cottages,[96] as in 1983. At the canal junction, opened 1835,[97] there was a public house in 1841 and a house by the wharf.[98] A few cottages were added near the junction before the 1880s[99] but by 1870 the public house was closed[1] and there was no further growth.

SOCIAL AND CULTURAL ACTIVITIES.
From the late 18th century Wellington town shared some of the social advantages of the county's ancient boroughs and had no rival in the country between Shrewsbury and Newport. On the eve of the First World War its attractions probably equalled those of many small market towns. In the mid 20th century, however, the

[61] Ibid. 22 Oct. 1965.
[62] *Shropshire Star*, 11 Nov. 1969.
[63] *Telford Jnl.* 23 Mar. 1979.
[64] 1981 census figs. compiled in S.C.C. Planning Dept.
[65] Below, Hadley, intro.
[66] D. G. Fenter, 'Bldg. Development carried out in Telford by the Development Corp.' (TS. in S.R.O. 3763); T.D.C. *Telford Street Plan* (1981); local inf.
[67] *Telford Jnl.* 16 Dec. 1977.
[68] *Shropshire Star*, 27 Jan. 1982.
[69] Ibid. 15 Dec. 1978.
[70] Ibid. 25 Oct. 1979; local inf.
[71] *Telford Jnl.* 16 Dec. 1977.
[72] *Shropshire Star*, 4 Feb. 1978.
[73] *Telford Jnl.* 19 June 1981.
[74] T.D.C. *Telford Street Plan* (1981).
[75] *Sir Chris. Hatton's Bk. of Seals*, ed. L. C. Loyd and D. M. Stenton (1950), p. 148.
[76] *Hearth Tax 1672*, 84.
[77] SA 719.   [78] Below, Econ. Hist. (Agric.).
[79] S.R.O. 1224/1/1.
[80] *Hearth Tax 1672*, 87–9; above plate 55.

[81] Eyton, ix. 45.
[82] *Hearth Tax 1672*, 86.
[83] Below, Econ. Hist. (Quarries, Mines, and Sandpits).
[84] Above, L. Wenlock, Growth of Settlement.
[85] S.R.O. 14, tithe appt.; 1856/5.
[86] Below, Local Govt.
[87] Below.
[88] Below, Man. and Other Est.
[89] S.R.O. 972, parcel 236, Leegomery and Wappenshall map.
[90] Below, Econ. Hist. (Agric.).
[91] S.R.O. 1856/2.
[92] O.S. Map 6″, Salop. XXXVI. SW. (1903 edn.).
[93] Above, intro.
[94] Below, Hadley, intro.; above, plate 47.
[95] Eyton, vii. 348.
[96] S.R.O. 972, parcel 236, Leegomery and Wappenshall map.
[97] Above, Communications.
[98] S.R.O. 14, tithe appt. (nos. 23–4); 1856/2.
[99] O.S. Map 6″, Salop. XXXVI. NW. (1890 edn.).
[1] *P.O. Dir. Salop.* (1856), 138; (1870), 160 (nil).

urban district council did not respond readily to pressure for increased and improved public leisure facilities.[2] Only with the creation of Telford in 1968 and Wrekin district in 1974 did it become likely that considerable public money would eventually be spent on cultural and social amenities.

Seventeen Wellington alesellers were licensed in 1615 and one at Leegomery.[3] In 1753 there were forty, concentrated in the town and on Watling Street. By 1822 numbers had fallen,[4] but after the Beer Act, 1830,[5] beer retailers proliferated. There were thirty in 1856 (twelve in New Street) as well as thirty public houses and inns.[6] Numbers were not reduced[7] before the Licensing Act, 1904.[8] In 1982 there were c. 25 public houses and licensed hotels in the town and one at Walcot.[9] In the 16th and 17th centuries cards, shovelboard, and nineholes were played[10] and cock fighting continued until the 19th century, but cruel sports did not flourish as in the coalfield.[11] Bowls were popular by the 1840s.[12]

Outdoor recreation was not highly organized before the 19th century. Hunting took place on the Wrekin in the 15th century[13] and a fox hunt occurred near Wellington in 1759.[14] The main annual events for the working class were the Wrekin wakes on the first four Sundays in May; traditionally they ended in a hilltop battle. In the early 19th century they were discouraged by the magistrates and died out.[15] Wellington had a wake on All Saints' Day (1 November), if a Sunday, or the Sunday following,[16] and there was another at Walcot in the 17th century.[17] In the 1770s an annual Whit Monday 'jubilee' was held in the town with an open-air breakfast, a pageant, and an assembly or ball.[18]

By the 1840s there were race meetings for a time and a cricket club.[19] In 1856 the old rowdy sports seemed 'unworthy of the enlightenment of the age' and the 1861 Shropshire Olympian Games, held at Wellington, consisted chiefly of serious athletics.[20] In 1874 Wellington Horticultural Society (founded 1850)[21] began its annual show and athletic sports.[22] Wellington Town football club, formed in 1879, had professional players and its own ground by the 1920s.[23] It was renamed Telford United in 1969.[24] Wellington (late Wrekin) Golf Club had a course at Steeraway until 1909, when it opened one at the Ercall.[25] After the Second World War there were clubs for most outdoor sports.[26]

Although no public recreation ground existed before the 20th century, the Wrekin was much frequented[27] and the grounds of neighbouring mansions were available for outdoor events.[28] In the town the Green (or Bowling Green) was used for open-air gatherings in the 1770s[29] and still in 1854.[30] In 1910 J. C. Bowring's widow left land in Haygate Road for a recreation ground in his memory and the U.D.C. became its trustees in 1926.[31] The council, jointly with other authorities, bought recreational land on the Ercall in 1939,[32] and in 1945 J. T. M. Johnston gave Limekiln Wood to the urban and rural district councils jointly.[33] The U.D.C. was given a playing field in Orleton Lane in 1949[34] and by 1981 Wrekin district council had several other open spaces in the parish.[35]

There was a corps of the Shropshire Volunteer Infantry by 1795. Called the Wellington Fencibles, their successors were disbanded in 1816. A Wellington troop of the Shropshire Yeomanry Cavalry was formed in 1795 and it served continuously in various forms until 1914. A second troop, formed 1798, was absorbed into the first in 1828. From 1859 there was a corps of the Shropshire Rifle Volunteers, later the 4th Bn. King's Shropshire Light Infantry T.A. and later still the 5th Bn. The Light Infantry (V). In 1889 a battery of the 1st Shropshire & Staffordshire Artillery Volunteers opened a drill hall in King Street, which the battery's successors used as H.Q. until 1946. From 1947 Wellington again provided a squadron or troop H.Q. of the Shropshire Yeomanry. In 1983 the King Street hall remained Wellington's T.A.V.R. centre.[36]

By the 1770s regular assemblies were held for subscribers.[37] Large indoor meetings and enter-

[2] Shropshire Star, 22 July, 20 Aug., 3 Nov. 1965; 6 Oct. 1966; 21 Apr. 1969.
[3] S.R.O., q. sess. rec. parcel 254, badgers', drovers', and alesellers' licensing bk. 1613–1714. Some of them may have lived in the coalfield townships.
[4] Ibid. parcels 255–9, regs. of alesellers' recognizances, 1753–1828.
[5] 1 Wm. IV, c. 64.
[6] P.O. Dir. Salop. (1856), 135–7.
[7] S.R.O., q. sess. rec. boxes 147–8, licensing returns 1891–1901.
[8] 4 Edw. VII, c. 23.
[9] Brit. Telecom, Dir. (1982), sect. 303 (YP), pp. 192–7, 252–4.
[10] P.R.O., SC 2/197/96; S.R.O. 112, box 90, nos. 24, 76.
[11] S.R.O. 1224, box 251, deed of 1727; Wellington Townswomen's Guild, Wellington Before Telford (1973), 27. Cf. above, Madeley, Social and Cultural Activities; below, Wombridge, Social and Cultural Activities.
[12] S.R.O. 14, tithe appt. and map (nos. 413, 694, 1145).
[13] S. Shaw, Hist. Staffs. i (1798), 168 and n.
[14] V.C.H. Salop. ii. 166.
[15] Burne, Salop. Folk Lore, 362–3.
[16] Eng. Topog. (Gent. Mag. Libr.), x. 155.
[17] S.R.O. 112, box 90, no. 96.
[18] Shrews. Chron. 27 Feb., 24 Apr., 15 May 1773; 10 May 1777.
[19] V.C.H. Salop. ii. 181 n., 183, 195.
[20] Ibid. 193; S.R.O. 359/6, 9.
[21] S. Bagshaw, Dir. Salop. (1851), 425.
[22] Wellington Jnl. 11 Aug. 1883.
[23] V.C.H. Salop. ii. 198, 200–1; O.S. Map 1/2,500, Salop. XXXVI. 10 (1902 edn.).
[24] Shropshire Star, 19 Apr. 1969.
[25] R. H. K. Browning, Wrekin Golf Club (Golf Clubs Assoc. [1954]), 5 (copy in S.P.L.).
[26] Wellington Before Telford, 34.
[27] S. Bagshaw, Dir. Salop. (1851), 426.
[28] e.g. New Centurion Publishing & Publicity Co. Ltd. Wellington Official Guide, 1950–1, 20; F. Neilson, My Life in Two Worlds, i (1952), 243; E. W. Gladstone, Salop. Yeomanry (1953), 9; J. H. Lenton, Methodism in Wellington, 1765–1982 (Wellington, 1982), 23; S.R.O. 359/9.
[29] Shrews. Chron. 24 Apr., 15 May 1773.
[30] S.R.O., DA 13/297 (S.R.O. 3172/5/9), poster.
[31] S.R.O., DA 13/134 (S.R.O. 3172/8/3/5), file P2(1), clk. of U.D.C. to Char. Com. 19 Feb. 1954; ibid. Min. of Educ. to clk. of U.D.C. 2 Mar. 1954.
[32] S.R.O., DA 13/100/22, p. 155.
[33] Ibid. /100/20, p. 384.
[34] Wellington Jnl. 16 July 1949.
[35] Telford Social Trends, i, ed. J. MacGuire (T.D.C. 1980), 226–7; T.D.C. Telford Street Plan (1981).
[36] G. A. Parfitt, Salop. Militia and Volunteers (Hist. of Corps of K.S.L.I. iv [1970]), 203, 237, 253; Gladstone, Salop. Yeomanry, 8, 24, 190, 441; Kelly's Dir. Salop. (1900), 259; inf. from Mr. G. Archer Parfitt.
[37] Shrews. Chron. 12 Mar. 1774.

tainments were held in the market hall,[38] demolished c. 1800,[39] and in the successive town halls,[40] opened 1848[41] and 1867,[42] until c. 1920.[43] Thereafter the lack of a large public hall was often regretted,[44] though halls belonging to churches, societies, and schools were sometimes available and functions could be held in the town hall's smaller hall[45] and at the privately owned Ercall Assembly Room, Market Street (opened 1880,[46] closed after 1937),[47] Forest Glen Pavilions, below the Wrekin (opened 1889),[48] and Wrekin Hall, Walker Street (opened 1908).[49] The Palais de Danse (later the Majestic ballroom; opened by 1934,[50] closed c. 1969), New Street,[51] and the nearby Town House (opened 1960)[52] were also available for social events.

Cultural societies were not numerous before the 20th century. The infantry volunteers had a band by 1798[53] as did the rifle volunteers in 1861.[54] There was a choral society in 1898[55] and an orchestral and operatic society in the 1930s.[56] A successful town band was remembered in 1973.[57] The Wellington Repertory Theatre Club, formed by 1943,[58] was moribund by 1966[59] and in the 1960s Wellington's cultural attractions were compared unfavourably with those of Oakengates.[60] In 1966, however, the Wellington Arts Association was formed and started an annual festival,[61] forerunner of the Wrekin and Telford Festival.[62] In 1971 the county council let the former Prince's Street school to the Wrekin Arts Association as an arts centre,[63] incorporating a small theatre,[64] and by 1973 the town had musical, choral and operatic, and dramatic societies.[65] A civic society started c. 1979.[66]

The short-lived Alhambra (later Playhouse) variety theatre, Tan Bank, opened in 1927; it became the Rechabite Hall.[67] There were two early cinemas: the Picture Pavilion, Mill Bank,[68] and the Rink Picture Palace, Tan Bank, both opened in 1911. The former closed in 1927.[69] The latter underwent two changes of name before becoming the Grand Theatre in 1914.[70] It became a bingo hall in 1975[71] and had over 2,500 weekly attendances in 1980.[72] The Town Hall cinema, opened in 1920,[73] closed in 1959.[74] From 1975 the Clifton, Bridge Road, opened in 1937,[75] was Telford's only cinema.[76] Like the Grand Theatre it was occasionally used for stage performances.[77] Weekly attendances averaged over 2,600 in 1979,[78] but in 1983 it closed.

The earliest men's social club was perhaps the news room and billiards room established in 1846 at a shop in the Market Place. It had 45 members in 1851[79] but closed after 1856.[80] A mechanics' institute in New Street, registered in 1848, included a library and had c. 70 members in 1851,[81] but by 1856 the town lacked 'any institution for the moral and intellectual elevation of the people'.[82] In 1859, however, the town's most enduring social organization outside the churches was formed, a branch of the Y.M.C.A. It took a lease of the Wrekin Buildings (including the Wrekin Hall) in 1913 and bought them in 1920.[83] In 1983 its wide ranging activities attracted c. 700 people every week.[84] By 1890 Richard Stone had opened a working men's hall[85] and in 1891 there was a Wellington Working Men's Union & Horticultural Society.[86] A working men's club met in King Street in 1900.[87] In the 1920s and 1930s ex-service men used the Comrades of the Great War Club, Haygate Road, and the British Legion.[88] During and after the Second World War the principal men's club was the Sir John Bayley Social Club,[89] which had licensed premises in Haygate Road in 1983.

There were Conservative and Liberal clubs by 1885[90] and a Socialist Society was formed in

[38] S.R.O. 1224, box 252, deed of 1759; P.R.O., RG 31/7, Salop. no. 131; Gladstone, Salop. Yeomanry, 10.
[39] Below, Econ. Hist. (Mkts. and Fairs).
[40] S. Bagshaw, Dir. Salop. (1851), 423; Hobson, Wellington Dir. (1898), 17; Wellington Jnl. 13 Apr. 1957; Wellington Before Telford, 29.
[41] Below, Econ. Hist. (Mkts. and Fairs).
[42] [U. B. M. Rayska,] 'Wellington Mkt.' (TS. [1981]; written for Wellington (Salop) Markets Co. Ltd.), p. 3. Thanks are due to Miss Rayska for providing a copy.
[43] When the main hall became a cinema: below.
[44] Wellington Jnl. 2 May 1947; 4 and 11 Feb. 1966; Shropshire Star, 3 Nov. 1965; Telford Observer, 24 June 1970.
[45] J. Jones & Son, Dir. of Wellington & Dist. (1934), 6.
[46] Date stone.
[47] Jones, Dir. Wellington (1937), 59.
[48] Shropshire Star, 3 Feb. 1979.
[49] Wellington Y.M.C.A. Handbk. 1959-60 (copy in Salop. Librs.).
[50] Jones, Dir. Wellington (1934), 57.
[51] G.P.O. Telephone Dir. (1969), sect. 72, p. 166.
[52] Inf. from Mr. T. Heath, owner in 1960.
[53] Gladstone, Salop. Yeomanry, 9.
[54] S.R.O. 359/6.
[55] Hobson, Wellington Dir. (1898), 11.
[56] Jones, Dir. Wellington (1937), 16.
[57] Wellington Before Telford, 28-9.
[58] Local inf.
[59] Shropshire Star, 1 July 1966.
[60] Ibid. 20 Aug., 3 Nov. 1965; Dawley Observer, 28 May 1969.
[61] Wellington Jnl. 25 Mar., 8 July 1966.
[62] Local inf.

[63] S.C.C. Mins. (Educ.) 1970-1, 359; Telford Observer, 8 Dec. 1971.
[64] Telford Jnl. 28 Jan. 1977.
[65] Wellington Before Telford, 34.
[66] Telford Jnl. 9 Feb. 1979.
[67] F. J. Brown, 'Cinemas of Telford 1910-83' (TS. in possession of Mr. Brown), 6. Mr. Brown is thanked for lending a copy.
[68] The former R.C. chapel: S.R.O. 4050/1, p. 8.
[69] Brown, op. cit. 2-3, 8.   [70] Ibid. 3.
[71] Shropshire Star, 4 Apr. 1975.
[72] Telford Social Trends, i. 213.
[73] Brown, 'Cinemas', 5.
[74] S.R.O., DA 34 (S.R.O. 3279/I), Town Hall file.
[75] Brown, op. cit. 13.
[76] Shropshire Star, 4 Apr. 1975.
[77] S.R.O., DA 34 (S.R.O. 3279/I), Clifton files of 1951-65; Wellington Before Telford, 29.
[78] Telford Social Trends, i. 213.
[79] S. Bagshaw, Dir. Salop. (1851), 424.
[80] P.O. Dir. Salop. (1856), 137.
[81] Orders of Q. Sess. iv. 65; S. Bagshaw, Dir. Salop. (1851), 424.
[82] P.O. Dir. Salop. (1856); S.R.O. 359/9
[83] Shropshire Mag. Nov. 1959, 21, 23, 35.
[84] Inf. from the gen. sec. Wellington & Dist. Y.M.C.A.
[85] S.C.C. Illustr. Official Handbk. (1890), unpaginated (copy in S.R.O.).
[86] Kelly's Dir. Salop. (1891), 461.
[87] Ibid. (1900), 341.
[88] Jones, Dir. Wellington (1934), 2, 12.
[89] New Centurion Publishing & Publicity Co. Ltd. Wellington Official Guide, 1950-1, 20; local inf.
[90] Kelly's Dir. Salop. (1885), 976, 978.

1897.[91] The *Shropshire Labour Reporter*, published in Wellington, was revived in 1904.[92] A Liberal and Labour Association existed *c.* 1912.[93] The Morris Hall, off Church Street, given by J. K. Morris of Shrewsbury in 1929 and rebuilt 1936, was the headquarters of Wrekin divisional (later constituency) Labour party[94] until it moved to Hadley *c.* 1971.[95]

In the 20th century indoor sport was enjoyed at the swimming pool, Walker Street, provided by the U.D.C. in 1910,[96] and at a privately run billiards hall on Tan Bank, opened by 1934,[97] where nationally known players sometimes competed.[98] In 1964 the county council opened the Wrekin Youth Centre at Bennetts Bank.[99] By 1976 Wrekin district council had plans for a combined sports, arts, and community centre south of Walker Street, and in 1981 a new swimming pool was completed.[1]

Newspapers were published in Wellington from 1849 to 1965. In 1849[2] Robert Hobson[3] founded the *Railway Messenger or Wellington Advertiser*, successively renamed the *Wellington Advertiser* in 1850 and the *Shropshire News and Mineral District Reporter* in 1855.[4] In 1854[5] Thomas Leake[6] founded the Conservative *Wellington Journal and General Advertiser*,[7] which absorbed its rival in 1874[8] and became the *Wellington Journal and Shrewsbury News*. From 1874 to 1876 the Liberal *Shropshire Examiner* was published in Wellington.[9] In 1885[10] the owners of the *Shropshire Guardian* (the county's leading Liberal paper) founded the *Wellington Standard*. In 1892, however, the *Journal* absorbed the *Standard* and its Liberal contemporaries published in Shrewsbury,[11] the *Guardian*, *Eddowes's Shrewsbury Journal*, and the *Shropshire Evening News*.[12] The *Wellington Journal*'s circulation grew from 4,550 in 1864 to over 40,000 by 1900[13] and stood at 48,000 in 1965,[14] when it passed from Leakes Ltd. to the Shropshire Star & Journal Ltd. (a subsidiary of the Midland News Association

Ltd.), moved to Ketley, and was renamed the *Shropshire Journal*.[15]

There were circulating libraries in the later 19th century[16] but in 1902 no reading room 'worthy of the name'.[17] In that year the U.D.C. adopted the Public Libraries Act, 1892,[18] and was given the former guardians' and parish offices in Walker Street by H. H. France-Hayhurst of Overley Hall.[19] The library's resources were inadequate by the 1940s[20] and complemented by Boots' and W.H. Smith's subscription libraries,[21] but the county council took it over in 1949[22] and in 1962 an extension was declared open by the poet Philip Larkin,[23] librarian 1943–6.[24] In 1980 the library had the biggest book stock in Telford.[25]

The earliest welfare clubs were the benefit societies recorded in Wellington from the later 18th century. In the later 19th their role passed to local branches of national or county organizations. A Union Society was formed in 1761 at the Bull's Head, and benevolent societies in 1772 and 1774.[26] A freemasons' lodge at the Talbot lasted from 1789 to 1798.[27] At least 15 friendly societies were registered in the earlier 19th century, usually at public houses.[28] A district of the Independent Order of Odd Fellows (Manchester Unity) was established in 1843; the town had three lodges and 506 members in 1898. By then there were two courts of the Ancient Order of Foresters, a lodge of the National United Order of Free Gardeners, and a tent of the Independent Order of Rechabites (Salford Unity),[29] which later had a hall on Tan Bank.[30] Several friendly society branches remained in the late 20th century.[31]

Wellington's three later lodges of freemasons were formed in 1852, 1934, and 1952, and by 1969 lodges from Ironbridge and Oakengates also met in the parish. In that year the five collaborated to open the former Constitution Hill school (bought 1966) as a masonic hall for east Shropshire. The three Wellington lodges had 187 members in 1980.[32]

[91] *V.C.H. Salop.* iii. 346.
[92] Shrews. Socialist Soc. *Salopian Socialist and Labour Annual* (1904), 20 (copy in S.R.O. 4433/1).
[93] S.R.O. 2475/2.
[94] S.R.O. 3251/1, pp. 341, 343–4, 346.
[95] P.O. *Telephone Dir.* (1971), sect. 303, p. 265; (1972), sect. 303, p. 284.
[96] *Shrews. Chron.* 2 Sept. 1910.
[97] Jones, *Dir. Wellington* (1934), 89. It was the former Rechabite Hall: Brown, 'Cinemas', 6.
[98] *Shropshire Mag.* Oct. 1956, 17; local inf.
[99] S.C.C. *Mins. (Educ.)* 1964–5, 103.
[1] *Shropshire Star*, 4 Mar. 1976; *Telford Jnl.* 20 Nov. 1981.
[2] *V.C.H. Salop.* iii. 313 n.
[3] S. Bagshaw, *Dir. Salop.* (1851), 429.
[4] The Times, *Tercentenary Handlist of Newspapers* (1920), 235.
[5] Ibid. 238.   [6] *P.O. Dir. Salop.* (1856), 136.
[7] *V.C.H. Salop.* iii. 313 and n.
[8] The Times, *Tercentenary Handlist*, 235.
[9] *Examiner*, 26 Dec. 1874; 28 Jan. 1876.
[10] The Times, *Tercentenary Handlist*, 281.
[11] Ibid. 273, 278.
[12] *Wellington Jnl.* 2 Jan. 1892; *V.C.H. Salop.* iii. 313, 345.
[13] Inf. from *Shropshire Star* libr., Ketley.
[14] Benn Bros. Ltd. *Newspaper Press Dir.* (1965), 222.
[15] Ibid. (1967), 206; *Wellington Jnl.* 12 Feb. 1965; *Shropshire Jnl.* 19 Feb. 1965; below, Ketley, Econ. Hist.

(Newspaper Printing and Publishing).
[16] e.g. *P.O. Dir. Salop.* (1856), 136; Review Publishing Co. *Industries of Salop. (and District) Business Review* [1891], 39 (copy in S.R.O.).
[17] *Shrews. Chron.* 18 July 1902.
[18] 55 & 56 Vic. c. 53: S.R.O., DA 13/100/5, p. 62.
[19] *Shrews. Chron.* 6 June, 22 Aug. 1902.
[20] P. Larkin, 'Single handed and Untrained', *Libr. Assoc. Record*, lxxix. 531, 533, 539.
[21] *Wellington Before Telford*, 23.
[22] *S.C.C. Mins. (Educ.)* 1948–9, 170.
[23] *Wellington Jnl.* 15 Sept. 1962.
[24] *Libr. Assoc. Record*, lxxix. 531, 533, 539.
[25] *Telford Social Trends*, i. 216.
[26] S.R.O., q. sess. rec. parcel 285, friendly socs. reg.
[27] H. Temperton, *Hist. of Craft Freemasonry in Salop. 1732–1982* [1982], 21–2.
[28] S.R.O., q. sess. rec. parcel 285, friendly socs. reg.; Registrar of Friendly Socs. *List of Friendly Socs. in Co. of Salop, 1793–1855* (H.M.S.O. 1857; copy in S.R.O.).
[29] Hobson, *Wellington Dir.* (1898), 35–6.
[30] The former Playhouse theatre: Brown, 'Cinemas', 6.
[31] *Wellington Before Telford*, 35.
[32] B. C. W. Johnson, *Brief Hist. of St. John's Lodge No. 601, Meeting at Wellington, Salop. 1852–1952* [c. 1952], 12, 21, 41, 43, 62; Temperton, *Freemasonry in Salop.* 78, 81, 89, 108; inf. from Mr. J. L. McFall, member of St. Milburga No. 1145 Lodge of Freemasons Council, 1966.

A savings bank flourished 1818–89[33] and had 692 depositors in 1851.[34] The Wellington, Dawley Green, Ketley, & Shropshire Building Society, registered 1851,[35] had 126 members in 1886[36] but closed *c.* 1893.[37]

In the late 19th century welfare work was done by the Ladies' Association for the Care of the Friendless, to rescue delinquent girls, and a division of the Shropshire Needlework Guild.[38] A Rotary Club started in 1929.[39] In 1961 an Old People's Welfare Committee built a social centre, the Belmont Hall, off New Street,[40] and in the late 20th century the usual welfare organizations had local branches.[41]

MANORS AND OTHER ESTATES. In 1066 *WELLINGTON*, with five berewicks, was held by Edwin, earl of Mercia (d. 1071). Roger of Montgomery, created earl of Shrewsbury by 1074, was tenant in chief by 1086, when Great Dawley was dependent.[42] Wellington was presumably forfeited to the Crown by Earl Roger's son Robert of Bellême in 1102.[43]

From 1177 to 1189 the king assigned lands in Wellington to Simon son of Simon, keeper of Stretton castle, with an annual allowance from Wellington's revenues. From 1192 to 1194 William and James, sons of Simon (presumably the abovenamed), were assigned Crown lands in Wellington on similar terms, as was Gwion, son of Jonas of Powys, from 1194 to 1210 when the manor was granted in fee farm to Thomas of Erdington, the sheriff.[44] From 1211 Thomas held by serjeanty and from 1212 by the service of one knight. He died in 1218 and in 1221 his son Giles[45] (d. *c.* 1268) was lord. Giles was succeeded by his son Sir Henry (d. *c.* 1282). Sir Henry's son, also Henry, was a minor,[46] and by 1283 Hugh Burnell (d. 1286) was lord. His widow Sibyl (d. by 1306) held Wellington in dower and was succeeded by their grandson Edward Burnell (d. 1315).[47] Until the forfeiture of Francis, Viscount Lovel, in 1485 the descent followed that of Acton Burnell.[48] In 1514 the Crown granted the manor to Sir Christopher Garneys of Kenton (Suff.) (d. 1534)[49] and

Jane his wife, in socage.[50] They had no children[51] and by 1550 the reversion had been settled on Michael Garneys, their nephew. In that year he sold the reversion to Arthur Dymoke and Robert Rychers, who sold it later in the year for £520 to Robert Allen[52] (d. after 1566),[53] a Shrewsbury draper. In the same year Allen sold the reversion of a moiety to John Steventon.[54] On Dame Jane's death *c.* 1551[55] Allen and Steventon came into possession.[56] Steventon (d. 1560) was succeeded by his son Richard[57] (d. without male issue 1587), who left the moiety to his nephew William Steventon.[58] In 1602 William re-unified the manor by buying the other moiety from Edward and Elizabeth Bridgman of Aston Eyre, Elizabeth being the granddaughter and legatee of Robert Allen.[59] Steventon (d. 1647)[60] was succeeded by his grandson Richard Steventon, who died in 1659 having left the manor for sixteen years to his aunts Eleanor Chelwood, Elizabeth Mytton, Mary Haughton, and Jane Lippesley, and to Cresswell Tayleur, and the heir of Abigail Sweetenham, in equal shares, with remainder to Richard's half-brother William Forester[61] (kt. 1689).[62] The Foresters had held land in Wellington township since the early 15th century.[63] After the death of Sir William's father, Francis, in 1692, the manor descended with Little Wenlock.[64] In 1842 Lord Forester, lord of the manor,[65] owned 110 a. in Wellington township[66] but by 1910 his descendant had virtually no property there.[67] No later record of the lordship has been found.

Wombridge priory held a virgate in Wellington township but alienated it *c.* 1230.[68]

Sir John Charlton (d. 1380) of Apley held four burgages, ½ a. of meadow, and ½ virgate of arable in Wellington of the lord of the manor.[69] The Charltons' Wellington estate comprised *c.* 175 a. *c.* 1676.[70] In 1842 St. John Chiverton Charlton had only 78 a. in the township[71] but in 1910 his heir Sir Thomas Meyrick owned over 100 a. of agricultural land there and many urban sites.[72]

By 1535 a burgage in Wellington belonged to St. Bartholomew's college, Tong.[73]

Edward Cludde (d. 1614) had an estate in Wellington[74] and in 1840 Edward Cludde of Orle-

[33] S.R.O. 119/41, rules of 1825; 507/3.
[34] R. M. Baxter, 'A Hist. of Wellington' (TS. 1949), 53 (copy in S.P.L.).
[35] *Orders of Q. Sess.* iv. 86.
[36] I. Gregory, 'E. Salop. Coalfield and the "Gt. Depression" 1873–96' (Keele Univ. M.A. thesis, 1978), 181.
[37] *Kelly's Dir. Salop.* (1891), 461.
[38] Hobson, *Wellington Dir.* (1898), 15, 25.
[39] *Shropshire Star*, 17 Feb. 1979.
[40] *Wellington Jnl.* 11 Nov. 1961.
[41] *Wellington Before Telford*, 34–5.
[42] *V.C.H. Salop.* i. 317; iii. 7.
[43] Ibid. iii. 10. It was in Crown hands by 1169: *Pipe R. 1169* (P.R.S. xiii), 110.
[44] For him see *V.C.H. Salop.* iii. 13.
[45] Eyton, ix. 41–3.
[46] *Plac. de Quo Warr.* (Rec. Com.), 680; S.P.L., MS. 2788, pp. 340–1, 343. In 1374 the Burnell title was said by Thos. of Erdington to derive from a demise by one of those Henrys to a Rog. Sprenchose: *Pedigrees from the Plea Rolls*, ed. G. Wrottesley (1905), 113.
[47] Eyton, viii. 44–5; *Cal. Inq. p.m.* v, pp. 393–4.
[48] *Cal. Pat. 1313–17*, 612; *Cal. Inq. p.m.* viii, p. 495; xv, pp. 288–9; *Cal. Pat. 1476–85*, 32; *Cal. Inq. p.m. Hen. VII*, i, p. 211. Cf. *V.C.H. Salop.* viii. 7.
[49] *D.N.B.*
[50] *L. & P. Hen. VIII*, i (2), p. 1400.

[51] *Suff. Manorial Fams.* ed. J. J. Muskett, i (Exeter, priv. print. 1900), 190.
[52] Barnard MSS., Raby Castle, abstr. of writings, pt. 4, f. 262.
[53] P.R.O., C 142/145, no. 33.
[54] S.R.O. 1681, box 44, deed.
[55] *Suff. Manorial Fams.* i. 190.
[56] In possession 1553: Barnard MSS., Raby Castle, abstr. of writings, pt. 5, f. 315.
[57] P.R.O., C 142/131, no. 190.
[58] Ibid. /218, no. 41.
[59] S.R.O. 1681, box 44, deed.
[60] *S.P.R. Lich.* viii (1), 28.
[61] S.P.L., Deeds 5658.
[62] W. A. Shaw, *Kts. of Eng.* (1906), ii. 265.
[63] S.R.O. 625, box 11, deed of 1433.
[64] S.R.O. 1224, box 268, deed of 1714; box 270, deed of 1735; box 272, will of 1805; box 291, wills of 1st and 2nd barons, 1821 and 1872; 1681, box 36, abstr. of title of 1918. Cf. above L. Wenlock, Man. and Other Est.
[65] S.R.O. 1224, box 206, maț ct. presentments.
[66] S.R.O. 14, tithe appt. His father had sold 110 hos. and over 230 a. there in 1822: *Shrews. Chron.* 13 Sept. 1822; S.R.O. 1224, box 175, acct.
[67] S.R.O. 4044/83–5.
[68] Eyton, ix. 45.
[69] *Cal. Inq. p.m.* xv, pp. 135–6.
[70] S.P.L., MS. 2340, ff. 46–72.
[71] S.R.O. 14, tithe appt.
[72] S.R.O. 4044/83–5.
[73] *Valor. Eccl.* (Rec. Com.), iii. 196; P.R.O., E 318/740.
[74] P.R.O., C 142/337, no. 102.

ton owned 97 a. in Wellington township.[75] In 1910 his descendant Col. E. W. Herbert owned a considerable estate there.[76]

DOTHILL is presumed to have been one of Wellington's berewicks in 1066;[77] it was still subject to that manor's court leet and court baron in 1823.[78] In 1248 Giles of Erdington, lord of Wellington, enfeoffed John de Praères with a carucate at Dothill for the service of ⅛ knight.[79] A John de Praères held the manor of Dothill in 1292[80] but by the late 14th century the Horton family seems to have been in possession. It was alleged in 1481 that Isabel, daughter and heir of John, son of a John de Praères of Dothill, had married Philip Horton, said to have held Dothill *temp.* Edward III.[81] John Horton of Dothill was a tax collector in 1383, as was Richard Horton of Dothill in 1419 and 1440.[82] It was said in 1623 that Richard's daughter and heir, Alice, married William Steventon *c.* 1431. From him Dothill descended from father to son until 1587, the following being lords:[83] William (II) (fl. 1473–1507),[84] Richard, John (d. 1560),[85] and Richard (1560–87). The last named left it to his nephew William[86] (d. 1647).[87] Thus from 1602 Dothill descended with Wellington manor, except that life tenancies were devised to Richard Steventon's mother Mary Forester (1659–61) and to George Townshend Forester (1811–45).[88] In 1917 Lord Forester was lord of the manor and owned most of the township[89] but by 1922 the chief landowner was Ernest Groom.[90] He died unmarried[91] and by 1952 most of the estate belonged to H. F. Hodgson,[92] who sold 197 a. to Wellington urban district council in 1956.[93]

In the later Middle Ages Dothill house occupied the north-west angle of a rectangular moat *c.* 50 metres by *c.* 70 metres. In 1626 it consisted of a five-bayed north–south range (with projecting two-storeyed porch on the east), incorporating a three-bayed hall (originally open) with a tall east-facing oriel at its solar end. Opposite the oriel a west-projecting wing had been added, and beyond the service end the main range had been extended southwards. The moat had been partly filled in. Agricultural buildings lay to the north.

In the grounds was an 'arbour' to the east and a pool to the west.[94] By 1734, and probably before 1726,[95] about 7 ha. of formal gardens surrounded the house, mostly on the west, providing vistas of nearby churches and mansions. Southwards the pool was formalized into a canal with a grassed amphitheatre beyond. The moat had been filled in except for the south arm, also made into a canal.[96] The formal gardens reverted to grass in the later 18th century.[97] Between 1763 and 1765[98] the house received a north extension in brick,[99] of five bays and three storeys.[1] In the earlier 19th century the rest was demolished, and the building of the 1760s was attached by 1841[2] to a former dairy[3] nearby, a brick building that had been standing since the early 17th century.[4] The house thus formed was demolished *c.* 1960[5] but in 1982 vestiges of the moat and of the garden walls remained.

APLEY was presumably one of the berewicks belonging to Wellington in 1066.[6] It was later termed a manor but was held of the lords of Wellington manor[7] and remained subject to the Wellington court leet and court baron in 1818.[8] John de Praères of Dothill was a freeholder in Apley in 1282.[9] Apley belonged to Sir Alan of Charlton (d. 1360)[10] by 1317[11] and later to his grandsons Sir John Charlton (d. 1380)[12] and Thomas Charlton (d. 1386).[13] In 1384 Thomas granted the manor to Sir John Atwood for life.[14] Atwood died in 1391 and it reverted to Thomas's son Thomas, a minor.[15] Thomas died a minor in 1397 when his coheirs were his sister Ellen and Thomas of Knightley, son of his sister Anne, who had married William of Knightley. Ellen died without issue in 1399, leaving Thomas, a minor, as sole heir.[16] Thomas received seisin in 1417[17] and by 1428 had assumed the surname Charlton.[18] He died in 1460.[19] Apley then descended from father to son until 1532, the following being lords: Robert (d. 1473),[20] Richard (d. *c.* 1522),[21] and William (d. 1532).[22] William's grandson Francis Charlton (d. 1557)[23] succeeded him[24] and, on the expiry of his widow's life interest, was followed successively by his sons William (d. 1566) and

[75] S.R.O. 14, tithe appt.
[76] S.R.O. 4044/83–5.
[77] Eyton, ix. 54.
[78] S.R.O. 1224, box 206, estreat of ct. r.
[79] Eyton, ix. 60–1.
[80] *Plac. de Quo Warr.* (Rec. Com.), 680.
[81] Wrottesley, *Pedigrees from the Plea Rolls*, 456–7.
[82] *Cal. Fine R.* 1383–91, 19; 1413–22, 301; 1437–45, 146.
[83] *Visit. Salop. 1623*, ii (Harl. Soc. xxix), 445.
[84] Wrottesley, *Pedigrees from the Plea Rolls*, 456; S.P.L., MS. 2795, p. 227.
[85] P.R.O., C 142/131, no. 190. [86] Ibid. /218, no. 41
[87] *S.P.R. Lich.* viii (1), 28.
[88] *T.S.A.S.* 4th ser. vii. 147–9; S.R.O. 1224, box 272, Geo. Forester's will; Burke, *Peerage* (1938), 1035.
[89] *Kelly's Dir. Salop.* (1917), 265.
[90] Ibid. (1922), 273; (1941), 275.
[91] Inf. from Mr. A. P. Baggs.
[92] S.R.O., DA 13/100/19, p. 207.
[93] Ibid. /100/24, pp. 85, 162.
[94] S.R.O. 1224/1/1, above, plates 3, 50.
[95] Above, Communications (Roads).
[96] S.R.O. 1224/1/2, above, plate 48.
[97] Ibid. /1/3, 6.
[98] S.R.O. 1224, box 299, acct. bk. of Wm. Haycock's work.
[99] *T.S.A.S.* 4th ser. vii. 149.
[1] Bodl. MS. Top. Salop. c. 2, p. 199.
[2] S.R.O. 1224/1/7; 1856/1.
[3] S.R.O. 1224/1/2.
[4] *T.S.A.S.* 4th ser. vii. 149, which refers to a date stone 1628. A large bldg. already occupied the site in 1626: S.R.O. 1224/1/1.
[5] S.R.O., DA 13/100/28, p. 68.
[6] Eyton, ix. 54.
[7] *Cal. Inq. p.m.* xv, pp. 135–6.
[8] S.R.O. 1224, box 206, estreat of ct. r.
[9] Eyton, ix. 61.
[10] *T.S.A.S.* liii. 258.
[11] *Cal. Chart. R.* 1300–26, 370.
[12] *Cal. Inq. p.m.* xv, pp. 135–6.
[13] P.R.O., C 137/67, no. 149; Wrottesley, *Pedigrees from the Plea Rolls*, 224.
[14] *Sir Chris. Hatton's Bk. of Seals*, ed. L. C. Loyd and D. M. Stenton (1950), p. 148.
[15] *Cal. Close*, 1402–5, 22–3.
[16] P.R.O., C 137/67, no. 149; Wrottesley, *Pedigrees from the Plea Rolls*, 224.
[17] *Cal. Close*, 1413–19, 393.
[18] L.J.R.O., B/A/1/9, f. 99v.
[19] *N. & Q.* 9th ser. xi. 131.
[20] Ibid.
[21] *Visit. Salop. 1623*, i (Harl. Soc. xxviii), 101.
[22] Ibid.; P.R.O., C 142/247, no. 32; *L. & P. Hen. VIII*, vi, p. 141.
[23] *T.S.A.S.* liii. 266.
[24] *L. & P. Hen. VIII*, vi, p. 141.

Andrew[25] (d. 1617).[26] The estate then passed from father to son until 1802, the following being lords: Francis (d. 1642),[27] Francis (d. 1698), John (d. 1720), St. John (d. 1742), St. John (d. 1776), and St. John (d. 1802). From the last named it passed successively to his brother William (d. 1838) and to William's son St. John Chiverton. At his death in 1873 St. John Chiverton Charlton was succeeded by his son Thomas, who had assumed the surname Meyrick in 1858. Sir Thomas (cr. bt. 1880) died in 1921 and Apley passed to his third son Rowland Francis (d. 1953), whose brother Walter Thomas died later in 1953.[28] The estate passed to W. T. Meyrick's son Walter James Charlton, who sold it in 1971 to Telford development corporation, the owner in 1981.[29]

Apley Castle was built c. 1327 following licence to crenellate,[30] perhaps on or near the site of an earlier building.[31] It included a 14th-century first-floor chapel, of which a piscina and other features were *in situ* in 1981, and a gatehouse, and was walled and probably moated. In the early 17th century the house was converted and greatly enlarged, but it was partly dismantled after capture by royalist forces in 1644[32] and restored after the Civil Wars.[33] A new house designed by Joseph Bromfield was built 1792–4[34] a little to the north-west, and the former house was converted into a stable block,[35] which remained in 1981. The new house, of brick, had seven bays and two and a half storeys and faced north-west, on which front was a stone portico of four unfluted giant Ionic columns. In 1856 the house was greatly enlarged at the rear to create an imposing new front facing south-east. The new work was in an eclectic style, mainly of brick with a stone portico of eight columns.[36] The former house was surrounded by trees in the early 17th century,[37] as was the latter one in the early 19th.[38] After 1856 St. John Chiverton Charlton had the woods extended, and created ornamental gardens on the north-west side.[39] By 1900 avenues had been planted from the house north-east and south-east to the estate boundaries.[40] W. J. C. Charlton-Meyrick sold the house in 1954[41] and it was demolished c. 1955.[42] The north-west portico was re-erected near Hodnet Hall in 1970.[43]

ARLESTON, termed a manor by 1317,[44] is believed to have been one of Wellington's berewicks in 1066[45] and was reckoned part of Wellington manor in 1383.[46] A substantial part of the land there descended with Wellington manor,[47] to whose great court Arleston was subject in 1345.[48] Lord Forester was virtually sole landowner in 1842,[49] but in 1918 the 6th baron sold the estate, including Arleston House farm, in separate lots to the sitting tenants or by auction.[50]

Arleston Manor (formerly Arleston House) is timber-framed but much of the exterior has been rendered and simulated framing painted on the plaster. The plan is of a late 16th-century[51] front range, facing south, with a central entry against the chimney stack, and behind it a contemporary shorter parallel range in which the larger room has a fireplace against the main stack. The interior retains a quantity of late 16th- and early 17th-century panelling, much of it reset, and two moulded plaster ceilings of similar date, and one of them has on the underside of a beam the badges of local families. The house was restored early in the 20th century, when a number of features in imitation of the original style were introduced, and again c. 1979[52] when the timberwork of the eastern elevation was exposed and restored.

Among other estates in Arleston township had been 40 a. granted by Henry II to Seburga of Hadley, to which Roger Corbet, her great-great-grandson, proved his title in 1253.[53] John Forester (d. 1591) and his heirs, lords of Wellington hay, held an estate of 43 a. at Arleston in free socage of the manor of Wellington,[54] which the Foresters themselves held from 1659.

In 975 King Edgar granted *ASTON* to his *minister* Ealhhelm.[55] In 1066 it was probably one of the berewicks of Wellington[56] and in 1190 was a member of that manor.[57] The Empress Maud granted Aston to Shrewsbury abbey c. 1144 but Henry II, as lord of Wellington, deprived the monks c. 1167. Richard I restored it to them by charter in 1190 but they did not regain full possession until c. 1195.[58] Aston thereafter remained abbey property until surrendered to the Crown in 1540.[59] By the later 13th century at least parts of the township lay within the manor of Eyton on Severn.[60] In 1540 the Crown sold Aston to Thomas Bromley (kt. by 1546)[61] to hold as a

[25] P.R.O., C 142/786, no. 67.
[26] Ibid. /361, no. 146.
[27] Ibid. /786, no. 67; T.S.A.S. liii. 271.
[28] T.S.A.S. liii. 280–91; Burke, *Peerage* (1970), 1803.
[29] Inf. from the archivist, T.D.C.
[30] *Cal. Pat.* 1327–30, 145.
[31] *T.S.A.S.* liii. 259.
[32] Ibid. l. 163.
[33] J. B. Blakeway, *Sheriffs of Salop.* (Shrews. 1831), 134. Descr. based on S.R.O. 625, box 20, inventories of 1659, 1663; Bodl. MS. Top. Salop. c. 2, ff. 66–7 (drawings of 1730).
[34] S.R.O. 625, box 20, certif. of completion; box 21, agreement of 1791.
[35] *T.S.A.S.* liii. 289.
[36] F. Leach, *County Seats of Salop.* (Shrews. 1891), 55–6; Pevsner, *Shropshire*, 59.
[37] S.R.O. 1224/1/1.
[38] S.R.O. 1856/2.
[39] Leach, *Co. Seats*, 55–6; O.S. Map 1/2,500, Salop. XXXVI. 5 (1882 edn.).
[40] O.S. Map 6″, Salop. XXXVI. NW. (1902 edn.).
[41] *Shrews. Chron.* 8 Oct. 1954.
[42] S.R.O. 711/1.
[43] Barbara Jones, *Follies and Grottoes* (1974), 277–8.

[44] *Cal. Pat.* 1313–17, 612.
[45] Eyton, ix. 54.
[46] *Cal. Inq. p.m.* xv, pp. 288–9.
[47] S.R.O. 1681, box 44, deed of 1550.
[48] S.R.O. 1224, box 204, ct. r.
[49] S.R.O. 14, tithe appt. Eight others had 1½ a. between them.
[50] S.R.O. 1681, box 44, sale plans and draft deeds; parcel 46, sale partic. Conveyance of the auctioned lots was completed in 1919.
[51] Dates 1614 and 1630 formerly on the E. gables were probably added in the 19th cent.
[52] *Shropshire Star*, 19 Sept. 1979; *W. Midlands Mag.* Nov. 1979, 58–9.
[53] Eyton, vii. 354–6.
[54] *T.S.A.S.* 4th ser. vii. 151.
[55] *Cart. Sax.* ed. Birch, iii, no. 1315.
[56] Eyton, ix. 54.
[57] *Pipe R.* 1190 (P.R.S. N.S. i), 124.
[58] *Cart. Shrews.* i, pp. 50–1, 54–5.
[59] *V.C.H. Salop.* ii. 36.
[60] Eyton, viii. 281; *T.S.A.S.* xi. 419; B.L. Add. MS. 6165, f. 43 and v.
[61] Cf. Shaw, *Kts. of Eng.* ii. 58; *Hist. Parl., Commons*, 1509–58, i. 508.

member of his manor of Eyton on Severn,[62] to which it still owed suit in 1810.[63] At his death in 1555 Aston passed with Eyton to his daughter Margaret[64] and her husband Richard Newport[65] (kt. 1560, d. 1570). At Dame Margaret's death in 1598[66] Aston passed with Eyton to their son Francis[67] (kt. 1603)[68] and thereafter followed the descent of Harley manor.[69]

Aston Hall, presumably the capital messuage of the Newports' Aston estate,[70] is probably late 16th- or early 17th-century in origin and the much altered back range, which is timber-framed, contained the hall and service end. Part of an original painted plaster wall of a first-floor room survives. In the late 17th century the parlour end was rebuilt in brick as a two-roomed cross wing and a new staircase with turned balusters was inserted. Most of the fenestration was renewed in the mid or late 19th century when the roof was partly reconstructed and minor additions were made.

About 1280 Richard of Charlton had land in Aston,[71] and Sir John Charlton (d. 1374) held a messuage and a virgate of Shrewsbury abbey. His widow Joan (d. 1397) held it in dower[72] and their son John (d. 1401) succeeded her.[73] The estate seems to have descended thereafter with Charlton (in Wrockwardine)[74] until 1588, when Edward Grey sold Charlton and his Aston estate (by then regarded as appurtenant to Charlton) to Francis Newport.[75] From 1598 it descended with the estate that Newport inherited from his mother.[76] A 16th-century claim by the Vernons to the former Charlton estate[77] seems to have been dropped in 1611.[78]

In 1548 Edward, Lord Grey, leased an estate at Aston to Robert Pemberton of Aston[79] (d. 1553). It was held by Pemberton's grandson Edward Pemberton at his death in 1617.[80] Later the family seems to have acquired a freehold. In 1840 the Pembertons' heir Edward Cludde of Orleton owned 511 a. at Aston and was the only substantial landowner besides the duke of Cleveland.[81] In 1983 the heirs of Cludde and Cleveland, the earl

of Powis and Lord Barnard, remained the principal landowners.[82]

WALCOT, probably a berewick of Wellington in 1066,[83] was granted to Haughmond abbey by both the Empress Maud in 1141 and King Stephen, and Maud's grant was confirmed by Duke Henry in 1153.[84] Walcot was said in 1255 to have been taken out of Wellington manor by Henry II.[85] Termed a manor by 1317,[86] it was held in chief by Haughmond until surrendered to the Crown in 1539.[87] In 1544 the Crown sold Walcot to Sir Rowland Hill[88] (d. 1561)[89] and it was from 1549, at latest, reckoned a member of Uckington manor,[90] though often itself described as a manor. It was still subject to Uckington in 1833.[91]

In 1666 the manorial estate was intact,[92] but soon thereafter the lords sold off parts of Walcot and there were seven freeholds in 1842.[93] Nevertheless the lords kept land there, and the Noel-Hills (Lords Berwick), to whom Uckington had passed,[94] remained principal landowners in Walcot until the mid 20th century.[95] In 1670 Samuel Garbet, of Cronkhill, bought freehold property in Walcot which descended in the Garbets[96] until James Garbet's bankruptcy.[97] Another freehold, belonging in 1715 to the Revd. Thomas Markham of Donnington (in Wroxeter), was sold in 1753 by his son the Revd. Timothy Markham to William Cludde of Orleton,[98] and the Orleton estate included land in Walcot until 1905 or later.[99] William Cludde (d. 1829), however, sold some land[1] and his family owned only 38 a. in Walcot in 1842.[2] A freehold bought from the lord of the manor by John Grice in 1671 descended to the Roe family 1747–91, thereafter to the sisters of the last Roe.[3] William Turner, husband of one of them, sold land to Roger Walmesley (d. 1833), who had also bought land from William Cludde and may have owned the former Garbet estate.[4] The Walmesley estate, 73 a. in 1842,[5] was sold under the will of George Walmesley, proved 1856.[6]

In 1835 the duke of Cleveland had an estate at

[62] L. & P. Hen. VIII, xvi, p. 54.
[63] S.R.O. 1011, box 169, ct. r.
[64] P.R.O., C 142/104, no. 94.
[65] Barnard MSS., Raby Castle, abstr. of writings, pt. 6, f. 355.
[66] T.S.A.S. 4th ser. xi. 38.
[67] Barnard MSS., Raby Castle, abstr. of writings, pt. 6, ff. 362–3, 378. [68] T.S.A.S. 4th ser. xi. 155.
[69] Barnard MSS., Raby Castle, abstr. of writings, pt. 7, ff. 399, 409–14; S.R.O., q. sess. rec. box 260, reg. of gamekeepers, 1742–79, 1 Dec. 1743; Kelly's Dir. Salop. (1891), 456; (1934), 298. Cf. V.C.H. Salop. viii. 88 (cf. below, Corrigenda).
[70] It belonged to the Barnard est. in 1983: local inf.
[71] Eyton, ix. 60. [72] P.R.O., C 136/98, no. 10.
[73] Cal. Close, 1396–9, 151; P.R.O., C 137/33, no. 40.
[74] e.g. P.R.O., C 137/33, no. 40; C 138/59, no. 53; C 142/128, no. 82; Barnard MSS., Raby Castle, box 12, bdle. 11, deed of 1576. Cf. below, Wrockwardine, Man. and Other Est.
[75] Barnard MSS., Raby Castle, box 1, bdle. 27, no. 62a.
[76] Above.
[77] P.R.O., C 142/128, no. 82. Cf. V.C.H. Salop. viii. 265.
[78] Barnard MSS., Raby Castle, box 1, bdle. 27, nos. 63–4.
[79] S.P.L., MS. 2345, no. 110.
[80] T.S.A.S. 4th ser. ix. 82–6.
[81] S.R.O. 14, tithe appt.
[82] Local inf. [83] Eyton, ix. 54.

[84] Reg. Regum Anglo-Norm. iii, nos. 376–7, 379.
[85] Rot. Hund. (Rec. Com.), ii. 57.
[86] Cal. Pat. 1313–17, 618.
[87] V.C.H. Salop. ii. 68.
[88] L. & P. Hen. VIII, xix (1), p. 278.
[89] P.R.O., C 142/132, no. 18.
[90] S.R.O. 112, box 90, estreats of ct. r.
[91] Ibid. box 89, suit r.
[92] S.P.L., Deeds 5894.
[93] S.R.O. 14, tithe appt.
[94] S.P.R. Lich. xiv (2), pp. vi–vii.
[95] S.R.O. 14, tithe appt., showing Ld. Berwick as the biggest landowner (152 a.); Kelly's Dir. Salop. (1941), 318.
[96] Two are noted in D.N.B.; cf. Alum. Cantab. 1752–1900, iii. 8.
[97] S.R.O. 112, box 119, deeds; S.P.L., Deeds 2512.
[98] S.R.O. 1011, box 223, abstr. of title.
[99] Ibid. will of 1782; Kelly's Dir. Salop. (1905), 306. Cf. below, Wrockwardine, Man. and Other Est.
[1] S.R.O. 1300/249.
[2] S.R.O. 14, tithe appt.
[3] S.R.O. 1493, box 310, abstr. of title. For some geneal. details of the Grices see par. reg. bur. 16 Jan. 1738/9; 15 Oct. 1747 (transcript in S.P.L.).
[4] S.R.O. 1300/249; S.P.L., Deeds 2512. Walmesley's father had been a tenant of the Garbets in Walcot.
[5] S.R.O. 14, tithe appt.
[6] S.R.O. 1300/250.

Walcot,[7] perhaps a recent acquisition,[8] which comprised 42 a. in 1842.[9] His heir, Lord Barnard, was named one of the chief landowners in 1941.[10]

Walcot Grange (formerly Walcot Grove) belonged to Lord Berwick in 1842[11] and may therefore have been on the site of a medieval capital messuage, but the buildings standing in 1982 were not earlier than 19th-century.

In 1066 and 1086 *LEE*, later called *LEEGOMERY* from the Cumbray family, was held by Toret; in 1086 he held it of the sheriff Reynold of Bailleul who held under Earl Roger.[12] The tenancy in chief could not survive beyond 1102,[13] and nothing more is known of Reynold's mesne lordship: the manor did not descend with most of his estates to the FitzAlans.[14]

By 1167 Leegomery belonged to Alfred de Cumbray (fl. 1180).[15] Later it was held in chief by John de Cumbray, at whose death (c. 1199) it passed to his son Roger (d. c. 1213), whose coheirs were Parnel (fl. 1218) and Agnes de Cumbray. Parnel was Simon Tuchet's widow, and by 1221 Leegomery had passed to their son Thomas (d. c. 1234), who held by serjeanty.[16] From him it descended successively to his sons Henry (d. c. 1241) and Robert (d. 1248). Robert's serjeanty was that of providing a mounted and armed man for 40 days in wars against Wales.[17] Thereafter it descended until the later 14th century from father to son, the following being lords: Thomas (d. c. 1315), Robert (d. c. 1341), Thomas (d. 1349), John (d. c. 1361), John (d. 1372), and John (cr. Baron Audley 1403, d. 1408).[18] Thereafter, apart from forfeiture to the Crown 1497–1512, the manor descended with the barony of Audley[19] until 1528 when Lord Audley sold it to James Leveson.[20] In 1544 Leveson settled it on his son Richard[21] (kt. 1553, d. 1560), who inherited Lilleshall in 1547. After Sir Richard's death the manor passed to his daughter Elizabeth[22] and her husband William Sheldon of Beoley (Worcs.).[23] They held it in 1579[24] but Sir Walter Leveson (Elizabeth's brother, a rival claimant)[25] had gained possession by 1584.[26] The descent thereafter followed that of Lilleshall,[27] except that

under the will of Sir Richard Leveson[28] (d. 1661) Leegomery passed successively to his grandnephew Francis Fowler[29] (d. 1667), to Fowler's son Francis (d. 1668),[30] and then to another grandnephew William Gower,[31] each of whom was required to assume the additional surname of Leveson on taking possession. The last named inherited Lilleshall in 1674.[32]

The manor included (in Wellington parish) the townships of Ketley,[33] Leegomery, and Wappenshall.[34] The duke of Sutherland's Leegomery and Wappenshall estates (but not the manorial rights) were sold in 1912, the former to R. F. Meyrick of Apley (on behalf of Sir Thomas Meyrick),[35] the latter to E. W. Bromley.[36]

Alan of Charlton had demesne land in Wappenshall in 1317,[37] which descended with Apley.[38] At his death in 1566 William Charlton of Apley had a small freehold at Leegomery.[39] About 1676 the Charltons owned 75 a. in Wappenshall (where they had a lease of 206 a. more) and 31 a. in Leegomery.[40] St. John Chiverton Charlton owned 59 a. in Wappenshall and 73 a. in Leegomery in 1842.[41] His heir R. F. Meyrick added the duke of Sutherland's Leegomery estate,[42] and owned land in Wappenshall in 1929.[43] In 1971 W.J.C. Charlton-Meyrick sold his Leegomery estate to Telford development corportion, the owner in 1981.[44]

Leegomery House, the capital messuage,[45] a brick farmhouse of the 18th and 19th centuries, became a community centre in 1979.[46] Wappenshall Farm was a 16th-century timber-framed house, perhaps of T plan. A room at the parlour end was subdivided in the 18th century and the whole was cased in brick c. 1800. In the 19th century brick lean-to additions were built.

In the late 12th century John de Cumbray gave a virgate and 8 a. of land at Wappenshall to Wombridge priory,[47] and Sir John Charlton of Apley (d. 1380) held ½ virgate of the priory.[48]

In the earlier 14th century the Burnells had land in Wappenshall that was subject to their manor court of Wellington,[49] and in the 17th the Steventons, also lords of Wellington, had land there,[50] perhaps including the 30 a. that William

---

[7] S.R.O. 112, box 119, sale plan.
[8] Not mentioned in an abstr. of title up to 1809 (S.R.O. 659/1).
[9] S.R.O. 14, tithe appt.
[10] *Kelly's Dir. Salop.* (1941), 318.
[11] S.R.O. 14, tithe appt.; 1856/7 (no. 47).
[12] *V.C.H. Salop.* i. 321
[13] Ibid. iii. 10.
[14] Eyton, vii. 340.
[15] Except where otherwise stated the following descent as far as John Tuchet (d. c. 1361) is based on ibid. 340–8.
[16] *Ex. e Rot. Fin.* (Rec. Com.), i. 271.
[17] *Rot. Hund.* (Rec. Com.), ii. 57.
[18] *Complete Peerage*, xii (2), 54–61.
[19] Ibid. i. 341–2. Cf. *Cal. Close*, 1454–61, 54.
[20] *L. & P. Hen. VIII*, iv (2), p. 2118.
[21] Ibid. xix (2), p. 321
[22] P.R.O., C 142/131, no. 186; Staffs. R.O., D. 593/A/1/20/2.
[23] Staffs. R.O., D. 593/B/2/5/4/1, deed.
[24] P.R.O., CP 25(2)/201/21 & 22 Eliz. I Mich. [no. 23].
[25] Staffs. R.O., D. 593/A/1/20/2.
[26] Ibid. /H/14/1/1.
[27] P.R.O., C 142/283, no. 90; /312, no. 158; CP 25(2)/528/22 Chas. I Hil. [no. 11]; CP 43/459, m. 188; /783, m. 382; /900, m. 228.
[28] S.R.O. 1378/18.

[29] *T.S.A.S.* i. 138.
[30] *S.H.C.* 1920 and 1922, 33.
[31] S.R.O. 38/332.
[32] Above, Lilleshall, Man. and Other Est.
[33] Below, Ketley.
[34] *Feud. Aids*, iv. 219; Eyton vii. 345–6.
[35] S.R.O. 3882/5, box 4, deed of 1913 (draft).
[36] S.R.O. 972, parcel 196, sale partic.; box 198, list of purchasers.
[37] *Cal. Chart. R.* 1300–26, 370.
[38] *Sir Chris. Hatton's Bk. of Seals*, p. 148; *Cal. Pat.* 1391–6, 23–4; *Cal. Close*, 1402–5, 22–3; *L. & P. Hen. VIII*, vi, p. 141; P.R.O., C 137/67, no. 149; C 142/786, no. 67; S.R.O. 625, box 21, deed of 1569.
[39] S.R.O. 625, box 21, deed of 1615.
[40] S.P.L., MS. 2340, ff. 19–24.
[41] S.R.O. 14, tithe appt.
[42] Above.
[43] *Kelly's Dir. Salop.* (1929), 103.
[44] Inf. from the archivist, T.D.C.
[45] S.R.O. 38/337; 972, parcel 236, map of 1723.
[46] D. G. Fenter, 'Bldg. Development carried out in Telford by the Development Corp.' (TS. in S.R.O. 3763).
[47] Eyton, vii. 341.
[48] *Cal. Inq. p.m.* xv, pp. 135–6.
[49] S.R.O. 1224, box 204, ct. r. of 1345.
[50] P.R.O., CP 43/131, m. 13; S.P.L., Deeds 5658.

Charlton of Apley acquired from George Forester in 1805 in exchange for property in Wellington township.[51]

King John seems to have kept WELLINGTON HAY in demesne after granting the rest of Wellington manor to Thomas of Erdington.[52] It was royal demesne in 1380[53] but was held by Richard FitzAlan, earl of Arundel, at his forfeiture in 1397.[54] By 1469 the estate was called a manor.[55] In 1398 it was described as a wood and a free chase[56] and in 1451 as wood and pasture.[57] It was reckoned at 1,000 a. in 1426.[58] In 1398 the king granted it for 20 years to William le Scrope, earl of Wiltshire.[59] He was executed in 1399[60] and the estate was restored in 1400 to Thomas, earl of Arundel. At his death without issue in 1415 the estate was divided between his sisters Elizabeth, duchess of Norfolk, Joan, Lady Bergavenny, and Margaret, the wife of Sir Roland Lenthall.[61] Elizabeth sold her third in 1425 to Norman Babyngton[62] (d. 1434)[63] and his wife Margaret (d. 1451).[64] It passed from Margaret to Norman's brother and heir Sir William[65] who held it in chief as $\frac{1}{30}$ knight's fee. When he died in 1454 his heir was his son William.[66] Lady Bergavenny died in 1435, and her third passed to her granddaughter Elizabeth, Lady Bergavenny, wife of Sir Edward Nevill. She died in 1448 and her third passed to their son George, later Lord Bergavenny (d. 1492).[67] Sir Roland Lenthall, surviving his wife and their son Edward, died in 1450 holding her third by the curtesy of England.[68] That third was then divided between Edward's heirs John de Mowbray, duke of Norfolk (d. 1461), grandnephew of Thomas, earl of Arundel, and George Nevill, the earl's great-grandnephew.[69] Thus George Nevill became holder of a moiety of the whole estate. The duke, at his death in 1461, held the other moiety,[70] having presumably acquired the Babyngton third since 1454. The whole estate seems eventually to have devolved upon Nevill's son George, Lord Bergavenny (d. 1535). He leased it for a term of years to John Forester (d. c. 1521) and his heirs,[71] perhaps in 1512.[72] The lease was still unexpired in 1535.[73] Since the 12th

century Forester's ancestors had been keepers in fee of Wellington hay within the forest of the Wrekin. In 1555 Henry Nevill, Lord Bergavenny, sold the hay to Sir Rowland Hill and Thomas Leigh, aldermen of London. In the same year Hill acquired Leigh's share and conveyed the whole estate to John Forester of Watling Street through the governors of Market Drayton grammar school, who thereby secured an annual rent charge of £22.[74]

Hugh Forester was mentioned between 1187 and 1197. Robert Forester, fl. c. 1200–1227, held $\frac{1}{2}$ virgate in chief by the serjeanty of keeping the king's hay. He seems to have been succeeded by another Robert (d. c. 1278). From him the serjeanty descended from father to son until 1350, the follwing being holders: Roger (d. by the end of 1283),[75] Roger (d. c. 1312),[76] Roger (fl. 1319),[77] and John[78] (d. 1350). John was succeeded by his brother William[79] (d. 1395).[80] From William the serjeanty (mentioned as late as 1443)[81] descended from father to son as follows: Roger (d. 1403), Roger (d. 1443), John (d. 1466), and Edward. Edward was probably succeeded by the John Forester[82] who became lessee of the Wellington hay estate. John seems to have had a son John[83] who may have been living in 1544 when a John Forester the younger, of Watling Street, was recorded.[84]

The younger John was probably the same John Forester who acquired the freehold of Wellington hay in 1555 and he who died in 1591. He was succeeded by his grandson Francis Forester.[85] In 1623 Francis bought Little Wenlock manor, whose descent Wellington hay thereafter followed.[86] The estate still bore that name in 1637[87] but by 1684 it had been changed to WATLING STREET[88] after the Foresters' seat. That was perhaps to avoid confusion with Wellington manor, acquired by the Foresters in 1659. Lord Forester was virtually sole landowner in Watling Street township in 1842,[89] as was the 5th baron in 1912.[90] He and his successor afterwards sold much of the estate,[91] including the Old Hall, which was bought before 1926 by Ralph Hickman.[92]

[51] S.R.O. 972, box 153, abstr. of title of 1828; S.R.O. 1224, parcel 318, rentals of 1805–6.
[52] Eyton, ix. 44.
[53] Cal. Pat. 1377–81, 552.
[54] Cal. Fine R. 1391–9, 253.
[55] Cal. Pat. 1467–77, 130.
[56] Ibid. 1396–9, 339; Cal. Inq. Misc. vi, p. 89.
[57] Cal. Fine R. 1445–52, 266.
[58] Cal. Pat. 1422–9, 341.
[59] Cal. Fine R. 1391–9, 253.   [60] D.N.B.
[61] Complete Peerage, i. 246.
[62] Cal. Pat. 1422–9, 341; Cal. Fine R. 1445–52, 222.
[63] P.R.O., C 139/62, no. 12.
[64] Ibid. /142, no. 18
[65] Cal. Fine R. 1445–52, 222.
[66] P.R.O., C 139/157, no. 23.
[67] Complete Peerage, i. 26–31; Cal. Fine R. 1445–52, 266.
[68] P.R.O., C 139/143, no. 27.
[69] Cal. Fine R. 1445–52, 266; Cal. Close, 1454–61, 231.
[70] P.R.O., C 140/5, no. 46.
[71] P.R.O., C 1/797, no. 57.
[72] S.P.L., MS. 2790, p. 277.
[73] P.R.O., C 1/797, no. 57.
[74] S.R.O. 1224, parcel 205, deed (at end).
[75] Eyton, ix. 46–8.

[76] Cal. Close, 1307–13, 475.
[77] Eyton, ix. 49.
[78] Cal. Inq. p.m. vii, pp. 479–80.
[79] Ibid. ix, p. 379.
[80] Cal. Fine R. 1391–9, 180.
[81] P.R.O., C 139/108, no. 15.
[82] T.S.A.S. 2nd ser. iii. 156–9.
[83] S.P.L., MS. 2790, p. 277.
[84] L. & P. Hen. VIII, xix (2), p. 197.
[85] P.R.O., C 142/228, no. 85.
[86] Ibid. /483, no. 46; S.R.O. 1224, box 208, deed of 1684; box 268, deed of 1714; box 270, deed of 1735; box 272, will of 1805; box 291, wills of 1st and 2nd barons, 1821 and 1872; S.R.O. 1681, box 36, abstr. of title of 1918. Cf. above, L. Wenlock, Man. and Other Est.
[87] P.R.O., C 142/483, no. 46.
[88] S.R.O. 1224, box 264, deed.
[89] S.R.O. 14, tithe appt. Three others had 7½ a. between them.
[90] S.R.O. 4011/84/1, no. 801; /84/3, nos. 2533, 2558, 2597, 2941; /84/4, no. 3059.
[91] S.R.O. 1681, box 44, deed of 1913; sale plans of 1918 and draft deeds; parcel 46, sale partic. of 1918.
[92] T.D.C. The Old Hall (Historic Bldgs. in Telford, no. 12).

The surviving timber-framed ranges of the Old Hall (formerly Watling Street hall)[93] are on the east and north and are probably early 17th-century. They still contain a quantity of reset panelling of that date. There were other ranges on the west[94] and south,[95] which may once have joined to enclose a courtyard.[96] By 1830 the south range was only a stump and the west range had been demolished and replaced by a wing in the former courtyard.[97] In the mid 19th century, after the house had become a school,[98] the north range was extended westwards in timber framing and a small brick block was added on the south-east. Buildings continued to be added on the south and west at various times in the later 19th century,[99] and c. 1932 a large laboratory and gymnasium block was erected on the frontage to Limekiln Lane.[1]

The rectory was appropriated in 1232 when the abbot of Shrewsbury and the bishop of Coventry and Lichfield agreed to divide the great tithes of the parish equally, though reserving to the abbey those already appropriated to it; the bishop's share was to endow a new prebend in Lichfield cathedral.[2] In 1249, after a dispute, it was agreed that the abbey should have all the hay tithes of the Aston demesne land and two thirds of the hay tithes of Arleston, Hadley, Walcot, and Wellington townships, and the prebendary all the hay tithes of thirteen bovates of villein arable at Aston.[3] In 1291 the abbey's share was valued at £6 a year, the prebendary's at £10.[4] In 1535 the abbey's share was worth £11 a year, the prebendary's £10.[5]

In 1538 the abbey leased the tithes of demesne land in Arleston, Hadley, Walcot, and Wellington townships to William Taylor of Little Wenlock for 60 years at 20s. rent, having formerly leased them to John Taylor of Wellington. Between 1557 and 1566 William Charlton of Apley bought from the Crown some of the abbey's tithes,[6] and by 1616 Andrew Charlton of Apley not only held those[7] but was also lessee of those leased to Taylor in 1538. In 1650 Parliament sold the leased tithes to Humphrey Hill of Riseley (Beds.).[8] By 1655, however, Francis Charlton of Apley owned all the former abbey's tithes in the parish,[9] and they seem thereafter to have descended with Apley.[10]

The prebendary's share was normally leased to a local person for three lives at a rent of £13 6s. 8d. In 1605 such a lease was granted to Matthew Steventon (d. 1633),[11] a Wellington tanner,[12] and was unexpired in 1649.[13] In 1665 Francis Charlton of Apley took a similar lease[14] and the lords of Apley were successive lessees thereafter,[15] thus possessing all the great tithes either as impropriators or lessees. In 1649 the great tithes were worth £194 a year.[16] By the early 17th century the prebendary's lessee usually sublet the tithes of particular townships or farms.[17] The practice was continued by the Charltons with their own tithes and the prebendary's.[18] In 1693–4 they received rents totalling £195 for the parish's great tithes,[19] in 1759–60 about the same.[20] When the Charltons leased their land in the parish, they sometimes included the tithes.[21] John Charlton also held 5½ a. of rectorial glebe c. 1676, which he sublet.[22]

Under the Cathedrals Act, 1840, the prebend's endowment was vested in the Ecclesiastical Commissioners.[23] On the eve of commutation all the great tithes were payable in kind except for moduses totalling £4 6s. 6d. in lieu of the hay tithes of Apley, Dothill, and Watling Street townships and of most of Aston township (all but 44½ a.).[24] In Eyton township 87 a. (partly in Eyton parish) were tithe free,[25] as were c. 43 a. in Aston, and throughout the parish there were parcels owing only vicarial tithes. The great tithes of each holding were split equally between the lessee of the prebend's endowment and St. John Chiverton Charlton (in practice the same person). In addition there was rectorial glebe of 6½ a., presumably in dual ownership, all in Wellington township and all let to tenants.

In the years 1838–42 the rectorial tithes of Wellington parish were commuted to £1,521 6s. 10d. (including £49 19s. 6d. in Eyton township and £36 in Preston township) divided equally as before.[26] By 1880 the Ecclesiastical Commissioners had assigned most of their share to the incumbents of Hadley, Ketley, Lawley, Christ Church,[27] and (apparently) Uppington with Aston.[28] In 1897 the commissioners were allowed to sell some property formerly belonging to the prebend,[29] presumably part of the rectorial glebe.

[93] S.R.O. 1224, box 297, hearth tax receipt of 1687; 999/36.2, deed of 1774.
[94] Mortices on NW. corner post of N. range.
[95] Bodl. MS. Top. Salop. c. 2, ff. 498, 500; S.P.L., J. H. Smith colln., no. 340.
[96] There was a 'chamber over the gate' in 1692: S.R.O. 1224, box 274, inventory.
[97] S.P.L., J. H. Smith colln., no. 340.
[98] Below, Educ.
[99] T.D.C. The Old Hall.
[1] Old Hall Sch. Record, 1934–7 (copy in possession of headmaster, 1982).
[2] Cart. Shrews. i, p. 66.
[3] Ibid. pp. 67–9.
[4] Tax. Eccl. (Rec. Com.), 243, 247.
[5] Valor. Eccl. (Rec. Com.), iii. 189–90, 526–7.
[6] S.R.O. 625, box 21, Wm. Charlton's i.p.m.
[7] P.R.O., C 142/786, no. 67.
[8] L.J.R.O., B/V/1/32, s.v. Wellington; S.R.O. 625, box 11, deed of 1650.
[9] Baxter, 'Wellington', 68.
[10] L.J.R.O., B/V/1/81, s.v. Wellington; S.R.O. 14, tithe appt.; S.R.O. 625, box 11, deed of 1676; box 21, deed of 1667; S.R.O. 1005/169; 3882/6/2.

[11] Par. reg. bur. 22 Feb. 1632/3 (transcript in S.P.L.).
[12] S.R.O. 625, box 10, deed of 1628.
[13] Baxter, 'Wellington', 68.
[14] S.R.O. 625, box 11, deed of 1676.
[15] Ibid. deeds of 1721, 1736; L.J.R.O., B/A/15, Eyton; Preston; S.R.O. 14, tithe appt.
[16] Baxter, 'Wellington', 68.
[17] S.R.O. 625, box 10, deeds of 1628, 1630.
[18] Ibid. deed of 1665; box 11, deed of 1726.
[19] S.P.L., Deeds 2498, rental.
[20] S.R.O. 625, parcel 22, rental.
[21] e.g. ibid. box 11, deed of 1784.
[22] S.P.L., MS. 2340, f. 61.
[23] 3 & 4 Vic. c. 113.
[24] The only modus mentioned in 1722 was 7s. 6d. a year for Aston hay tithes: S.R.O. 625, parcel 22, rental, Mich. 1722.
[25] L.J.R.O., B/A/15, Eyton.
[26] Ibid. Eyton; Preston; S.R.O. 14, tithe appt.
[27] Below, Church sections of Wellington; Hadley; Ketley; Lawley.
[28] S.R.O. 3916/1/33, Uppington with Aston.
[29] Lich. Dioc. Regy., bps.' reg. Q (Orders in Council), p. 351.

ECONOMIC HISTORY. Until the 19th century Wellington parish apart from the three coalfield townships depended on agriculture and its associated occupations, with Wellington town as the centre for marketing and professional services. Manufacturing firms established themselves in the town in the 19th century, encouraged by the arrival of main-line railways. Prominent in those new industries were Wesleyan Methodists,[30] especially the Grooms,[31] and early 20th-century Wellington had a numerous middle class.[32] In the mid 20th century, however, most of the Victorian manufactures ceased or moved away. In the 1960s Wellington town was still the chief shopping centre between Shrewsbury and Wolverhampton, but its retail trades were in decline and many of the inhabitants worked in Shrewsbury.[33] Under Telford new town (designated in 1968) it was planned that Wellington should continue as a shopping, professional, and business centre, though second to the new centre at Malinslee.[34] Shopkeepers' fears that Telford's new centres, especially that at Malinslee, would draw trade from Wellington town[35] seemed by 1982 to have been partly realized.[36]

Two southern townships, Arleston and Watling Street, lay partly on the coalfield and belonged to the Forester family. Mining there did not affect either place to the degree observable in the three coalfield townships. Nor was Aston's rural character altered by the establishment of F. L. Cox & Co.'s Overley chemical works[37] c. 1970.[38] Walcot, too, remained rural despite the presence from 1927 of the Allscott sugar factory.

AGRICULTURE. In 1086 Wellington manor with its berewicks, and Leegomery and Wappenshall, in Leegomery manor, included much land capable of supporting herds and crops, and was far more developed than nearby Lilleshall, an area of similar size.[39] On Wellington manor there were 6 ploughteams on the demesne and 9 among the tenants, who included 12 villeins, 12 oxherds, and 8 bordars. The manor was taxed at 14 hides, and its value, £18, had dropped little since 1066.[40] The number of bordars suggests that much woodland had been cleared,[41] probably most recently around Apley and Leegomery (as the name element *leah* indicates). The rest was probably open country much earlier, as the element *tun* in Arleston,

Aston, and Wellington suggests.[42]

Woodland still covered much of the Wrekin and Wellington hay in the late 12th century[43] (though Domesday did not record it) and it was continuous with that of Little Wenlock.[44] Moreover in 1611 the name 'Wellington forest' was still applicable to a large wooded area.[45] In 1190 Shrewsbury abbey and Wenlock priory, having held the Wrekin woods in common, divided the woods and pannage, nevertheless allowing intercommoning throughout the woods for certain vills, one of which, Aston, lay in Wellington parish. In 1234 Wenlock ceded its share to Shrewsbury.[46] In the 13th century the whole parish except Dothill, Walcot, and Wellington townships lay within the forest jurisdiction of Mount Gilbert[47] and agricultural improvement was therefore to some extent controlled though not prevented.[48] In 1301 the forest parts of the parish were disafforested except for Wellington hay.[49] The hay was the only woodland that the Crown had preserved and inclosed for hunting; nevertheless the keeper had been allowed an assart in it, the men of Wellington could pasture their livestock there most of the year, and pannage was sold.[50]

Wellington manor had land for 9 more ploughs in 1086,[51] presumably in the waste. At Aston a freeholder in the 1230s quitclaimed two wastes, 'Aylwyesmor' and 'Bradelemor', to Shrewsbury abbey, with liberty to ditch, inclose, and convert them, but reserved such arable and meadow as had already been reclaimed from them.[52]

By the later Middle Ages each township except Wellington hay (later Watling Street) and Apley had a set of open arable fields.[53] Wellington, the most populous, had three large fields:[54] Wrekin field on the west, Smallbrook field[55] on the north, and Poolyhill (or Pooly) field on the east, renamed Windmill field shortly before 1665.[56] The township seems to have contained virtually no woodland and the one considerable area of waste was probably Bradley moor,[57] between the town and Wrekin field. Arleston too had three fields: Windmill field on the east, Lawley field, presumably on the south-east, and Mill field, probably on the north-west.[58] On the south-west Arleston's steeply rising ground had some woodland and much rough grazing. Aston's open fields lay around the main settlement,[59] Down field north, Sich field west, and Wood field east.[60] In the

[30] e.g. the Clifts, Corbetts, Grooms, Isons, and Stones, some of whom were related: Review Publishing Co. *Inds. of Salop.* 36; W. Mate & Sons Ltd. *Shropshire: Historical, Descriptive, Biographical* (1906), pt. 2, p. 188; Lenton, *Methodism in Wellington*, 9–10, 15–16.

[31] H. W. Pooler, *My Life in General Practice* (1950), 13.

[32] *V.C.H. Salop.* iii. 345.

[33] *Shropshire Mag.* Oct. 1956, 14; local inf.

[34] T.D.C. *Basic Plan for Telford* (1973), 19.

[35] T.D.C. *Wellington Centre* [1972]; *Telford Observer*, 24 May 1972.

[36] *Shropshire Star*, 24 Feb. 1982.

[37] T.D.C. *Telford Ind. Dir.* [c. 1979], advt. facing p. 42; above plate 55.

[38] P.O. *Telephone Dir.* (1970), sect. 303, yellow p. 28.

[39] Above, Lilleshall, Econ. Hist.

[40] *V.C.H. Salop.* i. 317.

[41] S. P. J. Harvey, 'Evidence for Settlement Study: Domesday Bk.' *Medieval Settlement*, ed. P. H. Sawyer (1976), 197–9.

[42] On *leah* and *tun* see M. Gelling, *Signposts to the Past* (1978), 126–8.

[43] *Cart. Shrews.* ii, p. 354; Eyton, ix. 47–8.

[44] Above, L. Wenlock, Econ. Hist.

[45] J. Speed, *Map of Salop.* (1611).

[46] *Cart. Shrews.* ii, pp. 352–4.

[47] Eyton, ix. 144–9.

[48] e.g. ibid. vii. 341; ix. 45, 57; P.R.O., E 32/145.

[49] *Cart. Shrews.* ii, pp. 245–51.

[50] Eyton, ix. 46–9. On the keepership see above, Man. and Other Est.

[51] *V.C.H. Salop.* i. 317.

[52] *Cart. Shrews.* i, pp. 109–10.

[53] Early-medieval inclosure may have extinguished Apley's fields. This para. is based on (in addition to the sources cited) S.R.O. 14, tithe appt. and map; 1856/5–7.

[54] S.R.O. 999/Tt 1–2, deeds of 1601–5. Locations are deduced from S.P.L., MS. 2340, ff. 46–72.

[55] So called by 1433: S.R.O. 625, box 11, deed.

[56] S.R.O. 999/Tt 4.

[57] So called by 1315: S.R.O. 625, box 11, deed.

[58] S.R.O. 999/Qq 8, deed of 1603.

[59] O.S. aerial photos., film 70.071, frames 086–092 (copies in S.P.L.); above, plate 55.

[60] Barnard MSS., Raby Castle, box 12, bdle. 11, deed of 1653.

south-east of the township the steep western flank of the Wrekin, its summit, and the upper slopes descending on the east comprised extensive pastures, wastes, and woods.[61] Even Dothill, probably the smallest township, had three open fields.[62] Walcot had two, Bucknall field on the west and Mill field on the east,[63] with other land in Wide field,[64] an open field in Charlton township.[65] Walcot had virtually no woodland; waste and rough grazing seem to have lain in the far west around Clipsmoor[66] (which extended into Charlton)[67] and Walcot waste,[68] and in the east around Buttington hill.[69] Leegomery township had three open fields: Mack field on the north-west, Mill field on the north-east, and Wellington (or Dairy) field,[70] presumably on the south.[71] There was waste on the west side of the township at Lee Holme moor,[72] which extended into Apley,[73] and much on the rising ground south of the fields,[74] around Chockley.[75] Wappenshall had three open fields:[76] Brick Kiln (or Brick) field east of the main settlement, Park field, adjoining Apley park and so named by 1649, on the south-west,[77] and Middle field, perhaps on the south.[78] Northwards of Wappenshall's fields lay the Weald Moors, a waste where Wappenshall originally intercommoned with other townships and manors.[79] By 1520, however, Wappenshall had acquired exclusive rights over the nearest part, thus named Wappenshall moor,[80] which nevertheless had no visible boundary and was subject to claims of common by tenants of Wrockwardine manor.[81]

A variety of tenures co-existed in the earlier 14th century. In 1315 Edward Burnell had 12 free tenants paying rent in Wellington manor.[82] Even smallholdings might be held by feudal tenure. In 1346, for example, John, son of Thomas the shepherd, held ⅛ virgate of the lord of Wellington in fee, owing fealty, relief, and rent. A less privileged tenant of Wellington manor at Wappenshall c. 1315 held for life by deed in return for services. In 1345 his son fined to hold the land on the same terms after his father's death 'according to the custom of the manor'. Other tenants of the manor at that time, presumably copyholders, paid an entry fine, held for life, and owed heriot.[83] Burnell had 8 customary tenants at Arleston in 1315, owing 59s. rent between them.[84] There were 12 tenants for life at Apley in 1384.[85] Neifs were narrowly restricted to servile tenure: one of Wellington manor in 1346 buying from the lord land previously held freely was required to hold it unfreely (*native*).[86] In 1541 there were tenants at will on Haughmond abbey's former estate at Walcot,[87] but also at least one large leaseholder.[88] In 1540 there were tenants at will, copyholders, and two large leaseholders on Shrewsbury abbey's former estate at Aston.[89]

While every township seems to have included arable and pasture in the later Middle Ages, livestock was necessarily more important at Arleston, Aston, and Wappenshall, where woodland or pasture were most plentiful. Aston had a wood-ward in the earlier 14th century,[90] and it was presumably grazing and pannage that had almost denuded the Wrekin by the 1530s.[91] Seven townships had common rights, including pannage, on the Aston part of the Wrekin in 1583 and pannage was still let in 1651.[92] In 1598 arable exceeded permanent pasture by 2 to 1 on farms in Leegomery township[93] but farmers there could rent additional pasture at Wappenshall moor in the same manor.[94] The Wellington manorial estate favoured most kinds of farming, for it included parts of Arleston and Wappenshall and grazing and pannage in Wellington hay, as well as extensive arable in Wellington township.

During the 16th and 17th centuries commonable lands were consolidated and inclosed piecemeal, and by c. 1725 the open fields and commons had virtually disappeared. Conversion of arable to pasture was often the aim.[95] Gradual adjustments had to be made in open-field regulations. It was ordered c. 1638 that inquiry be made at Walcot whether exchanges and inclosures had left enough open land in the fields to sustain the old stint of sheep, 16 for each tenant.[96]

At Apley and Dothill, each with one principal freeholder, parks were created. At Apley a small park existed by 1610,[97] and in 1663 Francis Charlton kept it for grazing his horses.[98] By the early

[61] Barnard MSS., Raby Castle, abstr. of writings, pt. 1, f. 33.
[62] S.R.O. 1224, box 250, deed of 1610.
[63] S.R.O. 1502/4, deed of 1536.
[64] S.R.O. 112, box 90, ct. r. of 1585.
[65] Location from S.R.O. 3265/1–2.
[66] So called by 1617: S.R.O. 1011, box 167, ct. bk. 17 Oct. 1617.
[67] S.R.O. 3265/1–2.
[68] Mentioned in 1583: S.R.O. 112, box 90, ct. r.
[69] Ibid. ct. r. of 1594.
[70] Staffs. R.O., D. 593/J/11/2/1, ct. r. of 1603.
[71] S.P.L., MS. 2340, f. 19, survey of c. 1676; S.R.O. 972, parcel 236, Leegomery and Wappenshall map of 1723.
[72] So called by 1663: S.P.L., Deeds 2498, Mich. rental, s.v. Apley.
[73] Located from S.R.O. 972, parcel 236, Leegomery and Wappenshall map of 1723. [74] Field names ibid.
[75] Perhaps derived from OE. ceart, 'rough, infertile ground': H. D. G. Foxall, Salop. Field Names (Salop. Arch. Soc. 1980), 25.
[76] Staffs. R.O., D. 593/J/11/2/1, ct. r. of 1606. In this section most of the inf. from Staffs. R.O., D. 593, was kindly supplied by Dr. P. R. Edwards.
[77] Located from S.R.O. 972, parcel 236, Leegomery and Wappenshall map of 1723.

[78] S.R.O. 625, box 10, deed of 1654; S.P.L., MS. 2340, ff. 21–7, survey of c. 1676. Dodsich field and Wellington field, perhaps fragments of the main fields, were also mentioned; Wellington man. had jurisdiction over some Wappenshall land (above, Man. and Other Est.), perhaps in the latter field.
[79] T.S.A.S. lxiii. 3–4.
[80] S.R.O. 972, box 221, deed of 1520.
[81] T.S.A.S. lxiii. 3–4.
[82] Eyton, ix. 45.
[83] S.R.O. 1224, box 204, ct. r. of 1345–6.
[84] Eyton, ix. 45.
[85] Sir Chris. Hatton's Bk. of Seals, p. 148.
[86] S.R.O. 1224, box 204, ct. r.
[87] Eyton, ix. 62.
[88] S.R.O. 1502/4; P.R.O., SC 6/Hen. VIII/3009, m. 44.
[89] P.R.O., SC 6/Hen. VIII/3010, m. 51d.
[90] T.S.A.S. xi. 419.
[91] Leland, Itin. ed. Toulmin Smith, ii. 83.
[92] Barnard MSS., Raby Castle, box 12, bdle. 24, deeds.
[93] Staffs. R.O., D. 593/H/14/1/1.
[94] Ibid. /J/11/2/1, ct. r. of 1605.
[95] e.g. S.R.O. 112, box 90, Uckington ct. r. of 1585; 625, box 10, deed of 1717; 1224, box 250, deeds of 1610, 1638.
[96] S.R.O. 112, box 90, Uckington man. ct. presentments.
[97] S.R.O. 1224, box 250, deed; 1224/1/1.
[98] S.P.L., Deeds 2498, Mich. rental.

19th century it covered most of the township.[99] Dothill park was created after 1626. It contained *c.* 170 a., about half the demesne,[1] and in 1758 was stocked with deer.[2] At Arleston the name Park leasows, recorded in 1635,[3] probably referred to a small inclosure,[4] as perhaps did the Park in Wellington township, mentioned in 1663.[5]

Inclosure of arable was completed earliest in townships under single ownership: at Dothill by 1626,[6] at Walcot by 1666,[7] at Apley by *c.* 1676.[8] Aston had open fields in 1653.[9] Arleston, Leegomery township, and Wappenshall, each with more than one important freeholder, still had open fields *c.* 1676[10] but none fifty years later.[11] In Wellington township, with two large freehold estates and many smaller ones, the surviving open-field arable, a considerable acreage, was inclosed by agreement in 1702.[12]

Inclosure of common pastures likewise proceeded gradually towards their virtual extinction by the earlier 18th century. Parts of Wappenshall moor were held in severalty by 1520,[13] and the whole by 1605.[14] Further inclosures of the Weald Moors by Wappenshall inhabitants in the earlier 17th century were resisted by the commoners of Wrockwardine manor.[15] At Walcot at least part of the waste was inclosed by 1583,[16] and by 1666 all the permanent pasture was held in severalty.[17] At Aston pasture near the Wrekin called Abbot's moor was inclosed by 1577[18] and common rights on the Aston part of the Wrekin were disputed by the lord in the 1650s.[19] In Wellington township Bradley moor was at least partly inclosed by *c.* 1676,[20] and Lee Holme moor, in Apley and Leegomery, was held in severalty by 1680.[21] In the 1750s the only common in the parish was said to be that at the foot of the Wrekin,[22] in Aston township.[23] It seems to have been inclosed in 1811.[24]

By the early 18th century surviving woods had been inclosed by the manorial lords and were carefully managed. In 1726 William Forester had 448 a. of woodland in hand in Arleston and

Watling Street townships,[25] and by 1752 the lower slopes of the Wrekin, partly in Aston township, had been planted with conifers.[26] When letting farms the Foresters and Charltons normally reserved any wood or underwood to their own use.[27]

In the late 17th and early 18th century farms varied widely in size, but were often under 50 a. Walcot consisted almost wholly of five farms, of between 60 a. and 105 a. in 1666.[28] In 1664 Leegomery consisted mainly of seven farms between *c.* 40 a. and *c.* 100 a.,[29] but in 1734 three were amalgamated in one of *c.* 240 a.[30] At Wappenshall *c.* 1676 the Charltons had one farm of 206 a. (held of the Leveson-Gower estate) and two others of 29 a. and 16 a. The rest of their land there was let to farmers living in other townships, in amounts up to 14 a. In Wellington township the six biggest holdings on the Charlton estate ranged only from 11 a. to 41 a.[31] In Watling street township the Foresters had three large farms in 1726: 244 a. (part of the demesne, with other land), 162 a. (Newhouse farm), and 126 a. (Buckatree farm). In Arleston, Watling Street, and immediately adjacent parts of other townships they had ten other farms of between 32 a. and 96 a., and eight holdings, with resident tenants, of 5 a.–19 a. Other Forester land was held there by farmers living elsewhere, in amounts up to 18 a.[32]

By the early 18th century most agricultural land was probably held by lease. On the Wellington manorial estate copyhold tenure had ceased by the late 17th century.[33] Farms on the Charlton estate were usually held by lease *c.* 1721.[34] Other tenures nevertheless subsisted. At Walcot all but one of the farmers were tenants at will in 1666[35] and in Wellington township there were many small freeholders.[36] Early 16th-century leases seem often to have been for long terms of years,[37] but by the century's close were usually for three or fewer lives,[38] often subject to a long term of years,[39] fixed in the mid 17th century at 99.[40] In practice a lease for three lives was expected to last *c.* 21 years[41] on the assumption that each generation of the tenant

---

[99] O.S. Map 1″, sheet 61 NE. (1833 edn.).

[1] S.R.O. 1224/1/1, 3; 1224, box 295, survey *temp.* Wm. Steventon and later.

[2] *Eng. Topog.* (Gent. Mag. Libr.), x. 155.

[3] S.R.O. 1224, box 250, deed.

[4] A group of names with the element 'Park' occurred on the W. side of the tns. in 1842: S.R.O. 14, tithe appt.; 1856/5 (nos. 126, 228–30, 239).

[5] S.P.L., Deeds 2498, Mich. rental. The name occurred immediately NW. of the town in 1842: S.R.O. 14, Wellington tithe appt. and map (no. 555).

[6] S.R.O. 1224/1/1.   [7] S.P.L., Deeds 5894.

[8] S.P.L., MS. 2340, f. 9.

[9] Barnard MSS., Raby Castle, box 12, bdle. 11, deed.

[10] S.P.L., MS. 2340, ff. 19–27; S.R.O. 1224, box 250, deed of 1676.

[11] S.R.O. 972, parcel 236, Leegomery and Wappenshall map of 1723; 1224, box 295, survey of 1726.

[12] S.R.O. 739/1, survey of 1702; 1224, parcel 205, ct. bk. 26 Oct. 1702 (last ref. to open fields).

[13] S.R.O. 972, box 221, deed.

[14] Staffs. R.O., D. 593/J/11/2/1, ct. r.

[15] *T.S.A.S.* lxiii. 8.

[16] S.R.O. 112, box 90, Uckington ct. r.

[17] S.P.L., Deeds 5894.

[18] Barnard MSS., Raby Castle, box 12, bdle. 25, deed.

[19] Barnard MSS., Raby Castle, abstr. of writings, pt. 7, f. 424.

[20] S.P.L., MS. 2340, ff. 49, 59, 66.

[21] S.P.L., Deeds 2498, Mich. rental.

[22] *Eng. Topog.* (Gent. Mag. Libr.), x. 155.

[23] J. Rocque, *Map of Salop.* (1752).

[24] There is a MS. award (with map) in possession of Ld. Barnard, Raby Castle, press 13/5.

[25] S.R.O. 1224, box 295, survey, f. 27.

[26] Rocque, *Map of Salop.*

[27] e.g. S.R.O. 625, box 10, deed of 1717; 1224, box 250, deed of 1696.

[28] Barnard MSS., Raby Castle, box 12, bdle. 24, deed of 1610; S.P.L., Deeds 5894.

[29] Staffs. R.O., D. 593/J/11/6/2, ct. r.

[30] Ibid. /I/1/21a, deed.

[31] S.P.L., MS. 2340, ff. 19–27, 46–72.

[32] S.R.O. 1224, box 295, survey, ff. 1–27.

[33] None mentioned in S.R.O. 1224, parcel 205, ct. bk. of 1690–1704.

[34] S.R.O. 625, box 19, sched.

[35] S.P.L., Deeds 5894.

[36] S.R.O. 739/1.

[37] e.g. Staffs. R.O., D. 593/H/14/1/1, Leegomery deed of 1517 (99 yrs.); S.R.O. 972, box 221, deed of 1520 (61 yrs.); 1502/4, deed of 1536 (81 yrs.).

[38] e.g. S.R.O. 1681, box 44, deed of 1602 (with sched. of leases).

[39] e.g. Staffs. R.O., D. 593/B/2/5/4/1, deeds of 1569 (80 yrs.); S.R.O. 1224, box 250, deeds of 1602 (80 yrs.) and 1632 (80 yrs.).

[40] e.g. S.R.O. 38/337; 625, box 10, deed of 1654 (reciting one of 1649); 1224, box 250, deed of 1659.

[41] S.R.O. 1224, box 250, deed of 1629.

family would have it renewed well before expiry.[42] Leases on those terms remained usual for farms until the late 18th century.[43]

Except perhaps in Wellington township, most farmers in the later 17th and earlier 18th century had sheep, cattle, and arable crops together.[44] There seem to have been especially large flocks of sheep in Aston,[45] where the Wrekin afforded common grazing.[46] In Leegomery seven farmers had a total stint of 240 sheep in Mack field in 1664,[47] and as many as 142 sheep were kept by a Leegomery dyer in 1698.[48] Cattle were kept for milk rather than beef, and several farmers made cheese in commercial quantities. In Wellington township, however, a high proportion of the milk seems to have been drunk or made into butter. Many farmers also kept a few pigs. In the earlier 18th century arable cultivation was being improved by landlord regulations. By 1716 some leases required the land to be properly manured[49] and in 1741 an Apley lease forbade its impoverishment by 'over much tillage'.[50] In the 1750s both dung and lime were used on the land. A plough named after its inventor, one Lummis, was then in general use.[51] By the 1750s the Foresters' tenants had to cultivate 'in course and not out of turn', were forbidden to take more than four crops in one course, and had to sow clover with the fourth crop.[52] Clover was being sown at Wappenshall by the 1720s.[53] Turnips were being grown by the 1660s but were not an important rotation crop in the earlier 18th century. The usual arable crops in the later 17th and earlier 18th century were wheat, barley, oats, and peas; smaller amounts of rye, vetches, clover, beans, and potatoes were grown. Mixed grains, sown in spring, were commonly used in addition to autumn-sown wheat.[54]

The early 18th century disparity of farms remained in the earlier 19th, and in both periods reflected the nature and size of the different townships. In the larger ones, Aston, Arleston, Walcot, and Watling Street, arable exceeded pasture and meadow by about 2 to 1 in 1842.[55] In those townships the average size of tenant holdings over 25 a. was 83 a. and the biggest tenant holding in one township was 206 a., in Aston. A few tenants had land in more than one of those townships, up to 266 a. A third of single-township holdings over 25 a. were under 50 a.

In Apley, Dothill, and Wappenshall pasture and meadow exceeded arable by about 2 to 1 in 1842. At Apley the resident landlord kept 88 per cent of the land as a park, and the only holding over 25 a. had 37 a. At Dothill, where the landlord was not resident, 74 per cent (240 a.) was in one farm, with no other holdings over 25 a. Similarly at Wappenshall 94 per cent (372 a.) was in the hands of one tenant.

Leegomery resembled the larger townships in land use but was like the smaller ones in size, and like them had one large farm (245 a.) and no other holdings over 25 a.

Wellington township was unlike the others. The large arable fields of the 17th century were mostly pastoral by the 1750s.[56] In 1842 pasture and meadow exceeded arable by 6 to 1. There were 530 a. of agricultural land[57] but no large farms. A few tenants were purely agricultural[58] but at least two thirds had trades or professions in the town.[59] Farming may have provided some with a secondary income;[60] others needed a little pasture or meadow to carry on their trades[61] or for their horses.[62]

In the later 19th and earlier 20th century Apley, Dothill, Leegomery, and Wappenshall continued to consist mainly of one holding.[63] In the other townships there was a gradual increase in the average size of farms over 50 a.[64]

By c. 1800 the Forester and Leveson-Gower estates, and probably others, had adopted the principle of annual tenancies,[65] though some leases survived long: a 1737 lease of 222 a. at Leegomery was still in force in 1802, and a 1756 lease of 194 a. at Wappenshall lasted until c. 1829.[66]

In 1801 wheat accounted for 43 per cent of recorded cereal acreage, barley for 31 per cent, and oats for 26 per cent. Turnips and rape were then widely grown, as were potatoes.[67] Rotations on the Leveson-Gower farms were centrally recorded by 1820,[68] as on the Forester estate by the 1840s.[69] The 'Norfolk' rotation (wheat–turnips–barley–clover), with occasional variations, was generally used.

[42] C. Clay, 'Lifeleasehold in the Western Counties of Eng.' Ag. H.R. xxix. 83–4.

[43] e.g. S.R.O. 625, box 11, deed of 1664; 1224, box 251, deed of 1728; box 253, deed of 1775; Yeomen and Colliers in Telford, ed. B. Trinder and J. Cox (1980), pp. 17–18.

[44] Para. based on Trinder and Cox, op. cit. pp. 72–90.

[45] Ibid. p. 339; Barnard MSS., Raby Castle, box 12, bdle. 24, deeds of 1625, 1651; L.J.R.O., B/C/11, John Hall, 1675; Thos. Felton, 1697; Rob. Price, 1741.

[46] Trinder and Cox, op. cit. p. 249; above.

[47] Staffs. R.O., D. 593/J/11/6/2, ct. r.

[48] Trinder and Cox, op. cit. p. 309.

[49] e.g. S.R.O. 1224, box 250, deed of 1716.

[50] S.R.O. 625, box 19, deed.

[51] Eng. Topog. (Gent. Mag. Libr.), . 155.

[52] e.g. S.R.O. 1224, box 252, deed of 1757; box 253, deed of 1761.   [53] L.J.R.O., B/C/11, Wm. Poulford, 1721.

[54] e.g. Trinder and Cox, Yeomen and Colliers, pp. 339, 365, 387; S.R.O. 1224, box 251, deed of 1733.

[55] In the following paras. inf. dated 1842 is from S.R.O. 14, tithe appt., unless otherwise noted.

[56] Eng. Topog. (Gent. Mag. Libr.), x. 155.

[57] i.e. described as arable, pasture, or meadow.

[58] e.g. Edw. Churm.

[59] Pigot, Nat. Com. Dir. (1842), 44–8. There is evidence of a similar pattern in the 17th cent.: Trinder and Cox, Yeomen and Colliers, p. 74.

[60] e.g. for John Espley, who kept a public ho. and traded as a pork butcher, maltster, and nurseryman.

[61] e.g. Jos. Pickering, butcher.

[62] e.g. Jas. Evett, surgeon.

[63] S.R.O. 972, parcel 196, sale partic. of 1912, pp. 44, 46–7; O.S. Map 6″, Salop. XXXVI. NW. (1929 edn.).

[64] S.R.O. 14, tithe appt.; P.R.O., MAF 68/3880, Salop. nos. 232, 239–40; /4945, nos. 232, 239–40.

[65] Based on S.R.O. 1224, parcels 317–18, rentals of 1785–1813 (cf. above, L. Wenlock, Econ. Hist.); J. R. Wordie, 'Rent Movements and the Eng. Tenant Farmer, 1700–1839', Research in Econ. Hist. vi. 207; cf. above, Lilleshall, Econ. Hist.

[66] S.R.O. 972, parcel 150, abstr. of leases, ff. 33–4.

[67] P.R.O., HO 67/14, no. 275 (covering the whole par.).

[68] S.R.O. 972, parcel 93, cropping bk.

[69] S.R.O. 2443/1, ff. 2–6, 8–10, 29.

From the mid 19th century the area of agricultural land diminished considerably,[70] and in 1968 much of what remained lay in Apley home farm (469 a.) and Leegomery House farm (241 a.), which were mainly arable and Eyton farm (655 a.), a mixed enterprise that included Wappenshall.[71] In the late 19th and early 20th

TABLE IX

WELLINGTON: LAND USE, LIVESTOCK, AND CROPS

	1867	1891	1938	1965
Percentage of grassland	56	66	78	43
arable	44	34	22	57
Percentage of cattle	13	22	35	38
sheep	72	67	46	14
pigs	15	11	19	48
Percentage of wheat	58	47	52	32
barley	34	34	24	66
oats	8	19	23	2
mixed corn & rye	0	0	1	0
Percentage of agricultural land growing roots and vegetables	12	11	8	7

Sources: P.R.O., MAF 68/143, no. 14; /1340, no. 11; /3880, Salop. nos. 232, 239–40; /4945, nos. 232, 239–40.

century farmers moved from cereals to livestock, though sheep farming declined. From 1927 they were helped by the fodder by-products of Allscott sugar factory,[72] and turnips and swedes gave way to sugar beet as the main root crop. In the mid 20th century, although pig production increased, livestock farming was widely superseded by barley growing.

MILLS. In 1086 Wellington manor had a mill worth 12s.,[73] perhaps at Walcot.[74] By 1315 Wel-

lington township had a windmill,[75] and one stood by the 17th century on the west side of Mill Lane.[76] It closed in the later 19th century.[77]

Walcot had a mill by 1141.[78] In the 16th, 17th, and 18th centuries both fulling and corn milling took place at a site on the Tern.[79] The mills, which lay on the Rodington side of the parish boundary in 1842,[80] were rebuilt in 1761 and extended in 1886,[81] by which time fulling had ceased.[82] Corn milling finished c. 1927 and the buildings were demolished in 1961.[83]

Leegomery (or Lee)[84] mill was worth 12s. in 1258[85] and stood on a leat by Ketley brook.[86] In 1842 it was driven by both steam and water,[87] but in 1912 by water alone.[88] Flour milling ceased in 1914 but grinding for farmers continued until 1945.[89] The buildings were gutted by fire in 1978.[90]

Arleston had a water mill in 1603,[91] perhaps near Mill yard, north-west of the hamlet, but there was none by 1842.[92] Mills of Francis Forester 'in Watling Street' were mentioned in 1666.[93] A windmill near the Vineyard, Wellington, in 1808 may have been short-lived.[94]

Field names west of the town indicate two shelling mills,[95] perhaps of the 18th century.

MARKETS AND FAIRS. Wellington provided a convenient outlet for the surrounding countryside's surplus produce and supplied the area with craft goods. Those functions were greatly stimulated by the town's markets and fairs, which were favoured (at least until the 1920s) by road and rail communications. Wellington's market survived the early competition of Shrewsbury and Newport markets and impeded the rise of such potential rivals as High Ercall (market granted 1267) and Madeley (1269).

In 1244 Giles of Erdington was granted a Thursday market in Wellington manor, and the Crown renewed the grant to the lord in 1283,[96] 1514,[97] and 1692.[98] The 1514 and 1692 renewals included a court of pie powder, but no record of its business is known. In 1856 the Wellington Market Hall Co., formed in 1841,[99] bought the tolls from Lord Forester.[1] In 1864 it was superseded by the Wellington (Salop) Market Co. Ltd. and a subsidiary market, on Saturday, was

[70] Para. based on Table IX and sources there cited. The sources cover Wellington civil parish (1867 and 1891) and Wellington Urban, Wellington Rural, and Hadley C.P.s (1938 and 1965). They include the coalfield tns., for which no separate returns were made.
[71] S.R.O. 4417/1, pp. 10, 25, 31; /2.
[72] K. C. Riley, 'Changes in Population in the Wellington–Oakengates Conurbation 1801–1951' (London Univ. M.A. thesis, 1958), 167; below, Econ. Hist. (Sugar).
[73] *V.C.H. Salop*. i. 317.
[74] Below.
[75] *Cal. Pat.* 1313–17, 333.
[76] S.R.O. 999/Tt 4 (field name); 1931/3.
[77] S.R.O. 14, tithe map and appt. (no. 1379); S. Bagshaw, *Dir. Salop.* (1851), 433; O.S. Map 1/2,500, Salop. XXXVI. 9 (1882 edn.).
[78] *Reg. Regum Anglo-Norm.* iii, nos. 376, 378–9; above, Man. and Other Est.
[79] *L. & P. Hen. VIII*, xix (1), p. 278; S.R.O. 112, box 90, ct. r. of 1588; Walcot presentment of c. 1625; 999/EA 36, R 1, R 1A; S.P.L., Deeds 5894.
[80] S.R.O. 639/1.
[81] *Shropshire Mag.* Dec. 1961, 38.
[82] S. Bagshaw, *Dir. Salop.* (1851), 439; O.S. Map 1/2,500,

Salop. XXXV. 11 (1882 edn.).
[83] *Shropshire Mag.* Dec. 1961, 38.
[84] S.P.L., Deeds 2498, Mich. rental of 1680.
[85] *Cal. Inq. Misc.* i, pp. 83–4.
[86] S.R.O. 972, parcel 236, map of 1723.
[87] S.R.O. 14, tithe appt. (no. 167).
[88] S.R.O. 972, parcel 196, sale partic. p. 48.
[89] SA 15648.
[90] *Shropshire Star*, 29 Sept. 1978.
[91] S.R.O. 999/Qq 8. Windmill field (ibid.), and Windmill leasow occurred in 1842: ibid.; S.R.O. 14, tithe appt.; 1856/5 (nos. 42, 48). They were probably named from the nearby mill in Wellington tns. (above).
[92] S.R.O. 14, tithe appt.; 1856/5 (nos. 131, 134).
[93] S.R.O. 1224, box 250, deed.
[94] R. Baugh, *Map of Salop.* (1808); not on B.L. Maps, O.S.D. 208 (1817).
[95] S.R.O. 14, tithe appt. and map (nos. 90, 158).
[96] *Cal. Chart. R.* 1226–57, 277; 1257–1300, 267.
[97] *L. & P. Hen. VIII*, i (2), p. 1400.
[98] S.R.O. 604 (uncat.), letters patent (copy).
[99] [U. B. M. Rayska,] 'Wellington Mkt.' (TS. [1981]; written for Wellington (Salop) Markets Co. Ltd.), 2.
[1] S.R.O. 604 (uncat.), deed (copy).

authorized.[2] In 1960[3] the Wellington (Salop) Markets (Successors) Co. Ltd. superseded the 1864 company. Another subsidiary market day, Tuesday, was introduced in 1970.[4]

By 1680 a market hall, open beneath,[5] stood in the middle of the broad southern end of Church Street,[6] which then served as the market place.[7] The hall was c. 12 metres north–south and c. 6 metres east–west.[8] It was presumably timber-framed, for it was dismantled and sold[9] c. 1800.[10] There was afterwards no cover for women selling butter, eggs, etc.,[11] until 1848, when the company built a town hall[12] off Butchers Lane[13] with an open butter market beneath.[14] General markets remained in the street until 1866. The company then opened a large market hall and yard on the site of the town hall (then rebuilt), and in 1868 added a corn exchange. A covered potato market was included in the 1866 building[15] and there was a wholesale vegetable market in 1890.[16] Butter was being sold wholesale in 1927[17] and the corn exchange remained active until the eve of the Second World War.[18]

The general market had 105 permanent stall holders in 1975. It remained popular despite competition from Telford town centre's new hypermarket,[19] and Wellington retailers considered its drawing-power vital to Wellington's survival as a shopping centre.[20]

The market grant of 1244 included a fair on 10–12 June, and the renewal of 1283 mentioned a second on 28–30 August.[21] Under the renewal of 1514, however, the second fair was on 5–7 November,[22] presumably for fatstock. The renewal of 1692 mentioned only one fair, beginning 18 March,[23] presumably for store animals,[24] but the other fairs continued, being held in 1727 on 24 June and 10 November.[25] The June fair was noted for cart-horses. By 1772 the dates had changed to 29 March, 22 June, and 17 November.[26] The first was said in 1802 to be on 2 March,[27] but it was on 29 March again by 1825 and lasted three days.[28] By 1835 a fourth fair was added on 29 September

and was noted for butter and cheese. The fairs were otherwise mainly devoted to livestock.[29] In 1825 the cattle fair was on the Green[30] on the north side of the churchyard. The horse fair was held on a separate site, probably at the bottom of Tan Bank, by the late 17th century,[31] and at the 'top' of New Street in 1825.[32]

It became desirable to withdraw livestock from the weekly markets, and from c. 1840 the four traditional fairs were therefore supplemented by fairs on the last Thursdays of all other months (changed to Mondays in 1841).[33] By 1851 the December fair was held on the Monday week before Christmas.[34] From that year the fairs increasingly took the forms of auctions and in 1855 moved to a railside Smithfield[35] south-east of the station,[36] provided by the auctioneer John Barber. After the 1866 cattle plague it was replaced[37] in 1867 by a new Smithfield[38] next to the railway off Bridge Road,[39] provided by the market company.[40] By 1879 sales were held there every Monday and the traditional fairs had ceased.[41]

In the later 19th century Wellington's sales had the advantage over Newport's and Shifnal's of good rail links both to the stock fattening areas of south and east Shropshire and to the butchers of Birmingham and the Black Country,[42] and in 1890 Wellington was second only to Shrewsbury in frequency of sales.[43] In 1910 there were 22,000 cattle and 56,000 sheep sold, but by 1950 only 3,000 and 11,000.[44] With increasing use of motor transport Wellington lost its former advantage and was especially difficult of access by road from south of the Severn. Over the same period, having prospered as one of the leading Midland fatstock markets, Wellington's sales suffered from a movement in east Shropshire towards dairy and cereal farming.[45] Nevertheless in 1981 Wellington's remained predominantly a fatstock market; in that year 2,100 cattle were sold, 7,200 sheep, and 5,400 pigs.[46]

By 1927 there were sales of breeding ewes and store lambs every September.[47] From the 1850s

[2] Wellington (Salop) Market Act, 1864, 27 & 28 Vic. c. 103 (Local and Personal).
[3] *Shropshire Mag.* May 1975, 23.
[4] Inf. from the secretary, Wellington (Salop) Markets Co. Ltd. The word '(Successors)' was dropped in the 1960s.
[5] S.R.O. 1224, box 204, ct. r.
[6] S.R.O. 1224/1/6.
[7] Earlier mkt. places are described above, Growth of Settlement. [8] S.R.O. 1224/1/6.
[9] S.R.O. 604 (uncat.), petition of 1826.
[10] *Temp.* Geo. Forester: ibid. It was standing 1793 (S.R.O. 1224/1/6), gone by 1806 (1931/3).
[11] S.R.O. 604 (uncat.), petition of 1826.
[12] Rayska, 'Wellington Mkt.' 2.
[13] S.R.O., dep. plan 575.
[14] S. Bagshaw, *Dir. Salop.* (1851), 423–4.
[15] Rayska, 'Wellington Mkt.' 3.
[16] *Rep. R. Com. Mkt. Rights*, xiii (2) [C. 6268–VIa], p. 424, H.C. (1890–1), xl.
[17] Min. of Agric. & Fisheries, *Rep. on Mkts. & Fairs in Eng. & Wales*, ii (H.M.S.O. 1927), 53.
[18] Inf. from Mr. R. W. L. Oakes, partner in Messrs. Barber & Son.
[19] *Shropshire Mag.* May 1975, 23, 25.
[20] *Shropshire Jnl.* 7 Nov. 1969; *Telford Jnl.* 21 Aug. 1981.
[21] *Cal. Chart. R.* 1226–57, 277; 1257–1300, 267.
[22] *L. & P. Hen. VIII*, i. (2), p. 1400.
[23] S.R.O. 604 (uncat.), letters patent (copy).
[24] A cattle fair 1751 and 1752: S.R.O., q. sess. order bk.

1741–57, ff. 175v., 191.
[25] T. Cox and A. Hall, *Magna Britannia*, iv (1727), 632.
[26] *Shrews. Chron.* 12 Dec. 1772.
[27] J. Plymley, *Gen. View of Agric. of Salop.* (1803), 338.
[28] S.R.O. 1224, box 295, Wm. Pearce to Geo. Pritchard, 21 Mar. 1825.
[29] Pigot, *Nat. Com. Dir.* (1835), 380.
[30] S.R.O. 1224, box 295, Pearce to Pritchard, 21 Mar. 1825.
[31] Ibid. box 204, ct. r. of 1689. The Pool Head (below, Public Services) was in the same street.
[32] Ibid. box 295, Pearce to Pritchard, 21 Mar. 1825.
[33] *Shrews. News & Cambrian Reporter*, 6 Feb. 1841.
[34] S. Bagshaw, *Dir. Salop.* (1851), 422.
[35] W. M. Moisley, 'Mkts. of Salop.' (London Univ. M.Sc. thesis, 1951), 36, 38.
[36] Nr. Smithfield Pl. (later Victoria St.): O.S. Map 1/500, Salop. XXXVI. 9. 19 (1882 edn.).
[37] Inf. from Mr. Oakes.
[38] Rayska, 'Wellington Mkt.' 3.
[39] O.S. Map 1/500, Salop. XXXVI. 9. 12 (1882 edn.).
[40] Inf. from Mr. Oakes.
[41] *P.O. Dir. Salop.* (1879), 425.
[42] Moisley, 'Mkts. of Salop.' 46, 47 n., 72.
[43] Ibid. 40.
[44] Ibid. 70.
[45] Ibid. 47, 55, 72.
[46] Inf. from Mr. Oakes.
[47] Min. of Ag. & Fish. *Rep. Mkts. & Fairs*, ii. 55.

wool sales, the largest in the Midlands, had been held just outside the town[48] every June or July, with 50,000–60,000 fleeces a year in the 1920s,[49] but they ceased in 1938[50] and local sheep farming declined markedly thereafter.[51] Barber & Son held monthly horse sales at their Wrekin Horse Repository,[52] Market Street[53] (opened 1891),[54] but had ended them by 1927.[55]

TRADES AND INDUSTRIES. By the earlier 14th century cloth and leather trades were established in the town; they were to survive into the 18th and 19th centuries respectively.

The surnames Chaloner, Mercer, Shearman, Tailor, Teyntour, and Walker occurred in the town in the earlier 14th century,[56] and in the 17th and 18th there were many dyers, mercers, and tailors.[57] Walker Street[58] may have housed fullers, and by the late 17th century fulling was done at Allscott and Walcot mills.[59] In the 17th and 18th centuries spinning and weaving were carried on, mostly at a domestic level and outside the town, using local hemp, flax, and wool.[60] Hempen cloth was then among the chief commodities at Wellington markets and fairs.[61] In the earlier 19th century the town's drapers, tailors, and clothing retailers remained numerous but local cloth manufacture had probably ceased.[62]

The surnames Barker and Corvisor occurred in the town in the 14th century[63] and Shrewsbury tanners were selling hides at Wellington market in the early 15th.[64] Between the 16th and 18th centuries the town had many leather workers[65] and by the late 17th century manorial leather inspectors were elected.[66] There was a tannery in Walker Street in 1690.[67] Tan Bank[68] is said to have been the site of another.[69] The town had a tannery in 1804[70] but the office of leather sealer lapsed in 1811.[71] Other tanneries worked in the mid 19th

century but none later.[72]

The surnames Carpenter and Cooper in the 14th century[73] indicate the presence of another range of essential crafts. Other trades in the 16th, 17th, and 18th centuries were bell founding, rope making, and nailing. Bell founding was carried on by the Clibury family from c. 1590 to c. 1682 and their business continued into the next century under John Bradshaw.[74] The foundry was said to have been near the later Charlton Arms, Church Street.[75] There was more than one roper in Wellington manor by 1688.[76] John Barney set up in New Street in the 1820s[77] and Edward Barney succeeded him; his shop was in New Street, his ropewalk in Water Lane.[78] By 1842 Thomas Heywood had the business[79] and his family continued rope making until the 1900s.[80] The Wellington Rope Spinning, Saddlery, & Harness Co. were rope makers in Glebe Street from the 1900s to the 1920s.[81] Wellington was noted for nails by the 18th century.[82] There were workshops in 1724[83] and a Naylors Square in 1772.[84] Richard Emery was a lessee of nailers' shops in New Street in 1783, and his son was a nail manufacturer there from 1809[85] until at least 1828.[86] The town had ten shops in 1842, many of them in or near New Street,[87] off which lay Nailors Row.[88] Some nail making continued until late in the century.[89]

At the end of the 18th century there were no regular local banking services. In 1805, however, Thomas Eyton, receiver-general of Shropshire and a local landowner,[90] formed a banking partnership at Wellington with two industrial entrepreneurs, John Wilkinson and Joseph Reynolds.[91] The bank offered assistance to local industrialists.[92] By 1828 the firm was Reynolds, Charlton & Co., with premises in the Market Place.[93] In 1836 the bank united with others in Coalbrookdale, Newport, and Shifnal to form the

[48] *Wellington Before Telford*, 12.
[49] Min. of Ag. & Fish. *Rep. Mkts. & Fairs*, ii. 55, 136.
[50] Inf. from Mr. Oakes.
[51] Moisley, 'Mkts. of Salop.' 55–6.
[52] *Wellington Jnl.* 10 Mar. 1900.
[53] Inf. from Mr. Oakes.
[54] Rayska, 'Wellington Mkt.' 4.
[55] None mentioned in Min. of Ag. & Fish. *Rep. Mkts. & Fairs*, ii.
[56] S.R.O. 1224, box 204, ct. r. of 1345–6.
[57] Trinder and Cox, *Yeomen and Colliers*, pp. 47, 49, 120–59.
[58] So named by 1680: S.R.O. 1224, box 204, ct. r. Medieval streets of the same name were in Stratford upon Avon and Warwick: *P.N. Warws.* (E.P.N.S.), 237, 261.
[59] Above, Mills; below Wrockwardine, Econ. Hist.
[60] Trinder and Cox, *Yeomen and Colliers*, pp. 62–3.
[61] *Eng. Topog.* (Gent. Mag. Libr.), x. 155.
[62] Tibnam & Co. *Salop. Dir.* (1828), 119, 121, 123–4; Pigot, *Nat. Com. Dir.* (1835), 381–2.
[63] *T.S.A.S.* 2nd ser. i. 174; S.R.O. 1224, box 204, ct. r. of 1345.
[64] *Salop. Peace Roll, 1400–14*, ed. E. G. Kimball (1959), p. 115.
[65] *Cal. Pat.* 1553–4, 452; Baxter, 'Wellington', 55; B. Trinder, 'Two Probate Invs. from Industrial Salop.' *Ind. Arch. Rev.* iii. 239–42; L.J.R.O., B/C/11, Wm. Allen, 1628; Trinder and Cox, *Yeomen and Colliers*, pp. 120–59; S.R.O. 1224, box 204, ct. r. of 1688; par. reg. bur. 26 May 1758; marr. 11 Oct. 1772 (transcript in S.P.L.).
[66] Below, Local Govt.
[67] S.R.O. 1224, parcel 205, ct. bk. 26 Oct. 1690.
[68] So called by 1769: ibid. box 253, deed.
[69] *Wellington Before Telford*, 8.
[70] S.R.O. 625, box 11, deed.
[71] Below, Local Govt.
[72] Pigot, *Nat. Com. Dir.* (1835), 383; *P.O. Dir. Salop.* (1856), 213; (1870), 268–9.
[73] S.R.O. 1224, box 204, ct. r. of 1345.
[74] H. B. Walters, *Ch. Bells of Salop.* (Oswestry, 1915), 416–17, 426–31, 484; *Salop. News Letter*, xlv. 16–17.
[75] D. Mason, 'Churches of the Broseley Area', *Jnl. Wilkinson Soc.* ii. 4.
[76] S.R.O. 1224, box 204, ct. r.
[77] Tibnam & Co. *Salop. Dir.* (1828), 125; not mentioned in S.R.O. 3129/5/5.
[78] Pigot, *Nat. Com. Dir.* (1835), 383; S.R.O. 14, tithe appt. and map (nos. 308, 798); 746/5.
[79] Pigot, *Nat. Com. Dir.* (1842), 48.
[80] S. Bagshaw, *Dir. Salop.* (1851), 429; *P.O. Dir. Salop.* (1879), 428; *Kelly's Dir. Salop.* (1885), 976, and later edns. They continued as dealers until the 1930s.
[81] *Kelly's Dir. Salop.* (1909), 278, and later edns.
[82] *Eng. Topog.* (Gent. Mag. Libr.), x. 155.
[83] S.R.O. 4309, survey, f. 70.
[84] S.R.O. 81/482.
[85] S.R.O. 1224, box 254, deed of 1809.
[86] Tibnam & Co. *Salop. Dir.* (1828), 122.
[87] S.R.O. 14, tithe appt. and map; Pigot, *Nat. Com. Dir.* (1842), 46–7.
[88] S. Bagshaw, *Dir. Salop.* (1851), 427.
[89] *P.O. Dir. Salop.* (1870), 159.
[90] Above, Eyton, Man. and Other Est.
[91] R. S. Sayers, *Lloyd's Bank in the Hist. of Eng. Banking* (1957), 277; Trinder, *Ind. Rev. Salop.* (1981), 138.
[92] L. S. Pressnell, *Country Banking in the Ind. Rev.* (1956), 327; Sayers, op. cit. 20.
[93] Tibnam & Co. *Salop. Dir.* (1828), 118.

Shropshire Banking Co. (taken over by Lloyd's Banking Co. Ltd. in 1874),[94] with a branch in Church Street.[95] Three other banks (eventually incorporated in the main clearing banks) opened branches in the town between 1863 and 1926.[96] By 1856 there were five solicitors in the town, some of whom also undertook public business arising from Wellington's role as an administrative centre, such as clerkships to the divisional magistrates, the county court, and the canal and railway companies. One, for instance, was superintendent registrar, another county coroner and deputy steward of Bradford hundred court.[97]

Printing in Wellington began a little later than in some other Shropshire towns. F. Houlston & Son, booksellers, began printing and publishing c. 1805, specializing in religious and educational works.[98] Their best known authors were Mrs. Lucy Cameron and her sister Mrs. Mary Martha Sherwood. The firm transferred most of its publishing business to London in the 1820s[99] but (as Houlston & Son)[1] continued printing in Wellington.[2] Robert Hobson acquired the Wellington business (later Hobson & Co.)[3] c. 1850.[4] He started the town's first newspaper in 1849.[5] The printing side of the business ceased c. 1974.[6] Benjamin Smith was printing in New Street by 1821[7] and until the 1870s.[8] James Keay was a printer in the same street by 1851[9] and the business continued until c. 1907.[10] John Jones (later John Jones & Son)[11] began printing c. 1878 at the Lawns.[12] The firm moved to King Street c. 1930,[13] where it remained until c. 1973.[14] In 1982 there were at least three small printers in the town, all recent arrivals.[15]

In the 19th century industries on a larger scale than any previously known in Wellington began to establish themselves in the town and its outskirts. They comprised malting and brewing; the extensive timber yard and works of the Groom company, a business that contributed perhaps more than any other to Wellington's commercial growth in the 19th century;[16] several engineering firms, including one (S. Corbett & Son) with a national

reputation for agricultural machinery; and brick and tile manufacturers.

Malt was milled in Wellington in 1601[17] and malt mills were mentioned in 1663[18] and 1759.[19] Some 17th- and 18th-century public houses seem to have brewed for wholesale[20] and in 1771 John Espley gave his occupation as brewer.[21] There were fifteen maltsters in 1828[22] and malting was on a large scale in 1851,[23] when the first of several large brewing concerns, the Shropshire Brewery, was founded by Richard Taylor.[24] In the 1870s it passed to Anslow & Wackrill[25] (later J. G. Wackrill).[26] The premises were in Watling Street, opposite the Old Hall.[27] The brewery passed to Potter & Co. (later Potter & Cockburn) in the 1890s[28] and to N. Butler & Co. of Wolverhampton in 1912,[29] when it closed.[30] In 1877[31] Edwin Pitchford & Co. opened the Union Brewery[32] in the former workhouse, Walker Street.[33] The Union Brewery Co. belonged to Benjamin Garbett by 1891[34] and remained in business until c. 1920.[35] The Red Lion Brewery Co. opened premises in New Church Road c. 1907[36] and seems to have closed in the 1920s.[37] The last surviving brewery was the Wrekin Brewery established by Thomas Taylor in Market Street in 1870.[38] He sold the Wrekin Brewery Co.[39] in 1901[40] and the Murphy family controlled it 1921–66.[41] In 1921 it owned 24 licensed and 9 beer houses, mostly in east Shropshire;[42] in 1966 it had 201 houses. The brewery closed, however, in 1969.[43] Malting had long remained a significant local industry. There were four maltsters in the town in the later 19th and early 20th century, and in 1941 only Wellington, Shrewsbury, and Wem had more than one.[44] In Wellington, however, none remained by 1969.[45]

Herbert Phillips set up as a mineral-water manufacturer at Mill Bank c. 1890. H. Phillips & Co. may have passed c. 1907 to O. D. Murphy (later O. D. Murphy & Sons Ltd.) who moved the business in 1912 to the former Shropshire Brewery.[46] It closed in 1969.[47]

In the 1840s Wellington was the county's prin-

[94] Sayers, op. cit. 80, 242.
[95] Pigot, *Nat. Com. Dir.* (1842), 45.
[96] *Wellington Before Telford*, 13; *Kelly's Dir. Salop.* (1905), 274; date '1926' on rainwater head, Nat. Westminster Bank, Church St.
[97] *P.O. Dir. Salop.* (1856), 136–7, 210.
[98] *T.S.A.S.* xlviii. 87, 128.
[99] *Shropshire Mag.* Apr. 1959, 15–16.
[1] Tibnam & Co. *Salop. Dir.* (1828), 118; M. N. Cutt, *Mrs. Sherwood and her Books for Children* (1974), 111.
[2] Pigot, *Nat. Com. Dir.* (1835), 381.
[3] *P.O. Dir. Salop.* (1879), 428.
[4] S. Bagshaw, *Dir. Salop.* (1851), 432; Review Publishing Co. *Inds. of Salop.* 38.
[5] Above, Social and Cultural Activities.
[6] P.O. *Telephone Dir.* (1975), sect. 303, p. 145.
[7] S.R.O. 3129/5/5, p. 1.
[8] *P.O. Dir. Salop.* (1870), 137.
[9] S. Bagshaw, *Dir. Salop.* (1851), 430.
[10] *Kelly's Dir. Salop.* (1900), 264; (1905), 273.
[11] Ibid. (1917), 269.
[12] Review Publishing Co. *Inds. of Salop.* 39.
[13] *Kelly's Dir. Salop.* (1934), 304.
[14] P.O. *Telephone Dir.* (1972), sect. 303, yellow p. 138.
[15] Brit. Telecom, *Dir.* (1982), sect. 303 (YP), p. 251.
[16] Rev@w Publishing Co. *Inds. of Salop.* 36.
[17] S.R.O. 999/Tt 1.
[18] S.P.L., Deeds 2498, Mich. rental.
[19] S.R.O. 625, box 11, deed (draft).
[20] Trinder and Cox, *Yeomen and Colliers*, pp. 111–13.
[21] Par. reg. marr. 1 Apr. 1771 (transcript in S.P.L.).
[22] Tibnam & Co. *Salop. Dir.* (1828), 121–2.
[23] S. Bagshaw, *Dir. Salop.* (1851), 422.
[24] S.R.O. 3022/2.
[25] *P.O. Dir. Salop.* (1879), 427.
[26] S.R.O. 3022/2.
[27] O.S. Map 1/500, Salop. XXXVI. 9. 24 (1882 edn.).
[28] *Kelly's Dir. Salop.* (1895), 249; (1900), 264.
[29] S.R.O. 4011/84/1, no. 787.
[30] *Shropshire Mag.* May 1976, 21.
[31] Review Publishing Co. *Inds. of Salop.* 42.
[32] *P.O. Dir. Salop.* (1879), 429.
[33] *Shropshire Mag.* Nov. 1969, 28.
[34] Review Publishing Co. *Inds. of Salop.* 42.
[35] *Kelly's Dir. Salop.* (1917), 270.
[36] Ibid. (1909), 278.
[37] Ibid. (1922), 279.
[38] S.R.O. 436/7202.
[39] *Kelly's Dir. Salop.* (1895), 250.
[40] S.R.O. 436/7202.
[41] *Shropshire Mag.* May 1976, 21; above, Eyton, Man. and Other Est.
[42] S.R.O. 436/7202.
[43] *Shropshire Mag.* May 1976, 21.
[44] *P.O. Dir. Salop.* (1856 and later edns.); *Kelly's Dir. Salop.* (1885 and later edns.).
[45] G.P.O. *Telephone Dir.* (1969), sect. 72, yellow p. 94.
[46] *Kelly's Dir. Salop.* (1891 and later edns.); Jones, *Dir. Wellington* (1934), 41.
[47] *Shropshire Mag.* May 1976, 21.

cipal chair-making centre[48] and in 1842 at least sixteen men in New Street traded as chair makers, wood turners, coopers, joiners, cabinet makers, timber merchants, or wheelwrights.[49] One of them was R. G. Groom, a former basket maker[50] and by 1835 the founder of a timber business[51] that was to make the Grooms the town's leading family.[52] In the 1850s Groom & Sons became Richard & Thomas Groom,[53] the founder's sons[54] having succeeded him. In the 1870s, as Richard & Thomas Groom & Sons, the firm was also making turned goods,[55] and by 1882 had the railside Shropshire Works (formerly of John Dickson & Co.)[56] off Bridge Road, consisting of saw mills and a bendware and turnery factory.[57] In 1883 Thomas Groom founded the Wrekin Chemical works in Limekiln Lane to produce chemicals from wood. Complaints of stench caused removal of the works to Stirchley in 1886.[58] The products of R. Groom, Sons, & Co. ranged from clothes pegs to heavy civil engineering timbers, and Grooms were reputedly the country's largest timber buyers.[59] The firm remained at Bridge Road until c. 1970.[60]

Francis Stone set up as a cabinet maker and furniture broker in New Street c. 1845.[61] By 1870 he had moved to Crown Street[62] and was there succeeded by Richard Stone.[63] The latter also had the Crown Works, Cemetery Road, by 1891,[64] and another branch at Oakengates by 1900.[65] As Richard Stone & Sons Ltd., later the Crown Works (Wellington) Ltd.,[66] the firm set up c. 1910 as wholesale cabinet makers at a new Crown Works in Orleton Lane[67] beside the railway[68] and remained there until c. 1940.[69]

About 1895 Henry Addison & Co. (formerly H. & S. Addison), makers of church and school furniture, opened their railside Waterloo Works[70] in the former Springhill foundry in Orleton Lane,[71] remaining there until c. 1940.[72]

Engineering firms began to be established in the early 19th century. John Edge, a blacksmith in Walker Street in 1821,[73] was a brass founder by 1824,[74] and in 1842 William Edge was making agricultural machinery in the same street.[75]

By 1838 Margaret Jones & Son had an iron and brass foundry on the north side of Newhall Street (later Foundry Lane).[76] By 1851 it belonged to William Mansell.[77] Known as the Wrekin Foundry by 1891, it then occupied c. 2 a. and made industrial machinery.[78] In the 1900s it passed briefly to Duncan Sinclair[79] and then to James Clay & Co.,[80] agricultural engineers, later James Clay (Wellington) Ltd.,[81] who moved the Wrekin Foundry to the Ketleybrook area in 1924.[82]

By 1851 William Edwards & Son (later John Edwards & Co.)[83] had an iron foundry[84] on the other side of Foundry Lane.[85] In the 1890s it became a factory for bread-making machinery.[86] By 1913 the site seems to have passed to a firm of motor engineers.[87]

In the early 1850s Samuel Corbett, a blacksmith in King Street,[88] set up in Park Street as an agricultural implement maker.[89] By the 1870s, as S. Corbett & Son, the firm's agricultural machinery business was flourishing.[90] By the 1890s Corbetts were among the country's best known manufacturers[91] and they continued at Park Street until 1974.[92]

S. Corbett & Son had an ironmongery business in Church Street, which passed in the 1890s to W. Corbett & Co. By 1909 that firm was making galvanized iron tanks in Alexandra Road.[93] In the 1920s or 1930s it acquired new premises nearby,[94] the Alexandra works,[95] where it remained as W. Corbett & Co. (Wellington) Ltd. in 1982.[96]

William Botwood was a coach builder at Tan Bank in 1851,[97] and in 1870 E. C. Clift, formerly of Leominster,[98] was a partner in Clift & Dawson (later Clift & Son),[99] coach builders, also of Tan

[48] B. Cotton, 'Country chairs and their makers', *Antique Dealer & Collector's Guide*, May 1983, 48.
[49] Pigot, *Nat. Com. Dir.* (1842), 45–7.
[50] S.R.O. 3129/5/5, p. 2; Mate, *Salop.* pt. 2, p. 192.
[51] Pigot, *Nat. Com. Dir.* (1835), 382.
[52] Pooler, *My Life in General Practice*, 13.
[53] S. Bagshaw, *Dir. Salop.* (1851), 429; *P.O. Dir. Salop.* (1856), 136.
[54] S.R.O. 3129/5/5, p. 2.
[55] *P.O. Dir. Salop.* (1870), 158; (1879), 428.
[56] Ibid. (1856), 135.
[57] O.S. Map 1/500, Salop. XXXVI. 9. 17 (1882 edn.).
[58] *Wellington Jnl.* 30 Aug. 1884; W. Howard Williams, 'Dawley New Town Hist. Survey: Industries' (TS. 1964), p. 39 (copy in S.P.L., accession 5202); above, Stirchley, Econ. Hist.
[59] Review Publishing Co. *Inds. of Salop.* 36.
[60] G.P.O. *Telephone Dir.* (1969), sect. 72, p. 112.
[61] S. Bagshaw, *Dir. Salop.* (1851), 433; Review Publishing Co. *Inds. of Salop.* 41.
[62] *P.O. Dir. Salop.* (1870), 159.
[63] Ibid. (1879), 429.
[64] Review Publishing Co. *Inds. of Salop.* 41.
[65] *Kelly's Dir. Salop.* (1900), 265.
[66] Ibid. (1934), 303.
[67] Ibid. (1913), 285; S.R.O. 4011/84/5, no. 4049.
[68] O.S. Map 1/2,500, Salop. XXXVI. 9 (1927 edn.).
[69] *Kelly's Dir. Salop.* (1937), 283.
[70] *Guide to the Church Congress and Eccl. Art Exhibition to be held at Shrews.* (1896), 222 (copy in S.R.O. 2605/1).
[71] O.S. Map 1/2,500, Salop. XXXVI. 9 (1882 and 1902 edns.).
[72] *Kelly's Dir. Salop.* (1937), 282.

[73] S.R.O. 3129/5/5, p. 77.
[74] S.R.O. 1224, box 206, ct. r.
[75] Pigot, *Nat. Com. Dir.* (1842), 46.
h17[6] Ibid.; S.R.O. 746/5; S.R.O. 14, tithe appt. and map (no. 314).
[77] S. Bagshaw, *Dir. Salop.* (1851), 430. It was later claimed that he founded the business c. 1830: Review Publishing Co. *Inds. of Salop.* 39.
[78] Review Publishing Co. op. cit. 39.
[79] *Kelly's Dir. Salop.* (1900), 264; Riley, 'Population in Wellington–Oakengates', 142.
[80] S.R.O. 4011/84/1, no. 15.
[81] *Kelly's Dir. Salop.* (1909), 276; (1913), 283.
[82] Below, Hadley, Econ. Hist.
[83] *P.O. Dir. Salop.* (1870), 158.
[84] S. Bagshaw, *Dir. Salop.* (1851), 429.
[85] O.S. Map 1/500, Salop. XXXVI. 9. 18 (1882 edn.).
[86] *Kelly's Dir. Salop.* (1900), 264; S.R.O. 4011/84/3, no. 2099.
[87] *Kelly's Dir. Salop.* (1913), 285.
[88] S. Bagshaw, *Dir. Salop.* (1851), 428.
[89] *P.O. Dir. Salop.* (1856), 135.
[90] S.R.O. 3185/5.
[91] Review Publishing Co. *Inds. of Salop.* 37.
[92] Local inf.
[93] *Kelly's Dir. Salop.* (1891), 459; (1900), 263; (1909), 276.
[94] O.S. Map 1/2,500, Salop. XXXVI. 9 (1927 and 1939 edns.).
[95] County Assocs. Ltd. *Wellington & Dist. Dir.* [1950], 4.
[96] Brit. Telecom, *Dir.* (1982), sect. 303 (Alpha), p. 86.
[97] S. Bagshaw, *Dir. Salop.* (1851), 428.
[98] Mate, *Salop.* pt. 2, p. 188.
[99] *Kelly's Dir. Salop.* (1885), 976.

Bank[1] and perhaps successors to Botwood.[2] By the 1890s their Excelsior Carriage Works was exporting to the empire.[3] The firm made motor-car bodies by 1913 as the Excelsior Motor and Carriage Works. Duncan Campbell acquired it in the later 1920s[4] but ceased coach building in the 1940s.[5]

In the 1870s Richard and Thomas Haynes were making agricultural implements in Foundry Lane.[6] The firm (later Haynes & Bromley)[7] set up in Bridge Road in 1882[8] and by 1909 were ironmongers, agricultural implement dealers, and agricultural engineers.[9] By the 1960s as John Bromley & Co. (Wellington) Ltd., reputedly the county's oldest agricultural hardware merchants, they traded throughout Shropshire[10] but c. 1970 they closed.[11]

The Victoria Sheet Metal Co. began in Victoria Street[12] in 1921[13] and moved in the 1940s to the vacant Crown Works.[14] In 1949 the firm began to specialize in making tractor cabs and by the 1960s was one of the country's leading makers.[15] It left for Broseley c. 1972.[16]

By the mid 17th century bricks had been made at several sites[17] but probably intermittently. In 1738 St. John Charlton paid for the making of 50,000 bricks and 17,500 tiles at Apley.[18] In the later 18th century, however, demand justified continuously working kilns centrally sited. In 1763 Brooke Forester let a kiln in Wellington for 21 years to a tenant who would supply him with bricks and tiles for repairs anywhere in the parish.[19] In 1842 Wellington had at least six brick makers, most of them in New Street,[20] including Richard Corbett, who also owned a brick yard in Wrekin Road.[21] John Corbett occupied it in 1851[22] but it seems to have closed soon after.[23] In the 1870s another Richard founded the Haygate Brick Works in Haygate Road,[24] which remained in production until the 1890s.[25] By 1870 John Millington, a brick and tile maker and coal merchant at Ketley,[26] established the Marquis Coal & Tilery Co. with a railside brickworks off Orleton Lane[27]

but production ceased before 1891.[28]

In 1916 Johnson Bros., of Birmingham, bought the former Central Hall, New Street,[29] and it became the Wrekin Toy Factory.[30] By 1922 it belonged to the Chad Valley Co. Ltd. as the Wrekin Toy Works.[31] In 1972 there were over 150 employees[32] but by 1975, when it closed, only 78.[33] In 1926 Norah Wellings, a former designer at the Wrekin Toy Works,[34] began making dolls at the former Baptist chapel, King Street,[35] renamed the Victoria Toy Works.[36] It closed c. 1959.[37]

QUARRIES, MINES, AND SANDPITS. Carboniferous limestone outcropped in Watling Street township in a band stretching north-eastwards from the Little Wenlock boundary to Steeraway.[38] In 1240 the Shrewsbury Dominicans received lime from the king's new kiln under Mount Gilbert[39] and in 1255 the king had two oak-fired kilns in Wellington hay.[40]

In the later 17th century the Steeraway kilns, all on the Forester estate, were coal-fired. Lime was sent north as far as Cold Hatton (in Ercall Magna) and west as far as Hunkington (in Upton Magna). Production fluctuated widely: 120 'hundreds' were sold from Steeraway in 1685, but in the next year only 39.[41] In 1716 output was 121 hundreds (726 loads),[42] fewer than at the Little Wenlock kilns.[43] A railway linked Steeraway to the Watling Street by the late 1730s.[44]

In the 18th and 19th centuries management of the limeworks was in the same hands as at Little Wenlock.[45] Limestone extraction was stimulated by local iron making. In the 1800s there was at least one deep shaft. In 1842 a 45-ft. seam was being worked and 100 men and 20 boys were employed.[46] Fluxing limestone was probably exhausted by the mid 19th century; Ketley was importing it from Wales by 1837.[47] Agricultural and building lime was nevertheless still needed and in 1882, when mining resumed at Steeraway, there were several shafts, levels, and kilns.[48] There were 22 employees in 1883 and 4,400 tons

[1] P.O. Dir. Salop. (1870), 157.
[2] Clift's firm claimed c. 1890 to have been founded in 1845: S.R.O. 2390/5.
[3] Review Publishing Co. Inds. of Salop. 36.
[4] Kelly's Dir. Salop. (1913), 283; (1922), 277; (1929), 291.
[5] Ibid. (1941), 280; County Assocs. Ltd. Wellington & Dist. Dir. [1950], 45.
[6] P.O. Dir. Salop. (1879), 428.
[7] Kelly's Dir. Salop. (1891), 510.
[8] Ibid. (1885), 976; Ed. J. Burrow & Co. Ltd. Wellington R.D. Official Guide [1962], 31.
[9] Kelly's Dir. Salop. (1909), 275.
[10] Burrow, op. cit. 31.
[11] G.P.O. Telephone Dir. (1969), sect. 72, p. 50.
[12] Kelly's Dir. Salop. (1922), 280.
[13] Burrow, Wellington R.D. Official Guide [1967], 27.
[14] County Assocs. Ltd. Wellington & Dist. Dir. [1950], 51.
[15] Burrow, op. cit. 27-8.
[16] P.O. Telephone Dir. (1971), sect. 303, p. 243; (1972), sect. 303, p. 260, s.v. Victor Cabs Ltd.
[17] e.g. Brick furlong, Arleston, 1603 (S.R.O. 999/Qq 8); Brick Kiln leasow, Dothill, 1626 (1224/1/1); Brick field, Wappenshall, 1649 (625, box 10, deed of 1654).
[18] S.R.O. 676/12, p. 21.
[19] S.R.O. 1224, box 253, deed.
[20] Pigot, Nat. Com. Dir. (1842), 45-7.
[21] S.R.O. 14, tithe appt. and map (no. 1235).
[22] S. Bagshaw, Dir. Salop. (1851), 433.
[23] Not mentioned in P.O. Dir. Salop. (1856).
[24] Ibid. (1879), 428; O.S. Map 1/500, Salop. XXXVI. 9. 22

(1882 edn.).
[25] Kelly's Dir. Salop. (1891), 459; (1895), 247.
[26] P.O. Dir. Salop. (1856), 63.
[27] Ibid. (1870), 158; O.S. Map 1/500, Salop. XXXVI. 9. 12 (1882 edn.).
[28] Kelly's Dir. Salop. (1891), 460.
[29] Lenton, Methodism in Wellington, 28.
[30] S.R.O., DA 13/514/5, f. 39; /514/12, f. 35.
[31] Kelly's Dir. Salop. (1922), 277.
[32] Burrow, Wellington Official Guide [1972], 31.
[33] Shropshire Star, 13 Feb. 1976.
[34] C. E. King, Dolls and Dolls' Houses (1977), 130.
[35] Kelly's Dir. Salop. (1929), 294.
[36] Ibid. (1937), 287.
[37] Wargrave Press, Wrekin Civic & Commercial Dir. (1958), 61.
[38] Inst. Geol. Sciences Map 1/25,000, Telford (1978 edn.).
[39] Cal. Lib. 1226-40, 466.
[40] Rot. Hund. (Rec. Com.), ii. 56.
[41] S.R.O. 1224, box 296, Steeraway acct. bk. 1685-9. On the local customary measures of lime see p. 86 nn. 68-9.
[42] S.R.O. 1224, parcel 298, lime acct. bk. 1715-17.
[43] Above, L. Wenlock, Econ. Hist.
[44] M. J. T. Lewis, Early Wooden Rlys. (1970), 238, 240; Trinder, Ind. Rev. Salop. (1981), 86.
[45] Above, L. Wenlock, Econ. Hist.
[46] Trinder, op. cit. 215.
[47] Ibid. 147.
[48] O.S. Maps 1/2,500, Salop. XXXVI. 13; XLIII. 1 (1882 edn.).

of stone were extracted in 1886. In 1900, however, 7 workers remained and mining ceased.[49] The kilns closed c. 1918.[50]

Much of Arleston township, with the adjoining part of Watling Street township, all within the Forester estate, lay south of the Boundary fault[51] and thus on the coalfield. They were the only parts of the parish, outside the three coalfield townships, where coal and ironstone mining occurred.

In the 1680s there was mining at Arleston, Arleston sough, and Short Wood.[52] In 1690 Short Wood yielded at least 555 stacks of coal and 166 dozens of ironstone and in 1691 Arleston sough produced at least 446 stacks of coal. At both sites the pits were sometimes leased,[53] as in 1712 when Sir William Forester let pits near Short Wood to two colliers from Oakengates.[54] Short Wood, however, was excluded from Richard Hartshorne's lease of 1718;[55] its coal was probably reserved for the nearby limekilns or for landsale, for by the late 1730s the coal and lime works were linked to each other by a railway that led northwards to the Watling Street.[56] Clod coals from Upper Short Wood and Birch Coppice, both in Watling Street township,[57] were included in the Forester contracts of 1740, 1750, and 1756 with the Coalbrookdale partners.[58] Other coals were sent to Shrewsbury via the Watling Street until the Shrewsbury Canal opened in 1797.[59]

From 1798, and possibly from 1784, the coalpits at Short Wood and Upper Short Wood were leased to the tenants of the limeworks[60] but mining may have ceased in the earlier 19th century.[61] From 1798, perhaps from 1777, coal and ironstone north and east of Arleston hamlet were among minerals leased to the Coalbrookdale Co.[62] Pits were worked there in the early 19th century[63] but none by 1882.[64]

In the early 20th century some small private pits were opened. Two shafts and a level were in use at Short Wood in 1925[65] and there was a mine there in 1945.[66] In 1953 the Brandlee Colliery Co. opened an adit mine at Short Wood, which employed c. 25 men and produced c. 200 tons of coal a week. It closed in 1970, the last private mine in east Shropshire.[67] In the 1950s opencast

working began at Upper Short Wood[68] and in 1977 north-west at Limekiln Lane, where 400,000 tons of power-station coal were expected.[69]

Igneous rocks for hardcore and roadstone[70] were being quarried at the Ercall and Lawrence's Hill, both in Watling Street township, by 1882.[71] In 1982 there were similar quarries at the Ercall and at Maddock's Hill[72] nearby (opened 1936).[73] Sandpits at Ketleysands were exploited in the 19th and 20th centuries.[74]

SUGAR. The Shropshire Beet Sugar Co. Ltd. opened Allscott sugar beet mill in 1927[75] in Walcot township. It passed to the British Sugar Corporation Ltd. (later British Sugar P.L.C.) in 1936[76] and remained the county's only such factory in 1982. Its sugar output rose from 6,487 tons in 1927–8 to 19,555 tons in 1930–1 and beet-growing in north-east Shropshire expanded correspondingly. Thereafter acreages grown, and consequently tonnages of sugar refined, fluctuated with the weather and the market.[77] The factory underwent considerable expansion and technological improvement between the 1940s and the 1980s. In 1950 there were 200 permanent and c. 250 seasonal employees and annual sugar production was c. 25,000 tons, with large tonnages of molasses and pulp.[78] In 1981–2 annual production of sugar was c. 45,000 tonnes (c. 49,600 tons) with corresponding amounts of molasses and pulp. The increased output was achieved with only 220 permanent and 90 casual employees.[79]

LOCAL GOVERNMENT. Wellington, as a royal demesne manor,[80] had exemption from suit of Bradford hundred great court and was separately represented at the eyre of 1203.[81] After 1210 the manor was in private hands but the exemption was preserved: in 1255 Wellington was a free manor and its steward merely attended twice a year at the hundred court.[82] Wellington's separate great and little courts were mentioned in 1345 and 1481. By 1680 they had coalesced as the 'view of frankpledge with the court baron' and so continued until 1840 or later. Apley, Arleston, Dothill, and Wellington townships presented at

[49] I. J. Brown, *Hist. of Limestone Mining in Salop.* (Salop. Mining Club Acct. vi. 1967), 14.
[50] *Kelly's Dir. Salop.* (1917), 270.
[51] Inst. Geol. Sciences Map 1/25,000, *Telford* (1978 edn.).
[52] S.R.O. 1224, box 296, 'Warham's work and Coalmeadow' acct. bk. 7 Jan. 1684/5; ibid. coal accts. May and Sept. 1690.
[53] Ibid. coal accts. 1689–91.
[54] S.R.O. 1224, box 250, deed. Locations from S.R.O. 14, tithe appt.; 1856/5.
[55] S.R.O. 1224, box 256, deed; above, L. Wenlock, Econ. Hist.
[56] Lewis, *Early Wooden Rlys.* 238, 240, 279; Trinder, *Ind. Rev. Salop.* (1981), 86.
[57] Locations from S.R.O. 14, tithe appt. and map (nos. 74, 100); O.S. Map 6", Salop. XLIII. NW. (1889 edn.).
[58] S.R.O. 1224, boxes 259–60, deeds; above, L. Wenlock, Econ. Hist.
[59] Trinder, *Ind. Rev. Salop.* (1981), 86.
[60] S.R.O. 1224, box 255, deed of 1798; above, L. Wenlock, Econ. Hist.
[61] Pits shown on O.S. Map 1", sheet 61 NE. (1833 edn.); none in S.R.O. 14, tithe appt.
[62] S.R.O. 1224, box 259, deed of 1798; above, L. Wenlock, Econ. Hist.
[63] *Abstr. of Q. Sess. Rolls 1820–30*, ed. M. C. Hill (S.C.C.

1974), 314/100; S.R.O. 14, tithe appt.; 1856/5 (nos. 145, 147, 151, 154).
[64] O.S. Map 1/2,500, Salop. XXXVI. 14 (1882 edn.).
[65] Ibid. 6", Salop. XXXVI. SW. (1929 edn.).
[66] S.R.O. 1324/1.
[67] *Salop. News Letter*, xxxviii. 18; I. J. Brown, *Mines of Salop.* (Buxton, 1976), 48.
[68] O.S. Maps 1/25,000, SJ 60 (1958 edn.); 6", SJ 60 NE. (1966 edn.).
[69] *Shropshire Star*, 4 Aug. 1977.
[70] Inst. Geol. Sciences Map 1/25,000, *Telford* (1978 edn.).
[71] O.S. Maps 1/2,500, Salop. XXXVI. 13; XLIII. 1 (1882 edns.); R. W. Pocock and others, *Shrews. Dist.* (Geol. Surv. Memoir, 1938), 222–4.
[72] Brit. Telecom, *Dir.* (1982), sect. 303 (YP), p. 255.
[73] Pocock and others, op. cit. 223 n.
[74] Below, Ketley, Econ. Hist.
[75] E. J. Howell, *Shropshire* (Land of Britain, lxvi), 229.
[76] Inf. from the general manager, Allscott Sugar Factory.
[77] Howell, op. cit. 227, 229–30.
[78] S.R.O., DA 26/114/4, p. 987.
[79] Inf. from the general manager.
[80] Acct. based on ct. r. listed below.
[81] *V.C.H. Salop.* iii. 48–9.
[82] *Rot. Hund.* (Rec. Com.), ii. 56.

the great court in 1345 and 1481. By 1680 the court was held annually in October and sometimes, until 1704 or later, there was also an April session. From 1802 courts sat annually in October or November. In 1687 an adjourned session was held at the market hall, and the lord's right to hold manor courts there was reserved in 1739.[83] The hall was demolished c. 1800[84] and by 1824 the court always adjourned to the Talbot.[85] There are rolls for 1345–6, 1481, 1680, 1686–1704, 1745–6, 1752–7, and (with a few years missing) 1787–1840, and estreats of fines for 1723–9, 1755–6, 1773–4, 1776–7, and (with numerous gaps) 1787–1822.[86]

Wellington never became a corporate borough, and the lord's steward presided at its manor courts. There was by 1346 a distinct class of burgesses, presumably holders of burgages (mentioned by 1301)[87] and thus to some extent hereditary. Burgages were still so called in 1674.[88] By custom only burgesses were free to carry on a trade. In the Middle Ages residents who were not burgesses could purchase that freedom from the lord on an annual basis as tensers, and 'taintership money' was still demanded of them in the 1680s and 1750s. Non-burgesses in 1346 could buy the same right for life. From 1826 men setting up new businesses were amerced in nominal sums by the manor court, but paid less if they had served an apprenticeship within the manor.

By the late 17th century the court's verdicts, orders, and elections were made by the 12 jurors or homage, many of whom had earlier served as manorial officers. They were drawn from various occupations and economic levels[89] and the jury's composition varied from year to year. It was nevertheless controlled by a handful of regular attenders, who included some of the town's wealthiest men. Since they were not necessarily the Foresters' tenants[90] it is unlikely that the lord could exert much pressure on the court. In the mid and late 18th century there might be as many as 14 jurors, and by 1752 the position of foreman was recognized. There were up to 22 jurors in the 1830s and the average was then 15. Membership was less varied by then, however, and regular attendance more usual.

The highest appointment made by the jury was that of bailiff, an office that existed by 1315.[91] In 1345 there were two bailiffs for the 'town and liberty', elected and sworn annually at a great court; it is not known whether their bailiwicks were separate. There was only one bailiff in 1481, drawn from the jury and similarly sworn (and presumably elected). In the late 17th century the bailiff was drawn from the same men as were

juries, but some had yet to be jurors themselves. Usually, however, they had served at least one of the lower manorial offices, especially that of constable. In the 1830s the bailiff had usually served as a juror but not in any other office, and by 1835 he was unofficially styled mayor.[92]

There were two constables by 1481, drawn from the jury, and in the late 17th century most were potential jurors and even bailiffs. In the 1830s, however, they were unlikely to be jurors. From 1837 a third constable was also elected. The manorial constables disappeared after the formation of the county constabulary in 1840.[93]

Two aletasters (called clerks of the market by 1787) were elected annually by 1345 and still in 1840. Until the late 17th century, or later, they were potential jurors, though often younger than the constables.

In 1481, but not in 1345 or the late 17th century, a body of 'fivemen' (quinque homines) was drawn from the jury. Its role is not known.

In the late 17th century there were three, sometimes two, street surveyors for the town. They disposed of occasional rates for street repairs and were usually senior jurors. The office had disappeared by 1745.

The other elective offices created after 1481 were of lower standing; the holders were not usually potential jurors. There were two leather inspectors and sealers by the late 17th century and until 1811. Two, sometimes three, swine ringers and yokers were elected in the late 17th century, but were reduced to one by 1787. The office remained in 1840. Until the open fields were inclosed in 1702[94] a hayward was elected. There were also two street scavengers for the town by the late 17th century and still in 1840.

The manor had a common crier by 1697 and still in 1905[95] but it was not an elective office. In 1815 he collected the court's fines for the constables and received an allowance for each court attended.[96] He still appeared in uniform in the 1870s, ending his announcements with 'God save the queen and the lord of the manor!'[97]

In 1680 there were shooting butts and a common pound. In 1842 the pound lay on the east side of King Street.[98] The county magistrates provided a lock-up in 1779.[99] It was rebuilt c. 1831[1] and in 1842 stood in the churchyard.[2] In 1853, after the county police station opened,[3] it was offered to the parish.[4] Stocks were mentioned in 1818.[5] From the 18th century, copyhold tenures and open-field agriculture having ceased, the court's concerns were mostly with stray animals, obstructions to roads and watercourses, and regulation of the town's streets and pavements. By

[83] S.R.O. 1224, box 251, deed.
[84] Above, Econ. Hist. (Mkts. and Fairs).
[85] Described 1824–8 as the ho. of John Haynes (cf. Tibnam & Co. Salop. Dir. (1828), 125) and 1829–40 as that of Jas. Griffiths (cf. Pigot, Nat. Com. Dir. (1835), 382).
[86] In S.R.O. 1224, boxes 204, 206; parcel 205.
[87] Cart. Shrews. ii, p. 249.　[88] S.R.O. 999/Oo(1)/15.
[89] Many occur in Trinder and Cox, Yeomen and Colliers, pp. 120–59.
[90] S.R.O. 1224, box 297, Lady Day rental of 1688.
[91] S.R.O. 625, box 11, deed.
[92] Pigot, Nat. Com. Dir. (1835), 380.
[93] V.C.H. Salop. iii. 157.　[94] Above, Econ. Hist. (Agric.).

[95] Kelly's Dir. Salop. (1905), 270.
[96] S.R.O. 1224, box 206, crier's acct. He also collected the proceeds of L. Wenlock man. ct.
[97] Pooler, My Life in General Practice, 6.
[98] S.R.O. 14, tithe appt. and map (no. 1434).
[99] S.R.O., q. sess. order bk. 1772–82, ff. 213, 217v., 231; below, p. 234.
[1] S.R.O., q. sess. order bk. 1828–33, f. 198; S.R.O. 1560/5, 11 Nov. 1831.
[2] S.R.O. 14, tithe appt. and map (no. 683).
[3] Below, Public Services.
[4] S.R.O. 3129/5/6, 16 Dec. 1853.
[5] Baxter, 'Wellington', 47.

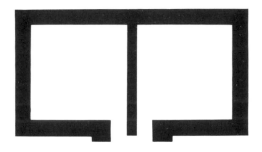

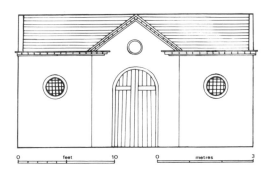

WELLINGTON LOCK-UP, 1779

court baron for Uckington, Norton, and Walcot, which was held at those places interchangeably until 1560 or later. By 1563 the same court was usually described as of Uckington 'with the members'. By 1575 and until 1833, or later, it regularly appointed a constable for Walcot and heard the township's presentments. There were stocks and a pound in 1583.[14]

By 1600 Little Dawley and Malinslee (in Dawley) were under separate courts baron,[15] leaving Leegomery, Wappenshall, and Ketley with one court baron, of which records from the 17th to the 19th century are preserved.[16] It met at Leegomery House in the mid 17th century[17] and a pound lay nearby in 1723.[18] Leegomery manor was in the leet jurisdiction of Bradford hundred in 1255[19] and 1592.[20]

By 1748 there was a parish workhouse in the town, farmed by Thomas Hazlehurst,[21] a tailor,[22] described in 1753 as manager.[23] The overseers paid him a fixed quarterly sum to cover inmates' food, clothes, medical care, and burial. He provided work and presumably sold the products, perhaps as part of his tailoring business, and paid for the apprenticing of children. From 1748 paupers from Newport were also admitted,[24] and from Berrington temporarily 1750–1.[25] By 1797 parish relief was controlled by a vestry committee or board, which employed a salaried workhouse governor and matron and sat fortnightly to receive applications for relief and examine the overseers' accounts. Two of the board, chosen in rotation, visited the house several times during the fortnight and reported at its end to their colleagues. In 1834 relief was still supervised by a select vestry; rating was left to the overseers and a professional valuation.[26]

In November 1797 the house contained 10 men, 14 women, and 20 children. There were also 40 children put out to nurse and 57 paupers on weekly out-relief. Numbers receiving indoor relief fluctuated rapidly. There were 186 in April 1801, but only 39 in October 1802. Of the paupers on out-relief a few were fed at the house.[27] Poor relief cost £1,503 in 1803.[28] In 1817, with pits and ironworks closed,[29] the sum was £7,916.[30] In the emergency the parish put 100–150 unemployed men to road work, as in Madeley,[31] and paid them wages. In the period 1819–22 some paupers were being paid by the parish as out-workers, sewing footwear.[32] After 1817 expenditure on the poor fell

the 1840s, however, its sanitary work was far from effective.[6] After 1854, when responsibility for the town's sanitary condition passed to improvement commissioners,[7] the court probably ceased to meet.

In Aston township before c. 1588 the Grey estate owed suit to Charlton Castle manor court[8] and the Newport estate to that of Eyton on Severn.[9] From c. 1588 Aston was all subject to Eyton.[10] In 1810 it remained subject to Eyton's court leet and court baron, which still appointed a constable for Aston.[11] Walcot township, before the suppression of Haughmond abbey in 1539, seems to have been subject to a joint court or courts held at Haughmond, Uffington, Downton, and Walcot interchangeably.[12] As late as 1563 Walcot presented, unusually, at the court leet and court baron for Uffington 'with the members' (also called Haughmond 'with the members').[13] By then, however, the redistribution of Haughmond abbey's former estates had been accompanied by a revision of manorial jurisdictions, for by 1549 Walcot usually presented at the court leet and

[6] R. A. Slaney, *Health of Towns Commission: Rep. on the State of Birmingham and other large Towns* (1845), 27 (copy in S.P.L.). [7] Below.
[8] S.P.L., MS. 2345, no. 110 (deed of 1548).
[9] Barnard MSS., Raby Castle, box 12, bdle. 11, deed of 1583.
[10] Below, Wrockwardine, Local Govt. and Public Services.
[11] S.R.O. 1011, box 169, ct. r.
[12] S.R.O. 1502/4; *V.C.H. Salop.* ii. 68.
[13] S.P.L., Deeds 6027. The 'Haughmond' ct. met at Uffington in 1563.
[14] Uckington ct. r., estreats, and suit r. in S.R.O. 112, boxes 89–90. Before the Dissolution Uckington and Norton presented at Atcham ct. leet and ct. baron: box 90, Atcham ct. r.
[15] Above, Dawley, Man. and Other Est.; Local Govt.
[16] Staffs. R.O., D. 593/J/11/6.
[17] S.R.O. 38/337.
[18] S.R.O. 972, parcel 236, Leegomery and Wappenshall map.
[19] *Rot. Hund.* (Rec. Com.), ii. 57.
[20] Staffs. R.O., D. 593/J/10, ct. r. of 1592.
[21] S.R.O. 3990/9.
[22] S.R.O. 4241/P/1 (formerly S.R.O. 714/10).
[23] S.R.O. 3331/1, f. 57v.; cf. below, Wrockwardine, Local Govt. and Public Services.
[24] S.R.O. 3990/9.
[25] S.R.O. 4241/P/1.
[26] *Rep. Poor Law Com.* H.C. 44, p. 395c (1834), xxxii.
[27] S.R.O. 88/1.
[28] *Rep. Poor Law Com.* H.C. 44, p. 394a (1834), xxx.
[29] *Some Facts, shewing the Vast Burthen of the Poor's Rate, by a member of the Salop. Co. Cttee. for the employment of the poor* (Holborn, 1817), 4 (copy in S.P.L.).
[30] *Poor Rate Returns*, H.C. 556, suppl. app. p. 141 (1822), v.
[31] Below, Madeley, Local Govt.
[32] S.R.O. 3129/5/3.

and in 1826 only £1,616 was spent.[33] There was a sharp rise between 1829 and 1831, when £3,059 was paid, then a gradual fall[34] as full employment returned. In 1834 the workhouse had *c.* 40 residents, none of them able-bodied, and it seems that most of the men on out-relief were colliers.[35] The parish was in Wellington poor-law union 1836–1930.[36]

In 1797[37] the workhouse moved from Street Lane[38] to the south side of Walker Street.[39] The guardians kept and enlarged the Walker Street premises for adults and used the former Ercall Magna parish workhouse, at Waters Upton, for children. The guardians also rented the former Wrockwardine parish workhouse 1838–41.[40] In 1851 the main workhouse could accommodate 160 residents and there was room for *c.* 100 children at Waters Upton.[41] In 1876 those houses were replaced by a new building[42] south-west of the town on the north side of Street Lane.[43] It had accommodation for 350 in 1885.[44] In 1930 ownership passed to the county council[45] and by 1948 the institution was occupied mainly by the sick. In that year, as Wrekin Hospital, it was vested in the minister of Health.[46] Some non-sick residents remained, however, and the hospital was therefore administered by both the county council and the Birmingham Regional Hospital Board until 1950, when the non-sick were taken elsewhere and the council's involvement ceased.[47]

Until 1897 the union's offices were the parish offices, Walker Street,[48] presumably inherited in 1836. The guardians met there[49] until 1883 and then at the improvement commissioners' new board room.[50] The board room at the workhouse of 1876 was not used because of its distance from the town.[51] The guardians bought Edgbaston House, Walker Street, in 1897[52] and moved their offices and board room to it.[53] The Wellington area guardians committee was meeting there in 1937.[54] In 1982 Edgbaston House was occupied by a firm of solicitors, of whom one was superintendent registrar of marriages for Wellington district.

Under the Lighting and Watching Act, 1833,[55] the parish chose to elect gas lighting inspectors for the town and under the Highway Act, 1835,[56]

chose to elect a board, whose district comprised Wellington, Watling Street, and Arleston townships.[57] By the 1840s the open vestry was concerned almost exclusively with ecclesiastical administration,[58] its other rates and responsibilities having been delegated to its own committees or taken over by other authorities.

In 1854 the Wellington (Salop) Improvement Act appointed 15 commissioners (thereafter to be elected by the ratepayers) with extensive powers within the improvement district, including those previously exercised by the highway board and the parish lighting inspectors. For most purposes the improvement district comprised the eastern part of Wellington township, with small adjacent parts of Watling Street and Arleston townships.[59]

In 1856 the commissioners' office was in New Street but by 1870 was in Walker Street,[60] where brick-built offices, including a board room, opened in 1883.[61] Wellington urban district council, which in 1894 replaced the commissioners (the urban sanitary authority under the Act of 1872), inherited the improvement commissioners' offices[62] and met there (except 1955–9)[63] until the urban district was abolished in 1974 and merged in Wrekin district.[64] In 1900 the U.D.C. was allegedly controlled by Wesleyans.[65] By the 1960s Conservatives and Independents predominated.[66]

The part of the parish outside the improvement area was added to the Wrekin highway district in 1865; that district was adjusted to coincide with Wellington rural sanitary district, formed in 1872, to which its powers were transferred in 1882.[67] In 1974 Wellington rural district was merged in Wrekin district.[68]

The commissioners' common seal was circular, 45 mm. in diameter, and depicted the Wrekin with INCORPORATED 1854 at the base. It was inscribed (roman) at the circumference: WELLINGTON IMPROVEMENT COMMISSIONERS.[69] The council's first common seal was circular, 50 mm. in diameter, and consisted of an inscription (black letter) across the face: THE SEAL OF THE URBAN DISTRICT COUNCIL OF WELLINGTON, SALOP.[70] A new seal incorporating the council's arms was provided in 1951.[71] The arms granted that year included a

[33] *Poor Rate Returns*, H.C. 556, suppl. app. p. 141 (1822), v; H.C. 334, p. 176 (1825), iv; H.C. 83, p. 164 (1830–1), xi.

[34] Ibid. H.C. 83, p. 164 (1830–1), xi; H.C. 444, p. 159 (1835), xlvii.

[35] *Rep. Poor Law Com.* H.C. 44, pp. 395b, 395d (1834), xxxi.

[36] V. J. Walsh, 'Admin. of Poor Laws in Salop. 1820–55' (Pennsylvania Univ. Ph.D. thesis, 1970), 150 (copy in S.R.O.); *Kelly's Dir Salop.* (1929), 286, 289.

[37] *Shropshire Mag.* Sept. 1960, 17.

[38] S. Bagshaw, *Dir. Salop.* (1851), 424; Baxter, 'Wellington', 53.

[39] S.R.O. 14, tithe appt. and map (no. 346); above, plate 51.

[40] Walsh, 'Admin. of Poor Laws', 150, 206–7, 211 n., 214.

[41] S. Bagshaw, *Dir. Salop.* (1851), 421, 424.

[42] S.R.O. 77/13, pp. 170, 175.

[43] O.S. Map 6", Salop. XXXVI. SW. (1887 edn.); above, plate 52.

[44] *Kelly's Dir. Salop.* (1885), 350.

[45] Under the Local Govt. Act, 1929, 19 Geo. V, c. 17.

[46] Under the National Assistance Act, 1948, 11 & 12 Geo. VI, c. 29.

[47] *S.C.C. Mins.* 1949–50, 286–7; 1950–1, 22.

[48] S.R.O. 88/3, p. 133; 507/3, 27 Nov. 1885.

[49] S.R.O. 77/12, p. 220; 88/3, pp. 126, 157.

[50] *Kelly's Dir. Salop.* (1885), 973; S.R.O. 77/12, p. 75. The

guardians called it the union board room: S.R.O. 77/12, pp. 100 sqq.

[51] S.R.O. 77/11, pp. 191–2; /12, p. 62.

[52] S.R.O. 88/4, p. 259.

[53] Ibid. p. 294; 507/3, 10 Dec. 1896.

[54] *Kelly's Dir. Salop.* (1941), 276.   [55] 3 & 4 Wm. IV, c. 90.

[56] 5 & 6 Wm. IV, c. 50.

[57] Wellington (Salop) Improvement Act, 1854, 17 & 18 Vic. c. 40 (Local and Personal).

[58] S.R.O. 3129/5/6.

[59] 17 & 18 Vic. c. 40 (Local and Personal); S.R.O., dep. plan 571. The district was conterminous with area A on map above, p. 199.

[60] *P.O. Dir. Salop.* (1856), 137; (1870), 156.

[61] *Wellington Jnl.* 12 May 1883.

[62] New Centurion Publishing & Publicity Co. Ltd. *Wellington Official Guide*, 1950–1, 6.

[63] S.R.O., DA 13/100/21, pp. 204, 220; /100/27, p. 449.

[64] Local inf.

[65] *Wellington Jnl.* 10 Nov. 1900.

[66] *Express & Star*, 14 Jan. 1964; *Shropshire Star*, 14 May 1966.

[67] S.R.O. 560/474, 667, 670.   [68] Local inf.

[69] Impression in S.R.O., DA 13/991, deed of 1884.

[70] Impression ibid. /154, deed of 1898.

[71] Ibid. /134, file V/3, Shaw & Sons Ltd. to B. H. J. Renshaw, 28 Sept. 1951.

crest (on a wreath of the colours in front of a portcullis chained sable a bugle horn stringed or) and the motto *Deo adjuvante*.[72] A chairman's jewel depicting the arms was presented by the retiring clerk in 1951[73] and the council provided a silver gilt chain for it in 1951.[74]

WELLINGTON URBAN DISTRICT. *Argent fretty gules, a lion rampant sable; on a chief sable a silver castle between two gold fleurs-de-lis* [Granted 1951]

PUBLIC SERVICES. By the late 17th century there was a conduit on high ground at the southern edge of the town, near a large pool[75] fed from streams that rose near the parish's southern boundary.[76] Thence the Town brook[77] descended, perhaps along the conduit,[78] to the west side of Tan Bank[79] (probably the former Pool Head Lane)[80] and reached the nearby[81] Pool Head,[82] presumably a public water supply.[83] The brook descended thence[84] to join the Vineyard brook.[85]

In 1851, through T. C. Eyton,[86] the Wellington Waterworks Co. was formed to supply an area 5 miles around the Market Place. The company was reconstituted in 1860 as the Wellington (Salop) Waterworks Co. and its area reduced to Wellington civil parish and that part of Wrockwardine parish already supplied.[87] Wellington urban sanitary authority bought the undertaking in 1884.[88]

In the early 1850s[89] the company made a reservoir at the Ercall pools[90] near Buckatree Hall, and by 1859 a main descended from it, entered the town along Walker Street, and terminated in the Market Place[91] at a drinking fountain.[92] A second reservoir, near Steeraway, was opened *c.* 1870[93] and by the 1880s the town's main streets were furnished with standpipes.[94] The water authority did not supply water beyond the town until the 1890s, when it laid a main eastwards along Watling Street.[95] From *c.* 1905 the reservoirs were supplemented by water pumped from boreholes.[96] In 1933 the supply area was enlarged.[97] In 1946, shortly before water supply passed to a regional authority,[98] the hamlets of Arleston, Aston, and Wappenshall still had no piped water.[99] By then the urban district council's principal water sources were boreholes at Woodfield (in Ercall Magna)[1] sunk 1930–2.[2] Within the rural district council's area of responsibility Walcot was still without piped water in 1946.[3]

Before 1892 all the town's sewage was piped north-westwards to Springhill where it flowed untreated into a watercourse that fed Bratton brook. From 1892 or 1893 some was also piped from the east side of the town into Haybridge brook. In 1898 those arrangements were superseded by the Admaston disposal works in Dothill township.[4] The Dothill works was later replaced by the new Rushmoor works (in Wrockwardine) opened 1975.[5]

The parish's first public medical service was a dispensary supported by subscribers, which was established in 1834 and revived in 1859. Through local doctors it gave treatment to people not on parish relief. In 1900 *c.* 700 patients a year were being seen.[6] After the National Health Service was introduced the funds were used to endow a charity for the sick poor.[7] By 1916 a maternity and child welfare centre had been established by a local society.[8] Later the county council supported it[9] and in 1936 opened a new clinic[10] in Haygate

[72] G. Briggs, *Civic and Corporate Heraldry* (1971), 408–9. The arms allude to the Charlton, Cludde, Eyton, and Forester fams. and to events of the Civil Wars: *Shropshire Mag.* Aug. 1951, 18.
[73] S.R.O., DA 13/134, file V/4, Thos. Fattorini Ltd. to J. S. Broad, 18 Apr. 1951; Broad to Fattorini, 24 Apr. 1951.
[74] Ibid. Shaw & Sons Ltd. to B. H. J. Renshaw, 9 Nov. 1951; 19 Mar. 1952; Renshaw to Shaw, 21 Nov. 1951.
[75] See S.R.O. 14, tithe appt. and map (nos. 1249, 1263), for fields called Conduit meadow, mentioned *c.* 1676 (S.P.L., MS. 2340, ff. 54, 61).
[76] O.S. Map 6″, Salop. XXXVI. SW. (1887 edn.); XLIII. NW. (1889 edn.).
[77] Mentioned 1745: S.R.O. 1224, box 204, ct. r. Descr. 1788 as reaching the 'top of the Conduit field': box 206, ct. r.
[78] The brook's first 150 metres seem to have been artificially straight in the 1830s (S.R.O. 746/5) and it was crossed by Conduit Alley at O.S. Nat. Grid SJ 660 112 in the 1920s (S.R.O., DA 13/135, draft deed).
[79] S.R.O. 746/5.
[80] In 1724 Pool Head La. was W. of the Tenter yard (which was S. of New St.): S.R.O. 4309, survey, f. 78.
[81] S. of the E. end of Walker St.: Baxter, 'Wellington', 56.
[82] S.R.O. 1224, box 206, ct. r. of 1756.
[83] The 'old town pump' was removed from the bottom of Tan Bank *c.* 1907: *Wellington Jnl.* 21 July 1906; 19 Dec. 1908.
[84] S.R.O. 1224, box 206, ct. r. of 1756.
[85] Ibid. ct. r. of 1788.
[86] S.R.O., DA 13/297 (S.R.O. 3172/5/3), 11 Feb. 1853.

[87] Wellington (Salop) Waterworks Act, 1860, 23 & 24 Vic. c. 95 (Local and Personal).
[88] S.R.O. 119/54, Wellington U.D.C. petition against E. Salop. Water Bill, 1900 (printed copy), p. 3.
[89] 23 & 24 Vic. c. 95 (Local and Personal).
[90] S. Bagshaw, *Dir. Salop.* (1851), 425.
[91] S.R.O., dep. plan. 535.
[92] O.S. Map 1/500, Salop. XXXVI. 9. 18 (1882 edn.).
[93] S.R.O., DA 13/991, deed of 1887 (copy).
[94] O.S. Maps 1/500, Salop. XXXVI. 9. 8, 9. 14, 9. 18–19, 9. 24 (1882 edns.).
[95] *S.C.C. Mins.* 1897–8, 589.
[96] Pocock and others, *Shrews. Dist.* 225.
[97] Min. of Health Prov. Order Conf. (Wellington Salop) Act, 1933, 23 & 24 Geo. V, c. 92 (Local); A. H. S. Waters, *Rep. on Water Supplies* (S.C.C. 1946), 99.
[98] *S.C.C. Mins.* 1948–9, 355.
[99] Waters, op. cit. 26, 95, 97–8.
[1] Ibid. 26.
[2] Pocock, *Shrews. Dist.* 245.
[3] Waters, op. cit. 99.
[4] S.R.O., DA 13/135 (S.R.O. 3172/9/TB1), brief of 1905, pp. 1–5 and plan no. 2.
[5] *Telford Jnl.* 7 Aug. 1975.
[6] Hobson, *Wellington Dir.* (1898), 16; *Kelly's Dir. Salop.* (1900), 259.
[7] Below, Chars.
[8] S.R.O., S.C.C. Public Health and Ho. Cttee. min. bk. 2, pp. 203, 226.
[9] Ibid. 4, p. 26.
[10] Ibid. 8, p. 328.

Road,[11] which was replaced in 1971 by the council's new health centre in Chapel Lane, the first such in Shropshire.[12]

The U.D.C. built a small isolation hospital at Steeraway in 1903, which it shared with the R.D.C.[13] From 1919 it was leased to the county council,[14] which still used it in 1947.[15] Birmingham Regional Hospital Board sold it in 1951.[16] Under the will of J. C. Bowring's widow[17] a cottage hospital in his memory was built in Haygate Road in 1912.[18] Ownership later passed, like that of the public-assistance institution (renamed Wrekin Hospital),[19] to the regional hospital board.[20] Construction of a Telford general hospital at Apley was expected to begin in 1984.[21]

In 1910 a committee of local ladies gave a horse ambulance to the U.D.C.[22] and the council maintained an ambulance service until 1948, when it was superseded by the county ambulance station at Donnington.[23] Wellington and Oakengates U.D.C.s provided a service for the rural district[24] until 1945, when the R.D.C. began a service from Donnington.[25]

In 1898 a public soup kitchen, paid for by voluntary contributions, was open twice weekly in winter in King Street, and an unendowed coal charity existed for the poor. The sick poor were helped by the Wellington Nursing Association and the Wellington Ladies' Charity.[26] A home for underfed babies was founded by Mrs. Flora Dugdale in Wrockwardine Road. The county council took it over in 1920,[27] and in 1945 converted it into a home for older children.[28] It closed in 1978.[29] By 1893 it was a probation and after-care centre. A children's home was created at the workhouse in 1914.[30] In 1916 the children were transferred to Brooklyn House[31] on Watling Street, and thence in 1928 to the Mount,[32] Haygate Road. The county council took over the home in 1930 and opened a second at the Vineyard in 1947.[33]

In 1873 the Wellington (Salop) Burial Board,

elected by the vestry,[34] bought land off Haygate Road that was consecrated a cemetery in 1875.[35] In 1894[36] the board's functions passed to the Wellington (Salop) Burial Joint Committee, composed of representatives of the C.P.s in which the old board's area lay: Wellington Urban, Wellington Rural, Hadley, and Eyton. In 1913 the committee's part of Eyton C.P. was excluded from its area.[37] The committee's functions passed to Wrekin district council in 1974.[38]

The earliest known postmaster, unsalaried, was mentioned in 1795. His office was then a sub-office of Shrewsbury[39] but Wellington was designated a post town in 1813.[40] The post office occupied several successive sites in the town until 1927 when a new building opened in Walker Street.[41] It became the Telford head post office c. 1970.[42] The town's first sub-post office opened in Mill Bank c. 1890.[43]

In 1823 William Edwards opened a gas works[44] on the east side of Tan Bank[45] and by 1835 the town was said to be well lit.[46] A dispute over street lighting[47] led to the formation, through T. C. Eyton,[48] of a rival Wellington Coal and Gas-Light Co. in 1851, to supply gas within a 5-mile radius of Wellington, especially in Wellington, Ketley, and Oakengates.[49] The company built a works between Tan Bank and Wrekin Road[50] but by 1870[51] had a railside works on the west side of the town.[52] Edwards died in 1863[53] and next year the company bought his undertaking.[54] In 1872 the company's supply area was reduced to the parts of Wellington and Wrockwardine C.P.s within 2 miles of All Saints' church but excluding almost the whole of Hadley township. In 1903 the company was reconstituted as the Wellington (Salop) Gas Co.[55] It took over the undertakings of the Oakengates Gas and Water Co. Ltd. in 1922,[56] of the Hadley, Trench, and Wrockwardine Wood Lighting Co. Ltd. in 1930, and of the Lilleshall Gas Co. in 1939.[57] From 1936 the Severn Valley

[11] Wargrave Press, *Wrekin Civic & Commercial Dir.* (1964), 17.

[12] *V.C.H. Salop.* iii. 210.

[13] S.R.O., DA 13/100/5, pp. 120, 128, 263.

[14] S.R.O., DA 13/154, box 13, deed; *V.C.H. Salop.* iii. 211 n.

[15] S.R.O., DA 13/889, clk. of U.D.C. to Co. M.O.H. 15 July 1947.

[16] Birm. Regional Hosp. Bd., *Birm. Regional Hosp. Bd. 1947–66* (1966), 210.

[17] *Wellington Before Telford*, 24–5.

[18] *Kelly's Dir. Salop.* (1929), 287.

[19] Above, Local Govt.

[20] *Birm. Regional Hosp. Bd. 1947–66*, 210.

[21] *Shropshire Star*, 22 July 1983.

[22] S.R.O., DA 13/100/6, pp. 310, 319–20; *Wellington Jnl.* 23 Apr. 1910.

[23] S.C.C. *Proposals for an Ambulance Service* (1947), 4, 13 (copy in S.R.O., DA 26/134 (S.R.O. 3070/15/5), file 221); *S.C.C. Mins.* 1947–8, 15.

[24] S.R.O., DA 26/134 (S.R.O. 3070/12/7), file 222, clk. of R.D.C. to H. V. Osmond, 3 May 1944; chief financial officer of Oakengates U.D.C. to clk. of R.D.C. 26 Feb. 1945.

[25] S.R.O., DA 26/112/2, p. 513; above, Lilleshall, Public Services.

[26] Hobson, *Wellington Dir.* (1898), 16, 24–5.

[27] *Shrews. Chron.* 30 July 1920.

[28] *S.C.C. Mins.* 1945–6, 85, 190.

[29] Ibid. 1977–8, 99, 137.

[30] S.R.O. 77/19, pp. 18, 301.

[31] Ibid. /20, p. 220.

[32] Ibid. /22, pp. 19, 38; *S.C.C. Mins.* 1927–8, 78; 1928–9, 9, 95.

[33] *V.C.H. Salop.* iii. 215–16.

[34] Under the Burial Act, 1853, 16 & 17 Vic. c. 134.

[35] Lich. Dioc. Regy., bps.' reg. S, pp. 76–80.

[36] Local Govt. Act, 1894, 56 & 57 Vic. c. 73.

[37] *Co. of Salop (Alteration of Wellington (Salop) Burial Area) Conf. Order, 1913* (Local Govt. Bd. order no. 59949).

[38] Inf. from Wrekin District Council.

[39] *Wellington Before Telford*, 20.

[40] Inf. from P.O. Archives, St. Martin's-le-Grand, kindly supplied by the departmental records officer.

[41] Ibid.; S.R.O. 14, tithe appt. and map (no. 1184); 3129/5/5, p. 59; Tibnam & Co. *Salop. Dir.* (1828), 117; *Wellington Before Telford*, 20–1; O.S. Map 1/500, Salop. XXXVI. 9. 18 (1882 edn.); *Kelly's Dir. Salop.* (1891), 456; (1895), 244.

[42] P.O. *Telephone Dir.* (1970), sect. 303, p. 176.

[43] *Kelly's Dir. Salop.* (1891), 457.

[44] *Wellington Jnl.* 3 June 1939.

[45] S.R.O. 746/5.

[46] Pigot, *Nat. Com. Dir.* (1835), 380.

[47] S. Bagshaw, *Dir. Salop.* (1851), 424.

[48] S.R.O., DA 13/297 (S.R.O. 3172/5/3), 11 Feb. 1853.

[49] S.R.O. 2936/1.

[50] Bagshaw, op. cit. 424; S.R.O., DA 13/991, brief of 1894.

[51] *P.O. Dir. Salop.* (1870), 159.

[52] O.S. Map 1/500, Salop. XXXVI. 9. 17 (1882 edn.).

[53] *Wellington Jnl.* 3 June 1939.

[54] S.R.O. 2199/11.

[55] Wellington (Salop) Gas Act, 1903, 3 Edw. VII, c. 29 (Local).

[56] *Wellington (Salop) Gas Order, 1922* (Stat. Rules & Orders 1922, no. 401).

[57] S.R.O. 1491/84, pp. 18, 209.

Gas Corporation owned a controlling interest in the company,[58] which was nationalized in 1949.[59]

The U.D.C. had electricity-supply powers from 1901[60] but, unused,[61] they were relinquished in 1928 to a regional authority,[62] which supplied the town by 1934.[63] Electric street lighting was introduced in 1944.[64]

Wellington had at least one fire engine in 1803[65] and more than one in 1843, when the vestry contributed to their maintenance.[66] From 1853 the inhabitants were allowed to keep them at the new police station[67] but in 1858 one old appliance was kept at the Sun inn. The brigade was controlled by the improvement commissioners from c. 1854.[68] The commissioners opened a fire station in Walker Street c. 1883.[69] Two engines were provided by the Shropshire & North Wales Assurance Co. (later the Alliance Assurance Co.).[70] In 1906 the brigade had eight operational members, all retained men. The U.D.C. bought a horse-drawn steam appliance in 1909 but kept one of the manual engines until 1924.[71] The station moved to Foundry Lane c. 1924.[72] In 1928 the U.D.C. and R.D.C. formed the Wellington and District Joint Fire Brigade[73] and bought the first motorized engine, its only vehicle in 1939.[74] Control passed to the National Fire Service in 1941 and the brigade was absorbed by the county council in 1948.[75] One of the county's two divisional headquarters was located in Wellington and a new fire station, manned by full-time officers, opened in 1953[76] in Haybridge Road. In 1980 it was superseded as divisional headquarters by the new Telford central fire station, Stafford Park.[77]

From 1840, when a county constabulary was formed, Wellington had a divisional headquarters.[78] The superintendent and two of the constables were stationed in the town in 1840.[79] They used the lock-up of c. 1831[80] but otherwise worked from home until 1848 when an

office was provided[81] in Walker Street.[82] In 1853[83] a new station with lock-up and court room was opened in Church Street near the Green.[84] Eight officers were stationed there in 1885.[85] The premises were replaced in 1897[86] by a new station at the corner of Church Street and Plough Road,[87] which had fourteen officers in 1926.[88] It remained in use as a station until 1955, when a new divisional headquarters opened[89] in Glebe Street, but it still housed a magistrates' court in 1982.

CHURCHES. There was a priest at Wellington by 1086[90] and Roger of Montgomery, earl of Shrewsbury (d. 1094), gave the church there to Shrewsbury abbey.[91] By the mid 12th century the incumbent received only part of the tithes, the rest having been appropriated by the abbey,[92] and in 1232 a vicarage was formally ordained by the bishop, the great tithes being divided between the abbey and a new prebend in Lichfield cathedral. Under the ordinance of 1232 the advowson of the vicarage was to be with the abbey,[93] with which it remained until surrendered to the Crown in 1540.[94] The Crown was patron in 1558,[95] but by 1561 the advowson belonged to Thomas Eyton[96] (d. 1582), and thereafter it descended with the manor of Eyton upon the Weald Moors[97] until 1881. In 1767 the vicarage was united with the rectory of Eyton upon the Weald Moors, then in the same patronage.[98] In 1881 T. S. Eyton conveyed the advowson to John Hotson.[99] It passed c. 1890 to Georgiana Hunt,[1] and c. 1900 to the incumbent, H. M. Marsh-Edwards.[2] It was vested in trustees c. 1904,[3] and in 1907 was bought by the evangelical Church Trust Fund Trust, with which it remained in 1981.[4] The patronage was suspended 1975–80 during a reconsideration of church organization in Telford, and a priest-in-charge served the cure.[5] In 1980 the

[58] S.R.O. 2719/3/596, p. 4.
[59] Gas (Areas of Area Boards) Order 1948 (Stat. Instr. 1948, no. 2773); Gas (Vesting Date) Order 1949 (Stat. Instr. 1949, no. 392).
[60] Electric Lighting Orders Conf. (No. 5) Act, 1901, 1 Edw. VII, c. 138 (Local).
[61] S.R.O., DA 13/150 (S.R.O. 3172/11/24), instructions of [1925].
[62] S.R.O., DA 13/100/11, pp. 54, 70.
[63] Jones, Dir. Wellington (1934), 6.
[64] S.R.O., DA 13/100/15, 23 Mar. 1944.
[65] Wellington Jnl. 8 May 1909.
[66] S.R.O. 3129/5/6, 28 July 1843.
[67] S.R.O., q. sess. Const. Cttee. rep. bk. 1839–53, pp. 501–2; P.O. Dir. Salop. (1856), 137.
[68] [H. D. G. Foxall,] 'A Century at Wellington', Salop. Fire Service Newsletter, Feb. 1968, 11 (copy in possession of Mr. Foxall).
[69] When the improvement comrs.' offices were built: Wellington Jnl. 27 Aug. 1910 (wrongly dating the bldgs. 1877: above, Local Govt.).
[70] Hobson, Wellington Dir. (1898), 18.
[71] Salop. Fire Service Newsletter, Feb. 1968, 10–13.
[72] Ibid. 17; Kelly's Dir. Salop. (1926), 294.
[73] S.R.O. 478, deed.
[74] Ibid. min. bk. 1 Nov. 1928; 7 Nov. 1939.
[75] V.C.H. Salop. iii. 221.
[76] [H. D. G. Foxall,] 'Short Hist. of Fire-Fighting in Salop.' (TS. 1973), 3–4 (copy in S.R.O. 3005/2).
[77] Telford Jnl. 20 June 1980; below, Wombridge, Public Services.
[78] S.R.O., q. sess. Const. Cttee. rep. bk. 1839–53, p. 69.
[79] Ibid. p. 76.
[80] Above, Local Govt.
[81] S.R.O., q. sess. Const. Cttee. rep. bk. 1839–53, pp. 341,

352.
[82] S. Bagshaw, Dir. Salop. (1851), 425.
[83] S.R.O., q. sess. Const. Cttee. rep. bk. 1839–53, p. 531.
[84] Ibid. p. 496; O.S. Map 1/500, Salop. XXXVI. 9. 13 (1882 edn.).
[85] Kelly's Dir. Salop. (1885), 457.
[86] S.R.O. 1818/7, pp. 92, 150; 1904/121.
[87] O.S. Map 1/2,500, Salop. XXXVI. 9 (1927 edn.).
[88] Kelly's Dir. Salop. (1926), 294.
[89] Ann. Rep. of Ch. Const. 1955, 7 (copy in S.R.O.).
[90] V.C.H. Salop. i. 317.
[91] Cart. Shrews. i, p. 37.
[92] Ibid. i, pp. 7–8; ii, pp. 296–7.
[93] Ibid. i, p. 66.
[94] L.J.R.O., B/A/1/13, f. 224; V.C.H. Salop. ii. 36.
[95] In Mar. the advowson was granted to John Johnson (or Antony) and Geo. Cotton (Cal. Pat. 1557–8, 287) but the king and queen were patrons in June (L.J.R.O., B/V/1/2, p. 41).
[96] L.J.R.O., B/V/1/3.
[97] e.g. ibid. B/A/1/19, f. 105.
[98] Above, Eyton, Church.
[99] Lich. Dioc. Regy., bps.' reg. S, p. 437.
[1] Ibid. benefice and inst. bk. 1868–1900, p. 81; Kelly's Dir. Salop. (1891), 456. She was presumably Georgiana Veronica (née Davidson,) wife of Rowland Hunt: Burke, Land. Gent. (18th edn.), ii (1969), 331.
[2] Lich. Dioc. Regy., benefice and inst. bk. 1868–1900, p. 104; 1900–29, p. 5.
[3] Kelly's Dir. Salop. (1905), 268. Marsh-Edwards was charged with immorality before a church ct. in 1904: Shrews. Chron. 15 Jan. 1904.
[4] Inf. from Mrs. J. C. Duxbury and the Church Trust Fund Trust.
[5] Lich. Dioc. Regy., benefice and inst. bk. 1968– (in use), p. 55; Lich. Dioc. Dir. (1981), 100.

patronage was restored and he was made vicar of Wellington and rector of Eyton.[6]

Until 1232 the incumbent received part of the great and small tithes, the tithes of some estates in the parish being wholly or partly reserved to Shrewsbury abbey.[7] From 1232 the vicar received the small tithes from all the parish but no great tithes. He was also entitled to altar dues, arable glebe, rents from tenants of 'church lands' (*terre de ecclesia*), tithes of mills, and pensions from chapels,[8] perhaps at Eyton and Preston.[9] In 1291 the vicar's income was given as £2 13s. 4d.[10] In 1535 the vicarage was valued at £9 5s. net.[11]

In 1639 the vicar had glebe and tithes.[12] In 1649 his income was £51[13] and his gross income from Wellington was about the same c. 1693.[14] In 1758 the vicarial glebe was valued at c. £50[15] and in 1767 the incumbent's gross income was c. £118 from Wellington and c. £45 from Eyton, the total being deemed hardly sufficient to maintain a minister.[16] By 1799, however, it was c. £400.[17] In 1807 the incumbent gave the Eyton rectorial glebe (almost 18 a.) and the site of Wellington vicarage to Thomas Eyton in exchange for a new vicarage in Wellington and c. 7½ a. of land there.[18] The vicar sold 2 a. to Thomas Eyton in 1808,[19] and in 1842 his glebe totalled 40½ a.[20]

On the eve of commutation all the vicarial tithes of Wellington parish were payable in kind except those of Apley and Dothill townships, from each of which an annual modus of £1 was paid. In Aston township 43 a. were prescriptively exempt from vicarial tithes[21] and in Eyton township (in Eyton and Wellington parishes) 87 a. were free of all tithes. In Eyton township within Eyton parish no tithes were payable for calves and 1d. for each sow, and the incumbent received a modus of 7s. 6d. for the hay tithes of Eyton moor (from which Eyton parish owed no other tithes). In Preston township within Wellington parish the vicar received 1d. for every stall of bees in lieu of tithe honey, 1d. for every colt, and eggs at Easter in lieu of tithe poultry. In the years 1838–42 the incumbent's tithes from Wellington and Eyton parishes were commuted to £708 12s. 3d.[22] and in 1843 his net income from both parishes was £842.[23] In 1856 he assigned £10 a year from tithe

rent charge to the incumbent of Hadley.[24] In 1884 tithe rent charge still provided most of his income, supplemented by c. £123 rent[25] from letting 17 a. of the 40½-a. vicarial glebe and c. £18 from offerings and fees. In 1915 the vicarial glebe was smaller by 13 a. but there was then investment income of £69 2s. 2d. a year from the Ecclesiastical Commissioners and £10 7s. 2d. from Queen Anne's Bounty. Offerings and fees averaged £45.[26] The united living was worth £519 in 1932.[27]

There was a vicarage house by 1419.[28] The ground floor consisted in 1689 of a hall, kitchen, pantry, buttery, and brew house.[29] In 1807 the old vicarage, immediately south of the church,[30] was deemed unfit. The patron had recently provided a new one just north of Watling Street.[31] The vicar moved to a house called Melrose, in Haygate Road, in 1920[32] and to 6 Queen Street c. 1922.[33] His successor lived at Crescent House, Park Street, from 1923 to c. 1931, when a new vicarage was built in the grounds.[34]

Only one medieval vicar is known to have been a graduate: William Grinshill, 1419 – c. 1430,[35] was an Oxford bachelor of canon law.[36] Like him, several others had local surnames: Philip of Berrington, 1302 – c. 1329,[37] John of Humphreston, fl. 1349,[38] Thomas Grinshill, 1403 – c. 1419,[39] and John Hussey, fl. 1498–1519.[40] John Hychecok, fl. 1366 – c. 1403,[41] was granted a year's leave of absence in 1366 and two years' in 1373.[42] Thomas Grinshill was previously vicar of Wrockwardine.[43] William Grinshill was also rector of Preston upon the Weald Moors, 1422–8,[44] and official to the dean of St. Mary's, Shrewsbury.[45] Hussey may have been the same man who was master of Battlefield college c. 1520.[46]

In 1437 there was a guild of the Holy Trinity and the Virgin Mary, which owned 26 messuages, 10 a. of heath, and 6 a. of meadow.[47] By 1548 all the property lay within the parish and consisted mostly of houses; there were also 3 a. of land in the open fields and several small enclosures.[48] The revenues were divided between the guild (67s. 4d. net) and the service of Our Lady (100s. 6d. net). Both maintained stipendiaries: the guild's priest celebrated masses and assisted the vicar, Our Lady's priest celebrated at the Lady altar. The

[6] Inf. from the vicar.
[7] *Cart. Shrews.* i, pp. 7–8; ii, pp. 296–7.
[8] Ibid. i, p. 66.
[9] Above, Eyton, Church; Preston, Church.
[10] *Tax. Eccl.* (Rec. Com.), 245.
[11] *Valor Eccl.* (Rec. Com.), iii. 185.
[12] L.J.R.O., B/V/1/65.
[13] Baxter, 'Wellington', 68.
[14] W.S.L., H.M. 36 (shorthand transcribed by Mr. N. W. Tildesley).
[15] *Eng. Topog.* (Gent. Mag. Libr.), x. 155.
[16] L.J.R.O., B/A/2(i)/A–D, f. 90.
[17] S.R.O. 3916/1/1, p. 24.
[18] L.J.R.O., B/A/2(i)/F, pp. 19–30.
[19] Ibid. /2(i)/E, pp. 375–7.
[20] S.R.O. 14, tithe appt.
[21] Throughout the par. there were parcels owing only rectorial tithes.
[22] L.J.R.O., B/A/15, Eyton; Hortons Wood; Preston; S.R.O. 14, tithe appt.
[23] S.R.O. 3916/1/6, nos. 14, 38.
[24] Below, Hadley, Churches.
[25] *Return of Glebe Land, 1887*, H.C. 307, p. 68 (1887), lxiv.
[26] S.R.O. 3916/1/33, s.v. Wellington, All Saints.
[27] *Crockford* (1932), 586.
[28] L.J.R.O., B/A/1/8, ff. 29v.–30.
[29] Trinder and Cox, *Yeomen and Colliers*, pp. 284–6.
[30] S.R.O. 14, tithe appt. and map.
[31] Above; O.S. Map 6″, Salop. XXXVI. SW. (1887 edn.).
[32] *Reg. of Electors, Spring 1920: Wrekin Divn.* 643; *Autumn 1920*, 640. [33] Ibid. *Autumn 1921*, 638; *Spring 1922*, 643.
[34] Inf. from Mrs. Duxbury.
[35] L.J.R.O., B/A/1/8, f. 16v.; /1/9, f. 101.
[36] A. B. Emden, *Biog. Reg. Univ. Oxf. to 1500*, ii. 835.
[37] L.J.R.O., B/A/1/1, f. 18v.; /1/2, f. 206v.; Staffs. R.O., D. 593/A/1/19/8.
[38] L.J.R.O., B/A/1/2, f. 224.
[39] Ibid. /1/7, f. 109v.; /1/8, f. 16v.
[40] Ibid. /1/13, f. 224; *S.P.R. Lich.* xxi (3), p. vii.
[41] L.J.R.O., B/A/1/7, f. 109v.
[42] *S.H.C.* N.S. viii. 31, 66.
[43] *T.S.A.S.* 3rd ser. x. 217–19. He was vicar of Wrockwardine again 1422–5: ibid. 219–20.
[44] Emden, *Biog. Reg. Oxf. to 1500*, ii. 835.
[45] S.P.L., Haughmond Cart. f. 193.
[46] *V.C.H. Salop.* ii. 131.
[47] T. F. Dukes, *Antiquities of Salop.* (1844), 185.
[48] P.R.O., E 36/258, ff. 129–30.

latter also had a living elsewhere and kept a free grammar school.[49] A small separate endowment, worth 3s. 10d. a year, maintained a lamp and some lights.[50] Those endowments were sold by the Crown in 1549 to John Cupper and Richard Trevor,[51] acting for Alan Charlton,[52] uncle of Francis Charlton of Apley[53] and mentioned as vicar in 1535.[54]

After the Reformation the incumbents often had a family connexion with the patrons. Four vicars were Eytons: Thomas, fl. 1558–62,[55] John, 1689–1709,[56] Robert, 1713–51,[57] and John, 1802–23.[58] Henry Wood, 1709–12,[59] was probably a relative of William Wood, the patron's guardian, and perhaps a 'warming pan' vicar to await the presentation of the patron's cousin[60] Robert. John Rocke, 1782–1802,[61] was the patron's uncle,[62] and Edward Pryce Owen, 1823–41,[63] was Rocke's nephew.[64] Between 1666 and 1802 the living was always held in plurality except 1709–13, 1751–60, and 1767–73. Before the union of the livings in 1767 Wellington was sometimes held with Eyton[65] but more often with other parishes.[66] The most conspicuous pluralist was Robert Eyton, concurrently vicar of Wem (from 1718),[67] a prebendary of Hereford (from 1728), and archdeacon of Ely (from 1742).[68] Some pluralists were probably non-resident in the later 17th and 18th century, especially if they held a living other than Eyton. William Langley, 1662–89,[69] was buried at Stoke upon Tern in 1689[70] and Robert Eyton died at Wem in 1751.[71] John Rocke was living in Shrewsbury in 1799 but stayed in Wellington parish at weekends to take the services.[72] On the other hand John Eyton resided c. 1693,[73] Richard Smith, 1751–73,[74] lived continuously in the parish,[75] and so, probably, did Stephen Panting, 1778–82.[76] John Eyton, instituted 1802, and his successors resided, at least from 1807 when the new vicarage was built.

A curate was often, perhaps usually, employed, whether or not the vicar resided. The earliest known was mentioned in 1558.[77] Henry Gauntlett, an Evangelical divine, was curate 1804–5,[78] Patrick Brontë was curate briefly in 1809,[79] and H. Johnson Marshall, curate in 1843,[80] wrote tracts on religion as applied to social issues.[81] In 1856 there were two curates at All Saints', a senior and a junior.[82] In 1981 a deaconess served part-time but the curacy, then vacant, was not filled until 1983.[83]

Seven days after Elizabeth I's accession three parishioners were presented for not receiving communion on Sundays and festivals; it is not known whether they were papists or protestant dissenters.[84] Puritanism was encouraged by Francis Wright,[85] vicar 1621–59,[86] and perhaps by William Langley,[87] 1662–89. John Eyton was said c. 1693 to be 'too free in conversation' and much in debt.[88] Richard Smith, 1751–73, did his best to discourage Methodists and Quakers.[89] In 1772 there were two Sunday services, with one sermon in winter and two in summer, and prayers every Wednesday and Friday and at festivals. Communion was administered monthly and at Easter, Whit Sunday, Christmas, and Good Friday. There were usually c. 70 communicants.[90] Thomas Warter, 1773–7, published a sermon.[91] Nevertheless the late 18th century in Wellington was said to have been a period of social immorality and religious indifference. A remarkable revival was effected by the young John Eyton, vicar 1802–23, who worked closely with the Wesleyans.[92] Nevertheless at the time of his early death there were usually only c. 40 communicants, though at Easter as many as 160.[93] Wellington's population growth since 1772 may have assisted nonconformity rather than the Anglican church.

Eyton's successor Owen was best known as a painter and etcher.[94] In 1843 there were three

[49] T.S.A.S. 3rd ser. x. 351; below, Educ.
[50] T.S.A.S. 3rd ser. x. 374.
[51] Cal. Pat. 1548–9, 395–6.
[52] S.P.R. Lich. xxi (3), p. vi.
[53] S.R.O. 625, box 19, i.p.m. of Wm. Charlton (copy).
[54] Valor Eccl. iii. 185.
[55] L.J.R.O., B/V/1/2, p. 41; /1/5, s.v. Wellington; B/A/1/15, f. 40.
[56] T.S.A.S. 4th ser. iv. 190; par. reg. bur. 25 Feb. 1708/9 (transcript in S.P.L.). He was the patron's uncle: above, Eyton, Man. and Other Est.
[57] T.S.A.S. 4th ser. v. 189, 202; S.P.R. Lich. x (1), 648.
[58] L.J.R.O., B/A/1/28, p. 23; Baxter, 'Wellington', 71. He was the patron's son: Burke, Land. Gent. (18th edn.), iii (1972), 308; above, Eyton, Man. and Other Est.
[59] T.S.A.S. 4th ser. v. 188; par. reg. bur. 22 Dec. 1712 (transcript in S.P.L.).
[60] S.P.L., MS. 2788, p. 287.
[61] T.S.A.S. 4th ser. vi. 298; L.J.R.O., B/A/1/28, p. 19.
[62] S.R.O. 1487/3; above, Eyton, Man. and Other Est.
[63] S.P.R. Lich. xxi (3), p. viii; Lich. Dioc. Regy., episc. reg. 30, p. 181.
[64] Baxter, 'Wellington', 71; D.N.B. s.v. Owen, Hugh.
[65] Above, Eyton, Church.
[66] Stoke upon Tern 1666–89, Cleobury North 1773–7, Wrockwardine 1778–82, and Clungunford 1782–1802: T.S.A.S. 3rd ser. x. 233; 4th ser. iv. 182, 185, 190; v. 205, 208; vi. 296, 298, 309, 316; S.R.O. 2181/1/2, bur. 11 May 1689; 3963/Rg/2, bur. 17 Dec. 1795; L.J.R.O., B/A/1/24, p. 10; Dioc. of Heref. Institutions (1539–1900), ed. A. T. Bannister (Heref. 1923), 139.
[67] T.S.A.S. 4th ser. v. 191; S.P.R. Lich. x (1), 648.
[68] Par. reg. 1701–43, p. 1.
[69] T.S.A.S. 4th ser. iv. 182, 190.

[70] S.R.O. 2181/1/2, bur. 11 May.
[71] S.P.R. Lich. x (1), 648.
[72] S.R.O. 3916/1/1, p. 24.
[73] W.S.L., H.M. 36, s.v. Eyton upon the Weald Moors.
[74] Above, Eyton, Church.
[75] L.J.R.O., B/V/5, visit. return of 1772.
[76] Ibid. B/A/1/24, pp. 10, 111. Signed par. reg. 1780 (bap. 19 Jan. 1772 (transcript in S.P.L.)) but bur. at Wrockwardine (T.S.A.S. 3rd ser. x. 233). Cf. below, Wrockwardine, Church.
[77] L.J.R.O., B/V/1/2, p. 41.   [78] D.N.B.
[79] C. Lowe, Story of Par. Ch. of All Sts. Wellington (Shifnal [1962]), [19] (copy in S.P.L.).
[80] S.R.O. 3916/1/6, no. 38.
[81] B.M. Gen. Cat. of Printed Bks. to 1955 (photolithographic edn. 1959–66), cliii, col. 602.
[82] S.R.O. 3916/1/16, loose sheet.
[83] Local inf.
[84] L.J.R.O., B/V/1/2, p. 161 (24 Nov. 1558). The Catholic Bp. Baynes of Coventry and Lichfield was not deprived until June 1559: D.N.B.
[85] Calamy Revised, ed. A. G. Matthews, 556; T.S.A.S. 2nd ser. i. 85.
[86] L.J.R.O., B/A/1/16, f. 16; par. reg. bur. 30 July 1659 (transcript in S.P.L.).
[87] Baxter, 'Wellington', 70A; below, Prot. Nonconf.
[88] W.S.L., H.M. 36.
[89] Below, Prot. Nonconf.
[90] L.J.R.O., B/V/5, visit. return.
[91] B.M. Gen. Cat. of Printed Bks. to 1955, ccliii, col. 374.
[92] Trinder, Ind. Rev. Salop. 299. For his published sermons see B.M. Gen. Cat. of Printed Bks. to 1955, lxix, col. 1058.
[93] S.R.O. 3916/1/3, no. 37.
[94] D.N.B.

services every Sunday and another on Wednesday evenings, but the proportion of communicants to the population had fallen further,[95] a decline presumably accelerated by the opening of Christ Church and Ketley chapels of ease during Owen's incumbency. Under his successor Benjamin Banning, 1841–80,[96] ecclesiastical parishes were formed for Hadley (1858), Christ Church (1859), Lawley (1867), and Ketley (1880).[97] Moreover in 1874 Walcot was transferred to Withington ecclesiastical parish and Aston to Uppington.[98]

In 1870 a proposal to establish a surpliced choir aroused controversy[99] but one existed by 1883 when John Slaney left stock for its maintenance.[1] Thereafter the services attained a high musical standard,[2] still evident in 1981.[3] A. Z. Grace, instituted as vicar in 1881,[4] lost five children from diphtheria, became ill, took to drink,[5] and was suspended in 1884.[6] He resigned four years later.[7] H. M. Marsh-Edwards, 1897–1901,[8] who was responsible for an ambitious restoration of the church's interior, resigned before his liaison with a local servant girl became public knowledge.[9] Soon afterwards he was made a bishop in the 'Old Catholic Church of the East'.[10] In the late 19th century All Saints' was considered 'higher' than Christ Church, but from J. S. Moore's incumbency, 1901–23,[11] the successive vicars were decidedly Evangelical. In 1981 congregations of c. 200 were usual at Sunday morning services and were twice as large at the monthly family service. A church hall immediately south of the churchyard, built in 1903 by Moore's efforts, was burned down by vandals in 1978. A new hall, used solely for church purposes, opened on the site in 1980. A church hall built at Dothill c. 1962 was used as a Sunday school and by children's and youth groups.[12]

The ancient parish church of ALL SAINTS[13] was demolished in 1787.[14] At least one window dated from the 12th century.[15] The building comprised a chancel and nave, probably undivided, to which broad north and south aisles had been added at different dates; there was an embattled tower at the west end of the north aisle. The east window of the chancel was of the earlier 14th century. The east windows of the aisles were perhaps 15th-century. A 16th-century monument with recumbent effigies, inscribed to William Charlton and his wife, stood in the chancel on the north side.[16] It was removed at the demolition and later placed in Holy Cross church, Shrewsbury.[17] There was a west gallery by 1726.[18] There were three bells in 1553[19] and six in 1758, all dated 1713.[20] Of the plate there survives a silver paten of 1717 given in 1733.[21]

In 1747 there were detailed plans for rebuilding the church.[22] It was not until 1788, however, that a new church designed by George Steuart was begun[23] east of the churchyard[24] on a site conveyed by George Forester. In 1790 the building was finished, consecrated, and dedicated to All Saints.[25] Built of stone in the classical style, it consists of an aisled nave of five bays with eastern apse. The west front of three bays has Tuscan pilasters and a pediment, above which is a square tower of two stages with domed roof. In 1981 there were five bells from the old church, another dated 1798, and two dated 1890.[26] There are north, south and west galleries supported by iron columns that were originally exposed. The pulpit was in the centre of the nave in 1823.[27] Choir stalls were built at the east end, perhaps in 1866.[28] In alterations of 1898–9 the interior was elaborately reordered; the iron columns of the galleries were encased in arcades[29] and a heavy chancel screen was erected. It was removed in 1956.[30]

A chapel of ease called CHRIST CHURCH was consecrated in 1839. The site, on the south-east side of the town, had been bought in 1837 by the Church Building Commissioners from Lord Forester and building costs, £3,600,[31] were met by voluntary contributions, augmented by £1,550 in grants.[32] The living was then a curacy in the gift of the vicar of Wellington.[33] The chapel was licensed for baptisms and burials from 1839 and for marriages from 1859,[34] when a district chapelry was assigned to it[35] comprising the south-east

[95] S.R.O. 3916/1/6, no. 38.
[96] Lich. Dioc. Regy., episc. reg. 30, p. 183; Baxter, 'Wellington', 72.
[97] Lond. Gaz. 4 Feb. 1858, p. 547; 2 Aug. 1859, p. 2968; 5 Feb. 1867, p. 620; 30 Apr. 1880, p. 2783.
[98] Ibid. 15 May 1874, p. 2572; 11 Aug. 1874, p. 3921. By 1908 Walcot had been transferred to Wrockwardine eccl. par.: S.R.O. 1149/1.
[99] Wellington Before Telford, 25.
[1] S.R.O. 1206/53, pp. 31–3.
[2] Lowe, Story of Par. Ch. of All Sts. [20]; local inf.
[3] Local inf.
[4] Salopian Shreds & Patches, iv. 149.
[5] Lowe, Story of Par. Ch. of All Sts. [19]; local inf.
[6] Par. rec., instrument of suspension.
[7] Lich. Dioc. Regy., benefice and inst. bk. 1868–1900, p. 81.
[8] Ibid. p. 104; 1900–29, p. 5.
[9] Shrews. Chron. 9 Aug. 1901; 24 Oct. 1902; 15 Jan. 1904.
[10] Ibid. 15 Jan. 1904. For the vagaries of his later career see P. F. Anson, Bishops at Large (1964), 121, 212, 269–71.
[11] Lich. Dioc. Regy., benefice and inst. bk. 1900–29, pp. 5, 82.
[12] Local inf.
[13] So dedicated by 1492: Hist. MSS. Com. 47, 15th Rep. X, Shrews. Corp. p. 47.
[14] S.P.L., Prints and Engravings W45; above, plate 33.
[15] Travels in Eng. of Dr. Ric. Pococke, ii (Camd. Soc. N.S. xliv), 291.

[16] Eng. Topog. (Gent. Mag. Libr.), x. 155; S.P.L., MS. 372, vol. iii, p. 91.
[17] H. Owen and J. B. Blakeway, Hist. Shrews. (1825), ii. 166–7. The inscription gives Wm.'s d. as 1544, a date irreconcilable with the known pedigree of the Charltons of Apley: above, Man. and Other Est.
[18] S.R.O. 999/K 6.
[19] T.S.A.S. 2nd ser. xii. 314, 331.
[20] Eng. Topog. (Gent. Mag. Libr.), x. 155.
[21] S. A. Jeavons, Ch. Plate Archd. Salop (Shrews. 1964), p. 56.
[22] S.R.O., q. sess. files, 2/220.
[23] H. Colvin, Biog. Dict. Brit. Architects, 1600–1840 (1978), 780.
[24] L.J.R.O., B/A/2(i)/A–D, f. 463v.; S.R.O. 3916/1/3, no. 37.
[25] L.J.R.O., B/A/2(i)/A–D, ff. 463v.–464v.; date stone.
[26] H. B. Walters, Ch. Bells of Salop. (Oswestry, 1915), 332–4; inf. from Mrs. Duxbury.
[27] S.R.O. 3916/1/3, no. 37.
[28] When the organ was removed from the W. gallery: par. rec., balance sheet of 1866.
[29] Cranage, vii. 632–3.
[30] Lowe, Story of Par. Ch. of All Sts. [10].
[31] S. Bagshaw, Dir. Salop. (1851), 423.
[32] Lich. Dioc. Regy., bps.' reg. L, pp. 469–74.
[33] S.R.O. 3916/1/6, no. 39.
[34] S.R.O. 3499/Rg/1–3.
[35] Lond. Gaz. 2 Aug. 1859, p. 2968.

quarter of Wellington township, most of Arleston township, and parts of Leegomery and Watling Street townships.[36] The living became a perpetual curacy in 1859 (from 1868 a titular vicarage)[37] with the vicar of All Saints' as patron.[38] The cure was served by a priest-in-charge 1972–80 and was thereafter a vicarage.[39] In 1975 part of the parish was transferred to the new parish of central Telford.[40]

In 1893 the curacy was endowed with £1,000 raised by voluntary contributions,[41] which yielded £35 a year in 1851. Pew rents were calculated at £105 in 1851.[42] The living was worth £197 net in 1865.[43] In 1874 the Ecclesiastical Commissioners gave annual tithe rent charge of £135 gross,[44] part of the former endowment of Wellington prebend.[45] In 1892 the Ecclesiastical Commissioners gave £120 capital to meet a benefaction,[46] and in 1895 the living's net value was £230.[47] A large parsonage house north-west of the church[48] had been built by 1843.[49] It was replaced in 1980 by a new vicarage in Church Walk.[50]

In 1843 there were two services every Sunday and at Christmas and Good Friday. Communion was given monthly and on Christmas Day.[51] In 1851 average adult attendances were 280 in the mornings and 550 in the evenings.[52] In 1856 there were 35 communicants on average.[53] An assistant curate was employed by 1879[54] but none after c. 1974.[55] Before the incumbency of Thomas Owen, 1887–1903, services were infrequent; he increased their number and their 'outward reverence', reordering the church's interior and introducing a surpliced choir.[56] In 1887 there were three and four services on alternate Sundays. Communion was weekly.[57] Owen was Evangelical and an eloquent preacher.[58] In the earlier 20th century the number of communicants rose.[59] J. P. Abbey, vicar 1913–62,[60] was at first assumed to be Evangelical but he soon became Anglo-Catholic, and his tradition remained in 1981.[61] Two years after his death the bishop collated by lapse,[62] the patron (the vicar of All Saints') being the nominee of an Evangelical body.

The church, designed by Thomas Smith of Madeley[63] in the lancet Gothic style, is of light yellow brick and resembles his earlier church at Ironbridge. As originally arranged it comprised a chancel (a mere recess with font attached to the wall),[64] a nave with integral north and south aisles, north lobby, and south vestry, and a west tower. In 1915 there was one bell of 1838.[65] There were north, south, and west galleries, the last occupied by the choir.[66] In 1888[67] the communion table was raised on steps and choir stalls were built at the east end.[68] A choir vestry was added at the west in 1893.[69] The north and south galleries were taken down c. 1970.[70]

Anglican chapels were built at Wellington cemetery (by 1882),[71] the Old Hall School (1922),[72] and Wrekin College (reconstructed 1936–7).[73]

ROMAN CATHOLICISM. In 1592 Francis, son of Edward Forester of Watling Street, was admitted to the English College in Rome, but only four papists were recorded in 1676[74] and none c. 1693[75] or in 1772.[76] At the French Revolution George Forester accommodated French priests at Dothill[77] and in 1806 a Roman Catholic chapel at Dothill Lodge was registered by its priest Stephen LeMaître.[78] In 1834 there was a temporary chapel behind the Duke's Head in New Street, and soon afterwards it moved to a nearby shop.[79] A new church opened in 1838 on the east side of Mill Bank. In 1851 average attendance was put at 300,[80] a numerical strength attributable to an influx of Irish workers since the late 18th century. The church, dedicated to St. Patrick, was replaced in 1906 by a new one in King Street built of stone and brick in the Gothic style. The old church served many uses before its demolition c. 1971, including those of a Catholic parish hall, a roller-skating rink, a cinema, a training centre for the unemployed, and a Catholic schoolroom. A convent of Sisters of St. Louis moved from Much Wenlock to Haygate Road in 1978 and undertook teaching, social work, and nursing for the Roman Catholic parish. In 1981 the parish served c. 1,800 people, some of whom lived as far north as Prees, and up to 800 attended Sunday mass.[81]

[36] S.R.O. 1149/1.
[37] S.R.O. 3499/1, pp. 63–4, 124–5.
[38] P.O. Dir. Salop. (1871), 155; Lich. Dioc. Dir. (1981), 100. The bp. exercised patronage during vacancy of All Saints' or by lapse: Lich. Dioc. Regy., benefice and inst. bk. 1868–1900, p. 78; below.
[39] Lich. Dioc. Regy., benefice and inst. bk. 1968– (in use), pp. 28, 94; local inf.
[40] Lich. Dioc. Regy., bps.' reg. R (Orders in Council), p. 350.
[41] Ibid. L, pp. 460, 471–2.
[42] P.R.O., HO 129/365, no. 14.
[43] Clergy List (1865), benefice list, 241.
[44] Lich. Dioc. Regy., bps.' reg. R, p. 701.
[45] Above, Man. and Other Est.
[46] Lich. Dioc. Regy., bps.' reg. T, p. 511.
[47] Kelly's Dir. Salop. (1895), 244.
[48] O.S. Map 1/500, Salop. XXXVI. 9. 24 (1882 edn.).
[49] S.R.O. 3916/1/6, no. 39.
[50] Inf. from Mrs. Duxbury.
[51] S.R.O. 3916/1/6, no. 39.
[52] P.R.O., HO 129/365, no. 14.
[53] S.R.O. 3916/1/16, loose sheet.
[54] S.R.O. 3499/Rg/1, p. 169.
[55] Inf. from Mrs. Duxbury.
[56] S.R.O. 3499/Rg/7, newscutting on front endpaper.
[57] Ibid. /Rg/5.
[58] Shrews. Chron. 18 Sept. 1903.
[59] S.R.O. 3499/Rg/7–10.
[60] Lich. Dioc. Regy., benefice and inst. bk. 1900–29, p. 40; 1952–68, p. 110.
[61] Local inf.
[62] Lich. Dioc. Regy., benefice and inst. bk. 1952–68, p. 110.
[63] Cranage, vii. 634.
[64] S.R.O. 3916/1/6, no. 39.
[65] Walters, Ch. Bells of Salop. 334.
[66] S.R.O. 3499/Rg/7, newscutting on front endpaper.
[67] Bye-Gones, ix (1), 277.
[68] S.R.O. 3499/Rg/7, newscutting on front endpaper.
[69] Kelly's Dir. Salop. (1900), 259.
[70] Inf. from Mrs. Duxbury.
[71] O.S. Map 1/2,500, Salop. XXXVI. 9 (1882 edn.).
[72] Local inf.
[73] V.C.H. Salop. ii. 163.
[74] T.S.A.S. 2nd ser. i. 85.
[75] W.S.L., H.M. 36.
[76] L.J.R.O., B/V/5, visit. return.
[77] Baxter, 'Wellington', 80–1.
[78] S.R.O., q. sess. files, 7/32.
[79] Acct. based on: S.R.O. 4050/1, p. 8; /2, pp. 5–6.
[80] P.R.O., HO 129/365, no. 18.
[81] Inf. from the Revd. M. Wagstaffe.

PROTESTANT NONCONFORMITY. There is little evidence of early protestant dissent apart from a few Presbyterians and Baptists in the late 17th and early 18th century. The puritan vicar Francis Wright, 1621–59, was an active Presbyterian in 1648 but was reckoned an Independent by 1654. In the 1660s the ejected ministers of Kynnersley and St. Alkmund's, Shrewsbury, whose allegiances had also been Presbyterian and Independent, retired to Wellington and were buried there.[82] Their presence presumably fostered dissent, though numbers were not great. There were 40 adult nonconformists (just over 1 in 40 of the adult population) in 1676[83] and only 2 families were known c. 1693.[84] Dissenters licensed meeting houses at Aston (1693) and Wellington (1701 and 1730).[85] They may have been Presbyterians: a house at Aston was licensed for their worship in 1715.[86] Richard Smith, vicar 1751–73, firmly opposed nonconformity and tried to spoil a Quaker meeting at the market hall in 1760 by ringing the church bells.[87] By 1799 about one in five of the parish's population were dissenters, mostly Methodists, with a few Quakers and Baptists.[88]

On Census Sunday 1851 many more nonconformists than Anglicans attended worship in the parish.[89] There were considerable differences between the coalfield townships (Hadley, Ketley, and Lawley)[90] and the rest of the parish. In the three coalfield townships some 83 per cent of recorded attendances (at eight places of worship) were Methodist, half of them Wesleyan. Anglicans and Baptists had only one place of worship each, with 12 and 5 per cent of recorded attendances respectively. In the rest of the parish the combined recorded attendances of all protestant nonconformists were only 35 per cent, while Anglicans and Roman Catholics recorded 46 and 19 per cent respectively. By 1981 only two churches in the area of the ancient parish outside the coalfield townships survived to represent the long established nonconformist denominations: a Union Free church in Constitution Hill formed by Congregationalists and Baptists, and a Methodist (formerly Wesleyan) church in New Street.

Benjamin Wright is said to have been the first Anabaptist in the town.[91] His house was licensed for worship in 1695[92] and there were Baptists in 1730.[93] Wright's son-in-law Robert Morris (d. 1746) left 20s. a year to the minister of the Baptist meeting in Stillyard Shut, Shrewsbury, to preach four sermons a year at his house in Wellington.[94] There were no Baptists or Presbyterians in the parish by 1772[95] but there were a few Baptists by 1799[96] as the result of a revival led by Dr. John Palmer, minister of the Shrewsbury Baptists.[97] They met at Chapel (later Portway) House in Chapel House (later Plough) Road.[98] In 1807 Particular Baptists opened a new chapel in Back Lane (later King Street).[99] There were 52 members in 1824[1] and the chapel is said to have been rebuilt in brick in 1828[2] with seats for 340. On Census Sunday 1851 morning attendance was 60, evening attendance 100.[3] The chapel was enlarged in 1897[4] but closed in 1920[5] when its members joined the Congregationalists at Constitution Hill.[6]

The Quakers, whose meeting in 1760 was well attended[7] and who licensed a meeting place in the town in 1768,[8] achieved no lasting success in the parish outside Lawley where the Darbys' and Reynoldses' influence was strong.[9] In 1980, however, a group of Quakers that had met at Lilleshall since the 1960s was meeting at a house in Wellington.[10]

Congregational worship in Wellington was established when an Independent congregation was founded in 1818.[11] A brick chapel was built at Tan Bank in 1825[12] with a donation from the publishers F. Houlston & Son.[13] The large building could hold c. 350[14] but there were only 28 members in 1828, and in 1834 the size of the congregation was discouraging. Despite a revival of support in the earlier 1840s, when Congregationalists from Wellington founded a church at Oakengates, there were only 32 members in 1845.[15] By 1851, however, adult attendances averaged 120 in the morning and 200 in the evening.[16] Another decline followed. There were 37 members in 1863 and the chapel was closed and sold c. 1880.[17] Another revival occurred in 1898.[18] Services in temporary premises were well attended and in 1900 an impressive new church

[82] *Calamy Revised*, ed. A. G. Matthews, 256, 549, 556; *T.S.A.S.* 3rd ser. vii. 269, 272, 284.

[83] *T.S.A.S.* 2nd ser. i. 85.

[84] W.S.L., H.M. 36.

[85] *Orders of Q. Sess.* i. 144, 193; ii. 73.

[86] S.R.O., q. sess. order bk. 1709–26, f. 81.

[87] P.R.O., RG 31/7, Salop. no. 131; R. F. Skinner, *Nonconformity in Salop.* (Shrews. 1964), 32.

[88] S.R.O. 3916/1/1, p. 24.

[89] Para. based on P.R.O., HO 129/365, nos. 13A–31, 45. An unknown number of small prot. nonconf. meetings made no return. Actual percentages of nonconf. attendances were therefore slightly higher than those recorded, and of Anglicans and Roman Catholics slightly smaller.

[90] For these see below, Nonconf. sections of Hadley; Ketley; Lawley.

[91] Owen and Blakeway, *Hist. Shrews.* ii. 486.

[92] *Orders of Q. Sess.* i. 154.

[93] Inf. from Dr. H. Foreman.

[94] Owen and Blakeway, *Hist. Shrews.* ii. 485–6. Ben. may have been the Revd. Fra. Wright's son: Trinder and Cox, *Yeomen and Colliers*, pp. 23–4.

[95] L.J.R.O., B/V/5, visit. return.

[96] S.R.O. 3916/1/1, p. 24.

[97] *V.C.H. Salop.* ii. 11 (as corr. below, Corrigenda).

[98] Inf. from Dr. Foreman.

[99] S.R.O. 1931/3; *Baptist Handbk. 1861*, 72.

[1] *Shropshire Circular Letter, 1824*, 10 (copy in S.P.L., class C 98.6 v.f.).

[2] S. Bagshaw, *Dir. Salop.* (1851), 423; above, plate 37.

[3] P.R.O., HO 129/365, no. 17.

[4] *Kelly's Dir. Salop.* (1917), 264.

[5] Inf. from Dr. Foreman.

[6] G.R.O., Worship Reg. no. 48574.

[7] Above.

[8] P.R.O., RG 31/7, Salop. no. 142.

[9] Below, Lawley, Nonconf.

[10] Inf. from Mr. A. E. Morris.

[11] *Cong. Yr. Bk.* 1967–8, 246.

[12] Date stone.

[13] Trinder, *Ind. Rev. Salop.* 303.

[14] In 1851: P.R.O., HO 129/365, no. 20.

[15] E. Elliot, *Hist. Congregationalism in Salop.* [1898], 215–16; S. Bagshaw, *Dir. Salop.* (1851), 441; *Shrews. Chron.* 25 May 1900; below, Wombridge, Nonconf.

[16] P.R.O., HO 129/365, no. 20.

[17] Elliot, op. cit. 217–18; *P.O. Dir. Salop.* (1879), 427; *Kelly's Dir. Salop.* (1885), 974.

[18] A. Clegg, *One Hundred and Fifty Years* [Shrews. 1946], 5 (copy in S.P.L.).

was opened at Constitution Hill. Built of brick with stone dressings, it was designed in the Gothic style by Ingall & Sons of Birmingham.[19] In 1920[20] the Baptists closed their King Street chapel and joined the Congregationalists, whose church was then registered as a Union Free church.[21] There were 41 members in 1983.[22]

In 1772 there were 10 Methodist families in the parish.[23] Their distribution is uncertain, but Methodism is likely to have grown rapidly in the coalfield townships. In the parish as a whole Methodists were the largest group of worshippers recorded in 1851, though outside the coalfield townships their combined strength only equalled the Anglicans'. The Wesleyans were the most numerous Methodists but their places of worship were less widely distributed than the Primitives'.[24] The New Connexion was represented outside the coalfield townships only by a preaching place at New Works recorded in 1839.[25] Between 1851 and 1885 more Methodist chapels were built than at any earlier period and some old ones were rebuilt or enlarged, but the movement's prosperity was less than it seemed,[26] especially as the area was entering a long economic and demographic decline. Most Methodist chapels nevertheless managed to remain open until the later 1960s; thereafter many closed.

Wellington people were attracted to Wesleyan meetings at Madeley held by the vicar, J. W. Fletcher.[27] In 1765 Fletcher preached in Wellington[28] but the vicar, Richard Smith, opposed him with some succeess.[29] In 1771 a house in New Street was registered for worship probably by Methodists,[30] but in 1772 numbers were allegedly declining.[31] After Smith's death in 1773 Methodism grew in strength. A chapel in Chapel Lane[32] was licensed in 1797,[33] and in 1799 there were c. 200 Methodists of 'Lady Huntingdon's sort'.[34] Wesleyans were supported by John Eyton, vicar 1802–23, who preached at their meetings.[35] In 1813 Wellington was the only Wesleyan preaching place in the parish outside the coalfield townships[36] but by 1823 a society had been formed at Arleston.[37] It expired in 1845 and

was briefly revived in 1856.[38] A preaching place at or near the Wrekin existed 1825–8.[39] A society existed at Steeraway from 1886 to 1892[40] and in the 1920s.[41]

The Wellington chapel was enlarged in 1811[42] and replaced in 1836[43] by a new brick building at the junction of New Street and St. John Street. On Census Sunday 1851 there were 277 adult attendances in the morning and 251 in the evening.[44] In 1866 accommodation was increased to 560 by the addition of galleries[45] and in 1883 the chapel was replaced by another[46] farther west along New Street, which remained in use in 1983. The chapel of 1883, designed by Herbert Isitt to seat 850, was of brick with stone dressings, with an imposing Italianate façade. The chapel of 1836 was kept as a Sunday school and lecture hall (sometimes called the Central Hall) until 1916, when it was sold.[47]

A Wesleyan meeting was formed at Watling Street in 1859,[48] and in 1861[49] a small brick mission chapel opened there immediately west of what was later the junction with Regent Street. It closed c. 1941 and was let as commercial premises.[50]

The first Primitive Methodist meeting was at 229 Watling Street.[51] In 1822 Edward Williams's house in Tan Bank was licensed and in 1823 a schoolroom in Elizabeth Lewis's house there.[52] A chapel said to have been built in 1826[53] stood in Tan Bank by 1835.[54] Rebuilt in that year,[55] it stood just off the street, south of the junction with Foundry Lane.[56] In 1898[57] it was replaced by a new chapel on the opposite side of Tan Bank, designed by Elijah Jones[58] in brick and terracotta with Gothic details, where there were 285 sittings in 1940.[59] The old chapel was kept as a Sunday school,[60] probably until a new school was built next to the new chapel in 1906,[61] and was demolished c. 1972.[62] The chapel of 1898 closed in 1966, when the congregation amalgamated with that at New Street; it was used as a Methodist youth club[63] until 1978 when it was bought by Muslims for a mosque.[64]

Outside the coalfield townships there were,

[19] *Shrews. Chron.* 25 May 1900.
[20] Inf. from Dr. Foreman.
[21] G.R.O., Worship Reg. no. 48574.
[22] Inf. from Dr. Foreman.
[23] L.J.R.O., B/V/5, visit. return.
[24] P.R.O., HO 129/365, nos. 13A–31, 45.
[25] S.R.O. 3677/1.
[26] B. Trinder, *Meth. New Connexion in Dawley and Madeley* (Wesley Hist. Soc., W. Midlands Branch, Occ. Publ. i [1968]), 15–16.   [27] Randall, *Madeley*, 164.
[28] Skinner, *Nonconf. in Salop.* 73 n.
[29] L.J.R.O., B/V/5, visit. return of 1772.
[30] P.R.O., RG 31/7, Salop. no. 150. The certif. was signed by Wm. Buttery, perhaps a relative of Geo. Buttery, owner of the Lawley Bank chapel (presumed Wesleyan) in 1818: *Orders of Q. Sess.* iii. 210; below, Lawley, Nonconf.
[31] L.J.R.O., B/V/5, visit. return of 1772.
[32] S. Bagshaw, *Dir. Salop.* (1851), 423.
[33] P.R.O., RG 31/7, Salop. no. 187.
[34] S.R.O. 3916/1/1, p. 24.
[35] Trinder, *Ind. Rev. Salop.* 299.
[36] S.P.L., C 98.7 v.f., Shrews. circuit plan.
[37] S.P.L., L 98.7 v.f., Wellington circuit plan.
[38] S.R.O. 3767/XVII/A. Perhaps at Wm. Cooper's ho., licensed for nonconf. worship 1814: P.R.O., RG 31/7, Salop. no. 342.
[39] Shrews. Sch. libr., Broseley circuit bk. 1815–41.

[40] S.R.O. 3767/XVII/E3.
[41] Inf. from Mr. J. H. Lenton.
[42] Lenton, *Methodism in Wellington*, 5.
[43] *Wesleyan Meth. Mag.* lix. 375. Ref. supplied by Mr. Lenton.
[44] P.R.O., HO 129/365, no. 19.
[45] Local inf. (recorded in S.M.R.).
[46] Opened 23 Mar. 1883: S.R.O. 3767/XX/A, p. 1. The date stones read 1882.
[47] S.R.O. 3767/XX/A, pp. 2–3, 9, 76, 300.
[48] Ibid. /XVII/I, circuit plan.
[49] Ibid. /XVII/E2, sched. of 1881.
[50] Ibid. /XXI/C; *Meth. Church Bldgs.: Statistical Returns* (1940), 270.
[51] Lenton, *Methodism in Wellington*, 33.
[52] Ibid.; *Orders of Q. Sess.* iii. 227, 239.
[53] Lenton, op. cit. 33.   [54] S.R.O. 3038/7/1.
[55] Lenton, op. cit. 34.
[56] S.R.O. 14, tithe appt. and map; O.S. Map 1/500, Salop. XXXVI. 9. 18 (1882 edn.).   [57] Date stone.
[58] Local inf. (recorded in S.M.R.).
[59] *Meth. Church Bldgs.: Statistical Returns* (1940), 270.
[60] O.S. Map 1/2,500, Salop. XXXVI. 9 (1902 edn.).
[61] Date stone.   [62] *Wellington Before Telford*, 15.
[63] S.R.O. 3767/XX/V, 17 May, 25 Oct. 1966; O.S. Map 1/1,250, SJ 6511 SW. (1974 edn.).
[64] S.R.O. 3767/XXXVII/C.

besides the Wellington chapel, Primitive Methodist societies at Street Lane and Arleston (by 1834),[65] New Works (by 1837),[66] Watling Street (from 1838), Aston (from 1840), Steeraway (from 1842),[67] and Leegomery (by 1846).[68] Such groups were not always long lived or continuously active. Arleston, Aston, and Steeraway were active 1849 and 1861.[69] On Census Sunday 1851 the Aston cottage meeting had 40 afternoon attenders and 35 evening attenders[70] and 20 attended the afternoon service at Leegomery.[71] By 1890 the only active societies were at Aston[72] and New Works[73] and by 1928 both were gone.[74]

Dr. J. E. Cranage, an unconventional Anglican, was inspired by a visit to Ireland in 1859 to lead an undenominational mission among the poorer people of Wellington. His preaching at the town hall and elsewhere attracted numerous followers and in 1862 he built New Hall,[75] a large plain brick building off High Street. In 1875 there were meetings at noon every day and three meetings on Sundays,[76] as well as twelve cottage meetings in and around Wellington. Since 1859 there had been weekly meetings at the workhouse. In 1889 a Children's Gospel Hall was added at the west end of the hall. Cranage's work was supported by the 3rd duke of Sutherland and by Millicent, marchioness of Stafford,[77] a noted philanthropist.[78] After Cranage's death in 1891 Robert Weston continued his work[79] but the mission closed c. 1899[80] and the hall was sold to the Y.M.C.A.,[81] which disposed of it within a few years.[82] Wellington cemetery had a nonconformist chapel by 1882.[83] A Gospel Army Mission room in New Square was registered in 1883 but had closed by 1896.[84] The Salvation Army had a barracks in Foundry Lane (registered 1887, closed by 1896)[85] and a hall in New Street (registered 1912, closed c. 1923).[86] An iron chapel at Wappenshall canal junction closed for worship in the early 20th century and was dismantled.[87]

Other sects had begun to appear by the 1930s, when Christadelphians had Sunday services at the Rechabite Hall, Tan Bank.[88] Jehovah's Witnesses met in assembly rooms in Station Road from c. 1952[89] and moved c. 1954 to a newly built Kingdom Hall near the junction of Regent Street and Watling Street.[90] They left it c. 1980[91] and in 1981 it was occupied by a church affiliated to the Spiritualists' National Union, which had previously used a hut on the opposite side of Regent Street.[92] Mormon open-air preachings had attracted hostility rather than converts in 1853[93] but c. 1972 a substantial new church in Glebe Street was opened.[94] A few years later[95] the First United Church of Jesus Christ (Apostolic) took over the former Primitive Methodist Sunday school, Tan Bank; it was a predominantly West Indian church that had previously met at the Belmont Hall, New Street.[96]

ISLAM. The Telford mosque opened c. 1978[97] in the former Primitive Methodist chapel, Tan Bank.

EDUCATION. Roger Kyrkbie, notary public, was master of a grammar school in 1534. In 1548 Our Lady's priest in the parish church was said always to have kept a free grammar school, and the Crown continued his stipend of £4 17s. 6d. a year to later schoolmasters.[98] In 1659 land in Ollerton, let for £5 a year, was left to the school.[99] Some masters served for many years.[1] By 1639, possibly by 1620, the master had an assistant.[2] Teaching of grammar was not recorded after the mid 17th century[3] but the Crown stipend was continued to later schoolmasters like Francis Ore,[4] who kept a school in the church c. 1693.[5]

Other early references to schools are rare[6] but Rowland Griffiths, constable of Walcot in 1625, was then and in the 1630s a schoolmaster[7] and John Powell had a private school c. 1693.[8] In 1750

[65] Lenton, *Methodism in Wellington*, 33.
[66] S.R.O. 3605/2.
[67] Ibid. /1, pp. 11, 48, 75, 91, 123, 166.
[68] Ibid. p. 158.
[69] S.R.O. 1861/5, p. 3; /12.
[70] P.R.O., HO 129/365, no. 16.
[71] Ibid. no. 28.
[72] S.R.O. 3038/1/3.
[73] S.R.O. 1936/2.
[74] S.R.O. 1861/169, p. 10.
[75] D. H. S. Cranage, *Not Only a Dean* (1952), 10, 20; *The Parish Church, Wellington: Monthly News Letter*, xcii. [3–4] (copy in S.P.L.).
[76] *Wellington Jnl.* 3 July 1875.
[77] *New Hall, Wellington: Rep. of Mission Work for 1875*, [2–3] (copy in S.P.L., class L 93 v.f.); *Shrews. Chron.* 2 Aug. 1889.
[78] *The Times*, 22 Aug. 1955.
[79] Cranage, *Not Only a Dean*, 20, 43.
[80] *Kelly's Dir. Salop.* (1895), 246; Hobson, *Wellington Dir.* (1898), 14.
[81] Cranage, op. cit. 20.
[82] *S.C.C. Mins.* 1902–3, Technical etc. Cttee. rep. 12 July 1902, 18; S.R.O. 1604/18, p. 262; S.R.O., S.C.C. Educ. Cttee. min. bk. 1903–12, pp. 88–9.
[83] O.S. Map 1/2,500, Salop. XXXVI. 9 (1882 edn.).
[84] G.R.O., Worship Reg. no. 26851.
[85] Ibid. no. 29991.
[86] Ibid. no. 45357.

[87] Local inf.
[88] Jones, *Dir. Wellington* (1934), 10, 69; (1937), 12.
[89] G.R.O., Worship Reg. no. 63416.
[90] Ibid. no. 64217.
[91] T.D.C. *Telford Street Plan* [1980]; local inf.
[92] Local inf.
[93] *Salopian Jnl.* 5 and 12 Oct. 1853; below, Ketley, Nonconf.
[94] G.R.O., Worship Reg. no. 72882.
[95] After 1973: O.S. Map 1/1,250, SJ 6511 SW. (1974 edn.).
[96] Local inf.   [97] S.R.O. 3767/XXXVII/C.
[98] Bodl. Salop. Rolls 3; *T.S.A.S.* 3rd ser. x. 274–5, 351; N. Carlisle, *Concise Descr. of Endowed Schs. in Eng. and Wales* (1818), 397.
[99] Bodl. MS. C.C.C. 390/ii, f. 157.
[1] e.g. Humph. Chambers by 1616 to 1639: L.J.R.O., B/V/1/32, 37, 57, 62.
[2] Ibid. /1/37, 62.
[3] L.J.R.O., B/A/4/5, 2 June 1665 (ref. supplied by Dr. R. Hume).
[4] Bodl. MS. C.C.C. 390/ii, f. 157; L.J.R.O., B/V/4, 8 Sept. 1701 (ref. from Dr. Hume).
[5] W.S.L., H.M. 36.
[6] S. Garbet, *Hist. Wem* (1818), 200; below, Hadley, Educ.
[7] S.R.O. 112, box 90, man. ct. presentments c. 1625 and c. 1638–9.
[8] W.S.L., H.M. 36. Cf. perh. par. reg. bur. 27 July 1677, John Poole of Arleston, schmaster (transcript in S.P.L.).

a clergyman called Smith kept a school.[9] He was perhaps Richard Smith, curate of Eyton, who became vicar of Wellington next year.[10]

In 1818 the two largest schools in the parish, the charity (later National) school near All Saints'[11] and Newdale School,[12] had between them 288 pupils with another 283 at Sunday school. Provision for the poor was then considered sufficient.[13] There was a Primitive Methodist schoolroom in Tan Bank by 1823.[14] By 1833 there were 13 day schools in the area, all except Wellington National Schools supported by fees.[15] They included a Methodist school with 36 boys and 28 girls, and a Baptist school with 35 boys and 20 girls in separate departments; both schools closed before 1851. The rest, except Newdale School,[16] were private schools, three of which had opened since 1818 and together had 64 pupils. There were nine Sunday schools in 1833, all supported by voluntary contributions. Two Anglican Sunday schools had a total attendance of 20 boys and 90 girls, three Methodist ones had 251 boys and 222 girls, two Baptist ones 103 boys and 93 girls, and two Independent ones 85 boys and 85 girls. From the 1840s day schools were opened in the coalfield townships[17] and in the 1850s two more were opened in the town, one by the Roman Catholics, one by the Wesleyans.

Wellington school board, formed for Eyton and Wellington parishes in 1872, was the first in Shropshire.[18] Its first chairman, Richard Groom, was a prominent Wesleyan, its vice-chairman Thomas Ragg, vicar of Lawley; the vicar of All Saints' and the Baptist minister of Wellington too were original members.[19] There was no sectarian division and the board tackled its responsibilities vigorously. Its survey of 1873 revealed a shortage of school places: in Wellington town the National, Wesleyan, and Roman Catholic schools (average weekly attendance 396, 313, and 56) were overcrowded, as were the schools in the coalfield townships.[20] Shortage of places persisted throughout the board's existence, as population growth[21] and stricter government requirements[22] countered its efforts. The board immediately provided for unschooled gutter children in the town[23] and then offered to take over all the voluntary schools. Except for the Wesleyans[24] and Roman Catholics in Wellington, the voluntary managers relin-quished their increasingly heavy responsibilities, confident that Anglicans and nonconformists on the board would protect denominational interests. Indeed the board allowed the schools to be used on Sundays and for evening meetings[25] and to have their own managers, though it kept control of teachers' appointments and expenditure on buildings.[26] The board, which improved and replaced existing buildings and built three new schools,[27] was enterprising[28] and efficient. School fees, standardized at 2d. a week in 1876, were abolished in 1891.[29] Central premises for teaching cookery and laundry work were provided[30] and by 1903 there were well built schools[31] for all elementary pupils except those in the town's Roman Catholic and Wesleyan schools, then the only voluntary schools. No other Shropshire town had such a majority of board schools or new schools,[32] and the success of the county council's technical instruction classes in Wellington[33] testified to the schools' efficiency.[34] In 1903 the board's clerk, as clerk also to the urban district council and secretary to Wellington Science and Art Committee,[35] was a unifying influence.

The county council, successor to the board in 1903,[36] soon provided secondary schools in the town. Despite the fees, demand for places, particularly girls', was high.[37] Secondary reorganization under the Hadow Report (1926) was facilitated in the town because only one voluntary school had survived, St. Patrick's R.C. School. In the poorer coalfield townships a senior school was formed at Ketley in 1931[38] but all-age schools continued in Lawley and Hadley as late as 1956 and 1958.[39]

After 1945 more places were urgently needed to provide free secondary education for all, to raise the school-leaving age to 15 in 1947 and 16 in 1972, and to introduce 'special' education. Between 1973 and 1978 secondary education was reorganized along comprehensive lines. Sixth forms grew larger as children's earnings mattered less to parents. Elementary school accommodation, inadequate in the 1930s,[40] was improved by new building from the 1950s. increase of population reinforced the effects of post-war bulges in the national school population to keep local schools overcrowded until the 1970s. By 1980, however, the only schools left in old buildings were in the

[9] L. Wenlock par. reg. 4 June 1750 (transcript in S.P.L.).
[10] Above, Churches; Eyton, Church.
[11] Below.
[12] Below, Lawley.
[13] *Digest Educ. Poor*, H.C. 224, p. 761 (1819), ix (2).
[14] *Orders of Q. Sess.* iii. 239; above, Prot. Nonconf.
[15] The rest of this para. is based on *Educ. Enq. Abstract*, H.C. 62, pp. 785, 788 (1835), xlii; S. Bagshaw, *Dir. Salop.* (1851), 423, 432, 437–9.
[16] Below, Lawley.
[17] Below, Hadley; Ketley.
[18] *V.C.H. Salop.* iii. 175; *List of Sch. Boards, 1902* [Cd. 1038], p. 75, H.C. (1902), lxxix.
[19] *Wellington Jnl.* 12 Feb. 1874. For Ragg see below, Lawley, Church.
[20] *Wellington Jnl.* 12 July 1873; below, Hadley; Ketley.
[21] *V.C.H. Salop.* ii. 223, 228.
[22] Concerning compulsory attendance (1876), raising of sch.-leaving age, and improvement of bldgs. (1890s): ibid. iii. 174, 176.
[23] At New Hall: below.
[24] *Wellington Jnl.* 12 Feb. 1874.

[25] Ibid. 9 Aug. 1873; 12 Feb. 1874.
[26] Ibid. 12 Feb. 1876.
[27] Below, Hadley; Ketley; Lawley.
[28] *V.C.H. Salop.* iii. 176 (proposals for joint industrial sch.).
[29] *Wellington Jnl.* 11 Dec. 1875; Lawley Bd. Sch. log bk. (at Lawley Co. Primary Sch.) 1 Sept. 1891.
[30] *V.C.H. Salop.* iii. 176.
[31] Evid. of surviving bldgs.
[32] *Kelly's Dir. Salop.* (1909, 1913).
[33] Organizing sec.'s ann. reps. to Intermediate Educ. Cttee. in *S.C.C. Mins.* 1901–3.
[34] By the 1890s Wellington sch. attendance cttee. seems to have been alone in Salop. in adopting Standard VI as the leaving standard: *V.C.H. Salop.* iii. 176.
[35] *S.C.C. Mins.* 1903–4, 89.
[36] *V.C.H. Salop.* iii. 177 (cf. below, Corrigenda).
[37] Ibid. iii. 200; *S.C.C. Mins.* 1903–4, 89, 259; S.C.C. *Seventeen Years of Secondary Educ. in Salop.* (1920), 10 (copy in S.R.O.).
[38] Cf. *V.C.H. Salop.* iii. 202.
[39] Below, Hadley; Ketley; Lawley.
[40] *S.C.C. Mins. (Educ.)* 1934–5, 36.

coalfield townships,[41] in two of which nursery classes had been created in 1967 and 1970.[42] A special school was opened in 1965 and a special class formed at another school in 1979.

Even before 1903 Wellington's educational facilities beyond the elementary standards were better than in most of Shropshire: there were private schools and, from 1891, the county council's technical instruction classes.[43] Of several private schools in 1850, Old Hall School, Watling Street, was founded by the Cranages before 1835[44] and in 1851 was a boarding school for 50 boys, including local boys.[45] It became a boys' preparatory school in 1894,[46] opened a junior department in 1976, and took girls from 1977.[47] The school later known as the Hiatt Ladies' College opened in 1847 in King Street, taking day girls and boarders.[48] In 1911 it had 15 teachers and was the largest of the three girls' schools in the town that were approved for county scholars from 1903; the others were Brooklyn House (Miss Sugden's) and Sunfield House.[49] In 1953 Hiatt's had 80 day girls and 60 boarders,[50] but it closed in 1959,[51] a year after the Girls' High School increased its intake.[52] Wellington College, founded in 1880,[53] was in 1903 the one boys' school in the town approved for county scholars, and like Hiatt's it prepared candidates for county scholarships in secondary and higher education.[54] When it was sold by its founding principal in 1920 it was no longer primarily local and all 200 boys boarded. Its name changed to Wrekin College in 1921.[55] In 1972 it resumed taking day boys; from 1975 sixth-form day girls were taken, and from 1983 day and boarding girls aged 13.[56]

Technical instruction classes organized by Wellington Science and Art Committee for the county council were especially important for technicians, teachers, and pupil teachers; all classes were free to teachers. In 1891 the council granted the committee £50 and appointed a master to teach drawing and technical subjects in its district.[57] Mathematics, science, business studies, cookery, dressmaking, hygiene, and nursing were also taught. Local headmasters and specialist lecturers took classes.[58] Special mathematics and art classes were held for teachers and pupil teachers;[59] the art classes enabled teachers to obtain a Drawing Certificate,[60] an important qualification to fulfil government requirements in the 1890s; at least one Wellington teacher gained the full Art Master's Certificate.[61] In 1893 there were more classes in Wellington union than in any other Shropshire district;[62] held at first mainly in the Wesleyan Central Hall[63] but from 1901 in New Hall,[64] they were consistently well taught and well attended.[65]

Science and art classes and technical instruction continued and were especially important for pupil teachers.[66] In 1924 42 out of 187 students took Union of Educational Institutions examinations. Thirty joined a new W.E.A. three-year philosophy course. Mining, woodwork, and building construction classes were very well attended. The area was served by the Walker Technical College opened at Oakengates in 1927.[67] By post-war standards the college's facilities, despite improvements, were inadequate, and in 1962 the engineering, science, and mining departments moved to new buildings on a 28-a. site between Bennetts Bank and Haybridge Road. By 1972 all departments were concentrated there.[68] In the late 1960s and 1970s more classrooms, a library, communal facilities, and extra workshops for new engineering courses were provided.[69] In 1979 the former premises at Oakengates were recommissioned as an annexe.[70] In 1980 there were full-time courses in engineering, business and management, and general studies, the last group including social care, hairdressing, and pre-nursing courses. A wide range of short courses was arranged, usually in conjunction with local industry, commerce, and other agencies. Non-vocational courses were organized, at the college and throughout east Shropshire, by an adult-education co-ordinator, first appointed in 1964.[71] In 1964–5, when Wellington Evening Institute was the largest in the county, there were 258 full-time, 972 part-time, and 1,453 evening students; in 1980 there were 360 full-timers, 1,693 part-timers, and c. 2,500 students attending leisure classes.[72] In 1983 the college was renamed

[41] Below, Ketley; Lawley. [42] Below, Hadley; Ketley.
[43] S.C.C. Mins. 1903–4, 89–90.
[44] Pigot, Nat. Com. Dir. (1835), 381.
[45] S. Bagshaw, Dir. Salop. (1851), 425, 428, 432.
[46] Advts. in Wellington Jnl.; Old Hall School [prospectus c. 1980], 2. [47] Old Hall Sch. 2.
[48] Centenary brochure (1947; copy in Shropshire Star libr., Ketley). Cf. Shrews. Chron. 9 Apr. 1909 (obit. of foundress, Mrs. Eliz. Hiatt).
[49] S.C.C. Mins. 1903–4, 89, 258; 1904–5, 152–5; 1905–6, 130–2; and later reps.; Wellington Jnl. 7 Jan. 1911.
[50] Wellington Jnl. 4 Apr. 1953.
[51] Express & Star, 30 Nov. 1959.
[52] S.C.C. Mins. (Educ.) 1958–9, 187.
[53] V.C.H. Salop. ii. 163.
[54] Ibid.; S.C.C. Mins. 1896–7, 350–2, 1903–4, 259; S.C.C. Rep. on After-Careers of Co. Council Univ. Scholarship Holders, 1894–1913, 2 (copy in S.R.O.).
[55] V.C.H. Salop. ii. 163.
[56] Inf. from Wrekin Coll.; Shropshire Star, 26 Jan. 1983.
[57] S.C.C. Mins. Intermediate Educ. Cttee. rep. 9 May 1891, 23, 26; 30 June 1894, 40; and later reps.; S.C.C. Mins. 1895–6, 109.
[58] Ibid. Intermediate Educ. Cttee. rep. 8 July 1893, 33, 38.
[59] Ibid. Intermediate Educ. Cttee. rep. 12 July 1892, 34, 40, 42; S.C.C. Mins. 1896–7, 319, 321, 325, 329.

[60] See e.g. S.C.C. Mins. Intermediate Educ. Cttee. rep. 8 July 1893, 27.
[61] Ibid. Intermediate Educ. Cttee. rep. 8 July 1893, 27; S.C.C. Mins. 1896–7, 321.
[62] Ibid. Intermediate Educ. Cttee. rep. 8 July 1893, 33, 38.
[63] S.C.C. Rep. on Tech. Instr. in Salop. (Science and Art) (1891), p. xviii (at end of S.C.C. Mins. 1891–2).
[64] Bought by S.C.C. in 1906: S.C.C. Mins. 1902–3, Intermediate Educ. Cttee. rep. 12 July 1902, 18; S.C.C. Mins. (Educ.), 1906–7, 108.
[65] S.C.C. Mins. Intermediate Educ. Cttee. rep. 8 July 1893, 27, 33; 30 June 1894, 42.
[66] S.C.C. Mins. 1903–4, 95; 1904–5, 106, 116–17.
[67] S.C.C. 21st Ann. Rep. Technical and Evening Classes, 1924–5, 8 (copy in S.R.O.); cf. S.C.C. Mins. (Educ.) 1919 20, 31. For the tech. coll. see below, Wombridge. Educ.
[68] S.C.C. Mins. (Educ.) 1966–7, 300; 1972–3, 34; S.C.C. Educ. in Salop. 1945–65, 68; Walker Tech. Coll. (n.d., brochure suppl. by coll. 1980).
[69] S.C.C. Mins. (Educ.) 1966–7, 300; 1972–3, 32–4.
[70] Ibid. 1978–9, following p. 326, Pol. and G.P. Subcttee. rep., App. p. 36.
[71] Ibid. 1963–4, 137–8; Walker Tech. Coll. Part Time Courses 1980–1 and Full Time Courses 1980–1.
[72] S.C.C. Mins. (Educ.) 1963–4, 136; Educ. in Salop. 1945–65, 69; inf. from the coll.

Telford College of Arts and Technology.[73]

Wellington National (from 1876 National Board) School originated in a charity school built on the north side of All Saints' churchyard. In 1799 the day school had 60 pupils, the Sunday school 100. On each of its two storeys the plain brick building had a classroom 44 × 30 ft. lit by two windows; boys and girls were in separate departments and there was no playground.[74] By 1818 numbers had increased to 135 boys and 64 girls with an additional 269 children on Sunday.[75] The school, then parochial[76] and on Dr. Bell's plan,[77] was a National school by 1835.[78] Until 1833 or later it was free, supported mainly by voluntary subscriptions[79] but also by small endowments which included, for the boys' school, the annual Crown grant of £4 6s. 10d. previously paid to the masters of the defunct grammar school.[80] By 1847 fees were charged, income that year including £56 in school pence as well as £40 in subscriptions, £40 from church collections, and £5 from the endowment. Clothing grants for poor boys and girls, amounting to £30, were being made. Salaries were low. The vicar was sole manager and the school had no trust deed.[81] By 1842 there was a separate infant school,[82] which remained in the churchyard school after the boys and girls moved to a new building at Constitution Hill in 1855.[83] There were 288 pupils in 1851.[84]

In 1876 the school board took over the school with its charities,[85] improving and enlarging it. By 1885 there were 240 places. In 1897 the infants moved to new buildings at Constitution Hill, where there were 440 places (including infants') by 1900.[86] There were 420 pupils in 1906.[87]

In 1928 the main building was converted to provide 210 places each for Wellington Senior Boys' and Senior Girls' Council schools, amalgamated in 1936 and moved to Orleton Lane in 1940.[88] The infant school continued until 1941 when, to relieve overcrowding at Prince's Street Council School, it became a junior and infant school; it had 151 pupils in 1951, 180 in 1956. Its juniors transferred to the new Park County Junior School in 1956, its infants to the new Dothill County Infant School in 1961. Thereafter the building was used for further education[89] until its sale in 1966.[90]

St. Patrick's R.C. School, Mill Bank, was established in 1850 in a room behind St. Patrick's church. In 1856 a brick schoolroom and teacher's house were built nearby: slated and unceiled but with a boarded floor, the room measured 36 × 20 ft. and was for 150 pupils. In 1856 annual income of £51 included £16 in voluntary contributions, £14 in school pence, and £6 from church collections; weekly fees varied from 1d. to 4d. according to parents' means. Teaching was on the monitorial system and the annual cost per child was 9s. Deficits were met by the priest (one of the six managers) and from fund-raising efforts.[91] Government grants were received by 1874.[92] In 1873 there were 56 pupils, and 1885–1913 attendance averaged c. 65.[93] Non-Catholics could attend until c. 1910,[94] probably to keep up numbers, then low. The number of places was reduced to 86 in 1903.[95] The building was reported unsafe in 1939 and was extensively altered, pupils moving temporarily to the parish hall. In 1940 Catholic evacuees from Liverpool increased numbers. Conditions were insanitary but the school and parish hall were used until 1964.[96] In 1956 one class was held in the parish hall, two others at Constitution Hill in classrooms made available by the county council.[97] Meanwhile, in 1955, the building of a new school in North Road had begun[98] and in 1957 one senior and two junior classes moved there.[99] By 1960, when 100 seniors were seriously overcrowded in two classrooms at Mill Bank, a third room was rented at Constitution Hill.[1] In 1963, however, all seniors moved to a new secondary school in Whitchurch Road,[2] and in 1965 the remaining juniors and infants to the North Road school, thereafter St. Patrick's R.C. (Aided) Primary School.[3] In 1982 St. Patrick's had 188 pupils.[4]

Wellington Wesleyan School, Prince's Street, with 200 places, opened in 1858. It was a tiled brick building with boarded floor. Its 1859 income of £75 included £10 in voluntary contributions and £40 in school fees of 3d. a week. An infant schoolroom for 80 and a master's house were added in 1866 at the expense of Richard and Thomas Groom, school trustees and later to become original and long-serving members of the school board. In 1867 weekly fees were 2d. or 3d.

[73] Inf. from S.C.C. Educ. Dept.
[74] S.R.O. 3916/1/1, p. 24; P.R.O., ED 7/103, ff. 108v.–109.
[75] Digest Educ. Poor, 761, 767.
[76] Salop. Char. for Elem. Educ. (S.C.C. 1906), 89.
[77] Carlisle, Endowed Schs. 397.
[78] Pigot, Nat. Com. Dir. (1835), 381.
[79] Educ. Enq. Abstract, 785.
[80] Carlisle, Endowed Schs. 397. For the other endowments see Salop. Char. for Elem. Educ. 89.
[81] P.R.O., ED 7/103, f. 109 and v.
[82] Pigot, Nat. Com. Dir. (1842), 45.
[83] S.R.O. 1167/13, 1 Feb. 1897; P.O. Dir. Salop. (1856), 134; E. Cassey & Co. Dir. Salop. (1874), 367.
[84] S. Bagshaw, Dir. Salop. (1851), 423.
[85] Income on legacies of £150 (Wm. Warham 1813), £50 (Steph. Panting 1850), and £180 (Jas. Oliver 1867): Salop. Char. for Elem. Educ. 89. They were later transferred to S.C.C.
[86] Wellington Jnl. 8 Jan. 1876 (bd. mtg. rep.); Kelly's Dir. Salop. (1885), 974; (1900), 261; S.R.O. 1167/13, 1 Feb. 1897.
[87] Public Elem. Schs. 1906 [Cd. 3182], p. 540, H.C. (1906), lxxxvi.
[88] S.C.C. Mins. (Educ.) 1928–9, 43; 1936–7, 27; 1939–40,

54; 1944–5, 21.
[89] Ibid. 1965–6, 94; S.R.O. 1167/14, pp. 222–3; /15, pp. 12, 117, 130, 202–3.
[90] Above, Social and Cultural Activities.
[91] P.R.O., ED 7/103, f. 110v.; St. Pat.'s Par. vi (May 1971), 5 (copy in S.R.O. 4050/2); S. Bagshaw, Dir. Salop. (1851), 427, 432.
[92] Log bk. (at St. Pat.'s R.C. (Aided) Primary Sch. 1980) ann. rep. 1874.
[93] Wellington Jnl. 12 July 1873 (bd. mtg. rep.); Kelly's Dir. Salop. (1885–1913).
[94] St. Pat.'s Par. vi. 5.
[95] Public Elem. Schs. 1906, 540.
[96] Managers' min. bks. (in possession of par. priest) mtgs. of 4 May, 2 Nov, 1939; S.C.C. Mins. (Educ.) 1939–40, 54; St. Pat.'s Par. v. 8 (copy in S.R.O. 4050/1); S.R.O., DA 13/100/1. pp. 35–6.
[97] S.C.C. Mins. (Educ.) 1955–6, 280.
[98] Ibid. 1953–4, 107; 1954–5, 136; 1955–6, 122.
[99] Log bk. 3 Sept. 1957.
[1] S.C.C. Mins. (Educ.) 1960–1, 97.
[2] Ibid. 1963–4, 31; below.
[3] S.C.C. Mins. (Educ.) 1965–6, 94.
[4] S.C.C. Educ. Cttee. Educ. Dir. (1980), 10.

according to parents' means,[5] but in 1883 they were raised to 4*d*., 6*d*., or 9*d*., probably according to age or class.[6] By 1903 it was one of only nine Shropshire schools still charging fees[7] and it was still doing so in 1906.[8] The school nevertheless remained popular under its two successive headmasters.[9] By 1873, with 313 pupils, it was overcrowded,[10] and in 1891 and 1909 it was full.[11] From 1866 South Kensington drawing examinations were held and in 1896 the mixed school was renamed Wellington Elementary and Higher Grade School. It had a cookery room in 1897, a woodwork room in 1900, and by 1901 a wide curriculum.[12] Alterations to the buildings were necessary by 1906[13] and the trustees sold the school to the county council in 1911, when it became Prince's Street Council School.[14] For most of 1912, while the building was reconstructed, the Wesleyan Central Hall was used. In November staff and pupils returned to the school,[15] which then had 200 mixed and 120 infant places.[16] The school's nonconformist traditions were perpetuated by the long service of staff.[17] Its good reputation continued[18] and from 1913 it was always overcrowded.[19] In 1928 the mixed school became a junior school, 49 seniors transferred to the new senior schools at Constitution Hill, and 49 infants were admitted from the infant school there.[20] Serious overcrowding in the junior and infant schools, due to council-house building, was temporarily relieved in 1941 by making Constitution Hill a junior and infant school.[21] In 1951 Prince's Street County Infant School closed when staff and pupils moved to a new school in Mount Gilbert. Prince's Street was then converted to a junior school;[22] it had 401 pupils by 1956[23] but closed in 1970 when staff and pupils transferred to a new school in Churchill Road.[24]

New Hall Temporary School was opened by the school board in 1873. It was for infants and older children whose poverty and dirt had excluded them from other schools. Twenty-eight were admitted on the first day and after six months attendance averaged 52.[25] Some parents withdrew their children, objecting to their mixing with gutter children.[26] Some pupils had no boots and were in rags,[27] many were undisciplined.[28] The building, though large and airy, was unsuitable[29] and the school closed in 1874 when Hadley Board School opened.[30]

A workhouse school was opened in 1876.[31] In 1884 its 34 pupils received satisfactory instruction in scripture, geography, and elementary subjects, and industrial training was good.[32] It closed in 1884, pupils transferring to the nearby board school.[33]

Wrekin Road Board School opened in 1881[34] with 376 places in mixed and infant departments; 26 mixed places were added in 1899. Attendance averaged 264 in 1885, 294 in 1903–4, and 282 in 1913.[35] In 1886 the school board halved weekly fees for under-fives to 1*d*.,[36] apparently to discourage parents from withdrawing them in winter, then a common practice. The infant department was overcrowded in 1908 and under-fives were excluded[37] for a time.[38] After the 1928 reorganization seniors transferred to Constitution Hill Senior Council Schools and Wrekin Road became a junior and infant school; a special class for backward children was then established.[39] Overcrowding in the 1940s[40] was relieved by the infants' transfer to a new school in Orleton Lane in 1950.[41] Wrekin Road County Junior School continued until Park County Junior School opened in 1956.[42]

Wellington Girls' High School opened with 51 pupils[43] in temporary premises at New Hall in 1908.[44] In 1910 fees were £8 a year; there were 104 pupils, of whom 30 (including 8 bursars and pupil teachers) had free places. Eight girls left in 1911 for training colleges, others (with Oxford School Certificates) for elementary-school posts.[45] Eighty-eight girls transferred in 1912 to the new dual secondary school in King Street,[46] with places for 125 girls and 125 boys;[47] just over half the girls came from Wellington.[48] The school was over-

[5] P.R.O., ED 7/103, ff. 112v.–114v. For the Grooms see bd. mtg. reps. in *Wellington Jnl.* 12 Feb. 1874 sqq.; log bk. (at Ercall Co. Jnr. Sch.) 28 Sept. 1866.

[6] Log bk. 9 Feb. 1883.

[7] *S.C.C. Mins.* 1903–4, 200. Other local schs. had abolished them in 1891 when govt. fee grants became available. Cf. *V.C.H. Salop.* iii. 176.

[8] *Public Elem. Schs. 1906*, 540.

[9] Jas. Fance 1858–97, and Chas. Smith 1897–1911 continuing at Prince's St. 1911–31: log bk. 16 July 1897; 22 Dec. 1931.

[10] *Wellington Jnl.* 8 Feb., 12 July 1873 (bd. mtg. reps.).

[11] *Kelly's Dir. Salop.* (1891), 458; (1909), 274.

[12] Log bk. 15 Feb. 1866; 20 Jan. 1896 (correcting *V.C.H. Salop.* iii. 176); 8 Jan. 1900; rep. on cookery class 2 July 1897; rep. 1901.

[13] *Public Elem. Schs. 1906*, 540.

[14] *S.C.C. Mins. (Educ.)* 1909–10, 7, 75; 1911–12, 57.

[15] Log bk. 14 Mar., 25 Nov. 1912.

[16] *S.C.C. Mins. (Educ.)* 1911–12, 93.

[17] Esp. Chas. Smith, 1897–1931, J. W. Clift, correspondent 1897–1939, Ada Patterson, 1897–1932, Edith Knowles, 1917–40, T. C. Buttrey, 1932–69, and F. J. MacGowan, 1948–70 (and at Ercall Co. Jnr. Sch. 1970–80): Wesleyan, Prince's St., and Ercall jnr. schs.' log bks.

[18] Ibid. H.M.I.s' reps.

[19] *Kelly's Dir. Salop.* (1913), 281; e.g. log. bk. 8 Sept. 1916; 25 July 1918; 1 July 1919; 3 Apr. 1922; 1 Apr. 1924; 6 Nov. 1940.

[20] Log bk. 1 Oct. 1928.

[21] *S.C.C. Mins. (Educ.)* 1941–2, 23–4.

[22] Ibid. 1951–2, 75.

[23] Log bk. 4 Sept. 1956.

[24] *S.C.C. Mins. (Educ.)* 1970–1, 275.

[25] Hadley Inf. Bd. Sch. log bk. (at Hadley Co. Jnr. Sch.) 3 Feb. 1873; *Wellington Jnl.* 8 Feb., 12 July 1873 (bd. mtg. reps.).

[26] Hadley Inf. Bd. Sch. log bk. 23 Sept. 1873.

[27] Ibid. 19 June 1874.

[28] Ibid. rep. 1873.

[29] *Wellington Jnl.* 12 July 1873 (bd. mtg. rep.).

[30] Hadley Inf. Bd. Sch. log bk. 6 July, 17 Aug. 1874.

[31] S.R.O. 77/11, pp. 152–3.

[32] S.R.O. 77/12, p. 143.

[33] Ibid. pp. 145, 149, 163–4.

[34] S.R.O. 3593/6, p. 1.

[35] *Kelly's Dir. Salop.* (1885), 974; (1913), 281; *Public Elem. Schs. 1906*, 540.

[36] S.R.O. 3593/6, p. 76.

[37] Ibid. /7, p. 73.

[38] Ibid. p. 168.

[39] *S.C.C. Mins. (Educ.)* 1928–9, 98.

[40] Ibid. 1941–2, 23; 1945–6, 89.

[41] S.R.O. 3593/7, p. 304.

[42] *S.C.C. Mins. (Educ.)* 1955–6, 280.

[43] *Wellington Jnl.* 25 Mar. 1911 (rep. of prize-giving).

[44] *S.C.C. Mins. (Educ.)* 1908–9, 67, 98–101, 114.

[45] S.C.C. *Public Secondary Schs. in Salop. 1903–10* (1911), 5–6 (copy in S.R.O.); *Wellington Jnl.* 25 Mar. 1911.

[46] *S.C.C. Mins. (Educ.)* 1912–13, 46.

[47] S.C.C. *Higher Educ. Dept. Rep. 1912–14*, 4.

[48] *S.C.C. Mins. (Educ.)* 1911–12, 107.

crowded by 61 in 1915 and New Hall was used again[49] until, by 1920, the King Street buildings had been extended to take 120 more.[50] From 1929, or earlier, to 1945 there was a preparatory department for girls aged 5–11 and boys aged 5–8;[51] fees were £4 10s. a year.[52] More temporary classrooms were provided in 1931 but overcrowding in the 1930s[53] was relieved only when the boys moved to a new school in 1940.[54] When 221 evacuees from Holly Lodge High School, Smethwick,[55] arrived in 1939, the school worked in shifts for many months, only fifth- and sixth-formers receiving full-time education.[56] By 1965 the school had been extended and given new technical facilities.[57] It took its first three-form entry in 1958, peak year of the 'bulge',[58] and by 1970 it had 580 places.[59] The school became a mixed comprehensive in 1974 but was phased out by 1978,[60] leaving the buildings exclusively for a comprehensive sixth-form college.[61]

Wellington Boys' High School, with 125 places, opened in the dual secondary school building in 1912. In 1920 there were 133 pupils, only 8 of whom were over 16, though the girls' school had 249 with 43 over 16.[62] Presumably many boys left at 14 for trade apprenticeships. From 1929, or earlier, to 1945 the school had a preparatory department for boys aged 8–11.[63] Overcrowding in the 1930s[64] was relieved in 1940 when the school moved to a new building (200 places) in Golf Links Lane[65] and was renamed a grammar school.[66] In 1945 it had 330 pupils, some in temporary classrooms.[67] In 1958, at the peak of the 'bulge', it took its first three-form entry[68] and was a complete three-form school by 1965;[69] there were 580 places in 1970.[70] In the late 1950s extensions included four science laboratories[71] and new woodwork, metalwork, and engineering workshops with a technical-drawing room,[72] as part of a plan to make the school a technical grammar school and to close Oakengates Junior Technical School.[73] With the reorganization of secondary education on comprehensive lines, however, the school closed in 1974.[74]

Wellington Senior Council School, an amalgamation of boys' and girls' senior schools at Constitution Hill in 1936, moved to Orleton Lane (400 places) in 1940. In 1945 it was renamed Wellington Modern School.[75] Post-war extensions included (1948) the county's first school metalwork shop.[76] By 1957 there were 670 pupils.[77] In 1962 the girls transferred to a new modern school and the school, renamed Wellington Boys' Modern School, admitted boys transferred from High Ercall Modern School, then closed.[78] In 1974, renamed Orleton Park School, it became a mixed comprehensive school for pupils aged 11–16; it had 832 pupils in 1982.[79]

Orleton Lane County Infant School, with 180 places,[80] opened in 1950, staff and pupils moving from Wrekin Road County Infant School, then closed.[81] The building's aluminium frame was an experiment in design and economical construction.[82] By 1953 the school was considerably overcrowded, owing to council-house building, and was extended. In 1982, however, it had only 149 pupils.[83]

Barn Farm County Infant School, Mount Gilbert, with 200 places, opened in 1951,[84] staff and pupils transferring from Prince's Street County Infant School, then closed. In 1982 it had 159 pupils.[85]

Park County Junior School, North Road, with 400 places, opened in 1956,[86] 112 juniors and two teachers transferring from Constitution Hill County Primary School, thereafter an infant school.[87] In 1963 the school was so overcrowded that Dothill County Infant School accepted juniors until the opening of Dothill County Junior School in 1965. A special class began in 1979. The school had 312 pupils in 1982.[88]

Dothill County Infant School, Severn Drive, with 250 places,[89] opened in 1961 on the new Dothill housing estate. It admitted the pupils from Constitution Hill County Infant School.[90] By 1963 it was accepting juniors from Park County Junior School until the opening of Dothill County Junior School in 1965; additional demountable classrooms were provided. In 1982 there were 169 pupils.[91]

[49] Ibid. 1915–16, 67.
[50] S.C.C. *Seventeen Years of Secondary Educ. in Salop.* (1920), 8 (copy in S.R.O.).
[51] *Kelly's Dir. Salop.* (1929), 289; (1941), 277; S.C.C. *Educ. in Salop. 1945–65*, 45.
[52] S.C.C. *Mins. (Educ.)* 1913–14, 16.
[53] Ibid. 1930–1, 96.
[54] *Educ. in Salop. 1945–65*, 43.
[55] Cf. *V.C.H. Staffs.* xvii. 140.
[56] S.C.C. *Mins. (Educ.)* 1939–40, 76.
[57] Ibid. 1951–2, 79; 1957–8, 91; 1959–60, 193; *Educ. in Salop. 1945–65*, 43.
[58] S.C.C. *Mins. (Educ.)* 1958–9, 187.
[59] Ibid. 1970–1, 98.
[60] Inf. from S.C.C. Educ. Dept.
[61] Below (New Coll.).
[62] *Seventeen Years of Secondary Educ.* 7, 9; S.C.C. *Higher Educ. Dept. Rep. 1912–14*, 4.
[63] *Kelly's Dir. Salop.* (1929), 289; (1941), 277; *Educ. in Salop. 1945–65*, 45.
[64] S.C.C. *Mins. (Educ.)* 1934–5, 77, 99.
[65] Ibid. 1944–5, 72; *Educ. in Salop. 1945–65*, 43.
[66] S.R.O. 2699/1, p. 122.
[67] S.C.C. *Mins. (Educ.)* 1944–5, 72.
[68] Ibid. 1958–9, 187. [69] *Educ. in Salop. 1945–65*, 43.
[70] S.C.C. *Mins. (Educ.)* 1970–1, 98.

[71] Ibid. 1956–7, 201, 216.
[72] This new craft 'suite' was the first in Salop.: *Educ. in Salop. 1945–65*, 54.
[73] S.C.C. *Mins. (Educ.)* 1958–9, 187.
[74] Inf. from S.C.C. Educ. Dept.
[75] S.C.C. *Mins. (Educ.)* 1936–7, 27; 1937–8, 130; 1939–40, 54; 1944–5, 21, 92.
[76] *Educ. in Salop. 1945–65*, 53.
[77] S.C.C. *Mins. (Educ.)* 1956–7, 103.
[78] Ibid. 1960–1, 68; 1961–2, 121; 1962–3, 35.
[79] S.C.C. Educ. Cttee. *Sch. List* (1974), 2; idem, *Educ. Dir.* (1982), 3.
[80] S.C.C. *Mins. (Educ.)* 1952–3, 146.
[81] S.R.O. 3593/7, p. 304.
[82] *Educ. in Salop. 1945–65*, 26. Cf. *V.C.H. Salop.* iii. 204.
[83] S.C.C. *Mins. (Educ.)* 1953–4, 74; *Educ. Dir.* (1982), 10.
[84] S.C.C. *Mins. (Educ.)* 1949–50, 105; 1951–2, 16.
[85] Prince's St. Co. Inf. Sch. log bk. 28 July 1951; *Educ. Dir.* (1982), 9.
[86] S.C.C. *Mins. (Educ.)* 1953–4, 72; 1955–6, 280.
[87] S.R.O. 1167/15, p. 132.
[88] S.C.C. *Mins. (Educ.)* 1963–4, 156; *Sch. List* (1979), 12; *Educ. Dir.* (1982), 10.
[89] Inf. from S.C.C. Educ. Dept.
[90] S.R.O. 1167/15, pp. 202–3.
[91] S.C.C. *Mins. (Educ.)* 1963–4, 156; *Educ. Dir* (1982), 9.

Dothill Girls' Modern School opened in 1962 and admitted the girls from Wellington Modern School, which then became a boys' school, and from High Ercall Modern School, then closed.[92] The building had been greatly enlarged by 1974 when, as the Charlton School, the school became a mixed comprehensive school for pupils aged 11–16. In 1982 there were 836 pupils.[93]

Blessed Robert Johnson R.C. (Aided) Modern School, Whitchurch Road, opened in 1963,[94] the first Roman Catholic secondary school in Shropshire. Originally a two-form entry school,[95] it was soon extended.[96] In 1973, as the Bl. Robert Johnson Catholic College, it became a comprehensive school for pupils aged 11–18.[97] In 1982 it had 735 pupils;[98] some came from as far away as Bridgnorth or by train from Shrewsbury and Albrighton and stations between.[99]

Dothill County Junior School, with 320 places, opened in 1965 and was considerably extended in 1968. It had 336 pupils in 1982.[1]

Wellington Junior Training Centre for the Mentally Handicapped, North Road, opened in 1965 but became the responsibility of the county education authority only in 1971. It was then renamed the Charles Darwin Special School and had 40 places for pupils aged 5–16; exceptionally, the places were for the moderately as well as the severely subnormal.[2] In 1982 there were 27 pupils[3] drawn from a wide area including Shrewsbury.[4]

Ercall County Junior School, Churchill Road, with 320 places, opened in 1970 to replace Prince's Street County Junior School. There were 263 pupils in 1982.[5]

New College, a comprehensive sixth-form college, opened in 1975 in the former High School.[6] In 1982 there were 541 students,[7] most studying for the General Certificate of Education.[8]

An observation and assessment centre for secondary-school pupils opened in 1978 at the Vineyard community home. In 1980 there were pupils resident for 3–4 weeks in groups of up to fifteen.[9]

Ercall Wood School opened in 1979 in the former grammar school, Golf Links Lane. With a first-form entry of 115 pupils, it was intended to develop into a mixed comprehensive school for pupils aged 11–16.[10] There were 367 pupils in 1982.[11]

CHARITIES FOR THE POOR. Andrew Charlton of Apley, by will proved 1617, left £20 stock to provide clothing in Wellington, Wombridge, and Preston upon the Weald Moors parishes[12] but it was lost by 1787.[13]

Richard Steventon (d. 1659)[14] left a rent charge of £10 which in 1830 and 1861 was being distributed in clothing.[15] It was redeemed in 1868 and by 1884 the income was given to the Wellington Clothing Club.[16] In 1962 the income was £8 6s. 8d.[17] Walter Marigold (by will dated 1666) and William Phillipps left a rent charge of £1, which was distributed in cash in 1830[18] and bread in 1861 and 1889,[19] and was last received in 1937.[20] Roger Pavier (or Pavior), by will dated 1745,[21] left a rent charge of £4; in 1830 it was distributed in cash to aged poor[22] and in 1861 and 1889 in bread.[23] In 1772 there were unendowed almshouses in the churchyard, said to have been founded by one Steventon,[24] which were allotted to paupers by the parish. They were demolished when the new church was built, and the parish put up new ones on the churchyard's northern edge; they were administered in the same way in 1830.[25] Standing in 1854[26] they had been demolished by 1882[27] and a charity was endowed from sale of the materials.[28] The income was 13s. 4d. in 1962.[29] The four preceding charities were jointly administered by 1897, when their beneficial area was redefined as that of the then Wellington urban district and the then Wellington Rural civil parish.[30] They were afterwards known as the Wellington Non-Ecclesiastical Charities.[31] In 1964 the three surviving benefactions were united as the Charity of Richard Stevinton and Others,[32] whose income in 1975 was £15[33] distributed in cash.[34]

[92] S.C.C. Mins. (Educ.) 1960–1, 68; 1961–2, 121; 1962–3, 35.
[93] Ibid. 1967–8, 81; 1970–1, 388, 391; Educ. Dir. (1982), 3.
[94] S.C.C. Mins. (Educ.) 1963–4, 31.
[95] Ibid. 1958–9, 190.
[96] Ibid. 1966–7, 304; 1970–1, 391.
[97] Ibid. 1970–1, 391; Sch. List (1973), 2.
[98] Educ. Dir. (1982), 3.
[99] S.C.C. Mins. (Educ.) 1970–1, 391; 1971–2, 308.
[1] Inf. from S.C.C. Educ. Dept. and the headmaster; Educ. Dir. (1982), 9.
[2] Inf. from S.C.C. Educ. Dept.; S.C.C. Mins. (Educ.) 1971–2, 69.
[3] Educ. Dir. (1982), 10.
[4] See e.g. Shropshire Star, 10 Dec. 1980.
[5] S.C.C. Mins. (Educ.) 1967–8, 246; Sch. List (1970), 9; Educ. Dir. (1982), 9.
[6] S.C.C. Mins. (Educ.) 1974–5, 186.
[7] Educ. Dir. (1982), 3.
[8] Coll. prospectus.
[9] Inf. from S.C.C. Educ. Dept. Boarding costs were paid by S.C.C. Social Services Dept. For community homes see V.C.H. Salop. iii. 216.
[10] Inf. from S.C.C. Educ. Dept.
[11] Educ. Dir. (1982), 3.
[12] S.R.O. 625, box 21, will and letters of probate.
[13] Char. Don. 1786–8, ii, H.C. 511–II, pp. 1016–17 (1816), xvi (2).
[14] S.P.R. Lich. viii (1), 34.

[15] 24th Rep. Com. Char. H.C. 231, p. 370 (1831), xi; S.R.O. 3129/5/6, at end.
[16] Extract supplied by Mr. R. G. Rushen from min. bk. of Stevinton's Char. and Others; S.R.O. 3916/1/33.
[17] S.R.O., DA 13/134, file W/32, registration application, 28 Nov. 1962.
[18] Char. Don. 1786–8, ii. 1016–17; 24th Rep. Com. Char. 370.
[19] S.R.O. 3129/5/6, at end; exact by Mr. Rushen from min. bk.
[20] S.R.O., DA 13/134, file W/32, C. Eade to R. G. Rushen, 22 Dec. 1960.
[21] Char. Don. 1786–8, ii. 1016–17.
[22] 24th Rep. Com. Char. 370.
[23] S.R.O. 3129/5/6, at end; extract by Mr. Rushen from min. bk.
[24] L.J.R.O., B/V/5, visit. return.
[25] 24th Rep. Com. Char. 370.
[26] S.R.O. 3129/5/6, 8 Sept. 1854.
[27] O.S. Map 6", Salop. XXXVI. SW. (1887 edn.).
[28] S.R.O. 3916/1/33.
[29] S.R.O., DA 13/134, file W/32, registration application, 28 Nov. 1962.
[30] Ibid. Char. Com. order of 1897.
[31] Ibid. [B. H. J. Renshaw] to W. H. Duffield, 28 Nov. 1951.
[32] Ibid. Char. Com. scheme.
[33] Review of Local Chars. (S.C.C. 1975), 68.
[34] S.R.O., DA 13/134, file W/32, passim.

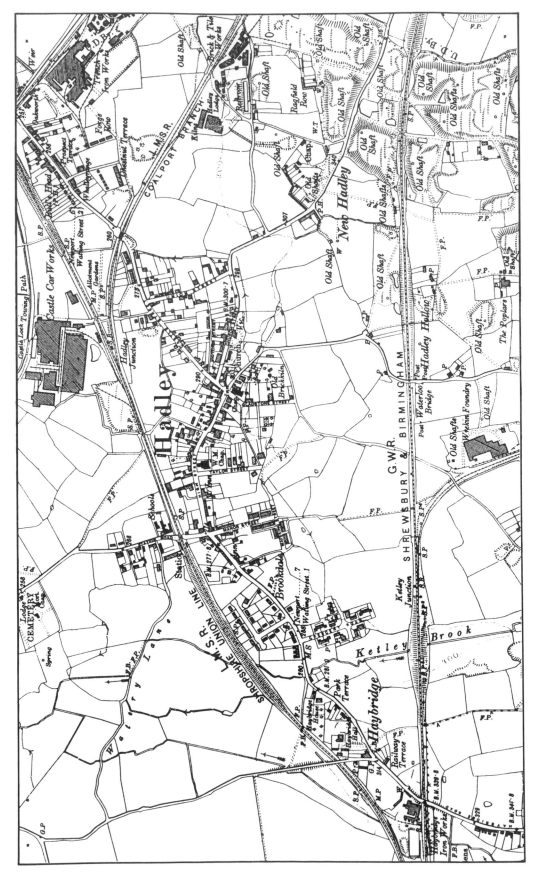

HADLEY c. 1925 (scale 6 in. to 1 mile)

A rent charge of 10s. left before 1787 by one Leeke was lost by 1830.[35]

In 1830 four or five cottages opposite the pound in Back Lane were said to have been built a century earlier as almshouses at the cost of one Icke. They were unendowed and by 1830 were occupied as private dwellings.[36]

Mrs. Margarette Noneley, by will proved 1852, left £450 stock[37] for members of the Church of England.[38] In 1861 it was distributed in clothing to worshippers at All Saints' and Christ Church.[39] The income in 1910 was £12 11s. 4d. James Oliver, by will proved 1867, left £225 stock[40] for bread doles in the parishes of All Saints and Christ Church; in 1910 the income was £5 19s. 8d. William Roberts, by will proved 1900, left stock for residents of Watling Street township; in 1910 the income was £7. Elizabeth Taylor, by will proved 1906, left stock for residents of the town of Wellington; the income was £38 4s. 8d. in 1910. In 1910 administration of the four preceding charities was combined as the Wellington United Charities. Their income in 1975 was £200[41] and in 1981 it was distributed both in cash and in kind.[42]

Henry Parker, by will proved 1898, left stock to provide food, clothing, and blankets in Christ Church parish;[43] the income in 1975 was £4. Mrs. Elizabeth Hiatt (d. 1909)[44] left stock for eleemosynary use in All Saints' parish and other stock for religious education or the relief of people associated with New Street Methodist chapel; in 1975 the former charity yielded £2, the latter £4. Henry Joseph Jones, by will proved 1953, left stock for relief in Christ Church parish and other stock for people associated with New Street Methodist chapel. In 1975 the former charity yielded £11, the latter £13.

After the National Health Service began the funds of the Wellington dispensary[45] were used to endow the Wellington and District Dispensary Charity for the sick of Wellington, Dawley, and Oakengates urban districts and Wellington rural district. In 1975 the income was £69.[46]

HADLEY AND HORTON

HADLEY township lies on the north-east side of Wellington ancient parish. In 1841 it was reckoned to contain 1,199 a. (485 ha.) and had roughly the shape of a tall rectangle.[47] Its southern boundary was Watling Street, its northern the old Newport–Shrewsbury road. Hadley brook[48] formed the eastern boundary; its southern part, called Springwell brook near Wombridge by the 12th century,[49] was called Beveley brook in the late 18th.[50] Hadley's western boundary mostly followed Ketley brook (called Hurley brook in its northern part)[51] but the Haybridge area extended westwards to its tributary Haybridge brook.[52] The area that adjoined the north side of Watling Street, although regarded locally as part of Ketley, was part of the ancient township of Hadley and is treated for most purposes in the present article; private houses along the north side of Watling Street that cannot be considered separately from those along the opposite side, in Ketley township, are treated in that article.[53]

Horton township, which adjoined Hadley on the east, was said in 1841 to have 354 a. (143 ha.). It was bounded on the south by the Newport–Wellington road and on the west by Hadley brook and the old Newport–Shrewsbury road. On the north and east, however, it had a tortuous outline that evidently reflected a complex division of tithes between Eyton, Preston, and Wellington parishes.[54]

In 1898 Horton township and most of Hadley township were included in the newly created Hadley civil parish.[55]

Hadley village lay on boulder clay, as did most of the township to the south and south-east. South-west and north of the village sand and gravel predominated, though much of Hadley park consisted of lake clay. South of the Boundary fault, which crossed the township's south-east quarter, lay workable coal and ironstone.[56] The land sloped downwards increasingly gently from c. 120 metres above O.D. in the south to c. 60 metres in the north. Hadley village lay at c. 85 metres. The township drained towards the Weald Moors.[57]

Most of Horton village stood on boulder clay, which also covered the area immediately south. Along the Hadley boundary, farther west, the land was predominantly sand and gravel in the south and lake clay in the north. North and east of the village boulder clay predominated, but there was much lake clay and alluvium.[58] The land sloped gently from south-east to north-west, falling from c. 75 metres to c. 60 metres. It

[35] Char. Don. 1786–8, ii. 1016–17; 24th Rep. Com. Char. 369–70.
[36] 24th Rep. Com. Char. 370.
[37] Kelly's Dir. Salop. (1885), 973. The Char. Com. scheme of 1910 gives Margaretta as her forename.
[38] Para. based on Char. Com. scheme of 1910; S.R.O., DA 13/134, file W/32, acct. [7 Dec. 1961].
[39] S.R.O. 3129/5/6, at end.
[40] Kelly's Dir. Salop. (1885), 973.
[41] Review of Local Chars. 68.
[42] Local inf.
[43] Para. based on S.C.C. chars. index; Review of Local Chars. 69.
[44] Shrews. Chron. 9 Apr. 1909.
[45] Above, Public Services.

[46] Review of Local Chars. 68 (citing Char. Com. scheme of 1956).
[47] Para. based on S.R.O. 14, tithe appt. and map.
[48] Ibid. Horton tithe appt. (no. 120); 1856/3.
[49] Below, Wombridge, Growth of Settlement.
[50] S.R.O. 972, parcel 245, Ketley map of 1794.
[51] O.S. Map 6", SJ 60 SE. (1966 edn.).
[52] Named in S.R.O., DA 13/135 (S.R.O. 3172/9/TB2), brief of 1894.   [53] Below, Ketley, intro.
[54] S.R.O. 14, tithe appt.; 1856/3.
[55] Changes are treated below, Local Govt. and Public Services.
[56] Inst. Geol. Sciences Map 1/25,000, Telford (1978 edn.).
[57] O.S. Map 1/25,000, SJ 61 (1957 edn.).
[58] Inst. Geol. Sciences Map 1/25,000, Telford (1978 edn.).

drained towards the Weald Moors along Crow brook, north of the village, and along its tributary Hadley brook.[59]

In 1979 there were traces of an oval earthwork enclosure near Blockleys' brickworks.[60] Incoherent linear crop marks in Hadley park[61] are the only other likely indications of early land use.

Lionel Murray, general secretary of the Trades Union Congress 1973–84,[62] was born at 3 Gladstone Street, Hadley, in 1922.[63]

The Roman Watling Street was turnpiked in 1726. Its Wellington–Newport branch passed through Hadley village and, as Trench Lane, formed Horton's southern boundary; presumably an early route, it was turnpiked in 1763. The old Newport–Shrewsbury road, along the northern boundary of both townships, was also presumably an early route. The Cotwall–Oakengates route (via Longdon upon Tern), turnpiked in 1726, also passed through Hadley village.[64] The first length of the Shrewsbury Canal (1794) crossed the northern part of Hadley township. It was disused from 1921 and formally abandoned in 1944.[65]

The Wellington–Stafford railway, built 1849,[66] crossed both townships; there was a station at Hadley, which closed to passengers and goods in 1964.[67] The Wellington–Wolverhampton line (1849) crossed Hadley township, with a halt at New Hadley by 1937.[68] In 1857 a branch of the Wellington–Wolverhampton railway was opened by the Wellington & Severn Junction Railway Co. (later G.W.R.) from Ketley Junction (in Hadley township) south to Horsehay, beyond which c. 1858 the company extended it to a terminus (in Madeley) near Lightmoor. Extensions beyond Lightmoor provided a direct route from Wellington, via Coalbrookdale, Buildwas, and Much Wenlock, to Presthope (from 1864) and Craven Arms (from 1867). From 1951 the passenger service ended at Much Wenlock. In 1962 the line from Ketley Junction to Ketley station was severed and all passenger traffic ceased. Thereafter goods from Wellington could reach Buildwas and Much Wenlock until 1963, and Coalbrookdale and Ketley until 1964, through Madeley Junction (on the Wellington–Wolverhampton line) and Lightmoor.[69] From 1964 that route was open only to sidings at Ironbridge B power station (in Buildwas).[70] The Coalport Branch Railway Co. (later L.N.W.R.) built a southward branch of the Wellington–Stafford line, from a point east of Hadley station to Coalport (in Madeley). It opened for goods in 1860 and passengers in 1861.[71] It closed to passengers in 1952, to goods beyond Stirchley in 1960, and entirely in 1964.[72]

Hadley and Horton were probably the only nucleated settlements until the later 18th century. In 1086 Hadley had 10 recorded inhabitants.[73] Numbers evidently increased a little before 1327 when there were 11 taxpayers,[74] but a mid 14th-century collapse followed by a slow recovery may be postulated.[75] In 1542 Hadley, like Aston, Lawley, and Walcot, had about one in seventeen of the 'able' men of the parish;[76] it may have had the same proportion of Wellington parish's 219 households in 1563.[77] By 1672, however, it had left those townships behind; 22 houses were liable to hearth tax.[78] The rapid increase since 1563 was almost certainly due to settlement of miners along the north side of Watling Street.[79] Mining and iron making flourished in Ketley and Hadley townships from the later 18th to the mid 19th century[80] and Hadley township had 1,280 inhabitants in 1841.[81]

Hadley village, little affected but for the opening of new shops, then consisted of houses grouped along c. 700 metres of the Newport–Wellington road, later called High Street. Soon after 1871, however, when the Castle Iron Works opened, new streets were laid out. When its successor opened, in 1900, 94 houses were immediately added in new streets that almost joined Hadley to Haybridge, and Castle Houses, 12 dwellings in two blocks, were built near the works; the new houses resembled some at Port Sunlight (Ches.).[82] The factory's failure caused many houses to be empty until it reopened in 1910.[83] Wellington rural district council enlarged the village with 204 houses at Brookdale (1921), Parkdale (1931–9), and Sunningdale (1936).[84] Parkdale extended northwards to a small settlement along Hadley Road known as Leegomery,[85] probably founded in the 1870s[86] for Castle Iron Works employees.

West of Hadley by 1817 lay Haybridge Hall and Haybridge House.[87] Two workmen's terraces were added,[88] presumably after the Haybridge ironworks opened in 1864.[89] In the 20th century Haybridge was gradually overrun by Hadley.

Between 1947 and 1968 the R.D.C. extended Hadley and Haybridge with 676 houses and flats[90]

[59] O.S. Map 1/25,000, SJ 61 (1957 edn.).

[60] SA 702.　　　　　　　　[61] SA 2001.

[62] Who's Who (1983), 1622; The Guardian, 8 Sept. 1984.

[63] Inf. from Mr. Murray.

[64] Above, Wellington, Communications.

[65] Ibid.; T.D.C. Hadley Park Lock (Hist. Bldgs. in Telford, no. 19).

[66] Above, Wellington, Communications.

[67] C. R. Clinker, Clinker's Reg. of Closed Stations 1830–1977 (Bristol, 1978), 58.

[68] Above, Wellington, Communications; O.S. Map 1/2,500, Salop. XXXVI. 10 (1939 edn.).

[69] E. T. MacDermot, Hist. of G.W.R. ed. C. R. Clinker, i (1964), 456; J. M. Tolson, 'In the Tracks of the Iron Masters', Railway Mag. xci. 373–8, 440–3.

[70] Clinker, op. cit. 21.

[71] Trinder, Ind. Rev. Salop. (1981), 153.

[72] Railway Mag. xci. 378.　　　[73] V.C.H. Salop. i. 321.

[74] T.S.A.S. 2nd ser. i. 182.

[75] Below, Econ. Hist. (Agric.).

[76] L. & P. Hen. VIII, xvii, pp. 507–8.

[77] i.e. c. 13: cf. above, p. 205 and n. 88.

[78] Hearth Tax 1672 (Salop. Arch. Soc.), 88.

[79] Below, Ketley, intro.

[80] Below, Econ. Hist.; Ketley, Econ. Hist.

[81] V.C.H. Salop. ii. 228.

[82] Below, Econ. Hist.; S.R.O. 14, tithe map; S.R.O., DA 26/100/1, pp. 280–1; O.S. Map 1/2,500, Salop. XXXVI. 10 (1882 and 1902 edns.); Telstar, Mar. 1981, 7; above, plate 18.

[83] Wellington Jnl. 11 Feb. 1905; Below, Econ. Hist.

[84] S.R.O., DA 26/100/2, pp. 218, 220; /100/5, pp. 48, 77; /100/6, p. 391; /114/1, p. 247; /114/2, p. 97.

[85] O.S. Map 6", SJ 61 SE. (1954 edn.).

[86] O.S. Map 1/2,500, Salop. XXXVI. 6 (1882 edn.).

[87] B.L. Maps, O.S.D. 208.

[88] O.S. Map 1/2,500, Salop. XXXVI. 10 (1882 edn.).

[89] Below, Econ. Hist.

[90] S.R.O., DA 26/114/3, p. 761; /114/4, pp. 867, 964–5, 1026; /114/5, pp. 1203, 1233; /114/6, pp. 1719, 1822, 1849, 1858, 1952, 1957; /101/9–12, 14, Ho. Cttee. mins. 10 Oct., 14 Nov. 1963; 16 July 1964; 16 Sept., 9 Dec. 1965; 8 Sept. 1966; 9 May 1968.

but further expansion could not proceed until the Rushmoor sewage works (in Wrockwardine) opened[91] in 1975.[92] Wrekin district council added 61 dwellings in 5 small schemes 1975–80,[93] but most house building after 1975 was on Telford development corporation's Leegomery estate (between Hadley Park Road and Haybridge Road),[94] which combined public (rented) and private housing.[95] The corporation contributed 1,059 rented houses and flats there 1978–c. 1981[96] and Wrekin district council 119 between 1978 and 1979.[97]

From 1978 a northern bypass diverted the Newport–Wellington road from the old centre of Hadley,[98] which was accordingly pedestrianized as a Telford 'district centre', declared open in 1981.[99]

South-east of Hadley, in the coal-bearing part of the township, lay two isolated rows of industrial workers' cottages by 1809, New Hadley and Ragfield Row.[1] The former, presumably occupied from the 1890s by B. P. Blockley's employees,[2] stood until replaced in 1930 by 20 council houses.[3] Extensions of Hadley council housing later absorbed the area.

Between Watling Street and the site of the Wellington–Wolverhampton railway there were scattered houses associated with coalpits until the mid 20th century,[4] when slum clearance[5] and the development of Allied Ironfounders' works[6] required more houses in that area. Wellington R.D.C. built 6 at Ketley Vallens in 1927[7] and 30 near Ketleybrook in 1935.[8] A private estate of 63 houses was completed off Ketley Vallens 1935–8.[9] Near Ketleybrook the council built 374 more houses and flats 1957–66.[10]

Horton village consisted in 1840 of some 20 farmhouses and cottages around the junction of Horton Lane and the old Newport–Shrewsbury road and along the north side of the lane.[11] The village had grown little by 1983 though there had been much rebuilding and modernization.

A short length of Trench Lane lay in Horton township. Only two houses there were in Wellington parish in 1840.[12] Nearby at Trench Lock, where the lane from Hadley crossed the Shrewsbury Canal and entered Horton township, settlement followed the opening of the Trench Iron Works in 1866.[13] By 1882 workers' housing on the Hadley side of the lock included 4 terraces (64 cottages),[14] and Wellington R.D.C. added 8 houses in 1921.[15] On the Horton side there was a terrace of 6 cottages by 1882,[16] near which Oakengates urban district council completed Jubilee Terrace c. 1935.[17]

Hadley had a fuller provision for social life than the other coalfield townships, and some of its amenities rivalled those of Wellington. Horton's, however, were negligible.

Hadley township had an aleseller in 1590 (his house perhaps the resort of those presented for illegal card playing that year) and at least two c. 1620, when Horton also had one.[18] From the 18th century road improvements and nearby industrial growth caused public houses to increase in Hadley village and on Watling Street and to open near pits and ironworks.[19] The principal inns were the Seven Stars on Watling Street, mentioned 1746,[20] and the Bush, Hadley, mentioned 1822.[21] At Horton the Horse Shoe, licensed before 1800, closed c. 1939[22] but the 19th-century Queen's Head[23] was open in 1983.

A Union Society at Hadley was registered in 1801 and a Brotherly Friendly Society began in 1823.[24] By 1898 the National Order of Free Gardeners had a lodge at the Granville Arms,[25] New Hadley, and in the 1930s the Ancient Order of Foresters had courts at Hadley and Horton.[26] The Independent Order of Rechabites had a tent c. 1940.[27]

A literary institute flourished in the 1870s and 1880s[28] and Trench Lock had reading rooms in 1898.[29] A Liberal and Labour Club was formed by 1913.[30] By 1922 it had been replaced by Hadley Working Men's Club & Institute.[31] A Comrades

[91] *Shropshire Star*, 30 Dec. 1971; 12 Aug. 1974.
[92] *Telford Jnl.* 7 Aug. 1975.
[93] Wrekin District Council, Tech. Resources file H.8/1 (1974–83) and completion bks.
[94] T.D.C. *Telford Street Plan* (1981).
[95] Inf. from S.C.C. Planning Dept.
[96] D. G. Fenter, 'Bldg. Development carried out in Telford by the Development Corp.' (TS. in S.R.O. 3763).
[97] Wrekin District Council, Tech. Resources file H.8/1 (1974–83) and completion bks.
[98] *Telford Jnl.* 2 Sept. 1977; *Shropshire Star*, 8 Feb. 1978.
[99] *Shropshire Star*, 3 Nov. 1981.
[1] N. J. Clarke, 'New Hadley colliery and ironworks', *Jnl. Wilkinson Soc.* vii. 13.
[2] Below, Econ. Hist.
[3] O.S. Map 1/2,500, Salop. XXXVI. 10 (1926 edn.); S.R.O., DA 26/100/4, pp. 295, 346. Date stone reads 1929.
[4] S.R.O. 14, tithe map; O.S. Map 1/2,500, Salop. XXXVI. 10 (1926 edn.).
[5] S.R.O., DA 26/114/1, pp. 156–7; *Dawley Observer*, 22 May 1968.   [6] Below, Econ. Hist.
[7] S.R.O., DA 26/100/3, p. 379.
[8] Ibid. /100/6, p. 327.
[9] Ibid. /505/1, Wellington Rural no. 2, pp. 36–42.
[10] Ibid. /114/7, pp. 1986, 2006; /114/8, pp. 2375, 2432; /101/9, 12, Ho. Cttee. mins. 12 Sept. 1963; 10 Nov. 1966.
[11] S.R.O. 1856/3.
[12] Ibid.
[13] Below, Econ. Hist.

[14] O.S. Map 1/2,500, Salop. XXXVI. 10 (1882 edn.).
[15] S.R.O., DA 26/100/2, p. 226.
[16] O.S. Map 1/2,500, Salop. XXXVI. 6 (1882 edn.).
[17] Ibid. (1939 edn.).
[18] P.R.O., SC 2/197/96; S.R.O., q. sess. rec. parcel 254, badgers', drovers', and alesellers' licensing bk. *s.a.* 16–17 Jas. I.
[19] S.R.O., q. sess. rec. parcel 257, reg. of alesellers' recognizances 1782–1801; S.R.O. 14, tithe appt. and map (nos. 176, 512, 518, 541, 619, 642, 821, 839); Co. of Salop, *Return of Licensed Hos. 1896*, 205–14 (copy in S.R.O., q. sess. rec. box 148); O.S. Map 1/2,500, Salop. XXXVI. 10 (1902 edn.).
[20] Trinder and Cox, *Yeomen and Colliers*, p. 398.
[21] S.R.O., q. sess. rec. parcel 259, reg. of alesellers' recognizances 1822–8.
[22] Co. of Salop, *Return of Licensed Hos. 1896*, 211; *Kelly's Dir. Salop.* (1937), 110.
[23] Co. of Salop, *Return of Licensed Hos. 1896*, 212.
[24] S.R.O., q. sess. rec. parcel 285, friendly socs. reg.
[25] Hobson & Co. *Wellington Dir., Almanack, and Diary* (1898), 36.
[26] J. Jones & Son, *Dir. of Wellington & Dist.* (1934), 141.
[27] Telford Community Arts Ltd. *The Hadley Book* (1982), 95.
[28] P.O. Dir. Salop. (1879), 327; *Kelly's Dir. Salop.* (1885), 857.
[29] Hobson, *Wellington Dir.* (1898), 52.
[30] *Kelly's Dir. Salop.* (1913), 108; (1917), 98.
[31] Ibid. (1922), 105; (1934), 111.

Club, mentioned 1934,[32] was apparently replaced before 1937 by the United Services & Village Club,[33] which had its own premises at Hadley centre in 1981.[34] An old people's rest room was opened by volunteers in 1953.[35] Wellington R.D.C. opened a children's play centre in 1964.[36] In 1980 Hadley parish council made Castle Farm a community centre[37] and premises in High Street were converted for West Indian use.[38] G.K.N. Sankey had its own sports and social club in 1981.[39]

In 1882 there was a cricket ground between Hadley village and Trench Lock.[40] The National Olympian Society held its 1883 athletics festival at Hadley.[41] The Hadley Blues football team flourished c. 1920,[42] and in the 1930s Ketley playing field, on the Hadley side of Watling Street, was opened by voluntary effort.[43] Wellington R.D.C. enlarged and improved it c. 1967[44] and by 1981 it included squash courts, a swimming pool, and a golf driving range.[45] In 1954 the R.D.C. opened another playing field at Sunningdale, laid out at the expense of Joseph Sankey & Sons Ltd.[46] It included a swimming pool and gymnasium by 1981. In addition the Glynwed and G.K.N. Sankey works had their own sports fields.[47] In the 1980s funfairs were held near the Seven Stars.[48]

Hadley and District Orpheus Male Voice Choir, formed 1901,[49] flourished in 1983, and the Wrekin Choral and Operatic Society, founded 1964, rehearsed at Hadley.[50] The Regal cinema, formerly the Primitive Methodist chapel,[51] opened in 1934[52] and closed c. 1957.[53] The county library opened a Hadley book centre in 1940[54] and a new branch library in 1968.[55] Ketley book centre was located in Hadley township 1946–55.[56]

MANORS AND OTHER ESTATES. In 1066 Witric and Elric held *HADLEY* as two manors. In 1086 Reynold of Bailleul, the sheriff, held it of Roger of Montgomery, earl of Shrewsbury.[57] By c. 1136 William FitzAlan was tenant in chief,[58]

the mesne lordship, merged with the tenancy in chief after 1102,[59] having presumably passed with the shrieval estates[60] to his father Alan son of Flaald.[61] In 1404,[62] 1444,[63] and 1548[64] the manor was held, with High Hatton (called a member of Hadley in 1404 but termed a manor in 1548), of the earl of Arundel's manor of Wroxeter by the annual render of a sparrowhawk. Hadley was still held of Wroxeter in 1614.[65]

In 1086 the demesne lord was Gosfrid.[56] William of Hadley, lord in Henry I's time, died c. 1136 and his widow Seburga held Hadley until after 1154. She was succeeded by their son Alan of Hadley (d. c. 1194), whose daughter and heir Cecily married Roger Corbet of Tasley[67] (d. c. 1204). The manor descended from father to son in the Corbets until the mid 14th century, the following being lords: Thomas (d. 1247), Roger (d. c. 1259), Thomas (d. c. 1300),[68] and Roger (d. c. 1349). The last named was succeeded by his son Robert, whose widow died in possession in 1353. In 1354 Robert's kinsman (probably his nephew) Sir Robert Corbet (d. 1404)[69] was lord. His son, another Sir Robert, succeeded,[70] and died in 1417, the manor passing to his daughter Sibyl, the wife of John Grevel of Sezincote (Glos.).[71] They were childless and by 1422 had settled the reversion on Guy Corbet, presumably a kinsman.[72] Grevel, surviving his wife and Guy, died in possession in 1444, when Guy's son Robert (d. 1495) succeeded.[73] The manor descended successively to Robert's son Richard (d. 1524) and grandson Richard Corbet.[74] The latter sold it in 1548 to Sir Rowland Hill.[75] At Sir Rowland's death in 1561 it passed for life to his nephew William Gratewood (d. c. 1583),[76] then to William's sister Alice, widow of Reynold Corbet of Stoke.[77] In 1583 she settled it on her son Richard (d. 1601)[78] and his wife Anne for their lives. Anne was in possession in 1617, and then or in 1618 the estate passed to their son John[79] (cr. bt. 1627, d. 1662).[80] In 1669 his son Sir John sold it to William Roe (d. 1679)[81] of Arleston. William's son, the Revd. Robert Roe, was in posses-

[32] Jones, *Dir. Wellington* (1934), 113.
[33] *Kelly's Dir. Salop.* (1937), 110.
[34] T.D.C. *Telford Street Plan* (1981).
[35] *Telford Jnl.* 4 Mar. 1977.
[36] *Telford Social Trends*, i, ed. J. MacGuire (T.D.C. 1980), 207–8.
[37] Fenter, 'Bldg. Development in Telford'.
[38] Ibid.
[39] T.D.C. *Telford Street Plan* (1981).
[40] O.S. Map 1/2,500, Salop. XXXVI. 10 (1882 edn.).
[41] *V.C.H. Salop.* ii. 193 and n.
[42] *The Hadley Bk.* 53.
[43] *Kelly's Dir. Salop.* (1937), 124; O.S. Map 1/2,500, Salop. XXXVI. 10 (1939 edn.).
[44] Ed. J. Burrow & Co. Ltd. *Wellington R.D. Official Guide* [1967], 22.
[45] T.D.C. *Telford Street Plan* (1981).
[46] S.R.O., DA 26/134 (S.R.O. 3172/8/13/11), file 171.
[47] T.D.C. *Telford Street Plan* (1981).
[48] Local inf.
[49] *Shropshire Mag.* Sept. 1964, 45.
[50] Ibid. Feb. 1972, 17.
[51] *The Hadley Bk.* 92.
[52] F. J. Brown, 'Cinemas of Telford 1910–83' (TS. in possession of Mr. Brown), 9.
[53] S.R.O., DA 34 (S.R.O. 3279/1), Regal file of 1957–8, memo. 7 Feb. 1958.
[54] *S.C.C. Mins. (Educ.)* 1940–1, 22.
[55] Ibid. 1968–9, 223.

[56] Ibid. 1946–7, 79, 126; S.R.O. 3767/X/K, G. C. Godber to Revd. H. M. Hart, 20 Sept. 1955.
[57] *V.C.H. Salop.* i. 321.   [58] Ibid. ii. 80.
[59] Ibid. iii. 10.
[60] Ibid. 9–10.   [61] Ibid. 10.
[62] P.R.O., C 137/46, no. 6.
[63] P.R.O., C 139/118, no. 23.
[64] P.R.O., CP 25(2)/62/496, no. 22.
[65] P.R.O., C 142/354, no. 126. Cf. *T.S.A.S.* 4th ser. iv. 107.
[66] *V.C.H. Salop.* i. 321.
[67] Eyton, vii. 354–5.
[68] Ibid. i. 88–97.
[69] P.R.O., C 137/46, no. 6.
[70] Eyton, vii. 360–2.
[71] P.R.O., C 138/26, no. 34.
[72] Guy was perhaps Sibyl's uncle: *S.P.R. Lich.* xxi (3), p. v.
[73] P.R.O., C 139/118, no. 23; *Cal. Inq. p.m. Hen. VII*, ii, p. 123.
[74] P.R.O., C 142/48, no. 100.
[75] P.R.O., CP 25(2)/62/496, no. 22.
[76] P.R.O., C 142/206, no. 32.
[77] Ibid. /132, no. 18.
[78] A. E. C[orbet], *The Fam. of Corbet: its Life and Times*, ii [1918], table facing p. 357.
[79] P.R.O., C 142/354, no. 126; CP 25(2)/343/16 Jas. I Mich. (2), no. 1.
[80] Corbet, op. cit. table facing p. 357.
[81] *Yeomen and Colliers in Telford*, ed. B. Trinder and J. Cox (1980), p. 150.

sion by 1700[82] and in 1710 he sold the manor to his son, the Revd. William Roe (d. 1741), who left it to his son William. The younger William died unmarried in 1761, when it passed to his brother, the Revd. Samuel Roe (d. 1780) of Stotfold (Beds.), whose sons Charles (d. 1816), John (d. 1838), and Henry Octavius (d. c. 1848)[83] were successive lords. H. O. Roe had no surviving relatives[84] and the manor was bought in 1848 by G. B. Thorneycroft,[85] a Wolverhampton ironmaster (d. 1851).[86] His son, Lt.-Col. Thomas Thorneycroft, seems to have held it until his death in 1903.[87] In 1905 the manor was said to belong to Sir Thomas Meyrick[88] and may have descended thereafter with Apley.

Hadley manor house lay off the south side of the village street opposite the junction with Station Road.[89] It was timber-framed, of three storeys, and aligned east–west, and seems to have been built in the earlier 17th century. There was a central chimney stack. A timber-framed range was later built out from the centre of the south front. The house was demolished c. 1965.[90]

By 1842 H. O. Roe had no land in Hadley, which was split between 88 freeholders. The largest estate was Hadley Park (273 a.), then owned by John Evans but later[91] by the Thorneycrofts; the brick-built house, of three bays and three storeys, was of the late 18th century. The next largest (122 a.) belonged to James Foster, the ironmaster.[92] Small estates belonged to Lord Forester (34 a.) and the duke of Sutherland (4 a.).[93]

In 1066 Erniet held HORTON. In 1086 it was held of Earl Roger by William Pantulf, with Warin as undertenant.[94] Pantulf's mesne lordship became a tenancy in chief, presumably in 1102.[95] The chief lordship presumably passed to Pantulf's successors, the barons of Wem, for Horton remained in the leet jurisdiction of Hinstock manor until 1851 or later.[96] The Hodnets and their successors had or claimed a chief lordship over Horton, or a part of it,[97] at least between c. 1285[98] and 1390;[99] their claims may have originated in the late 12th century if (as seems likely) Pain of Preston, an undertenant of the Hodnets in Preston,[1] then held Horton also. In the early 13th century Roger of Preston, probably the husband

of one of Pain's coheirs in Preston, held land in Horton of his nephew Otes of Hodnet.[2]

It seems likely that Pain of Preston was demesne lord of Horton in the late 12th century, for the scanty evidence suggests that Horton afterwards descended in quarters among the coheirs who inherited Pain's manor of Preston.[3] In 1353 Gillian, daughter of Hugh of the Heath, sold the reversions of a quarter of Horton and a quarter of Preston manors to Sir Alan of Charlton.[4] The Eytons owned woodland in Horton by 1271,[5] and by 1359 part at least of Horton was subject to the court baron of Eyton upon the Weald Moors,[6] whose lords (the Eytons) acquired an interest in a quarter of Preston manor at some time between 1350 and 1616. In 1616 the quarters of Horton manor were held by Andrew Charlton of Apley, Philip Eyton of Eyton, William Steventon of Dothill, and Sir Vincent Corbet, the coparceners of Preston. Some of those lords did not exercise manorial rights in Horton; Eyton said he had never heard of Steventon's lordship and Charlton admitted that he had never held a court for Horton and had no demesne there.[7] In 1620 Andrew Charlton's son Francis relinquished his property in Horton and in Horton's wood (alias the Trench) to Sir Philip Eyton in exchange for property in Preston upon the Weald Moors.[8] By 1631 Sir Philip claimed to be in sole possession of Horton manor and Horton's wood,[9] having presumably acquired the Corbet and Steventon quarters since 1616. Horton manor seems thereafter to have descended with Eyton; Thomas Eyton was lord of Horton in 1768,[10] and in the 19th century the family continued to appoint a gamekeeper[11] and to receive chief rents from two farms.[12]

By the mid 18th century, however, the Eytons had no land in the lordship,[13] and others sometimes claimed the manorial rights, perhaps in the belief that the Eytons' claim was extinct.[14] In 1766 the Revd. Samuel Roe regarded himself as lord of the manor of 'Hadley cum Horton'.[15] In 1813 Sir Corbet Corbet called himself lord of the manor of 'Horton and Trench Lane', apparently by virtue of his overlordship as lord of Hinstock.[16] His father had advanced similar claims in Great Dawley on the same grounds in 1781.[17] Sir Corbet's

[82] S.P.L., Deeds 1366.
[83] Inf. from Dr. G. D. Thompson.
[84] S.P.L., Deeds 18093. For Sam. see S.R.O., q. sess. rec. box 260, reg. of gamekeepers 1742–79, 15 Jan. 1766; Alum. Cantab. to 1751, iii. 493.
[85] S. Bagshaw, Dir. Salop. (1851), 437; inf. from Mrs. S. W. Thorneycroft.
[86] F. Boase, Mod. Eng. Biography, iii (1901), 958.
[87] P.O. Dir. Salop. (1856), 134; Kelly's Dir. Salop. (1900), 98; Burke, Land. Gent. (1952), 2503.
[88] Kelly's Dir. Salop. (1905), 101.
[89] Para. based on S.R.O. 14, tithe map; T.S.A.S. 4th ser. vii. 154 and facing pl.; Burrow, Wellington R.D. Official Guide [1962], 10 (lower illus., wrongly titled); The Hadley Bk. 97.
[90] S.R.O. 725/3, p. 256; 1490/4, p. 300.
[91] Kelly's Dir. Salop. (1891), 324.
[92] Below, Econ. Hist.
[93] S.R.O. 14, tithe appt.
[94] V.C.H. Salop. i. 332.
[95] Ibid. iii. 10. Cf. Eyton, ix. 160.
[96] Below, Local Govt. and Public Services. The 1316 Nomina Villarum wrongly entered the FitzAlans' Hopton (in Hodnet) as Horton: Eyton, ix. 285.

[97] Cf. below, Lawley.
[98] Collect. Topog. et Geneal. i. 119; Feud. Aids, iv. 221.
[99] Cal. Inq. p.m. xvi, pp. 407–8.
[1] Above, Preston, Man.
[2] Eyton, viii. 39.   [3] Above, Preston, Man.
[4] P.R.O., CP 25(1)/195/15, no. 2.
[5] P.R.O., E 32/147, m. 6.
[6] Below, Local Govt. and Public Services.
[7] S.R.O. 665/1/256.
[8] Ibid. /1/257–8.
[9] S.R.O. 513, box 8, deeds.
[10] S.R.O., q. sess. rec. box 260, reg. of gamekeepers 1742–79, 9 June 1768.
[11] Ibid. parcel 261, reg. of gamekeepers 1799–1807, p. 159.
[12] Eyton, viii. 39 n.
[13] The last known ref. is a deed of sale of 1695: Staffs. R.O., D. 1287/13/3/8.
[14] Horton was not included in the suit r. of Eyton man. 16 Nov. 1695: S.R.O. 665/1/1.
[15] S.R.O. 1155.
[16] S.R.O. 327, box 6, notice of 18 Jan. 1813.
[17] S.R.O. 2374, box 4, papers in Corbet and D'Avenant v. Slaney.

claim to Horton was still asserted in the 1820s.[18] In 1885 Lt.-Col. Thomas Thorneycroft, lord of Hadley, was named as lord of Horton.[19] By the 1980s, however, there were no known claims to the lordship.[20]

In the early 13th century Roger of Preston gave ½ virgate to Lilleshall abbey, and Sabin of Horton, perhaps his widow, gave a messuage, croft, and meadow.[21] The abbey may have lost the estate after c. 1280, when the abbot granted it for life to Sibyl, widow of Ralph, son of Eustace of Horton.[22]

In 1842 Horton township comprised fifteen freeholds (seven under 1 a.), none of which belonged to the families who had been lords.[23] In 1725 Walter Marigold had settled a freehold estate at Horton on his son William (d. c. 1731). It descended to his four daughters, one of whom married William Spearman.[24] In 1842 the estate (125 a.) was the biggest in Horton[25] and in 1856 belonged to William Spearman and others,[26] presumably descendants of William Marigold. By 1913 it belonged to C. E. Morris-Eyton, who then sold it.[27]

By 1726 William Icke the elder, of Leegomery, had settled an estate at Horton on his son William.[28] In 1842 Elizabeth Icke owned 37 a. in the township and William Icke 73 a.[29]

In 1731 the Preston hospital trustees acquired the Hoo Hall estate,[30] part of which lay in Horton township,[31] as did some of the land they bought from Humphrey Pitt in 1750.[32] The trustees, who owned 50 a. in the township in 1842, sold some of the land to the War Department in 1942,[33] and more land was sold c. 1953.[34]

ECONOMIC HISTORY. Weavers lived in Hadley township in the 17th and early 18th centuries.[35] James Burroughs was making rope by 1870[36] and the business continued until the 1930s.[37] His ropewalk was behind Ketley Wesleyan Methodist chapel.[38] Sandpits at Ketleysands were exploited in the 19th and 20th centuries.[39] By the mid 19th century there was some concentra-

tion of shops and public houses in Hadley village and a scattering along the north side of Watling Street.[40] Retailing grew in the village considerably in the 20th century.[41] A bank sub-branch opened c. 1920[42] and in the 1970s Hadley was developed as one of Telford's seven district shopping centres.[43] Coal and iron were exploited in Hadley from the later 18th century but in 1982 the main employers were engineering and brick works established in Hadley in the later 19th century. They faced severe difficulties, and unemployment ran high.[44] Some hope of improvement lay with Telford development corporation's industrial estates at Hortonwood (opened 1979)[45] and Trench Lock (opened 1982). At the former, much of which lay in Hadley and Horton,[46] it was estimated that 6,500 jobs could eventually be created.[47]

AGRICULTURE. In 1086 Hadley and Horton were poor and wooded.[48] Hadley had probably emerged through recent woodland clearance[49] and in 1086 a league of woodland remained, apparently over most of the township's northern and south-eastern parts.[50] Until the early 12th century Hadley wood extended eastwards beyond the later township boundary as far as the king's wood (later called Wrockwardine wood), but William of Hadley granted the eastern part to the canons of Wombridge[51] and it became part of Wombridge parish. In 1086 Hadley's recorded tenants were eight bordars, an indication of recent assarting.[52] The manor had been worth 37s. in 1066 but was waste soon afterwards, perhaps by destruction c. 1070.[53] By 1086, however, it was worth 15s. and taxed at 2 hides. There were two serfs and a ploughteam on the demesne, but only ½ ploughteam among the bordars and room for 2½ more teams. Horton was still waste in 1086 and taxed at 3 virgates. Horton had 1 ploughland but ½ league of woodland, apparently on the south and east,[54] and a hay (perhaps an inclosed wood).

Until 1301 both townships were within the jurisdiction of Mount Gilbert forest.[55] The arable nevertheless expanded. In 1262 and 1271 the

[18] S.R.O. 327, box 5, notices to quit, 17 Sept. 1828; Wm. Tayler to — Bratton, 19 Apr. 1829.

[19] Kelly's Dir. Salop. (1885), 788, 857.

[20] Inf. from Lt.-Col. R. C. G. Morris-Eyton and Mrs. S. W. Thorneycroft.

[21] Eyton, viii. 39.   [22] Ibid. 40.

[23] S.R.O. 14, tithe appt.

[24] S.R.O. 1493, box 310, abstr. of title and case for counsel's opinion.

[25] S.R.O. 14, tithe appt.

[26] P.O. Dir. Salop. (1856), 134.

[27] S.R.O. 3987/18.   [28] S.R.O. 999/K 6.

[29] S.R.O. 14, tithe appt.

[30] Above, Eyton, Man. and Other Est.; Preston, Man. For what follows see Staffs. R.O., D. 1287/13/11/1–2; S.R.O. 14, tithe appt.; Char. Com. files.

[31] e.g. Hinnersly piece.

[32] e.g. the Spinnings, the Bradleys.

[33] T.D.C., deed pkt. 1676.

[34] Ibid. 907, 1104.

[35] Trinder and Cox, Yeomen and Colliers, pp. 123, 127.

[36] P.O. Dir. Salop. (1870), 70.

[37] Kelly's Dir. Salop. (1934), 126.

[38] O.S. Map 1/2,500, Salop. XXXVI. 10 (1882 and 1926 edns.).

[39] For details see below, Ketley, Econ. Hist.

[40] S.R.O. 14, tithe appt. and map; P.O. Dir. Salop. (1856), 138.

[41] Kelly's Dir. Salop. (1900), 99; (1941), 109.

[42] Ibid. (1922), 104.

[43] T.D.C. Basic Plan for Telford (1973), 19.

[44] The Hadley Bk. 151.

[45] T.D.C. Telford: the Facts [1979].

[46] T.D.C. Telford Development Strategy, map (Feb. 1979).

[47] T.D.C. Telford Development Strategy: 1st Monitoring Rep. [1978], 30.

[48] Para. based on V.C.H. Salop. i. 321, 332.

[49] As the name-element leah suggests: M. Gelling, Signposts to the Past (1978), 126–8.

[50] Woodland and pasture names in S.R.O. 14, tithe appt. and map.

[51] T.S.A.S. 2nd ser. xi. 334–5; V.C.H. Salop. ii. 80.

[52] S. P. J. Harvey, 'Evidence for Settlement Study: Domesday Bk.' Medieval Settlement, ed. P. H. Sawyer (1976), 197–9.

[53] V.C.H. Salop. iii. 7.

[54] Above.

[55] Cartulary of Shrews. Abbey, ed. U. Rees (1975), ii, p. 249.

lord's widow was amerced for cultivating oats on an acre of land and another small parcel,[56] and in 1271 eight Horton tenants were amerced for asserting ½ a. of wood belonging to Peter of Eyton (III) in Horton (presumably at Horton's wood)[57] to enlarge one of their fields, and for sowing the assart with oats and winter corn.[58] In the later Middle Ages arable, probably in open fields, lay north-west, east, and south of Hadley village,[59] and at Horton arable fields[60] seem to have lain north and south of the village.[61] Both townships had considerable areas of meadow and pasture.[62] Most of the north-east part of Hadley was im-parked before *c.* 1277,[63] presumably from former woodland.

Hadley may have been slow to recover from the agrarian crises of the 14th century. In 1404 the underwood of the park was worth nothing; prob-ably there were no purchasers.[64] There were 80 a. of arable in demesne, all lying fallow, and 10 a. of meadow worth 10*s.* a year. Rents amounted to £10 13*s.* 4*d.* annually.[65] The lord leased the park before 1557,[66] and in 1623 it was leased as pasture;[67] parts, at least, were held by farmers a century later.[68]

In the later 17th and earlier 18th century the farmers of Hadley and Horton practised mixed husbandry.[69] All kept cattle, and herds averaged *c.* 12, rather more than in Wellington parish as a whole.[70] The largest recorded herd had 37 anim-als. The larger farmers usually made cheese and butter for sale. Some oxen were kept as draught animals. The larger farms had sheep too, in flocks averaging *c.* 30, near the parish average.[71] There were 57 sheep in the largest recorded flock. Two or three pigs were usually kept, and a few horses. The smaller farms were sometimes held by crafts-men. Concern for the arable's long-term fertility was reflected in a Hadley lease of 1725 forbidding its impoverishment by 'overmuch tillage'.[72]

By 1842 Hadley and Horton were wholly in-closed and still predominantly agricultural.[73] The two largest farms in Hadley were Hadley Park farm (273 a.) and Wheatley Grange farm (76 a.), which both lay in the north. They were compact and were run from houses standing amidst their fields: it therefore seems likely that both were formed by large-scale, late-medieval inclosure of former woodland.[74] Hadley Park farm, however, had been more than doubled in size since 1772.[75] Hadley had 12 other agricultural holdings over 25 a. in 1842; they averaged 42 a.[76] Those smaller farms were much fragmented and run from houses in the village street, and thus seem to have been formed by the gradual inclosure of dispersed open-field holdings, probably completed *c.* 1700.[77] The failure to rationalize the boundaries of the smaller farms[78] presumably implied a lack of co-operation among the township's many small freeholders:[79] in 1842 Hadley's 12 agricultural holdings between 25 a. and 75 a. were held of 23 different owners. There were 12 other agricul-tural holdings (6–21 a.) occupied by residents, of whom some were tradesmen. Seven small agri-cultural holdings (2–20 a.) were held by non-residents.

In Horton the three agricultural holdings over 25 a. in 1842 consisted of two farms (110 a. and 91 a.) run from houses in the village street and 35 a. held by a non-resident. The farms were frag-mented, but with pieces less dispersed than in Hadley. Four other agricultural holdings (4–17 a.) were occupied by residents (three of them in the village street) and three (14–24 a.) by non-residents.

Some improvement in the layout of farms was achieved later in the century. By 1861 Hadley Park farm had been further enlarged to 316 a.[80] Manor House farm, Hadley, which thereby lost an outlying 19 a., received by 1882 an additional 15 a., making it a compact unit.[81] At Horton John Hayward's farm lay in seven pieces in 1842, but by 1913 was compact.[82]

In Hadley arable exceeded meadow and pasture by about 3 to 2 in 1842, but on residents' farms over 25 a. the ratio was usually more than 2 to 1. In Horton it was about 3 to 1, and applied to all three holdings over 25 a. By the late 19th century a movement from arable to livestock had taken place. In 1842 arable formed 81 per cent of land on Manor House farm (34 a.), Hadley; forty years later it formed only 39 per cent.[83] The change was

---

[56] P.R.O., E 32/145, m. 6d.; /147, m. 6.

[57] Above, Eyton.

[58] P.R.O., E 32/147, m. 6.

[59] Field names, some with the element 'furlong', in S.R.O. 14, tithe appt. and map.

[60] A farm was descr. in 1686 and 1698 as in the 'township and fields' of Horton: S.R.O. 1709/56/1, 3.

[61] S.R.O. 14, tithe appt.; 1856/3.

[62] Field names in S.R.O. 14, tithe appts. and Hadley map; 1856/3.

[63] S.P.L., Deeds 16317 (datable from S.R.O. 972, box 220, deeds of 1277). Location from field names in S.R.O. 14, tithe appt. and map.

[64] Cf. above, Lilleshall, Econ. Hist.

[65] P.R.O., C 137/46, no. 6. The extent included High Hatton.

[66] S.R.O. 625, box 19, inq. p.m. of 1569 (copy).

[67] S.R.O. 327, box 268, deed.

[68] L.J.R.O., B/C/11, Jos. Icke, 1707; Ann Williams, 1714; Thos. Edge, 1728.

[69] Para. based on ibid. Rog. Golbourne, 1661; Jos. Grise, 1665; Thos. Bryan, 1667; Eliz. Grise, 1667; Eleanor Pickring, 1670; Wm. Barker, 1690; Thos. Nevall, 1692; Sarah Bayley, 1700; Wm. Bayley, 1701; Jos. Icke, 1707; Thos. Whitangam, 1711; Ann Williams, 1714; Jane Freeman, 1722; Thos.

Cooper, 1725; Alan Freeman, 1725; Thos. Edge, 1728; Thos. Prichard, 1729; Humph. Saven, 1729; Rob. Whitfield, 1747; Trinder and Cox, *Yeomen and Colliers*, pp. 257, 273–6, 312–13, 338, 356–7. Only 3 of these inventories were from Horton.

[70] Trinder and Cox, op. cit. p. 73.

[71] Ibid. p. 79.

[72] S.R.O. 1224, box 251, deed.

[73] Hadley 85 per cent, Horton 95 per cent. In the following paras. inf. dated 1842 is, unless otherwise stated, based on S.R.O. 14, tithe appts. and Hadley map; 1856/3.

[74] Wheatley may mean 'clearing for wheat': E. Ekwall, *Concise Oxf. Dict. Eng. P.N.* (4th edn.), 512.

[75] *Shrews. Chron.* 23 Nov. 1772.

[76] Of the 100 a. kept in hand by Jas. Foster only 41 per cent were agricultural (i.e. descr. as arable, pasture, or meadow) and they are not counted here.

[77] Cf. above, Wellington, Econ. Hist.

[78] Cf. above, L. Wenlock; Lilleshall; Wellington; below, Ketley; Lawley.

[79] Above, Man. and Other Est.

[80] S.R.O. 2069/1.

[81] S.R.O. 3129/16/16.

[82] S.R.O. 3987/18.

[83] S.R.O. 3129/16/16.

elsewhere less marked. In Horton, John Hayward's 91-a. farm was 78 per cent arable in 1842, 73 per cent in 1913.[84]

In the 1930s Hadley and Horton townships were still predominantly agricultural.[85] By 1940 Hadley Park farm had increased further, to 345 a. It was 41 per cent arable, compared with 64 per cent in 1842, and its livestock included c. 100 cattle and c. 300 pigs.[86] In 1941 Joseph Sankey & Sons Ltd. bought the farm in order to extend its works, and the house became the general manager's residence;[87] only a small proportion of the farmland, however, was converted to industrial use. In 1968 most of Horton lay in Hoo Hall farm (480 a.), which was devoted to livestock.[88] By 1980 there was hardly any agricultural land in Hadley south of Hadley park, but Horton had lost little.[89]

MILLS. A water mill at Hadley recorded in 1086[90] and 1590[91] was presumably on Ketley brook, but by 1842 it had gone.[92] A brick-built windmill at Hadley Park was converted to water power before 1792.[93] By 1842 it had been replaced by a steam mill east of the village,[94] which closed before 1882.[95]

BRICKS AND TILES. Tiles were being made at Horton in 1681.[96] In 1767 George Forester leased Brick Kiln leasow, Hadley,[97] to a Hadley brick maker.[98] Another brick yard lay near Watling Street in 1842[99] but by 1882 it had closed. There was then a brick and tile works immediately south-east of Hadley village, which closed before 1901. By that time[1] B. P. Blockley had opened the Ragfield Tileries[2] at New Hadley, next to the Coalport branch railway. The works specialized in blue and red bricks. Before 1912 Blockley built another works, the Hadley Tileries, nearby.[3] Blockleys Ltd.[4] added a third works in 1935. By 1963 the factory produced 20 million facing bricks a year,[5] and in 1964 there were 155 employees.[6] There were c. 500 by 1973.[7] Some signs of falling demand were noted[8] but in 1980 further expansion was planned.[9]

COAL, IRONSTONE, AND FIRECLAY. These occurred only in the south-eastern extremity of Hadley township, in deep strata,[10] but by 1766 the Revd. Samuel Roe, lord of Hadley, owned coal works in the manor.[11] In 1791 John Wilkinson (d. 1808) bought an estate in the coal area and developed mines in association with his New Hadley ironworks. By 1809 the estate had at least 24 active pits, some with pumping and winding engines.[12] By 1820 Thomas Jukes Collier & Co., in which James Foster was the active partner, were operating mines in Hadley. In 1825 the company bought 61 a. in Hadley Lodge farm and the Vallens, with their minerals, and in 1831 bought the Wilkinson estate (65 a.) and mines.[13] The New Hadley ironworks was closed but minerals were needed at the partners' Wombridge works.[14] By the 1840s, however, the Hadley mines, under Foster's sole ownership from 1837, were nearing exhaustion.[15] The Lilleshall Co. bought them with the estate in 1860 in order to expand its coal department but they proved uneconomic.[16] In 1870 most of the nine pairs of shafts produced only ironstone.[17] By 1882 there were only three working mines and at least 25 abandoned shafts.[18] Twenty years later one shaft was working, at New Hadley;[19] B. P. Blockley had acquired it from the company.[20] It closed, however, before 1925.[21]

IRON. John Wilkinson built an ironworks[22] in the coalfield part of Hadley, with two furnaces blown in c. 1804. Probably intended to replace the Willey works, it had little success.[23] In 1813 John Bradley & Co. (i.e. John Bradley and James Foster) agreed to buy all the iron for 7 years,[24] and from c. 1820 Thomas Jukes Collier & Co. seem to have operated the New Hadley works. It closed, however, before 1825.[25]

ENGINEERING. After the Wellington–Stafford railway was built in 1849 three firms established themselves at railside sites. The Haybridge and Trench works were managed in the 19th century by local Wesleyans, one of whom, Lt.-Col. James Patchett, ruled Hadley in the manner of a bene-

---

[84] S.R.O. 3987/18.
[85] [1st] Land Util. Surv. Map, sheet 61.
[86] S.P.L., Sale Cat. 9/41.
[87] Shropshire Mag. Sept. 1976, 22.
[88] S.R.O. 4417/1, p. 22; /2.
[89] T.D.C. Telford Street Plan (1980). See also above, Wellington, Econ. Hist. (Agric.), table.
[90] V.C.H. Salop. i. 321.
[91] P.R.O., SC 2/197/96.
[92] Field names in S.R.O. 14, tithe appt. and map (nos. 95–7, 109–10, 674).
[93] T.D.C. Hadley Park Windmill (Hist. Bldgs. in Telford, no. 18).
[94] S.R.O. 14, tithe appt. and map (no. 240).
[95] O.S. Map 1/2,500, Salop. XXXVI. 10 (1882 edn.).
[96] S.R.O. 739/1, f. 2.
[97] S.R.O. 14, tithe appt. and map (nos. 695, 710, 743).
[98] S.R.O. 1224, box 253, deed.
[99] S.R.O. 14, tithe appt. and map (no. 449).
[1] O.S. Map 1/2,500, Salop. XXXVI. 10 (1882 and 1902 edns.).
[2] Kelly's Dir. Salop. (1905), 101.
[3] Ibid. (1913), 107; S.R.O. 2079/XXXVI. 10; 4011/84/4, no. 3328.
[4] Kelly's Dir. Salop. (1926), 109.
[5] Telford Observer, 13 Jan. 1971.

[6] J. H. D. Madin & Partners, Dawley New Town Rep. No. 2: Interim Proposals (Sept. 1964), cap. 6, sect. 1, app.
[7] Shropshire Star, 27 Apr. 1973.
[8] Financial Times, 3 Aug. 1974.
[9] Telford Jnl. 28 Nov. 1980.
[10] I. J. Brown, Mines of Salop. (Buxton, 1976), 8–9; Inst. Geol. Sciences Map 1/25,000, Telford (1978 edn.).
[11] S.R.O. 1155/1.
[12] Trinder, Ind. Rev. Salop. (1981), 38, 100–2.
[13] N. Mutton, 'The Foster Fam.: a Study of a Midland Ind. Dynasty 1786–1899' (London Univ. Ph.D. thesis, 1974), 102, 197–8.
[14] Below, Wombridge, Econ. Hist.
[15] Mutton, op. cit. 113, 198.
[16] Ibid. 119; W. K. V. Gale and C. R. Nicholls, The Lilleshall Co. Ltd.: a Hist. 1764–1964 (1979), 42.
[17] Gale and Nicholls, op. cit. 51.
[18] O.S. Maps 1/2,500, Salop. XXXVI. 10–11 (1882 edn.).
[19] Ibid. 10 (1902 edn.).
[20] N. J. Clarke, 'Hadley in the Past' (TS. [c. 1975]), [3] (copy in S.P.L.).
[21] O.S. Map 1/2,500, Salop. XXXVI. 10 (1926 edn.).
[22] Marked on O.S. Map 1″, sheet 61 NE. (1833 edn.).
[23] Trinder, Ind. Rev. Salop. (1981), 38.
[24] Mutton, 'Foster Fam.' 100.
[25] Ibid. 110; Trinder, op. cit. 144.

volent squire.[26] His Trench Iron Works had worker shareholders[27] and, by the 1920s, trade-union representation. At the Hadley Castle Works, however, there was no union recognition until the 1940s.[28]

The Haybridge Iron Co. (later Flather Bright Steels Ltd.)[29] was formed in 1864 with Benjamin Talbot as managing director.[30] The Wellington timber merchants Richard Groom and his son R. A. Groom both served as chairman.[31] The works made wire rods[32] and by the 1930s iron and steel bars and sections.[33] In 1950 much of the output was for export.[34] There were 307 employees in 1964,[35] and in 1974 business was expanding,[36] but the works closed in 1983.

The Trench Iron Works opened in 1866. The company failed in 1869, and in 1872 the Shropshire Iron Co. bought the works and extended it. In 1879, using Lilleshall Co. pig iron, it was able to produce 400 tons of wire rods and 100–150 tons of wire a week.[37] The Patchett family had the controlling interest from 1873 and James Patchett was managing director from the 1870s[38] until the general strike of 1926.[39] The works closed in 1931, making c. 400 men redundant.[40] In 1942 K. J. & A. Sommerfeld Ltd. (later Sommerfeld Flexboard Ltd.)[41] acquired the works[42] and made emergency runways and portable roadways. From 1947 they also made steel building components and furniture.[43] There were 136 employees in 1964,[44] and by 1967 the firm had worldwide exports.[45] From c. 1973 part of the site was occupied by a firm dealing in scrap metal and motor spares,[46] which remained in 1982. Sommerfelds moved to Doseley c. 1979.[47]

In 1871 the Castle Iron Works,[48] based on designs by Karl Siemens, was opened by Nettlefold & Chamberlain[49] of Smethwick.[50] In 1879 it was making wire and 400–500 tons of bar iron a week.[51] In 1886, however, Nettlefolds Ltd. left Shropshire, where costs, especially wages, were

high, and sold the works to Benjamin Talbot, whose firm went bankrupt in 1888.[52]

In 1900 G. F. Milnes & Co. Ltd. of Birkenhead, tramcar builders, opened the new Castle Car Works on the site.[53] There were c. 700 employees,[54] and 701 tramcars were completed in 1901.[55] Demand fell, however, and the works shut in 1904. In 1905 the United Electric Car Co. Ltd. bought them and leased them to the Metropolitan Amalgamated Railway Carriage & Wagon Co. Ltd. of Birmingham. In 1908 falling orders again forced a closure but most of the employees were offered jobs in the Birmingham area.[56]

In 1910 Joseph Sankey & Sons Ltd. of Bilston (later G.K.N. Sankey Ltd.)[57] bought the works and imported 100 employees from the Black Country. The Hadley Castle Works specialized in motor vehicle wheels and bodies and expanded with the British motor industry. After the First World War additional products included chassis frames, office furniture, and washing machines.[58] There were c. 1,500 employees in 1939.[59] The works grew sevenfold in the years 1948–60, becoming Europe's biggest manufacturer of motor vehicle wheels.[60] From the early 1970s the wheel division suffered from falling demand[61] and in the late 1970s the works entered a sudden decline. In January 1978 the workforce, 6,250,[62] was the largest of any Telford firm.[63] Four years later it had been cut to 2,550.[64]

In 1924 James Clay (Wellington) Ltd., agricultural machinery and implement manufacturers, moved their Wrekin Foundry from Wellington to a site beside the Ketley branch railway. From 1929 the firm was a subsidiary of Allied Ironfounders Ltd.[65] By 1958 it had moved to part of the Sinclair Iron Co.'s site in Ketley township[66] and by 1960[67] Aga Heat Ltd., another Allied Ironfounders subsidiary, had moved from Smethwick to extended buildings at the Hadley site, to make solid-fuel cookers and domestic water heat-

[26] For the Grooms and Ben. Talbot see J. H. Lenton, *Methodism in Wellington, 1765–1982* (Wellington, 1982), 15–16. For Patchett see *The Hadley Bk.* 116, 118.
[27] I. Gregory, 'E. Salop. Coalfield and the "Gt. Depression" 1873–96' (Keele Univ. M.A. thesis, 1978), 101–2.
[28] *The Hadley Bk.* 40, 132.
[29] *Shropshire Star*, 19 Mar. 1974.   [30] S.R.O. 1265/243.
[31] S.C.C. *Illustr. Official Handbk.* (1890), unpaginated (copy in S.R.O.); W. Mate & Sons Ltd. *Shropshire: Historical, Descriptive, Biographical* (1906), pt. 2, p. 192.
[32] *P.O. Dir. Salop.* (1870), 158.
[33] *Kelly's Dir. Salop.* (1934), 111.
[34] New Centurion Publishing & Publicity Co. Ltd. *Wellington Official Guide, 1950–1*, 38.
[35] Madin, *Dawley Rep. No. 2: Interim Proposals*, cap. 6, sect. 1, app.   [36] *Shropshire Star*, 19 Mar. 1974.
[37] J. Randall, *Randall's Tom Moody Almanack* (1879), special edn. 11–12 (copy in S.P.L.).
[38] Gregory, 'E. Salop. Coalfield', 101.
[39] *The Hadley Bk.* 40.
[40] K. C. Riley, 'Changes in Population in the Wellington–Oakengates Conurbation 1801–1951' (London Univ. M.A. thesis, 1958), 163.
[41] *P.O. Telephone Dir.* (1972), sect. 303, p. 240.
[42] *Express & Star*, 30 May 1962.
[43] County Assocs. Ltd. *Wellington & Dist. Dir.* [1950], 2.
[44] Madin, *Dawley Rep. No. 2: Interim Proposals*, cap. 6, sect. 1, app.

[45] Burrow, *Wellington R.D. Official Guide* [1967], 3, 27.
[46] P.O. *Telephone Dir.* (1973), sect. 303, p. 192; T.D.C. *Telford Ind. Dir.* (1982), 39.
[47] P.O. *Telephone Dir.* (1980), sect. 303 (Alpha), p. 399.
[48] O.S. Map 1/2,500, Salop. XXXVI. 10 (1882 edn.). The 'castle' was the nearby derelict windmill: T.D.C. *Hadley Pk. Windmill*.
[49] Gregory, 'E. Salop. Coalfield', 20.
[50] *V.C.H. Staffs.* xvii. 112–13.
[51] *Randall's Tom Moody Almanack* (1879), special edn. 11.
[52] Gregory, 'E. Salop. Coalfield', 52–5.
[53] J. H. Price, 'Story of G. F. Milnes', pt. 4, *Modern Tramway*, Oct. 1964, 354; above, plate 11.
[54] *V.C.H. Salop.* i. 477.
[55] Price, op. cit. pt. 5, *Modern Tramway*, Nov. 1964, 372.
[56] Ibid. pt. 6, *Modern Tramway*, Dec. 1964, 431–6.
[57] G.P.O. *Telephone Dir.* (1968), sect. 72, p. 2204.
[58] *Shrews. Chron.* 4 Nov. 1960, suppl.
[59] Riley, 'Population in Wellington–Oakengates', 179.
[60] *Shrews. Chron.* 4 Nov. 1960, suppl.
[61] *Shropshire Star*, 17 Sept. 1971; 12 July 1975.
[62] Ibid. 5 Feb. 1981.
[63] *Birmingham Post*, 16 May 1980.
[64] *Telford Jnl.* 27 Nov. 1981.
[65] Inf. from Mr. J. Bernstein, managing director, Glynwed Foundries Ltd., above, Wellington, Econ. Hist.
[66] Riley, 'Population in Wellington–Oakengates', 181.
[67] G.P.O. *Telephone Dir.* (1960), sect. 72, p. 2016.

ers. In 1962 Allied Ironfounders Ltd. turned the factory into its Aga Works, to make motor-vehicle and other small castings as well as domestic appliances. There were 231 employees in 1964.[68] The company's Shropshire concerns became part of Glynwed Foundries Ltd. in 1969. In 1975 the foundry closed[69] but the works continued as the Aga–Rayburn division of Glynwed Appliances Ltd.[70]

LOCAL GOVERNMENT AND PUBLIC SERVICES. No records of Hadley court baron are known. In 1255 Hadley did suit to the sheriff's tourn in Bradford hundred but not to the small hundred courts.[71] In the 1590s Hadley was in the hundred's leet jurisdiction.[72] A separate view of frankpledge for Hadley was mentioned in 1667.[73] At least part of Horton, including Horton's wood[74] and apparently the Hoo,[75] was subject to Eyton upon the Weald Moors court baron by 1359[76] and remained so in the early 17th century.[77] By 1478 Horton was usually in the leet jurisdiction of Hinstock and so remained in 1851, though in 1506 Horton presented at a court leet held, unusually, for Eyton. Shooting butts were ordered to be provided at Horton in 1506. There were stocks in 1542 and a pound in 1606. Horton had a constable by 1506 and one was still being sworn at Hinstock in 1851.[78]

Hadley township and the part of Horton in Wellington parish were in Wellington civil parish until 1894, Wellington poor-law union 1836–1930, Wrekin highway district 1865–82, and Wellington rural sanitary district 1872–94. In 1894 Hadley and Horton became part of Wellington Rural C.P. and Wellington rural district. In 1898 the north-eastern part of Wellington Rural C.P., including Horton and most of Hadley (the part north of the Wellington–Wolverhampton railway), became Hadley C.P., Hadley township south of the railway remaining in Wellington Rural C.P. (renamed Ketley C.P. in 1976)[79] with only a minor boundary adjustment with Hadley

C.P. in 1934. Also in 1934 a small area of Horton, at Trench, was transferred from Hadley C.P. and Wellington R.D. to Oakengates C.P. and urban district.[80] Outside Hadley and Horton townships Hadley C.P. lost areas to the C.P.s of Wellington Urban in 1903[81] and 1934[82] and Eyton upon the Weald Moors in 1905[83] and 1934; it gained only very small areas of Wellington Rural and Urban C.P.s in 1934.[84] In 1974 Oakengates U.D. and Wellington R.D. were abolished, their areas becoming part of the district of the Wrekin.[85] In 1968 Horton township and all but the extreme north end of Hadley township were included in the designated area of Telford new town.[86]

Hadley township was served by wells until c. 1897 when Wellington U.D.C. extended a main along Watling Street to Beveley. Only houses on the main road benefited[87] and the council laid no main to Hadley village until 1905.[88] In 1884 Wellington rural sanitary authority laid a sewer northwards from Hadley village to an outfall on pasture land. The system was extended[89] but in 1911 Wellington R.D.C. replaced it[90] and opened a sewage farm north of the village and, at about the same time, another in Horton township, north of Trench.[91] The former was enlarged in 1938 to take sewage from the new Ketley system.[92] The Horton works closed in the 1950s.[93] Later the Hadley and Ketley combined works were superseded by the Rushmoor works (in Wrockwardine), opened 1975.[94] Hadley parish council opened a cemetery off Hadley Park Road in 1903.[95] A health centre opened in Hadley centre c. 1982.

Gas was probably introduced to Hadley when the Hadley & Trench Gas Works (in Wombridge) opened, before 1882.[96] A police constable of the Wellington division was stationed at Hadley from 1840.[97] A sub-post office opened in the 1870s.[98]

CHURCHES. In the 14th century Hadley manor house had a private chapel. William the chaplain of Hadley was mentioned in 1349.[99] In 1377 Sir

[68] Madin, *Dawley Rep. No. 2: Interim Proposals*, cap. 6, sect. 1, app.

[69] Inf. from Mr. Bernstein.

[70] T.D.C. *Telford Ind. Dir.* (1982), 27.

[71] *Rot. Hund.* (Rec. Com.), ii. 57.

[72] P.R.O., SC 2/197/96; Staffs. R.O., D. 593/J/10, ct. r. of 1592.

[73] P.R.O., CP 25(2)/713/19 Chas. II Mich. [no. 10].

[74] An offence 'in bosco de Horton' was dealt with at Eyton in 1362: S.R.O. 513, box 1, ct. r.

[75] In 1499 Lubstree moor, in Eyton parish and Horton lordship (S.P.L., Deeds 18633), presumably lay near the Lilleshall–Wrockwardine rd. (above, Lilleshall, Communications) and therefore at the Hoo, whose N. tip touched the rd. (L.J.R.O., B/A/15, Hortons Wood).

[76] S.R.O. 513, box 1, ct. r.

[77] Ibid. ct. r. of 1362, 1422, 1587; 665/1/256.

[78] S.R.O. 327, boxes 4–5, ct. r.; 513, box 1, ct. r. of 1506.

[79] Above, Wellington, intro.; Local Govt.

[80] *Salop Review Order, 1934* (Min. of Health order no. 77933); O.S. Map 6″, SJ 61 SE. (1954 edn.).

[81] *32nd Ann. Rep. Local Govt. Bd.* [Cd. 1700], p. 341, H.C. (1903), xxiv; O.S. Map 6″, Salop. XXXVI. SW. (1929 edn.).

[82] *Salop. Review Order, 1934*; O.S. Maps 6″, SJ 61 SE., SW. (1954 edn.).

[83] *35th Ann. Rep. Local Govt. Bd.* [Cd. 3105], p. 44, H.C.

[84] *Salop Review Order, 1934*; O.S. Maps 6″, Salop. XXX. SW. (1928 edn.); XXXVI. NW. (1929 edn.).

[85] *Census, 1971, Rep. for Co. of Salop as constituted on 1st Apr. 1974*, 2.

[86] *Dawley New Town (Designation) Amendment (Telford) Order 1968* (Stat. Instr. 1968, no. 1912), map accompanying Explanatory Note.

[87] S.C.C. *Mins.* 1897–8, 589; 31 Jan. 1903, 89, 93–4.

[88] S.C.C. *Mins.* Suppl. Rep. on Water Supplies of Pars. of Wellington Rural and Hadley, 28 June 1912, 5.

[89] S.C.C. *Mins.* Sanitary Cttee. rep. 31 Jan. 1903, 89; S.R.O., DA 26/743/2.

[90] S.C.C. *Rep. by Co. M.O.H. 1911*, 124 (copy in S.R.O.).

[91] O.S. Map 1/2,500, Salop. XXXVI. 6 (1926 edn.); S.R.O. 2079/XXXVI. 6.

[92] S.R.O., DA 26/743/4, memo. 25 Jan. 1949.

[93] Ibid. surveyor of R.D.C. to A. H. S. Waters, 9 May 1952; O.S. Map 6″, SJ 61 SE. (1966 edn.).

[94] *Telford Jnl.* 7 Aug. 1975.

[95] Lich. Dioc. Regy., bps.' reg. U, pp. 583–7.

[96] Above, Wellington, Public Services; below, Wombridge, Public Services.

[97] S.R.O., q. sess. Const. Cttee. rep. bk. 1839–53, p. 76.

[98] *P.O. Dir. Salop.* (1879), 327.

[99] S.R.O. 513, box 1, ct. r.

Robert Corbet leased ½ virgate and a mill in Hadley for 99 years to the prior of Wombridge, and in return one of the canons or a chaplain celebrated divine service for his and his family's souls on Sundays, Wednesdays, and Fridays in the chapel within the manor house gates.[1]

In 1856 a chapel of ease was completed and consecrated on a site at Hadley given by Miss Ellen Thorneycroft. The cost was met by £355 in voluntary contributions and £725 in grants. The patronage was vested in the bishop, the archdeacon, the vicars of Wellington and Wrockwardine, and the rector of Kynnersley,[2] and remained with them in 1981.[3] The chapel was licensed for baptisms and burials in 1856 and for marriages in 1858.[4] In 1858 a district chapelry was assigned[5] comprising Horton township, most of Hadley township, and a small part of Arleston township.[6] The curate[7] became a titular vicar in 1868.[8] The cure was served by a priest-in-charge 1975–80 and was thereafter a vicarage.[9]

In 1856 the vicar of Wellington assigned the incumbent £10 a year from vicarial tithe rent charge. Pew rents were also assigned,[10] worth £30 a year in 1884.[11] In 1857 the living was endowed with £700 mainly from subscribers.[12] It was augmented by £10 a year in 1861,[13] and in 1863 was endowed with £500 to match a benefaction of £500.[14] In 1864 St. John Chiverton Charlton assigned the incumbent £20 a year in perpetuity from Wellington rectorial tithe rent charge.[15] The curate's net income was put at £102 in 1865.[16] In 1874 the Ecclesiastical Commissioners assigned annual tithe rent charge of £225 gross[17] out of the former endowment of Wellington prebend[18] and in 1919 endowed the living with a further £300 to meet a benefaction of £300.[19] The vicar's net income in 1932 was £350.[20]

The vicarage house, built c. 1857,[21] stood east of the church.[22] From 1975, however, the incumbent lived in Manor Road.[23]

James Barton was incumbent 1858–94,[24] the only other long incumbency being that of H. J. Moreton, 1941–74,[25] who held Preston upon the Weald Moors in plurality from 1947.[26] W. B. MacNab, vicar 1903–17, and Arthur Peters, 1917–28[27] held high-church beliefs[28] and the same tradition was favoured in 1982.

The church of the *HOLY TRINITY*[29] was designed by T. E. Owen[30] in the Gothic style. It is of red and yellow brick with Grinshill stone dressings and consists of a chancel with south organ chamber (added c. 1904 in place of an original clergy vestry)[31] and nave with north-west bell turret and south porch (added after 1903).[32] In 1915 there was one bell.[33] In 1981 a brick 'parochial centre' was added at the west.[34]

A chapel was built at Hadley cemetery,[35] opened 1903.[36]

NONCONFORMITY. John Nott, ejected vicar of Sheriffhales and almost certainly a Presbyterian,[37] was said to have preached for three or four years in a chapel near 'Hadly' in the 1660s[38] but it is not certain that Hadley in Wellington parish was meant. Between 1715 and 1729 there was a monthly Presbyterian lecture at Horton, usually given by a Mr. Seddon of Newport,[39] but no Presbyterians were reported in 1772.[40]

The most numerous nonconformists in Hadley were the Methodists. In 1813 and 1823 there was regular Wesleyan preaching in Ketley and New Hadley, and in 1823 at Ragfield and Hadley village.[41] Ketley Wesleyan chapel was built in 1832[42] in Hadley township, on Watling Street (later Station Road) c. 100 metres west of the junction with Waterloo Road.[43] In 1851 there were 226 seats, which were nearly all filled morning and evening.[44] The chapel, rebuilt in brick c. 1883[45] to the design of Herbert Isitt,[46] closed c. 1961[47] and was demolished for road widening,[48] being one of three small Methodist chapels close together that were sold so that a new church could

[1] *T.S.A.S.* 2nd ser. x. 190–1.
[2] Lich. Dioc. Regy., bps.' reg. P, pp. 523–7.
[3] *Lich. Dioc. Dir.* (1981), 62.
[4] E. C. Peele and R. S. Clease, *Salop. Par. Doc.* (Shrews. [1903]), 175.
[5] *Lond. Gaz.* 4 Feb. 1858, pp. 547–8.
[6] S.R.O. 1149/1.
[7] Lich. Dioc. Regy., episc. reg. 32, p. 152.
[8] *P.O. Dir. Salop.* (1870), 156.
[9] Lich. Dioc. Regy., benefice and inst. bk. 1968– (in use), p. 57; *Lich. Dioc. Dir.* (1980), 55; (1981), 62.
[10] Lich. Dioc. Regy., bps.' reg. P, pp. 524, 526.
[11] S.R.O. 3916/1/33, s.v.
[12] With £200 from the Dioc. Soc. and £100 from Q. Anne's Bounty: C. Hodgson, *Q. Anne's Bounty* (2nd edn.), suppl. pp. xxxviii, lxvii.
[13] *Lond. Gaz.* 15 Oct. 1861, p. 4067.
[14] Ibid. 12 June 1863, p. 3023.
[15] Lich. Dioc. Regy., bps.' reg. R, p. 623; S.R.O. 4510/Ben/10.
[16] *Clergy List* (1865), benefice list, 241.
[17] Lich. Dioc. Regy., bps.' reg. R, p. 703.
[18] Above, Wellington, Man. and Other Est.
[19] S.R.O. 4510/Ben/55.
[20] *Crockford* (1932), 437.
[21] S.R.O. 4510/Ben/5.
[22] O.S. Map 1/2,500, Salop. XXXVI. 10 (1882 edn.).
[23] *Lich. Dioc. Dir.* (1974), 30; (1976), 16.
[24] Lich. Dioc. Regy., episc. reg. 32, p. 152; benefice and inst. bk. 1868–1900, p. 98.

[25] Ibid. benefice and inst. bk. 1929–52, p. 82; *Crockford* (1975–6), 681.
[26] Lich. Dioc. Regy., benefice and inst. bk. 1929–52, p. 122.
[27] Ibid. 1900–29, pp. 9, 51, 112.
[28] *The Hadley Bk.* 113.
[29] So dedicated in 1856: Lich. Dioc. Regy., bps.' reg. P, p. 527.
[30] H. Colvin, *Biog. Dict. Brit. Architects, 1600–1840* (1978), 604.
[31] S.R.O. 4510/ChF/25; /V/2, 6 Apr. 1904.
[32] Ibid. /V/2, 15 Apr. 1903.
[33] H. B. Walters, *Ch. Bells of Salop.* (Oswestry, 1915), 329.
[34] Inf. from the vicar.
[35] *Kelly's Dir. Salop.* (1909), 104.
[36] Above, Local Govt. and Public Services.
[37] *V.C.H. Oxon.* vii. 212.
[38] *Calamy Revised*, ed. A. G. Matthews, 368.
[39] Dr. Williams's Libr., Evans MS. (344), f. 97.
[40] L.J.R.O., B/V/5, Wellington visit. return.
[41] S.P.L., C 98.7 v.f., Shrews. circuit plan; L 98.7 v.f., Wellington circuit plan.
[42] S.R.O. 3763/XVII/E2, sched. of 1881.
[43] S.R.O. 14, tithe appt. and map.
[44] P.R.O., HO 129/365, no. 25.
[45] G.R.O., Worship Reg. no. 27201.
[46] Lenton, *Methodism in Wellington*, 17.
[47] Local inf. (recorded in S.M.R.); S.R.O. 3767/X/M, 8 Mar. 1963.
[48] S.R.O. 3767/X/M, 5 Nov. 1963; 16 Jan. 1964.

be built with the proceeds.[49] The new church opened in 1966[50] on the corner of Station Road and Waterloo Road.

In Hadley village a former Baptist schoolroom in High Street occupied by George Jones,[51] a Wesleyan local preacher,[52] was licensed for worship in 1840.[53] On Census Sunday 1851 there were 14 attendances in the afternoon and 25 in the evening.[54] Jones, leader of a reform movement within Wellington Wesleyan circuit, broke with the circuit[55] and ceased to lead the Hadley society c. 1852.[56] In 1866[57] the building was replaced nearby by a large brick chapel designed by G. Bidlake.[58] The new chapel had 280 seats in 1881.[59] It was greatly enlarged in 1890[60] and had 342 seats in 1940 as well as incorporating a Sunday school and other rooms.[61] It remained in use in 1981, but part of the building was occupied by Telford development corporation as an information bureau.

The secession of a reform group from the Wellington Wesleyan circuit in the 1850s led to the building of three chapels in Hadley and Horton townships, eventually joined to the United Methodist Free Churches. A small plain brick chapel called Mount Zion, Ketley, was opened by Wesleyan Reformers in 1853 on Watling Street near Pottersbank.[62] One of the United Methodist Free Churches by 1860,[63] it closed c. 1966[64] when the new Ketley Methodist church opened nearby. A Wesleyan society at Horton, formed by 1840, left the connexion in 1852,[65] and in 1858[66] built a small brick United Methodist Free chapel;[67] it closed in 1966.[68] A United Methodist Free Churches meeting existed at New Hadley in 1859[69] and Zion was built for it in 1868[70] north of Hadley Lane[71] (later Hadley Road). It was rebuilt in 1932[72] on the south side of the road with bricks provided by Blockleys Ltd., who acquired the old site for clay extraction.[73] It remained open in 1981.

There was regular Primitive Methodist

preaching at Hadley in 1838 but it ceased later that year. It was renewed in 1840,[74] and in 1841 a small chapel was built[75] at the east end of High Street. On Census Sunday 1851 there were 69 attendances in the afternoon and 97 in the evening.[76] The chapel was rebuilt in brick on a large scale in 1879[77] but by 1910 was poorly attended and seriously in debt.[78] In 1927 it was reported unsafe[79] and from 1928 services were held in the adjoining schoolroom.[80] The society, with only 9 members,[81] expired in 1933[82] and the chapel was sold.[83]

Beveley had Primitive preaching intermittently by 1837,[84] and in 1871 a small brick chapel was built[85] on Watling Street. It was closed and sold c. 1958 and the congregation moved to Mount Zion, Ketley, the former United Methodist chapel.[86]

A preaching place near the Ketley ironworks in 1839 and 1849[87] may have been the Primitive meeting in Hadley township with average attendances of 50 at its Sunday services in 1851[88] and was perhaps the 'Wesleyan' chapel 'fronting the iron forge' in 1854.[89]

A small plain brick Primitive chapel was built in 1878[90] on the west side of the Hadley–Shawbirch road (later Hadley Park Road) and remained in use in 1981.

Other Primitive efforts were made in the mid 19th century. There was a society at Horton in the 1840s.[91] It had 30 evening attendances on Census Sunday 1851.[92] Regular preaching at Pottersbank, recorded in 1841, ceased in 1845 on the opening of Oakengates chapel.[93] A society was meeting in New Hadley in 1844[94] and 1865.[95]

New Hadley had regular New Connexion preaching in 1839[96] and a meeting existed there briefly in 1853.[97]

In 1816 the house of George Dean, a Particular Baptist, was licensed for worship at Hadley.[98] In 1841 his house lay on the south side of High Street and meetings were probably still being held

[49] Ibid. 8 Mar. 1963; below, Ketley, Nonconf.
[50] S.R.O. 3767/XVIII/A. The date stone reads 1965.
[51] S.R.O. 14, tithe appt. and map (no. 604).
[52] O. A. Beckerlegge, *United Meth. Ministers and their Circuits* (1968), 131.
[53] *Orders of Q. Sess.* iv. 9.
[54] P.R.O., HO 129/365, no. 23.
[55] J. Lenton, 'The Snedshill affair, 1851–2', Wesley Hist. Soc., Salop. Branch, *Bulletin*, i (10), [2] (copy in S.R.O. 3543/11).
[56] S.R.O. 3767/XVII/E1.
[57] S.R.O. 3767/V/B, 16 Nov. 1866.
[58] Ibid. 13 June 1867.
[59] S.R.O. 3767/XVII/E2, sched.
[60] O.S. Map 6", Salop. XXXVI. SW. (1887 and 1903 edns.); *The Hadley Bk.* 114.
[61] *Meth. Church Bldgs.: Statistical Returns* (1940), 270.
[62] Trinder, *Ind. Rev. Salop.* 296; *Eddowes's Jnl.* 16 Feb. 1853. The date stone reads 1852.
[63] G.R.O., Worship Reg. no. 9314.
[64] S.R.O. 3767/VIII/I, [Revd. P. H. W. de Visme] to Revd. H. Simpson, 2 Apr. 1966.
[65] S.R.O. 3767/XVII/A, E1.
[66] Date stone.
[67] S.R.O. 1101, box 261A, agreement.
[68] S.R.O. 3767/XXII/G, [Revd. R. Hallam] to [Revd. H.] Simpson, 13 May 1972.
[69] Circuit plan in possession of Mr. J. H. Lenton.
[70] Date stone (on new chapel).
[71] O.S. Map 6", Salop. XXXVI. SW. (1887 edn.).
[72] Date stone.

[73] Inf. from Mr. Lenton.
[74] S.R.O. 3605/1, pp. 11, 15, 37.
[75] Ibid. pp. 66, 79–80.
[76] P.R.O., HO 129/365, no. 26.
[77] S.R.O. 3767/II/L, sched. of 1918.
[78] S.R.O. 3916/1/34, s.v. Hadley.
[79] S.R.O. 3767/II/E, 8 Nov. 1927.
[80] Ibid. /II/G2, 3 Sept. 1928.
[81] Ibid. 6 Mar. 1933.
[82] S.R.O. 3767/II/H.
[83] Ibid. /II/G2, 9 Oct. 1933.
[84] S.R.O. 3605/1, pp. 7, 11, 27, 58.
[85] S.R.O. 3038/1/1, 12 June, 18 Sept. 1871.
[86] S.R.O. 3767/XVIII/A, [Revd. P. H. W. de Visme] to Meth. Dept. for Chapel Affairs, 12 May 1965.
[87] S.R.O. 1861/5, p. 3; 3605/1, p. 27.
[88] P.R.O., HO 129/365, no. 24 (signed by a resident of Forge Row, Ketley).
[89] G.R.O., Worship Reg. no. 4829.
[90] Date stone.
[91] S.R.O. 1861/5, p. 3; 3605/1, p. 38.
[92] P.R.O., HO 129/365, no. 45.
[93] S.R.O. 3605/1, pp. 58, 154.
[94] Ibid. p. 123.
[95] S.R.O. 1861/15, p. 2.
[96] S.R.O. 3677/1.
[97] B. Trinder, *Meth. New Connexion in Dawley and Madeley* (Wesley Hist. Soc., W. Midlands Branch, Occ. Publ. i [1968]), 13.
[98] P.R.O., RG 31/7, Salop. no. 255; *Orders of Q. Sess.* iii. 156, 200.

there.[99] It was afterwards greatly enlarged at the rear,[1] probably soon after 1840, and in 1851 the Baptist meeting room, presumably the extension to Dean's house, was a building used exclusively for worship. It had 139 sittings and on Census Sunday there were 25 attendances in the afternoon and 45 in the evening.[2] By 1861, however, worship seems to have ceased.[3]

In 1828 Thomas Robinson's house on Watling Street, nearly opposite the later School Lane, was licensed for worship,[4] presumably of Congregationalists; by 1840 Robinson had let it to trustees as an Independent chapel.[5] It evidently closed soon after.[6]

From c. 1967 there was an Elim Pentecostal church at Brookdale[7] (with Sunday meetings in a wooden hut in 1981) and a New Testament Church of God[8] in the former Mount Zion United Methodist chapel.

SIKHS. Guru Nanak temple opened c. 1974[9] in the former Hadley County Junior School, Station Road.

EDUCATION. The Revd. Robert Roe[10] was keeping a school in Hadley manor house in the 1690s,[11] and between 1840, or earlier, and 1851 George Jones was keeping one in a former Baptist schoolroom at Hadley.[12] Mrs. Ann Jones kept a school c. 1870; it may have been the Hadley United School whose expansion was agreed upon by Anglicans and Wesleyans intent on preventing the formation of a school board;[13] the venture, however, seems to have been unsuccessful or brief[14] and Hadley was included in the area of the Wellington board in 1872.[15]

Hadley Board Schools, Station Road, were opened in 1874 with 232 places in mixed and infant departments; there was also a master's house. It was the first purpose-built board school

in Shropshire.[16] A girls' department was opened in 1876.[17] Enlargement in 1884 produced places for 230 boys, 220 girls, and 210 infants;[18] a gymnasium was built in 1885.[19] Average attendance rose from 244 in 1885 to 650 in 1913.[20] Annual reports during the period were consistently good despite irregular attendance,[21] poverty and inability to pay fees during times of industrial depression,[22] and long closures during epidemics.[23] From 1875 the drawing reports for the boys' school were exceptionally good[24] and in the 1880s pupils were taking examinations in machine construction and physics.[25]

Reorganization for secondary education, considered in 1937,[26] was delayed for over twenty years. In 1936 and 1937, however, cookery and woodwork centres were built for senior pupils from Hadley and neighbouring schools.[27] The railway close by caused dirt and noise interrupting work.[28] Overcrowding in the 1940s[29] was relieved in 1951 when the infants transferred to a new school in Crescent Road.[30] Hadley County Boys' and Girls' schools, each with junior and senior pupils, continued until 1958 when the seniors transferred to a new secondary modern school in Crescent Road. The school reopened as Hadley County Junior School with 285 boys and girls.[31] In 1973 staff and pupils transferred to a replacement school in Crescent Road.[32]

Hadley County Infant School, Crescent Road, opened in 1951.[33] In 1970 the first purpose-built nursery unit to be attached to a Shropshire infant school was built under the government's urban aid programme, mainly because a quarter of the children were Asian or West Indian.[34] In 1982 there were 130 pupils.[35]

Hadley Secondary Modern School, Crescent Road, with 450 places,[36] opened in 1958[37] to serve Hadley and Ketley. It was long overdue: the county council had accepted tenders for its erection in 1939.[38] It had been considerably extended by 1974 when, as the Manor School, it became a

[99] S.R.O. 14, tithe appt. and map (no. 602). No Baptist chapel was recorded.
[1] O.S. Map 1/2,500, Salop. XXXVI. 10 (1882 edn.).
[2] P.R.O., HO 129/365, no. 22.
[3] Baptist Handbk. 1861, 72 (nil).
[4] Lich. Dioc. Regy., bps.' reg. H, p. 61.
[5] S.R.O. 14, tithe appt. and map (no. 497).
[6] Not recorded in P.R.O., HO 129, or S. Bagshaw, Dir. Salop (1851).
[7] G.R.O., Worship Reg. no. 70974.
[8] Ibid. no. 71180.
[9] S.C.C. chars. index.
[10] Above, Man. and Other Est.
[11] S. Garbet, Hist. Wem (Wem, 1818), 200; Alum. Cantab. to 1751, ii. 393. A Rob. Roe had a sch. in Wellington par. in 1682: L.J.R.O., B/V/1/84.
[12] Orders of Q. Sess. iv. 9; S. Bagshaw, Dir. Salop. (1851), 437; above, Nonconf.
[13] P.O. Dir. Salop. (1870), 160; E. Cassey & Co. Dir. Salop. (1874), 373; T. D. M. Jones, 'Development of Educ. Provision in the Rural Co. of Salop. betw. 1870 and 1914' (Keele Univ. M.A. (Educ.) thesis, 1969), 6.
[14] Sch. not incl. in sch. bd.'s 1873 survey: Wellington Jnl. 12 July 1873.
[15] Above, Wellington, Educ.
[16] Kelly's Dir. Salop. (1885), 857.
[17] Hadley Mixed Bd. Sch. log bk. (at Hadley Co. Jnr. Sch.) 12 July 1876.
[18] Kelly's Dir. Salop. (1891), 324.

[19] Hadley Boys' Bd. Sch. log bk. (at Hadley Co. Jnr. Sch.) 17 Apr. 1885.
[20] Kelly's Dir. Salop. (1885, 1891, 1909, 1913).
[21] Log bks. of Hadley Mixed, Hadley Boys', Hadley Girls' (at Hadley Co. Jnr. Sch.), and Hadley Inf. (at Hadley Co. Inf. Sch.) bd. schs.
[22] Hadley Inf. Bd. Sch. log bk. 19 Oct., 16 Nov. 1877; 29 Mar. 1878; rep. 1886 and later. Cf. similar entries in log bks. of Hadley Boys' and Girls' bd. schs.
[23] e.g. Hadley Inf. Bd. Sch. log bk. esp. 1894–6; cf. similar entries in log bks. of other depts.
[24] Hadley Mixed Bd. Sch. log bk. ann. drawing reps. 1875, 1876; Hadley Boys' Bd. Sch. log bk. reps. 1877–1900.
[25] e.g. Hadley Boys' Bd. Sch. log bk. 6 and 17 May, 24 June 1882.
[26] Hadley Council Boys' Sch. log bk. 3 June 1937; S.C.C. Mins. (Educ.) 1937–8, 54, 91.
[27] Hadley Council Girls' Sch. log bk. 13 Jan. 1936; Boys' Sch. log bk. 24 May 1937.
[28] e.g. Boys' Sch. log bk. reps. 1911, 1923, 1952.
[29] Co. Inf. Sch. log bk. rep. 1949.
[30] Ibid. 3 Sept. 1951; Co. Boys' Sch. log bk. rep. 1952.
[31] Hadley Co. Girls' Sch. log bk. 25 July, 2 Sept. 1958.
[32] Inf. from the headmaster.   [33] Log bk. 3 Sept. 1951.
[34] Ibid. 13 Apr., 19 May 1970.
[35] S.C.C. Educ. Cttee. Educ. Dir. (1982), 10.
[36] Inf. from S.C.C. Educ. Dept.
[37] Hadley Co. Girls' Sch. log bk. 25 July 1958.
[38] S.C.C. Mins. (Educ.) 1937–8, 54; 1939–40, 18.

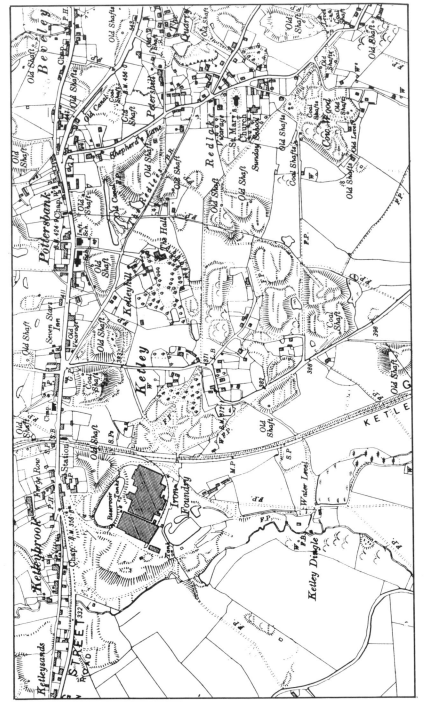

KETLEY AND REDLAKE c. 1925 (scale 6 in. to 1 mile)

266

comprehensive school for pupils aged 11–16.[39] In 1982 there were 833 pupils.[40]

Hadley County Junior School, Crescent Road, opened in 1973 and pupils and staff transferred there from the old board school in Station Road. In 1982 there were 294 pupils, many of them Asian or West Indian.[41]

Leegomery County Primary School, Grainger Drive, opened, at first for juniors only, in 1978 on the new Leegomery housing estate; infants were admitted in 1979. There were 241 pupils in 1982.[42]

Leegomery County Infant School, Grainger Drive, opened in 1982 with 142 pupils.[43]

CHARITY FOR THE POOR. In addition to those charities applicable to the whole of Wellington ancient parish, Hadley ecclesiastical parish benefited from John Millington's legacy (will proved 1875) of £30 stock for annual doles of cash to six widows being regular worshippers at Holy Trinity church.[44] The income in 1975 was £1.[45]

KETLEY

KETLEY township, south-east of Wellington town, had roughly the shape of an equilateral triangle, its apex to the south. A small part on the east lay in Wombridge ancient parish;[46] it was perhaps the part of Ketley wood where Thomas Tuchet granted perpetual quarrying rights to Wombridge priory c. 1269.[47] Much the greater part of Ketley township lay in Wellington ancient parish and forms the subject of the present article. Ketley, including the Wombridge part, was accounted a member of Leegomery manor[48] and was wholly owned by the marquess of Stafford in 1813.[49] The Ketley estate of his descendant, the 4th duke of Sutherland, was broken up and sold in 1894.[50]

The Wellington part of Ketley was reckoned to be 775 a. (314 ha.) in 1841.[51] Its northern boundary was Watling Street, its western Ketley brook and a tributary of that brook from the south-east. The eastern boundary (i.e. that of Wellington parish) ascended Hadley brook immediately south from Watling Street; thereafter it took a line southwards, turning several angles (to divide the Wellington and Wombridge parts of the township) and in part following Shrubbery Road, and reached the brook that marked Dawley's northern boundary. Thence it continued up that brook towards the south end of the township.[52] Ketley was included in Wellington Rural civil parish in 1894.[53]

The drift cover is mostly boulder clay except near Redlake and on the township's western edge, where sands and gravels predominate. Much of the township was underlain by workable coals of the Middle and Lower Coal Measures.[54] The land slopes down from south-east to north-west; the township's southern limit is at c. 195 metres above O.D., its north-western at c. 105 metres. Most of the township drains north-westwards into Ketley brook but the eastern edge drains eastwards into the boundary brook.[55]

Ketley and other parts of the coalfield had the custom of 'heaving' (groups lifting individuals of the opposite sex into the air) on Easter Monday and Tuesday, but it was in decline by the 1880s.[56]

The Roman Watling Street was turnpiked in 1726.[57] By the late 18th century many minor roads linked the scattered settlements.[58] A new section of the Holyhead–London road was built c. 1817 from Pottersbank on Watling Street to Snedshill (in Shifnal).[59]

The Ketley Canal, completed in 1788, brought coal and ironstone across the township to Ketley ironworks from Oakengates, where it later joined the Shropshire Canal.[60] The Ketley Canal may have been fed by the 'Derbyshire' underground drainage level dug from Old Park (in Dawley) to Ketley.[61] The canal included the first successful canal inclined plane in Britain, devised by William Reynolds[62] and situated immediately south-west of Ketley Hall.[63] The canal also took coal and iron via the Shropshire Canal to Horsehay and Coalbrookdale and brought in limestone from Lincoln Hill (in Madeley) and Buildwas.[64] The incline, however, was disused by 1818, probably because of the ironworks' recent closure.[65] East of the incline lay a coal wharf, which the canal apparently still served from Oakengates in 1842.[66]

[39] Ibid. 1972–3, 146, 271–2; 1974–5, 254; S.C.C. Educ. Cttee. Sch. List (1974), 2.
[40] Educ. Dir. (1982), 3.
[41] Ibid. 9; inf. from the headmaster; cf. Educ. Dir. (1980), 10.
[42] Sch. List (1977), 10; (1978), 10; Educ. Dir. (1982), 10.
[43] Educ. Dir. (1982), 10.
[44] S.R.O. 3916/1/33.
[45] Review of Local Chars. (S.C.C. 1975), 65.
[46] S.R.O. 972, parcel 245, map of 1794; S.R.O. 14, tithe map. Its hist. is treated below, Wombridge.
[47] Eyton, vii. 345.
[48] Ibid. 346; L. & P. Hen. VIII, iv (2), p. 2118; above, Wellington, Man. and Other Est.; Wellington, Local Govt.; below, Local Govt. and Public Services.
[49] S.R.O. 972, parcel 238, map.
[50] Ibid. parcel 187, sale partic.
[51] S.R.O. 14, tithe appt.
[52] Ibid. tithe map; 972, parcel 245, map of 1794.

[53] Changes are treated below, Local Govt. and Public Services.
[54] Inst. Geol. Sciences Map 1/25,000, Telford (1978 edn.).
[55] O.S. Maps 6", Salop. XXXVI. SW. (1929 edn.); XLIII. NW. (1928 edn.).
[56] C. S. Burne, Salop. Folk Lore (1883), 340.
[57] Above, Wellington, Communications.
[58] S.R.O. 972, parcel 245, map of 1794.
[59] Above, Wellington, Communications.
[60] C. Hadfield, Canals of W. Midlands (1969), 151–2.
[61] J. Prestwich, 'On the Geology of Coalbrook Dale', Trans. Geol. Soc. London, 2nd ser. v. 450 and n.
[62] Hadfield, op. cit. 151–2.
[63] S.R.O. 972, parcel 245, map of 1794; R. Russell, Lost Canals of Eng. and Wales (1971), 144.
[64] Trinder, Ind. Rev. Salop. (1981), 81, 83.
[65] Hadfield, Canals of W. Midlands, 152.
[66] C. & J. Greenwood, Map of Salop. (1827); S.R.O. 14, tithe appt. and map (no. 836); Trinder, op. cit. 138.

By the 1880s, however, that surviving length had been abandoned.[67]

The earliest part of the Wellington & Severn Junction railway, opened 1857,[68] passed through the township with a station at Ketley. In order to meet competition from buses[69] New Dale halt (in Ketley township) opened in 1934 and Ketley Town halt in 1936. In 1962 the halts closed and Ketley station closed to passengers; the station closed entirely in 1964.[71]

Ketley had 14 taxpayers in 1327[72] but only 3 'able' men 1542, fewer than Aston, Lawley, or Walcot.[73] There was growth before 1672, probably associated with inclosure of wastes and with mining;[74] 12 households then paid hearth tax.[75] Ketley town and Coalpit Bank (mostly in Wombridge parish) were apparently the only nucleated settlements.

Ketley town was presumably the Ketley mentioned c. 1180.[76] It remained small[77] until Sinclair Gardens, 40 private rented houses, were added westwards 1934–5.[78] Eastwards 136 council houses were completed 1967–9.[79] Ketley Hall, residence of the ironworks managers until the late 19th century,[80] stood nearby at Ketleyhill. The small late 18th-century house, with a main (west) front of three bays and two storeys, was symmetrically extended by a third storey and by two bays at each end c. 1820. At the same time the interior was remodelled, notably by the heightening of some ceilings and the insertion of a spacious new staircase hall.

Near Coalpit Bank[81] was Bank House, home of the Hartshornes and later of Richard and William Reynolds.[82] The older part is a tall 2-storeyed building of the early 18th century with fronts of four bays to the south and west. In 1721, for Richard Hartshorne,[83] the east side was lengthened and refronted as seven bays with a central entrance. A little later short single-storeyed walls were added at each end of that elevation: the northern one concealed a small extension, and later in the century it was enlarged and carried up to the same height as the main elevation. Several rooms behind the east and south fronts retain early to mid 18th-century fittings. The main

staircase was probably moved to its present position in the later 18th century. Before c. 1900 the house was more than once enlarged and redecorated.

On Watling Street (whose north side lay in Hadley township) a settlement called Staneford occupied the site of modern Beveley in 1447.[84] There were probably miners' cottages along the road by the late 17th century.[85] In 1794 four workmens' settlements, almost contiguous, occupied its length.[86] Ketleybrook (inhabited by 1672)[87] lay immediately north of the ironworks. Shepherd's Lane[88] was the length near the Seven Stars inn. Eastwards lay Pottersbank and Beveley Brook (later called Beveley). The roadside settlements ceased growing in the early 19th century[89] and the more decayed parts were cleared in the mid 20th.[90]

The Ketley wood recorded as inhabited in the 16th and 17th centuries[91] was probably an extensive and loosely defined area outside the centres of population.[92] By 1794, however, Ketley Wood was merely a small group of cottages east of the Rock.[93]

The rest of the township was sparsely inhabited before the 18th century, when mining gave rise to unconnected, but sometimes large, groups of cottages on the wastes. At first many were let by speculators but in the early 19th century the marquess of Stafford assumed direct management and carried out improvements.[94] In 1841 the township had 2,642 inhabitants.[95]

The largest colliers' settlement by 1794 was that later defined as Redlake, Petershill, and the Quarry, but then called Beveley.[96] At Redlake a brick and stone cottage dated 1769 was standing in 1983. The settlement had virtually ceased to grow by 1813[97] and in the 20th century was favoured as a quiet residential area. The speculative Castle View estate (29 houses) was built northwards 1938–40.[98]

Mannerley Lane and the Rock were by 1794 a loose north–south string of colliers' cottages south of Redlake.[99] By 1813 the cottages had spread northwards around Gorsy (later Cow) Wood and had reached Redlake.[1] Cow Wood dwindled in the

[67] O.S. Map 6″, Salop. XXXVI. SE. (1889 edn.).

[68] Above, Hadley, intro.

[69] R. Christiansen, *W. Midlands* (Regional Hist. of Rlys. of Gt. Brit. vii, 1973), 157.

[70] J. M. Tolson, 'In the Tracks of the Iron Masters', *Railway Mag.* xci. 377–8.

[71] C. R. Clinker, *Clinker's Reg. of Closed Stations 1830–1977* (Bristol, 1978), 69, 100.

[72] *T.S.A.S.* 2nd ser. i. 184.

[73] *L. & P. Hen. VIII*, xvii, pp. 507–8.

[74] Below, Econ. Hist.

[75] *Hearth Tax 1672* (Salop. Arch. Soc.), 86.

[76] P.R.O., E 32/143.

[77] S.R.O. 972, parcel 245, map of 1794; O.S. Map 1/2,500, Salop. XXXVI. 14 (1882 and 1926 edns.).

[78] S.R.O., DA 26/505/1, Wellington Rural no. 2, pp. 33–5.

[79] Ibid. /101/13, 15, Ho. Cttee. mins. 13 July 1967; 11 Sept. 1969.

[80] T.D.C. *Ketley Hall* (Hist. Bldgs. in Telford, no. 20).

[81] Below, Wombridge.

[82] T.D.C. *Bank House, Ketley* (Hist. Bldgs. in Telford, no. 21).

[83] Date stone.

[84] *T.S.A.S.* xi. 338. The name may not have referred to the

nearby crossing by Watling St. of the Springwell brook: below, Wombridge, Growth of Settlement.

[85] Above, Hadley, intro.

[86] S.R.O. 972, parcel 245, map.

[87] L.J.R.O., B/C/11, John Goulborne, 1671.

[88] The name was later given to the Pottersbank–Redlake road: O.S. Map 1/2,500, Salop. XXXVI. 14 (1882 edn.).

[89] Ibid. XXXVI. 10 (1882 and 1926 edns.); S.R.O. 14, Hadley and Ketley tithe maps.

[90] S.R.O., DA 26/505/1, Wellington Rural no. 2, pp. 7–17.

[91] Staffs. R.O., D. 593/H/14/1/1; /J/11/2/1, ct. r. of 1605 (refs. supplied by Dr. P. R. Edwards); *Hearth Tax 1672*, 86.

[92] Below, Econ. Hist. (Agric.).

[93] S.R.O. 972, parcel 238, map of 1813; parcel 245, map of 1794.

[94] B. Trinder, 'Open Village in Ind. Brit.' *Ind. Heritage: Trans. 3rd International Conf. on Conservation of Ind. Monuments*, iii, ed. M. Nisser (Stockholm, 1981), 374–5.

[95] *V.C.H. Salop.* ii. 228.

[96] S.R.O. 972, parcel 245, map.

[97] Ibid. parcel 238, map.

[98] S.R.O., DA 26/505/1, Wellington Rural no. 3, pp. 40–3.

[99] S.R.O. 972, parcel 245, map.

[1] Ibid. parcel 238, map.

late 19th century but there was otherwise little change[2] until 32 council houses were built at Mannerley Lane and the Rock 1930–6.[3] A further 213, the Overdale estate, transformed the area 1948–56[4] and more were added in the later 1970s.[5] In 1978 Telford development corporation planned an estate of over 600 public (rented) and private houses east of the Rock. By 1983 some of the private houses had been built.[6]

Lawley Bank had encroached on the township's southern edge by 1794.[7]

The dispersed and impoverished nature of Ketley's settlements inhibited organized social life, and in any case the proximity of Wellington, Hadley, and Oakengates rendered special provision for Ketley largely unnecessary. Moreover such amenities as Ketley acquired were often sited on the north side of Watling Street in Hadley township.[8] Public houses and friendly societies were popular in the earlier 19th century, but later industrial decline made many of them redundant.

There were few alesellers c. 1600.[9] They multiplied[10] with the growth of industry and the improvement of the London–Holyhead road, and in 1842 there were thirteen, six on Watling Street and the rest scattered among the settlements.[11] Many, however, were closed before 1900.[12]

A Brotherly Society was formed in 1784, a Union Society in 1806, and a Union Friendly Society in 1809,[13] as well as several societies at Ketley Bank,[14] but no later 19th-century friendly societies are known. An old people's club was built in 1959 by voluntary effort.[15] The Glynwed and *Shropshire Star* works had their own sports facilities.[16]

The county library sited a branch in Ketley town 1968–71,[17] but no other library is known.

ECONOMIC HISTORY.

Until the later 18th century the township supported a small agricultural population. By the later 17th century there was also some employment, not necessarily full-time, in the textile trades and coalpits. A Ketley clothier (d. 1676) seems to have been principally a farmer. A glover was mentioned in 1703 and there were weavers at Ketley and Ketleybrook.[18] Nevertheless some men already depended entirely on coalmining: about 1688 some inhabitants of Coalpit Bank complained that poverty forced them to send wives and children into the pits.[19] There were potters in Wellington parish in 1763,[20] perhaps in Ketley township where clay was abundant just under the surface near Pottersbank.[21] There were no potters by 1813[22] but industrial exploitation of the township's clay for bricks, tiles, and fireclay goods was well established.[23] Other large-scale industries were developing and by 1821 four fifths of the c. 560 employed people were colliers or industrial workers;[24] moreover the township had become dependent on one company. In 1841 full employment and good wages were enjoyed.[25] A small jam factory opened at Lawley Bank farm c. 1893. Later called the Wrekin Preserves Co., the business seems to have closed c. 1920.[26] In the 1920s slag from the former ironworks was got as road material.[27] In the mid 20th century, when the last collieries closed, there was still only one large employer, Glynwed Foundries Ltd. Telford development corporation planned that the township should otherwise be mainly residential by the end of the century.[28]

AGRICULTURE. In the earlier Middle Ages two thirds of the township, the higher ground that formed its eastern and southern parts, were predominantly wooded[29] and presumably accounted for a large proportion of the two leagues of woodland attached to Leegomery manor in 1086.[30] Clearance of the north-western third probably occurred during the Anglo-Saxon period, as the name Ketley suggests.[31] Further clearances, partly for arable, took place in the 12th[32] and 13th[33] centuries, probably in places as widely separated as Beveley, Mannerley Lane, Mosseygreen, and Redlees, but the township was not disafforested until 1301.[34] By the 16th century clearance was also creating inclosed pastures,[35] and the ancient woodland had probably been reduced to substan-

[2] O.S. Map 1/2,500, Salop. XXXVI. 14 (1882, 1902, and 1926 edns.).

[3] S.R.O., DA 26/100/5, pp. 18, 212, 231; /100/6, p. 392.

[4] Ibid. /114/4, pp. 841, 965, 1109; /114/5, pp. 1338, 1523; /114/6, pp. 1613, 1902.

[5] *Shropshire Star*, 31 July 1975.

[6] Inf. from S.C.C. Planning Dept.

[7] S.R.O. 972, parcel 238, map; below, Lawley, intro.

[8] Above, Hadley, intro., Nonconf.

[9] P.R.O., SC 2/197/96; S.R.O., q. sess rec. parcel 254, badgers', etc. licensing bk. Trin. 1613; Trin. 1615.

[10] S.R.O. q. sess. rec. parcels 255–9, regs. of alesellers' recognizances 1753–1828.

[11] S.R.O. 14, tithe appt. and map.

[12] Co. of Salop, *Return of Licensed Hos. 1896*, 227–9 (copy in S.R.O., q. sess. rec. box 148).

[13] S.R.O. q. sess. rec. parcel 285, friendly socs. reg.

[14] Below, Wombridge, Social and Cultural Activities.

[15] Ed. J. Burrow & Co. Ltd. *Wellington R.D. Official Guide* [1967], 22.

[16] *Telford Social Trends*, i, ed. J. MacGuire (T.D.C. 1980), 226–7; T.D.C. *Telford Street Plan* (1981).

[17] *S.C.C. Mins. (Educ.)* 1968–9, 223; inf. from Salop. Librs.

[18] Trinder and Cox, *Yeomen and Colliers*, pp. 64, 129, 138; L.J.R.O., B/C/11, Ric. Higgons, 1677; Thos. Mayden, 1703.

Sources earlier than the 19th cent. rarely distinguish between the Wellington par. and Wombridge par. parts of Ketley tns. From the 19th cent. the Wellington part alone is treated below.

[19] Trinder, *Ind. Rev. Salop.* (1981), 213.

[20] Par. reg. marr. 22 June 1763 (transcript in S.P.L.).

[21] Inst. Geol. Sciences Map 1/25,000, *Telford* (1978 edn.).

[22] S.R.O. 972, box 41, survey of 1813.

[23] Below.

[24] S.R.O. 3129/5/5.

[25] *1st Rep. Com. Child. Emp. App. Pt. I* [381], p. 82, H.C. (1842), xvi.

[26] S.R.O. 972, parcel 187, sale partic. of 1894, p. 21 (lot 59) and plan no. 2; *Kelly's Dir. Salop.* (1895), 112; (1917), 116.

[27] S.R.O., DA 26/100/3, pp. 124, 213.

[28] T.D.C. *Telford Development Strategy*, map (Feb. 1979).

[29] Field names in S.R.O. 14, tithe appt. and map.

[30] *V.C.H. Salop.* i. 321.

[31] E. Ekwall, *Concise Oxf. Dict. Eng. P.N.* (4th edn.), 273.

[32] P.R.O., E 32/143.

[33] Ibid. /147, m. 3.

[34] *Cartulary of Shrews. Abbey*, ed. U. Rees (1975), ii, p. 249.

[35] Staffs. R.O., D. 593/B/2/5/4/1, deed of 1553. In this section most of the inf. from Staffs. R.O., D. 593, was kindly supplied by Dr. P. R. Edwards.

tial fragments such as Gorsy wood.[36] The township's permanent pasture and meadow then exceeded its arable in area.[37]

In the 16th century there were three open fields[38] near Ketley town.[39] One may have been called Wellington field,[40] another Quite field.[41] Beyond the fields Allmoore and Humble moor[42] were probably common wastes; they lay respectively to the north-west and south-east.[43] It is likely that gradual consolidation and inclosure of strips had virtually extinguished the open fields by c. 1700.[44] By then the lord's policy was also to inclose commons.[45]

In 1598 there were six small farms: three copyholds for lives and three leaseholds for three lives. There were also smallholdings by 1598, each consisting of a dwelling and inclosed pastures in former woodland; they were usually leaseholds.[46] The last copyhold farms probably became leaseholds in the earlier 17th century. By the 1640s,[47] and until the later 18th century,[48] new farm leases were normally for 99 years terminable on three or fewer lives. On 20 October 1671 William Leveson-Gower granted at least five such leases,[49] for high entry fines and low reserved rents. In the earlier 18th century the Leveson-Gowers favoured annual tenancies. In 1755, however, an urgent need of capital induced Lord Gower to grant new leases to all tenants who wanted them. Annual tenancies were restored as the leases fell in,[50] mostly in the 1790s but not finally until after 1818.[51]

In the 17th and earlier 18th century the main farms practised a mixed husbandry. All had cereals and cattle in herds averaging six. Most had sheep, in flocks of c. 30. In 1705 one farmer also had 15 horses, probably as a dealer or carrier, but most had far fewer.[52] The smallholders, some of whom were tradesmen or labourers, usually had a few cattle, but rarely sheep or cereals.[53]

By the 1790s most of the former open-field area was occupied by industrial development. The township's farms over 25 a. were compact, and managed from houses within their boundaries: a pattern characteristic of assarted lands. In 1813 the two largest holdings were those of Reynolds & Co. (296 a.) and Thomas Freeman (140 a.), both more than half agricultural. There were six others over 25 a., the largest having 63 a.[54]

The disappearance of leaseholds by c. 1820 and the surrender of the Reynolds holding c. 1818[55] enabled James Loch, the marquess of Stafford's agent, to adjust the pattern.[56] The former Reynolds and Freeman holdings were broken up, and two of the others over 25 a. were dissolved. With land thus released Loch created pastoral smallholdings for deserving tenants[57] and adjusted the remaining farms. By 1842 there were six farms,[58] the largest having 58 a., and over thirty holdings between 1 a. and 25 a. compared with seven in 1813. Three fifths of the township were still agricultural, with equal acreages of arable and permanent grass and only 8 a. of woodland. On each farm over 25 a., however, arable exceeded permanent grass by at least 3 to 2.

In the later 19th century the farms increased in size and moved towards livestock.[59] In 1894 the five farms over 25 a. averaged 67 a. and together covered more land than the six of 1842. Their permanent grass exceeded their arable by 2 to 1.[60] Ketley's agriculture remained predominantly pastoral in the earlier 20th century[61] and was only moderately affected by urban encroachments.[62] In the 1970s Telford development corporation planned to cover the land with housing before 1986,[63] but little had been done by 1983.[64]

MILLS. In the 17th century Ketley farmers owed suit to Leegomery mill.[65] By 1794 William Reynolds had a windmill near the ironworks.[66] It seems to have closed between 1856 and 1870.[67]

COAL AND IRONSTONE. Over most of the north-east and south-east coal and ironstone occurred near the surface.[68] The lord had ironstone near Ketley wood in 1584.[69] Coalpit Bank was so called by 1613.[70]

From 1715 Lord Gower leased all the coal,

[36] Named on S.R.O. 972, parcel 238, map of 1813.
[37] Staffs. R.O., D. 593/H/14/1/1.
[38] Ibid.
[39] S.R.O. 972, parcel 238, map of 1813 ('Field ground').
[40] S.R.O. 38/331 ('Wellington Field leasow').
[41] Staffs. R.O., D. 593/I/1/21a, deed of 1673.
[42] Mentioned 1649–50: S.R.O. 38/330–1.
[43] Trinder, *Ind. Rev. Salop.* (1981), 23; S.R.O. 14, tithe appt. and map (no. 549).
[44] S.R.O. 38/332; Staffs. R.O., D. 593/B/2/5/26, deed; /I/1/21a, deeds.
[45] S.R.O. 38/332; 245/4.
[46] Staffs. R.O., D. 593/H/14/1/1.
[47] S.R.O. 38/329–31.
[48] S.R.O. 972, parcel 150, leases abstr. ff. 31–4.
[49] S.R.O. 38/332; Staffs. R.O., D. 593/B/2/5/26, deed; /I/1/21a, deeds.
[50] J. R. Wordie, 'Rent Movements and the Eng. Tenant Farmer, 1700–1839', *Research in Econ. Hist.* vi. 206–7.
[51] S.R.O. 972, parcel 150, leases abstr. ff. 31–4. Cf. above, Lilleshall, Econ. Hist. (Agric.).
[52] L.J.R.O., B/C/11, Thos. Davis, 1676; Ric. Higgons, 1677; Humph. Poole, 1745; Trinder and Cox, *Yeomen and Colliers*, pp. 327, 367–8.
[53] L.J.R.O., B/C/11, John Goulborne, 1671; Thos. Fieldhouse, 1688; Rog. Norton, 1694; Wm. Smith, 1699; Ric. Davis, 1701; Thos. Onions, 1702; Thos. Mayden, 1703;

Thos. Grifecke, 1708; John Houle, 1739; Wm. Clayton, 1745; Trinder and Cox, op. cit. pp. 354–6, 395–6, 398.
[54] S.R.O. 972, box 41, survey of 1813; parcel 238, map of 1813. The pattern was similar in 1794: ibid. parcel 245, map.
[55] Below, Iron and Engineering.
[56] Para. based on S.R.O. 14, tithe appt. and map; 972, box 41, survey of 1813; 972, parcel 238, map of 1813. Cf. Lilleshall, Econ. Hist. (Agric.).
[57] J. Loch, *Acct. of Improvements on Est. of Marquess of Stafford* (1820), app. p. 100.
[58] Defined as holdings with over 25 a. of productive land (arable, pasture, or meadow).
[59] See also above, Wellington, Econ. Hist. (Agric.), table.
[60] S.R.O. 972, parcel 187, sale partic. of 1894.
[61] [1st] Land Util. Surv. Map, sheet 61.
[62] T.D.C. *Telford Street Plan* [1980].
[63] T.D.C. *Telford Development Strategy*, map (Feb. 1979).
[64] T.D.C. *Telford Street Plan* (1981); inf. from S.C.C. Planning Dept.
[65] e.g. S.R.O. 999/EA 40.
[66] S.R.O. 14, tithe appt. and map (no. 168); 972, parcel 245, Ketley map.
[67] P.O. Dir. Salop. (1856), 63; (1870), 70.
[68] Inst. Geol. Sciences Map 1/25,000, *Telford* (1978 edn.).
[69] Staffs. R.O., D. 593/H/14/1/11.
[70] S.R.O., q. sess. rec. parcel 254, badgers', etc. licensing bk. Trin. 1613.

ironstone, and limestone to Richard Hartshorne of Ketley, master collier, for 21 years. The pits were mostly in Ketley wood and at Coalpit Bank.[71] From 1732 the lease was renewed, with permission to make coke at the pit heads and erect a steam engine.[72] Hartshorne died in 1733 and his widow Jane held the lease at her death in 1737. Her Ketley pits were then under five charter masters, with 376 stacks of coal lying on the banks.[73]

Until the later 19th century the landlord granted successive 21-year mineral leases. In 1754 Abraham Darby (II) had recently become lessee.[74] He seems to have found the mines in need of improvement.[75] Soon afterwards the Horsehay and Ketley ironworks began production, and thereafter Ketley coal and ironstone was mostly consumed there. By 1777 Darby's son-in-law Richard Reynolds was lessee. In that year Reynolds's Ketley mines (partly in Wombridge parish) produced 20,733 tons of Clod coal for coking and 2,741 tons of other coals.[76] Reynolds seems to have passed his interest, probably in 1789 with that in the ironworks, to his sons,[77] William (d. 1803)[78] and Joseph. To them alone the lease was renewed in 1797.[79] It seems likely, however, that in 1818, having given up the Ketley ironworks,[80] Joseph did not seek renewal of his mineral lease. In that year it was granted to the Ketley Co.,[81] new lessees of the ironworks, to whom it was renewed from 1839 and 1860.[82] The 1860 mineral rent was £1,000 plus royalties.[83] The Ketley Co. remained profitable until 1874[84] but by August 1876 liabilities exceeded assets by at least £12,000.[85] The iron and brick works were sold, the company surrendered its coal and ironstone lease c. 1879, and in 1881 dissolved itself.[86]

In 1879 the coal and ironstone were leased to Nettlefolds Ltd.,[87] purchasers of the brickworks.[88] In 1882 mining was concentrated immediately east and south-east of Ketley town. Nearly thirty abandoned shafts were recorded.[89] Nettlefolds left Shropshire in 1886 but their manager at Ketley (formerly manager of the Ketley Co.) continued mining until 1895 at the Rock.[90] The duke of Sutherland, at his sale of Ketley in 1894, included the mineral rights with the several lots,[91] and thereafter small independent mines operated in the coal-bearing parts. The last were the Rock collieries, which closed in 1964.[92]

Short-term opencast mining by the National Coal Board began in 1967 at Prince's End[93] and in 1975 at Clare's Lane (partly in Dawley), where the scheme was expected to yield 400,000 tons for Ironbridge 'B' power station and to reclaim the land for building by Telford development corporation.[94]

IRON AND ENGINEERING. From 1756 Lord Gower leased land next to Watling Street to Abraham Darby (II) and Thomas Goldney for an ironworks.[95] The first furnace came into blast in 1757 and a second in 1758. Coal and ironstone lay nearby, and limestone came from Benthall.[96] In 1757 Richard Reynolds joined the partnership and seems to have become manager. He bought the Goldney shares in 1775.[97] By 1776 there were three furnaces and in 1785 a forge began work. Reynolds resigned his shares to his sons William and Joseph in 1789, and in 1796 they became sole partners.[98]

William, especially gifted, was already manager[99] and keenly interested in the application of scientific discoveries.[1] Under the Reynolds brothers Ketley's was the fifth largest ironworks in Britain. In 1804 there were six blast furnaces, and output of pig in 1806 was c. 7,500 tons.[2] Coal and ironstone then came not only from Ketley but also from Little Wenlock[3] and Wrockwardine Wood[4] and limestone came from Buildwas, Lincoln Hill,[5] and Steeraway.[6] The foundry made large castings for civil and mechanical engineers and the forge made plates and rods.[7]

From William's death in 1803 the works prospered until 1816, when Joseph closed it because of falling demand.[8] Miners and ironworkers lost their jobs and for a time Ketley threatened to become an 'appendage to the Wellington workhouse'.[9] Early in 1818, however, the marquess of Stafford leased the site to Richard

[71] S.R.O. 38/342.

[72] Ibid. /343.

[73] Trinder and Cox, *Yeomen and Colliers*, pp. 70–1, 384. A stack in Ketley occupied customarily 140,608 cu. in.: S.R.O. 38/343. For other definitions of a stack see p. 85, n. 25.

[74] S.R.O. 1224, box 259, Wm. Ferriday to [Wm. Forester], 6 Dec. 1754.

[75] Ibid. 11 Feb., 7 Mar. 1755.

[76] Trinder, *Ind. Rev. Salop.* (1981), 22–3, 54.

[77] Below.   [78] Trinder, op. cit. 138.

[79] Staffs. R.O., D. 593/I/1/21a, deed.

[80] Trinder, op. cit. 138.

[81] Staffs. R.O., D. 593/I/1/34.

[82] S.R.O. 1101, box 116, deeds of 1842, 1863 (copies).

[83] S.R.O. 972, parcel 150, leases reg. 1853–92.

[84] S.R.O. 1101, box 116, brief in Evett v. Ogle, f. 5.

[85] Ibid. min. bk. (extracts), f. 3.

[86] Ibid. brief in Evett v. Ogle, ff. 6, 10.

[87] Staffs. R.O., D. 593/I/1/37.

[88] I. Gregory, 'E. Salop. Coalfield and the "Gt. Depression" 1873–96' (Keele Univ. M.A. thesis, 1978), 48–50.

[89] O.S. Maps 1/2,500, Salop. XXXVI. 14, 15; XLIII. 2, 3 (1882 edn.).

[90] S.R.O. 972, parcel 187, sale partic. p. 6 and plans nos. 2, 4; Gregory, op. cit. 47–53.

[91] S.R.O. 972, parcel 187, sale partic. p. 6.

[92] O.S. Maps 6", Salop. XXXVI. SE., SW.; XLIII. NW. (1903 and 1929 edns.); XLIII. NE. (1903 and 1928 edns.); *Kelly's Dir. Salop.* (1895 and later edns.); W. Howard Williams, 'Dawley New Town Hist. Survey: Industries' (TS. 1964), pp. 59–61, 70 (copy in S.P.L., accession 5202); I. J. Brown, *Mines of Salop.* (Buxton, 1976), 45–6, 54–5.

[93] *Shropshire Star*, 21 Jan. 1967.

[94] *Contract Jnl.* 23 Oct. 1975.

[95] Trinder, *Ind. Rev. Salop.* (1981), 23.

[96] S.P.L., MS. 332, p. 247.

[97] A. Raistrick, *Dynasty of Iron Founders* (1970), 83–5, 88, 90.

[98] Trinder, *Ind. Rev. Salop.* (1981), 42–3.

[99] Raistrick, op. cit. 89.

[1] Trinder, op. cit. 116–17; H. S. Torrens, 'The Reynolds–Anstice Shropshire geological collection, 1776–1981', *Archives of Nat. Hist.* x. 429–34.

[2] Trinder, op. cit. 43.

[3] S.R.O. 1224, box 259, deed of 1798.

[4] Trinder, op. cit. 33.   [5] Ibid. 59, 81.

[6] B.L. Maps, O.S.D. 208, shows a rly. (so described on O.S. Map 1", sheet 61 NE. (1833 edn.)) to Ketley.

[7] Trinder, op. cit. 42–4, 51–2, 97, 101.

[8] Ibid. 138; Raistrick, *Iron Founders*, 238.

[9] Trinder, op. cit. 137–8 (quoting a local contemporary).

Mountford, Henry Williams, William Shakeshaft, John Ogle, and William Hombersley. As the Ketley Co. they revived three blast furnaces and the forge. Annual production of pig was c. 5,000 tons in 1823 and c. 5,750 in 1830.[10] Some coal was bought from the Lawley Co.[11] By 1837 fluxing limestone was imported from north Wales.[12] In the 1850s pig and bar iron remained the chief products.[13] The Ketley Co. collapsed c. 1874, closed the works, and sold the plant in 1879 to Nettlefolds Ltd.[14] Nettlefolds did not, however, revive ironworking, and unemployment was severe.[15]

Engineering resumed at the site in 1903[16] when Duncan Sinclair, former manager of the Coalbrookdale works, established the Sinclair Iron Co. Ltd. to make light castings for the building trade. With c. 60 employees at first,[17] the firm had over 200 by 1912.[18] It became part of Light Castings Ltd. in 1922 and of Allied Ironfounders Ltd. in 1929.[19] By 1958 James Clay (Wellington) Ltd., another subsidiary of Allied Ironfounders, had moved from Hadley township to another part of the site.[20] In 1962 the combined plant, then one of Europe's biggest producers of rainwater goods,[21] became the Sinclair Works of Allied Ironfounders Ltd.[22] There were 1,212 employees in 1964.[23] Allied Ironfounders' Shropshire concerns became part of Glynwed Foundries Ltd. in 1969. From 1970 to 1978 the works made automobile castings on a large scale, but thereafter concentrated on cast-iron rainwater, soil, and drain pipes and gutters. There were c. 750 employees in September 1982.[24]

In 1809 Edward Cranage of Ketley was an iron founder[25] and by 1842 Mark Tipton, farmer and publican at Mosseygreen, was making chains, gates, and bedsteads.[26] He was described as an ironmaster in 1856, as was William Onions, publican at Redlake.[27] No small ironmasters were recorded in 1870[28] and light engineering seems to

have resumed only in the mid 20th century. C. A. Ensor (later Ensor Caravans Ltd.) was building caravans in the 1930s.[29] By the early 1950s several small firms had set up in Holyhead Road.[30] Of them, the Holway Tool & Engineering Co. Ltd. remained in 1982.[31] Others had recently arrived.[32]

BRICKS, TILES, AND FIRECLAY. Tiles were being made in 1755[33] and George Atkiss, brick maker at Redlake in 1821,[34] may have succeeded Nathaniel Atkiss, tile maker, and Thomas Atkiss, brick maker, recorded in the later 18th century.[35] In 1813 Reynolds & Co. had brickworks at Potters piece and Redlees, and Robert Pool another near Potters piece.[36] No brickworks were there in 1842 but the duke of Sutherland had clay pits in hand in Holyhead Road[37] and in the 1850s John Millington was making bricks and tiles[38] nearby.[39] By 1870 Millington had closed the works[40] and opened another in Wellington[41] but the pits remained in 1894.[42]

In the mid 18th century the ironworks and mines received fire bricks and clay from Horsehay,[43] but by 1794 the Reynoldses had a works making white bricks south of Ketley town.[44] Between 1813 and 1842 it closed; a new brickworks was built at the ironworks site.[45] It was the Ketley Co.'s only profitable department by 1876 and was acquired c. 1879 by Nettlefolds Ltd., who needed fireclay goods for their Castle Iron Works, Hadley.[46] After Nettlefolds left Shropshire in 1886[47] the brickworks closed.[48] The Rock collieries produced 150 tons of fireclay a week in the 1950s and 1960s[49] and fireclay was expected from the opencast coal workings of the 1960s and 1970s.[50]

QUARRIES AND SANDPITS. Sandstone occurred near the surface at Redlake and the Rock and was found elsewhere in the Coal Measures.[51] The lord of Leegomery manor had a quarry in Ketley

[10] Ibid. 138.
[11] S.R.O. 1224, box 295, royalty acct. of 1824.
[12] Trinder, op. cit. 147.
[13] P.O. Dir. Salop. (1856), 62.
[14] S.R.O. 1101, box 116, brief in Evett v. Ogle, f. 15; min. bk. (extracts), f. 10; above, Coal and Ironstone.
[15] Gregory, 'E. Salop. Coalfield', 170.
[16] Ed. J. Burrow & Co. Ltd. Salop. Co. Handbk. [1966], 39.
[17] K. C. Riley, 'Changes in Population in the Wellington–Oakengates Conurbation 1801–1951' (London Univ. M.A. thesis, 1958), 145, 181.
[18] Shrews. Chron. 8 Nov. 1912.
[19] Burrow, Salop. Co. Handbk. [1966], 39.
[20] Riley, 'Population in Wellington–Oakengates', 181–2.
[21] Burrow, Wellington R. D. Official Guide [1962], 24; [1967], 25.
[22] Inf. from Mr. J. Bernstein, managing director, Glynwed Foundries Ltd.
[23] J. H. D. Madin & Partners, Dawley New Town Rep. No. 2: Interim Proposals (Sept. 1964), cap. 6, sect. 1, app.
[24] Inf. from Mr. Bernstein.
[25] S.R.O. 1681, box 180, abstr. of conveyance, 28–9 Apr.
[26] Pigot, Nat. Com. Dir. (1842), 46–7; S.R.O. 14, tithe appt. and map.
[27] P.O. Dir. Salop. (1856), 63.
[28] Ibid. (1870).
[29] Kelly's Dir. Salop. (1934), 126; (1941), 124.
[30] County Assocs. Ltd. Oakengates, Newport & Shifnal Dir. (1952), 30–1, 37–8.

[31] T.D.C. Telford Ind. Dir. (1982), 31.
[32] e.g. P.O. Telephone Dir. (1971), sect. 303, p. 212 (S. & S. Structures); (1973), sect. 303, p. 162 (K.N. Engineering).
[33] S.P.L., MS. 332, p. 8.
[34] S.R.O. 3129/5/5, p. 256.
[35] Par. reg. marr. 23 Dec. 1764; 20 Apr. 1772 (transcript in S.P.L.).
[36] S.R.O. 972, box 41, survey of 1813, pp. 187, 194; parcel 238, map of 1813 (nos. 149, 200, 212).
[37] S.R.O. 14, tithe appt. and map (no. 959).
[38] S. Bagshaw, Dir. Salop. (1851), 439; P.O. Dir. Salop. (1856), 63.
[39] 'Old Brickkiln' on O.S Map 1/2,500, Salop. XXXVI. 14 (1882 edn.). Site occ. by R. and J. Millington 1894: S.R.O. 972, parcel 187, sale partic. p. 25 (lot 71) and plan no. 3.
[40] Not in P.O. Dir. Salop. (1870).
[41] Above, Wellington, Econ. Hist.
[42] S.R.O. 972, parcel 187, sale partic. p. 27 (lot 88) and plan no. 3.
[43] S.P.L., MSS. 332, p. 234; 333, pp. 8, 19.
[44] S.R.O. 972, box 41, survey of 1813, p. 185; parcel 238, map of 1813 (no. 80); parcel 245, map of 1794.
[45] S.R.O. 14, tithe appt. and map (no. 107).
[46] Gregory, 'E. Salop. Coalfield', 48–50; Staffs. R.O., D. 593/I/1/37.
[47] Gregory, op. cit. 52.
[48] Kelly's Dir. Salop. (1885), 868; not mentioned ibid. (1891).
[49] Brown, Mines of Salop. 54.
[50] Contract Jnl. 23 Oct. 1975.
[51] Inst. Geol. Sciences Map 1/25,000, Telford (1978 edn.).

wood[52] c. 1269.[53] In the 1760s and 1770s hearth stones for Horsehay ironworks came from Ketley.[54] In 1813 Reynolds & Co. held the quarries at Redlake and Ketley town and William Light those at the Rock[55] but by 1842 all were in the duke of Sutherland's hands.[56] The Rock quarries closed before 1882[57] but the 4th duke kept the Redlake and Ketley town ones until 1894.[58] Only the Redlake quarries remained in 1901 and they closed before 1925.[59]

Industrially useful sands occurred in the northeast, but more especially in the north-west at Ketleysands, which lay mostly in Arleston and partly in Hadley townships.[60] Until the 1770s only Ketley sand was used at Horsehay ironworks;[61] later Donnington Wood and Lawley sands were also used.[62] In the Arleston part of Ketleysands the Ketley Co. and the Botfields were lessees of separate sandpits in the earlier 19th century[63] and William Edwards[64] rented another in 1842.[65] The Botfields extracted 2,657 tons in the half-year to June 1825.[66] Two large pits remained at Ketleysands in 1912[67] but were disused by 1925.[68] Richard Griffiths owned a pit in the Hadley part of Ketleysands in 1842;[69] it closed before 1882[70] and another nearby lay disused by 1901.[71] At an adjoining site[72] C. W. Adey began commercial extraction c. 1935[73] but ceased in the 1940s.[74] Ketley township had no sandpits in the earlier 19th century[75] but in 1894 the duke of Sutherland had one in hand near Redlake and Edwin Pitchford rented one at Pottersbank.[76]

NEWSPAPER PRINTING AND PUBLISHING. In 1964 the Midland News Association Ltd. replaced the Shropshire edition of its Wolverhampton evening *Express & Star* with the *Shropshire Star*, printed and published by a subsidiary company at a new works in Ketley.[77] The *Star*'s circulation grew from 21,000 in 1964 to 88,000 in 1981.[78] From 1965 the subsidiary also printed and published the weekly *Shropshire Journal*, formerly the *Wellington Journal*.[79] In 1973 the parent company replaced its Ketley subsidiary with two others: the Shropshire Star Ltd. and Shropshire Weekly Newspapers Ltd. The latter, having acquired the *Telford Observer*, amalgamated it with the Wrekin editions of the *Shropshire Journal* as the *Telford Journal*.[80] The other editions were soon discontinued in favour of the subsidiary's other local weeklies, whose printing was also transferred to Ketley.[81] In 1981 the *Telford Journal* had a circulation of 10,400 and the eight newspapers printed by Shropshire Weekly Newspapers at Ketley a total of 52,000.[82]

LOCAL GOVERNMENT AND PUBLIC SERVICES. Ketley was subject to the court baron of Leegomery[83] and remained so in 1806.[84] The duke of Sutherland had a pound near Ketley town in 1842.[85] In 1590 Ketley was in the leet jurisdiction of Bradford hundred.[86]

The township (except for the part in Wombridge parish) was in Wellington civil parish until 1894, Wellington poor-law union 1836–1930, Wrekin highway district 1865–82, and Wellington rural sanitary district 1872–94. In 1894 it became part of Wellington Rural C.P. and Wellington rural district.[87] At Ketley Bank a small area was transferred to Oakengates C.P. and urban district in 1934,[88] and in 1966 the southern part of the township, including Overdale and the Rock, was transferred to Dawley C.P. and U.D.[89] In 1974 Dawley and Oakengates U.D.s and Wellington R.D. were dissolved, their areas becoming part of the district of the Wrekin.[90] In 1976 the surviving part of Wellington Rural C.P., which lay mostly in Ketley township, was renamed Ketley.[91] The part of the township taken into Dawley C.P. and

[52] *T.S.A.S.* xi 326. Possibly in Wombridge par.
[53] Eyton vii. 345.
[54] S.P.L., MS. 333, pp. 8, 480.
[55] S.R.O. 972, box 41, survey, pp. 185, 188, 201; parcel 238, map (nos. 102, 236, 395–6).
[56] S.R.O. 14, tithe appt. and map (nos. 206, 266, 500–1, 649, 952).
[57] O.S. Maps 1/2,500, Salop. XXXVI. 14; XLIII. 2 (1882 edn.).
[58] S.R.O. 972, parcel 187, sale partic. pp. 10 (lot 12), 32 (lot 112), and plans nos. 1, 3.
[59] O.S. Map 1/2,500, Salop. XXXVI. 14 (1902 and 1926 edns.).
[60] R. W. Pocock and others, *Shrews. Dist.* (Geol. Surv. Memoir, 1938), 224; Inst. Geol. Sciences Map 1/25,000, *Telford* (1978 edn.).
[61] S.P.L., MSS. 332–3.
[62] Ibid. 334, pp. 6, 377, 379.
[63] S.R.O. 14, tithe appt. (nos. 56, 74); 1101, box 116, deed of 1842 (copy), f. 5; 1224, box 254, deed of 1824; 1856/5 (nos. 56, 74).
[64] Perhaps the Wellington ironfounder: above, Wellington, Econ. Hist.
[65] S.R.O. 14, tithe appt.; 1856/5 (no. 67).
[66] S.R.O. 1224, box 295, royalty acct.
[67] S.R.O. 4011/84/3, nos. 2165, 2206.
[68] O.S. Maps 1/2,500, Salop. XXXVI. 10, 14 (1926 edn.).
[69] S.R.O. 14, tithe appt. and map (no. 836).
[70] O.S Map 1/2,500, Salop. XXXVI. 10 (1882 edn.).
[71] Ibid. (1902 edn.).
[72] Ibid. (1939 edn.).
[73] *Kelly's Dir. Salop.* (1937), 126.

[74] Ibid. (1941), 124; O.S. Map 6", SJ 61 SE. (1954 edn.).
[75] S.R.O. 14, tithe map and appt.; 972, box 41, survey of 1813.
[76] S.R.O. 972, parcel 187, sale partic. pp. 27 (lot 88), 32 (lot 112), and plan no. 3.
[77] *Birmingham Post*, 5 Oct. 1964.
[78] Benn Bros. Ltd. *Newspaper Press Dir.* (1965), 221–2; Benn Business Inf. Services Ltd. *Benn's Press Dir.* (1983), U.K. 100; *Sunday Times*, 28 Oct. 1984 (p. 13).
[79] *Wellington Jnl.* 12 Feb. 1965; *Shropshire Jnl.* 19 Feb. 1965.
[80] *Telford Jnl.* 5 Jan. 1973. A *Telford Jnl.* was formerly published as a monthly suppl. in Telford copies of the *Shropshire Jnl.*: *Shropshire Jnl.*, 5 June 1969.
[81] Inf. from *Shropshire Star* libr., Ketley.
[82] Benn Business Inf. Services Ltd. *Benn's Press Dir.* (1983), U.K. 62, 85, 87, 96, 100.
[83] Staffs. R.O., D. 593/J/11/6/1, ct. r.; above, Wellington, Local Govt.
[84] Staffs. R.O., D. 593/J/11/6/5, ct. r.
[85] S.R.O. 14, tithe appt. and map (no. 751).
[86] P.R.O., SC 2/197/96.
[87] Above, Wellington, intro.; Local Govt.
[88] *Salop Review Order, 1934* (Min. of Health order no. 77933); O.S. Map 6", SJ 61 SE. (1954 edn.).
[89] *Salop Order 1966* (Min. of Ho. & Local Govt. order no. 22958); O.S. *Map Referred to in The Salop Order 1966* (copy in S.R.O. 2981, parcel VI).
[90] *Census, 1971, Rep. for Co. of Salop as constituted on 1st Apr. 1974*, 2.
[91] S.C.C. Planning Dept. file no. 051001, Wrekin District Council sec. to co. sec. 15 July 1976.

U.D. in 1966 had been included in 1963 in the designated area of Dawley new town,[92] and in 1968 the whole township was included in that of Telford.[93]

Before 1897 many inhabitants drew water from Ketley spout, a pure spring near Ketley Dingle, and from Mosseygreen pool, a polluted pond. The former was superseded[94] in 1897 when Wellington U.D.C. extended a main eastwards along Watling Street to Beveley.[95] At first only houses on the main road benefited[96] but by 1912 the U.D.C. system also included Ketley town and Ketleyhill. From 1909 Dawley U.D.C. supplied Wellington R.D.C. with water for Mannerley Lane and the Rock,[97] an arrangement that eventually covered the rest of the old township.[98] Main sewerage was first provided in 1938 when Wellington R.D.C. completed a scheme that connected the township to the Hadley disposal works.[99] In 1952 Wellington Rural parish council opened a cemetery at Redlake.[1] There was a sub-post office by 1851.[2]

CHURCH. A chapel of ease at Redlake was completed in 1838[3] at the 2nd duke of Sutherland's expense[4] and licensed for baptisms and burials.[5] The living was then a curacy, filled at the duke's nomination. Chapel and graveyard were consecrated in 1839.[6] Owing to objections from the vicar of Wellington a licence for marriages was not granted until 1841.[7] In 1879 the 3rd duke conveyed the site and fabric to the Ecclesiastical Commissioners[8] and in 1880 surrendered the patronage to the bishop,[9] with whom it remained in 1981.[10] A district chapelry was assigned in 1880,[11] comprising the part of Ketley township in Wellington parish and a small part of Hadley township.[12] The incumbents were thereafter titular vicars. From 1969 the cure was served by a priest-in-charge.[13] In 1975 part of the parish was transferred to the new parish of Central Telford.[14] The priest-in-charge appointed in 1978 was already priest-in-charge (from 1980 vicar)[15] of Oakengates.[16] In 1983 Overdale was returned to Ketley parish from that of Central Telford.[17]

In 1838 the 2nd duke endowed the curacy with £1,000.[18] Endowments from various sources, totalling £2,600, were added in 1844 and 1847.[19] By 1851 the living was worth £131 a year gross; £20 came from pew rents, and there was glebe yielding £20 a year.[20] Between 1861 and 1881 the Ecclesiastical Commissioners augmented the living by £125 a year.[21] In 1880 they also assigned annual tithe rent charge of £62 gross[22] out of the former endowment of Wellington prebend.[23] In 1884 the vicar's gross income of £326 included £154 from the Ecclesiastical Commissioners, £61 from Queen Anne's Bounty, and £21 from 10 a. of glebe.[24]

By 1843 the curate was living in a house belonging to the duke.[25] In 1881 a brick vicarage house designed by Edward Haycock was completed[26] on a site given by the 3rd duke.[27] It was occupied by the incumbent[28] until the priest-in-charge of Oakengates took charge of Ketley in 1978, and was then sold.[29]

In 1839 the 2nd duke, attending a service incognito, found the sermon fair and unexaggerated and the singing reminiscent of the Kirk.[30] In 1843 there were two Sunday services and one each Wednesday evening. Communion was given eight times a year and there were c. 50 communicants.[31] In 1851 adult attendances averaged 130 in the morning and 115 in the evening.[32] Between 1878 and 1921 there were six incumbents. None remained more than 13 years and all but one resigned.[33]

The church of ST. MARY[34] was designed by James Trubshaw,[35] mainly in the Gothic style. It

[92] Dawley New Town (Designation) Order 1963 (Stat. Instr. 1963, no. 64), accompanying map (copy in S.R.O. 2981, parcel VI).
[93] Dawley New Town (Designation) Amendment (Telford) Order 1968 (Stat. Instr. 1968, no. 1912), map accompanying Explanatory Note.
[94] S.C.C. Mins. Sanitary Cttee. rep. 31 Jan. 1903, 95–6.
[95] Ibid. 1897–8, 589.
[96] Ibid. 31 Jan. 1903, 94.
[97] S.C.C. Mins. Suppl. Rep. on Water Supplies of Pars. of Wellington Rural and Hadley, 28 June 1912, 2–3.
[98] A. H. S. Waters, Rep. on Water Supplies (S.C.C. 1946), 98.
[99] S.R.O., DA 26/100/6, pp. 184–5; /100/7, p. 448.
[1] S.R.O., DA 26/134 (S.R.O. 3070/11/15), file 297, clk. of R.D.C. to Min. of Health & Local Govt. 16 Dec. 1952.
[2] S. Bagshaw, Dir. Salop. (1851), 438–9.
[3] Cranage, vii. 591.
[4] Lich. Dioc. Regy., bps.' reg. L, p. 500; episc. reg. 30, p. 114.
[5] E. C. Peele and R. S. Clease, Salop. Par. Doc. (Shrews. [1903]), 195.
[6] Lich. Dioc. Regy., bps.' reg. L, pp. 518–19.
[7] Ibid. pp. 233–5.
[8] Ibid. S, p. 364.
[9] Ibid. p. 360.
[10] Lich. Dioc. Dir. (1981), 68.
[11] Lich. Dioc. Regy., bps.' reg. Q (Orders in Council), p. 237.
[12] S.R.O. 1149/1.
[13] Lich. Dioc. Regy., benefice and inst. bk. 1968– (in use), p. 9.

[14] Ibid. bps.' reg. R, p. 350.
[15] Lich. Dioc. Dir. (1981), 79.
[16] Crockford (1977–9), 524.
[17] Inf. from the Revd. R. A. J. Hill, rector of Central Telford.
[18] Lich. Dioc. Regy., bps.' reg. L, pp. 504, 506.
[19] C. Hodgson, Q. Anne's Bounty (2nd edn.), pp. ccxxxv, ccxciv; suppl. pp. xv, lxvii.
[20] P.R.O., HO 129/365, no. 15.
[21] Lond. Gaz. 15 Oct. 1861, p. 4065; 21 May 1880, p. 3137; 4 Mar. 1881, p. 1021.
[22] Lich. Dioc. Regy., bps.' reg. S, p. 364.
[23] Above, Wellington, Man. and Other Est.
[24] S.R.O. 3916/1/33, s.v.
[25] Ibid. /1/6, no. 19.
[26] S.R.O. 4488/VR/1; Lond. Gaz. 21 May 1880, p. 3137; 4 Mar. 1881, p. 1021.
[27] Lich. Dioc. Regy., bps.' reg. S, p. 292.
[28] Lich. Dioc. Dir. (1976), 16.
[29] S.P.L., Sale Cat. 4/44.
[30] Trinder, Ind. Rev. Salop. 300.
[31] S.R.O. 3916/1/6, no. 19.
[32] P.R.O., HO 129/365, no. 15.
[33] S.R.O. 3499/Rg/7, newscutting on endpaper; Lich. Dioc. Regy., benefice and inst. bk. 1868–1900, pp. 78, 94, 102; 1900–29, pp. 28, 55, 67. For Thos. Owen, 1878–87, see Shrews. Chron. 18 Sept. 1903; for W. B. Gowan, 1887–93, D. Hudson, Munby: Man of Two Worlds (1972), 416–18; Shrews. Chron. 21 Oct. 1898.
[34] So dedicated in 1839: Lich. Dioc. Regy., bps.' reg. L., p. 519.
[35] Ibid. p. 500.

is built of dressed sandstone and consists of chancel and nave with transepts and west tower and west gallery. In 1915 there was one bell of 1836.[36]

NONCONFORMITY. The Methodists, mainly the Primitive Methodists, were the only nonconformists to enjoy any success in Ketley. A Quaker evangelist spoke there in 1759,[37] and in 1854 a Baptist at the Rock was reported to have joined the Mormons.[38] A Salvation Army barracks, registered in 1888, had closed by 1896.[39] An undenominational iron chapel was remembered in 1982.[40]

Sporadic Wesleyan efforts were made over some sixty years. There was regular Wesleyan preaching at the Rock in 1813,[41] and still in 1823 when Old Park (in Dawley) and Mannerley Lane were associated preaching places.[42] By 1840 the Rock and Mannerley Lane were still associated but in 1852 they separated and seem to have expired. The latter was revived from 1856 to c. 1866.[43] Redlake had a Wesleyan society by 1840. It seems to have lapsed in 1852,[44] but a house said to have been lent for Wesleyan worship in 1853 was still being used when the society ceased in 1874.[45]

A Primitive Methodist society at Coalpit Bank met in Wombridge parish in 1830.[46] By 1841 it used Robert Pocock's schoolroom south of Main Road, Ketley Bank, which it rebuilt as a brick chapel in 1859.[47] Altered in 1907,[48] it had 191 seats and was called St. Paul's by 1940.[49] It had a congregation of 31 in 1983.[50] The Rock too had regular Primitive preaching by 1835.[51] A small plain brick chapel was built in 1861[52] off the west side of Rock Road. In 1877[53] a larger chapel, with 300 seats in 1940,[54] was built in polychrome brick against the old chapel, which then became the Sunday school.[55] In 1981 the new chapel was still in use. There was regular Primitive preaching at Ketleybrook by 1834.[56] A small plain brick chapel called Ebenezer was built there in 1863[57] on the north side of the Holyhead road. Dr. S. Parkes

Cadman (1864–1936), a celebrated preacher in the United States,[58] was baptized there.[59] The chapel closed in 1963.[60] Other mid 19th-century efforts by the Primitives were shorter lived. There was regular preaching at Redlake in 1839 and 1849[61] and at Mannerley Lane in 1842, 1851 (48 afternoon attendances on Census Sunday), and 1861.[62]

A small plain brick chapel of the United Methodist Free Churches was built at Mosseygreen in 1873 and rebuilt or extended in 1904.[63] Worship ceased in 1971.[64]

EDUCATION. Richard Reynolds built a school at Ketley in the late 18th century, probably the Sunday school that in 1786 had 300 places.[65] A private school at Coalpit Bank was run by Robert Pocock from 1830, or earlier, until his death in 1858. Colliers' children, however, depended on Sunday schools, one of the largest in the district being that held by the Primitive Methodists in Pocock's school: it had 500–700 pupils in 1841.[66]

Ketley Parochial (later National) School, with 200 places, was opened in 1842 at the 2nd duke of Sutherland's expense. The slated brick building at Redlake, near the new St. Mary's church, was probably designed by Charles Barry[67] and had three classrooms; there was also a teacher's house. Annual income in 1849 was £80: £20 in fees, the rest from the duke, who largely maintained the school. The master and his wife were jointly salaried at £60 and half the fees. From 1865 or earlier there were government grants. By 1870 it was called a National school; there were then boys', girls', and infant departments, but by 1885 only mixed and infant. Attendance averaged c. 150 in 1851, 223 in 1885, and 153 in 1895.[68] In 1895 the school closed, probably because of the cost of repairs and improvements. It passed to the school board, which reopened it in 1896 as Ketley National Board School, and it continued in existence until 1898.[69]

Ketley Board School, Holyhead Road, with mixed and infant departments, was opened in

[36] H. B. Walters, *Ch. Bells of Salop.* (Oswestry, 1915), 329.
[37] Trinder, *Ind. Rev. Salop.* 305.
[38] Dawley Bank Baptist Ch. min. bk. 1848–84, 26 Apr. 1854 (in possession of ch. sec.); cf. above, Wellington, Prot. Nonconf.
[39] G.R.O., Worship Reg. no. 31125.
[40] Local inf.
[41] S.P.L., C 98.7 v.f., Shrews. circuit plan.
[42] S.P.L., L 98.7 v.f., Wellington circuit plan.
[43] S.R.O. 3767/XVII/A; /XVII/I, circuit plans of 1865–6.
[44] Ibid. /XVII/A.
[45] S.R.O. 3027/1/1, 4a.
[46] Below, Wombridge, Nonconf.
[47] S.R.O. 3038/6/1; date stone; below, Educ.
[48] Date stone.
[49] *Meth. Church Bldgs.: Statistical Returns* (1940), 268.
[50] Local inf.
[51] S.R.O. 3605/2, 28 Dec. 1835.
[52] S.R.O. 2533/130, 10 June 1861; date stone.
[53] Date stone.
[54] *Meth. Church Bldgs.: Statistical Returns* (1940), 270.
[55] Local inf. (recorded in S.M.R.).
[56] Inf. from Mr. J. H. Lenton.
[57] Date stone.
[58] *Dict. American Biog.* xxii. 85–6.
[59] S.R.O. 3767/XVIII/A, newscutting [of 1962].

[60] Ibid. /IX/I, 19 Mar., 30 Apr. 1963; /IX/H, 3 Dec. 1963.
[61] S.R.O. 1861/5, p. 3; 3605/1, p. 22. The mtg. did not survive to 1861: S.R.O. 1861/12.
[62] S.R.O. 1861/12; 3605/1, p. 81; P.R.O., HO 129/365, no. 30.
[63] Date stones.
[64] S.R.O. 4113/10/1, 23 Nov. 1971.
[65] R. F. Skinner, *Nonconformity in Salop.* (Shrews. 1964), 37 n., 39 n.
[66] J. E. G. Cartlidge, *The Vale and Gates of Usc-con* (Congleton, [1935]), 78, 103; S.R.O. 3038/6/1; *1st Rep. Com. Child. Emp. App. Pt. I* [381], pp. 39–40, 83, H.C. (1842), xvi.
[67] Inf. from Mr. D. Blissett.
[68] S. Bagshaw, *Dir. Salop.* (1851), 438; P.R.O., ED 7/103, f. 118; *Rep. of Educ. Cttee. of Council* [3666], pp. 84–5, H.C. (1866), xxvii; *P.O. Dir. Salop.* (1870), 70; *Kelly's Dir. Salop.* (1885), 868; (1895), 109.
[69] S.R.O. 4005/3, pp. 1, 20–1, 42–3, 54–5. Evelyn J. Green, 'Development of Educ. in the Oakengates Dist. of Salop. betw. 1830 and 1902' (Liverpool Univ. M.Ed. dissertation, 1975), 52. No early record of the receipt of a Nat. Soc. grant exists. A Nat. Soc. letter to the incumbent (1907) described the schs. as 'estate' schs. belonging to the duke of Sutherland.

1898 to replace the National Board School.[70] In 1905 a new infant school and teacher's house were built nearby. The mixed school was then adapted for older pupils; in 1907 it had 306 places, the infant school 236.[71] Attendance in 1909 averaged 290 mixed pupils, 180 infants.[72] In 1931 the former mixed school was used for the new Ketley Senior Council School (240 places), the former infant school for Ketley Junior Mixed and Infant Council School (230 places). That year the old National school was rented and adapted for temporary use as a domestic subjects centre, and in 1934 a room in the senior school was converted to a science laboratory.[73] Overcrowding in the 1950s in Ketley Primary School[74] (so called since 1945)[75] was relieved in 1958 when the seniors left their building for a new secondary modern school.[76] The juniors transferred to a new junior school in 1967, when the old school became Ketley County

Infant School[77] and the building of 1905 was converted to a nursery unit, the first to be attached to a Shropshire infant school.[78] In 1980 the infant school had only 109 pupils.[79]

Ketley Town County Junior School, Riddings Close, with 320 places, opened in 1966 and admitted pupils from Ketley County Junior School. In 1980 there were 226 pupils.[80]

CHARITIES FOR THE POOR. In addition to those charities applicable to the whole of Wellington ancient parish, Ketley had two of its own. By will proved 1887 William Slaney Lewis left £200 stock for blankets and clothing for widows in the ecclesiastical parish;[81] the income in 1975 was £5.[82] By will proved 1898[83] Henry Parker left stock for food, clothing, and blankets; the income in 1975 was £4.[84]

LAWLEY

LAWLEY township, south-south-east of Wellington town, was reckoned to be 708 a. (287 ha.) in 1841.[85] It was roughly lozenge-shaped, longer from north to south. Its boundaries, though fairly regular, did not for the most part follow roads or watercourses. On the north-west, however, Ketley brook was the boundary, and on the north-east a tributary of it; their confluence was the township's northern point. The southernmost parts of the south-west and south-east boundaries also followed valleys that converged at the township's extremity.[86] In 1894 Lawley was included in Wellington Rural civil parish.[87]

Lawley village stands on sand and gravel but most of the township consists of boulder clay beneath which were workable coals of the Middle and Lower Coal Measures.[88] The township's highest points (c. 200 metres above O.D.) were in the south, on Horsehay common, and south-east, at Lawley Bank; thence the township sloped down to c. 110 metres at its northern tip and to c. 175 metres at its southern. Northward drainage was into Ketley brook, southward was towards the Severn.[89]

The Wellington–Worcester road, turnpiked in 1764,[90] ran south-eastwards through the township to Dawley Bank[91] but by 1808 had been diverted[92] southwards across Lawley common by Ball's Hill to Dawley.[93] The Wellington–Coalbrookdale turnpike road, of which the part north of Horsehay was built c. 1817, also crossed the township. A new turnpike road linking the other two was built across the common c. 1827.[94] The earliest length of the Wellington & Severn Junction Railway, opened 1857,[95] passed through the township, with a station at Lawley Bank that closed to passengers and goods in 1962.[96]

In 1086 only 4 serfs and a villein were recorded[97] and 4 'able' men in 1542,[98] but 12 households paid hearth tax in 1672.[99]

Lawley village, which was centred by the 17th century on three farmsteads,[1] changed little[2] until 16 council houses were added 1930–2.[3] Another 58 were added 1947–61[4] and 33 in the later 1960s.[5] In 1983 Telford development corporation intended that housing should eventually cover the rest of the township.[6]

Lawley Bank, a mining settlement, was inha-

---

[70] S.R.O. 4005/1, p. 1.

[71] Ibid. p. 140; S.C.C. Mins. 1903–4, 219; ibid. (Educ.) 1905–6, 84; 1906–7, 143.

[72] Kelly's Dir. Salop. (1909), 119.

[73] S.C.C. Mins. (Educ.) 1930–1, 67; 1931–2, 12; 1932–3, 33; 1933–34, 86.

[74] Ibid. 1949–50,   [75] Inf. from S.C.C. Educ. Dept.

[76] Below, Hadley, Educ.; inf. from the headmaster.

[77] Inf. from the headmistress.

[78] Ketley Co. Inf. Sch. log bk. (at the sch.) 5 Oct. 1967.

[79] S.C.C. Educ. Cttee. Educ. Dir. (1980), 10.

[80] Ibid.; inf. from S.C.C. Educ. Dept. and the headmistress.

[81] S.R.O. 1206/61, pp. 534–5.

[82] Review of Local Chars. (S.C.C. 1975), 68.

[83] S.C.C. chars. index.   [84] Review of Local Chars. 68.

[85] S.R.O. 14, tithe appt.

[86] S.R.O. 1856/4; O.S. Maps 1/25,000, SJ 60, 61 (1957 edn.).

[87] Changes are treated below, Local Govt. and Public Services.

[88] Inst. Geol. Sciences Map 1/25,000, Telford (1978 edn.).

[89] O.S. Maps 1/25,000, SJ 60, 61 (1957 edn.).

[90] Above, Wellington, Communications.

[91] J. Rocque, Map of Salop. (1752).

[92] At O.S. Nat. Grid SJ 675 088.

[93] R. Baugh, Map of Salop. (1808); above, Dawley, Communications.

[94] Above, Dawley, Communications; Wellington, Communications.

[95] Above, Hadley intro.

[96] C. R. Clinker, Clinker's Reg. of Closed Stations, 1830–1977 (Bristol, 1978), 73.

[97] V.C.H. Salop. i. 332, 334.

[98] L. & P. Hen. VIII, xvii, p. 507.

[99] Hearth Tax 1672 (Salop. Arch. Soc.), 89.

[1] Below, Econ. Hist.

[2] S.R.O. 1856/4; O.S. Map 1/2,500, Salop. XLIII. 2 (1882 and 1927 edns.).

[3] S.R.O., DA 26/100/5, pp. 18, 172.

[4] Ibid. /114/3, p. 763; /114/4, p. 1081; /114/6, p. 1597; /114/7, pp. 2077, 2187; /114/8, p. 2460.

[5] Dawley U.D.C.: a Story, 1966–74, [9] (copy in S.R.O., DA 8/294).

[6] Inf. from S.C.C. Planning Dept.

bited by 1704.[7] By the end of the century it extended into Ketley township.[8] and was continuous with Dawley Bank.[9] During the 19th century it contracted slightly[10] but 22 council houses were built in 1939[11] and Telford development corporation added 55 dwellings in 1975.[12]

There were many miners' cottages by 1840 on the margins of Lawley common, the southern part of which was called Horsehay common.[13] The largest groups were near Lawley Bank and at Spring Village.[14] The cottages did not increase in number thereafter[15] but most were later rebuilt or modernized.

Newdale, in the north, was a mining settlement founded *c.* 1759 by the Coalbrookdale Co.[16] By 1794[17] there were 18 back-to-back houses[18] called the Long Row[19] and there were *c.* 12 other houses in 1840.[20] The population in 1841 was 196.[21] Newdale did not change significantly in extent until the later 20th century,[22] when many of the inhabitants moved to council houses in Lawley village.[23] The Long Row was demolished *c.* 1960[24] and only three houses were occupied by 1981.[25]

There were few alesellers in the early 17th century[26] but by 1753 there were five in Lawley or Lawley Bank.[27] In 1842 there were four at Lawley Bank and none elsewhere.[28] By 1901 only the Bull's Head and the Wrekin View remained,[29] as in 1983.

Lawley Bank Female Society was registered in 1806, and in 1835 the Malinslee Friendly Society met at the King's Head, Lawley Bank.[30] A church institute was built next to St. John's church in 1920[31] and replaced by a new church hall in 1962.[32] Wellington rural district council provided a playing field in Lawley village *c.* 1963[33] and there was a Lawley Athletic football club by 1964.[34]

MANORS AND OTHER ESTATES. There were originally two manors called *LAWLEY*, which had passed by 1300 into the same demesne lordship and came to be regarded as one manor.

The larger manor was held in 1086 of Earl Roger by Turold of Vesly, and of Turold by Hunnit, who is likely to have held it in 1066. As with other manors, Turold's mesne lordship appears to have passed to the Chetwynds, who evidently held their fee, following the extinction of the earldom of Shrewsbury, of the FitzAlans and whose undertenants were the descendants of the Anglo-Saxon Toret.[35] John of Chetwynd was lord of part of Lawley in 1255.[36] By 1285, however, William of Hodnet (fl. 1300)[37] held Lawley as tenant in chief and was the immediate lord of the tenant in demesne.[38] That part of Lawley was accounted a member of Hodnet manor,[39] with which the overlordship passed to William's son-in-law William of Ludlow (d. 1316) and to John of Ludlow (d. 1398).[40] The Domesday tenant in demesne, Hunnit, appears to have been succeeded by Toret.[41] Peter FitzToret (fl. 1160–94) was lord in 1180, and his son Bartholomew Toret (fl. 1196–1229) succeeded him. Bartholomew was dead by 1235, and the estate passed, presumably through his daughter Joan or grandson Richard Corbet (III), to the Corbets of Moreton Corbet. By 1255 Robert Corbet (d. 1300) was lord,[42] and after 1283 he acquired the smaller manor too.

That smaller manor, held in 1066, by Erniet, was held of the earl by William Pantulf.[43] Pantulf's mesne lordship became a tenancy in chief, presumably in 1102,[44] and descended to the barons of Wem,[45] to whose court leet of Hinstock part of Lawley continued to owe service.[46] A mesne lordship in that part had been acquired by the Eyton family of Eyton upon the Weald Moors by 1285,[47] and in 1606 Lawley was said to be held of Eyton manor.[48] A chief rent of 5s. was paid to the lords of Eyton by the demesne lords of Lawley at least until 1686.[49] The demesne lord in 1255 was Ralph of Stanton,[50] who was named as lord in 1284 or 1285.[51] Walter of Stanton later conveyed the manor to Robert Corbet of Moreton (d. 1300),[52] who was already lord of the larger manor.

The descent of both manors seems to have

[7] Wellington par. reg. bap. 5 Mar. 1703/4 (transcript in S.P.L.).
[8] S.R.O. 972, parcel 245, map.
[9] Above, Dawley, Growth of Settlement.
[10] S.R.O. 1856/4; O.S. Map 1/2,500, Salop. XLIII. 2 (1902 edn.).
[11] S.R.O., DA 26/114/2, p. 106.
[12] D. G. Fenter, 'Bldg. Development carried out in Telford by the Development Corp.' (TS. in S.R.O. 3763).
[13] O.S. Map 1/2,500, Salop. XLIII. 2 (1882 edn.).
[14] S.R.O. 1856/4.
[15] O.S. Maps 1/2,500, Salop. XLIII. 2, 6 (1882, 1902, and 1927 edns.); ibid. 6″, SJ 60 NE. (1966 edn.).
[16] Below, Econ. Hist.
[17] Trinder, *Ind. Rev. Salop.* (1981), 192.
[18] S.R.O. 1856/4.
[19] S.R.O., DA 26/100/2, pp. 323–4.   [20] S.R.O. 1856/4.
[21] *V.C.H. Salop.* ii. 228.
[22] O.S. Map 1/2,500, Salop. XXXVI. 14 (1882, 1902, and 1939 edns.); ibid. 6″, SJ 60 NE. (1966 edn.).
[23] S.R.O. 4105/Ch/51.
[24] *Salop. News Letter*, xxxiii. 1.
[25] S.R.O. 4345/4, dist. 1MA, p. 2.
[26] S.R.O., q. sess. rec. parcel 254, badgers', drovers', and alesellers' licensing bk. Trin. 1615.
[27] Ibid. parcel 255, reg. of alesellers' recognizances 1753–4.

[28] S.R.O. 14, tithe appt.; 1856/4.
[29] O.S. Map 1/2,500, Salop. XLIII. 2 (1902 edn.).
[30] S.R.O., q. sess. rec. parcel 285, friendly socs. reg.
[31] Ed. J. Burrow & Co. Ltd. *R.D. of Wellington Official Guide* [*c.* 1960], 20.
[32] S.R.O. 4105/ChH/1.
[33] S.R.O., DA 26/134 (S.R.O. 3172/8/15/3), file 550.
[34] *Dawley Observer*, 19 June 1964.
[35] *V.C.H. Salop.* i. 334; Eyton, ii. 48–9; viii. 82, 100.
[36] *Rot. Hund.* (Rec. Com.), ii. 56.
[37] Eyton, ix. 333.
[38] *Feud. Aids*, iv. 219.
[39] Eyton, viii. 100.
[40] Ibid. ix. 333–5; *Cat. Anct. D.* vi, C 4637.
[41] Eyton, ii. 48–9.
[42] Ibid. viii. 100; x. 182, 185–7.
[43] *V.C.H. Salop.* i. 332.
[44] Ibid. iii. 10.
[45] *Feud. Aids*, iv. 219.
[46] Below, Local Govt. and Public Services.
[47] *Feud. Aids*, iv. 219.
[48] P.R.O., C 142/303, no. 141.
[49] *Cal. Inq. p.m.* iii, pp. 504–5; Eyton, viii. 38 n.
[50] *Rot. Hund.* ii. 56.
[51] *Feud. Aids*, iv. 219.
[52] *Cal. Inq. p.m.* iii, pp. 504–5.

followed that of Moreton Corbet until the mid 17th century.[53] In 1649 Sir Vincent Corbet sold Lawley to Richard Browne[54] (d. 1677).[55] Browne left most of his estate to his son Robert (d. 1682), whose trustees sold that part of it to Thomas Burton of Longner in 1683.[56] It seems to have descended with Longner[57] until 1853 when Robert Burton sold it to the Coalbrookdale Co.[58] In 1910 the company sold its land in Lawley in small lots, but not the lordship of the manor.[59] The lordship was presumably implied in the company's conveyance in 1962 of all its assets to Allied Ironfounders Ltd., which in 1973 sold the same to Glynwed Foundries Ltd., of Bilston (Staffs.), the owners in 1981.[60]

Lawley House is a 19th-century brick building[61] perhaps on the site of a medieval capital messuage.

Bartholomew Toret granted a virgate to the canonesses of Brewood with his sister Gundred. They held it of Robert Corbet in 1255 but parted with it before the Dissolution.[62]

Richard Browne (d. 1677) left one estate at Lawley separately from the manorial estate, to his son Philip, who sold his Lawley property in 1733 to William Forester of Dothill.[63] In 1842 it was the only estate other than the Burtons' and comprised 107 a.[64] In 1918 Lord Forester sold it.[65]

ECONOMIC HISTORY. Like nearby Hadley[66] the two Lawley manors were not wealthy in 1086, and the name-element *leah* suggests that they had been created by woodland clearance in a period not far distant.[67] The manors were taxed at only 1½ hide. The smaller had land for one ploughteam but had been waste for some time, was worth nothing, and had no recorded tenants. The larger had one team in demesne, with four serfs, and another team in the hands of a villein. Since 1066 its value had fallen from 12s. to 10s.[68]

Domesday recorded no woodland, but in the early Middle Ages waste and woodland probably covered most of the higher parts of the township,

on the southern, western, and north-western sides, with arable lying lower down on the east and north-east.[69] The township lay within the forest jurisdiction of Mount Gilbert until 1301[70] and assarting was therefore controlled. In the late 12th century the men of Lawley were amerced for 3½ a. of wheat taken into cultivation.[71] In the later Middle Ages there were at least two open arable fields,[72] Synders field[73] on the north-east side of the village,[74] and Wall field,[75] perhaps on the north.

By the early 16th century it had become profitable to inclose open-field arable for pasture. In 1512 a tenant inclosed and converted 18 a.[76] By 1589 the landlord had inclosed the woodland and had let parcels of it to tenants in severalty, some of whom used them as pasture.[77] There were eight farms in 1615, three large ones owing rents between £1 2s. 8d. and £4 11s. 4d., the others owing between 9s. and 14s. 10d. each.[78] The same number of farms existed c. 1712, mostly 'very small'.[79]

At least five farms were held by lease in 1615. The two oldest leases then in force, dated 1581, were for 60 years terminable on the life of the landlord, Vincent Corbet (kt. 1607).[80] By 1605, the date of the next oldest lease, the term was invariably three lives. All lessees owed 2 capons a year, suit of court, and heriot.[81] In 1639 a lessee had to carry a stack of coal annually from Lawley to Moreton Corbet, and within Lawley each tenant had to carry annually a quantity of mine timber proportionate to the size of his farm.[82] In the late 17th and earlier 18th century the farmers had both cereals and cattle, and the larger ones usually had sheep and a few pigs.[83]

In the early 19th century, as in the early 17th, there were three large farms:[84] John Williams's (187 a.), Lawley farm (140 a.),[85] and Lawley House farm (107 a.).[86] In 1806 the three other agricultural holdings were between 11 a. and 26 a. Lawley common (including Horsehay common), in the extreme south of the township, then consisted of the Great common (131 a.) and Emery's

[53] Ibid.; *Cal. Close, 1381–5*, 20; *Cal. Inq. p.m. Hen. VII*, i, p. 476; P.R.O., C 142/187, no. 56; /205, no. 187; /303, no. 141; /399, no. 154; /554, no. 66; S.P.L., Deeds 18146. Cf. A. E. C[orbet], *The Fam. of Corbet: its Life and Times*, ii [1918], table facing p. 368.

[54] P.R.O., CP 25(2)/590/1649 East. no. [9]; S.R.O. 1224, box 223, pedigree of Ric. Browne.

[55] Wellington par. reg. bur. 26 May (transcript in S.P.L.).

[56] S.R.O. 1224, box 223, wills of Ric. and Rob. Browne (copies) and papers in Burton v. Cleaton and Cleaton.

[57] S.R.O., q. sess. rec. box 260, reg. of gamekeepers 1711–78, 14 Sept. 1725; P.R.O., CP 43/862, rot. 392. Cf. W. Hughes, *Sheriffs of Salop. 1831–86* (Shrews. 1886), 44–5.

[58] S.R.O. 1681, box 122, deed; T.D.C., deed pkt. 1372, abstr. of title.

[59] S.R.O. 1268/4. Conveyances were completed 1911: e.g. 1681, box 178, deed.

[60] Deeds in possession of Thorn-Pudsey & Derry, Ironbridge.

[61] SA 21141.

[62] *Rot. Hund.* ii. 56 (in which Bartholomew is called Bertram); Dugdale, *Mon.* v. 731.

[63] S.R.O. 1224, box 223, will (copy) and deed.

[64] S.R.O. 14, title appt.

[65] S.R.O. 1681, box 44, sale plan.

[66] Above, Hadley, Econ. Hist.

[67] See M. Gelling, *Signposts to the Past* (1978), 126–8.

[68] *V.C.H. Salop.* i. 332, 334.

[69] Field names in S.R.O. 14, tithe appt.; 1856/4.

[70] *Cartulary of Shrews. Abbey*, ed. U. Rees (1975), ii, p. 249.

[71] P.R.O., E 32/143.

[72] S.R.O. 1011, box 169, estreat of fines.

[73] So called in 1589: ibid.

[74] Lynaldes furlong (named ibid. as pt. of the field) recurs as Linell in S.R.O. 14, tithe appt.; 1856/4 (no. 97).

[75] S.R.O. 1224, box 223, deeds of 1688, 1726.

[76] I. S. Leadam, 'Inquisition of 1517: Inclosures and Evictions', *Trans. R.H.S.* N.S. viii. 324–5.

[77] S.R.O. 1011, box 169, estreat of fines.

[78] S.R.O. 322, box 2, ct. bk.

[79] S.R.O. 1224, box 223, brief in Burton v. Cleaton and Cleaton.

[80] W. A. Shaw, *Kts. of Eng.* (1906) ii. 143.

[81] S.R.O. 322, box 2, ct. bk. [82] S.R.O. 215/24.

[83] L.J.R.O., B/C/11, Rob. Corbett, 1679; Fra. Cleaton, 1686; Rob. Corbet, 1726; Wm. Hulett, 1727; Basil Davies, 1741.

[84] Para. based on S.R.O. 14, tithe appt.; 1224, box 295, survey of 1808; 3651, box 31, survey of 1806.

[85] So called by 1881: O.S. Map 6", Salop. XLIII. NW. (1889 edn.).

[86] Ibid. Called Lawley farm in 1808: S.R.O. 1224, box 295, survey, f. 40v.

common (36 a.), on which the farmers had grazing rights proportionate to their holdings. Inclosure and division among the farmers was then considered, and by 1842 a 62-a. parcel of common had been added to John Williams's farm and 71 a. (in three parcels) were let to the Coalbrookdale Co. Other farmers, however, received nothing of the former commons, the rest of whose area consisted mostly of cottages at the margins. The township's woodland had been used up since the 17th century, probably for mining timber, and none remained in 1842.

After c. 1857, when the railway bisected the township,[87] the farms of the manorial estate were radically reorganized.[88] Thomas Jones's former holding at Lawley Bank (21 a. in 1842) was enlarged to comprise all other farmland east of the railway (including the Coalbrookdale Co.'s former holding) and became Lawley Bank farm (113 a. in 1910). Lawley farm thereby lost a small acreage east of the railway, but was greatly enlarged north and south (to 203 a. by 1910), mainly at the expense of the former Williams farm, whose remaining land (126 a. in 1910) was put into the Coalbrookdale Co.'s Horsehay farm, administered from Dawley parish.[89] Lawley House farm, which included 106 a. outside the township in 1842, was unaltered by boundary changes within Lawley, but by 1918 had 187 a. outside the township.[90] Of the four smallholdings of 1842, only Newdale farm (38 a.) remained in 1910.

At the beginning of the 19th century arable exceeded permanent grass by about 3 to 1 on Lawley and Lawley House farms, and by about 2 to 1 on the Williams farm. Wheat accounted for by far the greatest cereal acreage on the three main farms. No turnips were recorded but clover, peas, and vetches were used.[91] In 1842 the township's agricultural land (c. 616 a.) was equally divided between arable (c. 315 a.) and pasture (including former commons) and meadow. The division was in those proportions on the Williams farm, which by then included much former common; farther north, however, on Lawley and Lawley House farms, arable still exceeded pasture and meadow by more than 2 to 1.[92] In the later 19th century the area of agricultural land decreased only slightly and the reorganized farms did not share uniformly in the parish's movement towards livestock.[93] By the 1910s the arable proportion of the township's farmland had fallen to

about 40 per cent but, in the north and centre, constituted about 80 per cent in Newdale farm and 69 per cent in Lawley farm. In the south arable formed only 34 per cent in the Lawley part of Horsehay farm and only 22 per cent in Lawley Bank farm,[94] and the Lawley part of Lawley House farm by then consisted almost entirely of pasture.[95]

In 1980 Lawley still had a high proportion of agricultural land[96] but Telford development corporation had designated most of the township for future housing, roads, and open spaces, with no industrial sites.[97] In the later 19th and earlier 20th century only Lawley Bank (straggling into Ketley township and Dawley parish) had had any appreciable concentration of shops and public houses,[98] and a little coalmining was then almost the only occupation outside agriculture.

Hugh the smith had a forge c. 1180.[99] Fields called Smithy Pool lay near Lawley village.[1] At Newdale the Coalbrookdale Co. seems to have started a small and short-lived foundry in 1759.[2] Some ironworking jobs were available in the 19th and 20th centuries on the borders of the township, for instance at Lawley Furnaces[3] and Horsehay. By 1957[4] the Birchfield Foundry Ltd., iron founders, were established near Lawley Bank station. The works employed 44 in 1964[5] but closed c. 1968.[6]

Coal and ironstone seams lay near the surface on Lawley common, at Lawley Bank, along the Little Wenlock boundary, and at Newdale.[7] The lord of the manor had mines in 1589 (at 'Coalpit Bank',[8] perhaps Lawley Bank), 1639,[9] and 1677.[10] Ironstone may have been sent to Coalbrookdale furnace in 1685.[11]

In 1705 Robert Burton leased all coal mines on the manorial estate to Gabriel and Roger Cleaton. By 1712 they had apparently raised several thousand stacks and were working near the Flat leasow[12] in the north.[13] By 1755 the Lawley Co. was supplying coal and ironstone to Horsehay ironworks.[14] In 1759 Robert Burton leased minerals in the manor to Thomas Goldney and Abraham Darby (II).[15] Large quantities of coal and ironstone went to Horsehay in the 1760s and 1770s,[16] and in 1793 coal was being sent to Coalbrookdale.[17] In 1806 the Coalbrookdale Co. had the mineral rights on Lawley common and Joseph Reynolds & Co. those around Newdale.[18] Active pits lay mainly on the north side of the

[87] Above, intro.
[88] Para. based on S.R.O. 14, tithe appt.; 1268/4; 1856/4.
[89] Above, Dawley, Econ. Hist.
[90] S.R.O. 1681, box 44, sale plan of 1918; parcel 46, sale partic.
[91] S.R.O. 1224, box 295, survey of 1808; 3651, box 31, survey of 1806.
[92] S.R.O. 14, tithe appt.
[93] Cf. above, Wellington, Econ. Hist.
[94] S.R.O. 1268/4 (sale partic. of 1910).
[95] S.R.O. 1681, parcel 46, sale partic. of 1918. For Lawley's agric. from 1867 see also above, Wellington, Econ. Hist. (Agric.), Table IX.
[96] T.D.C. Telford Street Plan (1980).
[97] T.D.C. Telford Development Strategy, map (Feb. 1979).
[98] P.O. Dir. Salop. (1856), 138; Kelly's Dir. Salop. (1941), 129.   [99] P.R.O., E 32/143.
[1] S.R.O. 14, tithe appt.; 1856/4 (nos. 161, 225, 227–8).
[2] Trinder, Ind. Rev. Salop. (1981), 23.

[3] Above, L. Wenlock, Econ. Hist.
[4] O.S. Map 6", SJ 60 NE. (1966 edn.).
[5] J. H. D. Madin & Partners, Dawley New Town Rep. No. 2: Interim Proposals (Sept. 1964), map 14 and cap. 6, sect. 1, app.
[6] G.P.O. Telephone Dir. (1968), sect. 72, p. 2025.
[7] Inst. Geol. Sciences Map 1/25,000, Telford (1978 edn.).
[8] S.R.O. 1011, box 169, estreat of ct. r.
[9] S.R.O. 215/24.
[10] S.R.O. 1224, box 223, Ric. Browne's will (copy).
[11] A. Raistrick, Dynasty of Iron Founders, (1970), 30.
[12] S.R.O. 1224, box 223, brief in Burton v. Cleaton and Cleaton.
[13] S.R.O. 14, tithe appt.; 1856/4 (nos. 106, 117–18).
[14] S.P.L., MS. 332, pp. 8, 23, 246.
[15] S.R.O. 81/483; 1987/34/1.
[16] S.P.L., MS. 333, pp. 4, 480.
[17] Trinder, Ind. Rev. Salop. (1981), 81.
[18] S.R.O. 3651, box 31, survey, ff. 11, 14, 18.

common and at Lawley Bank.[19] In 1853 the Coalbrookdale Co. bought the mineral rights with the manorial estate.[20]

On the Forester estate the coal, ironstone, and clay were leased from 1818[21] to the partners who in 1822 opened Lawley furnace nearby.[22] In the 1820s this Lawley Co. was selling some of the Clod coal to the Ketley Co.[23] but in the 1840s was using most of the coal at its own furnace.[24] In 1847 the Coalbrookdale Co. became lessees of the furnace and mines,[25] and in the half-year to March 1856 raised c. 10,000 tons of coal and c. 5,300 of ironstone from the mines (partly in Little Wenlock parish).[26] Lawley furnace closed c. 1870.[27]

By 1882 mining had almost ceased; there were over thirty abandoned shafts. Remaining pits on Lawley common and at Newdale[28] were closed by 1901.[29] Nevertheless by 1909[30] C. R. Jones & Sons were lessees of minerals near Lawley Furnaces at the Lawley colliery, partly on the manorial[31] and partly on the Forester estates.[32] They bought the Lawley colliery minerals from those estates in 1911[33] and 1919[34] respectively. The Wrekin Coal Co. operated the colliery in 1941[35] but the mines were shut by 1958.[36] The minerals elsewhere on the manorial estate were sold, when it was broken up in 1911, to the purchasers of the several lots,[37] and small-scale mining continued at Lawley Bank[38] and Lawley common.[39] The last mine near Lawley Bank closed c. 1954.[40]

Opencast mining was in progress near Lawley village in 1957[41] and ceased c. 1960.[42] Between 1973 and 1975 opencast working on 113 a. at Lawley common yielded c. 300,000 tons of coal for power station use and destroyed old shafts and tips in preparation for building.[43]

In 1589 the lord had a stone quarry in Thomas Maydon's pasture,[44] perhaps near the Ketley boundary,[45] and in 1839 it was said that limestone pits had formerly been worked.[46]

Slag from Lawley Furnaces was used for road material in the 1920s.[47]

From c. 1936 John A. Greenwood and Kathleen M. Ball produced high quality lead figurines in Spring Village, Horsehay. Miss Ball continued to paint figures there until 1952, and Greenwood moved to Scarborough in 1959. Production was mainly of military figures for sale, but special commissions ranging from single figures to major exhibition dioramas were also undertaken.[48]

LOCAL GOVERNMENT AND PUBLIC SERVICES. There was a court baron in the late 16th and earlier 17th century, of which an estreat of 1589 survives.[49] In 1255,[50] and still in 1615,[51] Lawley was partly in the leet jurisdiction of Hinstock and partly in that of Bradford hundred. In the mid 16th century one constable presented at Hinstock, and perhaps more than one in the early 17th.[52] In 1540 the inhabitants were required to make a pound for the lord of Hinstock.[53] Part of Lawley still owed suit to Hinstock in 1813.[54]

The township was in Wellington civil parish until 1894, Wellington poor-law union 1836–1930, Wrekin highway district 1865–82, and Wellington rural sanitary district 1872–94. In 1894 the township became part of Wellington Rural C.P. and Wellington rural district.[55] Much of the southern part, including Horsehay common and Spring Village, was taken into Dawley C.P. and urban district in 1934[56] and almost all the rest in 1966, leaving a tiny area at the northern tip in Wellington Rural C.P.[57] (renamed Ketley C.P. in 1976).[58] In 1974 the whole township became part of the district of the Wrekin.[59] In 1963 the parts in, or later added to, Dawley C.P. and U.D. were included in the designated area of Dawley new town,[60] and in 1968 the whole township was included in the designated area of Telford.[61]

[19] R. Baugh, *Map of Salop.* (1808); C. & J. Greenwood, *Map of Salop.* (1827).
[20] S.R.O. 1681, box 122, deed.
[21] S.R.O. 604 (uncat.), deed of 1817 (draft).
[22] Above, L. Wenlock, Econ. Hist.
[23] S.R.O. 1224, box 295, royalty acct. of 1824.
[24] S.R.O. 604 (uncat.), acct. of 1844.
[25] Ibid. deed (draft).
[26] Ibid. acct.
[27] Above, L. Wenlock, Econ. Hist.
[28] O.S. Maps 1/2,500, Salop. XXXVI. 14; XLIII. 2 (1882 edn.).
[29] Ibid. 6″, Salop. XXXVI. SW.; XLIII. NW. (1903 edn.).
[30] *Kelly's Dir. Salop.* (1909), 123.
[31] S.R.O. 1268/4, p. 9 and plan no. 1.
[32] S.R.O. 1681, box 44, sale plan; parcel 46, sale partic. p. 3.
[33] Ibid. box 178, deed.   [34] Ibid. parcel 46, deed.
[35] *Kelly's Dir. Salop.* (1941), 129.
[36] O.S. Map 1/2,500, SJ 6609 (1958 edn.).
[37] S.R.O. 1268/4, p. 2.
[38] *Kelly's Dir. Salop.* (1922), 123; (1929), 128; O.S. Map 6″, XLIII. NW. (1928 edn.).
[39] *Kelly's Dir. Salop.* (1941), 129.
[40] W. Howard Williams, 'Dawley New Town Hist. Survey: Industries' (TS. 1964), p. 62 (copy in S.P.L., accession 5202).
[41] O.S. Map 1/2,500, SJ 6608 (1958 edn.).
[42] *Shropshire Star*, 10 Sept. 1975.
[43] Ibid. 30 Jan. 1973; *Building*, 24 Oct. 1975.
[44] S.R.O. 1011, box 169, estreat of ct. r.

[45] Where Maidens meadow was in 1842: S.R.O. 14, tithe appt.; 1856/4 (no. 96).
[46] *V.C.H. Salop.* i. 29.
[47] Williams, 'Dawley Hist. Survey: Inds.' p. 43.
[48] Mrs. J. A. Nathaniel (*née* Kathleen M. Ball) kindly provided inf. and refs. to *Illustr. Lond. News*, 6 Apr. 1946, 372–3; 1 Nov. 1947, 500–1; *Express & Star*, 27 May 1955; *Northern Echo*, 24 Nov. 1959.
[49] S.R.O. 215/24; 1011, box 169, estreat.
[50] *Rot. Hund.* (Rec. Com.), ii. 56.
[51] S.R.O. 322, box 2, ct. bk., 'A note showing how the town of Lawley is divided in several leets'.
[52] S.R.O. 327, box 4, ct. r. of 1543, 1545; box 5, ct. r. of 1606, 1609.
[53] Ibid. box 4, ct. r. of 1540.
[54] Ibid. box 6, suit r. of 1813–20, p. 63.
[55] Above, Wellington, intro; Local Govt.
[56] *Salop Review Order, 1934* (Min. of Health order no. 77933); O.S. Map 6″, SJ 60 NE. (1954 edn.).
[57] *Salop Order 1966* (Min. of Ho. & Local Govt. order no. 22958); O.S. *Map Referred to in The Salop Order 1966* (copy in S.R.O. 2981, parcel VI).
[58] S.C.C. Planning Dept. file no. 051001, Wrekin District Council sec. to co sec. 15 July 1976.
[59] *Census, 1971, Rep. for Co. of Salop as constituted on 1st Apr. 1974*, 2.
[60] *Dawley New Town (Designation) Order 1963* (Stat. Instr. 1963, no. 64), accompanying map (copy in S.R.O. 2981, parcel VI).
[61] *Dawley New Town (Designation) Amendment (Telford) Order 1968* (Stat. Instr. 1968, no. 1912), map accompanying Explanatory Note.

From 1909 Dawley urban district council, by agreement with Wellington rural district council, supplied mains water to Lawley Bank and Horsehay Common from the U.D.C.'s Lawley Bank reservoir.[62] The system was later extended to the rest of the township,[63] reaching Newdale in 1924.[64] The R.D.C., with Dawley U.D.C., opened a small sewerage scheme at Lawley Bank in 1926.[65] In 1939 the R.D.C. completed a larger scheme serving Lawley Bank and Lawley village and opened a new disposal works at Lawley Bank.[66] The first sub-post office within the township boundary opened in Lawley village in the 1940s.[67]

CHURCH. In 1865, owing largely to the efforts of Bartholomew Yates of Lawley House farm,[68] a chapel of ease was completed on a site given by the Coalbrookdale Co. and Lord Forester.[69] Building costs were borne by Henry Dickinson, a partner in the Coalbrookdale Co.,[70] Mrs. Mary Jones (*née* Darby),[71] and others and the chapel was consecrated the same year.[72] From 1865 it was licensed for baptisms, marriages, and burials.[73] In 1867 a consolidated chapelry was assigned to it,[74] comprising Lawley township and the north-east part of Little Wenlock parish.[75] The living, a perpetual curacy in the bishop's gift,[76] became a titular vicarage in 1868.[77] The last vicar resigned in 1962. A priest-in-charge was appointed from 1965[78] to 1975, when Lawley became a district in the new parish of Central Telford.[79] Thereafter Lawley was in the immediate pastoral charge of the successive rectors of Central Telford.[80]

In 1864 Lord Forester and the Coalbrookdale Co. gave 12 a. of land[81] but by 1884 there was no glebe[82] other than the 3 a. of churchyard and vicarage grounds.[83] In 1867 the Ecclesiastical Commissioners granted £10 a year to meet a benefaction[84] and in 1870 the living was said to be worth £100 a year.[85] The Ecclesiastical Commissioners gave £85 a year in 1874 and tithe rent charge of £186 a year gross from the former

endowment of Wellington prebend.[86] The vicar's net income was given as £250 in 1885.[87] The Ecclesiastical Commissioners granted an augmentation in 1918[88] and his net income was £279 in 1932.[89] The vicarage house was built south of the church in 1865.[90] The priest-in-charge became rector of Central Telford in 1975 and moved to the new Hollinswood estate (in Dawley) in 1976. Thereafter the house remained in diocesan use, but became vacant in 1983.[91]

Thomas Ragg the first incumbent, 1865-81, was a self-educated divine and poet, already well known before his ordination in 1858. He had earlier been offered ministries by nonconformist congregations.[92] Two long incumbencies covered most of the succeeding period: G. H. White's 1882–1917[93] and Arnold Clay's 1935–62.[94] J. R. Edwards, 1917–29,[95] was Evangelical but his successors were Anglo-Catholic.[96]

The church of *ST. JOHN THE EVANGELIST*[97] was designed by John Ladds in the Gothic style. It is of red and yellow brick with stone dressings and comprises a chancel with apse, north chapel (used by 1905 as a vestry), south vestry (used as a boiler house), and south-west turret and spire, and a nave with gallery and south porch.[98] In 1915 there was one bell of 1865.[99]

NONCONFORMITY. It seems to have been the Darbys who introduced their employees at Newdale to the Society of Friends. Buildings there were licensed for Quaker meetings in 1762[1] but it may have been 1768 before a regular meeting was established.[2] In 1798 attendance was 24, mainly the Reynolds family and their senior employees.[3] A new meeting house at Newdale was built *c.* 1814[4] but closed in 1843 when the meeting united with that at Coalbrookdale.[5]

J. W. Fletcher, the Methodist vicar of Madeley 1760–85, preached at Horsehay,[6] which by 1813 was a Wesleyan preaching place associated with

[62] *S.C.C. Mins.* Suppl. Rep. on Water Supplies of Pars. of Wellington Rural and Hadley, 28 June 1912, 3. For reservoir site see O.S. Map 1/2,500, Salop. XLIII. 2 (1927 edn.).
[63] A. H. S. Waters, *Rep. on Water Supplies* (S.C.C. 1946), 98.
[64] S.R.O., DA 26/100/3, pp. 75, 79.
[65] Ibid. pp. 241, 291–2.
[66] S.R.O., DA 26/100/6, pp. 184–6; /112/1, p. 62.
[67] County Assocs. Ltd. *Wellington & Dist. Dir.* [1950], 115.
[68] Plaque in ch.
[69] S.R.O. 4105/Ch/1.   [70] Randall, *Madeley*, 299.
[71] S.R.O. 4105/Ch/5.
[72] Lich. Dioc. Regy., bps.' reg. R, pp. 25–30.
[73] E. C. Peele and R. S. Clease, *Salop. Par. Doc.* (Shrews. [1903]), 199.
[74] Lich. Dioc. Regy., bps.' reg. Q (Orders in Council), p. 120.
[75] S.R.O. 1149/1.
[76] Lich. Dioc. Regy., episc. reg. 32, p. 341.
[77] *P.O. Dir. Salop.* (1870), 156.
[78] Lich. Dioc. Regy., benefice and inst. bk. 1952–68, p. 123.
[79] Above, Dawley, Churches.
[80] Inf. from the Revd. R. A. J. Hill, rector.
[81] Lich. Dioc. Regy., bps.' reg. R, pp. 25–30.
[82] S.R.O. 3916/1/33, s.v.
[83] O.S. Map 1/2,500, Salop. XLIII. 2 (1927 edn.).

[84] Lich. Dioc. Regy., bps.' reg. R, p. 158.
[85] *P.O. Dir. Salop.* (1870), 156.
[86] Lich. Dioc. Regy., bps.' reg. R, p. 703. For an earlier, fruitless, scheme see ibid. pp. 25–30. For the prebend see above, Wellington, Man. and Other Est.
[87] *Kelly's Dir. Salop.* (1885), 871.
[88] Lich. Dioc. Regy., bps.' reg. V, p. 688.
[89] *Crockford* (1932), 561.
[90] S.R.O. 4105/Be/7.
[91] Inf. from the Revd. R. A. J. Hill.
[92] *D.N.B.*
[93] Lich. Dioc. Regy., benefice and inst. bk. 1868–1900, p. 61; 1900–29, p. 50.
[94] Ibid. 1929–52, p. 36; 1952–68, p. 123.
[95] Ibid. 1900–29, pp. 50, 119.
[96] S.R.O. 4105/Ve/14.
[97] So dedicated in 1865: Lich. Dioc. Regy., bps.' reg. R, pp. 25–30.
[98] Cranage, vii. 595.
[99] H. B. Walters, *Ch. Bells of Salop.* (Oswestry, 1915), 329.
[1] S.R.O., q. sess. order bk. 1757–72, f. 95.
[2] *Jnl. Friends' Hist. Soc.* li. 206.
[3] Trinder, *Ind. Rev. Salop.* 304–5.
[4] S.R.O., q. sess. files, 12/176.
[5] *V.C.H. Salop.* ii. 12.
[6] R. F. Skinner, *Nonconformity in Salop.* (Shrews. 1964), 72.

Little Wenlock.[7] A brick chapel was built *c.* 1816[8] at Spring Village, near Horsehay. On Census Sunday 1851 100 attended in the morning and 150 in the evening.[9] It closed in 1968 and the congregation joined the former Primitive society at Moreton's Coppice.[10] A Wesleyan society was formed at Lawley Bank in 1798[11] and a chapel, presumably Wesleyan, was built *c.* 1818[12] on the south side of the road from Lawley (later Station Road) near the junction with Milners Lane.[13] About 1840 the congregation moved to a new chapel nearby, just in Dawley parish.[14] By 1882 there was a Sunday school on the old site.[15] There was regular Wesleyan preaching at Newdale by 1813.[16] A society was active there in the 1840s,[17] and by 1881 used borrowed premises[18] as a chapel.[19] It expired in 1924[20] when only four members remained.[21] A Wesleyan society was formed at Lawley Furnaces *c.* 1840.[22] In 1881 there were regular services there in a borrowed room[23] but the society expired *c.* 1892.[24]

A New Connexion society formed at Lawley Bank *c.* 1837 and opened a chapel in 1839[25] on the east side of Milners Lane.[26] On Census Sunday 1851 100 attended in the morning and 130 in the evening.[27] Called Mount Gilead by 1875,[28] the chapel closed *c.* 1911,[29] became a Baptist Sunday school,[30] and was demolished in 1938.[31]

There were Primitive societies at Lawley Common, Newdale, Lawley Bank, and Lawley between 1838 and 1842.[32] Lawley Bank was active in 1845, when the 'chapel' was repaired.[33] At Lawley village in 1862 there were hopes of building a chapel;[34] they were not realized but the society still existed in 1890.[35]

EDUCATION. Newdale School was established by the Coalbrookdale Co. before 1818, when it had 89 pupils with 14 more on Sundays. The rectangular brick building, with tiled roof and wooden floors, contained a large schoolroom, a classroom, and an entrance lobby. In 1865 the buildings were in good repair and attendance averaged 60. The curate of Lawley managed the school but government grants were paid through the company, which defrayed the school's expenses and allocated the annual income (£16 in voluntary contributions and £15 in fees) to the mistress. Company employees' children paid 1*d.* a week, those of the Ketley Co.'s 2*d.*, and others 3*d.*[36] The school closed and its pupils transferred in 1877 to the new school built by the Wellington school board,[37] in whose area Lawley was included in 1872.[38]

Lawley Bank Wesleyan School was established in 1868 in a building of *c.* 1800 owned by the Coalbrookdale Co., which charged £1 rent. The first quarter's income comprised £13 15*s.* in voluntary contributions and £15 9*s.* 10*d.* in fees of 2*d.* or 3*d.* a week according to the pupil's class; five children were free. The master received £11 9*s.* 6*d.* for the quarter, the sewing mistress £1 9*s.* 9*d.*[39] The school, though well attended and very efficient, was in bad repair in 1873, when the trustees accepted the school board's offer to take it over. The board agreed to pay £10 a year rent and, though the school was to continue only temporarily, to spend £200 on repairs. The Wesleyans were allowed use on Sundays and for evening meetings and the master was allowed to hold an evening school.[40] By 1875 the day school was so overcrowded that admission was refused to children from outside Wellington parish. In 1876, with a maximum attendance at the annual inspection, H.M. Inspector had to examine pupils in the playground for want of space indoors. The school closed in 1876, pupils transferring to the new board school in 1877.[41]

Lawley Board School, built on the same plan as Hadley's[42] but with 274 places,[43] opened with 78 mixed pupils and 20 infants in 1877.[44] The school admitted pupils from Newdale School and Lawley Bank Wesleyan Board School.[45] Mixed and infant departments were combined in 1884[46] after the building was altered.[47] Attendance averaged 200 in 1885, 160 in 1891, 200 in 1909, and 220 in 1913.[48] H. M. Inspectors' reports, received annually until 1903, were excellent and the night school established in 1878 was also efficient. From

[7] S.P.L., C 98.7 v.f., Shrews. circuit plan.
[8] *Orders of Q. Sess.* iii. 201.
[9] P.R.O., HO 129/365, no. 31.
[10] Above, Dawley, Prot. Nonconf.
[11] W. H. Barclay, *Hist. of Wesleyan Methodism at Lawley Bank* (1858), 33 (ref. supplied by Mr. J. H. Lenton). For the earlier hist. of Methodism in the neighbourhood see above, Dawley, Prot. Nonconf.
[12] *Orders of Q. Sess.* iii. 210.
[13] S.R.O. 14, tithe appt.; 1856/4 (no. 340).
[14] L.J.R.O., B/A/15, Dawley Magna (no. 1100); above, Dawley, Prot. Nonconf.
[15] O.S. Map 1/2,500, Salop. XLIII. 2 (1882 edn.).
[16] S.P.L., C 98.7 v.f., Shrews. circuit plan.
[17] S.R.O. 3767/XVII/A, 7 Jan. 1840; /XVII/E1, 30 June 1846.
[18] Ibid. /XVII/E2, sched.
[19] O.S. Map 6", Salop. XXXVI. SW. (1887 edn.).
[20] S.R.O. 3767/XVII/E5, Mar.–June 1924.
[21] Ibid.
[22] Ibid. /XVII/A, 29 Sept. 1840; 5 Jan. 1841.
[23] Ibid. /XVII/E2, sched.
[24] Ibid. /XVII/E3, Dec. 1891; Mar. 1892.
[25] B. Trinder, *Meth. New Connexion in Dawley and Madeley* (Wesley Hist. Soc., W. Midlands Branch, Occ. Publ. i [1968]), 7.

[26] S.R.O. 14, tithe appt.; 1856/4 (no. 498).
[27] P.R.O., HO 129/365, no. 21.
[28] *Wellington Jnl.* 20 Feb. 1875.
[29] Trinder, *Meth. New Connexion*, 19.
[30] *Wellington Jnl.* 17 June 1922.
[31] SA 14400.
[32] S.R.O. 3605/1, pp. 9, 18, 27, 37.
[33] Ibid. p. 154.
[34] S.R.O. 2533/130, 9 June 1862.
[35] S.R.O. 1936/2.
[36] *Digest Educ. Poor*, H.C. 224, pp. 761, 767 (1819), ix (2); P.R.O., ED 7/103, ff. 149–50, stating (1865) that the sch. had been established for 50–100 yrs.
[37] Lawley Bd. Sch. log bk. (at Lawley Co. Primary Sch.).
[38] Above, Wellington, Educ.
[39] P.R.O., ED 7/103, f. 120 and v.
[40] *Wellington Jnl.* 9 Aug., 11 Oct. 1873 (bd. mtg. reps.).
[41] Lawley Bd. Sch. log bk. 17 Mar. 1875; 14 July 1876; 15 Jan. 1877.
[42] *Wellington Jnl.* 11 Dec. 1875 (bd. mtg. rep.).
[43] *Kelly's Dir. Salop.* (1885), 871.
[44] Log bk. 15 Jan. 1877.
[45] Ibid. rep. 1877.
[46] Ibid. 22 Apr. 1884.
[47] Ibid. rep. 1884.
[48] *Kelly's Dir. Salop.* (1885, 1891, 1909, 1913).

1878 the Science and Art Department's annual drawing reports were consistently favourable.[49] The school continued as an all-age school until 1956, when seniors transferred to a new secondary modern school.[50] In 1980 Lawley County Primary School (142 pupils),[51] used the original building, by then improved, and demountable classrooms.

CHARITY FOR THE POOR. In addition to those charities applicable to the whole of Wellington ancient parish, Lawley benefited from Henry Parker's legacy (by will proved 1898) of stock to provide food, clothing, and blankets for residents of the ecclesiastical parish.[52] In 1975 the income was £4.[53]

WOMBRIDGE, LATER OAKENGATES

WOMBRIDGE parish developed out of the demesnes of the Augustinian priory of St. Leonard, founded c. 1135 in a clearing in Hadley wood. The area was the centre of one of the two bailiwicks of the royal forest of Mount Gilbert (or the Wrekin); like the centre of the other — Haughmond, also a monastic site — it was extra-parochial.[54] The priory stood less than 1 km. north of Watling Street, which bisected the ancient parish. The parish extended to only 702 a.[55] Oakengates, a late medieval hamlet on its eastern edge, stood on Watling Street 4 km. east of Wellington.

Oakengates grew into a sizeable town in the mid 19th century, dwarfing the small settlement at Wombridge, and in 1895 Wombridge parish council tried, though unsuccessfully, to change the parish name to Oakengates. In 1898, however, Wombridge civil parish, conterminous with the ancient parish, was included in the new urban district of Oakengates, which also comprised Wrockwardine Wood C.P. (914 a.) and the new C.P.s of St. George's (129 a.) and Priorslee (584 a.).[56] In 1934 the U.D.'s component C.P.s were amalgamated into Oakengates C.P. At the same time small parts of the C.P.s of Hadley (at Trench), Wellington Rural (at Ketley Bank), and Shifnal (between Woodhouse colliery and Priorslee Hall) were added to Oakengates while a small part of Priorslee (Hollinswood) was transferred to Dawley U.D.[57] The area so formed contained 2,396 a.[58] Two small parts of Oakengates U.D and C.P., east of Hollinswood and south of Priorslee village, were included in the designated area of Dawley new town in 1963[59] and were transferred to Dawley U.D. in 1966.[60] Oakengates was included in Telford new town in 1968[61] and in the district of the Wrekin in 1974 when the U.D was abolished.[62]

The history of Wombridge parish and the growth of Oakengates town, treated in the present article, are inextricably bound up with the adjacent district of Priorslee (a remote corner of the manor and parish of Shifnal), where Wombridge

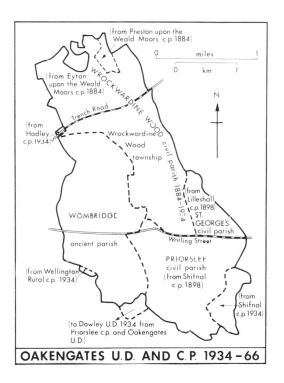

OAKENGATES U.D. AND C.P. 1934-66

priory built up an estate in the early Middle Ages.[63] Accordingly Priorslee's[64] industrial and urban involvement with Oakengates, with the gradual severance of its links with Shifnal, have formed complementary themes in modern times.

[49] Log bk. 14 Oct. 1878 and *passim*.
[50] *S.C.C. Mins. (Educ.)* 1955–6, 279; above, Dawley, Educ.
[51] S.C.C. Educ. Cttee. *Educ. Dir.* (1980), 10.
[52] S.C.C. chars. index.
[53] *Review of Local Chars.* (S.C.C. 1975), 65.
[54] *V.C.H. Salop.* i. 486 (corr. ibid. ii. 319); ii. 62, 66, 80, 223; Eyton, ix. 143–7. This art. was written 1982–3.
[55] L.J.R.O., B/A/15, Wombridge.
[56] S.R.O., S.C.C. Local Govt. etc. Cttee. min. bk. 1894–1903, pp. 56–7. Cf. *S.C.C. Mins.* Finance and Gen. Purp. Cttee. rep. 17 Apr. 1894, 26; ibid. council mins. 28 Apr. 1894, 5; below Local Govt.; *Kelly's Dir. Salop.* (1926), 176, 201, 208, 327, 333.

[57] *V.C.H. Salop.* ii. 225 n.
[58] *Kelly's Dir. Salop.* (1941), 176.
[59] *Dawley New Town (Designation) Order 1963* (Stat. Instr. 1963, no. 64), accompanying map (copy in S.R.O. 2981, parcel VI).
[60] *Census 1971, Co. Rep. Salop.* i. 8.
[61] *Dawley New Town (Designation) Amendment (Telford) Order 1968* (Stat. Instr. 1968, no. 1912), map accompanying Explanatory Note.   [62] Below, Local Govt.
[63] Eyton, ii. 313–14; *T.S.A.S.* ix. 378–80; xi. 325–39.
[64] Here conceived as Priorslee C.P. 1898–1943 with the small areas that in 1934 were lost to Dawley U.D. (Hollinswood) and gained from Shifnal C.P.

The bounds of Wombridge ancient parish appear to have been those to which Wombridge priory demesne had expanded by c. 1269. The western boundary partly followed Springwell brook, whose ancient course was largely obliterated by industry.[65] The other boundaries apparently did not follow major natural or man-made features. Priorslee lies almost 3 km. south-east of Wombridge church, and is bounded to the north by Watling Street.[66]

The area here treated, extending c. 3 km. from north to south and c. 3 km. from east to west, lies near the northern edge of the east Shropshire coalfield. Oakengates itself lies at c. 120 metres above O.D. in a shallow valley, flanked by the higher ground of Ketley Bank to the south and St. George's to the east, both over 150 metres above O.D. North of Oakengates the ground falls away towards the Weald Moors, to c. 75 metres above O.D. near Trench Pool. The location of the 'lake-ridge' referred to in the name Wombridge[67] is uncertain.

Oakengates town stands on a band of boulder clay and sand and gravel overlying the Middle Coal Measures. The coal measures outcrop either side of the band: to the south-west between Hartshill, Ketley Bank, and Hollinswood, and to the north-east between Newfield Farm and Sneds-hill. The Greyhound and Lightmoor faults cross the Coal Measures from south-west to north-east; south-east of the faults, on the eastern side of the dividing band of clay and gravel, the workable coal seams are overlain by the carboniferous sandstones, marl, and mudstones of the Hadley and Coalport formations.[68]

A hoard of 368 silver coins, deposited c. 1646, was unearthed at Priorslee in 1982 during construction of the M 54 motorway.[69]

COMMUNICATIONS. Few roads are likely to have been made before industry and settlement expanded in the 17th century, though there was presumably a way leading north from Watling Street to Wombridge priory, perhaps on the line of the later Hadley Road. Priorslee probably grew up beside the road from Watling Street to Shifnal, first mentioned in 1335.[70]

Watling Street and the road via Priorslee to Shifnal were turnpiked in 1726. The latter, bounding Snedshill coppice to the west, was replaced in 1730 by a 'new road', the later Canon-gate, running across the coppice.[71] About 1820 it in turn was replaced by a new road to the south-west as part of the Holyhead road improve-ments. The first part of the new road, built c. 1817, left Watling Street at Pottersbank, Ketley, and rejoined the existing Shifnal road at Snedshill along the later Church Road; about 1824 the new road was extended from Snedshill to Priorslee; and c. 1826 the length to Shifnal was completed.[72] Apparently associated with the Holyhead road improvement was the construction of a road running south-west from Watling Street at Pain's Lane to join it at Snedshill, the limit of the improvement of c. 1817. That road, the later Stafford Street, was apparently turnpiked by 1831, allowing traffic along Watling Street to bypass Oakengates to the south.[73]

At Teague's Bridge a sectional iron bridge was erected where the road (later Teague's Bridge Lane) crossed the Wombridge Canal, perhaps not long after the canal's construction in 1788.[74]

In 1931–2 the St. George's bypass was built under a government unemployment relief scheme.[75] Several major new roads were built following the designation of Telford new town in 1968. Queensway, partly built along the former Coalport branch railway, opened northwards to the Hollinswood interchange in 1971, to the Greyhound interchange, Ketley Bank, in 1975–6, and to the Wombridge interchange north of the church in 1981. A ring road around the centre of Oakengates was completed in 1975. The M 54 motorway, opened to the south of Oakengates, terminated in the east at Priorslee in 1975. Work to link it eastwards to the M 6 at Essington (Staffs.) was completed in 1983.[76]

A network of canals and railways linked mines and ironworks in the Oakengates area with each other and with outside markets. They were built over unsuitable terrain that necessitated the construction of frequent tunnels, bridges, and in-clined planes. In 1788 William Reynolds completed the 2½-km. Ketley Canal linking Ketley ironworks with mines near Oakengates, and c. 1788 he built the 3-km. Wombridge Canal con-necting mines near Wombridge church with the Donnington Wood furnaces and the Donnington Wood Canal. About 1790 the Shropshire Canal opened; it ran south from the junction of the Donnington Wood and Wombridge canals and linked up with the Ketley Canal before passing through Oakengates to the Severn. The coalfield was given access to the county town by the Shrewsbury Canal, which opened fully in 1797; a section from Trench Pool to Long Lane, linked to the existing Wombridge Canal by the 223-yd. long Trench inclined plane which allowed boats to descend 75 ft., opened in 1794.[77]

[65] Below, Growth of Settlement.
[66] O.S. Map 1/50,000, sheet 127 (1977 edn.).
[67] Ibid.; E. Ekwall, *Concise Oxf. Dict. Eng. P.N.* (4th edn.), 530.
[68] Inst. Geol. Sciences Map 1/25,000, *Telford* (1978 edn.).
[69] SA 2898.
[70] *Cal. Pat.* 1334–8, 188.
[71] 12 Geo. I, c. 9; 3 Geo. II, c. 6; B.L. Eg. MS. 2872, Oaken Gate Cottages, Sneds Hill Works and Coppice (copy in S.R.O. 3629); O.S. Map 6″, SJ 71 SW. (1967 edn.); *T.S.A.S.* xlix. 24.
[72] *6th Rep. Sel. Cttee. Holyhead Rd.* H.C. 549, p. 110 (1819), v; *1st Rep. R. Com. Holyhead Rd.* H.C. 305, p. 23 (1824), ix; *3rd Rep.* H.C. 129, p. 10 (1826), xi; *4th Rep.* H.C.

412, p. 11 (1826–7), vii.
[73] Not shown on B.L. Maps, O.S.D. 208; shown on O.S. Map 1″, sheet 61 NE. (1833 edn.).
[74] Below; S.R.O. 1664/1; bridge in I.G.M.T. store.
[75] S.R.O., S.C.C. Roads and Bridges Cttee. min. bk. 11, pp. 69–70; 12, pp. 117–18 (*Co. Surveyor's Rep.* Jan. 1932, p. 3).
[76] *Telford Jnl.* 12 Dec. 1975; inf. from Miss U. B. M. Rayska; T.D.C. *Telford Street Plan* (1981).
[77] Trinder, *Ind. Rev. Salop.* (1981), 75–85; SA 3404; *Salop. News Letter*, xxxiii. 14; xxxiv. 4; I. J. Brown, *Mines of Salop.* (Buxton, 1976), 63; R. Dean, 'Canal Inclined Planes — A Contemporary View', *Jnl. Rly. & Canal Hist. Soc.* xxvii. 198–200; above, plate 8.

The section of the Wombridge Canal not incorporated in the Shrewsbury Canal probably became disused *c.* 1819. The Ketley Canal was abandoned in the mid 19th century but the Ketley inclined plan had closed by 1818, preventing access past that point.[78] The Shropshire Canal required considerable attention in the early 1850s; leaks were common and the canal was said to have broken through into the underlying Wellington–Wolverhampton railway in 1855, draining the summit level and flooding Oakengates. It was replaced in 1860 by the Coalport branch railway.[79] The Trench inclined plane closed in 1921, effectively marking the end of the Shrewsbury Canal; latterly the only regular traffic carried by the canal was flour to the mill at Wrockwardine Wood.[80]

A horse-drawn railway was built in 1747 on the Charltons' Oakengates estate from the Horsepasture mines, north-east of the settlement, probably to a wharf on Watling Street.[81] Among many railways of the earlier 19th century was that running eight miles from Hollinswood to Sutton wharf on the Severn,[82] and those to the Shrewsbury Canal west of the Trench inclined plane,[83] and from Priorslee to the Wrockwardine Wood inclined plane.[84]

In 1849 the Shrewsbury & Birmingham (later G.W.R.) line from Wellington to Wolverhampton opened after completion of a tunnel 471 yd. long south of Oakengates.[85] In 1857 the Coalport Branch Railway Co. (later L.N.W.R.) obtained permission to buy the decaying Shropshire Canal, and replaced it with the Coalport branch line from Hadley junction, which opened for freight in 1860 and for passengers in 1861. The G.W.R.'s goods branch from Hollinswood to Stirchley, known at first as the Old Park line, opened in 1908 and closed in 1959. Both companies had stations in Oakengates: Oakengates Market Street (L.N.W.R.) closed for passengers in 1952 and for goods in 1964, while Oakengates (G.W.R.), known as Oakengates West between 1951 and 1956, closed for goods in 1965. Stops at Hollinswood on the lines of both former companies closed in 1964, Wombridge halt on the old L.N.W.R. line also shutting in that year.[86]

Railways were vital to the local extractive and manufacturing industries. Between 1851 and 1855

the basis of the Lilleshall Co.'s extensive private railway system was laid, linking Priorslee and Snedshill with the company's other enterprises in the area.[87] From 1856 Hollinswood, adjacent to Priorslee furnaces, became an important marshalling yard, linked to the G.W.R.[88] Many smaller firms also had sidings from the main lines.[89]

GROWTH OF SETTLEMENT. The original endowment of St. Leonard's priory seems to have consisted of the central part of what became the parish of Wombridge. About 1135 William and Seburga of Hadley and their son Alan gave land bounded on the east by a stream dividing Hadley wood from the king's wood (Wrockwardine wood), on the west by Springwell brook, and on the south by Watling Street.[90] Eastward and northward expansion by *c.* 1181 may have been indicated by Henry II's confirmation to the priory of 80 a. of assarts beyond the stream then bounding Wrockwardine wood. The king's grant was confirmed *c.* 1220 by John le Strange (II). South of Watling Street the lords of Leegomery (Ketley) and Wrockwardine and, evidently, the lord of Shifnal all had claims in 'the common wood of Wombridge'. About 1220 Thomas Tuchet, lord of Leegomery, gave the canons his rights in the wood, and boundary disputes with Shifnal manor were apparently settled *c.* 1269 when the lord of Shifnal granted the canons the whole of his bank of the stream dividing Snedshill wood from the canons' wood. The canons' parish evidently then extended well south of Watling Street,[91] perhaps to its full eventual extent and so including the north-eastern part of Ketley township.[92] In 1318 the Crown confirmed 30 a. of assarts to the priory.[93] By the earlier 16th century the priory was exploiting the local coal and ironstone reserves.[94]

Early lay settlement in the parish was perhaps along Watling Street. In the 13th century there may have been some settlement at a place called Staniford, on Watling Street where it was crossed by a stream flowing north from Hollinswood towards the priory and forming the western boundary of Snedshill wood. The stream was ponded there *c.* 1269,[95] when a Ralph of Stanford was mentioned[96] That area, on the eastern edge of

[78] Above, Ketley, intro.; C. Hadfield, *Canals of W. Midlands* (1969), 151–2.

[79] R. Christiansen, *W. Midlands* (Regional Hist. of Rlys. of Gt. Brit. vii. 1973), 158; J. H. Denton, *Tour of Rlys. and Canals between Oakengates and Coalbrookdale* (Rly. & Canal Hist. Soc., W. Midlands Group, 1961; copy in S.P.L.); above, Hadley, intro.

[80] Hadfield, op. cit. 251.

[81] Trinder, *Ind. Rev. Salop.* (1981), 31, 72; M. J. T. Lewis, *Early Wooden Rlys.* (1970), 240, 273–4.

[82] Trinder, op. cit. 84; R. F. Savage and L. D. W. Smith, 'Waggonways and Plateways of E. Salop.' (Birm. Sch. of Archit. dissertation, 1965), 93–4 (copy in S.P.L.).

[83] C. & J. Greenwood, *Map of Salop.* (1827); S.R.O. 3882/1/17.

[84] Savage and Smith, op. cit. 93–4.

[85] Following para. based on Trinder, *Ind. Rev. Salop.* (1981), 152–3; J. M. Tolson, 'In the Tracks of the Iron Masters', *Railway Mag.* xci. 373–8; Christiansen, *W. Midlands*, 86.

[86] C. R. Clinker, *Clinker's Reg. of Closed Stations 1830–1977* (Bristol, 1978), 64, 103, 150, 170 n. 2651.

[87] W. K. V. Gale and C. R. Nicholls, *The Lilleshall Co.*

Ltd.: a Hist. 1764–1964 (1979), 34–5; below, Wrockwardine Wood, intro.

[88] Christiansen, *W. Midlands*, 90.

[89] O.S. Maps 1/2,500, Salop. XXXVI. 11, 15 (1882 edn.); S.P.L., Rly. Plan 32.

[90] V.C.H. Salop. ii. 80; Eyton, vii. 363–4; T.S.A.S. 2nd ser. x. 192; xi. 334–5; above, Hadley, Man. and Other Est., and Econ. Hist. (Agric.). For the name Springwell brook see T.S.A.S. xi. 335; J. E. G. Cartlidge, *The Priory of SS. Mary and Leonard, Wombridge, Salop* [?1971], 10 (copy in S.P.L.), which, however, in describing its course, confuses it with a brook to the E.

[91] V.C.H. Salop. ii. 81; Eyton, ii. 298–9; vii. 343, 345; ix. 23; T.S.A.S. xi. 325–7, 329, 335; 2nd ser. xi. 335, 337.

[92] S.R.O. 972, parcel 245, Ketley map of 1794; L.J.R.O., B/A/15, Wombridge.

[93] Cal. Chart. R. 1300–26, 404–5.

[94] Below, Econ. Hist. (Coal and Ironstone; Iron and Steel).

[95] T.S.A.S. xi. 325, 329, 335 (readings checked from B.L. Eg. MS. 3712, ff. 39, 40v., 42v.); cf. Eyton, ii. 298–9; vii. 343; ix. 23.

[96] T.S.A.S. xi. 346; cf. B.L. Eg. MS. 3712, f. 49v. Eyton, giving no reason, suggested 'Sanford'.

the parish, was known as Oakengates by 1414,[97] and by 1447 the name Staneford apparently belonged to a settlement about 1 km. to the west just outside the parish;[98] the displacement of the name suggests that in the 13th and 14th centuries settlement straggled along the section of Watling Street that crossed the middle of the parish. At Oakengates,[99] perhaps so called because it lay at the edge of a large block of woodland, the priory owned four messuages and a cottage, overseen by a bailiff, in 1535–6.[1] Settlement grew with industry and mining between the 16th and 19th centuries, hamlets developing alongside mines and ironworks, notably at Ketley Bank. There was little cohesion, and only in the mid 19th century, when a market was established and the railways arrived, did Oakengates begin to assume an urban role.

In the 17th and 18th centuries Oakengates was a small hamlet, and at Wombridge there was probably little more than Wombridge Farm, on the priory site.[2] In 1672 hearth tax was paid by eleven householders in Oakengates and three in Wombridge; Ketley Bank householders may have been taxed with Ketley township. In the 1690s 80 families were said to live in Oakengates and Wombridge.[3] In the south of the parish the settlement at Ketley Bank, in existence by the early 17th century and then known as Coalpit Bank,[4] grew[5] to be the largest in the parish by the later 18th century. Most of its houses were probably built by the occupiers and were detached or semi-detached. There was some order to the western part of the settlement, with properties flanking the main road, but to the east the cottages sprawled up to the boundary of Ketley.[6]

In 1801 the population of Wombridge parish was 1,835 and it remained at that level until the 1830s when it began to rise, reaching 2,057 in 1841 and 3,113 in 1881. Increase was especially sharp in the 1850s[7] as the Lilleshall Co. began to develop the New Yard works.[8] In the 1880s population declined slightly. In 1898 Wombridge (pop. 2,876 in 1901) was the second most populous civil parish of the four that make up Oakengates urban district (pop. 10,906 in 1901); it was, however, the only one that did not continue to record slight declines after 1911 until all four C.P.s were amalgamated in 1934. In 1931 Wombridge had 3,405 inhabitants, Wrockwardine Wood 4,978, Priorslee 2,644, and St. George's 163. The U.D. as a whole did not record a higher population figure than that of 1911 (11,744) until 1961 (12,163).[9] Subsequently the trend was upward, particularly in the 1960s when much housing was built: within the area of the U.D. (abolished in 1974) population rose from 16,701 in 1971 to 17,552 in 1981.[10]

Between 1826 and 1850 Oakengates developed from a group of a dozen detached houses and public houses, some thatched, which were surrounded by a quagmire in wet weather, into a 'good street' of 40–50 houses. William Charlton of Apley, lord of the manor of Wombridge 1802–38, was credited in 1842 with having promoted the improvement through his patronage from c. 1826.[11] By 1856, as well as public houses, shops, cobblers, and blacksmiths, there were other tradesmen including a hairdresser, a watchmaker and jeweller, and a bookseller and stationer.[12] Probably most buildings were erected by local tradesmen: in 1854, for instance, a block including the Charlton Arms was erected by Andrew Peplow, a beer retailer and brick maker.[13]

The new status of Oakengates was enhanced by the arrival of the railways between 1849 and 1861. The railways made Oakengates, like Wellington, accessible to the large populations between it and the Severn.[14] The town's range of commercial and professional facilities continued to expand: there were banks and a plumber there by 1870; a fruiterer, photographer, and private school by 1891; a fried fish shop by 1895; and an architect by 1905.[15]

The population of Oakengates continued to grow, and the town to expand, in the third quarter of the 19th century, when New Street, Leonard Street, and Slaney Street were built north of the existing main street.[16] In 1898 the town became the centre of a new urban district which took in Wrockwardine Wood and St. George's to the east and Priorslee to the south and south-east.

Divided from Wombridge and Oakengates by Snedshill wood and Hollinswood ('holly wood'), Priorslee, like the two woods, was part of Shifnal manor.[17] At Priorslee the priory built up an estate in the Middle Ages[18] and there was a 12th-century chapel.[19] A moat north of Priorslee, close to

---

[97] P.R.O., JUST 1/753, rot. 12 (1).
[98] i.e. at the modern Beveley: above, Ketley, intro.
[99] Ekwall, Concise Oxf. Dict. Eng. P.N. 347.
[1] J. E. G. Cartlidge, The Vale and Gates of Usc-con (Congleton, [1935]), 44; V.C.H. Salop. ii. 82.
[2] S.R.O., q. sess. rec. parcel 254, badgers', drovers', and alesellers' licensing bk. s.a. 1619; Camden, Brit. (1806), iii. 6; T. Cox and A. Hall, Magna Britannia, iv (1727), 636; below, Man. and Other Est.
[3] Hearth Tax 1672 (Salop. Arch. Soc.), 87–8; Salop. News Letter, xxxiii. 12.
[4] S.R.O., q. sess. rec. parcel 254, badgers', etc. licensing bk. s.a. 1613, 1616.
[5] J. Rocque, Map of Salop. (1752); cf. Shrews. Chron. 12 Dec. 1772.
[6] S.R.O. 972, parcel 245, Ketley map of 1794; Trinder, Ind. Rev. Salop. (1981), 188.
[7] Twenty per cent 1851–61, double the rate 1841–81.
[8] Below, Wrockwardine Wood, Econ. Hist. (Iron and Steel).
[9] V.C.H. Salop. ii. 225–6, 229.
[10] Above; T.D.C. Oakengates: Plan for Central Area at 1991 (1971; copy in S.P.L.); Census, 1971; 1981 census figs. compiled in S.C.C. Planning Dept.
[11] Salopian Jnl. 11 May 1842 (p. 2); Trinder, Ind. Rev. Salop. (1981), 197; S. Bagshaw, Dir. Salop. (1851), 441; above, Wellington, Man. and Other Est.; above, plate 17.
[12] P.O. Dir. Salop. (1856), 93–4.
[13] Ibid.; S.R.O. 3098/4 (incl. notes by I. J. Brown).
[14] Above, Communications; Trinder, Ind. Rev. Salop. (1981), 153.
[15] P.O. Dir. Salop. (1870), 104; Kelly's Dir. Salop. (1891), 378–9; (1895), 157–8; (1905), 167–8; below, Educ.
[16] Below; S.R.O. 1335/4/1; 3093/2; O.S. Maps 1/2,500, Salop. XXXVI. 11, 15 (1882 and 1902 edns.).
[17] T.S.A.S. 2nd ser. xi. 337; Eng. P.N. Elements (E.P.N.S.), i. 258.
[18] T.S.A.S. ix. 378–80; xi. 325–39; 2nd ser. xi. 335–7; xii. 220–3; Eyton, ii. 273, 279, 313; Cartlidge, Priory of Wombridge, passim; Valor Eccl. (Rec. Com.), iii. 194.
[19] Below, Churches.

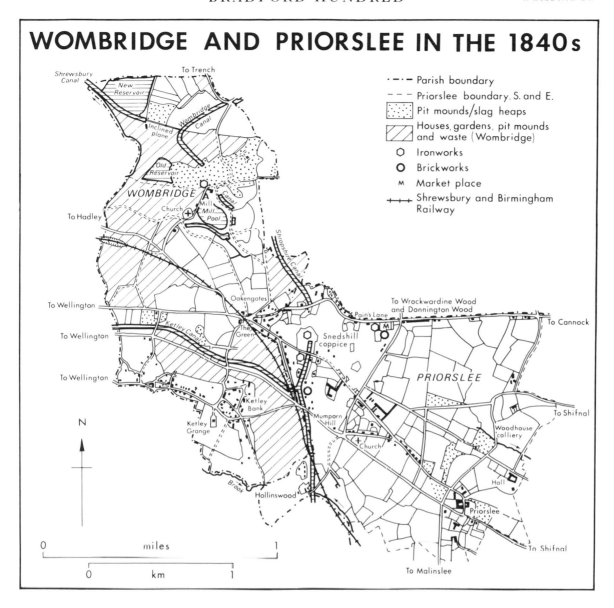

WOMBRIDGE AND PRIORSLEE IN THE 1840s

Houses, pitmounds, and waste, indicated only generally on the Wombridge parish tithe map, have been detailed in the Ketley Bank area from a map of Ketley manor of 1794 and the 1″ O.S. Map of 1833. For the significance of the SE. boundary of Priorslee see map of Parishes around Wellington *c.* 1831 on page 20.

Watling Street, probably marks the site of a medieval assart farm.[20] Priorslee Hall, north-east of the village, was the only major house in the area later defined as Oakengates U.D. It was probably built shortly before 1728, apparently by Edward Jorden; his father of the same name, of Dunsley (Staffs.), had married Sarah, daughter and heir of John Wyke, who owned land at Priorslee. The hall was used as the residence of the managing partner of the Lilleshall Co. from the early 19th century until 1964, when it became the headquarters of the new town development corporation.[21]

Priorslee village remained small in 1752.[22] By the later 18th century, however, houses had been built to the north-west, probably by squatters, down to the western edge of Snedshill coppice and probably on the Oakengates road around Mumporn Hill. A more coherent development, that apparently took place in the 1820s, was Snedshill Barracks on the south-eastern edge of Snedshill coppice;[23] probably built for John Horton & Co., the barracks formed a T-shaped group of 29 houses with gardens.[24] About 1839 a group of brick terraces was built in Priorslee village for colliers at the Lilleshall Co.'s Lawn and Rookery pits.[25] In the third quarter of the 19th

[20] SA 3120.

[21] T.D.C. *Priorslee Hall* (Hist. Bldgs. in Telford no. 1); SA 766.

[22] Rocque, *Map of Salop.*

[23] B.L. Eg. MS. 2872, Oaken Gate Cottages, Sneds Hill Works and Coppice (copy in S.R.O. 3629). St. Peter's,

Priorslee, was built nr. Snedshill Barracks in 1836: below, Churches; S.R.O. 1335/4/1; O.S. Map 1/2,500, Salop. XXXVI. 15 (1882 edn.).

[24] B.L. Maps, O.S.D. 208; Greenwood, *Map of Salop.*; S.R.O. 1335/4/1–2, nos. 292–3; O.S. Map 1/2,500, Salop, 15 (1882 edn.). [25] Brown, *Mines of Salop.* 62.

century building began to the south of Watling Street and St. George's, where School Street, Grove Street, and Lodge Road were laid out around Snowhill.[26]

In the last quarter of the 19th century there were no new developments[27] within the area defined in 1898 as Oakengates U.D. Two main settlements had grown up by c. 1875. The larger was Oakengates, four fifths in Wombridge parish and one fifth in Priorslee parish; half a mile to the east, separated from Oakengates by the Albion pit mounds, was St. George's, greatly expanded from the old hamlet of Pain's Lane (in Lilleshall parish) by new streets laid out at the south end of Wrockwardine Wood[28] and along the northern edge of Priorslee around Snowhill.[29] The two main settlements were distinguished by relatively well built terraced houses. In the area's subsidiary settlements accommodation was often worse: there was a preponderance of residual 18th- and 19th-century squatter, barrack, and speculative buildings. In 1896 the sanitary inspector was able to note that there was still overcrowding in the area, but that it was no longer of the former 'gross' kind with adults 'lodged promiscuously' together.[30]

The main subsidiary settlements lay to the south: at Ketley Bank, Snedshill, and Priorslee village. Northwards the only considerable settlements were two in Wrockwardine Wood, one straggling along New Road and Lincoln Road and another at Trench. In the 20th century those scattered settlements were expanded and drawn closer together by the growth of council and private housing estates; three of the main council estates were at Trench, Snedshill, and Ketley Bank; a fourth was built in the centre of Wombridge parish (around Walton Avenue, Hartshill, and Church Parade). Thus by 1981 only a few well defined areas remained unbuilt. In the north (Wrockwardine Wood) Cockshutt Piece and the extensive playing fields around the Oakengates Leisure Centre remained open, as did the area north of Wombridge church; in the south the overgrown pit mounds between Albion Hill and Snedshill still just separated Oakengates from the continuous housing between St. George's and Snedshill.

In 1918 the Lilleshall Co.'s houses in the district generally lacked proper sewerage and drainage and were often badly designed and built and in disrepair, lacking back doors or opening windows. Oakengates urban district council recommended that the company should immediately demolish some houses and modernize others.[31] Between 1919 and 1922 the U.D.C. itself built 185 houses in Woodhouse Crescent (at Trench, in Wrockwardine Wood), Walton Avenue (Wombridge), and Freeston Avenue (Snedshill) after an earlier scheme for 70 had been rejected by Dr. Christopher Addison, minister of Health, as 'completely inadequate'. The first two estates were on previously undeveloped land and the third replaced Snedshill Barracks, which were demolished.[32]

The Addison programme ended with demand for council housing in Oakengates U.D. still unsatisfied and rising, and in 1925 the council's rent collector was regularly offered bribes by would-be tenants.[33] In the later 1920s and early 1930s, following the 1923 and 1924 Housing Acts, about 50 more council houses were built at Hartshill, Walton Avenue, and Freeston Avenue and there was a little council-approved private building.[34] Slum clearance began after the 1930 Housing Act, with c. 50 houses initially listed for demolition over five years,[35] replacement houses being built at Church Parade, Freeston Avenue, and Priorslee Road and in Gower Street, Wrockwardine Wood. By c. 1935 the U.D.C. had built 313 houses.[36] Even so they relieved only the most acute cases of bad housing; families that did not live in grossly overcrowded accommodation had virtually no chance of being allotted a house, although representatives of organizations like the Salvation Army were at times given houses.[37] There were some local environmental improvements in the later 1930s, the most noticeable being the removal of the Charlton Mound from the town centre by the International Voluntary Service for Peace on the initiative of J. E G. Cartlidge, vicar of Oakengates 1928–47.[38]

A major scheme of 1939 to build 74 council houses was interrupted by the war with only 16 completed, and in 1943 over 200 new houses were still required.[39] In 1947–8 building was restarted with prefabricated dwellings: 66 'Dyke' (concrete panel) houses were built, mainly at Church Parade, and 34 aluminium bungalows in Hayward Avenue and Mart Avenue.[40] In the early 1950s the U.D.C. built 'Gregory' flats and the 26-house Grove estate at Snowhill;[41] they were followed in the mid 1950s by 70 houses at Hartshill and c. 150

[26] O.S. Map 6″, Salop. XXXVI. SE. (1889 edn.).

[27] S.R.O. 1335/4/1; 3093/2; O.S. Maps 1/2,500 Salop. XXXVI. 11, 15 (1882 and 1902 edns.).

[28] Below, Wrockwardine Wood, Growth of Settlement.

[29] Above.

[30] S.C.C. Mins. 1896–7, 277.

[31] I.G.M.T., Lilleshall Co. colln. 846.

[32] Gale and Nicholls, Lilleshall Co. 95; S.R.O., DA 12/100/10–14, Ho. Cttee. mins. 16 and 19 Dec. 1919; 1 Mar., 23 Apr., 1 Oct. 1920; 27 June, 16 Sept., 2 Nov., 16 Dec. 1921; 10 Feb., 29 Mar., 26 Apr. 1922; 10 Sept. 1924.

[33] S.R.O., DA 12/100/14, Ho. Cttee. mins. 23 Apr. 1924; 4 Mar. 1925; D.N.B. 1951–61, s.v. Addison.

[34] 13 & 14 Geo. V, c. 24; 14 & 15 Geo. V, c. 35; S.R.O., DA 12/100/15–17, Ho. Cttee. mins. 29 Apr. 1925; 6 May, 1 and 28 July, 14 Oct. 1931; 8 Feb. 1933.

[35] 20 & 21 Geo. V, c. 39; S.R.O., DA 12/100/16 and 18,

Ho. Cttee. mins. 9 Dec. 1931; 13 Sept. 1933; 7 Mar. 1934.

[36] Cartlidge, Usc-con, 112; S.R.O., DA 12/100/19–21, Ho. Cttee. mins. 30 May, 25 July, 10 Oct., 7 Nov., 5 Dec. 1934; 25 May, 11 Sept., 4 Dec. 1935; 16 June 1936.

[37] S.R.O., DA 12/100/21–3, Ho. Cttee. mins. 14 July 1936; 1 Sept., 6 and 27 Oct., 1 Dec. 1937; 23 Feb., 23 Mar. 1938; 13 Apr., 21 Sept., 19 Oct. 1938.

[38] Cartlidge, Usc-con, 115–19; Express & Star, 2 May 1947; S.R.O. 4667; below, Churches.

[39] S.R.O., DA 12/100/23–4, Ho. Cttee. mins. 19 Jan. 1939; 17 May, 13 Sept. 1939; /28, Ho. Cttee. mins.? [unheaded], May 1943.

[40] Ibid. /30, 32–4, Ho. Cttee. mins. 6 Dec. 1944; 6 Nov., 4 Dec. 1946; 5 Feb., 2 Apr., 31 Dec. 1947; 4 Feb., 7 Apr. 1948; 30 Mar. 1949; Wellington Jnl. 21 May 1949.

[41] S.R.O., DA 12/100/38–9, Ho. Cttee. mins. 30 July 1952; 28 Apr. 1954.

houses and 10 old-age pensioners' bungalows at Ketley Bank.[42]

During the 1960s there was extensive residential development around Oakengates as slum clearance continued. In 1962 the U.D.C. erected 34 of the Lilleshall Co.'s prefabricated 'Dorran' bungalows at Snedshill for old-age pensioners.[43] Wombridge Farm was demolished c. 1965 and the speculative Newfield Garden Village estate built. Speculative estates were also built to the north (east of Trench Pool) and south (off Canongate) at that time[44] and the U.D.C.'s Ketley Bank estate expanded to c. 450 houses.[45] In the 1970s and early 1980s more council housing was built in Wrockwardine Wood,[46] near St. George's,[47] and at Snedshill.[48] Telford development corporation's Wombridge Common estate, 165 dwellings 1975–8, was its first housing estate in the northern area added to the new town in 1968.[49] In the late 1970s Priorslee village was conserved and modernized as a speculation by the corporation and enlarged by private builders.[50]

SOCIAL AND CULTURAL ACTIVITIES.

As almost everywhere in the coalfield the alehouse was an integral and ever present part of the community. There was an alehouse at Ketley Bank in 1613, and three at Oakengates in 1618–19.[51] Four were licensed in Wombridge parish in 1753 and six in 1805; they probably lay in Oakengates.[52] In the earlier 19th century the number of public houses grew as the town expanded, and in 1846 the Methodists noted that on reckoning Mondays the Oakengates pubs were frequently crowded.[53] In 1856 there were sixteen public houses and eight beer sellers in Oakengates, those figures remaining roughly constant until after the First World War when the beer sellers began to be closed. There were fourteen public houses in 1941. There were two public houses in Priorslee by 1856,[54] two were open in 1983.

Oakengates wake took place in early October in 1801–6, the focus of activity being the pubs along the main street.[55] Bull baiting was among the more notorious entertainments, and the county's last baiting was reputedly at the 1833 wake.[56] As late as 1870 colliers' daughters who had spent the summer working in market gardens around London would traditionally return for the wakes, some with dowries.[57] Horse and donkey races and athletic competitions were held south of Pain's Lane in the mid to late 19th century during the wakes,[58] then usually held in early September during the annual works' holiday. Like Oakengates Saturday night market, a leading social and commercial attraction throughout the district, the wakes did not survive the Second World War.[59]

Fairs, probably during the wakes, took place on the Green until the construction of the Wellington–Wolverhampton railway across it c. 1849, and thereafter at the other end of Oakengates in Owen's field. There were four fairs in 1850, and an annual funfair visited Oakengates until c. 1980 when it moved to Donnington.[60]

Neither cock fighting nor bull baiting was confined to the wakes. In the early 19th century bulls were regularly baited on Sundays in Oakengates and before 1810 miners from Oakengates and Ketley regularly spent a week cock fighting at the Bull's Head inn at Rodington.[61] Cock fighting persisted locally until the 1850s or later.[62]

By 1808 there was a brotherly or friendly society at Oakengates, perhaps that which met in the Leopard public house in 1823,[63] and there were several societies at Ketley Bank.[64] The Ancient Order of Foresters was well established in St. George's by 1875 and had links with Ketley Bank Primitive Methodist chapel. In 1903 a new Foresters' Hall was erected on the south side of West Street near the junction with Stafford Street.[65] In 1898 the 51 members of 'Earl Granville' lodge of the Independent Order of Odd Fellows (Manchester Unity) met at the Bull's Head, Oakengates.[66] For many years after its foundation

[42] Ibid. /41, Ho. Cttee. mins. 17 Feb. 1956; /43, minute 165; DA 12/134, Hartshill file.
[43] Gale and Nicholls, Lilleshall Co. 114–15.
[44] Salop. News Letter, xxix. 5; below, Man. and Other Est.; S.R.O., DA 12/111, mins. various.
[45] S.C.C. Mins. (Educ.) 1959–60, 199.
[46] i.e. 147 dwellings 1973–9 in Briggs Way, Cappoquin Drive, etc., off Moss Rd.: Wrekin District Council, Tech. Resources file H.8/1 (1974–83) and completion bks.
[47] i.e. 63 flats 1979–82 in Roman Grove (New St.) and Eccleshall Ho. and Turnpike Ct. (Gower St.): ibid.
[48] i.e. 31 dwellings 1978–80 at the Shrubbery (Priorslee Rd., Hazel Way): ibid.
[49] D. G. Fenter, 'Bldg. Development carried out in Telford by the Development Corp.' (TS. in S.R.O. 3763).
[50] Shropshire Star, 29 July, 23 Sept. 1978; inf. from Miss U. B. M. Rayska.
[51] S.R.O., q. sess. rec. parcel 254, badgers', etc. licensing bk.
[52] Ibid. parcels 255–9, regs. of alesellers' recognizances, 1753–1828.
[53] Below; Trinder, Ind. Rev. Salop. (1981), 198; S.R.O. 3098/2 (naming many Snedshill pubs).
[54] P.O. Dir. Salop (1856), 93–4, 104; (1879), 373–4, 387; E. Cassey & Co. Dir. Salop. (1871), 256–7, 285; Kelly's Dir. Salop. (1891), 378–9, 396; (1905), 167–9, 190; (1917), 162–3,

185; (1929), 174–5, 197; (1941), 177–8.
[55] Trinder, op. cit. 214, 220.
[56] Ibid. 206, 220–1; V.C.H. Salop. ii. 192; T.S.A.S. xlix. 24.
[57] Trinder, op. cit. 214–15; D. Hudson, Munby: Man of Two Worlds (1972), 418.
[58] G.M. James, 'Here be Dragons': Brief Glimpse into Hist. of St. Geo.'s, Telford [1982], 43–4 (copy in S.P.L.).
[59] St. Geo.'s C. E. Boys' Sch. log bk. (at the sch.) 13 Sept. 1872; Wombridge Inf. Council Sch. log bk. (at Wombridge Co. Primary Sch.) passim; below, Econ. Hist. (Mkt. and Fairs).
[60] James, op. cit. 33; W. M. Moisley, 'Mkts. of Salop.' (London Univ. M.Sc. thesis, 1951), 33; inf. from Wrekin Dist. Council.
[61] Trinder, Ind. Rev. Salop. (1981), 221; G. F. Carter and H. Walcot, Hist. Notes on Par. of Rodington (n.d.; copy in S.P.L.), 15; V.C.H. Salop. ii. 191.
[62] S.R.O. 1904/2.
[63] Orders of Q. Sess. iii. 132, 157, 208; S.R.O. 673/1/6, 14 June 1823.
[64] S.R.O., q.sess. rec. parcel 285, friendly socs. reg.; Orders of Q. Sess iv. 32.
[65] Wellington Jnl. 17 July 1875 (p.8); James, 'Here be Dragons', 8; date stone.
[66] Hobson & Co. Wellington Dir., Almanack, & Diary (1898), 35.

in 1938 the Uxacona lodge of freemasons met at Wombridge. It subsequently moved to Wellington.[67]

Attempts to form a Chartist association in Oakengates in 1842 were apparently unsuccessful.[68] In 1883 and 1888 the Oakengates Gladstone Liberal Club met, and between c. 1909 and c. 1917 the Oakengates Liberal and Labour Club was active.[69] Between c. 1913 and c. 1926 there was also an Oakengates Unionist Club.[70]

A mechanics' institute was erected in 1855,[71] and in 1877 an Oakengates Literary Institute was meeting.[72] The Priorslee Institute was recorded between 1913 and 1941.[73] A county library book centre opened at Oakengates in 1930.[74] About 1951 the former Baptist chapel in Stafford Road was converted into a county branch library; it closed in 1975 when new premises in Limes Walk were acquired.[75] There was a circulating library at Ferriday's in Market Street in 1937.[76]

The Wolverhampton owners of the *Shropshire Examiner* published the paper weekly in Oakengates from 1876 to 1877 when it merged in their *Midland Examiner and Times*.[77]

In 1871 Priorslee cricket club shared a professional bowler and groundsman with the Shifnal club.[78] Oakengates Town Football & Sports Co. Ltd. ran a football team between c. 1926 and 1937, probably playing on Owen's field.[79] In 1927 the Miners' Welfare Fund was responsible for levelling a pit mound at the junction of Hartshill and Hadley roads, on which a public recreation ground opened.[80] A bowling green, football pitch, and tennis courts were among the facilities there in 1983. There was a bowling green at the George Hotel in West Street early in the 20th century.[81] Facilities in 1983 included football pitches at Oakengates Leisure Centre, the Oakengates 'outpost', and Priorslee.[82] Pigeon keeping remained a popular hobby, as it had been throughout the century.[83]

A large temperance meeting place, the Coffee Palace, served Oakengates between c. 1895 and c. 1913.[84] Oakengates Community Hall, provided in the late 1930s by the Charlton Mound committee, was taken over by the urban district council in 1948–9.[85] In 1962 Oakengates Old Folks' Rest Centre opened; it was also hired out for meetings and social gatherings.[86] Oakengates town hall, seating over 900, was opened in 1968 and from time to time provided a stage for entertainers of international reputation. It was the chief venue of the Wrekin and Telford Festival from its inception in 1974. The festival, under the patronage of the distinguished cellist Paul Tortelier, rapidly became renowned for the quality of the visiting artists and for the organizers' policy of encouraging participation by local amateur groups.[87]

The town's first cinema, the Picture House, opened in 1912 above the market hall. It was superseded in 1923 by the Grosvenor Cinema, which closed in 1967. Another early cinema, the Hippodrome, occupied what became Maddocks' offices in Station Road.[88]

MANOR AND OTHER ESTATES. St. Leonard's priory was dissolved in 1536 and its demesnes were leased next year to William Abbot for 21 years. In 1539 James Leveson bought the reversion and fee of Abbot's leasehold lands from the Crown.[89] Leveson bought more of the priory lands at Oakengates in 1543, and in 1547, the year he died, he sold the priory and its demesnes to William Charlton (d. 1567), the priory's chief steward at the time of the Dissolution.[90] Thereafter the descent of the manor[91] of WOMBRIDGE followed that of Apley (in Wellington)[92] until 1901 when Sir Thomas Meyrick's Wombridge estate was divided and sold.[93]

William Charlton (d. 1567) lived at Wombridge,[94] probably in the former priory's gatehouse, called Wombridge Hall in the 1690s.[95] Mary, the wife of Francis Charlton (lord 1617–42), apparently used the priory church as a coach house, and her tenants (presumably after Francis's death) pounded cattle there. In the years 1693–8 the 'steeple', formerly a burial place,

[67] H. Temperton, *Hist. of Craft Freemasonry in Salop. 1732–1982* [1982], 69.
[68] Trinder, *Ind. Rev. Salop.* (1981), 235; *Salopian Jnl.* 11 May 1842 (p.2).
[69] *Wellington Jnl.* 10 Mar., 21 Apr. 1883; *Liberal and Radical Yr. Bk. 1888*, 468; *Kelly's Dir. Salop.* (1909), 172; (1913), 175; (1917), 163.
[70] *Kelly's Dir. Salop.* (1913), 175; (1917), 163; (1922), 170; (1926), 178.   [71] *P.O. Dir. Salop.* (1856), 93.
[72] *Wellington Jnl.* 17 Feb., 17 Nov., 15 Dec. 1877.
[73] *Kelly's Dir. Salop.* (1913), 198; (1941), 203.
[74] R.C. Elliott, 'Development of Public Libraries in Salop.' (Loughborough Univ. M.A. thesis, 1970), 121 (copy in Salop. Librs.).
[75] *S.C.C. Mins. (Educ.)* 1950–1, 27; *Telford Jnl.* 3 May 1974; inf. from Salop. Librs.
[76] Elliott, op. cit. app. II.
[77] *Examiner*, 4 Feb. 1876; 5 Oct. 1877.
[78] *Wellington Jnl.* 11 June 1949.
[79] *Kelly's Dir. Salop.* (1926), 178; (1929), 175; (1934), 179; (1937), 180; M. Evans, *Childhood Memories* (T.D.C. 1981), 23 (copy in S.P.L.).   [80] Cartlidge, *Usc-con*, 122.
[81] James, '*Here be Dragons*', 24.
[82] *Telford Social Trends*, i, ed. J. MacGuire (T.D.C. 1980), 226–7; for the 'outpost' see below, Educ.
[83] S.R.O., DA 12/100, *passim*, for complaints, etc. re pigeons.

[84] *Kelly's Dir. Salop.* (1895), 197; (1913), 175; U. Rayska and A. Carr, *Telford Past and Present* (1978), 21.
[85] *S.C.C. Mins. (Educ.)* 1948–9, 21; 1949–50, 102.
[86] Wombridge Co. Primary Sch. log bk. (at the sch.) 8 Mar. 1962.
[87] *Shropshire Mag.* Oct. 1965, 32–3; S.R.O., DA 12/124, pp. 64–76; inf. from Mr. D. Vince, Wrekin District Council.
[88] S.R.O., DA 34 (S.R.O. 3279/1), Grosvenor file; *Kelly's Dir. Salop.* (1917), 351; (1922), 363; (1926), 389; Evans, *Childhood Memories*, 20, 25; F.J. Brown, 'Cinemas of Telford 1910–83' (TS. in possession of Mr. Brown), 3, 6.
[89] *V.C.H. Salop.* ii. 82; *L. & P. Hen. VIII*, xiv (2), p. 302.
[90] *Cal. Pat. 1547–8*, 98; *L. & P. Hen. VIII*, xviii (1), p. 535.   [91] Ct. r. survive from 1697: below, Local Govt.
[92] P.R.O., C 142/361, no. 146; /786, no. 67; CP 25(2)/201/20 Eliz. I Trin. [no. 8]; CP 43/337, rot. 44; /478, rot. 99; /605, rot. 89; /949, rot. 173; S.R.O. 625, box 12, Law & Tindal to Chas. Emery, 27 Apr. 1843; 672/2; 972, box 153, abstr. of title of 1828; 999/30.1; 1005/69; 2990/18; 3882/1/5; S.P.L., MS. 2340, ff. 36–8; *Cal. S.P. Dom.* Addenda 1580–1625, 476; Dugdale, *Mon.* vi. 388 n.; *T.S.A.S.* liii, 266–9; Cartlidge, *Priory of Wombridge*, 19; cf. above, Wellington, Man. and Other Est. (Apley).
[93] *Shrews. Chron.* 27 Sept. 1901 (p. 8); S.R.O. 3882/4/1.
[94] *T.S.A.S.* vi. 109, 114; Leland, *Itin.* ed. Toulmin Smith, iii. 67; *L. & P. Hen. VIII*, xvi, pp. 292–3.
[95] *Salop. News Letter*, xxxiii. 12–13.

was used by the tenant as a cart house. By then other parts of the priory, including the chancel, had fallen down or been demolished and the materials been employed in building work at Apley Castle.[96] Parts of the priory buildings remained incorporated in Wombridge Farm until its demolition in 1965–6.[97]

In 1695 Sir John Leveson-Gower owned property in Ketley, Coalpit Bank, Oakengates, and Wombridge.[98] That part of Ketley township in Wombridge parish remained with the Sutherland estate until, with the Wellington part of the 4th duke's Ketley estate, it was divided and sold in 1894.[99]

In 1537 the tithes, termed rectorial, were included in William Abbot's 21-year lease of the priory, the Crown's reserved rent for them being £2 6s. 8d.[1] His lease of the tithes passed to Richard Abbot.[2] In 1578 the tithes were acquired from the Crown by the earl of Lincoln and Christopher Gowffe for a fee farm rent of £2 6s. 8d.[3] By 1621 the fee farm was owed by Francis Charlton, who died owning the rectory and tithes of Wombridge in 1642. The tithes were worth £3 10s. 0d. in 1655[4] and £3 12s. 6d. in 1708.[5] In 1847 the parish's tithes were commuted to rent charges of £92 19s. 6d., of which £87 17s. 6d. belonged to St. John C. Charlton, the rest being divided between six other impropriators and the perpetual curate, who owned merely the rent charge on the churchyard.[6]

ECONOMIC HISTORY. AGRICULTURE. By the mid 16th century what woodland remained in Wombridge and Priorslee was probably coppiced;[7] in 1556 there were said to be 38 a. of wood in Wombridge, worth 10s. an acre.[8] Among the coppices in the later 17th and 18th century were Queenswood and Wallamoor wood in Wombridge, managed by a keeper, and Snedshill coppice (82 a.) in Priorslee.[9] By 1847 only 6 a. of wood remained in Wombridge and none in Priorslee.[10]

Atcham furlong, presumably once open-field land, lay 500 metres south-east of Wombridge church in 1847.[11] Four or five ploughteams belonged to William Charlton's Wombridge tenants in the years 1693–8; most of the parish's other inhabitants were cottagers and colliers.[12] Little is known of the cottage economy of Wombridge and Oakengates but it probably differed little from that of Wrockwardine Wood.[13] By the late 18th century the eastern edge of Snedshill coppice marked the eastern boundary of the main industrial area, and it remained so throughout the 19th century. That part of Priorslee east of Snedshill coppice remained as farmland and was little affected by mining or industry until a few deep pits were sunk around Priorslee village and near Lower Woodhouse Farm in the 19th century.[14]

Considerable changes in land ownership and management occurred in the early 20th century. In 1901 Sir Thomas Meyrick's Wombridge estate was sold. Rent levels had become unrealistically low: a cottage rented from the estate for £2 was sublet for £6 10s., and five cottages with a gross annual rent of £4 10s. were sold in 1901 for £360. Many tenants purchased their own properties.[15] In 1922, because of increasing unprofitability, the Lilleshall Co. leased out its Woodhouse and Priorslee farms, which until then had supplied the company's managers with milk and potatoes on advantageous terms.[16] By 1936 motor transport had become so common that there was reputedly no demand in Oakengates for accommodation grazing for tradesmen's horses.[17]

MILLS. There was an iron mill at Wombridge at the Dissolution, probably near the priory on the stream draining north-westwards through the parish. That was probably the site of later mills known in the parish.[18] In 1672 Richard Adney rented the upper and lower mills in Wombridge, almost certainly to grind corn; probably at least one of the mills was converted from the earlier iron mill.[19] By 1709 there were three mills or wheels at Wombridge, and they remained in use until at least 1760.[20] A mill lay immediately east of Wombridge church in 1847; it apparently closed between 1882 and 1902, when the mill pond was filled in.[21]

[96] Ibid.; T.S.A.S. liii. 269–72; above, Wellington, Man. and Other Est. (Apley).

[97] V.C.H. Salop. ii. 82; Salop. News Letter, xxix. 5; Salop. News Sheet, viii. 2; SA 1106; S.R.O. 3763/78/30.

[98] P.R.O., CP 43/451, rot. 188.

[99] S.R.O. 972, parcel 187, sale partic. and plan no. 5; parcel 245, Ketley map of 1794; above, Ketley, intro.

[1] Valor Eccl. (Rec. Com.), iii. 194; V.C.H. Salop. ii. 82; L. & P. Hen. VIII, xiii (1), p.587; xiv (2), p. 302.

[2] Staffs. R.O., D. 593/J/22/15.

[3] Cal. Pat. 1575–8, p. 470.

[4] P.R.O., C 142/786, no. 67; SC 12/32/32; T.S.A.S. xlvii. 11; below, Churches.

[5] S.R.O. 625, box 15, tithe accts. 1706–16.

[6] L.J.R.O., B/A/15, Wombridge.

[7] See above, intro., for details of medieval woodland.

[8] Cartlidge, Priory of Wombridge, 20.

[9] S.P.L., Deeds 2498, Mich. rental of 1663; MS. 2600, f. 17, Oakengates; S.R.O. 625, bdle. 22, rentals; 4462/CW/2, s.a. 1674–5; I.G.M.T., Lilleshall Co. colln. 83–4; Trinder, Ind. Rev. Salop. (1981), 31.

[10] S.R.O. 1335/4/1–2; L.J.R.O., B/A/15, Wombridge.

[11] L.J.R.O., B/A/15, Wombridge (nos. 11–13).

[12] Salop. News Letter, xxxiii. 13.

[13] Yeomen and Colliers in Telford, ed. B. Trinder and J. Cox (1980), pp. 3, 432–3; B. Trinder, 'Two Probate Invs. from Industrial Salop.' Ind. Arch. Rev iii. 239–42; below, Wrockwardine Wood, Econ. Hist.

[14] B.L. Eg. MS. 2872; S.R.O. 1335/4/1–2; fuller treatment of Priorslee agric. hist. is reserved for a later volume of this Hist.

[15] Shrews. Chron. 27 Sept. 1901 (p. 8).

[16] Gale and Nicholls, Lilleshall Co. 95.

[17] S.R.O. 4309, ecclesiastical box X, Wombridge, T. Balfour to C. Langley, 17 Sept. 1936.

[18] Below (Iron and Steel). Cartlidge, Priory of Wombridge, 10, claimed that a mid 13th-cent. licence to the priory to make a pond at Stanford marked the creation of the mill pond. That is highly improbable on topographical grounds. For Stanford see above, Ketley, intro.

[19] Below (Iron and Steel); S.P.L., Deeds 2498, Lady Day rental of 1672; Telford Jnl. 5 May 1978.

[20] S.R.O. 625, box XV, water mill lease of 1709; rentals of 1663–1760 in S.P.L., Deeds 2498; in S.R.O. 625, bdle. 22; and in S.R.O. 676.

[21] L.J.R.O., B/A/15, Wombridge; P.O. Dir. Salop. (1870), 176; (1879), 446; Kelly's Dir. Salop. (1885), 995; O.S. Map 1/2,500 XXXVI. 11 (1882 and 1902 edns.).

COAL AND IRONSTONE. In 1535–6 there were two mines on the Wombridge priory demesne, worth £5 a year.[22] It is likely that both coal and ironstone, found in alternate bands, were raised. James Leveson acquired the mines with the priory demesnes[23] and reserved them when he sold the lands to William Charlton in 1547.[24] By 1578 Andrew Charlton of Apley owned a mine in Oakengates or Wombridge.[25] Both Leland and Camden mentioned the mines, by then firmly associated with Oakengates.[26] By the third quarter of the 17th century mining was established at Coalpit (later Ketley) Bank and probably at Snedshill.[27]

By the early 1720s the Charltons' Wombridge mines were let to Robert Brooks and John Lummas for £250 a year. By 1728, however, they owed the Charltons £950 and then gave up the mines, which were leased to Richard Hartshorne for £200 a year.[28] Hartshorne, who had leased the Ketley Bank mines from Lord Gower since 1715,[29] improved and expanded the local mining industry: c. 1730 an atmospheric pumping engine was installed at Wombridge, and by the time of his death in 1733 he was mining in the Greenfields and New Sough areas of the Charltons' Wombridge estate, and probably at Hollinswood and Snedshill in Priorslee, the property of the earls of Stafford.[30]

After 1733 Hartshorne's widow Jane (d. 1737) apparently continued to work the Ketley Bank and Priorslee mines[31] while the Wombridge ones were brought directly under the control of the Charlton estate, administered by Thomas Dorsett. In 1747 the Charlton estate promoted exploratory borings around Greenfields and in the previously unexploited Horsepasture area northeast of Oakengates. In six months of 1748 coal amounting to 2,375 stacks was raised from Wombridge, 74 per cent coming from the new Horsepasture area. The success of the local ironworks led other estates to take an increased interest in their mineral resources, and in 1755 the 4th earl of Stafford's agent Francis Paddy suggested that the granting of long leases of the Priorslee mines would encourage the tenants to build pumping engines.[32]

On his succession in 1754 the 2nd Earl Gower (cr. marquess of Stafford 1786, d. 1803) expanded his family's existing holdings by long leases from the earl of Shrewsbury and St. John Charlton, and became the main mine owner in the district.[33] That interest became the Lilleshall Co. in 1802.[34] One of the initial Lilleshall partners was

John Bishton the elder (d. 1803), who in 1793 with Benjamin Rowley leased mines in Priorslee from the Beaufoy family. Bishton formed a partnership with other lessees soon after, and in 1793–4 they apparently acquired the Snedshill mines from John Wilkinson (d. 1808), who had held them since at least 1778. Those interests did not come into the Lilleshall Co. when Bishton became a partner in 1802, and were only brought into the company in 1807 when Bishton's sons and executors negotiated a new partnership with Lord Granville Leveson-Gower.[35] In the 1780s Richard Reynolds's Ketley Co. began to mine under Wombridge, gaining access from a shaft in Wrockwardine Wood. The enterprise had been made possible through the draining of the area by an underground level at Wrockwardine Wood.[36]

Although Richard Hartshorne had installed a Coalbrookdale pumping engine at Wombridge c. 1730, it was only in the late 18th and early 19th century, after major technological improvements, that steam engines came to be widely used in the coalfield.[37] One of John Wilkinson's Boulton & Watt engines was installed at his Snedshill mines in 1778; Richard Banks, who operated pits in Wombridge in 1796 in association with a group of entrepreneurs known as the Wombridge Co., owned the 'Wombridge water engine', and William Reynolds the 'Bank water engine' at Ketley Bank. All were draining engines. The first pit-winding engine known to have been installed in the coalfield began work at Wombridge c. 1789. Designed by Richard Reynolds, it was so successful that similar engines were rapidly erected elsewhere: at Hollinswood in 1790, and at least three at Wombridge in 1795–6.[38] By 1793 so much coal was being raised around Oakengates that its carriage by road to Shrewsbury had become a problem, and the construction of the Shrewsbury Canal was proposed.[39]

Deep mining began early in the 19th century. The Lilleshall Co. opened the Lawn pit near Priorslee on land it had purchased in 1809; in 1841, at 900 ft., it was the deepest pit in the coalfield. The two nearby Woodhouse mines were probably sunk in the second quarter of the century.[40] Most of Priorslee, however, was leased in 1840 to John Horton & Co.[41] During the earlier 19th century coal production came to be concentrated at those deep collieries although ironstone was still got from smaller pits; in 1870 five of the existing ten pairs of pits at Priorslee produced ironstone.[42] In 1818 the Charltons' Wombridge mines were leased to James Foster, and in 1852 to

[22] V.C.H. Salop. ii. 82.
[23] Above, Man. and other Est.; Staffs. R.O., D.593/J/22/15 (datable 1539 × 1547).   [24] Cal. Pat. 1547–8, 98.
[25] P.R.O., CP 25(2)/201/20 Eliz. I. Trin. [no. 8].
[26] Leland, Itin. ed. Toulmin Smith, v. 18; Camden, Brit. (1772), i. 474; Staffs. R.O., D. 593/G/4/1/2/1.
[27] S.R.O. 38/341; Staffs. R.O., D. 641/2/D/2/3.
[28] Trinder, Ind. Rev. Salop. (1981), 30; S.R.O. 625, bdle. 22, rent r. of 1722–8.   [29] S.R.O. 38/42–3.
[30] Trinder, op. cit. 30–2, 94–5; Trinder and Cox, Yeomen and Colliers, pp. 70–1.
[31] Trinder and Cox, op. cit. p. 384.
[32] Trinder, Ind. Rev. Salop. (1981), 26, 30–2, 94–5; S.R.O. 38/344.

[33] Gale and Nicholls, Lilleshall Co. 16.
[34] Above, Lilleshall, Econ. Hist. (Mines, Quarries, and Sandpits).
[35] Trinder, Ind. Rev. Salop. (1981), 38, 45; I.G.M.T., Lilleshall Co. colln. 112–13, 116–17.
[36] Staffs. R.O., D. 593/L/4/4; Salop. News Sheet, xvii. 7–8.
[37] Trinder, op. cit. 38, 45, 93–104.
[38] Ibid. 100–2.
[39] Ibid. 84; J. Plymley, Gen. View of Agric. of Salop. (1803), 297–8.
[40] Gale and Nicholls, Lilleshall Co. 28; I.J. Brown, Mines of Salop. (Buxton, 1976), 42; V.C.H. Salop. i. 456.
[41] S.R.O. 1335/4/1–2.
[42] Gale and Nicholls, op. cit. 40, 51.

John Bennett & Co.[43] Bennett died in 1870, and in 1884 his executors were working Wombridge colliery.[44] In the later 19th century the minerals were mainly leased to Hopley Bros.[45]

By the early 20th century there was little mining in Wombridge. In Priorslee the Lawn pit closed in 1906[46] and activity was concentrated at the two Woodhouse pits, where both coal and ironstone were raised from shafts up to 311 yd. deep by a workforce of over 740 in 1922. Those pits closed in 1931 and 1940.[47]

IRON AND STEEL. About 1414 Thomas Ferrour, a Wolverhampton ironmonger, was robbed near Oakengates of six 'sharys' and 200 horse nails, worth 12s.;[48] it seems probable that he had purchased them locally. At the Dissolution Wombridge priory had an iron mill (probably a water-powered bloomery) and possibly a smithy, which were let for £1 6s. 8d.[49]

Whether the priory's ironworks was linked in any way to the Foleys' mill and furnace at Wombridge, working by 1663, is unknown. The Foleys' furnace, run with their works in Brewood, sent pig iron to many of their other iron-making concerns in the Stour Valley area. Thomas Foley (1616–77) paid the Charltons £60 a year for the furnace and two mills until he transferred his interests to his son Philip (1653–1716) in 1669, when the stock and equipment were worth £1,739.[50] The furnace produced 239 tons in 1669 and 289 in 1670.[51] Philip does not appear in surviving Charlton rentals, and the two mills were apparently let in 1672 to Richard Adney, probably for corn milling. While the furnace was frequently listed in rentals with the mills until 1753, the low rental and lack of other evidence suggest that the furnace probably closed soon after 1670.[52]

Not until c. 1780 was iron making re-established in the Oakengates area. In that year John Wilkinson, the leading Shropshire ironmaster of the 1770s, installed a Boulton & Watt engine to blow his two new blast furnaces at Snedshill, the first in the county on a site completely independent of water power. By the late 1780s Wilkinson had opened another furnace nearby, on a brook at Hollinswood. It was associated with those at Snedshill, a Newcomen engine being installed at Hollinswood by 1793. After what was probably a business dispute with his brother William, Wilkinson sold the Snedshill ironworks to John Bishton the elder, John Onions, and others in 1793–4 and the Hollinswood furnace closed. It was the first purpose-built coke blast furnace to go out of use in the county; it had apparently not been commercially successful.[53]

Bishton subsequently consolidated his family's holding in the partnership. In 1796 the two Snedshill furnaces reputedly made 3,400 tons of iron, and in the quarter to midsummer 1799 there were 758 tons of iron sold from Snedshill: 158 of melting-pig, 533 of forge iron, and 40 of 'hard' iron. The principal customers were Crawshay & Co. and Boulton & Watt for melting-iron, and John Knight (Stour Valley), John Addenbrooke (Wollaston and Lightmoor), Wright & Jesson (Wren's Nest near Linley), and Pemberton & Stokes (Eardington forge) for forge iron.[54] Trade at Snedshill was apparently similar to that at Horsehay, where Snedshill blooms and slabs were occasionally rolled.[55] The Snedshill ironworks, of which at least one furnace was managed by John Horton, was brought into the Lilleshall Co. under a new partnership agreement negotiated in 1807.[56]

By then there was at least one other ironworks in Wombridge, at Queenswood at the southern extremity of the parish. A large blast furnace was built there by the Coalbrookdale partners c. 1800 to supply the Ketley works with pig iron. By 1802 iron was being made that Boulton & Watt 'found to answer very well'. The works' subsequent history is not known.[57]

A major new iron-making enterprise began in 1818 when James Foster, the eminent Midland ironmaster, leased mines at Wombridge with an obligation to build two blast furnaces within 18 months. The original two furnaces produced over 5,000 tons of iron in 1825, and a third had been added in 1824. In 1830 the three produced over 7,000 tons. The prosperity of the works was, however, short-lived; in 1837 Foster bought out his two partners in the Wombridge and the associated Hadley works, and in 1843 began to build his Madeley Court blast furnaces to replace those at Wombridge, perhaps already shut. Not the least of the problems with the Wombridge works was apparently the inability of the Windmill farm inclined plane (in Madeley) to raise fully laden boats; that effectively prevented

[43] Below (Iron and Steel); *P.O. Dir. Salop.* (1856), 149; I.G.M.T., Lilleshall Co. colln. 612–13; inf. from Miss J.V. Capewell.

[44] S.R.O. 3039/3–4; Johnson, Poole, & Bloomer, mining agents, Brierley Hill, plans of Wombridge colliery 1884.

[45] S.R.O. 382/4/1.

[46] Gale and Nicholls, *Lilleshall Co.* 62; *Rep. Insp. Mines, Stafford Dist. (No. 9), 1908* [Cd. 4672–viii], pp. 215–18, H.C. (1909), xxxiii.

[47] Brown, *Mines of Salop.* 42.

[48] P.R.O., JUST 1/753, rot. 12 (1). Thanks are due to Mr. W. K. V. Gale and Dr. B. S. Trinder who kindly read, and commented on, this section.

[49] *V.C.H. Salop.* ii. 82; Trinder, *Ind. Rev. Salop.* (1981), 10; P.R.O., E 315/406, f. 45; SC 6/Hen. VIII/3006, m. 21; above, Mills.

[50] *Sel. Rec. Phil. Foley's Stour Valley Iron Wks. 1668–74,* i (Worcs. Hist. Soc. N.S. ix), pp. xiii, 1, 12–14, 33, 39, 44–5, 84–6, 94; S.P.L., Deeds 2498, rentals of 1663–1701.

[51] H.W.R.O. (H.), F/VI/KBf/14; /46 (refs. supplied by Dr. B. S. Trinder).

[52] Above, Mills; S.P.L., Deeds 2498; S.R.O. 625, bdle. 22; S.R.O. 676, rentals of 1722–60; 4406/1, pp. 165–6; Trinder, *Ind. Rev. Salop.* (1981), 32; H.W.R.O. (H.), F/VI/KBf/49, acct. of yield 1674 (not mentioning Wombridge; ref from Dr. Trinder).

[53] Trinder, op. cit. 37–8; A.T. Arnott and M. Sayer, 'Beam Engines in Blast-Furnace Blowing', *Ind. Arch. Rev.* iii. 30; B.L. Eg. MS. 2872, Oaken Gate Cottages, Sneds Hill Works and Coppice; I.G.M.T., Lilleshall Co. colln. 118.

[54] Gale and Nicholls, *Lilleshall Co.* 24; Trinder, op. cit. 45, 49, 97.

[55] Trinder, op. cit. 48–50; see also *'The Most Extraordinary District in the World': Ironbridge and Coalbrookdale,* ed. B. Trinder (1977), 55–6.

[56] Trinder, *Ind. Rev. Salop.* (1981), 45; Gale and Nicholls, op. cit. 21; I.G.M.T., Lilleshall Co. colln. 216–17.

[57] Trinder, *Ind. Rev. Salop.* (1981), 30, 43.

Foster from supplying his Wombridge works and Shrewsbury with his own coal.[58]

Production at the Snedshill furnaces declined after the construction of the Old Lodge furnaces at Lilleshall in 1825; only 317 tons were made in 1830 and the works seems to have closed later that year.[59] It apparently soon reopened when a forge was built on the site to make wrought iron under the nominally independent partnership of Horton, Simms, & Bull, which had close links with the Lilleshall Co. and used its pig iron. In 1854 Samuel Horton became sole owner of the firm, which he brought into the Lilleshall Co. in 1855 when a new Snedshill Bar Iron Co. was founded. The firm rapidly became established as one of the country's leading wrought iron makers, its products including bar, flat, cable, rivet, and horseshoe iron, boiler plates, sheets, wire rods, and structural sections. In addition to 35 puddling furnaces, about eight charcoal hearths were retained until c. 1873 to produce — slowly, expensively, and wastefully — the charcoal iron demanded by conservative customers.[60]

In 1851 the Lilleshall Co. built four blast furnaces at Priorslee. Unlike the Donnington Wood and Old Lodge furnaces[61] they usually worked on hot blast, and they effectively doubled the company's pig iron production capacity. In 1870 three of the furnaces were using hot blast to produce 230 tons a week each while one used cold blast to produce 140 tons. Fuel came from 42 round coke ovens, and the blast from rotative beam engines known as David and Sampson (sic). A steam hoist lifted the charge.[62]

Three Basic Bessemer converters were installed soon after 1879 at Priorslee, producing c. 700 tons of 'Lilleshall Steel' ingots a week. By 1886 the primary rolling of steel was being undertaken, possibly using a mill moved from Snedshill, to produce structural sections as well as billets and blooms for re-rolling at Snedshill.[63] About that time the Snedshill company was absorbed into the Lilleshall Co.[64]

In the early 1900s the Lilleshall Co.'s iron and steel operations were rationalized. Thereafter pig iron and steel were made at integrated works at Priorslee while wrought iron was made at Snedshill. New plant installed at Priorslee at that time included a Siemens open-hearth furnace to supplement the Bessemer converters; it was slow but, unlike the Bessemer, would accept any amount of scrap in the raw material. In 1910 carbon refractories in the blast furnace hearths were installed, an innovative development.[65]

With the closure of Blists Hill (in Madeley) in 1912 the blast furnaces at Priorslee became the only ones left in Shropshire. That year the Lilleshall Co. made an agreement with the German company Distillation AG to erect coke ovens and a by-products and benzole plant. It was Shropshire's only 20th-century integrated coke-ovens and by-product plant to use chamber-type ovens in place of the open heaps or circular ovens that had served the iron industry since the days of Abraham Darby (I).[66]

While there was no similar investment at Snedshill, the works remained sufficiently important in 1916 to be one of only two outside the Black Country that were members of the Marked Bar Association, effectively a price-fixing body. By 1920 capital expenditure had been suspended at Priorslee, and by 1922 both works were on a three-day week as cheap foreign steel took over the home market. In 1922 the converters at Priorslee were shut, and thenceforth steel was only rolled there. Wrought iron too was being dumped in Britain, and c. 1925 the Snedshill works closed. Those measures, particularly the closure of the Priorslee steelworks, lowered demand for Priorslee iron and by 1926 only one furnace was in use.[67]

In 1948 a separate company, the Lilleshall Iron & Steel Co. Ltd., was set up in anticipation of iron and steel nationalization. The new company, which took over the blast furnaces and steel rolling mills, was in public ownership from 1951 until 1953 when the Lilleshall Co. re-purchased the works. After 1947, however, pig iron production nationally had become increasingly concentrated at a few large steelworks, and Priorslee changed over to foundry iron production, which used a large proportion of scrap, especially baled tin cans, in the charge. In 1959 the one furnace remaining in blast was blown out; like the whole works it would have required major structural refurbishment, and in general there had been little modernization at Priorslee after the early 1900s.[68]

The closure meant that the furnace's waste gas could no longer be burnt off to provide steam power to the Priorslee steel re-rolling mill. Accordingly the mill was electrified in 1960 in the same year that it was joined with Spartan Steel & Alloys Ltd. of Birmingham to form the Shropshire Steel Co. Ltd., which rolled stainless steel there.[69] The Priorslee rolling mill, the last in Shropshire, closed in 1982.

About 1951 the Fairmile Engineering Co. of Bradford, then under Lilleshall Co. ownership, took over the latter's bulletproof-rivet shop at Priorslee, which had been established in 1939. A steel stockholding business was established, and from the mid 1960s Lilleshall Stockholders Ltd. benefited from the rapid growth in steel's distribution through stockholders.[70]

In the later 19th and in the 20th century

---

[58] Ibid. 144; T.S.A.S. lviii. 241; N. Mutton, 'The Foster Fam.: a Study of a Midland Ind. Dynasty 1786–1899' (London Univ. Ph.D. thesis, 1974), 101, 113, 130, 197–8.

[59] Trinder, Ind. Rev. Salop. (1981), 141.

[60] Gale and Nicholls, Lilleshall Co. 28, 42–6; S. Griffiths, Griffiths' Guide to the Iron Trade of Gt. Brit. (1873), 108.

[61] Above, Lilleshall, Econ. Hist. (Iron and Engineering).

[62] Gale and Nicholls, op. cit. 31–4, 52; Colliery Guardian, 1 Apr. 1870. The engines are preserved by I.G.M.T. at Blists Hill.   [63] Gale and Nicholls, op. cit. 56–7.

[64] Ibid. 59; I.G.M.T., Lilleshall Co. colln. 727, 731.

[65] Gale and Nicholls, op. cit. 62–5.

[66] Ibid. 62.

[67] Ibid. 57, 64–5, 79–84; I.G.M.T. Libr., photo. A 651; see W. K. V. Gale, 'The Prior's Lee Blast Furnaces of the Lilleshall Iron and Steel Co. Ltd., near Oakengates' (TS., copy in S.P.L.) for the methods used at Priorslee.

[68] Gale and Nicholls, op. cit. 102–4; above, plates 29–30.

[69] Ibid. 105, 115.

[70] Ibid. 96, 107, 117.

companies other than the Lilleshall Co. engaged in iron making and iron founding in Wombridge and Oakengates, but in general their operations are ill-documented. In 1854 a forge was built for the Wombridge Iron Co. a little way north of Wombridge church on the former site of Foster's ironworks. The company was owned by John Bennett. Products included merchant bar, guide iron, and wire rod[71] and in 1873 the company reputedly had ten puddling furnaces and three mills and forges.[72] Between 1891 and 1895 ownership of the company probably passed to Rollason & Slater of Birmingham, wire manufacturers. The works closed in 1902.[73]

John Maddock manufactured nails in Stirchley in 1869 and moved to Oakengates in 1878 when John Maddock & Co. was founded. At the firm's Great Western Nail Works a wide variety of malleable iron products was made, such as boot protectors. Later bicycle parts, cylinder blocks, and axles were cast for the early cycle and motor trades, necessitating extensions of the works into Station Road. About 1938 the company bought the Lilleshall Co.'s old Snedshill works and laid down there what was reputedly one of the most modern casting foundries in Europe. After the war pipe fittings became the principal manufacture. In 1983 parts for commercial vehicles were the main product. William Lee Ltd. took the works over in 1980. There were 200 employees in 1891, 575 in 1960, and 86 in 1983.[74]

Other little-documented companies included the Hollinswood Iron Works (fl. 1856),[75] perhaps the predecessor of the Eagle Iron Co. (fl. 1870–91) that produced shovels in West Street, St. George's, and was one of the main local suppliers of iron to C. & W. Walker of Donnington. The Eagle Iron Co. was later taken over by the Snedshill Co.[76] Martin & Sons, iron founders, of Slaney Street, Oakengates, operated between 1879 and 1891 and were perhaps succeeded by the Nitram Foundry Co. (fl. 1909–26).[77] The Shropshire Iron Co.'s works in Hadley were extended into Wombridge in 1873.[78] The Capewell Horse Nail Co. Ltd. had a works at Trench Pool c. 1909– c. 1917.[79]

Gasel Ltd., iron founders, were open in Leonard Street, Oakengates, c. 1952,[80] and c. 1960 H. L. Cornaby Ltd. of Oakengates made grey iron and nickel alloy castings for all trades.[81] Both had ceased by 1983 but Boliver Preece & Co., a small engineering firm founded in 1923, remained at the Charlton forge, Oakengates.[82]

OTHER INDUSTRIES. Clay was available both as a local drift deposit and as a waste product from mining. Bricks were generally made locally on site as required, whether for industrial or housing construction. There were brick kilns in the mid 18th century at Oakengates and by the 1780s at Hollinswood, where two former ovens were inhabited in 1793.[83] In the early 19th century there were two groups of kilns at Mumporn Hill, known as the upper and lower brickworks, and a further kiln on the site later occupied by Chapel Street.[84] By 1850 the Lilleshall Co.'s Snedshill brickworks was established in that area, making not only red bricks but also tiles, quarries, white bricks, fire bricks, and land drainage pipes from fireclay.[85] The company got fireclay from its own pits.[86] In the early 1900s the brickworks was improved and salt-glazed pipes and refractory bricks were added to the product range; glazed bricks were made from 1917. 'Belfast' glazed sinks, used nationally in new council estates, were a profitable line from 1918. New kilns and glazing technology were introduced in the 1930s. Nevertheless coal nationalization in 1947 reduced the supply of deep mined clay, which became difficult to obtain although some was got from a private pit at Ketley Bank. Moreover the growing popularity of plastic and stainless steel sinks in the 1950s reduced demand, and c. 1960 the Snedshill works was one of the enterprises taken into the Lilleshall Co.'s Building Materials Division. Ceramic manufacture ended there in 1977.[87]

In 1878 the Lilleshall Co. was making concrete blocks at Snedshill, and in 1903 a concrete works was built on the site of the former Snedshill blast furnaces to make blocks, fencing posts, and slabs. Furnace slag from Priorslee was used as aggregate. In the 1920s the works expanded and a wide range of pre-formed blocks and other structural elements began to be produced. About 1960 the works was taken into the company's new Buildings Materials Division, and 'Dorran' bungalows began to be made. In 1977 Lilleshall Homes Ltd. was sold and concrete making by the Lilleshall Co. ended.[88]

Lime was produced at Snedshill before 1788 and in the early 19th century, and there were sandstone quarries east of St. George's.[89] Several sandpits were dug to get the drift sand between Trench Pool and Oakengates in the later 19th and 20th century.[90]

Glass making began in the coalfield in the mid 1670s when Abraham Bigod, a glass maker from

[71] P.O. Dir. Salop. (1856), 149; V.C.H. Salop. i. 455; O.S. Map 1/2,500, Salop. XXXVI. 11 (1927 edn.).

[72] T. C. Hancox, 'Notes on Ironwks. Formerly Located at Wombridge' (TS. 1959; copy in S.P.L.).

[73] Ibid.; Kelly's Dir. Salop. (1891), 481; (1895), 274.

[74] Kelly's Dir. Salop. (1891), 560; (1905), 401; Review Publishing Co. Industries of Salop (and District) Business Review [1891], 44; Ed. J. Burrow & Co. Ltd. Oakengates Official Guide [1960], 23–5; I.G.M.T. Libr., photo. 1982/91; S.R.O. 1862/1–2; inf. from Wm. Lee Ltd.

[75] P.O. Dir. Salop. (1856), 104, 194.

[76] Ibid. (1870), 242; (1879), 510; Kelly's Dir. Salop. (1885), 1070; inf. from Mr. C. R. Nicholls; I. Gregory, 'E. Salop. Coalfield and the "Gt. Depression" 1873–96' (Keele Univ. M.A. thesis, 1978), 66, 104.

[77] P.O. Dir. Salop. (1879), 510; Kelly's Dir. Salop. (1885), 1070; (1891), 560; (1909), 404; (1926), 443.

[78] Above, p. 261; S.R.O. 2079/ XXXVI. 11.

[79] Kelly's Dir. Salop. (1909); 105; (1917), 98.

[80] County Assocs. Ltd. Oakengates, Newport & Shifnal Dir. (1952), 34.

[81] Burrow, Oakengates Official Guide [1960], 25.

[82] Inf. from the firm.

[83] Trinder, Ind. Rev. Salop. (1981), 31, 60, 194.

[84] S.R.O. 3098/2.

[85] Gale and Nicholls, Lilleshall Co. 40–2; S.R.O. 3039/3–4; I.G.M.T., Lilleshall Co. colln. 723.

[86] Gale and Nicholls, op. cit. 65; Shropshire Mag. Aug. 1976, 17.

[87] Gale and Nicholls, op. cit. 65–6, 91, 102, 114; below.

[88] Gale and Nicholls, op. cit. 66, 90–1, 114.

[89] B.L. Eg. MS. 2872, Lower Woodhouse farm, fields 5 and 6; S.R.O. 3092/2; above, Lilleshall, Econ. Hist. (Mines, Quarries, and Sandpits).   [90] Cartlidge, Usc-con, 3.

Amblecote (Staffs.), built a glasshouse near Snedshill. Window panes and bottles were still made there in 1696,[91] but the glasshouse was 'decayed' and out of use by 1720.[92]

Products and by-products of the local mining and iron and steel industries were at times used by firms established to exploit them. In the late 18th century there was a sulphuric acid works at Wombridge, which used iron pyrites from local coal as the basic raw material. About 1799 John Biddle began to make alkali there using the process developed in France by Malherbe and Athénas. It was apparently unsuccessful and the works evidently closed about the time (1800–3) that Biddle's interest in the Wrockwardine Wood glassworks began.[93]

About 1890 a coal distillation plant was built at Priorslee, apparently with German backing. The Lilleshall Co. bought the plant in 1920 and established a new private subsidiary, the Lilleshall Coal Distillation Co. Ltd.; the products were coke, benzole, naphthalene, and ammonium sulphate. Demand for coke, the main product, fell as blast furnace output declined. The works closed c. 1928 and such coke as Priorslee needed was subsequently purchased from outside suppliers.[94]

In 1912 an asphalt plant was built at Priorslee; it used tar from the coke ovens. At the same time crushing and screening plant was built to convert slag to agricultural fertilizer.[95] The Lilleshall Co. also owned the Basic Slag Works, Trench Pool, which it bought from Sir Thomas Meyrick in 1901. The works was still open during the First World War.[96]

Between c. 1900 and c. 1909 a Chemical Works (late H. & E. Albert) made phosphate powder fertilizer next to the Basic Slag Works.[97]

In the 1940s Russells Rubber Co. Ltd. set up a factory in the former Capewell nail works, making rubber components for motor vehicles. In 1980 there were c. 400 employees.[98]

From 1973 Telford development corporation provided new factory sites on its Stafford Park industrial estate, Priorslee.[99]

MARKET AND FAIRS. About 1826, when William Charlton of Apley began to patronize Oakengates,[1] a market place was formed on the south (or Shifnal) side of Watling Street near Pain's Lane. Like so many developments around Oakengates at that time, the provision of a market owed much to entrepreneurs connected with the Lilleshall Co. The first market place and shambles belonged to John Horton of Priorslee Hall and by 1842 another, smaller, market had been built by Richard Corfield, publican of the Ewe and Lamb, on property let to Horton by the lord of Shifnal manor, the 8th Baron Stafford, in what was becoming the centre of the town.[2] The lords of Shifnal seem not to have enforced any market rights[3] in Oakengates.[4] In 1842 accommodation was said to be still insufficient and there were proposals to build another market in the town centre, opposite the Lion inn.[5] In 1869 the market hall was rebuilt,[6] probably by shareholders.[7] Four fairs a year evidently retained some commercial character c. 1850 but pleasure fairs eventually took their place.[8] From the 1850s, after the arrival of the railways, the town centre market too became a popular social occasion on Saturday evenings.[9] Traders also used Market Street, whose coincidence with the Shifnal–Wombridge boundary prevented the sanitary authorities from exercising due control over the market. Oakengates had a reputation as a good pig market, and industrial workers sold their pigs direct to the pork butchers. About 1890 butcher's meat and vegetables from the surrounding countryside were a staple. No tolls or dues were collected then, but c. 1935 the Green, at the west end of Market Street and in Wombridge manor, was said to be partly in private ownership and subject to market tolls.[10]

The Saturday night street market maintained its popularity throughout the district until extinguished in 1939. Saturday remained market day after the Second World War, and in 1963 the market was moved to a site off New Street that was owned by the urban district council and soon afterwards became the forecourt of the new town hall. An annual 'old tyme' market was instituted some years before 1975 and was still held in 1982.[11]

LOCAL GOVERNMENT. Records of Wombridge court baron survive from 1697, 1708, 1711, 1717, and 1747, the matters dealt with being mainly agricultural.[12] The manor court also

[91] Trinder, *Ind. Rev. Salop.* (1981), 8.
[92] S.P.L., MS. 2600, f. 17, Oakengates.
[93] Trinder, op. cit. 116, 133–4; Plymley, *Agric. of Salop.* 72; below, Wrockwardine Wood, Econ. Hist. (Glass).
[94] Gale and Nicholls, *Lilleshall Co.* 90; Brown, *Mines of Salop.* 44; I.G.M.T., Lilleshall Co. colln. 885, 906.
[95] Gale and Nicholls, op. cit. 65.
[96] Ibid. 76; *Shrews. Chron.* 27 Sept. 1901; S.R.O. 3882/4/1; 4044/87, f. 69v.
[97] *Kelly's Dir. Salop.* (1900), 99; (1905), 101; (1909), 105; S.R.O. 4044/87, f. 69v.
[98] County Assocs. Ltd. *Wellington & Dist. Dir.* [1950], 49; *Shropshire Star,* 22 Apr., 14 Oct. 1980.
[99] *Shropshire Star,* 31 Aug. 1972.
[1] *Salopian Jnl.* 11 May 1842 (p. 2).
[2] Ibid.; S.R.O. 1335/4/1–2 (nos. 49, 134, 380); Trinder, *Ind. Rev. Salop.* (1981), 45, 122–3; Pigot, *Nat. Com. Dir.* (1842), 33.
[3] Cf. Eyton, ii. 294.
[4] *Rep. R. Com. Mkt. Rights,* xiii (2) [C. 6268–VIa], pp.

432–3, 437–8, H.C. (1890–1), xl.
[5] *Salopian Jnl.* 11 May 1842 (p. 2).
[6] *P.O. Dir. Salop.* (1879), 373.
[7] *Rep. R. Com. Mkt. Rights,* xiii (2), 434.
[8] W. M. Moisley, 'Mkts. of Salop.' (London Univ. M.Sc. thesis, 1951), 33; S. Bagshaw, *Dir. Salop.* (1851), 441; above, Social and Cultural Activities.
[9] *Salopian and W. Midland Monthly Illustr. Jnl.* June 1875 (copy in S.P.L.); *Rep. R. Com. Mkt. Rights,* xiii (2), 433; Hudson, *Munby: Man of Two Worlds,* 418; S.R.O. 2108/7; cf. Trinder, *Ind. Rev. Salop.* (1981), 197.
[10] *Rep. R. Com. Mkt. Rights,* xiii (2), 432, 434, 437–8; Cartlidge, *Usc-con,* 115; Moisley, op. cit. 33; below, Local Govt.
[11] Evans, *Childhood Memories,* 23–4; S.R.O. 2108/7–8; County Assocs. Ltd. *Oakengates, Newport, & Shifnal Dir.* (1952), 22 (and later edns.); *Wellington Jnl.* 22 Nov. 1963; *Shropshire Mag.* Oct. 1975, 30–1; local inf.; deeds in possession of Wrekin District Council.
[12] S.R.O. 625, box 15, ct. r.; 676/16, p. 20.

exercised a peculiar probate jurisdiction until 1857.[13] Priorslee was part of Shifnal manor and parish[14] and Ketley Bank part of Leegomery manor.[15]

A lock-up built at Snedshill in 1829 was in use in 1841. Another was built at Oakengates in 1874.[16] The Priorslee District Association for the Prosecution of Felons, formed between 1879 and 1885, remained in existence until the First World War.[17]

As in all the coalfield parishes the number of poor rose markedly as economic activity slumped in the early 19th century,[18] and Wombridge parish expenditure on relief reached a peak in 1817, having doubled since 1816. The number of immigrant workers in Wombridge led to numerous settlement disputes.[19] Wombridge was included in Wellington poor-law union 1836–1930, and in 1838 the appointment of an assistant overseer was authorized.[20] Priorslee was in Shifnal union 1836–1930.[21]

By the early 1890s four fifths of Oakengates town lay in Wombridge parish, one fifth in Shifnal parish. Authorities whose boundaries crossed the town were responsible for sanitary affairs; highway repair; street lighting; weights and measures inspection; magistrates', police, and county court business; and the registration of vital statistics. Properties were variously rated and proposals for a new water supply were held up. Wombridge ratepayers had to deal with sewage and industrial effluent flowing in from Priorslee, and Priorslee children attended Ketley Bank Board School though their parents paid no education rate. The town's principal street, Market Street, was under two highway boards and usually had two different levels; street traders could evade the sanitary inspector's jurisdiction by crossing it. Ten authorities had local government powers in Oakengates, the result of their operations being 'chaos' and the town's reputation for dirt and neglect.[22]

The creation of Oakengates urban district in 1898 helped to improve municipal government, the U.D. comprising the civil parishes of Wombridge, Priorslee, St. George's, and Wrockwardine Wood.[23] Nevertheless Oakengates remained under four education authorities until 1903[24] and three

poor-law unions until 1930.[25] The urban district council first met at the Coffee Palace but soon moved to rented offices in Market Street. Its offices were in Oxford Street c. 1905–c. 1940, thereafter in Stafford Road.[26] Wellington U.D. medical officer of health was employed from c. 1966.[27] Arms were granted to the council in 1960 and included a crest (out of a coronet composed of four laurel leaves set upon a rim or a demi wolf argent collared and lined gold and holding in the forepaws a tower sable the battlements enflamed proper) and the motto *Haec sunt nostra robora*.[28]

OAKENGATES URBAN DISTRICT. *Or, an eagle displayed wings inverted azure grasping in the talons two abbots' crosiers sable, on a chief gules three acorns slipped and leaved gold.*
[Granted 1960]

The council's common seal was circular, 56 mm. in diameter, depicting an oak between gates and inscribed (roman) at the circumference THE SEAL OF THE OAKENGATES URBAN DISTRICT COUNCIL.[29] In the 1960s a new common seal was struck to incorporate the council's arms; it was circular, 50 mm. in diameter, and inscribed (roman) at the circumference OAKENGATES URBAN DISTRICT COUNCIL.[30] The U.D. was abolished in 1974; thereafter the area, not assigned to any C.P., coincided with three urban wards of the district of the Wrekin, except that the northern part of the former U.D. (Hortonwood) was included with adjoining C.P.s in Hadley ward.

In 1968 Oakengates was included in the designated area of Telford new town.[31]

PUBLIC SERVICES. A gas works was built west of New Street in 1849 by William Edwards (d. 1863).[32] It was sold in 1864 to the Oakengates and St. George's Gas and Water Co. Ltd.,[33]

[13] A. J. Camp, *Wills and their Whereabouts* (1974), 185; *T.S.A.S.* 4th ser. xii. 277, 296–8, 321–2; 'Cal. Salop. Wills' (app. to *T.S.A.S.* 4th ser. xii), 47; wills in L.J.R.O., PC 11, in 1982.

[14] Eyton, ii. 265–83, 313–14. The man. and local govt. of Shifnal are reserved for treatment in a later vol. of this *Hist*.

[15] Above, Wellington, Local Govt.; S.R.O. 972, parcel 245, Ketley map of 1794.

[16] *Orders of Q. Sess.* iii. 277; iv. 216; S.R.O. 2924/69, 102.

[17] *Kelly's Dir. Salop.* (1885), 924; (1913), 198.

[18] *Some Facts, shewing the Vast Burthen of the Poor's Rate, by a member of the Salop. Co. Cttee. for the employment of the poor* (Holborn, 1817), 5 (copy in S.P.L.); Staffs. R.O., D 593/N/3/10/17; *Poor Rate Returns*, H.C. 556, suppl. app. p. 176 (1822), v; H.C. 83, p. 164 (1830–1), xi; H.C. 444, p. 159 (1835), xlvii. [19] *Orders of Q. Sess.* iii. 206.

[20] V. J. Walsh, 'Admin. of Poor Laws in Salop. 1820–55' (Pennsylvania Univ. Ph.D. thesis, 1970), 149 (copy in S.R.O.); E. C. Peele and R. S. Clease, *Salop. Par. Doc.* (Shrews. [1903]), 367.

[21] *P.O. Dir. Salop.* (1856), 104, 149; *Kelly's Dir. Salop.* (1929), 174, 197.

[22] *S.C.C. Mins.* reps. of clk. 16 June 1894, 1–10.

[23] Above, intro.

[24] Wombridge and Wrockw. Wood sch. bds., Newport and Wellington sch. attendance cttees.: *List of Sch. Boards, 1902* [Cd. 1038], pp. 75, 123–4, 130, H.C. (1902), lxxix.

[25] Newport (St. Geo.'s C.P.), Shifnal (Priorslee C.P.), and Wellington (Wombridge and Wrockw. Wood C.P.s): *Kelly's Dir. Salop.* (1929), 4.

[26] Ibid. (1900), 162; (1905), 167; (1937), 179; (1941), 176; above, intro.

[27] G.P.O. *Telephone Dir.* (1967), sect. 72, p. 2160.

[28] S.R.O., DA 12/134 (S.R.O. 3172/8/15(13)), file on arms; G. Briggs, *Civic and Corporate Heraldry* (1971), 290–1. The arms allude to the area's hist.

[29] Impression in S.C.C. Sec.'s Dept., deed RB (M) 1452.

[30] Impression ibid. RB (M) 3984.

[31] *Dawley New Town (Designation) Amendment (Telford) Order 1968* (Stat. Instr. 1968, no. 1912), map accompanying Explanatory Note.

[32] *P.O. Dir. Salop.* (1856), 93; *Wellington Jnl.* 3 June 1949 (p. 14); S.R.O. 2990/10–22.

[33] S.R.O. 2990/14.

which was in turn bought by the Wellington (Salop) Gas Co. in 1922.[34] By 1882 the Hadley & Trench Gas Works stood on the south-western edge of Trench Pool, and in 1912 the Hadley, Trench, and Wrockwardine Wood Lighting Co. Ltd. supplied gas to Oakengates urban district council.[35] The company was bought by the Wellington (Salop) Gas Co. in 1930.[36]

Electricity became available in the 1930s.[37]

In 1892 water supply in Oakengates was said to be 'as bad as it can be, . . . scanty, . . . inaccessible, . . . contaminated or liable to it', coming from rainwater butts or 'dip' wells if it could not be begged from one of the few pump wells. Soft water was bought for washing. Ketley Bank was as ill-supplied as Oakengates. Houses belonging to the Lilleshall Co. tended to be better served and the company was at that time improving the water supply by tapping pit water. Contamination was unavoidable as the area was sewered either not at all or ineffectively: the more recently developed streets had sewers, but they generally discharged into open ditches that passed other houses before draining into settling tanks below the town. Most houses, many with shared closets, had cess pits, many of them open. Other households had pails and threw sewage into their yards or the street. The disposal of ash and domestic refuse was just as erratic. In general only the Lilleshall Co. properties enjoyed the attention, albeit irregular, of a scavenger.[38]

Water supply to Oakengates was improved in the 1900s despite the abandonment of a major scheme of 1904. The Lilleshall Co.'s supply was transferred to the U.D.C. between 1901 and 1918; from 1913 it included water from the duke of Sutherland's Redhill reservoir fed from Hilton (Staffs.).[39] For a time, before 1946, Ketley Bank was supplied with water purchased from the borough of Wenlock and conveyed through Dawley U.D.C. and Wellington rural district council mains, but that arrangement proved unsatisfactory and Ketley Bank was linked c. 1946 to the Oakengates main system.[40]

The U.D.C. built the Trench Farm sewage works, Hortonwood, in 1904–5;[41] it was one of those replaced by the Rushmoor works, Wrockwardine, opened in 1975.[42]

A child-health centre opened in Oakengates in 1918. In 1936 it moved to a site in Stafford Road, where it remained in 1983.[43] The U.D.C. helped to maintain an ambulance service for Wellington rural district until 1945.[44]

Fear of air raids led to the provision of several 'fire boxes' containing hoses, etc., in 1916; the nearest fire engine was then at Wellington.[45] After the Second World War the county council provided a retained fire station at Oakengates.[46] It closed in 1980 when Telford central fire station opened at Stafford Park industrial estate.[47]

Oakengates had one police constable in 1840[48] and a post office by 1856.[49]

CHURCHES. During the Middle Ages St. Leonard's priory presumably served the area that became Wombridge parish. No vicarage was endowed before the Dissolution, and afterwards the benefice (if there was one) seems to have been simply a donative and outside the bishop's ordinary jurisdiction.[50] It was evidently in the Crown's patronage until the earlier 17th century. Probably between 1621 and 1642 patronage was acquired by the Charltons with the impropriate tithes. In 1621 Francis Charlton still owed the Crown the 'king's rent' of £2 6s. 8d. for the maintenance of a minister,[51] but before his death in 1642 he may have been allowing £20 a year to the cure. In 1656 his son was called patron and the old 'king's rent' was then retained by the Charltons. The patronage remained with the family, W. J. C. Charlton-Meyrick being patron in 1982.[52] From 1693 curates were licensed to the cure but there was no formal institution until the perpetual curacy became a vicarage in 1866[53]

The first known minister was described as *lector* in 1609 and 1616.[54] There was no minister in 1656.[55] Before 1693 a minister built a house on the waste at Oakengates and lived there, but within a few years Francis Charlton (d. 1698) had let it to a lay tenant.[56] Nevertheless there was apparently glebe of 9 a. in the 1690s,[57] and in the early 18th century the curates of Wombridge received £5 from the Charltons and £3 from a legacy of James Rushbury (d. 1718), an agent of the family.[58] From that period there is evidence of

[34] Above, Wellington, Public Services.
[35] O.S. Map 1/2,500, Salop. XXXVI. 10 (1882 edn.); S.R.O., DA 12/134/51 (19 Aug. 1952); /134/52 (16 Aug. 1952).
[36] Above, Wellington, Public Services.
[37] *Kelly's Dir. Salop.* (1937), 179.
[38] *S.C.C. Mins.* rep. of Co. M.O.H. 31 Dec. 1892, 9–11; *S.C.C. Mins.* 1896–7, 273–82.
[39] Gale and Nicholls, *Lilleshall Co.* 72–4; S.R.O. 119/60; above, Dawley, Public Services; above, Lilleshall, Public Services.
[40] A. H. S. Waters, *Rep. on Water Supplies* (S.C.C. 1946), 24.
[41] Above, Eyton, intro.
[42] *Telford Jnl.* 7 Aug. 1975; inf. from Severn–Trent Water Auth., Wellington.
[43] Inf. from Salop Area Health Auth.
[44] Above, Wellington, Public Services.
[45] S.R.O., DA 12/100/7, pp. 448–53; Evans, *Childhood Memories*, 22.
[46] S.R.O. 3005/2.
[47] *Shropshire Star*, 31 Oct. 1980.

[48] S.R.O., q. sess. Const. Cttee. rep. bk. 1839–53, p. 76.
[49] *P.O. Dir. Salop.* (1856), 94.
[50] The man. ct. had right of probate: above, Local Govt.
[51] P.R.O., SC 12/32/32; above, Man. and Other Est.
[52] P.R.O., C 142/786, no. 67; *Salop. News Letter*, xxxiii. 12; *T.S.A.S.* xlvii. 11; S.R.O. 1005/69; 3882/4/1, p. 14; Lich. Dioc. Regy., benefice and inst. bk. 1900–29, p. 18; *Lich. Dioc. Dir.* (1982), 106.
[53] L.J.R.O., B/A/1/18, ff. 3, 30v.; /1/26, pp. 80–1; /1/28, pp. 59, 105; Lich. Dioc. Regy., episc. reg. 32, p. 109; bps.' reg. R, p. 123; benefice and inst. bk. 1868–1900, p. 13; S.R.O. 4162/Pa/3.
[54] L.J.R.O., B/V/1/25; /1/32.
[55] *T.S.A.S.* xlvii. 11.
[56] *Salop. News Letter*, xxxiii. 12; above, Wellington, Man. and Other Est. (Apley); S.R.O. 625, bdle. 22, Mich. rental of 1722, p. 11.
[57] *Salop. News Letter*, xxxiii. 12.
[58] S.R.O. 625, box 11, 'The annual charge to be pd. out of the est. of St. J. Charlton'; 676/8, loose sheet; 4309, box III, Thos. Dorsett to Jos. Shirke, 1 Feb. 1743/4; *9th Rep. Com. Char.* H.C. 258, p. 324 (1823), ix.

regular services at Wombridge, perhaps interrupted in the 1770s; baptisms and burials are recorded from 1721, marriages are recorded from 1802.[59]

Between 1746 and 1841 augmentations of the living totalling £2,200 were made from Queen Anne's Bounty, that of £200 in 1841 meeting a benefaction of St. John C. Charlton.[60] The living, worth £82 in 1856,[61] was improved by c. £50 a year between 1864 and 1867 by the Ecclesiastical Commissioners from £1,000 of subscriptions and grants. In 1879 the living was worth £170.[62] It had risen to £200 by 1913 and £378 by 1932.[63] During the 19th and 20th centuries the area of the glebe fluctuated between 3 a. and 10½ a.[64]

In 1841 St. John C. Charlton gave a site for a benefice house, and there was one in 1851.[65] In 1884, however, the vicarage was said to be a former farmhouse.[66] A new vicarage was built next to the old one c. 1982.

The earliest known ministers, Richard Wood (fl. 1609–16) and one Holmes (before 1693), lived in the parish[67] but Robert Bromhall, LL.D., lived at Hadley. When licensed in 1693, immediately after his ordination as deacon, Bromhall was aged c. 60; he was licensed as schoolmaster in the parish and from 1697 was also assistant curate in Dawley.[68] William Sockett, rector of Preston upon the Weald Moors from 1714, also served Wombridge from 1721.[69] William Laplain, Stephen Panting, and Joshua Gilpin, successive vicars of Wrockwardine, apparently served Wombridge for periods between 1743 and 1783.[70]

C. R. Cameron, perpetual curate 1808–56, was also perpetual curate of St. George's 1807–31.[71] Both he and his wife Lucy (1781–1858)[72] published numerous books and pamphlets of an improving nature, many illustrated with examples from the Oakengates area. In their works they frequently condemned self-indulgent and spendthrift miners, and in 1831 during the wages riots Cameron was active on behalf of the magistracy and yeomanry. At times the Camerons criticized standards of Methodist discipline and called in question the religious convictions of enthusiastic nonconformist preachers.[73] Cameron's successor, James Russell (1856–71), also published sermons and commentaries.[74]

The Lady chapel of the former priory church remained standing until 1756. There was no glass in its windows in the period 1693–8 and a repair brief was reputedly issued in 1723. The building was still in use c. 1741 but collapsed in 1756.[75] A brief was issued in 1757 and a new church was erected. Built of brick, with stone-dressed round-headed windows, the church of *ST. MARY AND ST. LEONARD* comprised a nave and small west tower. It seated 200. In 1824 a further brief was issued and north and south transepts, both with galleries, were added to the eastern end of the nave, increasing the seating to 500.[76] There was also an eastern apse, which was removed with the galleries in a major restoration of 1869.[77]

Additions of 1869, designed by George Bidlake of Wolverhampton, included a chancel with south transept, an organ chamber and vestry on the north side, and north and south nave aisles. The church was also reseated, the tower raised, and the roof replaced.[78] A legacy of James Oliver (d. 1867) of Wellington, the son of a former incumbent, provided £900 of the cost. In 1859 and 1866 plate was given in memory of James's sister, mother-in-law, and nephew. There is one bell, of 1899.[79] Sir Thomas Meyrick gave ½ a. to extend the graveyard in 1898.[80]

The register of baptisms and burials begins in 1721, that of marriages in 1802.[81] Between the collapse of the old church in 1756 and the completion of the replacement most baptisms were at Priorslee.[82]

The new church of *HOLY TRINITY*, Oakengates, was built in 1854 and immediately assigned its own parish from the parishes of Wombridge and Shifnal. That part of Wombridge south of Priory Farm was put in the new parish, largely depriving Wombridge of both population and parish. Accordingly in 1859 the area north of Hartshill and Market Street, on the Watling Street, and west of Harts Bridge Road, was returned to Wombridge.[83] In 1854 patronage of

[59] Cartlidge, *Usc-con*, 66–7; *S.P.R. Lich.* viii (1), c 282.
[60] C. Hodgson, *Q. Anne's Bounty* (2nd edn.), pp. ccxxix, ccxciv.
[61] *P.O. Dir. Salop.* (1856), 149.
[62] S.R.O. 3916/1/8, loose letter, Jas. Russell to archdcn. 25 May 1864; Lich. Dioc. Regy., bps.' reg. R, p. 253; *P.O. Dir. Salop.* (1879), 446.
[63] *Kelly's Dir. Salop.* (1913), 313; *Crockford* (1932), 599.
[64] Lich. Dioc. Regy., bps.' reg. Q, p. 754; R, p. 260; U, p. 301; S.R.O. 625, box 12, Law & Tindal to Chas. Emery, 28 Apr. 1841; 4309, ecclesiastical box XI, Wombridge; *Return of Glebe Land, 1887*, H.C. 307, p. 68 (1887), lxiv; *Kelly's Dir. Salop.* (1885–1922).
[65] S.R.O. 625, box 12, Law & Tindal to Chas. Emery, 28 Apr. 1841; S. Bagshaw, *Dir. Salop.* (1851), 442.
[66] S.R.O. 3916/1/26/56.
[67] Above.
[68] L.J.R.O., B/A/1/18, ff. 3, 30v.; *Salop. News Letter*, xxxiii. 12.
[69] Cartlidge, *Usc-con*, 66; above, Preston, Church.
[70] *S.P.R. Lich.* viii (1), 165–229; below, Wrockwardine, Church.
[71] L.J.R.O., B/A/1/28, p. 105; Lich. Dioc. Regy., episc. reg. 32, p. 107; above, Lilleshall, Churches.
[72] *D.N.B.*
[73] B.M. *Gen. Cat. of Printed Bks. to 1955* (photolitho-graphic edn. 1959–66), xxxii, cols. 668–9, 692–6; Trinder, *Ind. Rev. Salop.* (1981), 163–4, 205, 234.
[74] Lich. Dioc. Regy., episc. reg. 32, p. 109; benefice and inst. bk. 1868–1900, p. 13; B.M. *Gen. Cat. of Printed Bks. to 1955*, ccix, col. 485.
[75] B.L. Add. MS. 30316, f. 37; S. Bagshaw, *Dir. Salop.* (1851), 441; *Bye-Gones*, N.S. i. 73; Eyton, vii. 363–73; Cartlidge, *Priory of Wombridge*, 23; *Salop. News Letter*, xxxiii. 12; Birm. Univ. Libr., Mytton Papers, vii. 132.
[76] *Orders of Q. Sess.* ii. 161; iii. 244; W. A. Bewes, *Ch. Briefs* (1896), 360, 419; S.P.L., MS. 372, vol. ii, p. 75; S.P.L., J. H. Smith colln., no. 220; *P.O. Dir. Salop.* (1856), 149; above plate 36, showing the church before the alterations of 1824.
[77] S.R.O. 4162/Ch/1.
[78] Ibid.
[79] Ibid.; Cartlidge, *Priory of Wombridge*, 23; *Shropshire Mag.* Nov. 1969, 28; Cranage, vii. 637; S. A. Jeavons, *Ch. Plate Archd. Salop* (Shrews. 1964), pp. 56, 90, 94, 115; H. B. Walters, *Ch. Bells of Salop.* (Oswestry, 1915), 284–5, 448.
[80] Lich. Dioc. Regy., bps.' reg. U, p. 301.
[81] Peele and Clease, *Salop. Par. Doc.* 267; S.R.O. 4162/Rg/1–3.
[82] *Bye-Gones*, N.S. i. 73.
[83] Cartlidge, *Usc-con*, 70–3; Lich. Dioc. Regy., bps.' reg. P & QA (Orders in Council), pp. 109, 116 (2nd nos.).

the living was vested in the bishop of Lichfield, patron in 1982.[84]

In 1853 and 1855 the living, until 1868 a perpetual curacy, was endowed by grants and subscriptions and matching benefactions from Queen Anne's Bounty.[85] In 1870 the living was worth £70, and in 1881 £97 18s. 2d. made up of £41 18s. from the Ecclesiastical Commissioners, £30 11s. 7d. from Queen Anne's Bounty, and £25 8s. 7d. in fees and offerings.[86] Further grants were made in 1885, 1886, and 1887,[87] and in 1892 the living was worth £131.[88] Grants were again made in 1908 and 1910,[89] and in 1922 the living was valued at £300, in 1932 £308 net.[90]

The vicarage house was built next to the church in 1856 on land given in 1854 by St. John C. Charlton. The building was apparently financed from a residue in the church building fund.[91] J. E. G. Cartlidge (d. 1976), vicar 1928–47, published several books and pamphlets on the area's history, and was active in local government and the movement to improve the derelict industrial landscape of Oakengates in the 1930s.[92]

Holy Trinity church was built and consecrated in 1855, £3,103 having been raised by subscriptions and grants since 1850. Designed by Ewan Christian and built by John Millington, in the event it cost only £2,047[93] and seated 500.[94] It consisted of a nave with short north and south aisles, chancel and a central turret, and was built in banded red and blue brick; originally the roof was similarly striped.[95]

There is one bell, installed after 1885.[96] A churchyard extension was consecrated in 1930.[97]

The registers are complete from 1855.[98]

A chapel of ease at Priorslee in Shifnal parish, probably of 12th-century build, survived to serve the needs of the area's increasing industrial population in the later 18th century and, having been replaced by a new church of ST. PETER in 1836, was demolished in 1838.[99]

In the mid 18th century the old chapel was occasionally served (like Wombridge) by William Laplain and Stephen Panting, successive vicars of Wrockwardine (1740–87).[1] A set of plate was given in 1771.[2] In 1799 land bought by Queen

Anne's Bounty provided the minister serving the chapel with £20–£30 a year;[3] baptisms took place there.[4] E. Roberts was minister on the nomination of the vicar of Shifnal; Roberts, however, had moved to Wales and the one Sunday service there was then taken by Robert Smith, curate of Shifnal. Said to be inconveniently timed, at one o'clock, it attracted a poor congregation. There were eight to ten Easter and Christmas communicants.[5] By 1824 Smith was minister at Priorslee, residing at Coppice Green, 5 km. to the east. His living was then worth c. £120 a year. The frequency and time of services remained unaltered.[6]

Under J. T. Matthews, minister c. 1827–c. 1857 and headmaster of Shifnal grammar school,[7] services were more frequent and more conveniently timed and a new church was built. In 1829 there were Sunday services at one and three o'clock, one with a sermon, and communion was celebrated four times a year.[8] In 1843, after the new church had been built and consecrated, services remained the same and there were 20 communicants. Marriages and burials had begun in 1837 and 1839 respectively.[9]

William Angell, minister from Matthews's death until 1881, had been his curate for at least the last year of his life.[10] During Angell's time, in 1863, Priorslee became an ecclesiastical parish separate from Shifnal. The perpetual curate was styled vicar from 1868 and the benefice remained in the patronage of the vicar of Shifnal[11] until 1982 when[12] it was united with the benefice of St. George's; patronage of the united benefice was then vested in the vicar of Shifnal and the bishop of Lichfield jointly.[13] The living, worth £140 in 1843, was worth £224 in 1885 and £400 in 1932.[14] The glebe had comprised 23 a. in Shifnal and a 28-a. farm in Halesowen (Salop. and Worcs.) in 1843; by 1884 the latter had perhaps been exchanged for one near Oldbury (Worcs.).[15]

It is not clear when in the 19th century a benefice house was first provided. In 1926 an old six-bedroomed vicarage was sold and a new one built on adjoining land.[16]

The new brick church built at Snedshill, 1 km.

[84] Lich. Dioc. Regy., bps.' reg. P, p. 260; Lich. Dioc. Dir. (1982), 79.
[85] P.O. Dir. Salop. (1856), 93; C. Hodgson, Q. Anne's Bounty (2nd edn.), suppl. pp. xxxiii, lxvii, lxxxvi.
[86] P.O. Dir. Salop. (1870), 103; S.R.O. 3916/1/26/37.
[87] Lich. Dioc. Regy., bps.' reg. S, p. 723; T, pp. 55, 107.
[88] S.R.O. 3916/1/26/37.
[89] Lich. Dioc. Regy., bps.' reg. V, pp. 149, 259.
[90] Kelly's Dir. Salop. (1922), 169; Crockford (1932), 211.
[91] S.R.O. 4309, ecclesiastical box VI, Oakengates; Lich. Dioc. Regy., bps.' reg. P, p. 256; Cartlidge, Usc-con, 71; P.O. Dir. Salop. (1856œ), 93.
[92] See works cited in footnotes above and below; Shrews. Chron. 3 Dec. 1976 (p. 4); Cartlidge, op. cit. 115–19; above, intro.
[93] Cartlidge, op. cit. 70–1; cf., however, Lich. Dioc. Regy., bps.' reg. P, pp. 257, 267–72.
[94] P.O. Dir. Salop. (1856), 93.
[95] S.P.L., J. H. Smith colln., no. 151; S.R.O. 3916/1/8, photo. on verso of Norton in Hales; Cranage, i. 23.
[96] Walters, Ch. Bells of Salop. 281.
[97] Lich. Dioc. Regy., bps.' reg. W, pp. 384–6.
[98] Peele and Clease, Salop. Par. Doc. 251–2.
[99] B.L. Add. MS. 21180, f. 49; 21236, f. 19; S.P.L., MS.

372, vol. i, p. 71; S.P.L., MS. 3065, no. 117; S.R.O. 3916/1/4; Bodl. MS. Top. Salop. c.2, f. 422.
[1] Above; below, Wrockwardine, Church; S.P.R. Lich. viii (1), 160–226.
[2] Jeavons, Ch. Plate Archd. Salop, pp. 67, 119.
[3] S.R.O. 3916/1/1, p. 56.
[4] S.R.O. 3916/1/1; Peele and Clease, Salop. Par. Doc. 267; J. E. G. Cartlidge and N. S. Kidson, Short Acct. of Hist. of Par. of Priors Lee (Shifnal, 1937; copy in S.P.L.), pp. vi–vii.
[5] S.R.O. 3916/1/1, pp. 55–6.   [6] Ibid. /1/4.
[7] Cartlidge and Kidson, Hist. Priors Lee, pp. vi, xii.
[8] S.R.O. 3916/1/3.
[9] Ibid. /1/8; Peele and Clease, Salop. Par. Doc. 267.
[10] P.O. Dir. Salop. (1856), 104; (1879), 387; Kelly's Dir. Salop. (1885), 924.
[11] Cartlidge and Kidson, Hist. Priors Lee, pp. vi–vii.
[12] On resignation of vicar of St. Geo.'s: inf. from Revd. Preb. C. Hill.
[13] Church Com. scheme, 23 July 1981 (confirmed 31 July 1981: Lond. Gaz. 6 Aug. 1981, p. 10194).
[14] S.R.O. 3916/1/6; Kelly's Dir. Salop. (1885), 924; Crockford (1932), 742.
[15] S.R.O. 3916/1/6; /1/29, Priorslee terrier of 1884.
[16] Ibid. /1/3–4; 4309, ecclesiastical box VI, Priorslee.

north-west of the old chapel and closer to the population, was designed by Ewan Christian. It consisted of a nave seating 415, 200 seats being free. A west tower and vestries were added between 1843 and 1851.[17] In 1903 a south gallery was removed and a chancel designed by C. B. Dalgleish added.[18] A churchyard extension was consecrated in 1917.[19] The single bell was installed in 1958; another of 1726 survives unhung.[20]

The register of baptisms begins in 1813, marriages in 1837, and burials in 1867.[21]

NONCONFORMITY. WOMBRIDGE. William Charlton of Wombridge (d. 1567) was reputed a papist or sympathizer with papists.[22]

Samuel Campion, the minister ejected from Hodnet in 1660, held Sunday conventicles at Wombridge in 1669.[23] In 1691 the Presbyterians or Congregationalists considered holding meetings at Wombridge as the established church was so ineffectual at ministering to the expanding population.[24]

C. R. Cameron, perpetual curate of Wombridge 1808–56, resisted the nonconformists[25] and, save for the Wesleyan chapel at Ketley Bank, no nonconformist meeting house was ever established in his parish during his time. In the 1840s and 1850s, however, Primitive Methodist, Congregational, and New Connexion Methodist chapels opened on the southern (or Shifnal parish) side of Oakengates town, and the Primitives opened one in Ketley Bank. There were no chapels on the north side of Oakengates town until 1868 when the Methodist New Connexion moved to Slaney Street and the Baptists opened in Stafford Road. The Salvation Army began work in the town in 1882 and other sects arrived in the 20th century. A United Church was formed in 1981 by the Methodists and United Reformed Church.

About 1764 a Wesleyan society was established at Ketley Bank by J. W. Fletcher, vicar of Madeley.[26] A Wesleyan chapel built there in 1823 served a wide area including Lawley Bank. In 1878 the society bought Bethesda chapel in Station Road, Oakengates, from the Methodist New Connexion. Bethesda closed in 1908 and Ketley Bank chapel became once more the centre of local Wesleyan activity. In 1983 the chapel had a congregation of 30.[27]

A Wesleyan society met at Hollinswood in the 1840s and 1850s and there was reputedly a Wesleyan chapel there in 1897.[28]

Primitive Methodism was introduced to the Oakengates area, and to Shropshire, in 1821 when W. Saunders preached at Ketley Bank and Wrockwardine Wood. In 1822 James Bonser preached at Oakengates to almost 2,000 people, and Hugh Bourne also preached near the town that year. Oakengates bull ring was regularly used for open-air preaching until Wrockwardine Wood chapel opened in 1823, the incumbent of Wombridge, C. R. Cameron, apparently resisting the chapel's siting in his parish.[29]

A chapel for the Primitives was built on the south side of Market Street in 1845, only to be demolished in advance of the Wellington–Wolverhampton railway c. 1846. It was replaced by a chapel opened in 1847 in Station Hill. Measuring 39 × 36 ft., it had a west gallery and seated 500; there was an adjacent burial ground. In 1867 mining subsidence closed the chapel and a new one was built farther east in Station Hill in 1868. Originally three bays square, and of brown brick with blue brick dressings, the chapel was extended in 1905. In 1940 it seated 520 and had a schoolroom and three other rooms. In 1981, on the eve of the chapel's closure and the congregation's move to the United Reformed church, the Oakengates Methodist chapel had 41 members; an average of 20 attended the morning service and 30 that in the evening.[30]

There was regular Primitive Methodist preaching at Ketley Bank from 1830.[31] Before 1841, when it used Pocock's school, Ketley Bank,[32] the society met in East Road.[33] It was thus evidently not the dissenting body that met at the Lord Hill c. 1857.[34]

The New Connexion Methodists (or Reformers) opened Bethesda chapel in Station Road, Oakengates, in 1856. In 1878 they sold it to the Wesleyans.[35] In the mean time Zion chapel, Slaney Street, had opened: the New Connexion used that between 1868 and 1892.[36]

In 1843 the Wellington Congregationalists instituted services in Oakengates, the first being held in a room in the Charlton Arms, Market Street. A Sunday school began at the same time. Oakengates's first minister was appointed in 1846; a schoolroom in Lion Street opened in 1847, and the chapel that surmounted it in 1848. Of brown brick and slate, the chapel has a three-bayed front with brick pilasters, rendered entablature and pediment, and carved consoles to the windows. It was originally four bays deep, and a two-storeyed fifth bay was later added. In 1848 the congregation of 21 gained independence from Wellington.

[17] S.R.O. 3916/1/6; S. Bagshaw, *Dir. Salop.* (1851), 476.
[18] S.R.O. 3916/1/8; S.P.L., J. H. Smith colln., no. 161; Cartlidge and Kidson, *Hist. Priors Lee*, pp. vi, x, xiv; *P.O. Dir. Salop.* (1870), 118; I.G.M.T., Lilleshall Co. colln. 405.
[19] Cartlidge and Kidson, op. cit. p. xi.
[20] Ibid.
[21] Peele and Clease, *Salop. Par. Doc.* 267.
[22] *V.C.H. Salop.* iii. 60, 237; *Camden Misc.* ix (Camd. Soc. N.S. liii), 45.
[23] *Original Rec. of Early Nonconf.* ed. G. L. Turner (1911), i. 55; ii. 737.
[24] *Freedom After Ejection*, ed. A. Gordon (1917), 90.
[25] See above and below.
[26] Trinder, *Ind. Rev. Salop.* (1981), 158.
[27] Above, intro.; below; Cartlidge, *Usc-con*, 81; James *'Here be Dragons'*, 16; inf. from Mr. J. H. Lenton.

[28] Inf. from Mr. Lenton; *Wellington Jnl.* 12 June 1897.
[29] Cartlidge, op. cit. 77–8; Trinder, *Ind. Rev. Salop.* (1981), 167–71.
[30] S.R.O. 3038/4/6–8; SA 14438; inf. from Mr. Lenton; *Meth. Church Bldgs.: Statistical Returns* (1940), 267.
[31] Cartlidge, op. cit. 78, S.R.O. 3605/2, 28 Dec. 1835.
[32] Above, Ketley, Nonconf., Educ.
[33] Cartlidge, op. cit. 78.
[34] S.R.O. 972, parcel 235, plan of proposed schoolrm. (watermark 1857). Cf. *P.O. Dir. Salop.* (1856), 94; O.S. Map 1/2,500, Salop. XXXVI. 15 (1882 edn.).
[35] *Eddowes's Jnl.* 15 Sept. 1856; inf. from Mr. Lenton; above.
[36] *Return of Churches, 1882*, H.C. 401, p. 366 (1882), l; G.R.O., Worship Reg. no. 61435; James, *'Here be Dragons'*, 16.

The congregation grew during the later 19th century and between 1855 and 1868 side galleries and classrooms were built. In 1937 there were sittings for 500. The Congregationalists (United Reformed Church) began to share a building with the Methodists when Oakengates United church opened in 1981.[37]

Oakengates United church was designed in brick by R. Bellamy. Owned by the United Reformed Church, it was also used by the Methodists. It had 72 members in 1983.[38]

A Baptist chapel with 200 sittings was built in Stafford Road in 1868. It was apparently disused by 1948.[39]

The Salvation Army began to hold Sunday services in Oakengates town hall in 1882, with week-night meetings in a mission in Quob Lane (later Station Road) and open-air gatherings on the Green. The Army met in the town hall until the Bridge Street barracks opened in 1896. The barracks were used until 1967 when the Salvation Army Centre in Hartshill Road opened.[40]

The Christian or Plymouth Brethren met in the Gospel Room, New Street, in 1900 and later in the Foresters' Hall, West Street. By 1923 they had moved to premises in West Street, Wrockwardine Wood.[41] They may be identifiable with the Brotherhood that met in Slaney Street or Stafford Road.[42]

Jehovah's Witnesses had a Kingdom Hall in New Street between 1958 and 1967.[43]

PRIORSLEE. There was a cottage meeting at Priorslee in 1813 under the care of the Shifnal Wesleyan society. The meeting became independent in 1824 and in 1840 had connexions with the Snedshill society. The Snedshill Wesleyans' numbers declined markedly in the 1840s. Nevertheless in 1850 they opened a new chapel and schoolroom in Priorslee Road. On Census Sunday 1851 morning service was attended by 143 worshippers, afternoon service by 256. Already in 1850 there were strained relations with the circuit, and in 1852 the congregation broke away as a Wesleyan Reform church. It produced its own plan, the only such instance in the west Midlands. The chapel, later a United Methodist Free church, was rebuilt c. 1920, and its congregation joined the Oakengates United church in 1981.[44]

Trinity chapel in Chapel Street was built by the Wesleyans in 1863 to replace the Nabb chapel, Wrockwardine Wood. In 1940 it seated 220 in pews and had a school hall and one other room attached to it. It was de-registered in 1964.[45]

The Primitives had a chapel in Canongate, which was replaced c. 1900 by one in Priorslee Road. It closed in 1918 and was demolished in 1922.[46]

The New Connexion had a small chapel at Hollinswood built in 1832. In 1851 morning service was attended by 41 adults and 60 children and afternoon service by 89 and 71 respectively; 74 also attended evening service. A new chapel of 1854 was later known as Zoar. A schoolroom was added in 1866. Zoar had 8 members in 1900 and closed in 1901.[47]

In 1967 a new St. George's Methodist church opened in Church Street, replacing the Jubilee chapel. Designed by A.S.S.Q. Associates, of Birmingham, it was built by Patrick Smith.[48]

EDUCATION. WOMBRIDGE. In 1693 Robert Bromhall, LL.D., was licensed as deacon and schoolmaster in the parish.[49] By 1833 20 boys and 21 girls were attending two private day schools, 30 boys and 80 girls a church Sunday school, and 300 boys and 250 girls a Wesleyan Sunday school. The Sunday schools were supported by voluntary contributions.[50] A National school opened in 1846 and a short-lived British school in 1860.[51]

George Collins, vicar 1872–8,[52] tried in vain to raise money for a new church school at Ketley Bank where 250 children lacked school places in 1875,[53] when Wombridge school board was formed. A turbulent election returned a nonconformist majority; the board included the vicar but the Congregational minister became chairman.[54] The National school was offered to the board for a nominal rent but the board rejected the managers' conditions[55] and the offer was soon withdrawn.[56] Controversy raged over the board's intended school site at Ketley Bank, some ratepayers demanding a more central position. Anglicans, led by the vicar, still wanted a church school.[57] The Education Department, however, approved the Ketley Bank site[58] and the school opened in 1878. A continuing shortage of school places was relieved by enlargements of the board and National schools in the 1880s and 1890s and by the opening

---

[37] E. Elliot, *Hist. of Congregationalism in Salop.* [1898], 275–8; S.R.O. 2390/2; *P.O. Dir. Salop.* (1856), 93; *Kelly's Dir. Salop.* (1937), 179.

[38] *Shropshire Star*, 25 Mar. 1981; inf. from Mr. Lenton.

[39] Cartlidge, *Usc-con*, 81; G.R.O., Worship Reg. no. 19799; *Return of Churches, 1882*, 366; *S.C.C. Mins. (Educ.)* 1947–8, 80; 1950–1, 27; James, 'Here be Dragons', 16.

[40] Cartlidge, op. cit. 82; *Wellington Jnl.* 15 Sept. 1883 (p. 8); G.R.O., Worship Reg. nos. 27484, 35711, 70790.

[41] G.R.O., Worship Reg. no. 38026; James, op. cit. 17; below, Wrockwardine Wood, Nonconf.; O.S. Map 1/2,500, Salop. XXXVI. 11 (1927 edn.); *Kelly's Dir. Salop.* (1905), 167.

[42] James, op. cit. 16.

[43] G.R.O., Worship Reg. no. 67064.

[44] Wesley Hist. Soc., Salop. Branch, *Bulletin*, i (10) (copy in S.R.O. 3543/11); SA 14422; *Shropshire Star*, 21 Dec. 1981 (p. 11).

[45] *P.O. Dir. Salop.* (1856), 101; G.R.O., Worship Reg. no. 15957; *Meth. Church Bldgs.: Statistical Returns* (1940), 270;

below, Wrockwardine Wood, Nonconf.

[46] James, 'Here be Dragons', 17.

[47] Inf. from Mr. Lenton; B. Trinder, *Meth. New Connexion in Dawley and Madeley* (Wesley Hist. Soc., W. Midlands Branch, Occ. Publ. [1968]).

[48] SA 14421.

[49] L.J.R.O., B/A/1/18, f. 3.

[50] *Educ. Enq. Abstract*, H.C. 62, p. 787 (1835), xlii.

[51] Below.

[52] Lich. Dioc. Regy., benefice and inst. bk. 1868–1900, pp. 20, 46.

[53] *Wellington Jnl.* 27 Feb. 1875 (p. 5).

[54] Ibid. 20 Mar. (p. 7), 3 July (p. 4) 1875; *List of Sch. Boards, 1902* [Cd. 1038], p. 75, H.C. (1902), lxxix.

[55] Continued use of bldg. for the church Sun. sch. and choir practice.

[56] *Wellington Jnl.* 12 June 1875 (p. 8).

[57] Ibid. 24 July 1875 (p. 5: rep. of ratepayers' mtg. at which 'disorder prevailed').

[58] Ibid. 3 Feb. 1877 (p. 5).

of Ketley Board School in 1898 and Wombridge Infant Council School in 1910.[59]

There were two girls' private schools. One at Belle Vue House, Stafford Road, existed in 1891 and 1910.[60] By 1903 there was another called Oakengates High School; it was approved by the county council for minor scholarship holders and still existed in 1910.[61] One of the two may have been the private school at Oakengates mentioned in 1914.[62]

Elementary schools were reorganized when senior pupils transferred to senior council schools in Ketley[63] and in New Road[64] in 1931 and 1933. The old C.E. school closed in 1933 and the two remaining council schools in Wombridge became junior mixed and infant schools. Nursery education was established in 1945 and comprehensive secondary education (to the age of 16) in 1974.[65]

In 1891, at the instigation of C. C. Walker,[66] Oakengates Science and Art Committee was formed to promote technical education in the district. The first chairman was William Perrott, secretary of the Lilleshall Co.[67] He was soon succeeded by Dr. J. McC. McCarthy,[68] who served for thirty years, as did the committee's first secretary, R. L. Corbett.[69] The enrolment of 222 students at Oakengates Coffee Palace assembly rooms in 1892 was the beginning of continuous technical education in east Shropshire. In 1900 other rooms at the Coffee Palace were also rented, and by 1903 classes were being held five nights a week and on Saturdays for teachers and pupil-teachers.[70] Courses, ordinary and advanced, included mining, engineering, and commercial subjects.[71] When the Coffee Palace lease expired in 1915[72] senior classes were held at Wombridge Infant Council School and at the Primitive Methodist chapel. By 1924 sixty per cent of local boys leaving school attended courses jointly financed by the county council and the Walker Trust.

Walker Technical College, Hartsbridge Road, opened in 1927.[73] It became the county centre for mining engineering, and its wide range of courses included those for the Ordinary and Higher National Certificates in mechanical engineering. Student numbers increased more than tenfold between 1927 (227) and 1962 (2,580). There was a junior technical school with 27 full-time pupils (aged 13–16) in 1930, 69 in 1931, and 120 in 1935 when they were drawn from ten miles around. In 1939 it admitted 148 evacuees from Smethwick Junior Technical College and temporarily adopted double-shift working.[74] The junior technical school closed in 1959 when technical facilities were provided in Wellington at the Boys' Grammar School and Girls' High School.[75]

Extensions to the college in the late 1930s and after 1945 failed to keep pace with increases in student numbers,[76] and in 1962 the engineering, science, and mining departments moved into new buildings in Wellington.[77] The Oakengates building accommodated the college's commerce and general studies department until 1972[78] and its courses for unemployed young people from 1979.[79] Oakengates Teachers' Development Centre was located there from 1968[80] and Wolverhampton Day Teachers' College had an outpost there for mature students 1969–77.[81]

Wombridge National School, Bridge Street, was built in 1846, chiefly at James Oliver's[82] expense aided by parliamentary and National Society grants; Oliver (d. 1867) left the school an endowment of £1,000.[83] In 1851 attendance averaged 80 boys and 50 girls.[84] By 1865 government grants were being earned[85] and by 1875 the boys' department was qualifying for drawing grants.[86] The school was efficient: in 1880, when attendance averaged 263, the government grant reached £326.[87] In 1889 accommodation was increased to 290 places when a new classroom at each end of the school was built at Sir Thomas Meyrick's expense.[88] Attendance averaged 241 in 1892 and 290 in 1909.[89] In 1903 the school was reorganized in three departments.[90] Overcrowding, however, caused bad working conditions[91] and in 1910,

[59] Below.
[60] *Kelly's Dir. Salop.* (1891), 379, 577; (1909), 171, 425; S.R.O. 4044/87, f. 42v. (no. 848).
[61] Kept by Mrs. Bowler, later by Miss A. G. Corbett, at Carlyle Ho.: *S.C.C. Mins.* 1903–4, 188, 191; ibid. *(Educ.)* 1904–5, 85; 1905–6, 66; *Kelly's Dir. Salop.* (1905), 168, 424; (1909), 171, 425; S.R.O. 4044/87, f. 50v. (no. 1018).
[62] Though possibly no longer existing: cf. *Kelly's Dir. Salop* (1913), 174–6, 439 (no private sch. mentioned); S.R.O. 1240/12, p. 338.
[63] Above, Ketley, Educ.
[64] i.e. Wrockwardine Wood Snr. (Mixed) Council Sch.: below.
[65] Below.
[66] The iron founder: above, Lilleshall, Econ. Hist. This and the next two paras. based on S.C.C. *Walker Technical College* (bklet. for opening of new bldg. 6 Nov. 1962); *Technical Educ.* Nov. 1962, 18–19; Cartlidge, *Usc-con*, 105–8.
[67] *S.C.C. Mins.* Intermediate Educ. Cttee. rep. 31 Oct. 1891, 27; Gale and Nicholls, *Lilleshall Co.* 52, 59, 74–5. He became managing dir. in 1895.
[68] For him see *V.C.H. Salop.* iii. 208; *Shrews. Chron.* 9 Nov. 1923 (p. 5); 7 Nov. 1924 (p. 10).
[69] Sch. attendance offr., Wombridge sch. bd.: *Kelly's Dir. Salop.* (1891), 378.
[70] *S.C.C. Mins.* 1903–4, 93.
[71] Ibid. 102; *(Educ.)* 1904–5, 40.
[72] Ibid. *(Educ.)* 1914–15, 93.
[73] Ibid. 1926–7, 28; *V.C.H. Salop.* iii. 202.

[74] *S.C.C. Mins. (Educ.)* 1939–40, 77.
[75] Ibid. 1958–9, 187.
[76] e.g. ibid. 1936–7, 14; 1945–6, 35; 1950–1, 72–4; 1954–5, 23.
[77] Above, Wellington, Educ.
[78] *S.C.C. Mins. (Educ.)* 1972 3, 34.
[79] Under the Manpower Services Com.'s Youth Opportunities Scheme: ibid. 1978–9, app. (following p. 326), p. 36.
[80] Ibid. 1967–8, 221; S.C.C. Educ. Cttee. *Educ. Dir.* (1981), 13.
[81] *S.C.C. Mins. (Educ.)* 1968–9, 264; inf. from Mr. N. G. Herne, former lecturer at the coll.
[82] Son of Thos. Oliver, perp. cur. 1805–8: Cartlidge, *Usc-con*, 68, 104.
[83] *Salop. Char. for Elem. Educ.* (S.C.C. 1906), 101.
[84] S. Bagshaw, *Dir. Salop.* (1851), 441; S.R.O. 1564/420–1; P.R.O., ED 7/102, f. 481; *Rep. of Educ. Cttee. of Council, 1864–5* [3533], p. 506, H.C. (1865), xlii.
[85] *Rep. of Educ. Cttee. of Council, 1865–6* [3666], p. 85, H.C. (1866), xxvii.
[86] *Wellington Jnl.* 12 June 1875 (p. 8).
[87] *Rep. of Educ. Cttee. of Council, 1879–80* [C. 2562–I], p. 680, H.C. (1880), xxii.
[88] *Kelly's Dir. Salop.* (1913), 174; S.R.O. 1564/417–18.
[89] *Rep. of Educ. Cttee. of Council, 1891–2* [C. 6746–I], p. 694, H.C. (1892), xxviii; *Kelly's Dir. Salop.* (1909), 171.
[90] Wombridge Nat. Inf. Sch. log bk. (at Wombridge Co. Primary Sch.) 4 Dec. 1903.
[91] e.g. ibid. reps. 1904, 1905, 1907, 1908.

since expansion on the cramped site[92] was impossible, the infant department transferred to a new council school[93] at Hartshill,[94] and recognized accommodation was reduced to 236 places.[95] By 1913, however, the school was again overcrowded[96] and in 1925 the building was condemned.[97] It closed in 1933, staff and pupils transferring to the enlarged council school at Hartshill.[98]

Oakengates British School opened in 1860. It was re-established in 1864 at the Independent chapel,[99] a new master and mistress, man and wife, being appointed to teach at least 100 pupils.[1] It closed before 1870.[2]

Ketley Bank Board School, Main Road, opened in 1878 with 243 places in three departments; there was a master's house. Infants paid 2d. a week and older pupils 3d., more than in other board schools in the coalfield.[3] Enlargement provided 406 places by 1882, 477 by 1896.[4] Attendance averaged 237 in 1880, 386 in 1892, 425 in 1909, and 452 in 1913.[5] By 1930, however, there were only 327 pupils. Next year the boys' headmaster became head of the new Ketley Senior School,[6] to which Ketley Bank's senior pupils then transferred.[7] The girls' headmistress stayed as head of what then became Ketley Bank Junior Council School.[8] The number of pupils halved between 1932 and 1935,[9] when mixed and infant departments amalgamated and the school became Ketley Bank Junior Mixed and Infant Council School.[10] Numbers fell to 68 by 1949[11] but increased in the 1950s,[12] reaching 244 by 1965. As Ketley Bank County Primary School it then closed, staff and pupils transferring to the new Queenswood County Primary School.[13] The noted efficiency of the Ketley Bank schools[14] owed much to the long service of competent head teachers.[15]

Wombridge Infant Council School, Hartshill, opened in 1910, admitting the National school's infants; it had 160 places and was full by 1916 and in the 1920s.[16] Under its first headmistress (1910–31)[17] it became an excellent school where, in the 1920s, H. M. Inspector sent teachers to observe the methods and apparatus in use.[18] In 1933, when the church school closed, the school was reorganized as Wombridge Junior Mixed and Infant Council (from 1945 County Primary) School with 302 places.[19] Attendance averaged 243 in 1940.[20] In 1952, with 320 pupils, the school was overcrowded and admissions were restricted.[21] Numbers increased from 290 in 1969 to 382 in 1975;[22] the building was then extended and modernized.[23] There were 318 pupils in 1981.[24] Throughout the school's history there was notable stability of staffing and management, and church links were maintained by local incumbents' service as managers or correspondents.[25]

Wrockwardine Wood Senior (Mixed) Council School, New Road, opened on a 3-a. site in 1933 to serve an area extending from Priorslee and Wombridge to Donnington and Trench.[26] Its 400 places were not filled even by 1943,[27] but in the 1950s it became seriously overcrowded[28] until, in 1955, the boys transferred to the new Wrockwardine Wood Boys' Modern School.[29] Extensions to the Wrockwardine Wood Girls' Modern School (as it became) produced 600 places by 1969, 750 by 1972;[30] there were 459 girls in 1965, 637 in 1972.[31] In 1973, renamed Wrockwardine Wood School, it became mixed, and in 1974 comprehensive for pupils aged 11–16; there were 683 pupils in 1973.[32] By 1977 there were 900 places and by 1981 1,004 pupils.[33] From the early 1970s the school had a unit for educationally subnormal pupils.[34]

Oakengates Nursery School, Hartshill, with 40 places, was established in 1945 in a former wartime nursery.[35] Forty-two children were admitted

[92] Cartlidge, Usc-con, 104–5.
[93] S.C.C. Mins. (Educ.) 1907–8, 171.
[94] Wombridge Inf. Council Sch. log bk. (at Wombridge Co. Primary Sch.) 24 Oct. 1910.
[95] S.C.C. Mins. (Educ.) 1910–11, 84.
[96] Kelly's Dir. Salop. (1913), 174.
[97] S.C.C. Mins. (Educ.) 1925–6, 49.
[98] Ibid. 1933–4, 11.
[99] St. Geo.'s C.E. Boys' Sch. log bk. 5 Sept. 1864.
[1] Wellington Jnl. 3 Sept. 1864 (p. 2).
[2] Not mentioned in P.O. Dir. Salop. (1870) or E. Cassey & Co. Dir. Salop. (1871).
[3] P.R.O., ED 7/102, f. 484. Elsewhere they did not exceed 2d.: J. McFall, 'Educ. in Madeley Union of Salop. in 19th Cent.' (Keele Univ. M.A. (Educ.) thesis, 1973), 122–3; Wellington Jnl. 11 Dec. 1875.
[4] Kelly's Dir. Salop. (1891), 378; Wellington Jnl. 19 Sept. 1896 (p. 6).
[5] Rep. of Educ. Cttee. of Council 1879–80, 680; 1891–2, 694; Kelly's Dir. Salop. (1909), 171; (1913), 174.
[6] S.C.C. Mins. (Educ.) 1930–1, 67.
[7] Ibid. From 1933 snr. pupils also went to the new snr. sch. in New Rd. (below): Ketley Bank Jnr. Council Sch. log bk. (at Queenswood Co. Primary Sch.) 4 Aug. 1933.
[8] Ketley Bank Jnr. Council Sch. log bk. 21 Nov. 1930; 7 Jan. 1931.   [9] Ibid. rep. 1935.   [10] Ibid. 1 Nov. 1935.
[11] Ketley Bank Co. Primary Sch. log bk. (at Queenswood Co. Primary Sch.) rep. 1949.
[12] Ibid. rep. 1955; 30 Sept. 1956.
[13] Queenswood Co. Primary Sch. log bk. (at the sch.) 7 Sept. 1965.

[14] Ketley Bank sch. log bks. reps. 1893–8, 1901, 1903, 1911, 1922, 1924–5, 1928, 1932, 1935, 1949, 1955.
[15] Ibid. passim.
[16] Wombridge Inf. Council Sch. log bk. 24 Oct. 1910; 4 Aug. 1916 (173 on roll); 23 Mar. 1923 (173); 21 Dec. 1928 (164); 29 Aug. 1932 (160); S.C.C. Mins. (Educ.) 1910–11, 134.
[17] Nat. Sch. inf. mistress 1903–10: Nat. Inf. Sch. log bk. 4 Dec. 1903; Inf. Council Sch. log bk. 24 Oct. 1910; 8 Jan. 1913; 31 July 1931.
[18] See e.g. log bk. 19 Sept., 3 Oct., 29 Nov., 7 Dec. 1921; 28 Feb. 1922; sqq.
[19] S.C.C. Mins. (Educ.) 1933–4, 11.
[20] Log bk. 31 Mar. 1940.   [21] Ibid. 21 Mar. 1952.
[22] S.C.C. Educ. Cttee. Sch. List (1969), 9; (1975), 11.
[23] Log bk. 1 Oct., 6 Nov. 1969; 5 Feb., 17 June, 23 July 1970; S.C.C. Mins. (Educ.) 1970–1, 286.
[24] S.C.C. Educ. Cttee. Educ. Dir. (1981), 10.
[25] Log bks. passim.
[26] S.C.C. Mins. (Educ.) 1928–9, 30; 1933–4, 63.
[27] Ibid. 1939–40, 56; S.R.O. 2699/59, p. 190.
[28] S.C.C. Mins. (Educ.) 1951–2, 77; 1958–9, 165, 213, 217.
[29] Below, Wrockwardine Wood, educ.
[30] S.C.C. Mins. (Educ.) 1969–70, 167; 1972–3, 396.
[31] Sch. List (1965), 2; (1972), 3.
[32] Ibid. (1973), 3; S.C.C. Mins. (Educ.) 1972–3, 392–3; 1973–4, 23.
[33] S.C.C. Mins. (Educ.) 1976–7, 308; Educ. Dir. (1981), 3.
[34] S.C.C. Mins. (Educ.) 1971–2, 386–7; Educ. Dir. (1981), 11.
[35] S.C.C. Mins. (Educ.) 1945–6, 97, 128.

immediately but many were left waiting.[36] The school served an area stretching as far as Donnington Wood.[37] It was replaced by a new two-class building in 1967.[38] In 1975 a part-time system was introduced,[39] and 80 pupils attended morning or afternoon sessions in 1981.[40]

Teague's Bridge County Primary School, Teague's Crescent, opened in 1964[41] with 320 places.[42] It became a junior school in 1967 when the infants transferred to the new Teague's Bridge County Infant School.[43] There were 309 pupils in 1972 but only 269 in 1981.[44]

Queenswood County Primary School, Yates Way, opened in 1965 with 329 places, to replace Ketley Bank County Primary School.[45] In 1975 there were 281 pupils but in 1981 only 223.[46]

Teague's Bridge County Infant School, Teague's Crescent, opened in 1967[47] with 240 places.[48] In 1972 there were 217 pupils but in 1981 only 152.[49]

PRIORSLEE. By 1824 in addition to a National school there were three nonconformist schools in the area. By 1838 many of the National school's day pupils also attended Methodist Sunday schools, membership of which made a child eligible for a £2 burial grant from a local burial club.[50]

A National school, opened at Snedshill Coppice in 1818,[51] served the Pain's Lane (in Lilleshall) and Priorslee districts. Run on Dr. Bell's system, the school was supported by subscriptions and annual church collections. It seems always to have had about 100 pupils. Sunday scholars, though at first only 30, were soon more numerous: 120 in 1824, 150 in 1838.[52] The school, which was free,[53] continued until 1860 when a new one[54] opened at Snowhill.

St. George's church school, opened in 1860, was built on an extensive open site south of what became School Street, Snowhill; the cost was met by the Lilleshall Co. and a government grant. There were three departments and two adjoining

houses for the master and the girls' and infants' mistresses.[55] Enlargement produced 300 boys' places, 150 girls', and 200 infants' by 1885.[56] In 1894 the schools affiliated to the National Society to obtain a building-improvement grant;[57] they were not, however, called National schools.[58] Exceptionally the boys' school was, by 1863, supported entirely by capitation grant and fees;[59] the latter were high, though varied according to parents' means, and payable even during absence from school.[60] Its excellence was consistent and remarkable: under long-serving masters it was almost certainly the most efficient school in the coalfield. Attendance was high and the first master dismissed irregular boys. Boys did very well in the South Kensington drawing examinations and by 1884 there was a Standard VII examination.[61] The girls' school was overcrowded until at least 1917 and before 1900 no mistress stayed long;[62] fees were not high.[63] Boys' and girls' departments amalgamated in 1939.[64] From 1949 pupils aged 13 transferred to Wrockwardine Wood Modern School.[65] In the early 1950s boys aged 11–12 attended a woodwork centre at Ketley Bank County Primary School.[66] Only in 1955, however, did all senior pupils leave for secondary schools.[67] That year too the infants transferred to the new St. George's C.E. (Controlled) Infant School nearby,[68] and the school (itself controlled since 1957)[69] became a junior school. In 1971 a three-classroom extension on the site of the nearby C.E. Infant School added 120 junior places.[70] Junior and infant schools combined in 1981[71] and the old buildings were closed in 1982.

In 1872 the Lilleshall Co. paid for a new Priorslee National School, known in the 1880s as the Granville School, with 200 infant places; it was soon enlarged for 69 more places. In 1872 income included weekly fees of 2d. from 137 pupils and voluntary contributions,[72] and by 1876 church collections.[73] In 1881 a mixed school under a master was established[74] and the infants transfer-

[36] Ibid. 137.
[37] Ibid. 1964–5, 116.
[38] Wombridge Co. Primary Sch. log bk. 21 Apr. 1967.
[39] In accordance with a national trend. See Sch. List (1975), 3.
[40] Educ. Dir. (1981), 3.
[41] Log bk. (at the sch.) 7 Sept. 1964.
[42] S.C.C. Mins. (Educ.) 1960–1, 105.
[43] Log bk. 9 Jan. 1967.
[44] Sch. List (1972), 10; Educ. Dir. (1981), 10.
[45] Log bk. (at the sch.) 7 Sept. 1965.
[46] Sch. List (1975), 10; (1976), 10; Educ. Dir. (1981), 10.
[47] Teague's Br. Co. Jnr. Sch. log bk. 9 Jan. 1967.
[48] S.C.C. Mins. (Educ.) 1961–2, 255.
[49] Sch. List (1972), 10; Educ. Dir. (1981), 10.
[50] S.R.O. 3916/1/3, no. 11.
[51] Staffs. R.O., D. 593/N/3/11/4; S.R.O. 4462/Sch/1, 5 June 1818.
[52] S.R.O. 3916/1/3, no. 11; /1/8, no. 11; /1/20, s.v. Donnington Wood; Nat. Soc. file 169; Digest Educ. Poor, H.C. 224, p. 755 (1819), ix (2); S. Bagshaw, Dir. Salop. (1851), 476–7; P.O. Dir. Salop. (1856), 101, 104.
[53] P.O. Dir. Salop. (1856), 104.
[54] Below.
[55] P.R.O., ED 7/102, f. 479; P.O. Dir. Salop. (1870), 122.
[56] Kelly's Dir. Salop. (1885), 929.
[57] Nat. Soc. file 169, terms of union 26 Sept. 1894.
[58] In e.g. log bks. or reps., but P.O. Dir. Salop. (1879), 391, and Kelly's Dir. Salop. (to 1900) wrongly call it National.

[59] St. Geo.'s C.E. Boys' Sch. log bk. (at St. Geo.'s C.E. (Cont.) Jnr. Sch.) 1 Dec. 1863. Available log bks. of other schs. in the coalfield reveal no such state of affairs.
[60] P.R.O., ED 7/102, f. 479; St. Geo.'s C.E. Boys' Sch. log bk.
[61] St. Geo.'s C.E. Boys' Sch. log bk.
[62] St. Geo.'s C.E. Girls' Sch. log bk. (at St. Geo.'s C.E. (Cont.) Jnr. Sch.).
[63] See e.g. ibid. 14 Dec. 1888.
[64] St. Geo.'s C.E. Mixed Sch. log bk. (at St. Geo.'s C.E. (Cont.) Jnr. Sch.) 11 Sept. 1939.
[65] Ibid. rep. 1949.
[66] St. Geo.'s C.E. Sch. log bk. 23 Apr. 1953; Ketley Bank Co. Primary Sch. log bk. rep. 1955.
[67] When Trench Boys' Modern Sch. opened: St. Geo.'s C.E. Mixed Sch. admissions bk. (at the sch.).
[68] S.C.C. Mins. (Educ.) 1961–2, 48; below.
[69] St. Geo.'s C.E. Mixed Sch. log bk. 31 May 1937.
[70] Inf. from the headmistress, St. Geo.'s C.E. (Cont.) Primary Sch.
[71] Inf. from S.C.C. Educ. Dept.
[72] P.R.O., ED 7/102, f. 477; Wellington Jnl. 21 Aug. 1875 (p. 7); Cartlidge and Kidson, Hist. Priors Lee, pp. vi, xii; Nat. Soc. file on Priorslee Nat. Sch., managers' letters, 1 Dec. 1888; 16 and 22 July 1889.
[73] e.g. Wellington Jnl. 5 Aug. 1876 (p. 5).
[74] St. Geo.'s C.E. Boys' Sch. log bk. 31 Oct. 1881.

red to unsuitable accommodation rented from the United Methodist Free church. The withdrawal of government grant was threatened if infants remained in the condemned premises and in 1890 the Lilleshall Co. built a new school for 200 next to the existing school.[75] Attendance averaged 350 in 1885, 370 in 1895, and 299 in 1904. By 1906 the accommodation limit was 444.[76] By 1940 mixed and infant departments had combined. The school became controlled in 1956.[77] A fall in numbers (from 183 in 1955 to 104 in 1958) and the need for repairs caused the school's closure in 1958.[78]

St. George's C.E. (Controlled) Infant School, London Road, opened in 1961 with 120 places in four classes.[79] Infant numbers fell from 166 in 1975 to 101 in 1980,[80] and in 1981 the junior and infant schools combined as St. George's C.E. (Controlled) Primary School, with 320 pupils.[81]

CHARITIES FOR THE POOR. WOMBRIDGE. One pound a year from James Rushbury's legacy (1718) to the church was to be devoted to the poor of Wombridge. In the later 18th century 16s. was paid out each year, but by c. 1803 payments had ceased.[82]

W. H. Rushton's charity, established in 1890, produced an income of £6 from stock in 1975, used to buy clothing for widows.

PRIORSLEE. Priorslee benefited in 1975 from Shifnal united charities and from two charities confined to Priorslee ecclesiastical parish. Samuel Horton, the Priorslee ironmaster (d. 1865), left £300 stock for widows. In 1975 the charity's income was £14.

The charity of William Slaney Lewis, established in 1888, yielded £3 in 1975, spent on blankets and clothing for widows.[83]

WROCKWARDINE

WROCKWARDINE, a mainly rural parish, lies south and east of the river Tern and north of Watling Street; the western boundary is mostly with Wroxeter parish and to the east lies the northern part of Telford new town. The main part of the ancient parish, dealt with here, included the townships of Wrockwardine, Admaston, Allscott, Bratton, Charlton, Cluddley, Leaton, and Long Lane, the capital messuages of Burcot and Orleton, and the deserted settlement and former township of Nash.[84] A detached township of the ancient parish, Wrockwardine Wood, lay 7 km. to the east; its history is treated separately below.[85]

To the north the parish is bounded partly by Long Lane, the river Tern, and the road from Allscott to Watling Street at Norton. The western boundary of the parish and of Charlton township partly follows a stream. To the south the parish boundary largely follows the original line of Watling Street: the boundary – the 'king's boundary' – diverged northwards from the road at Overley Hill by 975, and southwards around Cluddley, probably by the Saxon period.[86] Bullocks brook, so called by 1580,[87] largely forms the eastern parish boundary, though Bratton and Orleton townships both extend east of it.[88]

In 1882 Wrockwardine civil parish contained 4,762 a. (1,927 ha.), including 515 a. in Wrockwardine Wood and 92 a. of detached moorland north of Eyton upon the Weald Moors.[89] In 1884 Wrockwardine Wood became a separate civil parish and the moorland was transferred to Eyton C.P. At the same time the transfer of Walcot township (414 a.) from Wellington C.P. with 13 a. from Rodington C.P. increased the length of the parish boundary formed by the river Tern.[90] In 1903 and 1934 3 a. and 165 a. respectively of land east and south of Cluddley and Orleton were transferred to Wellington Urban C.P.[91] The eastern part of the parish, including Admaston and Bratton villages, was included within the designated area of Telford new town in 1968.[92]

Crossing the parish from south-west to north-east are the Brockton and Burcot faults, c. 1 km. apart. Between them outcrop Uriconian Rhyolite, particularly between Overley Hill and Leaton and west of Wrockwardine, and tuff, on which Wrockwardine village lies.[93] From those high outcrops the ground falls away northwards to the Tern and the Weald Moors and southwards to low ground at the foot of the Wrekin. Cluddley extends southwards to the base of the Wrekin. It was presumably the commanding views obtained from Wrockwardine church tower that led to its seizure by Parliamentarian troops in 1645–6.[94]

[75] Nat. Soc. file on Priorslee Nat. Sch., managers' letters and applicn. for bldg. grant 15 Feb. 1890.

[76] Kelly's Dir. Salop. (1885), 924; (1895), 177; Public Elem. Schs. 1906 [Cd. 3182], p. 538, H.C. (1906), lxxxvi.

[77] Inf. from S.C.C. Educ. Dept.

[78] S.C.C. Mins. (Educ.) 1958–9, 46.

[79] Inf. from S.C.C. Educ. Dept.

[80] Sch. List (1975), 10; Educ. Dir. (1980), 10.

[81] Educ. Dir. (1981), 10; inf. from S.C.C. Educ. Dept.

[82] 9th Rep. Com. Char. H.C. 258, pp. 324–5 (1823), ix; 24th Rep. Com. Char. H.C. 231, p. 371 (1831), xi; above, Churches.

[83] Review of Local Chars. (S.C.C. 1975), 67; Cartlidge and Kidson, Hist. Priors Lee, p. xv.

[84] For townships at different periods see below, Man. and Other Est.; S.R.O. 14/1/5, MS. addn. at end; 4472/CW/2; S. Bagshaw, Dir. Salop. (1851), 443–8. This art. was written in 1982.

[85] Below, Wrockwardine Wood.

[86] T.S.A.S. lvi. 31–3; below; above, plate 55.

[87] S.R.O. 38/1.

[88] S.R.O. 14/1/4.

[89] O.S. Area Bk. (1882, with emendation slip).

[90] Ibid.; O.S. Area Bk. Wellington (1885); 14th Ann. Rep. Local Govt. Bd. [C. 4515], pp. xlvii, 191, 204, H.C. (1884–5), xxxii.

[91] V.C.H. Salop. ii. 229; Census 1891 and 1911 compared; Census 1931, Herefs. and Salop. (Part II) (1936), 8.

[92] Dawley New Town (Designation) Amendment (Telford) Order 1968 (Stat. Instr. 1968, no. 1912), map accompanying Explanatory Note.

[93] Inst. Geol. Sciences Map 1/25,000, Telford (1978 edn.).

[94] Diary of Marches of Royal Army (Camd. Soc. [1st ser.], lxxiv), 278.

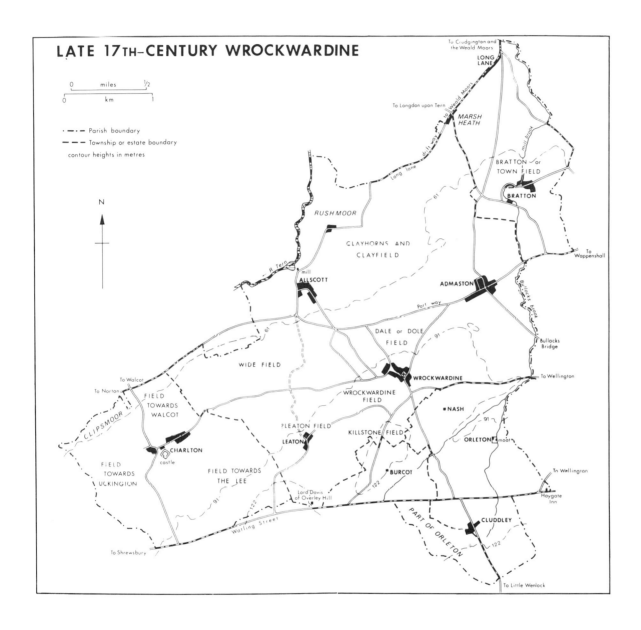

LATE 17TH-CENTURY WROCKWARDINE

0   miles   ½
0   km   1

·—·—· Parish boundary
— — Township or estate boundary
contour heights in metres

N

To Crudgington and
the Weald Moors
LONG LANE

To Longdon upon Tern

MARSH HEATH

BRATTON or TOWN FIELD

BRATTON

To Wappenshall

RUSHMOOR

CLAYHORNS AND CLAYFIELD

mill
ALLSCOTT

ADMASTON

Port way

Bullocks brook

Bullocks Bridge

R Tern

DALE or DOLE FIELD

91

To Wellington

WIDE FIELD

WROCKWARDINE

To Walcot

To Norton

FIELD TOWARDS WALCOT

WROCKWARDINE FIELD

NASH

91

CLIPSMOOR

?LEATON FIELD

KILLSTONE FIELD

ORLETON moat

To Wellington

LEATON

Haygate Inn

CHARLTON
castle

FIELD TOWARDS THE LEE

BURCOT

FIELD TOWARDS UCKINGTON

91

122

Lord Davis
of Overley Hill

PART OF ORLETON

122

CLUDDLEY

122

Watling Street

To Shrewsbury

To Little Wenlock

307

Most of the rest of the parish lies on boulder clay or sand and gravel, while some terrace gravel is associated with the river Tern and Rushmoor lies on lake clay.[95]

Domesday Book recorded 32 inhabitants in Wrockwardine and Bratton,[96] and 25 parishioners paid to the 1327 subsidy, but there is no indication that Charlton and Orleton were included in the latter total.[97] In 1349 manorial income had fallen 'because the tenants there are dead', but by 1367 it was back at the levels obtaining before the Black Death, a fact perhaps suggesting a population recovery.[98] In 1672 hearth tax was paid by 77 people: 12 in Wrockwardine, 16 in Charlton, 12 in Admaston, 10 in Allscott, 9 in Bratton, 9 in Leaton, Burcot, and Cluddley, 6 in Long Lane, and 3 at Orleton and Nash;[99] the proportions accord with those of the 1539 muster.[1] The population was 1,033 in 1841, 1,380 in 1961, and 2,105 in 1981,[2] Admaston's growth largely accounting for an increase in the 1960s.

South of Bratton is a multi-period prehistoric site with Bronze Age ring ditches and Iron Age or Romano-British ditches and enclosures.[3] Another possible prehistoric enclosure lies east of Charlton castle,[4] while other possible sites and scattered finds across the parish all attest to activity in the area before Watling Street was made in the initial phase of the Roman conquest.[5]

It has been suggested that Wrockwardine village was the site of Pengwern, the legendary sub-Roman centre of Powys, destroyed by the Mercians c. 660.[6] In 1066 it was the centre of a royal multiple estate, probably containing the $7\frac{1}{2}$ berewicks mentioned in 1086. It was a five-hide unit and a hundred meeting place.[7] Place-name evidence, reinforcing that of Domesday, suggests that Wrockwardine, 'the enclosure (*worthign*) by the Wrekin',[8] was an ancient centre around which subsidiary settlements were established. In the parish, lying 1–3 km. from the village, are five places with the element *tun* in their names, which may be English renamings of older settlements. There are also two with the element *cot* and three with *leah*, which may be settlements newly established in the 8th or 9th century in a period of expansion.[9]

Wrockwardine village is a loose agglomeration of 17th-century and later timber-framed and brick farmhouses and cottages grouped around the church and small green. After c. 1920 the village extended south and roughly doubled in size.

Admaston, 'Eadmund's *tun*',[10] grew in the mid 18th century from a rural village into a small spa.[11] Similar geological formations to those at Kingley Wych saltworks[12] produced a high saline content in the water. By 1750 Admaston Spa, sometimes known as Wellington Spa, had opened and in 1805 there was a hotel there, which was rebuilt in brick in the early 1840s. It had, roughly, a courtyard plan, with a colonnaded entrance and clock tower; the facilities included a bath house. The spa's profitability declined from the 1860s and it became a private residence in 1890. It was a hotel from c. 1928 to c. 1933 but later a chicken farm, then a lodging house. Telford development corporation bought it in 1975 and renovated it 1978–80, converting it to three substantial houses.[13] The presence of the spa and (by 1856) a railway halt led to the emergence of Admaston as a small, locally fashionable centre, and several large houses of the 18th and 19th century, such as Admaston Hall, Oaklands, and Donnerville, bear witness to that phase of prosperity. Speculative housing development began south-west of the village in the 1960s and continued after Admaston's inclusion in Telford new town in 1968.[14]

Bratton, the 'newly cultivated *tun*', was a small hamlet centred on Bratton Farm in 1839.[15] Houses were built on the west side of Bratton Road, half way from Bratton Farm to Admaston, before 1930 and on the east side of the road between 1947 and 1953.[16]

Charlton, 'the *tun* of the ceorls',[17] Leaton, 'the *tun* in the wood or clearing',[18] Allscott, 'Ælfwulf's[19] *cot*', and Cluddley, 'the *leah* where burdock grew',[20] remained in 1982, as they had been in 1839,[21] hamlets grouped around farmhouses. Leaton Grange incorporates a late medieval hall with crown-post roof.

Any hamlets that may have existed at Orleton, 'the *tun* of the earls', Burcot, 'the *cot* belonging to the *burg*' or 'the dwelling place or cottage',[22] and Nash, 'at the ash tree',[23] had disappeared before the early 18th century when only single messuages remained.[24] Orleton Hall and Burcot Farm remained in 1982 but Nash, a medieval township[25] where there had been a farm in the later 17th century and a single barn in 1839,[26] was completely deserted.

[95] Inst. Geol. Sciences Map 1/25,000, *Telford* (1978 edn.).

[96] *V.C.H. Salop.* i. 315, 332; below, Econ. Hist.

[97] *T.S.A.S.* 2nd ser. i. 181, 186–7.

[98] Ibid. 4th ser. i. 219–22; below, Econ. Hist.

[99] *Hearth Tax 1672* (Salop. Arch. Soc.), 96–8.

[1] *L. & P. Hen. VIII*, xiv (1), p. 288.

[2] *V.C.H. Salop.* ii. 229; 1981 census figs. compiled in S.C.C. Planning Dept.

[3] SA 102, 720, 2007.

[4] SA 36, 2028; *T.C.S.V.F.C.* xvi. 76.

[5] SA *passim*.

[6] G. Jones, 'Continuity Despite Calamity: The Heritage of Celtic Territorial Organization in Eng.' *Jnl. Celtic Studies*, iii. 22–30; below, Man. and Other Est.

[7] *V.C.H. Salop.* i. 315, 332; above, Bradford hundred.

[8] E. Ekwall, *Concise Oxf. Dict. Eng. P.N.* (4th edn.), 539.

[9] Map on p. 3; M. Gelling, 'On Looking into Smith's Elements', *Nomina*, v. 39–45. Dr. Gelling kindly commented on the place names.

[10] Ekwall, op. cit. 3.

[11] U. Rayska, *Brief Hist. of Admaston Spa* (1977; copy in S.P.L., class L 21.6 v.f.).

[12] Below, Preston, Econ. Hist.

[13] *Telford Jnl.* 22 Sept. 1978; *Shropshire Star*, 15 (p. 21) and 29 (p. 26) Nov. 1980.

[14] Above; below.

[15] Ekwall, *Concise Oxf. Dict. Eng. P.N.* 61; S.R.O. 14/1/4.

[16] O.S. Maps ½", sheet 16 (1930 edn.); 1", sheet 118 (1947 and 1953 edns.).

[17] Ekwall, op. cit. 96.

[18] Inf. from Dr. Gelling.

[19] Or Ælf's, Æthelwulf's, or Eanwulf's.

[20] Ekwall, *Concise Oxf. Dict. Eng. P.N.* 7, 113.

[21] S.R.O. 14/1/4–5.

[22] Ekwall, op. cit. 74, 351.

[23] Inf. from Dr. Gelling.

[24] S.R.O. 999/Pp (2) 11; S.R.O. 999, parcel 752, Burcot map c. 1690; Orleton and Nash map, 1728, at Orleton Hall.

[25] Eyton, ix. 26.

[26] *Yeomen and Colliers in Telford*, ed. B. Trinder and J. Cox (1980), p. 13; S.R.O. 999/Rr 43–51.

By 1650 squatters' cottages had been built along Long Lane, the drift way to the Weald Moors, and probably at Rushmoor.[27] In 1851 Long Lane was a straggling township of cottages 3 km. long but by 1982 few houses remained outside the hamlets of Long Lane and Rushmoor.[28] There was already a hamlet called Lea at Overley Hill in 1817.[29] Overley Hall, a 14-bedroomed red-brick house with 'Tudor' features and a gothic tower, set in 48 a. of grounds, was built in 1882 for Joseph Beattie, a Birmingham banker.[30] H. H. France-Hayhurst bought it in 1890[31] and lived there till 1907.[32]

Watling Street crosses the parish from east to west. Mentioned in 975,[33] it remained a major thoroughfare throughout the Middle Ages. The way to the Wrekin, probably the road running south from Wrockwardine village through Cluddley, was mentioned in 1411–12.[34] Some other roads, though not recorded before the 16th century, are likely to have been medieval; several apparently divided open fields. The drift way to the Weald Moors from Allscott via Long Lane was mapped c. 1580, as were the roads from Longdon upon Tern to Bratton and Wellington and from Wrockwardine to Wappenshall, and probably that leading due east from Wrockwardine.[35] The Admaston–Wellington road crossed Bullocks brook in 1626 at Bullocks bridge.[36] Noted in 1674 were the way from Wrockwardine to Burcot, the port or common highway from Admaston to Shrewsbury, the Allscott-Leaton bridleway, the Leaton–Wellington market way (perhaps one of the footpaths of 1839 leading east from Leaton),[37] the Allscott–Charlton and Wrockwardine–Charlton roads with Breadon bridge on the latter, and a footpath from Wrockwardine to 'Winshall' (probably Wappenshall).[38] A road running north to the Weald Moors from Bratton c. 1580 was disused by 1752.[39]

Watling Street was turnpiked in 1726. There was a tollgate south of Burcot in 1815.[40] In 1835–6 one of Thomas Telford's improvements to Watling Street was completed, a 3-km. diversion north to avoid Overley Hill. A new tollhouse was also built at Burcotgate.[41] The roads to Wellington (via Shawbirch) from Longdon upon Tern and Sleapford[42] were turnpiked with Watling Street;[43] both passed through the north-east of the parish, the former having a tollhouse at Bratton.[44]

In 1975 the interchange between Watling Street and the M 54 motorway was opened north of Cluddley.[45]

The Shrewsbury Canal passed through Long Lane; it was complete from Trench Pool to there by 1794 and the adjoining length to Shrewsbury opened in 1797. A wharf at Long Lane originally supplied coal and lime to the Shawbury area; in 1898 the Lilleshall Co. used it as a coal wharf and brick yard.[46] Traffic ceased on the canal in the 1920s.[47]

Two railway lines crossed the parish, converging on Wellington. That from Shrewsbury to Wellington opened in 1849.[48] Walcot station and Admaston halt were open by 1851[49] and closed in 1964.[50] The line from Wellington to Market Drayton opened in 1867. It closed to passengers in 1963 and to goods in 1967.[51] There was a halt north of Bratton.[52]

Most of the first recorded inns or public houses in the parish lay along Watling Street. The Haygate inn opened between 1625 and 1693. It became known as the Falcon inn c. 1829 and was also known as the Royal Oak. A leading coaching inn from the late 18th century or earlier, it closed c. 1856 after the railway reached Wellington. It then became a farmhouse but reopened as the Falcon hotel in 1971.[53] The Plume of Feathers, on Watling Street at Overley Hill, opened between c. 1690 and 1721 in, or on the site of, a house known between 1670 and c. 1690 as Lord Davis's.[54] Also on Watling Street, south of Charlton, was the Blue Bell in 1707; bannering took place there in 1721.[55] Both probably closed when the road was moved north in 1835; the Blue Bell was apparently out of business by 1838, the Plume of Feathers by 1851.[56] There was an alehouse at Charlton in 1613.[57] Most of the public houses open in 1982 dated from the earlier 19th century or before: the Buck's Head, Long Lane, existed by 1810; the

[27] S.P.L., MS. 110, Wrockwardine jury presentments 11 Oct. 1650, and 1654; S.R.O. 1011, box 233, plot and descr. of Marsh Heath, 1672.

[28] S. Bagshaw, Dir. Salop. (1851), 447; S.R.O. 14/1/4.

[29] B.L. Maps, O.S.D. 208.

[30] S.R.O. 3882/4/2; P.R.O., RG 11/2955, f. 5 (no. 242); S.R.O., q. sess. rec. box 299, file of corresp. re J.P.s 1877–92, letters re Beattie's appt. Feb.–Mar. 1883; Orders of Q. Sess. iv. 259; Kelly's Dir. Salop. (1885), 787, 999.

[31] S.R.O., q. sess. rec. box 299, file of corresp. re J.P.s 1877–92, letters re France-Hayhurst's appt. and change of address, Mar.–Apr. 1879; 24 Mar. 1890. He had earlier lived at Wrockwardine Hall.

[32] S.R.O. 3882/4/2. He d. at Leaton Grange: Shrews. Chron. 18 Feb. 1918; Burke, Land. Gent. (1952), 1190.

[33] T.S.A.S. lvi. 32–3.

[34] S.P.L., Deeds 19395.

[35] S.R.O. 38/1.

[36] S.R.O. 1224/1/1; O.S. Nat. Grid SJ 125 635.

[37] S.R.O. 14/1/4.

[38] S.R.O. 999/M 5–6; ibid. /Oo 6.

[39] S.R.O. 38/1; J. Rocque, Map of Salop. (1752).

[40] Trinder, Ind. Rev. Salop. (1981), 86; S.R.O. 665/2/6014; B.L. Maps, O.S.D. 208.

[41] 13th Rep. R. Com. Holyhead Rd. H.C. 437, p. 8 (1836), xxxvi; SA 15334; above, plate 7.

[42] Above, Wellington, Communications.

[43] 12 Geo. III, c. 9.

[44] S.R.O. 14/1/4–5 (no. 915).

[45] Inf. from the archivist, T.D.C.

[46] Trinder, Ind. Rev. Salop. (1981), 85; Hobson & Co. Wellington Dir., Almanack, & Diary (1898), 56.

[47] Salop. Librs. Shropshire Canals (1980), 67–8.

[48] Above, Wellington, Communications.

[49] S. Bagshaw, Dir. Salop. (1851), 439, 445.

[50] C. R. Clinker, Clinker's Reg. of Closed Stations 1830–1977 (Bristol, 1978), 2, 135.

[51] Above, Wellington, Communications.

[52] O.S. Map 1/25,000, SJ 61 (1957 edn.).

[53] T.D.C. Falcon Hotel (Hist. Bldgs. in Telford, no. 13).

[54] S.R.O. 999/Pp (2) 11; /GG 10; S.R.O. 999, parcel 752, Burcot map c. 1690; Rocque, Map of Salop.

[55] S.P.R. Lich. viii (1), 96; S.R.O. 4472/CW/1, s.a. 1721; Rocque, Map of Salop.

[56] Below; S.R.O. 14/1/4–5 (no. 139); S. Bagshaw, Dir. Salop. (1851), 443–7.

[57] S.R.O., q. sess. rec. parcel 254, badgers', drovers', and alesellers' licensing bk.

Gate inn, Bratton, by 1820, possibly by 1779;[58] the Fox and Duck near Walcot by 1817[59] and the Pheasant, Admaston, by 1846.[60]

Periodically in the 18th and 19th centuries Admaston Spa was a centre for local genteel society, and in 1851 the locality was known for its steeplechase meetings and field sports. The spa was the meeting place of a masonic lodge between 1852 and 1857.[61] Several friendly societies existed in the later 18th and 19th century. The Wrockwardine Friendly Society met in the Wheatsheaf inn between 1794 and 1822, and a Wrockwardine and Eyton Benefit Society was reputedly formed in 1795.[62] A society of the same name was founded or reformed in 1840; in 1841 its committee attempted to allay fears about its financial security, and announced plans for an annual festival with prizes for the best garden, neatest cottage, and other examples of industrious, orderly, and virtuous habits. It was apparently absorbed into the Shropshire Provident Society in 1850.[63] Between c. 1829 and c. 1836 a charity club met in Wrockwardine.[64] The Odd Fellows had a popular lodge in Admaston in 1898.[65] There was a militia club between at least 1796 and 1808.[66]

A. A. Turreff, vicar 1906–45, instigated various church-based social activities and organizations, such as a men's club in 1907, and a church hall was opened in 1909.[67] A coal and clothing club operated in 1925.[68] County library book centres were opened at Wrockwardine in 1928 and 1935, and at Admaston in 1933.[69] Admaston House community centre opened in 1970; it contained a branch library from 1970 to 1979.[70]

A bowling club was formed c. 1929 and was still playing in 1935.[71] There was a cricket club in 1887,[72] and in 1947 a cricket ground was made at Orleton hall. It was the home ground of Wellington cricket club and one of the grounds used by the Shropshire county side; in 1979 they played the Indian touring side there.[73]

MANORS AND OTHER ESTATES. In 975 the southern boundary of Wrockwardine was called the 'king's boundary'[74] and the king retained the manor of *WROCKWARDINE* in 1066. Roger of Montgomery, created earl of Shrewsbury by 1074, was tenant in chief by 1086, and the manor

contained 7½ berewicks,[75] which probably included Admaston, Allscott, Burcot, Charlton, Cluddley, Leaton, Nash, and Orleton.[76] It has been argued that the multiple estate was of considerable antiquity, perhaps succeeding Wroxeter in the 5th century as an administrative centre, and was perhaps the site of Cynddylan's hall of Pengwern, burnt by the Mercians c. 660.[77]

The manor was presumably forfeited after the rebellion of Earl Roger's son Robert of Bellême in 1102[78] and remained with the Crown until 1231. In 1172 Henry II granted half the manor's annual value to the brothers Roger and Jonas of Powys, the full value, £14, being assigned to them in 1175. Roger, one of the king's leading servants in north Wales and the marches, was sole beneficiary from 1176 to 1186 when his son Meredith was joined with him. Father and son were dead by Michaelmas 1187, but Meyrick, another son of Roger of Powys, received £10 a year out of the manor from 1195 until his death in 1200.[79]

In 1200 the manor was farmed to Hamon le Strange, whose elder brother, John (II) of Knockin, succeeded him as farmer in 1203.[80] In 1228 John became life tenant of the manor, previously held during pleasure.[81] In 1231, however, during John (II)'s lifetime, the manor was granted in fee to his son John (III) for £8 a year.[82] By 1255 John (III) who lived until 1269,[83] had enfeoffed his son Hamon in the manor.[84] Hamon granted it to his younger brother Robert before they left on Crusade in 1271. Early in 1273, when Hamon's death overseas became known, Wrockwardine was seized by the sheriff as an unlicensed alienation. Edward I regranted it to Robert in 1275 as $\frac{1}{20}$ knight's fee.[85] Robert was succeeded in 1276 by his son John, who was succeeded in 1289 by his brother Fulk, summoned from 1309 as Lord Strange of Blakemere (d. 1324). Fulk claimed free warren in Wrockwardine in 1292. Fulk's son and heir John, Lord Strange (d. 1349), who was granted free warren in his demesnes in 1333, granted the manor in 1347 to his son and heir Fulk, later Lord Strange (d. 1349), and Fulk's wife Elizabeth, who retained it during two later marriages until her death as Lady Cobham in 1376. The manor then descended with the barony of Strange of Blakemere to the Talbots, earls of Shrewsbury from 1442,[86] being held

[58] Co. of Salop, *Return of Licensed Hos. 1896*, 204 (copy in S.R.O., q. sess. rec. box 148); date stone reset in bar of Gate inn.

[59] B.L. Maps, O.S.D. 208.

[60] *Return of Licensed Hos. 1896*, 204.

[61] Rayska, *Admaston Spa*; S.R.O. 1536, A. Kynaston to L. Barnston, 23 Aug. 1751.

[62] Registrar of Friendly Socs. *List of Friendly Socs. in Co. of Salop, 1793–1855* (H.M.S.O. 1857; copy in S.R.O.), pp. 42–3.

[63] S.R.O. 436/6720.

[64] S.R.O. 673/1/7, 20 Nov. 1829; 20 Nov. 1836.

[65] Hobson, *Wellington Dir.* (1898), 35.

[66] S.R.O. 4472/P/1/3, 5.

[67] Below, Church; S.R.O. 4472/Par/8 (Jan. 1925); *Wellington Before Telford*, 38.

[68] S.R.O. 4472/Par/8 (Oct. 1925).

[69] R. C. Elliott, 'Development of Public Libraries in Salop.' (Loughborough Univ. M.A. thesis, 1970), app. II (copy in Salop. Librs.).

[70] *Shropshire Star*, 28 Sept. 1970; inf. from Salop. Librs.

[71] S.R.O. 4472/Par/13 (June 1929).

[72] S.R.O. 860/3, 17 Oct. 1887.

[73] Inf. from Mr. V. M. E. Holt.

[74] *T.S.A.S.* lvi. 32.

[75] *V.C.H. Salop.* i. 315.

[76] The medieval townships, apart from Bratton (which was listed separately in Domesday).

[77] *Jnl. of Celtic Studies*, iii. 22–6, 29–30.

[78] *V.C.H. Salop.* iii. 10.

[79] Eyton, ix. 19–20; xi. 31–4.

[80] H. le Strange, *Le Strange Records* (1916), 67, 70, 84–5.

[81] Ibid. 77–8.

[82] Ibid. 79–81, 99, 353.   [83] *D.N.B.*

[84] Le Strange, *Le Strange Records*, 139, 144.

[85] Ibid. 145, 165, 170–2.

[86] Ibid. 173, 186, 200, 206, 288–90, 298, 301, 304, 309, 317–18, 320; *T.S.A.S.* 4th ser. i. 208–27; *D.N.B.* s.v. Talbot, John, 1st earl of Shrews. The rest of this acct. is based on *T.S.A.S.* 4th ser. v. 225–76; inf. from Mr. V. M. E. Holt.

by dowager countesses 1473–6,[87] 1538–67,[88] and 1590–1608.[89] On the death of Edward, 8th earl of Shrewsbury, in 1618 the manor was divided into three, and so it remained until the early 19th century.

One third was settled on Alathea, countess of Arundel and Surrey (d. 1654), niece of the 8th earl of Shrewsbury,[90] who was succeeded by her younger son Sir William Howard, Viscount Stafford, impeached and executed 1680.[91] His son Henry Stafford-Howard, created earl of Stafford 1688, sold his interest in Wrockwardine to Richard Hill of Hawkstone, the statesman and diplomat, in 1715.[92] In 1722 Hill settled it in marriage on his nephew Samuel Barbour, who took the name Hill. He lived at Shenstone (Staffs.) and died in 1758, when his cousin Thomas Hill, of Tern, inherited the manor.[93] Hill (d. 1782) was succeeded by his son Noel, created Lord Berwick 1784 (d. 1789). In 1813 the 2nd Lord Berwick sold his third of the manor, apart from the Wrockwardine Wood mining rights, to William Cludde of Orleton.

Another third apparently passed in 1618 to George Saville (2nd bt. 1622) of Thornhill (Yorks. W.R.), grandnephew of the 8th earl of Shrewsbury. He died in 1626 and was succeeded by his brother Sir William (d. 1644), whose son Sir George[94] sold his third of the manor to Edward Revell in 1665, having previously disposed of the mining rights.[95] Revell held it until 1675. Rosamund Revell then held the third until her death in 1690[96] when it passed to Edward Revell who held it until 1696. Thereafter it passed successively to John Revell (d. 1729); John's daughter Sarah (d. 1757), wife of Robert Moreton; Sarah's nephew John Revell Phillips (d. probably in 1766); Phillips's widow Sarah; and in 1767 to their son Thomas Carter Phillips, a minor. He died in 1783 and Revell Phillips, his brother, held it thereafter until 1811 when he sold it to William Cludde.

Another third of the manor was held by the 8th earl of Shrewsbury's widow Jane. After her death in 1625 or 1626 it descended with the earldom (dukedom 1694–1718) until 1822 when the 15th earl sold it to William Cludde. Like Lord Berwick, the earl retained the Wrockwardine Wood mining rights.[97]

Thus by 1822 the manor had been reunited by William Cludde, mayor of Shrewsbury in 1795 and high sheriff in 1814. He died in 1829 and was succeeded by his son Edward (d. 1840). Edward's daughter Anna Maria (d. 1906) owned the manor, from 1854 jointly with her husband R. C. Herbert

(d. 1902). The manor was settled on their son Col. E. W. Herbert in 1901 and passed on his death in 1924 to his son Lt.-Col. E. R. H. Herbert, 5th earl of Powis 1952 (d. 1974). In 1982 Powis's nephew V. M. E. Holt owned the Orleton estate and possibly any manorial rights.

In 1324 the manor house was ruinous. It was said in 1650 formerly to have stood in the close called the Hall yard,[98] south-west of the church. A fishpond partly survived there in 1982. One of the main chimney stacks of Wrockwardine Hall, lying north-east of the church, bore a tablet placed there by Edward Pemberton to commemorate the building of the house in 1628 and his own completion of a new wing in 1750.[99] The limits of the 17th-century house cannot be defined with certainty but it probably lay in the range at the north-east corner of the surviving main block and extended eastwards from it. Much early 17th-century panelling was reset in the dining room and bedrooms in the mid 18th century and there is a richly decorated late 17th-century staircase, apparently *in situ*, in the centre of the old range. A map of 1742 depicts the hall, probably accurately, as a building of five bays and two storeys with four pairs of windows, central entrance, two chimney stacks, and three attic gables.[1] The mid 18th-century work greatly enlarged the house to the west and to the south (where there was a new front of seven bays) and added new kitchens on the north and east.[2] Several interior fittings of that date survive, including richly decorated ceilings to the hall and staircase, several fireplaces, and an oak staircase with slender twisted balusters. In the earlier 19th century some rooms were redecorated and nearly all the windows were renewed and many enlarged. The front may have been rendered, perhaps preserving earlier rusticated plaster quoins. During 20th-century restorations most of the rendering was removed and the brickwork renewed. The house, never occupied by the lords of the manor,[3] was bought by the War Department in 1948 and became the official residence of G.O.C. West Midland District (Commander Western District from 1980).[4]

From the later 12th century or earlier the Burnells of Acton Burnell held land in *ADMASTON*,[5] one of the members of Wrockwardine *c.* 1285.[6]

BURCOT was probably one of Wrockwardine's berewicks in 1086, and was one of its members *c.* 1285.[7] Its medieval holders are unknown. In 1650 and 1670 it was owned by Jonathan Langley of Shrewsbury Abbey (sheriff 1663, d. 1671);[8] he was succeeded by his son Peter, a draper, and

---

[87] Cath., widow of the 3rd earl.

[88] Eliz., widow of the 4th earl (*D.N.B.*).

[89] Eliz. ('Bess of Hardwick': *D.N.B.*), widow of the 6th earl (*D.N.B.*).

[90] *D.N.B.*

[91] *D.N.B.*

[92] *T.S.A.S.* lv. 148; cf. *D.N.B.*

[93] S. Shaw, *Hist. Staffs.* ii (1801), 37, 44–5.

[94] Halifax, the 'trimmer': *D.N.B.*

[95] Below, Wrockwardine Wood, Man.

[96] Above, Stirchley, Churches.

[97] Below, Wrockwardine Wood, Man.

[98] S.P.L., MS. 110, presentment of Wrockwardine jury 11 Oct. 1650, p. 10.

[99] TS. (n.d.) supplied by Maj.-Gen. J. A. Ward-Booth. In 1982 the tablet was illegible.

[1] S.R.O. 999, parcel 753, map of J. Pemberton's est. 1742.

[2] Two rainwater heads on the N. front are dated 1744 and have the Pemberton crest.

[3] Wm. Cludde (formerly Pemberton), who acquired the man. 1811–22, had inh. Orleton in 1785 (*T.S.A.S.* 4th ser. v. 275) and that remained the fam. home.

[4] Inf. from H.Q. Western Dist.

[5] Eyton, ix. 38–9.

[6] *Collect. Topog. et Geneal.* i. 117.

[7] Eyton, ix. 26.

[8] *T.S.A.S.* 4th ser. i. 230; H. Owen and J. B. Blakeway, *Hist. Shrews.* (1825), ii. 137; S.R.O. 999/Pp (2) 3, 6, 10, 11.

Peter in turn by his son Jonathan, who died childless in 1742. In 1785 Edward Cludde left it with the Orleton estate to his nephew William Pemberton (later Cludde) and Burcot remained part of the Orleton estate in 1982.[9]

In 1670 the capital messuage of Burcot was apparently an H-shaped timber-framed building with a central gable on the cross wing and three chimneys. To the south lay two long barns.[10] By c. 1690 a range forming a courtyard had been added east of the main house, and two further barns to the south.[11] Probably c. 1807 that house, or a successor, was replaced by one in brick on the site of the former barns, overlooking Watling Street.[12] Earthwork terraces to the north-east, traceable in 1982, may have been the remains of a 17th- or 18th-century formal garden.[13]

The manor of CLUDDLEY was a member of Wrockwardine c. 1285.[14] Several possible early lords are known: Walter of Cluddley (fl. 1175–80), Richard son of Ralph (fl. 1203), Robert of Cluddley (fl. c. 1235–c. 1250), Ralph of Cluddley (fl. 1256–60), John of Cluddley (fl. 1274). About 1285 Ralph of Cluddley, who was still living in 1300, was stated to hold the manor of John le Strange, lord of Wrockwardine.[15] Later a Richard Cludde of Cluddley occurred and his son and grandson, both William Cludde, inherited Cluddley. From soon after 1392 the manor descended with Orleton. The Orletons of Orleton had land in Cluddley by 1295.[16]

Between c. 1585 and c. 1642 the Forsters of Evelith (in Shifnal) held a messuage and 100 a. in Cluddley of the earl of Arundel.[17]

Although various possible earlier lords are known — Ralph of Orleton (fl. 1141–55), Adam of Orleton (fl. 1172–80), Ralph of Orleton (fl. 1186–c. 1225), and William of Orleton (fl. 1240–64)[18] — the manor of ORLETON first definitely appeared in 1295 when the last named William or another of the same name died as tenant in chief.[19] The manor then passed from father to son, the following being lords: Adam (d. 1305), John (fl. 1346), Richard (d. 1382), and Richard (d. 1388). It then passed to the younger Richard's cousin Giles of Orleton, who did not live there and sold the manor to Richard's widow Joan in 1392. Soon thereafter Orleton passed to Joan's kinsman William Cludde (II) of Cluddley, the son of Margaret of Orleton. William (II) styled of Cluddley and Orleton, a woolmonger,[20] appeared from 1382 to 1431 when he was said to hold Orleton as 1/10 knight's fee. William was succeeded by his son Thomas and the manor thereafter passed from father to son, the following being lords: Thomas

(II) (fl. 1485–90), Richard (d. 1545), Thomas (d. 1553), Edward (d. 1614), Charles (d. 1631), Edward (d. 1651), and Edward (d. 1721). The last named left it to his nephew William Cludde, on whose death in 1765 his son Edward became lord. Edward died in 1785 leaving the manor to his nephew William Pemberton of Wrockwardine Hall (d. 1829), who took the name Cludde under the terms of his uncle's will. From 1882 Orleton descended with Wrockwardine.

The medieval manor house of Orleton stood within a square moat; the moat remained complete in 1728.[21] In 1983 the surviving north-east arm of the moat was crossed by a possibly medieval stone bridge of two arches, which may have been contemporary with the stone foundations of the adjoining gatehouse. The later 16th-century superstructure of the gatehouse was timber-framed and the upper floor jettied on all sides; a datestone of 1588 in a chimney stack may relate to that rebuilding. Later alterations included the installation of chimney stacks, the underpinning of the jetties with brick, and the removal of the original ground-floor outer walls. A lantern and clock were added in the earlier 19th century.

The oldest part of Orleton Hall is at the centre of the north-east front, represented in 1983 on the ground floor by the central hall. The walls are in part timber-framed; a map of 1728[22] showed the site occupied by a triple-gabled house probably of the 17th century or earlier. The hall may have been entered through a porch in line with the gatehouse. In the later 18th century the house was greatly enlarged on the south-east, south-west, and north-west in a plain classical style with a main front of nine bays and three storeys.[23] The old hall was remodelled c. 1830 and fronted by a stone colonnade between the short 18th-century wings. There are extensive kitchen buildings and outbuildings along the north-east side of the house and beyond them farm buildings and stables, including a stable and coach-house range dated 1735.[24] To the east of the former moat there is an early 19th-century brick dovecot and a large walled garden with an elevated mid 18th-century gazebo in the Chinese style.[25]

Roger and Joan Child held a carucate in Orleton in chief in 1393–4. They were allowed to have a private oratory in their house in the parish in 1409.[26]

The rector of Wrockwardine, Odelerius of Orléans, gave 1 hide in CHARLTON, probably that held by his church in 1086, to Shrewsbury abbey before 1092.[27] The abbey retained the overlordship until 1540,[28] although the earl of

---

[9] Inf. from Mr. R. Kilvert-Minor-Adams.
[10] S.R.O. 999/Pp (2) 11.
[11] S.R.O. 999, parcel 752, Burcot map c. 1690.
[12] S.R.O. 665/2/5995. But the ho. is not shown on a map of 1808: S.R.O. 1267/3.
[13] SA 2963.
[14] Collect. Topog. et Geneal. i. 117.
[15] Eyton, ix. 39.
[16] Cal. Inq. p.m. iii, p. 202; T.S.A.S. 4th ser. viii. 155–206.
[17] Visit. Salop. 1623, i (Harl. Soc. xxviii), 186; P.R.O., C 142/337, no. 101; /351, no. 88; /496, no. 80.
[18] Eyton, viii. 276–7; Cartulary of Shrews. Abbey, ed. U. Rees (1975), i, p. 154.

[19] The following descent is based on T.S.A.S. 4th ser. viii. 155–208.
[20] P.R.O., JUST 1/753, rot. 11 (1) d.
[21] Orleton and Nash map, 1728, at Orleton Hall; above, plate 5.
[22] Orleton and Nash map, 1728.
[23] Painting of Orleton, 1792, at Orleton Hall; Bodl. MS. Top. Salop. c. 2, f. 123.
[24] Date stone; above, plate 5.
[25] Not shown on S.R.O. 1267/3; above, plate 49.
[26] T.S.A.S. 3rd ser. x. 218–19; L.J.R.O., B/A/1/7, f. 200v.
[27] Cart. Shrews. i, pp. xix, 39.
[28] P.R.O., C 137/33, no. 40, m. 4; Eyton, ix. 34.

Arundel was called overlord in 1494 and 1504.[29]

In the 12th century the Charlton family presumably held the manor of the abbey by subinfeudation.[30] By 1306 John Charlton (kt. *c.* 1307) was probably lord. He was a prominent servant of Edward II before and after his accession[31] and *c.* 1309 was granted the manor of Pontesbury, with which Charlton descended.[32] Free warren in both manors' demesnes was granted in 1307. In 1588 Edward Grey sold Charlton to Francis Newport[33] (kt. 1603),[34] and thereafter it descended with Harley and was a member of the manor of Eyton on Severn.[35] In 1611 the Vernons of Hodnet abandoned a claim, maintained since 1551, to a moiety of the manor.[36]

Before 1260 a virgate in Charlton was held of St. Mary's and St. Julian's, Shrewsbury, by William of Uppington (*alias* of Charlton). By 1284 it belonged to Master John of Charlton, who later occurred as rector of Wrockwardine.[37]

Sir John Charlton was licensed to crenellate his dwelling at Charlton in 1316,[38] and in 1341 was allowed to have mass celebrated in a chapel there.[39] The defended manor house, known as Charlton Castle, was apparently still used as a residence of the lords of Powys in the earlier 16th century[40] but following the manor's sale to Francis Newport in 1588 it fell into disuse.[41] Part of an apparently round corner tower and a length of curtain wall remained standing *c.* 1820.[42] In 1982 the site was marked by a quadrangular wet-moated enclosure, 68 × 54 metres, with some red sandstone walling visible on the island. To the south-east lay a fishpond, to the east a rabbit warren.[43]

Richard of Sugdon granted 4½ a. in Charlton to Haughmond abbey after 1274 for the maintenance of lights at St. Mary's altar in the abbey church.[44]

Before 1066 BRATTON was held by Erniet. In 1086 Warin held it of William Pantulf. William was also lord of Eyton upon the Weald Moors, and the two manors descended together in the Eyton family.[45] Mention of the chapel yard in 1784, and the presence of a large fishpond in 1839 may indicate the existence of a medieval capital messuage, perhaps on the site of the modern Bratton Farm. In 1784 the capital messuage was Bratton House, south-west of the farmhouse.[46]

In 1333 and 1350 the great tithes, with the tithes of hay in Allscott and Charlton, were appropriated to Shrewsbury abbey,[47] which already enjoyed two thirds of the manorial demesne tithes and had probably done so for two centuries or more.[48] The annual value of the rectorial tithes 1487–91 was £17 6s. 8d. and £14 in 1534–5.[49] In 1537 the abbot apparently leased all the tithes of wheat, barley, rye, peas, oats, muncorn, and hay, with the tithe barn at Allscott, to John Steventon of Dothill, although a similar lease to John Eyton is also known. The Steventons continued to lease the impropriate tithes after the rectory passed to the Crown in 1540, and in 1609 William Steventon bought the tithe estate from two speculators who had acquired it from the Crown shortly before; a fee farm of £18 was due to the Crown. In 1655 the rectorial tithes were worth £120 a year. They were then said to be in Richard Steventon's possession,[50] but had in fact been sold in six undivided shares in 1635. At least five of the shares were reunited in the Cluddes' hands between 1728 and 1790[51] and the Cluddes also bought the fee farm of £18, which by 1705 had belonged to Henry and Anne Brett.[52] Thomas Eyton apparently bought the rectorial tithes of Bratton from the Cluddes in 1813.[53]

In 1838 Edward Cludde, Thomas Eyton, and the half dozen smaller impropriators who owned parts of the hay tithes of Allscott merged almost two thirds of the rectorial tithes in the parish (excluding Charlton township) with the land that they owned. The unmerged rectorial tithes were commuted to £208 6s. 8d. a year: £9 12s. to the duke of Cleveland for part of the hay tithes of Allscott and £198 14s. 8d. to Edward Cludde. The great tithes in Charlton (except the corn tithes from the 'home closes') belonged to Cleveland and were commuted to £133 a year.[54] In 1847 Mrs. Edward Cludde, preferring not to own ecclesiastical property, sold the family's tithe rent charge to Queen Anne's Bounty for the incumbent of Wrockwardine Wood.[55]

ECONOMIC HISTORY. In 1086 the 7½ berewicks of Wrockwardine, for which geld was paid

[29] *Cal. Inq. p.m. Hen. VII*, i, pp. 420–1; ii, p. 745.

[30] Eyton, ix. 30–2, 34–5; R. Morgan, 'The Barony of Powys, 1275–1360', *Welsh Hist. Rev.* x. 12–14.

[31] *D.N.B.*

[32] *V.C.H. Salop.* viii. 264–5; cf. Eyton, ix. 32; *Cal. Pat.* 1313–17, 566; 1572–5, pp. 163–4; *Cal. Chart. R.* 1300–26, 107; *Cal. Close*, 1349–54, 576; 1396–9, 151; *Cal. Inq. Misc.* iii, p. 187; *Cal. Inq. p.m.* x, p. 111; xiv, pp. 19–22; *Cal. Inq. p.m. Hen. VII*, i, pp. 420–1; ii, pp. 484–5; *L. & P. Hen. VIII*, ii, p. 1121; P.R.O., C 1/1364/16; C 137/33, no. 40, m. 4; C 138/59, no. 53, m. 4; E 364/78.

[33] Barnard MSS., Raby Castle, box 1, bdle. 27, nos. 62a, 62b.

[34] *T.S.A.S.* 4th ser. xi. 155.

[35] L.J.R.O., B/A/15, Charlton; *Kelly's Dir. Salop.* (1941), 83, 318; cf. *V.C.H. Salop.* viii. 88; Barnard MSS., Raby Castle, box 12, bdle. 17, leases; S.R.O., q. sess. rec. box 260, reg. of gamekeepers, 1742–79, 1 Dec. 1743.

[36] *V.C.H. Salop.* viii. 265; Barnard MSS., Raby Castle, box 1, bdle. 27, nos. 63–4.

[37] Eyton, ix. 30, 34–6; *V.C.H. Salop.* ii. 119; *Feud. Aids*, iv. 22.

[38] *Cal. Pat.* 1313–17, 566.

[39] *D.N.B.*

[40] W. R. B. Robinson, 'Patronage and Hospitality in Early Tudor Wales: the Role of Hen., Earl of Worcester, 1526–49', *Bull. Inst. Hist. Res.* li. 21.

[41] Barnard MSS., Raby Castle, box 12, bdle. 7, leases of 2 Jan. 1610; 20 Feb. 1657.

[42] SA 37; S.P.L., accession 3065, no. 269.

[43] S.R.O. 14/1/4–5 (no. 90).

[44] S.P.L., Haughmond Cart. f. 42v.

[45] *V.C.H. Salop.* i. 332; below, Eyton, Man. and Other Est.

[46] S.R.O. 14/1/4; 1011, box 167, Eyton ct. r. 27 Oct. 1784.

[47] *V.C.H. Salop.* ii. 33; L.J.R.O., B/A/1/3, f. 126.

[48] *Cart. Shrews.* i, pp. 7–8, 11.

[49] Eyton, ix. 28; Owen and Blakeway, *Hist. Shrews.* ii. 508; *Valor Eccl.* (Rec. Com.), iii. 184, 189.

[50] S.P.L., MS. 110, tithes of Wrockwardine; MS. 4072, ii, pp. 668–79; *T.S.A.S.* 3rd ser. x. 208; xlvii. 8; P.R.O., E 310/23/244, nos. 4, 9, 31; STAC 8/266/18.

[51] S.P.L., MS. 110, tithes of Wrockwardine; deeds cited in S.R.O. 999 catalogue, p. 2. Cf. S.R.O. 659/1, p. 3.

[52] Deed cited in S.R.O. 999 catalogue, p. 3.

[53] S.R.O. 665/1/220, 234–5.

[54] S.R.O. 14/1/4–5; L.J.R.O., B/A/15, Charlton.

[55] R. M. Grier, *John Allen* (1889), 172–3.

on 5 hides, contained 17 ploughteams and there was land for another in Charlton. The four ploughteams in demesne were probably worked by the eight oxherds mentioned. Twelve teams belonged to 13 villeins, 4 bordars, a radman, and a priest. The presence of bordars with a share in the ploughteams probably implies the recent or continued expansion of cultivation, and Wrockwardine's value had risen from £6 13s. 8d. T.R.E. to £12 10s. in 1086. Charlton, which had one of the ploughteams and the potential for another, was worth 5s.; it belonged to the church. Wrockwardine's woodland lay 7 km. to the east in a detached block, which later became a township.[56] The 11th-century administrative status of this comparatively populous royal manor and hundred meeting place — leaving aside suggestions that it was the site of Pengwern[57] — was perhaps one reason why the manor had, or claimed, rights over a large part of the area's economic resources. Wrockwardine eventually obtained much the greatest part of the great area of woodland east of Wellington. It also had rights of common on the Wrekin and claimed uniquely extensive common rights over the whole of the Weald Moors. Exploitation of those valuable common rights may help to explain the exceptionally high proportion of Wrockwardine's territory occupied by openfield land in the Middle Ages.[58]

Areas of open field have been identified near Wrockwardine and the other villages and hamlets, a distribution clearly indicating that there were distinct groups of fields for the several settlements in the Middle Ages. In the 17th century Killstone field lay south-west of Wrockwardine, with Wrockwardine (or Town) field to the west, Dale (or Dole) field to the north, and Clay field and Clayhorns farther north still. Leaton field too was then reckoned one of Wrockwardine's fields but had perhaps originally been attached to Leaton.[59] Wide field, shared with Walcot township (in Uckington manor) in the 16th century, lay northwest of Wrockwardine and was apparently contiguous with Charlton's northern open field.[60] There were other areas of open-field land east of Allscott, north of Admaston,[61] and between Burcot, Orleton, and Cluddley.[62]

In Charlton the three main fields surrounded the hamlet and c. 1300 were usually known as the fields towards Walcot, Uckington, and the Lea.[63] A field towards Wrockwardine was mentioned in 1321,[64] and there may have been other small areas of open-field land elsewhere in the township.[65]

At Bratton, worth 24s. T.R.E., 1½ hide paid geld in 1086. There was land enough for four ploughteams but the manor was 'almost waste' and the five bordars there owned nothing.[66] Bratton field or fields (or Town field) adjoined the village.[67]

A three-course rotation was practised on the Wrockwardine demesne in 1367,[68] but arable cultivation had perhaps become less profitable in the earlier 14th century: 2 carucates of Orleton demesne land in Cluddley and Orleton were said to be very infertile in 1324[69] and much of Charlton's land was considered of poor quality in 1354.[70] So many tenants died in 1349 that income from rents fell by 90 per cent; the value of the demesnes halved. By 1367, however, land values and manorial income seem to have recovered fully.[71] Whatever the balance of arable and livestock farming in the parish before the Black Death, sheep farming seems not to have been of great importance, for in 1341 there was alleged to be little pasture for sheep.[72]

Some specialization may gradually have developed in the townships, for Charlton and Allscott seem to have been the two best townships for hay.[73] In the Middle Ages manorial tenants had grazing rights on the Wrekin.[74] The northern side of the parish also provided extensive areas of common pasture on low lying moors. Clipsmoor extended between Charlton and Walcot townships.[75] There was further common pasture in the parish on Rushmoor, Marsh heath, and Little moor[76] and rights were claimed all over the Weald Moors.[77] From 1560 or earlier, however, manors surrounding and intercommoning the Weald Moors began to inclose them. By force, later by litigation, the commoners of Wrockwardine attempted to assert their rights of common over all the moors as far east as Newport, 13 km. away. Lord Shrewsbury's sale of his rights in the Weald Moors in 1582 soon resulted in the inclosure of most of the remaining moorland between Wrockwardine and Kynnersley by Sir Walter Leveson's tenants. Only a small amount of reputedly poor, marshy soil was left uninclosed. The Levesons and their tenants were particularly active inclosers and, according to the men of Wrockwardine in 1650, had inclosed 300 a. in Eyton and Bratton. Altogether over 2,000 a. were said to have been inclosed in under a century. Loss of the moorland pasture may have greatly reduced the numbers of cattle, and especially of sheep, owned by the inhabitants of Wrockwardine. It was prob-

[56] V.C.H. Salop. i. 315. Cf. S. P. J. Harvey, 'Evidence for Settlement Study: Domesday Bk.' Medieval Settlement, ed. P. H. Sawyer (1976), 197–9; R. Lennard, Rural Eng. 1086–1135 (1959), 356; below, Wrockwardine Wood.

[57] Above, intro.

[58] Below.

[59] S.R.O. 999 passim, esp. /M 10.

[60] S.R.O. 112, box 90, ct. r. 1584–6; above, Wellington, Local Govt.

[61] Field-name evidence: S.R.O. 14/1/4–5.

[62] O.S. aerial photos., film 70.071, frames 086–92 (copies in S.P.L.).

[63] Eyton, ix. 32, 36; Barnard MSS., Raby Castle, box 1, bdle. 27, no. 32 and passim; ridge and furrow at O.S. Nat. Grid SJ 598 103.

[64] Barnard MSS., box 1, bdle. 27, no. 20.

[65] Ibid. no. 3.

[66] V.C.H. Salop. i. 332.

[67] S.R.O. 38/14; 513, box 1, Eyton ct. r. 1586–7.

[68] T.S.A.S. 4th ser. i. 221.

[69] Ibid. 4th ser. viii. 157.

[70] Eyton, ix. 33–4.

[71] T.S.A.S. 4th ser. i. 219–22.

[72] Inq. Non. (Rec. Com.), 182.

[73] L.J.R.O., B/A/1/2, f. 217v.; /1/3, f. 126; B/V/6, Wrockwardine, 1612.

[74] S.P.L., Deeds 19395.

[75] Above, Wellington, Econ. Hist. (Agric.).

[76] S.P.L., Deeds 19394; S.P.L., MS. 110, Wrockwardine ct. r. and copies; S.R.O. 924/389; 999/M 1–2, 9–10.

[77] For what follows see T.S.A.S. lxiii. 1–10; P. R. Edwards, 'Drainage Operations in the Wealdmoors', Evolution of Marshland Landscapes (Oxf. Univ. Dept. for External Studies, 1981), 136–43.

ably at the same time that the amount of wood-land pasture available in Wrockwardine wood began to decline as industry developed there.[78] At the time of the Wildmoors Inclosure Act, 1801, Wrockwardine retained some vestiges of common rights in the Weald Moors, in lieu of which 92 a. of moorland lying 1 km. north-east of Long Lane were allotted to the lord of the manor.[79]

Limited engrossment and conversion of open-field land to pasture occurred in the early 16th century.[80] Later, however, loss of commons may have stimulated open-field inclosure, most of which took place in the 17th century. Nevertheless remnants of open fields survived in 1808.[81]

In the later 16th and the 17th century, during and after inclosure, mixed farming was practised and probate inventories[82] showed the Wrockwardine farmers among the most prosperous in the area. In 1650, when some engrossment had already occurred, average farm size was 17–32 a.[83] A variety of cereals was grown, with wheat the commonest, and some peas and vetches. Clover was mentioned in 1729.[84] Cattle were kept primarily for milk; as in other parishes average herd sizes fell noticeably in the 1720s, but by the 1740s they had more than recovered. Most farms had stocks of hay; in 1612 it was said that Allscott and Charlton were the two best townships for hay in the parish.[85] Wrockwardine lay at the southern extremity of the Cheshire cheese country, and cheese for market as well as domestic consumption was widely produced. Many farmhouses, especially in Admaston, Allscott, and Bratton, had cheese store-chambers; Thomas Calcutt of Allscott had 121 cheeses in his when he died in 1744.[86]

All but the most insubstantial holdings had horses and most farms had some sheep. Flocks, generally small, averaged c. 30 sheep, although William Binnell of Cluddley had 160 in 1740.[87] Small numbers of pigs and poultry for domestic consumption were widely kept.

Hemp, and presumably flax, were already grown in the parish in the 16th century[88] and the amount produced probably increased in the late 18th century owing to the government bounty.[89] The crop was apparently concentrated immediately north-west of Wrockwardine village.[90]

In 1650 copyhold land descended by Borough English.[91] Copyhold tenure long survived in the manor, perhaps because of the divided lordship.[92] Certainly enfranchisement proceeded after William Cludde's reunion of the manorial shares

1811–22.[93] Some copyholds, however, survived until the abolition of the tenure in 1926.[94]

In 1810 87 per cent of the parish, apparently excluding Wrockwardine Wood, was occupied by 31 farms of 25 a. or more; the average size was 113 a., the largest 218 a. In addition there were 31 holdings of 5–25 a.[95] Farm sizes remained roughly the same in 1838 when, apart from land northwest and south-east of Admaston and some land around Allscott, the parish was divided into substantial, discrete farms.[96]

TABLE X

WROCKWARDINE: LAND USE, LIVESTOCK, AND CROPS

	1867	1891	1938	1965
Percentage of grassland	51	62	70	47
arable	49	38	30	53
Percentage of cattle	13	21	39	36
sheep	73	68	48	35
pigs	14	11	13	29
Percentage of wheat	66	43	46	32
barley	31	41	28	64
oats	3	16	26	3
mixed corn & rye	0	0	0	1
Percentage of agricultural land growing roots and vegetables	17	13	11	16

Sources: P.R.O. MAF 68/143, no. 14; /1340, no. 8; /3880, Salop. no. 243; /4945, no. 243.

In 1801 slightly more barley was grown than wheat; about half that quantity of oats was also produced and a little rye.[97] Slightly more than half the parish was under grass in 1838,[98] and during the later 19th and earlier 20th century grassland and cattle farming grew at the expense of arable. Later the trend reversed, barley becoming more important and, after the Allscott sugar factory opened in 1927, sugar beet became the preponderant root crop. From the mid 19th century cattle increased while sheep declined, and after 1938 the number of pigs grew.

[78] Below, Wrockwardine Wood, Econ. Hist.

[79] Wildmoors Inclosure and Drainage Act, 1801, 41 Geo. III, c. 77 (Local and Personal); S.R.O. 14/1/4–5; 665/1/301–29; 3121/1; S.P.L., MS 110, Wrockwardine, copy corresp. to Incl. Com. 1801. Cf. O.S. Area Bk. (1882).

[80] I. S. Leadam, 'Inquisition of 1517: Inclosures and Evictions', Trans. R.H.S. N.S. viii. 324.

[81] S.R.O. 1267/3.

[82] What follows is based on Yeomen and Colliers in Telford, ed. B. Trinder and J. Cox (1980).

[83] P. R. Edwards, 'Farming Econ. of NE. Salop. in 17th Cent.' (Oxf. Univ. D.Phil. thesis, 1976), 18–19.

[84] Trinder and Cox, op. cit. p. 440 (no. 252).

[85] L.J.R.O., B/V/6, Wrockwardine, 1612.

[86] Trinder and Cox, op. cit. p. 455 (no. 264).

[87] Ibid. (no. 261).

[88] S.R.O. 999/Pp 3. See Trinder and Cox, op. cit. for 17th-

and 18th-cent. examples.

[89] H. Green, 'The Linen Ind. of Salop.' Ind. Arch. Rev. v. 114–18; S.R.O., q. sess. order bk. 1783–9, pp. 41, 67.

[90] Field-name evidence: S.R.O. 14/1/4–5; 1267/3.

[91] S.R.O. 3651, box 193, customs of Wrockwardine man.; T.S.A.S. 4th ser. i. 228–31.

[92] S.R.O. 665/1/234.

[93] 2nd Rep. Sel. Cttee. on Inc. and Property Tax, H.C. 510, pp. 453–4 (1852), ix; 12th Rep. Copyhold Com. [1730], p. 6, H.C. (1854), xix, and subsequent reps. (13th–15th, 18th–21st); above, Man. and Other Est.

[94] S.P.L., MS. 110, Wrockwardine ct. r. and extracts; S.R.O. 3288/4/2–9; 12 & 13 Geo. V, c. 16, ss. 128, 191; 15 & 16 Geo. V, c. 4.

[95] S.P.L., MS. 5704.

[96] S.R.O. 14/1/4–5.

[97] P.R.O., HO 67/14, no. 218.   [98] S.R.O. 14/1/4–5.

In 1965 nine farms in the parish had 150–300 a., and a further two 300–500 a. Mechanization increased in the 1970s and ended the tradition of bringing in seasonal potato and beet pickers by bus from 'the works', as the Telford industrial area was known.[99]

The main mill in the parish was apparently always that at Allscott, on the river Tern. It was probably the mill worth 12s. in 1086.[1] In 1176 Henry II gave it to Haughmond abbey.[2] Control of the Tern in the area was clearly a problem,[3] and c. 1235 Haughmond gave Wrockwardine church 4 a. of land belonging to Allscott mill in exchange for the right to take turves and soil from 'Gretholers' moor to repair the mill pond. The mill was worth 4s. a year in 1291.[4]

In 1553, when John Steventon was tenant, the mill was acquired from the Crown by two London speculators[5] and in 1650 Richard Steventon owned three water corn mills, probably three wheels in one mill, at Allscott.[6] In 1689 a fulling mill was to be built in the mill yard[7] and in 1700 John Cope of Allscott was described as a fuller. There were three water corn and two fulling mills there in 1745.[8] By 1799 a skin mill had replaced the fulling mills.[9] The mill closed between 1856 and 1870.[10]

Ralph of Orleton held a mill worth one mark a year, probably at Orleton, in 1198.[11] A water mill at Orleton, mentioned in 1305, was ruinous in 1324.[12] It may have lain c. 400 metres north of the hall.[13] At Wrockwardine a windmill was noted as destroyed in 1349;[14] it or a successor probably stood c. 1 km. east of the village.[15] There may have been a water mill at Bratton, where the mill brook, presumably a stretch of Bullocks brook, was mentioned in 1586–7.[16] At Cluddley a brick windmill, probably of the late 18th century, had a steam mill added in the mid 19th century. It went out of use between 1885 and 1895.[17]

Activity in the parish not directly concerned with agriculture was always limited. In 1712 Thomas Binnell dug clay on Rushmoor for brick and tile making.[18] A brick kiln east of the Wrockwardine–Admaston road in 1827[19] had closed by 1838. Field names suggest the presence before 1838 of other kilns or clamps.[20] A brick kiln at Long Lane in 1838 apparently later closed, to

reopen c. 1885. About 1900 drain pipes became its main product; it closed c. 1937.[21]

Basalt and granite were quarried around Leaton and Overley Hill during the 19th century. Extraction continued on a small scale until c. 1960 when new plant was introduced and larger-scale quarrying began east of Leaton.[22]

There was a fertilizer factory south of Allscott from 1870 or earlier until c. 1958 when it became a fertilizer warehouse.[23] In 1982 a depot at Cluddley for Unigate Dairies received milk from a wide area for sale in Telford.[24]

LOCAL GOVERNMENT AND PUBLIC SERVICES. In 1255 Hamon le Strange did no suit to shire or hundred court, and c. 1285 John le Strange held a court with pleas of bloodshed, the hue and cry, and a gallows.[25] Two courts a year were said to be held in 1292.[26]

Court rolls of Wrockwardine manor, dealing mainly with agricultural regulation, survive for 1397–8, 1411–14, and 1456–7, and there are many later records.[27] In 1413–14 the townships of Wrockwardine, Admaston, Allscott, Bratton, Burcot, Cluddley, Leaton, Nash, and Quam Pool (in Wrockwardine Wood) presented, although Bratton was a member of Eyton manor and made presentments at courts there in the 16th century and answered with Eyton and Horton at Hinstock court leet from the 14th to the 19th centuries.[28] In the later 16th and in the 17th and 18th centuries courts for Wrockwardine dealt with the assize of bread and of ale, agricultural matters, and the transfer of copyholds.[29] By 1797, whence there are continuous records until 1936, the court leet and the court baron were combined. In the later 18th century the court usually met every April and October; later its meetings became increasingly irregular, apparently taking place as business demanded. The last court transactions dealt with the abolition of copyhold, following the Law of Property Act, 1922.[30]

In 1650 the customary bailiff was a copyholder who served as many years as he had nooks of land; he received a tree from the demesne for each year's service.[31] T. F. Dukes, the Shropshire

[99] Inf. from Mr. R. Kilvert-Minor-Adams.
[1] V.C.H. Salop. i. 315.
[2] Eyton, ix. 36.
[3] Ibid. 37; Cal. Pat. 1225–32, 223.
[4] Eyton, ix. 37.
[5] Cal. Pat. 1553, 63.
[6] S.R.O. 999/Rr 67.
[7] Ibid. /EA 26.
[8] Ibid. /D 4–6; Trinder and Cox, Yeomen and Colliers, p. 64.
[9] S.R.O. 999/D 10–11.
[10] P.O. Dir. Salop. (1856), 154; (1870), 180.
[11] Bk. of Fees, i. 6.
[12] T.S.A.S. 4th ser. viii. 156–8.
[13] S.R.O. 14/1/4–5 (nos. 310–11); 999/Pp 11; 3651, box 15, conveyance, 3 Nov. 1672.
[14] T.S.A.S. 4th ser. i. 219.
[15] Field names, 16th-cent. and later: S.R.O. 14/1/4–5 (nos. 326, 334–5, 842–3); 999/Rr 4.
[16] S.R.O. 513, box 1, Eyton ct. r. 1586–7.
[17] SA 724; S. Bagshaw, Dir. Salop. (1851), 447; Kelly's Dir. Salop. (1885), 999; (1895), 279.
[18] S.P.L., MS. 110, Wrockwadine ct. r. 6 Oct. 1712 (copy).

[19] C. & J. Greenwood, Map of Salop. (1827).
[20] S.R.O. 14/1/4–5.
[21] Ibid.; Kelly's Dir. Salop. (1885), 1000; (1909), 310; (1937), 322; (1941), 319. The wks. lay partly in Longdon upon Tern: O.S. Map 6", Salop. XXXV. NE. (1887 edn.).
[22] O.S. Map 6", Salop. XXXV. SE. (1887 edn.); local inf.
[23] P.O. Dir. Salop. (1870), 180; Wargrave Press, Wrekin Civic & Commercial Dir. (1958), 32.
[24] Inf. from the manager.
[25] Rot. Hund. (Rec. Com.), ii. 56; Collect. Topog. et Geneal. i. 117.
[26] T.S.A.S. 4th ser. i. 212.
[27] S.P.L., MS. 110, Wrockwardine; S.P.L., Deeds 19394–7; below.
[28] S.R.O. 327, boxes 4–5, Hinstock ct. leet verdicts; 513, box 1, Eyton ct. r. 1506–7, 1586–7.
[29] S.R.O. 14/3/74–5; 999/Nn, Rr; 1011, box 233, Wrockwardine man. jury presentment of 1650; 3390/6/115; 3651, box 193, ct. bks. and other ct. rec.
[30] S.P.L., MS. 110, Wrockwardine ct. r. and copies; S.R.O. 3288/4/2–9; 12 & 13 Geo. V, c. 16.
[31] S.R.O. 3651, box 193, customs of Wrockwardine man.; T.S.A.S. 4th ser. i. 228–31.

antiquary, was manorial steward 1817–39.[32] The office of crier was abolished in the mid 19th century.[33] A lock-up or crib, then apparently disused, was mentioned in 1842;[34] its site is unknown.

In 1305 the court of Orleton manor was said to be worth nothing.[35] Henry of Walcot, bailiff of Charlton, was mentioned in 1379.[36] A court may have been held at Charlton until c. 1588 when the manor was bought by Francis Newport. Thereafter Charlton was a member of the manor of Eyton on Severn.[37]

Three overseers of the poor were appointed in 1669 and disbursed £31 3s. 3d. on pensions, house repairs, paupers' burials, and the like.[38] Between 1725 and 1834 two overseers were normally appointed annually. In 1725–6 £59 18s. 4d. was disbursed, in 1760–1 £67 12s. 10d., although in 1755–6 expenditure had reached £94 13s. 4d.[39] In 1760–1 the poor were farmed to Thomas Hazlehurst for £50 a year.[40] By 1782, when the parish apparently resumed direct responsibility for the poor, a workhouse was rented. Expenditure that year totalled £194 1s. 8d. From 1790 it rose sharply, and in 1795 voluntary subscriptions to provide half-price bread and flour raised £122 13s. 4d.[41] In 1803 the indoor poor were farmed for £50, to John Hollis. About 1801 a new workhouse had been erected 1 km. west of Wrockwardine on land belonging to the Tiddicross charity, and Hollis was to provide its inmates with bread, cheese, and beer, and beef or mutton at least once a week. In 1803 £544 18s. 6d. was spent on the poor, mostly as out-relief.[42] In 1814 the workhouse, then under a salaried keeper, comprised a kitchen, paupers' kitchen, 5 bedrooms containing 13 beds, a 'dead room' with 3 spinning wheels and 1 long wheel, pantry, brewhouse, and cellar.[43]

Expenditure on poor relief was highest in 1816–17 when c. £1,620 was spent and there were up to thirty in the workhouse. The parish owed £1,980,[44] and 703 of the population of 1,938 were receiving parish relief, including 200 men completely unemployed. As ever, most of the poor lived in Wrockwardine Wood, the industrial part of the parish, which, however, contributed only a

seventh of the parish rate income.[45] Late in 1816 the unemployed were set to work on the parish roads.[46] Over the next five years expenditure fell rapidly to £1,052 in 1822–3. By 1827–8 it had risen again to £1,291.[47] A select vestry was formed, probably in 1819.[48]

In 1725 the overseers were allowed 5s. for performing their duties, increased to a guinea in 1809.[49] By 1814, when his salary was increased to £20, a workhouse keeper was employed;[50] his pay rose to £25 in 1819[51] and £30 in 1821.[52] By 1806 a doctor was retained, apparently for £10.[53]

Between 1836 and 1930 Wrockwardine was part of Wellington poor-law union, which rented the Wrockwardine parish workhouse in the period of high unemployment between 1838 and 1841.[54] Wrockwardine became part of Wrekin highway district in 1863,[55] and was part of Wellington rural district from its formation until 1974 when it became part of the district of the Wrekin.[56]

A Wrockwardine Association for the Prosecution of Felons was formed between 1814 and 1818.[57]

Admaston sewage works serving that village was built 1911–12.[58] About 1933 piped water was brought from Wellington to Admaston, Bratton, and Wrockwardine.[59] The Rushmoor sewage works serving northern Telford opened in 1975; several smaller works, including Admaston's, were phased out after that.[60] By 1885 post offices were open in Wrockwardine and Admaston.[61]

CHURCH. Parts of Wrockwardine church predate the mid 12th century[62] and there was a priest in 1086.[63] Shrewsbury abbey claimed the church itself as a gift of Roger, earl of Shrewsbury (d. 1094).[64] Dependent chapels, referred to generally in two mid 12th-century confirmations of abbey property,[65] were not mentioned thereafter.

The church, valued at £10 in 1291,[66] was appropriated to Shrewsbury abbey in 1333[67] but the first vicar was not instituted until 1341 and the vicarage was ordained only in 1351.[68] Patronage of the vicarage belonged to Shrewsbury abbey until 1540 when it passed to the Crown. In 1862 the

[32] *T.S.A.S.* 4th ser. v. 282; for his libr. see S.R.O. 665/3/166.
[33] S.R.O. 3288/4/6
[34] S.R.O. 999/33-4.
[35] *T.S.A.S.* 4th ser. viii. 156.
[36] Barnard MSS., Raby Castle, box 1, bdle. 27, no. 46.
[37] Ibid. box 12, bdle. 17, leases.
[38] S.R.O. 4472/P/1/1.
[39] Ibid. /P/1/2.
[40] Ibid. at end; cf. above, Wellington, Local Govt.
[41] S.R.O. 4472 /P/1/3.
[42] Ibid. /P/1/4; /P/2/12–13.
[43] Ibid. /P/1/5, at front and end. For spinning and long wheels see Trinder and Cox, *Yeomen and Colliers*, pp. 62–3.
[44] S.R.O. 4472/P/1/5, 1 Apr. 1817.
[45] *Some Facts, shewing the Vast Burthen of the Poor's Rate, by a member of the Salop. Co. Cttee. for the employment of the poor* (Holborn, 1817), 6 (copy in S.P.L.); below, Wrockwardine Wood.
[46] S.R.O. 4472/P/1/5, at end, resolutions of 22 Nov., 20 Dec. 1816.
[47] Ibid. /P/1/5–6.
[48] Ibid. /Ve/2.
[49] Ibid. /P/1/2, 5.

[50] Ibid. /P/1/5, at front.
[51] Ibid. /P/1/6, p. 181.
[52] Ibid. /Ve/2, 19 May 1821.
[53] Ibid. /P/1/4.
[54] V. J. Walsh, 'Admin. of Poor Laws in Salop. 1820–55' (Pennsylvania Univ. Ph.D. thesis, 1970), 150, 207, 211 n. (copy in S.R.O.); for the wkho.'s later hist. see below, Chars.; *Kelly's Dir. Salop.* (1929), 327.
[55] S.R.O., q. sess. order bk. 1861–9, p. 127.
[56] *V.C.H. Salop.* ii. 217; sources cited ibid. iii. 169, n. 29.
[57] *Shrews. Chron.* 27 May 1814, advt.; 23 Jan. 1818 (p. 1).
[58] S.R.O., DA 26/100/1, pp. 319, 385.
[59] S.R.O. 4472/Par/17 (Jan. 1934); A. H. S. Waters, *Rep. on Water Supplies* (S.C.C. 1946), 99.
[60] Local inf.
[61] *Kelly's Dir. Salop.* (1885), 999.
[62] Below.
[63] *T.S.A.S.* lvi. 253.
[64] *Cart. Shrews.* i, p. 5.
[65] Ibid. ii, pp. 297, 299.
[66] *Tax. Eccl.* (Rec. Com.), 247.
[67] Under a licence of 1329: *Cal. Pat. 1327–30*, 413; *V.C.H. Salop.* iii. 33; *Cal. Papal Reg.* ii. 410.
[68] L.J.R.O., B/A/1/2, f. 217v.; /1/3, f. 126.

lord chancellor exchanged it with the earl of Powis for the patronage of Holy Cross, Shrewsbury.[69] In 1889 Powis conveyed it to his brother R. C. Herbert,[70] whose great-grandson, V. M. E. Holt, owned it until 1981[71] when the living was united with those of Longdon upon Tern, Rodington, and Uppington; Holt, with Lord Barnard, the Martyrs' Memorial and Church of England Trust, and the bishop of Lichfield, then became a joint patron of the united benefice.[72]

After 1351 the vicar had all offerings of wax and money; tithes of wool, lambs, flax, hemp, chickens, piglets, pigeons, geese, calves, pasture, cheese, dairy products, bees, gardens, fishponds, and mills (built or to be built); 'pennies of charity'; tithes of hay, apart from those of Allscott and Charlton (which were reserved to the abbey); and all other small tithes.[73] About 1490 the vicarage was worth £8 a year.[74]

The vicar's income in 1612 consisted of tithes of wool, lambs, flax, geese, pigs, apples, and garden produce; the tithe corn of all 'home closes'; the tithe hay except from Allscott and Charlton; Easter offerings; and 1½d. for every cow and calf.[75] In 1655 the small tithes were worth £28 a year and the glebe £2.[76] Richard Steventon apparently procured the living for Joshua Barnet, vicar 1656–62, and allowed him £20 a year for life, which was afterwards settled on the vicarage.[77] Steventon further endowed the vicarage with a £10 rent charged on the great tithes under the terms of his will dated 1658, to provide an 'able orthodox minister'. Edward Pemberton (d. 1680) left a rent charge of £6 13s. 4d. for similar purposes; it was discharged for £200 in 1689.[78]

In 1701 the vicarial tithes were basically those of 1612, but owners of 5 or 6 calves paid 2s. every two years, and owners of 10 paid the same yearly. Tithes of wool and lambs were paid in kind: one in seven or two in seventeen lambs were customary, with 3d. extra for 8 to 10 or 18 to 20 lambs. The seventh pig and goose were customarily paid to the vicar, whereas for other produce a tenth was usual. Some of the hay tithe was compounded for a modus.[79]

About 1708 the living was worth £49 and in 1799 £120 a year.[80] By 1792 tithes were paid in cash, although Wrockwardine moor, when mowed, was tithable in kind in 1829.[81] The vicar's net income 1828–31 averaged £376.[82] In 1838, at commutation, the vicar owned most of the hay, clover, and rye-grass tithes, all small tithes, and agistment of unprofitable cattle. His tithes were commuted to £343 15s. a year. Then, as in 1612, there was only about an acre of glebe.[83] The net value of the living fell by 1891 to £250, and to £190 by 1900, at which level it apparently remained for some years. In 1917 the living was worth £300, in 1932 £346.[84]

In 1351, when the bishop ordained the vicarage, Shrewsbury abbey undertook to build a new vicarage house opposite the existing rectory in Allscott within two years. It was to have a hall, two chambers, a kitchen, stable, and outbuildings.[85] By 1537 there was also a tithe barn.[86] In the early 17th century the 14th-century vicarage was in disrepair, but it was apparently remodelled during that century to produce the building visible in 1982, which was timber-framed, two-bayed and two-storeyed, with a central stack.[87] That house was sold in 1806 and a new one bought opposite the church,[88] to which the house next door was added by the patron in 1832.[89] A new vicarage house was built south-east of the village in 1963.[90]

At Domesday and until c. 1095 Odelerius of Orléans, father of the historian Orderic Vitalis, was priest. Odelerius, one of the three learned clerks who accompanied Roger of Montgomery to England, also held Atcham church and probably lived in Shrewsbury where he served St. Peter's chapel. He was presumably given Wrockwardine in or after 1071.[91] Master John Charlton, rector by the 1290s and still in 1320, was apparently a married or widowed priest; he was probably related to the family who owned Charlton.[92] One pre-Reformation vicar is known to have been a graduate, John Dovy, 1463–72.[93]

In 1548 the service of Our Lady was suppressed. The 70-year-old stipendiary Thomas Fryer[94] had been receiving an annuity of 33s. 4d. from the abbot of Shrewsbury in 1534, when he was called dean of the church of Wrockwardine.[95] He was perhaps related to John Fryer, vicar from c. 1550

[69] Lich. Dioc. Regy., bps.' reg. Q (Orders in Council), p. 40; S.R.O. 3651, box 196, order in council re Wrockwardine patronage.
[70] S.R.O. 3651, box 196, conveyance of Wrockwardine patronage.
[71] Lich. Dioc. Dir. (1981), 106; Burke, Land. Gent. (18th edn.), ii (1969), 307–8.
[72] Church Com. scheme, 28 Oct. 1981 (confirmed 24 Nov. 1981: Lond. Gaz. 1 Dec. 1981, p. 15283).
[73] L.J.R.O., B/A/1/3, f. 126.
[74] Eyton, ix. 28; Owen and Blakeway, Hist. Shrews. ii. 508, 532; Valor Eccl. (Rec. Com.), iii. 184, 189.
[75] L.J.R.O., B/V/6, Wrockwardine, 1612.
[76] T.S.A.S. xlvii. 8.
[77] Calamy Revised, ed. A. G. Matthews, 29–30; Cal. S.P. Dom. 1657–8, 239.
[78] L.J.R.O., B/V/6, Wrockwardine, 1679 × ?1682, 1698; T.S.A.S. 4th ser. ix. 90–1.
[79] L.J.R.O., B/V/6, Wrockwardine, 1701.
[80] T. Cox and A. Hall, Magna Britannia, iv (1727), 718; S.R.O. 3916/1/1, p. 25.
[81] S.R.O. 665/1/251–5; 4472/T/6.

[82] Rep. Com. Eccl. Revenues [67], pp. 508–9, H.C. (1835), xxii.
[83] S.R.O. 14/1/5; L.J.R.O., B/A/15, Charlton; B/V/6, Wrockwardine, 1612.
[84] Kelly's Dir. Salop (1891), 484; (1900), 294; (1905), 305; (1913), 318; (1917), 301; Crockford (1932), 1331.
[85] L.J.R.O., B/A/1/3, f. 126.
[86] S.P.L., MS. 110, Wrockwardine, abstr. of lease of 1537. A 'tithe barn' was demolished in Allscott c. 1970: local inf.
[87] L.J.R.O., B/V/1/39, 60; B/V/6, Wrockwardine, 1701; SA 15504; Barnard MSS., Raby Castle, box 12, bdle. 25, lease, 20 Oct. 1597, for descr. of ho. then.
[88] L.J.R.O., B/V/6, Wrockwardine, deeds of 1806.
[89] S.R.O. 4472/Gl/7–10; Lich. Dioc. Regy., bps.' reg. I, pp. 265–6; S.R.O. 3916/1/33.
[90] Lich. Dioc. Regy., bps.' reg. X, pp. 553–6, 614–15.
[91] Eccl. Hist. of Ordericus Vitalis,, ed. M. Chibnall, i (1980), 1–4; cf. V.C.H. Salop. ii. 30; iii. 7.
[92] Eyton, ix. 29, 35–6.
[93] L.J.R.O., B/A/1/12, ff. 82v., 88.
[94] T.S.A.S. 3rd ser. x. 350–1.
[95] Valor Eccl. (Rec. Com.), iii. 191.

to 1573 or later, and Richard Freer, curate in 1579 and 1585.[96] In 1620 the vicar, Charles Duckworth, M.A., was not resident but there was a curate, William Holmes.[97] James Smyth, instituted 1635, 'deserted' the parish in the First Civil War.[98] Jonathan Gellibrand, minister from 1647, was ejected in 1655.[99] An inscription on the bell frame of 1656 prayed for the Church of England's deliverance from heresy, schism, 'self-opinion', and 'popish sanctity'.[1] In that year Joshua Barnet was appointed minister. After his ejection in 1662 he lived at Isombridge (in Ercall Magna) and preached both at home and elsewhere, being 'very moderate and . . . much beloved by the neighbouring clergy'.[2]

After 1662 almost all the vicars were graduates. Benjamin Reed, 1728–33, employed a curate in 1730.[3] Stephen Panting, 1765–82, resided at Wellington; he conducted two Sunday services with one sermon. There was communion on seven feast days, usually to fewer than 60 communicants.[4] Small sums were paid out of the sacrament money to the parish poor from the mid 18th century or earlier: £1 18s. 6d. in 1742 and £12 for the two years 1806 and 1807.[5] Joshua Gilpin, 1782–1828, was also incumbent of Buildwas 1796–1822;[6] he was presented through the personal interest of the Quaker Richard Reynolds.[7] For the sake of his son's education Gilpin lived at Newport c. 1799–1802. In 1799 he preached twice on Sundays in summer and once in winter, and administered communion every six weeks.[8] He was an admirer of Fletcher of Madeley, an Arminian Evangelical and Methodist of liberal opinions.[9] His works included an 'improved' edition of The Pilgrim's Progress, a collection of hymns, and a memorial to his son (d. 1806) that ran to many editions.[10] A good preacher, though with a weak voice, he drew only a small congregation. There were 80 communicants at Easter 1824.[11]

During Gilpin's incumbency the church was 'beautified' and repaired, a new gallery being added.[12] Between 1788, or earlier, and 1823 a parish orchestra was maintained, with violins, viola, bass viol, and clarinet, and there was a choir with up to 16 treble singers.[13]

Gilpin employed a curate.[14] So sometimes did his long-serving successor G. L. Yate, 1828–73; c. 1830 the curate was paid £50.[15] Yate maintained the same services and frequency of communion as Gilpin. Attendance was no higher than in the later 18th century; in 1843 there were only 39 regular communicants, with c. 63 at festivals. In 1843 the seating – with 63 free seats and 110 children's seats, apparently in the galleries – sufficed for the parish, servants sitting in appropriated seats.[16] In 1884 a small majority of seat holders voted to retain the 56 rented places.[17]

An iron mission chapel was built at Charlton after 1875. In 1898 there were Sunday afternoon services but by 1927 it was disused and items from it were given to Wellington workhouse. The building was sold c. 1932 and later converted to a house.[18] By 1908 Walcot, formerly in Withington ecclesiastical parish, had been transferred to Wrockwardine parish.[19]

A. A. Turreff, vicar 1906–45,[20] increased the Sunday services from three to four and there was monthly communion.[21] The church became more active in the village and a parish magazine was started; in the later 1920s and 30s there were c. 200 Easter communicants.[22]

Miss E. M. Clay, dissatisfied with the ministry and witness of the vicar in the 1950s,[23] began to hold meetings in Admaston, and in 1957 she devised St. Christopher's Hall there for Christian work. She had built the hall c. 1947 as a centre for women's devotional work.[24] Her friend Miss Norah Shoebotham continued the work, and in the early 1960s, under a later vicar, communion was celebrated there monthly. Norah Shoebotham subsequently left the residue of her estate to the hall, and part of the income was put towards the cost of a deaconess, who also worked in All Saints' parish, Wellington. In 1982 the hall, which remained closely connected with the two Anglican parishes[25] and with the Methodists of

[96] L.J.R.O., B/V/1/8, 11; Barnard MSS., Raby Castle, box 12, bdle. 24, lease, 16 Nov. 1585; [L. Marshall], St. Peter's Church, Wrockwardine: A Brief Acct. of its Hist., Architecture, and Contents, ed. T. J. Shotton (Shifnal, 1972).
[97] Marshall, St. Peter's Ch.; L.J.R.O., B/V/1/39.
[98] S.R.O. 4472/Rg/1, s.a. 1635, 1640, 1645.
[99] Walker Revised, ed. A. G. Matthews, 305; Calamy Revised, ed A. G. Matthews, 29–30.
[1] H. B. Walters, Ch. Bells of Salop. (Oswestry, 1915), 336.
[2] T.S.A.S. 2nd ser. i. 83.
[3] Marshall, St. Peter's Ch.; L.J.R.O., B/V/6, Wrockwardine, 1730.
[4] L.J.R.O., B/A/1/21, p. 115; /1/24, p. 112; B/V/5, visit. return of 1772.
[5] S.R.O. 4472/Ve/1.
[6] L.J.R.O., B/A/1/24, p. 112; Lich. Dioc. Regy., episc. reg. 29, p. 146; S.P.R. Lich. xiv (3), p. viii.
[7] M. P. Hack, Ric. Reynolds (1896), 51.
[8] S.R.O. 665/2/5972; 3916/1/1, no. 25.
[9] C. Hulbert, Hist. and Descr. of Co. of Salop. ii (1837), 158; J. Benson, Life of Rev. J. W. de la Flechere (1805), p. iii; S.R.O. 665/2/5972.
[10] B.M. Gen. Cat. of Printed Bks. to 1955 (photolithographic edn. 1959–66), lxxxvi. 289–90.
[11] Hulbert, op. cit. 158; S.R.O. 665/2/5980, 6036; 3916/1/4.
[12] Below.

[13] S.R.O. 4472/CW/3, s.a. 1788, 1789; /CW/4, 1 Oct. 1821; 13 Apr., 14 May 1822; 5 and 8 Feb. 1823.
[14] S.R.O. 665/2/6036; 3916/1/4.
[15] Lich. Dioc. Regy., episc. reg. 29, p. 146; 32, p. 200; benefice and inst. bk. 1868–1900, p. 28; P.O. Dir. Salop. (1856), 154; Rep. Com. Eccl. Revenues, 508–9.
[16] S.R.O. 3916/1/5.
[17] S.R.O. 4472/ChP/2.
[18] Ibid. /Mch/1–14; /Par/15 (Jan. 1932); Hobson, Wellington Dir. (1898), 58; P. M. Thomas, 'Influence of Ch. of St. Peter on Par. of Wrockwardine' (St. Katherine's Coll., Liverpool, dissertation, 1964). Thanks are due to Mrs. P. M. Bradburn for the loan of her dissertation.
[19] Above, Wellington, Churches; S.R.O. 3966/Misc/1/9.
[20] Lich. Dioc. Regy., benefice and inst. bk. 1900–29, p. 20; 1929–52, p. 106.
[21] S.R.O. 4472/SRg/1.
[22] Ibid. /Par/8–24.
[23] This para. based on Review of Local Chars. (S.C.C. 1975), 69; corresp. in possession of Revd. Preb. W. S. Frost; inf. from Deaconess Joyce Mitson; Thomas, 'Influence of Ch. of St. Peter', 54, 146, 148.
[24] M. McCrea, 'A Pair of Shoes: An Acct. of the Lives and Time of Jessie and Norah Shoebotham' (TS.; copy in S.P.L.).
[25] i.e. All Saints', Wellington (whose vicar was a trustee), and St. Peter's, Wrockwardine.

Admaston, was the meeting place of several groups and societies with Christian links.

For much of the period 1600–1900 the parish clerk was a member of the Houlston family.[26]

The church of *ST. PETER*, so named by 1435,[27] is cruciform with a central tower and stair turret, and north and south chapels.[28]

The lower part of the eastern 6 metres of the nave, constructed of large stone blocks, probably predates the mid 12th century. That early church had centrally placed, but not quite opposing, north and south doorways; the latter was the main entrance until 1854. No indications remain of the early Norman church's east end or fenestration.

Probably in the later 12th century the church was rebuilt with rubble walling on a cruciform plan with a central tower. The chancel was lit by three round-headed east windows and a north and a south one. Only the south window survives open, largely reconstructed in 1854; until then a square window occupied the space. The central tower was supported on four pointed arches, the piers being formed of ten columns that have been much altered by repairs after subsidences. Four pointed windows lit its upper storey. The transepts apparently had doorways of differing late Norman styles in their end walls near the western angles; only the northern one was open in 1982. Aisles were apparently planned, for doorways, again in differing late Norman styles, were provided in the west walls of the transepts; a straight joint in the north wall of the nave, close to the north-west pier, may echo the intention. The continuous masonry of the lower nave walls, however, shows that the plan was never executed.

Probably in the 14th century the nave was extended 5 metres west and had its north doorway blocked to allow the insertion of a two-light window, one possibly also being inserted in the south wall.[29] An east window, with image brackets below to either side, replaced the three 12th-century windows in the chancel, which also received angle buttresses and a new plain trussed-rafter roof. Probably in the later 14th century the north, or Cludde, chapel was built with openings from the chancel and north transept, the latter possibly screened. The chapel may have replaced an earlier one, the arch into the transept being possibly 13th-century. Traces of medieval painting have survived on the apex of the east wall. The south chapel was built in the late 15th or early 16th century, access to the chancel and transept being through half-arches, which acted as tower buttresses. In 1751 Samuel Fowler, vicar of Atcham, sold the chapel to Edward Pemberton[30] and it was thenceforth known as the Pemberton chapel. Fowler had a freehold estate in Wrockwardine that had belonged in 1650 to Eleanor, widow of Thomas Salter (d. 1623) and

daughter of Edward Cludde the elder (d. 1614) of Orleton.[31]

At least three major restoration programmes were proposed in the 19th century but it is not clear how fully any of them was executed. In 1808 John Carline reported on the fabric and Samuel Smith of Madeley was asked to estimate the cost of repairs and building works including the erection of a new gallery, probably to replace an existing one at the west end.[32] David Parkes, the antiquary and artist, visited the church in 1812 and noted that the chancel had been 'beautified' and that overall the church had been repaired in 'an incongruous . . . fantastic Gothic' style.[33] By 1838 there was a south gallery, by 1854 a north one.

In 1854 Ewan Christian suggested radical alterations and repairs. His main proposal, the erection of a north aisle,[34] was not adopted, and others may have been similarly unfruitful. Work that was undertaken included the blocking of the south door and the opening of a west one; probably the insertion of north and south windows in the western part of the nave; the blocking of the south chapel's east door; the partial reroofing of the nave; the reflooring of the chancel; the removal of the north gallery; and the replacement of the pews by benches, some old pew panelling being used as wainscot. The pulpit, rebuilt to incorporate 17th-century panelling, was probably moved from the north-east corner of the nave into the chancel, and new communion rails were put in. The south chapel became the vestry, replacing one under the west gallery.

In 1879 it was again unsuccessfully proposed to build a north aisle, but during 1881–91 major work was done to designs by S. Pountney Smith and by Mr. Bowdler, both of Shrewsbury. The church was stripped of plaster and internally repointed; the tower was underpinned and the bells rehung; the nave was reroofed on the south side; windows were renewed. Either then or in 1854 a rood light was inserted high in the south wall; no predecessor is known, and it was apparently a purely antiquarian addition.[35]

In 1901 the west and south galleries were removed.[36] Further major repairs were done 1906–7 to designs by T. L. Moore, the north chapel being restored and the chancel and tower underpinned.[37] A chancel screen was installed in 1913. In 1931 communion rails dated 1685 were reinstated after being found at Wrockwardine Hall.[38]

The plate is all 19th-century or later.[39] There were four bells in 1549, five in 1686. Four remained in use in 1981, two of the early 14th century, one of 1616, and one of 1678. The fifth, of 1650, was dismounted in 1951 and replaced by a new bell. A sixth bell is of 1828.[40] A font,

[26] S. Bagshaw, *Dir. Salop.* (1851), 443; S.R.O. 4472/CW/5; Hobson, *Wellington Dir.* (1898), 58.

[27] Barnard MSS., Raby Castle, box 1, bdle. 27, no. 45.

[28] Acct. based on Cranage, vii. 639–49; see above, plate 35.

[29] Drawing by W. Burton in S.P.L., Prints and Engravings W95; Bodl. MS. Top. Salop. c. 2, f. 572.

[30] S.R.O. 999/Oo (1) 12–13.

[31] Ibid. /Rr 67; *T.S.A.S.* 4th ser. viii. 175.

[32] S.R.O. 4472/CW/3, 21 May 1808 (at end); see also S.R.O. 665/2/6000.

[33] B.L. Add. MS. 21180, p. 60.

[34] S.R.O. 4472/ChF/1.

[35] Ibid. /ChF/2; *Kelly's Dir. Salop.* (1900), p. 294; *Salopian Shreds & Patches*, iv. 255; v. 3; viii. 82.

[36] S.R.O. 4472/ChFac/5.

[37] *T.S.A.S.* 3rd ser. x. 242.

[38] Marshall, *St. Peter's Ch.*

[39] S. A. Jeavons, *Ch. Plate Archd. Salop* (Shrews. 1964), pp. 73–4, 101, 109, 111.

[40] Walters, *Ch. Bells of Salop.* 334–6; *Shropshire Mag.* Nov. 1951, 18–19; S.R.O. 4472/Ch/1.

perhaps contemporary with the oldest parts of the church, was turned out in 1808. A pillar font or piscina, also 12th-century, was perhaps removed then too. Another font, probably late 12th-century and previously in a Wellington garden, was given to the church in 1934.[41] The church also has two 19th-century fonts, and a portable one (given *c.* 1931) formerly the property of Bishop King of Lincoln.[42] The chest may be 14th-century.[43] The sundial in the churchyard was made in 1750; a cast-iron base replaced a stone one in 1932.

The registers are complete from 1591.[45] A new graveyard south-west of the village was consecrated in 1864.[46]

NONCONFORMITY. In 1676 one papist lived in the parish and in 1767 David Clifford, a farmer, was listed as a papist.[47] In 1772 one or two women who were frequent churchgoers also attended local Methodist meetings, but there was no dissenters' meeting house.[48] 'Very few' parishioners were dissenters in 1799.[49] Meeting houses were licensed at Long Lane in 1818[50] and at Wrockwardine in 1823.[51] Wesleyans met at Allscott between 1828 and 1836.[52] Wrockwardine and Admaston both joined the Wrockwardine Wood Primitive Methodist circuit in 1840.[53] No nonconformists were meeting in 1851.

United Free Methodists had a chapel at Overley Hill from 1862. It was de-registered in 1935 and demolished after 1945.[54]

In 1873 a building in Admaston was used by Wesleyan Methodists. It was apparently replaced by a 150-seat chapel built in 1874; by 1940 it had a schoolroom and two other rooms attached to it.[55] In 1982 average attendance was 60 in the morning and 30 in the afternoon.[56] The Methodists also maintained connexions with St. Christopher's Hall.[57]

EDUCATION. John Poole (or Pole) and Henry Bynnell were schoolmasters in the late 17th century[58] and Richard Poyner from 1702.[59] Elizabeth Bullock (d. 1681) and Jane Schofield (d. 1705) kept schools in their houses. A 'schoolhouse' at Allscott was mentioned in 1732.[60] By 1799 the parish had a Sunday school and a day school 'by subscription' and by 1818 two well conducted schools for *c.* 63 cottagers' children, poor pupils' fees being paid by richer neighbours.[62]

The Cludde family built and supported separate boys' and girls' schools on their property;[63] both were closely associated with the church and by 1852 were designated C.E. schools.[64] As early as 1849 they had certificated teachers and were earning government grants; by 1883 they were earning drawing grants. Exceptionally for small rural schools, they regularly trained pupil teachers, even from 1851, and usually received good reports.[65]

The girls' school with 40 pupils was founded in 1823.[66] It had 60 pupils in 1851 and was supported by Anna Maria Cludde.[67] It was held in an old cottage until temporarily accommodated in the boys' school in 1852.[68] The following year a new St. Peter's Girls' School (with 100 places in schoolroom and classroom) and a new teacher's house were built opposite the church at Miss Cludde's expense. She, from 1854 as Mrs. R. C. Herbert (d. 1906), and her mother (d. 1859) were managers and they defrayed the school's expenses, amounting in 1853 to £45 including the mistress's salary of £35.[69] In 1885 an infant department (60 places) was added but by 1900 girls' and infant departments had amalgamated. Attendance averaged 89 in 1891 and 97 in 1913.[70] From 1931 girls aged 12–14 attended Wellington cookery centre.[71] There were 90 places and 73 pupils (including 14 infant boys) in 1935.[72] Smethwick evacuees attended 1939–44.[73] In 1940 it became a junior mixed and infant school with 93 pupils: seniors transferred to Wellington Senior Council School and boys came from the closed C.E. Boys' School.[74] The school became controlled in 1949

[41] *Salop. Arch. Soc. News Bull.* xvi. 4–7; Bodl. MS. Top. Salop . c.2, f. 571.
[42] S.P.L., MS. 3397, nos. 6–8, 29; S.R.O. 4472/Par/14 (Jan. 1931).
[43] S.P.L., MS. 6767, no. 32.
[44] Marshall, *St. Peter's Ch.*; S.R.O. 4472/CW/2, s.a. 1750.
[45] S.R.O. 4472/Rg/1 sqq.; *S.P.R. Lich.* viii (1).
[46] Lich. Dioc. Regy., bps.' reg. Q, pp. 687 sqq.
[47] *T.S.A.S.* 2nd ser. i. 83; L.J.R.O., B/A/12(i), f. 94.
[48] L.J.R.O., B/V/5, visit. return of 1772.
[49] S.R.O. 3916/1, p. 25.
[50] P.R.O., RG 31/7, Salop. no. 365; *Orders of Q. Sess.* iii. 209.
[51] Lich. Dioc. Regy., bps.' reg. G, p. 340; P.R.O., RG 31/2, Lich. no. 992.
[52] Shrews. Sch. libr., Broseley circuit bk. 1815–41.
[53] S.R.O. 3605/1, p. 37.
[54] G.R.O., Worship reg. nos. 14862, 22814; *Return of Churches, 1882,* H.C. 401, p. 366 (1882), l; SA 14436.
[55] G.R.O., Worship reg. nos. 21324, 22435; *Return of Accom. Provided in Wesleyan Meth. Chapels, 1901* (Wesleyan Conference Office, 1902), 49; *Meth. Church Bldgs.: Statistical Returns* (1940), 270; SA 14403.
[56] Inf. from Mr. J. H. Lenton.
[57] Above, Church.
[58] L.J.R.O., B/V/1/77, f. 8v.; /1/80, f. 9v.; /1/81.
[59] L.J.R.O., B/A/4/13, 7 May 1702.
[60] Trinder and Cox, *Yeomen and Colliers,* pp. 43–4, 409, 426–7, 443.
[61] S.R.O. 3916/1/1 p. 25, which does not indicate whether either sch. was in Wrockwardine Wood.
[62] *Digest Educ. Poor,* H.C. 224, p. 764 (1819), ix (2).
[63] Marshall, *St. Peter's Ch.,* intro. by the Revd. A. A. Turreff (1937).
[64] S.R.O. 4472/Sch/1/1–29, 37. The schs. were not National Schs. though called so in *Kelly's Dir. Salop* (1885), 999; (1900), 295.
[65] S.R.O. 4472/Sch/1/1–106; /2/1–16.
[66] S.R.O. 3916/1/4.
[67] S. Bagshaw, *Dir. Salop.* (1851), 444.
[68] *Mins. of Educ. Cttee. of Council, 1851–2,* ii [1480], p. 419, H.C. (1852), xl.
[69] P.R.O., ED 7/103, f. 255; *T.S.A.S.* 4th ser. viii. 195–6.
[70] *Kelly's Dir. Salop.* (1885), 999; (1891), 485; (1900), 295; (1913), 318.
[71] Log bk. (at the sch.) 9 Jan. 1931.
[72] Ibid. 7 Jan. 1935.
[73] e.g. ibid. 12 Sept., 7 Dec. 1939; Wrockwardine C.E. Jnr. Mixed and Inf. Sch. log bk. (at the sch.) 1 Aug. 1941; 13 Mar. 1942; 17 Sept. 1944.
[74] Log bk. 1 and 5 Apr. 1940.

and was immediately improved. In 1950 there were 115 pupils in three classes.[75] Numbers were higher in the 1970s[76] owing to housing development at Admaston, and by 1981 two demountable classrooms had been added and the teacher's house was being used as an extension; by then, however, there were only 114 pupils.[77]

Wrockwardine Boys' School, with 103 places, was built in 1837 at Mrs. Edward Cludde's expense;[78] her husband provided the site.[79] Income in 1848 consisted of £32 17s. 6d. in subscriptions and collections, £24 11s. in fees. Mrs. Cludde supported the school generously; the master, whose salary was then £45, had a cottage of hers rent-free.[80] By 1856 a teacher's house had been built.[81] In 1878 the efficient master was well paid for his school of 65 pupils: he received £75 a year, the government grant, and a third of the school pence.[82] There were 75 pupils in 1851 and attendance averaged 78 in 1891 and 63 in 1913.[83] A twice weekly night school in 1877 had ten pupils.[84] The school closed in 1940, seniors transferring to Wellington Senior Council School and juniors to the former girls' and infant school.[85]

In the 1850s there were three boarding schools: a boys' school at Admaston (still open in 1879) and girls' schools at Admaston and Wrockwardine.[86] In 1870 there was a private girls' school at Allscott[87] and in 1885 another at Admaston.[88] From 1891 to c. 1905 the Colonial Training Home for Girls at Leaton Grange prepared destitute girls for domestic service in the colonies.[89] The Royal National Institute for the Blind ran a Sunshine Home for retarded blind babies at Overley Hall from 1950 to 1980.[90] In 1981 Overley Hall School opened as a private boarding school for mentally and physically handicapped pupils aged 5–19 years.[91]

CHARITIES FOR THE POOR. Various benefactions made between 1616 and 1657 totalling £60 were used to buy a field called Tiddicross, of which the rent was distributed annually. Edward Pemberton improved the land's value in 1670 by building a house and barn on it. The parish workhouse was built on the site c. 1801 but the rent of £4 10s. was not increased; it was paid out annually as the Tiddicross charity from the poor rate. In 1830 the charity's income was raised to £8,

closer to a realistic rent.[92] In 1907 it was £35 a year, from the four cottages[93] to which the old workhouse had been converted.[94]

By her will of 1675 Margaret Langley of Burcot left £10. It was probably the bequest that was being honoured in 1821 by Edward Cludde and Mr. Stainer, who had charges of 10s. a year on their estates. Cludde's 10s. provided two bushels of flour distributed annually; Stainer's, with an additional 10s. from the sacrament money, provided bread given with the flour. Usually c. 80 people, widows receiving preference, benefited.[95] In 1897 the charity's income was £2 10s. distributed as a hundred 6d. loaves.[96]

A £3 rent charge was left by Edward Pemberton (d. 1680) for apprenticing one child a year. Between 1804 and 1821 it paid for nine apprentices. In 1897 the income, £4 4s. 4d. from stock, was paid to the girls' school. Under a scheme of 1922 the charity was widened to include general assistance to young and other poor persons.[97]

Thomas Ore (d. 1798) left a 40s. rent charge. The vicar was to have £1 1s. and the parish clerk 1s. for administering it. By 1821, and still in 1897, it was given to the same sixteen recipients each year.[98]

Joshua Gilpin, vicar (d. 1828), left the interest on £50 to be divided equally between eight of the poorest families. Until her death in 1856 Gilpin's widow personally supervised the distribution. In the later 19th century beneficiaries received between 3s. 9d. and 4s. 6d.[99]

A charitable clothing club, founded by donations and subscriptions, was established in 1832. Members of the society, numbering 57 in 1853 and 68 in 1875, paid in small sums over the year. To their savings a sum from the charity's capital was added, the whole being paid out in tickets redeemable by a Wellington tailor.[1]

Sir W. S. R. Cockburn (d. 1858)[2] left a cottage and garden at Rushmoor. It was sold for £70, to which £20 was added by G. L. Yate, vicar 1828–73, and £2 by Mrs. R. C. Herbert. In 1895 the charity's income was £2 17s.; 10s. was given to each of the two occupants of Cludde's almshouses and the remainder distributed to twelve poor people.[3]

Under schemes of 1922 Cludde's, Cockburn's, and the clothing charities were combined in one group, Pemberton's, Ore's, Gilpin's, and the

[75] Ibid. rep. 1950.
[76] S.C.C. Educ. Cttee. *Sch. List* (1979), 8 (134 pupils).
[77] Inf. from the headmaster; S.C.C. Educ. Cttee. *Educ. Dir.* (1981), 8.   [78] *Kelly's Dir. Salop.* (1891), 485.
[79] Plaque in Wrockwardine P.O. (the former sch.).
[80] P.R.O., ED 7/103, f. 255.
[81] *P.O. Dir. Salop.* (1856), 153.
[82] S.R.O. 4472/Sch/1/5, 55; /2/7–8.
[83] S. Bagshaw, *Dir. Salop.*p (1851), 444; *Kelly's Dir. Salop.* (1891), 485; (1913), 310.   [84] S.R.O. 4472/Sch/1/3.
[85] Wrockwardine C.E. Jnr. Mixed and Inf. Sch. log bk. 1 Apr. 1940.
[86] S. Bagshaw, *Dir. Salop.* (1851), 445; *P.O. Dir. Salop* (1856), 154; (1879), 450; [J. Randall], *Randall's Tourist's Guide to Wenlock* ([Madeley] 1875), advt.
[87] *P.O. Dir. Salop.* (1870), 180, 258.
[88] *Kelly's Dir. Salop.* (1885), 999.
[89] Ibid. (1900), 295; (1905), 306; advt. in *Penny Illustr. Paper*, 1891 (copy in S.P.L., class L 33.7 v.f.).

[90] Inf. from R.N.I.B.
[91] Inf. from Mr. and Mrs. P. Brown, sch. principals.
[92] *5th Rep. Com. Char.* H.C. 159, pp. 371–2 (1821), xii; *T.S.A.S.* 4th ser. viii. 206–8; above, Local Govt. and Public Services.
[93] S.R.O. 4472/Cy/7/4.
[94] The bldg. (at O.S. Nat. Grid SJ 613 119) still stood in 1982.
[95] *5th Rep. Com. Char.* 371; S.R.O. 999/Pp (2) 1.
[96] S.R.O. 4472/Cy/1/4.
[97] Ibid.; *5th Rep. Com. Char.* 371; *T.S.A.S.* 4th ser. ix. 90–1; *Review of Local Chars.* (S.C.C. 1975), 69.
[98] *5th Rep. Com. Char.* 372; S.R.O. 4472/Cy/1/4; /Cy/8/1; /Rg/3, s.a. 1798.
[99] Above, Church; *5th Rep. Com. Char.* 372; S.R.O. 4472/Cy/4/5, esp. p. 1.
[1] S.R.O. 4472/Cy/2/1–2.
[2] Burke, *Peerage* (1949), 442.
[3] S.R.O. 4472/Cy/1/7–8.

bread charity in another. The combined annual income of the two groups and of the Tiddicross charity was £55 in 1975.[4]

A pair of almshouses was erected in Wrockwardine village in 1841 as a memorial to Edward Cludde (d. 1840) of Orleton. The houses were designed by Edward Haycock, built by Thomas Smith of Madeley, and paid for by subscriptions.[5] Two widows were housed, and in 1895 £10 8s. from stock was distributed between them.[6] From c. 1980 the almshouses were occupied by married couples.[7]

WROCKWARDINE WOOD

WROCKWARDINE Wood, north-east of Oakengates town centre, was originally a detached piece of woodland, later a township, belonging to the manor and parish of Wrockwardine, the rest of which lay 7 km. to the west. The township, the area here treated, contained 515 a. in 1882.[8] Its eastern and western boundaries followed no natural features or roads for any significant distance. On the south it was bounded by Watling Street. The northern boundary was that part of the ancient Wellington–Newport road known by 1288 as Trench Way (later Trench Road),[9] a name suggesting that the wood was cleared back from it in the early Middle Ages.[10] From Watling Street the ground falls sharply, giving extensive views north across the township. In 1884 the township became a civil parish and was enlarged to 914 a. by the transfer of Hortonwood and part of Trench from the parish of Eyton upon the Weald Moors, and of an adjoining detachment from Preston upon the Weald Moors.[11] In 1898 the civil parish was included in the new urban district of Oakengates.[12] Wrockwardine Wood was included within the designated area of Telford new town in 1968.[13]

The Middle Coal Measures, lying close to the surface across most of the southern half of the township, were intensively mined from the 17th to the 19th century. Across the lower, northern half of the township boulder clay and small outcrops of sandstone from the Hadley and Coalport formations occur. Some sand and gravel lies along Trench Road.[14]

There was little settlement in the township in the Middle Ages. Part of the settlement at Quam Pool apparently lay in Wrockwardine Wood, and Quam Pool township made presentments at Wrockwardine manor courts between 1397 and 1457.[15] A moat in the north part of the township probably marked the site of the farm or lodge of a medieval assart.[16] By the mid 17th century there were settlements along the roads bounding the township to north and south. The development of coal and ironstone mining in the 18th and 19th centuries may have accounted for the scatters of squatters' cottages south-west of Cockshutt Piece and north-east of Ball's coppice. In the earlier 19th century there was some building in the north part of the township around the glassworks and the new church. In the later 19th century, however, much more extensive building began to cover the centre and south part of the township with new streets and works. Much of the north remained undeveloped until the 20th century when new estates were built there by the Oakengates urban district council and, from the 1960s, speculative builders and Wrekin district council.

In 1650 there were 12 cottagers at Pain's Lane on Watling Street. In 1836 the place was said to have risen in eminence; there were then 33 householders in that part of Wrockwardine Wood.[17] Even in 1847, however, Pain's Lane remained a crossroads settlement and the laying out of new streets there began only in the 1850s when terraces were built in various styles, largely for workers at the Lilleshall Co.'s Priorslee blast furnaces and, from 1861, at the New Yard. Many of the terraces in Granville Street, and particularly in Church Street were relatively spacious and well built, and in New Street small groups of houses have the style of a freehold land society estate. More cramped terraces were erected east of the Priorslee–Donnington road north of Granville Street. Albion Street was developed from the 1860s, when Pain's Lane began to be known as St. George's.[18]

Trench, like Pain's Lane, was only partly in Wrockwardine Wood. Settlement probably began in the mid 17th century. It remained a straggling roadside settlement, although considerable infilling and linear expansion occurred in the 19th century, when Trench became one of the few villages in the east Shropshire coalfield to have any concentration of shops and public houses. The public houses had apparently been an integral part of the settlement from the start.[19]

[4] Review of Local Chars. 69.

[5] T.S.A.S. 4th ser. viii. 206; S.R.O. 4472/Cy/3/2; above, plate 54.

[6] S.R.O. 4472/Cy/1/7–8.

[7] Inf. from Revd. Preb. W. S. Frost.

[8] O.S. Area Bk. Wrockwardine (1882). This art. was written 1982.

[9] S.P.L., MS. 110, Wrockwardine jury presentment, 11 Oct. 1650, p. 14.

[10] Above, Eyton; Lilleshall; O. Rackham, Ancient Woodland (1980), 155; inf. from Dr. M. Gelling.

[11] 14th Ann. Rep. Local Govt. Bd. [C. 4515], pp. xlvii, 191, 204, H.C. (1884–5), xxxii; V.C.H. Salop. ii. 229; Kelly's Dir. Salop. (1900), 296.

[12] J. E. G. Cartlidge, The Vale and Gates of Usc-con (Congleton, [1935]), 111.

[13] Dawley New Town (Designation) Amendment (Telford) Order 1968 (Stat. Instr. 1968, no. 1912), map accompanying Explanatory Note.

[14] Inst. Geol. Sciences Map 1/25,000, Telford (1978 edn.).

[15] Above, Lilleshall, Growth of Settlement; S.P.L., Deeds 19394–7.

[16] SA 2848.

[17] S.P.L., MS. 110, Wrockwardine jury presentment, 11 Oct. 1650, p. 15; C. Hulbert, Hist. and Descr. of Salop. ii (1837), 173; S.R.O. 1011/231; Trinder, Ind. Rev. Salop. (1981), 195.

[18] Trinder, op. cit. 195–6; analyses of 1851 and 1861 censuses in possession of Dr. B. S. Trinder; O.S. Maps 1/2,500, Salop. XXXVI. 11, 15 (1882 edn.); above, Lilleshall, Churches.

[19] Above, Eyton; Trinder, op. cit. 198; S.R.O., q. sess. rec. parcels 255–7, regs. of alesellers' recognizances 1753–1801; S. Bagshaw, Dir. Salop. (1851), 448.

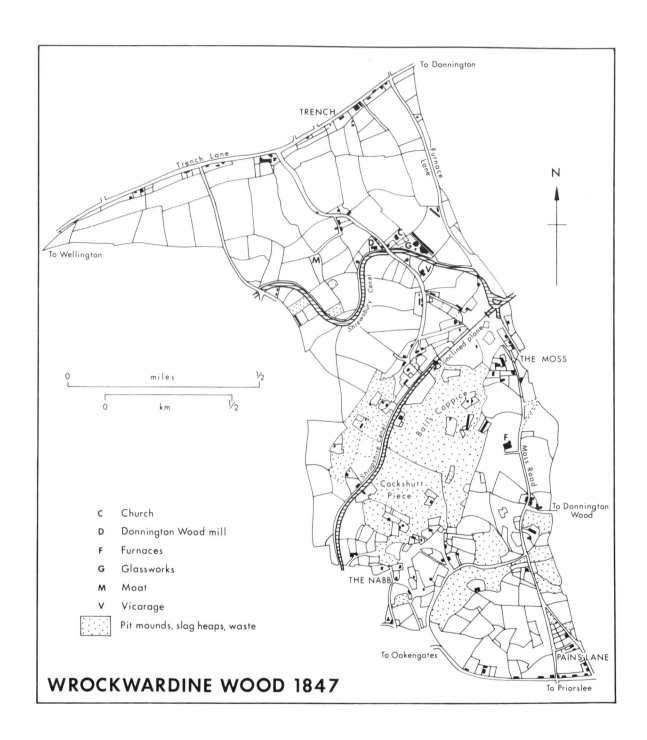

To Donnington

TRENCH

Trench Lane

Furnace Lane

To Wellington

N

C
D
G
M
V

Shrewsbury Canal

Inclined plane

THE MOSS

Ball's Coppice

miles
0   ½

km
0   ½

Shropshire Canal

F

Moss Road

Cockshutt Piece

To Donnington Wood

C   Church
D   Donnington Wood mill
F   Furnaces
G   Glassworks
M   Moat
V   Vicarage
         Pit mounds, slag heaps, waste

THE NABB

To Oakengates

PAINS LANE

WROCKWARDINE WOOD 1847

To Priorslee

Two sprawling industrial settlements developed either side of Cockshutt Piece, apparently in the 18th century. At the Nabb scattered squatters' cottages were erected, to which some terraces, like Diamond Row, were added in the 19th century. At the Moss and around the church, there were, as well as squatter properties, some single-storeyed terraces, like Moss barracks, and some terraces of c. 1800, like Glasshouse Row.

Other early 19th-century terraces, like Bonser's Row and Bunter's Row, some of them speculatively built, were scattered elsewhere in the township south of the Wombridge Canal.[20] As elsewhere in the coalfield housing demand occasionally caused the conversion of industrial buildings to tenements. Wrockwardine Wood furnaces closed in the 1820s and were later made into 16 dwellings, and the glassworks into 10 dwellings in 1856.[21] Until the growth of St. George's in the 1850s there were few good quality artisans' dwellings in Wrockwardine Wood; most buildings were small and poorly constructed. They were, however, usually well spaced, and there were no concentrations of barrack dwellings similar to those in Donnington Wood.[22]

Lincoln Road and New Road, like St. George's, were laid out in the third quarter of the 19th century, short terraces again being the dominant form of housing.

After the First World War Oakengates urban district council built housing in the north-east corner of the township, the inner part of Woodhouse Crescent being finished in 1922.[23] Council houses were built in Gower Street to accommodate families cleared from slums under the 1930 Housing Act.[24] By 1946 the remainder of the Woodhouse Crescent estate was built, with the neighbouring Gibbons Road estate being added in the mid 1950s.[25] In the 1970s and early 1980s over 200 council dwellings were built at the south end of Moss Road and near St. George's in New Street and Gower Street.[26] Speculative building of the 1960s or early 1970s filled the area south of Trench Road around Teague's Bridge Lane. By 1973 a large area between Albion Street and the Nabb had been scheduled for private housing,[27] and building was in progress there in 1982.

In 1650, as well as 16 tenants occupying 14 holdings in the township, there were 35 cottagers, 12 of them at Pain's Lane. Sixteen householders paid hearth tax in 1672.[28] By 1817 the township had 1,938 inhabitants; 703 of them were receiving poor relief.[29] By 1841 population had fallen to 1,698, but it had risen to 2,099 by 1851, and in 1861 the figure was 3,317, an increase of 58 per cent over the decade. By 1871 it was 3,794, and over the next forty years population grew, though more slowly, to a peak of 5,276 in 1911. Thereafter it fell[30] perhaps for fifty years.[31] Between 1851 and 1861 the number of miners increased from 309 to 476, and that of ironworkers and engineers from 84 to 486. The number of pit bank girls rose too, from 63 to 128. Many of the new workers were immigrants from the more rural parts of the county: 90 per cent of the township's population was native to the coalfield in 1851, only 64 per cent in 1871.[32]

From the growth of mining and industry in the 17th century until the building of council and private housing estates in the 1960s and 1970s most of the township's inhabitants were employed in the local coal, iron, and steel works. The changing methods or fortunes of those industries directly affected the employees. In 1791 the introduction of a new system of regulating wages and hours by the Coalbrookdale partners led to riots at Coalpit Bank and Wrockwardine Wood. In 1816–17, during the post-war depression, 36 per cent of the inhabitants received poor relief,[33] and in 1931 the old-fashioned New Yard works closed with the loss of 1,000 jobs.[34]

Apart from Watling Street and Trench Road, turnpiked in 1726 and 1763,[35] and probably what were known by the 19th century as Teague's Bridge Lane, Church Road, and Furnace Lane, all roads in the township seem to be later than the 17th-century expansion of mining.

The Wombridge Canal, probably completed in 1788, and the Shropshire Canal, completed c. 1793, crossed Wrockwardine Wood and met on its eastern boundary. About 1794 the Wombridge Canal was linked to the new Shrewsbury Canal. An inclined plane on the Shropshire Canal rose 122 ft. in 320 yd. from the junction to a summit level on Cockshutt Piece. The Shropshire Canal closed in 1857, the Shrewsbury c. 1921.[36] An underground level, perhaps navigable, ran between Donnington Wood furnaces and the area north-west of the Nabb by c. 1800.[37]

There were horse-drawn railways in the township in the mid 19th century. The Coalbrookdale partners were authorized to build one c. 1758, just west of what became Furnace Lane.[38] Others ran towards Donnington Wood furnaces

[20] Trinder, op. cit. 195–6; analyses of 1841–71 censuses in possession of Dr. Trinder.

[21] Above, Dawley, Growth of Settlement; W. K. V. Gale and C. R. Nicholls, The Lilleshall Co. Ltd.: a Hist. 1764–1964 (1979), 53.

[22] Above, Lilleshall, Growth of Settlement; I.G.M.T., Lilleshall Co. colln. 846.

[23] W. Howard Williams, A Brief Hist. of Wrockwardine Wood Church and Parish (1974), 25.

[24] Cartlidge, Usc-con, 112; S.R.O., DA 12/100/19–21, Ho. Cttee. mins. 30 May, 25 July, 10 Oct., 7 Nov., 5 Dec. 1934; 25 May, 11 Sept., 4 Dec. 1935; 16 June 1936.

[25] O.S. Map 1", sheet 119 (1946 edn.); Reg. of Electors, Wrekin Constituency, Mar. 1954, p. 105; Feb. 1958, p. 97.

[26] Wrekin District Council, Tech. Resources file H.8/1 (1974–83) and completion bks.

[27] S.R.O., DA 12/134, T.D.C., St. Geo.'s local plan, 1973; S.C.C. Mins. (Educ.) 1972–3, 251.

[28] S.P.L., MS. 110, Wrockwardine jury presentment, 11 Oct. 1650, p. 15; Hearth Tax 1672 (Salop. Arch. Soc.), 98.

[29] Trinder, Ind. Rev. Salop. (1981), 137.

[30] V.C.H. Salop. ii. 229.

[31] Above, Wombridge, Growth of Settlement.

[32] Trinder, Ind. Rev. Salop. (1981), 195–6.

[33] Ibid. 137, 229.

[34] Gale and Nicholls, Lilleshall Co. 89; cf. V.C.H. Salop. ii. 229. [35] 12 Geo. I, c. 9; 3 Geo. III, c. 59.

[36] C. Hadfield, Canals of W. Midlands (1969), 40, 151, 251, 328–9; I.G.M.T., Lilleshall Co. colln. 106, 110; Trinder, Ind. Rev. Salop. (1981), 76, 84–5, 153.

[37] S.R.O. 691/1; Salop. News Sheet, xvii. 7–8.

[38] S.R.O. 1270/1.

from the township's western boundary[39] and from east of the Nabb.[40] In 1851 the Lilleshall Co. began to replace the old railways with a private standard-gauge network, which linked most of the company's interests by 1855. The network reached its peak during the First World War when 26 miles of track carried 1½ million tons of goods a year. It linked with the G.W.R. line at Oakengates and the L.N.W.R. line at Donnington. The system closed in 1959.[41]

Until the later 19th century social life apparently centred on alehouse and chapel. About 1650 nine people were presented for selling ale in Wrockwardine Wood.[42] In the mid 18th century up to seven alehouse keepers were licensed in Trench, a settlement only partly in the township, and up to five in the rest of the township.[43] There were eight public houses and seven beer sellers in 1856. By the later 19th century there were up to 14 beer sellers but the number of public houses had remained fairly constant.[44]

Cockpit yard at the Moss was mentioned in 1802.[45]

The Gentleman's Club of Pain's Lane, begun for senior Lilleshall Co. employees in 1812, met monthly on Saturday evenings in the Shaw Birch or the King's Arms public houses, Trench Lane. Sick benefit and death grants were withheld from those afflicted as a result of fighting, drunkenness, or venereal disease.[46] In 1840 a friendly society began to meet at the White Horse inn.[47] In 1843 there was a school clothing society and a missionary society, in 1844 a general clothing society.[48] In 1871–2 there were two lodges of Odd Fellows (Manchester Unity) in Trench: 'Miners' Glory' with 21 members, 'Marquis of Stafford' with 270.[49] Several friendly societies existed in 1904.[50]

Much of the local welfare provision was by the Lilleshall Co. for its employees. A soup kitchen, opened in 1878, excluded Lilleshall Co. employees as they were fed by the company at the New Yard.[51] A dining room provided in 1900 for workers at the New Yard was available after work for 'socials'. About the same time the company bought the Bird in Hand public house at the Nabb 'to safeguard the workers' beer'.[52]

In 1875 a reading room and library opened in Matthews Buildings under the auspices of the rector and others.[53] There was a Wrockwardine Wood Liberal Association in 1885, a Liberal and Labour Club in 1917.[54]

Wrockwardine Wood was said to have had one of the earliest professional football clubs in the country, playing first on Wade's field (later Wade Road) and later on the White Horse field, where by 1974 there was a licensed clubhouse. Trench Athletic also enjoyed considerable success in the early 20th century, playing on the Shawbirch field, at times against teams like Aston Villa reserves.[55] Wrockwardine Wood Bowling Club was formed in 1922 with a green on the White Horse field. The Nabb Bowling Club was formed in the same year, when part of an old pit mound was levelled and grassed.[56] The Trench and District Electric Theatre was open in 1917, in the building known as Trench Billiard Hall in 1937 and 1941.[57] The Regent cinema, Wrockwardine Wood, popularly known as the 'Ranch House', opened in 1946 and closed c. 1958.[58] With the designation of Telford new town in 1968 and the subsequent housing developments within the parish the range of social facilities increased. In 1982 Trench Road community centre, the Oakengates Leisure Centre (opened 1974), and a social centre for the unemployed were in use, and schools' facilities were increasingly available for public use out of school hours.[59]

MANOR. Wrockwardine Wood originally formed part of Wrockwardine manor[60] but the lord of the manor's mineral rights in the township were gradually separated from the other manorial rights. Sir George Saville began the process in 1660 by conveying his mining rights five years before he sold his third interest in the rest of the manor. Most of the rights formerly Saville's were owned by the Charltons of Apley from 1673. In 1813 and 1822 respectively Lord Berwick and the earl of Shrewsbury retained the mining rights when they sold their third shares of Wrockwardine manor. In 1822 Berwick sold his mines in Wrockwardine Wood to Viscount Granville (cr. Earl Granville 1833); he evidently still owned them in 1839[61] but by 1851 they were said to be the duke of Sutherland's property.[62] The dukes of Sutherland and the earls of Shrewsbury were said to own the manorial rights in the township in the early 20th century, the collieries being principally the dukes' property.[63]

[39] S.R.O., dep. plan 289a; S.R.O. 691/1.

[40] I.G.M.T., Lilleshall Co. colln. 228, 235; Williams, *Wrockwardine Wood*, 10.

[41] Gale and Nicholls, *Lilleshall Co.* 76.

[42] S.P.L., MS. 110, Wrockwardine Wood jury presentment, c. 1650.

[43] S.R.O., q. sess. rec. parcel 254, badgers', drovers', and alesellers' licensing bk. 1613–1714; 255, reg. of alesellers' recognizances, 1753–69.

[44] P.O. Dir. Salop. (1856), 154; Kelly's Dir. Salop. (1885), 1000; (1917), 303.

[45] I.G.M.T., Lilleshall Co. colln., 182.

[46] Ibid., Pain's Lane Gentleman's Club rule bk. [? 1818]; Gale and Nicholls, *Lilleshall Co.* 38.

[47] S.R.O., q. sess. rec. parcel 285, friendly socs. reg.

[48] S.R.O. 673/1/16, 20 Nov. 1843; 20 Nov. 1844.

[49] Rep. Registrar Friendly Socs. 1871, H.C. 394, p. 108 (1872), liv; 1872, H.C. 323, pp. 133–4 (1873), lxi.

[50] 'The Advertiser' Almanack and Dir (Shifnal and Oakengates edn. 1904; copy in S.P.L.).

[51] I. Gregory, 'E. Salop. Coalfield and the "Gt. Depression" 1873–96' (Keele Univ. M.A. thesis, 1978), 170.

[52] Gale and Nicholls, *Lilleshall Co.* 74.

[53] Wellington Jnl. 16 Jan. 1875; S.R.O. 1604/19, p. 23.

[54] Kelly's Dir. Salop. (1885), 1000; (1917), 303.

[55] Williams, *Wrockwardine Wood*, 25; V.C.H. Salop. ii. 200.

[56] Williams, op. cit. 25.

[57] Kelly's Dir. Salop. (1917), 303; (1937), 323; (1941), 320; SA 15909; F. J. Brown, 'Cinemas of Telford 1910–83' (TS. in possession of Mr. Brown), 3.

[58] S.R.O., DA 34 (S.R.O. 3279/I), Town Hall (Wellington) file, memo. 20 Sept. 1958; Brown, op. cit. 9.

[59] Shropshire Star, 29 June 1974.   [60] Above.

[61] Above, Wrockwardine, Man. and Other Est.; Staffs. R.O., D. 593/B/2/5/18, deeds of 1839 (copies); S.R.O. 1634 (uncat.), deed of 1 May 1824.

[62] S. Bagshaw, Dir. Salop. (1851), 447.

[63] Kelly's Dir. Salop. (1900), 296; (1941), 319.

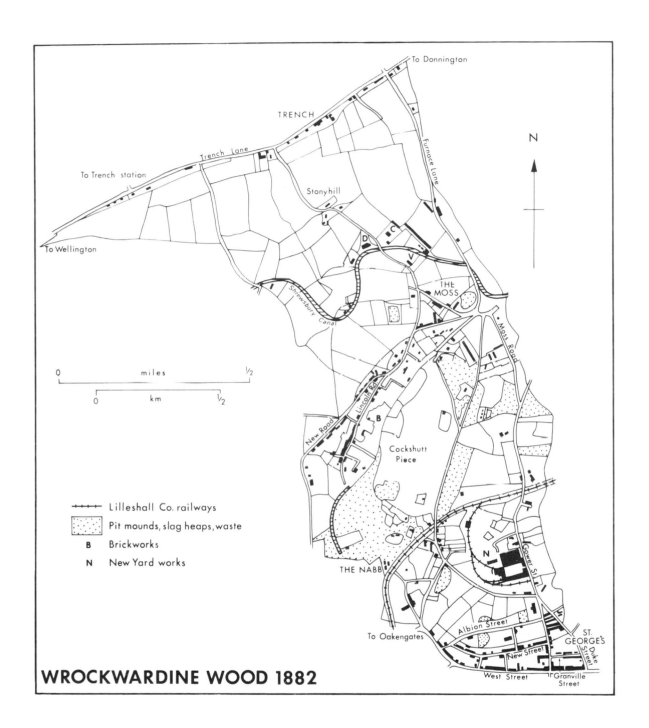

To Donnington

TRENCH

Trench Lane

To Trench station

Furnace Lane

Stonyhill

To Wellington

N

C

D

V

THE
MOSS

Shrewsbury Canal

Moss Road

| 0 | miles | 1/2 |
| 0 | km | 1/2 |

New Road

Lincoln Rd

B

Cockshutt
Piece

Lilleshall Co. railways

Pit mounds, slag heaps, waste

B   Brickworks

N   New Yard works

N

Gower St.

THE NABB

To Oakengates

Albion Street

ST.
GEORGE'S

New Street

Duke Street

West Street

Granville
Street

WROCKWARDINE WOOD 1882

ECONOMIC HISTORY. Wrockwardine Wood was probably identical with the woodland 1 league long and ½ league broad recorded in Domesday.[64] Referred to as the king's wood c. 1130, it was claimed in 1235 to be well stocked with oaks and underwood.[65] It was within the royal forest of Mount Gilbert or the Wrekin. By c. 1290 assarting had begun, and it may have increased following disafforestation in 1301.[66] Pigs were pastured in 'Kingshay' in 1397–8 and 1413–14.[67] The area was still known as King's wood c. 1577.[68] Much of the surviving woodland was probably cleared in the century after 1650 as mining expanded. A great deal of timber was sold to the Coalbrookdale Co. for the building of the Horsehay ironworks in 1754.[69] The woodland then remaining, at the Nabb and on Cockshutt Piece, was coppiced[70] but by 1847 virtually no woodland remained. In the later 19th century, with the decline of mining, woodland began to reappear on Cockshutt Piece, which was partly wooded in 1982.[71]

In 1650 almost 38 per cent of the township was let to 16 tenants in 14 holdings; three were of 60 a., 50 a., and 30 a., the rest varying between 14 a. and 4 a. Thirty-two cottages (three of them divided) were occupied by 35 cottagers, 12 of them at Pain's Lane. By the early 18th century smallholdings probably occupied most of the northern half of the township. Yeomen, colliers, and labourers all engaged in mixed farming, and there was also some small-scale textile production.[72] In 1847 about half the land north of the Shropshire Canal was under arable cultivation, while some pasture and meadow lay at either end of the township.[73] Agricultural land shrank as housing expanded in the 1860s and 1870s. In 1891, however, c. 240 a. remained under arable cultivation with a further 330 a. under grass.[74] After the First World War house building south of Trench Road further reduced those totals, and building by the district council and private developers in the 1970s took most of the remaining agricultural land.

MILL. Between 1818 and 1821 a partnership was formed to mill, bake, and deal in grain, and a four-storeyed brick steam mill was built in 1818 on the north bank of the Shrewsbury Canal. The mill, generally known as Donnington Wood mill, closed in the 1970s.[75]

COAL AND IRONSTONE. The township's mineral resources were exploited in the Middle Ages; an iron ore mine was noted in 1324. Regular extraction, however, probably began in the early 17th century.[76] In 1650 a coal delf was noted;[77] it was probably an opencast mine extracting coal, and almost certainly ironstone too, from the Middle Coal Measures that lay near the surface over most of the southern half of the township.[78] In 1767 the traveller Joseph Banks described a pit in the Wrockwardine Wood area where there were three layers of ironstone between the coal beds. Uppermost were smooth ironstone balls about the size of potatoes, next a regular stratum of stone, and below that large lumps of ironstone weighing up to ½ cwt. set in blue clay or shale known as 'crows' or 'hatter's blocks'.[79]

Sir George Saville, one of the lords of Wrockwardine manor, sold his third interest in the Wrockwardine Wood mines to Francis Butler in 1660. At the same time he sold his interest in various holdings in Wrockwardine and Wrockwardine Wood to the ground tenants, omitting to reserve the mineral rights. Ownership of the rights was at once disputed and similar problems arose several times over the next two centuries.[80] In 1673 Butler sold his third interest in the mines to Francis Charlton, who leased the adjoining Lilleshall mining rights next year.[81] The Charlton mines were leased to, or operated by, the Pitts family, whose rights were challenged in 1696 when several independent charter masters began mining.[82]

Underground mining probably began about then. Lord Gower's agent William Cartwright had apparently worked the mines on his own account after Francis Charlton's extraction of most of the easily available surface coal, and in 1699 he reported that he had found a potentially good mine 22 yards deep.[83] The industry was still small in scale: Richard Vickers of Wrockwardine Wood (d. 1705) made part of his living carrying coal on two pack horses and part from working a smallholding.[84] In 1715, however, large stocks of coal lay unsold at Donnington Wood and Wrockwardine Wood.[85]

In 1731 Richard Hartshorne (d. 1733), the leading Shropshire coal entrepreneur, had a lease of the Charlton mining interests, and new pits were being sunk in Wrockwardine Wood. In 1736–7 the mines were let to Walter Stubbs of Beckbury. By then there were mines at the Nabb and the Moss; a third group, possibly distinct, was known as the 'little pits'.[86] By the 1750s colliers who had earlier worked farther south in

---

[64] V.C.H. Salop. i. 315. The township measured c. 1½ mile N.–S. by c. ½ mile E.–W., which accords with the Domesday fig.: Rackham, Ancient Woodland, 113, 115.

[65] B.L. Add. MS. 50121, p. 105; Eyton, ix. 145.

[66] V.C.H. Salop. i. 486; Cartulary of Shrews. Abbey, ed. U. Rees (1975), ii, p. 249; T.S.A.S. 4th ser. i. 211.

[67] S.P.L., Deeds 19394, 19396.

[68] C. Saxton, Map of Salop. (1577).

[69] Trinder, Ind. Rev. Salop. (1981), 22.

[70] Ibid. 31–2; S.R.O. 676/24; 4309, box 2, survey of 1724.

[71] L.J.R.O., B/A/15, Wrockwardine Wood; O.S. Map 1/2,500, Salop. XXXVI. 11 (1882 edn.).

[72] S.P.L., MS. 110, Wrockwardine jury presentment, 11 Oct. 1650, p. 15; Yeomen and Colliers in Telford, ed. B. Trinder and J. Cox (1980), p. 481, for index to Wrockwardine Wood inventories.

[73] L.J.R.O., B/A/15, Wrockwardine Wood.

[74] P.R.O., MAF 68/1340, no. 10.

[75] S.R.O. 1101/XXV/12; 2288/1–2.

[76] S.R.O. 999/Uu 4 (evid. of J. Mountford, J. ap Richard, R. Ward); T.S.A.S. 4th ser. i. 214; v. 282.

[77] S.P.L., MS. 110, Wrockwardine jury presentment, 11 Oct. 1650, p. 14.

[78] Inst. Geol. Sciences Map 1/25,000, Telford (1978 edn.).

[79] S. R. Broadridge, 'Jos. Banks and W. Midlands Ind.' Staffs. Industrial Arch. Jnl. ii. 6.

[80] S.P.L., MS. 4072, p. 651; T.S.A.S. 4th ser. v. 283–6.

[81] T.S.A.S. 4th ser. v. 282–7; above, Lilleshall, Econ. Hist. (Mines, Quarries, and Sandpits).

[82] S.R.O. 2842/1–2.

[83] Staffs. R.O., D. 593/P/13/3, Cartwright to Sir J. Leveson-Gower, 1 Aug. 1699.

[84] Trinder and Cox, Yeomen and Colliers, pp. 428–9.

[85] Staffs. R.O., D. 593/L/1/1.

[86] Trinder, Ind. Rev. Salop. (1981), 30–1; S.R.O. 676/24–5, 27.

the coalfield were finding employment in the Wrockwardine Wood mines.[87]

Extraction was stimulated by the expansion of Shropshire's coke-iron industry. In 1757 the township's mines began to supply ironstone to the Coalbrookdale partners' works at Coalbrookdale, Horsehay, and Ketley, and in the next three years it amounted to some 2,000, 5,000, and 4,300 dozens of 'black' and 'bald' ironstone. In 1761 Richard Reynolds of Ketley began to work the mines on the Charlton estate, including those in Wrockwardine Wood, on his own account. Thereafter most of the ore was sent to Ketley where Reynolds held larger interests than in the other works.[88]

Ironstone made greater profits than coal for landlord and tenant alike. In 1758–9 St. John Charlton received £232 as his share of the royalties: £199 for ironstone and £33 for coal.[89] In the years 1748–54 Earl Gower invested an average of £1,714 a year in mines in the township, averaging 14 per cent profit.[90] Between 30 and 100 dozens of ironstone a month were raised in 1764–5.[91] The Gower interest increased, the 2nd Earl Gower buying land in 1771. By 1780 ironstone production was running at nearly 300 dozens a month,[92] and in the 1780s Joseph Rathbone and Richard Reynolds's son William took an under-lease of ironstone mines from Earl Gower & Co., who between 1781 and 1783 had obtained the lease of all the township's minerals. Rathbone and Reynolds sent the ore to be smelted in their Donnington Wood furnaces, blown in in 1785.[93] During the 1780s ironstone production rose to over 400 dozens a month, and in 1782 a pumping engine was installed, probably at the Nabb.[94]

Between the mid 18th century and the mid 19th virtually all the land south of the Wombridge Canal was covered by mines, tips, and houses. There were steam-wound deep pits on Cockshutt Piece. Mining was almost monopolized by the Lilleshall Co.[95] On the disentanglement of the Reynolds interests from the Coalbrookdale partners' concerns the leased Wrockwardine Wood mines (and Donnington Wood ironworks) were given up and taken over by John Bishton the elder and his partners in 1797. Those interests of Bishton's were put into the Lilleshall Co. in 1802.[96] The Lilleshall Co. worked the minerals bought in 1822 by Lord Granville from Lord Berwick.[97]

Between 1805 and late 1807 approximately 400 dozens of ironstone a month were still being raised from the Wrockwardine Wood mines by about nine charter masters. Production fell to half that level by early 1810, to a quarter by mid 1812. In the summer of 1813 only 90–100 dozens monthly were produced by two or three charter masters. The decline heralded the general recession in the Shropshire iron trade after the boom it enjoyed during the early years of the Napoleonic wars.[98] In 1854 the Lilleshall Co. leased the right to mine coal between the two canals, except tops and clods, to John Bennett.[99] In 1865 his lease was extended to include the ironstone rights. In 1900 there was still some commercial mining in the parish, but it had ceased by 1908.[1]

IRON AND STEEL. In 1801 John Bishton, lessee of the Wrockwardine Wood mines and the Donnington Wood ironworks,[2] built two blast furnaces on the west side of what was later known as Moss Road. In 1802 he took them into the newly formed Lilleshall Co. The furnaces were closed down in 1826, about the time that the Donnington Wood Old Lodge furnaces were blown in.[3]

In 1861 the Lilleshall Co. began to build the Phoenix Foundry, an engineering works that replaced the Donnington Wood Old Yard works and soon became known as the New Yard.[4] Engineering rapidly became as important to the company as its coal, iron, and brick production, and it was well enough established by 1862 to allow the company to exhibit and win prizes at the London International Exhibition. From the start locomotives and blowing engines were manufactured, largely from the company's raw materials, and production in general was centred on the needs of the iron and coal industries. From c. 1870, after doing similar work on its own plants, the company began to modernize blast furnaces and construct new ones for other firms. Those, like most of the company's products, were for both the home and export markets.

In the early 20th century railway engine manufacture ceased, but large gas engines began to be produced to the Nürnberg design. German engineers in general played an important part in the company in the decade before the First World War. By 1904 at the works there were pattern shops, a foundry capable of making castings weighing up to 60 tons, a smithy with steam and pneumatic hammers, and machine, fitting, erecting, structural engineering, and boiler shops, all equipped with overhead electric travelling cranes. The entire plant was powered by its own generat-

[87] P.R.O., E 134/27 Geo. II Hil./8, m. 8.

[88] Trinder, op. cit. 33; S.R.O. 676/28.

[89] Trinder, op. cit. 33.

[90] J. R. Wordie, 'A Great Landed Estate in the 18th Cent.' (Reading Univ. Ph.D. thesis, 1967), 191.

[91] I.G.M.T., Lilleshall Co. colln. 941.

[92] Ibid.; Trinder, Ind. Rev. Salop. (1981), 28.

[93] I.G.M.T., Lilleshall Co. colln. 72–3, 76, 81; S.R.O., q. sess. rec. parcel 281, reg. of papist deeds 1717–88, f. 281v.; Staffs. R.O., D. 593/M/2/1/2; /I/1/22; above, Lilleshall, Econ. Hist. (Iron and Engineering).

[94] I.G.M.T., Lilleshall Co. colln. 114, 941; Trinder op. cit. 100.

[95] Trinder, op. cit. 197; Gale and Nicholls, Lilleshall Co. 29.

[96] Trinder, op. cit. 43, 45; Gale and Nicholls, op. cit. 26; Raistrick, Iron Founders, 216–18.

[97] Staffs. R.O., D. 593/B/2/5/18, deed of 19 Mar. 1839 (copy).

[98] I.G.M.T., Lilleshall Co. colln. 942; Trinder, op. cit. 137.

[99] I.G.M.T., Lilleshall Co. colln. 548, 612; S.R.O. 3882/1/46.

[1] S.R.O. 3882/1/46; Rep. Insp. Mines, Stafford Dist. (No. 9), 1908 [Cd. 4672–viii], H.C. (1909), xxxiii (no mention); I. J. Brown, Mines of Salop. (Buxton, 1976), 45.   [2] Above.

[3] Trinder, Ind. Rev. Salop. (1981), 45; Gale and Nicholls. Lilleshall Co. 26.

[4] Acct. of Lilleshall Co. based on Gale and Nicholls, op. cit.; see above, plate 10.

ing station. About 1912 the works reached a peak in the range of products manufactured and the number of workers employed (*c.* 4,000).

Munitions were produced during the First World War but thereafter a period of unprofitability began; the plant was old, and there were difficulties in getting, and then fulfilling, orders. The works closed in 1931. From 1937 the buildings began to be let out in sections to other companies, and it remained in multiple occupation in 1982.

CLAY INDUSTRIES. In 1764 Richard Jones, a Wellington brick and tile maker, took the lease of a clay mine in Brick Kiln field in order to make bricks and tiles. John Jones made 209,000 bricks in 1783 at the Moss, and by 1793 a group of kilns at the Nabb and the Moss was supplying the Donnington Wood industries.[5]

Bricks were probably produced in the township throughout the 19th century, the Lilleshall Co. owning a brickworks there by the 1850s. In 1882 a brickworks stood between Lincoln Road and Cockshutt Piece and there was also a kiln at the Nabb. The brickworks had apparently closed by 1902.[6]

GLASS. The establishment of a glassworks, often known as the Donnington Wood glassworks, on the north bank of the Wombridge Canal in Wrockwardine Wood[7] was one of the few attempts to expand the coalfield's range of industries.[8] Glass had been produced in the coalfield in the late 17th century but there is no evidence that its manufacture continued into the 18th century.

In 1792 William Reynolds, the Ketley ironmaster, and his brother Joseph agreed with William Phillips to construct a glassworks. In 1796 the glasshouse was being managed by Richard Mountford, and between 1800 and 1803 its ownership passed to a partnership of Mountford, William and Henry Cope, and John Biddle. All were connected with glasshouses in the Birmingham and Stourbridge areas. William Cope left the partnership in 1814[9] and the firm traded under the name of Biddle, Mountford, & Co. The glassworks, like the whole east Shropshire coalfield, was badly affected by the post-war depression and closed for a time in late 1816.[10] It closed finally in 1841, after Mountford's death, as a consequence of the Glass Duties Act, 1838.[11] Only eight glassworkers then lived in Wrockwardine Wood: six blowers, a packer, and a labourer.[12]

Production may have started before the end of 1792 when a circular glasshouse was shown on a map.[13] In 1794 Stourbridge clay was apparently used for crucibles, while refractory bricks came from Horsehay, and slag for the glass itself from the nearby Donnington Wood blast furnaces. In 1805 'black rock stone' was brought from Lord Craven's land in Little Dawley. By 1833 two English glass cones were operating, and there were two glasshouses at closure.[14] A cone illustrated on a bill of 1840 from Biddle, Mountford, & Co. may have been a standardized representation.[15] The principal products were crown glass and dark green bottles for the French wine trade. Some table ware was also manufactured as well as fancy goods such as rolling pins, walking sticks, and buttons. A 70-gallon bottle blown at the works was reputedly displayed at Reynolds's house.

In the 1790s a manager's house was built south of the canal. It later became the rectory. Glasshouse Row adjacent to the works was built *c.* 1800, perhaps by the owners to house the workforce. In 1856 the glass furnaces themselves were converted to working class housing known as Glassworks Square.[16]

LOCAL GOVERNMENT AND PUBLIC SERVICES. Wrockwardine Wood was part of the manor, and until 1884 the civil parish, of Wrockwardine. In spite of its isolation it seems to have been treated exactly as the other constituent townships, although special journeys had to be made to relieve the poor. The township, later parish, was in Wellington poor-law union 1836–1930.[17]

Wrockwardine Wood C.P. was formed in 1884, as part of Wellington rural sanitary district, becoming a ward of Oakengates urban district on its creation in 1898.[18] Wrockwardine Wood C.P. was abolished in 1934 when it became part of Oakengates C.P.[19]

The Granville hospital, Gower Street, was built for its employees by the Lilleshall Co. It opened in 1873 but by 1879 a smaller, eight-bed building in Albion Street had been provided. An ambulance service was added to the hospital's facilities in 1917.[20]

CHURCH. The inhabitants of Wrockwardine Wood appear at times to have used churches and chapels of ease nearer than the parish church 7 km. away.[21] In the early 19th century the success

[5] S.R.O. 303/71; Trinder, op. cit. 60.
[6] Gale and Nicholls, op. cit. 38; O.S. Map 1/2,500, Salop. XXXVI. 11 (1882 and 1902 edns.).
[7] O.S. Nat. Grid SJ 700 126.
[8] Acct. based on Trinder, *Ind. Rev. Salop.* (1981), 132–3.
[9] H. Chance, 'Donnington Wood Glasshouses', *The Glass Circle,* Nov. 1964, 3 (copy in S.P.L.).
[10] Trinder, op. cit. 137.
[11] I.G.M.T., Lilleshall Co. colln. 473b; Glass Duties Act, 1838, 1 & 2 Vic. c. 44.   [12] *Census,* 1841.
[13] S.R.O., dep. plan 289b and bk. of ref. dated 10 Nov. 1792.
[14] O.S. Map 1", sheet 61 NE. (1833 edn.); *The Glass Circle,* Nov. 1964, 3; I.G.M.T., Lilleshall Co. colln., Mr. Ashdown's [glassho.] valuation.

[15] S.R.O. 1172/13. The block was made by T. Radcliffe & Co., Birm.
[16] Below, Church; Trinder, *Ind. Rev. Salop.* (1981), 196; Gale and Nicholls, *Lilleshall Co.* 53.
[17] Above, Wrockwardine, Local Govt. and Public Services; below, Church; *P.O. Dir. Salop.* (1856), 154; *Kelly's Dir. Salop.* (1929), 328.
[18] *14th Ann. Rep. Local Govt. Bd.* pp. xlvii, 191, 204; *V.C.H. Salop.* ii. 229; *Kelly's Dir. Salop.* (1900), 295.
[19] Cartlidge, *Usc-con,* 111.
[20] Gale and Nicholls, *Lilleshall Co.* 74; G. M. James, 'Here be Dragons': Brief Glimpse into Hist. of St. Geo.'s, Telford [1982], 19–20 (copy in S.P.L.).
[21] Williams, *Wrockwardine Wood,* 12; Lilleshall par. reg. (transcripts in S.P.L.).

of Methodism in the area apparently stimulated Joshua Gilpin, vicar of Wrockwardine 1782–1828[22] and a friend of John Fletcher, the Methodist vicar of Madeley, to introduce cottage lectures in Wrockwardine Wood. They were initially given by Matthew Wishton and R. W. Kyle, curate for Wrockwardine Wood, in a cottage in Furnace Lane.[23] The National school, built near the glassworks and opened in 1831, was licensed for preaching and held up to 250 adults.[24] Wrockwardine Wood church, built next to the school, was consecrated in 1833. It was paid for by public subscription of £990 and grants totalling £600.[25]

Wrockwardine Wood became a separate ecclesiastical parish in 1834. The patronage was the Crown's until 1887 when it was conveyed to the bishop of Lichfield, the patron in 1982.[26] The living formally became a rectory in 1868, although from the acquisition of the great tithes in 1847 Reginald Yonge frequently signed himself rector.[27] In 1861 the southern part of the parish containing part of the Nabb and Pain's Lane was transferred to the new consolidated chapelry later known as St. George's.[28]

The incumbent of Wrockwardine Wood enjoyed a stipend of £81 c. 1834. G. L. Yate, vicar of Wrockwardine, had given up the small tithes, other offerings, and pew rents from Wrockwardine Wood to endow the living.[29] By 1856 the value of the living had risen to c. £140, augmentations totalling £1,000 having been made from Queen Anne's Bounty to match private subscriptions and other grants in 1835, 1836, 1842 (two), and 1849. Additionally, lands worth £300 were given by Yate in 1842 and £770 by subscribers in 1849.[30] In 1847 Queen Anne's Bounty bought the great tithes that belonged to Mrs. Cludde of Orleton, on behalf of the incumbent.[31] By 1871 the living was worth c. £200 and by 1884 £230 including £89 in tithe rent charges and £9 in pew rents and surplice fees. There were also 4 a. of glebe,[32] whose rent was estimated in 1887 to be worth £10.[33] By 1900 the living's value had fallen to £180; it remained at that level in 1917. By 1932 it had risen to £360.[34]

In 1835 G. L. Yate acquired a third interest in the glassworks manager's house, the rest being bought in 1843 after the works had closed.[35]

Profits from R. W. Kyle's *Sermons Doctrinal and Practical* (1837) were devoted to the house fund.[36] Until the purchase of the house the incumbents had apparently not resided near the church: Kyle lived in Trench in 1837 and Henry Bagnall lived in Priorslee in 1843.[37] The incumbents of Wrockwardine Wood seem usually to have had a curate.[38]

In 1843 there were two Sunday services, with others at Christmas and on Good Friday, communion being given four times a year to 20 parishioners. On Census Sunday 1851 44 adults worshipped in the afternoon and 82 in the evening.[39] In 1889, in the wake of their building restorations, Gilbert Todd (rector 1874–92) and his curate were attempting to improve the character of the services and they formed a surpliced choir.[40] A bell of 1891 was hung in the tower.[41]

In 1884 the Nabb mission was built on land given by the Lilleshall Co., the building costs being raised through subscriptions. The iron building was enlarged in 1892 to provide 170 sittings.[42]

The church of *HOLY TRINITY* was built in 1833 to a design by Samuel and Thomas Smith of Madeley.[43] Initially it consisted of a west tower, nave, and chancel, of red brick with some stone dressing. Of plain Georgian design with round-headed windows, it had a large west gallery and seated 610, 430 seats being free.[44] Much of the initial seating was in square pews, which were replaced by benches in 1889 when considerable alterations, designed by Joseph Farmer of Shifnal, were made.[45] Between 1876 and 1890 the chancel was enlarged and an apse added, also a vestry and organ chamber. In 1902 four sandstone balls surmounting the tower were replaced by pinnacles.[46] In 1936 a choir vestry was built on the west side of the tower. In 1970–1 extensive repairs to the church were necessary after a fire.[47]

The registers are complete from 1833.

Land was given to extend the churchyard in 1897, 1921, and 1938, the last ground being consecrated in 1943. The churchyard was levelled in 1967.[48]

NONCONFORMITY. A Wesleyan Methodist society associated with John Fletcher, the

[22] L.J.R.O., B/A/1/24, p. 112.
[23] Williams, op. cit. 12.
[24] Below, Educ.; Lich. Dioc. Regy., bps.' reg. I, pp. 687–91, 695, 702–6; S.R.O. 3916/1/2, no. 61; ibid. /1/6.
[25] From Inc. Ch. Bldg. Soc. and Eccl. Com.: Lich. Dioc. Regy., bps.' reg. I, pp. 702–6.
[26] Ibid. Q, pp. 296–301; Lich. Dioc. Dir. (1982), 107.
[27] Lich. Dioc. Regy., bps.' reg. I, p. 700; R, p. 274; Williams, *Wrockwardine Wood*, 15.
[28] Above, Lilleshall, Churches.
[29] *Rep. Com. Eccl. Revenues* [67], pp. 508–9, H.C. (1835), xxii; R. W. Kyle, *Sermons Doctrinal and Practical* (1837), p. xii.
[30] C. Hodgson, *Q. Anne's Bounty* (2nd edn.), pp. ccxx, ccxxii, ccxxx, ccxcv; suppl. pp. xviii, lxvii.
[31] R. M. Grier, *John Allen* (1889), 172–3; above, Wrockwardine, Man. and Other Est.
[32] E. Cassey & Co. *Dir. Salop.* (1871), 410; S.R.O. 3916/1/26.
[33] *Return of Glebe Land, 1887*, H.C. 307, p. 68 (1887), lxiv.
[34] *Kelly's Dir. Salop.* (1900), 1000; (1917), 302; (1926),

333; *Crockford* (1932), 177.
[35] Williams, *Wrockwardine Wood*, 13–14.
[36] Kyle, *Sermons*, title page.
[37] Ibid. p. xvi; S.R.O. 3916/1/8, no. 44.
[38] Williams, *Wrockwardine Wood*, 20.
[39] P.R.O., HO 129/365, no. 78.
[40] *Salopian Shreds & Patches*, ix. 134–5; Lich. Dioc. Regy., benefice and inst. bk. 1868–1900, pp. 30, 93.
[41] H. B. Walters, *Ch. Bells of Salop.* (Oswestry, 1915), 285.
[42] *Kelly's Dir. Salop.* (1885), 1000; (1900), 296; Gale and Nicholls, *Lilleshall Co.* 53.
[43] H. M. Colvin, *Biog. Dict. Brit. Architects, 1600–1840* (1978), 762.
[44] S.R.O. 3916/1/8, no. 44.
[45] *Salopian Shreds & Patches*, ix. 134.
[46] *Kelly's Dir. Salop.* (1900), 295–6; Williams, *Wrockwardine Wood*, 15.
[47] *Kelly's Dir. Salop.* (1929), 328; (1941), 319; Williams, op. cit. 17–19.
[48] Lich. Dioc. Regy., bps.' reg. U, pp. 275, 312–13; W, pp. 46, 639; X, p. 66; Williams, op. cit. 19.

Evangelical vicar of Madeley, apparently met at Trench in 1765.[49] Wesleyans were meeting at the Nabb in 1813, and by 1815 there was a chapel there.[50] On Census Sunday 1851 afternoon service was attended by 130 adults, evening service by 70; afternoon attendance was said to average 180.[51] In 1863 the Wesleyans moved to St. George's and the Nabb chapel closed.[52]

In 1824 St. John's Wesleyan chapel, Trench Road, opened. Society membership grew from 8 in 1821 to 71 in 1824, and more than doubled between 1826 and 1828 to 134. On Census Sunday 1851 services were attended by 99 adults in the morning and 333 in the evening, although there were only 140 free and 146 rented seats. Attendance was said to average 150 adults and 70 children.[53] There were 50 adherents in 1910 and 1920, and 80 in 1930.[54] In 1948 membership was small and the chapel closed, being replaced by the Methodist church hall, New Donnington.[55]

The first Primitive Methodist society in the county was established at Oakengates in 1821. In 1823 it became a circuit centre and the first circuit chapel was built at the Moss next to the inclined plane. It replaced Oakengates in 1828 as the circuit centre.[56] On Census Sunday 1851 there were 405 adult worshippers in the afternoon and 303 in the evening, apparently average numbers. The chapel had 500 seats, 300 of them free.[57] In 1864 it was rebuilt in diapered red and blue brick to seat 700, and in 1869 there were said to be 204 society members and a congregation of 550. A schoolroom was built next to the chapel in 1879.[58] In 1904 the congregation split when W. H. Stones, a leading church member and a circuit steward, supported Dr. J. McC. McCarthy, a Conservative candidate in the county council elections, contrary to connexional policy over the 1902 Education Act. Reprimanded by the circuit, Stones resigned office and later defied the circuit by accepting the trustees' invitation to preach in the chapel. A scuffle involving the minister ensued, and the dispute caused Stones and his followers to establish the Wrockwardine Wood Central Hall in Donnington Wood.[59] Between 1903 and 1905 the congregation of Wrockwardine Wood chapel fell from 550 to 400, and membership from c. 100 to 83.[60] There were said to be 250 adherents in 1910 and 1920, 150 in 1930.[61] A

burial ground opened in 1927.[62] The chapel had 51 members in 1982.[63]

A Primitive Methodist chapel at the Nabb known as the Rough[64] was demolished in 1864 and rebuilt in stone in 1869 to seat 170; 100 attended the principal services in 1871.[65] Numbers soon fell, to 40 in 1875 and 20 in 1890. Although they recovered between 1900 and 1910, there were only 20 adherents in 1926 when the chapel was last listed.[66] It was demolished in 1930.[67]

The Primitive Methodist Jubilee chapel, built of red brick in 1860 on the north side of Church Street, St. George's, seated 400; half the seats were free. The principal services were attended by 250 in 1869, a number that remained fairly constant until 1900. By 1920 there were only 150 adherents. In 1867 a 'double decker' schoolroom was added and in 1886 a Sunday school.[68] The chapel and schoolroom were sold in 1965, having been replaced by a new chapel on the opposite side of the road.[69]

Bethesda chapel, Trench, on the corner of Trench and Church roads, was built in 1866 in diapered red and blue brick. It seated 200, half the seats being free; 150 attended the main services in 1875, but only 60–70 between 1880 and 1890.[70] Attendance averaged 20 in 1982.[71]

In 1870 a brick mission in Lincoln Road opened, reputedly for poor people reluctant to attend the main Primitive chapel at the Moss. It had c. 150 free seats; 50 people attended the principal services in 1871, 125 in 1880. Between 1900 and 1920 there were 60–70 adherents, and 100 in 1930.[72] It was de-registered in 1954.[73] Primitive Methodists also met in 1861 at a house in Bunter's Row, south of the Shrewsbury Canal on the western boundary of the township.[74]

The Wesleyan Reformers' Ebenezer chapel, New Street, was built in 1855. It seated 230. It closed in 1963 and was sold in 1965.[75] The New Connexion met at Glasshouse Row in 1845.[76]

By 1923 the Brethren had moved from Oakengates to a Gospel Hall in West Street, which they still used in 1983.[77] Jehovah's Witnesses had a Kingdom Hall in Plough Road from 1967.[78]

EDUCATION. In 1833 a Primitive Methodist Sunday school, started in 1823, had 177 pupils,

[49] Trinder, *Ind. Rev. Salop.* (1981), 158.
[50] S.R.O., q. sess. order bk. 1808–19, f. 174v.; inf. from Mr. J. H. Lenton.
[51] P.R.O., HO 129/365, no. 76.
[52] S.R.O. 1963/2; above, Wombridge, Nonconf.
[53] P.R.O., HO 129/365, no. 78.
[54] S.R.O. 1861/107, 137, 153.
[55] S.R.O. 3767/XXIII/A, H. I. Powell to Mr. Mason, 28 July 1943; inf. from Mr. Lenton; above, Lilleshall, Prot. Nonconf.
[56] *V.C.H. Salop.* ii. 14.
[57] P.R.O., HO 129/365, no. 77.
[58] S.R.O. 1861/19, 79.
[59] S.R.O. 2123/632; *Wellington Jnl.* 1 Oct. 1904; Wesley Hist. Soc., Salop. Branch, *Bulletin*, i (7) (1976; copy in S.R.O. 3543/9); above, Lilleshall, Prot. Nonconf.
[60] S.R.O. 1861/98, 100–2.
[61] Ibid. 107, 137, 153.
[62] S.R.O. 3511/24–5.
[63] Inf. from Mr. Lenton.
[64] Ibid.

[65] Williams, *Wrockwardine Wood*, 20; S.R.O. 1861/22.
[66] S.R.O. 1861/29, 79, 96, 107, 146.
[67] Williams, op. cit. 20.
[68] *Jubilee Methodist Church, St. Geo.'s: Centenary Bk. 1860–1960* (copy in S.R.O. 3038/9/30); S.R.O. 1861/19, 79, 96, 137.
[69] G.R.O., Worship Reg. nos. 14084, 71040; S.R.O. 3038/9/47; above, Wombridge, Nonconf.
[70] S.R.O. 1861/30, 44, 79, 96; inf. from Mr. Lenton.
[71] Inf. from Mr. Lenton.
[72] S.R.O. 1861/22, 44, 96, 107, 137, 153; Wesley Hist. Soc., Salop. Branch, *Bull.* i (7).
[73] Inf. from Mr. Lenton.
[74] S.R.O. 1861/12.
[75] *Kelly's Dir. Salop.* (1909), 200; *Meth. Church Bldgs.: Statistical Returns* (1940), 268; SA 14435.
[76] James, '*Here be Dragons*', 17; G.R.O., Worship Reg. no. 7173; *Return of Churches, 1882*, H.C. 401, p. 366 (1882), l.
[77] Above, Wombridge, Nonconf.; G.R.O., Worship Reg. no. 49042.
[78] Ibid. no. 71036.

and a Wesleyan one had 326.[79] In 1828 Thomas Davies kept school in his house at the Nabb.[80] In 1826 there was Anglican concern because in that 'nursery of sectarianism' upwards of 280 children aged 7–13 were still without instruction,[81] and in 1831 a National school opened, albeit with only 109 places, for day and Sunday pupils.[82]

Wrockwardine Wood school board, formed in 1875, consisted of three nonconformists, the rector, and another Anglican; the Primitive Methodist minister became chairman.[83] At first a most disorderly board[84] torn by sectarian strife,[85] it achieved nothing in its first three-year term beyond preparing proposals and plans,[86] although it was aware that c. 400 children had no schooling. Anglicans petitioned against the board in 1875 and 1876, but its refusal to build near the National school was widely supported. The rector,[87] who was alleged to have acted subversively,[88] extended the National school,[89] though insufficiently to satisfy the Education Department.[90] The 1878 election, in which many illiterates[91] voted, produced an Anglican majority on the board,[92] which, under pressure from the Education Department, opened boys' and girls' and infant schools in 1879. A small Standard I boys' school was built in 1890[93] and school accommodation was ample in 1894.[94]

After 1878 the board was competent, even showing initiative,[95] and its schools were usually efficient.[96] Weekly fees of 2d.[97] were often waived, as many as 44 at a time, to encourage attendance.[98] The board accepted the government fee grant in 1891[99] and was exceptionally good at enforcing attendance.[1] In 1893 the board welcomed a proposal for evening continuation classes in the board schools.[2] From 1891 there were cookery and drawing classes; later geometry, physics, shorthand, mining, arithmetic, and other subjects were taught.[3] Students could progress to advanced courses at Oakengates.[4] Evening continuation classes were held until at least 1914.[5] From

1961 evening classes were held at the new Trench Modern School.[6]

All the 19th-century schools were in use until a reorganization in 1933 when Wrockwardine Wood Senior (Mixed) Council School opened, the boys' and junior boys' council schools closed,[7] and the C.E. and Gower Street Council schools became junior mixed and infant schools. In the 1960s the two last named closed, as did a temporary school opened in 1943; the church school was rebuilt on a new site. Between 1953 and 1977 a new infant school, a new (Roman Catholic) primary school, and a new modern school opened[8] to fulfil government policies, to accommodate the 'bulge', and to take more children from new housing; in 1974 the modern school became comprehensive, for pupils aged 11–16. From the late 1970s the falling birth rate reduced numbers in primary schools.[9]

Wrockwardine Wood National School, built on the edge of the churchyard,[10] opened with 109 places[11] in 1831: 92 pupils (including infants) occupied the single, brick-floored room. Attendance averaged 79 in 1853. Income in 1849 was largely from fees of 1d. a week and subscriptions. By 1865 120 pupils paid 2d. a week. That year £50 was spent on repairs, a deficit of £47 4s. 3½d. being met by the rector, who owned the master's house; his salary was £27 2s. 10d. The first master served at least 26 years.[12] The appointment of a certificated master in 1865 qualified the school to be inspected for government grants.[13] The rector secured 100 more infant places[14] in 1878,[15] and by 1885 the school had been further enlarged for 400 pupils but had only girls' and infant departments, attendance averaging 230. In 1905 attendance averaged 368[16] and by 1911 the school was overcrowded.[17] The building, extensively repaired in 1921, was condemned in 1926.[18] In the reorganization of 1933 the county council let an adjoining building (the former Junior Boys' Council School) to the managers for £1 a year and contributed to the cost of alterations; Betton's charity

[79] *Educ. Enq. Abstract*, H.C. 62, p. 787 (1835), xlii.
[80] S.R.O. 303/79–80.
[81] Nat. Soc. file 173.
[82] P.R.O., ED 7/102, f. 492.
[83] *List of Sch. Boards, 1902* [Cd. 1038], p. 75 (1902), lxxix; *Wellington Jnl.* 16 Jan. 1875 (p. 5).
[84] *Wenlock and Ludlow Express*, 8 Sept. 1877 (cutting in Nat. Soc. file 173).
[85] e.g. S.R.O. 1604/19, pp. 69–79; cf. *V.C.H. Salop.* iii. 176.
[86] S.R.O. 1604/19, pp. 180–2.
[87] He seems to have been chmn. of the bd. 1881–90: ibid. /20, 10 Jan. 1881; /21, 3 and 14 Jan. 1890.
[88] *Inter alia* by securing the dismissal of the bd.'s vice-chmn. from his post with the Lilleshall Co.: ibid. /19, pp. 10–12, 38–9, 70–2, 95–8, 101–2, 158–60.
[89] *Wellington Jnl.* 29 June 1878 (p. 8).
[90] S.R.O. 1604/19, p. 181.
[91] i.e. 200 out of 585 voters and 930 electors.
[92] *Wellington Jnl.* 5 Jan. 1878.
[93] Below.
[94] S.R.O. 1604/21, 13 Feb. 1894.
[95] Ibid. 11 Aug., 8 Sept. 1891 (proposal for joint cookery centre).
[96] S.R.O. 1240/9–12; 1604/19–21.
[97] S.R.O. 1604/19, p. 215.
[98] e.g. ibid. /20, 8 Jan., 14 May 1880; /21, 13 May 1890.
[99] Ibid. /21, 11 Aug. 1891.

[1] St. Geo.'s Boys' Nat. Sch. log bk. (at the sch.) 17 Sept. 1891.
[2] S.R.O. 1604/21, 11 July 1893.
[3] Ibid. 12 Jan. 1892; *S.C.C. Mins.* 1891–1903, organizing sec.'s ann. reps. to Intermediate Educ. Cttee.
[4] e.g. *S.C.C. Mins. (Educ.)* 1904–5, 40; 1906–7, 45.
[5] *S.C.C. Higher Educ. Dept. Rep. 1912–14*, 24–7.
[6] Inf. from the John Hunt Sch.
[7] *S.C.C. Mins. (Educ.)* 1932–3, 94; above, Wombridge, Educ. (for the snr. sch.).
[8] Below.
[9] *S.C.C. Mins. (Educ.)* 1956–80; S.C.C. Educ. Cttee. *Sch. List* (1970–9); S.C.C. Educ. Cttee. *Educ. Dir.* (1980–1); inf. from S.C.C. Educ. Dept.
[10] On a site given by Lds. Shrews. and Berwick: Lich. Dioc. Regy., bps.' reg. I, pp. 687–91; S.R.O. 1604/19, p. 70.
[11] *Wellington Jnl.* 29 June 1878 (p. 8).
[12] P.R.O., ED 7/102, f. 492; *Educ. Enq. Abstract*, 787; *Mins. of Educ. Cttee. of Council, 1853–4*, ii [1788], p. 558, H.C. (1854), lii; *P.O. Dir. Salop.* (1856), 154. Cf. S.R.O. 3916/1/2, 8.
[13] St. Geo.'s C.E. Boys' Sch. log bk. (at the sch.) 9 Jan. 1865.
[14] S.R.O. 1604/19.
[15] Nat. Soc. file 173; *Wellington Jnl.* 29 June 1878 (p. 8).
[16] *Kelly's Dir. Salop.* (1885), 1000; (1905), 307.
[17] Ketley Bank Girls' Council Sch. log bk. (at Queenswood Co. Primary Sch.) 27 Jan. 1911.
[18] S.R.O. 2699/58, p. 104.

also made a small grant. A new junior mixed and infant school with 320 places then opened.[19] In 1948, when further repairs were needed, the school became controlled.[20] It then had too few teachers, and even in 1956 only two of its eight teachers were college-trained and certificated.[21] In the 1950s the school (275 places) was overcrowded.[22] In 1953 it became a junior school.[23] In 1961 Wrockwardine Wood (Temporary) County Primary School merged with it but continued to use its separate premises.[24] That year the C.E. school building was again black-listed, and in 1964 the new Wrockwardine Wood C.E. (Controlled) Junior School, with 320 places, was erected in Church Road, Trench.[25] Numbers rose and the school was extended in the 1970s. In 1981 it had 382 pupils.[26]

Wrockwardine Wood Girls' and Infant Board School, Gower Street, opened in 1879 to accommodate 99 girls and 136 infants in separate departments; it occupied the extended premises of the former Granville hospital. The first year's income comprised £150 in government grant, £56 in fees, and only £25 from the rates. Weekly fees of 2d.[27] were reduced in 1887 and abolished in 1891.[28] After extensions in 1895 there were 140 girls' places and 185 infants'.[29] The girls' school was full from 1885 until 1909, when attendance averaged 118. Infant attendance averaged 102 in 1885, 140 in 1909.[30] The school's normal efficiency[31] was disrupted 1911-15 owing mainly to the mistresses' incompetence.[32] In 1927 the schools were renamed Gower Street Girls' and Infants' Council Schools.[33] By then numbers were falling notably.[34] In the 1933 reorganization the departments amalgamated, senior girls left,[35] and junior boys were admitted from the closed council school; the school, with 305 places, was renamed Wrockwardine Wood Junior Mixed and Infant Council School. In 1936 it had 256 places but only 111 pupils;[36] by 1941, owing to house building at Donnington Wood, it was full.[37] In 1943 a

nursery class was formed but, being almost unused, closed.[38] Numbers fell to 72 in 1952[39] and 36 in 1957 but had risen to 70 when the school, its building condemned, closed in 1961; pupils transferred to St. George's C.E. junior and infant schools.[40]

Wrockwardine Wood Boys' Board School opened in 1879 with 180 places in the newly built Primitive Methodist Sunday school. The weekly fee was 2d.[41] The school was efficient under its four successive masters,[42] one of whom, Thomas Barlow (appointed 1881), earned it the excellent merit grant six times.[43] The Education Department rejected plans to extend it, and in 1890 Standard I boys transferred to the new Wrockwardine Wood Junior Boys' Board School.[44] Attendance averaged 189 in 1885, 180 in 1891,[45] and 200 in 1905. To relieve overcrowding, yet again, Standard II boys were accommodated at the junior boys' school from 1905 to 1915, by which time numbers had fallen considerably.[46] Improved in 1915,[47] the school closed in 1933 when its pupils transferred to other schools including the new senior council school in Wombridge.[48]

Wrockwardine Wood Junior (or Standard I) Boys' Board School, built on the National School, opened in 1890 with 100 places to relieve overcrowding at the boys' board school. It also took Standard II boys 1905-15.[49] Attendance averaged 70 in 1891, 38 in 1904, and 86 in 1909.[50] The school closed in 1933.[51] Thereafter the buildings were used by the adjoining C.E. school.[52]

Wrockwardine Wood (Temporary) Junior Mixed and Infant Council School opened in 1943 in the Methodist schoolroom previously let to the boys' council school.[53] It admitted 27 pupils from the overcrowded Donnington Wood C.E. School.[54] In 1944 there were 36 pupils.[55] The infants transferred to the new Wrockwardine Wood County Infant School in 1953.[56] In 1961 the school became part of Wrockwardine Wood C.E.

---

[19] Ibid. pp. 122-4, 127-8; S.C.C. Mins. (Educ.) 1928-9, 20; 1932-3, 94; 1934-5, 37.

[20] S.R.O. 2699/58, p. 138; S.C.C. Mins. (Educ.) 1948-9, 19. [21] S.R.O. 2699/58, pp. 137, 170.

[22] Ibid. pp. 140, 166, 182; S.C.C. Mins. (Educ.) 1949-50, 233; 1957-8, 34.

[23] Wrockwardine Wood C.E. (Cont.) Jnr. Sch. log bk. (at the sch.) 14 Sept. 1953.

[24] i.e. the Methodist schoolrm.: S.C.C. Mins. (Educ.) 1960-1, 163; 1962-3, 17; below.

[25] S.C.C. Mins. (Educ.) 1960-1, 105; 1961-2, 135; log bk. 7 Jan. 1964.

[26] S.C.C. Mins. (Educ.) 1970-1, 379; 1971-2, 177, 363; Sch. List (1970-9); Educ. Dir. (1981), 10.

[27] S.R.O. 1604/19, pp. 160-1, 194-5, 223 sqq.; P.R.O., ED 7/102, f. 486.

[28] SR.O. 1240/9, pp. 106-7; 1604/21, 11 Aug. 1891.

[29] S.R.O. 1240/12, pp. 19, 186-7.

[30] Kelly's Dir. Salop. (1885), 1000; (1891), 486; (1905), 307; (1909), 311.

[31] Reps. 1922-32 in S.R.O. 1240/10, 12.

[32] Ibid. reps., etc., 1911-15. Cf. (for resignations) S.R.O. 1240/12, p. 352; 2699/59, pp. 92, 113, 115.

[33] S.R.O. 2699/59, p. 151.

[34] S.R.O. 1240/10, p. 386; /12, pp. 412, 425.

[35] Some going to St. Geo.'s C.E. Sch., some to Wrockwardine Wood Snr. Council Sch. (above, Wombridge, Educ.).

[36] S.R.O. 1240/12, pp. 443, 464; S.C.C. Mins. (Educ.) 1933-4, 63; 1934-5, 37.

[37] S.C.C. Mins. (Educ.) 1939-40, 15-16; 1940-1, 38; above, Lilleshall, Growth of Settlement.

[38] S.R.O. 1240/13, pp. 14, 18.

[39] Ibid. p. 75.

[40] S.C.C. Mins. (Educ.) 1957-8, 34; 1961-2, 48.

[41] P.R.O., ED 7/102, f. 492. It was nr. the end of the later Chapel Terr.

[42] No adverse reps. in S.R.O. 1604/20-1; 2699/59.

[43] S.R.O. 1604/20, 25 Oct. 1881; /21, 8 Jan., 12 Feb. 1889.

[44] Ibid. /21, 5 Nov., 10 Dec. 1889.

[45] Kelly's Dir. Salop. (1885), 1000; (1891), 486.

[46] S.R.O. 2699/59, pp. 9, 13, 16-17, 110.

[47] S.C.C. Mins. (Educ.) 1914-15, 47, 110; 1915-16, 66.

[48] i.e. Wrockwardine Wood Snr. Council Sch. See ibid. 1933-4, 12, 63; above, Wombridge, Educ.

[49] S.R.O. 1604/21, 10 Dec. 1889; 2699/59, pp. 16-17, 110.

[50] Kelly's Dir. Salop. (1891), 486; (1909), 311; Public Elem. Schs. 1906 [Cd. 3182], p. 538, H.C. (1906), lxxxvi.

[51] S.C.C. Mins. (Educ.) 1933-4, 63.

[52] Ibid. 1934-5, 37.

[53] Ibid. 1941-2, 56, 84.

[54] Ibid. 1943-4, 36.

[55] S.R.O. 2699/59, p. 194.

[56] Inf. from Miss E. Downing, first headmistress of the co. inf. sch.

(Controlled) Junior School, which continued to use the building.[57]

Wrockwardine Wood County Infant School, Church Road, opened in 1953 with 200 places.[58] It was extended in 1961[59] but there were only 200 pupils by 1981.[60]

Trench Boys' Modern School, Gibbons Road, opened in 1955 with 360 places.[61] It had 553 pupils in 1965 and 702 in 1972[62] when extensions had provided 750 places.[63] Named the John Hunt School in 1973, it then became mixed,[64] with 704 pupils.[65] In 1974 it became comprehensive, for pupils aged 11–16.[66] Extensions had provided 1,050 places by 1976 and there were 1,116 pupils in 1981.[67] From the early 1970s the school had a unit for educationally subnormal pupils.[68]

St. Luke's R.C. (Aided) Primary School, Church Road, Trench, opened in 1977 with 280 places and 116 pupils. In 1981 it had 115 pupils.[69]

CHARITIES FOR THE POOR. Wrockwardine Wood was entitled to a share in the Wrockwardine parish charities.[70]

[57] S.C.C. Mins. (Educ.) 1960–1, 163; 1962–3, 17.
[58] Wrockwardine Wood C.E. (Cont.) Jnr. Sch. log bk. 14 Sept. 1953.
[59] S.C.C. Mins. (Educ.) 1960–1, 110; 1961–2, 44.
[60] Educ. Dir. (1981), 10.
[61] S.C.C. Mins. (Educ.) 1951–2, 31, 77, 79; inf. from the headmaster.
[62] Sch. List (1965), 2; (1972), 3.
[63] S.C.C. Mins. (Educ.) 1969–70, 167; 1972–3, 396.

[64] Ibid. 1972–3, 392–3. It was named after Ld. Hunt.
[65] Sch. List (1973), 3.
[66] S.C.C. Mins. (Educ.) 1974–5, 173.
[67] Ibid. 1975–6, 199; Educ. Dir. (1981), 3.
[68] S.C.C. Mins. (Educ.) 1971–2, 386–7; Educ. Dir. (1981), 11.
[69] S.C.C. (Educ.) 1974–5, 334; Sch. List (1977), 10; Educ. Dir. (1981), 10; inf. from the sch.
[70] Review of Local Chars. (S.C.C. 1975), 69.

INDEX

Among the abbreviations used the following, sometimes with -s added to form a plural, may need elucidation: adv., advowson; archd., archdeacon; bdy., boundary; bro., brother; bur., buried; C.P., civil parish; ch., church; char., charity; co., company, county; ct., court; dau., daughter; fl., flourished; ho., house; hund., hundred; inc., inclosure; ind., industry; lib., liberty; m., married; n, note; pk., park; R.D., rural district; R.S.D., rural sanitary district; rem., remains; Rom., Roman; s., son; sis., sister; U.D., urban district; U.S.D., urban sanitary district; w., wife. A page number in italics denotes an illustration on or facing that page.

INDEX

CORRIGENDA TO VOLUMES I–III, VIII

Earlier corrigenda to Volumes I and II were published in Volumes II and III. In references to pages printed in more than one column 'a', 'b', and 'c' following a page number denote the first, second, and third column.

Vol. I, page 54, line 10, *for* 'was born 13 May, 1835' *read* 'inherited his father's property 1855'
"   "   59, paragraph on the Roden, line 4, *for* 'Dee' *read* 'Mersey'
"   "   152, line 15, *for* 'vicar' *read* 'rector'
"   "   276, line 38, *for* '37' *read* '87'
"   "   321b, line 19, *for* '3' *read* '4'
"   "   426a, lines 40, 51–2, *for* 'Telford' *read* 'Jessop'
"   "   426b, line 55, *for* '1778' *read* '1788'
"   "   444a, line 31, *for* 'These were' *read* 'One of these was'
"   "   444a, line 33, *for* 'afterwards' *read* 'the present works nearby was carried on'
"   "   455b, line 9, *for* 'Bennet' *read* 'Bennett'
"   "   460a, line 22, *for* 'were two furnaces' *read* 'was a furnace'
"   "   460a, line 39, *for* 'successor' *read* 'great-grandson'
"   "   460b, line 18, *after* 'to' *insert* 'Richard Corfield, father of'
"   "   460b, line 18, *after* 'Pitchford' *delete* ','
"   "   460b, line 47, *for* '1676' *read* '1677 or 1678'
"   "   460, note 4, *for* '7–9' *read* '7–8'
"   "   461a, line 27, *for* '1708' *read* '1707'
"   "   461a, line 30, *after* 'only,' *insert* '. . .'
"   "   461a, lines 30–1, *for* 'such articles could' *read* 'iron pots and other ware may'
"   "   461a, line 31, *for* 'better and more easily and' *read* 'fine and with more ease and . . .'
"   "   461a, line 32, *for* 'could' *read* 'they can'
"   "   461a, line 53, *for* '1709' *read* '1709/10'
"   "   462a, line 46, *for* 'Upper' *read* 'Lower'
"   "   462b, line 30, *after* 'in' *insert* 'helping to run'
"   "   463a, line 4, *for* 'August' *read* 'October'
"   "   463a, line 17, *for* '1758' *read* 'the 1750s'
"   "   463a, lines 18–19, *delete* 'for a term of ninety-nine years'
"   "   463a, line 23, *for* '1753' *read* '1754'
"   "   463a, line 24, *for* 'Plowden' *read* 'R. A.'
"   "   463a, line 25, *for* 'Robert' *read* 'Plowden'
"   "   463a, line 26, *delete* 'A.'
"   "   463a, line 38, *after* '1755' *insert* 'and 1757'
"   "   463b, line 2, *for* '1750' *read* '1755'
"   "   463b, line 44, *before* 'to' *insert* 'that year likely'
"   "   464a, line 17, *after* 'furnaces' *insert* ', eventually'
"   "   464a, line 21, *for* '1759' *read* '1757'
"   "   464a, lines 22–3, *for* 'Shrewsbury' *read* 'Bersham'
"   "   464b, line 23, *for* 'N.' *read* 'U.'
"   "   464b, lines 48–9, *delete* 'Rev. William Hinton and'
"   "   464b, line 49, *after* 'Elwell' *insert* 'and his brothers'
"   "   464b, line 49, *for* '1774' *read* '1775'
"   "   464b, lines 49–50, *for* 'It is doubtful, however, whether the' *read* 'The'
"   "   464b, line 51, *for* 'at this time' *read* 'in 1757–8'
"   "   465a, line 10, *before* 'J.' *insert* 'John Wilkinson who later sold them to'
"   "   465b, line 14, *for* 'Humphry' *read* 'Humphrey'
"   "   465, note 13, line 4, *for* 'beginning' *read* 'have begun'
"   "   465, note 13, line 5, *after* 'and' *insert* 'are'
"   "   465, note 15, *move the source cited in note 16 to the beginning of this note, changing* '1768' *to* '1768–9'
"   "   465, note 15, *for* '202' *read* '203'
"   "   465, note 16, *for existing note read* 'Case of Sir Humph. Mackworth [?1707].'
"   "   466a, line 13, *for* 'got to work' *read* 'incorporated in the Coalbrookdale partners' enterprises'
"   "   466a, line 57, *after* 'introduced' *insert* 'rapidly'
"   "   466b, line 27, *for* ', or' *read* 'and'
"   "   466b, line 28, *for* 'then' *read* 'the former'
"   "   466b, line 40, *for* 'the works' *read* 'Upton'
"   "   466b, line 49, *for* 'Upper' *read* 'Lower'
"   "   467b, line 34, *for* 'bronze' *read* 'cast iron, bronzed,'
"   "   467, note 23, *for* 'Warrington' *read* 'Warington'
"   "   470a, line 33, *for* 'Donnington were' *read* 'Snedshill had been'
"   "   470a, line 34, *for* 'Company.' ' *read* 'Company' in 1807 from successors of Wilkinson.'
"   "   479a, line 28, *for* 'Stirchley' *read* 'Old Park'
Vol. II, page 2, line 22, *after* 'places' *insert* '(except Woore)' *and after* 'were' *insert* 'all'
"   "   11, line 29, *for* 'James' *read* 'John'
"   "   30b, line 6, *for,* 'in' *read* 'shortly after'
"   "   35b, lines 4, 6, *delete* 'Sir'
"   "   71a, line 26, *for full stop read comma*
"   "   71, note 8, *for* '346' *read* '336'
"   "   72a, line 29, *for* 'abbey' *read* 'manor'
"   "   73a, line 3, *for* 'Atcham' *read* 'Ercall Magna'
"   "   76, note 18, *for* '1518' *read* '1517'
"   "   77, note 33, *for existing note read* 'L.J.R.O., B/c 5.'
"   "   78, note 59, line 3, *for* '40/2' *read* '2/40'

Vol. II, page 79b, line 42, *for* 'occurs' *read* 'resigned'
"   "   79b, line 43, *for* '1518' *read* '1517'
"   "   79, note 5, *after* '1516' *add* '; L. & P. Hen. VIII*, ii, no. 2717'
"   "   79, note 6, *after* '2717' *add* '; S.H.C.* 4th ser. vii. 179'
"   "   81a, line 2, *for* 'dispossessors' *read* 'successors'
"   "   81a, line 9, *for* 'Broctkon' *read* 'Brockton'
"   "   82b, line 30, *for* '20' *read* '21'
"   "   93, note 13, *for* '3rd' *read* '4th'
"   "   106a, note 1, *before* 'de' *insert* 'C.'
"   "   146a, line 32, *before* 'Newports' *insert* 'sane'
"   "   152a, lines 29, 41, *for* 'Holbach' *read* 'Holbache'
"   "   152, note 3, *for* 'Holbach' *read* 'Holbache'
"   "   163, note 10, *for* '82' *read* '89'
"   "   205, lines 8, 16, 27, *after* '1966' *insert* 'and 1967'
"   "   212, line 6, *after* '1966' *insert* 'and 1967'
"   "   212, *s.v.* 'Atcham R.D.', *for* '1966' *read* '1967' *(six times)*
"   "   213, *s.v.* 'Bridgnorth', *delete* 'and U.D.' *and for* '1966' *read* '1967'
"   "   213, *s.v.* 'Oldbury', *delete* 'and U.D.'
"   "   214, *s.v.* 'Clun R.D.', line 3, *for* '1966' *read* '1967'
"   "   214, *s.v.* 'Bishop's Castle', *delete* 'and U.D.' *and for* '1966' *read* '1967'
"   "   214, *s.v.* 'Drayton ... R.D.', line 3, *for* 'to' *read* 'from'
"   "   214, *s.v.* 'Ellesmere R.D.', line 3, *for* '1966' *read* '1967'
"   "   215, *s.v.* 'Ludlow R.D.', six of the eight references '1966' *should read* '1967', *the reference s.vv.* 'Stretton, Church'
               and 'Stretton, Little' *to remain unaltered*
"   "   215, *s.v.* 'Ludlow', *delete* 'and U.D.'
"   "   215, *s.v.* 'Ludlow Castle', *for* 'U.D.' *read* 'M.B.'
"   "   215, last line, *for* 'U.D.' *read* 'M.B.'
"   "   216, *s.v.* 'Newport R.D.', *for* '1934' *read* '1936'
"   "   216, *s.v.* 'North Shropshire R.D.', *for* '1966' *read* '1967'
"   "   216, *s.v.* 'Oswestry R.D.', *for* '1966' *read* '1967' *(five times)*
"   "   216, *s.v.* 'Oswestry Urban', *for* 'U.D.' *read* 'M.B.'
"   "   217, *s.v.* 'Shifnal R.D.', two of the three references to '1966' *should read* '1967', *the reference s.v.* 'Stirchley' *to remain*
               unaltered
"   "   217, *s.v.* 'Teme R.D.', *for* 'Act.' *read* 'Act,'
"   "   217, *s.v.* 'Wellington R.D.', *for* '1934' *read* '1936' *(nine times)*
"   "   218, *s.v.* 'Wem R.D.', *for* '1966' *read* '1967'
"   "   220, notes (n) and (w), *delete* 'and U.D.'
"   "   226, notes (s) and (t), *delete* 'and U.D.' *(three times)*
"   "   235, line 3, *for* 'and' *read* ', and 1967, under'
"   "   235, line 7, *delete* 'chap. and'
"   "   235, line 9, *for* 'See' *read* 'Part transferred to Pimhill C.P. And see'
"   "   235, lines 10–11, 16, 30, 32, 37, 39, 46, 48, 50–1, 53, and 55, *delete* 'A.P. and'
"   "   235, line 19, *delete* 'and U.D.' *(bis)*
"   "   235, line 21, *for* 'and U.D.: M.B. and U.D. dissolved' *read* 'Dissolved'
"   "   236, lines 1, 3–5, 12, 15, 23, 25, 27, 29, 33, 35, 38–42, 46, 49, 51, *delete* 'A.P. and'
"   "   236, lines 8, 55, *for* 'and U.D.: M.B. and U.D. dissolved' *read* 'Dissolved'
"   "   236, line 18, *delete* 'and U.D.' *(bis)*
"   "   236, line 22, *after* 'Albrighton' *add* '; Astley'
"   "   237, lines 11–12, 14, 18, 23–4, *delete* 'A.P. and'
"   "   241c, *transpose* 'Letone, see Leaton' *and* 'Lestune, see Leighton'
"   "   243b, *move* 'Savintune, see Shavington' *to its correct alphabetical position before* 'Saward'
"   "   244b, *s.v.* 'Wadelestun', *for* 'unidentified' *read* '? Woodluston in Forden, Mont.'
"   "   245b, *before* 'Woolstaston' *insert* 'Woodluston, see Wadelestun'
"   "   245c, *s.v.* 'Yagdon', *for* 'Shrewsbury St. Chad' *read* 'Baschurch'
"   "   246b, *s.v.* 'Acton Round', *after* '3' *add* ', 210'
"   "   247b, *s.v.* 'Albrighton, in St. Mary's, Shrewsbury, chap.', *delete* ', 235'
"   "   247c, *s.v.* 'Alveley', *between* 'man.' *and* 'par.' *insert* 'mill, ii. 63'
"   "   250c, *s.v.* 'Bennet', *delete* 'John, i. 455'
"   "   250c, *s.v.* 'Bennett', *read* 'Bennett:' *and insert thereunder* 'John, i. 455' *above* 'Ric., ii. 153'
"   "   251c, *s.v.* 'Bishop's Castle', *delete* 'U.D.' *and following references*
"   "   253c, *s.v.* 'Bridgnorth, M.B.', *after* '220' *add* 'and n'
"   "   253c, *s.v.* 'Bridgnorth', *delete* 'U.D.' *and following references*
"   "   256a, *s.v.* 'Burton-upon-Trent', *for* '(Staffs.)' *read* '(Derb. and Staffs.)'
"   "   258a, *s.v.* 'Charlton', *below* 'Thos.' *insert new entry* 'Wm. (d. 1532), ii. 35'
"   "   258a, *s.v.* 'Charlton', *delete the entry for* 'Sir Wm.'
"   "   260b, *s.v.* 'Coalbrookdale, in Madeley', *before* 'Meadow Wharf' *insert* 'Lower Forge, i. 462, 466'
"   "   260b, *s.v.* 'Coalbrookdale, in Madeley', *delete entry for* 'Upper Forge'
"   "   261b, *s.v.* 'Corfield', *before* 'Thos.' *insert* 'Ric., i. 460'
"   "   263a, *s.v.* 'Dawley, cock-fighting', *for* '193' *read* '192'
"   "   264a, *s.v.* 'Donnington, in Lilleshall, iron ind.' *delete* '470,'
"   "   267c, *s.v.* 'FitzAlan, Ric., Earl of Arundel (d. 1397)', *for* '97' *read* '96'
"   "   273a, *s.v.* 'Highley, coalmining', *for* '454' *read* '452–4'
"   "   273a, *s.v.* 'Highley, geol.', *for* '454' *read* '452–4'
"   "   273a, *s.v.* 'Highley, rlwy.' *before* 'ii' *insert* 'i. 454;'
"   "   273c, *s.v.* 'Holbach', *read* 'Holbache' *and for* 'his' *read* 'David's'
"   "   273c, *s.v.* 'Holbache', *delete* 'Holbache,' *and insert rest of entry beneath* 'David, ii. 152'
"   "   275c, *after entry* 'Jesson', *add new entry* 'Jessop, Wm., i. 426'
"   "   279b, *s.v.* 'Lilleshall, tannery', *for* '20' *read* '21'
"   "   282a, *s.v.* 'Ludlow', *delete* 'U.D.' *and following references*
"   "   283a, *s.v.* 'Mackworth', *for* 'Humphry' *read* 'Humph.'
"   "   284c, *s.v.* 'Mersey', *after* 'i.' *insert* '59,'
"   "   287c, *s.v.* 'Newport, Hen.', *for* '1762' *read* '1734'
"   "   289c, *s.v.* 'Oswestry', *delete* 'U.D.' *and following references*
"   "   290b, *s.v.* 'Palmer', *for* 'Jas.' *read* 'John'
"   "   292c, *s.v.* 'Prees, geol.', *after* '40' *add* ', 59'
"   "   294a, *s.v.* 'Red Hill', *after* 'Lilleshall' *insert* ', Sheriffhales,'
"   "   298a, *s.v.* 'Sheriffhales (Hales)', *after* 'Burlington' *insert* 'Red Hill;'
"   "   298c, *s.v.* 'Shrewsbury, athletics, County Youth Sports', *before* '194 n' *insert* 'ii.'

Vol. II, page	302a, s.v. 'Slaney, Rob. Aglionby (d. 1757), *add* 'i. 463;'
" "	302a, s.v. 'Slaney, Rob. Aglionby (d. 1862)', *delete* 'i. 463;'
" "	302b, s.v. 'Smitheman', *for* 'N.' *read* 'U.'
" "	302c, s.v. 'sports and games', *after* 'swimming;' *insert* 'tilting;'
" "	303b, s.v. 'Stirchley', *for* 'chain making, i. 479' *read* 'chemical wks., i. 479 *n*'
" "	305b, s.v. 'Telford', *delete* '426,'
" "	305b, s.v. 'Tern, in Atcham', *delete* '68, 73'
" "	305b, s.v. 'Tern, in Ercall Magna', *after* 'ii.' *insert* '68, 73,'
" "	306a, s.v. 'Trefeglwys', *add* '(Mont.)'
" "	309b, s.v. 'Wenlock, M.B.', *after* '213,' *insert* '215,'
" "	309b, s.v. 'Wenlock', *delete* 'U.D.' *and following references*
" "	311c, s.v. 'Wilkinson, John', *for* '464,' *read* '464–5,'
Vol. III, page	8, *map should show Little Buildwas in Wrockwardine hundred not Condover hundred*
" "	11, lines 29, 31, *for* '1138' *read* '1139'
" "	12, line 25, *for* 'cousins' *read* 'kinsmen'
" "	29, line 16, *for* 'Eudes' *read* 'Otes'
" "	45, line 5, *after* 'granted' *insert* 'or confirmed'
" "	45, note 62, *for* 'escheated to' *read* 'was briefly resumed by'
" "	53, line 24, *for* '1255' *read* '1274'
" "	168, line 6, *before* 'steward' *insert* 'deputy'
" "	176, line 24, *for* 'one' *read* 'ones'
" "	176, line 25, *after* 'Shrewsbury' *add* 'and the Wesleyan school in Wellington'
" "	176, note 27, *after* '73–8 *add* '; Wellington Wesleyan Sch. log bk. 20 Jan. 1896'
" "	176, note 28, *for* 'Ibid.' *read* 'Jones, op. cit.'
" "	177, line 29, *after* 'Shrewsbury' *insert* 'and Wenlock'
" "	177, note 41, *after* 'S.R.O.' *insert* '2699/7, p. 273;'
" "	178, line 14, *for* '1895' *read* '1894–5'
" "	296, line 32, *for* 'Forester' *read* 'Weld-Forester'
" "	364b, s.v. 'Atcham', *delete* 'Tern;'
" "	369b, *between* ' 'Condetret' hundred' *and* 'Condover' *insert new entry* ' 'Conditre', *see* Walton'
" "	372c, s.v. 'Ercall, High', *after* 'Haughton' *add* '; Tern'
" "	373c, s.v. 'Forester, Cecil Weld', *for* 'Weld' *read* '(d. 1828)'
" "	373c, s.v. 'Forester, Cecil', *after* 'Cecil' *insert* '(d. 1774)'
" "	376b, s.v. 'Hodnet' [*surname*], *for* 'Eudes' *read* 'Otes'
" "	392b, s.v. 'Stottesdon', *after* 'Farlow' *add* '; Walton'
" "	392c, s.v. 'Sutherland', *for* 'Suthecland' *read* 'Sutherland'
" "	393a, s.v. 'Tern', *for* 'Atcham' *read* 'High Ercall'
" "	394c, *between* 'Walsh' *and* 'Ward' *insert new entry* 'Walton, in Stottesdon: 'Conditre', 2 *n*'
" "	395a, s.v. 'Weld-Forester, Cecil Weld', *delete* 'Weld'
" "	395a, s.v. 'Weld-Forester, Geo. Cecil Weld', *delete* 'Weld'
Vol. VIII, page	88a, lines 22–3, *for* 'mistress . . . Harrison' *read* 'illegitimate son John Harrison with remainder to Harrison's
" "	mother Mrs. Anne Smyth'
" "	270b, line 25, *for* '54' *read* '51'
" "	270b, line 26, *after* 'Thomas' *insert* 'Porter'
" "	270b, line 26, *for* '1754' *read* '1751'
" "	270b, line 27, *after* 'Thomas' *insert* 'Porter'
" "	270b, line 27, *delete* 'Sir'
" "	270b, line 28, *for* '1771' *read* '1770'
" "	270b, line 30, *after* '1826' *insert* '(cr. bt. 1795)'
" "	270b, line 30, *after* ';' *insert* 'Sir'
" "	270b, line 31, *before* 'Joseph' *insert* 'Sir'